Important Internal Revenue Code Sections

The United States income tax was authorized by the Sixteenth Amendment to the U.S. Constitution on March 1, 1913. The Internal Revenue Code (IRC) is the detailed tax law as passed by the U.S. Congress. Some of the most important sections (adapted from Raabe, et.al. *Federal Tax Research*, 8th Ed.) of the code are summarized below, along with the chapter (and, where appropriate, specific learning objective numbers) of the text in which the section is covered.

Code Section	Contents	Text Chapter
1	Individual Tax Rates	Chapter 1 *(LO 1.5 and Appendix A)*
11	Corporate Tax Rates	Chapters 1 & 11 *(LO 1.2 and LO 11.1)*
36B	Premium Tax Credit	Chapters 6 *(LO 6.4)*
61	Definition of Gross Income	Chapter 2 *(LO 2.1)*
62	Deductions for Gross Income	Chapters 3 & 4
162	Trade or Business Deductions	Chapters 3 & 4
163	Interest Deduction	Chapter 5 *(LO 5.3)*
164	Deduction for Taxes	Chapter 5 *(LO 5.2)*
165	Losses	Chapters 3 & 8 *(LO 3.8 and LO 8.3)*
167, 168, 179	Depreciation, Election to Expense	Chapter 7 *(LOs 7.3 through 7.7)*
212	Production of Income Expenses	Chapter 5 *(LO 5.6)*
351	Forming a Corporation	Chapter 11 *(LO 11.7)*
469	Passive Activities	Chapter 4 *(LO 4.2)*
721	Forming a Partnership	Chapter 10 *(LO 10.2)*
904	Foreign Tax Credit	Chapter 6 *(LO 6.6)*
1245	Depreciation Recapture	Chapter 8 *(LO 8.7)*
5000A	Minimum Essential Care	Chapter 6 *(LO 6.4)*
6662	Penalties for Tax Filings	Chapter 12 *(LO 12.3)*

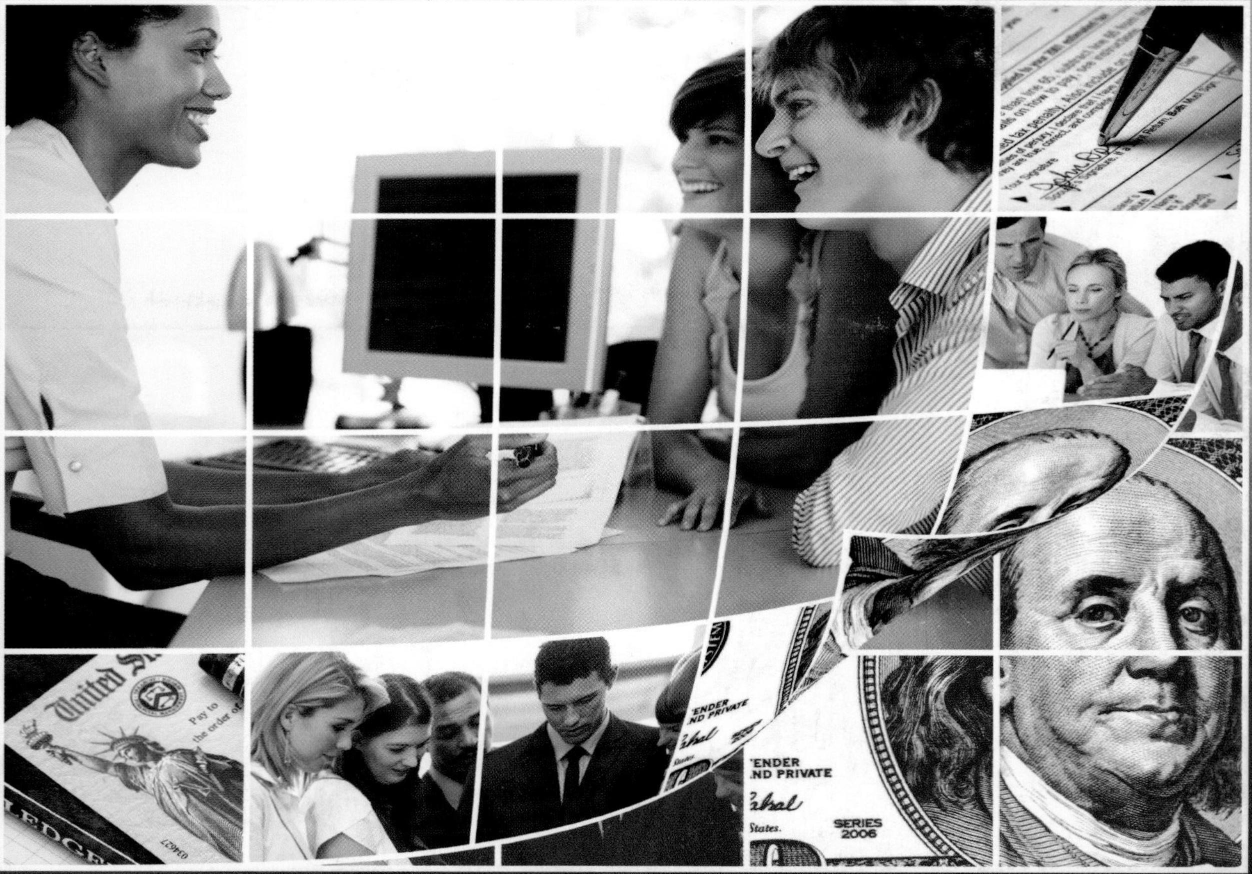

© Yuri Arcurs/Shutterstock; © Garry L./Shutterstock; © NoDerog/iStockphoto.com; © spxChrome/iStockphoto.com; © Peter Firus/iStockphoto.com

Over

QUICK TAX REFERENCE 2014

The Tax Formula for Individuals

	Gross Income
–	Deductions for Adjusted Gross Income
=	Adjusted Gross Income
–	Greater of Itemized Deductions or the Standard Deduction
–	Exemptions
=	Taxable Income
x	Tax Rate *(using appropriate tax tables or rate schedules)*
=	Gross Tax Liability
–	Tax Credits and Prepayments
=	Tax Due or Refund

Social Security, Medicare & Self-Employment Taxes

	Social Security	Medicare	Total
Employer	6.20%	1.45%	7.65%
Employee	6.20%	1.45%	7.65%
Self-Employed	12.40%	2.90%	15.30%

Wage Base for Social Security and Self-Employment Tax $117,000

Wage Base for Medicare No cap

2014 Federal Tax Rate Schedule

If Taxable Income is Over:	But Not Over:	The Tax is:
SINGLE INDIVIDUAL		
$0	$9,075	10% of taxable income
$9,075	$36,900	$907.50 plus 15% of the excess over $9,075
$36,900	$89,350	$5,081.25 plus 25% of the excess over $36,900
$89,350	$186,350	$18,193.75 plus 28% of the excess over $89,350
$186,350	$405,100	$45,353.75 plus 33% of the excess over $186,350
$405,100	$406,750	$117,541.25 plus 35% of the excess over $405,100
$406,750		$118,118.75 plus 39.6% of the excess over $406,750
MARRIED FILING JOINTLY OR QUALIFYING WIDOW(ER)		
$0	$18,150	10% of taxable income
$18,150	$73,800	$1,815.00 plus 15% of the excess over $18,150
$73,800	$148,850	$10,162.50 plus 25% of the excess over $73,800
$148,850	$226,850	$28,925.00 plus 28% of the excess over $148,850
$226,850	$405,100	$50,765.00 plus 33% of the excess over $226,850
$405,100	$457,600	$109,587.50 plus 35% of the excess over $405,100
$457,600		$127,962.50 plus 39.6% of the excess over $457,600
MARRIED FILING SEPARATELY		
$0	$9,075	10% of taxable income
$9,075	$36,900	$907.50 plus 15% of the excess over $9,075
$36,900	$74,425	$5,081.25 plus 25% of the excess over $36,900
$74,425	$113,425	$14,462.50 plus 28% of the excess over $74,425
$113,425	$202,550	$25,382.50 plus 33% of the excess over $113,425
$202,550	$228,800	$54,793.75 plus 35% of the excess over $202,550
$228,800		$63,981.25 plus 39.6% of the excess over $228,800
HEAD OF HOUSEHOLD		
$0	$12,950	10% of taxable income
$12,950	$49,400	$1,295.00 plus 15% of the excess over $12,950
$49,400	$127,550	$6,762.50 plus 25% of the excess over $49,400
$127,550	$206,600	$26,300.00 plus 28% of the excess over $127,550
$206,600	$405,100	$48,434.00 plus 33% of the excess over $206,600
$405,100	$432,200	$113,939.00 plus 35% of the excess over $405,100
$432,200		$123,424.00 plus 39.6% of the excess over $432,200

Child Tax Credit

Amount per child under 17	$1,000
Credit reduction of $50 per $1,000 of modified AGI:	
joint filers, in excess of	$110,000
single or head of household filers, in excess of	$75,000
married filing separately filers, in excess of	$55,000

Standard Deductions

Single	$6,200
Married Filing Jointly or Surviving Spouse	$12,400
Married Filing Separately	$6,200
Head of Household	$9,100
Additional for 65 and Older or Blind—Married	$1,200
Additional for 65 and Older or Blind—Unmarried	$1,550

(per individual and for each situation: age or blind)

The basic standard deduction for employed dependents equals the lesser of:

- $6,200 **or**

The greater of

- $1,000 or the individual's earned income plus $350

Personal/Dependent Exemption $3,950

Auto Standard Mileage Allowances

Business: **$0.56** Charity Work: **$0.14** Medical/Moving: **$0.235**

Traditional IRA Deduction

- If neither individual nor spouse is a participant in another plan, the maximum deduction is $5,500 if under age 50, or $6,500 if age 50 or over
- If the individual is an active participant in another plan:

Married/Joint AGI	Single AGI	Max. Deduction
Up to $96,000	Up to $60,000	$5,500 (under 50) $6,500 (50 or over)
$96,000–$115,999	$60,000–$69,999	Phased-out
$116,000 and Over	$70,000 and Over	No deduction

- If the individual is not an active participant in a qualified retirement plan (but spouse is), allowable contributions are fully deductible up to $181,000 and phased-out at $191,000 of joint income

Roth IRA Requirements

- Individuals and spouses can contribute a maximum $5,500 plus $1,000 for taxpayers age 50 or over
- Contribution amount is phased-out when AGI is between:
  - – $114,000 and $129,000 for single filers
  - – $181,000 and $191,000 for joint filers
- Contributions are not tax-deductible
- Like traditional IRAs, contributions are limited to amount of earned income

Concise, Current, & Practical!

Income Tax Fundamentals' Winning Forms Approach Is Time-Tested

Income Tax Fundamentals 2015 Edition is designed as a self-contained book for an introductory course in individual income taxation. We take pride in the concise, current, and practical coverage of the income tax return preparation process. Whittenburg/Altus-Buller/Gill continues to be the **market-leading text** with a forms approach and is a reliable choice, with an experienced author team that offers a commitment to accuracy. The text workbook format presents materials in practical sections with multiple examples, Internet activities, and review problems. The presentation of the material does not assume that the reader has taken a course in accounting, making it appropriate for use as a self-study guide to federal income tax. Whittenburg/Altus-Buller/Gill adopters tell us:

> *Great text. I have used it for years mostly because of its simple and straightforward approach to the basic income tax elements.*
>
> — Jerold K. Braun, Daytona State College

> *This text provides an excellent overview for community tax classes. The software gives these students good hands-on experience with the concepts.*
>
> — Jay Wright, New River Community College

> *I love this book with all its comprehensive problems that progress from easy to difficult.*
>
> — LoAnn Nelson, PhD, CPA, Lake Region State College

> *The layout of the chapters is well-thought out.*
>
> — James Hromadka, San Jacinto College

> *I enjoy using the Whittenburg text...it is the best I have found.*
>
> — Jana Hosmer, Blue Ridge Community College

Whittenburg/Altus-Buller/Gill's hallmark "**Forms Approach**" allows students to practice filling out tax returns right in the book without having to download tax forms online. The forms approach is supported by an **annotated 1040 map**. The 1040 map is an expanded tax formula, showing where each piece of the tax formula is covered in the book. It is a helpful visual tool for instructors who like to reference the tax formula in class. The 1040 map helps students understand how all of the elements of the text fit together. To see the annotated 1040 map, please turn to Pages x–xi.

H&R BLOCK TAX SOFTWARE

Each individual tax form needed to complete the problems in the text is included within ***Income Tax Fundamentals*** and within the complimentary **Premium & Business® software from H&R Block**. H&R Block Premium & Business® is practical and remarkably easy to use, with many helpful features available to new users. The H&R Block website (**www.hrblock.com**) offers useful tips, calculators, and other current tax information. All of the 2014 Individual Income Tax Return problems in the text may be solved using this software, or students may prepare the tax returns by hand. If you would like to use H&R Block Premium & Business® on your campus computers, please contact the publishing team.

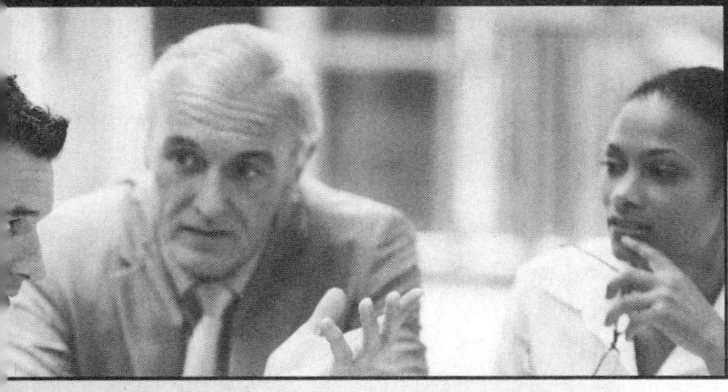

Income Tax Fundamentals

Evolves Each Year to Benefit You

New to This Edition

Updated for recent changes under the Affordable Care Act

The Affordable Care Act, also known as the ACA and, more popularly as, "Obamacare," introduced two new important provisions in 2014 as part of its ongoing implementation: the individual shared responsibility and the premium tax credit. We include a discussion of the complex calculation of the individual shared responsibility, which is the tax for failing to carry appropriate health insurance (or "minimum essential coverage") under the ACA requirements. In addition, the calculation of the premium tax credit and the reconciliation process when the credit is advanced during the year are covered with detailed examples. We have provided coverage on both elements in Chapter 6 under Learning Objectives 6.4.

The ACA elements introduced in 2013, such as the 3.8 percent net investment income tax and the 0.9 percent Medicare surtax continue to be considered and examples now include the 2014 tax forms used to report these two additional taxes on high income earners.

We also cover the new voluntary Annual Filing Season Program intended to serve as the replacement for the now-defunct Registered Tax Return Preparer program and the new options for use of unused medical flexible spending account balanced at year end.

Updated for the Affordable Care Act Changes Related to the 2014 Tax Year

The Affordable Care Act, also known as the ACA and, more popularly as, "Obamacare," added a Medicare surtax on net investment income and the earned income of individuals with income over certain limits. We have provided tables in Chapters One, Two, Eight, and Nine showing the cumulative effect of the tax increases passed by ATRA and the tax increases passed under the ACA for 2013. These changes are covered in new Learning Objectives 1.9 and 9.9.

In addition to the complex new rate calculations, the ACA surtaxes, and the itemized deduction and exemption phase-outs added by the two new laws already mentioned, we cover smaller changes in the tax law such as:

- The landmark Supreme Court decision allowing same-sex couples to file joint returns for the first time
- The new 10% threshold for medical expenses for filers under age 65
- The newly available simplified home office deduction
- The IRS First Time Penalty Abatement Program
- The Annual Filing Season Program intended to substitute for the cancelled RTRP designation

And more...

Cost of Living Changes

The entire text and thousands of ancillary problems and examples were updated to reflect the annual cost of living increases required by the tax law. Every Form and Schedule in the text was updated to draft or final 2014 forms, except two, which were unavailable as we went to press.

A Complete Learning System—CengageNOW

CENGAGENOW

CengageNOW for Taxation takes students from motivation to mastery. Built on principles of learning, designed and created hand-in-hand with educators, Cengage Learning digital solutions focus on engagement, taking students through levels of application, analysis, and critical thinking with depth and context unmatched in the market.

CengageNOW elevates thinking by providing superior content designed with the entire student workflow in mind. Students learn more efficiently with the variety of engaging assessments and learning tools. For instructors, CengageNOW provides ultimate control and customization and a clear view into student performance that allows for the opportunity to tailor the learning experience to improve outcomes.

Motivation

Many instructors find that students come to class unmotivated and unprepared. To help with engagement and preparedness, CengageNOW for Whittenburg offers the following feature:

Self-Study Questions based on the questions in the text, these problems help students prepare for class lectures or review prior to an exam. Self-Study Questions provide ample practice for the students while providing them with valuable feedback and checks along the way.

Application

Students need to learn problem-solving skills in order to complete taxation problems on their own. However, as students try to work through homework problems, sometimes they become stuck and need guidance. To help reinforce concepts and keep students on the right track, CengageNOW for Whittenburg offers the following:

- **End-of-chapter homework: Group 1 and 2 problems**
- **Algorithmic versions** of end-of-chapter homework are available for at least 10-15 problems per chapter.
- **Detailed feedback for each homework question.** Homework questions include enhanced, immediate feedback so students can learn as they go. Levels of feedback include an option for "check my work" prior to submission of an assignment. Then, after submitting an assignment, students receive even more extensive feedback explaining why their answers were incorrect. Instructors can decide how much feedback their students receive and when, including the full solution, if they wish.
- **"Show Me How" demo's provide help when students need it most.** All the Group 2 Problems include a Show Me How link that takes students to an example from the text that can be used to help solve it.
- Built-in **Test Bank** for online assessment.

For students who need additional support, CengageNOW's **Personalized Study Plan** is complete with pre-tests and post-tests, an eBook, practice quizzes, and more.

Mastery

Finally, students need to make the leap from memorizing concepts to actual critical thinking. They need to be able to connect multiple topics and master the material. To help students grasp the big picture of taxation and achieve the end goal of mastery, CengageNOW for Whittenburg offers the following:

Comprehensive Problems Students will now be able to complete the problems by providing information on tax forms and schedules.

Cengage Learning Testing Powered by Cognero®

Cognero® is a flexible, online system that allows instructors to:

- author, edit, and manage test bank content from multiple Cengage Learning solutions
- create multiple test versions in an instant
- deliver tests from your LMS, your classroom or wherever you want
- Simplicity at every step. A desktop-inspired interface features drop-down menus and familiar, intuitive tools.
- Full-featured test generator. Choose from 15 question types (including true/false, multiple choice, and essay). Multi-language support, an equation editor, and unlimited metadata help ensure your tests are complete and compliant.
- Cross-compatible capability. Import and export content into other systems.

CL Testing Powered by Cognero® is accessible through the instructor companion site, **www.cengage.com/login.**

Key Terms

Key Terms with page references are located at the end of Chapters 1 through 8 and reinforce the important tax terms introduced in each chapter.

Comprehensive Instructor Companion Website

In order to expedite the availability of all instructor materials in a timely manner and to make changes, when necessary, all instructor materials, including Cognero® testing software, will be offered exclusively on the password-protected website, **www.cengage.com/login.**

As We Go to Press

To access tax law information after the publication of this text, please visit **www.cengagebrain.com**. At the CengageBrain home page, fill the ISBN of your textbook (from the back cover of your book). This will take you to the product page where free companion resources can be found.

Reliable Instructor Resources Are Convenient

Solutions Manual

The printed manual contains detailed solutions to the problems in the text and the Additional Comprehensive Problems that are located in Appendix D, chapter outlines, and suggested minimum assignments (ISBN 13: 978-1-305-38878-9).

Instructor Companion Website

This password-protected site contains instructor resources: the Solutions Manual, Chapter Outlines and Suggested Minimum Assignments, the Test Bank, Cognero® testing tools, Solutions to the Cumulative Tax Return Problems, H&R Block software solutions and instructions, Instructor PowerPoints, and more: **www.cengage.com/login**

Step-by-Step Format Builds Student Confidence

The practical, step-by-step format in ***Income Tax Fundamentals 2015 Edition*** builds from simple to complex topics. The authors are careful to lead students down a path of understanding rather than overwhelming them with excessive detail and multiple Internal Revenue Code references.

- Helpful examples within each chapter provide realistic scenarios for students to consider.

EXAMPLE Scott provides all of the support for an unrelated family friend who lives with him for the entire tax year. He also supports a cousin who lives in another state. The family friend can qualify as Scott's dependent, but the cousin cannot. The family friend meets the member of the household test. Even though the cousin is not considered a relative, he could have been a dependent if he met the member of the household part of the test. ♦

- The short sections within each chapter offer numerous examples, supported by the "Self-Study Problems" throughout. The Self-Study Problems encourage students to answer a series of short questions in a fill-in-the-blank or multiple-choice format. The solutions to the Self-Study Problems are provided at the end of the text, offering immediate solutions to students to help build confidence.

- The Quick Tax Reference Guide on the inside of the back cover of the textbook includes the Tax Equation.

If Taxable Income is Over:	But Not Over:	The Tax is:
SINGLE INDIVIDUALS		
$0	$8,925	10% of taxable income
$8,925	$36,250	$892.50 plus 15% of the excess over $8,925
$36,250	$87,850	$4,991.25 plus 25% of the excess over $36,250
$87,850	$183,250	$17,891.25 plus 28% of the excess over $87,850
$183,250	$398,350	$44,603.25 plus 33% of the excess over $183,250
$398,350	$400,000	$115,586.25 plus 35% of the excess over $398,350
$400,000		$116,163.75 plus 39.6% of the excess over $400,000
MARRIED FILING JOINT RETURNS OR QUALIFYING WIDOW(ER)S		
$0	$17,850	10% of taxable income
$17,850	$72,500	$1,785.00 plus 15% of the excess over $17,850
$72,500	$146,400	$9,982.50 plus 25% of the excess over $72,500
$146,400	$223,050	$28,457.50 plus 28% of the excess over $146,400
$223,050	[illegible]	$49,919.50 plus 33% of the excess over $223,050
$398,350	[illegible]	$107,768.50 plus 35% of the excess over $398,350
[illegible]0,000	[illegible]	[illegible]lus 39.6% of the excess over [illegible]

LEARNING OBJECTIVES

After completing this chapter, you should be able to:

- **LO 1.1** Understand the history and objectives of U.S. tax law.
- **LO 1.2** Describe the different entities subject to tax and reporting requirements.
- **LO 1.3** Understand and apply the tax formula for individuals.
- **LO 1.4** Identify individuals who must file tax returns.
- **LO 1.5** Determine filing status and understand the calculation of tax according to

- Learning Objectives help organize information and are referenced by the end-of-chapter exercises.

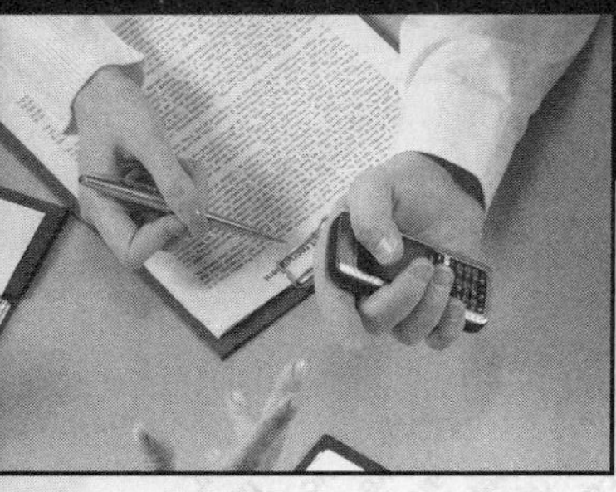

Real-World Applications Keep Students Engaged

- The "Would You Sign This Tax Return?" feature places readers in the office of a tax preparer with interesting and even humorous real-world tax ethics questions that will intrigue students. Many of these features are inspired by the authors' own experiences working with various clients in tax preparation. As part of each scenario, students decide if they would sign the tax return. You, as the instructor, can use the cases to spark group discussions on basic tax preparation ethics.

Would You Sign This Tax Return?

Paid Preparer Use Only	Print/Type preparer's name	Preparer's signature	Date	Check ☐ if self-employed	PTIN
	Firm's name ▶		Firm's EIN ▶		
	Firm's address ▶		Phone no.		

Your client, William Warrant, was hired for a management position at an Internet company planning to start a Web portal called "indulgedanimals.com" for dogs, cats, and other pets. When he was hired, William was given an incentive stock option (ISO) worth $500,000, which he exercised during the year. Exercise of the ISO creates a tax preference item for the alternative minimum tax (AMT) and causes him to have to pay substantial additional tax when combined with his other tax items for the year. He is livid about the extra tax and refuses to file the AMT Form 6251 with his tax return because the AMT tax is "unfair" and "un-American" according to him. Would you sign this tax return?

© IlYA AKINSHIN/Shutterstock.com; © Zhukov Oleg/Shutterstock.com.

- Real-world examples within Tax Break segments provide actual, effective examples of tax-planning strategies that clearly illustrate the concepts discussed throughout the book and cover nearly every basic tax-planning technique used by tax preparers.

TAX BREAK

Taxpayers may provide information with their individual tax return authorizing the IRS to deposit refunds directly into their bank account. Taxpayers with a balance due may pay their tax bill with a credit card, subject to an IRS fee.

- High-interest tax facts within "Would You Believe?" sections grab students' attention with interesting asides, including captivating facts and stories about tax laws and preparation.

Would You Believe?

The following quotation is often attributed to Albert Einstein: "The hardest thing in the world to understand is the income tax."

- New Law Alert boxes throughout the text draw students' attention to specific areas affected by new tax legislation.

NEW LAW ALERT

In 2013, the U.S. Supreme Court struck down parts of the Defense of Marriage Act enabling same-sex couples to file joint federal tax returns. The general rule recognizes a marriage that was validly entered into in a state or foreign jurisdiction whose laws authorize same-sex marriages, even when the married couple resides currently in a jurisdiction that does not recognize the validity of same-sex marriages.

Income Tax Fundamentals

Delivers Proven End-of-Chapter Strengths

- The pages are perforated, allowing students to complete end-of-chapter problems and submit them for homework. Students can also tear out tax forms as needed.
- Several question types ensure a variety of assignment options:
  - Multiple Choice Questions
  - Problems
  - Writing Assignments
  - Comprehensive Problems
  - The Cumulative Software Problem gives students the flexibility to use multiple resources, such as the tax forms within the book, H&R Block Premium & Business®, or alternative tax preparation software.

Digital Tools Enhance Student Understanding

CengageNow is a powerful online homework tool. CengageNow includes an interactive eBook, end-of-chapter homework, detailed student feedback, interactive quizzing, testing with Pre- and Post-tests, videos with quizzing that covers the most challenging topics, a lab guide for using the H&R Block software, flashcards, games, and much more.

The student companion website offers—*at no additional costs*—study resources for students. Go to **www.cengagebrain.com**, and fill in the ISBN number of your textbook (from the back cover of your book). This will take you to the product page where free companion resources can be found.

The H&R Block Premium & Business® CD is included with each text. A detailed reference lab guide will help the student use the software for solving end-of-chapter problems.

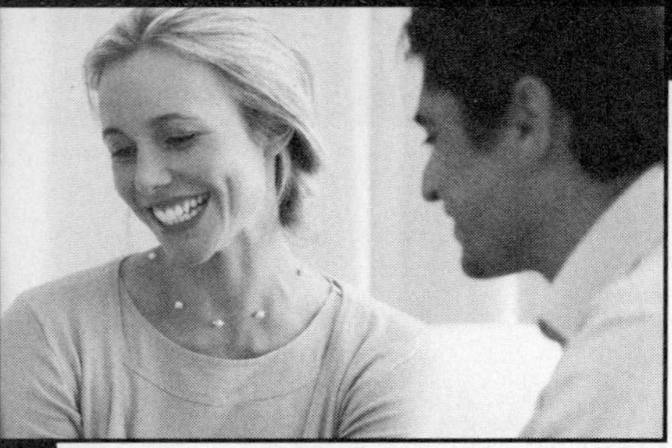

Note to Students: Maximize Your Reading Experience

This book includes many examples to help illustrate learning objectives. After reading each section, including the examples, answer the corresponding Self-Study Problems. You can find the solutions to the Self-Study Problems at the end of the text to check your accuracy. Use your performance to measure your understanding, and re-read the Learning Objective section if needed. Many key tax terms are defined in each chapter, which will help improve your overall comprehension.

USING TAX SOFTWARE

Numerous tax return problems in the text can be solved using either tax preparation software or hand preparation. The popular software, H&R Block Premium & Business®, is included in a CD with the text. A student guide to H&R Block Premium & Business® is provided at the companion website. Your college may offer additional tax preparation software, such as Intuit's ProSeries®, but remember that you can always work the problems by hand.

USING THE FEATURE "WOULD YOU SIGN THIS TAX RETURN?"

A practitioner who knows when to say "I cannot sign this tax return," even if it means losing a client, is exercising the most basic ethical wisdom. Chapters 1–9 each contain a "Would You Sign This Tax Return?" case reflecting a common client issue. Each issue corresponds to an obvious concept illustrated in the previous section. However, how to handle the client is not obvious. The art of explaining tax rules to a client who does not understand them, or, worse, wants to break them, requires not only a good understanding of the rules, but good interpersonal skills and sometimes the gift of persuasion. The news in the last several years has shown reports of respected CPA firms with members who failed to say the simple words, "I cannot sign this tax return," showing us that simple ethical practice is not always easy. We hope instructors will use these cases to spark group discussions or contemplation, and, perhaps, add examples from their own experience.

USING THE CUMULATIVE SOFTWARE PROBLEM

The Cumulative Software Problem can be found at the end of Chapters 1–8. The case information provided in each chapter builds on the information from previous chapters, resulting in a lengthy and complex tax return by the conclusion of the problem in Chapter 8. Your professor may have you work in groups to prepare each of the tax returns. The groups can follow the real-world accounting firm model using a preparer, a reviewer, and a firm owner who takes responsibility for the accuracy of the return and signs it. All of the issues in the problem are commonly seen by tax preparers and are covered in the text. The full return is difficult to prepare by hand, so tax software is recommended. If the problem is prepared using tax software, the data should be saved so the additional information in the succeeding chapters can be added without duplicating input from previous chapters.

USING THE ALTERNATE TAX RETURN PROBLEMS

Each of the first six chapters contains an alternate tax return problem numbered "2B." The problems have been added to increase the variety of full tax returns available for added practice. Problem "2B" is similar in coverage to problem "2A" in each chapter and uses the same forms. Forms are provided at the end of the chapter and, if desired, additional forms may be easily obtained from the IRS website (**www.irs.gov**).

The Annotated 1040 Map

The annotated 1040 map is an expanded tax formula, showing you where each piece of the tax formula is covered in the book. The 1040 map helps you understand how all of the elements of the text and the tax formula fit together. Use this as a reference and bookmark this page.

Form 1040 Department of the Treasury—Internal Revenue Service (99)
U.S. Individual Income Tax Return **2014** OMB No. 1545-0074 IRS Use Only—Do not write or staple in this space.

For the year Jan. 1–Dec. 31, 2014, or other tax year beginning , 2014, ending , 20 — See separate instructions.

Your first name and initial	Last name	**Your social security number**
If a joint return, spouse's first name and initial	Last name	**Spouse's social security number**
Home address (number and street). If you have a P.O. box, see instructions.	Apt. no.	▲ Make sure the SSN(s) above and on line 6c are correct.
City, town or post office, state, and ZIP code. If you have a foreign address, also complete spaces below (see instructions).		**Presidential Election Campaign** Check here if you, or your spouse if filing jointly, want $3 to go to this fund. Checking a box below will not change your tax or refund. ☐ You ☐ Spouse
Foreign country name	Foreign province/state/county — Foreign postal code	

Filing Status
LO 1.5
Check only one box.

1 ☐ Single
2 ☐ Married filing jointly (even if only one had income)
3 ☐ Married filing separately. Enter spouse's SSN above and full name here. ▶
4 ☐ Head of household (with qualifying person). (See instructions.) If the qualifying person is a child but not your dependent, enter this child's name here. ▶
5 ☐ Qualifying widow(er) with dependent child

Exemptions
LO 1.6

6a ☐ **Yourself.** If someone can claim you as a dependent, **do not** check box 6a
b ☐ **Spouse**
c **Dependents:**

(1) First name Last name	(2) Dependent's social security number	(3) Dependent's relationship to you	(4) ✓ if child under age 17 qualifying for child tax credit (see instructions)
			☐
			☐
			☐
			☐

If more than four dependents, see instructions and check here ▶ ☐

d Total number of exemptions claimed

Boxes checked on 6a and 6b
No. of children on 6c who:
• lived with you
• did not live with you due to divorce or separation (see instructions)
Dependents on 6c not entered above
Add numbers on lines above ▶

Income

Attach Form(s) W-2 here. Also attach Forms W-2G and 1099-R if tax was withheld.

If you did not get a W-2, see instructions.

Line	Description		Line	Annotation
7	Wages, salaries, tips, etc. Attach Form(s) W-2		7	*Chapters 1, 2, & 9*
8a	**Taxable** interest. Attach Schedule B if required		8a	*LO 2.2*
b	**Tax-exempt** interest. **Do not** include on line 8a	8b *LO 2.11*		
9a	Ordinary dividends. Attach Schedule B if required		9a	*LO 2.2*
b	Qualified dividends	9b *LO 2.2*		
10	Taxable refunds, credits, or offsets of state and local income taxes		10	*LO 5.2*
11	Alimony received		11	*LO 2.3*
12	Business income or (loss). Attach Schedule C or C-EZ		12	*LO 3.1*
13	Capital gain or (loss). Attach Schedule D if required. If not required, check here ▶ ☐		13	*Line 1.8, Chapter 8*
14	Other gains or (losses). Attach Form 4797		14	*Chapter 8*
15a	IRA distributions 15a	b Taxable amount	15b	*LO 4.6*
16a	Pensions and annuities 16a	b Taxable amount	16b	*LOs 2.5 & 4.8*
17	Rental real estate, royalties, partnerships, S corporations, trusts, etc. Attach Schedule E		17	*LO 4.1, Chapters 10 & 11*
18	Farm income or (loss). Attach Schedule F		18	*LO 1.2, Chapter 3 overview*
19	Unemployment compensation		19	*LO 2.12*
20a	Social security benefits 20a	b Taxable amount	20b	*LO 2.14*
21	Other income. List type and amount		21	*LO 2.1*
22	Combine the amounts in the far right column for lines 7 through 21. This is your **total income** ▶		22	*TOTAL INCOME*

Adjusted Gross Income

Line	Description	Line	Annotation	Line	Annotation
23	Reserved	23	*Educator expenses (if extended)*		
24	Certain business expenses of reservists, performing artists, and fee-basis government officials. Attach Form 2106 or 2106-EZ	24			
25	Health savings account deduction. Attach Form 8889	25	*LO 4.4*		
26	Moving expenses. Attach Form 3903	26	*LO 4.5*		
27	Deductible part of self-employment tax. Attach Schedule SE	27	*LO 9.6*		
28	Self-employed SEP, SIMPLE, and qualified plans	28	*LOs 4.7–4.9*		
29	Self-employed health insurance deduction	29	*LO 4.3*		
30	Penalty on early withdrawal of savings	30	*LO 2.2*		
31a	Alimony paid b Recipient's SSN ▶	31a	*LO 2.3*		
32	IRA deduction	32	*LO 4.6*		
33	Student loan interest deduction	33	*LO 5.3*		
34	Reserved	34	*LO 5.8 (if extended)*		
35	Domestic production activities deduction. Attach Form 8903	35			
36	Add lines 23 through 35			36	*DEDUCTIONS FOR AGI*
37	Subtract line 36 from line 22. This is your **adjusted gross income** ▶			37	*AGI*

For Disclosure, Privacy Act, and Paperwork Reduction Act Notice, see separate instructions. Cat. No. 11320B Form **1040** (2014)

DRAFT AS O
August 28, 20
DO NOT FIL

DRAFT AS OF August 28, 2014 DO NOT FILE

Section	Line	Description	Box	Entry	Box	Entry
Tax and Credits	38	Amount from line 37 (adjusted gross income)			38	*AGI*
	39a	Check if: ☐ **You** were born before January 2, 1950, ☐ Blind. ☐ **Spouse** was born before January 2, 1950, ☐ Blind. } **Total boxes checked** ▶ **39a** ☐				*ITEMIZED OR STANDARD DEDUCTION*
	b	If your spouse itemizes on a separate return or you were a dual-status alien, check here ▶ **39b** ☐				
	40	**Itemized deductions** (from Schedule A) **or** your **standard deduction** (see left margin)			40	*LO 1.7, Chapter 5*
	41	Subtract line 40 from line 38			41	
	42	**Exemptions.** If line 38 is $152,525 or less, multiply $3,950 by the number on line 6d. Otherwise, see instructions			42	*LO 1.6, LO 5.9*
	43	**Taxable income.** Subtract line 42 from line 41. If line 42 is more than line 41, enter -0-			43	*TAXABLE INCOME*
	44	**Tax** (see instructions). Check if any from: **a** ☐ Form(s) 8814 **b** ☐ Form 4972 **c** ☐			44	*LOs 1.5, 2.2, 6.10, 8.4*
	45	**Alternative minimum tax** (see instructions). Attach Form 6251			45	*LO 6.9*
	46	Excess advance premium tax credit repayment. Attach Form 8962			46	*LO 6.4*
	47	Add lines 44, 45, and 46 ▶			47	*TAX BEFORE CREDITS AND OTHER TAXES*
	48	Foreign tax credit. Attach Form 1116 if required	48	*LO 6.6*		
	49	Credit for child and dependent care expenses. Attach Form 2441	49	*LO 6.3*		
	50	Education credits from Form 8863, line 19	50	*LO 6.5*		
	51	Retirement savings contributions credit. Attach Form 8880	51	*LO 4.8*		
	52	Child tax credit. Attach Schedule 8812, if required	52	*LO 6.1*		
	53	Residential energy credit. Attach Form 5695	53	*LO 6.8*		
	54	Other credits from Form: **a** ☐ 3800 **b** ☐ 8801 **c** ☐	54	*LO 6.7*		
	55	Add lines 48 through 54. These are your **total credits**			55	*TOTAL CREDITS*
	56	Subtract line 55 from line 47. If line 55 is more than line 47, enter -0- ▶			56	
Other Taxes	57	Self-employment tax. Attach Schedule SE			57	*LO 9.6*
	58	Unreported social security and Medicare tax from Form: **a** ☐ 4137 **b** ☐ 8919			58	
	59	Additional tax on IRAs, other qualified retirement plans, etc. Attach Form 5329 if required			59	*LO 4.6*
	60a	Household employment taxes from Schedule H			60a	*LO 9.8*
	b	First-time homebuyer credit repayment. Attach Form 5405 if required			60b	
	61	Health care: individual responsibility (see instructions) Full-year coverage ☐			61	*LO 6.4*
	62	Taxes from: **a** ☐ Form 8959 **b** ☐ Form 8960 **c** ☐ Instructions; enter code(s)			62	*LO 1.9, LO 9.9*
	63	Add lines 56 through 62. This is your **total tax** ▶			63	*TOTAL TAX*
Payments	64	Federal income tax withheld from Forms W-2 and 1099	64	*LO 9.1, Chapter 1*		
	65	2014 estimated tax payments and amount applied from 2013 return	65	*LO 9.2, Chapter 1*		
	66a	**Earned income credit (EIC)**	66a	*LO 6.2*		
	b	Nontaxable combat pay election **66b**				
	67	Additional child tax credit. Attach Schedule 8812	67			
	68	American opportunity credit from Form 8863, line 8	68	*LO 6.5*		
	69	Net premium tax credit. Attach Form 8962	69	*LO 6.4*		
	70	Amount paid with request for extension to file	70	*LO 1.4*		
	71	Excess social security and tier 1 RRTA tax withheld	71			
	72	Credit for federal tax on fuels. Attach Form 4136	72			
	73	Credits from Form: **a** ☐ 2439 **b** ☐ Reserved **c** ☐ Reserved **d** ☐	73			
	74	Add lines 64, 65, 66a, and 67 through 73. These are your **total payments** ▶			74	*PAYMENTS*
Refund	75	If line 74 is more than line 63, subtract line 63 from line 74. This is the amount you **overpaid**			75	*REFUND*
	76a	Amount of line 75 you want **refunded to you.** If Form 8888 is attached, check here ▶ ☐			76a	
Direct deposit? See instructions.	▶ b	Routing number ▶ **c** Type: ☐ Checking ☐ Savings				
	▶ d	Account number				
	77	Amount of line 75 you want **applied to your 2015 estimated tax** ▶	77			*-OR-*
Amount You Owe	78	**Amount you owe.** Subtract line 74 from line 63. For details on how to pay, see instructions ▶			78	*AMOUNT DUE*
	79	Estimated tax penalty (see instructions)	79			

Standard Deduction for—
- People who check any box on line 39a or 39b **or** who can be claimed as a dependent, see instructions.
- All others:

Single or Married filing separately, $6,200
Married filing jointly or Qualifying widow(er), $12,400
Head of household, $9,100

If you have a qualifying child, attach Schedule EIC.

Third Party Designee
Do you want to allow another person to discuss this return with the IRS (see instructions)? ☐ **Yes.** Complete below. ☐ **No**
Designee's name ▶ Phone no. ▶ Personal identification number (PIN) ▶

Sign Here
Under penalties of perjury, I declare that I have examined this return and accompanying schedules and statements, and to the best of my knowledge and belief, they are true, correct, and complete. Declaration of preparer (other than taxpayer) is based on all information of which preparer has any knowledge.
Joint return? See instructions. Keep a copy for your records.

Your signature	Date	Your occupation	Daytime phone number
Spouse's signature. If a joint return, **both** must sign.	Date	Spouse's occupation	If the IRS sent you an Identity Protection PIN, enter it here (see inst.)

Paid Preparer Use Only

Print/Type preparer's name	Preparer's signature	Date	Check ☐ if self-employed	PTIN
Firm's name ▶			Firm's EIN ▶	
Firm's address ▶			Phone no.	

About the Authors

Gerald E. Whittenburg is a professor of accounting and taxation at San Diego State University. He received his PhD from the University of Houston. Dr. Whittenburg's professional designations include Certified Public Accountant, Certified Management Accountant, and Enrolled Agent. His research interests have focused on corporate and individual taxation, as well as the tax research process. His articles on these and other topics have appeared in journals such as the *Accounting Review, Advances in Taxation, Journal of Taxation, Taxation for Accountants, Taxes, Management Accounting, Practical Tax Strategies, Journal of Taxation of Investments, Valuation Strategies, Journal of Small Business Strategy, Journal of Taxation of Financial Institutions, The Tax Adviser, Tax Notes, Real Estate Accounting and Taxation,* and *Journal of Accounting Education.* Dr. Whittenburg has authored several tax textbooks, including *Income Tax Fundamentals, California Income Tax Fundamentals,* and *Federal Tax Research.* His books are used in more than 300 colleges and universities throughout the United States. He received a California State University (CSU) Trustee's Outstanding Faculty Award in 1991. This award was a competitive one across the entire 20-campus CSU system. Dr. Whittenburg was a visiting scholar at the University of Adelaide (Australia) in 1999 and 2005. In 2003, he received a Fulbright Senior Specialist grant at the Academy of Tax Services of Ukraine. While in Ukraine, he lectured students and conferred with the faculty and staff on income taxation in the United States.

Martha Altus-Buller is a Certified Public Accountant with more than 25 years of experience in tax practice in San Diego, California. She attended Reed College in Portland, Oregon, for two years and holds a BA in Mathematics from the University of California at San Diego and an MS in Accounting from San Diego State University. She won a Sells award for scoring among the top in the country on the May 1983 CPA exam. Her practical experience includes work as a tax manager for Arthur Young, now Ernst & Young, one of the (then) Big 8 accounting firms.

Steven L. Gill is an associate professor of accounting and taxation in the Charles W. Lamden School of Accountancy at San Diego State University. He received a BS in Accounting from the University of Florida, an MS in Taxation from Northeastern University, and a PhD in Accounting from the University of Massachusetts. Prior to entering academia, he worked for almost 12 years in the field of tax and accounting, including roles in public accounting, internal audit, corporate accounting, and, ultimately, vice president of finance. Although currently in inactive status, he holds a Certified Public Accountant designation. His research interests include a concentration in taxation, encompassing mutual funds and college savings ("529") plans as well as a wider interest in corporate internal control structure and weaknesses, management overconfidence, and earnings quality. He has published a wide variety of articles in various academic and practitioner journals, and has taught at both the undergraduate and graduate levels, including taxation and financial accounting.

Reviewers

Janice Akao, *Butler Community College*
Sandra Augustine, *Hilbert College*
George Barbi, *Lanier Technical College*
Lydia Botsford, *DeAnza College*
Mike Bowyer, *Montgomery Community College*
Jerold Braun, *Daytona State College*
Lindy Byrd, *Augusta Technical College*
Greg Carlton, *Davidson County Community College*
Jerry Chaney, *Southside Virginia Community College*
John Chappel, *Northland Community and Technical College*
Marilyn Ciolino, *Delgado Community College*
Diane Clugston, *Cambria-Rowe Business College*
Thomas Confrey, *SUNY Orange*
Amy Conley, *Genesee Community College*
Salle Crutaire, *Central Lakes College*
Eric DaGragnano, *City College*
William Dams, *Lenoir Community College*
Geoffrey Danzig, *Miami Dade College – Hialeah Campus*
Susan Davis, *Green River Community College*
Vaun Day, *Central Arizona College*
Men Dennis, *San Diego City College*
Kerry Dolan, *Great Falls College Montana State University*
Vicky C. Dominguez, *College of Southern Nevada*
John Fasler, *Whatcom Community College*
Brian Fink, *Danville Area Community College*
Brenda Fowler, *Central Carolina Community College*
George Frankel, *San Francisco State University*
Alan Fudge, *Linn-Benton Community College*
Gregory Gosman, *Keiser University*
Jeffery Haig, *Copper Mountain College*
Tracie Hayes, *Randolph Community College*
Michael Heath, *River Parishes Community College*
Keith Hendrick, *Georgia Piedmont Technical College*
Rob Hochschild, *Ivy Tech Community College*
Japan Holmes, Jr., *Savannah Technical College*
Jana Hosmer, *Blue Ridge Community College*
James Hromadka, *San Jacinto College*
Adrian Jarrell, *James Sprunt Community College*
Paul Johnson, *Mississippi Gulf Coast Community College*
Jessica Jones, *Mesa Community College*
Dieter Kiefer, *American River College*
Christopher Kinney, *Mount Wachusett Community College*
Mark Klamrzynski, *Phoenix College*
Raymond Kreiner, *Piedmont College*

Linda Lane, *Walla Walla Community College*
Christie Lee, *Lanier Technical College*
Susan Logorda, *Lehigh Carbon Community College*
Anthony Masino, *East Tennessee State University*
Diania McRae, *Southwestern Community College*
Deanne Michaelson, *Pellissippi State Community College*
Jennifer Morton, *Ivy Tech Community College*
Robert Nabhan, *Berks Technical Institute*
LoAnn Nelson, *Lake Region State College*
Michael O'Connell, *River Valley Community College*
Sharon O'Reilly, *Gateway Technical College*
Kevin Parker, *York Technical College*
Roxanne Phillips, *Everest College*
Mike Prockton, *Finger Lakes CC*
John Ribezzo, *Community College of Rhode Island*
Hanna Sahebifard, *Golden West College*
Larry Sayler, *Greenville College*
Charley Sherman, *Oakland Community College*
James Shimko, *Jackson Community College*
Kimberly Sipes, *Kentucky State University*
Amy Smith, *Pearl River Community College*
Joanie Sompayrc, *UT-Chattanooga*
Todd Stowe, *Southwest Florida College*
Gracelyn Stuart-Tuggle, *Palm Beach State College*
Robert Taylor, *Lees-McRae College*
Teresa Thamer, *Brenau University*
Stan Walker, *Georgia Northwestern Technical School*
Jerry Weese, *Southwestern Community College*
Mary Ann, *Whitehurst Southern Crescent Technical College*
Sharon Williams, *Sullivan University*
Douglas Woods, *Wayne College*
Patricia Worsham, *Norco College*
Jay Wright, *New River Community College*
Douglas Yentsch, *South Central College*
Jane Zlojutro, *Northwestern Michigan College*

Acknowledgments

The authors wish to thank all of the instructors who provided feedback for the 2015 edition via surveys as well as the following supplement authors and verifiers for their most valuable suggestions and support:

D. Elizabeth Stone Atkins—*High Point University, High Point, NC*
Bernie Hill—*Pima Community College, Tucson, AZ*
Paul Shinal—*Cayga Community College, Auburn, NY*
Lisa Swallow—*University of Montana, Missoula, MT*
David Candelaria—*Mt. San Jacinto College, Menifee, CA*
Jim Clarkson—*San Jacinto College South, Houston, TX*
Susan Snow Davis—*Green River Community College, Auburn, WA*
Pennie Eddy—*Appalachian Technical College, Jasper, GA*

In addition, gratitude is expressed to Susan Gill, Steve Smith, and Kathleen Smith for their expert assistance reviewing chapters of this text. We also appreciate Susan Snow Davis from Green River Community College, who wrote the helpful guide about how to use H&R Block Premium & Business® in the tax course, which may be found on the companion website.

We appreciate your continued support in advising us of any revisions or corrections you feel are appropriate.

Gerald E. Whittenburg
Martha Altus-Buller
Steven Gill

TABLE OF CONTENTS

CHAPTER 1 The Individual Income Tax Return

LO 1.1 History and Objectives of the Tax System 1-2
LO 1.2 Reporting and Taxable Entities 1-3
LO 1.3 The Tax Formula for Individuals 1-5
LO 1.4 Who Must File 1-7
LO 1.5 Filing Status and Tax Computation 1-9
LO 1.6 Personal and Dependency Exemptions 1-13
LO 1.7 The Standard Deduction 1-19
LO 1.8 A Brief Overview of Capital Gains and Losses 1-21
LO 1.9 Special Rules for High-Income Taxpayers 1-23
LO 1.10 Tax and the Internet 1-29
LO 1.11 Electronic Filing (E-Filing) 1-31
Questions and Problems 1-34

CHAPTER 2 Gross Income and Exclusions

LO 2.1 The Nature of Gross Income 2-2
LO 2.2 Interest and Dividend Income 2-4
LO 2.3 Alimony 2-6
LO 2.4 Prizes and Awards 2-11
LO 2.5 Annuities 2-12
LO 2.6 Life Insurance 2-15
LO 2.7 Gifts and Inheritances 2-16
LO 2.8 Scholarships 2-16
LO 2.9 Accident and Health Insurance 2-17
LO 2.10 Meals and Lodging 2-18
LO 2.11 Municipal Bond Interest 2-19
LO 2.12 Unemployment Compensation 2-19
LO 2.13 Employee Fringe Benefits 2-20
LO 2.14 Social Security Benefits 2-23
Questions and Problems 2-29

CHAPTER 3 Business Income and Expenses, Part I

LO 3.1 Schedule C 3-2
LO 3.2 Inventories 3-7
LO 3.3 Transportation 3-11
LO 3.4 Travel Expenses 3-14
LO 3.5 Meals and Entertainment 3-16
LO 3.6 Educational Expenses 3-17
LO 3.7 Dues, Subscriptions, and Publications 3-19
LO 3.8 Special Clothing and Uniforms 3-20
LO 3.9 Business Gifts 3-21
LO 3.10 Bad Debts 3-22
LO 3.11 Office in the Home 3-23
LO 3.12 Net Operating Losses 3-26
LO 3.13 Hobby Losses 3-27
Questions and Problems 3-31

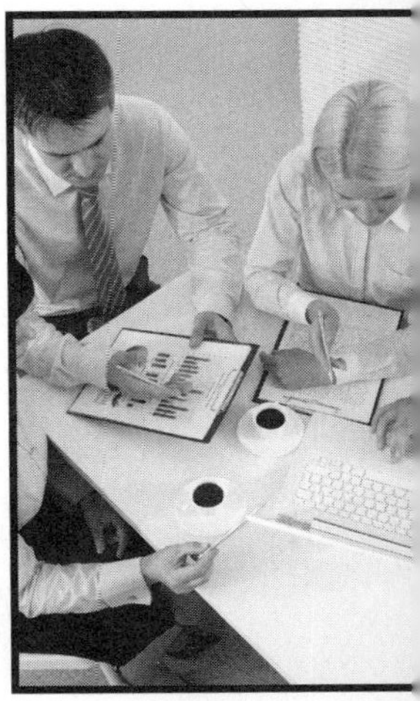

CHAPTER 4 Business Income and Expenses, Part II

LO 4.1 Rental Income and Expenses 4-2
LO 4.2 Passive Loss Limitations 4-5
LO 4.3 Self-Employed Health Insurance Deduction 4-9
LO 4.4 Health Savings Accounts 4-13
LO 4.5 Moving Expenses 4-14
LO 4.6 Individual Retirement Accounts 4-16
LO 4.7 Keogh Plans and Simplified Employee Pensions 4-23
LO 4.8 Qualified Retirement Plans Including Section 401(k) Plans 4-24
LO 4.9 Rollovers 4-27
Questions and Problems 4-32

CHAPTER 5 Itemized Deductions and Other Incentives

LO 5.1 Medical Expenses 5-2
LO 5.2 Taxes 5-5
LO 5.3 Interest 5-8
LO 5.4 Contributions 5-12
LO 5.5 Casualty and Theft Losses 5-17
LO 5.6 Miscellaneous Deductions 5-19
LO 5.7 Classification of Deductions—Employees 5-23
LO 5.8 Educational Incentives 5-24
LO 5.9 Phase-Out of Itemized Deductions and Exemptions for High-Income Taxpayers 5-30
Questions and Problems 5-34

CHAPTER 6 Credits and Special Taxes

LO 6.1 Child Tax Credit 6-2
LO 6.2 Earned Income Credit 6-2
LO 6.3 Child and Dependent Care Credit 6-3
LO 6.4 The Affordable Care Act 6-6
LO 6.5 Education Tax Credits 6-12
LO 6.6 Foreign Tax Credit 6-15
LO 6.7 Adoption Expenses 6-16
LO 6.8 Energy Credits 6-18
LO 6.9 The Individual Alternative Minimum Tax (AMT) 6-22
LO 6.10 Unearned Income of Minor Children and Certain Students 6-26
LO 6.11 Community Property 6-30
Questions and Problems 6-37

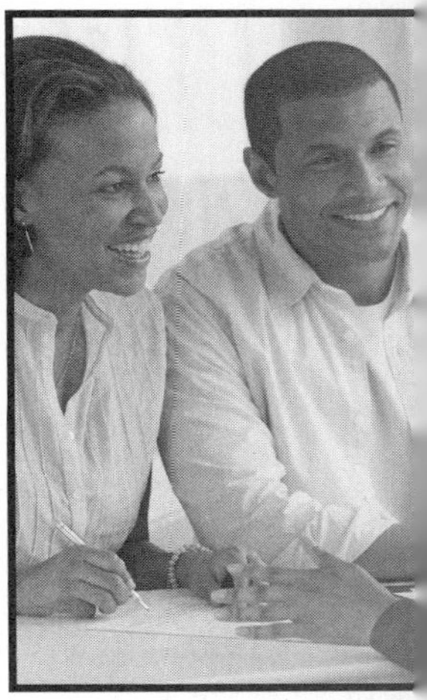

CHAPTER 7 Accounting Periods and Methods and Depreciation

LO 7.1 Accounting Periods 7-2
LO 7.2 Accounting Methods 7-3
LO 7.3 Depreciation 7-5
LO 7.4 Modified Accelerated Cost Recovery System (MACRS) 7-6
LO 7.5 Election to Expense 7-12
LO 7.6 Listed Property 7-14
LO 7.7 Limitation on Depreciation of Luxury Automobiles 7-17
LO 7.8 Intangibles 7-20
LO 7.9 Related Parties (Section 267) 7-21
Questions and Problems 7-26

CHAPTER 8 Capital Gains and Losses

LO 8.1 What Is a Capital Asset? 8-2
LO 8.2 Holding Period 8-3
LO 8.3 Calculation of Gain or Loss 8-3
LO 8.4 Net Capital Gains 8-7
LO 8.5 Net Capital Losses 8-9
LO 8.6 Section 1231 Gains and Losses 8-11
LO 8.7 Depreciation Recapture 8-12
LO 8.8 Capital Gains and Casualty Gains and Losses 8-22
LO 8.9 Installment Sales 8-25
LO 8.10 Like-Kind Exchanges 8-29
LO 8.11 Involuntary Conversions 8-31
LO 8.12 Sale of a Personal Residence 8-32
Questions and Problems 8-38

CHAPTER 9 Withholding, Estimated Payments, and Payroll Taxes

LO 9.1 Withholding Methods 9-2
LO 9.2 Estimated Payments 9-8
LO 9.3 The FICA Tax 9-9
LO 9.4 Federal Tax Deposit System 9-11
LO 9.5 Employer Reporting Requirements 9-15
LO 9.6 Self-Employment Tax 9-17
LO 9.7 The FUTA Tax 9-19
LO 9.8 The Nanny Tax 9-25
LO 9.9 Computing the 0.9 Percent Medicare Surtax for High-Income Taxpayers 9-26
Questions and Problems 9-35

CHAPTER 10 Partnership Taxation

LO 10.1 Nature of Partnership Taxation 10-2
LO 10.2 Partnership Formation 10-3
LO 10.3 Partnership Income Reporting 10-5
LO 10.4 Current Distributions and Guaranteed Payments 10-15
LO 10.5 Tax Years 10-16

LO 10.6 Transactions between Partners and the Partnership 10-16
LO 10.7 The At-Risk Rule 10-17
LO 10.8 Limited Liability Companies 10-19
Questions and Problems 10-22

CHAPTER 11 The Corporate Income Tax

LO 11.1 Corporate Tax Rates 11-2
LO 11.2 Corporate Capital Gains and Losses 11-3
LO 11.3 Special Deductions and Limitations 11-3
LO 11.4 Schedule M-1 11-6
LO 11.5 Filing Requirements and Estimated Tax 11-7
LO 11.6 S Corporations 11-15
LO 11.7 Corporate Formation 11-17
LO 11.8 Corporate Accumulations 11-25
LO 11.9 The Corporate Alternative Minimum Tax 11-25
Questions and Problems 11-29

CHAPTER 12 Tax Administration and Tax Planning

LO 12.1 The Internal Revenue Service 12-2
LO 12.2 The Audit Process 12-6
LO 12.3 Interest and Penalties 12-10
LO 12.4 Statute of Limitations 12-14
LO 12.5 Preparers, Proof, and Privilege 12-15
LO 12.6 The Taxpayer Bill of Rights 12-18
LO 12.7 Tax Planning 12-21
Questions and Problems 12-26

Appendices

Appendix A Tax Rate Schedules and Tax Tables A-1
Appendix B Earned Income Credit Table B-1
Appendix C Withholding Tables C-1
Appendix D Additional Comprehensive Tax Return Problems D-1
Appendix E Solutions to Self-Study Problems E-1
Glossary of Tax Terms G-1
Index I-1
List of Forms L-1
List of Schedules L-2

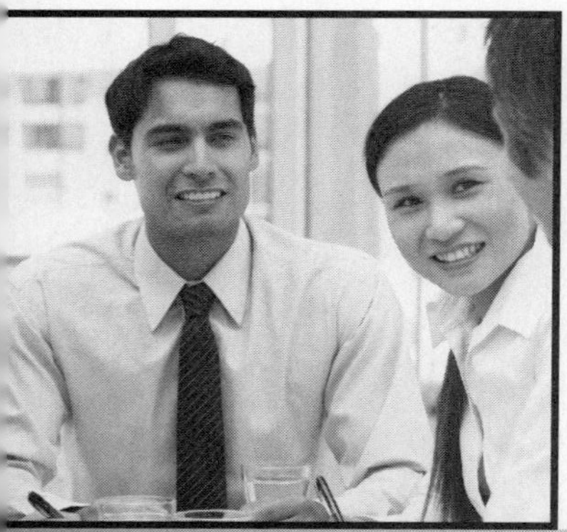

QUESTIONS

Please contact the Cengage Learning Taxation publishing team if you have any questions:

Mike Schenk, Product Director: mike.schenk@cengage.com
Sharon Oblinger, Sr. Product Manager: sharon.oblinger@cengage.com
Charisse Darin, Marketing Manager: charisse.darin@cengage.com
Kendra Brown, Sr. Content Developer: k.brown@cengage.com
Lysa Kosins, Media Content Developer: lysa.kosins@cengage.com

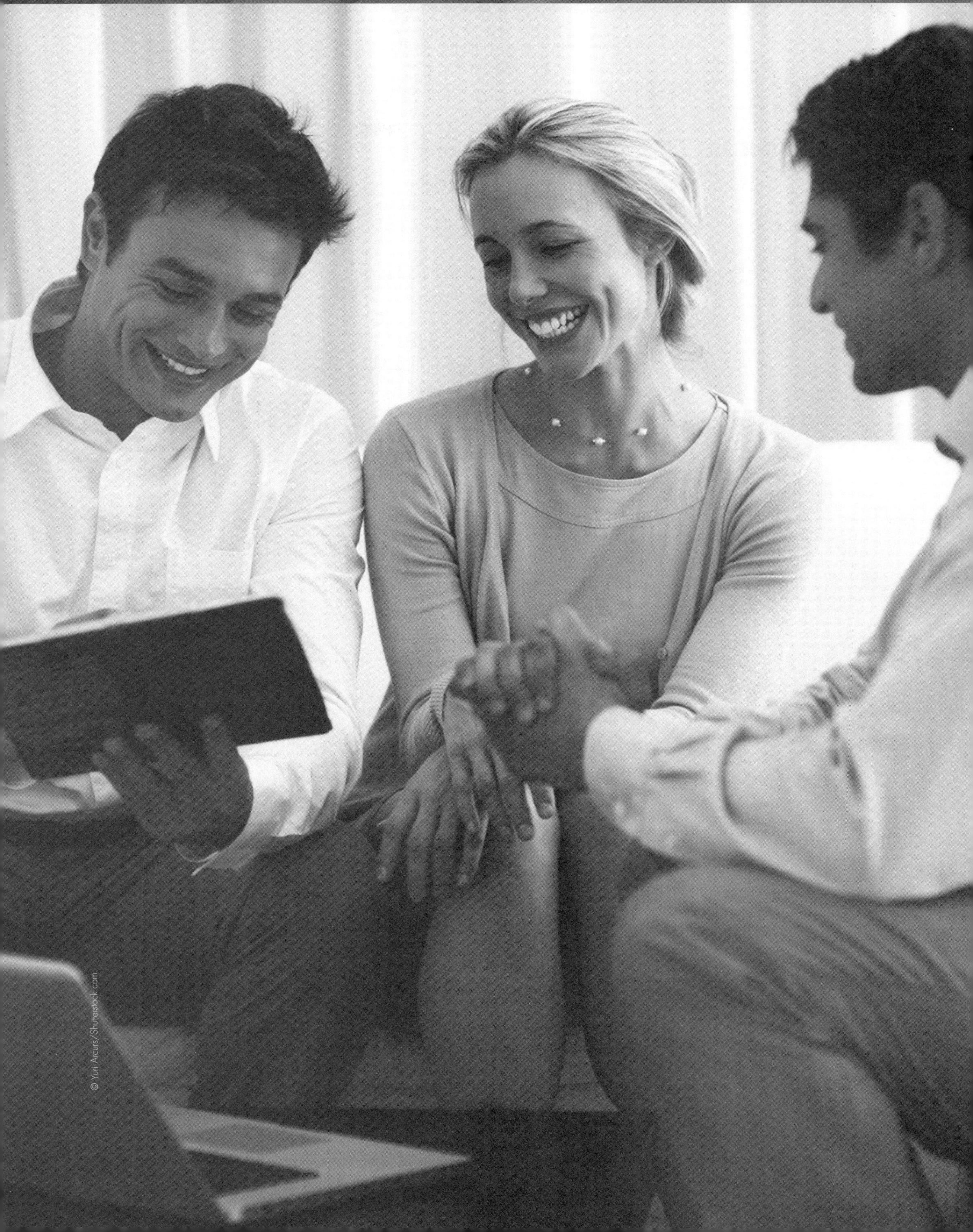

© Yuri Arcurs/Shutterstock.com

CHAPTER 1

The Individual Income Tax Return

LEARNING OBJECTIVES

After completing this chapter, you should be able to:

LO 1.1 Understand the history and objectives of U.S. tax law.

LO 1.2 Describe the different entities subject to tax and reporting requirements.

LO 1.3 Understand and apply the tax formula for individuals.

LO 1.4 Identify individuals who must file tax returns.

LO 1.5 Determine filing status and understand the calculation of tax according to filing status.

LO 1.6 Calculate the number of exemptions and the exemption amounts for taxpayers.

LO 1.7 Calculate the correct standard or itemized deduction amount for taxpayers.

LO 1.8 Compute basic capital gains and losses.

LO 1.9 Identify the new tax rules for high-income taxpayers.

LO 1.10 Access and use various Internet tax resources.

LO 1.11 Understand the basics of electronic filing (e-filing).

OVERVIEW

This chapter introduces the U.S. individual income tax system. Important elements of the individual tax formula are covered. These include the tax calculation, who must file, filing status, exemptions, and the interaction of itemized deductions and the standard deduction. The chapter illustrates all the steps required for completion of Form 1040EZ, Income Tax Return for Single and Joint Filers With No Dependents, and Form 1040A, U.S. Individual Income Tax return (short form). Also included is a discussion of reporting and taxable entities.

An introduction to capital gains and losses is included to provide a basic understanding of capital transactions prior to the detailed coverage in Chapter 8. An overview of tax information available at the IRS website and other helpful tax websites is also included. A discussion of the process for electronic filing (e-filing) of an individual tax return completes the chapter.

Learning Objective 1.1

Understand the history and objectives of U.S. tax law.

HISTORY AND OBJECTIVES OF THE TAX SYSTEM

The U.S. income tax was authorized by the Sixteenth Amendment to the Constitution on March 1, 1913. Prior to the adoption of this amendment, the U.S. government had levied various income taxes for limited periods of time. For example, an income tax was used to help finance the Civil War. The finding by the courts that the income tax law enacted in 1894 was unconstitutional eventually led to the adoption of the Sixteenth Amendment. Since adoption of the amendment, the constitutionality of the income tax has not been questioned by the federal courts.

Many people believe the sole purpose of the income tax is to raise revenue to operate the government. This belief is not accurate. The tax law has many goals other than raising revenue. These goals fall into two general categories—economic goals and social goals—and it is often unclear which goal a specific tax provision was written to meet. Tax provisions have been used for such economic motives as reduction of unemployment, expansion of investment in productive (capital) assets, and control of inflation. Specific examples of economic tax provisions are the limited allowance for expensing of capital expenditures and the accelerated cost recovery system (ACRS or MACRS) of depreciation. In addition to pure economic goals, the tax law is used to encourage certain business activities and industries. For example, an income tax credit encourages businesses to engage in research and development activities, the energy credits encourage investment in solar and wind energy businesses, and a special deduction for soil and water conservation expenditures related to farm land benefits farmers.

Social goals have also resulted in the adoption of many specific tax provisions. The child and dependent care credit, the earned income credit, and the charitable contribution deduction are examples of tax provisions designed to meet social goals. Social provisions may influence economic activities, but they are written primarily to encourage taxpayers to undertake activities to benefit themselves and society.

An example of a provision that has both economic and social objectives is the provision allowing the gain on the sale of a personal residence up to $250,000 ($500,000 if married) to be excluded from taxable income. From a social standpoint, this helps a family afford a new home, but it also helps achieve the economic goal of ensuring that the United States has a mobile workforce.

The use of the income tax as a tool to promote economic and social policies has increased in recent years. Keeping this in mind, the beginning tax student can better understand how and why the tax law has become so complex.

TAX BREAK

Every year, Congress passes laws to assist taxpayers living in disaster areas. For example, in 2014 victims of mud slides in Washington and tornados, storms and flooding in parts of Alabama, Arkansas, Florida, and Mississippi were all granted relief from various payment and filing deadlines. An abundance of information related to specific disaster relief provisions is available at the IRS website (**www.irs.gov**).

Self-Study Problem 1.1 *See Appendix E for Solutions to Self-Study Problems*

Which of the following is not a goal of the income tax system?

a. Raising revenue to operate the government.
b. Providing incentives for certain business and economic goals, such as higher employment rates, through business-favorable tax provisions.
c. Providing incentives for certain social goals, such as charitable giving, by allowing tax deductions, exclusions, or credits for selected activities.
d. All the above are goals of the income tax system.

REPORTING AND TAXABLE ENTITIES

Learning Objective 1.2

Describe the different entities subject to tax and reporting requirements.

Under U.S. tax law, there are five basic taxable or reporting entities. They are individuals, corporations, partnerships, estates, and trusts. The taxation of individuals is the major topic of this text; an overview of the taxation of partnerships and corporations is presented in Chapters 10 and 11, respectively. Taxation of estates and trusts is a specialized area not covered in this text.

The Individual

The most familiar taxable entity is the individual. Taxable income for individuals generally includes wages, salary, self-employment earnings, rent, interest, and dividends. Individual taxpayers file Form 1040EZ, Form 1040A, or Form 1040. Form 1040X is used to amend any of these three individual tax returns for changes or errors discovered after filing. Form 1040EZ is the simplest tax form, but may be used, in general, only by taxpayers who have the following characteristics:

1. The taxpayer must be single or married filing a joint return.
2. The taxpayer must not be age 65 or over and/or blind.
3. The taxpayer must not claim any dependents.
4. The taxpayer's taxable income must be less than $100,000.
5. The taxpayer's income must include only wages, salaries, certain reported tips, taxable scholarship or fellowship grants, unemployment compensation, Alaska Permanent Fund dividends, and not more than $1,500 of taxable interest income.
6. The taxpayer must not claim any credits other than the earned income credit.

Many taxpayers who cannot file Form 1040EZ file Form 1040A. Generally, Form 1040A is filed by taxpayers who are not self-employed and do not benefit from itemizing their deductions.

Form 1040, the long form, is used by all individual taxpayers who must file a tax return and do not qualify to file Form 1040EZ or Form 1040A.

An individual taxpayer's interest income (over $1,500) and dividend income (over $1,500) are reported on Schedule B of Form 1040 and Form 1040A, while self-employment income from a trade or business, other than farm or ranch activities, is included on Schedule C. Farm or ranch income is reported on Schedule F. The supplemental income schedule, Schedule E, is used to report rental or royalty income and pass-through income from partnerships, S corporations, and estates and trusts. If an individual taxpayer has capital gains or losses, he or she must generally file Schedule D to report those gains or losses. Schedule A is completed by individuals who itemize their deductions. Itemized deductions on Schedule A include medical expenses, certain taxes, certain interest, charitable contributions, casualty and theft losses, and other miscellaneous deductions. These tax forms and schedules and some less common forms are presented in this text.

The Corporation

Corporations are subject to the U.S. income tax and must report income annually on Form 1120. The tax rate schedule for corporations is:

Taxable Income Over	*But Not Over*	*The Tax Is*	*Of the Amount Over*
$ 0	$ 50,000	15%	$ 0
50,000	75,000	$ 7,500 + 25%	50,000
75,000	100,000	13,750 + 34%	75,000
100,000	335,000	22,250 + 39%	100,000
335,000	10,000,000	113,900 + 34%	335,000
10,000,000	15,000,000	3,400,000 + 35%	10,000,000
15,000,000	18,333,333	5,150,000 + 38%	15,000,000
18,333,333	—	6,416,667 + 35%	18,333,333

Some corporations may elect S corporation status. An S corporation does not pay regular corporate income taxes; instead, the corporation's income passes through to the shareholders and is included on their individual returns. Chapter 11 covers the basics of corporate taxation, including a discussion of S corporations.

The Partnership

The partnership is not a taxable entity; instead it is a reporting entity. Generally, all income or loss of a partnership is included on the individual tax returns of the partners. However, a partnership must file Form 1065 to report the amount of income or loss and show the allocation of the income or loss to the partners. The partners, in turn, report their share of ordinary income or loss on their tax returns. Other special gains, losses, income, and deductions of the partnership are reported and allocated to the partners separately, since the items are given special tax treatment at the partner level. Capital gains and losses, for example, are reported and allocated separately, and the partners report their share on Schedule D of their individual income tax returns. See Chapter 10 for a discussion of partnerships, including limited partnerships and limited liability companies.

SUMMARY OF MAJOR TAX FORMS AND SCHEDULES

Form or Schedule	*Description*
1040EZ	Individual return—single and joint filers with no dependents
1040A	Individual return, short form
1040	Individual return, long form
1040X	Amended individual return
Schedule A	Itemized deductions
Schedule B	Interest and dividend income
Schedule C	Profit or loss from business or profession (sole proprietorship)
Schedule D	Capital gains and losses
Schedule E	Supplemental income and loss (rent, royalty, and pass-through income from Forms 1065, 1120S, and 1041)
Schedule F	Farm and ranch income
1041	Fiduciary (estates and trusts) tax return
1120	Corporate tax return
1120S	S corporation tax return
1065	Partnership information return
Schedule K-1 (Form 1065)	Partner's share of partnership results

All of the forms listed here, and more, are available at the IRS website (**www.irs.gov**).

Self-Study Problem 1.2 ***See Appendix E for Solutions to Self-Study Problems***

Indicate which is the most appropriate form or schedule for each of the following items. Unless otherwise indicated in the problem, assume the taxpayer is an individual.

ITEM	*Form or Schedule*
1. Bank interest income of $1,600 received by a taxpayer who itemizes deductions	________
2. Capital gain on the sale of AT&T stock	________
3. Income from a farm	________
4. Trust's income	________
5. An individual partner's share of partnership income reported by the partnership	________
6. Salary of $70,000 for a taxpayer who itemizes deductions	________
7. Income from a sole proprietorship business	________
8. Income from rental property	________
9. Dividends of $2,000 received by a taxpayer who does not itemize deductions	________
10. Income of a large corporation	________
11. Partnership's loss	________
12. Charitable contribution deduction for an individual who itemizes deductions	________
13. Single individual with no dependents whose only income is $18,000 (all from wages) and who does not itemize deductions	________

THE TAX FORMULA FOR INDIVIDUALS

Learning Objective 1.3

Understand and apply the tax formula for individuals.

Individual taxpayers calculate their tax in accordance with a tax formula. Understanding the formula is important, since all tax determinations are based on the result. The formula is:

Gross Income
− Deductions for Adjusted Gross Income
= Adjusted Gross Income
− Greater of Itemized Deductions or the Standard Deduction
− Exemptions
= Taxable Income
× Tax Rate (using appropriate tax tables or rate schedules)
= Gross Tax Liability
− Tax Credits and Prepayments
= Tax Due or Refund

Would You Believe?

In 2013, the income tax turned 100 years old. In 1913, the basic income tax rate was 1 percent and increased up to 6 percent on incomes over $500,000 (that would be almost $12 million today). The Form 1040 was three pages long with an additional one page of instructions.

Gross Income

The calculation of taxable income begins with gross income. Gross income includes all income, unless the tax law provides for a specific exclusion. The exclusions from gross income are discussed in Chapter 2.

Deductions for Adjusted Gross Income

The first category of deductions includes the deductions for adjusted gross income. These deductions include trade or business expenses, certain reimbursed employee business expenses paid under an accountable plan, alimony payments, moving expenses, student loan interest, the penalty on early withdrawal from savings, contributions to qualified retirement plans, and if extended in 2014, certain educator expenses and a deduction for tuition and fees. Later chapters explain these deductions in detail.

Adjusted Gross Income (AGI)

The amount of adjusted gross income is sometimes referred to as the "magic line," since it is the basis for several deduction limitations, such as the limitation on medical expenses. A taxpayer's adjusted gross income is also used to determine limits on certain charitable contributions and contributions to certain individual retirement accounts.

Would You Believe?

The Wall Street Journal reported: "Humorist Dave Barry says the IRS is making progress in 'its mission to develop a tax form so scary that merely reading it will cause the ordinary tax-payer's brain to explode.'" He cites Schedule J, Form 1118: "Adjustments to Separate Limitation Income (Loss) Categories for Determining Numerators of Limitation Fractions, Year-End Recharacterization Balances, and Overall Foreign and Domestic Loss Account Balances."

Standard Deduction or Itemized Deductions

Itemized deductions are personal items that Congress has allowed as deductions. Included in this category are medical expenses, certain interest expenses, certain taxes, charitable contributions, casualty losses, and other miscellaneous items. Taxpayers should itemize their deductions only if the total amount exceeds their standard deduction amount. The following table gives the standard deduction amounts for 2014.

Filing Status	*2014 Standard Deduction*
Single	$ 6,200
Married, filing jointly	12,400
Married, filing separately	6,200
Head of Household	9,100
Qualifying widow(er)	12,400

Taxpayers who are 65 years of age or older or blind are entitled to an additional standard deduction amount. For 2014, the additional standard deduction amount is $1,550 for unmarried taxpayers and $1,200 for married taxpayers and surviving spouses. Taxpayers who are both 65 years of age or older and blind are entitled to two additional standard deduction amounts. See LO 1.7 for a complete discussion of the basic and additional standard deduction amounts.

Exemptions

Exemptions are worth $3,950 each for 2014. The two types of exemptions, personal and dependency, are described later in this chapter.

The Gross Tax Liability

A taxpayer's gross tax liability is obtained by reference to the tax table or by use of a tax rate schedule. Tax credits and prepayments are subtracted from gross tax liability to calculate the net tax due the government or the refund due the taxpayer.

TAX BREAK

Taxpayers may provide information with their individual tax return authorizing the IRS to deposit refunds directly into their bank account. Taxpayers with a balance due may pay their tax bill with a credit card, subject to an IRS fee.

Self-Study Problem 1.3 *See Appendix E for Solutions to Self-Study Problems*

Bill is a single taxpayer. In 2014, his salary is $28,500 and he has interest income of $1,500. In addition, he has deductions for adjusted gross income of $2,100 and he has $6,400 of itemized deductions. If Bill claims one exemption for this year, calculate the following amounts:

1. Gross income $________
2. Adjusted gross income $________
3. Standard deduction or itemized deduction amount $________
4. Taxable income $________

WHO MUST FILE

Learning Objective 1.4

Identify individuals who must file tax returns.

Several conditions must exist before a taxpayer is required to file a U.S. income tax return. These conditions primarily relate to the amount of the taxpayer's income and the taxpayer's filing status. Figures 1.1 through 1.3 summarize the filing requirements for taxpayers in 2014. If a taxpayer has any nontaxable income, the amount should be excluded in determining whether the taxpayer must file a return.

Taxpayers are also required to file a return if they have net earnings from self-employment of $400 or more, or owe taxes such as Social Security taxes on unreported tips. When a taxpayer is not required to file but is due a refund for overpayment of taxes, a return must be filed to obtain the refund.

A taxpayer who is required to file a return should mail the return to the appropriate IRS Campus Processing Site listed on the IRS website (**www.irs.gov**). Generally, individual returns are due on the fifteenth day of the fourth month of the year following the close of the tax year. For a calendar year taxpayer, therefore, the due date is April 15, unless the fifteenth falls on a weekend or holiday, in which case the due date is the next business day. An extension of time to file until October 15 may be requested on Form 4868 by April 15. However, all tax due must be paid by April 15 or penalties and interest will apply.

FIGURE 1.1 WHO MUST FILE

Chart A—For Most People

IF your filing status is . . .	AND at the end of 2014 you were* . . .	THEN file a return if your gross income** was at least . . .
Single (see the instructions for line 1)	under 65 65 or older	$10,150 11,700
Married filing jointly*** (see the instructions for line 2)	under 65 (both spouses) 65 or older (one spouse) 65 or older (both spouses)	$20,300 21,500 22,700
Married filing separately (see the instructions for line 3)	any age	$3,950
Head of household (see the instructions for line 4)	under 65 65 or older	$13,050 14,600
Qualifying widow(er) with dependent child (see the instructions for line 5)	under 65 65 or older	$16,350 17,550

**If you were born on January 1, 1950, you are considered to be age 65 at the end of 2014. (If your spouse died in 2014 or if you are preparing a return for someone who died in 2014, see Pub. 501.)*

*****Gross income** means all income you received in the form of money, goods, property, and services that is not exempt from tax, including any income from sources outside the United States or from the sale of your main home (even if you can exclude part or all of it). Do not include any social security benefits unless (a) you are married filing a separate return and you lived with your spouse at any time in 2014 or (b) one-half of your social security benefits plus your other gross income and any tax-exempt interest is more than $25,000 ($32,000 if married filing jointly). If (a) or (b) applies, see the instructions for lines 20a and 20b to figure the taxable part of social security benefits you must include in gross income. Gross income includes gains, but not losses, reported on Form 8949 or Schedule D. Gross income from a business means, for example, the amount on Schedule C, line 7, or Schedule F, line 9. But, in figuring gross income, do not reduce your income by any losses, including any loss on Schedule C, line 7, or Schedule F, line 9.*

****If you did not live with your spouse at the end of 2014 (or on the date your spouse died) and your gross income was at least $3,950, you must file a return regardless of your age.*

FIGURE 1.2

Chart B—For Children and Other Dependents (See the instructions for line 6c to find out if someone can claim you as a dependent.)

If your parent (or someone else) can claim you as a dependent, use this chart to see if you must file a return.

In this chart, **unearned income** includes taxable interest, ordinary dividends, and capital gain distributions. It also includes unemployment compensation, taxable social security benefits, pensions, annuities, and distributions of unearned income from a trust. **Earned income** includes salaries, wages, tips, professional fees, and taxable scholarship and fellowship grants. **Gross income** is the total of your unearned and earned income.

Single dependents. Were you **either** age 65 or older **or** blind?

☐ **No.** You must file a return if **any** of the following apply.
- Your unearned income was over $1,000.
- Your earned income was over $6,200.
- Your gross income was more than the **larger** of—
  - $1,000, or
  - Your earned income (up to $5,850) plus $350.

☐ **Yes.** You must file a return if **any** of the following apply.
- Your unearned income was over $2,550 ($4,100 if 65 or older **and** blind).
- Your earned income was over $7,750 ($9,300 if 65 or older **and** blind).
- Your gross income was more than the **larger** of—
  - $2,550 ($4,100 if 65 or older **and** blind), or
  - Your earned income (up to $5,850) plus $1,900 ($3,450 if 65 or older **and** blind).

Married dependents. Were you **either** age 65 or older **or** blind?

☐ **No.** You must file a return if **any** of the following apply.
- Your unearned income was over $1,000.
- Your earned income was over $6,200.
- Your gross income was at least $5 and your spouse files a separate return and itemizes deductions.
- Your gross income was more than the **larger** of—
  - $1,000, or
  - Your earned income (up to $5,850) plus $350.

☐ **Yes.** You must file a return if **any** of the following apply.
- Your unearned income was over $2,200 ($3,400 if 65 or older **and** blind).
- Your earned income was over $7,400 ($8,600 if 65 or older **and** blind).
- Your gross income was at least $5 and your spouse files a separate return and itemizes deductions.
- Your gross income was more than the **larger** of—
  - $2,200 ($3,400 if 65 or older **and** blind), or
  - Your earned income (up to $5,850) plus $1,550 ($2,750 if 65 or older **and** blind).

FIGURE 1.3

Chart C—Other Situations When You Must File

You must file a return if any of the five conditions below apply for 2014.

1. You owe any special taxes, including any of the following.

a. Alternative minimum tax.

b. Additional tax on a qualified plan, including an individual retirement arrangement (IRA), or other tax-favored account. But if you are filing a return only because you owe this tax, you can file **Form 5329** by itself.

c. Household employment taxes. But if you are filing a return only because you owe this tax, you can file **Schedule H** by itself.

d. Social security and Medicare tax on tips you did not report to your employer or on wages you received from an employer who did not withhold these taxes.

e. Recapture of first-time homebuyer credit. See the instructions for line 60b.

f. Write-in taxes, including uncollected social security and Medicare or RRTA tax on tips you reported to your employer or on group-term life insurance and additional taxes on health savings accounts. See the instructions for line 62.

g. Recapture taxes. See the instructions for line 44 and line 62.

2. You (or your spouse, if filing jointly) received HSA, Archer MSA, or Medicare Advantage MSA distributions.

3. You had net earnings from self-employment of at least $400.

4. You had wages of $108.28 or more from a church or qualified church-controlled organization that is exempt from employer social security and Medicare taxes.

5. Advance payments of the premium tax credit were made for you, your spouse, or a dependent who enrolled in coverage through the Health Insurance Marketplace. You should have received Form(s) 1095-A showing the amount of the advance payments, if any.

TAX BREAK

More than 8 million people file tax returns every year even though their wages and other income are too low to require filing according to the Treasury Inspector General for Tax Administration (TIGTA). TIGTA estimated that taxpayers spend $390 million and 75 million hours preparing and filing unnecessary tax returns each year. Therefore, the first step in preparing a tax return should be to determine if the taxpayer is actually required to file.

Self-Study Problem 1.4 *See Appendix E for Solutions to Self-Study Problems*

Indicate by a check mark whether the following taxpayers are required to file a return for 2014 in each of the following independent situations:

	Filing Required? Yes	No
1. Taxpayer (age 45) is single with income of $8,300.	_____	_____
2. Husband (age 67) and wife (age 64) have an income of $18,000 and file a joint return.	_____	_____
3. Taxpayer is a college student with a salary from a part-time job of $6,500. She is claimed as a dependent by her parents.	_____	_____
4. Taxpayer has net earnings from self-employment of $4,000.	_____	_____
5. Taxpayers are married with income of $15,900 and file a joint return. They expect a refund of $600 from excess withholding.	_____	_____
6. Taxpayer is a waiter and has unreported tips of $450.	_____	_____
7. Taxpayer is a qualifying widow (age 48) with a dependent son (age 18) and income of $16,800.	_____	_____

FILING STATUS AND TAX COMPUTATION

Learning Objective 1.5
Determine filing status and understand the calculation of tax according to filing status.

An important step in calculating the amount of a taxpayer's tax is the determination of the taxpayer's correct filing status. The tax law has five different filing statuses: single; married, filing jointly; married, filing separately; head of household; and qualifying widow(er). A tax table that must be used by most taxpayers, showing the tax liability for all five statuses, is provided in Appendix A. The tax table must be used unless the taxpayer's taxable income is $100,000 or over or the taxpayer is using a special method to calculate the tax liability. If taxpayers can use the tax table to determine their tax, they must do so; otherwise, a tax rate schedule is used. Each filing status has a separate tax rate schedule as presented in Appendix A.

Single Filing Status

A taxpayer who does not meet the definition of married, qualifying widow(er), or head of household status must file as single. This status must be used by any taxpayer who is unmarried or legally separated from his/her spouse by divorce or separate maintenance decree as of December 31 of the tax year. State law governs whether a taxpayer is married, divorced,

or legally separated. If a taxpayer's spouse dies during the year, the taxpayer's status is married for that year.

Married Filing Jointly

Taxpayers are considered married for tax purposes if they are married on December 31 of the tax year. Also, in the year of one spouse's death, the spouses are considered married for the full year. In most situations, married taxpayers pay less tax by filing jointly than by filing separately. Married taxpayers may file a joint return even if they did not live together for the entire year.

© ER_09/Shutterstock.com

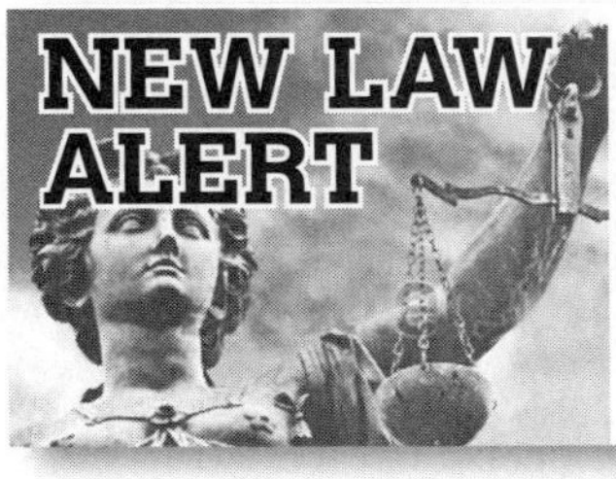

In 2013, the U.S. Supreme Court struck down parts of the Defense of Marriage Act enabling same-sex couples to file joint federal tax returns. The general rule recognizes a marriage that was validly entered into in a state or foreign jurisdiction whose laws authorize same-sex marriages, even when the married couple resides currently in a jurisdiction that does not recognize the validity of same-sex marriages.

Married Filing Separately

Married taxpayers may file separate returns and should do so if it reduces their total tax liability. They may file separately if one or both had income during the year. If separate returns are filed, both taxpayers must compute their tax in the same manner. For example, if one spouse itemizes deductions, the other spouse must also itemize deductions. Each taxpayer reports his or her income, deductions, and credits and is responsible only for the tax due on his or her return. If the taxpayers live in a community property state, they must follow state law to determine community income and separate income. The community property states include Arizona, California, Idaho, Louisiana, Nevada, New Mexico, Texas, Washington, and Wisconsin. See Chapter 6 for additional discussion regarding income and losses from community property.

A legally married taxpayer may file as head of household (based on the general filing status rules) if he or she qualifies as an abandoned spouse. A taxpayer qualifies as an abandoned spouse only if *all* of the following requirements are met:

1. A separate return is filed,
2. The taxpayer paid more than half the cost (rent, utilities, etc.) to maintain his or her home during the year,
3. The spouse did not live with the taxpayer at any time in the last 6 months of the year, and
4. For over 6 months during the year the home was the principal residence for a dependent child, stepchild, or adopted child. Under certain conditions a foster child may qualify as a dependent.

In certain circumstances, married couples may be able to reduce their total tax liability by filing separately. For instance, since some itemized deductions, such as medical expenses and casualty losses, are reduced by a percentage of adjusted gross income (discussed in Chapter 5), a spouse with a casualty loss and low separate adjusted gross income may be better off filing separately.

Head of Household

If an unmarried taxpayer can meet special tests, he or she is allowed to file as head of household. Head of household rates are lower than rates for single or married filing separately. A taxpayer qualifies for head of household status if both of the following conditions exist:

1. The taxpayer was unmarried or an abandoned spouse as of December 31 of the tax year, and
2. The taxpayer paid more than half of the cost of keeping a home that was the principal place of residence of a dependent child or other qualifying dependent relative. An unrelated dependent or a dependent, such as a cousin, who is too distantly related, will not qualify the taxpayer for head of household status. If the dependent is the taxpayer's parent, the parent need not live with the taxpayer. In all cases other than dependent parents, who may maintain a separate residence, the qualifying dependent relative must actually live in the same household as the taxpayer. A divorced parent who meets the above requirements, but has signed an IRS form or a qualifying legal agreement shifting the dependency deduction to his or her ex-spouse, may still file using head of household status.

TAX BREAK

Divorcing couples may save significant taxes if one or both of the spouses qualifies as an "abandoned spouse" and can use the head of household filing status. The combination of head of household filing status for one spouse with married filing separately filing status for the other spouse is commonly seen in the year (or years) leading up to a divorce. In cases where each spouse has custody of a child, the separated taxpayers may each claim head of household status.

Qualifying Widow(er) with Dependent Child

A taxpayer may continue to benefit from the joint return rates for 2 years after the death of his or her spouse. To qualify to use the joint return rates, the widow(er) must pay over half the cost of maintaining a household where a dependent child, stepchild, adopted child, or foster child lives. After the 2-year period, these taxpayers usually qualify for the head of household filing status.

Tax Computation

For 2014, there are seven income tax brackets (10 percent, 15 percent, 25 percent, 28 percent, 33 percent, 35 percent, and 39.6 percent). The individual tax rates for 2014 are presented in the tax rate schedules in Appendix A. The tax rate schedule for single taxpayers is summarized below. Certain high-income taxpayers are subject to additional taxes discussed in LO 1.9.

Single Tax Rate Schedule

If taxable income is over—	But not over—	The tax is:	Of the amount over—
$ 0	$ 9,075	---------- + 10%	$ 0
9,075	36,900	$ 907.50 + 15%	9,075
36,900	89,350	5,081.25 + 25%	36,900
89,350	186,350	18,193.75 + 28%	89,350
186,350	405,100	45,353.75 + 33%	186,350
405,100	406,750	117,541.25 + 35%	405,100
406,750	----------	118,188.75 + 39.6%	406,750

Tax Tables

The tax rates applicable to net long-term capital gains currently range from 0 percent to 31.8 percent depending on the taxpayer's tax bracket and the kind of capital asset. The

calculation of the tax on capital gains is discussed in detail in Chapter 8, and the applicable tax rates are discussed in LO 1.8 of this chapter.

The tax rates for qualifying dividends, discussed in detail in Chapter 2, range from 0 percent to 23.8 percent in 2014.

EXAMPLE Carol, a single taxpayer claiming one exemption, has adjusted gross income of $120,000 and taxable income of $105,000 for 2014. Her tax is calculated using the 2014 tax rate schedule from Appendix A as follows:

$22,575.75 = $18,193.75 + 28% × ($105,000 − $89,350) ♦

EXAMPLE Meg is a single taxpayer during 2014. Her taxable income for the year is $27,530. Using the tax table in Appendix A, her gross tax liability for the year is found to be $3,675. ♦

TAX BREAK

Taxpayers considering marriage may be able to save thousands of dollars by engaging in tax planning prior to setting a date. If the couple would pay less in taxes by filing as married rather than as single (which will frequently happen if one spouse has low earnings for the year), they may prefer a December wedding. They can take advantage of the rule that requires taxpayers to file as married for the full year if they were married on the last day of the year. On the other hand, if filing a joint return would cause the couple to pay more in taxes (which frequently happens if both spouses have high incomes), they may prefer a January wedding.

Self-Study Problem 1.5 *See Appendix E for Solutions to Self-Study Problems*

Indicate the filing status (or statuses) in each of the following independent cases, using this legend:

A – Single
B – Married, filing a joint return
C – Married, filing separate returns
D – Head of household
E – Qualifying widow(er)

Case	***Filing Status***
1. The taxpayers are married on December 31 of the tax year.	__________
2. The taxpayer is single, with a dependent child living in her home.	__________
3. The taxpayer is unmarried and is living with his girlfriend.	__________
4. The taxpayer is married and his spouse left midyear and has disappeared. The taxpayer has no dependents.	__________
5. The unmarried taxpayer supports her dependent mother, who lives in her own home.	__________
6. The taxpayer's wife died last year. His 15-year-old dependent son lives with him.	__________

PERSONAL AND DEPENDENCY EXEMPTIONS

Learning Objective 1.6

Calculate the number of exemptions and the exemption amounts for taxpayers.

Taxpayers are allowed two types of exemptions: personal and dependency. For 2014, each exemption reduces adjusted gross income by $3,950.

Personal Exemptions

Personal exemptions are granted to taxpayers for themselves; almost all taxpayers and spouses are entitled to one personal exemption each. Children who may be claimed as dependents on their parents' tax returns are not allowed to claim a personal exemption for themselves on their own tax returns.

Would You Believe?

The IRS started requiring the disclosure of Social Security numbers for each dependent claimed by a taxpayer to stop dishonest taxpayers from making up extra dependents or even claiming pets. Before this change, listing phony dependents was one of the most common forms of tax fraud. Reportedly, 7 million dependents disappeared from the tax rolls after Congress required taxpayers to include dependents' Social Security numbers on tax returns.

Dependency Exemptions

Dependency exemptions are granted for each person, other than the taxpayer or spouse who qualifies as a dependent. A dependent is an individual who meets the tests discussed below to be considered either a *qualifying child* or a *qualifying relative*.

Qualifying Child

For a child to be a dependent, he or she must meet the following tests:

1. **Relationship Test**
   The child must be the taxpayer's child, stepchild, or adopted child, or the taxpayer's brother or sister, half brother or half sister, or stepsibling, or a descendant of any of these. Under certain circumstances, a foster child can also qualify. The child must be younger than the person claiming him or her unless the child is permanently disabled.
2. **Domicile Test**
   The child must have the same principal place of abode as the taxpayer for more than half of the taxable year. In satisfying this requirement, temporary absences from the household due to special circumstances such as illness, education, and vacation are not considered.
3. **Age Test**
   The child must be under age 19 or a full-time student under the age of 24. A child is considered a full-time student if enrolled full-time for at least 5 months of the year. Thus, a college senior graduating in May or June can qualify in the year of graduation.
4. **Joint Return Test**
   The child must not file a joint return with his or her spouse. If neither the spouse nor the child is required to file, but they file a return merely to claim a refund of tax, they are not considered to have filed a return for purposes of this test.

5. **Citizenship Test**
   The dependent must be a U.S. citizen, a resident of the United States, Canada, or Mexico, or an alien child adopted by and living with a U.S. citizen.
6. **Self-Support Test**
   A child who provides more than one-half of his or her own support cannot be claimed as a dependent of someone else. Support includes expenditures for items such as food, lodging, clothes, medical and dental care, and education. To calculate support, the taxpayer uses the actual cost of the above items, except lodging. The value of lodging is calculated at its fair rental value. Funds received by students as scholarships are excluded from the support test.

In the event that a child satisfies the requirements of dependency for more than one taxpayer, the following tie-breaking rules apply:

- If one of the individuals eligible to claim the child is a parent, that person will be allowed the exemption.
- If both parents qualify (separate returns are filed), then the parent with whom the child resides the longest during the year prevails. If the residence period is the same or is not ascertainable, then the parent with the highest AGI (Adjusted Gross Income) prevails.
- If no parents are involved, the taxpayer with the highest AGI prevails.

EXAMPLE Bill, age 12, lives in the same household with Irene, his mother, and Darlene, his aunt. Bill qualifies as a dependent of both Irene and Darlene. Since Irene is Bill's mother, she has the right to claim Bill as a dependent. The tie-breaking rules are not necessary if the taxpayer who would get the exemption does not claim the exemption. Hence, Darlene can claim Bill as a dependent if Irene does not claim him. ♦

In the case of divorced or legally separated parents with children, the dependency exemption for a child belongs to the parent with whom the child lived for more than 6 months out of the year. The exemption can be shifted to the noncustodial parent if the custodial parent signs IRS Form 8332, and the form is attached to the noncustodial parent's tax return.

Figure 1.4 illustrates the interaction of the qualifying child dependency tests described above.

Qualifying Relative

A person who is not a qualifying child can be a qualifying relative if the following five-part test is met. A child of a taxpayer who does not meet the tests to be a qualifying child can still qualify as a dependent under the qualifying relative tests described below.

1. **Relationship or Member of Household Test**
   The individual must either be a relative of the taxpayer or a member of the household. The list of qualifying relatives is broad and includes parents, grandparents, children, grandchildren, siblings, aunts and uncles by blood, nephews and nieces, "in-laws," and adopted children. Foster children may also qualify in certain circumstances. If the potential dependent is a more distant relative, additional information is available at the IRS website (**www.irs.gov**). For example, cousins are not considered relatives for this purpose.

FIGURE 1.4 **DEPENDENCY EXEMPTION TESTS FLOW CHART FOR QUALIFYING CHILD**

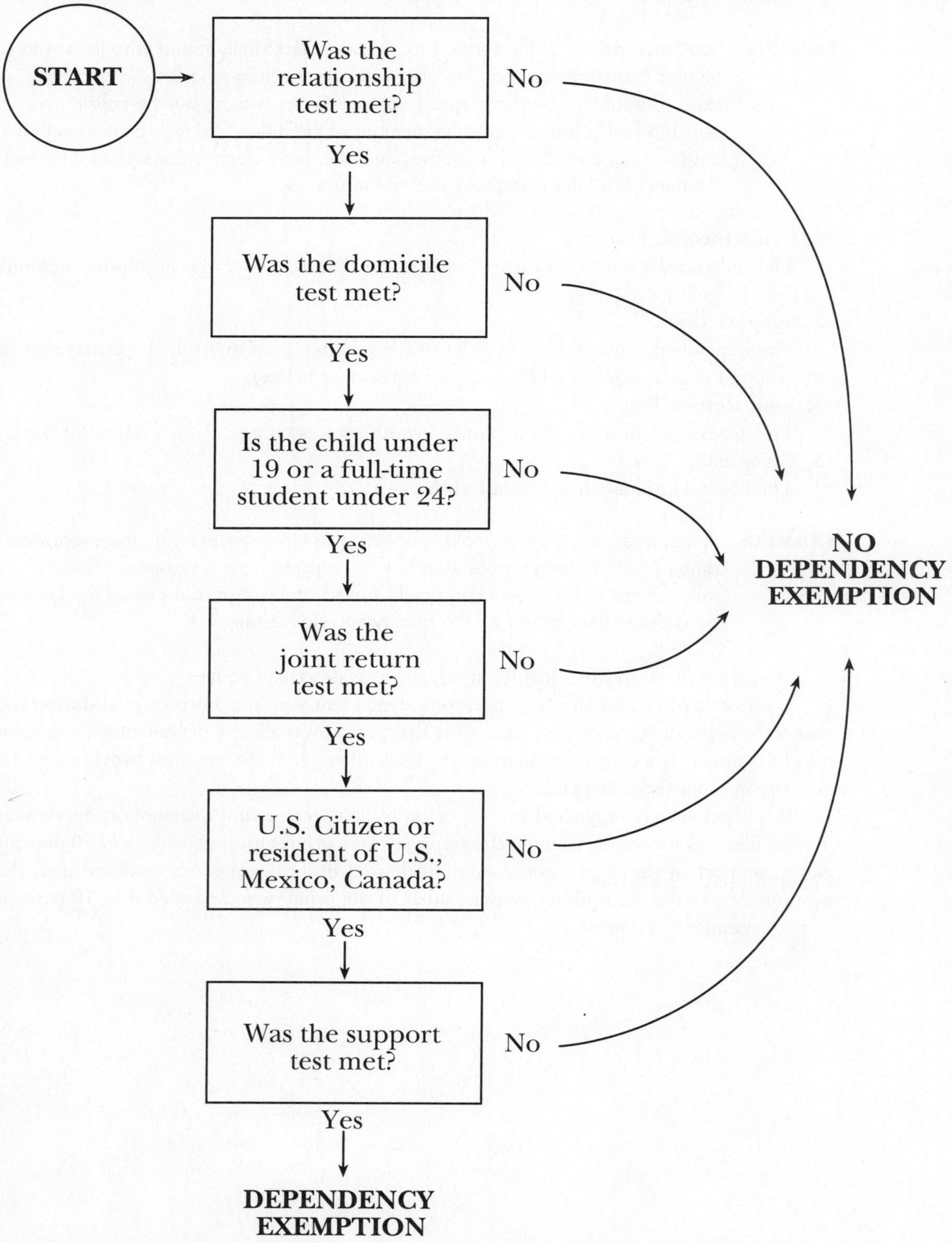

© Cengage Learning

In addition to the relatives listed, any person who lived in the taxpayer's home as a member of the household for the entire year meets the relationship test. A person is not considered a member of the household if at any time during the year the relationship between the taxpayer and the dependent was in violation of local law.

EXAMPLE Scott provides all of the support for an unrelated family friend who lives with him for the entire tax year. He also supports a cousin who lives in another state. The family friend can qualify as Scott's dependent, but the cousin cannot. The family friend meets the member of the household test. Even though the cousin is not considered a relative, he could have been a dependent if he met the member of the household part of the test. ♦

2. **Gross Income Test**
   The individual cannot have gross income equal to or above the exemption amount ($3,950 in 2014).
3. **Support Test**
   The dependent must receive over half of his or her support from the taxpayer or a group of taxpayers (see multiple support agreement below).
4. **Joint Return Test**
   The dependent must not file a joint return unless it is only to claim a refund of taxes.
5. **Citizenship Test**
   The dependent must meet the citizenship test.

EXAMPLE A taxpayer has a 26-year-old son with gross income less than the exemption amount who receives more than half his support from his parents. The son fails the test to be a qualifying child based on his age, but passes the test to be a dependent based on the qualifying relative rules. ♦

Figure 1.5 illustrates the qualifying relative tests described above.

A taxpayer can claim an exemption for a dependent who was born or died during the year if the dependency tests were met while that person was alive. A dependency exemption may be claimed for a baby born on or before December 31. Taxpayers must provide a Social Security number for all dependents.

If a dependent is supported by two or more taxpayers, a multiple support agreement may be filed. To file the agreement, the taxpayers (as a group) must provide over 50 percent of the support of the dependent. Assuming that all other dependency tests are met, the group may give the exemption to any member of the group who provided over 10 percent of the dependent's support.

FIGURE 1.5 DEPENDENCY EXEMPTION TESTS FLOW CHART FOR QUALIFYING RELATIVE

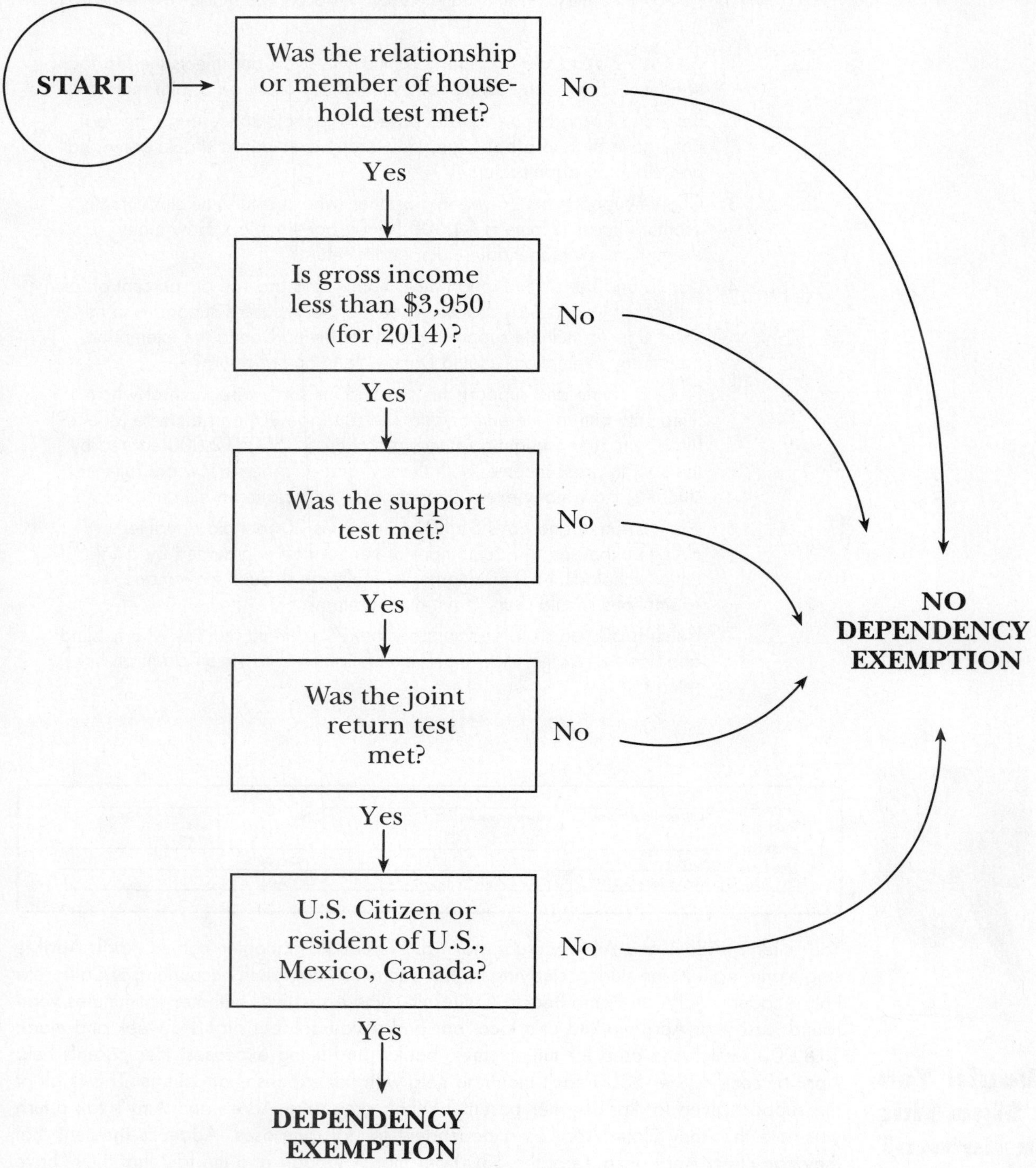

© Cengage Learning

Self-Study Problem 1.6

See Appendix E for Solutions to Self-Study Problems

Indicate in each of the following independent situations the number of exemptions the taxpayer should claim on his 2014 income tax return. If a test is not mentioned, you should consider that it is met.

_______ 1. Abel is 72 years old and married. His wife is 64 and meets the test for blindness. How many exemptions should they claim on a joint return?

_______ 2. Betty and Bob are married and have a 4-year-old son. During the year Betty gave birth to a baby girl. How many exemptions should Betty and Bob claim on a joint return?

_______ 3. Charlie supports his 26-year-old brother, who is a full-time student. His brother's gross income is $4,500 from a part-time job. How many exemptions should Charlie claim on his return?

_______ 4. Donna and her sister support their mother and provide 60 percent of her support. If Donna provides 25 percent of her mother's support and her sister signs a multiple support agreement giving Donna the exemption, how many exemptions should Donna claim on her return?

_______ 5. Frank is single and supports his son and his son's wife, both of whom lived with him for the entire year. The son (age 20) and his wife (age 19) file a joint return to get a refund, reporting $2,500 ($2,000 earned by the son) in gross income. Both the son and daughter-in-law are full-time students. How many exemptions should Frank claim on his return?

_______ 6. Gary is single and pays $5,000 toward his 20-year-old daughter's college expenses. The remainder of her support is provided by a $9,500 tuition scholarship. The daughter is a full-time student. How many exemptions should Gary claim on his return?

_______ 7. Helen is 50 years old and supports her 72-year-old mother, who is blind and has no income. How many exemptions should Helen claim on her return?

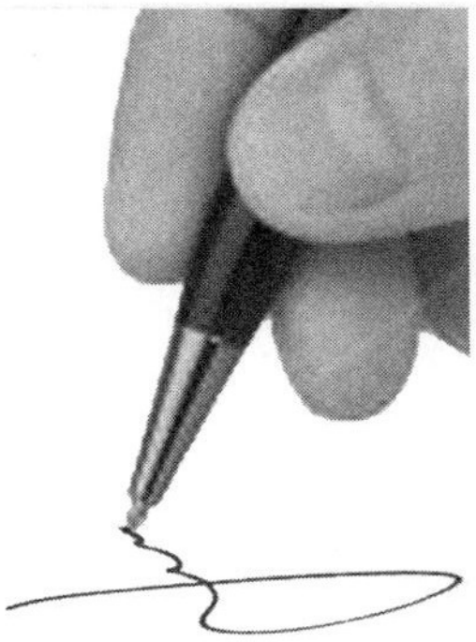

© Ilya Akinshin/Shutterstock.com; © Zhukov Oleg/Shutterstock.com

Would You Sign This Tax Return?

Paid Preparer Use Only	Print/Type preparer's name	Preparer's signature	Date	Check ☐ if self-employed	PTIN
	Firm's name ▶		Firm's EIN ▶		
	Firm's address ▶		Phone no.		

Your clients, Adam and Amy Accrual, have a 21-year-old daughter named April. April is single and is a full-time student studying for her bachelor's degree in accounting at California Poly Academy (CPA) in Pismo Beach, California, where she lives with her roommates year-round. Last year April worked at a local bar and restaurant four nights a week and made $18,000, which she used for tuition, fees, books, and living expenses. Her parents help April by sending her $300 each month to help with her expenses at college. This is all of the support given to April by her parents. When preparing Adam and Amy's tax return you note that they claim April as a dependent for tax purposes. Adam is insistent that they can claim April because of the $300 per month support and the fact that they "have claimed her since she was born." He will not let you take April off his return as a dependent. Would you sign the Paid Preparer's declaration (see example above) on this return? Why or why not?

THE STANDARD DEDUCTION

Learning Objective 1.7

Calculate the correct standard or itemized deduction amount for taxpayers.

The standard deduction was placed in the tax law to provide relief for taxpayers with few itemized deductions. The amount of the standard deduction is subtracted from adjusted gross income by taxpayers who do not itemize their deductions. If a taxpayer's gross income is less than the standard deduction amount, the taxpayer has no taxable income. The standard deduction amounts are presented below:

Filing Status	*2014 Standard Deduction*
Single	$ 6,200
Married, filing jointly	12,400
Married, filing separately	6,200
Head of household	9,100
Qualifying widow(er)	12,400

TAX BREAK

Taxpayers may be able to reduce taxes by itemizing deductions on Schedule A of Form 1040 rather than claiming the standard deduction. The U.S. General Accounting Office has estimated that close to a billion dollars a year may be lost by taxpayers who fail to itemize their deductions.

Additional Amounts for Old Age and Blindness

Taxpayers who are 65 years of age or older or blind are entitled to an additional standard deduction amount. For 2014, the additional standard deduction amount is $1,550 for unmarried taxpayers and $1,200 for married taxpayers and qualifying widows or widowers. Taxpayers who are both at least 65 years old and blind are entitled to two additional standard deduction amounts. The additional standard deduction amounts are also available for the taxpayer's spouse, but not for dependents. An individual is considered blind for purposes of receiving an additional standard deduction amount if:

1. Central visual acuity does not exceed 20/200 in the better eye with correcting lenses, or
2. Visual acuity is greater than 20/200 but is limited to a field of vision not greater than 20 degrees.

EXAMPLE John is single and 70 years old in 2014. His standard deduction is $7,750 ($6,200 plus an additional $1,550 for being 65 years of age or older). ♦

EXAMPLE Bob and Mary are married in 2014 and file a joint return. Bob is age 68, and Mary is 63 and meets the test for blindness. Their standard deduction is $14,800 ($12,400 plus $1,200 for Bob being 65 years or older and another $1,200 for Mary's blindness). ♦

Individuals Not Eligible for the Standard Deduction

The following taxpayers cannot use the standard deduction, but must itemize instead:

1. A married individual filing a separate return, whose spouse itemizes deductions.
2. A nonresident alien.
3. An individual filing a short-period tax return because of a change in the annual accounting period.

EXAMPLE Ed and Ann are married individuals who file separate returns for 2014. Ed itemizes his deductions on his return. Ann's adjusted gross income is $12,000, and she has itemized deductions of $900. Ann's taxable income is calculated as follows:

Adjusted gross income	$ 12,000
Itemized deductions	(900)
Exemption amount	(3,950)
Taxable income	$ 7,150

Since Ed itemizes his deductions, Ann must also itemize deductions and is not entitled to use the standard deduction amount. ♦

Special Limitations for Dependents

The standard deduction is limited for the tax return of a dependent. The total standard deduction may not exceed the greater of $1,000 or the sum of $350 plus the dependent's earned income up to the basic standard deduction amount in total (e.g., $6,200 for single taxpayers), plus any additional standard deduction amount for old age or blindness. The standard deduction amount for old age and blindness is only allowed when a dependent files a tax return. It is not allowed to increase the standard deduction of the taxpayer claiming the dependent. Also, remember that a dependent may not claim a personal exemption on his or her own return.

EXAMPLE Penzer, who is 8 years old, earned $6,600 as a child model during 2014. A dependency exemption for Penzer is claimed by his parents on their tax return. Penzer is required to file a tax return, and his taxable income will be $400 ($6,600 less $6,200, the standard deduction amount). He is not allowed to claim an exemption for himself. If Penzer had earned only $400, his standard deduction would be $1,000 (the greater of $1,000 or $750 [$400 + $350]), and he would not owe any tax or be required to file a return. ♦

EXAMPLE Geoffrey, who is 4 years old, earned $6,500 of interest income on a large bank account left to him by his grandmother. He had no earned income. His standard deduction is $1,000 (the greater of $1,000 or $350). He is not allowed an exemption, because he is a dependent. His taxable income will be $5,500 ($6,500 less $1,000, the standard deduction amount). Dependent children may be taxed at their parents' tax rates when their taxable income is made up of unearned income, such as interest. The special "kiddie tax" calculations are covered in Chapter 6. ♦

Self-Study Problem 1.7 ***See Appendix E for Solutions to Self-Study Problems***

Indicate in each of the following independent situations the amount of the standard deduction the taxpayers should claim on their 2014 income tax returns.

________ 1. Adam is 45 years old, in good health, and single.

________ 2. Bill and Betty are married and file a joint return. Bill is 66 years old, and Betty is 60.

________ 3. Charlie is 70, single, and blind.

________ 4. Debbie qualifies for head of household filing status, is 35 years old, and is in good health.

________ 5. Elizabeth is 9 years old, and her only income is $3,600 of interest on a savings account. She is claimed as a dependent on her parents' tax return.

________ 6. Frank and Frieda are married with two dependent children. They file a joint return, are in good health, and both of them are under 65 years of age.

A BRIEF OVERVIEW OF CAPITAL GAINS AND LOSSES

Learning Objective 1.8

Compute basic capital gains and losses.

When a taxpayer sells an asset, there is normally a gain or loss on the transaction. Depending on the kind of asset sold, this gain or loss will have different tax consequences. Chapter 8 of this text has detailed coverage of the effect of gains and losses on a taxpayer's tax liability. Because of their importance to the understanding of the calculation of an individual's tax liability, however, a brief overview of gains and losses will be discussed here.

The amount of gain or loss realized by a taxpayer is determined by subtracting the *adjusted basis* of the asset from the *amount realized*. Generally, the adjusted basis of an asset is its cost less any depreciation (covered in Chapter 7) taken on the asset. The amount realized is generally what the taxpayer receives from the sale (e.g., the sales price less any cost of the sale). The formula for calculation of gain or loss can be stated as follows:

Gain (or loss) = Amount realized − Adjusted basis

Most gains and losses realized are also recognized for tax purposes. That is, most gains or losses that occur are included in the taxpayer's taxable income. The exceptions to this general tax recognition rule are discussed in Chapter 8.

EXAMPLE Lisa purchased a rental house a few years ago for $100,000. Total depreciation to date on the house is $25,000. In the current year she sells the house for $155,000 and receives $147,000 after paying selling expenses of $8,000. Her gain on the sale is $72,000, calculated as follows:

Amount realized ($155,000 − $8,000)	$ 147,000
Adjusted basis ($100,000 − $25,000)	(75,000)
Gain realized	$ 72,000

This gain realized will be recognized as a taxable gain. ♦

Capital Gains and Losses

Gains and losses can be either *ordinary* or *capital*. Ordinary gains and losses are treated for tax purposes just like other items of income such as salaries and interest, and they are taxed at ordinary rates. Capital gains and losses receive special tax treatment.

In general, a capital asset is any property (either personal or investment) held by a taxpayer, with certain exceptions as listed in the tax law (see Chapter 8). Examples of capital assets held by individual taxpayers include stocks, bonds, land, cars, boats, and other items held as investments or for personal use. Typical assets that are not capital assets are inventory and accounts receivable.

The rates on long-term (held more than 12 months) capital gains are summarized as follows:

Ordinary Tax Bracket	*2014 Capital Gains Tax Rates**
10% and 15%	0%
25% through 35%	15%
39.6%	20%

*Special higher rates for "high-income" taxpayers are covered in LO 1.9.

Gain from property held 12 months or less is deemed to be short-term capital gain and is taxed at ordinary income rates. Capital gains from the sale of assets that have been depreciated, or capital gains from "collectibles," may be taxed at higher rates as discussed in Chapter 8.

EXAMPLE In 2014, Chris sells AT&T stock for $25,000. He purchased the stock 5 years ago for $15,000, giving him an adjusted basis of $15,000 and a long-term gain of $10,000. Chris' taxable income without the sale of the stock is $150,000, which puts him in the 28 percent tax bracket. The tax due on the long-term capital gain would be $1,500 (15% × $10,000) instead of $2,800 (28% × $10,000) if the gain on the stock were treated as ordinary income. ♦

When calculating capital gain or loss, the taxpayer must net all capital asset transactions to determine the nature of the final gain or loss (see LO 8.4 for a discussion of this calculation). If an individual taxpayer ends up with a net capital loss (short-term or long-term), up to $3,000 per year can be deducted against ordinary income. The net loss not used in the current year may be carried forward and used to reduce taxable income in future years (see LO 8.5 for a discussion of capital losses). Losses from capital assets held for personal purposes, such as a nonbusiness auto or a personal residence, are not deductible, even though gains on personal assets are taxable.

TAX BREAK

Taxpayers may wish to postpone the sale of capital assets until the holding period is met to qualify for the preferential long-term capital gains rate. Of course, there is always the risk that postponing the sale of a capital asset such as stock may result in a loss if the price of the stock decreases below its cost during volatile markets. The economic risks of a transaction should always be considered along with the tax benefits.

EXAMPLE Amy purchased gold coins as an investment. She paid $50,000 for the coins. This year she sells the coins to a dealer for $35,000. As a result, Amy has a $15,000 capital loss. She may deduct $3,000 of the loss against her other income this year. The remaining unused loss of $12,000 ($15,000 − $3,000) is carried forward and may be deducted against other income in future years. Of course, the carryover is subject to the $3,000 annual limitation in future years. ♦

TAX BREAK

Volunteer Income Tax Assistance (VITA) Program

Many universities and colleges run VITA sites in conjunction with their accounting programs. This is a small but vital part of the VITA program run by the IRS. The majority of the VITA sites are not run by schools, but rather by community groups, such as churches, senior groups (AARP), military bases, etc. If a student has a chance to participate in a VITA program, he or she should do so if at all possible. The experience provides valuable insight into preparing tax returns for others.

The Volunteer Income Tax Assistance (VITA) program offers free tax help to people who generally make $52,000 or less, persons with disabilities, the elderly and limited English speaking taxpayers who need assistance in preparing their own tax returns. IRS-certified volunteers provide free basic income tax return preparation with electronic filing to qualified individuals. VITA sites are generally located at community and neighborhood centers, libraries, schools, shopping malls and other convenient locations across the country. Please see the IRS website to locate the nearest VITA site and for more information.

Self-Study Problem 1.8 *See Appendix E for Solutions to Self-Study Problems*

Erin purchased stock in JKL Corporation several years ago for $8,750. In the current year, she sold the same stock for $12,800. She paid a $200 sales commission to her stockbroker.

1. What is Erin's amount realized? $__________
2. What is Erin's adjusted basis? $__________
3. What is Erin's *realized* gain or loss? $__________
4. What is Erin's *recognized* gain or loss? $__________
5. How is any gain or loss treated for tax purposes?

____

____

____

SPECIAL RULES FOR HIGH-INCOME TAXPAYERS

Learning Objective 1.9

Identify the new tax rules for high-income taxpayers.

In 2013, two separate laws went into effect increasing taxes for high-income taxpayers. The first increases were part of the sweeping health care legislation passed in the spring of 2010, which has been called by various abbreviated names including "The Affordable Care Act," or ACA, and "Obamacare." The term Obamacare began as an uncomplimentary term, but has since been accepted widely as a descriptive term, and even used by President Obama himself. ACA will be used to refer to this law.

The second set of tax increases for high-income taxpayers were passed as part of the American Taxpayer Relief Act (ATRA) of 2012. This act is also known as the "fiscal cliff" legislation, since it was passed in the first hours of 2013 just as many of the previous decade's tax laws expired. The following is a summary of significant tax increases for taxpayers with income of $200,000 to $450,000 and more.

The 3.8 Percent Medicare Tax on Net Investment Income

Beginning in 2013, the ACA imposes a new 3.8 percent Medicare tax on the net investment income of individuals with modified AGI over $250,000 for joint filers ($125,000 if married filing separate), and $200,000 for single filers (note that these amounts are not indexed for inflation). Modified AGI is adjusted gross income increased by certain foreign earned income amounts not covered in this text. Investment income subject to the additional 3.8 percent tax includes the following:

- Interest and dividends
- Royalties
- Annuities
- Net rental income, with some exceptions
- Passive activities
- Most gains on the sale of capital and other assets

Income not subject to the 3.8 percent tax includes the following:

- Tax-exempt interest
- Excluded gain on the sale of a principal residence
- Distributions from retirement plans and individual retirement accounts
- Wages and self-employment income (earned income) subject to a new 0.9 percent tax

Deductions allowed in arriving at net investment income subject to tax include:

- State income taxes reasonably allocated to the investment income
- Investment interest expense
- Allocable investment expenses exceeding the 2 percent of AGI floor

The $3,000 net deduction allowed for capital losses in excess of capital gains for regular tax purposes and net operating losses are not allowed to reduce net investment income. Additional rules govern which income and deductions are included in calculating net investment income. The net investment income tax is reported on Form 8960.

EXAMPLE Dan is single and has $60,000 of dividend income and $190,000 of wage income. His additional tax is computed as follows:

Modified AGI	$ 250,000
Threshold	200,000
Excess	50,000
Investment income	60,000
Lesser of the above amounts	50,000
Tax rate	3.8%
Additional tax	$ 1,900 ♦

The 0.9 Percent Additional Medicare Tax on Earned Income

Beginning in 2013, the ACA imposes a new 0.9 percent Medicare surtax on earned income such as wages and self-employment income which is not included in the calculation of the 3.8 percent tax on net investment income. Because individuals pay Medicare tax of 2.9 percent of wages (in conjunction with their employers), and self-employed taxpayers pay Medicare tax of 2.9 percent on their earnings, the extra 0.9 percent tax will bring the total percentage up to the same amount as the new 3.8 percent Medicare tax levied on net investment income. Detailed examples of the calculation of the 0.9 percent tax will be presented in Chapter 9 (LO 9.9) along with the coverage of wage withholding and self-employment taxes. The 0.9 percent tax applies to earned income exceeding the thresholds for the 3.8 percent tax.

EXAMPLE Kathy is single and earns wages of $300,000 in 2014 from her work at a surgery center. Her employer must withhold 0.9 percent, or $900, on the $100,000 of income she earns in excess of $200,000. This amount is reported with Kathy's total Medicare taxes on her Form W-2. If Kathy were self-employed as a doctor and earned the same income, she would report and pay the $900 with the tax calculated on her Form 1040, Individual Income Tax Return. ♦

ATRA Top Rates for Qualified Dividends and Capital Gains Increased to 20 Percent

Starting in 2013, ATRA imposes a 20 percent tax on qualified dividends and long-term capital gains for taxpayers in the new 39.6 percent tax bracket discussed above. Therefore, the tax applies to taxpayers with taxable income above $406,750 for single taxpayers, $432,200 for head of household taxpayers, and $457,600 for married taxpayers filing jointly.

Form **8960**

Department of the Treasury
Internal Revenue Service (99)

Net Investment Income Tax— Individuals, Estates, and Trusts

▶ Attach to Form 1040 or Form 1041.

▶ Information about Form 8960 and its separate instructions is at *www.irs.gov/form8960.*

OMB No. 1545-2227

2013*

Attachment Sequence No. **72**

Name(s) shown on Form 1040 or Form 1041 | **Your social security number or EIN**

Part I Investment Income ☐ Section 6013(g) election (see instructions)
☐ Regulations section 1.1411-10(g) election (see instructions)

Line	Description	Box	Amount	Box	Amount
1	Taxable interest (Form 1040, line 8a; or Form 1041, line 1)			1	
2	Ordinary dividends (Form 1040, line 9a; or Form 1041, line 2a)			2	
3	Annuities from nonqualified plans (see instructions)			3	
4a	Rental real estate, royalties, partnerships, S corporations, trusts, etc. (Form 1040, line 17; or Form 1041, line 5)	4a			
b	Adjustment for net income or loss derived in the ordinary course of a non-section 1411 trade or business (see instructions)	4b			
c	Combine lines 4a and 4b			4c	
5a	Net gain or loss from disposition of property from Form 1040, combine lines 13 and 14; or from Form 1041, combine lines 4 and 7	5a			
b	Net gain or loss from disposition of property that is not subject to net investment income tax (see instructions)	5b			
c	Adjustment from disposition of partnership interest or S corporation stock (see instructions)	5c			
d	Combine lines 5a through 5c			5d	
6	Changes to investment income for certain CFCs and PFICs (see instructions)			6	
7	Other modifications to investment income (see instructions)			7	
8	Total investment income. Combine lines 1, 2, 3, 4c, 5d, 6, and 7			8	

Part II Investment Expenses Allocable to Investment Income and Modifications

Line	Description	Box	Amount	Box	Amount
9a	Investment interest expenses (see instructions)	9a			
b	State income tax (see instructions)	9b			
c	Miscellaneous investment expenses (see instructions)	9c			
d	Add lines 9a, 9b, and 9c			9d	
10	Additional modifications (see instructions)			10	
11	Total deductions and modifications. Add lines 9d and 10			11	

Part III Tax Computation

Line	Description	Box	Amount	Box	Amount
12	Net investment income. Subtract Part II, line 11 from Part I, line 8. Individuals complete lines 13–17. Estates and trusts complete lines 18a–21. If zero or less, enter -0-			12	
	Individuals:				
13	Modified adjusted gross income (see instructions)	13			
14	Threshold based on filing status (see instructions)	14			
15	Subtract line 14 from line 13. If zero or less, enter -0-	15			
16	Enter the smaller of line 12 or line 15			16	
17	Net investment income tax for individuals. Multiply line 16 by 3.8% (.038). Enter here and on Form 1040, line 60			17	
	Estates and Trusts:				
18a	Net investment income (line 12 above)	18a			
b	Deductions for distributions of net investment income and deductions under section 642(c) (see instructions)	18b			
c	Undistributed net investment income. Subtract line 18b from 18a (see instructions)	18c			
19a	Adjusted gross income (see instructions)	19a			
b	Highest tax bracket for estates and trusts for the year (see instructions)	19b			
c	Subtract line 19b from line 19a. If zero or less, enter -0-	19c			
20	Enter the smaller of line 18c or line 19c			20	
21	Net investment income tax for estates and trusts. Multiply line 20 by 3.8% (.038). Enter here and on Form 1041, Schedule G, line 4			21	

For Paperwork Reduction Act Notice, see your tax return instructions. Cat. No. 59474M Form **8960** (2013)

***The 2014 version of this form was not available as we went to press. Please check the IRS website (www.irs.gov) for updates.**

Form **8959**

Department of the Treasury
Internal Revenue Service

Additional Medicare Tax

▶ **If any line does not apply to you, leave it blank. See separate instructions.**
▶ **Attach to Form 1040, 1040NR, 1040-PR, or 1040-SS.**
▶ **Information about Form 8959 and its instructions is at *www.irs.gov/form8959*.**

OMB No. 1545-0074
2014
Attachment Sequence No. 71

DRAFT AS OF October 6, 2014 DO NOT FILE

Name(s) shown on return | **Your social security number**

Part I Additional Medicare Tax on Medicare Wages

1 Medicare wages and tips from Form W-2, box 5. If you have more than one Form W-2, enter the total of the amounts from box 5 . . . . . **1**
2 Unreported tips from Form 4137, line 6 . . . . . **2**
3 Wages from Form 8919, line 6 . . . . . **3**
4 Add lines 1 through 3 . . . . . **4**
5 Enter the following amount for your filing status:
Married filing jointly $250,000
Married filing separately $125,000
Single, Head of household, or Qualifying widow(er) $200,000 **5**
6 Subtract line 5 from line 4. If zero or less, enter -0- **6**
7 Additional Medicare Tax on Medicare wages. Multiply line 6 by 0.9% (.009). Enter here and go to Part II **7**

Part II Additional Medicare Tax on Self-Employment Income

8 Self-employment income from Schedule SE (Form 1040), Section A, line 4, or Section B, line 6. If you had a loss, enter -0- (Form 1040-PR and Form 1040-SS filers, see instructions.) **8**
9 Enter the following amount for your filing status:
Married filing jointly $250,000
Married filing separately $125,000
Single, Head of household, or Qualifying widow(er) $200,000 **9**
10 Enter the amount from line 4 . . . . . **10**
11 Subtract line 10 from line 9. If zero or less, enter -0- . . . **11**
12 Subtract line 11 from line 8. If zero or less, enter -0- **12**
13 Additional Medicare Tax on self-employment income. Multiply line 12 by 0.9% (.009). Enter here and go to Part III **13**

Part III Additional Medicare Tax on Railroad Retirement Tax Act (RRTA) Compensation

14 Railroad retirement (RRTA) compensation and tips from Form(s) W-2, box 14 (see instructions) **14**
15 Enter the following amount for your filing status:
Married filing jointly $250,000
Married filing separately $125,000
Single, Head of household, or Qualifying widow(er) $200,000 **15**
16 Subtract line 15 from line 14. If zero or less, enter -0- **16**
17 Additional Medicare Tax on railroad retirement (RRTA) compensation. Multiply line 16 by 0.9% (.009). Enter here and go to Part IV **17**

Part IV Total Additional Medicare Tax

18 Add lines 7, 13, and 17. Also include this amount on Form 1040, line 62, (Form 1040NR, 1040-PR, and 1040-SS filers, see instructions) and go to Part V **18**

Part V Withholding Reconciliation

19 Medicare tax withheld from Form W-2, box 6. If you have more than one Form W-2, enter the total of the amounts from box 6 . . . . . **19**
20 Enter the amount from line 1 . . . . . **20**
21 Multiply line 20 by 1.45% (.0145). This is your regular Medicare tax withholding on Medicare wages **21**
22 Subtract line 21 from line 19. If zero or less, enter -0-. This is your Additional Medicare Tax withholding on Medicare wages **22**
23 Additional Medicare Tax withholding on railroad retirement (RRTA) compensation from Form W-2, box 14 (see instructions) **23**
24 **Total Additional Medicare Tax withholding.** Add lines 22 and 23. Also include this amount with federal income tax withholding on Form 1040, line 64 (Form 1040NR, 1040-PR, and 1040-SS filers, see instructions) **24**

Self-Study Problem 1.9 ***See Appendix E for Solutions to Self-Study Problems***

______ 1. Ronald Trunk is single and independently wealthy. His only income in 2014 is taxable interest totaling $450,000. He has no investment expenses associated with this income and lives where there is no state income tax. Complete Form 8960 on Page 1-25 to calculate Ronald's 2014 net investment income tax.

______ 2. Marcie and Scott Chang are married. Scott takes care of their three children while Marcie is self-employed selling commercial real estate. Her income in 2014 is $330,000. Marcie and Scott have no other earned or unearned income. Complete Form 8959 on Page 1-27 to determine how much additional Medicare tax on earned income must Marcie pay with their joint tax return in 2014?

"Play or Pay" Penalty for Large Employers Not offering Required Health Insurance Beginning in 2015, large employers will be assessed penalties for not offering health coverage. The calculation of the penalty is complex and depends on many variables such as type of coverage provided by the employer and income levels of the employees.

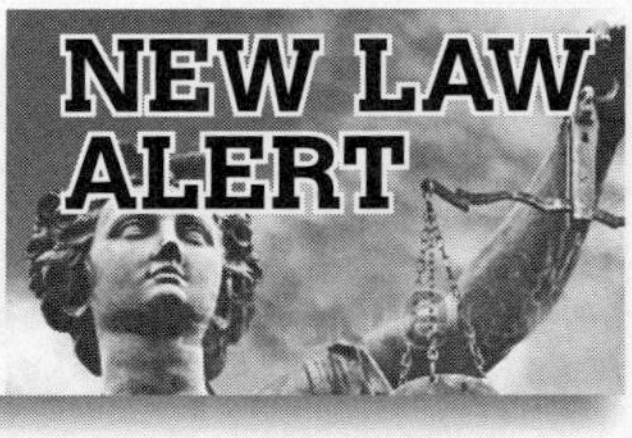

© ER_09/Shutterstock.com

TAX AND THE INTERNET

Learning Objective 1.10
Access and use various Internet tax resources.

Taxpayers and tax practitioners can find a substantial amount of useful information on the Internet. Government agencies, businesses, organizations, and groups (e.g., the IRS, H&R Block, and Cengage Learning) maintain sites that contain information of interest to the public.

The information available on various websites is subject to rapid change. Discussed below are some current Internet sites that are of interest to taxpayers. Taxpayers should be aware that the locations and information provided on the Internet are subject to change by the site organizer without notice.

The IRS Site, www.irs.gov

One of the most useful sites containing tax information is the one maintained by the IRS. The IRS website was accessed more than 300 million times in the first half of 2014. The IRS site has a search function to assist users in locating information. A wealth of free tools and other information is available under "Tools" on the home page. The Forms and Publications search function is particularly useful and allows the user to locate and download almost any tax form or publication available from the IRS. A help function is available to aid users of the IRS site. E-mail access to the IRS is provided for users who have questions or want to communicate with the IRS. The IRS has also launched a YouTube video site and an iTunes podcast site. The YouTube site has numerous educational videos covering a number of tax-related topics, including how to check on a refund and how to file a tax return extension. The IRS news feed on Twitter, @IRSnews is also a good source of tax information. The IRS also offers IRS2GO—a mobile phone app.

The following is a 2014 screenshot of the IRS website, **www.irs.gov**:

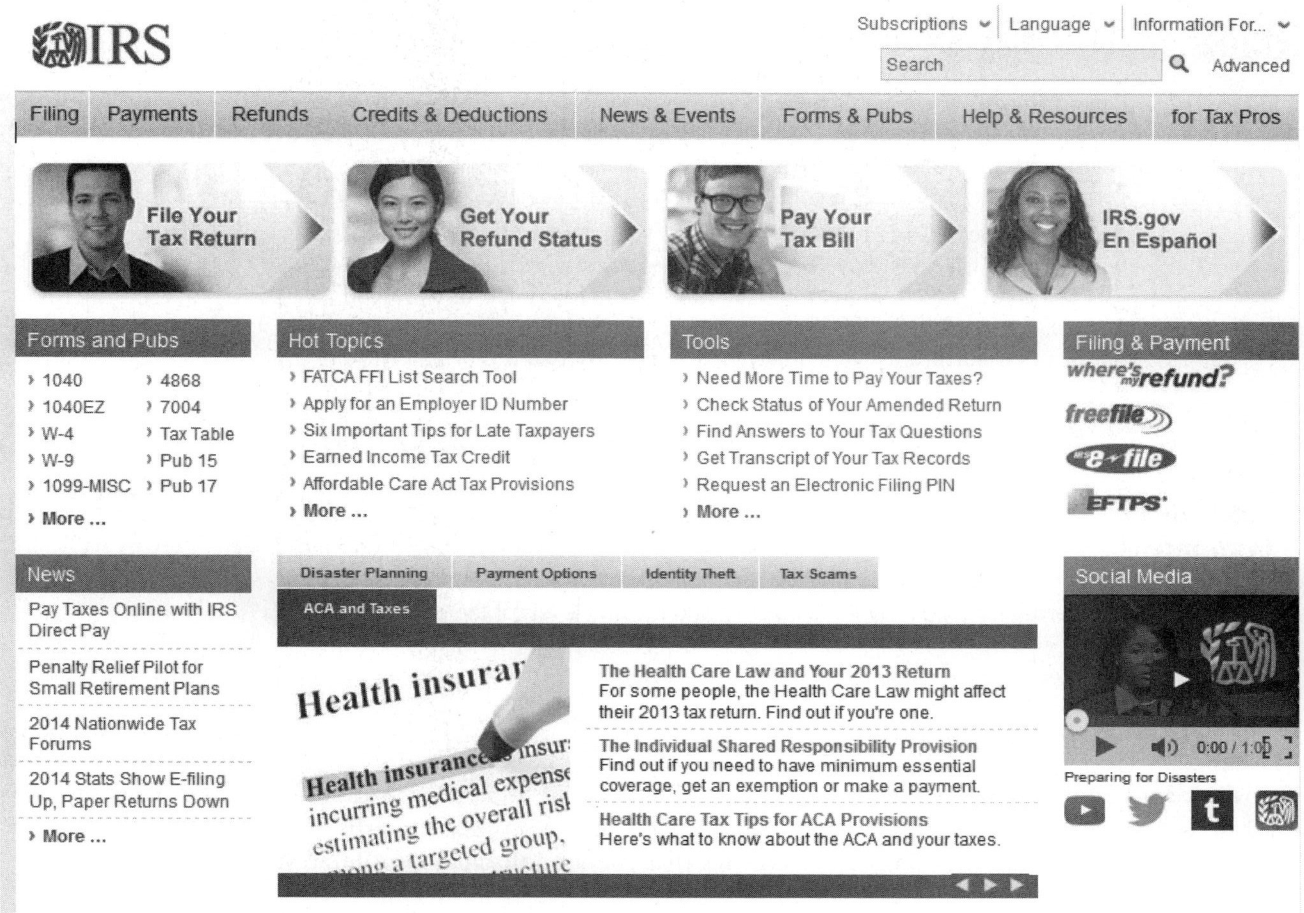

Reproduced courtesy of the Internal Revenue Service (www.irs.gov).

H&R Block, www.hrblock.com

Another excellent Internet site for taxpayers is the one maintained by the tax software company, H&R Block. The site contains information on law changes, tax planning, tax terms, and more.

Will Yancey's Home Page, www.willyancey.com

This site is one of the best indexes available with links to other tax, accounting, and legal Internet sites. The site has hundreds of links to commercial websites, federal government websites, state and local websites, and international websites.

Would You Believe?

The IRS issues warnings to taxpayers each year about identity theft scams via e-mail knows as "phishing" scams. The e-mails look official and may even have a link to a bogus website that looks almost identical to www.irs.gov (and may even mention USA.gov or IRS.gov). The fake e-mails may also appear to have been sent by the IRS Taxpayer Advocate's Office. Taxpayers who get these messages should not respond to the e-mail or click on the links. Although the IRS maintains Twitter and Facebook accounts, the IRS does not initiate contact with taxpayers by e-mail, texting or any social media.

Self-Study Problem 1.10 *See Appendix E for Solutions to Self-Study Problems*

Indicate whether the following statements are true or false by circling the appropriate letter.

T F 1. Taxpayers can download tax forms and IRS publications from the IRS website.
T F 2. A help function is available to aid users of the IRS website.
T F 3. The IRS has a mobile phone app

ELECTRONIC FILING (E-FILING)

Learning Objective 1.11
Understand the basics of electronic filing (e-filing).

Electronic filing (e-filing) is the process of transmitting federal income tax return information to the IRS Service Center using a computer with Internet access. For the taxpayer, electronic filing offers a faster refund, either through a direct deposit to the taxpayer's bank account or by check. IRS statistics show an error rate of less than 1 percent on electronically filed returns, compared with more than 20 percent on paper returns.

Electronic filing of individual income tax returns may be done with the IRS by using one of two methods.

The first electronic filing method is e-filing using a personal computer and tax preparation software such as H&R Block's At Home which is included with this text. Individual taxpayers may transmit their returns from home, workplaces, libraries, retail outlets, or, in some limited situations, even using a mobile phone app. The IRS website contains detailed information on this process as the IRS is constantly working to make e-filing more user-friendly and widely available. The IRS provides free tax preparation and e-filing software to individuals with income below certain thresholds (see **www.irs.gov/freefile**). Individuals with higher income may still e-file free, using IRS fill-in forms (see **www.freefilefillableforms.com**). The fillable forms program performs calculations but will not provide the tax preparation guidance that standard tax software programs provide.

The second e-filing option is to use the services of a tax professional, including certified public accountants, tax attorneys, IRS-enrolled agents, and tax preparation businesses qualifying for the IRS tax professional e-filing program.

Electronic filing represents a significant growth area in computerized tax services. Approximately 80 percent of all individual taxpayers now e-file. Mandatory electronic filing is currently in the process of being phased in for the professional tax return preparation industry. In the future, electronic filing will likely be required for most tax returns filed.

Would You Believe?

In 2006, General Electric Co. electronically filed their corporate tax return. If printed, it was estimated at 24,000 pages and expected to stack up to 8 feet tall. In 2010, GE enjoyed a 7 percent effective tax rate but filed a federal income tax return estimated at a whopping 57,000 pages or 19 feet tall.

Self-Study Problem 1.11 *See Appendix E for Solutions to Self-Study Problems*

Indicate whether the following statements are true or false by circling the appropriate letter.

T F 1. Compared to paper returns, electronic filings significantly reduce the error rate for tax returns filed.
T F 2. Individuals may not use electronic filing for their own personal tax returns, but must engage a tax professional if they wish to e-file.
T F 3. Taxpayers who e-file generally receive faster refunds.
T F 4. Taxpayers who e-file can only request their refund in the form of a check.

KEY TERMS

Individual, 1-3
Form 1040EZ, 1-3
Form 1040A, 1-3
Form 1040, 1-3
Corporation, 1-4
Partnership, 1-4
gross income, 1-5
adjusted gross income, 1-6
standard deductions, 1-6, 1-19
itemized deductions, 1-6
exemptions, 1-6
single filing status, 1-9
married filing jointly, 1-10
married filing separately, 1-10
head of household, 1-10
qualifying widow(er), 1-11
exemptions, 1-13
qualifying child, 1-13
qualifying relative, 1-14
capital assets, 1-21
capital gains, 1-21
net investment income tax 1-23
Medicare surtax 1-24

KEY POINTS

Learning Objectives	Key Points
LO 1.1: Understand the history and objectives of U.S. tax law.	• The income tax was authorized by the Sixteenth Amendment to the Constitution on March 1, 1913. • In addition to raising money to run the government's programs, the income tax is used as a tool of economic and social policies. • Examples of economic tax provisions are the limited allowance for expensing capital expenditures and the accelerated cost recovery system (ACRS or MACRS) of depreciation. The charitable contribution deduction is an example of a social tax provision.
LO 1.2: Describe the different entities subject to tax and reporting requirements.	• Individual taxpayers file Form 1040EZ, Form 1040A, or Form 1040. • Corporations must report income annually on Form 1120 and pay taxes. • An S corporation generally does not pay regular corporate income taxes; instead, the corporation's income passes through to its shareholders and is included in their individual tax returns. • A partnership files Form 1065 to report the amount of income or loss and show the allocation of the income or loss to the partners. • Generally, all income or loss of a partnership is included in the tax returns of the partners.
LO 1.3: Understand and apply the tax formula for individuals.	• AGI (adjusted gross income) is gross income less deductions for adjusted gross income. • AGI less the larger of itemized deductions or the standard deduction and less exemption amounts equals taxable income. • Appropriate tax tables or rate schedules are applied to taxable income to calculate the gross tax liability. • The gross tax liability less credits and prepayments equals the tax due or refund.
LO 1.4: Identify individuals who must file tax returns.	• Conditions relating to the amount of the taxpayer's income must exist before a taxpayer is required to file a U.S. income tax return. • Taxpayers are also required to file a return if they have net earnings from self-employment of $400 or more, or owe taxes such as Social Security taxes on unreported tips.
LO 1.5: Determine filing status and understand the calculation of tax according to filing status.	• There are five filing statuses: single; married, filing jointly; married, filing separately; head of household; and qualifying widow(er). • Tax is calculated using the appropriate tax table or rate schedule for the taxpayer's filing status.

LO 1.6: Calculate the number of exemptions and the exemption amounts for taxpayers.	• Taxpayers are allowed two types of exemptions: personal and dependency. • For 2014, each exemption reduces adjusted gross income by $3,950. • Personal exemptions are granted to taxpayers for themselves and their spouse. • Extra exemptions may be claimed for each person other than the taxpayer or spouse who qualifies as a dependent. A dependent is an individual who is either a qualifying child or a qualifying relative.
LO 1.7: Calculate the correct standard or itemized deduction amount for taxpayers.	• The standard deduction was placed in the tax law to provide relief for taxpayers with few itemized deductions. • For 2014, the standard deduction amounts are: Single $6,200; Married, filing jointly $12,400; Married, filing separately $6,200; Head of household $9,100; Qualifying widow(er) $12,400. • Taxpayers who are 65 years of age or older or blind are entitled to additional standard deduction amounts of $1,550 for unmarried taxpayers and $1,200 for married taxpayers and surviving spouses in 2014.
LO 1.8: Compute basic capital gains and losses.	• The amount of gain or loss realized by a taxpayer is determined by subtracting the adjusted basis of the asset from the amount realized. • Gains and losses can be either ordinary or capital. • Ordinary gains and losses are treated for tax purposes like other items such as salary and interest. • Capital gains and losses result from the sale or exchange of capital assets. • Common capital assets held by individual taxpayers include stocks, bonds, land, cars, boats, and other items held as investments. • Gain from property held 12 months or less is deemed to be short-term capital gain and is taxed at ordinary income tax rates. • Gain from property held more than 12 months is deemed to be long-term capital gain and is taxed at preferential income tax rates. • The long-term capital gains rate for 2014 for taxpayers in the 10 percent and 15 percent tax brackets is 0 percent; it is 15 percent for most other brackets. High-income taxpayers have higher rates (see LO 1.9). • If an individual taxpayer ends up with a net capital loss (short-term or long-term), up to $3,000 per year can be deducted against ordinary income. Losses from personal-use assets are not deductible.
LO 1.9: Identify the new tax rules for high-income taxpayers.	• The Affordable Care Act (ACA) added a 3.8 percent Medicare tax on net investment income and a 0.9 percent tax on earned income beginning in 2013 for certain high-income taxpayers. • The top tax rate was increased from 15 percent to 20 percent for certain capital gains and dividends of high-income individuals beginning in 2013.
LO 1.10: Access and use various Internet tax resources.	• Taxpayers and tax practitioners can find a substantial amount of useful information on the Internet. • Some of the most useful sites containing tax information are the IRS (**www.irs.gov**), H&R Block (**www.hrblock.com**), and Will Yancey's home page (**www.willyancey.com**).
LO 1.11: Understand the basics of electronic filing (e-filing).	• Electronic filing (e-filing) is the process of transmitting federal income tax return information to the IRS Service Center using a device with Internet access. • Electronic filing offers a faster refund, either through a direct deposit to the taxpayer's bank account or by check.

© Dusit/Shutterstock.com

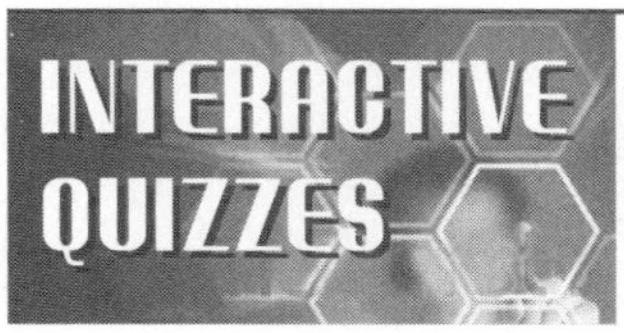

Interactive quizzes are available as an optional online resource for Income Tax Fundamentals. Visit **www.cengagebrain.com** for more information.

QUESTIONS and PROBLEMS

GROUP 1:
MULTIPLE CHOICE QUESTIONS

LO 1.1 ______ 1. The current income tax system was:
  a. Designed solely to raise money to run the government
  b. Authorized by the founding fathers when the government was formed
  c. Not designed with social objectives in mind
  d. Authorized by the Sixteenth Amendment to the Constitution in 1913
  e. None of the above

LO 1.2 ______ 2. Partnership income is reported on:
  a. Form 1040
  b. Form 1120
  c. Form 1040X
  d. Form 1065

LO 1.3 ______ 3. Which of the following is a deduction for adjusted gross income in 2014?
  a. Personal casualty losses
  b. Medical expenses
  c. Student loan interest
  d. Charitable contributions
  e. None of the above

LO 1.3 ______ 4. All of the following are itemized deductions in 2014 except:
  a. Charitable contributions
  b. Alimony payments
  c. Casualty losses
  d. Medical expenses
  e. All of the above are itemized deductions

LO 1.3 ______ 5. Ramon, a single taxpayer with no dependents, has adjusted gross income for 2014 of $98,000 and his itemized deductions total $19,000. What taxable income will Ramon show in 2014?
  a. $79,000
  b. $75,100
  c. $75,050
  d. $81,650
  e. $85,600

LO 1.4

6. Ben is a single taxpayer with no dependents who is 32 years old. What is the minimum amount of income that he must have to be required to file a tax return for 2014?
   a. $6,200
   b. $12,400
   c. $10,000
   d. $10,150
   e. None of the above

LO 1.5

7. Joan, who was divorced in 2014, had filed a joint tax return with her husband in 2013. During 2014, she did not remarry and continued to maintain her home in which her five dependent children lived. In the preparation of her tax return for 2014, Joan should file as:
   a. A single individual
   b. A qualifying widow(er)
   c. Head of household
   d. Married, filing separately
   e. None of the above

LO 1.6

8. Margaret and her sister support their mother and together provide 85 percent of their mother's support. If Margaret provides 40 percent of her mother's support:
   a. Her sister is the only one who can claim their mother as a dependent.
   b. Neither Margaret nor her sister may claim their mother as a dependent.
   c. Both Margaret and her sister may claim their mother as a dependent.
   d. Margaret and her sister may split the dependency exemption.
   e. Margaret may claim her mother as a dependent if her sister agrees in a multiple support agreement.

LO 1.6

9. Margaret, age 65, and John, age 62, are married with a 23-year-old daughter who lives in their home. They provide over half of their daughter's support, and their daughter earned $4,000 this year from a part-time job. Their daughter is not a full-time student. How many exemptions should Margaret and John claim on a joint return for 2014?
   a. 2
   b. 3
   c. 4
   d. 5
   e. 6

LO 1.6

10. Lyn, age 65, and Robert, age 66, are married and support Lyn's father (no taxable income) and Robert's mother, who has $2,200 of gross income. If they file a joint return for 2014, how many exemptions may Lyn and Robert claim?
    a. 2
    b. 3
    c. 4
    d. 5
    e. 6

LO 1.6

11. Arthur is 65 years old. He supports his father, who is 90 years old, blind, and has no income. For 2014, how many exemptions should Arthur claim on his tax return?
    a. 1
    b. 2
    c. 3
    d. 4
    e. 5

______________ **LO 1.7**

12. Taxpayers who are 65 or older get the benefit of:
    a. An additional exemption
    b. An additional amount added to their standard deduction
    c. An additional amount added to their itemized deductions
    d. None of the above

______________ **LO 1.7**

13. Taxpayers who are blind get the benefit of:
    a. An additional exemption
    b. An additional amount added to their standard deduction
    c. An additional amount added to their itemized deductions
    d. None of the above

______________ **LO 1.8**

14. Which of the following is *not* a capital asset to an individual taxpayer?
    a. Stocks
    b. A 48-foot sailboat
    c. Raw land held as an investment
    d. Inventory in the taxpayer's business
    e. All of the above are capital assets

______________ **LO 1.8**

15. Jayne purchased General Motors stock 6 years ago for $20,000. In 2014, she sells the stock for $35,000. What is Jayne's gain or loss?
    a. $15,000 short-term
    b. $15,000 long-term
    c. $15,000 ordinary
    d. $15,000 extraordinary
    e. No gain or loss is recognized on this transaction

______________ **LO 1.8**

16. Alexis purchased a rental house 3 years ago for $285,000. Her depreciation to date is $35,000. Due to a decrease in real estate prices, she sells the house for only $275,000 in 2014. What is her gain or loss for tax purposes?
    a. $0
    b. $10,000 loss
    c. $10,000 gain
    d. $35,000 loss
    e. $25,000 gain

______________ **LO 1.8**

17. Shannon has a long-term capital loss of $7,000 on the sale of bonds in 2014. Her taxable income without this transaction is $48,000. What is her taxable income considering this capital loss?
    a. $41,000
    b. $45,000
    c. $48,000
    d. $55,000
    e. Some other amount

______________ **LO 1.9**

18. The 3.8 percent Medicare tax on net investment income applies to:
    a. Tax-exempt interest income
    b. Interest and dividends
    c. IRA distributions
    d. Wages

__________ **LO 1.9** 19. The top ATRA tax rate for long-term capital gains was increased to ___ percent, and the ACA added a net investment income Medicare surtax for high-income taxpayers of ___ percent, for a maximum long-term capital gain tax rate of ___ percent in 2013. Fill in the blanks.

a. 25; 3.8; 28.8
b. 20; 0.9; 20.9
c. 20; 3.8; 23.8
d. 39.6; 0.9; 40.5

__________ **LO 1.11** 20. Electronically filed tax returns:

a. May not be transmitted from a taxpayer's home computer
b. Constitute more than 90 percent of the returns filed with the IRS
c. Have error rates similar to paper returns
d. Offer faster refunds than paper returns

GROUP 2: PROBLEMS

LO 1.1 1. List three major purposes the tax system is meant to serve:

a. ____________________
b. ____________________
c. ____________________

LO 1.3 2. Jason and Mary are married taxpayers in 2014. They are both under age 65 and in good health. For this tax year, they have a total of $41,000 in wages and $500 in interest income. Jason and Mary's deductions for adjusted gross income amount to $5,000 and their itemized deductions equal $7,950. They claim two exemptions for the year on their joint tax return.

a. What is the amount of Jason and Mary's adjusted gross income?

$__________

b. What is the amount of their itemized deductions or standard deduction?

$__________

c. What is their 2014 taxable income?

$__________

LO 1.3 3. Leslie is a single taxpayer who is under age 65 and in good health. For 2014, she has a salary of $23,000 and itemized deductions of $1,000. Leslie is entitled to one exemption on her tax return.

a. How much is Leslie's adjusted gross income?

$__________

b. What amount of itemized or standard deduction(s) should she claim?

$__________

c. What is the amount of Leslie's taxable income?

$__________

LO 1.3
LO 1.8 4. In 2014, Lou has a salary of $54,000 from her job. She also has interest income of $1,700. Lou is single and has no dependents. During the year, Lou sold silver coins held as an investment for a $7,000 loss. Calculate the following amounts for Lou:

a. Adjusted gross income

$____________

b. Standard deduction

$____________

c. Exemption

$____________

d. Taxable income

$____________

LO 1.3

5. What is the formula for computing taxable income as summarized in the text?

____

____

____

LO 1.3
LO 1.5

6. Diego, age 28, married Dolores, age 27, in 2014. Their salaries for the year amounted to $46,479 and they had interest income of $3,500. Diego and Dolores' deductions for adjusted gross income amounted to $1,900, their itemized deductions were $10,172, and they claimed two exemptions on their return.
   a. What is the amount of their adjusted gross income?

   $____________

   b. What is the amount of their itemized deductions or standard deduction?

   $____________

   c. What is the amount of their taxable income?

   $____________

   d. What is their tax liability for 2014?

   $____________

LO 1.3
LO 1.5

7. Ulysses and Penelope are married and file separate returns for 2014. Penelope itemizes her deductions on her return. Ulysses' adjusted gross income was $17,400, his itemized deductions were $2,250, and he is entitled to one exemption. Calculate Ulysses' income tax liability.

   $____________

LO 1.3
LO 1.5
LO 1.6

8. Alicia (age 27) is a single, full-time college student. She earns $13,000 from a part-time job and has taxable interest income of $1,400. Her itemized deductions are $690. Calculate Alicia's taxable income for 2014. (Please note: Chapter 6 will cover the computation of tax for dependent college students under age 24.)

   $____________

LO 1.3
LO 1.5
LO 1.6

9. Jonathan is a 35-year-old single taxpayer with adjusted gross income of $45,000. He uses the standard deduction and has no dependents.
   a. Calculate Jonathan's taxable income. Please show your work. ____________

   ____

   ____

b. When you calculate Jonathan's tax liability are you required to use the tax tables or the tax rate schedules, or does it matter? ____________

____

c. What is Jonathan's tax liability? ____________

____

LO 1.3 **LO 1.5** **LO 1.6** **LO 1.7**

10. Jim (age 50) and Martha (age 49) are married with three dependent children. They file a joint return for 2014. Their income from salaries totals $50,000, and they received $10,000 in taxable interest, $5,000 in royalties, and $3,000 in other ordinary income. Jim and Martha's deductions for adjusted gross income amount to $3,200, and they have itemized deductions totalling $13,000. Calculate the following amounts:

a. Gross income

$____________

b. Adjusted gross income

$____________

c. Itemized deduction or standard deduction amount

$____________

d. Number of exemptions

$____________

e. Taxable income

$____________

f. Income tax liability (Do not consider the alternative minimum tax covered in Chapter 6 or any credits.)

$____________

LO 1.3 **LO 1.5** **LO 1.6** **LO 1.7**

11. Frank, age 35, and Joyce, age 34, are married and file a joint income tax return for 2014. Their salaries for the year total $83,000 and they have taxable interest income of $4,000. They have no deductions for adjusted gross income. Their itemized deductions are $12,500. Frank and Joyce do not have any dependents.

a. What is the amount of their adjusted gross income?

$____________

b. What is their deduction for personal exemptions?

$____________

c. What is the amount of their taxable income?

$____________

LO 1.3 **LO 1.5** **LO 1.6** **LO 1.7**

12. Christine is a single 50-year-old taxpayer with no dependents. Her only income is $40,000 of wages. Calculate her taxable income and her tax liability. Please show your work.

____

____

____

LO 1.4

13. Nicoula waits tables in a La Jolla restaurant. Nicoula received $1,200 in unreported tips during 2014 and owes Social Security taxes on these tips. Her total income for the year, including the tips, is $4,300. Is Nicoula required to file an income tax return for 2014 ? Why or why not?

____

____

____

LO 1.4

14. For each of the following situations, indicate whether the taxpayer(s) is (are) required to file a tax return for 2014. Explain your answer.
    a. Helen is a single taxpayer with interest income in 2014 of $8,750.

    ____

    ____

    ____

    b. Joan is a single college student who is claimed as a dependent by her parents. She earned $1,550 from a part-time job and has $1,150 in interest income.

    ____

    ____

    ____

    c. Leslie (age 64) and Mark (age 66) are married and file a joint return. They received $17,800 in interest income from a savings account.

    ____

    ____

    ____

    d. Ray (age 60) and Jean (age 57) are married and file a joint tax return. They had $14,700 in interest income.

    ____

    ____

    ____

    e. Harry, a 19-year-old single taxpayer, had net earnings from self-employment of $1,500.

    ____

    ____

    ____

LO 1.5

15. Determine from the tax table in Appendix A the amount of the income tax for each of the following taxpayers for 2014:

Taxpayer(s)	*Filing Status*	*Taxable Income*	*Income Tax*
Allen	Single	$21,000	$__________
Boyd	MFS	24,545	$__________
Caldwell	MFJ	35,784	$__________
Dell	H of H	27,450	$__________
Evans	Single	45,000	$__________

LO 1.5

16. For each of the following cases, indicate the filing status for the taxpayer(s) for 2014 using the following legend:

A – Single
B – Married, filing a joint return
C – Married, filing separate returns
D – Head of household
E – Qualifying widow(er)

Case	Filing Status
a. Linda is single and she supports her mother (who has no income), including paying all the costs of her housing in an apartment across town.	____________
b. Frank is single and he has a dependent child living in his home.	____________
c. Arthur is single and he supports his 30-year-old brother, who lives in his own home.	____________
d. Leslie's final decree of divorce was granted on June 18, 2014. She has no dependents.	____________
e. Tom and Carry were married on December 31, 2014.	____________

LO 1.5

17. Melissa and Aaron are married taxpayers with taxable income of $102,000.
    a. When you calculate their tax liability are you required to use the tax tables or the tax rate schedules, or does it matter? ____________
    b. What is their 2014 tax liability? ____________

LO 1.5

18. Jessica and Carl were married on July 1, 2014. What are their options for filing status for their 2014 taxes? ____________

LO 1.5

19. Maggie is single and supports her 85-year-old parents who live in a home rented for them by Maggie and who have no income. What is Maggie's filing status and why? ____________

LO 1.5

20. List each alternative filing status available to unmarried individual taxpayers and the circumstances under which the alternatives can be used. ____________

LO 1.5
LO 1.6

21. Mary is single and supports her 30-year-old son who has income of $2,000 and lives in his own apartment.
    a. Can she claim him as a dependent? ____________
    b. Can she claim head of household filing status? Why or why not? ____________

LO 1.6

22. Indicate, in each of the following situations, the number of exemptions the taxpayers are entitled to claim on their 2014 income tax returns.

	Number of Exemptions
a. Donna, a 20-year-old single taxpayer, supports her mother, who lives in her own home. Her mother has income of $1,350.	____________

b. William, age 43, and Mary, age 45, are married and support William's 19-year-old sister, who is not a student. The sister's income from a part-time job is $3,950. __________

c. Devi was divorced in 2014 and receives child support of $250 per month from her ex-husband for the support of their 8-year-old son, John, who lives with her. Devi is 45 and provides more than half of her son's support. __________

d. Wendell, an 89-year-old single taxpayer, supports his son, who is 67 years old, lives with him, and earns no income. __________

e. Wilma, age 65, and Morris, age 66, are married. They file a joint return. __________

LO 1.6

23. What is the total dollar amount of personal and dependency exemptions which a married couple with one child and $80,000 of adjusted gross income would claim in 2014? __________

LO 1.6

24. If Charles, a 16-year-old child model, earns $50,000 a year and is completely self-supporting even though he lives with his parents, can his parents claim him as a dependent? Why or why not?

LO 1.6

25. Marc's brother, Phillip, who is a 20-year-old French citizen, lives in France for the full year. Marc supports Phillip while he attends college. Can Marc claim Phillip as a dependent? Why or why not?

LO 1.7

26. Describe the difference between the standard deduction and itemized deductions. How should a taxpayer decide whether to take the standard deduction or claim itemized deductions?

LO 1.9

27. Rachel is single and has wages of $150,000 and dividend income of $90,000. She has no investment expenses. Calculate the amount of the 3.8 percent net investment income tax she must pay.

LO 1.10

28. Go to the IRS website (**www.irs.gov/newsroom**) and note the name of the most recent news release.

LO 1.10

29. Go to the IRS website (**www.irs.gov**) and print out a copy of the most recent *Schedule F* of *Form 1040*.

LO 1.10

30. Go to the IRS website (**www.irs.gov**) and print out a copy of the most recent *Instructions* for *Schedule R* of *Form 1040*.

LO 1.10

31. Go to Will Yancey's home page (**www.willyancey.com**) and give the complete Web address for each of the following sites:
    a. The California Franchise Tax Board
    b. The New York Department of Taxation and Finance

GROUP 3: WRITING ASSIGNMENTS

RESEARCH

1. Jerry, age 23, a full-time student and not disabled, lives with William and Sheila Carson. Jerry is William's older brother. Jerry is single, a U.S. citizen, and does not provide more than one-half of his own support. William and Sheila are both 21 and file a joint return. Can William and Sheila claim a dependency exemption for Jerry as a qualifying child?
   Required: Go to the IRS website (**www.irs.gov**) and review Publication 501. Write a letter to William and Sheila stating if they can claim Jerry as a qualifying child. (An example of a client letter is available at the website for this text.)

ETHICS

2. Jason and Mary Wells, friends of yours, were married on December 30, 2014. They know you are studying taxes and have come to you with a question concerning their filing status. Jason and Mary would each like to file single for tax year 2014. Jason has prepared their taxes both as single and married filing jointly, and he has realized that the couple will get a larger combined refund if they each file single. Jason argues "that it's not as if we were married for very long in 2014." What would you say to Jason and Mary?

GROUP 4: COMPREHENSIVE PROBLEMS

Instructions for working all Group 4 Comprehensive Tax Return Problems in the text are as follows:

Birthdays: If you are using the tax software, make up birthdates for taxpayers and dependents. Adult taxpayers should have ages between 25 and 64 unless a different age is specified.

Wages: Assume the wages subject to income tax in the problems are the same as Social Security wages and Medicare wages. Make up employer names and other information which may be required by your tax software package.

Missing Data: Please make realistic assumptions about any missing data.

A student guide to H&R Block At Home software is available at the companion website.

1. Patty Bayan is a single taxpayer living at 543 Space Drive, Houston, TX 77099. Her Social Security number is 466-33-1234. For 2014, Patty has no dependents, and her W-2 from her job at a local restaurant where she parks cars contains the following information:

22222	a Employee's social security number 466-33-1234	OMB No. 1545-0008	
b Employer identification number (EIN) 33-0714916		1 Wages, tips, other compensation 19,400	2 Federal income tax withheld 3,000
c Employer's name, address, and ZIP code Burger Box 1234 Mountain Road Houston, TX 77099		3 Social security wages 19,400	4 Social security tax withheld 1,203
		5 Medicare wages and tips 19,400	6 Medicare tax withheld 281
		7 Social security tips	8 Allocated tips
d Control number		9	10 Dependent care benefits
e Employee's first name and initial Patty / Last name Bayan / Suff. 543 Space Drive Houston, TX 77099 f Employee's address and ZIP code		11 Nonqualified plans	12a
		13 Statutory employee ☐ Retirement plan ☐ Third-party sick pay ☐	12b
		14 Other	12c
			12d

15 State	Employer's state ID number	16 State wages, tips, etc.	17 State income tax	18 Local wages, tips, etc.	19 Local income tax	20 Locality name
TX						

Form **W-2** Wage and Tax Statement 2014 Department of the Treasury—Internal Revenue Service

Copy 1—For State, City, or Local Tax Department

These wages are Patty's only income for 2014. Please make your own assumption regarding the election to donate $3 to the Presidential Election Campaign Fund on this and subsequent problems. The election to donate does not affect tax liability in any way.

Required: Complete Form 1040EZ on Pages 1-47 and 1-48 for Patty Bayan for the 2014 tax year.

2A. Leslie and Leon Lazo are married and file a joint return for 2014. Leslie's Social Security number is 466-47-3311 and Leon's is 467-74-4451. They live at 143 Snapdragon Drive, Reno, NV 82102. For 2014, Leslie did not work, and Leon's W-2 from his butcher's job showed the following:

22222	a Employee's social security number 467-74-4451	OMB No. 1545-0008	
b Employer identification number (EIN) 33-0711 111		1 Wages, tips, other compensation 50,000	2 Federal income tax withheld 4,600
c Employer's name, address, and ZIP code Super Deal Grocery 2200 Meas Blvd. Reno, NV 82102		3 Social security wages 50,000	4 Social security tax withheld 3,100
		5 Medicare wages and tips 50,000	6 Medicare tax withheld 725
		7 Social security tips	8 Allocated tips
d Control number		9	10 Dependent care benefits
e Employee's first name and initial Leon / Last name Lazo / Suff. 143 Snapdragon Drive Reno, NV 82102 f Employee's address and ZIP code		11 Nonqualified plans	12a
		13 Statutory employee ☐ Retirement plan ☐ Third-party sick pay ☐	12b
		14 Other	12c
			12d

15 State	Employer's state ID number	16 State wages, tips, etc.	17 State income tax	18 Local wages, tips, etc.	19 Local income tax	20 Locality name
NV						

Form **W-2** Wage and Tax Statement 2014 Department of the Treasury—Internal Revenue Service

Copy 1—For State, City, or Local Tax Department

Leslie and Leon have an 18-year-old son named Lyle (Social Security number 552-52-5552), who is a dependent, is a full-time student, and does not qualify for the child tax credit due to his age.

Required: Complete Form 1040A on Pages 1-49 and 1-50 for Leslie and Leon for the 2014 tax year.

2B. Abigail (Abby) Boxer is a single mother working as a civilian accountant for the U.S. Army. Her Social Security number is 676-73-3311 and she lives at 3456 Alamo Way, San Antonio, TX 78249. Helen, Abby's 18-year-old daughter (Social Security number 676-73-3312), is a dependent child living with her mother, and she does not qualify for the child tax credit due to her age. For 2014, Abby's W-2 from the U.S. Department of Defense shows the following:

Wages	$42,500
Withholding (federal income tax)	5,160

Abby also has taxable interest from Arroyo Seco Bank of $230.

Required: Complete Form 1040A on Pages 1-49 and 1-50 for Abigail for the 2014 tax year.

GROUP 5: CUMULATIVE SOFTWARE PROBLEM

1. Dr. Ivan I. Incisor and his wife Irene are married and file a joint return for 2014. Ivan's Social Security number is 477-34-4321 and he is 48 years old. Irene I. Incisor's Social Security number is 637-34-4927 and she is 45 years old. They live at 468 Mule Deer Lane, Spokane, WA 99206.

Dr. Incisor is a dentist and he took 6 months off work to attend a cosmetic dentistry training program in 2014. His 2014 Form W-2 from his job at Bitewing Dental Clinic, Inc., showed the following:

Wages	$65,000
Withholding (federal income tax)	6,000

The Incisors have a 17-year-old son, Ira, who is enrolled in the eleventh grade at the Perpetual Perpetuity School. Ira's Social Security number is 690-99-9999. The Incisors also have an 18-year-old daughter, Iris, who is a part-time freshman student at Snow Mass Community College (SMCC). Iris' Social Security number is 899-99-9999. Iris is married to Sean Slacker (SS No. 896-33-0954), who is 19 years old and a part-time student at SMCC. Sean and Iris have a 1-year-old child, Seth Slacker (SS No. 648-99-4306). Sean, Iris, and Seth all live in an apartment up the street from Ivan and Irene during the entire current calendar year. Sean and Iris both work for Sean's wealthy grandfather as apprentices in his business. Their wages for the year were a combined $50,000, which allowed them to pay all the personal expenses for themselves and their son.

Ivan and Irene have savings account interest income of $380 from the Pacific Northwest Bank.

Required: Use a computer software package to complete Form 1040 for Ivan and Irene Incisor for 2014. Be sure to save your data input files since this case will be expanded with more tax information in later chapters. Make assumptions regarding any information not given.

Form **1040EZ**

Department of the Treasury—Internal Revenue Service

Income Tax Return for Single and Joint Filers With No Dependents (99) **2014**

OMB No. 1545-0074

Your first name and initial	Last name	**Your social security number**
If a joint return, spouse's first name and initial	Last name	**Spouse's social security number**
Home address (number and street). If you have a P.O. box, see instructions.	Apt. no.	▲ Make sure the SSN(s) above are correct.
City, town or post office, state, and ZIP code. If you have a foreign address, also complete spaces below (see instructions).		**Presidential Election Campaign** Check here if you, or your spouse if filing jointly, want $3 to go to this fund. Checking a box below will not change your tax or refund. ☐ You ☐ Spouse
Foreign country name	Foreign province/state/county	Foreign postal code

DRAFT AS OF July 24, 2014 DO NOT FILE

Income

Attach Form(s) W-2 here.

Enclose, but do not attach, any payment.

1	Wages, salaries, and tips. This should be shown in box 1 of your Form(s) W-2. Attach your Form(s) W-2.	1	
2	Taxable interest. If the total is over $1,500, you cannot use Form 1040EZ.	2	
3	Unemployment compensation and Alaska Permanent Fund dividends (see instructions).	3	
4	Add lines 1, 2, and 3. This is your **adjusted gross income.**	4	
5	If someone can claim you (or your spouse if a joint return) as a dependent, check the applicable box(es) below and enter the amount from the worksheet on back. ☐ **You** ☐ **Spouse** If no one can claim you (or your spouse if a joint return), enter $10,150 if **single;** $20,300 if **married filing jointly.** See back for explanation.	5	
6	Subtract line 5 from line 4. If line 5 is larger than line 4, enter -0-. This is your **taxable income.** ▶	6	

Payments, Credits, and Tax

7	Federal income tax withheld from Form(s) W-2 and 1099.	7	
8a	**Earned income credit (EIC)** (see instructions)	8a	
b	Nontaxable combat pay election. 8b		
9	Add lines 7 and 8a. These are your **total payments and credits.** ▶	9	
10	**Tax.** Use the amount on **line 6 above** to find your tax in the tax table in the instructions. Then, enter the tax from the table on this line.	10	
11	Health care: individual responsibility (see instructions) Full-year coverage ☐	11	
12	Add lines 10 and 11. This is your **total tax.**	12	

Refund

Have it directly deposited! See instructions and fill in 13b, 13c, and 13d, or Form 8888.

13a	If line 9 is larger than line 12, subtract line 12 from line 9. This is your **refund.** If Form 8888 is attached, check here ▶ ☐	13a	
▶ b	Routing number ▶ **c** Type: ☐ Checking ☐ Savings		
▶ d	Account number		

Amount You Owe

14	If line 12 is larger than line 9, subtract line 9 from line 12. This is the **amount you owe.** For details on how to pay, see instructions. ▶	14	

Third Party Designee

Do you want to allow another person to discuss this return with the IRS (see instructions)? ☐ **Yes.** Complete below. ☐ **No**

Designee's name ▶ Phone no. ▶ Personal identification number (PIN) ▶

Sign Here

Under penalties of perjury, I declare that I have examined this return and, to the best of my knowledge and belief, it is true, correct, and accurately lists all amounts and sources of income I received during the tax year. Declaration of preparer (other than the taxpayer) is based on all information of which the preparer has any knowledge.

Joint return? See instructions.

Keep a copy for your records.

Your signature	Date	Your occupation	Daytime phone number
Spouse's signature. If a joint return, **both** must sign.	Date	Spouse's occupation	If the IRS sent you an Identity Protection PIN, enter it here (see inst.)

Paid Preparer Use Only

Print/Type preparer's name	Preparer's signature	Date	Check ☐ if self-employed	PTIN
Firm's name ▶		Firm's EIN ▶		
Firm's address ▶		Phone no.		

For Disclosure, Privacy Act, and Paperwork Reduction Act Notice, see instructions. Cat. No. 11329W Form **1040EZ** (2014)

DRAFT AS OF
July 24, 2014
DO NOT FILE

Use this form if

- Your filing status is single or married filing jointly. If you are not sure about your filing status, see instructions.
- You (and your spouse if married filing jointly) were under age 65 and not blind at the end of 2014. If you were born on January 1, 1950, you are considered to be age 65 at the end of 2014.
- You do not claim any dependents. For information on dependents, see Pub. 501.
- Your taxable income (line 6) is less than $100,000.
- You do not claim any adjustments to income. For information on adjustments to income, use the TeleTax topics listed under *Adjustments to Income* at *www.irs.gov/taxtopics* (see instructions).
- The only tax credit you can claim is the earned income credit (EIC). The credit may give you a refund even if you do not owe any tax. You do not need a qualifying child to claim the EIC. For information on credits, use the TeleTax topics listed under *Tax Credits* at *www.irs.gov/taxtopics* (see instructions). If you received a Form 1098-T or paid higher education expenses, you may be eligible for a tax credit or deduction that you must claim on Form 1040A or Form 1040. For more information on tax benefits for education, see Pub. 970. If you can claim the premium tax credit or you received or benefited from payments of the advance premium tax credit, you must use Form 1040A or Form 1040.
- You had only wages, salaries, tips, taxable scholarship or fellowship grants, unemployment compensation, or Alaska Permanent Fund dividends, and your taxable interest was not over $1,500. But if you earned tips, including allocated tips, that are not included in box 5 and box 7 of your Form W-2, you may not be able to use Form 1040EZ (see instructions). If you are planning to use Form 1040EZ for a child who received Alaska Permanent Fund dividends, see instructions.

Filling in your return

If you received a scholarship or fellowship grant or tax-exempt interest income, such as on municipal bonds, see the instructions before filling in the form. Also, see the instructions if you received a Form 1099-INT showing federal income tax withheld or if federal income tax was withheld from your unemployment compensation or Alaska Permanent Fund dividends.

For tips on how to avoid common mistakes, see instructions.

Remember, you must report all wages, salaries, and tips even if you do not get a Form W-2 from your employer. You must also report all your taxable interest, including interest from banks, savings and loans, credit unions, etc., even if you do not get a Form 1099-INT.

Worksheet for Line 5 — Dependents Who Checked One or Both Boxes

Use this worksheet to figure the amount to enter on line 5 if someone can claim you (or your spouse if married filing jointly) as a dependent, even if that person chooses not to do so. To find out if someone can claim you as a dependent, see Pub. 501.

A. Amount, if any, from line 1 on front . . . . . . ______
\+ 350.00 Enter total ▶ **A.** ______

B. Minimum standard deduction . . . . . . **B.** 1,000

C. Enter the **larger** of line A or line B here . . . . . . **C.** ______

D. Maximum standard deduction. If **single,** enter $6,200; if **married filing jointly,** enter $12,400 . **D.** ______

E. Enter the **smaller** of line C or line D here. This is your standard deduction . . . . . . **E.** ______

F. Exemption amount.
- If single, enter -0-.
- If married filing jointly and —
  - —both you and your spouse can be claimed as dependents, enter -0-.
  - —only one of you can be claimed as a dependent, enter $3,950.

} **F.** ______

G. Add lines E and F. Enter the total here and on line 5 on the front . . . . . . **G.** ______

(keep a copy for your records)

If you did not check any boxes on line 5, enter on line 5 the amount shown below that applies to you.
- Single, enter $10,150. This is the total of your standard deduction ($6,200) and your exemption ($3,950).
- Married filing jointly, enter $20,300. This is the total of your standard deduction ($12,400), your exemption ($3,950), and your spouse's exemption ($3,950).

Mailing Return

Mail your return by **April 15, 2015.** Mail it to the address shown on the last page of the instructions.

Form **1040A** Department of the Treasury—Internal Revenue Service
U.S. Individual Income Tax Return (99) **2014** IRS Use Only—Do not write or staple in this space.

DRAFT AS OF July 24, 2014 DO NOT FILE

Your first name and initial	Last name	OMB No. 1545-0074 **Your social security number**
If a joint return, spouse's first name and initial	Last name	**Spouse's social security number**
Home address (number and street). If you have a P.O. box, see instructions.	Apt. no.	▲ Make sure the SSN(s) above and on line 6c are correct.
City, town or post office, state, and ZIP code. If you have a foreign address, also complete spaces below (see instructions).		**Presidential Election Campaign** Check here if you, or your spouse if filing jointly, want $3 to go to this fund. Checking a box below will not change your tax or refund. ☐ You ☐ Spouse
Foreign country name	Foreign province/state/county	Foreign postal code

Filing status
Check only one box.

1 ☐ Single
2 ☐ Married filing jointly (even if only one had income)
3 ☐ Married filing separately. Enter spouse's SSN above and full name here. ▶
4 ☐ Head of household (with qualifying person). (See instructions.) If the qualifying person is a child but not your dependent, enter this child's name here. ▶
5 ☐ Qualifying widow(er) with dependent child (see instructions)

Exemptions

6a ☐ **Yourself.** If someone can claim you as a dependent, **do not** check box 6a.
b ☐ **Spouse**
} **Boxes checked on 6a and 6b**

c **Dependents:**

If more than six dependents, see instructions.

(1) First name Last name	(2) Dependent's social security number	(3) Dependent's relationship to you	(4) ✓ if child under age 17 qualifying for child tax credit (see instructions)
			☐
			☐
			☐
			☐
			☐
			☐

No. of children on 6c who:
• lived with you
• did not live with you due to divorce or separation (see instructions)
Dependents on 6c not entered above

d Total number of exemptions claimed. **Add numbers on lines above ▶**

Income

Attach Form(s) W-2 here. Also attach Form(s) 1099-R if tax was withheld.

If you did not get a W-2, see instructions.

Line	Description		
7	Wages, salaries, tips, etc. Attach Form(s) W-2.		7
8a	**Taxable** interest. Attach Schedule B if required.		8a
b	**Tax-exempt** interest. **Do not** include on line 8a.	8b	
9a	Ordinary dividends. Attach Schedule B if required.		9a
b	Qualified dividends (see instructions).	9b	
10	Capital gain distributions (see instructions).		10
11a	IRA distributions.	11a	**11b** Taxable amount (see instructions). 11b
12a	Pensions and annuities.	12a	**12b** Taxable amount (see instructions). 12b
13	Unemployment compensation and Alaska Permanent Fund dividends.		13
14a	Social security benefits.	14a	**14b** Taxable amount (see instructions). 14b
15	Add lines 7 through 14b (far right column). This is your **total income.** ▶		15

Adjusted gross income

Line	Description		
16	Reserved	16	
17	IRA deduction (see instructions).	17	
18	Student loan interest deduction (see instructions).	18	
19	Reserved	19	
20	Add lines 16 through 19. These are your **total adjustments.**		20
21	Subtract line 20 from line 15. This is your **adjusted gross income.** ▶		21

For Disclosure, Privacy Act, and Paperwork Reduction Act Notice, see separate instructions. Cat. No. 11327A Form **1040A** (2014)

Form 1040A (2014) Page **2**

DRAFT AS OF July 24, 2014 DO NOT FILE

Tax, credits, and payments

Standard Deduction for—
- People who check any box on line 23a or 23b **or** who can be claimed as a dependent, see instructions.
- All others:

Single or Married filing separately, $6,200
Married filing jointly or Qualifying widow(er), $12,400
Head of household, $9,100

22 Enter the amount from line 21 (adjusted gross income). 22

23a Check if: { ☐ **You** were born before January 2, 1950, ☐ Blind / ☐ **Spouse** was born before January 2, 1950, ☐ Blind } **Total boxes checked** ▶ 23a ☐

b If you are married filing separately and your spouse itemizes deductions, check here ▶ 23b ☐

24 Enter your **standard deduction.** 24

25 Subtract line 24 from line 22. If line 24 is more than line 22, enter -0-. 25

26 **Exemptions.** Multiply $3,950 by the number on line 6d. 26

27 Subtract line 26 from line 25. If line 26 is more than line 25, enter -0-. This is your **taxable income.** ▶ 27

28 **Tax,** including any alternative minimum tax (see instructions). 28

29 Excess advance premium tax credit repayment. Attach Form 8962. 29

30 Add lines 28 and 29. 30

31 Credit for child and dependent care expenses. Attach Form 2441. 31

32 Credit for the elderly or the disabled. Attach Schedule R. 32

33 Education credits from Form 8863, line 19. 33

34 Retirement savings contributions credit. Attach Form 8880. 34

35 Child tax credit. Attach Schedule 8812, if required. 35

36 Add lines 31 through 35. These are your **total credits.** 36

37 Subtract line 36 from line 30. If line 36 is more than line 30, enter -0-. 37

38 Health care: individual responsibility (see instructions). Full-year coverage ☐ 38

39 Add line 37 and line 38. This is your **total tax.** 39

40 Federal income tax withheld from Forms W-2 and 1099. 40

41 2014 estimated tax payments and amount applied from 2013 return. 41

If you have a qualifying child, attach Schedule EIC.

42a **Earned income credit (EIC).** 42a

b Nontaxable combat pay election. 42b

43 Additional child tax credit. Attach Schedule 8812. 43

44 American opportunity credit from Form 8863, line 8. 44

45 Net premium tax credit. Attach Form 8962. 45

46 Add lines 40, 41, 42a, 43, 44, and 45. These are your **total payments.** ▶ 46

Refund

Direct deposit? See instructions and fill in 48b, 48c, and 48d or Form 8888.

47 If line 46 is more than line 39, subtract line 39 from line 46. This is the amount you **overpaid.** 47

48a Amount of line 47 you want **refunded to you.** If Form 8888 is attached, check here ▶ ☐ 48a

▶ b Routing number ▶ c Type: ☐ Checking ☐ Savings

▶ d Account number

49 Amount of line 47 you want **applied to your 2015 estimated tax.** 49

Amount you owe

50 **Amount you owe.** Subtract line 46 from line 39. For details on how to pay, see instructions. ▶ 50

51 Estimated tax penalty (see instructions). 51

Third party designee

Do you want to allow another person to discuss this return with the IRS (see instructions)? ☐ **Yes.** Complete the following. ☐ **No**

Designee's name ▶ Phone no. ▶ Personal identification number (PIN) ▶

Sign here

Joint return? See instructions. Keep a copy for your records.

Under penalties of perjury, I declare that I have examined this return and accompanying schedules and statements, and to the best of my knowledge and belief, they are true, correct, and accurately list all amounts and sources of income I received during the tax year. Declaration of preparer (other than the taxpayer) is based on all information of which the preparer has any knowledge.

Your signature	Date	Your occupation	Daytime phone number
Spouse's signature. If a joint return, **both** must sign.	Date	Spouse's occupation	If the IRS sent you an Identity Protection PIN, enter it here (see inst.)

Paid preparer use only

Print/type preparer's name	Preparer's signature	Date	Check ▶ ☐ if self-employed	PTIN
Firm's name ▶			Firm's EIN ▶	
Firm's address ▶			Phone no.	

Form **1040A** (2014)

Student Name ______________________

Class/Section ______________________

Date ______________________

KEY NUMBER TAX RETURN SUMMARY

CHAPTER 1

Comprehensive Problem 1

Adjusted Gross Income (Line 4) ______________

Taxable Income (Line 6) ______________

Tax Liability (Line 12) ______________

Tax Overpaid (Line 13a) ______________

Comprehensive Problem 2A

Adjusted Gross Income (Line 21) ______________

Deductions (Line 24) ______________

Exemptions (Line 26) ______________

Tax Liability (Line 39) ______________

Tax Overpaid (Line 47) ______________

Comprehensive Problem 2B

Adjusted Gross Income (Line 21) ______________

Deductions (Line 24) ______________

Exemptions (Line 26) ______________

Tax Liability (Line 39) ______________

Tax Overpaid (Line 47) ______________

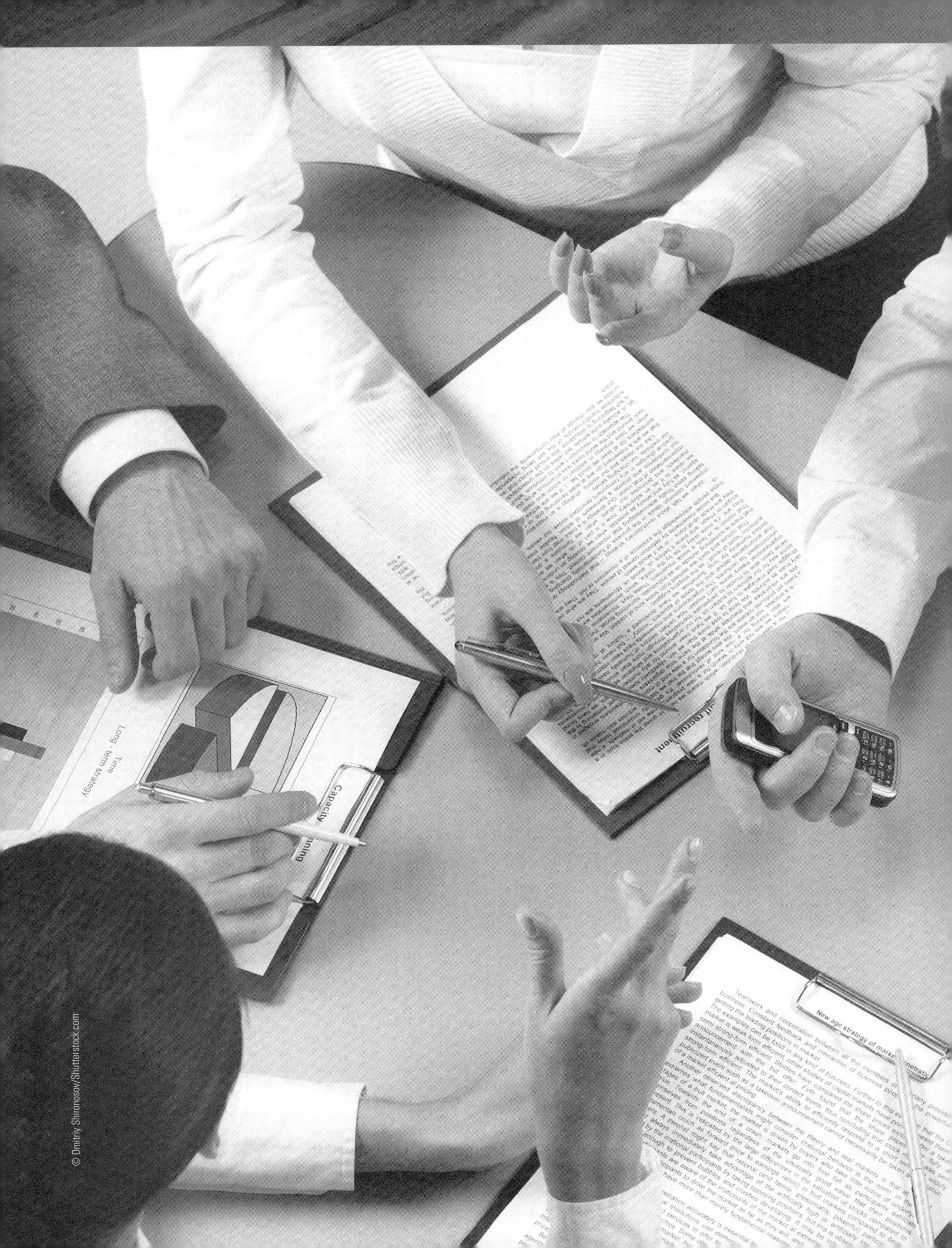

© Dmitriy Shironosov/Shutterstock.com

CHAPTER 2

Gross Income and Exclusions

LEARNING OBJECTIVES

After completing this chapter, you should be able to:

LO 2.1 Understand and apply the definition of gross income.
LO 2.2 Identify the tax treatment of interest and dividend income.
LO 2.3 Describe the tax treatment of alimony and child support.
LO 2.4 Determine when prizes and awards are included in income.
LO 2.5 Calculate the taxable and nontaxable portions of annuity payments.
LO 2.6 Understand the tax treatment of life insurance proceeds.
LO 2.7 Identify the general rules for the tax treatment of gifts and inheritances.
LO 2.8 Describe the elements of scholarship income that are excluded from tax.
LO 2.9 Understand the general tax treatment of health insurance.
LO 2.10 Determine when meals and lodging may be excluded from taxable income.
LO 2.11 Understand the tax treatment of municipal bond interest.
LO 2.12 Describe the tax treatment of unemployment compensation.
LO 2.13 Identify the common employee fringe benefit income exclusions.
LO 2.14 Apply the rules governing inclusion of Social Security benefits as income.

OVERVIEW

This chapter starts with the definition of gross income. Tables 2.1 and 2.2 list the common inclusions in and exclusions from gross income. Detailed coverage is provided for inclusions and exclusions that may present specific problems to taxpayers. The coverage includes the special tax treatment for interest and dividends, alimony, prizes and awards, annuities, life insurance proceeds, and gifts and inheritances. Coverage of important exclusions includes scholarships, accident and health insurance benefits, certain meals and lodging, municipal bond interest, and the special treatment of Social Security benefits. The elements of gross income discussed here represent much of what is included in the first line of the individual tax formula.

Learning Objective 2.1

Understand and apply the definition of gross income.

THE NATURE OF GROSS INCOME

Gross income is the starting point for calculating a taxpayer's tax liability. The tax law states that gross income is:

... all income from whatever source derived, including (but not limited to) the following items:

1. Compensation for services, including fees, commissions, fringe benefits, and similar items
2. Gross income derived from business
3. Gains derived from dealings in property
4. Interest
5. Rents
6. Royalties
7. Dividends
8. Alimony and separate maintenance payments
9. Annuities
10. Income from life insurance and endowment contracts
11. Pensions
12. Income from discharge of indebtedness
13. Distributive share of partnership gross income
14. Income in respect of a decedent
15. Income from an interest in an estate or trust

Would You Believe?

Income earned illegally from any source, including drug sales and organized crime, is taxable. Al Capone, who headed an enormous, violent, and profitable crime organization, eluded conviction for criminal activities until 1930 when he was sent to prison for tax evasion.

The definition of gross income as **"all income from whatever source derived"** is perhaps the most well-known definition in the tax law. Under this definition, unless there is an exception in the law, the U.S. government considers all income taxable. Therefore, prizes and awards, cash and noncash payments for goods and services, payments made in trade or *barter* (such as car repairs traded for tax preparation services), and illegal income not generally reported to the IRS are all still taxable income.

Table 2.1 provides an expanded list of items that are included in gross income. When in doubt, the general rule is that everything a taxpayer receives must be included in gross income unless specifically excluded. Any noncash items must be included in gross income at the fair market value of the items received.

The tax law provides that certain items of income are exempt from taxation; these items are referred to as *exclusions*. The exclusions include items such as life insurance proceeds, gifts, and veterans' benefits. A more complete list of exclusions from gross income is provided in Table 2.2.

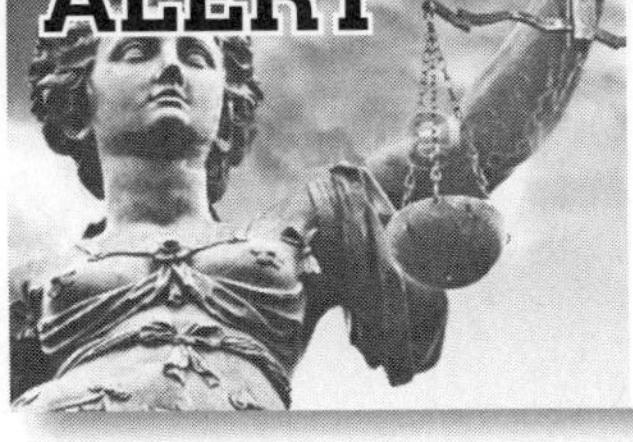

© ER_09/Shutterstock.com

In 2014, the Internal Revenue Service decided that virtual currencies such as bitcoin should be treated as property for federal tax purposes. This means that wages paid using virtual currency are taxable to the employee and must be reported on a Form W-2. Payments using virtual currency made to independent contractors and other service providers are taxable and self-employment tax rules generally apply. Normally, payers must issue Form 1099.

TABLE 2.1 2014 INCLUSIONS IN GROSS INCOME—PARTIAL LIST

Alimony
Amounts recovered after being deducted in prior years
Annuities
Awards
Back pay
Bargain purchase from employer
Bonuses
Breach of contract damages
Business income
Clergy fees and contributions
Commissions
Compensation for services
Contributions received by members of the clergy
Damages for nonphysical personal injury
Death benefits
Debts forgiven
Directors' fees
Dividends
Embezzled funds
Employee awards
Employee benefits (except certain fringe benefits)
Employee bonuses
Employee stock options
Estate and trust income
Farm income
Fees
Gains from illegal activities
Gains from sale of property
Gambling winnings
Group-term life insurance premiums paid by employer for coverage over $50,000
Hobby income
Incentive awards
Interest income
Jury duty fees
Living quarters, meals (unless furnished for employer's convenience, etc.)
Military pay (unless combat pay)
Notary fees
Partnership income
Pensions
Prizes
Professional fees
Punitive damages
Rents
Retirement pay
Rewards
Royalties
Salaries
Scholarships (room and board)
Severance pay
Strike and lockout benefits
Supplemental unemployment benefits
Tips and gratuities
Unemployment compensation
Wages

© Cengage Learning

TABLE 2.2 2014 EXCLUSIONS FROM GROSS INCOME—PARTIAL LIST

Accident insurance proceeds
Annuities (to a limited extent)
Bequests
Casualty insurance proceeds
Child support payments
Damages for physical personal injury or sickness
Disability benefits (generally, but not always)
Gifts
Group-term life insurance premiums paid by employer (coverage not over $50,000)
Health insurance proceeds
Inheritances
Life insurance proceeds
Meals and lodging (furnished for employer's convenience, etc.)
Military allowances
Minister's dwelling rental value allowance
Municipal bond interest
Relocation payments
Scholarships (tuition and books)
Social Security benefits (with limits)
Veterans' benefits
Welfare payments
Workers' compensation

© Cengage Learning

Self-Study Problem 2.1

See Appendix E for Solutions to Self-Study Problems

Indicate whether each of the items listed below should be included in gross income or excluded from gross income in 2014.

	Included	***Excluded***
1. Prizes and awards	________	________
2. Embezzled funds	________	________
3. Child support payments	________	________
4. Alimony	________	________
5. Pensions	________	________
6. Inheritances	________	________
7. Welfare payments	________	________
8. Bequests	________	________
9. Jury duty fees	________	________
10. Royalties	________	________
11. Life insurance proceeds paid at death	________	________
12. Hobby income	________	________
13. Rewards	________	________
14. Partnership income	________	________
15. Casualty insurance proceeds	________	________
16. G.I. Bill benefits	________	________
17. Scholarships for room and board	________	________
18. Business income	________	________
19. Gifts	________	________

Learning Objective 2.2

Identify the tax treatment of interest and dividend income.

INTEREST AND DIVIDEND INCOME

Any interest or dividend income a taxpayer receives or that is credited to his or her account is taxable income, unless it is specifically exempt from tax such as state or municipal bond interest (discussed further in LO 2.11). If the interest or dividends total more than $1,500, the taxpayer is required to file Schedule B of Form 1040, which lists the amounts and sources of the income.

The fair market value of gifts or services a taxpayer receives for making long-term deposits or opening accounts in savings institutions is also taxable interest income. Interest is reported in the year it is received by a cash basis taxpayer.

TAX BREAK

Taxpayers may defer reporting interest income on a bank certificate of deposit (CD) if the CD has a maturity of 1 year or less and there is a substantial penalty for early withdrawal. For example, assume an investor purchases a 6-month CD on September 1, 2014, which matures on March 1, 2015, and the bank charges a penalty equal to 2 months of interest in the event of early withdrawal. In this case, the 4 months of interest earned on the account during 2014 will not have to be reported until the investor's 2015 tax return is filed.

When a taxpayer withdraws funds early from a CD and must pay a penalty as described above, the full amount of the interest is reported as income and the penalty may be deducted on Form 1040 as a deduction for adjusted gross income.

U.S. Savings Bonds

The U.S. government issues three basic types of savings bonds to individuals: Series EE Bonds, Series HH Bonds, and Series I Bonds. Series EE Bonds increase in value over their life, and the increase in redemption value is generally taxable when the bond is redeemed and the interest is paid. The second type of savings bond, Series HH Bond, is issued at face value and pays interest twice a year by check. Interest on Series HH Bonds is reported in the year received by a cash basis taxpayer. (Note: As of August 31, 2004, the Treasury stopped issuing Series HH bonds. HH bonds sold before August 31, 2004, are still outstanding and paying interest.) Series I Bonds, like Series EE Bonds, do not pay interest until maturity, but earnings are adjusted for inflation on a semiannual basis.

Cash basis taxpayers report the increase in redemption value (interest) on a Series EE Bond or a Series I Bond using one of the following methods:

1. The interest may be reported in the year the bonds are cashed or in the year they mature, whichever is earlier (no election is required to use this method), or
2. The taxpayer may elect to report the increase in redemption value each year.

If the taxpayer wants to change from method (1) to method (2), he or she may do so without the permission of the IRS. In the year of change, all interest earned to date and not previously reported must be reported on all Series EE Bonds and Series I Bonds held by the taxpayer. Once method (2) is selected, the taxpayer must continue to use it for all Series EE Bonds currently held or acquired in the future. Taxpayers cannot change back to method (1) without permission of the IRS.

Dividends

Dividends are one type of distribution paid to a taxpayer by a corporation. Taxpayers may receive the following types of distributions from a corporation:

1. Ordinary dividends
2. Nontaxable distributions
3. Capital gain distributions

Ordinary dividends are by far the most common type of corporate distribution. They are paid from the earnings and profits of the corporation.

Nontaxable distributions are a return of invested capital and are not paid from the earnings and profits of the corporation. They are considered a return of the taxpayer's investment in the corporation and are not included in the taxpayer's income. Instead, the taxpayer's basis in the stock is reduced by nontaxable distributions until the basis reaches zero.[1] After the stock has reached a zero basis, distributions that represent a return of capital are taxed as capital gains. Capital gain distributions are reported either on Page 1 of Form 1040 or on Schedule D.

Current Tax Rates for Dividends

For years, experts have argued that corporate dividends are taxed twice, once when the corporation pays tax on profits, and once when the dividend is received by the shareholder.

[1] A taxpayer's basis in an investment is usually the cost of the investment. The basis is used to determine the gain or loss when the investment is sold.

To provide some tax relief for individual taxpayers who receive corporate dividends, the tax rates on qualifying dividends are as follows:

Ordinary Tax Bracket	*Qualifying Dividend Tax Rate for 2014**
10% and 15%	0%
25% through 35%	15%
39.6%	20%

*Beginning in 2013, an additional 3.8 percent Medicare surtax on net investment income, including qualifying dividends, applies to high-income taxpayers with income over certain thresholds. Please see Chapter 1, LO 1.9, for further details.

Corporations issuing dividends and brokerage companies holding stock investments for taxpayers are required to classify and report the amount of qualifying dividends to investors.

Self-Study Problem 2.2

See Appendix E for Solutions to Self-Study Problems

Bill and Betty Brown received the following dividend and interest income during 2014:

	Received by		
	Bill	***Betty***	***Jointly***
Dividends (all qualified for lower tax rates):			
IBM	$275	$175	
GM			$ 450
AT&T	450	300	
Interest:			
Ford Bonds		425	
Big Savings and Loan			2,150
U.S. Bonds			175
Nontaxable Distribution:			
Western Gas & Electric			875
Totals	$725	$900	$3,650

The Browns have taxable income, including dividends and interest, of $40,000.

Complete Form 1040, Schedule B, and the tax calculation worksheet on Pages 2–7 and 2–8 for the Brown's 2014 tax year.

Learning Objective 2.3

Describe the tax treatment of alimony and child support.

ALIMONY

Alimony payments are deductible by the individual making the payments, and they are taxable income to the person receiving the payments. The term *alimony*, for income tax purposes, includes separate maintenance payments or similar periodic payments made to a spouse or former spouse. Payments must meet certain requirements to be considered alimony. These requirements depend on whether the divorce or separation agreement was executed before 1985 or after 1984. The post-1984 tax rules for divorce agreements are discussed below.

For divorce agreements executed after 1984, alimony payments must meet the following requirements:

1. The payments must be in cash and must be received by the spouse (or former spouse).
2. The payments must be made under a decree of divorce or separate maintenance or under a written instrument incident to the divorce.

Self-Study Problem 2.2

SCHEDULE B
(Form 1040A or 1040)
Department of the Treasury
Internal Revenue Service (99)

Interest and Ordinary Dividends

► Attach to Form 1040A or 1040.
► Information about Schedule B and its instructions is at *www.irs.gov/scheduleb.*

OMB No. 1545-0074
2014
Attachment Sequence No. 08

Name(s) shown on return | **Your social security number**

DRAFT AS OF
June 18, 2014
DO NOT FILE

Part I Interest

(See instructions on back and the instructions for Form 1040A, or Form 1040, line 8a.)

Note. If you received a Form 1099-INT, Form 1099-OID, or substitute statement from a brokerage firm, list the firm's name as the payer and enter the total interest shown on that form.

			Amount
1	List name of payer. If any interest is from a seller-financed mortgage and the buyer used the property as a personal residence, see instructions on back and list this interest first. Also, show that buyer's social security number and address ►	1	
2	Add the amounts on line 1	2	
3	Excludable interest on series EE and I U.S. savings bonds issued after 1989. Attach Form 8815	3	
4	Subtract line 3 from line 2. Enter the result here and on Form 1040A, or Form 1040, line 8a ►	4	

Note. If line 4 is over $1,500, you must complete Part III.

Part II Ordinary Dividends

(See instructions on back and the instructions for Form 1040A, or Form 1040, line 9a.)

Note. If you received a Form 1099-DIV or substitute statement from a brokerage firm, list the firm's name as the payer and enter the ordinary dividends shown on that form.

			Amount
5	List name of payer ►	5	
6	Add the amounts on line 5. Enter the total here and on Form 1040A, or Form 1040, line 9a ►	6	

Note. If line 6 is over $1,500, you must complete Part III.

Part III Foreign Accounts and Trusts

(See instructions on back.)

You must complete this part if you **(a)** had over $1,500 of taxable interest or ordinary dividends; **(b)** had a foreign account; or **(c)** received a distribution from, or were a grantor of, or a transferor to, a foreign trust.

		Yes	No
7a	At any time during 2014, did you have a financial interest in or signature authority over a financial account (such as a bank account, securities account, or brokerage account) located in a foreign country? See instructions		
	If "Yes," are you required to file FinCEN Form 114, Report of Foreign Bank and Financial Accounts (FBAR), to report that financial interest or signature authority? See FinCEN Form 114 and its instructions for filing requirements and exceptions to those requirements		
b	If you are required to file FinCEN Form 114, enter the name of the foreign country where the financial account is located ►		
8	During 2014, did you receive a distribution from, or were you the grantor of, or transferor to, a foreign trust? If "Yes," you may have to file Form 3520. See instructions on back		

Qualified Dividends and Capital Gain Tax Worksheet—Line 44

Keep for Your Records

Before you begin:
- √ See the earlier instructions for line 44 to see if you can use this worksheet to figure your tax.
- √ Before completing this worksheet, complete Form 1040 through line 43.
- √ If you do not have to file Schedule D and you received capital gain distributions, be sure you checked the box on line 13 of Form 1040.

1. Enter the amount from Form 1040, line 43. However, if you are filing Form 2555 or 2555-EZ (relating to foreign earned income), enter the amount from line 3 of the Foreign Earned Income Tax Worksheet ..... 1. ______
2. Enter the amount from Form 1040, line 9b* ..... 2. ______
3. Are you filing Schedule D?*
   ☐ **Yes.** Enter the **smaller** of line 15 or 16 of Schedule D. If either line 15 or line 16 is blank or a loss, enter -0-
   ☐ **No.** Enter the amount from Form 1040, line 13 ..... 3. ______
4. Add lines 2 and 3 ..... 4. ______
5. If filing Form 4952 (used to figure investment interest expense deduction), enter any amount from line 4g of that form. Otherwise, enter -0- ..... 5. ______
6. Subtract line 5 from line 4. If zero or less, enter -0- ..... 6. ______
7. Subtract line 6 from line 1. If zero or less, enter -0- ..... 7. ______
8. Enter:
   $36,900 if single or married filing separately,
   $73,800 if married filing jointly or qualifying widow(er),
   $49,400 if head of household. ..... 8. ______
9. Enter the smaller of line 1 or line 8 ..... 9. ______
10. Enter the smaller of line 7 or line 9 ..... 10. ______
11. Subtract line 10 from line 9. This amount is taxed at 0% ..... 11. ______
12. Enter the smaller of line 1 or line 6 ..... 12. ______
13. Enter the amount from line 11 ..... 13. ______
14. Subtract line 13 from line 12 ..... 14. ______
15. Enter:
    $406,750 if single,
    $228,800 if married filing separately,
    $457,600 if married filing jointly or qualifying widow(er),
    $432,200 if head of household. ..... 15. ______
16. Enter the smaller of line 1 or line 15 ..... 16. ______
17. Add lines 7 and 11 ..... 17. ______
18. Subtract line 17 from line 16. If zero or less, enter -0- ..... 18. ______
19. Enter the smaller of line 14 or line 18 ..... 19. ______
20. Multiply line 19 by 15% (.15) ..... 20. ______
21. Add lines 11 and 19 ..... 21. ______
22. Subtract line 21 from line 12 ..... 22. ______
23. Multiply line 22 by 20% (.20) ..... 23. ______
24. Figure the tax on the amount on line 7. If the amount on line 7 is less than $100,000, use the Tax Table to figure the tax. If the amount on line 7 is $100,000 or more, use the Tax Computation Worksheet ..... 24. ______
25. Add lines 20, 23, and 24 ..... 25. ______
26. Figure the tax on the amount on line 1. If the amount on line 1 is less than $100,000, use the Tax Table to figure the tax. If the amount on line 1 is $100,000 or more, use the Tax Computation Worksheet ..... 26. ______
27. **Tax on all taxable income.** Enter the **smaller** of line 25 or line 26. Also include this amount on Form 1040, line 44. If you are filing Form 2555 or 2555-EZ, do not enter this amount on Form 1040, line 44. Instead, enter it on line 4 of the Foreign Earned Income Tax Worksheet ..... 27. ______

**If you are filing Form 2555 or 2555-EZ, see the footnote in the Foreign Earned Income Tax Worksheet before completing this line.*

3. The payor must have no liability to make payments for any period following the death of the spouse receiving the payments.
4. The payments must not be designated in the written agreement as anything other than alimony.
5. If the parties are divorced or legally separated, they must not be members of the same household at the time the payments are made.

Disguised child support payments may not be treated as alimony. Payments contingent on the status of a child, such as the age or marital status of the child, are not considered alimony.

EXAMPLE Under a 2008 divorce agreement, Sam has agreed to pay his former spouse, Silvia, $1,000 per month. The payments meet all the tests for classification as alimony, but they will be reduced to $600 per month when their child, in Silvia's custody, becomes 18 years of age. In this situation, $400 of each payment must be treated as nondeductible child support and cannot be considered alimony. ♦

Would You Believe?

In 2014 the Treasury Inspector General for Tax Administration (TIGTA) issued a report detailing their study to attempt to match alimony deducted with alimony included in income for tax year 2010. They found that the amount of alimony deducted exceeded the amount of alimony reported as income by about $2.3 billion. Of the approximately 568,000 taxpayers that reported an alimony deduction, about 47 percent had no corresponding alimony income or the amounts did not match.

Alimony Recapture

Congress has enacted provisions to prevent "front-end loading" of alimony payments. The tax law may require taxpayers paying alimony to include previously deducted payments in income if the payments significantly decrease in amount during the first few years. The rules for alimony recapture are complex and vary depending on the year the divorce decree was granted.

TAX BREAK

During a divorce, the tax impact of structuring payments as alimony rather than as property settlement payments should be carefully considered. If one spouse is in a lower tax bracket than the other spouse, both spouses may be better off structuring payments made to the lower-income spouse as alimony. The tax savings to the high-income spouse will be larger than the taxes paid by the low-income spouse. The benefit of the tax savings can then be shared with the low-income spouse in the form of higher alimony payments, resulting in a win–win situation.

Property Transfers

A spouse who transfers property in settlement of a marital obligation is not required to recognize any gain as a result of the property's appreciation. Thus, if in a divorce settlement a wife transfers property with a fair market value of $10,000 and a tax basis of $3,000 to her husband, she will not be required to recognize the gain of $7,000 ($10,000 – $3,000). Of course, the husband would be required to assume the wife's tax basis ($3,000) in the property.

Child Support

Payments made for child support are not deductible by the taxpayer making them, nor are they income to the recipient. However, they may be an important factor in determining which spouse is entitled to claim the dependency exemption for the child (see Chapter 1). Child support payments must be up to date before any amount paid may be treated as alimony. That is, if a taxpayer is obligated to pay both child support and alimony, he or she must

first meet the child support obligation before obtaining a deduction for alimony payments. Payments for child support include payments designated as such in the marital settlement agreement, plus any alimony payments that are contingent upon the status of a child.

EXAMPLE Jim is required under a 2008 divorce decree to pay $400 alimony and $250 child support per month. Since the decree separately states that $250 is child support, only $400 per month is deductible by Jim and counts as income to his ex-wife. ♦

Would You Believe?

The IRS treats an annulled marriage as though it never existed. Therefore, the IRS requires couples who have received an annulment to refile their tax returns as unmarried persons for as many as 3 years back. In some cases, this can be a very expensive procedure.

Self-Study Problem 2.3

See Appendix E for Solutions to Self-Study Problems

Answer the following questions, assuming the divorce agreements were executed after 1984.

1. A husband is required to pay his former wife $12,000 in alimony in the current year. Since he is short of cash, he gives her an automobile worth $12,000, which she accepts in place of the alimony. How much may the husband deduct as alimony?

   $__________

2. A husband is required to pay alimony of $2,000 per month to his ex-wife. However, the alimony is reduced to $1,200 per month when their son, who lives with his mother, becomes 18. How much of the monthly payment is alimony income to the wife?

   $__________

3. A wife is required to transfer $100,000 worth of property to her ex-husband as a property settlement. The property has a basis to the wife of $20,000. How much taxable gain must the wife recognize on this transfer?

   $__________

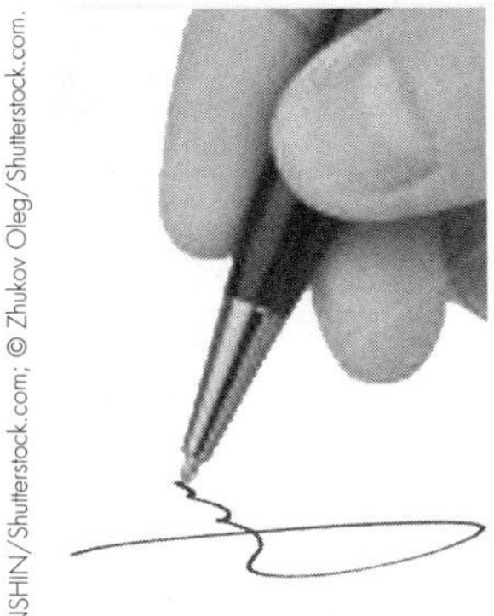

© ILYA AKINSHIN/Shutterstock.com; © Zhukov Oleg/Shutterstock.com.

Would You Sign This Tax Return?

Paid Preparer Use Only	Print/Type preparer's name	Preparer's signature	Date	Check ☐ if self-employed	PTIN
	Firm's name ▶		Firm's EIN ▶		
	Firm's address ▶		Phone no.		

For the last 10 years, you prepared the joint tax returns for Dominic (husband; age 40) and Dulce (wife; age 35) Divorcio. Last year they got a divorce and remained as your separate tax clients. Under the dissolution decree, Dominic has to pay Dulce $2,500 per month alimony, which he does for the current year. You have completed Dominic's tax return for the current year and you deducted the required alimony payments to Dulce on Dominic's Form 1040. Dulce came in to have you prepare her tax return and refused to report her alimony received as income. She stated, "I am not going to pay tax on the $30,000 from Dominic." She views the payments as "a gift for putting up with him for all those years of marriage." Dulce will not budge on excluding this alimony from income. Would you sign the Paid Preparer's declaration (see example above) on this return? Why or why not?

PRIZES AND AWARDS

Learning Objective 2.4

Determine when prizes and awards are included in income.

Prizes and awards are taxable income to the recipient. Winnings from television or radio shows, door prizes, lotteries, and other contest winnings are income to taxpayers. In addition, all other awards are generally taxable, even if they are awards given for accomplishments and with no action on the part of the taxpayer. Even a Nobel prize is taxable. If the prize or award is received in property instead of cash, the fair market value of the property is included in the taxpayer's income. For example, the gift bags given to the attendees at the Academy Awards include items such as expensive jewelry and vacations worth more than $100,000. The value of these gift bags is included in taxable income. Taxpayers may refuse a prize and exclude its value from income.

An exception is provided for certain employee achievement awards in the form of tangible personal property, such as a gold watch for 25 years of service. If the award is made in recognition of length of service or safety achievement, the value of the property may be excluded from income. Generally, the maximum amount excludable is $400. However, if the award is a "qualified plan award," the maximum exclusion is increased to $1,600.

Would You Believe?

Former *Survivor* star Richard Hatch turned himself in to federal marshals in March of 2011 to begin serving a 9-month prison sentence for failure to pay taxes on his $1 million prize from the television show.

EXAMPLE Van enters a drawing and wins a new automobile. The automobile has a sticker price of $20,200. The fair market value of the prize should be included in Van's gross income, but the fair market value is probably not the sticker price; instead, it is the price at which a similar car normally would be sold. ♦

Self-Study Problem 2.4

See Appendix E for Solutions to Self-Study Problems

For each of the following independent cases, indicate the amount of gross income that should be included on the taxpayer's return.

	Gross Income
1. Helen enters a radio contest and wins $2,000.	$________
2. In 2014, Professor Deborah wins an award of $10,000 for a book on literature she published 4 years ago. The award was presented in recognition of her past literary achievements.	$________
3. Bill is a professional baseball player. Because he has hit 50 home runs this season, he was given a new wrist watch worth $2,500.	$________
4. John is an employee of Big Corporation. He is awarded $5,000 for a suggestion to improve the plant layout.	$________
5. Martha received a desk clock worth $350 from her employer in recognition of her 15 years of loyal service as an employee.	$________

Learning Objective 2.5

Calculate the taxable and nontaxable portions of annuity payments.

ANNUITIES

When taxpayers consider retirement, they often purchase annuities. An annuity is a type of investment in which the taxpayer purchases the right to receive periodic payments for the remainder of his or her life. The amount of each periodic payment is based on the annuity purchase price and the life expectancy of the annuitant. Standard mortality tables, based on the current age of the annuitant, are used to calculate the annuity amount.

The Simplified Method

Individual taxpayers generally must use the "simplified" method to calculate the taxable amount from an annuity for annuities starting after November 18, 1996. Nonqualified plan annuities and certain annuitants age 75 and over must still use the general rule discussed below.

To calculate the excluded amount, the IRS provides the following worksheet.

Simplified Method Worksheet

1. Enter total amount received this year. 1. ____________
2. Enter cost in the plan at the annuity starting date. 2. ____________
3. Age at annuity starting date

	Enter
55 and under	360
56–60	310
61–65	260
66–70	210
71 and older	160

3. ____________

4. Divide line 2 by line 3. 4. ____________
5. Multiply line 4 by the number of monthly payments this year. If the annuity starting date was before 1987, also enter this amount on line 8, and skip lines 6 and 7. Otherwise, go to line 6. 5. ____________
6. Enter the amount, if any, recovered tax free in prior years. 6. ____________
7. Subtract line 6 from line 2. 7. ____________
8. Enter the smaller of line 5 or 7. 8. ____________
9. Taxable amount this year: Subtract line 8 from line 1. Do not enter less than zero. 9. ____________

Note 1: The denominators provided in step 3 above are effective for annuity starting dates after November 18, 1996. For annuity starting dates prior to November 18, 1996, see any standard tax service.

Note 2: When annuity benefits with starting dates after 1997 are paid over two lives (joint and survivor annuities), a different set of denominators must be used in step 3.

Combined Age of Annuitants	Number of Payments
110 or less	410
111–120	360
121–130	310
131–140	260
141 and over	210

EXAMPLE Joey, age 67, began receiving benefits under a joint and survivor annuity to be paid over the joint lives of himself and his wife Jody, who is 64. He received his first annuity payment in March of the current year. Joey contributed $38,000 to the annuity and he had no distributions from the plan before the current year. The monthly payment to Joey is $1,700.

Joey must use the simplified method to calculate his taxable amount. Using the worksheet, Joey's taxable amount for the current year would be:

Simplified Method Worksheet

1. Enter total amount received this year. — 1. *$17,000.00*
2. Enter cost in the plan at the annuity starting date. — 2. *$38,000.00*
3. Combined age at annuity starting date

	Enter
110 or less	410
111–120	360
121–130	310
131–140	260
141 and over	210

3. *260*

4. Divide line 2 by line 3. — 4. *$ 146.15*
5. Multiply line 4 by the number of monthly payments this year. — 5. *$ 1,461.50*
6. Enter the amount, if any, recovered tax free in prior years. — 6. *$ 0.00*
7. Subtract line 6 from line 2. — 7. *$38,000.00*
8. Enter the smaller of line 5 or 7. — 8. *$ 1,461.50*
9. Taxable amount this year: Subtract line 8 from line 1. Do not enter less than zero. ♦ — 9. *$15,538.50*

The exclusion ratio is calculated at the start of the annuity and remains constant. For annuities starting after 1986, the maximum amount excludable is limited to the taxpayer's investment in the annuity. After the taxpayer's investment is recovered, all additional amounts received are fully taxable. If the taxpayer dies before the entire investment is recovered, any unrecovered amount is permitted as a miscellaneous itemized deduction (not subject to the 2 percent floor) at the time of the annuitant's death. For annuities starting before 1987, the exclusion ratio is used for the life of the annuitant, even after full recovery of the investment. For these earlier annuities, if the annuitant dies prior to recovering the entire investment, the unrecovered portion is lost.

The General Rule

Prior to implementation of the Simplified Method discussed above, the General Rule was used for most annuities. Rather than use the denominators provided in Step 3 of the Simplified Method Worksheet, the life expectancy of the annuitant was determined based on mortality tables provided by the IRS. The excluded amount under the general rule can be calculated as follows:

$$\text{Amount Excluded} = \frac{\text{Investment in Contract}}{\text{Annual Payment} \times \text{Life Expectancy}} \times \text{Amount Received}$$

Employee Annuities

Many employees participate in retirement plans organized by their employers. Employers generally make periodic payments to the plans on behalf of their employees. If the payments are made to qualified retirement plans, contributions by the employer are not taxable to the employees in the current year. Since the contributions are not taxable when made, they are not considered part of the employee's investment in the contract when calculating the exclusion ratio.

Self-Study Problem 2.5

See Appendix E for Solutions to Self-Study Problems

Part a

Phil retired in January 2014 at age 63. His pension is $1,500 per month from a retirement plan to which Phil contributed $42,500. Phil's life expectancy is 21 years, and this year he received eleven payments for a total pension income of $16,500. Calculate Phil's taxable income from the annuity in the current year, using the general rule.

$__________

Part b

Calculate Phil's taxable income using the following Simplified Method Worksheet.

Simplified Method Worksheet

1. Enter total amount received this year. 1. __________
2. Enter cost in the plan at the annuity starting date. 2. __________
3. Age at annuity starting date

	Enter
55 and under	360
56–60	310
61–65	260
66–70	210
71 and older	160

3. __________

4. Divide line 2 by line 3. 4. __________
5. Multiply line 4 by the number of monthly payments this year. If the annuity starting date was before 1987, also enter this amount on line 8, and skip lines 6 and 7. Otherwise, go to line 6. 5. __________
6. Enter the amount, if any, recovered tax free in prior years. 6. __________
7. Subtract line 6 from line 2. 7. __________
8. Enter the smaller of line 5 or 7. 8. __________
9. Taxable amount this year: Subtract line 8 from line 1. Do not enter less than zero. 9. __________

LIFE INSURANCE

Learning Objective 2.6

Understand the tax treatment of life insurance proceeds.

Life insurance proceeds are excluded from gross income based on the premise that it would be inappropriate in a time of need to tax the proceeds from a life insurance policy. Therefore, a major exclusion from gross income is provided for life insurance proceeds. To be excluded, the proceeds must be paid to the beneficiary by reason of the death of the insured. If the proceeds are taken over several years instead of in a lump sum, the insurance company pays interest on the unpaid proceeds. The interest is generally taxable income.

Early payouts of life insurance, also called accelerated death benefits or viatical settlements, are excluded from gross income for certain terminally or chronically ill taxpayers. The taxpayer may either collect an early payout from the insurance company or sell or assign the policy to a viatical settlement provider. A terminally ill individual must be certified by a medical doctor to have an illness which is reasonably expected to cause death within 24 months. A chronically ill individual must be certified by a medical doctor as unable to perform daily living activities without assistance. Chronically ill taxpayers may only exclude gain on accelerated death benefits to the extent proceeds are used for long-term care.

If an insurance policy is transferred to another person for valuable consideration, all or a portion of the proceeds from the life insurance policy may be taxable to the recipient. For example, taxable proceeds result when a policy is transferred to a creditor in payment of a debt. When a transfer for value occurs, the proceeds at the death of the insured are taxable to the extent they exceed the cash surrender value of the policy at the time it was transferred, plus the amount of the insurance premiums paid by the purchaser. There is an exception to the rule that policies transferred for valuable consideration result in taxable proceeds. Transfers to a partner of the insured, a partnership in which the insured is a partner, or a corporation in which the insured is an officer or a shareholder do not cause the policy proceeds to be taxable.

EXAMPLE Howard dies on January 15, 2011, and leaves Wanda, his wife, a $50,000 insurance policy, the proceeds of which she elects to receive as $10,000 per year plus interest for 5 years. In the current year, Wanda receives $12,200 ($10,000 + $2,200 interest). She must include the $2,200 of interest in income. ♦

EXAMPLE David owns a life insurance policy at the time he is diagnosed with a terminal illness. After his diagnosis, he sells the policy to Viatical Settlements, Inc., for $100,000. David is not required to include the gain on the sale of the insurance in his gross income. ♦

EXAMPLE Amy transfers to Bill an insurance policy with a face value of $40,000 and a cash surrender value of $10,000 for the cancellation of a debt owed to Bill. Bill continues to make payments, and after 2 years Bill has paid $2,000 in premiums. Amy dies and Bill collects the $40,000. Since the transfer was for valuable consideration, Bill must include $28,000 in taxable income, which is equal to the $40,000 total proceeds less $10,000 value at the time of transfer and $2,000 of premiums paid. If Amy and Bill were partners in the same partnership, the entire proceeds ($40,000) would be tax free. ♦

Self-Study Problem 2.6 *See Appendix E for Solutions to Self-Study Problems*

On March 19, 2009, Karen dies and leaves Larry an insurance policy with a face value of $100,000. Karen is Larry's sister, and Larry elects to take the proceeds over 10 years ($10,000 plus interest each year). This year Larry receives $13,250 from the insurance company. How much income must Larry report for the current year?

$____________

Learning Objective 2.7

Identify the general rules for the tax treatment of gifts and inheritances.

GIFTS AND INHERITANCES

Taxpayers are allowed to exclude from income the fair market value of gifts and inheritances received, but income received from the property after such a transfer is taxable. Normally, the gift tax or estate tax is paid by the donor or the decedent's estate; such property is, therefore, usually tax free to the person receiving the gift or inheritance.

One tax problem that may arise concerning a gift is the definition of what constitutes a gift. The courts define a gift as a voluntary transfer of property without adequate consideration. Gifts made in a business setting are suspect since they may be disguised payments for goods or services. The courts are likely to rule that gifts in a business setting are taxable income, even if there was no obligation to make the payment. Also, if the recipient renders services for the gift, it will be presumed to be income for the services performed.

EXAMPLE In January of the current year, Richard inherits shares of Birch Corporation stock worth $22,000. After receiving the stock, he is paid $1,300 in dividends during the current year. His gross income from the inheritance in the current year would be $1,300. The $22,000 fair market value of the stock is excluded from gross income. ♦

Self-Study Problem 2.7 *See Appendix E for Solutions to Self-Study Problems*

Don is an attorney who supplied a list of potential clients to a new attorney, Lori. This list aided in the success of Lori's practice. Lori was very pleased and decided to do something for Don. In the current year, Lori gives Don a new car worth $40,000. Lori was not obligated to give this gift to Don, and she did not expect Don to perform future services for the gift. How much income, if any, should Don report from this transaction? Explain your answer.

Income $____________

Explain ____

____

Learning Objective 2.8

Describe the elements of scholarship income that are excluded from tax.

SCHOLARSHIPS

A scholarship is an amount paid or awarded to, or for the benefit of, a student to aid the student in the pursuit of his or her studies. Scholarships granted to degree candidates are taxable income, with the exception of amounts spent for tuition, fees, books, and course-required supplies and equipment. Therefore, scholarship amounts received for items such as room and board are taxable to the recipient.

EXAMPLE In 2014, Diane receives a $5,000 scholarship to study accounting at Big State University. Diane's expenses for tuition and books amount to $1,200 during the fall semester; therefore, she would have taxable income of $3,800 ($5,000 − $1,200) from the scholarship. ♦

Payments received by students for part-time employment are not excludable; they are taxable as compensation. For example, students in work–study programs must include their compensation in gross income.

Self-Study Problem 2.8 ***See Appendix E for Solutions to Self-Study Problems***

Indicate whether each item below would be included in or excluded from the income of the recipient in 2014.

	Included	Excluded
1. A $2,000 National Merit Scholarship for tuition	______	______
2. A basketball scholarship for room and board	______	______
3. Payments under a work–study program	______	______
4. Salary for working at Beech Research Laboratory	______	______
5. A stipend for a graduate teaching assistant	______	______
6. Payment received from an employer while on leave working on a research project	______	______

ACCIDENT AND HEALTH INSURANCE

Learning Objective 2.9

Understand the general tax treatment of health insurance.

Many taxpayers are covered by accident and health insurance plans. These plans pay for the cost of medical care of the taxpayer and any dependents who are insured under the plan. The taxpayer may pay the total premiums of the plan, or his or her employer may pay part or all of the premiums. Taxpayers are allowed liberal exclusions for payments received from these accident and health plans. The taxpayer may exclude the total amount received for payment of medical care. This exclusion applies to any amount paid for the medical care of the taxpayer, his or her spouse, or dependents. The payment may be made to the doctor, the hospital, or the taxpayer as reimbursement for the payment of the expenses. In addition, any premiums paid by a taxpayer's employer are excluded from the taxpayer's income, and the premium payments may be deducted by the employer.

Most accident and health care policies also pay fixed amounts to the insured for loss of the use of a member or function of the body. These amounts may also be excluded from income. For example, a taxpayer who receives $25,000 because he or she is blinded in one eye may exclude the $25,000 from income.

EXAMPLE Bob is a married taxpayer. His employer pays a $250 per month premium on a policy covering Bob and his family. Jean, Bob's wife, is sick during the year and her medical bills amount to $6,500; the insurance company paid $6,000 for the bills. Bob and Jean may exclude from income the $250 per month premium paid by Bob's employer and the $6,000 paid by the insurance company. The $500 not paid by the insurance company is deductible on Bob and Jean's return, subject to the medical expense deduction limitations (see Chapter 5). ♦

Self-Study Problem 2.9 *See Appendix E for Solutions to Self-Study Problems*

Marjorie, a single taxpayer, is an employee of Big State Corporation. Big State Corporation pays premiums of $1,000 on her health insurance for the current year. Also, during the current year, Marjorie has an operation for which the insurance company pays $5,000 to her hospital and doctor. Of the above amounts, how much must Marjorie include in her gross income?

$__________

Learning Objective 2.10

Determine when meals and lodging may be excluded from taxable income.

MEALS AND LODGING

If certain tests are met, employers may exclude the value of meals and lodging from an employee's taxable income. The exclusion is granted for any meals and lodging furnished by the employer for the convenience of the employer, but only if:

1. The meals are furnished on the business premises of the employer during working hours because the taxpayer must be available for emergency calls or the employer limits the employee to short meal periods, and
2. The lodging is on the business premises and must be accepted as a requirement for employment.

To exclude the value of lodging provided by the employer, the employee must be required to accept the lodging to perform the duties of the job properly. For example, a taxpayer who receives lodging on an offshore oil rig may exclude the value of the lodging from income, since the employee cannot go home at night. The exclusion for lodging also includes the value of utilities such as electricity, water, heat, gas, and similar items that make the lodging habitable.

The value of meals or lodging provided by the employer in other situations, and cash allowances for meals or lodging, must be included in the employee's gross income.

Self-Study Problem 2.10 *See Appendix E for Solutions to Self-Study Problems*

In each of the following independent cases, indicate whether the value of the meals or lodging should be included in or excluded from the taxpayer's income.

	Included	***Excluded***
1. A waiter is required to eat lunch, furnished by his employer, on the premises during a busy lunch hour.	______	______
2. A police officer receives a cash allowance to pay for meals while on duty.	______	______
3. A worker receives lodging at a remote construction site in Alaska.	______	______
4. A taxpayer manages a motel and, although the owner does not require it, she lives at the motel rent free.	______	______
5. A bank teller is furnished meals on the premises to limit the time she is away during busy hours.	______	______
6. A hospital provides a free lunchroom for its staff; the staff is not required to eat there, but the hospital's administration wants to encourage the employees to be on the premises for emergencies.	______	______

MUNICIPAL BOND INTEREST

Learning Objective 2.11

Understand the tax treatment of municipal bond interest.

In 1913 when the Sixteenth Amendment was enacted, Congress questioned the constitutionality of taxing the interest earned on state and local government obligations. Congress provided an exclusion from taxpayers' income for the interest on such bonds. To qualify for the exclusion, the interest must be from an obligation of a state, territory, or possession of the United States, or a political subdivision of the foregoing or of the District of Columbia. For example, Puerto Rico bonds qualify for the exclusion. Federal obligations, such as treasury bills and treasury bonds, do not qualify.

The interest exclusion allows high-income taxpayers to lend money to state and local governments at lower interest rates (discounts). For example, a taxpayer in the 33 percent tax bracket can receive the same after-tax return on a 6 percent municipal bond as he or she can receive on an 8.96 percent corporate bond. This equivalent after-tax return rate for a tax-free bond can be calculated as follows:

$$\text{After-tax return} = \frac{\text{Tax-free interest rate}}{1 - \text{the taxpayer's tax rate}}$$

TAX BREAK

Taxpayers in low tax brackets are likely to find that they earn a higher overall return investing in taxable bonds rather than comparable tax-free municipal bonds. This is because the smaller tax benefit from the municipal bonds does not make up for the reduced interest rate paid on municipal bonds. Municipal bonds are also generally not appropriate investments for IRAs or other retirement accounts since income on these accounts is excluded from tax until withdrawn, anyway.

Self-Study Problem 2.11 *See Appendix E for Solutions to Self-Study Problems*

Calculate the taxable interest rate that will provide the equivalent after-tax return in the cases that follow.

1. A taxpayer is in the 28 percent tax bracket and invests in a San Diego City Bond paying 7 percent. What taxable interest rate will provide the same after-tax return?

   ____________%

2. A taxpayer is in the 33 percent tax bracket and invests in a New York State Bond paying 6.5 percent. What taxable interest rate will provide the same after-tax return?

   ____________%

UNEMPLOYMENT COMPENSATION

Learning Objective 2.12

Describe the tax treatment of unemployment compensation.

Unemployment compensation payments are fully taxable in 2014.

EXAMPLE Genny was unemployed for several months during 2014 and received unemployment compensation of $4,000. The $4,000 is included in Genny's taxable income for 2014. ♦

Self-Study Problem 2.12 *See Appendix E for Solutions to Self-Study Problems*

Christi was unemployed during part of 2014. She received $3,000 in unemployment compensation. How much of the $3,000 must be included in Christi's gross income?

$__________

Learning Objective 2.13

Identify the common employee fringe benefit income exclusions.

EMPLOYEE FRINGE BENEFITS

The tax law provides that all fringe benefits must be included in the employee's gross income, unless specifically excluded by law. The primary types of fringe benefits that may be excluded from gross income are described below.

Employer-Provided Spending Accounts

Many employers, especially larger employers, form plans that allow employees to set aside money periodically from their salary before it is taxed to pay for one or more of the expenses listed below. If all the requirements of the plan are met and the employee provides receipts for the expenses incurred, the full amount of expenses reimbursed out of the employee's account will be treated as a tax-free reduction in salary. These accounts may provide significant tax savings for employees, with only a small administrative cost to employers. Employees must be aware, however, of the "use-it-or-lose-it" rule for dependent care accounts (e.g., any balance remaining in the employee's account at December 31 is lost). Medical spending account plans have the option to allow the carryover of up to $500 of unused amounts at December 31 or a 3-month grace period after year-end to incur additional medical expenses before the employee loses his balance in the account.

Dependent Care Accounts

Employers may offer a dependent care plan in which employees can set aside up to $5,000 of their salary to cover the costs of caring for a dependent child or aging parent. Such costs may include day care, day camp, in-home care for a parent living with the taxpayer, and preschool.

Medical Flexible Spending Accounts

Employers may offer medical flexible spending accounts of up to $2,500 in which employees can set aside funds from their salary to cover medical expenses which they anticipate incurring during the year. These expenses may include eyeglasses, laser-eye surgery, necessary dental work, and health insurance copayments.

Public Transportation, Parking at Work, and Bicycle Commuting

Employers may make tax-free payments of up to $130 per month to employees to cover the costs of public transportation to work and up to $250 per month to cover parking at work. Bicycle commuters are allowed a special tax-free fringe benefit. Up to $20 per month may be reimbursed to employees for the cost of purchasing, repairing, and storing their bicycles.

TAX BREAK

Previously, medical flexible spending accounts did not permit taxpayers to carryover any funds set aside that were left unspent at the end of the year ("use it or lose it"). Some plans allowed a grace period after year end to submit claims on money set aside the previous year. Starting in 2013, instead of a grace period, a plan can permit a taxpayer to carryover up to $500 of unspent funds into the next year.

Group Term Life Insurance

Employers may pay for up to $50,000 of group term life insurance for employees as a tax-free fringe benefit. Providing group term life insurance to employees must not favor officers, shareholders, or highly paid personnel.

No-Additional-Cost Services

This category of fringe benefits includes services that are provided to employees and their families at little or no additional cost to the employer, and which would otherwise have remained unused. An airline employee who is allowed to fly at no cost on a standby basis is an example. The value of the airfare may be excluded from the employee's gross income.

Employees are only allowed to receive tax-free services in the major line of business in which they are employed. For example, if an airline company also owns a rental car agency, the employees working in the airline division would not be entitled to the tax-free use of rental cars.

Qualified Employee Discounts

The value of employee discounts may be excluded from gross income if the discounts are available on a nondiscriminatory basis. That is, the discounts must be available to substantially all full-time employees. However, an employee discount is not tax free if the discount:

1. Is on real estate or personal property of the type held for investment,
2. Exceeds 20 percent of the customer price, for services,
3. Exceeds the employer's gross markup for merchandise, or
4. Is for a line of business in which the employee is not employed.

EXAMPLE R. J. works for a company that owns two separate businesses, a chain of auto parts stores and a chain of sporting goods stores. If R. J. works for the auto parts chain, she is not allowed a tax-free discount on merchandise purchased at the sporting goods stores. ♦

Working Condition Fringe Benefits

An employee may exclude the value of property or services provided by an employer to the extent that the cost of the property or services would be a deductible expense of the employee. Examples of this type of exclusion include the use of a company car for business (not personal) purposes and a subscription to a tax journal paid for by a CPA firm. The working condition fringe benefit rules also allow several expenses which would not be deductible if paid by the employee. These include the value of parking provided to an employee and certain personal use of demonstrator autos by automobile salespeople.

De Minimis Fringe Benefits

The value of small fringe benefits may be excluded from an employee's gross income if accounting for the benefits would be impractical. Examples of this type of exclusion include occasional personal use of an office copy machine, personal letters typed by a company secretary, a company picnic for the employees, and small holiday gifts provided to employees (e.g., a Christmas turkey).

If an employer provides a subsidized lunchroom for its employees, the value of the meals may be excluded from the employees' income if (1) the facility is on or near the employer's place of business, (2) the revenue from the lunchroom normally exceeds direct operating costs, and (3) the meals are provided without discrimination to all employees.

Cell phones provided to employees primarily for business purposes are considered tax-free de minimus fringe benefits. Examples of cell phones which qualify include those provided to allow employees to communicate with clients, or to allow employers to contact employees in the field or at home.

Tuition Reduction

All employees of educational institutions may exclude from their income the value of a tuition reduction, if the plan is for an undergraduate education and available to all employees. The exclusion applies to the employees, their spouses, and their dependents. The value of a graduate education tuition reduction plan can only be excluded by graduate students of the institution who are teaching or doing research at that institution.

Athletic Facilities

Employees may exclude from gross income the value of the use of an athletic facility located on the premises of their employer. The facility must be used primarily by employees.

Retirement Planning Fringe Benefit

Qualified retirement planning services constitute a fringe benefit that is excluded from income. This change was made to encourage employers to provide retirement planning services for their employees to assist them in preparing for retirement. Qualified retirement planning services are any retirement planning services provided to an employee and his or her spouse by an employer maintaining a "qualified employer plan." The exclusion also applies to advice and information on retirement income planning for an individual and his or her spouse, including how the employer's plan fits into the individual's overall retirement income plan. The exclusion, however, does not apply to services that may be related to tax preparation, accounting, legal, or brokerage services.

EXAMPLE As part of its qualified plan, Linda's employer provides retirement planning services. Linda has a meeting with a financial planner to review her retirement plan. The cost of the meeting ($600) is paid for by her employer's qualified plan. The $600 is not income to Linda and is deductible to the employer. ♦

Self-Study Problem 2.13

See Appendix E for Solutions to Self-Study Problems

Indicate in each of the following cases whether the value of the employee fringe benefit is included (I) in or excluded (E) from the employee's gross income.

_____ 1. An employee of a railroad receives a free train-trip pass.

_____ 2. An employee of a department store receives a 25 percent discount on a shirt. The department store's markup is 15 percent.

_____ 3. An employee attends a New Year's party paid for by her employer.

_____ 4. An employee of a stock brokerage firm receives a subscription to a financial newsletter paid for by his employer.

_____ 5. An employee's wife regularly uses a company car to go shopping.

_____ 6. An airline employee receives a 50 percent discount at a hotel chain owned by her employer while traveling on vacation.

_____ 7. An employee uses the company's employee fitness room.

SOCIAL SECURITY BENEFITS

Learning Objective 2.14

Apply the rules governing inclusion of Social Security benefits as income.

Many taxpayers may exclude all of their Social Security benefits from gross income. Middle-income and upper-income Social Security recipients, however, may have to include up to 85 percent of their benefits in gross income. The formula to determine taxable Social Security income is based on *modified adjusted gross income* (MAGI). Generally, MAGI is the taxpayer's adjusted gross income (without Social Security benefits) plus any tax-free interest income. On rare occasions, taxpayers will also have to add back unusual items such as the foreign earned income exclusion, employer-provided adoption benefits, or interest on education loans. If MAGI plus 50 percent of Social Security benefits is less than the base amount shown below (base amounts are not adjusted for inflation), benefits are excluded from income.

Base Amounts	*Applies To*
$32,000	Married filing jointly
$ 0	Married taxpayers who did not live apart for the entire year and still filed separate returns
$25,000	All other taxpayers

The formula for calculating the taxable amount of Social Security is complex and time-consuming. Many taxpayers rely on tax-preparation software to perform the calculation. For preparation by hand, the Form 1040 Instructions include a full-page worksheet that takes taxpayers through the calculation one step at a time.

EXAMPLE For the 2014 tax year, Nancy, a single taxpayer, receives $7,000 in Social Security benefits. She has adjusted gross income of $20,000, not including any Social Security income, and receives $10,000 of tax-exempt municipal bond interest. Nancy must include $3,500 of her Social Security benefits in income. The amount included in gross income is determined as follows:

Simplified Taxable Social Security Worksheet (for most people)

1.	Enter the total amount of Social Security income.	1. $ 7,000
2.	Enter one-half of line 1.	2. 3,500
3.	Enter the total of taxable income items on Form 1040 except Social Security income.	3. 20,000
4.	Enter the amount of tax-exempt interest income.	4. 10,000
5.	Add lines 2, 3, and 4.	5. 33,500
6.	Enter all adjustments for AGI except for student loan interest, the domestic production activities deduction, and the tuition and fees deduction.	6. –0–
7.	Subtract line 6 from line 5. If zero or less, stop here, none of the Social Security benefits are taxable.	7. 33,500
8.	Enter $25,000 ($32,000 if married filing jointly; $0 if married filing separately and living with spouse at any time during the year).	8. 25,000
9.	Subtract line 8 from line 7. If zero or less, enter –0–.	9. 8,500

Note: *If line 9 is zero or less, stop here;* ***none of your benefits are taxable.*** *Otherwise, go on to line 10.*

10.	Enter $9,000 ($12,000 if married filing jointly; $0 if married filing separately and living with spouse at any time during the year).	10. 9,000
11.	Subtract line 10 from line 9. If zero or less, enter –0–.	11. –0–
12.	Enter the **smaller** of line 9 or line 10.	12. 8,500
13.	Enter one-half of line 12.	13. 4,250
14.	Enter the **smaller** of line 2 or line 13.	14. 3,500
15.	Multiply line 11 by 85% (.85). If line 11 is zero, enter –0–.	15. –0–
16.	Add lines 14 and 15.	16. 3,500
17.	Multiply line 1 by 85% (.85).	17. 5,950
18.	**Taxable benefits.** Enter the **smaller** of line 16 or line 17.	18. $ 3,500

♦

EXAMPLE Linda, a widow, is retired and receives Social Security benefits of $14,000 in 2014. She has MAGI of $47,000. Linda must include $11,900 of her Social Security benefits in income. The amount included in income is determined as follows:

Simplified Taxable Social Security Worksheet (for most people)

1.	Enter the total amount of Social Security income.	1. $14,000
2.	Enter one-half of line 1.	2. 7,000
3.	Enter the total of taxable income items on Form 1040 except Social Security income.	3. 47,000
4.	Enter the amount of tax-exempt interest income.	4. –0–
5.	Add lines 2, 3, and 4.	5. 54,000
6.	Enter all adjustments for AGI except for student loan interest, the domestic production activities deduction, and the tuition and fees deduction.	6. –0–
7.	Subtract line 6 from line 5. If zero or less, stop here, none of the Social Security benefits are taxable.	7. 54,000
8.	Enter $25,000 ($32,000 if married filing jointly; $0 if married filing separately and living with spouse at any time during the year).	8. 25,000
9.	Subtract line 8 from line 7. If zero or less, enter –0–.	9. 29,000
	Note: *If line 9 is zero or less, stop here;* ***none of your benefits are taxable.*** *Otherwise, go on to line 10.*	
10.	Enter $9,000 ($12,000 if married filing jointly; $0 if married filing separately and living with spouse at any time during the year).	10. 9,000
11.	Subtract line 10 from line 9. If zero or less, enter –0–.	11. 20,000
12.	Enter the **smaller** of line 9 or line 10.	12. 9,000
13.	Enter one-half of line 12.	13. 4,500
14.	Enter the **smaller** of line 2 or line 13.	14. 4,500
15.	Multiply line 11 by 85% (.85). If line 11 is zero, enter –0–.	15. 17,000
16.	Add lines 14 and 15.	16. 21,500

17. Multiply line 1 by 85% (.85). 17. 11,900

18. **Taxable benefits.** Enter the **smaller** of line 16 or line 17. 18. $11,900

♦

TAX BREAK

Many tax professionals and taxpayers use search engines such as Google for assistance with tax questions and to access relevant articles and timely discussions of the tax law, as it changes due to new laws passed by Congress, court cases deciding uncertain areas of the law, and new IRS rules explaining the law. Because not all information on the Internet is accurate, any tax information site should be evaluated for reliability, timeliness, and other limitations. To access a multitude of websites providing information on the taxability of Social Security, including worksheets and calculators, enter "taxable Social Security" into your search engine.

Social Security Income Inclusion Formulas

Filling Status	*MAGI + 50% SS*	*Amount of SS That Is Included in Taxable Income*
Single, HOH, Surviving Spouse, MFS (Living apart)	Under $25,000	No SS benefits included in taxable income
	$25,000 – $34,000	The lesser of: 50% of SS benefits, or 50% of (MAGI + 50%SS, over $25,000)
	Over $34,000	The lesser of: 85% of SS benefits, or (lesser of box above or $4,500) + 85% of (MAGI + 50%SS, over $34,000)
Married Filing Jointly	Under $32,000	No SS benefits included in taxable income
	$32,000 – $44,000	The lesser of: 50% of SS benefits, or 50% of (MAGI + 50%SS, over $32,000)
	Over $44,000	The lesser of: 85% of SS benefits, or (lesser of box above or $6,000) + 85% of (MAGI + 50%SS, over $44,000)

Note: The Social Security income inclusion formulas in the table above are shown for information only. No problems in the text will require the use of these formulas.

Self-Study Problem 2.14 ***See Appendix E for Solutions to Self-Study Problems***

For the 2014 tax year, Kim and Edward are married and file a joint return. They have Social Security benefits of $13,000 and their adjusted gross income is $20,000, not including any Social Security income. They also receive $30,000 in tax-free municipal bond interest. How much, if any, of the Social Security benefits should Kim and Edward include in gross income? Use the worksheet below to compute your answer.

$ ________

Simplified Taxable Social Security Worksheet (for most people)

1.	Enter the total amount of Social Security income.	1. $________
2.	Enter one-half of line 1.	2. ________
3.	Enter the total of taxable income items on Form 1040 except Social Security income.	3. ________
4.	Enter the amount of tax-exempt interest income.	4. ________
5.	Add lines 2, 3, and 4.	5. ________
6.	Enter all adjustments for AGI except for student loan interest, the domestic production activities deduction, and the tuition and fees deduction.	6. ________
7.	Subtract line 6 from line 5. If zero or less, stop here, none of the Social Security benefits are taxable.	7. ________
8.	Enter $25,000 ($32,000 if married filing jointly; $0 if married filing separately and living with spouse at any time during the year).	8. ________
9.	Subtract line 8 from line 7. If zero or less, enter –0–.	9. ________
	Note: *If line 9 is zero or less, stop here;* ***none of your benefits are taxable.*** *Otherwise, go on to line 10.*	
10.	Enter $9,000 ($12,000 if married filing jointly; $0 if married filing separately and living with spouse at any time during the year).	10. ________
11.	Subtract line 10 from line 9. If zero or less, enter –0–.	11. ________
12.	Enter the **smaller** of line 9 or line 10.	12. ________
13.	Enter one-half of line 12.	13. ________
14.	Enter the **smaller** of line 2 or line 13.	14. ________
15.	Multiply line 11 by 85% (.85). If line 11 is zero, enter –0–.	15. ________
16.	Add lines 14 and 15.	16. ________
17.	Multiply line 1 by 85% (.85).	17. ________
18.	**Taxable benefits.** Enter the **smaller** of line 16 or line 17.	18. $________

KEY TERMS

gross income, 2-2
inclusions – gross income, 2-3
exclusions – gross income, 2-3
alimony recapture, 2-9
property transfers, 2-9
qualified plan award, 2-11
annuities, 2-12
the simplified method, 2-12
the general rule, 2-14
employee annuities, 2-14
accelerated death benefits, 2-15
viatical settlements, 2-15
employee fringe benefits, 2-20
employer-provided spending accounts, 2-20
dependent care accounts, 2-20
medical flexible spending accounts, 2-20
no-additional-cost service, 2-21
qualified employee discounts, 2-21
working condition fringe benefit, 2-21
retirement planning fringe benefits, 2-22

KEY POINTS

Learning Objectives	Key Points
LO 2.1: Understand and apply the definition of gross income.	• Gross income means "all income from whatever source derived." • Gross income includes everything a taxpayer receives unless it is specifically excluded from gross income by the tax law.
LO 2.2: Identify the tax treatment of interest and dividend income.	• Interest income is taxable except for certain state and municipal bond interest. Interest or dividend income exceeding $1,500 per year must be reported in detail on Schedule B of Form 1040. • Series EE Savings Bond interest is taxable in the year the bonds are cashed unless a taxpayer elects to report the Series EE Savings Bond interest each year as it accrues. • Series HH Savings Bond interest is taxable each year as it is paid to the taxpayer. • Ordinary dividends are taxable in the year received. • In 2014, qualified dividends are taxed at rates ranging from 0 percent to 20 percent and possibly included in the 3.8 percent net investment income tax.
LO 2.3: Describe the tax treatment of alimony and child support.	• Alimony paid in cash is taxable to the person who receives it and is deductible to the person who pays it. • Child support is not alimony and therefore is not taxable when received nor deductible when paid.
LO 2.4: Determine when prizes and awards are included in income.	• Amounts received from prizes and awards are normally taxable income unless refused by the taxpayer. • Certain small prizes (generally under $400) for length of service and safety achievement are excluded from gross income.
LO 2.5: Calculate the taxable and nontaxable portions of annuity payments.	• Annuity payments received by a taxpayer have an element of taxable income and an element of tax-free return of the original purchase price. • The part of the payment that is excluded from income is the ratio of the investment in the contract to the total expected return. • The total expected return is the annual payment multiplied by the life expectancy of the annuitant, based on mortality tables provided by the IRS. • Individual taxpayers generally must use the "simplified" method to calculate the taxable amount from a qualified annuity starting after November 18, 1996.

LO 2.6: Understand the tax treatment of life insurance proceeds.	• Life insurance proceeds are excluded from gross income. If the proceeds are taken over several years instead of in a lump sum, any interest on the unpaid proceeds is generally taxable income. • Early payouts of life insurance are excluded from gross income for certain terminally or chronically ill taxpayers. • All or a portion of the proceeds from a life insurance policy transferred to another person for valuable consideration is generally taxable to the recipient.
LO 2.7: Identify the general rules for the tax treatment of gifts and inheritances.	• The fair market value of gifts and inheritances received is excluded from gross income, although income received from the property after the transfer is taxable.
LO 2.8: Describe the elements of scholarship income that are excluded from tax.	• Scholarships granted to degree candidates are excluded from gross income if spent for tuition, fees, books, and course-required supplies and equipment. Amounts received for items such as room and board are taxable to the recipient.
LO 2.9: Understand the general tax treatment of health insurance.	• Taxpayers are allowed an exclusion for payments received from accident and health plans. The taxpayer may exclude the total amount received for payment of medical care, including any amount paid for the medical care of the taxpayer, his or her spouse, or dependents.
LO 2.10: Determine when meals and lodging may be excluded from taxable income.	• Meals and lodging are excluded from gross income provided they are for the convenience of the employer and they are furnished on the business premises. Lodging must be a condition of employment to be excluded.
LO 2.11: Understand the tax treatment of municipal bond interest.	• Interest from an obligation of a state, territory, or possession of the United States, or of a political subdivision of the foregoing, or of the District of Columbia, is excluded from gross income.
LO 2.12: Describe the tax treatment of unemployment compensation.	• Unemployment compensation is taxable.
LO 2.13: Identify the common employee fringe benefit income exclusions.	• Certain fringe benefits provided to employees may be excluded from the employees' gross income. These include dependent care and medical flexible spending accounts.
LO 2.14: Apply the rules governing inclusion of Social Security benefits as income.	• Taxpayers with income under $25,000 ($32,000 for Married Filing Jointly) exclude all of their Social Security benefits from gross income. • Middle-income and upper-income Social Security recipients, however, may have to include up to 85 percent of their benefits in gross income. • Calculating the taxable amount of Social Security is complex and most easily done using a worksheet, such as the one provided in this chapter, or a tax program such as H&R Block's At Home.

© Dusit/Shutterstock.com

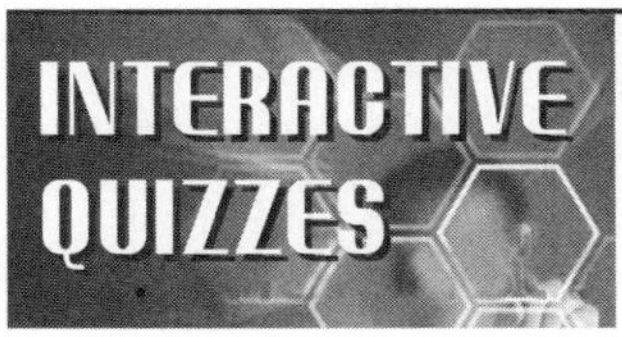

Interactive quizzes are available as an optional online resource for Income Tax Fundamentals. Visit **www.cengagebrain.com** for more information.

QUESTIONS and PROBLEMS

GROUP 1: MULTIPLE CHOICE QUESTIONS

_______ **LO 2.1**

1. The definition of gross income in the tax law is:
   a. All items specifically listed as income in the tax law
   b. All cash payments received for goods provided and services performed
   c. All income from whatever source derived
   d. All income from whatever source derived unless the income is earned illegally

_______ **LO 2.1**

2. Which of the following is not taxable for income tax purposes?
   a. Interest income on savings accounts
   b. Income from real estate investments
   c. Child support
   d. Dividend income from stock
   e. All of the above are taxable

_______ **LO 2.1**

3. All of the following items are taxable to the taxpayer receiving them, except:
   a. Bonuses
   b. Unemployment compensation
   c. Gifts
   d. Prizes
   e. Gambling winnings

_______ **LO 2.1**

4. Which of the following types of income is tax exempt?
   a. Worker's compensation
   b. Income earned illegally
   c. Dividends from foreign corporations
   d. Dividends from closely held corporations
   e. Dividends from utility corporations' stock

_______ **LO 2.1**

5. Which of the following is included in gross income?
   a. Loans
   b. Inheritances
   c. Tuition and books scholarships
   d. Rewards
   e. None of the above

_______ **LO 2.4**

6. Which of the following prizes or awards is taxable?
   a. Professional sports awards
   b. Prizes from a television game show
   c. Awards for superior performance on the job
   d. A one-acre lot received as a prize
   e. All of the above are taxable

_______ **LO 2.5**

7. A 58-year-old taxpayer retires this year and receives the first payment on an annuity that was purchased several years ago. The taxpayer's investment in the annuity is $74,400, and the annuity pays $1,000 per month for the remainder of the taxpayer's life. Based on IRS mortality tables, the taxpayer is expected to live another 20 years.

If the taxpayer receives $4,000 in annuity payments in the current year, the nontaxable portion calculated using the simplified method is:

a. $0
b. $960
c. $1,240
d. $4,000
e. None of the above

LO 2.6

8. Which of the following might result in life insurance proceeds that are taxable to the recipient?
   a. A life insurance policy in which the insured is the son of the taxpayer and the beneficiary is the taxpayer
   b. A life insurance policy transferred by a partner to the partnership
   c. A life insurance policy transferred to a creditor in payment of a debt
   d. A life insurance policy purchased by a taxpayer insuring his or her spouse
   e. A life insurance policy purchased by a corporation insuring an officer

LO 2.7

9. Which of the following gifts would probably be held to be taxable to the person receiving the gift?
   a. One thousand dollars given to a taxpayer by his or her father
   b. A trip to Mexico given to a purchasing agent by one of the company's suppliers
   c. A house given to a taxpayer by a friend
   d. A Mercedes-Benz given to a taxpayer by his cousin
   e. An interest in a partnership given to a taxpayer by his or her uncle

LO 2.7
LO 2.9
LO 2.10
LO 2.11

10. Which of the following items would be includable in the gross income of the recipient?
    a. Insurance payments for medical care of a dependent child
    b. Insurance payments for loss of the taxpayer's sight
    c. Season tickets given by a salesperson to a customer
    d. Interest from bonds issued by the state of Texas
    e. Lodging provided to a worker on a remote oil rig

LO 2.14

11. For 2014, the maximum percentage of Social Security benefits that must be included in a taxpayer's gross income is:
    a. 85%
    b. 75%
    c. 65%
    d. 50%
    e. 25%

LO 2.14

12. Generally, modified adjusted gross income (MAGI) is adjusted gross income (without Social Security benefits):
    a. Less tax-exempt interest
    b. Less personal and dependency exemptions
    c. Less itemized deductions
    d. Less tax-exempt interest plus any foreign income exclusion
    e. Plus tax-exempt interest income

GROUP 2: PROBLEMS

LO 2.1 1. Indicate whether each of the items listed below would be included (I) in or excluded (E) from gross income for the 2014 tax year.

_______ a. Welfare payments
_______ b. Commissions
_______ c. Hobby income
_______ d. Scholarships for room and board
_______ e. $300 set of golf clubs, an employee award for length of service
_______ f. Severance pay
_______ g. Ordinary dividend of $50
_______ h. Accident insurance proceeds
_______ i. Inheritances
_______ j. Gifts
_______ k. Tips and gratuities

LO 2.1 2. John installed a new roof on his friend's house in return for a used truck worth $8,000. How much income must John report on his tax return for his services? _______________

LO 2.1 3. Larry is a tax accountant and Sheila is a hairdresser. Larry prepares Sheila's tax return for free and Sheila agrees to style Larry's hair six times for free in return for the tax return. The value of the tax return is approximately $300 and the hair styling work is approximately $300.

a. How much of the $300 is includable income to Larry? Why? _______________

b. How much of the $300 is includable income to Sheila? Why? _______________

LO 2.1 4. Kerry and Jim have a successful marijuana farm in the woods around Humboldt County, California. Growing marijuana is illegal for federal purposes. Are Kerry and Jim required by law to report the income from their farm on their tax return? Why? _______________

LO 2.2 5. How are qualified dividends taxed in 2014? Please give the three rates of tax which apply to qualified dividends, and specify when each of these rates applies. _______________

LO 2.2 6. If a taxpayer holding Series EE Bonds does not make an election with respect to the taxation of the bonds, how is the interest that accrues each year on the bonds taxed?
____

LO 2.2

7. Sally and Charles Heck received the following dividends and interest during 2014:

	Sally	*Charles*	*Jointly*
Qualifying dividends:			
General Motors	$850		
IBM		$2,100	
Gene Corporation			$3,250
Wilson Corporation		750	
Interest:			
Dime Box Bank			1,250
First National Bank			750

Assuming the Hecks file a joint tax return, complete Schedule B of Form 1040 (on Page 2-33) for them for the 2014 tax year. Do not attempt to complete the Qualified Dividends and Capital Gain Tax Worksheet.

LO 2.3

8. Answer the following questions, assuming that the related divorce agreements were executed during 2014.
   a. Under a divorce agreement, Joan is required to pay her ex-husband, Bill, $700 a month until their daughter is 18 years of age. At that time, the required payments are reduced to $500 per month.
      1. How much of each $700 payment may be deducted as alimony by Joan? $________
      2. How much of each $700 payment must be included in Bill's taxable income? $________
   b. Under the terms of a property settlement executed during 2014, Jane transferred property worth $500,000 to her ex-husband, Tom. The property has a tax basis to Jane of $400,000.
      1. How much taxable gain must be recognized by Jane at the time of the transfer? $________
      2. What is the amount of Tom's tax basis in the property he received from Jane? $________

LO 2.3

9. Arlen is required by his divorce agreement to pay alimony of $2,000 a month and child support of $2,000 a month to his ex-wife Jane. What is the tax treatment of these two payments for Arlen? What is the tax treatment of these two payments for Jane?
   Arlen ____________________

   Jane ____________________

LO 2.3

10. As part of the property settlement related to their divorce, Cindy must give Allen the house that they have been living in, while she gets 100 percent of their savings accounts. The house was purchased for $100,000 15 years ago in Southern California and is now worth $500,000. How much gain must Cindy recognize on the transfer of the house to Allen? What is Allen's tax basis in the house for calculating tax on any future sale of the house?
    Cindy ____________________

    Allen ____________________

SCHEDULE B
(Form 1040A or 1040)

Department of the Treasury
Internal Revenue Service (99)

Interest and Ordinary Dividends

▶ Attach to Form 1040A or 1040.
▶ Information about Schedule B and its instructions is at *www.irs.gov/scheduleb*.

OMB No. 1545-0074
2014
Attachment Sequence No. 08

Name(s) shown on return | Your social security number

DRAFT AS OF
June 18, 2014
DO NOT FILE

Part I Interest

(See instructions on back and the instructions for Form 1040A, or Form 1040, line 8a.)

Note. If you received a Form 1099-INT, Form 1099-OID, or substitute statement from a brokerage firm, list the firm's name as the payer and enter the total interest shown on that form.

			Amount
1	List name of payer. If any interest is from a seller-financed mortgage and the buyer used the property as a personal residence, see instructions on back and list this interest first. Also, show that buyer's social security number and address ▶	1	
2	Add the amounts on line 1	2	
3	Excludable interest on series EE and I U.S. savings bonds issued after 1989. Attach Form 8815	3	
4	Subtract line 3 from line 2. Enter the result here and on Form 1040A, or Form 1040, line 8a ▶	4	

Note. If line 4 is over $1,500, you must complete Part III.

Part II Ordinary Dividends

(See instructions on back and the instructions for Form 1040A, or Form 1040, line 9a.)

Note. If you received a Form 1099-DIV or substitute statement from a brokerage firm, list the firm's name as the payer and enter the ordinary dividends shown on that form.

			Amount
5	List name of payer ▶	5	
6	Add the amounts on line 5. Enter the total here and on Form 1040A, or Form 1040, line 9a ▶	6	

Note. If line 6 is over $1,500, you must complete Part III.

Part III Foreign Accounts and Trusts

(See instructions on back.)

	You must complete this part if you **(a)** had over $1,500 of taxable interest or ordinary dividends; **(b)** had a foreign account; or **(c)** received a distribution from, or were a grantor of, or a transferor to, a foreign trust.	Yes	No
7a	At any time during 2014, did you have a financial interest in or signature authority over a financial account (such as a bank account, securities account, or brokerage account) located in a foreign country? See instructions		
	If "Yes," are you required to file FinCEN Form 114, Report of Foreign Bank and Financial Accounts (FBAR), to report that financial interest or signature authority? See FinCEN Form 114 and its instructions for filing requirements and exceptions to those requirements		
b	If you are required to file FinCEN Form 114, enter the name of the foreign country where the financial account is located ▶		
8	During 2014, did you receive a distribution from, or were you the grantor of, or transferor to, a foreign trust? If "Yes," you may have to file Form 3520. See instructions on back		

For Paperwork Reduction Act Notice, see your tax return instructions. Cat. No. 17146N **Schedule B (Form 1040A or 1040) 2014**

LO 2.4

11. How much of each of the following is taxable?
    a. Cheline received a $50,000 gift bag at the Oscars in 2014.
    b. Jon received a gold watch worth $350 for 25 years of service to his accounting firm.
    c. Kerry won $1,000,000 in her state lottery.
    d. Deborah is a professor who received $50,000 as an award for her scientific research from the university that employs her.

LO 2.4
LO 2.8

12. For each of the following independent cases, indicate the amount of gross income that must be included on the taxpayer's 2014 income tax return.
    a. Malchia won a $4,000 humanitarian award.
    $______________
    b. Rob won a new automobile (with a sticker price of $15,700 and a market value of $14,500) for being the best junior tennis player in 2014.
    $______________
    c. George received a $3,500 room and board scholarship to attend Western University.
    $______________

LO 2.5

13. Lola, age 62, began receiving a $2,000 monthly annuity in the current year upon the death of her husband. She received eight payments in the current year. Her husband contributed $40,000 to the qualified employee plan. Use the Simplified Method Worksheet below to calculate Lola's taxable amount from the annuity.

Simplified Method Worksheet

1. Enter total amount received this year. 1. ____________
2. Enter cost in the plan at the annuity starting date. 2. ____________
3. Age at annuity starting date

	Enter
55 and under	360
56–60	310
61–65	260
66–70	210
71 and older	160

3. ____________

4. Divide line 2 by line 3. 4. ____________
5. Multiply line 4 by the number of monthly payments this year. If the annuity starting date was before 1987, also enter this amount on line 8, and skip lines 6 and 7. Otherwise, go to line 6. 5. ____________

6. Enter the amount, if any, recovered tax free in prior years. 6. ____________
7. Subtract line 6 from line 2. 7. ____________
8. Enter the smaller of line 5 or 7. 8. ____________
9. Taxable amount this year: Subtract line 8 from line 1. Do not enter less than zero. 9. ____________

LO 2.6

14. Sharon transfers to Russ a life insurance policy with a cash surrender value of $30,000 and a face value of $100,000 in exchange for real estate. Russ continues to pay the premiums on the policy until Sharon dies 7 years later. At that time, Russ has paid $14,000 in premiums, and he collects the $100,000 face value. How much of the proceeds is taxable to Russ?

$____________

Why? ____

____

LO 2.6

15. Greg died on July 1, 2014, and left Lea, his wife, a $50,000 life insurance policy which she elects to receive at $5,000 per year plus interest for 10 years. In the current year, Lea receives $6,200. How much should Lea include in her gross income?

$____________

LO 2.6

16. David is certified by his doctor as terminally ill with liver disease. His doctor certifies that he cannot reasonably be expected to live for more than a year. He sells his life insurance policy to Viatical Settlements, Inc., for $250,000. He has paid $20,000 so far for the policy. How much of the $250,000 must David include in his taxable income? ____

____

LO 2.6

17. Helen receives a $200,000 lump sum life insurance payment when her friend Alice dies. How much of the payment is taxable to Helen? ____________________

____

LO 2.7

18. In June of 2014, Kevin inherits stock worth $125,000. During the year, he collects $7,500 in dividends. How much of these amounts, if any, should Kevin include in his gross income for 2014?

$____________

Why? ____

____

LO 2.7

19. Gwen is a tax accountant who works very hard for a large corporate client. The client is pleased and gives her a gift of $10,000 at year-end. How much of the gift is taxable to Gwen? ____

____

LO 2.7

20. Charlene receives a gift from her boyfriend of $10,000. He knows she is having financial problems and wants to help her. How much of the gift is taxable to Charlene? ____

____

LO 2.8

21. Robbie receives a scholarship of $20,000 to an elite private college. $10,000 of the scholarship is earmarked for tuition, and $10,000 covers his room and board. How much of the scholarship, if any, is taxable to Robbie? ____________________

____

LO 2.9 22. Skyler is covered by his company's health insurance plan. The health insurance costs his company $3,500 a year. During the year, Skyler is diagnosed with a serious illness and the health insurance pays $100,000 for surgery and treatment. How much of the insurance and treatment costs are taxable to Skyler? ____________

____

LO 2.9 23. Ellen is a single taxpayer. Ellen's employer pays $150 per month ($1,800 this year) for her health insurance. During the year, Ellen had medical expenses of $3,500 and the insurance company paid $2,000 of the expenses. How much of the above amounts, if any, must be included in Ellen's gross income?

$____________

Why? ____________

____

LO 2.10 24. a. Milton is a nurse whose employer provided meals for him on the employer's premises, since he is given only 30 minutes for lunch. Is the value of these meals taxable income to Milton?
Explain ____________

____

b. Mary is a San Diego ambulance driver. The city provides Mary with meals while she is working so she will be available for emergencies. Is the value of these meals taxable income to Mary?
Explain ____________

____

LO 2.11 25. Vandell is a taxpayer in the 28 percent tax bracket. He invests in Otay Mesa Water District Bonds that pay 6 percent interest. What taxable interest rate will provide the same after-tax return to Vandell?

____________%

LO 2.11 26. Karen is a well-off retired investment advisor who is in the 35 percent tax bracket. She has a choice between investing in a high-quality municipal bond paying 5 percent or a high-quality corporate bond paying 7 percent. Which investment do you think she will make and why? ____________

____

____

LO 2.12 27. Lydia, a married individual, was unemployed for a few months during 2014. During the year, she received $3,250 in unemployment compensation payments. How much of her unemployment compensation payments must be included in gross income?

$____________

LO 2.13 28. Linda and Richard are married and file a joint return for 2014. During the year, Linda, who works as an accountant for a national airline, used $2,100 worth of free passes for travel on the airline; Richard used the same amount. Linda and Richard also used $750 worth of employee discount coupons for hotel rooms at the hotel chain that is also owned by the airline. Richard is employed at State University as an accounting clerk. Under a tuition reduction plan, Richard saved $1,000 in tuition fees during 2014. He is studying for a master's degree in business. Richard also had $30 worth of personal typing done by his secretary at the University. What is the amount of fringe benefits that should be included in Linda and Richard's gross income on their 2014 tax return?

$____________

LO 2.13

29. Ellen's tax client is employed at a large company that offers medical flexible spending accounts to its employees. Tom must decide at the beginning of the year whether he wants to put as much as $2,500 of his salary into the medical spending account. He expects that he will have to pay for at least $8,000 of medical expenses for his family during the year since his wife is seeing a psychiatrist every week and his daughter and son are both having their teeth straightened. Tom does not itemize deductions. Should Ellen recommend that Tom put the maximum in his medical flexible spending account, and if so, why? ____________________________________

____

____

____

LO 2.14

30. During the 2014 tax year, Brian, a single taxpayer, received $6,000 in Social Security benefits. His adjusted gross income for the year was $18,000 (not including the Social Security benefits) and he received $30,000 in tax-exempt interest income. Calculate the amount of the Social Security benefits that Brian must include in his gross income for 2014.

Simplified Taxable Social Security Worksheet (for most people)

1. Enter the total amount of Social Security income.	1. ________
2. Enter one-half of line 1.	2. ________
3. Enter the total of taxable income items on Form 1040 except Social Security income.	3. ________
4. Enter the amount of tax-exempt interest income.	4. ________
5. Add lines 2, 3, and 4.	5. ________
6. Enter all adjustments for AGI except for student loan interest, the domestic production activities deduction, and the tuition and fees deduction.	6. ________
7. Subtract line 6 from line 5. If zero or less, stop here, none of the Social Security benefits are taxable.	7. ________
8. Enter $25,000 ($32,000 if married filing jointly; $0 if married filing separately and living with spouse at any time during the year).	8. ________
9. Subtract line 8 from line 7. If zero or less, enter –0–.	9. ________
Note: *If line 9 is zero or less, stop here;* ***none of your benefits are taxable.*** *Otherwise, go on to line 10.*	
10. Enter $9,000 ($12,000 if married filing jointly; $0 if married filing separately and living with spouse at any time during the year).	10. ________
11. Subtract line 10 from line 9. If zero or less, enter –0–.	11. ________
12. Enter the **smaller** of line 9 or line 10.	12. ________
13. Enter one-half of line 12.	13. ________
14. Enter the **smaller** of line 2 or line 13.	14. ________
15. Multiply line 11 by 85% (.85). If line 11 is zero, enter –0–.	15. ________
16. Add lines 14 and 15.	16. ________
17. Multiply line 1 by 85% (.85).	17. ________
18. **Taxable benefits**. Enter the **smaller** of line 16 or line 17.	18. ________

LO 2.14

31. Please answer the following questions regarding the taxability of Social Security:
    a. A 68-year-old taxpayer has $20,000 in Social Security income and $100,000 in tax-free municipal bond income. Does the municipal bond income affect the amount of Social Security the taxpayer must include in income? ______________
    ____
    b. A 68-year-old taxpayer has $20,000 in Social Security income and no other taxable or tax-free income. How much of the Social Security income must the taxpayer include in taxable income? ______________
    ____
    ____
    c. A 68-year-old taxpayer has $20,000 in Social Security income and has significant other taxable retirement income. What is the maximum percentage of Social Security that the taxpayer might be required to include in taxable income? ______
    ____
    ____

32. Go to the IRS website (**www.irs.gov**) and print out a copy of *Worksheet 1. Recapture of Alimony* in the most recent IRS Publication 504, Divorced or Separated Individuals.

33. Go to the IRS website (**www.irs.gov**) and redo Problem 7, using the most recent interactive "Fill-in Forms" Schedule B. Print out the *completed Schedule B.*

GROUP 3: WRITING ASSIGNMENT

RESEARCH

1. Professor Vanessa Lazo received a free tour to Costa Rica in a drawing at a professional conference. Professor Lazo has asked for your help in determining whether the free tour that she received is taxable. She understands that prizes and awards are taxable income to the recipient, but she does not think the free tour qualifies as a prize or award and is, therefore, not taxable.

   Required: Go to the IRS website (**www.irs.gov**) and locate Publication 525. Review the chapter on Other Income. Write a letter to Professor Vanessa Lazo stating whether the free tour is taxable. If it is taxable, be sure to include in your letter where the income must be reported and the dollar amount.
   (An example of a client letter is available at the website for this text, located at **www.cengagebrain.com.**)

GROUP 4: COMPREHENSIVE PROBLEMS

1. Bev and Ken Hair have been married for 3 years. They live at 3567 River Street, Springfield, MO 63126. Ken is a full-time student at Southwest Missouri State University (SMSU) and Bev works as an accountant at Cypress Corporation. Bev's

Social Security number is 465-74-3321 and Ken's is 465-57-9934. Bev's earnings and income tax withholdings for 2014 are:

Earnings from Cypress Corp.	$50,000
Federal income tax withheld	5,500
State income tax withheld	675

The Hairs have interest income of $1,000 on City of St. Louis bonds. During 2014, Bev and Ken received the following 1099-INT and DIV:

9292 ☐ VOID ☐ CORRECTED

PAYER'S name, street address, city or town, state or province, country, ZIP or foreign postal code, and telephone no.
Boatman's Bank
300 City Avenue
Springfield, MO 63126

Payer's RTN (optional)

OMB No. 1545-0112

2014 Form **1099-INT**

Interest Income

1 Interest income $ 577

2 Early withdrawal penalty $

Copy A

For Internal Revenue Service Center

File with Form 1096.

For Privacy Act and Paperwork Reduction Act Notice, see the **2014 General Instructions for Certain Information Returns.**

PAYER'S federal identification number	RECIPIENT'S identification number
XX-XXXXXXX	*465-57-9934*

RECIPIENT'S name
Ken & Bev Hair

Street address (including apt. no.)
3567 River Street

City or town, state or province, country, and ZIP or foreign postal code
Springfield, MO 63126

Account number (see instructions)

2nd TIN not. ☐

3 Interest on U.S. Savings Bonds and Treas. obligations $	
4 Federal income tax withheld $	5 Investment expenses $
6 Foreign tax paid $	7 Foreign country or U.S. possession
8 Tax-exempt interest $	9 Specified private activity bond interest $
10 Market discount $	11 Bond premium $
12 Tax-exempt bond CUSIP no.	13 State / 14 State identification no. / 15 State tax withheld $ $

Form **1099-INT** Cat. No. 14410K www.irs.gov/form1099int Department of the Treasury - Internal Revenue Service

Do Not Cut or Separate Forms on This Page — Do Not Cut or Separate Forms on This Page

9191 ☐ VOID ☐ CORRECTED

PAYER'S name, street address, city or town, state or province, country, ZIP or foreign postal code, and telephone no.
Green Corporation
900 South Orange Ave
Springfield, MD 63126

1a Total ordinary dividends $ 287

1b Qualified dividends $ 287

OMB No. 1545-0110

2014 Form **1099-DIV**

Dividends and Distributions

Copy A

For Internal Revenue Service Center

File with Form 1096.

For Privacy Act and Paperwork Reduction Act Notice, see the **2014 General Instructions for Certain Information Returns.**

PAYER'S federal identification number	RECIPIENT'S identification number
XX-XXXXXXX	*465-57-9934*

RECIPIENT'S name
Ken & Bev Hair

Street address (including apt. no.)
3567 River Street

City or town, state or province, country, and ZIP or foreign postal code
Springfield, MO 63126

Account number (see instructions)

2nd TIN not. ☐

2a Total capital gain distr. $	2b Unrecap. Sec. 1250 gain $
2c Section 1202 gain $	2d Collectibles (28%) gain $
3 Nondividend distributions $	4 Federal income tax withheld $
	5 Investment expenses $
6 Foreign tax paid $	7 Foreign country or U.S. possession
8 Cash liquidation distributions $	9 Noncash liquidation distributions $
10 Exempt-interest dividends $	11 Specified private activity bond interest dividends $
12 State / 13 State identification no.	14 State tax withheld $ $

Form **1099-DIV** Cat. No. 14415N www.irs.gov/form1099div Department of the Treasury - Internal Revenue Service

Do Not Cut or Separate Forms on This Page — Do Not Cut or Separate Forms on This Page

Ken is an excellent student at SMSU. He was given a $1,750 scholarship by the university to help pay educational expenses. The scholarship funds were used by

Ken for tuition and books. Ken also had a part-time job at SMSU. He was paid $2,525 on a W-2 for helping out in the Dean's office. There was no income tax withheld on the amount paid to Ken from this job.

Last year, Bev was laid off from her former job and was unemployed during January 2014. She was paid $1,825 of unemployment compensation until she started work with her current employer, Cypress Corporation.

Ken has a 4-year-old son, Robert R. Hair, from a prior marriage. During 2014, he paid his ex-wife $300 per month in child support. Robert is claimed as a dependent by Ken's ex-wife.

During 2014, Ken's aunt died. The aunt, in her will, left Ken $15,000 in cash. Ken deposited this money in the SMSU Credit Union account.

Required: Complete the Hair's federal tax return for 2014. Use Form 1040A and the worksheet on Pages 2-45 through 2-47. Make realistic assumptions about any missing data.

2A. Ray and Maria Gomez have been married for 3 years. They live at 1610 Quince Ave., McAllen, TX 78701. Ray works for Palm Oil Corporation and Maria works for the City of McAllen. Maria's Social Security number is 444-65-9912 and Ray's is 469-21-5523. Ray and Maria's earnings and income tax withheld for 2014 are:

Ray:	Earnings from Palm Oil Corp.	$29,420
	Federal income tax withheld	4,320
	State income tax withheld	0
Maria:	Earnings from the City of McAllen	$31,300
	Federal income tax withheld	5,300
	State income tax withheld	0

Ray and Maria have interest income of $577 from a savings account at McAllen State Bank. In addition, they own U.S. Savings bonds (Series EE). The bonds had a value of $10,000 on January 1, 2014, and their value is $10,700 on December 31, 2014. They have not made an election with respect to these bonds.

Ray has an ex-wife named Judy Gomez. Pursuant to their divorce decree, Ray pays her $400 per month in alimony. All payments were made on time in 2014. Judy's Social Security number is 566-74-8765.

During 2014, Ray was in the hospital for a successful operation. His health insurance company reimbursed Ray $4,732 for all of his hospital and doctor bills.

In June of 2014, Maria's father died. Under a life insurance policy owned and paid for by her father, Maria was paid death benefits of $25,000.

Maria bought a Texas lottery ticket on impulse during 2014. Her ticket was lucky and she won $3,000. The winning amount was paid to Maria in November 2014, with no income tax withheld.

Palm Oil Corporation provides Ray with a company car to drive while he is working. The Corporation spent $5,000 to maintain this vehicle during 2014. Ray never uses the car for personal purposes.

Required: Complete the Gomez's federal tax return for 2014. Use Form 1040 on Pages 2-49 and 2-50. Make realistic assumptions about any missing data.

2B. Carl Conch and Mary Duval are married and file a joint return. They live at 1234 Mallory Sq. Apt. 64, Key West, FL 33040. Carl works for the Key Lime Pie Company and Mary is a homemaker after losing her job in 2013. Mary's Social Security

number is 633-65-7912 and Carl's is 835-21-5423. Carl's earnings and income tax withheld for 2014 are:

Earnings from Key Lime Pie Company	$67,000
Federal income tax withheld	9,726
State income tax withheld	0

Carl and Mary have interest income of $283 from a savings account at Coral Reef State Bank.

Carl owns stock in Southwest Airlines. Southwest paid Carl $125 in nonqualified dividends in 2014.

Mary is divorced and she pays her ex-husband (Tom Tortuga) child support. Pursuant to their divorce decree, Mary pays Tom $525 per month in child support. All payments were made on time in 2014.

In June of 2014, Mary's father gave her a cash gift of $75,000. Mary also received unemployment compensation of $2,600 during 2014. Mary won a $1,000 prize in a women's club raffle in 2014. No income tax was withheld from the prize.

The Key Lime Pie Company provides Carl with a company car to drive while he is working. The Company spent $6,475 to maintain this vehicle during 2014. Carl never uses the car for personal purposes.

Required: Complete Carl and Mary's federal tax return for 2014. Use Form 1040 on Pages 2-49 and 2-50. Make realistic assumptions about any missing data.

GROUP 5: CUMULATIVE SOFTWARE PROBLEM

1. The following additional information is available for the Dr. Ivan and Irene Incisor family.

   Ivan and Irene have the following investment income, in addition to that reported in Chapter 1:

Dividends (qualified) on Big Bank stock	$850
Dividends (qualified) on Big Gas Company stock	470
Dividends (nonqualified) from Mango Mutual Fund	145
Interest on Washington State Municipal Bonds	650
Interest on Big Electric Company Bonds	650

Ivan went to a local Indian casino and won $6,000 playing Keno. Ivan had no other gambling income or loss for the year.

In February, Irene received $50,000 in life insurance proceeds from the death of her friend Sharon.

In July, Ivan's uncle Igor died and left him real estate (undeveloped land) worth $72,000.

Five years ago, Ivan and Irene were divorced. Ivan married Mary Molar, but that marriage did not work out and they were divorced a year later. Under their divorce decree, Ivan pays Mary $13,000 per year alimony. All payments were made on time during 2014. Mary's Social Security number is 667-34-9224. Three years ago, Ivan and Irene were remarried.

Bitewing Dental Clinic, Inc. pays Ivan's dental license fees and membership dues to dental organizations. During 2014, Bitewing paid $1,240 for such dues and fees for Ivan.

Irene was laid off from her job on January 2, 2014. For 2014, she received $3,750 in unemployment benefits.

Ivan and his family are covered by an employer-sponsored health insurance plan at work. Bitewing pays $700 per month premiums for Ivan and his family. During the year, Irene was in the hospital for a few days to have her appendix removed. The bill for the surgery was $5,100 of which the health insurance plan reimbursed Ivan the full $5,100.

Required: Combine this new information about the Incisor family with the information from Chapter 1 and complete a revised 2014 tax return for Ivan and Irene. Be sure to save your data input files since this case will be expanded with more tax information in later chapters.

Form **1040A** Department of the Treasury—Internal Revenue Service
U.S. Individual Income Tax Return (99) **2014** IRS Use Only—Do not write or staple in this space.

DRAFT AS OF July 24, 2014

Your first name and initial	Last name	OMB No. 1545-0074 **Your social security number**
If a joint return, spouse's first name and initial	Last name	**Spouse's social security number**
Home address (number and street). If you have a P.O. box, see instructions.	Apt. no.	▲ Make sure the SSN(s) above and on line 6c are correct.
City, town or post office, state, and ZIP code. If you have a foreign address, also complete spaces below (see instructions).		**Presidential Election Campaign** Check here if you, or your spouse if filing jointly, want $3 to go to this fund. Checking a box below will not change your tax or refund. ☐ You ☐ Spouse
Foreign country name	Foreign province/state/county	Foreign postal code

Filing status
Check only one box.

1 ☐ Single
2 ☐ Married filing jointly (even if only one had income)
3 ☐ Married filing separately. Enter spouse's SSN above and full name here. ▶
4 ☐ Head of household (with qualifying person). (See instructions.) If the qualifying person is a child but not your dependent, enter this child's name here. ▶
5 ☐ Qualifying widow(er) with dependent child (see instructions)

Exemptions

6a ☐ **Yourself.** If someone can claim you as a dependent, **do not** check box 6a.
b ☐ **Spouse**

Boxes checked on 6a and 6b

c **Dependents:**

If more than six dependents, see instructions.

(1) First name	Last name	(2) Dependent's social security number	(3) Dependent's relationship to you	(4) ✓ if child under age 17 qualifying for child tax credit (see instructions)
				☐
				☐
				☐
				☐
				☐
				☐

No. of children on 6c who:
- **lived with you**
- **did not live with you due to divorce or separation (see instructions)**

Dependents on 6c not entered above

d Total number of exemptions claimed.

Add numbers on lines above ▶

Income

Attach Form(s) W-2 here. Also attach Form(s) 1099-R if tax was withheld.

If you did not get a W-2, see instructions.

Line	Description			
7	Wages, salaries, tips, etc. Attach Form(s) W-2.			7
8a	**Taxable** interest. Attach Schedule B if required.			8a
b	**Tax-exempt** interest. **Do not** include on line 8a.	8b		
9a	Ordinary dividends. Attach Schedule B if required.			9a
b	Qualified dividends (see instructions).	9b		
10	Capital gain distributions (see instructions).			10
11a	IRA distributions.	11a	**11b** Taxable amount (see instructions).	11b
12a	Pensions and annuities.	12a	**12b** Taxable amount (see instructions).	12b
13	Unemployment compensation and Alaska Permanent Fund dividends.			13
14a	Social security benefits.	14a	**14b** Taxable amount (see instructions).	14b
15	Add lines 7 through 14b (far right column). This is your **total income.** ▶			15

Adjusted gross income

Line	Description		
16	Reserved	16	
17	IRA deduction (see instructions).	17	
18	Student loan interest deduction (see instructions).	18	
19	Reserved	19	
20	Add lines 16 through 19. These are your **total adjustments.**		20
21	Subtract line 20 from line 15. This is your **adjusted gross income.** ▶		21

For Disclosure, Privacy Act, and Paperwork Reduction Act Notice, see separate instructions. Cat. No. 11327A Form **1040A** (2014)

Form 1040A (2014) Page **2**

DRAFT AS OF July 24, 2014 DO NOT FILE

Tax, credits, and payments

22	Enter the amount from line 21 (adjusted gross income).		22
23a	Check if: ☐ **You** were born before January 2, 1950, ☐ Blind; ☐ **Spouse** was born before January 2, 1950, ☐ Blind } **Total boxes checked** ▶ 23a ☐		
b	If you are married filing separately and your spouse itemizes deductions, check here ▶ 23b ☐		
24	Enter your **standard deduction**.		24
25	Subtract line 24 from line 22. If line 24 is more than line 22, enter -0-.		25
26	**Exemptions.** Multiply $3,950 by the number on line 6d.		26
27	Subtract line 26 from line 25. If line 26 is more than line 25, enter -0-. This is your **taxable income.** ▶		27
28	**Tax,** including any alternative minimum tax (see instructions).	28	
29	Excess advance premium tax credit repayment. Attach Form 8962.	29	
30	Add lines 28 and 29.		30
31	Credit for child and dependent care expenses. Attach Form 2441.	31	
32	Credit for the elderly or the disabled. Attach Schedule R.	32	
33	Education credits from Form 8863, line 19.	33	
34	Retirement savings contributions credit. Attach Form 8880.	34	
35	Child tax credit. Attach Schedule 8812, if required.	35	
36	Add lines 31 through 35. These are your **total credits.**		36
37	Subtract line 36 from line 30. If line 36 is more than line 30, enter -0-.		37
38	Health care: individual responsibility (see instructions). Full-year coverage ☐		38
39	Add line 37 and line 38. This is your **total tax.**		39
40	Federal income tax withheld from Forms W-2 and 1099.	40	
41	2014 estimated tax payments and amount applied from 2013 return.	41	
42a	**Earned income credit (EIC).**	42a	
b	Nontaxable combat pay election. 42b		
43	Additional child tax credit. Attach Schedule 8812.	43	
44	American opportunity credit from Form 8863, line 8.	44	
45	Net premium tax credit. Attach Form 8962.	45	
46	Add lines 40, 41, 42a, 43, 44, and 45. These are your **total payments.** ▶		46

Standard Deduction for—
- People who check any box on line 23a or 23b **or** who can be claimed as a dependent, see instructions.
- All others:

Single or Married filing separately, $6,200

Married filing jointly or Qualifying widow(er), $12,400

Head of household, $9,100

If you have a qualifying child, attach Schedule EIC.

Refund

47	If line 46 is more than line 39, subtract line 39 from line 46. This is the amount you **overpaid.**		47
48a	Amount of line 47 you want **refunded to you.** If Form 8888 is attached, check here ▶ ☐		48a
▶ b	Routing number ☐☐☐☐☐☐☐☐☐ ▶ **c** Type: ☐ Checking ☐ Savings		
▶ d	Account number ☐☐☐☐☐☐☐☐☐☐☐☐☐☐☐☐☐		
49	Amount of line 47 you want **applied to your 2015 estimated tax.**	49	

Direct deposit? See instructions and fill in 48b, 48c, and 48d or Form 8888.

Amount you owe

50	**Amount you owe.** Subtract line 46 from line 39. For details on how to pay, see instructions. ▶		50
51	Estimated tax penalty (see instructions).	51	

Third party designee

Do you want to allow another person to discuss this return with the IRS (see instructions)? ☐ **Yes.** Complete the following. ☐ **No**

Designee's name ▶ Phone no. ▶ Personal identification number (PIN) ▶ ☐☐☐☐☐

Sign here

Joint return? See instructions. Keep a copy for your records.

Under penalties of perjury, I declare that I have examined this return and accompanying schedules and statements, and to the best of my knowledge and belief, they are true, correct, and accurately list all amounts and sources of income I received during the tax year. Declaration of preparer (other than the taxpayer) is based on all information of which the preparer has any knowledge.

Your signature	Date	Your occupation	Daytime phone number
Spouse's signature. If a joint return, **both** must sign.	Date	Spouse's occupation	If the IRS sent you an Identity Protection PIN, enter it here (see inst.) ☐☐☐☐☐☐

Paid preparer use only

Print/type preparer's name	Preparer's signature	Date	Check ▶ ☐ if self-employed	PTIN
Firm's name ▶			Firm's EIN ▶	
Firm's address ▶			Phone no.	

Qualified Dividends and Capital Gain Tax Worksheet—Line 28*

Keep for Your Records

Before you begin: ✓ Be sure you do not have to file Form 1040 (see the Instructions for Form 1040A, line 10).

1. Enter the amount from Form 1040A, line 27 . . . . . 1. ______
2. Enter the amount from Form 1040A, line 9b . . . . . 2. ______
3. Enter the amount from Form 1040A, line 10 . . . . . 3. ______
4. Add lines 2 and 3 . . . . . 4. ______
5. Subtract line 4 from line 1. If zero or less, enter -0- . . . . . 5. ______
6. Enter the **smaller** of:
   - The amount on line 1, or
   - $36,900 if single or married filing separately, $73,800 if married filing jointly or qualifying widow(er), or $49,400 if head of household. . . . . 6. ______
7. Enter the smaller of line 5 or line 6 . . . . . 7. ______
8. Subtract line 7 from line 6. This amount is taxed at 0% . . . . . 8. ______
9. Enter the smaller of line 1 or line 4 . . . . . 9. ______
10. Enter the amount from line 8 . . . . . 10. ______
11. Subtract line 10 from line 9 . . . . . 11. ______
12. Multiply line 11 by 15% (.15) . . . . . 12. ______
13. Use the Tax Table to figure the tax on the amount on line 5. Enter the tax here . . . . . 13. ______
14. Add lines 12 and 13 . . . . . 14. ______
15. Use the Tax Table to figure the tax on the amount on line 1. Enter the tax here . . . . . 15. ______
16. **Tax on all taxable income.** Enter the **smaller** of line 14 or line 15 here and on Form 1040A, line 28 . . . . . 16. ______

***Note: This worksheet does not apply for high-income taxpayers under the ACA or ATRA provisions (See LO 1.9).**

Form **1040** Department of the Treasury—Internal Revenue Service (99)
U.S. Individual Income Tax Return **2014** OMB No. 1545-0074 IRS Use Only—Do not write or staple in this space.

For the year Jan. 1–Dec. 31, 2014, or other tax year beginning , 2014, ending , 20 See separate instructions.

Your first name and initial	Last name	**Your social security number**
If a joint return, spouse's first name and initial	Last name	**Spouse's social security number**
Home address (number and street). If you have a P.O. box, see instructions.	Apt. no.	▲ Make sure the SSN(s) above and on line 6c are correct.
City, town or post office, state, and ZIP code. If you have a foreign address, also complete spaces below (see instructions).		**Presidential Election Campaign** Check here if you, or your spouse if filing jointly, want $3 to go to this fund. Checking a box below will not change your tax or refund. ☐ You ☐ Spouse
Foreign country name	Foreign province/state/county / Foreign postal code	

Filing Status

Check only one box.

1 ☐ Single
2 ☐ Married filing jointly (even if only one had income)
3 ☐ Married filing separately. Enter spouse's SSN above and full name here. ▶
4 ☐ Head of household (with qualifying person). (See instructions.) If the qualifying person is a child but not your dependent, enter this child's name here. ▶
5 ☐ Qualifying widow(er) with dependent child

Exemptions

6a ☐ **Yourself.** If someone can claim you as a dependent, **do not** check box 6a . . . . .
b ☐ **Spouse** . . . .

Boxes checked on 6a and 6b

c **Dependents:**

(1) First name Last name	(2) Dependent's social security number	(3) Dependent's relationship to you	(4) ✓ if child under age 17 qualifying for child tax credit (see instructions)
			☐
			☐
			☐
			☐

If more than four dependents, see instructions and check here ▶ ☐

No. of children on 6c who:
- lived with you
- did not live with you due to divorce or separation (see instructions)

Dependents on 6c not entered above

d Total number of exemptions claimed . . . .

Add numbers on lines above ▶

Income

Attach Form(s) W-2 here. Also attach Forms W-2G and 1099-R if tax was withheld.

If you did not get a W-2, see instructions.

7	Wages, salaries, tips, etc. Attach Form(s) W-2		7
8a	**Taxable** interest. Attach Schedule B if required		8a
b	**Tax-exempt** interest. **Do not** include on line 8a . . .	8b	
9a	Ordinary dividends. Attach Schedule B if required		9a
b	Qualified dividends	9b	
10	Taxable refunds, credits, or offsets of state and local income taxes		10
11	Alimony received		11
12	Business income or (loss). Attach Schedule C or C-EZ		12
13	Capital gain or (loss). Attach Schedule D if required. If not required, check here ▶ ☐		13
14	Other gains or (losses). Attach Form 4797		14
15a	IRA distributions . 15a	b Taxable amount . . .	15b
16a	Pensions and annuities 16a	b Taxable amount . . .	16b
17	Rental real estate, royalties, partnerships, S corporations, trusts, etc. Attach Schedule E		17
18	Farm income or (loss). Attach Schedule F		18
19	Unemployment compensation		19
20a	Social security benefits 20a	b Taxable amount . . .	20b
21	Other income. List type and amount		21
22	Combine the amounts in the far right column for lines 7 through 21. This is your **total income** ▶		22

DRAFT AS OF August 28, 20 DO NOT FIL

Adjusted Gross Income

23	Reserved	23	
24	Certain business expenses of reservists, performing artists, and fee-basis government officials. Attach Form 2106 or 2106-EZ	24	
25	Health savings account deduction. Attach Form 8889 .	25	
26	Moving expenses. Attach Form 3903	26	
27	Deductible part of self-employment tax. Attach Schedule SE .	27	
28	Self-employed SEP, SIMPLE, and qualified plans . .	28	
29	Self-employed health insurance deduction	29	
30	Penalty on early withdrawal of savings	30	
31a	Alimony paid b Recipient's SSN ▶	31a	
32	IRA deduction	32	
33	Student loan interest deduction	33	
34	Reserved	34	
35	Domestic production activities deduction. Attach Form 8903	35	
36	Add lines 23 through 35		36
37	Subtract line 36 from line 22. This is your **adjusted gross income** . . . . . ▶		37

For Disclosure, Privacy Act, and Paperwork Reduction Act Notice, see separate instructions. Cat. No. 11320B Form **1040** (2014)

Form 1040 (2014) Page **2**

DRAFT AS OF August 28, 2014 DO NOT FILE

Section	Line	Description	Line box	Amount	Line box	Amount
	38	Amount from line 37 (adjusted gross income)			38	
Tax and Credits	39a	Check if: { ☐ **You** were born before January 2, 1950, ☐ Blind. / ☐ **Spouse** was born before January 2, 1950, ☐ Blind. } **Total boxes checked** ▶ **39a** ☐				
	b	If your spouse itemizes on a separate return or you were a dual-status alien, check here ▶ 39b☐				
	40	**Itemized deductions** (from Schedule A) **or** your **standard deduction** (see left margin)			40	
	41	Subtract line 40 from line 38			41	
	42	**Exemptions.** If line 38 is $152,525 or less, multiply $3,950 by the number on line 6d. Otherwise, see instructions			42	
	43	**Taxable income.** Subtract line 42 from line 41. If line 42 is more than line 41, enter -0-			43	
	44	**Tax** (see instructions). Check if any from: **a** ☐ Form(s) 8814 **b** ☐ Form 4972 **c** ☐			44	
	45	**Alternative minimum tax** (see instructions). Attach Form 6251			45	
	46	Excess advance premium tax credit repayment. Attach Form 8962			46	
	47	Add lines 44, 45, and 46 ▶			47	
	48	Foreign tax credit. Attach Form 1116 if required	48			
	49	Credit for child and dependent care expenses. Attach Form 2441	49			
	50	Education credits from Form 8863, line 19	50			
	51	Retirement savings contributions credit. Attach Form 8880	51			
	52	Child tax credit. Attach Schedule 8812, if required	52			
	53	Residential energy credit. Attach Form 5695	53			
	54	Other credits from Form: **a** ☐ 3800 **b** ☐ 8801 **c** ☐	54			
	55	Add lines 48 through 54. These are your **total credits**			55	
	56	Subtract line 55 from line 47. If line 55 is more than line 47, enter -0- ▶			56	
Other Taxes	57	Self-employment tax. Attach Schedule SE			57	
	58	Unreported social security and Medicare tax from Form: **a** ☐ 4137 **b** ☐ 8919			58	
	59	Additional tax on IRAs, other qualified retirement plans, etc. Attach Form 5329 if required			59	
	60a	Household employment taxes from Schedule H			60a	
	b	First-time homebuyer credit repayment. Attach Form 5405 if required			60b	
	61	Health care: individual responsibility (see instructions) Full-year coverage ☐			61	
	62	Taxes from: **a** ☐ Form 8959 **b** ☐ Form 8960 **c** ☐ Instructions; enter code(s)			62	
	63	Add lines 56 through 62. This is your **total tax** ▶			63	
Payments	64	Federal income tax withheld from Forms W-2 and 1099	64			
	65	2014 estimated tax payments and amount applied from 2013 return	65			
	66a	**Earned income credit (EIC)**	66a			
	b	Nontaxable combat pay election 66b				
	67	Additional child tax credit. Attach Schedule 8812	67			
	68	American opportunity credit from Form 8863, line 8	68			
	69	Net premium tax credit. Attach Form 8962	69			
	70	Amount paid with request for extension to file	70			
	71	Excess social security and tier 1 RRTA tax withheld	71			
	72	Credit for federal tax on fuels. Attach Form 4136	72			
	73	Credits from Form: **a** ☐ 2439 **b** ☐ Reserved **c** ☐ Reserved **d** ☐	73			
	74	Add lines 64, 65, 66a, and 67 through 73. These are your **total payments** ▶			74	
Refund	75	If line 74 is more than line 63, subtract line 63 from line 74. This is the amount you **overpaid**			75	
	76a	Amount of line 75 you want **refunded to you.** If Form 8888 is attached, check here ▶☐			76a	
Direct deposit? See instructions.	▶ b	Routing number ▶ **c** Type: ☐ Checking ☐ Savings				
	▶ d	Account number				
	77	Amount of line 75 you want **applied to your 2015 estimated tax** ▶	77			
Amount You Owe	78	**Amount you owe.** Subtract line 74 from line 63. For details on how to pay, see instructions ▶			78	
	79	Estimated tax penalty (see instructions)	79			

Standard Deduction for—

- People who check any box on line 39a or 39b **or** who can be claimed as a dependent, see instructions.
- All others:

Single or Married filing separately, $6,200

Married filing jointly or Qualifying widow(er), $12,400

Head of household, $9,100

If you have a qualifying child, attach Schedule EIC.

Third Party Designee

Do you want to allow another person to discuss this return with the IRS (see instructions)? ☐ **Yes.** Complete below. ☐ **No**

Designee's name ▶ Phone no. ▶ Personal identification number (PIN) ▶

Sign Here

Joint return? See instructions. Keep a copy for your records.

Under penalties of perjury, I declare that I have examined this return and accompanying schedules and statements, and to the best of my knowledge and belief, they are true, correct, and complete. Declaration of preparer (other than taxpayer) is based on all information of which preparer has any knowledge.

Your signature	Date	Your occupation	Daytime phone number
Spouse's signature. If a joint return, **both** must sign.	Date	Spouse's occupation	If the IRS sent you an Identity Protection PIN, enter it here (see inst.)

Paid Preparer Use Only

Print/Type preparer's name	Preparer's signature	Date	Check ☐ if self-employed	PTIN
Firm's name ▶			Firm's EIN ▶	
Firm's address ▶			Phone no.	

www.irs.gov/form1040 Form **1040** (2014)

Student Name ______________________

Class/Section ______________________

Date ______________________

KEY NUMBER TAX RETURN SUMMARY

CHAPTER 2

Comprehensive Problem 1

Adjusted Gross Income (Line 21) ______________

Taxable Income (Line 27) ______________

Tax Liability (Line 39) ______________

Tax Overpaid (Line 47) ______________

Comprehensive Problem 2A

Adjusted Gross Income (Line 37) ______________

Taxable Income (Line 43) ______________

Tax Liability (Line 63) ______________

Tax Overpaid (Line 75) ______________

Comprehensive Problem 2B

Adjusted Gross Income (Line 37) ______________

Taxable Income (Line 43) ______________

Tax Liability (Line 63) ______________

Tax Overpaid (Line 75) ______________

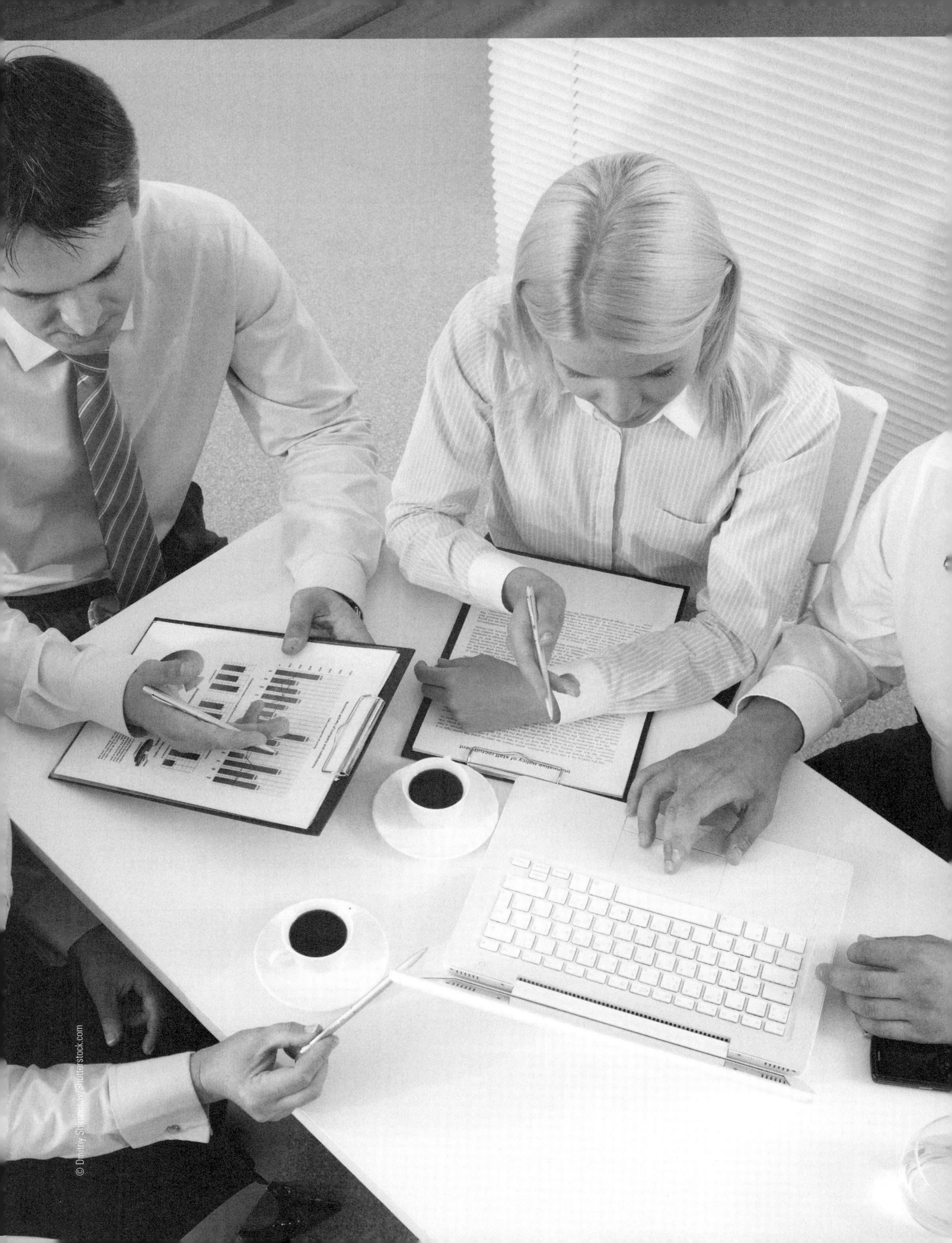

© Dmitriy Shironosov/Shutterstock.com

CHAPTER 3

Business Income and Expenses, Part I

LEARNING OBJECTIVES

After completing this chapter, you should be able to:

LO 3.1 Complete a basic Schedule C (Profit or Loss from Business).

LO 3.2 Understand the tax treatment of inventories and cost of goods sold.

LO 3.3 Identify the requirements for deducting transportation expenses.

LO 3.4 Identify the requirements for deducting travel expenses.

LO 3.5 Determine the requirements for claiming meals and entertainment deductions.

LO 3.6 Identify the requirements for claiming business education expenses.

LO 3.7 Identify the tax treatment of dues and subscriptions.

LO 3.8 Determine which clothing and uniforms may be treated as tax deductions.

LO 3.9 Explain the special limits for business gift deductions.

LO 3.10 Explain the tax treatment of bad debt deductions.

LO 3.11 Ascertain when a home office deduction may be claimed and how the deduction is computed.

LO 3.12 Describe the basic tax treatment of deductions for net operating losses.

LO 3.13 Apply the factors used to determine whether an activity is a hobby, and understand the tax treatment of hobby losses.

OVERVIEW

This chapter covers Schedule C, "Profit or Loss from Business (Sole Proprietorship)," and many of the common business expenses allowed as deductions in arriving at net taxable business income. Schedule C is filed by self-employed taxpayers, such as accountants, doctors, lawyers, architects, consultants, small manufacturers, restaurateurs, store owners, gardeners, event planners, bookkeepers, and other small businesses. This form is one of the most commonly used tax forms and, for many taxpayers, the net income reported on Schedule C is the primary component in their adjusted gross income.

The common business expenses covered in this chapter are travel, transportation, bad debts, inventory, net operating losses, home office, entertainment, business education, dues, subscriptions, publications, special clothing, uniforms, and business gifts. While these expenses are often associated with Schedule C (Sole Proprietorship income), they may also be associated with rental and royalty income deducted on Schedule E, or farm and ranch

income deducted on Schedule F. In addition, some of these expenses might be incurred by employees in connection with their employment. Employee business expenses are covered in Chapter 5.

Learning Objective 3.1

Complete a basic Schedule C (Profit or Loss from Business).

SCHEDULE C

A taxpayer who operates a trade or business or practices a profession as a sole proprietorship must file a tax return reporting his or her taxable income or loss from the activity. Schedule C is similar to the income statement in financial accounting. Taxable income from a business or profession is reported on either Schedule C-EZ (short form), Schedule C (long form), or Schedule F (a specialized version of Schedule C for farmers and ranchers).

Trade or Business

The term *trade or business* is not formally defined, although the term is used often in the Internal Revenue Code. For example, Section 162 of the Code states that a taxpayer is allowed to deduct all the ordinary and necessary expenses in carrying on a trade or business. Generally, a "trade or business" for tax purposes is any activity engaged in for profit. Note that a taxpayer does not have to actually make a profit, but he or she should be seeking to make a profit through regular and continual effort. Intermittent activities (e.g., casual craft sales) or leisure pursuits (e.g., wine making) may not meet the tax definition of a trade or business and may require reporting under the hobby loss rules discussed later in this chapter.

Tests for Deductibility

Expenses must meet several general tests to qualify as a tax deduction. Listed below are three common tests for deductibility. These tests give guidelines for deductibility, but often in practice it is a matter of judgment as to whether an expense is considered a legitimate business expense. Taxpayers and IRS agents frequently disagree as to whether specific expenses pass the following tests, and many court cases have been devoted to these disagreements. The tests below overlap and an expense may fail more than one test.

- **The Ordinary & Necessary Test:** Under the tax law, for trade or business expenses to be deductible they must be ordinary and necessary. Generally, this means that the type of expense is commonly found in the specific business, and is helpful and appropriate in running the business. For example, Rob is a CPA who goes to a "tax boot camp" which offers intensive training on tax return preparation every year. Rob also hires a trainer at his local gym to work out with him to help him maintain the strength and endurance needed to handle the rigors of tax season. The cost of the "tax boot camp" would be deductible. The cost of the personal trainer is not a common or ordinary expense of CPA firms and is not necessary for preparing tax returns and therefore would not be deductible.
- **The Business Purpose Test:** Expenses must have a legitimate business purpose to be considered deductible. Larry is an independent consultant who maintains an office in his home, although he always meets with clients at their place of business. He spent $75,000 upgrading his office to include a large attached glass sunroom and a display area for his orchid collection. This home office upgrade would likely be considered to serve no business purpose, so the expenses related to the improvements would not be allowed.
- **The Reasonableness Test:** The tax law requires that deductions be reasonable to be deducted. For example, Derek owns a small business and takes one of his clients, who is also a friend, to an expensive business dinner every week. They enjoy a variety of restaurants and fine wines, and always spend some time talking about their joint business interests. The yearly cost of the entertainment is $20,000, and Derek generates $15,000 of fees from his friend each year. This lavish and extravagant business entertainment would

likely not be considered reasonable given the circumstances. If they had met for pizza and a business discussion every week, the expense would likely be considered reasonable and deductible.

Schedule C-EZ

Taxpayers must file Schedule C unless they qualify to file Schedule C-EZ. To use the short form, Schedule C-EZ, the taxpayer must meet the following requirements:

1. Business expenses must be $5,000 or less,
2. There must be no inventory during the year,
3. The business must not have had a net loss for the year,
4. The taxpayer must have only one business as a sole proprietor,
5. The business must have had no employees during the year,
6. The taxpayer must not be required to complete Form 4562 to report depreciation,
7. The business must not include a home office deduction,
8. The business must not have had disallowed passive losses in a prior year(s), and
9. The business must use the cash method of accounting.

Schedule C-EZ of Form 1040 is straightforward. It is one page long and consists of three parts. The three parts are General Information (Part I), Net Profit (Part II), and Vehicle Information (Part III). The general information section includes information such as the business name and address. The net profit section of Schedule C-EZ Part II (see Figure 3.1) is only three lines long: gross receipts (line 1), total expenses (line 2), and net profit (line 3). Taxpayers claiming car or truck expenses must also complete Part III of Schedule C-EZ, giving information about the vehicle used in the business or profession.

Schedule C

Schedule C is required for more complex businesses and requires a taxpayer to provide more information. The first section (lines A to J) of Schedule C requires disclosure of basic information such as the business name and location, the accounting method (cash, accrual, or other, as covered in Chapter 7), material participation in the business (for passive activity loss classification purposes), and whether the business was started or acquired during the year.

FIGURE 3.1 SCHEDULE C-EZ PART II

Part II **Figure Your Net Profit**

1	**Gross receipts. Caution.** If this income was reported to you on Form W-2 and the "Statutory employee" box on that form was checked, see *Statutory employees* in the instructions for Schedule C, line 1, and check here . . . . ▶ ☐	1	
2	**Total expenses** (see page 2). If more than $5,000, you **must** use Schedule C	2	
3	**Net profit.** Subtract line 2 from line 1. If less than zero, you **must** use Schedule C. Enter on both **Form 1040, line 12,** and **Schedule SE, line 2,** or on **Form 1040NR, line 13** and **Schedule SE, line 2** (see instructions). (Statutory employees **do not** report this amount on Schedule SE, line 2.) Estates and trusts, enter on **Form 1041, line 3**	3	

FIGURE 3.2 PRINCIPAL BUSINESS OR PROFESSIONAL ACTIVITY CODES EXCERPT

Principal Business or Professional Activity Codes

These codes for the Principal Business or Professional Activity classify sole proprietorships by the type of activity they are engaged in to facilitate the administration of the Internal Revenue Code. These six-digit codes are based on the North American Industry Classification System (NAICS).

Select the category that best describes your primary business activity (for example, Real Estate). Then select the activity that best identifies the principal source of your sales or receipts (for example, real estate agent). Now find the six-digit code assigned to this activity (for example, 531210, the code for offices of real estate agents and brokers) and enter it on Schedule C or C-EZ, line B.

Note. If your principal source of income is from farming activities, you should file Schedule F.

Accommodation, Food Services, & Drinking Places

Accommodation

721310 Rooming & boarding houses
721210 RV (recreational vehicle) parks & recreational camps
721100 Traveler accommodation (including hotels, motels, & bed & breakfast inns)

Food Services & Drinking Places

722514 Cafeterias & buffets
722410 Drinking places (alcoholic beverages)
722511 Full-service restaurants
722513 Limited-service restaurants
722515 Snack & non-alcoholic beverage bars

115310 Support activities for forestry

Arts, Entertainment, & Recreation

Amusement, Gambling, & Recreation Industries

713100 Amusement parks & arcades
713200 Gambling industries
713900 Other amusement & recreation services (including golf courses, skiing facilities, marinas, fitness centers, bowling centers, skating rinks, miniature golf courses)

Museums, Historical Sites, & Similar Institutions

712100 Museums, historical sites, & similar institutions

Performing Arts, Spectator Sports, & Related Industries

Finance & Insurance

Credit Intermediation & Related Activities

522100 Depository credit intermediation (including commercial banking, savings institutions, & credit unions)
522200 Nondepository credit intermediation (including sales financing & consumer lending)
522300 Activities related to credit intermediation (including loan brokers)

Insurance Agents, Brokers, & Related Activities

524210 Insurance agencies & brokerages
524290 Other insurance related activities

517000 Telecommunications & Internet service providers

Data Processing Services

518210 Data processing, hosting, & related services
519100 Other information services (including news syndicates & libraries, Internet publishing & broadcasting)

Motion Picture & Sound Recording

512100 Motion picture & video industries (except video rental)
512200 Sound recording industries

Manufacturing

315000 Apparel mfg.
312000 Beverage & tobacco product mfg.
334000 Computer & electronic product

Both Schedule C and Schedule C-EZ ask that the taxpayer supply a principal business or professional activity code (see Figure 3.2). These codes are used to classify sole proprietorships by the type of business activity. For example, a full-service restaurant is code 722511, as shown in Figure 3.2.

Schedule C Income (Part I)

Part I of Schedule C (Figure 3.3) contains the calculation of the taxpayer's gross income from the business or profession. The calculation starts with gross receipts or sales (line 1). Returns and allowances (line 2) and cost of goods sold (line 4) are subtracted to arrive at the gross profit from the activity. Other related income from the business (line 6) is added to the gross profit to produce the Schedule C gross income (line 7).

Schedule C Expenses (Part II)

The taxpayer reports the expenses from his or her business or profession in Part II of Schedule C (Figure 3.4). Expenses such as advertising, insurance, interest, rent, travel, wages, and utilities are reported on lines 8 through 27. Some expenses such as depreciation may require additional supporting information from another schedule. The expenses are totaled on line 28 and subtracted from gross income (line 7) to arrive at the tentative profit from the activity (line 29). An expense for business use of a taxpayer's home (see LO 3.11) is computed on Form 8829 or using the simplified method. The deductible portion of home office expenses is entered on line 30 and subtracted from tentative profit, resulting in the net profit or loss (line 31) from the activity. Common business expenses are covered in detail later in this chapter.

FIGURE 3.3 SCHEDULE C INCOME (PART I)

DO NOT FILE

Part I Income

1	Gross receipts or sales. See instructions for line 1 and check the box if this income was reported to you on Form W-2 and the "Statutory employee" box on that form was checked . . . . ▶ ☐	1	
2	Returns and allowances	2	
3	Subtract line 2 from line 1	3	
4	Cost of goods sold (from line 42)	4	
5	**Gross profit.** Subtract line 4 from line 3	5	
6	Other income, including federal and state gasoline or fuel tax credit or refund (see instructions)	6	
7	**Gross income.** Add lines 5 and 6 . . . . ▶	7	

FIGURE 3.4 **SCHEDULE C EXPENSES (PART II)**

Part II Expenses. Enter expenses for business use of your home **only** on line 30.

8	Advertising	8		18	Office expense (see instructions)	18	
9	Car and truck expenses (see instructions)	9		19	Pension and profit-sharing plans	19	
				20	Rent or lease (see instructions):		
10	Commissions and fees	10		a	Vehicles, machinery, and equipment	20a	
11	Contract labor (see instructions)	11		b	Other business property	20b	
12	Depletion	12		21	Repairs and maintenance	21	
13	Depreciation and section 179 expense deduction (not included in Part III) (see instructions)	13		22	Supplies (not included in Part III)	22	
				23	Taxes and licenses	23	
				24	Travel, meals, and entertainment:		
14	Employee benefit programs (other than on line 19)	14		a	Travel	24a	
15	Insurance (other than health)	15		b	Deductible meals and entertainment (see instructions)	24b	
16	Interest:			25	Utilities	25	
a	Mortgage (paid to banks, etc.)	16a		26	Wages (less employment credits)	26	
b	Other	16b		27a	Other expenses (from line 48)	27a	
17	Legal and professional services	17		b	**Reserved for future use**	27b	

28 **Total expenses** before expenses for business use of home. Add lines 8 through 27a ▶ 28

29 Tentative profit or (loss). Subtract line 28 from line 7 . . . 29

30 Expenses for business use of your home. Do not report these expenses elsewhere. Attach Form 8829 unless using the simplified method (see instructions).
Simplified method filers only: enter the total square footage of: (a) your home: ________
and (b) the part of your home used for business: ________ . Use the Simplified Method Worksheet in the instructions to figure the amount to enter on line 30 . . . 30

31 **Net profit or (loss).** Subtract line 30 from line 29.
• If a profit, enter on both **Form 1040, line 12** (or **Form 1040NR, line 13**) and on **Schedule SE, line 2.** (If you checked the box on line 1, see instructions). Estates and trusts, enter on **Form 1041, line 3.**
• If a loss, you **must** go to line 32. 31

32 If you have a loss, check the box that describes your investment in this activity (see instructions).
• If you checked 32a, enter the loss on both **Form 1040, line 12,** (or **Form 1040NR, line 13**) and on **Schedule SE, line 2.** (If you checked the box on line 1, see the line 31 instructions). Estates and trusts, enter on **Form 1041, line 3.**
• If you checked 32b, you **must** attach **Form 6198.** Your loss may be limited.
32a ☐ All investment is at risk.
32b ☐ Some investment is not at risk.

Schedule C Cost of Goods Sold (Part III)

The calculation of cost of goods sold is reported in Part III (Figure 3.5) of Schedule C. In Part III lines 33 and 34, taxpayers must answer questions about the methods used to calculate inventory. Cost of goods sold is equal to the beginning inventory (line 35) plus

FIGURE 3.5 **COST OF GOODS SOLD (PART III)**

Part III Cost of Goods Sold (see instructions)

33 Method(s) used to value closing inventory: **a** ☐ Cost **b** ☐ Lower of cost or market **c** ☐ Other (attach explanation)

34 Was there any change in determining quantities, costs, or valuations between opening and closing inventory? If "Yes," attach explanation . . . ☐ **Yes** ☐ **No**

35	Inventory at beginning of year. If different from last year's closing inventory, attach explanation	35	
36	Purchases less cost of items withdrawn for personal use	36	
37	Cost of labor. Do not include any amounts paid to yourself	37	
38	Materials and supplies	38	
39	Other costs	39	
40	Add lines 35 through 39	40	
41	Inventory at end of year	41	
42	**Cost of goods sold.** Subtract line 41 from line 40. Enter the result here and on line 4	42	

DRAFT AS OF June 19, 2014 DO NOT FILE

purchases (line 36), labor (line 37), materials and supplies (line 38), and other costs (line 39) less ending inventory (line 41). Please see LO 3.2 for a more detailed discussion of inventories.

Schedule C Vehicle Information (Part IV)

If a taxpayer uses a car or truck in his or her sole proprietorship, then Part IV of Schedule C (Figure 3.6) must be completed to provide the IRS with supplemental vehicle information. In Part IV, a taxpayer should provide the date the vehicle was placed in business service (line 43), the business miles driven (line 44a), the commuting miles driven (line 44b), and other miles driven (line 44c). On lines 45 to 47 of Part IV, taxpayers must answer questions relevant to obtaining a deduction for business use of a vehicle.

Schedule C Other Expenses (Part V)

In the expense section of Schedule C (Part II), line 27 contains an entry for other miscellaneous expenses. These other expenses must be itemized in Part V of Schedule C and include deductible items which do not have specific lines already assigned in the expenses section (Part II). Expenses for business gifts, education, professional dues, and consulting fees are commonly listed.

Gambling Winnings

Gambling winnings are not reported on Schedule C unless the taxpayer is a professional gambler. Net casual gambling winnings are reported as "other income" on Form 1040. Gambling losses, limited to the amount of winnings, are deducted as a miscellaneous itemized deduction (see Chapter 5).

Self-Employment Tax

Self-employed taxpayers, sole proprietors, and independent contractors with net earnings of $400 or more, many of whom report income on Schedule C, must pay a self-employment tax calculated on Schedule SE with their Form 1040. For new business owners, the self-employment tax may come as a particularly unpleasant and costly surprise if they are not aware of its existence.

The self-employment tax is made up of two taxes, the Social Security tax, which is meant to fund old age and disability insurance payments, and the Medicare tax. For 2014, the Social Security tax rate of 12.4 percent applies to the first $117,000 of net

FIGURE 3.6 **VEHICLE INFORMATION (PART IV)**

Part IV **Information on Your Vehicle.** Complete this part **only** if you are claiming car or truck expenses on line 9 and are not required to file Form 4562 for this business. See the instructions for line 13 to find out if you must file Form 4562.

43 When did you place your vehicle in service for business purposes? (month, day, year) ▶ ____ / ____ / ____

44 Of the total number of miles you drove your vehicle during 2014, enter the number of miles you used your vehicle for:

a Business ____________ b Commuting (see instructions) ____________ c Other ____________

45 Was your vehicle available for personal use during off-duty hours? . . . . ☐ Yes ☐ No

46 Do you (or your spouse) have another vehicle available for personal use?. . . . . ☐ Yes ☐ No

47a Do you have evidence to support your deduction? . . . . ☐ Yes ☐ No

b If "Yes," is the evidence written? . . . . ☐ Yes ☐ No

self-employment income, while the Medicare tax rate of 2.9 percent applies to all net self-employment income, with no ceiling. Half of the self-employment tax is allowed as a deduction on the front page of Form 1040 in arriving at adjusted gross income. A similar tax is levied on employees partly through payroll withholding and partly through employer contributions, so it is not actually paid with Form 1040 as it is for self-employed taxpayers. Self-employed Social Security and Medicare taxes are covered in detail in Chapter 9. Beginning in 2013, a 0.9 percent Medicare surtax applies to certain high-income taxpayers (see LO 9.9).

TAX BREAK

Self-employed taxpayers are subject to higher risk of IRS audit than wage earners and must be able to substantiate income and expenses reported on Schedule C if audited. A good accounting and record-keeping system is recommended for all self-employed taxpayers, no matter how small the business. The high audit rate is due to government reports showing significant underreporting of net business income among sole proprietors.

Self-Study Problem 3.1 *See Appendix E for Solutions to Self-Study Problems*

Teri Kataoka is self-employed as a professional golf instructor. She uses the cash method of accounting and her Social Security number is 466-47-8833. Her principal business code is 812990. Teri's business is located at 1234 Golfcrest Dr., Palm Springs, CA 92262. During 2014, Teri had the following income and expenses:

Fees from golf lessons	$39,250
Expenses:	
Car mileage (5,407 business miles)	3,028
Business liability insurance	450
Office expense	640
Rent on office space	2,700
City business license	250
Travel expense	3,100
Meals and entertainment (deductible portion)	895
Utilities	975

Teri bought her car on January 1, 2014. She used it to commute 3,000 miles and she drove 6,000 miles for nonbusiness purposes.

Complete Schedule C on Pages 3-9 and 3-10 for Teri showing her net income from self-employment. Make realistic assumptions about any missing data.

INVENTORIES

Learning Objective 3.2

Understand the tax treatment of inventories and cost of goods sold.

The cost of inventory a taxpayer owns has a significant impact on the taxable income of the taxpayer. The deduction for the cost of goods sold of a retail business is a direct function of the amount of the beginning and ending inventories. Cost of goods sold, which is the largest single deduction for many businesses, is calculated as follows:

Beginning inventory	$ 75,000
Add: purchases	250,000
Costs of goods available for sale	$ 325,000
Less: ending inventory	(100,000)
Cost of goods sold	$ 225,000

Valuation of inventories used in calculating the cost of goods sold is necessary to clearly reflect the income of the taxpayer.

To calculate cost of goods sold, the taxpayer must value the beginning and ending inventories of the business. He or she must determine the cost of the items on hand. This process is not as easy as it seems, since the taxpayer will often have paid different prices during the year for the same item. There are two common methods of inventory valuation used by taxpayers: first in, first out (FIFO) and last in, first out (LIFO). The FIFO method is based on the assumption that the first merchandise acquired is the first to be sold. Accordingly, the inventory on hand consists of the most recently acquired goods. Alternatively, when the taxpayer uses the LIFO method, it is assumed that the most recently acquired goods are sold first and the inventory on hand consists of the earliest purchases. FIFO and LIFO are simply calculation assumptions; the goods that are actually on hand do not have to correspond to the assumptions of the method selected. In addition to the LIFO and FIFO methods which are commonly used by taxpayers in valuing beginning and ending inventories, taxpayers may specifically identify the goods that are sold and the goods that are in ending inventory. However, the process of specifically identifying items sold and on hand is not a practical alternative for most taxpayers.

EXAMPLE Page made the following purchases of a particular inventory item during 2014:

March 1	50 units at $120 per unit	$ 6,000
August 1	40 units at $130 per unit	5,200
December 1	25 units at $140 per unit	3,500
Total		$14,700

If the ending inventory is 60 units, it is valued under the FIFO method as illustrated below:

25 units at $140 each	$3,500
35 units at $130 each	4,550
Ending inventory	$8,050

Assuming that Page had no beginning inventory of the item, the same ending inventory (60 units) would be valued using the LIFO method as follows:

50 units at $120 each	$6,000
10 units at $130 each	1,300
Ending inventory	$7,300

The cost of goods sold for both the FIFO and LIFO methods are presented below:

	FIFO	***LIFO***
Beginning inventory	$ 0	$ 0
Add: purchases	14,700	14,700
Cost of goods available for sale	$14,700	$14,700
Less: ending inventory	(8,050)	(7,300)
Cost of goods sold	$ 6,650	$ 7,400

Notice that taxable income will be $750 more when the FIFO method is used instead of the LIFO method. During periods of inflation, taxpayers pay less tax if they use the LIFO inventory valuation method. ♦

A taxpayer may adopt the LIFO method by using it in a tax return and attaching Form 970 to make the election. Once the election is made, the method may be changed only with the consent of the IRS. Also, if the LIFO election is made for reporting taxable income, taxpayers must use the same method for preparing their financial statements. In other words, a

Self-Study Problem 3.1

SCHEDULE C (Form 1040)
Department of the Treasury
Internal Revenue Service (99)

Profit or Loss From Business
(Sole Proprietorship)

▶ Information about Schedule C and its separate instructions is at *www.irs.gov/schedulec.*
▶ Attach to Form 1040, 1040NR, or 1041; partnerships generally must file Form 1065.

OMB No. 1545-0074
2014
Attachment Sequence No. 09

DRAFT AS OF June 19, 2014 DO NOT FILE

Name of proprietor | **Social security number (SSN)**

A Principal business or profession, including product or service (see instructions) | **B Enter code from instructions** ▶

C Business name. If no separate business name, leave blank. | **D Employer ID number (EIN),** (see instr.)

E Business address (including suite or room no.) ▶
City, town or post office, state, and ZIP code

F Accounting method: **(1)** ☐ Cash **(2)** ☐ Accrual **(3)** ☐ Other (specify) ▶

G Did you "materially participate" in the operation of this business during 2014? If "No," see instructions for limit on losses . ☐ Yes ☐ No

H If you started or acquired this business during 2014, check here ▶ ☐

I Did you make any payments in 2014 that would require you to file Form(s) 1099? (see instructions) ☐ Yes ☐ No

J If "Yes," did you or will you file required Forms 1099? ☐ Yes ☐ No

Part I Income

1	Gross receipts or sales. See instructions for line 1 and check the box if this income was reported to you on Form W-2 and the "Statutory employee" box on that form was checked ▶ ☐	1	
2	Returns and allowances	2	
3	Subtract line 2 from line 1	3	
4	Cost of goods sold (from line 42)	4	
5	**Gross profit.** Subtract line 4 from line 3	5	
6	Other income, including federal and state gasoline or fuel tax credit or refund (see instructions)	6	
7	**Gross income.** Add lines 5 and 6 ▶	7	

Part II Expenses. Enter expenses for business use of your home **only** on line 30.

8	Advertising	8		18	Office expense (see instructions)	18	
9	Car and truck expenses (see instructions)	9		19	Pension and profit-sharing plans	19	
10	Commissions and fees	10		20	Rent or lease (see instructions):		
11	Contract labor (see instructions)	11		a	Vehicles, machinery, and equipment	20a	
12	Depletion	12		b	Other business property	20b	
13	Depreciation and section 179 expense deduction (not included in Part III) (see instructions)	13		21	Repairs and maintenance	21	
				22	Supplies (not included in Part III)	22	
				23	Taxes and licenses	23	
				24	Travel, meals, and entertainment:		
14	Employee benefit programs (other than on line 19)	14		a	Travel	24a	
15	Insurance (other than health)	15		b	Deductible meals and entertainment (see instructions)	24b	
16	Interest:			25	Utilities	25	
a	Mortgage (paid to banks, etc.)	16a		26	Wages (less employment credits)	26	
b	Other	16b		27a	Other expenses (from line 48)	27a	
17	Legal and professional services	17		b	**Reserved for future use**	27b	

28	**Total expenses** before expenses for business use of home. Add lines 8 through 27a ▶	28	
29	Tentative profit or (loss). Subtract line 28 from line 7	29	
30	Expenses for business use of your home. Do not report these expenses elsewhere. Attach Form 8829 unless using the simplified method (see instructions). **Simplified method filers only:** enter the total square footage of: (a) your home: ____ and (b) the part of your home used for business: ____ . Use the Simplified Method Worksheet in the instructions to figure the amount to enter on line 30	30	
31	**Net profit or (loss).** Subtract line 30 from line 29. • If a profit, enter on both **Form 1040, line 12** (or **Form 1040NR, line 13**) and on **Schedule SE, line 2.** (If you checked the box on line 1, see instructions). Estates and trusts, enter on **Form 1041, line 3.** • If a loss, you **must** go to line 32.	31	

32 If you have a loss, check the box that describes your investment in this activity (see instructions).
- If you checked 32a, enter the loss on both **Form 1040, line 12,** (or **Form 1040NR, line 13**) and on **Schedule SE, line 2.** (If you checked the box on line 1, see the line 31 instructions). Estates and trusts, enter on **Form 1041, line 3.**
- If you checked 32b, you **must** attach **Form 6198.** Your loss may be limited.

32a ☐ All investment is at risk.
32b ☐ Some investment is not at risk.

Schedule C (Form 1040) 2014 Page **2**

Part III Cost of Goods Sold (see instructions)

33 Method(s) used to value closing inventory: a ☐ Cost b ☐ Lower of cost or market c ☐ Other (attach explanation)

34 Was there any change in determining quantities, costs, or valuations between opening and closing inventory? If "Yes," attach explanation . . . ☐ Yes ☐ No

DRAFT AS OF June 19, 2014 DO NOT FILE

35	Inventory at beginning of year. If different from last year's closing inventory, attach explanation	35	
36	Purchases less cost of items withdrawn for personal use	36	
37	Cost of labor. Do not include any amounts paid to yourself	37	
38	Materials and supplies	38	
39	Other costs	39	
40	Add lines 35 through 39	40	
41	Inventory at end of year	41	
42	**Cost of goods sold.** Subtract line 41 from line 40. Enter the result here and on line 4	42	

Part IV Information on Your Vehicle.

Complete this part **only** if you are claiming car or truck expenses on line 9 and are not required to file Form 4562 for this business. See the instructions for line 13 to find out if you must file Form 4562.

43 When did you place your vehicle in service for business purposes? (month, day, year) ▶ ____/____/____

44 Of the total number of miles you drove your vehicle during 2014, enter the number of miles you used your vehicle for:

a Business ______________ b Commuting (see instructions) ______________ c Other ______________

45 Was your vehicle available for personal use during off-duty hours? . . . ☐ Yes ☐ No

46 Do you (or your spouse) have another vehicle available for personal use? . . . ☐ Yes ☐ No

47a Do you have evidence to support your deduction? . . . ☐ Yes ☐ No

b If "Yes," is the evidence written? . . . ☐ Yes ☐ No

Part V Other Expenses.

List below business expenses not included on lines 8–26 or line 30.

48 **Total other expenses.** Enter here and on line 27a	48	

Schedule C (Form 1040) 2014

taxpayer may not use LIFO for his or her tax return and use FIFO for financial statements presented to a bank. This rule is strictly enforced by the IRS.

Generally, if a taxpayer produces, purchases, or sells merchandise as part of the business, inventory must be kept and the accrual method for purchases and sales of merchandise must be used. However, certain taxpayers can use the cash method of accounting even if they produce, purchase, or sell merchandise:

- If the average annual gross receipts is $1 million or less (average annual gross receipts for a tax year is figured by adding the gross receipts for that tax year and the 2 preceding tax years and dividing by 3), or
- If the average annual gross receipts is more than $1 million but not more than $10 million and the principal business activity is an eligible business. An eligible business is (1) a business not involved in mining, manufacturing, wholesale trade, retail trade, or information industries, or (2) a service business, or (3) a custom manufacturer.

Self-Study Problem 3.2

See Appendix E for Solutions to Self-Study Problems

Kelly owns a small retail store. During the year, Kelly purchases $175,000 worth of inventory. Her beginning inventory is $62,500 and her ending inventory is $57,200. Also, she withdrew $4,500 in inventory for her personal use during the year. Use Part III of Schedule C below to calculate Kelly's cost of goods sold for the year.

Part III **Cost of Goods Sold** (see instructions)

33	Method(s) used to value closing inventory: a ☐ Cost b ☐ Lower of cost or market c ☐ Other (attach explanation)		
34	Was there any change in determining quantities, costs, or valuations between opening and closing inventory? If "Yes," attach explanation ☐ Yes ☐ No		
35	Inventory at beginning of year. If different from last year's closing inventory, attach explanation	35	
36	Purchases less cost of items withdrawn for personal use	36	
37	Cost of labor. Do not include any amounts paid to yourself	37	
38	Materials and supplies	38	
39	Other costs	39	
40	Add lines 35 through 39	40	
41	Inventory at end of year	41	
42	**Cost of goods sold.** Subtract line 41 from line 40. Enter the result here and on line 4	42	

DRAFT AS OF June 19, 2014 DO NOT FILE

TRANSPORTATION

Learning Objective 3.3

Identify the requirements for deducting transportation expenses.

Certain transportation expenses for business purposes are deductible by taxpayers. Deductible expenses include travel by airplane, rail, and bus, and the cost of operating and maintaining an automobile. Meals and lodging are *not* included in the transportation expense deduction; those expenses may be deducted as travel expenses. Transportation expenses may be deducted even if the taxpayer is not away from his or her tax home.

Deductible transportation costs do not include the normal costs of commuting to and from the taxpayer's place of regular employment. Commuting includes the expenses of buses, subways, taxis, and operating a private car between home and the taxpayer's principal place of work, and is generally a nondeductible personal expense. The cost of transportation between the taxpayer's home and a work location is generally not deductible, except in the three sets of circumstances described below:

1. A taxpayer is allowed to deduct daily transportation expenses incurred in going between the taxpayer's residence and work locations outside the metropolitan area where the taxpayer lives and normally works.

2. If the taxpayer has a regular place of business, daily expenses for transportation between the taxpayer's home and temporary work locations are deductible.
3. A taxpayer may deduct daily expenses for transportation between the taxpayer's home and other regular or temporary work locations if the taxpayer's residence is the taxpayer's principal place of business, based on the home office rules, which are discussed later in this chapter.

In all cases, the additional costs of hauling tools and instruments are deductible. For example, the cost of renting a trailer to haul tools to a job site is deductible.

If the taxpayer works at two or more jobs during the same day, he or she may deduct the cost of going from one job to the other or from one business location to another. The deductible expense is based on the cost of travel by the shortest, most normally traveled route, even if the taxpayer uses another route. If the taxpayer works at a second job on a day that he or she does not work at the first job, the commuting expenses to the second job are not deductible.

EXAMPLE Walter is a self-employed CPA working full-time Monday through Friday. On Tuesday night he teaches an accounting class at a local university. Walter leaves the office at 5:30 p.m. on his class day and, after dinner at a local cafe, teaches his class from 7:00 p.m. to 10:00 p.m. The distance from Walter's home to his office is 12 miles, the distance from his office to the university is 15 miles, and the distance from the university to his home is 18 miles. If Walter teaches the class thirty-two times a year, his mileage deduction is based on 480 miles (32 × 15 miles). While he is traveling from home to the office (12 miles) and from the university to home (18 miles), he is commuting and the mileage is not deductible. If Walter taught the class in the afternoon and returned to his regular job before going home, he could claim a deduction based on the round-trip mileage from his office to and from the university, 30 miles (2 × 15 miles). Alternatively, if he taught the course on a day (Saturday) when he did not work at his full-time job, Walter would not be entitled to any mileage deduction. ♦

Taxpayers may deduct the actual expenses of transportation, or they may be entitled to use a standard mileage rate to calculate their deduction for transportation costs. The standard mileage rate for 2014 is 56 cents per mile. Most costs associated with the operation of an automobile, such as gasoline, oil, insurance, repairs, and maintenance, as well as depreciation, are built into the standard mileage rate. The deduction for parking and toll fees related to business transportation (not commuting) and the deduction for interest on car loans and state and local personal property taxes on the automobile are determined separately. Self-employed taxpayers deduct the business portion of the state and local personal property taxes and interest on automobile loans on Schedule C or F. To use the standard mileage method, the taxpayer must:

1. own or lease the automobile,
2. not operate a fleet of automobiles, using five or more at the same time,
3. not have claimed depreciation on the automobile using any method other than straight-line depreciation, and
4. not have claimed Section 179 (expense election) depreciation or bonus depreciation on the automobile (see Chapter 7 for a complete discussion of depreciation).

If the taxpayer is entitled to use either the actual cost or the standard mileage method, he or she may select the method that results in the largest tax deduction for the first year. If the taxpayer does not use the standard mileage method in the first year, the method is not available for any subsequent year. A change to the actual cost method can be made any year. If, after using the standard mileage method, the taxpayer uses actual costs to determine the

automobile expense deduction, depreciation on the automobile must be calculated using straight-line depreciation (see Chapter 7). The standard mileage method may be used for a car for hire, such as a taxi, if the automobile meets the other requirements for use of this method.

Taxpayers who use actual cost to calculate their transportation deductions must keep adequate cost records. The deductible portion of the total automobile expenses is based on the ratio of the number of business miles driven during the year to the total miles driven during the tax year multiplied by the total automobile expenses for the year. The business-use percentage is applied to the total automobile expenses for the year, including depreciation, but excluding any expenses which are directly attributable to business use of the automobile, such as business parking fees and tolls. The deduction for interest and personal property taxes is also separately computed.

EXAMPLE T.J. is a new salesman who drove his automobile 22,500 total miles during the 2014 tax year. The business use of the automobile was 80 percent of the total miles driven. The actual cost of gasoline, oil, repairs, depreciation, and insurance for the year was $10,000. The automobile expense deduction is calculated as follows:

1. Standard mileage method:	
Business mileage = 18,000 miles (22,500 miles × 80%)	
18,000 miles × 56 cents/mile	$10,080
2. Actual cost method:	
80% × $10,000 (total actual cost)	$8,000

Since the deduction is larger using the standard mileage method, T.J. should deduct that amount. ♦

Would You Believe?

In 2004, the IRS reported that 18,000 fraudulent tax returns were filed using prisoner taxpayer identification. In 2008, the Inmate Fraud Prevention Act expanded the IRS access to prisoner information to curb fraudulent returns. The Homebuyer Assistance and Improvement Act of 2010 provided the IRS with more authority and additional expansion was provided in the American Taxpayer Relief Act of 2012. In 2014, the Treasury Inspector General reported that the number of fraudulent prisoner returns has increased to 186,000 returns and refunds totaling $3.7 billion.

Self-Study Problem 3.3

See Appendix E for Solutions to Self-Study Problems

Marc Lusebrink, sole proprietor of Oak Company, bought a used automobile and drove it 17,944 miles on business during 2014 and a total (including business miles) of 23,925 miles. His total expenses for his automobile for the year are:

Gasoline	$4,475
Oil changes	150
Insurance	570
Tires	225
Repairs	620
Total	$6,040

The automobile cost $14,000 on January 1, and depreciation expense for the year, including business use, was $2,800. His business parking and toll fees for business amount to $316. Calculate Marc's transportation expense deduction for the year.

Learning Objective 3.4

Identify the requirements for deducting travel expenses.

TRAVEL EXPENSES

Travel expenses are defined as ordinary and necessary expenses incurred in traveling away from home in pursuit of the taxpayer's trade or business. These expenses are deductible as long as they can be substantiated and are not lavish or extravagant. Transportation expenses incurred while not away from home, business gifts, and business entertainment are not included as travel expenses, although these items are separately deductible, subject to certain limitations. Expenses included as part of the travel deduction include the cost of such items as meals, lodging, taxis, tips, and laundry. Most travel expenses are fully deductible, but Congress decided that a portion of the cost of meals is a personal expense. Therefore, only 50 percent of the cost of meals is deductible. If an employer reimburses an employee for the cost of business meals, then the 50 percent limitation applies to the employer so that the employer can deduct only 50 percent of the expense.

To deduct travel expenses, a taxpayer must be in travel status. The taxpayer must be away from home "overnight." Overnight does not literally mean 24 hours; it is a period of time longer than an ordinary work day in which rest or relief from work is required. Also, the taxpayer must be away from his or her "tax home" to be on travel status. A tax home is the taxpayer's principal place of business or employment, and not necessarily the same location as his or her family residence. If the taxpayer has two or more places of business, the taxpayer's tax home is at the principal place of business. Factors that determine the principal place of business include total time spent in each location, the degree of business activity, and the relative amount of income from each location.

Expenses of a temporary assignment are deductible if it is not practical to return home at the end of each day's work or if the employer requires the employee's attendance at a business meeting, training activity, or other overnight business function. If the assignment is for a long period of time or indefinite (generally more than 1 year), the new location may be considered the taxpayer's new tax home and he or she may lose the travel deduction. If the travel deduction is lost, an employee must include as income any reimbursements of travel expenses.

Taxpayers who make a combined business and pleasure trip within the United States may deduct all of the costs incurred in traveling to and from the business destination provided the trip is primarily for business. Once at the destination, only the business portion of the travel costs for meals, lodging, local transportation, and incidental expenses may be deducted; any costs which are not associated with the taxpayer's business are not deductible. If a taxpayer makes a trip which is primarily for pleasure, the travel expenses to and from the destination are not deductible even though the taxpayer engages in some business activity while at the destination. Although the traveling expenses to and from the destination are not deductible, any expenses incurred while at the destination that are related to the taxpayer's business are deductible.

Special rules and limitations apply to combined business and pleasure travel outside the United States. Even though a trip is primarily for business, if the trip has any element of pleasure, the cost of traveling to and from the destination must be allocated between the business and personal portions of the trip. The travel expenses for transportation to and from the destination must be allocated based on the number of business days compared to the total number of days outside the United States. The rules for travel costs to and from the destination where the trip is primarily for pleasure are the same as the rules for travel within the United States; none of the travel costs are deductible. Once at the destination, the taxpayer's expenses directly related to the taxpayer's business are deductible. For a complete explanation of travel outside the United States, see IRS Publication 463.

No deduction for travel expenses is allowed unless the taxpayer keeps proper expense records. Taxpayers must substantiate the following:

1. The amount of each separate expenditure, such as airfare and lodging. Expenses such as meals and taxi fares may be accumulated and reported in reasonable categories. As an alternative to reporting actual expenses, a per diem method may be used in certain circumstances.
2. The dates of departure and return for each trip and the number of business days on the trip.
3. The destination or locality of the travel described by the name of the city or town.
4. The business reason for the travel or the business benefit expected to be gained from the travel.

Per Diem Substantiation

Instead of requiring actual expense records, small business employers who reimburse employees for travel expenses can choose a per diem method of substantiation. The primary advantage of using a per diem method to substantiate expenses is that it eliminates much of the record keeping usually associated with travel expenses. The IRS has approved three per diem methods to substantiate travel expenses. The first two methods are for travel expenses, including lodging, meals, and incidentals, for employee reimbursement. The third method is only for meals and incidentals and is the only per diem method allowed directly to self-employed taxpayers.

1. *The Regular Federal Rate Method.* Under this method the employee is allowed a per diem amount for travel equal to the current federal per diem rate which varies based on the travel location. A complete list of the regular per diem rates in effect for each area of the United States is available at the U.S. General Services Administration website (GSA).
2. *The High-Low Method.* The high-low method provides a simplified way of computing the federal per diem rate for travel within the United States. This method avoids the need to keep a current list of the per diem rates for all localities in the United States. Under this method a small number of locations are designated as high-cost localities and all other locations are deemed to be low-cost areas. In 2014, the high-cost allowance is $251 per day and the low-cost amount is $170 per day. If an employer uses this method to reimburse an employee any time during a calendar year, this method must be used for all travel for that employee in the same calendar year.
3. *The Meals and Incidental Expenses* (M&IE) *Method.* Under this method the employee uses a current per diem amount for M&IE only. Actual cost records are required for lodging expenses. The M&IE rate may be taken from the per diem rate tables or the high-low method may be used. For 2014, the M&IE allowance is $65 per day for high-cost localities and $52 per day for low-cost localities. The M&IE method is the only per diem method that can be used by self-employed taxpayers to substantiate travel expenses. Employees and self-employed taxpayers who do not incur meal expenses when traveling are allowed an incidental expense allowance of $5 per day.

Per diem rates are revised on October 1 every year with additional revisions made for specific locations throughout the year. For purposes of illustration and problems, the rates above are assumed to be chosen for the full year. Different rates than those shown above may apply.

EXAMPLE During 2014, Susan travels from Los Angeles to Hawaii for a 3-day business trip and pays $450 for the airfare. While in Hawaii, Susan spends 3 days on business and an additional 2 days on vacation. The lodging and meal costs are $300 and $120, respectively, for the business portion of the trip. The total cost of meals and lodging for the personal portion of the trip is $260. Susan may deduct $450 for the airfare, $300 for the business lodging, and $60 (50 percent of $120) for the business meals. None of the $260 of personal expenses is deductible. ♦

Self-Study Problem 3.4 *See Appendix E for Solutions to Self-Study Problems*

Byron is a certified public accountant who is self-employed. He is required to make a 5-day business trip to Salt Lake City for an audit. Since he is going to be in Utah, Byron decides to stay for the weekend and go skiing. His expenses for the trip are as follows:

Airfare to Salt Lake City and return	$ 190
Hotel while on the audit (5 nights at $65 per night)	325
Total cost of meals while on the audit	136
Laundry in Salt Lake City	22
Taxi fares in Salt Lake City	72
Transportation from Salt Lake City to and from Park City ski resort	100
Lodging at Park City ski resort	190
Lift tickets	27
Ski rental	24
Meals at Park City	82
Total	$1,168

If Byron has proper records to substantiate the above expenses, how much may he deduct as travel expenses for the 7-day trip?

$__________

Learning Objective 3.5

Determine the requirements for claiming meals and entertainment deductions.

MEALS AND ENTERTAINMENT

Self-employed taxpayers are allowed to deduct 50 percent of the cost of meals and entertainment incurred in connection with their trade or business. To obtain a deduction, certain conditions must be satisfied. The entertainment expenses must be (1) directly related to or (2) associated with the active conduct of the taxpayer's trade or business. Expenses directly related to the taxpayer's trade or business are costs related to an actual business meeting, such as the expense of a sales luncheon where a salesperson is making a sale to a client. It is not necessary that the sale is actually made, but the parties must discuss business and the taxpayer must have a reasonable expectation of making the sale.

Expenses associated with the conduct of the taxpayer's trade or business are generally those expenses which serve a specific business purpose, such as obtaining new business. The entertainment must take place immediately before or after a bona fide business discussion. For example, a sales presentation may be made in the morning before lunch. The client may be taken to lunch after the meeting, and business need not be the primary topic of the lunch since the parties involved just attended the sales meeting. Entertainment includes activities such as attending sports events, playing golf or tennis, and attending plays.

The deduction of the costs of entertainment facilities, such as yachts, hunting or fishing camps, recreational vehicles, and airplanes, is strictly limited. A taxpayer may not deduct

the cost of depreciation, maintenance, and annual fees for such facilities. However, other business expenses are not affected by this limitation. For example, the cost of qualified entertainment on a yacht is deductible, even though the cost of the yacht is not.

Generally, club dues are not deductible. Nondeductible club dues include dues paid to country clubs, business luncheon clubs, and airline and hotel clubs. Dues paid to professional organizations, such as bar or medical organizations, are deductible. Dues paid to civic or public organizations, such as Chambers of Commerce, Kiwanis, and Rotary, are also allowed as legitimate business deductions. These clubs do public service work, and are not organizations like country clubs which are entertainment or pleasure driven. Many business people belong to clubs such as Kiwanis or Rotary to network, meet potential clients, and increase their visibility in the community, but the club must do significant service work for the members' dues to qualify as deductions.

Self-Study Problem 3.5 *See Appendix E for Solutions to Self-Study Problems*

Eugene is a self-employed salesman who specializes in selling life insurance to wealthy customers. During 2014, Eugene joins and uses the Country Club as a place to entertain customers and sell insurance to new and existing clients. During the year, Eugene paid the following amounts at the club:

Annual dues	$2,000
Business meals, directly related (84 days)	1,700
Personal meals (36 days)	400
Greens fees (personal use)	600
Total	$4,700

Calculate the amount of the $4,700 spent by Eugene that he is allowed as a deduction for entertainment.

$__________

EDUCATIONAL EXPENSES

Learning Objective 3.6

Identify the requirements for claiming business education expenses.

Please note: Educational incentives such as qualified tuition programs, educational savings accounts, and the deduction for higher education expenses are discussed in LO 5.8. The deduction for education loan interest is discussed in LO 5.3. Education tax credits are discussed in LO 6.5. Because numerous education incentives have been added in the last several years, the tax law in this area has become very complex. There may be more than one tax option for treating a particular education expense. This section deals primarily with the deduction of continuing education expenses incurred by taxpayers already employed or self-employed.

Taxpayers may deduct educational expenses if specific conditions are met. The tax law is silent with respect to educational expense deductions, therefore we must look to the IRS regulations for the allowable deductions. There are two tests related to the deduction of educational expenses, at least one of which must be met to deduct the expenses. The tests are:

1. the educational expenses must be paid to meet *the requirements of the taxpayer's employer or the requirements of law or regulation* for keeping the taxpayer's salary, status, or job, or
2. the educational expenses must be paid to *maintain* or *improve existing skills* required in performing the duties of the taxpayer's present work.

Educational expenses meeting one of the above tests, which have a bona fide business purpose, may be deducted even if the education leads to a college degree.

Educational expenses are not deductible, even if one of the above tests is met, if (1) the education is required to meet the minimum requirements for the taxpayer's current job, or (2) the education is part of a program that will lead to a new trade or business even if the taxpayer does not intend to enter that new trade or business.

Education Required by Employer or Law

Taxpayers who are required to meet educational standards beyond minimum requirements may deduct the expenses of the education. However, the expenses must be paid for education to maintain the taxpayer's current job, not to meet the minimum requirements for that job. If the education qualifies the taxpayer for a new trade or business, the expenses are not deductible.

EXAMPLE Jenny is a high school teacher working under a temporary teaching certificate. The state in which she teaches requires a master's degree to receive a permanent certificate, and Jenny only has a bachelor's degree. Her expenses to obtain a master's degree are not deductible even though the degree is required by her school district, since she has not yet met the minimum educational requirements to be a permanent teacher.

However, Jenny may qualify for the deduction for higher education expenses discussed in LO 5.8 or the lifetime learning credit discussed in LO 6.5. ♦

Maintaining or Improving Existing Skills

Expenses that are paid by a taxpayer for education to maintain or improve existing skills are deductible. Expenses deductible under this category include the costs of continuing education courses and academic work at a college or university. However, the education must not lead to qualification in a new trade or business. The deduction of CPA exam and bar exam review courses is consistently disallowed by the IRS.

EXAMPLE John is a certified public accountant (CPA) in practice with a CPA firm. He decides a law degree would be helpful to him in his present job since he does a lot of income tax planning for clients. He enrolls in a night program at a local law school. John's educational expenses are not deductible since the program leads to a new trade or business, the practice of law. Whether or not John plans to practice law is not relevant.

However, John may qualify for the deduction for higher education expenses discussed in LO 5.8, or the lifetime learning credit discussed in LO 6.5. ♦

EXAMPLE Kenzie recently completed her degree in accounting and went to work for a local CPA firm. She spends $1,000 for a CPA exam review course to help her pass the exam. The $1,000 is not deductible since passing the CPA exam leads to a new trade or business, that of being a licensed CPA as opposed to an accountant.

Depending on whether Kenzie takes this course at a qualified institution of higher education, and other circumstances, she may qualify for the lifetime learning credit discussed in LO 6.5. ♦

Expenses of Travel for Educational Purposes

Travel expenses incurred while away from home for trips that are primarily to obtain qualifying education are also deductible. For example, a taxpayer may deduct travel expenses for attending a continuing education course in a distant city. Whether a trip is primarily personal or primarily educational depends on the relative amount of time devoted to each activity. If the trip qualifies as primarily for educational purposes, the cost of transportation to and from the destination is fully deductible. The lodging and meal expenses directly connected with the educational activity are also deductible. As is the case with travel expenses, the cost of meals is only 50 percent deductible. Expenses for "travel as a form of education" are not deductible.

EXAMPLE Jay is a doctor who attended a continuing education seminar in New York in 2014. His expenses related to attendance at the program are as follows:

Lodging in New York	$ 350
Transportation	700
Meals	150
Fee for the course	250
Total	$1,450

Jay's educational expense deduction for the seminar would be $1,375 including lodging of $350, transportation of $700, meals of $75 (50 percent of the cost of the meals), and the course fee of $250. ♦

EXAMPLE Natalie is an instructor of Japanese at Big State University. She spends the summer traveling in Japan to improve her understanding of the Japanese language and culture. Although Natalie arranges her trip to improve her ability to teach the Japanese language, no education deduction is allowed for the travel expenses. ♦

Educator Expenses

Please note: As we go to press it is expected that in late 2014 Congress will extend the deduction for educator expenses retroactively for all of 2014. Check the Whittenburg companion website for updates.

Eligible educators may deduct up to $250 for classroom materials such as books, supplies, computer equipment, and supplementary materials as a deduction in arriving at AGI. An eligible educator is a kindergarten through grade-twelve teacher, counselor, or principal who works at least 900 hours during the school year.

Self-Study Problem 3.6 *See Appendix E for Solutions to Self-Study Problems*

Nadine is a self-employed attorney. Her expenses for continuing legal education are as follows:

Lodging in Tempe, Arizona	$1,200
Transportation	350
Meals	200
Books	175
Tuition	550
Weekend trip to the Grand Canyon	175
Total	$2,650

Calculate Nadine's educational expense deduction for the current year. Assume Nadine's household income is too high for her to qualify for the new deduction for higher education expenses discussed in LO 5.8 or the lifetime learning credit discussed in LO 6.5.

$__________

DUES, SUBSCRIPTIONS, AND PUBLICATIONS

Learning Objective 3.7
Identify the tax treatment of dues and subscriptions.

Doctors, lawyers, accountants, engineers, teachers, and other professionals engaged in practice or employed may deduct certain dues and the cost of certain subscriptions and publications. Included in this category of deductions are items such as membership to the local bar for a lawyer, dues to the American Institute of Certified Public Accountants (AICPA) for an accountant, and the cost of subscriptions to any journal that is directly related to the taxpayer's profession.

EXAMPLE Hal is a federal law enforcement officer who pays $200 per year for a subscription to the official agency work manual. The agency provides a manual in the office for its employees, but Hal spends a lot of time on the road away from the office. Hal may deduct the cost of the subscription. ♦

Self-Study Problem 3.7 *See Appendix E for Solutions to Self-Study Problems*

Indicate which of the following dues, subscriptions, and publications are deductible (D) and which are not deductible (ND) by circling the correct answer.

1.	Dues to the American Medical Association paid by a physician.	D	ND
2.	A subscription to a tax journal paid for by an accounting professor.	D	ND
3.	Dues to a health spa paid by a lawyer.	D	ND
4.	Subscription to an education journal paid for by a high school teacher.	D	ND
5.	Subscription to *Motor Trend* magazine paid for by a registered nurse.	D	ND

Learning Objective 3.8

Determine which clothing and uniforms may be treated as tax deductions.

SPECIAL CLOTHING AND UNIFORMS

Employees and self-employed individuals are allowed a deduction for the costs of special work clothing or uniforms. The deduction is not allowed for the general cost and upkeep of normal work clothes; the clothing must be specialized. To be deductible, the clothing or uniforms must (1) be required as a condition of employment, and (2) not be suitable for everyday use. Both conditions must be met for the deduction to be allowed. It is not enough that the employee is required to wear special clothing if the clothing can be worn while the employee is not on the job. If the clothing or uniforms qualify, the costs of purchase, alterations, laundry, and their maintenance are deductible.

The uniforms worn by police officers, firefighters, nurses, and letter carriers qualify for the deduction. The costs of uniforms of transportation workers, such as bus drivers, train conductors, and airline pilots, are deductible if the uniforms are used for work only. The uniforms must not be worn when the employee is not working. Uniforms that can be converted to clothes suitable for general wear never qualify for the deduction.

Taxpayers who are in the armed forces reserves may deduct the unreimbursed cost of their uniforms if military regulations restrict their wear to duty time as a reservist. Generally, members of the armed forces may *not* deduct the cost of their uniforms, as the member is usually required to wear his or her uniform during off-duty hours or the uniforms are suitable for off-duty wear. However, if local regulations prohibit wearing fatigues off-duty, the cost of uniforms is deductible to the extent the cost exceeds any uniform allowances.

The costs of protective clothing, such as safety shoes, hard hats, and rubber boots, required on the job are also deductible. However, the cost of regular work clothing and standard shoes may not be deducted even if required by the employer or union rules, since the clothing is suitable for general wear. For example, a lawyer may not deduct the cost of suits that an employer requires him or her to wear. Self-employed taxpayers deduct special clothing and uniforms on Schedule C. Employees deduct unreimbursed amounts on Schedule A as a miscellaneous itemized deduction as discussed in Chapter 5.

Would You Believe?

In his book, Bjorn Ulvaeus, one of the founders of 1970s megahit band Abba, states that the costumes that the band wore were intended to be so outrageous that they could not be considered suitable for general attire and thus garner a Swedish tax deduction (the tax laws are very similar to those in the U.S. on uniforms). Lady Gaga's "meat dress" worn at the 2010 Video Music Awards is likely to qualify for a deduction as well.

Self-Study Problem 3.8 *See Appendix E for Solutions to Self-Study Problems*

Steve has his own business as an installer for the light company, and he wears regular work clothes that cost $400 during the year. Also, Steve must wear safety shoes and an orange neon vest on the job that cost $650 this year, and he purchased pole-climbing equipment, spikes, and a safety belt that cost $275. What is Steve's deduction on Schedule C for these items.

$________

BUSINESS GIFTS

Learning Objective 3.9

Explain the special limits for business gift deductions.

Within limits, taxpayers are allowed a deduction for business gifts. Salespersons and other taxpayers may deduct up to $25 per year per donee. For purposes of this limitation, a husband and wife count as one donee. Thus, the maximum that a taxpayer could deduct for gifts to a client or potential client and his or her spouse is a total of $25 per year, unless the spouse is also a client, in which case the spouse may receive a separate $25 gift. Incidental expenses such as gift wrapping and shipping may be excluded from the limitation and are fully deductible. There is no limitation for small business gifts costing up to $4 each that have the taxpayer's name or company name imprinted on them, such as pencils and calendars, and no limitation on promotional materials, such as signs and display racks. Also, the cost of gifts of tangible personal property made to employees for length of service on the job and safety achievement may be deducted up to a limit of $400 per employee per year. If the gift is made in conjunction with a "qualified plan," the limit is raised to $1,600. Gifts made to a taxpayer's supervisor (or individuals at a higher employment level) are not deductible. Those gifts are considered nondeductible personal expenses.

EXAMPLE Marc is a salesperson who gives gifts to his clients. During the year, Marc gives Mr. Alford a gift costing $20 and Mrs. Alford (not a client) a gift costing $15. He also gives Ms. Bland a gift that cost $24 plus $2 for wrapping. Marc may deduct a total of $25 for the two gifts to Mr. and Mrs. Alford, and $26 for the gift to Ms. Bland. The $2 gift-wrapping charge is not included as part of the $25 limitation on the gift to Ms. Bland. ♦

Substantiation Requirement

To deduct entertainment expenses (discussed in LO 3.5) and business gifts, taxpayers must be able to substantiate the deduction. The four items that must be substantiated to deduct entertainment expenses and gifts are the:

1. Amount of the expense (entertainment and gifts),
2. Time and place (entertainment) or date and description (gifts),
3. Business purpose (entertainment and gifts), and
4. Business relationship (entertainment and gifts).

If any of the above information is not available, the IRS will disallow the deduction for entertainment expenses or gifts.

Self-Study Problem 3.9 *See Appendix E for Solutions to Self-Study Problems*

Carol makes the following business gifts during 2014:

Donee	*Amount*	*Deduction*
1. Mr. Jones (a client)	$ 20	$________
2. Mr. Brown (a client)	32	________
3. Mrs. Green (a client)	15	________
4. Mr. Green (the nonclient husband of Mrs. Green)	18	________
5. Ms. Gray (Carol's supervisor)	45	________
6. Mr. Edwards (a client receiving a display rack with Carol's company name on it)	75	________
7. Various customers (receiving ball point pens with the company name on them)	140	________
Total Business Gift Deduction		$________

Calculate Carol's allowed deduction for each business gift and her total allowed deduction.

Learning Objective 3.10

Explain the tax treatment of bad debt deductions.

BAD DEBTS

When a taxpayer sells goods or services on credit and the accounts receivable subsequently become worthless (uncollectible), a bad debt deduction is allowed to the extent that income arising from the sales was previously included in income. Currently, taxpayers must use the specific charge-off method and are allowed deductions for bad debts only after the debts are determined to be partially or completely worthless.

A taxpayer who uses the specific charge-off method must be able to satisfy the IRS that the debt is worthless and demonstrate the amount of the worthlessness. For a totally worthless account, a deduction is allowed for the entire amount of the taxpayer's basis in the account in the year the debt becomes worthless. The taxpayer's basis in the debt is the amount of income recognized from the recording of the debt, or the amount paid for the debt if it was purchased.

EXAMPLE Todd owns a small retail store. During the current tax year, Todd has $8,500 worth of uncollectible accounts receivable. Assuming he reported $7,800 in sales income from the accounts, that amount is his basis in the accounts receivable. Therefore, Todd's deduction for bad debts is limited to $7,800 for the year. ♦

Business and Nonbusiness Bad Debts

Bad debts fall into two categories, business bad debts and nonbusiness bad debts. Debts that arise from the taxpayer's trade or business are classified as business bad debts, while all other debts are considered nonbusiness bad debts. The distinction between the two types of debts is important, since business bad debts are ordinary deductions and nonbusiness bad debts are short-term capital losses. Short-term and long-term capital gains may be offset by short-term capital losses. If there are net capital losses, only $3,000 of net capital losses may be deducted against ordinary income in any one tax year. Unused short-term capital losses are carried forward and may be deductible in future years, subject to the $3,000 annual limitation. The treatment of capital gains and losses is discussed in Chapter 8.

EXAMPLE Robert loaned his friend, Calvin, $5,000 to start a business. In the current year, Calvin went bankrupt and the debt became completely worthless. Since the debt is a nonbusiness debt, Robert may claim only a $3,000 short-term capital loss deduction this year (assuming no other capital transactions). The $2,000 unused deduction may be carried forward to the next year. This is not a business bad-debt deduction, because Robert is not in the business of loaning funds. ♦

Self-Study Problem 3.10 ***See Appendix E for Solutions to Self-Study Problems***

Indicate whether the debt in each of the following cases is a business or nonbusiness debt.

	Business	Nonbusiness
1. Accounts receivable of a doctor from patients	________	________
2. A father loans his son $2,000 to buy a car	________	________
3. A corporate president loans another corporation $100,000	________	________
4. Loans by a bank to its customers	________	________
5. A taxpayer loans her sister $15,000 to start a business	________	________

Paid Preparer Use Only	Print/Type preparer's name	Preparer's signature	Date	Check ☐ if self-employed	PTIN
	Firm's name ▶		Firm's EIN ▶		
	Firm's address ▶		Phone no.		

Your clients, Tom (age 48) and Teri (age 45) Trendy, have a son, Tim (age 27). Tim lives in Hawaii where he studies the effects of various sunscreens on his ability to surf. Last year, Tim was out of money and wanted to move back home and live with Tom and Teri. To prevent this, Tom lent Tim $20,000 with the understanding that he would stay in Hawaii and not come home. Tom had Tim sign a formal note, including a stated interest rate and due date. Tom has a substantial portfolio of stocks and bonds with a number of capital gains and losses in the current year. He concluded that Tim is a deadbeat and the $20,000 note is worthless. Consequently, Tom wants to report Tim's bad debt on his and Teri's current tax return and net it against his other capital gains and losses. Tom is adamant about this. Would you sign the Paid Preparer's declaration (see example above) on this return? Why or why not?

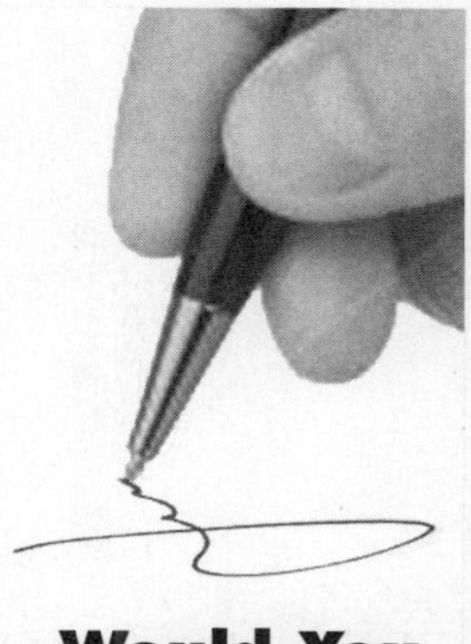

Would You Sign This Tax Return?

©ILYA AKINSHIN/Shutterstock.com; ©Zhukov Oleg/Shutterstock.com.

OFFICE IN THE HOME

Learning Objective 3.11

Ascertain when a home office deduction may be claimed and how the deduction is computed.

Some taxpayers operate a trade or business in their homes and qualify for home office deductions. The tax law imposes strict limits on the availability of the deduction. In fact, the deduction for an office in the home is allowed by exception. The general rule for a home office deduction states that a taxpayer will not be allowed a deduction for the use of a dwelling unit used by the taxpayer as a residence. The law provides four exceptions to the general rule under which a deduction may be allowed.

Under the first exception, a deduction is allowed if the home office is used on a regular basis and exclusively as the taxpayer's principal place of business. An employee may qualify under this exception, provided the business use of his or her home office is for "the convenience of

the employer" when the employer does not provide a regular office. A home office qualifies as a principal place of business if it is used in the conduct of administrative or management activities of a trade or business that are not substantially performed at a different fixed location.

A second exception states that a deduction is allowed if the home office is used exclusively and on a regular basis by patients, clients, or customers in meetings or dealings with the taxpayer in the normal course of a trade or business. That exception allows doctors and sales-people to deduct home office expenses even though they maintain another office away from their residence, and even though the office is not the taxpayer's principal place of business.

Under the third exception, the deduction of home office expenses is allowed if the home office is a separate structure not attached to the dwelling unit and is used exclusively and on a regular basis in the taxpayer's trade or business.

The fourth and final exception to the rule allows a deduction of a portion of the cost of a dwelling unit if it is used on a regular basis for the storage of business inventory or product samples held for use in the taxpayer's trade or business of selling products. Under this fourth exception, the taxpayer's home must be the taxpayer's sole place of business.

The Gross Income Limitation

The home office deduction may not reduce the net income from the business below zero, except for mortgage interest and property taxes allocable to the office, which are generally tax deductible anyway. The other costs of operating a home, which are included in the home office allocation, include rent, home insurance, repairs, cleaning, gardening, home-owners' association dues, and depreciation on the cost of the home. Depreciation expense is considered only after all other expenses have been allowed. Any unused deductions may be carried over to offset income in future years.

EXAMPLE Jane, an accounting professor, maintains an office in her apartment where she conducts a small tax practice. Jane properly allocates $1,500 in rent to the home office, and during the year she collects $1,400 in fees from various clients. Assuming Jane has no other expenses associated with her practice, only $1,400 of the rent may be claimed as a home office deduction, since she may not show a loss from the practice due to the gross income limitation. The unused portion is carried over to the next taxable year. ♦

EXAMPLE Assume the same facts as those in the previous example, except Jane owns her home. She has real estate taxes of $100, mortgage interest of $600, maintenance expenses of $200, and depreciation of $1,000 attributable to the home office. Her deduction for home office expenses is calculated as follows:

Gross income from tax practice	$1,400
Less: mortgage interest and real estate taxes	(700)
Balance	$ 700
Less: maintenance expense	(200)
Balance	$ 500
Depreciation (maximum allowed)	(500)
Net income from tax practice	$ 0

Please note that the only way the home office can generate an overall business loss for Jane is if her home office mortgage interest and taxes exceed her gross business income. ♦

If a home office is used for both business and personal purposes, no deduction is allowed. For example, Professor Jane in the previous example would not be allowed a

deduction for any expenses associated with the office in her home if the office was also used for personal activities, such as watching television.

The Home Office Allocation

The calculation of home office expenses involves the allocation of the total expenses of a taxpayer's dwelling between business and personal use. This allocation is usually made on the basis of the number of square feet of business space as a percentage of the total number of square feet in the residence, or on the basis of the number of rooms devoted to business use as a percentage of the total number of rooms in the dwelling.

EXAMPLE Lois operates a hair-styling salon in her home. The salon occupies 400 square feet of her residence, which has a total of 1,600 square feet. Her expenses for her residence are presented below and allocated as shown.

Expenses	*Total Amount*	*Business Percentage**	*Business Portion*
Rent	$10,000	25%	$2,500
Utilities	4,000	25%	1,000
Cleaning	2,000	25%	500

*400 sq. ft./1,600 sq. ft. ♦

Self-employed taxpayers filing Schedule C and claiming a deduction for home office expenses are required to file Form 8829, Expenses for Business Use of Your Home. Comprehensive problems 2A and 2B at the end of this chapter provide an opportunity to use this form.

Optional Safe Harbor Method

In an effort to reduce the complexity of the home office deduction, the IRS introduced a simplified method in 2013. Under the safe harbor, the taxpayer may deduct home office expenses at the applicable rate ($5 in 2014) multiplied by the number of square feet used in the home office, up to a maximum of 300 square feet, thus limiting the safe harbor to $1,500 in 2014. The deduction is still limited to the gross income from the business and actual home office expenses are not deducted. Any safe harbor deduction in excess of the income limit may be carried forward. The same home office qualifications apply but no allocations are required.

EXAMPLE Martha operates a business that generates $6,700 of income before the home office deduction. She has a qualifying home office of 350 square feet in her home. She properly allocates $1,200 of household expenses to her home office. Under the safeharbor method, Martha's home office deduction is $1,500 ($5 per square foot × maximum 300 square feet). No deduction is taken for the actual allocated expenses. ♦

Self-Study Problem 3.11

See Appendix E for Solutions to Self-Study Problems

Terry is a self-employed lawyer who maintains an office in her home. The office is used exclusively for client work, and clients regularly visit her home office. The mortgage interest and real estate taxes allocated to the business use of the home amount to $2,100, and maintenance, utilities, and cleaning service allocable to the business use of the home total $1,400. If gross billings of Terry's practice are $2,800 for this year and Terry has no other expenses allocable to the business, calculate the net income or loss she may report from the practice.

$________

Learning Objective 3.12

Describe the basic tax treatment of deductions for net operating losses.

NET OPERATING LOSSES

Under the U.S. tax law, a taxpayer is required to file an annual tax return. The pattern of a taxpayer's income, however, can lead to inequities among taxpayers with the same total amount of taxable income over a number of years. The inequities arise because of the progressive rates involved in the tax calculation. The higher the taxpayer's income, the higher the tax rate paid (see Chapter 12 for a discussion of tax rates). To alleviate this problem, Congress enacted the Net Operating Loss (NOL) provision. The following example shows inequities that could result if the net operating loss provision were not in the tax law.

EXAMPLE A and B are both single taxpayers with one exemption. Their taxable income or loss over a 3-year period is as shown in the following table. Notice their total taxable income for the 3-year period is the same ($150,000 each). However, the pattern of income is very different. As a result, without relief, B's tax liability is $20,099 ($45,386 – $25,287) more than A's tax liability.

Year	A's Income	A's Tax Liability	B's Income or Loss	B's Tax Liability
1	$ 50,000	$ 8,429	$120,000	$26,893
2	50,000	8,429	(60,000)	0
3	50,000	8,429	90,000	18,493
Total	$150,000	$25,287	$150,000	$45,386

♦

To provide taxpayer B relief from this inequitable tax situation, a deduction for NOLs is allowed by the tax law. Under this provision, a net operating loss from one tax year can be used as a deduction in another tax year. The net operating loss provision is primarily designed to provide relief for trade or business losses. Generally, only losses from the operation of a trade or business, casualty and theft losses, or confiscation losses can generate a net operating loss. Thus, individual taxpayers with only wages, itemized deductions (except casualty losses), and personal exemptions cannot generate a net operating loss.

Carrybacks and Carryovers

Under the general rule, a net operating loss is carried back 2 years and forward 20 years. The NOL is first carried back to the second prior year and then to the prior year (or until the NOL is used in full). If there is still unused NOL, the loss is carried forward to future tax years in chronological order. Taxpayers may make an irrevocable election to forgo the 2-year carryback and only use the 20-year carryover. When a taxpayer has two different NOL deductions available in a tax year, then the earliest year's loss is used first.

Where there is a net operating loss carryback, the taxpayer must file an amended tax return on Form 1040X or a quick claim for refund Form 1045. In future tax years, the net operating loss deduction is shown as a current deduction on the tax return for that year. Calculation of NOLs for individual taxpayers is very complex and beyond the scope of this text.

EXAMPLE Desiree has a net operating loss of $20,000 in 2014. She uses this NOL deduction in the following order: 2012, 2013, 2015 through 2034. Note she could elect not to carryback to the 2012 and 2013 tax years but rather just deduct the loss in 2015 and future years. ♦

Self-Study Problem 3.12 *See Appendix E for Solutions to Self-Study Problems*

Indicate whether the following statements are true or false by circling the appropriate letter.

T F 1. NOL deductions are first carried back 3 years and then forward 15 years.

T F 2. The itemized deduction for home mortgage interest can generate an NOL for an individual taxpayer.

T F 3. The purpose of the NOL provision in the tax law is to alleviate some of the inequities caused by the progressive tax rate structure.

T F 4. The election not to carry back an NOL deduction is irrevocable.

T F 5. When taxpayers have an NOL deduction, they can use it any year they choose, as long as the tax year is within the prescribed deduction period.

TAX BREAK

A taxpayer with a net operating loss who was in a low tax bracket for the carryback period, but expects to be in a high tax bracket the following year, may wish to elect out of the carryback period. The taxpayer will get a bigger tax benefit from deducting the NOL in the high-income year.

HOBBY LOSSES

Learning Objective 3.13

Apply the factors used to determine whether an activity is a hobby, and understand the tax treatment of hobby losses.

If a taxpayer enters into an activity without a profit motive, the tax law limits the amount of tax deductions available. Under the hobby loss provisions, a taxpayer may not show a loss from an activity that is not engaged in for profit. For example, the breeding of race horses is an activity which might not be considered a trade or business when carried on by a full-time dentist. The IRS might contend that the activity was for personal enjoyment and disallow any loss for tax purposes. Despite the limitation on losses, any profits from hobbies must be included in taxable income. Hobby income is reported on Line 21, Other Income on Form 1040.

Operational Rules

Individual taxpayers (or S corporations) can avoid the hobby loss rules if they can show that the activity was conducted with the intent to earn a profit. To determine whether the activity was engaged in for profit, the IRS will look at the following factors:

1. Whether the activity is conducted like a business,
2. The expertise of the taxpayer,
3. The time and effort expended,
4. Previous success of the taxpayer in similar activities,
5. Income and loss history from the activity,
6. Relationship of income to losses in the activity,
7. Financial status of the taxpayer, and
8. Elements of personal recreation in the activity.

The tax law provides a rebuttable presumption that if an activity shows a profit for 3 of the 5 previous years (2 of the 7 previous years for activities involving horses), the activity is engaged in for profit. For example, if an activity shows a profit for 3 of the previous 5 years, it is presumed to be a trade or business, and the IRS must establish that it is a hobby.

Loss Limitations

For a business activity that is not a hobby, there is no limitation on the amount of expenses allocable to the activity that the taxpayer may claim as deductions against the income of the activity. If an activity is determined to be a hobby, it is subject to the hobby loss rules and expenses may be allowed as deductions only to the extent of income from the activity. Expenses otherwise deductible on Schedule A, such as certain interest (e.g., home mortgage interest) and taxes, may be allowed without regard to the nature of the activity. Therefore, a taxpayer could have a loss on a hobby to the extent the amount of otherwise deductible interest and taxes paid exceeds the amount of income from the activity. Other allowed expenses attributable to the hobby activity are considered miscellaneous itemized deductions, subject to the 2 percent of adjusted gross income limitation (see Chapter 5).

EXAMPLE Fred, the president of a bank, decides that he wants to be a famous wine maker. He has the following expenses related to this activity:

Depreciation on wine-making equipment	$2,000
Personal property taxes on equipment	2,500
Wine-making supplies	4,600

During the year, Fred sells 200 cases of wine for $7,500. If the activity is not a hobby, then Fred may take a loss, against his other income, of $1,600 ($7,500 − $2,000 − $2,500 − $4,600). However, if the activity is deemed to be a hobby, the deductions are limited to the income from the activity. Fred would be allowed to deduct the property taxes of $2,500 which would leave income of $5,000. Only $5,000 of the $6,600 of depreciation and supplies is deductible (subject to the limitation on miscellaneous itemized deductions). ♦

Self-Study Problem 3.13

See Appendix E for Solutions to Self-Study Problems

Linda is a CPA who decides that she wants to be an artist. During 2014, she sells $250 worth of paintings and incurs the following expenses:

Painting supplies	$ 300
Transportation to locations for painting	2,500

If this activity is deemed to be a hobby, what amount of the expenses may Linda deduct on her 2014 tax return?

$ __________

KEY TERMS

Schedule C, 3-2
trade or business, 3-2
cost of goods sold, 3-5
self-employment tax, 3-6
inventories, 3-7
first in, first out (FIFO), 3-8
last in, first out (LIFO), 3-8
standard mileage rate, 3-12
actual cost method, 3-12
standard mileage method, 3-12
tax home, 3-14
per diem substantiation, 3-15
bona fide business discussion, 3-16
business gifts, 3-21
business and nonbusiness bad debts, 3-22
home office, 3-23
net operating losses, 3-26
carrybacks and carryovers, 3-26
hobby losses, 3-27

KEY POINTS

Learning Objectives	Key Points
LO 3.1: Complete a basic Schedule C (Profit or Loss from Business).	• Taxpayers who operate a business or practice a profession as a sole proprietorship must file a Schedule C (long form) or a Schedule C-EZ (short form) to report the net profit or loss from the sole proprietorship. • Deductions taken on Schedule C must be ordinary and necessary, reasonable, and have a business purpose. • If the taxpayer cannot meet the requirements for filing the simple Schedule C-EZ, then he or she must file a standard Schedule C. • Schedule C filers such as sole proprietors and independent contractors with net earnings of $400 or more must pay a self-employment tax calculated on Schedule SE with their Form 1040.
LO 3.2: Understand the tax treatment of inventories and cost of goods sold.	• Cost of goods sold, which is the largest single deduction for many businesses, is calculated as follows: beginning inventory + purchases − ending inventory. • There are two common methods of inventory valuation used by taxpayers: first in, first out (FIFO) and last in, first out (LIFO).
LO 3.3: Identify the requirements for deducting transportation expenses.	• Deductible transportation expenses include travel by airplane, rail, bus, and automobile. • If the taxpayer works at two or more jobs during the same day, he or she may deduct the cost of going from one job to the other or from one business location to another. • The standard mileage rate for 2014 is 56 cents per mile.
LO 3.4: Identify the requirements for deducting travel expenses.	• Travel expenses are defined as ordinary and necessary expenses incurred in traveling away from home in pursuit of the taxpayer's trade or business. • Deductible travel expenses include the cost of such items as meals, lodging, taxis, tips, and laundry. • A taxpayer must be away from home "overnight" in order to deduct travel expenses. Overnight is a period of time longer than an ordinary work day in which rest or relief from work is required. Also, the taxpayer must be away from his or her "tax home" to be on travel status. • Taxpayers must substantiate the following: the amount of each separate expenditure, the dates of departure and return for each trip and the number of business days on the trip, the destination or locality of the travel, and the business reason for the travel. • As an alternative to reporting actual expenses, a per diem method may be used in certain circumstances.
LO 3.5: Determine the requirements for claiming meals and entertainment deductions.	• Self-employed taxpayers and employees are allowed deductions for 50 percent of the cost of entertainment incurred in connection with their trade or business. • To be deductible, entertainment expenses must be (1) directly related to or (2) associated with the active conduct of the taxpayer's trade or business. • Expenses directly related to the taxpayer's trade or business are costs related to an actual business meeting, such as the expense of a sales luncheon where a salesperson is making a sale to a client. • Expenses associated with the conduct of the taxpayer's trade or business are generally those expenses that serve a specific business purpose. The entertainment must take place immediately before or after a bona fide business discussion.

LO 3.6: Identify the requirements for claiming business education expenses.	• To be deductible as a business expense, education expenditures must be paid to meet the requirements of the taxpayer's employer or the requirements of law or regulation for keeping the taxpayer's salary, status, or job, or the expenses must be paid to maintain or improve existing skills required in performing the duties of the taxpayer's work.
LO 3.7: Identify the tax treatment of dues and subscriptions.	• Professionals may deduct dues and the cost of subscriptions and publications. Included are items such as membership to the local bar for a lawyer, dues to the AICPA for an accountant, and the cost of subscriptions to any journal that is directly related to the taxpayer's profession.
LO 3.8: Determine which clothing and uniforms may be treated as tax deductions.	• In order to be deductible, clothing or uniforms must (1) be required as a condition of employment, and (2) not be suitable for everyday use.
LO 3.9: Explain the special limits for business gift deductions.	• Taxpayers are allowed a deduction for business gifts up to $25 per year per donee. For purposes of this limitation, a husband and wife count as one donee, unless the husband and wife are both clients.
LO 3.10: Explain the tax treatment of bad debt deductions.	• Bad debts are classified as either business bad debts or nonbusiness bad debts. Debts arising from a taxpayer's trade or business are classified as business bad debts, while all other debts are considered nonbusiness bad debts. • Business bad debts are treated as ordinary deductions and nonbusiness bad debts are treated as short-term capital losses, of which only $3,000 can be deducted against ordinary income each year.
LO 3.11: Ascertain when a home office deduction may be claimed and how the deduction is computed.	• A home office is generally not deductible. However, there are four exceptions to the general rule. • A home office deduction is allowed if the home office is used on a regular basis and exclusively as the taxpayer's principal place of business. An employee may qualify under this exception, provided the business use of his or her home office is for "the convenience of the employer" when the employer does not provide a regular office. • A home office deduction is allowed if the home office is used exclusively and on a regular basis by patients, clients, or customers in meetings or dealings with the taxpayer in the normal course of a trade or business. • The deduction of home office expenses is allowed if the home office is a separate structure not attached to the dwelling unit and is used exclusively and on a regular basis in the taxpayer's trade or business. • A home office deduction of a portion of the cost of a dwelling unit is allowed if it is used on a regular basis for the storage of business inventory or product samples. • The home office deduction is limited by the amount of net income from the associated trade or business. • A simplified home office deduction is also available at $5 per square foot up to a maximum of $1,500 in 2014.
LO 3.12: Describe the basic tax treatment of deductions for net operating losses.	• Net operating losses allow taxpayers to "smooth out" their income over a multiyear period thereby avoiding high marginal tax rates in high income years. • A net operating loss is carried back 2 years and forward 20 years allowing taxpayers to claim a refund of taxes in a year other than the year in which the loss occurred.
LO 3.13: Apply the factors used to determine whether an activity is a hobby, and understand the tax treatment of hobby losses.	• Under the hobby loss provisions, a taxpayer may not show a loss from an activity that is not engaged in for profit. • To determine whether the activity was engaged in for profit, the IRS will look at numerous factors including whether the activity is conducted like a business.

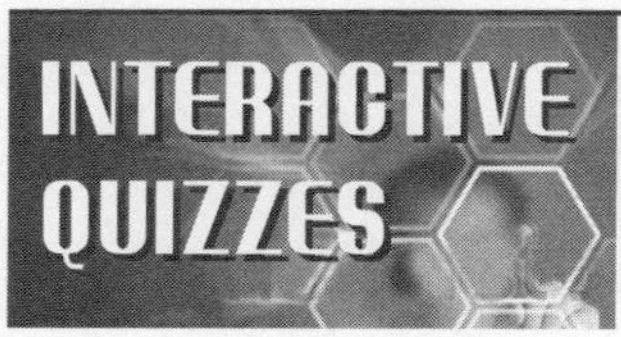

© Dusit/Shutterstock.com

Interactive quizzes are available as an optional online resource for Income Tax Fundamentals. Visit **www.cengagebrain.com** for more information.

QUESTIONS and PROBLEMS

GROUP 1: MULTIPLE CHOICE QUESTIONS

LO 3.1

______ 1. What form does a self-employed sole proprietor usually use to report income and expenses from business?
   a. Schedule C
   b. Schedule D
   c. Schedule A, Miscellaneous Itemized Deductions
   d. Form 2106, Employee Business Expenses
   e. None of the above

LO 3.1

______ 2. In the current year, Mary started a profitable housekeeping business as a sole proprietor. She has ten housekeepers working for her and spends her time selling their services and coordinating her employees' time. Mary made $50,000 in her first year of operations. In addition to filing a Schedule C to report her business earnings, Mary *must* also file:
   a. Schedule A
   b. Schedule SE
   c. Schedule B
   d. Schedule D
   e. None of the above

LO 3.1
LO 3.5

______ 3. Daniel is a self-employed consultant. Until this year he was always an employee. He comes to discuss his new business with you. As his tax accountant, you should:
   a. Discuss setting up a good record-keeping system for his new business
   b. Discuss the substantiation requirements for meals and entertainment
   c. Discuss the self-employment tax, as well as the income tax, on business earnings in order to help Daniel estimate what he might owe in taxes for the year
   d. Discuss the rules for deducting automobile expenses
   e. Discuss all of the above

LO 3.2

______ 4. Which of the following formulas represents the proper method of calculating cost of goods sold?
   a. Beginning inventory + Ending inventory − Purchases
   b. Ending inventory − Purchases − Beginning inventory
   c. Purchases − Beginning inventory − Ending inventory
   d. Beginning inventory + Purchases − Ending inventory
   e. None of the above

LO 3.2

______ 5. If a taxpayer has beginning inventory of $25,000, purchases of $185,000, and ending inventory of $30,000, what is the amount of the cost of goods sold for the current year?
   a. $155,000
   b. $180,000

c. $190,000
d. $185,000
e. None of the above

______ **LO 3.3**

6. Which of the following taxpayers may use the standard mileage method of calculating transportation costs?
   a. A taxi driver who owns a fleet of six cars for hire
   b. A taxpayer who used accelerated depreciation on his automobile
   c. A business executive who claimed bonus depreciation in the first year she used the car
   d. An attorney who uses his Porsche for calling on clients
   e. None of the above

______ **LO 3.4**

7. Which of the following taxpayers is entitled to a travel expense deduction?
   a. An employee, who worked in the Salt Lake City plant of a company, who is assigned to the Denver plant of the company for 4 years
   b. An employee who travels between several business locations within the same city each day
   c. A manager of a chain of department stores who works in the main store 3 weeks out of every month and visits distant branch locations on overnight trips during the remainder of the month
   d. An employee who resigns from his current job and accepts a new job in a city 500 miles away from his current residence
   e. A bank employee who travels to a branch office for a couple of hours of work and decides to stay overnight to attend a play

______ **LO 3.4**

8. Which of the following expenses incurred while the taxpayer is away from home "overnight" is not included as a travel expense?
   a. Laundry expenses
   b. Transportation expenses
   c. Meal expenses
   d. Business gifts
   e. Lodging expenses

______ **LO 3.4**

9. Under the high-low method, the federal per diem amount given in the text for 2014 for a high-cost locality for travel in the United States is:
   a. $163 per day
   b. $242 per day
   c. $251 per day
   d. $300 per day
   e. Some other amount

______ **LO 3.4**

10. Joe is a self-employed information technology consultant from San Francisco, CA. He takes a trip to Chicago primarily for business. He takes two personal days to go to museums and see the sights of Chicago. How should he treat the expenses related to this trip?
    a. One hundred percent of the trip should be deducted as a business expense since the trip was primarily for business.
    b. Fifty percent of the trip should be deducted as a business expense since the IRS limits such business expenses to 50 percent of the actual cost.
    c. The cost of all of the airfare and the business days should be deducted, while the cost of the personal days are not deductible.
    d. None of the expenses are deductible since there was an element of personal enjoyment in the trip.

LO 3.5

11. Which of the following expenses is deductible as an entertainment expense?
    a. The depreciation on an airplane used to entertain customers
    b. The cost of a hunting camp used to entertain customers
    c. The dues of a racket club used to keep in shape
    d. The cost of a cocktail party for clients paid for by a computer salesman at a computer fair
    e. The cost of a meal at the taxpayer's country club with a potential client during which they discussed golf

LO 3.6

12. Which of the following taxpayers may *not* deduct their educational expense?
    a. A CPA who attends a course to review for the real estate agents' exam
    b. A corporate president who attends a management course at a local university
    c. An attorney who attends a course on computing legal damages
    d. A real estate broker who attends a college course on real estate law
    e. All of the above are deductible

LO 3.7

13. Which of the following is not deductible by the taxpayer?
    a. A subscription to *The CPA Journal* by a CPA
    b. A subscription to *The Yale Medical Journal* by a doctor
    c. A subscription to *Financial Management* by a chief financial officer
    d. A subscription to *The Harvard Law Review* by a lawyer
    e. All of the above are deductible

LO 3.8

14. Which of the following employees are most likely permitted to deduct the cost of their uniform?
    a. A lawyer who is required by her employer to wear a business suit
    b. A furnace repairman who must wear overalls while on the job
    c. A nurse who can wear casual clothes while on duty
    d. A marine who must purchase uniforms for on-duty and off-duty hours
    e. A cheerleader for the San Diego Chargers football team who purchases her own costume

LO 3.9

15. Which of the following business gifts are fully deductible?
    a. A gift to a client costing $35
    b. A gift to an employee, for 10 years of continued service, costing $250
    c. A gift to a client and her nonclient spouse costing $45
    d. A gift to an employee paid under a qualified plan, for not having an on-the-job injury for 25 years, costing $1,650
    e. None of the above are fully deductible

LO 3.10

16. Loren loaned a friend $9,000 as financing for a new business venture. In the current year, Loren's friend declares bankruptcy and the debt is considered totally worthless. What amount may Loren deduct on his individual income tax return for the current year as a result of the worthless debt, assuming he has no other capital gains or losses for the year?
    a. $9,000 ordinary loss
    b. $9,000 short-term capital loss
    c. $3,000 short-term capital loss
    d. $3,000 ordinary loss
    e. $6,000 short-term capital loss

_______________ 17. Kathy is a self-employed taxpayer working exclusively from her home office. Before the home office deduction, Kathy has $3,000 of net income. Her allocable home office expenses are $5,000 in total (includes $2,000 of allocated interest and property taxes). How are the home office expenses treated on her current year tax return?

LO 3.11

a. All home office expenses may be deducted, resulting in a business loss of $2,000.
b. Only $3,000 of home office expenses may be deducted, resulting in net business income of zero. None of the extra $2,000 of home office expenses may be carried forward or deducted.
c. Only $3,000 of home office expenses may be deducted, resulting in net business income of zero. The extra $2,000 of home office expenses may be carried forward and deducted in a future year against home office income.
d. None of the home office expenses may be deducted since Kathy's income is too low.

_______________ 18. Which of the following taxpayers qualifies for a home office deduction?

LO 3.11

a. An attorney who is employed by a law firm and has a home office in which to read cases
b. A doctor who has a regular office downtown and a library at home to store medical journals
c. An accounting student who maintains a home office used exclusively to prepare tax returns
d. A nurse who maintains a home office to pay bills and read nursing journals
e. A corporate president who uses his home office to entertain friends and customers

_______________ 19. Carol maintains an office in her home where she conducts a dressmaking business. During the year she collects $4,000 from sales, pays $1,300 for various materials and supplies, and properly allocates $2,500 of rent expense and $500 of her utilities expense to the use of her home office. What amount of the rent and utilities expense may Carol deduct in the current year in computing her net income or loss from the dressmaking business?

LO 3.11

a. $0
b. $500
c. $2,500
d. $2,700
e. $3,000

_______________ 20. Bonita earns $31,000 from her job, and she has $1,000 of interest income. She has itemized deductions and personal exemptions of $35,000. There are no casualty or theft losses in the itemized deductions. What is Bonita's net operating loss for the current year?

LO 3.12

a. $0
b. $1,000
c. $3,000
d. $4,000
e. Some other amount

_______________ 21. Jim has a net operating loss in 2014. If he does not make any special elections, what is the first year to which Jim carries the net operating loss?

LO 3.12

a. 2011
b. 2012
c. 2013
d. 2015
e. 2016

LO 3.13

22. Which of the following factors is not considered by the IRS in determining whether an activity is a hobby?
    a. Whether the activity is conducted like a business
    b. The time and effort expended by the taxpayer
    c. Elements of personal recreation in the activity
    d. Financial status of the taxpayer
    e. All of the above are considered to determine if an activity is a hobby

GROUP 2: PROBLEMS

LO 3.1

1. Scott Butterfield is self-employed as a CPA. He uses the cash method of accounting, and his Social Security number is 644-47-7833. His principal business code is 541211. Scott's CPA practice is located at 678 Peso Dr., La Mesa, CA 92041. During 2014, Scott had the following income and expenses:

Fees from CPA practice	$128,250
Expenses:	
Car mileage (3,202 business miles)	1,793
Business insurance	870
Office expense	3,450
Rent on office space	8,400
City business license	150
Travel expense	4,100
Meals and entertainment (100%)	4,780
Utilities	1,625
Wages of secretary	25,700

Scott placed his car in service on January 1, 2009. This year, he commuted 2,000 miles in it and drove it 4,000 miles for nonbusiness purposes. His wife has a car for personal use.

Complete Schedule C on Pages 3-41 and 3-42 for Scott showing Scott's net income from self-employment.

LO 3.1

2. Go to the IRS website (**www.irs.gov**) and redo Problem 1 (Chapter 3, Group 2) using the most recent interactive Schedule C (Form 1040) on the IRS website that will allow the required information to be input. Print out the *completed Schedule C.*

LO 3.1

3. Margaret started her own business in the current year and will report a profit for her first year. Her results of operations are as follows:

Gross income	$50,000
Travel	1,000
Transportation 6,009 miles, using standard mileage method	
Entertainment in total	4,000
Seven gifts at $50 each	350
Rent and utilities for apartment in total (20% is used for a home office)	10,000

What is the net income Margaret should show on her Schedule C? Show the calculation of her taxable business income.

Gross income	______
Expenses (describe each)	______
	______
	______
	______
	______
	______
Taxable business income	______

LO 3.2

4. Lawrence owns a small candy store that sells one type of candy. His beginning inventory of candy was made up of 10,000 boxes costing $1.50 per box ($15,000), and he made the following purchases of candy during the year:

March 1	10,000 boxes at $1.60	$16,000
August 15	20,000 boxes at $1.60	32,000
November 20	10,000 boxes at $1.75	17,500

At the end of the year, Lawrence's inventory consisted of 15,000 boxes of candy.

a. Calculate Lawrence's ending inventory and cost of goods sold using the FIFO inventory valuation method.

Ending inventory $ ______
Cost of goods sold $ ______

b. Calculate Lawrence's ending inventory and cost of goods sold using the LIFO inventory valuation method.

Ending inventory $ ______
Cost of goods sold $ ______

LO 3.2

5. Kevin owns a retail store, and during the current year he purchased $600,000 worth of inventory. Kevin's beginning inventory was $65,000, and his ending inventory is $75,000. During the year, Kevin withdrew $15,000 in inventory for his personal use. Use Part III of Schedule C below to calculate Kevin's cost of goods sold for the year.

Part III **Cost of Goods Sold** (see instructions)

33	Method(s) used to value closing inventory: a ☐ Cost b ☐ Lower of cost or market c ☐ Other (attach explanation)		
34	Was there any change in determining quantities, costs, or valuations between opening and closing inventory? If "Yes," attach explanation . . . ☐ Yes ☐ No		
35	Inventory at beginning of year. If different from last year's closing inventory, attach explanation	35	
36	Purchases less cost of items withdrawn for personal use	36	
37	Cost of labor. Do not include any amounts paid to yourself	37	
38	Materials and supplies	38	
39	Other costs	39	
40	Add lines 35 through 39	40	
41	Inventory at end of year	41	
42	**Cost of goods sold.** Subtract line 41 from line 40. Enter the result here and on line 4	42	

DRAFT AS OF June 19, 2014 DO NOT FILE

LO 3.2

6. Go to the IRS website (**www.irs.gov**) and find the most recent IRS Publication 538, Accounting Periods and Methods; Inventories. Print out the *first two pages of the part on inventories*.

LO 3.2

7. Go to the IRS website (**www.irs.gov**) and redo Problem 5, using the most recent interactive Cost of Goods Sold Schedule on Page 2 of Schedule C (Form 1040). Print out the *completed Cost of Goods Sold schedule*.

LO 3.3

8. Teresa is a civil engineer who uses her automobile for business. Teresa drove her automobile a total of 21,732 miles during 2014, of which 95 percent was business mileage. The actual cost of gasoline, oil, depreciation, repairs, and insurance for the year was $8,300.
   a. How much is Teresa's transportation deduction based on the standard mileage method?

      $ ____________

   b. How much is Teresa's transportation deduction based on the actual cost method?

      $ ____________

   c. Which method should Teresa use to calculate her transportation deduction?

      ____

      Why? ____________

      ____

LO 3.3

9. Art is a self-employed installer of home entertainment systems, and he drives his car frequently to installation locations. Art drove his car 15,000 miles for business purposes and 20,000 miles in total. His actual expenses, including depreciation, for operating the auto are $10,000 since he had to have the car repaired several times. Art has always used the actual cost method in the past. How much is Art's deductible auto expense for the year?

   ____

   ____

LO 3.3

10. Martha is a self-employed tax accountant who drives her car to visit clients on a regular basis. She drives her car 4,000 miles for business and 10,000 for commuting and other personal use. Assuming Martha uses the standard mileage method, how much is her auto expense for the year? Where in her tax return should Martha claim this deduction? ____________

    ____

    ____

LO 3.4

11. Joan is a self-employed attorney in New York City. Joan took a trip to San Diego, CA, primarily for business, to consult with a client and take a short vacation. On the trip, Joan incurred the following expenses:

Airfare to and from San Diego	$ 575
Hotel charges while on business	340
Meals while on business	210
Car rental while on business	120
Hotel charges while on vacation	460
Meals while on vacation	290
Car rental while on vacation	180
Total	$2,175

    Calculate Joan's travel expense deduction for the trip, assuming the trip was made in 2014.

    $ ____________

LO 3.4

12. Go to the U.S. General Services Administration (GSA) website. What is the per diem rate for lodging and M&IE for each of the following towns:
    a. Flagstaff, AZ
    b. Palm Springs, CA
    c. Denver, CO

LO 3.4
LO 3.6

13. Bob is a self-employed lawyer and is required to take a week of continuing legal education every year to keep his license. This year he paid $1,000 in course fees for his continuing legal education in a different city. He also paid $500 for airfare and a hotel room and paid $260 for meals. What is the total amount he can deduct on his Schedule C related to these expenses?

____

____

____

LO 3.5

14. Grace is a self-employed sales consultant who spends significant time entertaining potential customers. She keeps all the appropriate records to substantiate her entertainment. She has the following expenses in the current year:

Restaurant meals	$5,000
Greens fees (all business)	500
Tickets to baseball games	500
Country Club dues (all business use)	6,000

What is the tax-deductible entertainment expense Grace may claim in the current year? On which tax form should she claim the deduction?

____

____

LO 3.5

15. Marty is a sales consultant. Marty incurs the following expenses related to the entertainment of his clients in 2014:

Dues to a country club (The country club was used for business 25 days of the total 75 days that it was used.)	$4,500
Business meals at the country club	850
Dues to a tennis club (The club was used 75 percent for directly related business.)	1,000
Tennis fees (personal use)	260
Business meals at various restaurants	2,250

a. How much is Marty's deduction for entertainment expenses for 2014?

$ ____________

b. For each item listed above that you believe is not allowed as a deduction, explain the reason it is not allowed.

____

____

____

____

LO 3.6

16. a. Loren is a secretary in a lawyer's office. Since he often deals with legal matters, Loren feels that a law degree will be beneficial to him. May Loren deduct his educational expenses for law school as a miscellaneous itemized deduction?

____

Explain ____

____

b. Alicia is an international salesperson who wishes to learn Spanish to improve her ability to communicate with foreign clients. May Alicia deduct her educational expenses for language school as a miscellaneous itemized deduction?

____

Explain ______________________________

____

c. Joan is a practicing lawyer. She enrolls in a local medical school and works toward a medical degree in her spare time. May Joan deduct her educational expenses for the medical classes as a miscellaneous itemized deduction?

____

Explain ______________________________

____

LO 3.7

17. Carey opens a law office in Chicago on January 1, 2014. On January 1, 2014, Carey purchases an annual subscription to a law journal for $170 and a 1-year legal reference service for $1,500. Calculate Carey's deduction for the above items for the 2014 tax year.

$ ______________

LO 3.8

18. Cooper and Brandy are married and file a joint income tax return with two separate Schedule Cs. Cooper is an independent security specialist who spent $400 on uniforms during the year. His laundry expenses for the uniforms were $75 for this year, plus $65 for altering them. Brandy works as a drill press operator and wears jeans and a work shirt on the job, which cost $175 this year. Her laundry costs were $50 for the work clothes. Brandy is also required by state regulators to wear safety glasses and safety shoes when working, which cost a total of $95. How much is their total deduction on their Schedule Cs for special clothing and uniforms?

$ ______________

LO 3.9

19. Sam owns an insurance agency and makes the following business gifts during the year. Calculate Sam's deduction for business gifts.

Donee	*Amount*	*Amount Allowed*
Ms. Sears (a client)	$35, plus $4 shipping	$ ______________
Mr. Williams (a tennis partner, not a business prospect or client)	55	$ ______________
Mr. Sample (a client)	22	$ ______________
Mrs. Sample (nonclient wife of Mr. Sample)	20	$ ______________
Various customers (calendars costing $3 each with the company name on them)	300	$ ______________
Mr. Shiver (an employee gift, a watch, for 25 years of continuous service)	175	$ ______________
Total business gift deduction		$ ______________

LO 3.10

20. Steinar loaned a friend $9,500 to buy some stock 3 years ago. In the current year the debt became worthless.

a. How much is Steinar's deduction for the bad debt for this year? (Assume he has no other capital gains or losses.)

$ ______________

b. What can Steinar do with the deduction not used this year?

____

____

____

____

LO 3.10

21. Sharon is an orthopedic surgeon. She performed a surgery 2 years ago and billed $10,000 to her patient. After 2 years of attempting to collect the money, it is clear that she will not be able to collect anything. Sharon reports income on her tax return on the cash basis, so she only reports the income she actually receives in cash each year. Can she claim a bad debt deduction for the $10,000?

____

____

____

____

LO 3.10

22. Carrie loaned her friend $4,500 to buy a used car. She had her friend sign a note with repayment terms and set a reasonable interest rate on the note because the $4,500 was most of her savings. Her friend left town without a forwarding address, and nobody Carrie knows has heard from her in the last year. How should Carrie treat the bad loan for tax purposes?

____

____

____

____

LO 3.11

23. Cindy operates a computerized engineering drawing business from her home. Cindy maintains a home office and properly allocates the following expenses to her office:

Depreciation	$1,500
Utilities	500
Real estate taxes	325
Mortgage interest (100 percent deductible)	500

a. Assume that Cindy earns income of $2,400 from her business for the year before deducting home office expenses. She has no other expenses associated with the business. Calculate Cindy's deduction for home office expenses.

$ __________

b. Assume that Cindy earns income of $2,600 from her business during the year before deducting home office expenses. Calculate Cindy's deduction for home office expenses.

$ __________

LO 3.11

24. Pete qualifies for a home office deduction. The amount of space devoted to business use is 300 square feet of the total 1,200 square feet in his apartment. Pete's total rent for the year is $9,600, and he pays utilities (other than telephone) of $2,500 for the year. Calculate Pete's deduction for home office expenses before the gross income limitation.

Rent	$ __________
Utilities other than telephone	__________
Total home office expenses	$ __________

SCHEDULE C (Form 1040)

Department of the Treasury
Internal Revenue Service (99)

Profit or Loss From Business

(Sole Proprietorship)

▶ Information about Schedule C and its separate instructions is at *www.irs.gov/schedulec*.
▶ Attach to Form 1040, 1040NR, or 1041; partnerships generally must file Form 1065.

OMB No. 1545-0074
2014
Attachment Sequence No. 09

DRAFT AS OF June 19, 2014 DO NOT FILE

Name of proprietor | **Social security number (SSN)**

A Principal business or profession, including product or service (see instructions) | **B Enter code from instructions** ▶

C Business name. If no separate business name, leave blank. | **D Employer ID number (EIN),** (see instr.)

E Business address (including suite or room no.) ▶
City, town or post office, state, and ZIP code

F Accounting method: **(1)** ☐ Cash **(2)** ☐ Accrual **(3)** ☐ Other (specify) ▶

G Did you "materially participate" in the operation of this business during 2014? If "No," see instructions for limit on losses ☐ **Yes** ☐ **No**

H If you started or acquired this business during 2014, check here ▶ ☐

I Did you make any payments in 2014 that would require you to file Form(s) 1099? (see instructions) ☐ **Yes** ☐ **No**

J If "Yes," did you or will you file required Forms 1099? ☐ **Yes** ☐ **No**

Part I Income

1	Gross receipts or sales. See instructions for line 1 and check the box if this income was reported to you on Form W-2 and the "Statutory employee" box on that form was checked ▶ ☐	1	
2	Returns and allowances	2	
3	Subtract line 2 from line 1	3	
4	Cost of goods sold (from line 42)	4	
5	**Gross profit.** Subtract line 4 from line 3	5	
6	Other income, including federal and state gasoline or fuel tax credit or refund (see instructions)	6	
7	**Gross income.** Add lines 5 and 6 ▶	7	

Part II Expenses. Enter expenses for business use of your home only on line 30.

8	Advertising	8		18	Office expense (see instructions)	18	
9	Car and truck expenses (see instructions)	9		19	Pension and profit-sharing plans	19	
10	Commissions and fees	10		20	Rent or lease (see instructions):		
11	Contract labor (see instructions)	11		a	Vehicles, machinery, and equipment	20a	
12	Depletion	12		b	Other business property	20b	
13	Depreciation and section 179 expense deduction (not included in Part III) (see instructions)	13		21	Repairs and maintenance	21	
				22	Supplies (not included in Part III)	22	
				23	Taxes and licenses	23	
14	Employee benefit programs (other than on line 19)	14		24	Travel, meals, and entertainment:		
				a	Travel	24a	
15	Insurance (other than health)	15		b	Deductible meals and entertainment (see instructions)	24b	
16	Interest:			25	Utilities	25	
a	Mortgage (paid to banks, etc.)	16a		26	Wages (less employment credits)	26	
b	Other	16b		27a	Other expenses (from line 48)	27a	
17	Legal and professional services	17		b	**Reserved for future use**	27b	

28	**Total expenses** before expenses for business use of home. Add lines 8 through 27a ▶	28	
29	Tentative profit or (loss). Subtract line 28 from line 7	29	
30	Expenses for business use of your home. Do not report these expenses elsewhere. Attach Form 8829 unless using the simplified method (see instructions). **Simplified method filers only:** enter the total square footage of: (a) your home: ______ and (b) the part of your home used for business: ______. Use the Simplified Method Worksheet in the instructions to figure the amount to enter on line 30	30	
31	**Net profit or (loss).** Subtract line 30 from line 29. • If a profit, enter on both **Form 1040, line 12** (or **Form 1040NR, line 13**) and on **Schedule SE, line 2.** (If you checked the box on line 1, see instructions). Estates and trusts, enter on **Form 1041, line 3.** • If a loss, you **must** go to line 32.	31	

32 If you have a loss, check the box that describes your investment in this activity (see instructions).
- If you checked 32a, enter the loss on both **Form 1040, line 12,** (or **Form 1040NR, line 13**) and on **Schedule SE, line 2.** (If you checked the box on line 1, see the line 31 instructions). Estates and trusts, enter on **Form 1041, line 3.**
- If you checked 32b, you **must** attach **Form 6198.** Your loss may be limited.

32a ☐ All investment is at risk.
32b ☐ Some investment is not at risk.

Schedule C (Form 1040) 2014 Page **2**

Part III **Cost of Goods Sold** (see instructions)

33 Method(s) used to value closing inventory: a ☐ Cost b ☐ Lower of cost or market c ☐ Other (attach explanation)

34 Was there any change in determining quantities, costs, or valuations between opening and closing inventory? If "Yes," attach explanation . . . ☐ Yes ☐ No

DRAFT AS OF June 19, 2014 DO NOT FILE

35	Inventory at beginning of year. If different from last year's closing inventory, attach explanation	35	
36	Purchases less cost of items withdrawn for personal use	36	
37	Cost of labor. Do not include any amounts paid to yourself	37	
38	Materials and supplies	38	
39	Other costs	39	
40	Add lines 35 through 39	40	
41	Inventory at end of year	41	
42	**Cost of goods sold.** Subtract line 41 from line 40. Enter the result here and on line 4	42	

Part IV **Information on Your Vehicle.** Complete this part **only** if you are claiming car or truck expenses on line 9 and are not required to file Form 4562 for this business. See the instructions for line 13 to find out if you must file Form 4562.

43 When did you place your vehicle in service for business purposes? (month, day, year) ► ____ / ____ / ____

44 Of the total number of miles you drove your vehicle during 2014, enter the number of miles you used your vehicle for:

a Business ____________ b Commuting (see instructions) ____________ c Other ____________

45 Was your vehicle available for personal use during off-duty hours? . . . ☐ Yes ☐ No

46 Do you (or your spouse) have another vehicle available for personal use? . . . ☐ Yes ☐ No

47a Do you have evidence to support your deduction? . . . ☐ Yes ☐ No

b If "Yes," is the evidence written? . . . ☐ Yes ☐ No

Part V **Other Expenses.** List below business expenses not included on lines 8–26 or line 30.

48 **Total other expenses.** Enter here and on line 27a	48	

Schedule C (Form 1040) 2014

LO 3.11 25. Randi qualifies for a home deduction. The amount of space devoted to business use is 400 square feet of the total 2,000 square feet of her home. Randi's mortgage interest and property taxes in total are $1,600. Other deductions properly allocated to the home office total $300. In addition, Randi purchases and uses supplies costing $200 during the year. Assume Randi earns income of $3,400 for the year before deducting any home office or supplies deduction. Calculate Randi's home office deduction (ignore self-employment taxes).

$__________

LO 3.11 26. Ann is a self-employed restaurant critic who does her work exclusively from a home office. Ann's income is $25,000 before the home office deduction this year. Her office takes up 200 square feet of her 1,000-square-foot apartment. The total expenses for her apartment are $6,000 for rent, $1,000 for utilities, $200 for renter's insurance, and $800 for pest control and other maintenance. What is Ann's home office deduction? Please show your calculations.

LO 3.12 27. Carl has had a couple of good years in his new business. However, in the current year he has a net operating loss of $80,000. He does not feel that the future of his business is very bright. As his tax accountant, how would you recommend Carl treat his net operating loss?

LO 3.12 28. Maggie lost her job in the current year. She paid the expenses of owning her home, interest on the mortgage, and property taxes out of savings. Her tax return shows negative taxable income of $20,000. How should this loss be treated?

LO 3.13 29. Lew is a practicing CPA who decides to raise bonsai as a business. Lew engages in the activity and has the following revenue and expenses:

Sales	$ 5,000
Depreciation on greenhouse	10,000
Fertilizer, soil, pots	1,500

a. What are the factors that the IRS will consider when evaluating whether the activity is a hobby?

b. If the activity is deemed to be a regular business, what is the amount of Lew's loss from the activity?

$__________

c. If the activity is deemed to be a hobby, what is the amount of Lew's expenses (if any) from the activity that may be deducted?

$__________

GROUP 3: WRITING ASSIGNMENTS

ETHICS

1. Robert, a new client of yours, is a self-employed caterer in Santa Fe, New Mexico. Robert drives his personal van when delivering catered meals to customers. You have asked him to provide the amount of business miles driven using his vehicle. You are planning on using the standard mileage method to calculate Robert's deduction for transportation costs. Robert has responded by saying, "Well, I don't really keep track of my miles. I guess I drove around 3,000 miles last year for the business." What would you say to Robert?

RESEARCH

2. Your supervisor has asked you to research the following situation concerning Aurora Browning. Aurora is a self-employed attorney practicing in Seattle, Washington. Aurora attended a legal convention that was held on an Alaskan cruise departing from and returning to Seattle, Washington. The cruise ship was a vessel registered in the United States. Aurora's associated expenses were:

Cost of cruise (not including meals)	$2,734
Total cost of meals while on the cruise	350
Cost of seminars while on the cruise	500
Total	$3,584

Required: Go to the IRS website (**www.irs.gov**) and locate Publication 463. Review the chapter on Travel. Write a letter to Aurora Browning stating the amount, if any, of travel expenses she can deduct related to the convention cruise. If she is allowed any travel expenses, make sure to include in your letter the substantiation requirements. (An example of a client letter is available at the website for this text located at **www.cengagebrain.com**.)

GROUP 4: COMPREHENSIVE PROBLEMS

1. Ken (age 31) and Amy (age 28) Booth have brought you the following information regarding their income, expenses, and withholding for the year. They are unsure which of these items must be used to calculate taxable income.

Income:	
Ken's salary (salesman)	$27,200
Amy's wages (part-time nurse)	18,200
Insurance reimbursement for repairs from an auto accident	500
Gift from Uncle George	2,000
Interest income from Lodge State Bank	640
Federal income taxes withheld:	
From Ken's salary	1,200
From Amy's wages	650

Amy owns and operates a computer bookstore named "The Disk Drive." The store is located at 2000 Park Ave, Bellview, ME 04104. During 2014, Amy had the following income and expenses:

Sales of books	$320,400
Expenses	
Store rental	15,000
Office expense	6,000
Advertising	14,000
City business license	1,000
Payroll	89,000
Payroll taxes	9,100
Utilities	8,000
Other	3,000
Inventory	
January 1	250,000
December 31	235,000
Purchases during the year	165,000

The previous year was Amy's first year of operating the bookstore. Amy and Ken elected to carry forward a $5,000 net operating loss from the first year of business into 2014. (Note: Net operating losses are reported on the "Other Income" line of Form 1040.)

This year, Amy loaned a friend $20,000 so that he could make an investment. Instead of making the investment, the friend lost all the money gambling and left for parts unknown. Amy has no hope of ever collecting on this bad debt.

Ken, who ordinarily never gambles, won $25,000 at a casino birthday party for one of his friends. This amount should be reported on the "Other Income" line of Form 1040.

The Booths support Ken's parents, Rod (Social Security number 124-80-9050) and Mary (Social Security number 489-37-6676) Booth, who live in their own home. Ken and Amy live at 2345 Park Ave, Bellview, ME 04104, and their Social Security numbers are 343-75-3456 (Ken) and 123-45-7890 (Amy).

Required: Complete the Booths' federal income tax return for 2014. Use Form 1040, Schedule C, Schedule D, and Form 8949, on Pages 3-49 to 3-56, and any other appropriate schedule(s) you need to complete this tax return. A statement is required to be attached to a return for a nonbusiness bad debt, but this requirement may be ignored for this problem. Assume no 1099-B is filed in association with the bad debt when filling out Schedule D.

2A. Russell (age 50) and Linda (age 45) Long have brought you the following information regarding their income and expenses for the current year. Russell owns and operates a landscaping business called Lawns and Landscapes Unlimited. The business is operated out of their home, located at 1234 Katy Rd., Katy, TX 77493. Russell Long had the following income and expenses from the landscaping business:

Income	$132,400
Expenses:	
Business insurance	3,800
Office supplies	2,600
Payroll	83,000
Payroll taxes	8,100
Meals and entertainment	2,350

Contract labor	7,290
Maintenance	8,300
Equipment rent	12,300
Telephone	2,300
Business gifts (no gift over $22)	770
Special clothing and safety shoes	600
Subscription to *Green Lawns* magazine	120
Educational seminar on bug control	350
Other expenses	1,830

The business uses the cash method of accounting and has no accounts receivable or inventory held for resale.

In addition to the above expenses, the Longs have set aside one room of their house as a home office. The room is 150 square feet and their house has a total of 1,500 square feet. They pay $12,000 per year rental on their house, and the utilities amount to $3,000 for the year.

The Longs also have the following interest income for the year:

Interest from Morgan Bank bond portfolio	$42,520

The Longs have two dependent children, Bill (Social Security number 123-23-7654) and Martha (Social Security number 345-67-8654). Both Bill and Martha are full-time high school students, ages 17 and 18, respectively, so they do not qualify for the child credit. Russell's Social Security number is 664-98-5678 and Linda's is 554-98-3946. They made an estimated tax payment to the IRS of $4,500 on April 15, 2014.

Required: Complete the Longs' federal tax return for 2014. Use Form 1040, Schedule B, Schedule C, and Form 8829, on Pages 3-57 to 3-63, and any other appropriate schedule(s) to complete this tax return. Do not complete Form 4562 (depreciation). Make realistic assumptions about any missing data.

2B. Frederick (Freddy) Freeweights (age 42) owns and operates a health club called "Treadmills West." The business is located at 4321 Arnold Street, Alpine, CA 91901. Freddy had the following income and expenses from the health club:

Income	$214,900
Expenses:	
Business insurance	3,800
Office supplies	3,335
Payroll	97,200
Payroll taxes	9,180
Travel	2,420
Equipment & club maintenance	10,666
Cleaning service	8,500
Equipment rent	22,820
Telephone	2,780
Utilities (electric, water, gas)	13,975
Rent	30,000
Advertising	4,750
Special workout clothing and boxing gloves	750
Subscription to *Biceps Monthly* magazine	120
Educational seminar on weight training	775
Other expenses	1,830

The business uses the cash method of accounting and has no accounts receivable or inventory held for resale.

Freddy has the following interest income for the year:

Cuyamaça Bank savings account	$12,831
Morgan Bank bond portfolio interest	10,825

Freddy has been a widower for 10 years with a dependent son, Arnold (Social Security number 276-23-3954), and he files his tax return as head-of-household. Arnold is an 18-year-old high school student; he does not qualify for the child credit. They live next door to the health club at 4323 Arnold Street. Freddy does all the administrative work for the health club out of an office in his home. The room is 150 square feet and the house has a total of 1,800 square feet. Freddy pays $20,000 per year in rent and $4,000 in utilities.

Freddy's Social Security number is 565-12-6789. He made an estimated tax payment to the IRS of $1,000 on April 15, 2014.

Required: Complete Freddy's federal tax return for 2014. Use Form 1040, Schedule B, Schedule C, and Form 8829, on Pages 3-57 to 3-63, and any other appropriate schedule(s) to complete this tax return. Do not complete Form 4562 (depreciation). Make realistic assumptions about any missing data.

GROUP 5: CUMULATIVE SOFTWARE PROBLEM

The following additional information is available for the Dr. Ivan and Irene Incisor family from Chapters 1 and 2.

On September 1, Irene opened a retail store that specializes in sports car accessories. The name of the store is "Plus Two Cones." The store is located at 617 Main Street, Spokane, WA. The store uses the cash method of accounting. Her income and expenses for the year are as follows:

Sales of merchandise	$62,300
Inventory, September 1 (purchased in August)	62,500
Inventory, December 31	58,700
Purchases during the year	35,300
Sales returns and allowances	525
Store rental	7,500
Office expense	1,400
Insurance	1,000
Advertising	3,000
Employee wages	3,350
Payroll and other business taxes	505
Interest on bank loan to open store	2,740
Accounting fees	300
Utilities	1,000
Telephone	800
Maintenance	480
Miscellaneous	175

In addition to the above items, Irene incurred travel expenses to attend a seminar on sports car accessories. She spent $300 on airfare, $400 on lodging, $100 on a rental car, and $150 on meals. Irene has proper receipts for these amounts.

Irene drove her 2005 Ford Explorer 1,459 miles for business related to Plus Two Cones. The Explorer was driven a total of 17,000 miles for the year. Included in the total 17,000 miles is 5,000 miles spent commuting to the store. Irene has the required substantiation for this business mileage. She uses the standard mileage method.

In July, Ivan loaned a friend $7,000 so he could buy a car. Ivan's friend lost his job in 2014 and stopped making payments on the loan. He plans to start making payments again, however, with additional interest as soon as he has new employment.

Required: Combine this new information about the Incisor family with the information from Chapters 1 and 2 and complete a revised 2014 tax return for Ivan and Irene. Be sure to save your data input files since this case will be expanded with more tax information in later chapters.

Form **1040** Department of the Treasury—Internal Revenue Service (99)
U.S. Individual Income Tax Return **2014** OMB No. 1545-0074 IRS Use Only—Do not write or staple in this space.

For the year Jan. 1–Dec. 31, 2014, or other tax year beginning , 2014, ending , 20 See separate instructions.

Your first name and initial	Last name	**Your social security number**
If a joint return, spouse's first name and initial	Last name	**Spouse's social security number**
Home address (number and street). If you have a P.O. box, see instructions.	Apt. no.	▲ Make sure the SSN(s) above and on line 6c are correct.
City, town or post office, state, and ZIP code. If you have a foreign address, also complete spaces below (see instructions).		**Presidential Election Campaign** Check here if you, or your spouse if filing jointly, want $3 to go to this fund. Checking a box below will not change your tax or refund. ☐ You ☐ Spouse
Foreign country name	Foreign province/state/county / Foreign postal code	

Filing Status

Check only one box.

1 ☐ Single
2 ☐ Married filing jointly (even if only one had income)
3 ☐ Married filing separately. Enter spouse's SSN above and full name here. ▶
4 ☐ Head of household (with qualifying person). (See instructions.) If the qualifying person is a child but not your dependent, enter this child's name here. ▶
5 ☐ Qualifying widow(er) with dependent child

Exemptions

6a ☐ **Yourself.** If someone can claim you as a dependent, **do not** check box 6a
b ☐ **Spouse**
c **Dependents:**

(1) First name Last name	(2) Dependent's social security number	(3) Dependent's relationship to you	(4) ✓ if child under age 17 qualifying for child tax credit (see instructions)
			☐
			☐
			☐
			☐

If more than four dependents, see instructions and check here ▶ ☐

d Total number of exemptions claimed

Boxes checked on 6a and 6b
No. of children on 6c who:
• lived with you
• did not live with you due to divorce or separation (see instructions)
Dependents on 6c not entered above
Add numbers on lines above ▶

Income

Attach Form(s) W-2 here. Also attach Forms W-2G and 1099-R if tax was withheld.

If you did not get a W-2, see instructions.

Line	Description		
7	Wages, salaries, tips, etc. Attach Form(s) W-2		7
8a	**Taxable** interest. Attach Schedule B if required		8a
b	**Tax-exempt** interest. **Do not** include on line 8a	8b	
9a	Ordinary dividends. Attach Schedule B if required		9a
b	Qualified dividends	9b	
10	Taxable refunds, credits, or offsets of state and local income taxes		10
11	Alimony received		11
12	Business income or (loss). Attach Schedule C or C-EZ		12
13	Capital gain or (loss). Attach Schedule D if required. If not required, check here ▶ ☐		13
14	Other gains or (losses). Attach Form 4797		14
15a	IRA distributions 15a	b Taxable amount	15b
16a	Pensions and annuities 16a	b Taxable amount	16b
17	Rental real estate, royalties, partnerships, S corporations, trusts, etc. Attach Schedule E		17
18	Farm income or (loss). Attach Schedule F		18
19	Unemployment compensation		19
20a	Social security benefits 20a	b Taxable amount	20b
21	Other income. List type and amount		21
22	Combine the amounts in the far right column for lines 7 through 21. This is your **total income** ▶		22

Adjusted Gross Income

Line	Description		
23	Reserved	23	
24	Certain business expenses of reservists, performing artists, and fee-basis government officials. Attach Form 2106 or 2106-EZ	24	
25	Health savings account deduction. Attach Form 8889	25	
26	Moving expenses. Attach Form 3903	26	
27	Deductible part of self-employment tax. Attach Schedule SE	27	
28	Self-employed SEP, SIMPLE, and qualified plans	28	
29	Self-employed health insurance deduction	29	
30	Penalty on early withdrawal of savings	30	
31a	Alimony paid b Recipient's SSN ▶	31a	
32	IRA deduction	32	
33	Student loan interest deduction	33	
34	Reserved	34	
35	Domestic production activities deduction. Attach Form 8903	35	
36	Add lines 23 through 35		36
37	Subtract line 36 from line 22. This is your **adjusted gross income** ▶		37

DRAFT AS OF August 28, 201 DO NOT FILE

For Disclosure, Privacy Act, and Paperwork Reduction Act Notice, see separate instructions. Cat. No. 11320B Form **1040** (2014)

Form 1040 (2014) Page **2**

DRAFT AS OF August 28, 2014 DO NOT FILE

Tax and Credits

Standard Deduction for—
- People who check any box on line 39a or 39b **or** who can be claimed as a dependent, see instructions.
- All others:

Single or Married filing separately, $6,200

Married filing jointly or Qualifying widow(er), $12,400

Head of household, $9,100

38	Amount from line 37 (adjusted gross income)	38
39a	Check if: ☐ **You** were born before January 2, 1950, ☐ Blind. ☐ **Spouse** was born before January 2, 1950, ☐ Blind. **Total boxes checked ▶ 39a**	
b	If your spouse itemizes on a separate return or you were a dual-status alien, check here ▶ 39b ☐	
40	**Itemized deductions** (from Schedule A) **or** your **standard deduction** (see left margin)	40
41	Subtract line 40 from line 38	41
42	**Exemptions.** If line 38 is $152,525 or less, multiply $3,950 by the number on line 6d. Otherwise, see instructions	42
43	**Taxable income.** Subtract line 42 from line 41. If line 42 is more than line 41, enter -0-	43
44	**Tax** (see instructions). Check if any from: **a** ☐ Form(s) 8814 **b** ☐ Form 4972 **c** ☐	44
45	**Alternative minimum tax** (see instructions). Attach Form 6251	45
46	Excess advance premium tax credit repayment. Attach Form 8962	46
47	Add lines 44, 45, and 46 ▶	47
48	Foreign tax credit. Attach Form 1116 if required — 48	
49	Credit for child and dependent care expenses. Attach Form 2441 — 49	
50	Education credits from Form 8863, line 19 — 50	
51	Retirement savings contributions credit. Attach Form 8880 — 51	
52	Child tax credit. Attach Schedule 8812, if required — 52	
53	Residential energy credit. Attach Form 5695 — 53	
54	Other credits from Form: **a** ☐ 3800 **b** ☐ 8801 **c** ☐ — 54	
55	Add lines 48 through 54. These are your **total credits**	55
56	Subtract line 55 from line 47. If line 55 is more than line 47, enter -0- ▶	56

Other Taxes

57	Self-employment tax. Attach Schedule SE	57
58	Unreported social security and Medicare tax from Form: **a** ☐ 4137 **b** ☐ 8919	58
59	Additional tax on IRAs, other qualified retirement plans, etc. Attach Form 5329 if required	59
60a	Household employment taxes from Schedule H	60a
b	First-time homebuyer credit repayment. Attach Form 5405 if required	60b
61	Health care: individual responsibility (see instructions) Full-year coverage ☐	61
62	Taxes from: **a** ☐ Form 8959 **b** ☐ Form 8960 **c** ☐ Instructions; enter code(s)	62
63	Add lines 56 through 62. This is your **total tax** ▶	63

Payments

If you have a qualifying child, attach Schedule EIC.

64	Federal income tax withheld from Forms W-2 and 1099 — 64	
65	2014 estimated tax payments and amount applied from 2013 return — 65	
66a	**Earned income credit (EIC)** — 66a	
b	Nontaxable combat pay election — 66b	
67	Additional child tax credit. Attach Schedule 8812 — 67	
68	American opportunity credit from Form 8863, line 8 — 68	
69	Net premium tax credit. Attach Form 8962 — 69	
70	Amount paid with request for extension to file — 70	
71	Excess social security and tier 1 RRTA tax withheld — 71	
72	Credit for federal tax on fuels. Attach Form 4136 — 72	
73	Credits from Form: **a** ☐ 2439 **b** ☐ Reserved **c** ☐ Reserved **d** ☐ — 73	
74	Add lines 64, 65, 66a, and 67 through 73. These are your **total payments** ▶	74

Refund

Direct deposit? See instructions.

75	If line 74 is more than line 63, subtract line 63 from line 74. This is the amount you **overpaid**	75
76a	Amount of line 75 you want **refunded to you.** If Form 8888 is attached, check here ▶ ☐	76a
▶ b	Routing number ▶ **c** Type: ☐ Checking ☐ Savings	
▶ d	Account number	
77	Amount of line 75 you want **applied to your 2015 estimated tax** ▶ 77	

Amount You Owe

78	**Amount you owe.** Subtract line 74 from line 63. For details on how to pay, see instructions ▶	78
79	Estimated tax penalty (see instructions) — 79	

Third Party Designee

Do you want to allow another person to discuss this return with the IRS (see instructions)? ☐ **Yes.** Complete below. ☐ **No**

Designee's name ▶ Phone no. ▶ Personal identification number (PIN) ▶

Sign Here

Joint return? See instructions. Keep a copy for your records.

Under penalties of perjury, I declare that I have examined this return and accompanying schedules and statements, and to the best of my knowledge and belief, they are true, correct, and complete. Declaration of preparer (other than taxpayer) is based on all information of which preparer has any knowledge.

Your signature	Date	Your occupation	Daytime phone number
Spouse's signature. If a joint return, **both** must sign.	Date	Spouse's occupation	If the IRS sent you an Identity Protection PIN, enter it here (see inst.)

Paid Preparer Use Only

Print/Type preparer's name	Preparer's signature	Date	Check ☐ if self-employed	PTIN
Firm's name ▶			Firm's EIN ▶	
Firm's address ▶			Phone no.	

www.irs.gov/form1040 Form **1040** (2014)

SCHEDULE C (Form 1040)

Department of the Treasury Internal Revenue Service (99)

Profit or Loss From Business
(Sole Proprietorship)

► Information about Schedule C and its separate instructions is at *www.irs.gov/schedulec*.
► Attach to Form 1040, 1040NR, or 1041; partnerships generally must file Form 1065.

OMB No. 1545-0074
2014
Attachment Sequence No. 09

DRAFT AS OF June 19, 2014 DO NOT FILE

Name of proprietor | **Social security number (SSN)**

A Principal business or profession, including product or service (see instructions) | **B Enter code from instructions** ►

C Business name. If no separate business name, leave blank. | **D Employer ID number (EIN),** (see instr.)

E Business address (including suite or room no.) ►
City, town or post office, state, and ZIP code

F Accounting method: **(1)** ☐ Cash **(2)** ☐ Accrual **(3)** ☐ Other (specify) ►

G Did you "materially participate" in the operation of this business during 2014? If "No," see instructions for limit on losses . ☐ **Yes** ☐ **No**

H If you started or acquired this business during 2014, check here . . . . . . ► ☐

I Did you make any payments in 2014 that would require you to file Form(s) 1099? (see instructions) . . . ☐ **Yes** ☐ **No**

J If "Yes," did you or will you file required Forms 1099? . . . . . ☐ **Yes** ☐ **No**

Part I Income

1	Gross receipts or sales. See instructions for line 1 and check the box if this income was reported to you on Form W-2 and the "Statutory employee" box on that form was checked . . . ► ☐	1	
2	Returns and allowances . . .	2	
3	Subtract line 2 from line 1 . . .	3	
4	Cost of goods sold (from line 42) . . .	4	
5	**Gross profit.** Subtract line 4 from line 3 . . .	5	
6	Other income, including federal and state gasoline or fuel tax credit or refund (see instructions)	6	
7	**Gross income.** Add lines 5 and 6 . . . ►	7	

Part II Expenses. Enter expenses for business use of your home **only** on line 30.

8	Advertising	8		18	Office expense (see instructions)	18	
9	Car and truck expenses (see instructions)	9		19	Pension and profit-sharing plans .	19	
				20	Rent or lease (see instructions):		
10	Commissions and fees .	10		a	Vehicles, machinery, and equipment	20a	
11	Contract labor (see instructions)	11		b	Other business property . . .	20b	
12	Depletion	12		21	Repairs and maintenance . . .	21	
13	Depreciation and section 179 expense deduction (not included in Part III) (see instructions)	13		22	Supplies (not included in Part III) .	22	
				23	Taxes and licenses	23	
				24	Travel, meals, and entertainment:		
14	Employee benefit programs (other than on line 19) . .	14		a	Travel	24a	
15	Insurance (other than health)	15		b	Deductible meals and entertainment (see instructions) .	24b	
16	Interest:			25	Utilities	25	
a	Mortgage (paid to banks, etc.)	16a		26	Wages (less employment credits) .	26	
b	Other	16b		27a	Other expenses (from line 48) . .	27a	
17	Legal and professional services	17		b	**Reserved for future use** . . .	27b	

28	**Total expenses** before expenses for business use of home. Add lines 8 through 27a . . . . ►	28	
29	Tentative profit or (loss). Subtract line 28 from line 7 . . .	29	
30	Expenses for business use of your home. Do not report these expenses elsewhere. Attach Form 8829 unless using the simplified method (see instructions). **Simplified method filers only:** enter the total square footage of: (a) your home: ______ and (b) the part of your home used for business: ______ . Use the Simplified Method Worksheet in the instructions to figure the amount to enter on line 30	30	
31	**Net profit or (loss).** Subtract line 30 from line 29. • If a profit, enter on both **Form 1040, line 12** (or **Form 1040NR, line 13**) and on **Schedule SE, line 2.** (If you checked the box on line 1, see instructions). Estates and trusts, enter on **Form 1041, line 3.** • If a loss, you **must** go to line 32.	31	

32 If you have a loss, check the box that describes your investment in this activity (see instructions).
- If you checked 32a, enter the loss on both **Form 1040, line 12,** (or **Form 1040NR, line 13**) and on **Schedule SE, line 2.** (If you checked the box on line 1, see the line 31 instructions). Estates and trusts, enter on **Form 1041, line 3.**
- If you checked 32b, you **must** attach **Form 6198.** Your loss may be limited.

32a ☐ All investment is at risk.
32b ☐ Some investment is not at risk.

Schedule C (Form 1040) 2014 Page **2**

Part III Cost of Goods Sold (see instructions)

33 Method(s) used to value closing inventory: **a** ☑ Cost **b** ☐ Lower of cost or market **c** ☐ Other (attach explanation)

34 Was there any change in determining quantities, costs, or valuations between opening and closing inventory? If "Yes," attach explanation . . . ☐ **Yes** ☑ **No**

35	Inventory at beginning of year. If different from last year's closing inventory, attach explanation	35	65,000
36	Purchases less cost of items withdrawn for personal use	36	585,000
37	Cost of labor. Do not include any amounts paid to yourself	37	
38	Materials and supplies	38	
39	Other costs	39	
40	Add lines 35 through 39	40	650,000
41	Inventory at end of year	41	75,000
42	**Cost of goods sold.** Subtract line 41 from line 40. Enter the result here and on line 4	42	575,000

DRAFT AS OF June 19, 2014 DO NOT FILE

Part IV Information on Your Vehicle.

Complete this part **only** if you are claiming car or truck expenses on line 9 and are not required to file Form 4562 for this business. See the instructions for line 13 to find out if you must file Form 4562.

43 When did you place your vehicle in service for business purposes? (month, day, year) ► / /

44 Of the total number of miles you drove your vehicle during 2014, enter the number of miles you used your vehicle for:

a Business ______ **b** Commuting (see instructions) ______ **c** Other ______

45 Was your vehicle available for personal use during off-duty hours? . . . ☐ **Yes** ☐ **No**

46 Do you (or your spouse) have another vehicle available for personal use? . . . ☐ **Yes** ☐ **No**

47a Do you have evidence to support your deduction? . . . ☐ **Yes** ☐ **No**

b If "Yes," is the evidence written? . . . ☐ **Yes** ☐ **No**

Part V Other Expenses.

List below business expenses not included on lines 8–26 or line 30.

48 **Total other expenses.** Enter here and on line 27a	48	

Schedule C (Form 1040) 2014

SCHEDULE D (Form 1040) Department of the Treasury Internal Revenue Service (99)	**Capital Gains and Losses** ▶ Attach to Form 1040 or Form 1040NR. ▶ Information about Schedule D and its separate instructions is at *www.irs.gov/scheduled*. ▶ Use Form 8949 to list your transactions for lines 1b, 2, 3, 8b, 9, and 10.	OMB No. 1545-0074 2014 Attachment Sequence No. 12

Name(s) shown on return	Your social security number

DRAFT AS OF June 9, 2014 DO NOT FILE

Part I Short-Term Capital Gains and Losses—Assets Held One Year or Less

See instructions for how to figure the amounts to enter on the lines below. This form may be easier to complete if you round off cents to whole dollars.	(d) Proceeds (sales price)	(e) Cost (or other basis)	(g) Adjustments to gain or loss from Form(s) 8949, Part I, line 2, column (g)	(h) Gain or (loss) Subtract column (e) from column (d) and combine the result with column (g)
1a Totals for all short-term transactions reported on Form 1099-B for which basis was reported to the IRS and for which you have no adjustments (see instructions). However, if you choose to report all these transactions on Form 8949, leave this line blank and go to line 1b				
1b Totals for all transactions reported on Form(s) 8949 with **Box A** checked				
2 Totals for all transactions reported on Form(s) 8949 with **Box B** checked				
3 Totals for all transactions reported on Form(s) 8949 with **Box C** checked				

4 Short-term gain from Form 6252 and short-term gain or (loss) from Forms 4684, 6781, and 8824	4	
5 Net short-term gain or (loss) from partnerships, S corporations, estates, and trusts from Schedule(s) K-1	5	
6 Short-term capital loss carryover. Enter the amount, if any, from line 8 of your **Capital Loss Carryover Worksheet** in the instructions	6	( )
7 **Net short-term capital gain or (loss).** Combine lines 1a through 6 in column (h). If you have any long-term capital gains or losses, go to Part II below. Otherwise, go to Part III on the back	7	

Part II Long-Term Capital Gains and Losses—Assets Held More Than One Year

See instructions for how to figure the amounts to enter on the lines below. This form may be easier to complete if you round off cents to whole dollars.	(d) Proceeds (sales price)	(e) Cost (or other basis)	(g) Adjustments to gain or loss from Form(s) 8949, Part II, line 2, column (g)	(h) Gain or (loss) Subtract column (e) from column (d) and combine the result with column (g)
8a Totals for all long-term transactions reported on Form 1099-B for which basis was reported to the IRS and for which you have no adjustments (see instructions). However, if you choose to report all these transactions on Form 8949, leave this line blank and go to line 8b				
8b Totals for all transactions reported on Form(s) 8949 with **Box D** checked				
9 Totals for all transactions reported on Form(s) 8949 with **Box E** checked				
10 Totals for all transactions reported on Form(s) 8949 with **Box F** checked				

11 Gain from Form 4797, Part I; long-term gain from Forms 2439 and 6252; and long-term gain or (loss) from Forms 4684, 6781, and 8824	11	
12 Net long-term gain or (loss) from partnerships, S corporations, estates, and trusts from Schedule(s) K-1	12	
13 Capital gain distributions. See the instructions	13	
14 Long-term capital loss carryover. Enter the amount, if any, from line 13 of your **Capital Loss Carryover Worksheet** in the instructions	14	( )
15 **Net long-term capital gain or (loss).** Combine lines 8a through 14 in column (h). Then go to Part III on the back	15	

Schedule D (Form 1040) 2014 — Page **2**

DRAFT AS OF June 9, 2014 DO NOT FILE

Part III Summary

16 Combine lines 7 and 15 and enter the result . . . . | 16 |

- If line 16 is a **gain,** enter the amount from line 16 on Form 1040, line 13, or Form 1040NR, line 14. Then go to line 17 below.
- If line 16 is a **loss,** skip lines 17 through 20 below. Then go to line 21. Also be sure to complete line 22.
- If line 16 is **zero,** skip lines 17 through 21 below and enter -0- on Form 1040, line 13, or Form 1040NR, line 14. Then go to line 22.

17 Are lines 15 and 16 **both** gains?

☐ **Yes.** Go to line 18.

☐ **No.** Skip lines 18 through 21, and go to line 22.

18 Enter the amount, if any, from line 7 of the **28% Rate Gain Worksheet** in the instructions . . ▶ | 18 |

19 Enter the amount, if any, from line 18 of the **Unrecaptured Section 1250 Gain Worksheet** in the instructions . . . . ▶ | 19 |

20 Are lines 18 and 19 **both** zero or blank?

☐ **Yes.** Complete the **Qualified Dividends and Capital Gain Tax Worksheet** in the instructions for Form 1040, line 44 (or in the instructions for Form 1040NR, line 42). **Do not** complete lines 21 and 22 below.

☐ **No.** Complete the **Schedule D Tax Worksheet** in the instructions. **Do not** complete lines 21 and 22 below.

21 If line 16 is a loss, enter here and on Form 1040, line 13, or Form 1040NR, line 14, the **smaller** of:

- The loss on line 16 or
- ($3,000), or if married filing separately, ($1,500)

} . . . . | 21 | ( ) |

Note. When figuring which amount is smaller, treat both amounts as positive numbers.

22 Do you have qualified dividends on Form 1040, line 9b, or Form 1040NR, line 10b?

☐ **Yes.** Complete the **Qualified Dividends and Capital Gain Tax Worksheet** in the instructions for Form 1040, line 44 (or in the instructions for Form 1040NR, line 42).

☐ **No.** Complete the rest of Form 1040 or Form 1040NR.

Form **8949** Department of the Treasury Internal Revenue Service

Sales and Other Dispositions of Capital Assets

▶ **Information about Form 8949 and its separate instructions is at** ***www.irs.gov/form8949.***

▶ **File with your Schedule D to list your transactions for lines 1b, 2, 3, 8b, 9, and 10 of Schedule D.**

OMB No. 1545-0123

2014

Attachment Sequence No. **12A**

Name(s) shown on return	**Social security number or taxpayer identification number**

Before you check Box A, B, or C below, see whether you received any Form(s) 1099-B or substitute statement(s) from your broker. A substitute statement will have the same information as Form 1099-B. Either may show your basis (usually your cost) even if your broker did not report it to the IRS. Brokers must report basis to the IRS for most stock you bought in 2011 or later (and for certain debt instruments you bought in 2014 or later).

DRAFT AS OF June 12, 2014 DO NOT FILE

Part I **Short-Term.** Transactions involving capital assets you held 1 year or less are short term. For long-term transactions, see page 2.

Note. You may aggregate all short-term transactions reported on Form(s) 1099-B showing basis was reported to the IRS and for which no adjustments or codes are required. Enter the total directly on Schedule D, line 1a; you are not required to report these transactions on Form 8949 (see instructions).

You *must* check Box A, B, *or* C below. Check only one box. If more than one box applies for your short-term transactions, complete a separate Form 8949, page 1, for each applicable box. If you have more short-term transactions than will fit on this page for one or more of the boxes, complete as many forms with the same box checked as you need.

☐ **(A)** Short-term transactions reported on Form(s) 1099-B showing basis was reported to the IRS (see **Note** above)

☐ **(B)** Short-term transactions reported on Form(s) 1099-B showing basis was **not** reported to the IRS

☐ **(C)** Short-term transactions not reported to you on Form 1099-B

1 (a) Description of property (Example: 100 sh. XYZ Co.)	(b) Date acquired (Mo., day, yr.)	(c) Date sold or disposed (Mo., day, yr.)	(d) Proceeds (sales price) (see instructions)	(e) Cost or other basis. See the **Note** below and see *Column (e)* in the separate instructions	**Adjustment, if any, to gain or loss.** If you enter an amount in column (g), enter a code in column (f). **See the separate instructions.** (f) Code(s) from instructions	(g) Amount of adjustment	(h) **Gain or (loss).** Subtract column (e) from column (d) and combine the result with column (g)
2 Totals. Add the amounts in columns (d), (e), (g), and (h) (subtract negative amounts). Enter each total here and include on your Schedule D, **line 1b** (if **Box A** above is checked), **line 2** (if **Box B** above is checked), or **line 3** (if **Box C** above is checked) ▶							

Note. If you checked Box A above but the basis reported to the IRS was incorrect, enter in column (e) the basis as reported to the IRS, and enter an adjustment in column (g) to correct the basis. See *Column (g)* in the separate instructions for how to figure the amount of the adjustment.

For Paperwork Reduction Act Notice, see instructions. Cat. No. 37768Z Form **8949** (2014)

Form 8949 (2014) Attachment Sequence No. **12A** Page **2**

Name(s) shown on return. Name and SSN or taxpayer identification no. not required if shown on other side	**Social security number or taxpayer identification number**

Before you check Box D, E, or F below, see whether you received any Form(s) 1099-B or substitute statement(s) from your broker. A substitute statement will have the same information as Form 1099-B. Either may show your basis (usually your cost) even if your broker did not report it to the IRS. Brokers must report basis to the IRS for most stock you bought in 2011 or later (and for certain debt instruments you bought in 2014 or later).

Part II **Long-Term.** Transactions involving capital assets you held more than 1 year are long term. For short-term transactions, see page 1.

Note. You may aggregate all long-term transactions reported on Form(s) 1099-B showing basis was reported to the IRS and for which no adjustments or codes are required. Enter the total directly on Schedule D, line 8a; you are not required to report these transactions on Form 8949 (see instructions).

DRAFT AS OF June 12, 2014 DO NOT FILE

You *must* check Box D, E, *or* F below. Check only one box. If more than one box applies for your long-term transactions, complete a separate Form 8949, page 2, for each applicable box. If you have more long-term transactions than will fit on this page for one or more of the boxes, complete as many forms with the same box checked as you need.

☐ **(D)** Long-term transactions reported on Form(s) 1099-B showing basis was reported to the IRS (see **Note** above)
☐ **(E)** Long-term transactions reported on Form(s) 1099-B showing basis was **not** reported to the IRS
☐ **(F)** Long-term transactions not reported to you on Form 1099-B

1 (a) Description of property (Example: 100 sh. XYZ Co.)	(b) Date acquired (Mo., day, yr.)	(c) Date sold or disposed (Mo., day, yr.)	(d) Proceeds (sales price) (see instructions)	(e) Cost or other basis. See the **Note** below and see *Column (e)* in the separate instructions	**Adjustment, if any, to gain or loss.** If you enter an amount in column (g), enter a code in column (f). **See the separate instructions.**		(h) **Gain or (loss).** Subtract column (e) from column (d) and combine the result with column (g)
					(f) Code(s) from instructions	(g) Amount of adjustment	
2 Totals. Add the amounts in columns (d), (e), (g), and (h) (subtract negative amounts). Enter each total here and include on your Schedule D, **line 8b** (if **Box D** above is checked), **line 9** (if **Box E** above is checked), or **line 10** (if **Box F** above is checked) ▶							

Note. If you checked Box D above but the basis reported to the IRS was incorrect, enter in column (e) the basis as reported to the IRS, and enter an adjustment in column (g) to correct the basis. See *Column (g)* in the separate instructions for how to figure the amount of the adjustment.

Form **8949** (2014)

Form **1040** Department of the Treasury—Internal Revenue Service (99)
U.S. Individual Income Tax Return **2014** OMB No. 1545-0074 IRS Use Only—Do not write or staple in this space.

For the year Jan. 1–Dec. 31, 2014, or other tax year beginning , 2014, ending , 20 See separate instructions.

Your first name and initial	Last name	**Your social security number**
If a joint return, spouse's first name and initial	Last name	**Spouse's social security number**
Home address (number and street). If you have a P.O. box, see instructions.	Apt. no.	▲ Make sure the SSN(s) above and on line 6c are correct.
City, town or post office, state, and ZIP code. If you have a foreign address, also complete spaces below (see instructions).		**Presidential Election Campaign** Check here if you, or your spouse if filing jointly, want $3 to go to this fund. Checking a box below will not change your tax or refund. ☐ You ☐ Spouse
Foreign country name	Foreign province/state/county	Foreign postal code

Filing Status

Check only one box.

1 ☐ Single
2 ☐ Married filing jointly (even if only one had income)
3 ☐ Married filing separately. Enter spouse's SSN above and full name here. ▶
4 ☐ Head of household (with qualifying person). (See instructions.) If the qualifying person is a child but not your dependent, enter this child's name here. ▶
5 ☐ Qualifying widow(er) with dependent child

Exemptions

6a ☐ **Yourself.** If someone can claim you as a dependent, **do not** check box 6a
b ☐ **Spouse**
} **Boxes checked on 6a and 6b**

c **Dependents:**

(1) First name Last name	(2) Dependent's social security number	(3) Dependent's relationship to you	(4) ✓ if child under age 17 qualifying for child tax credit (see instructions)
			☐
			☐
			☐
			☐

If more than four dependents, see instructions and check here ▶ ☐

No. of children on 6c who:
• **lived with you**
• **did not live with you due to divorce or separation (see instructions)**
Dependents on 6c not entered above

d Total number of exemptions claimed . . . **Add numbers on lines above** ▶

Income

Attach Form(s) W-2 here. Also attach Forms W-2G and 1099-R if tax was withheld.

If you did not get a W-2, see instructions.

Line	Description			Line	Amount
7	Wages, salaries, tips, etc. Attach Form(s) W-2			7	
8a	**Taxable** interest. Attach Schedule B if required			8a	
b	**Tax-exempt** interest. **Do not** include on line 8a	8b			
9a	Ordinary dividends. Attach Schedule B if required			9a	
b	Qualified dividends	9b			
10	Taxable refunds, credits, or offsets of state and local income taxes			10	
11	Alimony received			11	
12	Business income or (loss). Attach Schedule C or C-EZ			12	
13	Capital gain or (loss). Attach Schedule D if required. If not required, check here ▶ ☐			13	
14	Other gains or (losses). Attach Form 4797			14	
15a	IRA distributions	15a	b Taxable amount	15b	
16a	Pensions and annuities	16a	b Taxable amount	16b	
17	Rental real estate, royalties, partnerships, S corporations, trusts, etc. Attach Schedule E			17	
18	Farm income or (loss). Attach Schedule F			18	
19	Unemployment compensation			19	
20a	Social security benefits	20a	b Taxable amount	20b	
21	Other income. List type and amount			21	
22	Combine the amounts in the far right column for lines 7 through 21. This is your **total income** ▶			22	

DRAFT AS OF August 28, 20 DO NOT FILE

Adjusted Gross Income

Line	Description			Line	Amount
23	Reserved	23			
24	Certain business expenses of reservists, performing artists, and fee-basis government officials. Attach Form 2106 or 2106-EZ	24			
25	Health savings account deduction. Attach Form 8889	25			
26	Moving expenses. Attach Form 3903	26			
27	Deductible part of self-employment tax. Attach Schedule SE	27			
28	Self-employed SEP, SIMPLE, and qualified plans	28			
29	Self-employed health insurance deduction	29			
30	Penalty on early withdrawal of savings	30			
31a	Alimony paid b Recipient's SSN ▶	31a			
32	IRA deduction	32			
33	Student loan interest deduction	33			
34	Reserved	34			
35	Domestic production activities deduction. Attach Form 8903	35			
36	Add lines 23 through 35			36	
37	Subtract line 36 from line 22. This is your **adjusted gross income** ▶			37	

For Disclosure, Privacy Act, and Paperwork Reduction Act Notice, see separate instructions. Cat. No. 11320B Form **1040** (2014)

DRAFT AS OF August 28, 2014 DO NOT FILE

Form 1040 (2014) Page **2**

	Line	Description	Box
	38	Amount from line 37 (adjusted gross income)	38
Tax and Credits	39a	Check if: ☐ **You** were born before January 2, 1950, ☐ Blind. ☐ **Spouse** was born before January 2, 1950, ☐ Blind. } **Total boxes checked ▶ 39a** ☐	
	b	If your spouse itemizes on a separate return or you were a dual-status alien, check here ▶ 39b ☐	
	40	**Itemized deductions** (from Schedule A) **or** your **standard deduction** (see left margin)	40
	41	Subtract line 40 from line 38	41
	42	**Exemptions.** If line 38 is $152,525 or less, multiply $3,950 by the number on line 6d. Otherwise, see instructions	42
	43	**Taxable income.** Subtract line 42 from line 41. If line 42 is more than line 41, enter -0-	43
	44	**Tax** (see instructions). Check if any from: **a** ☐ Form(s) 8814 **b** ☐ Form 4972 **c** ☐	44
	45	**Alternative minimum tax** (see instructions). Attach Form 6251	45
	46	Excess advance premium tax credit repayment. Attach Form 8962	46
	47	Add lines 44, 45, and 46 ▶	47
	48	Foreign tax credit. Attach Form 1116 if required	48
	49	Credit for child and dependent care expenses. Attach Form 2441	49
	50	Education credits from Form 8863, line 19	50
	51	Retirement savings contributions credit. Attach Form 8880	51
	52	Child tax credit. Attach Schedule 8812, if required	52
	53	Residential energy credit. Attach Form 5695	53
	54	Other credits from Form: **a** ☐ 3800 **b** ☐ 8801 **c** ☐	54
	55	Add lines 48 through 54. These are your **total credits**	55
	56	Subtract line 55 from line 47. If line 55 is more than line 47, enter -0- ▶	56
Other Taxes	57	Self-employment tax. Attach Schedule SE	57
	58	Unreported social security and Medicare tax from Form: **a** ☐ 4137 **b** ☐ 8919	58
	59	Additional tax on IRAs, other qualified retirement plans, etc. Attach Form 5329 if required	59
	60a	Household employment taxes from Schedule H	60a
	b	First-time homebuyer credit repayment. Attach Form 5405 if required	60b
	61	Health care: individual responsibility (see instructions) Full-year coverage ☐	61
	62	Taxes from: **a** ☐ Form 8959 **b** ☐ Form 8960 **c** ☐ Instructions; enter code(s)	62
	63	Add lines 56 through 62. This is your **total tax** ▶	63
Payments	64	Federal income tax withheld from Forms W-2 and 1099	64
	65	2014 estimated tax payments and amount applied from 2013 return	65
	66a	**Earned income credit (EIC)**	66a
	b	Nontaxable combat pay election 66b	
	67	Additional child tax credit. Attach Schedule 8812	67
	68	American opportunity credit from Form 8863, line 8	68
	69	Net premium tax credit. Attach Form 8962	69
	70	Amount paid with request for extension to file	70
	71	Excess social security and tier 1 RRTA tax withheld	71
	72	Credit for federal tax on fuels. Attach Form 4136	72
	73	Credits from Form: **a** ☐ 2439 **b** ■ Reserved **c** ■ Reserved **d** ☐	73
	74	Add lines 64, 65, 66a, and 67 through 73. These are your **total payments** ▶	74
Refund	75	If line 74 is more than line 63, subtract line 63 from line 74. This is the amount you **overpaid**	75
	76a	Amount of line 75 you want **refunded to you.** If Form 8888 is attached, check here ▶ ☐	76a
	▶ b	Routing number ▶ **c** Type: ☐ Checking ☐ Savings	
	▶ d	Account number	
	77	Amount of line 75 you want **applied to your 2015 estimated tax** ▶	77
Amount You Owe	78	**Amount you owe.** Subtract line 74 from line 63. For details on how to pay, see instructions ▶	78
	79	Estimated tax penalty (see instructions)	79

Standard Deduction for—
- People who check any box on line 39a or 39b **or** who can be claimed as a dependent, see instructions.
- All others:

Single or Married filing separately, $6,200

Married filing jointly or Qualifying widow(er), $12,400

Head of household, $9,100

If you have a qualifying child, attach Schedule EIC.

Direct deposit? See instructions.

Third Party Designee

Do you want to allow another person to discuss this return with the IRS (see instructions)? ☐ **Yes.** Complete below. ☐ **No**

Designee's name ▶ Phone no. ▶ Personal identification number (PIN) ▶

Sign Here

Under penalties of perjury, I declare that I have examined this return and accompanying schedules and statements, and to the best of my knowledge and belief, they are true, correct, and complete. Declaration of preparer (other than taxpayer) is based on all information of which preparer has any knowledge.

Joint return? See instructions. Keep a copy for your records.

Your signature	Date	Your occupation	Daytime phone number
Spouse's signature. If a joint return, **both** must sign.	Date	Spouse's occupation	If the IRS sent you an Identity Protection PIN, enter it here (see inst.)

Paid Preparer Use Only

Print/Type preparer's name	Preparer's signature	Date	Check ☐ if self-employed	PTIN
Firm's name ▶			Firm's EIN ▶	
Firm's address ▶			Phone no.	

www.irs.gov/form1040 Form **1040** (2014)

SCHEDULE B
(Form 1040A or 1040)

Department of the Treasury
Internal Revenue Service (99)

Interest and Ordinary Dividends

► Attach to Form 1040A or 1040.
► Information about Schedule B and its instructions is at *www.irs.gov/scheduleb*.

OMB No. 1545-0074
2014
Attachment Sequence No. **08**

DRAFT AS OF June 18, 2014 DO NOT FILE

Name(s) shown on return | **Your social security number**

Part I Interest

(See instructions on back and the instructions for Form 1040A, or Form 1040, line 8a.)

Note. If you received a Form 1099-INT, Form 1099-OID, or substitute statement from a brokerage firm, list the firm's name as the payer and enter the total interest shown on that form.

			Amount
1	List name of payer. If any interest is from a seller-financed mortgage and the buyer used the property as a personal residence, see instructions on back and list this interest first. Also, show that buyer's social security number and address ►	1	
2	Add the amounts on line 1	2	
3	Excludable interest on series EE and I U.S. savings bonds issued after 1989. Attach Form 8815	3	
4	Subtract line 3 from line 2. Enter the result here and on Form 1040A, or Form 1040, line 8a ►	4	

Note. If line 4 is over $1,500, you must complete Part III.

Part II Ordinary Dividends

(See instructions on back and the instructions for Form 1040A, or Form 1040, line 9a.)

Note. If you received a Form 1099-DIV or substitute statement from a brokerage firm, list the firm's name as the payer and enter the ordinary dividends shown on that form.

			Amount
5	List name of payer ►	5	
6	Add the amounts on line 5. Enter the total here and on Form 1040A, or Form 1040, line 9a ►	6	

Note. If line 6 is over $1,500, you must complete Part III.

Part III Foreign Accounts and Trusts

(See instructions on back.)

You must complete this part if you **(a)** had over $1,500 of taxable interest or ordinary dividends; **(b)** had a foreign account; or **(c)** received a distribution from, or were a grantor of, or a transferor to, a foreign trust.

		Yes	No
7a	At any time during 2014, did you have a financial interest in or signature authority over a financial account (such as a bank account, securities account, or brokerage account) located in a foreign country? See instructions		
	If "Yes," are you required to file FinCEN Form 114, Report of Foreign Bank and Financial Accounts (FBAR), to report that financial interest or signature authority? See FinCEN Form 114 and its instructions for filing requirements and exceptions to those requirements		
b	If you are required to file FinCEN Form 114, enter the name of the foreign country where the financial account is located ►		
8	During 2014, did you receive a distribution from, or were you the grantor of, or transferor to, a foreign trust? If "Yes," you may have to file Form 3520. See instructions on back		

For Paperwork Reduction Act Notice, see your tax return instructions. Cat. No. 17146N **Schedule B (Form 1040A or 1040) 2014**

SCHEDULE C (Form 1040)

Department of the Treasury Internal Revenue Service (99)

Profit or Loss From Business
(Sole Proprietorship)

▶ **Information about Schedule C and its separate instructions is at *www.irs.gov/schedulec.***
▶ **Attach to Form 1040, 1040NR, or 1041; partnerships generally must file Form 1065.**

OMB No. 1545-0074
2014
Attachment Sequence No. 09

DRAFT AS OF June 19, 2014 DO NOT FILE

Name of proprietor | **Social security number (SSN)**

A Principal business or profession, including product or service (see instructions) | **B Enter code from instructions** ▶

C Business name. If no separate business name, leave blank. | **D Employer ID number (EIN),** (see instr.)

E Business address (including suite or room no.) ▶
City, town or post office, state, and ZIP code

F Accounting method: **(1)** ☐ Cash **(2)** ☐ Accrual **(3)** ☐ Other (specify) ▶

G Did you "materially participate" in the operation of this business during 2014? If "No," see instructions for limit on losses . ☐ Yes ☐ No

H If you started or acquired this business during 2014, check here . . . ▶ ☐

I Did you make any payments in 2014 that would require you to file Form(s) 1099? (see instructions) . ☐ Yes ☐ No

J If "Yes," did you or will you file required Forms 1099? . ☐ Yes ☐ No

Part I Income

1	Gross receipts or sales. See instructions for line 1 and check the box if this income was reported to you on Form W-2 and the "Statutory employee" box on that form was checked . . . ▶ ☐	1	
2	Returns and allowances	2	
3	Subtract line 2 from line 1	3	
4	Cost of goods sold (from line 42)	4	
5	**Gross profit.** Subtract line 4 from line 3	5	
6	Other income, including federal and state gasoline or fuel tax credit or refund (see instructions)	6	
7	**Gross income.** Add lines 5 and 6 . . . ▶	7	

Part II Expenses. Enter expenses for business use of your home only on line 30.

8	Advertising	8		18	Office expense (see instructions)	18	
9	Car and truck expenses (see instructions)	9		19	Pension and profit-sharing plans	19	
10	Commissions and fees	10		20	Rent or lease (see instructions):		
11	Contract labor (see instructions)	11		a	Vehicles, machinery, and equipment	20a	
12	Depletion	12		b	Other business property	20b	
13	Depreciation and section 179 expense deduction (not included in Part III) (see instructions)	13		21	Repairs and maintenance	21	
				22	Supplies (not included in Part III)	22	
				23	Taxes and licenses	23	
				24	Travel, meals, and entertainment:		
14	Employee benefit programs (other than on line 19)	14		a	Travel	24a	
15	Insurance (other than health)	15		b	Deductible meals and entertainment (see instructions)	24b	
16	Interest:			25	Utilities	25	
a	Mortgage (paid to banks, etc.)	16a		26	Wages (less employment credits)	26	
b	Other	16b		27a	Other expenses (from line 48)	27a	
17	Legal and professional services	17		b	**Reserved for future use**	27b	

28	**Total expenses** before expenses for business use of home. Add lines 8 through 27a . . . ▶	28	
29	Tentative profit or (loss). Subtract line 28 from line 7	29	
30	Expenses for business use of your home. Do not report these expenses elsewhere. Attach Form 8829 unless using the simplified method (see instructions). **Simplified method filers only:** enter the total square footage of: (a) your home: ______ and (b) the part of your home used for business: ______ . Use the Simplified Method Worksheet in the instructions to figure the amount to enter on line 30	30	
31	**Net profit or (loss).** Subtract line 30 from line 29. • If a profit, enter on both **Form 1040, line 12** (or **Form 1040NR, line 13**) and on **Schedule SE, line 2.** (If you checked the box on line 1, see instructions). Estates and trusts, enter on **Form 1041, line 3.** • If a loss, you **must** go to line 32.	31	

32 If you have a loss, check the box that describes your investment in this activity (see instructions).

- If you checked 32a, enter the loss on both **Form 1040, line 12,** (or **Form 1040NR, line 13**) and on **Schedule SE, line 2.** (If you checked the box on line 1, see the line 31 instructions). Estates and trusts, enter on **Form 1041, line 3.**
- If you checked 32b, you **must** attach **Form 6198.** Your loss may be limited.

32a ☐ All investment is at risk.
32b ☐ Some investment is not at risk.

For Paperwork Reduction Act Notice, see the separate instructions. Cat. No. 11334P **Schedule C (Form 1040) 2014**

Schedule C (Form 1040) 2014 Page **2**

Part III Cost of Goods Sold (see instructions)

DRAFT AS OF June 19, 2014 DO NOT FILE

33	Method(s) used to value closing inventory: **a** ☐ Cost **b** ☐ Lower of cost or market **c** ☐ Other (attach explanation)		
34	Was there any change in determining quantities, costs, or valuations between opening and closing inventory? If "Yes," attach explanation . . . ☐ **Yes** ☐ **No**		
35	Inventory at beginning of year. If different from last year's closing inventory, attach explanation . . .	35	
36	Purchases less cost of items withdrawn for personal use . . .	36	
37	Cost of labor. Do not include any amounts paid to yourself . . .	37	
38	Materials and supplies . . .	38	
39	Other costs . . .	39	
40	Add lines 35 through 39 . . .	40	
41	Inventory at end of year . . .	41	
42	**Cost of goods sold.** Subtract line 41 from line 40. Enter the result here and on line 4 . . .	42	

Part IV Information on Your Vehicle.

Complete this part **only** if you are claiming car or truck expenses on line 9 and are not required to file Form 4562 for this business. See the instructions for line 13 to find out if you must file Form 4562.

43 When did you place your vehicle in service for business purposes? (month, day, year) ► ____ / ____ / ____

44 Of the total number of miles you drove your vehicle during 2014, enter the number of miles you used your vehicle for:

a Business ____________ **b** Commuting (see instructions) ____________ **c** Other ____________

45 Was your vehicle available for personal use during off-duty hours? . . . ☐ **Yes** ☐ **No**

46 Do you (or your spouse) have another vehicle available for personal use?. . . ☐ **Yes** ☐ **No**

47a Do you have evidence to support your deduction? . . . ☐ **Yes** ☐ **No**

b If "Yes," is the evidence written? . . . ☐ **Yes** ☐ **No**

Part V Other Expenses.

List below business expenses not included on lines 8–26 or line 30.

48 **Total other expenses.** Enter here and on line 27a . . .	48	

Schedule C (Form 1040) 2014

Form **8829**

Department of the Treasury
Internal Revenue Service (99)

Expenses for Business Use of Your Home

▶ File only with Schedule C (Form 1040). Use a separate Form 8829 for each home you used for business during the year.

▶ Information about Form 8829 and its separate instructions is at *www.irs.gov/form8829.*

OMB No. 1545-0074

2014

Attachment Sequence No. 176

Name(s) of proprietor(s) | Your social security number

Part I Part of Your Home Used for Business

Line	Description				Box	Amount
1	Area used regularly and exclusively for business, regularly for daycare, or for storage of inventory or product samples (see instructions)				1	
2	Total area of home				2	
3	Divide line 1 by line 2. Enter the result as a percentage				3	%
	For daycare facilities not used exclusively for business, go to line 4. All others, go to line 7.					
4	Multiply days used for daycare during year by hours used per day	4	hr.			
5	Total hours available for use during the year (365 days x 24 hours) (see instructions)	5	8,760 hr.			
6	Divide line 4 by line 5. Enter the result as a decimal amount	6	.			
7	Business percentage. For daycare facilities not used exclusively for business, multiply line 6 by line 3 (enter the result as a percentage). All others, enter the amount from line 3 ▶				7	%

Part II Figure Your Allowable Deduction

Line	Description	Box	(a) Direct expenses	(b) Indirect expenses	Box	Amount
8	Enter the amount from Schedule C, line 29, **plus** any gain derived from the business use of your home, **minus** any loss from the trade or business not derived from the business use of your home (see instructions)				8	
	See instructions for columns (a) and (b) before completing lines 9–21.					
9	Casualty losses (see instructions)	9				
10	Deductible mortgage interest (see instructions)	10				
11	Real estate taxes (see instructions)	11				
12	Add lines 9, 10, and 11	12				
13	Multiply line 12, column (b) by line 7			13		
14	Add line 12, column (a) and line 13				14	
15	Subtract line 14 from line 8. If zero or less, enter -0-				15	
16	Excess mortgage interest (see instructions)	16				
17	Insurance	17				
18	Rent	18				
19	Repairs and maintenance	19				
20	Utilities	20				
21	Other expenses (see instructions)	21				
22	Add lines 16 through 21	22				
23	Multiply line 22, column (b) by line 7			23		
24	Carryover of prior year operating expenses (see instructions)			24		
25	Add line 22, column (a), line 23, and line 24				25	
26	Allowable operating expenses. Enter the **smaller** of line 15 or line 25				26	
27	Limit on excess casualty losses and depreciation. Subtract line 26 from line 15				27	
28	Excess casualty losses (see instructions)			28		
29	Depreciation of your home from line 41 below			29		
30	Carryover of prior year excess casualty losses and depreciation (see instructions)			30		
31	Add lines 28 through 30				31	
32	Allowable excess casualty losses and depreciation. Enter the **smaller** of line 27 or line 31				32	
33	Add lines 14, 26, and 32				33	
34	Casualty loss portion, if any, from lines 14 and 32. Carry amount to **Form 4684** (see instructions)				34	
35	**Allowable expenses for business use of your home.** Subtract line 34 from line 33. Enter here and on Schedule C, line 30. If your home was used for more than one business, see instructions ▶				35	

Part III Depreciation of Your Home

Line	Description	Box	Amount
36	Enter the **smaller** of your home's adjusted basis or its fair market value (see instructions)	36	
37	Value of land included on line 36	37	
38	Basis of building. Subtract line 37 from line 36	38	
39	Business basis of building. Multiply line 38 by line 7	39	
40	Depreciation percentage (see instructions)	40	%
41	Depreciation allowable (see instructions). Multiply line 39 by line 40. Enter here and on line 29 above	41	

Part IV Carryover of Unallowed Expenses to 2015

Line	Description	Box	Amount
42	Operating expenses. Subtract line 26 from line 25. If less than zero, enter -0-	42	
43	Excess casualty losses and depreciation. Subtract line 32 from line 31. If less than zero, enter -0-	43	

For Paperwork Reduction Act Notice, see your tax return instructions. Cat. No. 13232M Form **8829** (2014)

Student Name ______________________

Class/Section ______________________

Date ______________________

KEY NUMBER TAX RETURN SUMMARY

CHAPTER 3

Comprehensive Problem 1

Adjusted Gross Income (Line 37) ______________

Standard Deduction (Line 40) ______________

Taxable Income (Line 43) ______________

Tax Liability (Line 63) ______________

Comprehensive Problem 2A

Adjusted Gross Income (Line 37) ______________

Profit or (Loss) from Business, Schedule C (Line 31) ______________

Expenses for Business Use of Your Home, Form 8829 (Line 35) ______________

Tax Liability (Line 63) ______________

Tax Overpaid (Line 75) ______________

Comprehensive Problem 2B

Adjusted Gross Income (Line 37) ______________

Profit or (Loss) from Business, Schedule C (Line 31) ______________

Expenses for Business Use of Your Home, Form 8829 (Line 35) ______________

Tax Liability (Line 63) ______________

Tax Overpaid (Line 75) ______________

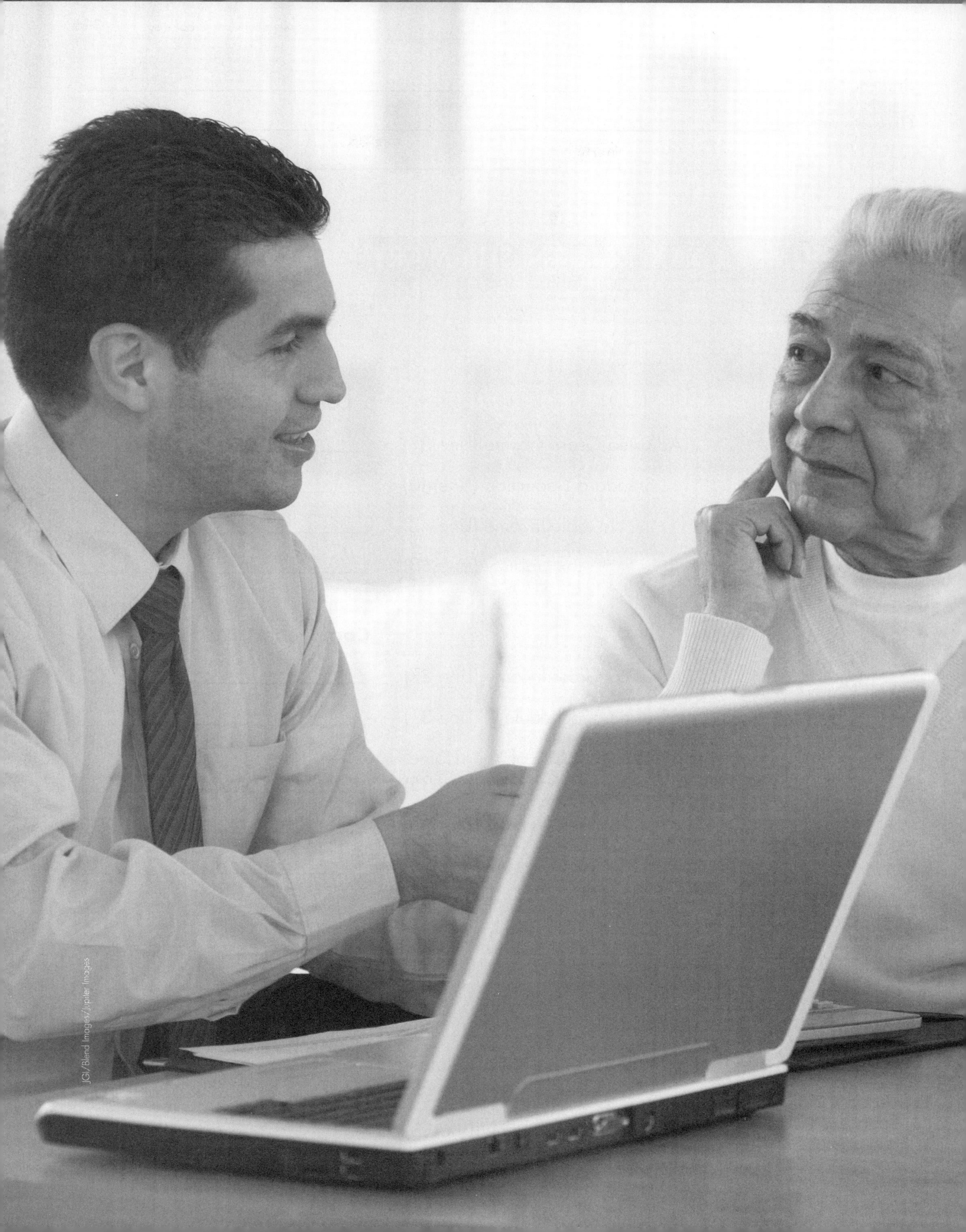

JGI/Blend Images/Jupiter Images

CHAPTER 4

Business Income and Expenses, Part II

LEARNING OBJECTIVES

After completing this chapter, you should be able to:

LO 4.1 Apply the tax rules for rental property and vacation homes.

LO 4.2 Explain the treatment of passive income and losses.

LO 4.3 Describe the self-employed health insurance deduction.

LO 4.4 Understand how Health Savings Accounts (HSAs) can be used for tax-advantaged medical care.

LO 4.5 Know the special rules applicable to moving expenses.

LO 4.6 Understand the treatment of Individual Retirement Accounts (IRAs), including Roth IRAs.

LO 4.7 Explain the general contribution rules for Keogh and Simplified Employee Pension (SEP) plans.

LO 4.8 Describe the general rules for qualified retirement plans and 401(k) plans.

LO 4.9 Explain the pension plan rollover rules.

OVERVIEW

Chapter 4 continues the discussion started in Chapter 3, covering additional important elements of income and expense which enter into the calculation of AGI. The first part of this chapter includes material on rental income and expenses, passive income and losses, self-employed health insurance, and Health Savings Accounts (HSAs). The second part of the chapter covers retirement plans and retirement plan deductions associated with business and wage income. The retirement plans covered include IRAs, Qualified and Section 401(k) plans, Keogh plans, and Simplified Employee Pension (SEP) plans. The business income and expenses included in this chapter are all part of the calculation of a taxpayer's adjusted gross income (AGI).

Learning Objective 4.1

Apply the tax rules for rental property and vacation homes.

RENTAL INCOME AND EXPENSES

The net income from rental property is taxable income to the taxpayer. In most cases, rental income is reported with the related expenses on Part I of Schedule E. If services are provided to the tenant beyond those customarily provided, such as cleaning and maid services, the income is reported on Schedule C and is subject to the self-employment tax. Expenditures deductible as rental expenses include real estate taxes, mortgage interest, insurance, commissions, repairs, and depreciation.

EXAMPLE June Sanchez owns a house that she rents for to a tenant $600 per month. The following are her expenses for the year:

Real estate taxes	$ 800
Mortgage interest	2,000
Insurance	200
Rent collection commissions	432
General repairs	350

June bought the property on July 1, 1999, and her original basis for depreciation of the house is $55,000. She uses straight-line depreciation with a 27.5 year life.

In 2014, June bought a new stove for the rental house that cost $500. The stove has a 5-year life, and 20 percent of the stove's cost is depreciated this year. June's net rental income for the year is calculated as follows:

Rental income ($600 × 12)		$ 7,200
Less expenses:		
Real estate taxes	$ 800	
Mortgage interest	2,000	
Insurance	200	
Commissions	432	
General repairs	350	
Depreciation:		
House ($55,000/27.5)	$2,000	
Stove ($500 × 20%)	100	
Total expenses		(5,882)
Net rental income		$ 1,318

Please note that depreciation is an advanced topic which will be covered in detail in Chapter 7. ♦

Vacation Homes

Many taxpayers own residences which they use personally as part-year residences and rent during the remainder of the year. Such part-year rental properties are often referred to as "vacation homes." The tax law limits the deduction of expenses associated with the rental of vacation homes.

EXAMPLE Jean owns a condo in Vail, Colorado. The condo is rented for 3 months during the year and is used by Jean for 1 month. If there were no vacation home limitations, Jean could deduct 11 months' worth of depreciation, maintenance, and other costs associated with the property. The resulting loss could then be deducted against Jean's other taxable income. ♦

To prevent taxpayers from claiming a deduction for expenses effectively personal in nature (associated with a personal residence), the tax law limits the deductions a taxpayer can claim for expenses associated with a vacation home. Deductions attributable to vacation homes used primarily as personal residences are limited to the income generated from the rental of the property. In general, only profit or breakeven (no loss) tax situations are allowed on the rental of vacation homes.

The expenses associated with the rental of a residence used for both personal and rental purposes are subject to three possible tax treatments. The tax treatment depends on the period of time the residence is used for personal versus rental purposes.

1. Primarily Personal Use

If a residence is rented for fewer than 15 days during the year, the rental period is disregarded and it is treated as a personal residence for tax purposes. The rental income is not taxable and the mortgage interest and real estate taxes may be allowed as itemized deductions. Other expenses, such as utilities and maintenance, are considered nondeductible personal expenses.

EXAMPLE Glenn owns a lake home. During the year he rented the home for $1,800 for 2 weeks, lived in the home for 3 months, and left the home vacant during the remainder of the year. The expenses for the lake home included $5,000 in mortgage interest, $700 in property taxes, $2,100 in utilities and maintenance, and $3,000 in depreciation. Since the lake home was rented for fewer than 15 days, Glenn would not report the $1,800 of income and would deduct only the interest and taxes as itemized deductions on Schedule A. The other expenses are nondeductible personal expenses. ♦

2. Primarily Rental Use

If the residence is rented for 15 days or more and is used for personal purposes for not more than *14 days or 10 percent of the days rented, whichever is greater*, the residence is treated as rental property. The expenses must then be allocated between the personal and rental days. If this is the case, the rental expenses may exceed the rental income, and the resulting loss would be deducted against other income, subject to the passive loss rules. (See LO 4.2 for further details.)

EXAMPLE Assume the same facts as in the preceding example except that the $1,800 rental fee is for 20 days and Glenn uses the lake home for only 10 days during the year. Since the lake home is now rented for 15 days or more and Glenn's use of the home is not more than 14 days (or 10 percent of the days rented, if greater), the property is treated partially as rental property and partially as a personal residence. Allocation of expenses associated with the home is based on the number of days of rental or personal use compared to

the total number of days of use. Glenn's personal use percentage is 33.33 percent (10 days/30 days) and the rental portion is 66.67 percent (20 days/30 days). For tax purposes, the rental income or loss is calculated as follows:

	Rental (66.67%)	Personal (33.33%)
Income	$ 1,800	$ 0
Interest and taxes	(3,800)	(1,900)
Utilities and maintenance	(1,400)	(700)
Depreciation	(2,000)	(1,000)
Rental Loss	($ 5,400)	$ 0

♦

3. Rental/Personal Use

If the residence is rented for 15 days or more and is used for personal purposes for more than *14 days or 10 percent of the days rented, whichever is greater*, allocable rental expenses are allowed only to the extent of rental income. Allocable rental expenses are deducted in three separate steps: first, the interest and taxes are deducted; second, utilities and maintenance expenses are deducted; and third, depreciation expense is deducted. For utilities, maintenance, and depreciation expenses to be deductible, there must be positive income following the deduction of items in the preceding step(s). In addition, the expenses, other than interest and taxes, are only deductible to the extent of that positive income. Expenses are allocated between the rental and personal days before the limits are applied. The IRS requires that the allocation be on the basis of the total days of rental use or personal use divided by the total days of use.

EXAMPLE Assume Glenn rents the lake home for $2,500 for 20 days and uses it for personal purposes for 60 days. Assume Glenn has the same operating expenses as in the previous examples. Since the lake home is rented for 15 days or more and Glenn uses the home for personal purposes for more than 14 days (or 10 percent of the days rented, if greater), the property is subject to the vacation home limitations. Glenn's personal use percentage is 75 percent (60 days/80 days) and the rental portion is 25 percent (20 days/80 days). The IRS requires that the rental income or loss be calculated as follows:

Gross rental income	$ 2,500
Less: interest and taxes (25%)	(1,425)
Balance	1,075
Less: utilities and maintenance (25%)	(525)
Balance	550
Less: depreciation (25%, limited to $550)	(550)
Net income	$ 0

The interest and taxes allocable to Glenn's personal use of the property in both examples are deductible as itemized deductions on Schedule A.

The personal portion of the utilities, maintenance, and depreciation is a nondeductible personal expense. ♦

It should be noted that the U.S. Tax Court has allowed taxpayers to use 365 days for the allocation of interest and taxes. Under the Tax Court rules, the interest and taxes allocable to the rental use of the property in the above example would be 5.5 percent (20/365) instead of 25 percent (20/80). The allocation of utilities and maintenance would remain unchanged, while a full $750 of depreciation (25% of $3,000) would be allowed and the remaining interest and taxes (345/365) would be included in itemized deductions. This controversy between the Tax Court decisions and the IRS has not been resolved.

TAX BREAK

Taxpayers may pay for their vacation with tax-free income by renting out their homes while they are away. If a home is rented fewer than 15 days a year, the rental income is tax-exempt. For example, a taxpayer with a home near the beach in San Diego could advertise a two-week winter rental, or a taxpayer with a home near a Super Bowl could advertise a short rental.

Self-Study Problem 4.1 *See Appendix E for Solutions to Self-Study Problems*

Janet Randolf lives in a duplex that she owns at 14 Randolf St., San Diego, CA 92111. Janet rents one-half of her duplex and lives in the other half. Her rental income for the year is $6,000. Janet's basis for depreciation in the rental portion is $15,000, and she uses straight-line depreciation with a 27.5 year useful life. On the whole duplex, real estate taxes are $1,200, interest on the mortgage is $3,400, utilities are $1,800, and insurance is $450. Use Part I of Schedule E on Page 4-7 to report Janet's income from rental of part of the duplex.

PASSIVE LOSS LIMITATIONS

Learning Objective 4.2

Explain the treatment of passive income and losses.

Because of past abuses primarily involving tax shelters and loss deductions from rental real estate, Congress enacted legislation limiting the deduction of certain "passive" losses from other taxable income. A passive activity is a trade or business in which the taxpayer does not materially participate and most rental real estate activity. Because the most common passive loss seen on tax returns is from ordinary real estate rental activities, many taxpayers with an investment in a real estate rental property are affected by these rules. In establishing the limitations, the tax law classifies individual income into three categories. These categories are (1) active income (e.g., wages, self-employment income, and salaries), (2) portfolio income (e.g., dividends and interest), and (3) passive income and losses (e.g., rental real estate income and loss and income and loss passed through from limited partnerships and other ventures in which the taxpayer has minimal or no involvement).

Generally, passive losses cannot be used to offset either active or portfolio income. Also, any tax credits derived from passive activities can only offset income taxes attributable to passive income. Any unused passive losses and credits are carried over and may be used to offset future passive income or taxes attributable to such income, respectively. Generally, losses remaining when the taxpayer disposes of his or her entire interest in the passive activity may be used in full; however, the taxpayer can only use remaining credits to offset the income tax arising from any gain recognized on the disposition of the activity.

EXAMPLE Mike's income items for 2014 are:

Salary	$40,000
Sales commissions	15,000
Dividends on Exxon stock	2,000
Rental income from real estate	5,000
Loss from limited partnership	(9,000)
Interest on savings account	4,000

Mike's active income for the year is $55,000 ($40,000 + $15,000), his portfolio income is $6,000 ($2,000 + $4,000), and his passive loss is $4,000 ($5,000 − $9,000). Mike must report gross income of $61,000 ($55,000 + $6,000), since the passive loss cannot be used to offset his active or portfolio income. The net passive loss of $4,000 will be carried over to 2015. ♦

Under the passive loss rules, real estate rental activities are specifically defined as passive, even if the taxpayer actively manages the property and even if the activity is not conducted as a partnership. Individual taxpayers, however, may deduct up to $25,000 of rental property losses against other income, if they are actively involved in the management of the property and their income does not exceed certain limits. The $25,000 loss deduction is phased out when the taxpayer's modified adjusted gross income (adjusted gross income before passive losses and Individual Retirement Account deductions) exceeds $100,000. The $25,000 is reduced by 50 cents for each $1.00 the taxpayer's modified adjusted gross income exceeds that amount. Therefore, no deduction is allowed when the taxpayer's modified adjusted gross income reaches $150,000. Special limitations apply to taxpayers filing as Married, Filing Separately and claiming a deduction for real estate rental losses under this special rule.

EXAMPLE Mary has modified AGI before passive losses of $120,000. In addition, she has a rental house which shows a loss of $18,000 for the year. She may deduct only $15,000 ($25,000 − 50% of $20,000) of the loss because of the phase-out of the $25,000 allowance for passive rental losses where modified AGI is over $100,000. ♦

Real Estate Rental as Trade or Business

Taxpayers heavily involved in real estate rental activities may qualify as having an active business rather than a passive activity. If so, the income and losses from qualified rental activities will no longer be subject to passive loss limitations. For a real estate rental to be considered active, the taxpayer must materially participate in the activity. An individual will satisfy this requirement if:

1. More than 50 percent of the individual's personal service during the tax year is performed in real property trades or businesses, and
2. The individual performs more than 750 hours of service in the real property trade or business in which he or she claims material participation.

EXAMPLE In 2014, Allan owns eighteen rental houses and spends 100 percent of his personal service time (1,800 hours in 2014) managing them. Allan spends his 1,800 hours of management time doing repairs, gardening, collecting rents,

Self-Study Problem 4.1

SCHEDULE E (Form 1040)
Department of the Treasury
Internal Revenue Service (99)

Supplemental Income and Loss
(From rental real estate, royalties, partnerships, S corporations, estates, trusts, REMICs, etc.)
► **Attach to Form 1040, 1040NR, or Form 1041.**
► **Information about Schedule E and its separate instructions is at *www.irs.gov/schedulee*.**

OMB No. 1545-0074
2014
Attachment Sequence No. **13**

Name(s) shown on return | **Your social security number**

DRAFT AS OF June 6, 2014 DO NOT FILE

Part I **Income or Loss From Rental Real Estate and Royalties** **Note.** If you are in the business of renting personal property, use **Schedule C** or **C-EZ** (see instructions). If you are an individual, report farm rental income or loss from **Form 4835** on page 2, line 40.

A Did you make any payments in 2014 that would require you to file Form(s) 1099? (see instructions) ☐ Yes ☐ No
B If "Yes," did you or will you file required Forms 1099? ☐ Yes ☐ No

1a	Physical address of each property (street, city, state, ZIP code)
A	
B	
C	

1b	Type of Property (from list below)	**2** For each rental real estate property listed above, report the number of fair rental and personal use days. Check the **QJV** box only if you meet the requirements to file as a qualified joint venture. See instructions.		**Fair Rental Days**	**Personal Use Days**	**QJV**
A			**A**			☐
B			**B**			☐
C			**C**			☐

Type of Property:
1 Single Family Residence 3 Vacation/Short-Term Rental 5 Land 7 Self-Rental
2 Multi-Family Residence 4 Commercial 6 Royalties 8 Other (describe)

Income: **Properties:**		**A**	**B**	**C**
3 Rents received	**3**			
4 Royalties received	**4**			
Expenses:				
5 Advertising	**5**			
6 Auto and travel (see instructions)	**6**			
7 Cleaning and maintenance	**7**			
8 Commissions	**8**			
9 Insurance	**9**			
10 Legal and other professional fees	**10**			
11 Management fees	**11**			
12 Mortgage interest paid to banks, etc. (see instructions)	**12**			
13 Other interest	**13**			
14 Repairs	**14**			
15 Supplies	**15**			
16 Taxes	**16**			
17 Utilities	**17**			
18 Depreciation expense or depletion	**18**			
19 Other (list) ►	**19**			
20 Total expenses. Add lines 5 through 19	**20**			
21 Subtract line 20 from line 3 (rents) and/or 4 (royalties). If result is a (loss), see instructions to find out if you must file **Form 6198**	**21**			
22 Deductible rental real estate loss after limitation, if any, on **Form 8582** (see instructions)	**22**	( )	( )	( )

23a Total of all amounts reported on line 3 for all rental properties	**23a**	
b Total of all amounts reported on line 4 for all royalty properties	**23b**	
c Total of all amounts reported on line 12 for all properties	**23c**	
d Total of all amounts reported on line 18 for all properties	**23d**	
e Total of all amounts reported on line 20 for all properties	**23e**	
24 **Income.** Add positive amounts shown on line 21. **Do not** include any losses	**24**	
25 **Losses.** Add royalty losses from line 21 and rental real estate losses from line 22. Enter total losses here	**25**	( )
26 **Total rental real estate and royalty income or (loss).** Combine lines 24 and 25. Enter the result here. If Parts II, III, IV, and line 40 on page 2 do not apply to you, also enter this amount on Form 1040, line 17, or Form 1040NR, line 18. Otherwise, include this amount in the total on line 41 on page 2	**26**	

For Paperwork Reduction Act Notice, see the separate instructions. Cat. No. 11344L **Schedule E (Form 1040) 2014**

cleaning and painting vacant houses, advertising for and interviewing new tenants, doing bookkeeping, and purchasing/installing new appliances, drapes, carpets, and toilets. He keeps a log to prove how many hours he works on his property in case he is audited. Since both the above tests are met, Allan's real estate rental activity is not a passive activity. If Allan has an overall loss of $40,000 on the real estate rentals, he can deduct the entire loss on his tax return as an active business, not a passive loss. ♦

Income from passive activities can be used by taxpayers to absorb passive losses that would otherwise be disallowed. The passive loss limitations are very complex. Certain oil and gas investments are not subject to the passive loss limitations, and special rules apply to investments in qualified low-income housing.

Would You Believe?

According to *Amazing But True Elvis Facts* by Bruce Nash and Allan Zullo (published by Andrews McMeel, May 1995), Elvis hated dealing with accountants, so he let the IRS handle his taxes. Never having a single tax shelter, one year he reportedly handed over 90 percent of his income.

Self-Study Problem 4.2 ***See Appendix E for Solutions to Self-Study Problems***

Sherry Moore has a limited partnership investment in a commercial rental project in which she has no personal involvement. During 2014, her share of the partnership loss equals $15,000. Sherry also has a rental house that she actively manages, and this activity generated a $21,000 loss for 2014. Sherry had no passive loss carryover from prior years. If Sherry's modified adjusted gross income before passive losses is $102,000, calculate the deduction amounts for Sherry's 2014 tax return using Form 8582 on Page 4-11.

SELF-EMPLOYED HEALTH INSURANCE DEDUCTION

Learning Objective 4.3
Describe the self-employed health insurance deduction.

Self-employed taxpayers are allowed an above-the-line deduction for the cost of providing health insurance for themselves and their families. This deduction is meant to give self-employed taxpayers the same tax treatment available to employees who are offered health insurance as a tax-free benefit of employment. Deductible insurance includes the following:

- Medical and dental insurance paid to cover the self-employed taxpayer, spouse, and dependent children;
- Medical and dental insurance paid for children under the age of 27 who are not dependents;
- Medicare premiums;
- Long-term care insurance paid for the taxpayer and the family of the taxpayer, within certain dollar limitations shown below.

EXAMPLE Joe has a barbershop and earns $60,000 in 2014 which he reports on Schedule C. Joe pays $10,000 in health and dental insurance costs for himself, his unemployed wife, and his 10-year-old daughter. The full $10,000 is a deduction for Joe's AGI. ♦

Special Rules

The following special rules limit the treatment of health insurance as a deduction for AGI:

- Other Health Care Plan Available: The self-employed health insurance deduction is not allowed for any months in which the taxpayer is eligible to participate in a subsidized health care plan offered by an employer of either the taxpayer or the spouse of the taxpayer.
- Earned Income Limitation: The deduction for self-employed health insurance is only allowed to the extent of the taxpayer's net earned income. For example, a taxpayer with a Schedule C business loss would not be allowed to claim a self-employed health insurance deduction even though he or she paid for health insurance. The deduction would instead be allowed as an itemized medical deduction subject to the limits discussed in Chapter 5.
- Long-Term Care Premium Limitation: The limitations on the deduction of long-term care premiums are as follows:

Attained Age Before the Close of the Taxable Year	*2014 Limitation on Premiums*
40 or less	$ 370
More than 40 but not more than 50	$ 700
More than 50 but not more than 60	$1,400
More than 60 but not more than 70	$3,720
More than 70	$4,660

- Definition of Self-Employment: Taxpayers with income reportable on Schedule C are generally considered self-employed. However, taxpayers with earnings from certain partnerships, S corporations, LLCs, and farm businesses may also be considered self-employed and may be allowed the above-the-line deduction for self-employed health insurance. Taxpayers with income from these sources sometimes present more complex health insurance deduction issues which should be researched as they appear.
- Deductible Portion: Self-employed taxpayers that receive advance premium credits under the Affordable Care Act may deduct only the portion paid out of pocket, not the portion covered by the premium tax credit.

EXAMPLE Candace is a 55-year-old massage therapist who earns $40,000 of net self-employment income in 2014. She pays $6,000 for medical insurance and $1,500 for long-term care insurance. Candace can take $7,400 ($6,000 + $1,400) as a deduction for AGI. ♦

Self-Study Problem 4.3 *See Appendix E for Solutions to Self-Study Problems*

During the 2014 tax year, Gwen supports her family as a physical therapist. She reports $90,000 of earned income on her Schedule C and paid the following insurance premiums:

- Family health insurance: $15,000
- Family dental insurance: $2,000
- Health insurance for her 24-year-old son who is not a dependent: $3,000
- Long-term care insurance for her 49-year-old husband: $750

What is Gwen's self-employed health insurance deduction for 2014? $__________

Self-Study Problem 4.2

Form **8582** — Department of the Treasury, Internal Revenue Service (99)

Passive Activity Loss Limitations

▶ See separate instructions.
▶ Attach to Form 1040 or Form 1041.
▶ Information about Form 8582 and its instructions is available at *www.irs.gov/form8582.*

OMB No. 1545-1008 — 2013* — Attachment Sequence No. 88

Name(s) shown on return | Identifying number

Part I — 2013 Passive Activity Loss

Caution: *Complete Worksheets 1, 2, and 3 before completing Part I.*

Rental Real Estate Activities With Active Participation (For the definition of active participation, see **Special Allowance for Rental Real Estate Activities** in the instructions.)

1a	Activities with net income (enter the amount from Worksheet 1, column (a))	1a	
b	Activities with net loss (enter the amount from Worksheet 1, column (b))	1b	( )
c	Prior years unallowed losses (enter the amount from Worksheet 1, column (c))	1c	( )
d	Combine lines 1a, 1b, and 1c	1d	

Commercial Revitalization Deductions From Rental Real Estate Activities

2a	Commercial revitalization deductions from Worksheet 2, column (a)	2a	( )
b	Prior year unallowed commercial revitalization deductions from Worksheet 2, column (b)	2b	( )
c	Add lines 2a and 2b	2c	( )

All Other Passive Activities

3a	Activities with net income (enter the amount from Worksheet 3, column (a))	3a	
b	Activities with net loss (enter the amount from Worksheet 3, column (b))	3b	( )
c	Prior years unallowed losses (enter the amount from Worksheet 3, column (c))	3c	( )
d	Combine lines 3a, 3b, and 3c	3d	
4	Combine lines 1d, 2c, and 3d. If this line is zero or more, stop here and include this form with your return; all losses are allowed, including any prior year unallowed losses entered on line 1c, 2b, or 3c. Report the losses on the forms and schedules normally used	4	

If line 4 is a loss and:
- Line 1d is a loss, go to Part II.
- Line 2c is a loss (and line 1d is zero or more), skip Part II and go to Part III.
- Line 3d is a loss (and lines 1d and 2c are zero or more), skip Parts II and III and go to line 15.

Caution: *If your filing status is married filing separately and you lived with your spouse at any time during the year,* ***do not*** *complete Part II or Part III. Instead, go to line 15.*

Part II — Special Allowance for Rental Real Estate Activities With Active Participation

Note: *Enter all numbers in Part II as positive amounts. See instructions for an example.*

5	Enter the **smaller** of the loss on line 1d or the loss on line 4	5	
6	Enter $150,000. If married filing separately, see instructions	6	
7	Enter modified adjusted gross income, but not less than zero (see instructions)	7	
	Note: *If line 7 is greater than or equal to line 6, skip lines 8 and 9, enter -0- on line 10. Otherwise, go to line 8.*		
8	Subtract line 7 from line 6	8	
9	Multiply line 8 by 50% (.5). **Do not** enter more than $25,000. If married filing separately, see instructions	9	
10	Enter the **smaller** of line 5 or line 9	10	

If line 2c is a loss, go to Part III. Otherwise, go to line 15.

Part III — Special Allowance for Commercial Revitalization Deductions From Rental Real Estate Activities

Note: *Enter all numbers in Part III as positive amounts. See the example for Part II in the instructions.*

11	Enter $25,000 reduced by the amount, if any, on line 10. If married filing separately, see instructions	11	
12	Enter the loss from line 4	12	
13	Reduce line 12 by the amount on line 10	13	
14	Enter the **smallest** of line 2c (treated as a positive amount), line 11, or line 13	14	

Part IV — Total Losses Allowed

15	Add the income, if any, on lines 1a and 3a and enter the total	15	
16	**Total losses allowed from all passive activities for 2013.** Add lines 10, 14, and 15. See instructions to find out how to report the losses on your tax return	16	

For Paperwork Reduction Act Notice, see instructions. Cat. No. 63704F Form **8582** (2013)

***The 2014 version of this form was not available as we went to press. Please check the IRS website for updates.**

HEALTH SAVINGS ACCOUNTS

Learning Objective 4.4

Understand how Health Savings Accounts (HSAs) can be used for tax-advantaged medical care.

Health Savings Accounts (HSAs) are a relatively new type of savings account which may be established for the purpose of paying unreimbursed medical expenses by taxpayers who carry qualifying high-deductible medical insurance. Contributions to HSAs are a deduction for AGI and are limited to certain dollar amounts depending on age and whether the high-deductible insurance covers an individual or a family. Earnings and unused contributions accumulated in an HSA are not taxed, and distributions to cover medical expenses are not taxed or penalized.

Health insurance with a high deductible is less expensive than standard health insurance since the issuing insurance company does not have to pay any of the taxpayer's medical expenses until a certain threshold (the deductible plus any other required out-of-pocket medical costs) is reached. The funds contributed to the HSA may then be used by the taxpayer to pay medical expenses not covered by the insurance. This popular combination of tax benefits and less expensive insurance is meant to encourage taxpayers to carry health insurance.

Deductions for Contributions to HSAs

The following table shows the contribution limits for HSA deductions for 2014. The table also shows the additional "catch-up" contributions allowed for individuals beginning at age 55 and ending at age 65, the age for Medicare eligibility. Individuals are not allowed to make contributions to HSAs once they attain the age of 65 and qualify for Medicare coverage. Finally, the table shows the lower and upper deductible and out-of-pocket medical expense limits (excluding the actual cost of insurance) required for insurance to qualify as a high-deductible health plan.

2014 Limits for HSAs

	Family	*Self-Only*
Contribution limit	$ 6,550	$3,300
Additional catch-up contribution for taxpayer age 55 or older	$ 1,000 per qualifying spouse	$1,000
Minimum health insurance deductible	$ 2,500	$1,250
Maximum health insurance out-of-pocket	$12,700	$6,350

Contributions to HSAs must generally be made by April 15 of the year following the year for which the contribution is made. IRS Form 8889 is used to provide information to the IRS regarding HSA deductions claimed on Form 1040 and to compute the deduction amount.

EXAMPLE Gary is 35 years old and carries self-only coverage in a qualifying high-deductible health insurance plan during 2014. Gary may contribute up to $3,300 to his HSA account and take this amount as a deduction for AGI. Gary may use some or all of the contribution to pay medical expenses he has incurred. Any amount he leaves in the HSA account will accumulate earnings tax free and carry forward to be used in the future. ♦

Distributions

Distributions from HSAs are free of tax when used to pay for qualified medical expenses. For 2014, distributions which are not used to pay for medical expenses are subject to both income tax and a 20 percent penalty. Once a taxpayer is 65 years old, distributions may be taken for nonmedical expenses and will be subject to income tax, but not the 20 percent penalty.

EXAMPLE Debbie is 66 years old and has $30,000 in her HSA. She can withdraw the $30,000 to purchase a new car, but will have to pay income tax on the distribution. If she takes the distribution to pay medical expenses, no income tax will be due. If Debbie were 55 years old and took a distribution from her HSA to buy a car, she would owe both income tax and a 20 percent penalty on the distribution. ♦

Guidance

The rules governing HSAs are more detailed and lengthy than the summaries above. IRS Publication 969 is a good source of information on a range of additional issues related to HSAs and their operation.

Self-Study Problem 4.4 *See Appendix E for Solutions to Self-Study Problems*

Give the deductible HSA amount for each of the following taxpayers for 2014:

1. Amy is 40 years old, has a qualifying high-deductible health plan, carries family coverage, and contributes the maximum amount to her family HSA. Deductible HSA amount: $____________
2. Cary is 60 years old, has self-only health insurance with no deductible, and contributes $1,200 to an HSA. Deductible HSA amount: $____________
3. Annabelle is 52 years old and contributes $2,000 to her HSA. She has qualifying self-only coverage in a high-deductible health plan. Deductible HSA amount: $____________
4. Lucille is 70 years old and covered by Medicare. She contributes $3,050 to her HSA. Deductible HSA amount: $____________

Learning Objective 4.5

Know the special rules applicable to moving expenses.

MOVING EXPENSES

Congress, recognizing the importance of having a mobile work force, felt taxpayers should not be penalized if forced to move to cities where better employment opportunities exist. Thus, the tax law provides a deduction for moving expenses to help relieve taxpayers of a portion of the financial burden of moving from one job location to another. Moving expenses are deductible in arriving at adjusted gross income.

To qualify for the moving expense deduction, three tests must be met. These tests are:

1. The taxpayer must change job sites. The taxpayer does not have to change employers. A job transfer with the same employer meets this test.
2. The taxpayer must move a certain minimum distance. The distance from the taxpayer's former residence to the new job location must be at least 50 miles more than the distance from the former residence to the former job location.

3. The taxpayer must remain at the new job location for a certain period of time. Generally, employees must work at least 39 weeks at the new job location during the 12 months following the move. Taxpayers who are self-employed must work at least 78 weeks at the new location during the 24 months after the move.

Taxpayers who are in the military or employees who are involuntarily transferred are still allowed the moving expense deduction even if the time or distance test is not met.

EXAMPLE Daniel works in San Diego and lives in Del Mar, a distance of 20 miles. He accepts a new position with his current firm in Rancho Cucamonga and moves there. Rancho Cucamonga is 110 miles from Del Mar. Daniel meets the distance test because the distance from his new place of employment, Rancho Cucamonga, to his former residence, Del Mar (110 miles), less the distance from his former place of employment to his former residence, Del Mar (20 miles), is at least 50 miles. ♦

Qualified moving expenses fall into two categories. These two categories are:

1. Moving household goods and personal effects.
2. Traveling from the former residence to the new place of residence. For purposes of the moving expense deduction, traveling includes lodging, but not meals, for the taxpayer and household members. The standard mileage rate for moving is 23.5 cents per mile in 2014.

Moving expenses must be reasonable to be deductible. For example, traveling expenses of going through Seattle on a move from Los Angeles to Miami would not be allowed. Qualified moving expenses reimbursed by an employer are not reported as part of the gross income of the employee. However, nonqualified moving expense reimbursements (e.g., employer reimbursement for meals during a move) are included in the gross income of an employee.

EXAMPLE John, an employee of Pine Corporation, is hired by Oak Corporation. His new job requires that he move from Denver to Houston. During the move, John incurs the following expenses:

Cost of moving furniture	$3,600
Transportation	500
Meals	200
Lodging	300
Total	$4,600

John's total qualified moving expense is $4,400 ($3,600 + $500 + $300). ♦

Self-Study Problem 4.5 *See Appendix E for Solutions to Self-Study Problems*

During May 2014, Maureen Motsinger is transferred to a new job by her employer. The transfer requires her to move from Phoenix to New York. The distance from her former residence to her new job location is 2,632 miles, and the distance from her former residence to her former job location is 20 miles. She incurs packing and moving expenses of $4,100. The cost of her lodging during the move is $650. Also, she spends $200 for meals during the move. She drives the 2,689 miles to New York in her automobile (the moving expense mileage rate for 2014 is 23.5 cents per mile). After her arrival in New York, Maureen's employer reimburses her $5,382 for the moving expenses. Calculate Maureen's moving expense deduction using Form 3903 on Page 4-17.

©ILYA AKINSHIN/Shutterstock.com; ©Zhukov Oleg/Shutterstock.com.

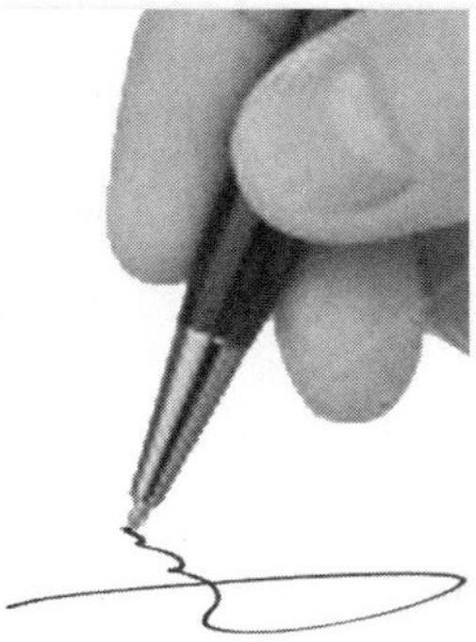

Would You Sign This Tax Return?

Paid Preparer Use Only	Print/Type preparer's name	Preparer's signature	Date	Check ☐ if self-employed	PTIN
	Firm's name ▶		Firm's EIN ▶		
	Firm's address ▶		Phone no.		

Mark (age 44) and Mary (age 41) Mower are your tax clients. They have two children, Matthew (age 20) and Mindy (age 17), who live at home. Mindy is a senior in high school and Matthew commutes to a local college where he is studying soil management. Mark owns and operates a successful lawn maintenance and landscaping business. He has six employees and three pick-up trucks used for transportation to the job sites. The business has a credit card in its name for use by the employees and Mark, who fills the trucks with gas almost daily. Mark gave a business credit card to Mary, Matthew, and Mindy and told them to use it to buy gas for their automobiles used for shopping, going to school, and short trips. In the current year, his wife and children put $5,210 of gasoline in their automobiles using the business credit card. Mark is adamant that the $5,210 be deducted on his Schedule C. He feels the amount is small compared to the business gas purchases of approximately $28,000. Mark says the amounts charged are spread throughout the credit card statements and would be very difficult for the IRS to detect on audit. Would you sign the Paid Preparer's declaration (see example above) on this return? Why or why not?

Learning Objective 4.6

Understand the treatment of Individual Retirement Accounts (IRAs), including Roth IRAs.

INDIVIDUAL RETIREMENT ACCOUNTS

There are two principal types of IRAs in the U.S. tax law. One is the *traditional IRA* and the other is the *Roth IRA*. Annual contributions to a traditional IRA are deductible, and retirement distributions are taxable. Annual contributions to a Roth IRA are not deductible, and retirement distributions are nontaxable. Earnings in both types of IRAs are not taxable in the current year.

Self-Study Problem 4.5

Form **3903**

Department of the Treasury
Internal Revenue Service (99)

Moving Expenses

► Information about Form 3903 and its instructions is available at *www.irs.gov/form3903.*

► Attach to Form 1040 or Form 1040NR.

OMB No. 1545-0074

2014

Attachment Sequence No. 170

Name(s) shown on return	Your social security number

Before you begin: ✓ See the **Distance Test** and **Time Test** in the instructions to find out if you can deduct your moving expenses.

✓ See **Members of the Armed Forces** in the instructions, if applicable.

DRAFT AS OF July 3, 2014 DO NOT FILE

1	Transportation and storage of household goods and personal effects (see instructions)	1	
2	Travel (including lodging) from your old home to your new home (see instructions). **Do not** include the cost of meals	2	
3	Add lines 1 and 2	3	
4	Enter the total amount your employer paid you for the expenses listed on lines 1 and 2 that is **not** included in box 1 of your Form W-2 (wages). This amount should be shown in box 12 of your Form W-2 with code **P**	4	
5	Is line 3 **more than** line 4? ☐ **No.** You **cannot** deduct your moving expenses. If line 3 is less than line 4, subtract line 3 from line 4 and include the result on Form 1040, line 7, or Form 1040NR, line 8. ☐ **Yes.** Subtract line 4 from line 3. Enter the result here and on Form 1040, line 26, or Form 1040NR, line 26. This is your **moving expense deduction**	5	

For Paperwork Reduction Act Notice, see your tax return instructions. Cat. No. 12490K Form **3903** (2014)

EXAMPLE Gene has $30,000 in his IRA in 2014. The earnings for the year on this IRA are $1,600. These earnings are not taxed to Gene in the current year. ♦

IRA Annual Contributions

There are annual contribution limits for both traditional and Roth IRAs. In 2014, the maximum annual contribution that may be made to either type of IRA is equal to the lesser of (1) 100 percent of the taxpayer's compensation or self-employment income (earned income) or (2) $5,500 (or $11,000 if an additional $5,500 is contributed to a spouse's IRA, and the spouse has no earned income). The maximum contribution to a spouse's IRA may not exceed $5,500. In 2014, there is an additional "catch-up" $1,000 annual contribution allowed for taxpayers and spouses age 50 and over, increasing the maximum contribution to $6,500.

EXAMPLE Quincy, age 31, works for Big Corporation and has a salary of $40,000 for 2014. Quincy is eligible to contribute the maximum $5,500 to his traditional or Roth IRA for 2014. If Quincy has a spouse who does not work, he could also contribute $5,500 into her IRA or Roth IRA. If Quincy is 55 years old instead of 31 years old, he could contribute $6,500 to his traditional or Roth IRA, and $5,500 or $6,500 for his spouse depending on whether she is old enough to qualify for the $1,000 "catch-up" contribution. ♦

TAX BREAK

The IRA limitation calculations discussed below are quite complex and change every year. Most taxpayers and tax preparers use tax software to assist them in calculating allowable IRA deductions. It is a standard belief in the tax community that computer software has paved the way for the enormous complexity we see in today's tax law. Although it is important to understand the rules for calculating IRA contributions, please also take solace in the fact that these calculations, as well as many others shown in this text, are not often done by hand in practice.

The annual deduction maximums above are reduced for traditional IRAs if the taxpayer is an active participant in another qualified retirement plan. The annual contribution allowed for a Roth IRA is reduced for all taxpayers over certain income levels, but is not affected by whether the taxpayer or spouse is an active participant in another retirement plan. In each case, the maximum annual contribution is phased out proportionately between certain adjusted gross income ranges, as shown below.

2014 AGI Phase-Out Ranges for Roth IRA Contributions

Filing Status	*AGI Phase-Out Range*
Single or HOH	$114,000–$129,000
Married, Joint	$181,000–$191,000

Note: Active plan participation status is not relevant to the Roth IRA phase-out calculation.

2014 AGI Phase-Out Ranges for Traditional IRA Contributions

Type of Taxpayer	*Phase-Out Range*
Single or HOH, not a plan participant	No phase-out
Single or HOH, active plan participant	\$60,000–\$70,000
Married, Joint, both active participants	\$96,000–\$116,000
Married, Joint, neither active plan participants	No phase-out
Married, Joint, one an active participant:	(See Note 1 below)
Active participant spouse	\$96,000–\$116,000 (Joint AGI)
Nonactive participant spouse	\$181,000–\$191,000 (Joint AGI)

Note 1: When one spouse is an active participant in a retirement plan and the other is not, two separate income limitations apply. The active participant spouse may make a full deductible IRA contribution unless the \$96,000–\$116,000 phase-out range applies to the couple's joint income. The spouse who is not an active participant may make a full deductible IRA contribution unless the higher \$181,000–\$191,000 phase-out range applies to the couple's joint income.

If a taxpayer contributes to both a traditional IRA and a Roth IRA, the combined contributions cannot exceed the normal annual limit (\$5,500 or \$6,500 if age 50 or older in 2014).

A nondeductible traditional IRA contribution may be made by taxpayers with income over the phase-out ranges shown above. Although the taxpayer cannot deduct the contribution, all income earned in the IRA account is sheltered from tax until the earnings are withdrawn, similar to the treatment of annuities discussed in Chapter 2. Many high-income taxpayers make nondeductible traditional IRA contributions each year because of the deferral of tax on the earnings of the IRA.

EXAMPLE Ed, age 31, is single and is covered by a retirement plan. If his modified adjusted gross income is \$65,000, Ed's maximum deductible traditional IRA contribution is \$2,750. With income of \$65,000, his \$5,500 contribution is proportionately phased out by dividing the amount remaining in his phase-out range, \$70,000 − \$65,000, or \$5,000, by the \$10,000 phase-out range (the difference between the bottom and top of the \$60,000 and \$70,000 phase-out range) and multiplying this by the \$5,500 maximum IRA deduction as follows:

$$\frac{(\$70,000 - \$65,000)}{\$10,000} \times \$5,500 = \$2,750 \text{ allowed IRA deduction}$$

Ed may choose to contribute the \$5,500 maximum to a traditional IRA, but the remaining \$2,750 will not be deductible. Alternatively, he may contribute the remaining \$2,750 to a Roth IRA since his income is below the phase-out range for Roth IRA contributions. He could also choose to ignore the allowed traditional IRA contribution and contribute the full \$5,500 to a Roth IRA. In any event, he cannot contribute more than \$5,500 in total to IRAs, and his maximum allowed tax deduction for a traditional IRA contribution will be \$2,750. ♦

EXAMPLE Ann, who is 36 and single, would like to contribute $5,500 to her Roth IRA. However, her AGI is $117,000, so her contribution is limited to $4,400, calculated as follows:

$$\frac{(\$129{,}000 - \$117{,}000)}{\$15{,}000} \times \$5{,}500 = \$4{,}400 \text{ allowed Roth IRA}$$

The $15,000 denominator in the calculation above is the amount of the phase-out range between $114,000 and $129,000. If she were 56 and wanted to contribute $6,500, her contribution would be limited to $5,200. ♦

EXAMPLE Paul and Lucy are married and are both 36 years old. Lucy is covered by a retirement plan and earns $61,000. Paul is not covered by a retirement plan and earns $57,000. Lucy cannot make a deductible contribution to a traditional IRA since the income on their joint tax return is greater than the $116,000 maximum phase-out range for married couples. Paul, however, can make a fully deductible IRA contribution of $5,500 since he qualifies for the $181,000–$191,000 phase-out range used when one spouse is an active participant in a plan and the other is not. Lucy could still choose to make a $5,500 contribution to a Roth IRA since their joint income is below the Roth IRA phase-out range for married couples. Paul would have a choice between making a $5,500 deductible contribution to a traditional IRA or a contribution of $5,500 to a Roth IRA or some combination thereof, not greater than $5,500. ♦

An IRA contribution may be made at any time before the original due date of the tax return for the year in which the deduction is to be claimed. This means, for example, that an individual can contribute to an IRA as late as April 15, 2015, and still deduct the amount on the 2014 tax return.

Roth IRA Conversions

Taxpayers may benefit from a rule allowing conversions of regular IRAs into Roth IRAs. Although the income generated by the conversion is subject to a current income tax, taxpayers with certain factors in their favor such as many years to retirement, a low current tax bracket, or a high expected tax bracket in retirement may wish to convert. Also, taxpayers with negative taxable income due to large personal deductions may wish to convert enough of their regular IRAs to Roth IRAs to bring taxable income to zero. This way the conversion can be done with no tax cost since deductions which would otherwise be lost are used to offset the taxable IRA income.

For tax years 2010 and beyond, a rule that required taxpayers to have $100,000 or less in AGI to convert regular IRA accounts to Roth IRA accounts was eliminated. Congress expects that many high-income taxpayers will take advantage of this opportunity and pay income tax due up-front on conversions.

Traditional IRA Distributions

Money removed from a traditional IRA is taxable as ordinary income and may be subject to a 10 percent penalty for early withdrawal. To avoid the 10 percent penalty, distributions from an IRA generally cannot begin before age 59½. However, penalty-free withdrawals from IRAs may be made by taxpayers under age 59½ who are:

1. Disabled
2. Using a special level payment option
3. Using the withdrawals for medical expenses in excess of 10 percent (7.5 percent if age 65 or older) of their AGI
4. The recipients of at least 12 weeks of unemployment compensation and to the extent they are paying medical insurance premiums for their dependents
5. Paying the costs of higher education, including tuition, fees, books, and room and board for the taxpayers or their spouses, children, or grandchildren
6. Withdrawing up to $10,000 for first-time home-buying expenses

While withdrawals made by these taxpayers are penalty free, they are still subject to income taxes. Also, taxpayers must start taking minimum annual distributions from their IRA at age 70½. The IRS provides tables for calculating the required minimum annual distributions based on the taxpayer's life expectancy.

EXAMPLE Tomas is 48 years old and has a midlife crisis and decides he has to have a red sports car. He withdraws $35,000 from his traditional IRA to pay for it. Tomas does not qualify for any of the penalty-free withdrawals listed earlier. The $35,000 is taxable to Tomas as ordinary income and he is subject to a $3,500 (10% × $35,000) penalty for removing the funds before age 59½. ♦

Roth IRA Distributions

A taxpayer can make tax-free withdrawals from a Roth IRA after a 5-year holding period if any of the following requirements are satisfied:

1. The distribution is made on or after the date on which the participant attains age 59½.
2. The distribution is made to a beneficiary (or the participant's estate) on or after the participant's death.
3. The participant becomes disabled.
4. The distribution is used to pay for qualified first-time home-buyer's expenses.

EXAMPLE Bob establishes a Roth IRA at age 50 and contributes the maximum each year for 10 years. The account is now worth $61,000, consisting of $35,000 of nondeductible contributions and $26,000 in earnings that have not been taxed. Bob may withdraw the $61,000 tax-free from the Roth IRA because he is over 59½ and has met the 5-year holding period requirement. ♦

The distributions may be taxable if the taxpayer receives distributions from a Roth IRA and does not satisfy the above requirements. The part of the distributions that represents a return of capital is tax free, and the part that represents a payout of earnings is taxable. Under the ordering rules for Roth IRA distributions, distributions are treated as first made from contributions (return of capital) and then from earnings.

EXAMPLE Assume the same facts in the previous example, except that Bob is only age 56 and receives distributions of $10,000. Assume his adjusted basis for the Roth IRA is $12,000 (contributions made of $2,000 × 6 years). The distribution is tax free and his adjusted basis is reduced to $2,000 ($12,000 − $10,000). ♦

TAX BREAK

A gift to a Roth IRA for a child or grandchild with a summer job can grow into a very large gift over time. The amount that may be contributed to a child's Roth IRA is the lesser of $5,500 or the child's earnings. A child with $5,500 in a Roth IRA at age 16 will have well over $100,000 at age 65 if the Roth IRA investment earns 7 percent.

Self-Study Problem 4.6 ***See Appendix E for Solutions to Self-Study Problems***

a. During 2014, George (a 24-year-old single taxpayer) has a salary of $43,000, dividend income of $14,000, and interest income of $3,000. In addition, he has rental income of $1,000. George is covered by a qualified retirement plan. Calculate the maximum regular IRA deduction that George is allowed.

$__________

b. During 2014, Irene (a single taxpayer, under age 50) has a salary of $107,000 and dividend income of $10,000. Calculate Irene's maximum contribution to a Roth IRA.

$__________

KEOGH PLANS AND SIMPLIFIED EMPLOYEE PENSIONS

Learning Objective 4.7

Explain the general contribution rules for Keogh and Simplified Employee Pension (SEP) plans.

Keogh plans are the unincorporated business's equivalent of the qualified retirement plans discussed in LO 4.8. The array of retirement plans available for self-employed taxpayers is now very similar to the retirement plans available to corporate taxpayers, and includes 401(k) plans, defined contribution plans, and defined benefit plans. The retirement plan area has become one of the most complex areas of the tax law. Many tax accountants refer taxpayers to a specialist for help in choosing a plan and for guidance through the ongoing employee coverage, tax reporting, and contribution requirements. The coverage in this text is meant to give a simple overview of several common options available to taxpayers for tax-deferred retirement plans, which remain one of the best completely legal tax shelters available.

Keogh Plans

For 2014, contributions to Keogh plans by self-employed taxpayers are generally limited to the lesser of 20 percent of their net earned income (before the Keogh deduction) or $52,000. A taxpayer's net earned income includes profits from a business if a material part of the profits from the business is from the taxpayer's personal services. Earned income must be reduced by one-half of the self-employment tax on the income (see Chapter 9) to arrive at net earned income used in the pension calculation.

EXAMPLE Dan is a self-employed doctor, and the net earned income (Schedule C net income less one-half of self-employment tax) from his practice is $125,000. Under the terms of his Keogh plan, Dan contributes 20 percent of net earned income (up to the maximum allowable) to the plan. Dan's contribution to the plan is calculated as follows:

The lesser of 20% of $125,000 ($25,000) or $52,000	$25,000 ♦

Simplified Employee Pensions (SEPs)

Simplified Employee Pensions, or SEPs, are one of the most popular retirement plans for self-employed taxpayers. The contribution limits for 2014 are the same as the limits for Keogh plans discussed above, that is, the lesser of 20 percent of net earned income before the SEP deduction or $52,000. The contributions are made into "SEP-IRAs," which are special IRA accounts with the higher funding limits allowed for Keogh plans. Participants in both SEPs and Keogh plans must meet requirements for minimum age and years of service. An employer must cover employees if the employees meet the requirements for coverage.

To avoid penalties, taxpayers generally may not receive distributions from a Keogh plan or SEP prior to age 59½ and must start drawing amounts by the age of 70½.

Self-Study Problem 4.7 ***See Appendix E for Solutions to Self-Study Problems***

Lewis, a self-employed individual, has net earned income of $50,000 in 2014. If Lewis has no employees, calculate the maximum contribution to a Keogh plan that he may deduct from his adjusted gross income.

$____________

Learning Objective 4.8

Describe the general rules for qualified retirement plans and 401(k) plans.

QUALIFIED RETIREMENT PLANS INCLUDING SECTION 401(K) PLANS

The tax law provides taxpayers and their employers with an incentive to plan for retirement through qualified retirement plans. Under the tax law, favorable tax treatment is granted to contributions, by or for employees, to qualified retirement plans. Employers may claim a deduction in the current year for contributions to qualified retirement plans on the employees' behalf, while the employees do not include the employer contributions in income until the contributed amounts are distributed. Tax on earnings on the amounts contributed to the plan is also deferred. This deferral of income taxation is a significant benefit to most taxpayers.

EXAMPLE In the current year, Polly's employer makes a $2,000 contribution to a qualified plan for Polly's retirement. The $2,000 is deductible to the employer in the current year and is not taxable to Polly until she withdraws the money from the plan. Any earnings on the money contributed to the plan are also taxable only upon withdrawal from the plan (usually many years later). ♦

Qualified Plans

For a retirement plan to be a qualified plan for income tax purposes, it must meet the following general requirements:

1. A plan must be created by an employer for the *exclusive benefit* of employees or their beneficiaries.
2. The contributions and benefits under a plan must *not discriminate in* favor of highly compensated employees.
3. A plan must meet certain *participation and coverage requirements*. The plan must provide that all employees who are 21 years old and who have completed at least 1 year of service with the employer are eligible to participate. If the plan provides for 100 percent vesting of accrued benefits upon commencement of participation in the plan, the 1 year of service requirement may be replaced with a requirement that the employee has completed at least 2 years of service.

4. *Minimum vesting* requirements must be met with respect to both employee and employer contributions.
5. *Uniform minimum distribution* rules must be met.

Types of Qualified Plans

The tax law provides for several types of qualified plans: pension plans, profit-sharing plans, stock bonus plans, and Employee Stock Ownership Plans (ESOPs). The pension plan can take one of two forms: the defined contribution plan or the defined benefit plan. Under a defined contribution plan, the amount of contribution for the employee is determined by reference to a formula based on the employee's current compensation. The employee's retirement benefits will be dependent upon the accumulated contributions and earnings in the account at the time of retirement. Under a defined benefit plan, the future retirement benefits of the employee are specified, and a formula is used to determine the contributions necessary to provide for the defined benefit. Profit-sharing plans are structured to allow the employee to share in company profits through employer contributions from such profits. Under a stock bonus plan, employer contributions on behalf of the employee consist of stock of the employer company.

EXAMPLE Heather is an employee who earned $30,000 during the current year. Her employer contributed $1,200 (4 percent of Heather's salary) to a qualified retirement plan. This plan is a defined contribution plan. ♦

EXAMPLE Alan works for an employer whose qualified retirement plan states that Alan will receive a retirement benefit at age 65 equal to 40 percent of his last year's salary. The employer must make adequate contributions to the plan to enable the stated retirement benefit to be paid (a sufficient amount of money must be in the plan upon Alan's retirement to pay for Alan's defined retirement benefit). This plan is a defined benefit plan. ♦

Limitations on Contributions to and Benefits from Qualified Plans

Employee and employer contributions to qualified plans are subject to certain dollar or percentage limitations. Under a defined contribution plan, the annual addition to an employee's account is generally not allowed to exceed the lesser of $52,000 or 25 percent of the employee's compensation. Under a defined benefit plan, the annual benefit payable to an employee upon retirement is limited to the lesser of $210,000 (for 2014) or 100 percent of the employee's average compensation for the highest three consecutive years of employment. The operational rules for qualified pension plans and the other types of qualified plans are complex.

Section 401(k) Plans

One of the more popular qualified retirement plans is the Section 401(k) plan, which permits an employee to choose to receive a direct payment of compensation in cash or to defer the amount through an employer contribution on behalf of the employee to a profit-sharing or stock bonus plan. Such a plan may be structured as a salary reduction agreement. The agreement may allow the employee to reduce his or her compensation or forgo an increase in compensation, with the amount contributed to the qualified retirement plan, thereby deferring tax on the compensation. Employees choose the percentage of their pay which will be withheld and contributed to the plan. Some employers match employee contributions up to a certain percentage in order to encourage participation.

For 2014, an employee may elect to make an annual contribution up to $17,500 ($23,000 for taxpayers age 50 or older) to a Section 401(k) plan. The amount of any contributions made to the Section 401(k) plan are also subject to the limitations applicable to all qualified plans. Any matching amount contributed to the plan by the employer on behalf of the employee is excluded from the employee's gross income. The contributions and the earnings on the amounts invested in the plan are taxable only when withdrawn.

EXAMPLE Carol, age 48, participates in a Section 401(k) plan. Carol's salary is $30,000 per year and she chooses to contribute 15 percent to the 401(k) plan. The maximum amount she may contribute on a tax-deferred basis to the Section 401(k) plan under a salary reduction agreement is $4,500 (15% × $30,000, not to exceed $17,500, in 2014). ♦

The annual maximum ($17,500, or $23,000 if age 50 or over, in 2014) is reduced dollar for dollar by amounts contributed as a result of the employee's participation in other salary reduction plans of any employer. Contributions in excess of the maximum allowed may be subject to a 10 percent excise tax imposed on the employer. Also, if the excess contributions are not withdrawn within a specified time period, the plan will lose its status as a qualified arrangement.

Finally, Section 401(k) plans must meet certain requirements in addition to the general qualification requirements for all qualified plans. The amount deferred must be 100 percent vested and may be distributed only upon retirement, death, disability, or other separation from service, attainment of age 59½, or hardship. The plan must also meet stringent anti-discrimination provisions in order to maintain its tax-deferred status.

Beginning in 2006, employers were allowed to set up Roth 401(k)s for their employees. The amounts allowed to be set aside are the same as for regular 401(k)s, but the dollars paid in do not reduce the employees' taxable income, which is similar to the tax treatment of Roth IRAs. Withdrawals, including earnings, are generally tax free based on rules similar to those for Roth IRA withdrawals. Roth 401(k)s are expected to be popular because they allow a significantly higher Roth contribution than a Roth IRA and because there is no AGI limitation, so they may be used by high-income taxpayers.

Low Income Retirement Plan Contribution Credit

Certain low-income taxpayers may claim a "Low Income Retirement Plan Contribution Credit," also called the "Saver's Credit," to encourage them to participate in tax saving retirement plans, including IRAs. The credit rate is 50 percent, 20 percent, or 10 percent depending on the taxpayer's filing status and adjusted gross income. The credit is a direct deduction from income taxes otherwise payable, and the cash saved may be used to make part of the contribution to the plan. Taxpayers receive up to a 50 percent credit for contribution amounts up to $2,000 or a maximum credit of $1,000. The credit phases out for adjusted gross income over certain income limits, as shown below.

Filing Status/Adjusted Gross Income for 2014 — Saver's Credit

Amount of Credit	*Joint*	*Head of Household*	*Single/Others*
50% of first $2,000 deferred	$0 to $36,000	$0 to $27,000	$0 to $18,000
20% of first $2,000 deferred	$36,001 to $39,000	$27,001 to $29,250	$18,001 to $19,500
10% of first $2,000 deferred	$39,001 to $60,000	$29,251 to $45,000	$19,501 to $30,000

EXAMPLE In 2014, Teddy and Abby file a joint tax return with AGI of $27,000. Teddy contributes $1,500 to a Section 401(k) plan at work. Teddy and Abby are entitled to a $750 (50% × $1,500) retirement plan contribution credit. The credit is in addition to any deduction or exclusion allowed for the contribution.

For more information regarding the calculation of the credit, see IRS Form 8880, "Credit for Qualified Retirement Savings Contributions." ♦

Self-Study Problem 4.8 *See Appendix E for Solutions to Self-Study Problems*

During 2014, Linda, age 32, has a salary of $40,000. She participates in a Section 401(k) plan and chooses to defer 20 percent of her compensation.

a. What is the maximum amount Linda can contribute to the Section 401(k) plan on a tax-deferred basis?

$____________

b. If Linda's salary was $125,000, instead of $40,000, what is the maximum amount that she could contribute to the Section 401(k) plan on a tax-deferred basis?

$____________

ROLLOVERS

Learning Objective 4.9

Explain the pension plan rollover rules.

In many situations, taxpayers need to transfer assets from one retirement plan to another plan of the same or different type. For example, the taxpayer may change jobs, take early retirement, or simply seek a better retirement fund manager. There are two ways this transfer can be accomplished: (1) direct transfer, also known as a trustee-to-trustee transfer, and (2) rollover of the distribution, in whole or in part, to an IRA or other qualified plan. There are potentially different tax treatments for the two types of transfers.

Direct Transfers

In direct transfers, the taxpayer instructs the trustee of the retirement plan to transfer assets to the trustee of another plan. There are no current-year tax consequences for this transaction. Also, there is no limit to the number of times a taxpayer can do this in a single tax year.

EXAMPLE Juan has $90,000 in a Section 401(k) plan with his employer. He also has two IRAs, one with ABC Bank ($20,000) and one with XYZ Mutual Fund ($30,000). In March of 20XX, Juan instructs ABC Bank to make a direct transfer to XYZ Mutual Fund of all of his funds ($20,000). In August of 20XX, Juan quits his job and instructs the trustee of the Section 401(k) plan to transfer his $90,000 directly to XYZ Mutual Fund. On December 31, 20XX, Juan has $140,000 in his XYZ Mutual Fund IRA. Since these were direct transfers, there are no tax consequences to Juan in the current year. ♦

Distribution Rollovers

In a distribution rollover, the taxpayer receives a distribution of funds from a retirement plan and then transfers part or all of the funds to the new retirement plan trustee. The taxpayer has a maximum of 60 days in which to transfer funds to the new plan and avoid taxes and penalties. The 60-day rollover period may be waived in cases of casualty, disaster, and other events beyond the reasonable control of the taxpayer such as death, disability,

incarceration, and postal error. The 60-day time limit is extended to 120 days for first-time home buyers.

The major drawback to distribution rollovers is that the trustee must withhold 20 percent of the amount distributed for federal income taxes, giving the employee only 80 percent of the amount in his or her plan. However, the employee must contribute 100 percent of the amount in the old plan to the new trustee within the required 60-day period to avoid tax on the distribution. Amounts that are not placed in a new plan within the required period are taxable as ordinary income in the current year. Also, if the taxpayer is under 59½ years old, the portion of the retirement plan distribution not transferred will be subject to a 10 percent penalty tax.

The exception to mandatory withholding is a distribution from an IRA; such distributions are not subject to the 20 percent withholding tax. Also, taxpayers are allowed only one distribution rollover each year for transfers from one IRA to another IRA. There are many other complex rules concerning retirement plan rollovers.

EXAMPLE Bea is 50 years old, has worked for Gold Company for 25 years, and has $200,000 in her retirement plan. This year, Gold Company is purchased by Green Company. As a result of the takeover, Bea was laid off. Bea requests a distribution of her $200,000 from Gold Company's retirement plan. The trustee of Gold's retirement plan must withhold $40,000 (20% of $200,000) from the distribution. Bea only receives $160,000 from her retirement plan distribution. If Bea wants to roll her funds into an IRA and avoid taxes, she must contribute $200,000, even though she only received $160,000. If Bea has no other resources and cannot make up the $40,000, the amount not contributed to the IRA will be taxable income to her and subject to a 10 percent penalty. If she does make up the $40,000 from other sources, she will receive the $40,000 withheld as a refund after her tax return is filed. ♦

Self-Study Problem 4.9

See Appendix E for Solutions to Self-Study Problems

Carol, age 40, has an IRA with Blue Mutual Fund. Her balance in the fund is $150,000. She has heard good things about the management of Red Mutual Fund, so she opens a Red Fund IRA. Carol requests her balance from the Blue Fund on July 1, 20XX.

a. How much will Carol receive from the Blue Fund IRA?

$__________

b. If the funds were distributed from a qualified retirement plan (not an IRA), how much would Carol receive?

$__________

c. When is the last day Carol can roll over the amount received into the Red Fund IRA and avoid taxation in the current year?

$__________

d. Assuming the funds were distributed from a qualified retirement plan, not from an IRA, how much will Carol have to contribute to the Red Fund IRA to avoid taxable income and any penalties?

$__________

Would You Believe?

The *Wall Street Journal* reported (February 19, 1998, Tax Report, Front Page) on an IRS "blooper" which scared thousands of taxpayers. In early 1998, the IRS sent out 3,000 erroneous notices, each showing a balance due of over $300 million and stating that all or a part of the taxpayer's expected refunds had been withheld to offset a federal tax debt. The IRS mailed corrections and apologies to all recipients, and blamed a "human programming error" for the problem.

In an even grander error reported in the *Wall Street Journal* (May 13, 1998, Tax Report, Front Page), a taxpayer received a notice showing a balance due of $40 billion plus change. Later, the IRS sent a corrected notice showing that the taxpayer only owed about $1,500.

KEY TERMS

passive income and losses, 4-5
Health Savings Accounts (HSAs), 4-13
traditional IRA, 4-16
Roth IRA, 4-16
annual contribution limits, 4-19
"catch-up" contribution, 4-19
nondeductible traditional IRA, 4-20
conversions, 4-21
early withdrawal, 4-22
distributions, 4-22
Keogh plans, 4-23
Simplified Employee Pensions, or SEPs, 4-24
qualified plan, 4-24
profit-sharing plans, 4-25
stock bonus plans, 4-25
Employee Stock Ownership Plans (ESOPs), 4-25
defined contribution plan, 4-25
defined benefit plan, 4-25
section 401(k) plan, 4-25
saver's credit, 4-26
trustee-to-trustee transfer, 4-27
rollover, 4-27

KEY POINTS

Learning Objectives	Key Points
LO 4.1: Apply the tax rules for rental property and vacation homes.	• Rental income and related expenses are reported on Schedule E. • Primary rental expenses include real estate taxes, mortgage interest, insurance, commissions, repairs, and depreciation. • If a residence is rented for fewer than 15 days during the year, the rental income is disregarded and the property is treated as a personal residence for tax purposes. • If the residence is rented for 15 days or more and is used for personal purposes for not more than 14 days or 10 percent of the days rented, whichever is greater, the residence is treated as a rental property. • If the residence is rented for 15 days or more and is used for personal purposes for more than 14 days or 10 percent of the days rented, whichever is greater, allocable rental expenses are allowed only to the extent of rental income.
LO 4.2: Explain the treatment of passive income and losses.	• The passive loss rules define three categories of income: (1) active income, (2) portfolio income, and (3) passive income and losses. • Normally, passive losses cannot be used to offset either active or portfolio income. Passive losses not used to offset passive income are carried forward indefinitely. • Generally, losses remaining when the taxpayer disposes of his or her entire interest in a passive activity may be used in full. • Under the passive loss rules, real estate rental activities are specifically defined as passive, even if the taxpayer actively manages the property.

	• Individual taxpayers may deduct up to $25,000 of rental property losses against other income if they are actively involved in the management of the property and their income does not exceed certain limits. • Taxpayers heavily involved in real estate rental activities may qualify as running a trade or business rather than a passive activity and fully deduct all rental losses.
LO 4.3: Describe the self-employed health insurance deduction.	• Deductible insurance includes: (1) medical and dental insurance paid to cover the self-employed taxpayer, spouse, and dependent children; (2) medical and dental insurance paid for children under the age of 27 who are not dependents; (3) long-term care insurance paid for the taxpayer and the family of the taxpayer; and (4) medicare premiums. • Taxpayers with income reportable on Schedule C are generally considered self-employed. • Taxpayers with earnings from certain partnerships, S corporations, LLCs, and farm businesses may also be considered self-employed and may be allowed the deduction for self-employed health insurance.
LO 4.4: Understand how Health Savings Accounts (HSAs) can be used for tax-advantaged medical care.	• Health Savings Accounts (HSAs) are used for the purpose of paying unreimbursed medical expenses by taxpayers who carry qualifying high-deductible medical insurance. • HSAs have an annual age-based contribution dollar limitation for deductions for individuals and families (see text for current limits). There is an additional "catch-up" contribution allowed for individuals beginning at age 55 and ending at age 65, the age for Medicare eligibility. • Distributions from HSAs are free of tax when used to pay for qualified medical expenses. Distributions which are not used to pay for medical expenses are subject to both income tax and a 20 percent penalty. • Once a taxpayer is 65 years old, distributions may be taken for nonmedical expenses and will be subject to income tax, but not to the 20 percent penalty.
LO 4.5: Know the special rules applicable to moving expenses.	• To qualify for the moving expense deduction, the taxpayer must change job sites, although the taxpayer does not have to change employers. A job transfer with the same employer meets this test. • The taxpayer must move a certain minimum distance. The distance from the taxpayer's former residence to the new job location must be at least 50 miles more than the distance from the former residence to the former job location. • The taxpayer must remain at the new job location for a certain period of time. Generally, employees must work at least 39 weeks at the new job location during the 12 months following the move or 78 weeks at the new location during the 24 months following the move, if self-employed.
LO 4.6: Understand the treatment of Individual Retirement Accounts (IRAs), including Roth IRAs.	• Annual contributions to a traditional IRA are deductible and retirement distributions are taxable, while annual contributions to a Roth IRA are not deductible and retirement distributions are nontaxable. • Earnings in both types of IRAs are not taxable in the current year. • In 2014, the maximum annual contribution that may be made to either type of IRA is equal to the lesser of (1) 100 percent of the taxpayer's compensation (earned income) or (2) $5,500 (plus an additional $5,500 which may be contributed on behalf of a spouse with no earned income). An additional catch-up $1,000 annual contribution is allowed for taxpayers age 50 and over.

	• Contributions to traditional IRAs are limited for taxpayers who are active participants in pension plans and have income over certain limits. Contributions to Roth IRAs are limited for taxpayers with income over certain limits, but they are not affected by taxpayer participation in other retirement plans. See text for specific rules and limits. • Money distributed from a traditional IRA is taxable as ordinary income and may be subject to a 10 percent penalty for early withdrawal (before age 59½). Some types of early withdrawals may be made without penalty. • A taxpayer can make tax-free withdrawals from a Roth IRA after a 5-year holding period if the distribution is made on or after the date on which the participant attains age 59½. Other tax-free withdrawals may also apply.
LO 4.7: Explain the general contribution rules for Keogh and Simplified Employee Pension (SEP) plans.	• For 2014, contributions to Keogh plans by self-employed taxpayers are generally limited to the lesser of 20 percent of their net earned income before the Keogh deduction or $52,000. • For 2014, the contribution to an SEP is also the lesser of 20 percent of net earned income before the SEP deduction or $52,000.
LO 4.8: Describe the general rules for qualified retirement plans and 401(k) plans.	• Employers may claim a deduction in the current year for contributions to qualified retirement plans on employees' behalf. The employees do not include the employer contributions in income until the contributed amounts are distributed. • For 2014, an employee may elect to make an annual contribution up to $17,500 ($23,000 for taxpayers age 50 or older) to a Section 401(k) plan. In addition, any matching amount contributed to the plan by the employer on behalf of the employee is excluded from the employee's gross income. • The low-income retirement "Savers Credit" rate is a maximum of 50 percent of up to $2,000 of retirement savings, phased out depending on the taxpayer's filing status and adjusted gross income.
LO 4.9: Explain the pension plan rollover rules.	• There are two ways to transfer assets from one retirement plan to another of the same or different type: (1) a direct transfer, also known as a trustee-to-trustee transfer, and (2) a rollover of an actual cash distribution, in whole or in part, to an IRA or other qualified plan. • There are no current-year tax consequences for a direct trustee-to-trustee transfer. • Distribution rollovers are subject to a 60-day time limit for completion and may also be subject to income tax withholding.

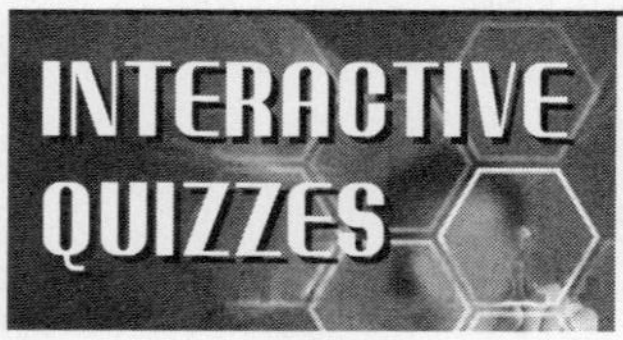

© Dusit/Shutterstock.com

Interactive quizzes are available as an optional online resource for Income Tax Fundamentals. Visit **www.cengagebrain.com** for more information.

QUESTIONS and PROBLEMS

GROUP 1: MULTIPLE CHOICE QUESTIONS

LO 4.1

1. Which of the following is true about the rental of real estate?
   a. Depreciation and maintenance expenses for an apartment complex are deductible.
   b. A vacation home is a home that is rented for 15 days or more and is used by the taxpayer for personal use for more than the greater of 14 days or 10 percent of the days it is rented for fair value during the year.
   c. If a home is rented for less than 15 days a year, the rent is not taxable.
   d. Repairs on rental property are deductible by the taxpayer.
   e. All of the above.

LO 4.1

2. John owns a second home in Palm Springs, CA. During the year, he rented the house for $4,000 for 30 days and used the house for 10 days during the summer. The house remained vacant during the remainder of the year. The expenses for the home included $5,000 in mortgage interest, $600 in property taxes, $900 for utilities and maintenance, and $3,500 of depreciation. What is John's deductible rental loss, before considering the passive loss limitations?
   a. $200
   b. $875
   c. $1,600
   d. $3,500
   e. $0

LO 4.2

3. Helen, a single taxpayer, has modified adjusted gross income (before passive losses) of $140,000. During 2014, Helen's rental house generated a loss of $15,000. Assuming Helen is actively involved in the management of the property, what is the amount of Helen's passive loss deduction from the rental house?
   a. $0
   b. $5,000
   c. $10,000
   d. $15,000
   e. None of the above

LO 4.2

4. Which of the following is not classified as portfolio income for tax purposes?
   a. Interest income on savings accounts
   b. Income from real estate investments
   c. Interest on taxable bonds
   d. Dividend income from stock
   e. None of the above

LO 4.2

5. Which of the following types of income is passive income?
   a. Net rental income from real estate limited partnership investments
   b. Dividends from domestic corporations
   c. Wages
   d. Interest income from certificates of deposit
   e. None of the above

LO 4.2

6. Which of the following is classified as active income?
   a. Salary income
   b. Interest income
   c. Limited partnership income
   d. Dividend income
   e. None of the above

LO 4.2

7. Nancy has active modified adjusted gross income before passive losses of $75,000. She has a loss of $10,000 on a rental property she actively manages. How much of the loss is she allowed to take against the $75,000 of other income?
   a. None
   b. $2,500
   c. $5,000
   d. $10,000

LO 4.2

8. Ned has active modified adjusted gross income before passive losses of $250,000. He has a loss of $15,000 on rental property he actively manages. How much of the loss is he allowed to take against the $250,000 of other income?
   a. None
   b. $10,000
   c. $15,000
   d. $5,000

LO 4.2

9. Norm is a real estate professional with a real estate trade or business as defined in the tax law. He has $80,000 of business income and $40,000 of losses from actively managed real estate rentals. How much of the $40,000 in losses is he allowed to claim on his tax return?
   a. $25,000
   b. None
   c. $40,000
   d. $20,000

LO 4.3

10. Which type of insurance is not deductible as self-employed health insurance?
    a. Medical insurance
    b. Disability insurance
    c. Dental insurance
    d. Long-term care insurance
    e. Spousal medical insurance

LO 4.3

11. Which of the following is false about the self-employed health insurance deduction?
    a. The deduction cannot be claimed when a subsidized employer health insurance plan is also available.
    b. The deduction cannot be claimed if the taxpayer has an overall business loss from self-employment.
    c. Long-term care premiums may be deducted within specified dollar limitations based on age.
    d. The self-employed health insurance deduction is an itemized deduction.
    e. Dental insurance is included as deductible self-employed health insurance.

LO 4.4

12. Which of the following is a false statement about Health Savings Accounts (HSAs)?
    a. Taxpayers who contribute to an HSA must carry qualifying high-deductible health insurance.
    b. Contributions to HSAs are deductible for AGI subject to dollar limits.
    c. Distributions from HSAs are not taxable when used to pay qualifying medical expenses.
    d. Taxpayers covered by Medicare may contribute to HSAs.
    e. Distributions from HSAs which are not used to pay qualifying medical expenses are generally subjected to a 20 percent penalty as well as income taxes.

LO 4.4

13. Charlene has self-only coverage in qualifying high-deductible health insurance. She is 57 years old and wishes to contribute the maximum amount to her HSA. How much is she allowed to contribute and deduct in 2014?
    a. $1,000
    b. $1,250
    c. $3,300
    d. $4,300
    e. $6,550

LO 4.5

14. All of the following are deductible as moving expenses in 2014, except:
    a. The cost of moving household goods
    b. Transportation to the new job location
    c. Packing expenses
    d. Lodging during the move
    e. All of the above are deductible moving expenses

LO 4.6

15. Lyndon, age 24, has a nonworking spouse and earns wages of $36,000 for 2014. He also received rental income of $5,000 and dividend income of $900 for the year. What is the maximum amount Lyndon can deduct for contributions to his and his wife's individual retirement accounts for the 2014 tax year?
    a. $11,000
    b. $3,600
    c. $4,500
    d. $5,500
    e. None of the above

LO 4.6

16. Martha and Rob, a married couple, under 50 years of age, have adjusted gross income on their 2014 joint income tax return of $45,000, before considering any IRA deduction. Martha and Rob have no earned income. What is the amount of Martha's maximum deductible IRA contribution?
    a. $3,500
    b. $3,000
    c. $2,700
    d. $5,000
    e. $0

LO 4.6

17. Donna, age 42 and a single taxpayer, has a salary of $98,000 and interest income of $19,000. What is the maximum amount Donna can contribute to a Roth IRA?
    a. $4,000
    b. $4,400
    c. $4,840
    d. $5,500
    e. Some other amount

LO 4.6

18. Mary has a Roth IRA held more than 5 years to which she has contributed $30,000. The IRA has a current value of $62,000. Mary is 55 years old and she takes a distribution of $38,000. How much of the distribution will be taxable to Mary?
    a. $0
    b. $8,000
    c. $30,000
    d. $38,000
    e. Some other amount

LO 4.6

19. Marge has a Roth IRA held more than 5 years to which she has contributed $30,000. The IRA has a current value of $62,000. Marge is 65 years old and she takes a distribution of $38,000. How much of the distribution will be taxable to Marge?
    a. $0
    b. $8,000
    c. $30,000
    d. $38,000
    e. Some other amount

LO 4.6

20. Mindy has a Roth IRA held longer than 5 years to which she has contributed $30,000. The IRA has a current value of $62,000. Mindy is 55 years old and she takes a distribution of $38,000 after retiring on disability. How much of the distribution will be taxable to Mindy?
    a. $0
    b. $8,000
    c. $30,000
    d. $38,000
    e. Some other amount

LO 4.6

21. What is the deadline for making a contribution to a traditional IRA or a Roth IRA for 2014?
    a. April 15, 2015
    b. April 15, 2014
    c. December 31, 2014
    d. October 15, 2015

LO 4.7

22. Which of the following statements with respect to a Keogh Plan is *not* accurate?
    a. Self-employed individuals are eligible to be members of a Keogh Retirement Plan.
    b. Contributions to Keogh Plans are limited to 15 percent of the taxpayer's net earned income or $50,000, whichever is greater.
    c. "Net earned income" includes profits from the taxpayer's business.
    d. Taxpayers must begin receiving distributions from a Keogh plan by the age of 70½.
    e. All of the above statements are accurate.

LO 4.8

23. Bob earns $40,000 during the current year. His employer contributes $2,000 (5 percent of Bob's salary) to a qualified retirement plan for Bob. This pension plan is what kind of plan?
    a. Defined benefit plan
    b. Defined contribution plan
    c. Employee Stock Ownership Plan
    d. Profit-sharing plan
    e. None of the above

_______________ 24. What is the maximum tax-deferred contribution that can be made to a Section 401(k) plan for an employee under age 50?

LO 4.8

a. $7,500
b. $10,000
c. $15,000
d. $17,500
e. $23,000

_______________ 25. Paul, age 37, participates in a Section 401(k) plan which allows employees to contribute up to 15 percent of their salary. His annual salary is $90,000 in 2014. What is the maximum he can contribute, on a tax-deferred basis under a salary reduction agreement, to this plan?

LO 4.8

a. $15,500
b. $20,500
c. $17,500
d. $13,500
e. None of the above

_______________ 26. James' employer makes a $2,000 contribution to a qualified retirement plan for James in the current year. James is only 45 years old and does not expect to retire until age 65, 20 years from now. What is the proper tax treatment of the $2,000 contribution for James' employer?

LO 4.8

a. The $2,000 is never deductible.
b. The $2,000 is deductible in the current year by the employer.
c. The $2,000 is deductible in the year James retires by the employer.
d. Only one-twentieth ($100) is deductible in the current year by the employer.
e. None of the above.

_______________ 27. When taxpayers receive distributions from individual retirement plans, how much time is allowed to roll over the amount received into a new plan to avoid paying taxes on the distribution in the current year, assuming there are no unusual events?

LO 4.9

a. 60 days
b. 90 days
c. 180 days
d. 1 year
e. There is no time limit

_______________ 28. Tom quits his job with $120,000 in his employer's qualified retirement plan. Since he is broke, Tom instructs the plan trustee to pay him the balance in his retirement account. How much will Tom receive when he gets his check from the retirement plan?

LO 4.9

a. $120,000
b. $100,000
c. $96,000
d. $24,000
e. Some other amount

_______________ 29. What is the maximum number of distribution rollovers a taxpayer can make during a tax year from one IRA to another?

LO 4.9

a. One
b. Two
c. Four
d. Ten
e. There is no limit

GROUP 2: PROBLEMS

LO 4.1 1. Dick owns a house that he rents to college students. Dick receives $750 per month rent and incurs the following expenses during the year:

Real estate taxes	$1,250
Mortgage interest	1,500
Insurance	375
Repairs	562
Association dues	1,600

Dick purchased the house in 1975 for $48,000. The house is fully depreciated. Calculate Dick's net rental income for the year, assuming the house was rented for a full 12 months.

Rental income $________

Expenses:

________ ________

________ ________

________ ________

________ ________

________ ________

Net rental income $________

LO 4.1 2. Sherry rents her vacation home for 6 months and lives in it for 6 months during the year. Her gross rental income during the year is $4,000. Total real estate taxes for the home are $950, and interest on the home mortgage is $3,000. Annual utilities and maintenance expenses total $1,800, and depreciation expense is $4,500. Calculate Sherry's net income or loss from the vacation home for this tax year.

$________

LO 4.2 3. Walter, a single taxpayer, purchased a limited partnership interest in a tax shelter in 1985. He also acquired a rental house in 2014, which he actively manages. During 2014, Walter's share of the partnership's losses was $30,000, and his rental house generated $20,000 in losses. Walter's modified adjusted gross income before passive losses is $120,000.

a. Calculate the amount of Walter's allowable deduction for rental house activities for 2014.

$________

b. Calculate the amount of Walter's allowable deduction for the partnership losses for 2014.

$________

c. What may be done with the unused losses, if anything?

____

____

____

____

LO 4.2 4. Clifford Johnson has a limited partnership investment and a rental condominium. Clifford actively manages the rental condominium. During 2014, his share of the loss from the limited partnership was $12,000, and his loss from the rental condo was $16,000. Assuming Clifford's modified adjusted gross income is $120,000 for 2014, and he has no prior year unallowed losses from either activity, complete Form 8582 on Page 4-39.

LO 4.5

5. In June of 2014, Keith accepts a new job with the same employer in San Diego. He formerly commuted 12 miles to a job in Canton, OH; San Diego is 2,150 miles from his old home. He incurs the following expenses in his move from Ohio in 2014:

Moving and packing charges	$ 5,100
Travel during the move (includes mileage at $0.235 per mile)	600
Lodging during the move	900
Meals during the move	300
Total	$ 6,900

Keith is not reimbursed for any of these expenses by his employer. What is the amount of Keith's moving expense deduction?

$____________

LO 4.5

6. Assume Keith's employer reimburses him $4,200 for the move. Using the information from Problem 5, calculate Keith's moving expenses deduction using Form 3903 on Page 4-49.

LO 4.5

7. Go to the IRS website (**www.irs.gov**) and redo Problem 6 using the most recent interactive Form 3903, Moving Expenses. Print out the *completed Form 3903.*

LO 4.5

8. Sherry moved to Chicago in the current year to take a new job after being laid off from her job in San Diego. She incurred $5,000 of costs moving her household goods, $300 for a one-way airplane ticket to Chicago, $800 for her first month's rent, and $500 for restaurant meals while looking for the apartment and staying with a friend. How much can Sherry claim as a moving expense?

____

____

____

LO 4.6

9. Karen, 28 years old and a single taxpayer, has a salary of $29,000 and rental income of $33,000 for the 2014 calendar tax year. Karen is covered by a pension through her employer.
   a. What is the maximum amount that Karen may deduct for contributions to her IRA for 2014?

      $____________

   b. If Karen is a calendar year taxpayer and files her tax return on August 15, what is the last date on which she can make her contribution to the IRA and deduct it for 2014?

      $____________

LO 4.6

10. Phil and Linda are 25-year-old newlyweds and file a joint tax return. Linda is covered by a retirement plan at work, but Phil is not.
    a. Assuming Phil's wages were $27,000 and Linda's wages were $18,500 for 2014 and they had no other income, what is the maximum amount of their deductible contributions to an IRA for 2014?

       Phil $____________
       Linda $____________

    b. Assuming Phil's wages were $49,000 and Linda's wages were $68,000 for 2014 and they had no other income, what is the maximum amount of their deductible contributions to an IRA for 2014?

       Phil $____________
       Linda $____________

Form **8582**

Department of the Treasury
Internal Revenue Service (99)

Passive Activity Loss Limitations

▶ See separate instructions.
▶ Attach to Form 1040 or Form 1041.
▶ Information about Form 8582 and its instructions is available at *www.irs.gov/form8582.*

OMB No. 1545-1008
2013*
Attachment Sequence No. **88**

Name(s) shown on return | **Identifying number**

Part I **2013 Passive Activity Loss**
Caution: *Complete Worksheets 1, 2, and 3 before completing Part I.*

Rental Real Estate Activities With Active Participation (For the definition of active participation, see **Special Allowance for Rental Real Estate Activities** in the instructions.)			
1a Activities with net income (enter the amount from Worksheet 1, column (a))	1a		
b Activities with net loss (enter the amount from Worksheet 1, column (b))	1b	( )	
c Prior years unallowed losses (enter the amount from Worksheet 1, column (c))	1c	( )	
d Combine lines 1a, 1b, and 1c			1d
Commercial Revitalization Deductions From Rental Real Estate Activities			
2a Commercial revitalization deductions from Worksheet 2, column (a)	2a	( )	
b Prior year unallowed commercial revitalization deductions from Worksheet 2, column (b)	2b	( )	
c Add lines 2a and 2b			2c ( )
All Other Passive Activities			
3a Activities with net income (enter the amount from Worksheet 3, column (a))	3a		
b Activities with net loss (enter the amount from Worksheet 3, column (b))	3b	( )	
c Prior years unallowed losses (enter the amount from Worksheet 3, column (c))	3c	( )	
d Combine lines 3a, 3b, and 3c			3d
4 Combine lines 1d, 2c, and 3d. If this line is zero or more, stop here and include this form with your return; all losses are allowed, including any prior year unallowed losses entered on line 1c, 2b, or 3c. Report the losses on the forms and schedules normally used			4

If line 4 is a loss and:
- Line 1d is a loss, go to Part II.
- Line 2c is a loss (and line 1d is zero or more), skip Part II and go to Part III.
- Line 3d is a loss (and lines 1d and 2c are zero or more), skip Parts II and III and go to line 15.

Caution: *If your filing status is married filing separately and you lived with your spouse at any time during the year,* **do not** *complete Part II or Part III. Instead, go to line 15.*

Part II **Special Allowance for Rental Real Estate Activities With Active Participation**
Note: *Enter all numbers in Part II as positive amounts. See instructions for an example.*

5 Enter the **smaller** of the loss on line 1d or the loss on line 4			5
6 Enter $150,000. If married filing separately, see instructions	6		
7 Enter modified adjusted gross income, but not less than zero (see instructions)	7		
Note: *If line 7 is greater than or equal to line 6, skip lines 8 and 9, enter -0- on line 10. Otherwise, go to line 8.*			
8 Subtract line 7 from line 6	8		
9 Multiply line 8 by 50% (.5). **Do not** enter more than $25,000. If married filing separately, see instructions			9
10 Enter the **smaller** of line 5 or line 9			10

If line 2c is a loss, go to Part III. Otherwise, go to line 15.

Part III **Special Allowance for Commercial Revitalization Deductions From Rental Real Estate Activities**
Note: *Enter all numbers in Part III as positive amounts. See the example for Part II in the instructions.*

11 Enter $25,000 reduced by the amount, if any, on line 10. If married filing separately, see instructions	11
12 Enter the loss from line 4	12
13 Reduce line 12 by the amount on line 10	13
14 Enter the **smallest** of line 2c (treated as a positive amount), line 11, or line 13	14

Part IV **Total Losses Allowed**

15 Add the income, if any, on lines 1a and 3a and enter the total	15
16 **Total losses allowed from all passive activities for 2013.** Add lines 10, 14, and 15. See instructions to find out how to report the losses on your tax return	16

For Paperwork Reduction Act Notice, see instructions. Cat. No. 63704F Form **8582** (2013)

***The 2014 version of this form was not available as we went to press. Please check the IRS website for updates.**

LO 4.6 11. What is the maximum amount a 45-year-old taxpayer and 45-year-old spouse can put into a Traditional or Roth IRA for 2014 (assuming they have sufficient earned income, but do not have an income limitation and are not covered by another pension plan)? ___________

LO 4.6 12. What is the maximum amount a 55-year-old taxpayer and 52-year-old spouse can put into a Traditional or Roth IRA for 2014, assuming they earn $70,000 in total and are not participants in pension plans? ___________

LO 4.6 13. Barry is a single, 40-year-old software engineer earning $190,000 a year and is not covered by a pension plan at work. How much can he put into a Roth IRA in 2014? ___________

LO 4.6 14. Bob is a single, 40-year-old doctor earning $190,000 a year and is not covered by a pension plan at work. How much can he put into a deductible Traditional IRA in 2014? ___________

LO 4.6 15. Dori is 58 years old and retired in 2014. She receives a pension of $25,000 a year and no other income. She wishes to put the maximum allowed into an IRA. How much can she contribute to her IRA? ___________

LO 4.7 16. During 2014, Jerry is a self-employed therapist, and his net earned income is $160,000 from his practice. Jerry's Keogh Plan, a defined contribution plan, states that he will contribute the maximum amount allowable. Calculate Jerry's contribution.

$___________

LO 4.7 17. Tony is a 45-year-old psychiatrist who has net earned income of $300,000 in 2014. What is the maximum amount he can contribute to his Simplified Employee Pension (SEP) for the year? ___________

LO 4.7 18. Anthony, a self-employed plumber, makes a maximum contribution to his SEP. His net earned income is $40,000. How much is he allowed to contribute to the plan?

$___________

LO 4.8 19. During 2014, Jill, age 39, participated in a Section 401(k) plan which provides for maximum employee contributions of 12 percent. Jill's salary was $90,000 for the year. Jill elects to make the maximum contribution. What is Jill's maximum tax-deferred contribution to the plan for the year?

$___________

LO 4.9 20. Telly, age 38, has a $140,000 IRA with Blue Mutual Fund. He has read good things about the management of Green Mutual Fund, so he opens a Green Fund IRA. Telly asked for and received his balance from the Blue Fund on May 1, 2014.

a. What amount will Telly receive from the Blue Fund IRA?

$___________

b. What amount must Telly contribute to the Green Fund IRA to avoid having taxable income and penalties for early withdrawal?

$___________

c. When is the last day Telly can roll over the amount received into the Green Fund IRA and avoid taxation in the current year, assuming no unusual circumstances?

____

d. What amount would Telly receive if the distribution were from his employer's qualified retirement plan?

$___________

LO 4.9

21. Allen (age 32) takes a distribution of $20,000 from his Traditional IRA account which he plans to deposit into an IRA with a different bank. During the 60-day rollover period, he gambles and loses the entire IRA balance. What income and/or penalties must he show on his tax return related to the failed rollover?

____

____

____

____

GROUP 3:
WRITING ASSIGNMENT

RESEARCH

Your supervisor has asked you to research the following situation concerning Shanita Mauer. Shanita worked and lived in Los Angeles, CA. She accepted a new position with her firm in Dallas, TX. During the move, Shanita incurred the following expenses:

Cost of moving furniture	$4,200
Transportation	750
Lodging	300
Cost of breaking lease on Los Angeles apartment	1,000
Security deposit on Dallas apartment	1,250
Total	$7,500

Required: Go to the IRS website (**www.irs.gov**). Locate and review Publication 521. Write a file memorandum stating the amount of moving expense that Shanita can claim. (An example of a file memorandum is available at the website for this text located at **www.cengagebrain.com.**)

GROUP 4:
COMPREHENSIVE PROBLEMS

1. Rebecca and Walter Bunge have been married for 5 years. They live at 883 Scrub Brush Street, Apt. 52B, Las Vegas, NV 89125. Rebecca is a homemaker and Walt is a high school teacher. Rebecca's Social Security number is 222-43-7690 and Walt's is 700-01-0002. Walt's earnings from teaching are:

Earnings from Las Vegas School Dist.	$50,000
Federal income tax withheld	5,000
State income tax withheld	0

The Bunges incurred the following expenses during their move from Maine to Nevada in January of 2014:

Cost of moving furniture	$4,300
Travel (3,166 miles at $0.235)	744
Lodging en route	150
Meals en route	90
House-hunting trip before the move	750

Walter's previous job, as a high school teacher in Maine, was only 5 miles from his home. Rebecca was unemployed prior to the move.

The Bunges own a ski condo in Utah. The condo was rented for 40 days during 2014 and used by the Bunges for 10 days. Pertinent information about the condo rental is as follows:

Rental income	$6,000
Mortgage interest	4,800
Homeowners' association dues	2,000
Utilities	1,000
Maintenance	2,800
Depreciation (assume fully depreciated)	0

The above amounts do not reflect any allocation between rental and personal use of the condo. The Bunges are active managers of the condo.

Required: Complete the Bunge's federal tax return for 2014. Use Form 1040, Schedule E, and Form 3903 on Pages 4-45 through 4-48 to complete their tax return.

2A. Dr. George E. Beeper is a single taxpayer. He lives at 45 Mountain View Dr., Apt. 321, Spokane, WA 99210. Dr. Beeper's Social Security number is 775-88-9531. Dr. Beeper works for the Pine Medical Group, and his earnings and income tax withholding for 2014 are:

Earnings from Pine Medical	$116,000
Federal tax withheld	25,000
State tax withheld	0

Dr. Beeper owns a rental house located at 672 Lake Street, Spokane, WA 99212. The house rents for $1,000 per month and was rented for the entire year. The following are the related expenses for the rental house:

Real estate taxes	$ 3,500
Mortgage interest	12,500
Insurance	900
Depreciation (assume fully depreciated)	0
Gardening	1,000
Repairs	600
Maintenance	3,636

The house was purchased on July 5, 1980. Dr. Beeper handles all rental activities (e.g., rent collection, finding tenants, etc.) himself.

During May 2014, Dr. Beeper transferred $67,000 out of his Section 401(k) plan from a former employer (Elm Medical Group) to an individual retirement account with the Spokane State Bank. The transfer was made directly from the Section 401(k) plan trustee to the bank.

Required: Complete Dr. Beeper's federal tax return for 2014. Use Form 1040, Schedule E, and Form 8582 on Pages 4-51 through 4-55 to complete this tax return. Do not complete Form 4562 for reporting depreciation. Make realistic assumptions about any missing data.

2B. Professor Patricia (Patty) Pâté is retired from the Palm Springs Culinary Arts Academy (PSCAA). She is a single taxpayer and is 68 years old. Patty lives at 98 Colander Street, Henderson, NV 89052. Professor Pâté's Social Security number is 565-66-9378. Patty receives monthly retirement benefits from her PSCAA retirement plan. Earnings and income tax withholding shown on her retirement 2014 Form 1099-R are:

Gross distribution and taxable amount	$61,200
Federal tax withheld	7,350
State tax withheld	0

Patricia owns a rental condo located at 392 Spatula Way, The Lakes, NV 88905. The condo rents for $850 per month and was rented for the entire year. The following are the related expenses for the rental house:

Real estate taxes	$2,725
Mortgage interest	7,500
Insurance	410
Depreciation (assume fully depreciated)	0
Homeowners' Association dues	1,540
Repairs	1,300
Gardening	2,090

The condo was purchased on August 31, 1977. Professor Pâté handles all rental activities (e.g., rent collection, finding tenants, etc.) herself.

During March 2014, Patricia took a $75,000 distribution from her 401(k) plan. Patricia received only $60,000 because the 401(k) plan administrators withheld $15,000 federal income tax from the distribution. Forty-five days after the distribution, Patricia deposited $50,000 in a rollover IRA, keeping $10,000 of the $60,000 received in order to remodel her kitchen.

Required: Complete Professor Pâté's federal tax return for 2014. Use Form 1040, Schedule E, and Form 8582 on Pages 4-51 through 4-55 to complete this tax return. Do not complete Form 4562 for reporting depreciation. Make realistic assumptions about any missing data.

GROUP 5: CUMULATIVE SOFTWARE PROBLEM

The following additional information is available for the Dr. Ivan and Irene Incisor family.

The Incisors own a rental beach house in Hawaii. The beach house was rented for the full year during 2014 and was not used by the Incisors during the year. The Incisors were active participants in the management of the rental. Pertinent information about the rental house is as follows:

Address: 1237 Pineapple St., Lihue, HI 96766	
Net rental income	$20,350
Mortgage interest	7,800
Real estate taxes	2,400
Utilities	1,825
Maintenance	3,000

The house is fully depreciated so there is no depreciation expense.

For the 2014 tax year, on March 15, 2015, Ivan contributes $5,500 to a traditional IRA for himself and $5,500 to a traditional IRA for his wife. He is not covered by a qualified retirement plan at work.

Irene had a retirement plan at the job from which she was laid off on January 2, 2014. The plan had a balance of $24,000. On May 10, 2014, Irene had the entire retirement plan balance rolled directly into an IRA at Timador & Embaucar Brokerage, Inc.

Required: Combine this new information about the Incisor family with the information from Chapters 1–3 and complete a revised 2014 tax return for Ivan and Irene. Be sure to save your data input files since this case will be expanded with more tax information in later chapters. Note that the "Saver's Credit" discussed in LO 4.8, also known as the "Surprise Credit," may apply.

Form **1040** Department of the Treasury—Internal Revenue Service (99)
U.S. Individual Income Tax Return 2014
OMB No. 1545-0074 IRS Use Only—Do not write or staple in this space.

For the year Jan. 1–Dec. 31, 2014, or other tax year beginning , 2014, ending , 20 See separate instructions.

Your first name and initial	Last name	**Your social security number**
If a joint return, spouse's first name and initial	Last name	**Spouse's social security number**
Home address (number and street). If you have a P.O. box, see instructions.	Apt. no.	▲ Make sure the SSN(s) above and on line 6c are correct.
City, town or post office, state, and ZIP code. If you have a foreign address, also complete spaces below (see instructions).		**Presidential Election Campaign** Check here if you, or your spouse if filing jointly, want $3 to go to this fund. Checking a box below will not change your tax or refund. ☐ You ☐ Spouse
Foreign country name	Foreign province/state/county · Foreign postal code	

Filing Status

Check only one box.

1 ☐ Single
2 ☐ Married filing jointly (even if only one had income)
3 ☐ Married filing separately. Enter spouse's SSN above and full name here. ▶
4 ☐ Head of household (with qualifying person). (See instructions.) If the qualifying person is a child but not your dependent, enter this child's name here. ▶
5 ☐ Qualifying widow(er) with dependent child

Exemptions

6a ☐ **Yourself.** If someone can claim you as a dependent, **do not** check box 6a
b ☐ **Spouse**
Boxes checked on 6a and 6b

c **Dependents:**

(1) First name Last name	(2) Dependent's social security number	(3) Dependent's relationship to you	(4) ✓ if child under age 17 qualifying for child tax credit (see instructions)
			☐
			☐
			☐
			☐

No. of children on 6c who:
• lived with you
• did not live with you due to divorce or separation (see instructions)
Dependents on 6c not entered above

If more than four dependents, see instructions and check here ▶ ☐

d Total number of exemptions claimed **Add numbers on lines above ▶**

Income

Attach Form(s) W-2 here. Also attach Forms W-2G and 1099-R if tax was withheld.

If you did not get a W-2, see instructions.

Line	Description		
7	Wages, salaries, tips, etc. Attach Form(s) W-2		7
8a	**Taxable** interest. Attach Schedule B if required		8a
b	**Tax-exempt** interest. **Do not** include on line 8a	8b	
9a	Ordinary dividends. Attach Schedule B if required		9a
b	Qualified dividends	9b	
10	Taxable refunds, credits, or offsets of state and local income taxes		10
11	Alimony received		11
12	Business income or (loss). Attach Schedule C or C-EZ		12
13	Capital gain or (loss). Attach Schedule D if required. If not required, check here ▶ ☐		13
14	Other gains or (losses). Attach Form 4797		14
15a	IRA distributions	15a	b Taxable amount 15b
16a	Pensions and annuities	16a	b Taxable amount 16b
17	Rental real estate, royalties, partnerships, S corporations, trusts, etc. Attach Schedule E		17
18	Farm income or (loss). Attach Schedule F		18
19	Unemployment compensation		19
20a	Social security benefits	20a	b Taxable amount 20b
21	Other income. List type and amount		21
22	Combine the amounts in the far right column for lines 7 through 21. This is your **total income** ▶		22

DRAFT AS OF August 28, 20 DO NOT FILE

Adjusted Gross Income

Line	Description		
23	Reserved	23	
24	Certain business expenses of reservists, performing artists, and fee-basis government officials. Attach Form 2106 or 2106-EZ	24	
25	Health savings account deduction. Attach Form 8889	25	
26	Moving expenses. Attach Form 3903	26	
27	Deductible part of self-employment tax. Attach Schedule SE	27	
28	Self-employed SEP, SIMPLE, and qualified plans	28	
29	Self-employed health insurance deduction	29	
30	Penalty on early withdrawal of savings	30	
31a	Alimony paid b Recipient's SSN ▶	31a	
32	IRA deduction	32	
33	Student loan interest deduction	33	
34	Reserved	34	
35	Domestic production activities deduction. Attach Form 8903	35	
36	Add lines 23 through 35		36
37	Subtract line 36 from line 22. This is your **adjusted gross income** ▶		37

For Disclosure, Privacy Act, and Paperwork Reduction Act Notice, see separate instructions. Cat. No. 11320B Form **1040** (2014)

Form 1040 (2014) Page **2**

DRAFT AS OF August 28, 2014 DO NOT FILE

Tax and Credits

Line	Description	Box
38	Amount from line 37 (adjusted gross income)	38
39a	Check if: ☐ **You** were born before January 2, 1950, ☐ Blind. ☐ **Spouse** was born before January 2, 1950, ☐ Blind. **Total boxes checked ▶ 39a** ☐	
b	If your spouse itemizes on a separate return or you were a dual-status alien, check here ▶ **39b** ☐	
40	**Itemized deductions** (from Schedule A) **or** your **standard deduction** (see left margin)	40
41	Subtract line 40 from line 38	41
42	**Exemptions.** If line 38 is $152,525 or less, multiply $3,950 by the number on line 6d. Otherwise, see instructions	42
43	**Taxable income.** Subtract line 42 from line 41. If line 42 is more than line 41, enter -0-	43
44	**Tax** (see instructions). Check if any from: **a** ☐ Form(s) 8814 **b** ☐ Form 4972 **c** ☐	44
45	**Alternative minimum tax** (see instructions). Attach Form 6251	45
46	Excess advance premium tax credit repayment. Attach Form 8962	46
47	Add lines 44, 45, and 46 ▶	47
48	Foreign tax credit. Attach Form 1116 if required — 48	
49	Credit for child and dependent care expenses. Attach Form 2441 — 49	
50	Education credits from Form 8863, line 19 — 50	
51	Retirement savings contributions credit. Attach Form 8880 — 51	
52	Child tax credit. Attach Schedule 8812, if required — 52	
53	Residential energy credit. Attach Form 5695 — 53	
54	Other credits from Form: **a** ☐ 3800 **b** ☐ 8801 **c** ☐ — 54	
55	Add lines 48 through 54. These are your **total credits**	55
56	Subtract line 55 from line 47. If line 55 is more than line 47, enter -0- ▶	56

Standard Deduction for—
- People who check any box on line 39a or 39b **or** who can be claimed as a dependent, see instructions.
- All others:

Single or Married filing separately, $6,200

Married filing jointly or Qualifying widow(er), $12,400

Head of household, $9,100

Other Taxes

Line	Description	Box
57	Self-employment tax. Attach Schedule SE	57
58	Unreported social security and Medicare tax from Form: **a** ☐ 4137 **b** ☐ 8919	58
59	Additional tax on IRAs, other qualified retirement plans, etc. Attach Form 5329 if required	59
60a	Household employment taxes from Schedule H	60a
b	First-time homebuyer credit repayment. Attach Form 5405 if required	60b
61	Health care: individual responsibility (see instructions) Full-year coverage ☐	61
62	Taxes from: **a** ☐ Form 8959 **b** ☐ Form 8960 **c** ☐ Instructions; enter code(s)	62
63	Add lines 56 through 62. This is your **total tax** ▶	63

Payments

Line	Description	Box
64	Federal income tax withheld from Forms W-2 and 1099 — 64	
65	2014 estimated tax payments and amount applied from 2013 return — 65	
66a	**Earned income credit (EIC)** — 66a	
b	Nontaxable combat pay election — 66b	
67	Additional child tax credit. Attach Schedule 8812 — 67	
68	American opportunity credit from Form 8863, line 8 — 68	
69	Net premium tax credit. Attach Form 8962 — 69	
70	Amount paid with request for extension to file — 70	
71	Excess social security and tier 1 RRTA tax withheld — 71	
72	Credit for federal tax on fuels. Attach Form 4136 — 72	
73	Credits from Form: **a** ☐ 2439 **b** Reserved **c** Reserved **d** ☐ — 73	
74	Add lines 64, 65, 66a, and 67 through 73. These are your **total payments** ▶	74

If you have a qualifying child, attach Schedule EIC.

Refund

Line	Description	Box
75	If line 74 is more than line 63, subtract line 63 from line 74. This is the amount you **overpaid**	75
76a	Amount of line 75 you want **refunded to you.** If Form 8888 is attached, check here ▶ ☐	76a
▶ b	Routing number ▶ **c** Type: ☐ Checking ☐ Savings	
▶ d	Account number	
77	Amount of line 75 you want **applied to your 2015 estimated tax** ▶ 77	

Direct deposit? See instructions.

Amount You Owe

Line	Description	Box
78	**Amount you owe.** Subtract line 74 from line 63. For details on how to pay, see instructions ▶	78
79	Estimated tax penalty (see instructions) — 79	

Third Party Designee

Do you want to allow another person to discuss this return with the IRS (see instructions)? ☐ **Yes.** Complete below. ☐ **No**

Designee's name ▶ Phone no. ▶ Personal identification number (PIN) ▶

Sign Here

Under penalties of perjury, I declare that I have examined this return and accompanying schedules and statements, and to the best of my knowledge and belief, they are true, correct, and complete. Declaration of preparer (other than taxpayer) is based on all information of which preparer has any knowledge.

Joint return? See instructions. Keep a copy for your records.

Your signature	Date	Your occupation	Daytime phone number
Spouse's signature. If a joint return, **both** must sign.	Date	Spouse's occupation	If the IRS sent you an Identity Protection PIN, enter it here (see inst.)

Paid Preparer Use Only

Print/Type preparer's name	Preparer's signature	Date	Check ☐ if self-employed	PTIN
Firm's name ▶			Firm's EIN ▶	
Firm's address ▶			Phone no.	

SCHEDULE E (Form 1040)

Department of the Treasury Internal Revenue Service (99)

Supplemental Income and Loss

(From rental real estate, royalties, partnerships, S corporations, estates, trusts, REMICs, etc.)

▶ **Attach to Form 1040, 1040NR, or Form 1041.**

▶ **Information about Schedule E and its separate instructions is at *www.irs.gov/schedulee.***

OMB No. 1545-0074

2014

Attachment Sequence No. **13**

DRAFT AS OF June 6, 2014 DO NOT FILE

Name(s) shown on return | **Your social security number**

Part I **Income or Loss From Rental Real Estate and Royalties** **Note.** If you are in the business of renting personal property, use **Schedule C** or **C-EZ** (see instructions). If you are an individual, report farm rental income or loss from **Form 4835** on page 2, line 40.

A Did you make any payments in 2014 that would require you to file Form(s) 1099? (see instructions) ☐ Yes ☐ No

B If "Yes," did you or will you file required Forms 1099? ☐ Yes ☐ No

1a	Physical address of each property (street, city, state, ZIP code)
A	
B	
C	

1b	Type of Property (from list below)	**2** For each rental real estate property listed above, report the number of fair rental and personal use days. Check the **QJV** box only if you meet the requirements to file as a qualified joint venture. See instructions.		**Fair Rental Days**	**Personal Use Days**	**QJV**
A			**A**			☐
B			**B**			☐
C			**C**			☐

Type of Property:
1 Single Family Residence
2 Multi-Family Residence
3 Vacation/Short-Term Rental
4 Commercial
5 Land
6 Royalties
7 Self-Rental
8 Other (describe)

Income:	**Properties:**	**A**	**B**	**C**
3 Rents received	**3**			
4 Royalties received	**4**			
Expenses:				
5 Advertising	**5**			
6 Auto and travel (see instructions)	**6**			
7 Cleaning and maintenance	**7**			
8 Commissions	**8**			
9 Insurance	**9**			
10 Legal and other professional fees	**10**			
11 Management fees	**11**			
12 Mortgage interest paid to banks, etc. (see instructions)	**12**			
13 Other interest	**13**			
14 Repairs	**14**			
15 Supplies	**15**			
16 Taxes	**16**			
17 Utilities	**17**			
18 Depreciation expense or depletion	**18**			
19 Other (list) ▶	**19**			
20 Total expenses. Add lines 5 through 19	**20**			
21 Subtract line 20 from line 3 (rents) and/or 4 (royalties). If result is a (loss), see instructions to find out if you must file **Form 6198**	**21**			
22 Deductible rental real estate loss after limitation, if any, on **Form 8582** (see instructions)	**22**	( )	( )	( )

23a Total of all amounts reported on line 3 for all rental properties	**23a**	
b Total of all amounts reported on line 4 for all royalty properties	**23b**	
c Total of all amounts reported on line 12 for all properties	**23c**	
d Total of all amounts reported on line 18 for all properties	**23d**	
e Total of all amounts reported on line 20 for all properties	**23e**	
24 **Income.** Add positive amounts shown on line 21. **Do not** include any losses	**24**	
25 **Losses.** Add royalty losses from line 21 and rental real estate losses from line 22. Enter total losses here	**25**	( )
26 **Total rental real estate and royalty income or (loss).** Combine lines 24 and 25. Enter the result here. If Parts II, III, IV, and line 40 on page 2 do not apply to you, also enter this amount on Form 1040, line 17, or Form 1040NR, line 18. Otherwise, include this amount in the total on line 41 on page 2	**26**	

For Paperwork Reduction Act Notice, see the separate instructions. Cat. No. 11344L **Schedule E (Form 1040) 2014**

Form **3903**

Department of the Treasury
Internal Revenue Service (99)

Moving Expenses

► **Information about Form 3903 and its instructions is available at *www.irs.gov/form3903.***
► **Attach to Form 1040 or Form 1040NR.**

OMB No. 1545-0074
2014
Attachment Sequence No. **170**

Name(s) shown on return	**Your social security number**

Before you begin: ✓ See the **Distance Test** and **Time Test** in the instructions to find out if you can deduct your moving expenses.
✓ See **Members of the Armed Forces** in the instructions, if applicable.

DRAFT AS OF July 3, 2014 DO NOT FILE

1	Transportation and storage of household goods and personal effects (see instructions) . . .	**1**	
2	Travel (including lodging) from your old home to your new home (see instructions). **Do not** include the cost of meals . . .	**2**	
3	Add lines 1 and 2 . . .	**3**	
4	Enter the total amount your employer paid you for the expenses listed on lines 1 and 2 that is **not** included in box 1 of your Form W-2 (wages). This amount should be shown in box 12 of your Form W-2 with code **P** . . .	**4**	
5	Is line 3 **more than** line 4? ☐ **No.** You **cannot** deduct your moving expenses. If line 3 is less than line 4, subtract line 3 from line 4 and include the result on Form 1040, line 7, or Form 1040NR, line 8. ☐ **Yes.** Subtract line 4 from line 3. Enter the result here and on Form 1040, line 26, or Form 1040NR, line 26. This is your **moving expense deduction** . . .	**5**	

For Paperwork Reduction Act Notice, see your tax return instructions. Cat. No. 12490K Form **3903** (2014)

Form **3903**

Department of the Treasury
Internal Revenue Service (99)

Moving Expenses

► **Information about Form 3903 and its instructions is available at *www.irs.gov/form3903*.**

► **Attach to Form 1040 or Form 1040NR.**

OMB No. 1545-0074

2014

Attachment Sequence No. **170**

Name(s) shown on return	**Your social security number**

Before you begin: ✓ See the **Distance Test** and **Time Test** in the instructions to find out if you can deduct your moving expenses.

✓ See **Members of the Armed Forces** in the instructions, if applicable.

DRAFT AS OF July 3, 2014 DO NOT FILE

1	Transportation and storage of household goods and personal effects (see instructions) . . .	**1**	
2	Travel (including lodging) from your old home to your new home (see instructions). **Do not** include the cost of meals	**2**	
3	Add lines 1 and 2	**3**	
4	Enter the total amount your employer paid you for the expenses listed on lines 1 and 2 that is **not** included in box 1 of your Form W-2 (wages). This amount should be shown in box 12 of your Form W-2 with code **P**	**4**	
5	Is line 3 **more than** line 4?		
	☐ **No.** You **cannot** deduct your moving expenses. If line 3 is less than line 4, subtract line 3 from line 4 and include the result on Form 1040, line 7, or Form 1040NR, line 8.		
	☐ **Yes.** Subtract line 4 from line 3. Enter the result here and on Form 1040, line 26, or Form 1040NR, line 26. This is your **moving expense deduction**	**5**	

For Paperwork Reduction Act Notice, see your tax return instructions. Cat. No. 12490K Form **3903** (2014)

Form **1040** Department of the Treasury—Internal Revenue Service (99)
U.S. Individual Income Tax Return **2014** OMB No. 1545-0074 IRS Use Only—Do not write or staple in this space.

DRAFT AS OF August 28, 2014 DO NOT FILE

For the year Jan. 1–Dec. 31, 2014, or other tax year beginning , 2014, ending , 20 — See separate instructions.

Your first name and initial	Last name	**Your social security number**
If a joint return, spouse's first name and initial	Last name	**Spouse's social security number**
Home address (number and street). If you have a P.O. box, see instructions.	Apt. no.	▲ Make sure the SSN(s) above and on line 6c are correct.
City, town or post office, state, and ZIP code. If you have a foreign address, also complete spaces below (see instructions).		**Presidential Election Campaign** Check here if you, or your spouse if filing jointly, want $3 to go to this fund. Checking a box below will not change your tax or refund. ☐ You ☐ Spouse
Foreign country name	Foreign province/state/county	Foreign postal code

Filing Status

Check only one box.

1 ☐ Single
2 ☐ Married filing jointly (even if only one had income)
3 ☐ Married filing separately. Enter spouse's SSN above and full name here. ▶
4 ☐ Head of household (with qualifying person). (See instructions.) If the qualifying person is a child but not your dependent, enter this child's name here. ▶
5 ☐ Qualifying widow(er) with dependent child

Exemptions

6a ☐ **Yourself.** If someone can claim you as a dependent, **do not** check box 6a
b ☐ **Spouse**

Boxes checked on 6a and 6b

c **Dependents:**

(1) First name Last name	(2) Dependent's social security number	(3) Dependent's relationship to you	(4) ✓ if child under age 17 qualifying for child tax credit (see instructions)
			☐
			☐
			☐
			☐

If more than four dependents, see instructions and check here ▶ ☐

No. of children on 6c who:
• lived with you
• did not live with you due to divorce or separation (see instructions)
Dependents on 6c not entered above

d Total number of exemptions claimed — **Add numbers on lines above ▶**

Income

Attach Form(s) W-2 here. Also attach Forms W-2G and 1099-R if tax was withheld.

If you did not get a W-2, see instructions.

Line	Description		Line	Amount
7	Wages, salaries, tips, etc. Attach Form(s) W-2		7	
8a	**Taxable** interest. Attach Schedule B if required		8a	
b	**Tax-exempt** interest. **Do not** include on line 8a	8b		
9a	Ordinary dividends. Attach Schedule B if required		9a	
b	Qualified dividends	9b		
10	Taxable refunds, credits, or offsets of state and local income taxes		10	
11	Alimony received		11	
12	Business income or (loss). Attach Schedule C or C-EZ		12	
13	Capital gain or (loss). Attach Schedule D if required. If not required, check here ▶ ☐		13	
14	Other gains or (losses). Attach Form 4797		14	
15a	IRA distributions 15a	b Taxable amount	15b	
16a	Pensions and annuities 16a	b Taxable amount	16b	
17	Rental real estate, royalties, partnerships, S corporations, trusts, etc. Attach Schedule E		17	
18	Farm income or (loss). Attach Schedule F		18	
19	Unemployment compensation		19	
20a	Social security benefits 20a	b Taxable amount	20b	
21	Other income. List type and amount		21	
22	Combine the amounts in the far right column for lines 7 through 21. This is your **total income** ▶		22	

Adjusted Gross Income

Line	Description	Line	Amount	Line	Amount
23	Reserved	23			
24	Certain business expenses of reservists, performing artists, and fee-basis government officials. Attach Form 2106 or 2106-EZ	24			
25	Health savings account deduction. Attach Form 8889	25			
26	Moving expenses. Attach Form 3903	26			
27	Deductible part of self-employment tax. Attach Schedule SE	27			
28	Self-employed SEP, SIMPLE, and qualified plans	28			
29	Self-employed health insurance deduction	29			
30	Penalty on early withdrawal of savings	30			
31a	Alimony paid b Recipient's SSN ▶	31a			
32	IRA deduction	32			
33	Student loan interest deduction	33			
34	Reserved	34			
35	Domestic production activities deduction. Attach Form 8903	35			
36	Add lines 23 through 35			36	
37	Subtract line 36 from line 22. This is your **adjusted gross income** ▶			37	

For Disclosure, Privacy Act, and Paperwork Reduction Act Notice, see separate instructions. Cat. No. 11320B Form **1040** (2014)

Form 1040 (2014) Page **2**

DRAFT AS OF August 28, 2014 DO NOT FILE

Tax and Credits

38 Amount from line 37 (adjusted gross income) 38

39a Check if: { ☐ **You** were born before January 2, 1950, ☐ Blind. } **Total boxes checked ▶ 39a** ☐
{ ☐ **Spouse** was born before January 2, 1950, ☐ Blind. }

b If your spouse itemizes on a separate return or you were a dual-status alien, check here ▶ 39b ☐

Standard Deduction for—
• People who check any box on line 39a or 39b **or** who can be claimed as a dependent, see instructions.
• All others:
Single or Married filing separately, $6,200
Married filing jointly or Qualifying widow(er), $12,400
Head of household, $9,100

40 **Itemized deductions** (from Schedule A) **or** your **standard deduction** (see left margin) . . 40

41 Subtract line 40 from line 38 41

42 **Exemptions.** If line 38 is $152,525 or less, multiply $3,950 by the number on line 6d. Otherwise, see instructions 42

43 **Taxable income.** Subtract line 42 from line 41. If line 42 is more than line 41, enter -0- . . 43

44 **Tax** (see instructions). Check if any from: **a** ☐ Form(s) 8814 **b** ☐ Form 4972 **c** ☐ ______ 44

45 **Alternative minimum tax** (see instructions). Attach Form 6251 45

46 Excess advance premium tax credit repayment. Attach Form 8962 46

47 Add lines 44, 45, and 46 . . . . ▶ 47

48 Foreign tax credit. Attach Form 1116 if required 48

49 Credit for child and dependent care expenses. Attach Form 2441 49

50 Education credits from Form 8863, line 19 50

51 Retirement savings contributions credit. Attach Form 8880 51

52 Child tax credit. Attach Schedule 8812, if required . . . 52

53 Residential energy credit. Attach Form 5695 . . . 53

54 Other credits from Form: **a** ☐ 3800 **b** ☐ 8801 **c** ☐ ______ 54

55 Add lines 48 through 54. These are your **total credits** 55

56 Subtract line 55 from line 47. If line 55 is more than line 47, enter -0- . . . . ▶ 56

Other Taxes

57 Self-employment tax. Attach Schedule SE 57

58 Unreported social security and Medicare tax from Form: **a** ☐ 4137 **b** ☐ 8919 . . 58

59 Additional tax on IRAs, other qualified retirement plans, etc. Attach Form 5329 if required . . 59

60a Household employment taxes from Schedule H 60a

b First-time homebuyer credit repayment. Attach Form 5405 if required 60b

61 Health care: individual responsibility (see instructions) Full-year coverage ☐ 61

62 Taxes from: **a** ☐ Form 8959 **b** ☐ Form 8960 **c** ☐ Instructions; enter code(s) ______ 62

63 Add lines 56 through 62. This is your **total tax** . . . . ▶ 63

Payments

64 Federal income tax withheld from Forms W-2 and 1099 . . 64

65 2014 estimated tax payments and amount applied from 2013 return 65

If you have a qualifying child, attach Schedule EIC.

66a **Earned income credit (EIC)** 66a

b Nontaxable combat pay election 66b

67 Additional child tax credit. Attach Schedule 8812 67

68 American opportunity credit from Form 8863, line 8 . . . 68

69 Net premium tax credit. Attach Form 8962 69

70 Amount paid with request for extension to file 70

71 Excess social security and tier 1 RRTA tax withheld 71

72 Credit for federal tax on fuels. Attach Form 4136 72

73 Credits from Form: **a** ☐ 2439 **b** ☐ Reserved **c** ☐ Reserved **d** ☐ ______ 73

74 Add lines 64, 65, 66a, and 67 through 73. These are your **total payments** . . . . ▶ 74

Refund

75 If line 74 is more than line 63, subtract line 63 from line 74. This is the amount you **overpaid** 75

76a Amount of line 75 you want **refunded to you.** If Form 8888 is attached, check here . ▶ ☐ 76a

Direct deposit? See instructions.

▶ b Routing number ______ ▶ c Type: ☐ Checking ☐ Savings

▶ d Account number ______

77 Amount of line 75 you want **applied to your 2015 estimated tax** ▶ 77

Amount You Owe

78 **Amount you owe.** Subtract line 74 from line 63. For details on how to pay, see instructions ▶ 78

79 Estimated tax penalty (see instructions) 79

Third Party Designee

Do you want to allow another person to discuss this return with the IRS (see instructions)? ☐ **Yes.** Complete below. ☐ **No**

Designee's name ▶ Phone no. ▶ Personal identification number (PIN) ▶

Sign Here

Joint return? See instructions. Keep a copy for your records.

Under penalties of perjury, I declare that I have examined this return and accompanying schedules and statements, and to the best of my knowledge and belief, they are true, correct, and complete. Declaration of preparer (other than taxpayer) is based on all information of which preparer has any knowledge.

Your signature	Date	Your occupation	Daytime phone number
Spouse's signature. If a joint return, **both** must sign.	Date	Spouse's occupation	If the IRS sent you an Identity Protection PIN, enter it here (see inst.)

Paid Preparer Use Only

Print/Type preparer's name	Preparer's signature	Date	Check ☐ if self-employed	PTIN
Firm's name ▶			Firm's EIN ▶	
Firm's address ▶			Phone no.	

www.irs.gov/form1040 Form **1040** (2014)

SCHEDULE E (Form 1040)

Department of the Treasury Internal Revenue Service (99)

Supplemental Income and Loss

(From rental real estate, royalties, partnerships, S corporations, estates, trusts, REMICs, etc.)

► **Attach to Form 1040, 1040NR, or Form 1041.**

► **Information about Schedule E and its separate instructions is at *www.irs.gov/schedulee*.**

OMB No. 1545-0074

2014

Attachment Sequence No. 13

Name(s) shown on return | **Your social security number**

DRAFT AS OF June 6, 2014 DO NOT FILE

Part I **Income or Loss From Rental Real Estate and Royalties** **Note.** If you are in the business of renting personal property, use **Schedule C** or **C-EZ** (see instructions). If you are an individual, report farm rental income or loss from **Form 4835** on page 2, line 40.

A Did you make any payments in 2014 that would require you to file Form(s) 1099? (see instructions) ☐ Yes ☐ No

B If "Yes," did you or will you file required Forms 1099? ☐ Yes ☐ No

1a	Physical address of each property (street, city, state, ZIP code)
A	
B	
C	

1b	Type of Property (from list below)	**2** For each rental real estate property listed above, report the number of fair rental and personal use days. Check the **QJV** box only if you meet the requirements to file as a qualified joint venture. See instructions.		**Fair Rental Days**	**Personal Use Days**	**QJV**
A			**A**			☐
B			**B**			☐
C			**C**			☐

Type of Property:

1 Single Family Residence 3 Vacation/Short-Term Rental 5 Land 7 Self-Rental

2 Multi-Family Residence 4 Commercial 6 Royalties 8 Other (describe)

Income:	**Properties:**		**A**	**B**	**C**
3	Rents received	**3**			
4	Royalties received	**4**			
Expenses:					
5	Advertising	**5**			
6	Auto and travel (see instructions)	**6**			
7	Cleaning and maintenance	**7**			
8	Commissions.	**8**			
9	Insurance	**9**			
10	Legal and other professional fees	**10**			
11	Management fees	**11**			
12	Mortgage interest paid to banks, etc. (see instructions)	**12**			
13	Other interest.	**13**			
14	Repairs.	**14**			
15	Supplies	**15**			
16	Taxes	**16**			
17	Utilities	**17**			
18	Depreciation expense or depletion	**18**			
19	Other (list) ►	**19**			
20	Total expenses. Add lines 5 through 19	**20**			
21	Subtract line 20 from line 3 (rents) and/or 4 (royalties). If result is a (loss), see instructions to find out if you must file **Form 6198**	**21**			
22	Deductible rental real estate loss after limitation, if any, on **Form 8582** (see instructions)	**22**	( )	( )	( )

23a	Total of all amounts reported on line 3 for all rental properties	**23a**	
b	Total of all amounts reported on line 4 for all royalty properties	**23b**	
c	Total of all amounts reported on line 12 for all properties	**23c**	
d	Total of all amounts reported on line 18 for all properties	**23d**	
e	Total of all amounts reported on line 20 for all properties	**23e**	
24	**Income.** Add positive amounts shown on line 21. **Do not** include any losses	**24**	
25	**Losses.** Add royalty losses from line 21 and rental real estate losses from line 22. Enter total losses here	**25**	( )
26	**Total rental real estate and royalty income or (loss).** Combine lines 24 and 25. Enter the result here. If Parts II, III, IV, and line 40 on page 2 do not apply to you, also enter this amount on Form 1040, line 17, or Form 1040NR, line 18. Otherwise, include this amount in the total on line 41 on page 2	**26**	

For Paperwork Reduction Act Notice, see the separate instructions. Cat. No. 11344L **Schedule E (Form 1040) 2014**

Form **8582**

Department of the Treasury
Internal Revenue Service (99)

Passive Activity Loss Limitations

▶ See separate instructions.
▶ Attach to Form 1040 or Form 1041.
▶ Information about Form 8582 and its instructions is available at *www.irs.gov/form8582.*

OMB No. 1545-1008
2013*
Attachment Sequence No. **88**

Name(s) shown on return | Identifying number

Part I **2013 Passive Activity Loss**

Caution: *Complete Worksheets 1, 2, and 3 before completing Part I.*

Rental Real Estate Activities With Active Participation (For the definition of active participation, see **Special Allowance for Rental Real Estate Activities** in the instructions.)			
1a Activities with net income (enter the amount from Worksheet 1, column (a))	1a		
b Activities with net loss (enter the amount from Worksheet 1, column (b))	1b	( )	
c Prior years unallowed losses (enter the amount from Worksheet 1, column (c))	1c	( )	
d Combine lines 1a, 1b, and 1c			1d
Commercial Revitalization Deductions From Rental Real Estate Activities			
2a Commercial revitalization deductions from Worksheet 2, column (a)	2a	( )	
b Prior year unallowed commercial revitalization deductions from Worksheet 2, column (b)	2b	( )	
c Add lines 2a and 2b			2c ( )
All Other Passive Activities			
3a Activities with net income (enter the amount from Worksheet 3, column (a))	3a		
b Activities with net loss (enter the amount from Worksheet 3, column (b))	3b	( )	
c Prior years unallowed losses (enter the amount from Worksheet 3, column (c))	3c	( )	
d Combine lines 3a, 3b, and 3c			3d
4 Combine lines 1d, 2c, and 3d. If this line is zero or more, stop here and include this form with your return; all losses are allowed, including any prior year unallowed losses entered on line 1c, 2b, or 3c. Report the losses on the forms and schedules normally used			4

If line 4 is a loss and:
- Line 1d is a loss, go to Part II.
- Line 2c is a loss (and line 1d is zero or more), skip Part II and go to Part III.
- Line 3d is a loss (and lines 1d and 2c are zero or more), skip Parts II and III and go to line 15.

Caution: *If your filing status is married filing separately and you lived with your spouse at any time during the year,* ***do not*** *complete Part II or Part III. Instead, go to line 15.*

Part II **Special Allowance for Rental Real Estate Activities With Active Participation**

Note: *Enter all numbers in Part II as positive amounts. See instructions for an example.*

5 Enter the **smaller** of the loss on line 1d or the loss on line 4			5
6 Enter $150,000. If married filing separately, see instructions	6		
7 Enter modified adjusted gross income, but not less than zero (see instructions)	7		
Note: *If line 7 is greater than or equal to line 6, skip lines 8 and 9, enter -0- on line 10. Otherwise, go to line 8.*			
8 Subtract line 7 from line 6	8		
9 Multiply line 8 by 50% (.5). **Do not** enter more than $25,000. If married filing separately, see instructions			9
10 Enter the **smaller** of line 5 or line 9			10

If line 2c is a loss, go to Part III. Otherwise, go to line 15.

Part III **Special Allowance for Commercial Revitalization Deductions From Rental Real Estate Activities**

Note: *Enter all numbers in Part III as positive amounts. See the example for Part II in the instructions.*

11 Enter $25,000 reduced by the amount, if any, on line 10. If married filing separately, see instructions	11
12 Enter the loss from line 4	12
13 Reduce line 12 by the amount on line 10	13
14 Enter the **smallest** of line 2c (treated as a positive amount), line 11, or line 13	14

Part IV **Total Losses Allowed**

15 Add the income, if any, on lines 1a and 3a and enter the total	15
16 **Total losses allowed from all passive activities for 2013.** Add lines 10, 14, and 15. See instructions to find out how to report the losses on your tax return	16

For Paperwork Reduction Act Notice, see instructions. Cat. No. 63704F Form **8582** (2013)

***The 2014 version of this form was not available as we went to press. Please check the IRS website for updates.**

Student Name ______________________________

Class/Section ______________________________

Date ______________________________

KEY NUMBER TAX RETURN SUMMARY

CHAPTER 4

Comprehensive Problem 1

Rental Real Estate (Line 17) ____________

Adjusted Gross Income (Line 37) ____________

Tax Liability (Line 63) ____________

Amount Overpaid (Line 75) ____________

Comprehensive Problem 2A

Adjusted Gross Income (Line 37) ____________

Exemptions (Line 42) ____________

Tax Liability (Line 63) ____________

Tax Overpaid (Line 75) ____________

Comprehensive Problem 2B

Pensions and Annuities (Line 16b) ____________

Adjusted Gross Income (Line 37) ____________

Itemized Deductions (Line 40) ____________

Tax Liability (Line 63) ____________

Tax Overpaid (Line 75) ____________

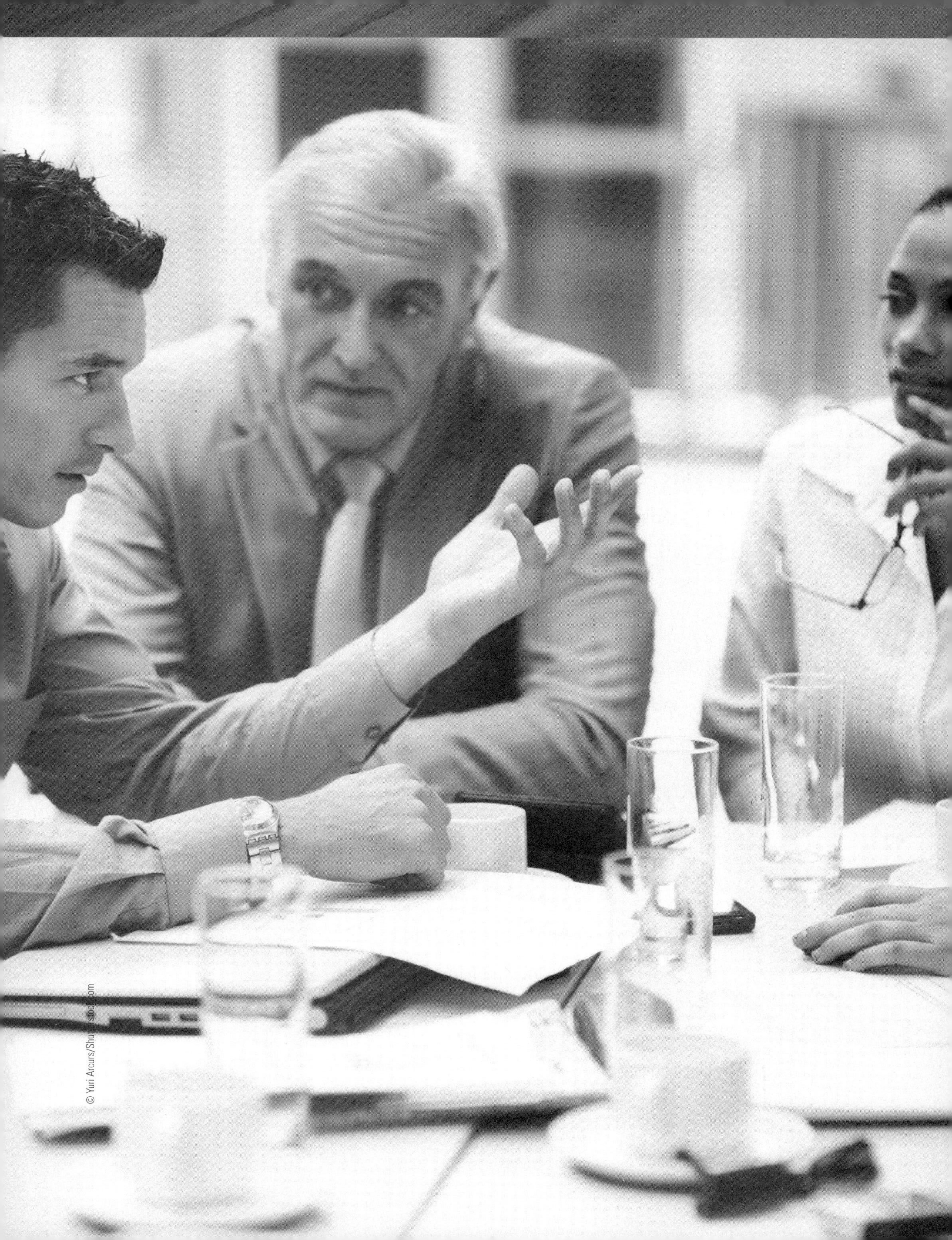

© Yuri Arcurs/Shutterstock.com

CHAPTER 5

Itemized Deductions and Other Incentives

LEARNING OBJECTIVES

After completing this chapter, you should be able to:

LO 5.1 Understand the nature and treatment of medical expenses.

LO 5.2 Calculate the itemized deduction for taxes.

LO 5.3 Apply the rules for an individual taxpayer's interest deduction.

LO 5.4 Determine the charitable contributions deduction.

LO 5.5 Compute the deduction for casualty and theft losses.

LO 5.6 Identify miscellaneous itemized deductions.

LO 5.7 Understand the treatment of employee business expenses.

LO 5.8 Understand the tax implications of using educational savings vehicles.

LO 5.9 Calculate itemized deduction and exemption phase-outs for high-income taxpayers.

OVERVIEW

The tax law allows individual taxpayers to deduct certain items from gross income when calculating taxable income. One kind of deduction is the *deduction for* (above-the-line) AGI such as alimony paid, deductible IRAs, and the expenses of self-employed persons (on Schedule C) or landlords (on Schedule E). These deductions are discussed in Chapters 1–4.

The other type of deduction in the individual tax formula is the *deduction from* AGI. The standard deduction in Chapter 1 is an example of a deduction from AGI. This chapter will introduce Schedule A itemized deductions. Itemized deductions fall into six categories: medical, state and local taxes, interest, charitable contributions, casualty and theft losses, and miscellaneous deductions. Unreimbursed employee expenses are deductible as a miscellaneous itemized deduction.

Most itemized deductions are personal expenses which Congress has deemed to be deductible for various social or economic policy purposes. For example, in order to encourage home ownership, the tax law allows a deduction (within certain limits) for personal home mortgage interest.

When calculating taxable income, individuals determine their standard deduction and their allowable itemized deductions, and use the larger of the two. For example, if a taxpayer's standard deduction is $9,100 and her itemized deductions are $14,200, she would use her itemized

deductions in calculating taxable income. On the other hand, if her itemized deductions were $6,500, she would use the larger standard deduction of $9,100 in computing taxable income.

Learning Objective 5.1

Understand the nature and treatment of medical expenses.

MEDICAL EXPENSES

Medical expenses are the first itemized deduction on Schedule A. Taxpayers are allowed a deduction for the medical expenses paid for themselves, their spouse, and dependents. Unreimbursed medical expenses for taxpayers under 65 can only be deducted to the extent that they exceed 10 percent of the taxpayer's AGI. The threshold of 10 percent replaces the 7.5 percent threshold which was in place for many years prior to 2013. For years 2013 through 2016, the 7.5 percent threshold will still apply to taxpayers who have reached age 65 by the end of the tax year. For married couples, the 7.5 percent threshold applies if at least one spouse has reached age 65 by the end of the tax year. The formula for calculating a taxpayer's medical expense deduction is as follows:

Prescription medicines and drugs, insulin, doctors, dentists, hospitals, medical insurance premiums	$ xxx
Other medical and dental expenses, such as lodging, transportation, eyeglasses, contact lenses, etc.	xxx
Less: insurance reimbursements	(xxx)
Subtotal	xxx
Less: 10 percent of adjusted gross income (7.5 percent for taxpayers age 65 or older)	(xxx)
Excess expenses qualifying for the medical deduction	$ xxx

What Qualifies as a Medical Expense?

Expenses that are deductible as medical expenses include the cost of items for the diagnosis, cure, mitigation, treatment, and prevention of disease. Also included are expenditures incurred that affect any structure or function of the body. Therefore, amounts for all of the following categories of expenditures qualify as medical expenses:

Prescription medicines and drugs and insulin
Fees for doctors, dentists, nurses, and other medical professionals
Hospital fees
Hearing aids, dentures, eyeglasses, and contact lenses
Medical transportation and lodging
Medical aids, such as crutches, wheelchairs, and guide dogs
Birth control prescriptions
Acupuncture
Psychiatric care
Medical insurance premiums, including Medicare premiums
Certain capital expenditures
Nursing home care for the chronically ill (e.g., Alzheimer's disease care)

Would You Believe?

The IRS has allowed the following unusual medical expenses:

- Long-distance phone calls made to a psychological counselor
- New siding replacing old siding on a home because the taxpayer was allergic to mold growing on the old siding
- A wig prescribed by a psychiatrist for a taxpayer upset by hair loss
- A cell phone for a taxpayer who may need instantaneous medical help
- Treatments provided by a Native American medicine man

Certain medical expenses are not deductible. For example, the cost of travel for the general improvement of the taxpayer's health is not deductible. The expense of a swimming pool is not deductible unless the pool is designed specially for the hydrotherapeutic treatment of the taxpayer's illness. No deduction is allowed for the cost of weight-loss programs (unless prescribed by a doctor; diet foods do not qualify) or marriage counseling. Medical expenses for unnecessary cosmetic surgery or similar procedures are not deductible. Cosmetic surgery is considered unnecessary unless it corrects (1) a congenital abnormality, (2) a personal injury resulting from an accident or trauma, or (3) a disfiguring disease. In general, unnecessary cosmetic surgery is any procedure which is directed at improving the patient's appearance and does not meaningfully promote the proper function of the body or prevent or treat illness or disease.

Would You Believe?

While several states have legalized marijuana for medical use in some instances, the IRS has ruled that taxpayers cannot deduct the cost of marijuana as a medical expense.

Medical Insurance

Medical insurance includes standard health policies, whether the benefits are paid to the taxpayer or to the provider of the services directly. In addition, the premiums paid for membership in health maintenance plans are deductible as medical insurance, as are supplemental payments for optional Medicare coverage. Insurance policies that pay a specific amount each day or week the taxpayer is hospitalized are not considered medical insurance and the premiums are not deductible. Premiums paid for qualified long-term care insurance policies are also deductible medical expenses up to specified limits which change each year and are based on the age of the taxpayer.

Self-employed taxpayers are allowed, subject to certain limitations, a deduction in arriving at adjusted gross income equal to 100 percent of the medical insurance premiums paid for themselves and their families. Long-term care insurance premiums, up to a specified amount based on the taxpayer's age, are considered health insurance for this purpose. These deductions are covered in detail in Chapter 4. If a deduction is taken for these items in arriving at AGI, then these same expenses are excluded from the medical expense deduction on Schedule A. However, if the self-employed insurance deduction is limited by net self-employment income, the excess medical insurance expenses can be included on Schedule A.

Medicines and Drugs

Prescription medicines and drugs and insulin are the only drugs deductible as medical expenses. No deduction is allowed for drugs purchased illegally from abroad, including Canada and Mexico. Nonprescription medicines such as over-the-counter antacids, allergy medications, and pain relievers, even if recommended by a physician, are not deductible as a medical expense.

Capital Expenditures

Payments for special equipment purchased and installed in the taxpayer's home for medical reasons may also be deductible. Unlike other capital expenditures, allowable amounts are deducted fully in the year the item is purchased. If the expenditure is for an improvement

that increases the value of the taxpayer's property, the deduction is limited to the amount by which the expenditure exceeds the increase in the value of the property. If the value of the property does not increase as a result of the expenditure, the entire cost is deductible. The cost of upkeep and operation of an item, the cost of which qualified as a medical expense, is also deductible, provided the medical reason for the improvement or special equipment still exists.

EXAMPLE A taxpayer has a heart condition and installs an elevator in his home at a cost of $6,000. The value of the home is increased by $4,000 as a result of the improvement. The taxpayer is allowed a deduction of $2,000 ($6,000 – $4,000), the excess of the cost of the equipment over the increase in the value of the taxpayer's home. ♦

Transportation

Transportation expenses primarily and necessary for medical care are deductible, including amounts paid for taxis, trains, buses, airplanes, and ambulances. Taxpayers may also claim a deduction for the use of their personal automobile for medical transportation. However, only out-of-pocket expenses such as the cost of gas and oil are deductible. Maintenance, insurance, general repair, and depreciation expenses are not deductible. If the taxpayer does not wish to deduct actual costs of transportation by personal automobile, the standard mileage rate is 23.5 cents per mile for 2014. In addition to the deduction for actual automobile costs or the standard mileage amount, parking and toll fees for medical transportation are deductible medical expenses. If the transportation expenses are for the medical care of a dependent child, the amounts are deductible by the parent.

Lodging for Medical Care

Taxpayers may deduct the cost of lodging up to $50 per night, per person, on a trip primarily for and essential to medical care provided by a physician or a licensed hospital. The deduction is allowed for the patient and an individual accompanying the patient, such as the parent of a child. However, no deduction is allowed if the trip involves a significant element of recreation or vacation. No deduction is allowed for meal costs.

Would You Believe?

A Las Vegas dentist admitted he provided free dental work to an IRS revenue officer in exchange for reductions of his $100,000 tax debt. Both men were indicted on conspiracy and bribery charges.

Self-Study Problem 5.1

See Appendix E for Solutions to Self-Study Problems

During the 2014 tax year, Frank (age 65) and Betty (age 63) paid the following medical expenses:

Medical insurance	$ 425
Prescription medicines and drugs	364
Hospital bills	2,424
Doctor bills	725
Eyeglasses for Frank's dependent mother	75
Doctor bills for Betty's sister, who is claimed as a dependent by Frank and Betty	220

In addition, in 2014, they drove 610 miles for medical transportation in their personal automobile. Their insurance company reimbursed Frank and Betty $1,420 during the year for the medical expenses. If their adjusted gross income for the year is $25,400, calculate their medical expense deduction. Use the segment of Schedule A of Form 1040 reproduced below.

Medical and Dental Expenses		**Caution.** Do not include expenses reimbursed or paid by others.		
	1	Medical and dental expenses (see instructions)	1	
	2	Enter amount from Form 1040, line 38 [2]		
	3	Multiply line 2 by 10% (.10). But if either you or your spouse was born before January 2, 1950, multiply line 2 by 7.5% (.075) instead	3	
	4	Subtract line 3 from line 1. If line 3 is more than line 1, enter -0-	4	

DRAFT AS OF

TAXES

Learning Objective 5.2

Calculate the itemized deduction for taxes.

Taxpayers are allowed to deduct certain state, local, and foreign taxes paid during the year. The purpose of the deduction for taxes is to relieve the burden of multiple taxation of the same income. However, the tax law distinguishes between a "tax" and a "fee." A tax is imposed by a government to raise revenue for general public purposes, and a fee is a charge with a direct benefit to the person paying the fee. Taxes are generally deductible; fees are not deductible. For example, postage, fishing licenses, and dog tags are not deductible as taxes.

If a taxpayer itemizes his or her deductions on Schedule A, the following taxes are deductible for 2014:

Income taxes (state, local, and foreign)
Sales taxes (by election in lieu of deducting state and local income tax; however, see note on next page)
Real estate property taxes (state, local, and foreign)
Personal property taxes (state and local)

The following taxes are *not* deductible:

Federal income taxes
Employee portion of Social Security taxes
Estate, inheritance, and gift taxes (except in unusual situations not discussed here)
Gasoline taxes
Excise taxes
Foreign taxes if the taxpayer elects a foreign tax credit

Taxes paid in connection with a trade or business or any activity for the production of income, such as payroll taxes, personal property taxes, etc., are deductible for adjusted gross income by the taxpayer on Schedule C, E, or F, instead of Schedule A.

Income Taxes and Sales Taxes

Please note: As we go to press it is expected that in late 2014, Congress will extend the deduction for sales taxes retroactively for all of 2014. Check the Whittenburg companion website for updates.

Taxpayers may elect to take either state and local sales and use taxes or state and local income taxes as itemized deductions. The election to take a deduction for state sales tax instead of state income tax primarily benefits taxpayers in states with no income taxes or low income tax rates.

For taxpayers electing to deduct state and local income taxes paid during 2014, the amount of the deduction is the total amount of state and local taxes withheld from wages plus any amounts actually paid during the year, even if the tax payments are for a prior year's tax liability. If the taxpayer receives a refund of taxes deducted in a previous year, the refund must generally be included in gross income (e.g., Line 10 of the Form 1040) in the year the refund is received. Taxes which did not provide any tax benefit (reduction in taxes) in the year paid are not required to be included in income in the year received as a refund. For example, a taxpayer claiming the standard deduction in the year taxes are paid does not receive a tax benefit for the payment and is not required to include a tax refund received the following year in income.

EXAMPLE For 2014, Mary elects to deduct state income taxes rather than state sales taxes as an itemized deduction. Mary has $1,800 of state income taxes withheld from her wages during 2014. In April of 2014, she paid an additional $250 on her 2013 state income tax return. Mary's deduction for state income taxes is $2,050 ($1,800 + $250). Her state income tax liability for the 2014 year was $1,650, resulting in a $150 refund ($1,800 − $1,650) that was received in 2015. The $150 refund is reported as income in the 2015 return, assuming Mary received a benefit from the state tax deduction for 2014. ♦

For taxpayers electing to deduct sales taxes in 2014, the deduction may be calculated by using either (a) actual sales taxes paid or (b) sales taxes from IRS tables plus the actual amount of sales tax for motor vehicles, boats, airplanes, and building materials (not appliances or furnishings) for building or improving a residence. Taxpayers choosing to deduct actual sales taxes paid are required to keep extensive records to support the amount of the deduction claimed including receipts for every item purchased during the year subject to sales tax.

Property Taxes

Taxes that are levied on state, local, or foreign real property for the general public welfare are deductible. However, special assessments charged to provide local benefit to property owners are not deductible; these amounts increase the basis of the taxpayer's property. Also, service fees, such as garbage fees and homeowner association fees, are not deductible as property taxes.

If real estate is sold during the year, the taxes must be divided between the buyer and the seller, and the division must be made according to the number of days in the year that each taxpayer held the property.

EXAMPLE Sally sells her home to Patty on March 2, 2014. The taxes for 2014 are paid by Patty and they total $1,825, or $5.00 per day ($1,825/365 days). The purchaser is treated as the owner on the day of sale. Sally is entitled to deduct 61 days of real property taxes or $305 (61 days × $5.00 per day). Patty deducts $1,520 (304 days × $5.00 per day). ♦

Generally, the escrow company or closing agent handling the sale of the property will make the allocation of taxes for the buyer and the seller and the result will be reflected in the settlement charges on the transfer of the title. These amounts are itemized on closing statements for the sale, which are provided to the buyer and the seller.

EXAMPLE William purchased a new residence from John in 2014. William's closing statement shows that he receives a credit for $299.80 in taxes that he will pay later in the year for the seller. Assuming that William pays $525.00 in total taxes on the property later in 2014, his property tax deduction for 2014 would be $225.20 ($525.00 − $299.80). John, the seller, would be allowed a deduction for $299.80 plus any other taxes he paid during the year prior to selling the property. ♦

Personal Property Taxes

To be deductible as an itemized deduction, personal property taxes must be levied based on the value of the property. Taxes of a fixed amount, or those calculated on a basis other than value, are not deductible. For example, automobile fees that are calculated on the basis of the automobile's weight are not deductible.

EXAMPLE Rich lives in a state that charges $20 per year plus 2 percent of the value of the automobile for vehicle registration. If Rich pays $160 [$20 + (2% × $7,000)] for his automobile registration, he may deduct only $140, the amount that is based on the value of the automobile. ♦

Self-Study Problem 5.2 ***See Appendix E for Solutions to Self-Study Problems***

Sharon is single, lives in Idaho, and has adjusted gross income of $21,150 for 2014. Sharon elects to deduct state income tax rather than state sales tax. The tax withheld from her salary for state income taxes is $1,050, and in May of the same year she received a $225 refund on her state income tax return for the prior year. Sharon paid real estate taxes on her house of $825 for the year and an automobile registration fee of $110, of which $25 is based on the weight of the automobile and the balance on the value of the property. Use the taxes section of Schedule A below to report Sharon's deduction for state and local taxes.

Taxes You Paid	**5** State and local				
	a ☐ Income taxes				
	b ☐ RESERVED	5			
	6 Real estate taxes (see instructions)	6			
	7 Personal property taxes	7			
	8 Other taxes. List type and amount ▶				
		8			
	9 Add lines 5 through 8			9	

August 15, 2014
DO NOT FILE

Learning Objective 5.3

Apply the rules for an individual taxpayer's interest deduction.

INTEREST

Taxpayers are allowed a deduction for certain interest paid or accrued during the tax year. Interest is defined as an amount paid for the use of borrowed funds. The type and amount of the deduction depend on the purpose for which the money is borrowed. Interest on loans for business, rent, and royalty activities is deducted for adjusted gross income. Certain interest on loans for personal purposes is deductible as an itemized deduction. The following types of personal interest are deductible:

Qualified residence interest (mortgage interest)
Mortgage interest prepayment penalties
Investment interest
Certain interest associated with a passive activity

Interest on other loans for personal purposes which do not fall into one of the above categories is generally referred to as consumer interest and is not deductible. Consumer interest includes interest on any loan, the proceeds of which are used for personal purposes, such as credit card interest, finance charges, and automobile loan interest. Interest on loans used to acquire assets generating tax-exempt income is also not deductible.

The following items are not considered "interest" and, therefore, are also not deductible:

Service charges
Credit investigation fees
Loan fees other than "points" discussed later under Prepaid Interest
Interest paid to carry single premium life insurance
Premium on convertible bonds

Many lenders require that home mortgage borrowers purchase private mortgage insurance (PMI) to protect the lender. Mortgage insurance issued related to debt used to acquire a principal residence is fully deductible in years 2007 through 2013 for taxpayers with AGI of $100,000 or less.

Please note: As we go to press it is not known whether Congress will extend the deduction for PMI in 2014. Be sure and check the Whittenburg companion website for updates.

Taxpayer's Obligation

To deduct interest on a debt, the taxpayer must be legally liable for the debt. No deduction is allowed for payments made for another's obligation, where the taxpayer is not liable for payment. Also, both the lender and the borrower must intend for the loan to be repaid.

EXAMPLE Bill makes a payment on his son's home mortgage since his son is unable to make the current payment. The interest included in the mortgage payment is not deductible by Bill since the mortgage is not his obligation. Bill's son cannot deduct the interest since he did not make the payment. ♦

A taxpayer who assumes the benefits and burdens of ownership, and is considered to essentially be an owner under state law, may be allowed to deduct mortgage interest on a residence even if not directly liable on the mortgage. This situation is not standard and the deduction is allowed only on a case-by-case basis.

EXAMPLE Mary loans her daughter $50,000 to start a business. The daughter is 19 years old and unsophisticated in business. No note is signed and no repayment date is mentioned. Mary would be surprised if the daughter's business venture is a success. In all likelihood, a true debtor-creditor relationship is not created. ♦

Prepaid Interest

Cash basis taxpayers are required to use the accrual basis for deducting prepaid interest. Prepaid interest must be capitalized and the deduction spread over the life of the loan. This requirement does not apply to points paid on a mortgage loan for purchasing or improving a taxpayer's principal residence, provided points are customarily charged and they do not exceed the normal rate. Such points paid on a mortgage for the purchase of a personal residence may be deducted in the year they are paid. Points paid to refinance a home mortgage are not deductible when paid, but must be capitalized and the deduction spread over the life of the loan. Points charged for specific loan services, such as the lender's appraisal fee and other settlement fees, are not deductible.

EXAMPLE On November 1, 2014, Allen, a cash basis taxpayer, obtains a 6-month loan of $500,000 on a new apartment building. On November 1, Allen prepays $36,000 interest on the loan. He must capitalize the prepaid interest and deduct it over the 6-month loan period. Therefore, his interest deduction for 2014 is $12,000 ($36,000/6 months × 2 months). ♦

Qualified Residence, Home Equity, and Consumer Interest

No deduction is available for consumer (personal) interest, such as interest on credit cards and loans for personal automobiles. Qualified residence interest, however, is a type of personal interest specifically allowed as a deduction. The term "qualified residence interest" is the sum of the interest paid on "qualified residence acquisition debt" plus "qualified home equity debt." The aggregate amount of qualified acquisition debt may not exceed $1,000,000 ($500,000 for married, filing separately), and the aggregate amount of qualified home equity debt may not exceed $100,000 ($50,000 for married, filing separately). Thus, the total amount of acquisition and home equity debt on the taxpayer's residence may not exceed $1,100,000 ($550,000 for married, filing separately).

The term "acquisition debt" is defined as debt secured by the taxpayer's principal or second residence incurred in acquiring, constructing, or substantially improving that residence. Refinanced debt is treated as acquisition debt only to the extent it does not exceed the principal amount of acquisition debt immediately before the refinancing. The term "home equity debt" is defined as debt secured by the taxpayer's principal or second residence, and which is not acquisition debt. Interest on qualifying home equity debt is deductible even if the proceeds are used for personal purposes.

EXAMPLE Vicky's residence has a fair market value of $300,000. The first mortgage, used to buy the house 10 years ago, is $125,000. She borrows $115,000 on a second mortgage secured by the house to send her children to college. The interest paid on the first mortgage is fully deductible, but interest on only $100,000 of the second mortgage is deductible.

Assume $8,000 of interest is paid by Vicky on the first mortgage and $7,000 is paid on the second mortgage. Vicky's mortgage interest deduction is calculated as follows:

Interest on acquisition debt	$ 8,000
Interest on home equity debt	
$7,000 × $100,000/$115,000	6,087
Mortgage interest deduction allowed	$14,087

The remaining interest on the home equity debt ($7,000 − $6,087 = $913) is considered nondeductible personal interest. ♦

An additional limit on the $100,000 qualified home equity debt allowed is the fair market value of the residence. For example, assume a taxpayer has the maximum $1,000,000 of acquisition debt and $100,000 of home equity debt. If the fair market value of the residence goes down to $1,050,000, only $50,000 of the home equity debt will qualify for an interest deduction. The reduction in home values during the recent recession has made this limitation more relevant than in past years.

Deduction for consumer interest, including any excess mortgage interest, automobile loan interest, and interest on credit cards, is not allowed.

TAX BREAK

If the sum of mortgage interest and other itemized deductions is less than the standard deduction, no tax benefit is received from the mortgage interest payments. In this case, a taxpayer may wish to pay the mortgage off as quickly as possible since few investments earn a guaranteed tax-free return equal to the interest rate on a home mortgage.

Education Loan Interest

Taxpayers are allowed a deduction **for** adjusted gross income for certain interest paid on qualified education loans. The deduction is limited to $2,500 for 2014, and is phased out for single taxpayers with modified AGI of $65,000 to $80,000 and for married taxpayers with modified AGI of $130,000 to $160,000. Qualified higher education expenses include tuition, room and board, and related expenses.

EXAMPLE Sam graduated from college in 2013, taking a job with a salary of $55,000 per year. During 2014, he pays $2,500 interest on qualified education loans. Because his income is below the $65,000 phase-out amount for individual taxpayers, he can deduct the full $2,500 of the interest in arriving at adjusted gross income on his 2014 tax return. If he had paid more than $2,500 in interest, the excess would be considered nondeductible consumer interest. ♦

TAX BREAK

If taxpayers borrow for personal purposes, such as buying a new automobile, they will likely be better off taking out a home equity loan rather than consumer debt. The interest on a home equity loan will be deductible (so long as there is no more than $100,000 of total home equity debt and the fair market value of the residence exceeds the acquisition debt and the home equity debt combined), while the interest on a consumer loan for the same purpose will not be deductible.

Investment Interest

To prevent abuses by taxpayers, the Internal Revenue Code includes a provision limiting the deduction of investment interest expense. This provision limits the amount of deductible interest on loans to finance investments. The investment interest deduction is limited to the taxpayer's net investment income. Net investment income is income such as dividends and interest, less investment expenses other than interest. Special rules apply to dividends and capital gains included as investment income due to their preferential tax rates. The general rule is that they may only be included as investment income if the taxpayer chooses to calculate tax on them at ordinary income rates. Any disallowed interest expense is carried over and may be deducted in succeeding years, but only to the extent that the taxpayer's net investment income exceeds investment interest expense for the year.

EXAMPLE Karen borrows $150,000 at 12 percent interest on January 1, 2014. The proceeds are used to purchase $100,000 worth of raw land and a $50,000 CD. During 2014, the CD pays interest of $1,500. Karen incurs expenses attributable to the investment property of $500. Of the $18,000 (12% of $150,000) interest incurred in 2014, $1,000 is deductible as limited to the total net investment income in 2014. The deduction is computed as follows:

Investment income	$1,500
Less: investment expenses	(500)
Net investment income	$1,000
Interest deductible in 2014	$1,000

The unused deduction of $17,000 ($18,000 − $1,000) is carried forward and may be used as an interest deduction in future years, subject to the net investment income limitation. ♦

Self-Study Problem 5.3 ***See Appendix E for Solutions to Self-Study Problems***

Dorothie paid the following amounts during 2014:

Interest on her home mortgage	$9,250
Service charges on her checking account	48
Visa and Mastercard interest	168
Automobile loan interest	675
Interest on a loan to buy stock	1,600
Credit investigation fee for a loan	75

Dorothie's residence has a fair market value of $150,000. The mortgage balance is $125,000, which is a loan that was acquired in 1998 when she purchased her home. Dorothie has $1,000 of net investment income. Use the following interest section of Schedule A to calculate Dorothie's interest deduction for the current year.

Interest You Paid	10	Home mortgage interest and points reported to you on Form 1098	10	
Note. Your mortgage interest deduction may be limited (see instructions).	11	Home mortgage interest not reported to you on Form 1098. If paid to the person from whom you bought the home, see instructions and show that person's name, identifying no., and address ▶	11	
	12	Points not reported to you on Form 1098. See instructions for special rules	12	
	13	RESERVED	13	
	14	Investment interest. Attach Form 4952 if required. (See instructions.)	14	
	15	Add lines 10 through 14		15

Learning Objective 5.4

Determine the charitable contributions deduction.

CONTRIBUTIONS

To encourage individuals to be socially responsible, the Internal Revenue Code allows a deduction for charitable contributions. To be deductible, the donation must be made in cash or property; the value of free use of the taxpayer's property by the charitable organization does not qualify. In addition, out-of-pocket expenses related to qualified charitable activities are deductible as charitable contributions. For example, a taxpayer who drives his car 200 miles during 2014 to take a church group to a meeting out of town would be allowed a charitable deduction of $28 (200 miles × 14 cents per mile).

EXAMPLE Lucille allows the Red Cross to use her building rent-free for 8 months. The building normally rents for $600 per month. There is no deduction allowed for the free use of the building. ♦

To be deductible, the donation must be made to a qualified recipient as listed in the tax law, including:

1. the United States, a state, or political subdivision thereof, if the donation is made for exclusively public purposes (such as a contribution to pay down the federal debt);
2. domestic organizations formed and operated exclusively for charitable, religious, educational, scientific, or literary purposes, or for the prevention of cruelty to children or animals;
3. church, synagogue, or other religious organizations;
4. war veterans' organizations;
5. civil defense organizations;
6. fraternal societies operating under the lodge system, but only if the contribution is used for one or more of the charitable purposes listed in (2) above; and
7. certain nonprofit cemetery companies.

The following contributions are not deductible:

1. Gifts to nonqualified recipients, for example, needy individuals, social clubs, labor unions, international organizations, and political parties;
2. Contributions of time, service, the use of property, or blood;
3. Contributions where benefit is received from the contribution, for example, tuition at a parochial school; and
4. Wagering losses, such as church bingo and raffle tickets.

If a taxpayer has doubt as to the deductibility of a payment to a specific organization, he or she should review the IRS's online search tool called "Exempt Organizations Select Check."

If cash is donated, the deduction is equal to the amount of the cash. For donated property other than cash, the general rule is that the deduction is equal to the fair market value of the property at the time of the donation. The fair market value is the price at which the property would be sold between a willing buyer and seller. There is an exception to this general rule for property that would have resulted in ordinary income or short-term capital gain had it been sold on the date of the contribution. In that situation, the deduction for the contribution is equal to the property's fair market value less the amount of the ordinary income or short-term capital gain that would have resulted from sale of the property. If sale of the property would have produced a long-term capital gain, the deduction is generally equal to the fair market value of the property. However, the fair market value is reduced by the amount of the potential long-term capital gain, if the donation is made to certain private nonoperating foundations or the donation is a contribution of tangible personal property to an organization that uses the property for a purpose unrelated to the organization's primary purpose.

EXAMPLE Jeano B. donates a painting acquired 5 years ago at a cost of $4,000 to a museum for exhibition. The painting's fair market value is $12,000. If Jeano had sold the painting, the difference between the sales price ($12,000) and its cost ($4,000) would have been a long-term capital gain. The deduction is $12,000, and it is not reduced by the amount of the appreciation, since the painting was put to a use related to the museum's primary purpose. If the painting had been donated to a hospital, the deduction would be $4,000, which is $12,000 less $8,000 ($12,000 − $4,000), the amount of the long-term capital gain that would have resulted if the painting had been sold. ♦

TAX BREAK

Rather than donate cash, taxpayers may wish to donate appreciated stock or other appreciated property to charity. If the gift is properly structured, a full deduction may be taken for the fair market value of the donated property, while tax on the appreciation is avoided completely.

Percentage Limitations

Generally, a taxpayer may not deduct total contributions in excess of 50 percent of the taxpayer's adjusted gross income. This 50 percent limitation applies to donations to all public charities, all private operating foundations, and private nonoperating foundations if they

distribute their contributions to public charities within a specified time period. Gifts to other qualified organizations, such as certain private nonoperating foundations, fraternal societies, and veterans' organizations, as well as gifts for the use of an organization, are limited to 30 percent of adjusted gross income. Special rules apply to contributions of long-term capital gain property. If the full fair market value of a gift of long-term capital gain property is deducted, and the contribution is to a 50 percent organization, the contribution is subject to the 30 percent limit. Taxpayers may avoid the 30 percent limit on contributions of long-term capital gain property by electing to reduce the value of the property by the appreciation that would otherwise be a long-term capital gain, in which case the 50 percent limitation applies. Long-term capital gain property donated to other than a 50 percent organization is subject to a 20 percent of adjusted gross income limitation.

EXAMPLE Carol donates publicly traded stock worth $15,000 to a qualified 50 percent charity. The original purchase price of the stock, 10 years ago, was $10,000. Because the stock is a gift of long-term capital gain property, Carol's deduction is limited to 30 percent of her adjusted gross income. Given that Carol's AGI is $20,000, she may take a deduction for $6,000 (30% of $20,000) and may carry the remaining $9,000 ($15,000 − $6,000) forward to the following year. Alternatively, Carol may deduct the original $10,000 cost of the stock using the 50 percent of AGI rule, which would give her a $10,000 deduction in the current year. Even though she would have a larger deduction in the current year, she would lose $5,000 of her potential charitable contribution deduction by choosing this alternative. ♦

Generally, contributions to 50 percent organizations are deducted first, followed by contributions subject to the 30 percent and 20 percent limitations, respectively. Contributions subject to the 30 percent and 20 percent of adjusted gross income limitations are allowed only to the extent that they do not exceed 50 percent of adjusted gross income reduced by the amount of contributions subject to the 50 percent limitation.

EXAMPLE In March of 2014, Grace contributes $15,000 in cash to a public university. In addition, at the same time she donates $7,000 in cash to an organization subject to the 30 percent of adjusted gross income limitation. Grace has adjusted gross income in 2014 of $35,000. Her contribution deduction is determined as follows:

Adjusted gross income	$35,000
	×50%
50% limitation	17,500
Allowable 50% limitation contributions	(15,000)
Excess 50% limitation	2,500
Maximum 30% contributions:	
Lesser of $2,500 or 30% of adjusted gross income, $10,500	2,500
Total deductible contributions:	
50% contributions	15,000
30% contributions	2,500
Total	$17,500

♦

In general, any contributions not allowed due to the adjusted gross income limitations may be carried forward for 5 years. The contributions may be deducted in the carryover years subject to the same percentage of income limitations which were applicable to the contributions in the year they originated. Contribution carryovers are allowed only after taking into account the current year contributions in the same category.

Would You Believe?

A tax lawyer pleaded guilty to tax evasion in Federal District Court for substantially overstating his charitable contributions. He told an IRS agent that he put $500 in cash into the church collection basket each week. His pastor, however, said that the parish didn't receive $500 in currency at all of its masses combined.

Substantiation Rules

Taxpayers should keep records, receipts, cancelled checks, and other proof of charitable contributions. For gifts of property, for example clothes and household goods given to the Salvation Army, totaling over $500, the taxpayer must attach a Form 8283 to his or her return giving the name and address of the donee, the date of the contribution, a description of the property, the approximate date of acquisition of the property, and certain other required information. For large gifts of property worth $5,000 or more, the donor must also obtain and submit an appraisal.

No charitable deduction is allowed for contributions of $250 or more unless the taxpayer substantiates the contributions with written acknowledgments from the recipient charitable organizations. The acknowledgments must contain this information:

- The amount of cash and a description (but not the value) of property other than cash contributed.
- Whether the charitable organization provided any goods or services in consideration, in whole or in part, for any property contributed. (If a payment is partly a gift and partly in consideration for goods or services provided to the donor, it is a "quid pro quo contribution" and special rules apply.)
- A description and good-faith estimate of the value of any goods or services provided by the donor, or, if the goods and services consist solely of intangible religious benefits, a statement to that effect. Intangible religious benefits are any benefits provided by organizations formed exclusively for religious purposes and not generally sold in a commercial setting. For example, attendance at church is considered an intangible religious benefit while attendance at a private religious school is not. A donation made at a church service is generally considered a charitable contribution while tuition paid to a private religious school is not considered a charitable contribution.

Taxpayers donating amounts of cash smaller than the $250 limit are required to keep a bank record (cancelled check) or a written communication from the charity. Taxpayers who itemize deductions should use checks instead of cash for church and similar cash donations.

Gifts of clothing and household items (including furnishings, electronics, appliances, and linens) are also subject to another requirement. They must be in "good" condition or better to qualify for a deduction. Also, charitable deductions may be denied for contributions of items with minimal value, such as used socks and undergarments. The rules for noncash contributions were passed because some taxpayers significantly overstated the value of noncash contributions deducted.

No particular form is prescribed for the written acknowledgment, nor does the donor's Social Security number have to be contained on the acknowledgment. It may be a receipt, letter, postcard, or computer form. The acknowledgment must be obtained on or before

the date on which the tax return for the tax year of the contribution is filed, or by the due date (plus extensions) if it is earlier than the actual filing date.

Taxpayers donating used vehicles to charity cannot claim a deduction greater than the amount for which the charity actually sells the vehicle. The charity will be required to provide the resale information on Form 1098-C to taxpayers donating vehicles. The same rule also applies to boats and planes donated to charity. Taxpayers must attach Form 1098-C to their tax return to substantiate the deduction. Taxpayers may claim an estimated value for the automobile if the charity does not sell it but rather uses it or gives it to a needy individual. The charity must certify that an exception applies if no resale amount is provided on Form 1098-C.

Would You Believe?

Tightening the rules for the charitable donations of cars caused the dollar value of the deductions to drop by 80 percent in 2005, the first year under the new rules. The dollar amount of charitable deductions for automobiles was approximately $2.4 billion in 2004 and only $470 million in 2005.

For quid pro quo contributions (donations involving the receipt of goods or services by the donee), written statements (disclosures) are required from the charitable organization to donors making contributions of more than $75. The disclosures need not be individual letters to donors; they simply provide the donors with good-faith estimates of the value of the goods or services and inform the donors that only the amounts of the contributions in excess of the value of the goods or services are deductible for federal income tax purposes.

A charitable organization knowingly providing false written acknowledgments is subject to penalty (generally $1,000) for aiding and abetting in the understatement of tax liability. A penalty of $10 per contribution per event, capped at $5,000, may be imposed on charities failing to make the required disclosures for quid pro quo contributions.

TAX BREAK

A cash basis taxpayer may charge year-end expenses on a credit card and still deduct the expenses even when payment on the credit card is not made until the next year. Instead of paying medical bills, charitable contributions, or even property taxes by check at year-end, the taxpayer may prefer to charge the expense. Note, however, that the credit card may not be one issued by the company supplying the deductible goods or services, but must be a card issued by a third party.

Self-Study Problem 5.4

See Appendix E for Solutions to Self-Study Problems

During 2014, Eric gave $260 to his church for which he received a written acknowledgement. He also has receipts for $75 given to the Boy Scouts of America and $125 given to the Mexican Red Cross. Eric gave the Salvation Army old clothes worth $150 (original cost $1,700). Last year Eric had a large contribution and could not deduct $800 of it due to the 50 percent limitation. This year Eric's adjusted gross income is $21,325. Use the Gifts to Charity section of Schedule A below to calculate Eric's deduction for the current year.

Gifts to Charity	16	Gifts by cash or check. If you made any gift of $250 or more, see instructions	16			
If you made a gift and got a benefit for it, see instructions.	17	Other than by cash or check. If any gift of $250 or more, see instructions. You **must** attach Form 8283 if over $500 . . .	17			
	18	Carryover from prior year	18			
	19	Add lines 16 through 18			19	

CASUALTY AND THEFT LOSSES

Learning Objective 5.5

Compute the deduction for casualty and theft losses.

Taxpayers are allowed deductions for casualty and theft losses. The deductions may be itemized deductions or, if related to a business, deductions for adjusted gross income. A casualty is a complete or partial destruction of property resulting from an identifiable event of a sudden, unexpected, or unusual nature. Examples of casualties include property damage from storms, floods, shipwrecks, fires, automobile accidents, and vandalism. For damage from weather conditions to be deductible, the condition must be unusual for the particular region. To qualify as a casualty, an automobile accident must not be caused by the taxpayer's willful act or willful negligence.

EXAMPLE A taxpayer has an automobile that he decides is a lemon, and he wants to get rid of it. He drives the automobile to the top of a cliff and pushes it off. There is no casualty loss deduction since the act is willful. ♦

Many events do not qualify as casualties. For example, progressive deterioration from rust or corrosion and disease or insect damage are usually not "sudden" enough to qualify as casualties. The IRS has held that termite damage is not deductible as a casualty; however, several courts have in the past allowed the deduction. Indirect losses, such as losses in property value due to damage to neighboring property, also are not deductible.

Would You Believe?

A taxpayer left his car in a tow-away zone near his building while he went on vacation for 2 weeks. When he came back, he discovered that the city had not only towed his car, but had it crushed. The IRS disallowed his casualty loss because, it claimed, the taxpayer could have prevented the loss by not parking in a tow-away zone. Fortunately for the taxpayer, the Tax Court overturned the IRS determination, saying he could not have known that the city would destroy his car.

If the taxpayer can establish that theft occurred, theft losses are deductible. It is important to show that the item was not simply misplaced. Theft losses are deductible in the year the theft is discovered, not in the year the theft took place. This is important in cases of embezzlement, where the theft has gone on over many years and the statute of limitations has run out on earlier years, otherwise preventing the taxpayer from amending returns for those years.

As a general rule, casualty losses are deductible in the year of occurrence, but there is an exception for federally declared disaster area losses. Taxpayers may elect to treat the losses in a disaster area as a deduction in the year prior to the year the casualty occurred. If a return has already been filed for the prior year, an amended return may be filed and a refund claimed for the prior year's taxes paid. This provision is designed to provide taxpayers with cash on a more timely basis when they have suffered severe casualties.

EXAMPLE In May of 2014, Amy's house is damaged by flooding. Shortly thereafter, the president of the United States declares the region a disaster area. The damage to the house is $6,000 and the loss may be deducted in 2013 or 2014, even if the 2013 return has already been filed. If Amy elects to take the deduction in 2013, she may immediately file an amended tax return for that year, and collect a refund of previously paid taxes. ♦

Measuring the Loss

The amount of the casualty or theft loss is measured by one of the following two rules:

Rule A—The deduction is based on the decrease in fair market value of the property, not to exceed the adjusted basis of the property.
Rule B—The deduction is based on the adjusted basis of the property.

Rule A applies to the partial destruction of business or investment property and the partial or complete destruction of personal property, while Rule B applies to the complete destruction of business and investment property. The cost of repairs is usually used for the measurement of loss from automobile damage. Repair costs may also be used to measure losses involving other types of property, but it is not controlling. Indirect costs, such as cleanup costs, are part of the loss, provided the payments do not restore the property to better than its previous condition.

EXAMPLE A taxpayer purchased his house 15 years ago for $25,000. Today it is worth $160,000, and heavy rains cause the house to slide into a canyon and be completely destroyed. The taxpayer's casualty loss deduction under Rule A is the decrease in fair market value ($160,000 – $0) not to exceed the taxpayer's basis ($25,000). Thus, the deduction is limited to $25,000. ♦

Deduction Limitations

The tax law includes limitations on the amount of the deduction for casualty and theft losses related to personal property. Of course, all casualty and theft losses are reduced by amounts of insurance proceeds. In addition, the amount of each personal casualty loss is reduced by $100 (the floor); the floor applies to each casualty or theft, not each year. In determining the casualty loss deduction, a taxpayer with three separate casualties occurring during the year must reduce each separate loss by the $100 amount; therefore, no deduction is allowed for a loss of $100 or less. In addition, taxpayers are allowed a deduction for personal casualty losses only to the extent the total losses for the year (less floor amounts) exceed 10 percent of the taxpayer's adjusted gross income, and then only if the taxpayer itemizes deductions.

If related to business property, there is no adjusted gross income limitation or dollar reduction applicable to casualty and theft losses; such losses are deductions for adjusted gross income. Chapter 8 discusses the reporting of casualty losses on business properties as well as the reporting of casualty gains where insurance proceeds exceed the basis of the damaged or stolen property.

EXAMPLE In 2014, John discovers a theft of personal property which had a fair market value and an adjusted basis of $4,000. For the year, his adjusted gross income is $24,000. His casualty loss deduction of $1,500 is calculated as follows:

Gross loss	$ 4,000
Floor limitation	(100)
Net loss	$ 3,900
Less: 10% of $24,000 AGI	(2,400)
John's casualty loss deduction	$ 1,500

♦

Self-Study Problem 5.5 *See Appendix E for Solutions to Self-Study Problems*

Vivian Walker (AGI of $25,000) has a personal coin collection (acquired 8 years ago) that has a fair market value of $9,000 and a basis of $6,000. The collection is stolen by a burglar. Vivian's insurance pays her $2,900 for the theft loss. Use Form 4684, Casualties and Thefts, on Page 5-21 to report Vivian's deduction.

MISCELLANEOUS DEDUCTIONS

Learning Objective 5.6

Identify miscellaneous itemized deductions.

Miscellaneous deductions fall into two categories, those allowed only to the extent the total exceeds 2 percent of adjusted gross income and those with no limitation. The following common miscellaneous deductions are examples of items which are **not** subject to the 2 percent of adjusted gross income limitation:

1. Handicapped "impairment-related work expenses"
2. Certain estate taxes
3. Amortizable bond premiums (on bonds acquired before October 23, 1986)
4. Unrecovered annuity costs at death
5. Gambling losses to the extent of gambling winnings

The common miscellaneous deductions that are subject to the 2 percent limitation include:

1. Unreimbursed employee business expenses and employee business expenses reimbursed under a nonaccountable plan (e.g., mileage and travel), covered in LO 5.7
2. Investment expenses (e.g., investment advice and fees for safe deposit boxes used to store investment-related papers)
3. Other general miscellaneous itemized deductions (e.g., tax return preparation fees, union dues, job-hunting expenses, and professional subscriptions)

Investment Expenses

Taxpayers are allowed a deduction for investment expenses directly related to taxable income or taxable income-producing property. Clerical help and office rent expenses incurred in caring for investments qualify for this deduction. Custodian fees are also deductible, including fees for holding stocks and bonds, collecting and reinvesting cash dividends and interest, and record keeping and providing a statement of accounts. Fees paid to a broker or similar agent to collect taxable interest or dividends are deductible, but fees paid to a broker to acquire stocks or bonds are not deductible; they are added to the cost of the stocks or bonds. No deduction is allowed for investment expenses related to tax-exempt income.

Tax Return Preparation Fees

Amounts paid for the preparation of tax returns are deductible in the year paid. For example, fees paid in 2014 for preparation of a taxpayer's 2013 tax return are deductible on the 2014 tax return. Included in this deduction are all regular fees for tax advice and audit representation, and such items as appraisal expenses to establish the amount of a casualty loss or the fair market value of donated property. Credit card convenience fees on tax payments are also included.

Job-Hunting Expenses

In some cases, taxpayers may deduct the cost of seeking employment, including travel and employment agency fees. To deduct job-hunting expenses, the taxpayer must be seeking employment in a trade or business in which he or she is currently employed, or, if

unemployed, there can be no lack of continuity since the taxpayer's last job. For example, the taxpayer may not terminate employment, get a college degree, and then deduct the cost of seeking employment after obtaining the degree. The deduction is allowed even if the attempt to obtain a new job is unsuccessful, but it is not allowed for first-time job seekers or taxpayers seeking employment in a new trade or business.

Self-Study Problem 5.6

See Appendix E for Solutions to Self-Study Problems

During the current year, Robert has AGI of $35,000 and incurs the following expenses:

Safe-deposit box rental fee (for stocks and bonds)	$ 25
Tax return preparation fee	450
Professional dues	175
Trade journals	125
Bank trust fees	1,055
Job-hunting expenses, for employment in the same profession	1,400
Total	$3,230

Assuming Robert is not self-employed, calculate his miscellaneous deductions on Schedule A of Form 1040.

Job Expenses and Certain Miscellaneous Deductions	21	Unreimbursed employee expenses—job travel, union dues, job education, etc. Attach Form 2106 or 2106-EZ if required. (See instructions.) ▶	21		
	22	Tax preparation fees	22		
	23	Other expenses—investment, safe deposit box, etc. List type and amount ▶	23		
	24	Add lines 21 through 23	24		
	25	Enter amount from Form 1040, line 38 | 25 |			
	26	Multiply line 25 by 2% (.02)	26		
	27	Subtract line 26 from line 24. If line 26 is more than line 24, enter -0-		27	

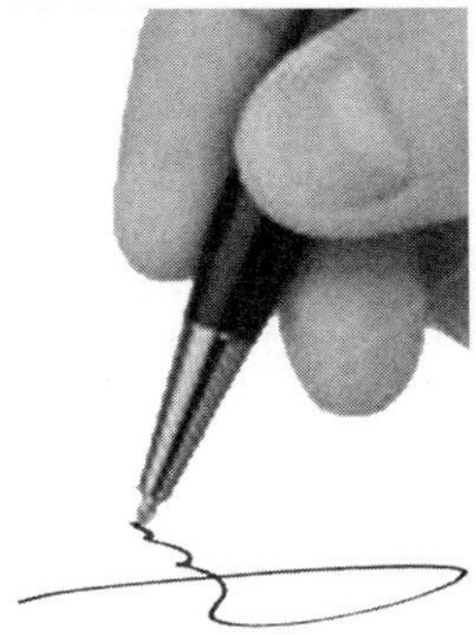

© ILYA AKINSHIN/Shutterstock.com; © Zhukov Oleg/Shutterstock.com

Would You Sign This Tax Return?

Paid Preparer Use Only	Print/Type preparer's name	Preparer's signature	Date	Check ☐ if self-employed	PTIN
	Firm's name ▶		Firm's EIN ▶		
	Firm's address ▶		Phone no.		

Sam Shiraz (age 45), one of your tax clients, is single and the manager of a bank in Cleveland, OH. Sam feels his life is stagnant and decides to go to Napa Valley, CA, to look for a job at a bank there. Sam is also a wine collector. He flies out to Napa Valley and spends 2 weeks looking for a job there. While in Napa Valley, he looks in the local newspaper's want ads every day, talks to an employment agency, and makes a few cold calls to various banks to see if they might have any openings for someone with his skills. Sam spends most of each day visiting wineries. After 2 weeks, Sam cannot find a job in Napa Valley, so he returns to his old job in Cleveland. The total cost (transportation, meals, lodging, and wine tasting) of the trip is $3,700. Sam has receipts and can substantiate these expenses. He is resolute in claiming the $3,700 as "job-hunting" expenses on Schedule A (subject to any 2 percent limitation) on his current year's tax return. Would you sign the Paid Preparer's declaration (see example above) on this return? Why or why not?

Self-Study Problem 5.5

Form **4684** | **Casualties and Thefts** | OMB No. 1545-0177

Department of the Treasury
Internal Revenue Service

► Information about Form 4684 and its separate instructions is at *www.irs.gov/form4684.*
► Attach to your tax return.
► Use a separate Form 4684 for each casualty or theft.

2014
Attachment
Sequence No. **26**

Name(s) shown on tax return | **Identifying number**

DRAFT AS OF
June 12, 2014
DO NOT FILE

SECTION A—Personal Use Property (Use this section to report casualties and thefts of property **not** used in a trade or business or for income-producing purposes.)

1 Description of properties (show type, location, and date acquired for each property). Use a separate line for each property lost or damaged from the same casualty or theft.

Property **A** ______
Property **B** ______
Property **C** ______
Property **D** ______

	Line	Properties A	Properties B	Properties C	Properties D
2 Cost or other basis of each property	2				
3 Insurance or other reimbursement (whether or not you filed a claim) (see instructions)	3				
Note: *If line 2 is* ***more*** *than line 3, skip line 4.*					
4 Gain from casualty or theft. If line 3 is **more** than line 2, enter the difference here and skip lines 5 through 9 for that column. See instructions if line 3 includes insurance or other reimbursement you did not claim, or you received payment for your loss in a later tax year	4				
5 Fair market value **before** casualty or theft	5				
6 Fair market value **after** casualty or theft	6				
7 Subtract line 6 from line 5	7				
8 Enter the **smaller** of line 2 or line 7	8				
9 Subtract line 3 from line 8. If zero or less, enter -0-	9				

	Line	Amount
10 Casualty or theft loss. Add the amounts on line 9 in columns A through D	10	
11 Enter the **smaller** of line 10 or $100	11	
12 Subtract line 11 from line 10	12	
Caution: *Use only one Form 4684 for lines 13 through 18.*		
13 Add the amounts on line 12 of all Forms 4684	13	
14 Add the amounts on line 4 of all Forms 4684.	14	
15 • If line 14 is **more** than line 13, enter the difference here and on Schedule D. **Do not** complete the rest of this section (see instructions). • If line 14 is **less** than line 13, enter -0- here and go to line 16. • If line 14 is **equal** to line 13, enter -0- here. **Do not** complete the rest of this section.	15	
16 If line 14 is **less** than line 13, enter the difference	16	
17 Enter 10% of your adjusted gross income from Form 1040, line 38, or Form 1040NR, line 37. Estates and trusts, see instructions	17	
18 Subtract line 17 from line 16. If zero or less, enter -0-. Also enter the result on Schedule A (Form 1040), line 20, or Form 1040NR, Schedule A, line 6. Estates and trusts, enter the result on the "Other deductions" line of your tax return	18	

For Paperwork Reduction Act Notice, see instructions. Cat. No. 12997O Form **4684** (2014)

CLASSIFICATION OF DEDUCTIONS—EMPLOYEES

Learning Objective 5.7

Understand the treatment of employee business expenses.

Business expenses incurred by an employee in performing services for his or her employer are generally considered miscellaneous itemized deductions, subject to the 2 percent of adjusted gross income limitation. As such, the expenses are deductible only if the taxpayer itemizes deductions and only if the taxpayer's total miscellaneous deductions exceed 2 percent of adjusted gross income.

In some cases, however, reimbursed employee business expenses may be treated as deductions in arriving at adjusted gross income. If an employee receives a reimbursement for employee business expenses under an accountable plan, the reimbursement is not included in gross income and the expenses are not included as deductions on the taxpayer's return. As a result of this treatment, the expenses are effectively treated as deductions in arriving at adjusted gross income. An accountable plan requires the employee to substantiate expenses (e.g., with receipts) and to return amounts reimbursed in excess of the substantiated expenses. Where such a plan exists, and an employee fails to substantiate the entire amount of his or her expenses or fails to return any excess reimbursement within a reasonable period of time, the excess amounts are not considered to have been reimbursed under an accountable plan. As such, the reimbursement is included in wages, and the expenses, even though reimbursed, are deductible only as miscellaneous itemized deductions, subject to the 2 percent of adjusted gross income limitation.

EXAMPLE During 2014, Kelly receives from her employer $4,500 as a reimbursement of travel expenses under an expense account reimbursement plan. Under the reimbursement plan, Kelly is required to substantiate her expenditures and to return any excess reimbursement to her employer, and in fact she satisfies both these requirements. None of the reimbursement is included in income and Kelly does not include any of the expenses as deductions on her return. This treatment of the reimbursed expenses results in the direct deduction of the expenses against the reimbursement income, effectively treating the expenses as deductions in arriving at adjusted gross income. ♦

EXAMPLE Assume that Kelly is reimbursed under a plan which does not require her to substantiate her expenses to her employer. The reimbursement will be included as wages and she will be able to deduct the expenses only if she itemizes deductions and only as miscellaneous itemized deductions subject to the 2 percent of adjusted gross income limitation. ♦

TAX BREAK

Employers can provide tax benefits to their employees for a small administrative cost by replacing a nonaccountable plan for employee expense reimbursement with an accountable plan. By using an accountable plan, the employee receives a reimbursement of business expenses without having to include those amounts in taxable income.

Form 2106

Employee business expenses are reported on Form 2106 or Form 2106-EZ, which is included with the taxpayer's Form 1040 for the year. Any employee business expenses that the employer would have reimbursed are not deductible if the employee does not seek reimbursement.

EXAMPLE Tracie Johnson is a salesperson for Very Big Insurance Company. Her job is to sell insurance policies to new and current policyholders. As part of her job during the year, Tracie incurs parking fees of $675, spends $2,500 on client meals, and drives 12,500 miles for business. Her car was purchased on February 11, 2010, and is driven 5,000 miles for commuting and 7,000 miles for personal purposes. She uses the standard mileage method. Tracie's employer does not reimburse employee expenses. Tracie can deduct these expenses on Form 2106-EZ as shown on Page 5-25. ♦

Self-Study Problem 5.7 *See Appendix E for Solutions to Self-Study Problems*

For each of the following independent situations, indicate whether the deduction should be classified as a deduction for adjusted gross income (DFOR) or a deduction from adjusted gross income (DFROM).

	DFOR	DFROM
1. Abel, an employee of Rose Corporation, is reimbursed for $5,000 of auto expenses every year. Rose Corporation does not require any substantiation and includes the $5,000 in Abel's wages. Abel's actual business auto expense is $950.	________	________
2. Lola, an employee of Elm Corporation, pays $50 for a subscription to a professional journal. Lola's employer does not have an expense reimbursement plan.	________	________
3. Frank, an employee of Azalea, Inc., pays $675 for travel expenses. Frank substantiates his expenses and submits a timely request for reimbursement under his employer's accountable plan.	________	________

Learning Objective 5.8

Understand the tax implications of using educational savings vehicles.

EDUCATIONAL INCENTIVES

Qualified Tuition Programs (QTP)

A Qualified Tuition Program (sometimes called a Section 529 tuition plan) allows taxpayers (1) to buy in-kind tuition credits or certificates for qualified higher education expenses or (2) to contribute to an account established to meet qualified higher education expenses. Such Qualified Tuition Programs may be sponsored by a state government or a private institution of higher learning. Distributions are generally not taxable if the funds are used to pay qualified higher education expenses. Qualified higher education expenses include tuition, fees, books, supplies, and equipment required for the enrollment or

Form **2106-EZ**

Department of the Treasury
Internal Revenue Service (99)

Unreimbursed Employee Business Expenses

▶ Attach to Form 1040 or Form 1040NR.

▶ Information about Form 2106 and its separate instructions is available at *www.irs.gov/form2106.*

OMB No. 1545-0074

2014

Attachment Sequence No. **129A**

Your name	Occupation in which you incurred expenses	Social security number
Tracie Johnson	Salesperson	

You Can Use This Form Only if All of the Following Apply.

- You are an employee deducting ordinary and necessary expenses attributable to your job. An ordinary expense is one that is common and accepted in your field of trade, business, or profession. A necessary expense is one that is helpful and appropriate for your business. An expense does not have to be required to be considered necessary.
- You **do not** get reimbursed by your employer for any expenses (amounts your employer included in box 1 of your Form W-2 are not considered reimbursements for this purpose).
- If you are claiming vehicle expense, you are using the standard mileage rate for 2014.

Caution: *You can use the standard mileage rate for 2014* ***only if: (a)*** *you owned the vehicle and used the standard mileage rate for the first year you placed the vehicle in service,* ***or (b)*** *you leased the vehicle and used the standard mileage rate for the portion of the lease period after 1997.*

DRAFT AS OF
July 31, 2014
DO NOT FILE

Part I — Figure Your Expenses

1	Complete Part II. Multiply line 8a by 56¢ (.56). Enter the result here	1	7,000
2	Parking fees, tolls, and transportation, including train, bus, etc., that **did not** involve overnight travel or commuting to and from work	2	675
3	Travel expense while away from home overnight, including lodging, airplane, car rental, etc. **Do not** include meals and entertainment	3	
4	Business expenses not included on lines 1 through 3. **Do not** include meals and entertainment	4	
5	Meals and entertainment expenses: $ 2,500 × 50% (.50). (Employees subject to Department of Transportation (DOT) hours of service limits: Multiply meal expenses incurred while away from home on business by 80% (.80) instead of 50%. For details, see instructions.)	5	1,250
6	**Total expenses.** Add lines 1 through 5. Enter here and on **Schedule A (Form 1040), line 21** (or on **Schedule A (Form 1040NR), line 7**). (Armed Forces reservists, fee-basis state or local government officials, qualified performing artists, and individuals with disabilities: See the instructions for special rules on where to enter this amount.)	6	8,925

Part II — Information on Your Vehicle. Complete this part **only** if you are claiming vehicle expense on line 1.

7 When did you place your vehicle in service for business use? (month, day, year) ▶ 02 / 11 / 2010

8 Of the total number of miles you drove your vehicle during 2014, enter the number of miles you used your vehicle for:

a Business 12,500 **b** Commuting (see instructions) 5,000 **c** Other 7,000

9 Was your vehicle available for personal use during off-duty hours? ☒ **Yes** ☐ **No**

10 Do you (or your spouse) have another vehicle available for personal use? ☐ **Yes** ☒ **No**

11a Do you have evidence to support your deduction? ☒ **Yes** ☐ **No**

b If "Yes," is the evidence written? ☒ **Yes** ☐ **No**

attendance at an eligible educational institution. In addition, taxpayers are allowed reasonable room and board costs, subject to certain limitations. The earnings portion of distributions that are not used for qualified tuition expenses are includable in the distributee's gross income under the annuity income rules and are subject to a 10 percent early withdrawal penalty.

EXAMPLE In 2014, Karen uses in-kind credits of $5,000 that were purchased through a state-qualified tuition program for her son's college tuition. The tuition is a qualified higher education expense of the son. Therefore, the $5,000 distribution will be excluded from Karen's or her son's income. ♦

EXAMPLE In 2014, Ken uses a distribution from a state QTP of $9,000 (of which $2,000 is earnings) to pay for his son's qualified higher education expenses. None of the $9,000 is taxable to Ken or his son. ♦

Unlike Educational Savings Accounts, discussed on the next page, there is no income limit on the amount of contributions to a Qualified Tuition Program. Like an Educational Savings Account, however, the contributions are not deductible. Any contributions are gifts, however, and thus subject to the gift tax rules. In addition, most programs impose some form of overall maximum contribution for each beneficiary based on estimated future higher education expenses.

EXAMPLE Bill has AGI of $275,000 and has two children. He chooses to contribute $9,000 (he is allowed to contribute any amount up to the limit imposed by his state's law) to a QTP for each of his children in 2014, even with his high AGI. The $18,000 is not deductible to Bill, but any earnings on the contribution accumulate tax free and are not taxable if used for future qualified higher education expenses. ♦

A taxpayer may claim an American Opportunity credit or lifetime learning credit (discussed in detail in Chapter 6) for a tax year and exclude from gross income amounts distributed (both the principal and the earnings portions) from a qualified tuition program on behalf of the same student. This is true as long as the distribution is not used for the same expenses for which a credit was claimed. However, the amount of qualified higher education expenses for a tax year for purposes of calculating the exclusion from income must be reduced by scholarships, veterans' benefits, military reserve benefits, employer-provided educational assistance amounts, and American Opportunity and lifetime learning credits amounts.

EXAMPLE In 2014, Sammy receives $15,000 from a qualified tuition program. He uses the funds to pay for his college tuition and other qualified higher education expenses. Sammy also claims an American Opportunity credit of $1,500 for the year, based on the same expenses. For purposes of the QTP exclusion calculation, the $15,000 must be reduced to $13,500 ($15,000 – $1,500). ♦

The tax law provides that if the total distributions from a qualified tuition program and from an educational savings account exceed the total amount of qualified higher education expenses, the taxpayer will have to allocate the expenses among the distributions for purposes of determining how much of each distribution is excludable.

TAX BREAK

There are billions of dollars invested in the increasingly popular Section 529 Qualified Tuition Programs across the country. The plans offered by different states vary significantly and it is possible for a taxpayer to invest in the plan of a state other than the state that he lives in. The following two websites offer information comparing state plans and answers to questions regarding plan operations: **www.collegesavings.org** and **www.savingforcollege.com**.

Educational Savings Accounts

Taxpayers are allowed to set up educational savings accounts, also known as Coverdell Education Savings Accounts, to pay for qualified higher education expenses. The maximum amount a taxpayer can contribute annually to an educational savings account for a beneficiary is $2,000. Contributions are not deductible and are subject to income limits. Contributions cannot be made to an educational savings account after the date on which the designated beneficiary becomes 18 years old. In addition, contributions cannot be made to a beneficiary's educational savings account during any year in which contributions are made to a qualified state tuition program on behalf of the same beneficiary. The educational savings account exclusion for distributions of income is available in any tax year in which the beneficiary claims the American Opportunity credit or the lifetime learning credit (see Chapter 6), provided the distribution is not used for the same expenses for which the credit was claimed.

Contributions to educational savings accounts are phased out between AGIs of $95,000 and $110,000 for single taxpayers and $190,000 and $220,000 for married couples who file a joint return. Like regular and Roth IRAs, contributions must be made by April 15 (or the following business day, if April 15 falls on a weekend or holiday) of the following year.

EXAMPLE Joe, who is single, would like to contribute $2,000 to an educational savings account for his 12-year-old son. However, his AGI is $105,000, so his contribution is limited to $667, calculated as follows:

$$\frac{(\$110{,}000 \text{ upper limit} - \$105{,}000 \text{ AGI})}{\$15{,}000} \times \$2{,}000 = \$667 \text{ contribution}$$

$15,000 is the spread between the upper and lower phase-out limits. ♦

TAX BREAK

For parents with income above the allowable limit, a gift may be made to a child and the child may make the contribution to an educational savings account. There is no requirement that the contributor should have earned income as there is for IRAs.

Amounts received from an educational savings account are tax free if they are used for qualified education expenses. Qualified education expenses include tuition, fees, books, supplies, and related equipment for private, elementary, and secondary school expenses as well as for college. Room and board also qualify if the student's course load is at least 50 percent of the full-time course load. If the distributions during a tax year exceed qualified education expenses, part of the excess is treated as a return of capital (the contributions), and part is

treated as a distribution of earnings. The distribution is presumed to be pro rata from each category. The exclusion for the distribution of earnings is calculated as follows:

$$\frac{\text{Qualified education expenses}}{\text{Total distribution}} \times \text{Earnings} = \text{Exclusion}$$

EXAMPLE Amy receives a $2,000 distribution from her educational savings account. She uses $1,800 to pay for qualified education expenses. Immediately prior to the distribution, Amy's account balance is $5,000, $3,000 of which are her contributions. Because 60 percent ($3,000/$5,000) of her account balance represents her contributions, $1,200 ($2,000 × 60%) of the distribution is a tax-free return of capital and $800 ($2,000 × 40%) is a distribution of earnings. The excludable amount of the earnings is calculated as follows:

$$\frac{\$1,800}{\$2,000} \times \$800 = \$720 \text{ (thus, the amount taxable is \$80, or \$800} - \text{\$720).}$$

Amy's adjusted basis for her savings account is reduced to $1,800 ($3,000 − $1,200). ♦

Higher Education Expenses Deduction

Please note: As we go to press in late 2014, it is not known whether Congress will extend the deduction for higher education expenses retroactively for all of 2014. Additionally, if extended, the phaseout thresholds may not be the same as 2013 described below. Check the Whittenburg companion website for updates.

Taxpayers are allowed an "above-the-line" deduction for qualified tuition and related expenses incurred during the tax year. The deduction will be allowed for qualified tuition and related expenses for enrollment at an institution of higher education during the tax year. In addition, the deduction will be allowed for qualified expenses paid during a tax year if those expenses are in connection with an academic term beginning during the tax year or during the first 3 months of the next tax year.

EXAMPLE Jerry pays $2,000 for his son's college tuition in November 2014 for the spring 2015 term. The spring term starts in January 2015. The $2,000 is deductible in 2014, even though it is for education provided in a later tax year. ♦

The total amount of qualified tuition and related expenses for the higher education expense deduction must be reduced by certain items. The reduction applies to (1) excludable interest from higher education savings bonds, (2) excludable distributions from qualified state tuition plans, and (3) excludable distributions from educational savings accounts.

EXAMPLE Matty pays $20,000 in tuition for her children to attend college in 2014. Included in that amount is $5,000 she received from a qualified state tuition plan and $3,000 excluded interest from educational saving bonds. Matty's qualified tuition expense for purposes of the higher education expense deduction is $12,000 ($20,000 − $5,000 − $3,000). ♦

The deduction may not exceed a specified annual amount. The deduction is $4,000 for single and head of household taxpayers with modified AGI below $65,000 and for married filing jointly taxpayers with modified AGI below $130,000. The amount is $2,000 for single taxpayers with modified AGI between $65,000 and $80,000 and for married joint filers with modified AGI between $130,000 and $160,000. Taxpayers with AGI exceeding the limits are not allowed a deduction.

EXAMPLE In 2014, Juan is single and has qualified higher education expenses of $7,000. His modified AGI is $62,000. He gets a $4,000 above-the-line deduction. If his modified AGI were $66,000, he would get a $2,000 deduction. ♦

Self-Study Problem 5.8 *See Appendix E for Solutions to Self-Study Problems*

a. Abby has a distribution of $10,000 from a qualified tuition program, of which $3,000 represents earnings. The funds are used to pay for her daughter's qualified higher education expenses. How much of the $10,000 distribution is taxable to the daughter?

$__________

b. During 2014, Henry (a single taxpayer) has a salary of $85,000 and interest income of $4,000. Calculate the maximum contribution Henry is allowed for an educational savings account.

$__________

Learning Objective 5.9

Calculate itemized deduction and exemption phase-outs for high-income tax payers.

PHASE-OUT OF ITEMIZED DEDUCTIONS AND EXEMPTIONS FOR HIGH-INCOME TAXPAYERS

This section covers the calculation of the itemized deduction and exemption phase-outs for high-income individuals. Commercial tax software preparation programs calculate the phase-outs automatically, so few tax preparers actually calculate these manually. This section is useful for students who wish to understand how the phase-outs work and for anyone preparing high-income tax returns without software.

Limitation on Total Itemized Deductions

In 2014, taxpayers with AGI over the following threshold amounts are subject to both the itemized deduction and the exemption phase-outs:

Filing Status	*Amount*
Single	$254,200
Head of household	279,650
Married filing jointly	305,050
Married filling separately	152,525

Itemized deductions are reduced by the lesser of 3 percent of the excess of the taxpayer's AGI over the threshold amount or 80 percent of itemized deductions other than the deductions for medical expenses, investment interest expense, casualty and theft losses, and gambling losses to the extent of gambling income.

EXAMPLE Francis and Marcia are married taxpayers who file a joint income tax return for 2014. They have AGI of $408,383 and itemized deductions of $20,000. The itemized deductions are from charitable contributions and state income taxes. Only $16,900 ($20,000 − $3,100) of the itemized

deduction amount is allowed in calculating taxable income. The reduction in the amount of itemized deductions claimed by Francis and Marcia is calculated as follows:

Lesser of:

$3,100 = 3% × ($408,383 − $305,050), or
$16,000 = 80% × $20,000 ♦

EXAMPLE Use the same facts as in the preceding example, but assume that the itemized deductions consist of $18,000 in casualty losses (after the $100 floor and after applying the 10 percent of AGI limitation) and $2,000 in state income taxes. In 2014, Francis and Marcia may deduct $18,400 ($20,000 − $1,600) of itemized deductions, with the $1,600 reduction calculated as follows:

Lesser of:

$3,100 = 3% × ($408,383 − $305,050), or
$1,600 = 80% × ($20,000 − $18,000) ♦

Personal and Dependency Exemption Phase-Out

Taxpayers are allowed two types of exemptions: personal and dependency, as covered in Chapter 1. For 2014, each exemption reduces AGI by $3,950. If a taxpayer's AGI exceeds the threshold amount, the exemption deduction is reduced by 2 percent for each $2,500 ($1,250 for married taxpayers filing separately) or fraction thereof by which the taxpayer's AGI exceeds the threshold amount.

EXAMPLE In 2014, Heather is a single taxpayer with AGI of $298,000. She is entitled to one exemption worth $3,950. Heather's exemption must be reduced by $1,422 (36% × $3,950). The 36% is calculated as follows:

1. ($298,000 − $254,200)/$2,500 = 17.5, which is rounded up to 18.
2. 2% × 18 = 36%, the exemption reduction percentage.

Heather's allowed exemption amount is $2,528 ($3,950 − $1,422). If Heather had an exemption for a dependent, this exemption would also be reduced. ♦

Self-Study Problem 5.9

Elvis and Greta are married taxpayers who file a joint income tax return for 2014. On their 2014 income tax return they have AGI of $421,550 and total itemized deductions of $30,000 which consist of $10,000 of state income taxes and $20,000 of medical expenses (after applying the 10 percent of AGI limitation). Of the $30,000 of itemized deductions, what amount is allowed as a deduction in calculating taxable income on Elvis and Greta's 2014 federal income tax return?

KEY TERMS

qualified residence interest (mortgage interest), 5-8
mortgage interest prepayment penalties, 5-8
private mortgage insurance (PMI), 5-8
prepaid interest, 5-9
qualified residence acquisition debt, 5-9
qualified home equity debt, 5-9
charitable contributions, 5-12
qualified recipient, 5-12
nonqualified recipients, 5-13
exempt organizations select check, 5-13
50 percent limitation, 5-13
30 percent limitation, 5-14
20 percent limitation, 5-14
substantiation rules, 5-15
casualty, 5-17
accountable plan, 5-23
qualified tuition program, 5-24
section 529 tuition plan, 5-24
educational savings accounts, 5-28
Coverdell Educational Savings Accounts, 5-28
itemized deduction and exemption phase-outs, 5-30

KEY POINTS

Learning Objectives	Key Points
LO 5.1: Understand the nature and treatment of medical expenses.	• Taxpayers are allowed an itemized deduction on Schedule A for medical expenses paid for themselves, their spouses, and their dependents. • Qualified medical expenses are deductible only to the extent they exceed 10 percent of a taxpayer's adjusted gross income (7.5 percent if age 65 or over). • Qualified medical expenses include such items as prescription medicines and drugs, insulin, fees for doctors, dentists, nurses, and other medical professionals, hospital fees, hearing aids, dentures, eyeglasses, contact lenses, medical transportation and lodging, crutches, wheelchairs, guide dogs, birth control prescriptions, acupuncture, psychiatric care, medical and Medicare insurance premiums, and various other listed medical expenses.
LO 5.2: Calculate the itemized deduction for taxes.	• The following taxes are deductible on Schedule A: income taxes (state, local, and foreign), sales taxes (through 2013 unless extended by Congress and by election in lieu of state and local income tax), real property taxes (state, local, and foreign), and personal property taxes (state and local). • Nondeductible taxes include the following: federal income taxes, employee portion of Social Security taxes, estate, inheritance, and gift taxes (except in unusual situations not discussed here), gasoline taxes, excise taxes, and foreign taxes if the taxpayer elects a foreign tax credit. • If real estate is sold during the year, the taxes must be divided between the buyer and seller based on the number of days in the year that each taxpayer held the property. • To be deductible, personal property taxes must be levied based on the value of the property. Personal property taxes of a fixed amount, or those calculated on a basis other than value, are not deductible.
LO 5.3: Apply the rules for an individual taxpayer's interest deduction.	• Deductible personal interest includes qualified residence interest (mortgage interest), mortgage interest prepayment penalties, investment interest, and certain interest associated with a passive activity. • Nondeductible consumer interest includes interest on any loan, the proceeds of which are used for personal purposes, such as credit card interest, finance charges, and automobile loan interest, with the exception of the interest on qualifying home equity debt used for these purposes. • "Qualified residence interest" is the sum of the interest paid on "qualified residence acquisition debt" plus "qualified home equity debt." • Deductible investment interest is limited to the taxpayer's net investment income, which is investment income such as dividends and interest, less investment expenses other than interest. • Taxpayers are allowed a deduction for AGI for certain qualified education loan interest.
LO 5.4: Determine the charitable contributions deduction.	• To be deductible, the donation must be made in cash or property. • Donations must be made to a qualified recipient. • The following contributions are not deductible: gifts to needy individuals, social clubs, labor unions, international organizations, and political parties; contributions of time, service, the use of property, or blood; contributions where benefit is received from the contribution, for example, tuition at a parochial school; and wagering losses, such as church bingo and raffle tickets. • For donated property other than cash, the general rule is that the deduction is equal to the fair market value of the property at the time of the donation. • Donations are limited to 50 percent (or 30 or 20 percent in some cases) of AGI.

LO 5.5: Compute the deduction for casualty and theft losses.	• A casualty is a complete or partial destruction of property resulting from an identifiable event of a sudden, unexpected, or unusual nature. Examples include property damage from storms, floods, shipwrecks, fires, automobile accidents, and vandalism. • For the partial destruction of business or investment property and the partial or complete destruction of personal property, the deduction is based on the decrease in fair market value of the property, not to exceed the adjusted basis of the property. • For the complete destruction of business and investment property, the deduction is based on the adjusted basis of the property. • The amount of each personal casualty loss is reduced by $100 and only the excess over 10 percent of the taxpayer's adjusted gross income is deductible.
LO 5.6: Identify miscellaneous itemized deductions.	• Miscellaneous deductions fall into two categories, those limited to the extent the total exceeds 2 percent of adjusted gross income and those with no limitation. • Examples of items which are not subject to the 2 percent of adjusted gross income limitation are handicapped "impairment-related work expenses," certain estate taxes, amortizable bond premiums, unrecovered annuity costs at death, and gambling losses to the extent of gambling winnings. • Common miscellaneous deductions that are subject to the 2 percent limitation include unreimbursed employee business expenses and employee business expenses reimbursed under a nonaccountable plan, investment expenses, tax return preparation fees, union dues, job-hunting expenses, and professional subscriptions.
LO 5.7: Understand the treatment of employee business expenses.	• Business expenses incurred by an employee are generally considered miscellaneous itemized deductions, subject to the 2 percent of adjusted gross income limitation. • Accountable-plan reimbursed employee business expenses may be effectively treated as deductions in arriving at adjusted gross income. • An accountable plan is one that requires the employee to substantiate expenses to the employer and to return amounts in excess of the substantiated amounts.
LO 5.8: Understand the tax implications of using educational savings vehicles.	• A Qualified Tuition Program (a Section 529 plan) allows taxpayers (1) to buy in-kind tuition credits or certificates for qualified higher education expenses or (2) to contribute to an account established to meet qualified higher education expenses. Distributions from the account are not taxable if the account is used for qualified higher education expenses. • Qualified higher education expenses include tuition, fees, books, supplies, and equipment required for the enrollment or attendance at an eligible educational institution. In addition, taxpayers are allowed reasonable room and board costs, subject to certain limitations. • The maximum amount a taxpayer can contribute annually to an educational savings account for a beneficiary is $2,000. The contribution is not deductible, and if the amounts received are used for qualified education expenses, the distributions are not taxable.
LO 5.9: Calculate itemized deduction and exemption phase-outs for high-income taxpayers.	• In 2014, an individual taxpayer whose adjusted gross income exceeds a threshold amount must reduce the amount of his or her total itemized deductions by the lesser of 3 percent of the excess of AGI over the threshold amount, or 80 percent of certain itemized deductions. • The 2014 exemption deduction is phased out gradually, although not completely, for taxpayers with AGI exceeding certain threshold amounts.

© Dusit/Shutterstock.com

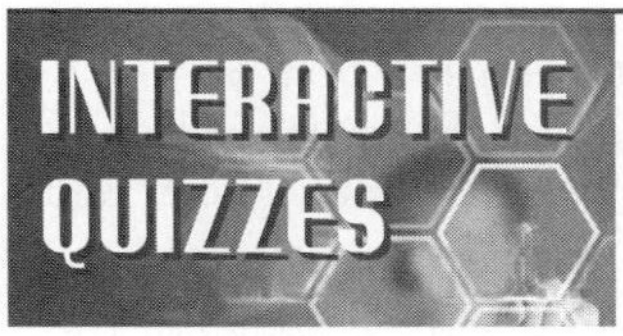

Interactive quizzes are available as an optional online resource for Income Tax Fundamentals. Visit **www.cengagebrain.com** for more information.

QUESTIONS and PROBLEMS

GROUP 1: MULTIPLE CHOICE QUESTIONS

LO 5.1

1. The cost of which of the following expenses is *not* deductible as a medical expense on Schedule A, before the 10 percent of adjusted gross income limitation?
   a. A psychiatrist
   b. Birth control prescriptions
   c. Acupuncture
   d. Marriage counseling

LO 5.1

2. The cost of which of the following is deductible as a medical expense?
   a. Travel to a warm climate
   b. Birth control pills
   c. A disability insurance policy that pays $200 for each day the taxpayer is in the hospital
   d. Liposuction to reduce waist size

LO 5.1

3. Which of the following is not considered a deductible medical expense?
   a. Dental work
   b. Eyeglasses
   c. Acupuncture
   d. Diet foods

LO 5.2

4. Which of the following taxes may be deducted as itemized deductions for 2014?
   a. State gasoline taxes
   b. Fishing license fee
   c. Federal income taxes
   d. Social Security taxes
   e. Local income taxes

LO 5.2

5. Wilma had $3,100 in state income taxes withheld from her paychecks during 2014. In April of 2014, Wilma paid the $300 due for her 2013 state tax return. Wilma's total tax liability on her state tax return for 2014 is $2,850. How much should Wilma deduct as an itemized deduction for state income taxes on her 2014 federal income tax return?
   a. $3,400
   b. $3,150
   c. $3,100
   d. $2,850
   e. None of the above

LO 5.2

6. Which of the following taxes are not deductible as an itemized deduction:
   a. Property tax on land held for investment
   b. State income taxes
   c. Auto registration fees based on the value of the auto
   d. Federal income taxes

LO 5.2
LO 5.4
LO 5.9

7. Ramon, a single taxpayer, has adjusted gross income for 2014 of $164,000 and his itemized deductions total $19,000. The itemized deductions consist of $11,000 in state income taxes and $8,000 of charitable contributions. What amount of itemized deductions will Ramon be allowed to deduct in 2014?
   a. $40
   b. $10,133
   c. $5,450
   d. $18,959
   e. $19,000

LO 5.3

8. Which of the following is deductible as interest on Schedule A?
   a. Loan fees that are not "points"
   b. Service charges
   c. Investment interest expense, subject to the net investment income limitation
   d. Interest on loans to finance tax-exempt bonds
   e. None of the above are deductible as interest

LO 5.3

9. Carrie finished her undergraduate degree using money from a student loan. She earned $36,000 her first year and paid $2,600 in interest. She can take a deduction for student loan interest in the amount of:
   a. $2,600
   b. $2,500
   c. $1,500
   d. $0
   e. None of the above

LO 5.3

10. Which of the following interest expense amounts is *not* deductible in the current year:
    a. Education loan interest of $2,000, assuming the taxpayer has income of $30,000.
    b. Home equity loan interest of $6,000, on a loan of $90,000, the proceeds of which were used to purchase a sports car and designer clothes.
    c. Investment interest expense of $10,000, assuming the taxpayer has no investment income.
    d. Qualified residence interest of $70,000 on a $1 million loan used to purchase a luxury apartment in downtown San Diego.

LO 5.4

11. Which of the following donations are *not* deductible as a charitable contribution?
    a. A donation of clothing to Goodwill Industries
    b. A contribution to a church
    c. A contribution to a public university
    d. A contribution to a labor union
    e. A contribution to a museum

LO 5.4

12. Stanley donates a hotel to a university for use as a conference center. The building cost $1,500,000 3 months ago and has a fair market value of $1,900,000 on the date the contribution is made. If Stanley had sold the building, the $400,000 difference between the sales price and cost would have been a short-term capital gain. What

is the amount of Stanley's deduction for this contribution, before considering any limitation based on adjusted gross income?
a. $2,300,000
b. $1,500,000
c. $1,900,000
d. $0
e. The amount cannot be determined from the information given

______ 13. In March of 2014, Thomas makes a $5,000 cash contribution to a public university. In that month, he also donates $20,000 to an organization subject to the 30 percent limitation. Thomas has adjusted gross income for 2014 of $35,000. What is the amount of Thomas's 2014 charitable contribution deduction?

LO 5.4

a. $5,000
b. $23,000
c. $10,500
d. $15,500
e. None of the above

______ 14. Which of the following gifts is a deductible contribution:

LO 5.4

a. A gift of $100 to a homeless person
b. A $500 gift to the Democratic National Committee
c. $1,000 spent on church bingo games
d. A $200 contribution to the federal government to pay down the national debt

______ 15. Which of the following is *not* a qualified casualty loss?

LO 5.5

a. Damage to an automobile from rust
b. An automobile accident
c. A fire loss
d. A tornado loss
e. A flood loss

______ 16. Which of the following is not a miscellaneous itemized deduction:

LO 5.6

a. Tax preparation fees
b. Professional dues
c. Investment interest expense
d. Job-hunting expenses

______ 17. Which of the following items is *not* deductible as a miscellaneous deduction on Schedule A?

LO 5.6

a. Investment expenses
b. Gambling losses to the extent of gambling winnings
c. Unreimbursed business expenses
d. Subscriptions to professional publications
e. Charitable contributions

______ 18. Which of the following statements is true with regard to the classification of employment-related expenses?

LO 5.7

a. A self-employed taxpayer's business travel expenses are deductible as itemized deductions.
b. Reimbursed employee business expenses are always deductible as deductions for adjusted gross income.
c. Unreimbursed employee business expenses are deductible as deductions for adjusted gross income.

d. Unreimbursed employee business expenses are deductible as deductions from adjusted gross income.
e. All of the above are true.

LO 5.7

19. What form does an employee use to report expenses that are fully reimbursed by an employer under an accountable plan?
 a. Schedule D
 b. Schedule A, Miscellaneous Itemized Deductions
 c. Schedule C
 d. Form 2106, Employee Business Expenses
 e. No form; the expenses are not reported as income to the employee, so they are not deducted on an IRS form in the employee's tax return

LO 5.8

20. Gina receives a $2,000 distribution from her educational savings account. She uses $1,600 to pay for qualified higher education expenses and $400 on a vacation. Immediately prior to the distribution, Gina's account balance is $5,000, $2,500 of which is her contributions. What is Gina's taxable income (after any exclusion) from the distribution?
 a. $1,600
 b. $1,000
 c. $800
 d. $200
 e. Some other amount

LO 5.8

21. Which of the following is correct for Qualified Tuition Programs?
 a. Contributions are deductible, and qualified educational expense distributions are tax free.
 b. Contributions are not deductible, and qualified educational expense distributions are tax free.
 c. Contributions are deductible, and qualified educational expense distributions are taxable.
 d. Contributions are not deductible, and qualified educational expense distributions are taxable.

LO 5.8

22. In 2014, Amy receives $15,000 (of which $4,000 is earnings) from a qualified tuition program. She does not use the funds to pay for tuition or other qualified higher education expenses. What amount is taxable to Amy?
 a. $0
 b. $4,000
 c. $11,000
 d. $15,000

LO 5.8

23. For married taxpayers filing a joint return in 2014, at what AGI level does the phase-out limit for contributions to Qualified Tuition Programs start?
 a. $110,000
 b. $190,000
 c. $220,000
 d. There is no phase-out limit on QTP contributions

LO 5.8

24. Which of the following is not true with respect to education incentives:
 a. The contributions to qualified tuition programs (Section 529 plans) are not deductible.
 b. The contributions to educational savings accounts (Coverdell ESA) are not deductible.

c. Tuition paid by a taxpayer earning $300,000 of income is not deductible.
d. Married taxpayers must have income less than $100,000 to contribute to a qualified tuition program (Section 529 plan).

LO 5.8

____________ 25. During 2014, Carl (a single taxpayer) has a salary of $90,500 and interest income of $15,500. Calculate the maximum contribution Carl is allowed for an educational savings account.
a. $2,000
b. $1,467
c. $533
d. $0
e. Some other amount

LO 5.8

____________ 26. George receives a $1,500 distribution from his educational savings account. He uses $1,200 to pay for qualified higher education expenses. Immediately prior to the distribution, George's account balance is $5,000, $3,000 of which is his contributions. What is George's tax-free return of capital from the distribution?
a. $1,500
b. $1,200
c. $900
d. $750
e. $600

LO 5.2
LO 5.4
LO 5.9

____________ 27. Ramon, a single taxpayer, has adjusted gross income for 2014 of $350,000. His itemized deductions total $50,000 consisting of $30,000 of state income taxes and $20,000 of charitable contributions. What is the amount of itemized deductions Ramon can claim after reduction for the itemized deduction phase-out for high-income taxpayers?
a. $2,874
b. $10,000
c. $47,000
d. $47,126
e. $50,000

LO 5.9

____________ 28. Jim and Martha are married taxpayers with $400,000 of adjusted gross income in 2014. They are allowed two personal exemptions. What is the amount of each of their $3,950 exemption deductions after applying the phase-out for high-income taxpayers?
a. $0
b. $780
c. $948
d. $3,002
e. $1,027

GROUP 2: PROBLEMS

LO 5.1

1. Linda installed a special pool for the hydrotherapeutic treatment of severe arthritis, as prescribed by her doctor. The cost of installing the pool was $20,000, and her insurance company paid $5,000 toward its cost. The pool increased the value of Linda's

house by $7,000, and it has a useful life of 10 years. How much of a deduction is Linda entitled to in the year of installation of the pool?

$ ____________

Explain____

____

____

LO 5.1

2. In 2014, Margaret and John Murphy (both over age 65) are married taxpayers who file a joint tax return with AGI of $25,000. During the year they incurred the following expenses:

Medical insurance premiums	$1,050
Premiums on an insurance policy that pays $100 per day for each day Margaret is hospitalized	300
Medical care lodging (two people, one night)	65
Hospital bills	2,200
Doctor bills	850
Dentist bills	175
Prescription drugs and medicines	340
Psychiatric care	300

In addition, they drove 78 miles for medical transportation, and their insurance company reimbursed them $900 for the above expenses. On the following segment of Schedule A of Form 1040, calculate the Murphy's medical expense deduction.

Medical and Dental Expenses		**Caution.** Do not include expenses reimbursed or paid by others.		
	1	Medical and dental expenses (see instructions)	1	
	2	Enter amount from Form 1040, line 38 [2]		
	3	Multiply line 2 by 10% (.10). But if either you or your spouse was born before January 2, 1950, multiply line 2 by 7.5% (.075) instead	3	
	4	Subtract line 3 from line 1. If line 3 is more than line 1, enter -0-		4

DRAFT AS OF

LO 5.1

3. Janet needs an elevator seat attached to her stairs since she has a medical condition that makes her unable to climb the stairs in her house. The $10,000 spent on the elevator seat does not increase the value of her house according to a local appraiser. How much of the capital asset is deductible in Janet's tax return as a medical expense?

____

____

____

____

LO 5.2

4. Lyndon's employer withheld $1,800 in state income taxes from Lyndon's wages. Lyndon obtained a refund of $200 this year for overpayment of state income taxes for last year. State income taxes were an itemized deduction on his 2013 return. His liability for this year's state income tax is $1,400. Indicate the amount of Lyndon's deduction for state income taxes on his federal tax return assuming he elects to deduct state income taxes for 2014.

$ ____________

LO 5.2

5. Mike sells his home to Jane on April 2, 2014. Jane pays the property taxes covering the full calendar year in October, which amount to $2,500. How much may Mike and Jane each deduct for property taxes in 2014?

Mike's deduction $ ____________

Jane's deduction $ ____________

LO 5.2

6. Laura is a single taxpayer living in New Jersey with adjusted gross income for the 2014 tax year of $35,550. Laura's employer withheld $3,300 in state income tax from her salary. In April of 2014, she pays $850 in additional state taxes for her prior year's tax return. The real estate taxes on her home are $1,600 for 2014, and her personal property taxes, based on the value of the property, amount to $380. Also, she paid $75 for state gasoline taxes for the year. Complete the taxes section of Schedule A below to report Laura's deduction assuming she elects to deduct state and local income taxes.

Taxes You Paid	5 State and local a ☐ Income taxes b ☐ RESERVED	5		
	6 Real estate taxes (see instructions)	6		
	7 Personal property taxes	7		
	8 Other taxes. List type and amount ▶ ______	8		
	9 Add lines 5 through 8		9	

August 15, 2014
DO NOT FILE

LO 5.2

7. Mary paid $2,000 of state income taxes in 2014. The total sales tax she paid during 2014 was $5,500, which included $3,000 for the cost of a new car. How should Mary treat the taxes paid on her 2014 tax return?

____

____

____

____

LO 5.3

8. Mary's mother defaults on a home loan and Mary pays $600 in loan payments, including $175 in interest. Mary is not legally obligated on the loan and has no ownership interest in her mother's home.
   a. What amount, if any, may Mary claim as an itemized deduction for 2014?

   $__________

   b. Why? ______________________________

   ____

LO 5.3

9. Matthew borrows $250,000 to invest in bonds. During 2014, his interest on the loan is $30,000. Matthew's interest income from the bonds is $10,000. This is Matthew's only investment income.
   a. Calculate Matthew's itemized deduction for investment interest expense for this year.

   $__________

   b. Is Matthew entitled to a deduction in future years? __________
   Explain ______________________________

   ____

LO 5.3

10. Ken paid the following amounts for interest during 2014:

Qualified interest on home mortgage	$4,700
Auto loan interest	850
"Points" on the mortgage for acquisition of his personal residence	300
Service charges on his checking account	40
Mastercard interest	300

Calculate Ken's itemized deduction for interest on the following portion of Schedule A.

Interest You Paid	10	Home mortgage interest and points reported to you on Form 1098	10
Note. Your mortgage interest deduction may be limited (see instructions).	11	Home mortgage interest not reported to you on Form 1098. If paid to the person from whom you bought the home, see instructions and show that person's name, identifying no., and address ▶	11
	12	Points not reported to you on Form 1098. See instructions for special rules	12
	13	RESERVED	13
	14	Investment interest. Attach Form 4952 if required. (See instructions.)	14
	15	Add lines 10 through 14	15

LO 5.3

11. Janet and James purchased their personal residence 15 years ago for $300,000. For the current year, they have an $80,000 first mortgage on their home, on which they paid $5,600 in interest. They also have a home equity loan secured by their home with a balance throughout the year of $150,000. They paid interest on the home equity loan of $12,000 for the year. Calculate the amount of their deduction for interest paid on qualified residence acquisition debt and qualified home equity debt for 2014.

Qualified residence acquisition debt interest $ 5,600

Qualified home equity debt interest $ 8,000

LO 5.3

12. Helen paid the following amounts of interest during the 2014 tax year:

Mortgage interest on Dallas residence (loan balance $50,000)	$2,025
Automobile loan interest (personal use only)	440
Mortgage interest on Vail residence (loan balance $50,000)	3,050
Visa and Mastercard interest	165

Calculate the amount of Helen's itemized deduction for interest (after limitations) for 2014.

$ 5,075

LO 5.3

13. Mark owns his home and has a $250,000 mortgage related to his purchase of the residence. When his daughter went to college in the fall of 2014, he borrowed $20,000 through a home equity loan on his house to help pay for her education. The interest expense on the main mortgage is $15,000, and the interest expense on the home equity loan is $1,500. How much of the interest is deductible as an itemized deduction and why?

____

LO 5.4

14. Barbara donates a painting that cost $5,000 3 years ago to a university for display in the president's office. The fair market value of the painting on the date of the gift is $7,000. If Barbara had sold the painting, the difference between the sales price and her cost would have been a long-term capital gain.

a. How much is Barbara's charitable contribution deduction for this donation?

$ ________

b. Explain ____________________

LO 5.4

15. Jerry made the following contributions during 2014:

His synagogue (by check)	$680
The Democratic Party (by check)	180
The American Red Cross (by check)	150
His lodge for a holiday party	100

In addition, Jerry donated used furniture to the Salvation Army that he purchased years ago for $2,000 with a fair market value of $400. Assuming Jerry has adjusted gross income of $45,000, has the necessary written acknowledgments, and itemizes deductions, complete the Gifts to Charity section of Schedule A below to show Jerry's deduction for 2014.

Gifts to Charity	16	Gifts by cash or check. If you made any gift of $250 or more, see instructions	16	830		
If you made a gift and got a benefit for it, see instructions.	17	Other than by cash or check. If any gift of $250 or more, see instructions. You **must** attach Form 8283 if over $500 . . .	17	400		
	18	Carryover from prior year	18			
	19	Add lines 16 through 18			19	1230

LO 5.4 16. Richard donates publicly traded Gold Company stock with a basis of $1,000 and a fair market value of $15,000 to the college he attended, which is considered a public charity. Richard has owned the shares for 10 years. How is this contribution treated on Richard's tax return?

____

____

____

____

LO 5.5 17. In June of 2014, Maureen's house is vandalized during a long-term power failure after a hurricane hit the city. The president of the United States declares Maureen's city a disaster area as a result of the wide-scale vandalism. In which tax year may Maureen take her casualty loss deduction?

____

Explain: __________________________________

____

____

LO 5.5 18. On January 3, 2014, Carey discovers his diamond bracelet has been stolen. The bracelet had a fair market value and adjusted basis of $8,000. Assuming Carey had no insurance coverage on the bracelet and his adjusted gross income for 2014 is $52,000, calculate the amount of his theft loss deduction.

$____________

LO 5.5 19. Wilbur DuVal has an apartment full of antique furniture. A fire in the apartment destroys a large part of his furnishings. The destroyed furnishings had a fair market value of $40,000, and Wilbur's original basis in the furnishings was $33,750. He recovers $13,000 from his insurance company. Wilbur's adjusted gross income for 2014 is $43,000. Use Form 4684 on Page 5-43 to report Wilbur's loss.

LO 5.5 20. Go to the IRS website **(www.irs.gov)** and print out a copy of the most recent *Instructions* for Form 4684, Casualties and Thefts.

LO 5.5 21. Kerry's car is totaled in an auto accident. The car originally cost $18,000, but is worth $7,500 at the time of the accident. Kerry's insurance company gives her a check for $7,500. Kerry has $30,000 of adjusted gross income. How much can Kerry claim as a casualty loss on her tax return? Please explain.

____

____

____

____

Form **4684**

Department of the Treasury
Internal Revenue Service

Casualties and Thefts

► Information about Form 4684 and its separate instructions is at *www.irs.gov/form4684.*
► Attach to your tax return.
► Use a separate Form 4684 for each casualty or theft.

OMB No. 1545-0177
2014
Attachment Sequence No. **26**

Name(s) shown on tax return | **Identifying number**

DRAFT AS OF
June 12, 2014
DO NOT FILE

SECTION A—Personal Use Property (Use this section to report casualties and thefts of property **not** used in a trade or business or for income-producing purposes.)

1 Description of properties (show type, location, and date acquired for each property). Use a separate line for each property lost or damaged from the same casualty or theft.

Property **A** __________

Property **B** __________

Property **C** __________

Property **D** __________

		Properties			
		A	**B**	**C**	**D**
2 Cost or other basis of each property	2				
3 Insurance or other reimbursement (whether or not you filed a claim) (see instructions)	3				
Note: *If line 2 is* ***more*** *than line 3, skip line 4.*					
4 Gain from casualty or theft. If line 3 is **more** than line 2, enter the difference here and skip lines 5 through 9 for that column. See instructions if line 3 includes insurance or other reimbursement you did not claim, or you received payment for your loss in a later tax year	4				
5 Fair market value **before** casualty or theft	5				
6 Fair market value **after** casualty or theft	6				
7 Subtract line 6 from line 5	7				
8 Enter the **smaller** of line 2 or line 7	8				
9 Subtract line 3 from line 8. If zero or less, enter -0-	9				

10 Casualty or theft loss. Add the amounts on line 9 in columns A through D	10	
11 Enter the **smaller** of line 10 or $100	11	
12 Subtract line 11 from line 10	12	
Caution: *Use only one Form 4684 for lines 13 through 18.*		
13 Add the amounts on line 12 of all Forms 4684	13	
14 Add the amounts on line 4 of all Forms 4684.	14	
15 • If line 14 is **more** than line 13, enter the difference here and on Schedule D. **Do not** complete the rest of this section (see instructions). • If line 14 is **less** than line 13, enter -0- here and go to line 16. • If line 14 is **equal** to line 13, enter -0- here. **Do not** complete the rest of this section.	15	
16 If line 14 is **less** than line 13, enter the difference	16	
17 Enter 10% of your adjusted gross income from Form 1040, line 38, or Form 1040NR, line 37. Estates and trusts, see instructions	17	
18 Subtract line 17 from line 16. If zero or less, enter -0-. Also enter the result on Schedule A (Form 1040), line 20, or Form 1040NR, Schedule A, line 6. Estates and trusts, enter the result on the "Other deductions" line of your tax return	18	

For Paperwork Reduction Act Notice, see instructions. Cat. No. 12997O Form **4684** (2014)

LO 5.5

22. Dan has a 20-year-old vintage car behind his residence. He has rarely used it. This year he discovers that it has been completely destroyed by rust. The car originally cost $5,000 and had a fair market value of that amount before the rust destroyed it. Dan has $25,000 of adjusted gross income. What is his casualty loss? Please explain.

LO 5.6

23. Jim is fired from his job as a waiter and decides to take an extended trip to Europe. After touring Europe for 3 months, Jim returns to look for a new job as a waiter. Are his job-hunting expenses deductible for 2014? ________

Please explain: ________

LO 5.6

24. During the 2014 tax year, Irma incurred the following expenses:

Union dues	$275
Tax return preparation fee	125
Brokerage fees for the purchase of stocks	35
Uniform expenses not reimbursed by her employer	300

If Irma's adjusted gross income is $22,000, calculate her miscellaneous deductions on the section of Schedule A of Form 1040 below.

Job Expenses and Certain Miscellaneous Deductions	21	Unreimbursed employee expenses—job travel, union dues, job education, etc. Attach Form 2106 or 2106-EZ if required. (See instructions.) ▶	21	
	22	Tax preparation fees	22	
	23	Other expenses—investment, safe deposit box, etc. List type and amount ▶	23	
	24	Add lines 21 through 23	24	
	25	Enter amount from Form 1040, line 38 [25]		
	26	Multiply line 25 by 2% (.02)	26	
	27	Subtract line 26 from line 24. If line 26 is more than line 24, enter -0-		27

LO 5.7

25. George is employed as a sales manager for a computer manufacturer. His employer does not have an accountable expense reimbursement plan. George is reimbursed by his employer for $3,000 of travel expenses. How will the travel expenses and reimbursement be treated in George's tax return?

LO 5.7

26. Josh is a judge employed by the county. He must purchase and maintain his judicial robes. The total cost of purchasing a new robe and dry cleaning for the current year is $750, which is not reimbursed by his employer. How much may he deduct on his tax return? Why? Where does he deduct this on his tax return?

LO 5.8

27. Jose paid the following amounts for his son to attend Big State University in 2014:

Tuition	$6,000
Room and board	5,000
Books	500
A car to use at school	2,000
Student football tickets	200
Spending money	4,000

How much of the above is a qualified higher education expense for purposes of his Qualified Tuition Program?

$ ____________

LO 5.8

28. In 2014, Van receives $20,000 (of which $4,000 is earnings) from a qualified tuition program. He uses the funds to pay for his college tuition and other qualified higher education expenses. How much of the $20,000 is taxable to Van?

$ ____________

LO 5.2
LO 5.4
LO 5.9

29. Steve and Sue are married with three dependent children. Their 2014 joint income tax return shows $390,000 of AGI and $60,000 of itemized deductions made up of $30,000 of state income taxes and $30,000 of charitable contributions. Calculate the following amounts:
    a. Itemized deduction or standard deduction amount $ 57,452
    b. Number of exemptions and total deduction amount $ 6,320
    c. Taxable income $ 326,228

GROUP 3: WRITING ASSIGNMENT

ETHICS

1. While preparing Massie Miller's 2014 Schedule A, you review the following list of possible charitable deductions provided by Massie:

Cash contribution to a family whose house burned down	$1,000
Time while working as a volunteer at Food Bank (5 hours × $50/hour)	250
Cash contribution to United Methodist Church (receipt provided)	800
Cash contribution to Salvation Army (*note from Massie: "I can't remember exactly the amount that I gave and I can't find the receipt. I think it was around $500."*)	500
Total	$2,550

What would you say to Massie regarding her listed deductions? How much of the deduction is allowed for charitable contributions?

RESEARCH

2. In 2014, Gale and Cathy Alexander hosted an exchange student, Axel Muller, for 9 months. Axel was part of International Student Exchange Programs (a qualified organization). Axel attended tenth grade at the local high school. Gale and Cathy did not claim Axel as a dependent but paid the following items for Axel's well-being:

Food and clothing	$1,500
Medical care	200
Fair market value of lodging	2,700
Entertainment	100
Total	$4,500

Gale and Cathy have asked for your help in determining if any of the $4,500 can be deducted as a charitable contribution.

Required: Go to the IRS website **(www.irs.gov)** and locate Publication 526. Write a letter to Gale and Cathy answering their question. If they can claim a deduction, be sure to include in your letter the amount that can be deducted and any substantiation requirements. (An example of a client letter is available at the website for this text located at **www.cengagebrain.com.**)

GROUP 4: COMPREHENSIVE PROBLEMS

1. John Williams (age 42) is a single taxpayer, and he lives at 1324 Forest Dr., Reno, NV 89501. His Social Security number is 555-94-9358. John's earnings and withholdings as the manager of a local casino for 2014 are:

Earnings from the Lucky Ace Casino	$195,000
Federal income tax withheld	32,000
State income tax withheld	0

John's other income includes interest on a savings account at Nevada National Bank of $13,075.

John pays his ex-wife $4,000 per month. When their 12-year-old child (in the wife's custody) reaches 18, the payments are reduced to $2,800 per month. His ex-wife's Social Security number is 554-44-5555.

During the year, John paid the following amounts (all of which can be substantiated):

Credit card interest	1,760
Auto loan interest	4,300
Auto insurance	900
Property taxes on personal residence	6,200
Blue Cross health insurance premiums	1,800
Other medical expenses	790
Income tax preparation fee	900
Charitable contributions:	
Boy Scouts	800
St. Matthews Church	300
U. of Nevada (Reno) Medical School	30,000
Nevada Democratic Party	250
Fund-raising dinner for the Reno Auto Museum (value of dinner is $50)	100

John also received the following Form 1098:

☐ CORRECTED (if checked)

RECIPIENT'S/LENDER'S name, street address, city or town, state or province, country, ZIP or foreign postal code, and telephone number **Reno Bank & Trust** **49 Commerce Street** **Reno, NV 89501**	* **Caution:** *The amount shown may not be fully deductible by you. Limits based on the loan amount and the cost and value of the secured property may apply. Also, you may only deduct interest to the extent it was incurred by you, actually paid by you, and not reimbursed by another person.*	OMB No. 1545-0901 **2014** Form **1098**	**Mortgage Interest Statement**
RECIPIENT'S federal identification no. *XX-XXXXXXX* / PAYER'S social security number *555-94-9358*	1 Mortgage interest received from payer(s)/borrower(s)* $ *19,700*		**Copy B** **For Payer/Borrower**
PAYER'S/BORROWER'S name *John Williams*	2 Points paid on purchase of principal residence $		The information in boxes 1, 2, 3, and 4 is important tax information and is being furnished to the Internal Revenue Service. If you are required to file a return, a negligence penalty or other sanction may be imposed on you if the IRS determines that an underpayment of tax results because you overstated a deduction for this mortgage interest or for these points or because you did not report this refund of interest on your return.
Street address (including apt. no.) *1324 Forest Dr.*	3 Refund of overpaid interest $		
City or town, state or province, country, and ZIP or foreign postal code *Reno, NV 89501*	4		
Account number (see instructions)	5		

Form **1098** (keep for your records) www.irs.gov/form1098 Department of the Treasury - Internal Revenue Service

Required: Complete John's federal tax return for 2014. Use Form 1040, Schedule A, and Schedule B, from Pages 5-51 through 5-54 to complete this tax return. Make realistic assumptions about any missing data.

Would You Believe?

The IRS is considering using Form 1098 to catch tax cheats. The IRS is looking for individuals who receive Form 1098 for mortgage interest paid but who are not filing tax returns. The IRS believes that a large number of taxpayers who are earning enough income to pay mortgage interest and living expenses are failing to file tax returns. Matching Form 1098 to tax returns **not** filed will likely provide a fruitful source for IRS audits.

2A. Bea Jones (age 32) moved from Texas to Florida in December 2013. She lives at 654 Ocean Way, Gulfport, FL 33707. Bea's Social Security number is 466-78-7359 and she is single. Her earnings and income tax withholding for 2014 for her job as a manager at a Florida shrimp-processing plant are:

Earnings from the Gulf Shrimp Co.	$42,000
Federal income tax withheld	7,800
State income tax withheld	0

Bea's other income includes interest on a savings account at Beach National Bank of $2,200 and $600 per month alimony from her ex-husband.

During 2014, Bea paid the following amounts (all of which can be substantiated):

Home mortgage interest	$9,700
Auto loan interest	2,300
Property taxes on personal residence	3,200
Unreimbursed hospital bills	3,200
Doctor bills	2,550
Other medical expenses	720
Income tax preparation fee	600
Job-hunting expenses	925
Union dues	800

In July 2014, someone broke into Bea's house and stole a diamond ring. The diamond ring had a fair market value of $10,000 and a tax basis to Bea of $7,600. The ring was uninsured.

Required: Complete Bea's federal tax return for 2014. Use Form 1040, Schedule A, Schedule B, and Form 4684, from Pages 5-55 through 5-59 to complete this tax return. Make realistic assumptions about any missing data.

2B. John Fuji (age 37) moved from California to Washington in December 2013. He lives at 468 Cameo Street, Yakima, WA 98901. John's Social Security number is 571-78-5974 and he is single. His earnings and income tax withholding for 2014 for his job as a manager at a Washington apple-processing plant are:

Earnings from the Granny Smith Apple Co.	$75,000
Federal income tax withheld	9,100
State income tax withheld	0

John's other income includes interest on a Certificate of Deposit at Braeburn National Bank of $1,285. Also, he paid $600 per month alimony to his ex-wife (Dora Fuji, Social Security number 573-79-6075).

During 2014, John paid the following amounts (all of which can be substantiated):

Home mortgage interest	$8,350
Auto loan interest	1,575
Credit card interest	655
Property taxes on personal residence	2,700
Unreimbursed hospital bills	5,200
Doctor bills	2,550
Other medical expenses	720
Income tax preparation fee	500
Job-hunting expenses	925
Cash charitable gift to the Jonagold Research Center	500

In July 2014, someone broke into John's house and stole a coin collection. The collection had a fair market value of $12,000 and a tax basis to John of $4,000. The collection was uninsured.

Required: Complete John's federal tax return for 2014. Use Form 1040, Schedule A, Schedule B, and Form 4684, on Pages 5-55 through 5-59 to complete this tax return. Make realistic assumptions about any missing data.

GROUP 5: CUMULATIVE SOFTWARE PROBLEM

The following additional information is available for the Dr. Ivan and Irene Incisor family from Chapters 1–4.

Ivan and Irene paid the following in 2014 (all by check or can otherwise be substantiated):

Contributions to Perpetual Perpetuity Catholic Church	$ 400
Tuition to Perpetual Perpetuity Catholic School for Ira	6,000

Clothes to Salvation Army (10 bags in good condition)	350
Contributions to George Kerry's Congressional campaign	250
Psychotherapy for Irene	2,000
Eyeglasses for Ira	375
Prescription medication and drugs	1,800
Credit card interest	1,345
Interest on Ivan's dental school loans	3,000
Investment interest on stock margin account	325
Auto loan interest (auto was paid for by a home equity loan on residence)	900
Auto insurance	1,600
Dave Deduction, CPA, for preparation of last year's tax return	700
Safe-deposit box for storage of stocks and tax data	100
Contribution to an educational savings account for Ira	1,000
Home mortgage interest	10,875
Home property taxes	8,100
Unreimbursed business expense (seminar on tooth polishing)	700

In June, Ivan purchased a new professional HDV camcorder for $7,000. While the Incisors were on vacation in August, someone broke into their residence and stole the camcorder. Ivan's homeowners' insurance did not reimburse him for any part of the loss since he declined the special premium add-on for high value items required by his policy.

Required: Combine this new information about the Incisor family with the information from Chapters 1–4 and complete a revised 2014 tax return for Ivan and Irene. Be sure to save your data input files since this case will be expanded with more tax information in later chapters.

Form **1040** Department of the Treasury—Internal Revenue Service (99)
U.S. Individual Income Tax Return **2014** OMB No. 1545-0074 IRS Use Only—Do not write or staple in this space.

For the year Jan. 1–Dec. 31, 2014, or other tax year beginning , 2014, ending , 20 See separate instructions.

Your first name and initial	Last name	**Your social security number**
If a joint return, spouse's first name and initial	Last name	**Spouse's social security number**
Home address (number and street). If you have a P.O. box, see instructions.	Apt. no.	▲ Make sure the SSN(s) above and on line 6c are correct.
City, town or post office, state, and ZIP code. If you have a foreign address, also complete spaces below (see instructions).		**Presidential Election Campaign** Check here if you, or your spouse if filing jointly, want $3 to go to this fund. Checking a box below will not change your tax or refund. ☐ You ☐ Spouse
Foreign country name	Foreign province/state/county	Foreign postal code

Filing Status

Check only one box.

1 ☐ Single
2 ☐ Married filing jointly (even if only one had income)
3 ☐ Married filing separately. Enter spouse's SSN above and full name here. ▶
4 ☐ Head of household (with qualifying person). (See instructions.) If the qualifying person is a child but not your dependent, enter this child's name here. ▶
5 ☐ Qualifying widow(er) with dependent child

Exemptions

6a ☐ **Yourself.** If someone can claim you as a dependent, **do not** check box 6a
b ☐ **Spouse**

Boxes checked on 6a and 6b

c **Dependents:**

(1) First name Last name	(2) Dependent's social security number	(3) Dependent's relationship to you	(4) ✓ if child under age 17 qualifying for child tax credit (see instructions)
			☐
			☐
			☐
			☐

If more than four dependents, see instructions and check here ▶ ☐

No. of children on 6c who:
• lived with you
• did not live with you due to divorce or separation (see instructions)
Dependents on 6c not entered above

d Total number of exemptions claimed

Add numbers on lines above ▶

Income

Attach Form(s) W-2 here. Also attach Forms W-2G and 1099-R if tax was withheld.

If you did not get a W-2, see instructions.

Line	Description		
7	Wages, salaries, tips, etc. Attach Form(s) W-2		7
8a	**Taxable** interest. Attach Schedule B if required		8a
b	**Tax-exempt** interest. **Do not** include on line 8a	8b	
9a	Ordinary dividends. Attach Schedule B if required		9a
b	Qualified dividends	9b	
10	Taxable refunds, credits, or offsets of state and local income taxes		10
11	Alimony received		11
12	Business income or (loss). Attach Schedule C or C-EZ		12
13	Capital gain or (loss). Attach Schedule D if required. If not required, check here ▶ ☐		13
14	Other gains or (losses). Attach Form 4797		14
15a	IRA distributions 15a	b Taxable amount	15b
16a	Pensions and annuities 16a	b Taxable amount	16b
17	Rental real estate, royalties, partnerships, S corporations, trusts, etc. Attach Schedule E		17
18	Farm income or (loss). Attach Schedule F		18
19	Unemployment compensation		19
20a	Social security benefits 20a	b Taxable amount	20b
21	Other income. List type and amount		21
22	Combine the amounts in the far right column for lines 7 through 21. This is your **total income** ▶		22

Adjusted Gross Income

Line	Description		
23	Reserved	23	
24	Certain business expenses of reservists, performing artists, and fee-basis government officials. Attach Form 2106 or 2106-EZ	24	
25	Health savings account deduction. Attach Form 8889	25	
26	Moving expenses. Attach Form 3903	26	
27	Deductible part of self-employment tax. Attach Schedule SE	27	
28	Self-employed SEP, SIMPLE, and qualified plans	28	
29	Self-employed health insurance deduction	29	
30	Penalty on early withdrawal of savings	30	
31a	Alimony paid b Recipient's SSN ▶	31a	
32	IRA deduction	32	
33	Student loan interest deduction	33	
34	Reserved	34	
35	Domestic production activities deduction. Attach Form 8903	35	
36	Add lines 23 through 35		36
37	Subtract line 36 from line 22. This is your **adjusted gross income** ▶		37

DRAFT AS OF August 28, 20 DO NOT FILE

Form 1040 (2014) Page **2**

Tax and Credits

38	Amount from line 37 (adjusted gross income)		38	
39a	Check if: ☐ **You** were born before January 2, 1950, ☐ Blind. ☐ **Spouse** was born before January 2, 1950, ☐ Blind. **Total boxes checked ▶ 39a** ☐			
b	If your spouse itemizes on a separate return or you were a dual-status alien, check here ▶ 39b☐			
40	**Itemized deductions** (from Schedule A) **or** your **standard deduction** (see left margin)		40	
41	Subtract line 40 from line 38		41	
42	**Exemptions.** If line 38 is $152,525 or less, multiply $3,950 by the number on line 6d. Otherwise, see instructions		42	
43	**Taxable income.** Subtract line 42 from line 41. If line 42 is more than line 41, enter -0-		43	
44	**Tax** (see instructions). Check if any from: **a** ☐ Form(s) 8814 **b** ☐ Form 4972 **c** ☐		44	
45	**Alternative minimum tax** (see instructions). Attach Form 6251		45	
46	Excess advance premium tax credit repayment. Attach Form 8962		46	
47	Add lines 44, 45, and 46 ▶		47	
48	Foreign tax credit. Attach Form 1116 if required	48		
49	Credit for child and dependent care expenses. Attach Form 2441	49		
50	Education credits from Form 8863, line 19	50		
51	Retirement savings contributions credit. Attach Form 8880	51		
52	Child tax credit. Attach Schedule 8812, if required	52		
53	Residential energy credit. Attach Form 5695	53		
54	Other credits from Form: **a** ☐ 3800 **b** ☐ 8801 **c** ☐	54		
55	Add lines 48 through 54. These are your **total credits**		55	
56	Subtract line 55 from line 47. If line 55 is more than line 47, enter -0- ▶		56	

Standard Deduction for—
- People who check any box on line 39a or 39b **or** who can be claimed as a dependent, see instructions.
- All others:

Single or Married filing separately, $6,200

Married filing jointly or Qualifying widow(er), $12,400

Head of household, $9,100

Other Taxes

57	Self-employment tax. Attach Schedule SE		57	
58	Unreported social security and Medicare tax from Form: **a** ☐ 4137 **b** ☐ 8919		58	
59	Additional tax on IRAs, other qualified retirement plans, etc. Attach Form 5329 if required		59	
60a	Household employment taxes from Schedule H		60a	
b	First-time homebuyer credit repayment. Attach Form 5405 if required		60b	
61	Health care: individual responsibility (see instructions) Full-year coverage ☐		61	
62	Taxes from: **a** ☐ Form 8959 **b** ☐ Form 8960 **c** ☐ Instructions; enter code(s)		62	
63	Add lines 56 through 62. This is your **total tax** ▶		63	

Payments

64	Federal income tax withheld from Forms W-2 and 1099	64		
65	2014 estimated tax payments and amount applied from 2013 return	65		
66a	**Earned income credit (EIC)**	66a		
b	Nontaxable combat pay election 66b			
67	Additional child tax credit. Attach Schedule 8812	67		
68	American opportunity credit from Form 8863, line 8	68		
69	Net premium tax credit. Attach Form 8962	69		
70	Amount paid with request for extension to file	70		
71	Excess social security and tier 1 RRTA tax withheld	71		
72	Credit for federal tax on fuels. Attach Form 4136	72		
73	Credits from Form: **a** ☐ 2439 **b** ☐ Reserved **c** ☐ Reserved **d** ☐	73		
74	Add lines 64, 65, 66a, and 67 through 73. These are your **total payments** ▶		74	

If you have a qualifying child, attach Schedule EIC.

Refund

75	If line 74 is more than line 63, subtract line 63 from line 74. This is the amount you **overpaid**		75	
76a	Amount of line 75 you want **refunded to you.** If Form 8888 is attached, check here ▶ ☐		76a	
▶ b	Routing number ▶ **c** Type: ☐ Checking ☐ Savings			
▶ d	Account number			
77	Amount of line 75 you want **applied to your 2015 estimated tax** ▶	77		

Direct deposit? See instructions.

Amount You Owe

78	**Amount you owe.** Subtract line 74 from line 63. For details on how to pay, see instructions ▶		78	
79	Estimated tax penalty (see instructions)	79		

Third Party Designee

Do you want to allow another person to discuss this return with the IRS (see instructions)? ☐ **Yes.** Complete below. ☐ **No**

Designee's name ▶ Phone no. ▶ Personal identification number (PIN) ▶

Sign Here

Under penalties of perjury, I declare that I have examined this return and accompanying schedules and statements, and to the best of my knowledge and belief, they are true, correct, and complete. Declaration of preparer (other than taxpayer) is based on all information of which preparer has any knowledge.

Joint return? See instructions. Keep a copy for your records.

Your signature	Date	Your occupation	Daytime phone number
Spouse's signature. If a joint return, **both** must sign.	Date	Spouse's occupation	If the IRS sent you an Identity Protection PIN, enter it here (see inst.)

Paid Preparer Use Only

Print/Type preparer's name	Preparer's signature	Date	Check ☐ if self-employed	PTIN
Firm's name ▶			Firm's EIN ▶	
Firm's address ▶			Phone no.	

www.irs.gov/form1040 Form **1040** (2014)

DRAFT AS OF August 28, 2014 DO NOT FILE

SCHEDULE A (Form 1040)

Department of the Treasury
Internal Revenue Service (99)

Itemized Deductions

► Information about Schedule A and its separate instructions is at *www.irs.gov/schedulea*.
► Attach to Form 1040.

OMB No. 1545-0074
2014
Attachment Sequence No. 07

Name(s) shown on Form 1040 | **Your social security number**

DRAFT AS OF August 15, 2014 DO NOT FILE

Section	Line	Description		
		Caution. Do not include expenses reimbursed or paid by others.		
Medical and Dental Expenses	1	Medical and dental expenses (see instructions)	1	
	2	Enter amount from Form 1040, line 38 [2]		
	3	Multiply line 2 by 10% (.10). But if either you or your spouse was born before January 2, 1950, multiply line 2 by 7.5% (.075) instead	3	
	4	Subtract line 3 from line 1. If line 3 is more than line 1, enter -0-		4
Taxes You Paid	5	State and local		
		a ☐ Income taxes b ☐ RESERVED	5	
	6	Real estate taxes (see instructions)	6	
	7	Personal property taxes	7	
	8	Other taxes. List type and amount ►	8	
	9	Add lines 5 through 8		9
Interest You Paid	10	Home mortgage interest and points reported to you on Form 1098	10	
Note. Your mortgage interest deduction may be limited (see instructions).	11	Home mortgage interest not reported to you on Form 1098. If paid to the person from whom you bought the home, see instructions and show that person's name, identifying no., and address ►	11	
	12	Points not reported to you on Form 1098. See instructions for special rules	12	
	13	RESERVED	13	
	14	Investment interest. Attach Form 4952 if required. (See instructions.)	14	
	15	Add lines 10 through 14		15
Gifts to Charity	16	Gifts by cash or check. If you made any gift of $250 or more, see instructions	16	
If you made a gift and got a benefit for it, see instructions.	17	Other than by cash or check. If any gift of $250 or more, see instructions. You **must** attach Form 8283 if over $500	17	
	18	Carryover from prior year	18	
	19	Add lines 16 through 18		19
Casualty and Theft Losses	20	Casualty or theft loss(es). Attach Form 4684. (See instructions.)		20
Job Expenses and Certain Miscellaneous Deductions	21	Unreimbursed employee expenses—job travel, union dues, job education, etc. Attach Form 2106 or 2106-EZ if required. (See instructions.) ►	21	
	22	Tax preparation fees	22	
	23	Other expenses—investment, safe deposit box, etc. List type and amount ►	23	
	24	Add lines 21 through 23	24	
	25	Enter amount from Form 1040, line 38 [25]		
	26	Multiply line 25 by 2% (.02)	26	
	27	Subtract line 26 from line 24. If line 26 is more than line 24, enter -0-		27
Other Miscellaneous Deductions	28	Other—from list in instructions. List type and amount ►		28
Total Itemized Deductions	29	Is Form 1040, line 38, over $152,525? ☐ **No.** Your deduction is not limited. Add the amounts in the far right column for lines 4 through 28. Also, enter this amount on Form 1040, line 40. ☐ **Yes.** Your deduction may be limited. See the Itemized Deductions Worksheet in the instructions to figure the amount to enter.		29
	30	If you elect to itemize deductions even though they are less than your standard deduction, check here ► ☐		

For Paperwork Reduction Act Notice, see Form 1040 instructions. Cat. No. 17145C **Schedule A (Form 1040) 2014**

SCHEDULE B
(Form 1040A or 1040)

Department of the Treasury
Internal Revenue Service (99)

Interest and Ordinary Dividends

▶ Attach to Form 1040A or 1040.
▶ Information about Schedule B and its instructions is at *www.irs.gov/scheduleb*.

OMB No. 1545-0074

2014

Attachment Sequence No. **08**

Name(s) shown on return | **Your social security number**

DRAFT AS OF June 18, 2014 DO NOT FILE

Part I Interest

(See instructions on back and the instructions for Form 1040A, or Form 1040, line 8a.)

Note. If you received a Form 1099-INT, Form 1099-OID, or substitute statement from a brokerage firm, list the firm's name as the payer and enter the total interest shown on that form.

			Amount
1	List name of payer. If any interest is from a seller-financed mortgage and the buyer used the property as a personal residence, see instructions on back and list this interest first. Also, show that buyer's social security number and address ▶	1	
2	Add the amounts on line 1	2	
3	Excludable interest on series EE and I U.S. savings bonds issued after 1989. Attach Form 8815	3	
4	Subtract line 3 from line 2. Enter the result here and on Form 1040A, or Form 1040, line 8a . . . . ▶	4	

Note. If line 4 is over $1,500, you must complete Part III.

Part II Ordinary Dividends

(See instructions on back and the instructions for Form 1040A, or Form 1040, line 9a.)

Note. If you received a Form 1099-DIV or substitute statement from a brokerage firm, list the firm's name as the payer and enter the ordinary dividends shown on that form.

			Amount
5	List name of payer ▶	5	
6	Add the amounts on line 5. Enter the total here and on Form 1040A, or Form 1040, line 9a . . . . ▶	6	

Note. If line 6 is over $1,500, you must complete Part III.

Part III Foreign Accounts and Trusts

(See instructions on back.)

You must complete this part if you **(a)** had over $1,500 of taxable interest or ordinary dividends; **(b)** had a foreign account; or **(c)** received a distribution from, or were a grantor of, or a transferor to, a foreign trust.

		Yes	No
7a	At any time during 2014, did you have a financial interest in or signature authority over a financial account (such as a bank account, securities account, or brokerage account) located in a foreign country? See instructions		
	If "Yes," are you required to file FinCEN Form 114, Report of Foreign Bank and Financial Accounts (FBAR), to report that financial interest or signature authority? See FinCEN Form 114 and its instructions for filing requirements and exceptions to those requirements		
b	If you are required to file FinCEN Form 114, enter the name of the foreign country where the financial account is located ▶		
8	During 2014, did you receive a distribution from, or were you the grantor of, or transferor to, a foreign trust? If "Yes," you may have to file Form 3520. See instructions on back		

Form **1040** Department of the Treasury—Internal Revenue Service (99)
U.S. Individual Income Tax Return **2014** OMB No. 1545-0074 IRS Use Only—Do not write or staple in this space.

For the year Jan. 1–Dec. 31, 2014, or other tax year beginning , 2014, ending , 20 See separate instructions.

Your first name and initial | Last name | **Your social security number**

If a joint return, spouse's first name and initial | Last name | **Spouse's social security number**

Home address (number and street). If you have a P.O. box, see instructions. | Apt. no. | ▲ Make sure the SSN(s) above and on line 6c are correct.

City, town or post office, state, and ZIP code. If you have a foreign address, also complete spaces below (see instructions).

Foreign country name | Foreign province/state/county | Foreign postal code

Presidential Election Campaign
Check here if you, or your spouse if filing jointly, want $3 to go to this fund. Checking a box below will not change your tax or refund. ☐ You ☐ Spouse

Filing Status

Check only one box.

1 ☐ Single
2 ☐ Married filing jointly (even if only one had income)
3 ☐ Married filing separately. Enter spouse's SSN above and full name here. ▶
4 ☐ Head of household (with qualifying person). (See instructions.) If the qualifying person is a child but not your dependent, enter this child's name here. ▶
5 ☐ Qualifying widow(er) with dependent child

Exemptions

6a ☐ **Yourself.** If someone can claim you as a dependent, **do not** check box 6a
b ☐ **Spouse**
} **Boxes checked on 6a and 6b**

c **Dependents:**

(1) First name Last name	(2) Dependent's social security number	(3) Dependent's relationship to you	(4) ✓ if child under age 17 qualifying for child tax credit (see instructions)
			☐
			☐
			☐
			☐

If more than four dependents, see instructions and check here ▶ ☐

No. of children on 6c who:
• lived with you
• did not live with you due to divorce or separation (see instructions)
Dependents on 6c not entered above

d Total number of exemptions claimed

Add numbers on lines above ▶

Income

Attach Form(s) W-2 here. Also attach Forms W-2G and 1099-R if tax was withheld.

If you did not get a W-2, see instructions.

7	Wages, salaries, tips, etc. Attach Form(s) W-2		7
8a	**Taxable** interest. Attach Schedule B if required		8a
b	**Tax-exempt** interest. **Do not** include on line 8a	8b	
9a	Ordinary dividends. Attach Schedule B if required		9a
b	Qualified dividends	9b	
10	Taxable refunds, credits, or offsets of state and local income taxes		10
11	Alimony received		11
12	Business income or (loss). Attach Schedule C or C-EZ		12
13	Capital gain or (loss). Attach Schedule D if required. If not required, check here ▶ ☐		13
14	Other gains or (losses). Attach Form 4797		14
15a	IRA distributions 15a	b Taxable amount	15b
16a	Pensions and annuities 16a	b Taxable amount	16b
17	Rental real estate, royalties, partnerships, S corporations, trusts, etc. Attach Schedule E		17
18	Farm income or (loss). Attach Schedule F		18
19	Unemployment compensation		19
20a	Social security benefits 20a	b Taxable amount	20b
21	Other income. List type and amount		21
22	Combine the amounts in the far right column for lines 7 through 21. This is your **total income** ▶		22

DRAFT AS OF August 28, 201 DO NOT FILE

Adjusted Gross Income

23	Reserved	23	
24	Certain business expenses of reservists, performing artists, and fee-basis government officials. Attach Form 2106 or 2106-EZ	24	
25	Health savings account deduction. Attach Form 8889	25	
26	Moving expenses. Attach Form 3903	26	
27	Deductible part of self-employment tax. Attach Schedule SE	27	
28	Self-employed SEP, SIMPLE, and qualified plans	28	
29	Self-employed health insurance deduction	29	
30	Penalty on early withdrawal of savings	30	
31a	Alimony paid b Recipient's SSN ▶	31a	
32	IRA deduction	32	
33	Student loan interest deduction	33	
34	Reserved	34	
35	Domestic production activities deduction. Attach Form 8903	35	
36	Add lines 23 through 35		36
37	Subtract line 36 from line 22. This is your **adjusted gross income** ▶		37

For Disclosure, Privacy Act, and Paperwork Reduction Act Notice, see separate instructions. Cat. No. 11320B Form **1040** (2014)

Form 1040 (2014) Page **2**

DRAFT AS OF August 28, 2014 DO NOT FILE

Tax and Credits

38	Amount from line 37 (adjusted gross income)	38	
39a	Check if: { ☐ **You** were born before January 2, 1950, ☐ Blind. / ☐ **Spouse** was born before January 2, 1950, ☐ Blind. } **Total boxes checked ▶ 39a** ☐		
b	If your spouse itemizes on a separate return or you were a dual-status alien, check here ▶ **39b** ☐		
40	**Itemized deductions** (from Schedule A) **or** your **standard deduction** (see left margin)	40	
41	Subtract line 40 from line 38	41	
42	**Exemptions.** If line 38 is $152,525 or less, multiply $3,950 by the number on line 6d. Otherwise, see instructions	42	
43	**Taxable income.** Subtract line 42 from line 41. If line 42 is more than line 41, enter -0-	43	
44	**Tax** (see instructions). Check if any from: **a** ☐ Form(s) 8814 **b** ☐ Form 4972 **c** ☐ ______	44	
45	**Alternative minimum tax** (see instructions). Attach Form 6251	45	
46	Excess advance premium tax credit repayment. Attach Form 8962	46	
47	Add lines 44, 45, and 46 ▶	47	
48	Foreign tax credit. Attach Form 1116 if required — 48		
49	Credit for child and dependent care expenses. Attach Form 2441 — 49		
50	Education credits from Form 8863, line 19 — 50		
51	Retirement savings contributions credit. Attach Form 8880 — 51		
52	Child tax credit. Attach Schedule 8812, if required — 52		
53	Residential energy credit. Attach Form 5695 — 53		
54	Other credits from Form: **a** ☐ 3800 **b** ☐ 8801 **c** ☐ ______ — 54		
55	Add lines 48 through 54. These are your **total credits**	55	
56	Subtract line 55 from line 47. If line 55 is more than line 47, enter -0- ▶	56	

Standard Deduction for—
• People who check any box on line 39a or 39b **or** who can be claimed as a dependent, see instructions.
• All others:
Single or Married filing separately, $6,200
Married filing jointly or Qualifying widow(er), $12,400
Head of household, $9,100

Other Taxes

57	Self-employment tax. Attach Schedule SE	57	
58	Unreported social security and Medicare tax from Form: **a** ☐ 4137 **b** ☐ 8919	58	
59	Additional tax on IRAs, other qualified retirement plans, etc. Attach Form 5329 if required	59	
60a	Household employment taxes from Schedule H	60a	
b	First-time homebuyer credit repayment. Attach Form 5405 if required	60b	
61	Health care: individual responsibility (see instructions) Full-year coverage ☐	61	
62	Taxes from: **a** ☐ Form 8959 **b** ☐ Form 8960 **c** ☐ Instructions; enter code(s) ______	62	
63	Add lines 56 through 62. This is your **total tax** ▶	63	

Payments

If you have a qualifying child, attach Schedule EIC.

64	Federal income tax withheld from Forms W-2 and 1099 — 64		
65	2014 estimated tax payments and amount applied from 2013 return — 65		
66a	**Earned income credit (EIC)** — 66a		
b	Nontaxable combat pay election — 66b		
67	Additional child tax credit. Attach Schedule 8812 — 67		
68	American opportunity credit from Form 8863, line 8 — 68		
69	Net premium tax credit. Attach Form 8962 — 69		
70	Amount paid with request for extension to file — 70		
71	Excess social security and tier 1 RRTA tax withheld — 71		
72	Credit for federal tax on fuels. Attach Form 4136 — 72		
73	Credits from Form: **a** ☐ 2439 **b** ☐ Reserved **c** ☐ Reserved **d** ☐ ______ — 73		
74	Add lines 64, 65, 66a, and 67 through 73. These are your **total payments** ▶	74	

Refund

75	If line 74 is more than line 63, subtract line 63 from line 74. This is the amount you **overpaid**	75	
76a	Amount of line 75 you want **refunded to you.** If Form 8888 is attached, check here ▶ ☐	76a	
▶ b	Routing number ______ ▶ **c** Type: ☐ Checking ☐ Savings		
▶ d	Account number ______		
77	Amount of line 75 you want **applied to your 2015 estimated tax** ▶ 77		

Direct deposit? See instructions.

Amount You Owe

78	**Amount you owe.** Subtract line 74 from line 63. For details on how to pay, see instructions ▶	78	
79	Estimated tax penalty (see instructions) — 79		

Third Party Designee

Do you want to allow another person to discuss this return with the IRS (see instructions)? ☐ **Yes.** Complete below. ☐ **No**

Designee's name ▶ Phone no. ▶ Personal identification number (PIN) ▶

Sign Here

Joint return? See instructions. Keep a copy for your records.

Under penalties of perjury, I declare that I have examined this return and accompanying schedules and statements, and to the best of my knowledge and belief, they are true, correct, and complete. Declaration of preparer (other than taxpayer) is based on all information of which preparer has any knowledge.

Your signature	Date	Your occupation	Daytime phone number
Spouse's signature. If a joint return, **both** must sign.	Date	Spouse's occupation	If the IRS sent you an Identity Protection PIN, enter it here (see inst.)

Paid Preparer Use Only

Print/Type preparer's name	Preparer's signature	Date	Check ☐ if self-employed	PTIN
Firm's name ▶			Firm's EIN ▶	
Firm's address ▶			Phone no.	

www.irs.gov/form1040 Form **1040** (2014)

SCHEDULE A (Form 1040)

Department of the Treasury
Internal Revenue Service (99)

Itemized Deductions

► Information about Schedule A and its separate instructions is at *www.irs.gov/schedulea*.

► Attach to Form 1040.

OMB No. 1545-0074

2014

Attachment Sequence No. 07

DRAFT AS OF August 15, 2014 DO NOT FILE

Name(s) shown on Form 1040 | **Your social security number**

Section	Line	Description	Box	
		Caution. Do not include expenses reimbursed or paid by others.		
Medical and Dental Expenses	1	Medical and dental expenses (see instructions)	1	
	2	Enter amount from Form 1040, line 38 [2]		
	3	Multiply line 2 by 10% (.10). But if either you or your spouse was born before January 2, 1950, multiply line 2 by 7.5% (.075) instead	3	
	4	Subtract line 3 from line 1. If line 3 is more than line 1, enter -0-		4
Taxes You Paid	5	State and local a ☐ Income taxes b ☐ RESERVED	5	
	6	Real estate taxes (see instructions)	6	
	7	Personal property taxes	7	
	8	Other taxes. List type and amount ►	8	
	9	Add lines 5 through 8		9
Interest You Paid	10	Home mortgage interest and points reported to you on Form 1098	10	
Note. Your mortgage interest deduction may be limited (see instructions).	11	Home mortgage interest not reported to you on Form 1098. If paid to the person from whom you bought the home, see instructions and show that person's name, identifying no., and address ►	11	
	12	Points not reported to you on Form 1098. See instructions for special rules	12	
	13	RESERVED	13	
	14	Investment interest. Attach Form 4952 if required. (See instructions.)	14	
	15	Add lines 10 through 14		15
Gifts to Charity	16	Gifts by cash or check. If you made any gift of $250 or more, see instructions	16	
If you made a gift and got a benefit for it, see instructions.	17	Other than by cash or check. If any gift of $250 or more, see instructions. You **must** attach Form 8283 if over $500	17	
	18	Carryover from prior year	18	
	19	Add lines 16 through 18		19
Casualty and Theft Losses	20	Casualty or theft loss(es). Attach Form 4684. (See instructions.)		20
Job Expenses and Certain Miscellaneous Deductions	21	Unreimbursed employee expenses—job travel, union dues, job education, etc. Attach Form 2106 or 2106-EZ if required. (See instructions.) ►	21	
	22	Tax preparation fees	22	
	23	Other expenses—investment, safe deposit box, etc. List type and amount ►	23	
	24	Add lines 21 through 23	24	
	25	Enter amount from Form 1040, line 38 [25]		
	26	Multiply line 25 by 2% (.02)	26	
	27	Subtract line 26 from line 24. If line 26 is more than line 24, enter -0-		27
Other Miscellaneous Deductions	28	Other—from list in instructions. List type and amount ►		28
Total Itemized Deductions	29	Is Form 1040, line 38, over $152,525? ☐ **No.** Your deduction is not limited. Add the amounts in the far right column for lines 4 through 28. Also, enter this amount on Form 1040, line 40. ☐ **Yes.** Your deduction may be limited. See the Itemized Deductions Worksheet in the instructions to figure the amount to enter.		29
	30	If you elect to itemize deductions even though they are less than your standard deduction, check here ► ☐		

For Paperwork Reduction Act Notice, see Form 1040 instructions. Cat. No. 17145C **Schedule A (Form 1040) 2014**

SCHEDULE B
(Form 1040A or 1040)

Department of the Treasury
Internal Revenue Service (99)

Interest and Ordinary Dividends

▶ Attach to Form 1040A or 1040.
▶ Information about Schedule B and its instructions is at *www.irs.gov/scheduleb*.

OMB No. 1545-0074
2014
Attachment Sequence No. **08**

Name(s) shown on return | **Your social security number**

DRAFT AS OF June 18, 2014 DO NOT FILE

Part I Interest

(See instructions on back and the instructions for Form 1040A, or Form 1040, line 8a.)

Note. If you received a Form 1099-INT, Form 1099-OID, or substitute statement from a brokerage firm, list the firm's name as the payer and enter the total interest shown on that form.

			Amount
1	List name of payer. If any interest is from a seller-financed mortgage and the buyer used the property as a personal residence, see instructions on back and list this interest first. Also, show that buyer's social security number and address ▶	1	
2	Add the amounts on line 1	2	
3	Excludable interest on series EE and I U.S. savings bonds issued after 1989. Attach Form 8815	3	
4	Subtract line 3 from line 2. Enter the result here and on Form 1040A, or Form 1040, line 8a ▶	4	

Note. If line 4 is over $1,500, you must complete Part III.

Part II Ordinary Dividends

(See instructions on back and the instructions for Form 1040A, or Form 1040, line 9a.)

Note. If you received a Form 1099-DIV or substitute statement from a brokerage firm, list the firm's name as the payer and enter the ordinary dividends shown on that form.

			Amount
5	List name of payer ▶	5	
6	Add the amounts on line 5. Enter the total here and on Form 1040A, or Form 1040, line 9a ▶	6	

Note. If line 6 is over $1,500, you must complete Part III.

Part III Foreign Accounts and Trusts

(See instructions on back.)

You must complete this part if you **(a)** had over $1,500 of taxable interest or ordinary dividends; **(b)** had a foreign account; or **(c)** received a distribution from, or were a grantor of, or a transferor to, a foreign trust.

		Yes	No
7a	At any time during 2014, did you have a financial interest in or signature authority over a financial account (such as a bank account, securities account, or brokerage account) located in a foreign country? See instructions		
	If "Yes," are you required to file FinCEN Form 114, Report of Foreign Bank and Financial Accounts (FBAR), to report that financial interest or signature authority? See FinCEN Form 114 and its instructions for filing requirements and exceptions to those requirements		
b	If you are required to file FinCEN Form 114, enter the name of the foreign country where the financial account is located ▶		
8	During 2014, did you receive a distribution from, or were you the grantor of, or transferor to, a foreign trust? If "Yes," you may have to file Form 3520. See instructions on back		

Form **4684**

Department of the Treasury
Internal Revenue Service

Casualties and Thefts

► **Information about Form 4684 and its separate instructions is at *www.irs.gov/form4684.***
► **Attach to your tax return.**
► **Use a separate Form 4684 for each casualty or theft.**

OMB No. 1545-0177

2014

Attachment
Sequence No. **26**

Name(s) shown on tax return | **Identifying number**

DRAFT AS OF
June 12, 2014
DO NOT FILE

SECTION A—Personal Use Property (Use this section to report casualties and thefts of property **not** used in a trade or business or for income-producing purposes.)

1 Description of properties (show type, location, and date acquired for each property). Use a separate line for each property lost or damaged from the same casualty or theft.

Property **A** ______

Property **B** ______

Property **C** ______

Property **D** ______

		Properties			
		A	**B**	**C**	**D**
2 Cost or other basis of each property	2				
3 Insurance or other reimbursement (whether or not you filed a claim) (see instructions)	3				
Note: *If line 2 is **more** than line 3, skip line 4.*					
4 Gain from casualty or theft. If line 3 is **more** than line 2, enter the difference here and skip lines 5 through 9 for that column. See instructions if line 3 includes insurance or other reimbursement you did not claim, or you received payment for your loss in a later tax year	4				
5 Fair market value **before** casualty or theft	5				
6 Fair market value **after** casualty or theft	6				
7 Subtract line 6 from line 5	7				
8 Enter the **smaller** of line 2 or line 7	8				
9 Subtract line 3 from line 8. If zero or less, enter -0-	9				

10 Casualty or theft loss. Add the amounts on line 9 in columns A through D	10	
11 Enter the **smaller** of line 10 or $100	11	
12 Subtract line 11 from line 10	12	
Caution: *Use only one Form 4684 for lines 13 through 18.*		
13 Add the amounts on line 12 of all Forms 4684	13	
14 Add the amounts on line 4 of all Forms 4684.	14	
15 • If line 14 is **more** than line 13, enter the difference here and on Schedule D. **Do not** complete the rest of this section (see instructions). • If line 14 is **less** than line 13, enter -0- here and go to line 16. • If line 14 is **equal** to line 13, enter -0- here. **Do not** complete the rest of this section.	15	
16 If line 14 is **less** than line 13, enter the difference	16	
17 Enter 10% of your adjusted gross income from Form 1040, line 38, or Form 1040NR, line 37. Estates and trusts, see instructions	17	
18 Subtract line 17 from line 16. If zero or less, enter -0-. Also enter the result on Schedule A (Form 1040), line 20, or Form 1040NR, Schedule A, line 6. Estates and trusts, enter the result on the "Other deductions" line of your tax return	18	

For Paperwork Reduction Act Notice, see instructions. Cat. No. 12997O Form **4684** (2014)

Student Name ______________________

Class/Section ______________________

Date ______________________

KEY NUMBER TAX RETURN SUMMARY

CHAPTER 5

Comprehensive Problem 1

Adjusted Gross Income (Line 37) ______________

Itemized Deductions (Line 40) ______________

Exemptions (Line 42) ______________

Tax Liability (Line 63) ______________

Tax Overpaid (Line 75) ______________

Comprehensive Problem 2A

Adjusted Gross Income (Line 37) ______________

Itemized Deductions (Line 40) ______________

Casualties and Thefts (Form 4684, Line 18) ______________

Tax Liability (Line 63) ______________

Tax Overpaid (Line 75) ______________

Comprehensive Problem 2B

Adjusted Gross Income (Line 37) ______________

Itemized Deductions (Line 40) ______________

Casualties and Thefts (Form 4684, Line 18) ______________

Tax Liability (Line 63) ______________

Tax Overpaid (Line 75) ______________

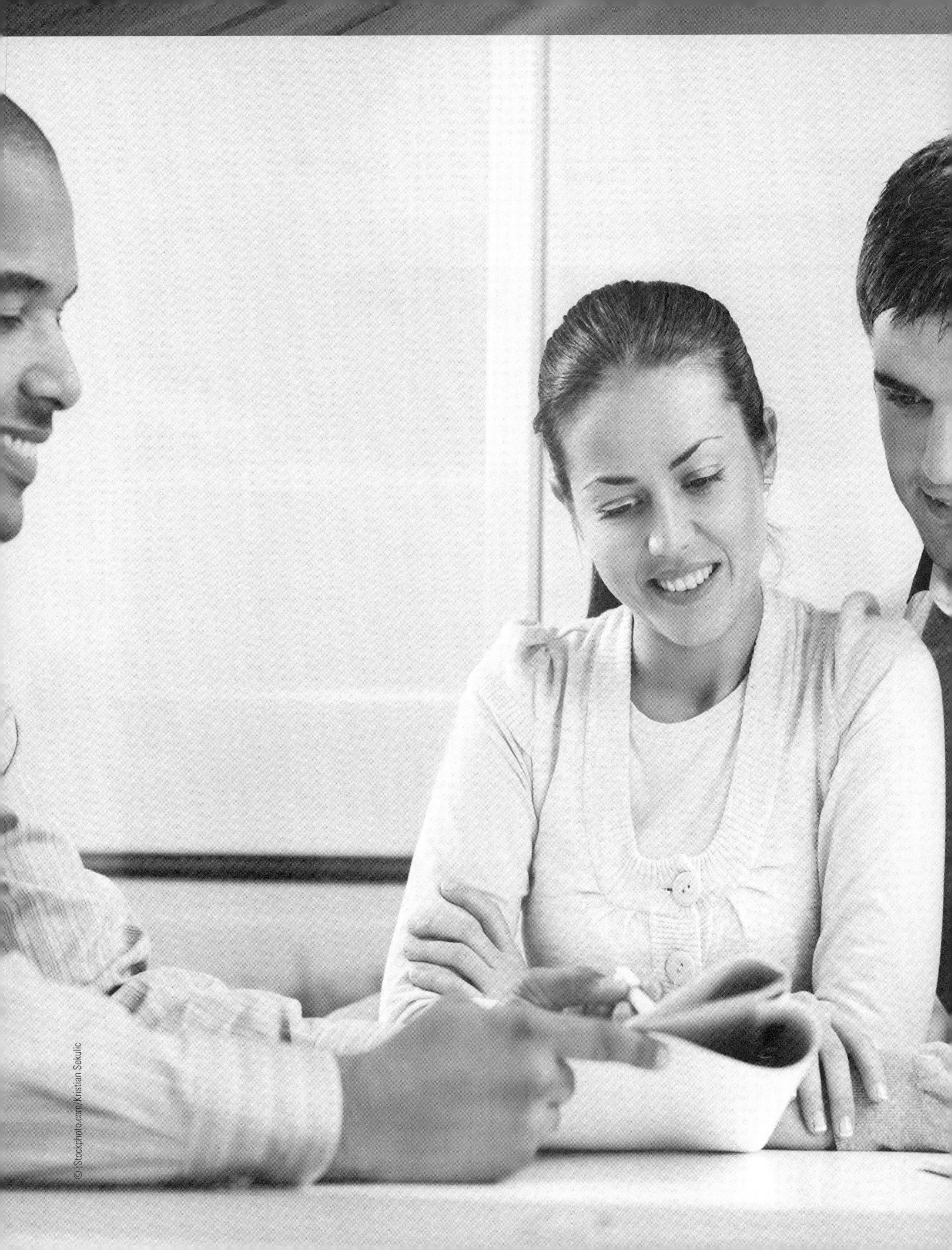

© iStockphoto.com/Kristian Sekulic

CHAPTER 6

Credits and Special Taxes

LEARNING OBJECTIVES

After completing this chapter, you should be able to:

LO 6.1 Calculate the child tax credit.

LO 6.2 Determine the earned income credit (EIC).

LO 6.3 Compute the child and dependent care credit for an individual taxpayer.

LO 6.4 Describe minimum essential coverage, the individual shared responsibility provision, and calculate the premium tax credit available under the Affordable Care Act.

LO 6.5 Apply the special rules applicable to the American Opportunity tax credit and lifetime learning credit.

LO 6.6 Understand the operation of the foreign tax credit.

LO 6.7 Determine the proper use and calculation of the adoption credit.

LO 6.8 Recognize the basic individual credits for energy efficiency.

LO 6.9 Understand the basic alternative minimum tax calculation.

LO 6.10 Apply the rules for computing tax on the unearned income of minor children and certain students.

LO 6.11 Distinguish between the different rules for married taxpayers residing in community property states when filing separate returns.

OVERVIEW

This chapter covers the most commonly seen tax credits and several special methods of calculating tax. A credit is a direct reduction in tax liability instead of a deduction from income. Credits are used because they target tax relief to certain groups of taxpayers. Because of the progressive rate structure of the income tax, a deduction provides greater benefit to higher-income taxpayers, while a tax credit provides equal benefit, regardless of the taxpayer's income level. Many credits exist in the tax law that are not covered here, such as the credit for research and development, the Work Opportunity Tax Credit, and the credit for the elderly and disabled.

The second part of this chapter covers the alternative minimum tax (AMT), the tax on unearned income of minor children (the "kiddie tax"), and an overview of community property law as it applies to the individual income tax. Each of these provisions can add substantial complexity to the individual income tax calculation. For example, if a taxpayer is

subject to the "kiddie tax," he or she must calculate tax liability in an alternative manner, using the marginal tax rates of his or her parents.

Learning Objective 6.1

Calculate the child tax credit.

CHILD TAX CREDIT

Individual taxpayers are permitted to take a tax credit based on the number of their dependent children. The children must be under age 17, U.S. citizens, claimed as dependents on the taxpayer's return, and meet the definition of "qualifying child" discussed in Chapter 1.

Maximum Credit and Phase-Outs

For 2014, the child tax credit is $1,000 per qualifying child. The available credit begins phasing out when AGI reaches $110,000 for joint filers ($55,000 for married taxpayers filing separately) and $75,000 for single or head of household taxpayers. The credit is phased out by $50 for each $1,000 (or part thereof) of AGI above the threshold amounts. Since the maximum credit available depends on the number of qualifying children, the income level at which the credit is fully phased out also depends on the number of children qualifying for the credit.

EXAMPLE Hilary and Patrick are married and file a joint tax return claiming their two children, ages 5 and 7, as dependents. Their adjusted gross income (AGI) for 2014 is $118,700. Hilary and Patrick's available child tax credit for 2014 is $1,550, computed as their maximum credit of $2,000 ($1,000 × 2 children) reduced by a $450 phase-out. Since Hilary and Patrick's AGI is in excess of the $110,000 threshold, the maximum credit must be reduced by $50 for every $1,000 (or part thereof) above the threshold amount {$50 × [($118,700 − $110,000)/$1,000]}. Thus, the credit reduction equals $450 [$50 × 9 (rounded from 8.7)]. ♦

Self-Study Problem 6.1 *See Appendix E for Solutions to Self-Study Problems*

a. Jose and Jane are married and file a joint tax return claiming their three children, ages 4, 5, and 18, as dependents. Their AGI for 2014 is $105,600. What is Jose and Jane's child credit for 2014?

$__________

b. Herb and Carol are married and file a joint tax return claiming their three children, ages 4, 5, and 18, as dependents. Their AGI for 2014 is $125,400. What is Herb and Carol's child credit for 2014?

$__________

Learning Objective 6.2

Determine the earned income credit (EIC).

EARNED INCOME CREDIT

The earned income credit (EIC) is available to qualifying individuals with earned income and AGI below certain levels. The earned income credit is meant to assist the working poor. Taxpayers with "disqualified income" (certain types of investment income) exceeding $3,350 in 2014 are not allowed to claim the earned income credit. The earned income credit is one of the few credits that is refundable. In other words, the taxpayer is eligible to claim the credit and receive a refund equal to the amount of the credit, even if no tax is owed to the federal government. The credit in effect can produce a "negative" income tax.

The formula for calculating the credit is based on the *adjusted gross income* of the taxpayer and the number of *qualifying* children of the taxpayer. The IRS issues an earned income credit table to assist taxpayers in computing the credit (see Appendix B). To compute the credit, the taxpayer must fill out a form calculating the credit from the tables based on earned income from wages, salaries, and self-employment income. If the taxpayer's adjusted gross income is different from earned income and exceeds certain threshhold amounts shown below, the credit must also be calculated from the tables based on adjusted gross income, and the smaller of the two credits calculated will be the credit allowed. This calculation is illustrated in Self-Study Problem 6.2.

Earned Income Credit Phase-Out Ranges

	Number of Qualifying Children			
Item	*One*	*Two*	*Three or More*	*None*
Earned Income Amount	$ 9,720	$13,650	$13,650	$ 6,480
Maximum Amount of Credit	$ 3,305	$ 5,460	$ 6,143	$ 496
Threshold Phase-out Amount (Single, Surviving Spouse, or Head of Household)	$17,830	$17,830	$17,830	$ 8,110
Completed Phase-out Amount (Single, Surviving Spouse, or Head of Household)	$38,511	$43,756	$46,997	$14,590
Threshold Phase-out Amount (Married Filing Jointly)	$23,260	$23,260	$23,260	$13,540
Completed Phase-out Amount (Married Filing Jointly)	$43,941	$49,186	$52,427	$20,020

Appendix B, at the back of the text, provides tables showing the amount of the earned income credit for each type of taxpayer.

To be eligible for the credit with no qualifying children, a worker must be over 25 and under 65 years old and not be claimed as a dependent by another taxpayer. There is no age requirement for taxpayers with qualifying children. In 2014, investment income may not exceed $3,350. Also, married taxpayers must file a joint return in order to receive any earned income credit.

As of 2014, a child must generally meet the tests to be a qualifying child as discussed in Chapter 1, with some special variations primarily related to support and divorced taxpayers. In previous years the IRS determined the number of errors associated with the preparation and calculation of the EIC was unacceptably high. In order to address the error rate in EICs filed by paid preparers, the IRS developed a checklist that paid preparers must complete. The new Form 8867 is intended to ensure that preparers have exercised due diligence with respect to the EIC. Any preparer that is paid to complete a tax return for any taxpayer claiming the EIC must submit this form with the return whether paper filing or e-filing. Failure to file Form 8867 could result in a $500 penalty. Please see the IRS website for additional information if necessary.

CHILD AND DEPENDENT CARE CREDIT

Learning Objective 6.3

Compute the child and dependent care credit for an individual taxpayer.

Congress enacted tax laws to provide benefits to taxpayers with dependents who must be provided with care and supervision while the taxpayers work. Taxpayers are allowed a credit for expenses for the care of their children and certain other dependents. To be eligible for the child

Self-Study Problem 6.2

See Appendix E for Solutions to Self-Study Problems

Dennis and Lynne have a 5-year-old child. Dennis has a salary of $16,200. Lynne is self-employed with a loss of $400 from her business. Dennis and Lynne receive $100 of taxable interest income during the year. Their earned income for the year is $15,800 and their adjusted gross income is $15,900 ($16,200 − $400 + $100).

Use the worksheet below and calculate their earned income credit from the EIC table in Appendix B.

$____________

Worksheet A—2014 EIC—Lines 66a and 66b *Keep for Your Records*

Before you begin: √ Be sure you are using the correct worksheet. Use this worksheet only if you answered "No" to Step 5, question 2. Otherwise, use Worksheet B.

RAFT AS OF
ctober 8, 2014

Part 1

All Filers Using Worksheet A

1. Enter your earned income from Step 5. *(Wages, Salaries)* [1] ______

2. Look up the amount on line 1 above in the EIC Table (right after Worksheet B) to find the credit. Be sure you use the correct column for your filing status and the number of children you have. Enter the credit here. [2] ______

If line 2 is zero, STOP You cannot take the credit. Enter "No" on the dotted line next to line 66a.

3. Enter the amount from Form 1040, line 38. *(Adjusted Gross Income)* [3] ______

4. Are the amounts on lines 3 and 1 the same?

☐ **Yes.** Skip line 5; enter the amount from line 2 on line 6.

☐ **No.** Go to line 5.

Part 2

Filers Who Answered "No" on Line 4

5. If you have:

- No qualifying children, is the amount on line 3 less than $8,150 ($13,550 if married filing jointly)?
- 1 or more qualifying children, is the amount on line 3 less than $17,850 ($23,300 if married filing jointly)?

☐ **Yes.** Leave line 5 blank; enter the amount from line 2 on line 6.

☐ **No.** Look up the amount on line 3 in the EIC Table to find the credit. Be sure you use the correct column for your filing status and the number of children you have. Enter the credit here. [5] ______
Look at the amounts on lines 5 and 2.
Then, enter the **smaller** amount on line 6.

Part 3

Your Earned Income Credit

6. This is your earned income credit. [6] ______

Enter this amount on Form 1040, line 66a.

Reminder—

√ If you have a qualifying child, complete and attach Schedule EIC.

1040 EIC 1040

CAUTION *If your EIC for a year after 1996 was reduced or disallowed, see* Form 8862, who must file, *earlier, to find out if you must file Form 8862 to take the credit for 2014.*

and dependent care credit, the dependent must either be under the age of 13 or be a dependent or spouse of any age who is incapable of self-care. If a child's parents are divorced, the child need not be the dependent of the taxpayer claiming the credit, but the child must live with that parent more than he or she lives with the other parent. For example, a divorced mother with custody of a child may be entitled to the credit even though the child is a dependent of the father.

Qualified Expenses

The expenses that qualify for the credit include amounts paid to enable both the taxpayer and his or her spouse to be employed. Qualified expenses include amounts paid for in-home care, such as a housekeeper, as well as out-of-home care, such as a day care center. Overnight camps do not qualify for the credit, nor do activities providing standard education such as kindergarten. Day camps such as soccer camps, music camps, math camps, and dinosaur camps do qualify for the credit since they are not considered standard education. Payments to relatives are eligible for the credit, unless the payments are to a dependent of the taxpayer or to the taxpayer's child who is under the age of 19 at the end of the tax year. To claim the credit, the taxpayer must include on his or her tax return, the name, address, and taxpayer identification number of the person or organization providing the care.

Allowable Credit

For taxpayers with AGI of less than $15,000, the child and dependent care credit is equal to 35 percent of the qualified expenses. For taxpayers with AGI of $15,000 or more, see Table 6.1 below for the applicable credit percentage. In determining the credit, the maximum amount of qualified expenses to which the applicable percentage is applied is $3,000 for one dependent and $6,000 for two or more dependents.

Married taxpayers must file a joint return to claim the child and dependent care credit, and the qualifying dependent care expenses are limited to the lesser of either spouse's earned income. For example, if a wife makes $22,000 and her husband earns $1,500, and

TABLE 6.1 CHILD AND DEPENDENT CARE CREDIT PERCENTAGES

Adjusted Gross Income			Applicable Percentage
Over		But Not Over	
$ 0	–	$15,000	35%
15,000	–	17,000	34%
17,000	–	19,000	33%
19,000	–	21,000	32%
21,000	–	23,000	31%
23,000	–	25,000	30%
25,000	–	27,000	29%
27,000	–	29,000	28%
29,000	–	31,000	27%
31,000	–	33,000	26%
33,000	–	35,000	25%
35,000	–	37,000	24%
37,000	–	39,000	23%
39,000	–	41,000	22%
41,000	–	43,000	21%
43,000	–	No limit	20%

© Cengage Learning

they spend $1,900 on child care, the maximum qualifying expenses are $1,500. A special rule applies when a taxpayer or their spouse is a full-time student or disabled. Full-time students or disabled taxpayers with little or no income are deemed to have earned income of $250 per month for one dependent and $500 per month for two or more dependents for purposes of calculating this limitation. For example, if a taxpayer's spouse is a full-time student for 9 months of the year and has no income, the maximum amount of the qualifying expenses for the care of one dependent is $2,250 ($250 per month × 9 months).

EXAMPLE Harry and Molly Grant are married and file a joint return. They have one child and pay $4,000 for child care expenses during the year. Harry earns $16,000 and Molly earns $8,500 during the year, resulting in adjusted gross income of $24,500. The Grant's child care credit is calculated as follows:

Qualified expenses	$4,000
Maximum for one dependent	3,000
Credit percentage from Table 6.1	× 30%
Credit allowed	$ 900

♦

EXAMPLE Assume the same facts as in the example above, except the qualified expenses are $2,100 (instead of $4,000). The credit is 30 percent of $2,100, or $630. ♦

Self-Study Problem 6.3 ***See Appendix E for Solutions to Self-Study Problems***

Julie Brown has been widowed for 5 years and has one dependent child. Her adjusted gross income and her earned income are $90,000. Assume her taxable income is $45,500, and her regular tax is $6,178 (line 10 on Form 2441). Julie has child care expenses of $1,500 and expenses for the care of her disabled dependent mother of $2,400. Calculate Julie's child and dependent care credit for 2014 using Page 1 of Form 2441 on Page 6-7.

Learning Objective 6.4

Describe minimum essential coverage, the individual shared responsibility provision, and calculate the premium tax credit available under the Affordable Care Act.

THE AFFORDABLE CARE ACT

The Affordable Care Act (also called the ACA or Obamacare) was passed in 2010; however, significant provisions of the law are being implemented over time. For example, Chapter 1 covers the 3.8 percent Net Investment Income tax and the 0.9 percent Medicare surtax on earned income, both of which are part of the ACA and started affecting taxpayers in 2013. In late 2013, the purchase of health care through state or federal exchanges began with the highly publicized issues with the federal website, healthcare.gov. Health insurance options available on the exchanges are classified as Platinum (highest levels of coverage), Gold, Silver, and Bronze (lowest levels of coverage).

Many of the numerous provisions of the ACA are beyond the scope of this text (e.g., the employer's shared responsibility provision); however, two important tax-related provisions affecting average taxpayers begin in 2014: (1) the Individual Shared Responsibility Provision (sometimes also known as the individual mandate) and (2) Health Insurance Premium Tax Credits.

Self-Study Problem 6.3

Form **2441** — **Child and Dependent Care Expenses**

Department of the Treasury
Internal Revenue Service (99)

► Attach to Form 1040, Form 1040A, or Form 1040NR.

► Information about Form 2441 and its separate instructions is at *www.irs.gov/form2441*.

OMB No. 1545-0074

2014

Attachment Sequence No. 21

Name(s) shown on return | **Your social security number**

DRAFT AS OF July 2, 2014 DO NOT FILE

Part I Persons or Organizations Who Provided the Care—You **must** complete this part.
(If you have more than two care providers, see the instructions.)

1 (a) Care provider's name	(b) Address (number, street, apt. no., city, state, and ZIP code)	(c) Identifying number (SSN or EIN)	(d) Amount paid (see instructions)

Did you receive **dependent care benefits?**
- **No** → Complete only Part II below.
- **Yes** → Complete Part III on the back next.

Caution. If the care was provided in your home, you may owe employment taxes. If you do, you cannot file Form 1040A. For details, see the instructions for Form 1040, line 60a, or Form 1040NR, line 59a.

Part II Credit for Child and Dependent Care Expenses

2 Information about your **qualifying person(s).** If you have more than two qualifying persons, see the instructions.

(a) Qualifying person's name — First	Last	(b) Qualifying person's social security number	**(c) Qualified expenses** you incurred and paid in 2014 for the person listed in column (a)

3 Add the amounts in column (c) of line 2. **Do not** enter more than $3,000 for one qualifying person or $6,000 for two or more persons. If you completed Part III, enter the amount from line 31 . . . . . **3**

4 Enter your **earned income.** See instructions **4**

5 If married filing jointly, enter your spouse's earned income (if you or your spouse was a student or was disabled, see the instructions); **all others**, enter the amount from line 4 . **5**

6 Enter the **smallest** of line 3, 4, or 5 . . . . . **6**

7 Enter the amount from Form 1040, line 38; Form 1040A, line 22; or Form 1040NR, line 37. . . . . **7**

8 Enter on line 8 the decimal amount shown below that applies to the amount on line 7

If line 7 is: Over	But not over	Decimal amount is	If line 7 is: Over	But not over	Decimal amount is
$0	15,000	.35	$29,000	31,000	.27
15,000	17,000	.34	31,000	33,000	.26
17,000	19,000	.33	33,000	35,000	.25
19,000	21,000	.32	35,000	37,000	.24
21,000	23,000	.31	37,000	39,000	.23
23,000	25,000	.30	39,000	41,000	.22
25,000	27,000	.29	41,000	43,000	.21
27,000	29,000	.28	43,000	No limit	.20

8 X.

9 Multiply line 6 by the decimal amount on line 8. If you paid 2013 expenses in 2014, see the instructions **9**

10 Tax liability limit. Enter the amount from the Credit Limit Worksheet in the instructions. **10**

11 **Credit for child and dependent care expenses.** Enter the **smaller** of line 9 or line 10 here and on Form 1040, line 49; Form 1040A, line 31; or Form 1040NR, line 47 . . . . **11**

Individual Shared Responsibility

Beginning in 2014, there is a "penalty tax" for failing to carry health insurance at a minimum level. The individual shared responsibility provisions require a taxpayer and members of the taxpayer's family to have minimum essential coverage (MEC) or an exemption from MEC. Alternatively, the taxpayer must pay a tax (referred to as the individual shared responsibility) when filing the 2014 federal income tax return in 2015. MEC is the level of coverage required by the ACA and is intended to ensure that the health insurance purchased by taxpayers covers essential health benefits that might be needed by taxpayers and their families. Taxpayers will typically obtain MEC health insurance through their employer, by purchasing directly from an insurance company or by purchasing coverage through one of the health insurance marketplaces (or exchanges) operated by a state or the federal government. Eventually, taxpayers will be notified as to whether their insurance meets the MEC by receiving informational reporting from their employer (Form 1095-C), health care insurance provider (Form 1095-B), or health care exchange (Form 1095-A). The informational reporting on Form 1095 is voluntary in 2014 but becomes mandatory in 2015. Note that a taxpayer is considered to have MEC for an entire month even if the taxpayer has MEC for only one day during that month.

If the minimum premiums for MEC are more than 8 percent of the taxpayer's income, then the taxpayer is exempt from the shared responsibility tax. In addition, a gap in MEC of less than three consecutive months does not require a payment of the shared responsibility. There are also other hardship exemptions from the payment available. Taxpayers using an exemption to avoid the individual shared responsibility should file Form 8965.

The shared responsibility is intended to increase over the first few years of the implementation of the MEC provisions. For 2014, the annual individual shared responsibility is the greater of (1) 1% of the household income above the required filing threshold for the taxpayer's filing status (covered in LO 1.4 in Chapter 1) or (2) the 2014 flat annual dollar amount of $95 per adult and $47.50 per child limited to a family maximum of $285. Both of these are subject to a cap of the national average premium for a bronze level health plan available on the federal exchange in 2014. The *monthly* premium for one adult for a bronze plan in 2014 is set at $204. The maximum monthly bronze premium for a family of five or more is $1,020. The percentages, the caps, and likely the average bronze premium will increase in 2015 and 2016. Household income for purposes of the shared responsibility calculation is defined as the total adjusted gross income of all household members for which a personal exemption is claimed modified by adding back any tax-exempt income (but not exempt Social Security benefits as in the premium tax credit discussed below). The individual shared responsibility is reported on line 61 of the 2014 Form 1040, line 38 of the Form 1040A, or line 11 of the Form 1040-EZ.

EXAMPLE Elijah and Maria are both under age 65, married, and have two children under 18. The 2014 AGI for Elijah, Maria, and one of the dependent children is $23,000, $44,000, and $1,000, respectively. No person in the household had minimum essential coverage and they did not qualify for an exemption. The monthly payment for the individual shared responsibility is $39.75 calculated as follows:

Shared responsibility is the greater of:

Income formula: (household AGI) $68,000 − (filing threshold) $20,300 = $47,700 × 1% = $477 or $39.75 per month

Flat dollar amount for two adults and two children: $95 + $95 + $47.50 + $47.50 = $285

The monthly payment is less than the bronze premium ($204 per month per adult) thus the shared responsibility is $39.75 per month or $477 for the year. ♦

Self-Study Problem 6.4A *See Appendix E for Solutions to Self-Study Problems*

Calculate the individual shared responsibility for each of the following taxpayers:

1. Meg, a single 37-year-old taxpayer, has AGI of $34,000 in 2014. She did not have minimum essential coverage for any of 2014.
2. Jill, a single 25-year-old taxpayer, has AGI of $56,000 in 2014. In May of 2014, Jill lost her job and was unable to continue coverage with her employer for June and July. Fortunately Jill found new work and MEC on August 30.
3. Carlos and Ted are both under 65 and legally married under state law for all of 2014. Carlos has AGI of $14,000 and Ted has AGI of $7,000 in 2014. Carlos received MEC from his employer for all of 2014; however, Ted lost his job in July of 2014 and failed to obtain MEC through either Carlos' plan or the state health care exchange. As a result, starting August 1, 2014, Ted did not have MEC. In spite of their low income, assume that Carlos and Ted do not qualify for an exemption.
4. Dave and Sue are both under 65, married and have four children all under the age of 18. Dave is a stay-at-home father and Sue had AGI of $340,000 in 2014. Because Dave and Sue are reasonably affluent, they decided to "self-insure" for all of 2014 and did not have MEC for the entire year.

Premium Tax Credit

Starting in 2014, under the ACA, eligible taxpayers may receive a tax credit intended to lower the cost of health care. To be eligible a taxpayer must meet all of the following requirements:

- Health insurance is purchased through one of the state exchanges or the federal exchange
- The taxpayer is not eligible for coverage through an employer or government plan
- The taxpayer's income falls below certain limits
- The taxpayer does not file Married Filing Separately except under very limited conditions
- The taxpayer cannot be claimed as a dependent by another

The income eligibility is based on household income (similar to the individual shared responsibility as described in the previous section); however, modified AGI requires the add-back of tax-exempt interest and any nontaxable social security. The maximum household income is 400 percent of the federal poverty line for the taxpayer's family size. Taxpayers below the federal poverty line are eligible for Medicaid and thus not eligible for the credit.

Calculating the premium tax credit is similar to the EITC in that specific tables are required to compute the allowable credit. The credit is intended to take the form of the lesser of (1) actual health care premiums paid or (2) a benchmark premium less the taxpayer's income. To calculate the premium credit requires the following steps:

Step 1. Calculate modified gross income for all members of the household. This is AGI for all individuals for which a personal exemption is claimed adjusted for a number of items including tax-exempt interest and nontaxable social security benefits.

Step 2. Compare the household income to the previous year's federal poverty line (FPL). Under the ACA, the FPL is set in the previous year during open enrollment (around October). The FPL is defined in three ways: (a) the 48 contiguous states and the District of Columbia, (b) Alaska, or (c) Hawaii. The FPL selected is based on the household's state of residence.

Persons in Family/Household	*2014 FPL for 48 States and DC*
1	$11,490
2	15,510
3	19,530
4	23,550
5	27,570
6	31,590
7	35,610
8	$39,630
Each addt'l person	+ $ 4,020

The household income is then expressed as a percentage of the FPL.

EXAMPLE Ed and Milly are married with two children under the age of 21. Household income is $47,100. Ed and Milly's household income is at 200 percent of the FPL ($47,100 ÷ $23,550 = 2.0 or 200 percent). ♦

Step 3. The amount of income deemed appropriately spent on health care premiums is then identified on the "applicable figure" table for 2014. The applicable figure is designed to represent the maximum percentage of income a household will spend on health care premiums. For example, a household of four with income of $47,100 has an applicable percentage of 6.3; thus the amounts intended to or deemed be paid for premiums is $47,100 × 6.3 percent or $2,967.

Household Income as % of FPL	*Initial %*	*Final %*
Less than 133%	0.0%	2.0%
At least 133% but less than 150%	3.0	4.0
At least 150% but less than 200%	4.0	6.3
At least 200% but less than 250%	6.3	8.05
At least 250% but less than 300%	8.05	9.5
At least 300% but less than 400%	9.5	9.5

If the household income falls between the stated percentages of the FPL, then the applicable percentage must be imputed.

EXAMPLE Eddie and Lindy are married with two children under 21 years of age and household income of $52,000. The percentage of FPL is $52,000 ÷ $23,550 = 2.21 or 221%. The applicable percentage is then calculated as [(% of FPL − Bottom of FPL range) divided by (Top of FPL range − Bottom of FPL range)] × (Final % − Initial %) + Initial %. Thus for Eddie and Lindy's household of 4 the applicable percentage is:

$$(221 - 200)/(250 - 200) \times (8.05 - 6.3) = 0.735 + 6.3 = 7.035$$

The amount of deemed premiums is $52,000 × 7.035% or $3,658. ♦

Step 4. The amount of the credit is based on comparing the cost of premiums for a designated silver plan in the taxpayer's state with the deemed premium cost calculated above. For example, if the deemed premium to be paid is $3,658 and the cost of a silver plan for that household is $10,000 then the premium tax credit is $6,342 ($10,000 − $3,658). For households that did not have coverage for the entire year, the credit is prorated based on the number of months coverage was maintained.

Step 5. Lastly, the amount calculated in steps 1-4 is compared to the actual premiums paid and the lesser of the two is the premium tax credit (i.e., the credit cannot exceed the actual premiums paid).

The premium tax credit can be obtained at two different times: (1) upfront (i.e., at the time of enrollment) or (2) at the end of the year when the tax return is filed. If the taxpayer elects to have the credit paid at the time of enrollment, the exchange will automatically adjust the premiums to reflect an estimated credit based on estimated household income. Since the actual premium credit is not known until household income can be computed after the end of the tax year, Form 8962 also provides a reconciliation of the estimated credit and the actual credit. If the actual credit is greater than the estimated credit, the additional credit is taken against any income tax liability at year end on the return. If the estimated credit taken throughout the year is greater than the actual credit, the difference is treated as additional tax due at year-end. However, as long as the household income remains below 400 percent of the FPL, the repayment amount of the credit is limited:

	Single	*Taxpayers Other Than Single*
Less than 200%	$300	$600
At least 200% but less than 300%	750	1,500
At least 300% but less than 400%	1,250	2,500
At least 400%	No limit	No limit

Taxpayers will receive the actual premiums paid, the cost of the silver plan, and any advance credits on Form 1095-A from the exchange on which they purchased the insurance.

Self-Study Problem 6.4B

See Appendix E for Solutions to Self-Study Problems

Mary and Harold Killington live in South Carolina, are married, and have three children ages 14, 16, and 26; however, the oldest child is not claimed as a dependent and does not live at home. Mary's adjusted gross income is $44,000 and Harold's is $22,000 and both are self-employed. They also have $2,000 in interest income from tax-exempt bonds. The Killingtons are enrolled in health insurance for all of 2014 through their state exchange and elected to have the credit paid in advance. The 2014 year-end Form 1095-A the Killingtons received from the exchange lists the following information:

Annual premiums	$11,200
Annual premium for the designated silver plan in the state	9,800
Annual advance payment of premium tax credit	5,800

Calculate the following for the Killingtons:

1. The actual premium tax credit
2. The reconciliation between the advance premium tax credit and actual premium tax credit
3. The repayment amount required

EDUCATION TAX CREDITS

Learning Objective 6.5

Apply the special rules applicable to the American Opportunity tax credit and lifetime learning credit.

The HOPE credit, expanded and renamed the American Opportunity tax credit for 2009 through 2017, and the lifetime learning credit are the education credits available to help qualifying low-income and middle-income individuals defray the cost of higher education.

American Opportunity Tax Credit

The American Opportunity tax credit is calculated as 100 percent of the first $2,000 of tuition, fees, books, and course materials paid, and 25 percent of the next $2,000, for a maximum annual credit of $2,500 per student. This credit is available for the first 4 years of postsecondary education. The American Opportunity tax credit may be claimed for the expenses of students pursuing bachelor's or associate's degrees or vocational training. Room and board, transportation costs, and personal living expenses are not qualifying expenses.

Tuition, fees, books, and course material expenses that qualify for the American Opportunity tax credit can be paid on behalf of the taxpayer, his or her spouse, or dependents.
The student must carry at least one-half the normal course load for one term during the tax year to qualify for the credit. In addition, the American Opportunity tax credit is not available for any student convicted of a federal or state drug felony.

For 2014, the American Opportunity tax credit is phased out ratably for joint returns with income between $160,000 and $180,000 and for single (or head of household) filers with income between $80,000 and $90,000. The American Opportunity tax credit is 40 percent refundable, so up to $1,000 (40 percent of $2,500) may be refunded to the taxpayer if the credit exceeds the taxpayer's tax liability.

EXAMPLE Jenny graduates from high school in June 2014. In the fall, she enrolls for twelve units at Big State University. Big State University considers students who take twelve or more units to be full-time students. Jenny's father pays her tuition and fees of $2,300. In 2014, the American Opportunity tax credit for Jenny is $2,075 [(100% × $2,000) + (25% × $300)]. ♦

EXAMPLE Jason, a single father, has AGI of $85,000 in 2014. In 2014, he pays $5,000 in qualified tuition for his son, who just started at Party-On University. Without any limitations, Jason would be entitled to a maximum American Opportunity tax credit of $2,500. However, after applying the AGI limitations, Jason's American Opportunity tax credit is reduced by $1,250 ($2,500 × ($90,000 − $85,000)/$10,000), resulting in a credit of $1,250. ♦

Qualifying expenses must be paid during the tax year for education during an academic year beginning within that tax year. If tuition expenses are paid during the tax year for an academic period beginning during the first 3 months of the following tax year, the expenses may be claimed during the payment year.

Lifetime Learning Credit

Taxpayers can elect a nonrefundable tax credit of 20 percent of tuition and fees up to $10,000 of qualified expenses in 2014. Books are qualified expenses under the American Opportunity tax credit, but not for the lifetime learning credit. The lifetime learning credit is available for expenses paid for education of the taxpayer, his or her spouse, or dependents. The credit is available for undergraduate, graduate, or professional courses at eligible educational institutions. The student can be enrolled in just one course and still get the credit. The credit is not subject to felony drug offense restrictions. The purpose of this credit is to encourage taxpayers to take courses at eligible institutions to acquire or improve job skills.

EXAMPLE In September 2014, Scott pays $1,200 to take a course to improve his job skills to qualify for a new position at work. His lifetime learning credit for 2014 is $240 (20% × $1,200). ♦

The lifetime learning credit is phased out at different levels than the American Opportunity tax credit. Married taxpayers with income between $108,000 and $128,000, and single (or head of household) taxpayers with income between $54,000 and $64,000, must phase the credit out evenly over the phase-out range for 2014.

EXAMPLE During 2014, Jason, a single father with AGI of $85,000, paid $2,500 of tuition for a master's degree program in the fine arts which he has been attending with the hope of eventually becoming a writer. Without any limitations, Jason would be entitled to a maximum lifetime learning credit of $500 (20% × $2,500). However, due to the income phase-out ranges for the lifetime learning credit, none of the credit may be claimed on his tax return. ♦

Limitations

The use of the American Opportunity tax credit and lifetime learning credit is limited in the following situations:

- Married taxpayers who do not file joint returns may not claim the credits.
- Expenses paid for room and board do not qualify.
- Expenses paid for nonacademic fees or for expenses that are not related to the student's course of instruction do not qualify. Also, expenses for courses that involve sports, games, and hobbies do not qualify for the credit unless the course is part of a degree program.
- Qualified educational expenses must be reduced by tax-free scholarships or employer reimbursements received by students before calculating credits. However, expenses paid from a gift or inheritance (which is tax-free) do qualify for credits.
- The credits cannot be used for expenses that are deducted from taxable income on a tax return for education costs (e.g., unreimbursed job-related educational expenses).
- Students claimed as dependents of other taxpayers are not eligible for educational credits. The persons who claim the students as dependents can claim the educational credit.

EXAMPLE Brenda, a college student, works part-time and pays part of her college expenses; her parents pay the rest. Although Brenda files her own tax return, her parents claim her as a dependent on their tax return. Brenda cannot claim a credit for the qualified amounts she paid, but her parents can claim a credit both for expenses they paid and expenses paid by Brenda. ♦

EXAMPLE Gary, a college student, works part-time and pays part of his college expenses. His parents pay for the rest. His parents have a high income and would not be able to claim an education credit for Gary. If Gary's parents decide not to claim Gary as a dependent, even though he qualifies as a dependent, Gary can claim an education credit on his own tax return for the expenses he paid and also for the expenses his parents paid. Since Gary could have been claimed as a dependent by his parents, he is not allowed to claim a dependency exemption on his own tax return. ♦

Using Both Credits

Taxpayers cannot take both the American Opportunity tax credit and the lifetime learning credit for the same student in the same tax year. An American Opportunity tax credit can be claimed for one or more students, and the lifetime learning credit can be claimed for other students in the same tax year. Also, the choice in one year does not bind the taxpayer for future years. For example, a taxpayer can claim the American Opportunity tax credit for a student in one tax year and take the lifetime learning credit for the same student the following year. Taxpayers should claim the credit or combination of credits that gives the best tax benefit.

Self-Study Problem 6.5 ***See Appendix E for Solutions to Self-Study Problems***

a. Judy graduates from high school in June 2014. In the fall, she enrolls for twelve units in Big State University. Big State University considers students who take twelve or more units to be full-time students. Judy's parents pay her tuition and fees of $1,900, have AGI of $78,000, and claim Judy as a dependent. What is the American Opportunity tax credit Judy's parents can claim for Judy if they file a joint return?

$__________

b. In September 2014, Gene pays $5,200 to take a course to improve his job skills at work. Gene's AGI is $35,000 for 2014. What is Gene's lifetime learning credit for 2014?

$__________

FOREIGN TAX CREDIT

Learning Objective 6.6

Understand the operation of the foreign tax credit.

U.S. taxpayers are allowed to claim a foreign tax credit on income earned in a foreign country and subject to income taxes in that country. The purpose of this credit is to eliminate double taxation on income earned in a foreign country. Taxpayers may make an annual election to claim a deduction instead of a credit for the foreign taxes, but most taxpayers receive a greater tax benefit by claiming the foreign tax credit. Generally, the foreign tax credit is equal to the amount of the taxes paid to foreign governments; however, there is an "overall" limitation on the amount of the credit, which is calculated as follows:

$$\frac{\text{Net foreign income}}{\text{U.S. taxable income}} \times \text{U.S. tax liability}$$

EXAMPLE Taxpayer Z has net income of $20,000 from Country K, which imposes a 15 percent income tax, and $30,000 from Country L, which imposes a 50 percent income tax. Z has taxable income in 2014 from U.S. sources of $80,000, and U.S. tax liability before the credit of $35,000. Taxpayer Z's foreign tax credit is calculated as follows:

Foreign taxes:	
Country K, $20,000 × 15%	$ 3,000
Country L, $30,000 × 50%	15,000
Total foreign taxes paid	$18,000

Overall limitation:

$$\frac{\text{Net foreign income}}{\text{U.S. taxable income}} \times \text{U.S. tax liability}$$

$$\frac{\$50,000}{\$20,000 + \$30,000 + \$80,000} \times \$35,000 = \$13,462$$

The foreign tax credit is $13,462, the lesser of the foreign taxes paid or the overall limitation. ♦

Unused foreign tax credits may be carried back 1 year and forward 10 years to reduce any tax liability in those years. Different rules apply to income earned in a U.S. possession. These rules are explained in the instructions to Form 1116, Foreign Tax Credit.

The foreign tax credit most commonly seen in practice is the credit U.S. taxpayers claim for foreign taxes withheld on dividends from foreign stock investments. Such investments are frequently held in mutual funds. The foreign withholding is generally reported to the IRS and to the taxpayer along with the dividend income from the stock or the mutual fund. The foreign tax credit for small amounts of withholding (up to $300, if single and $600, if married) may be claimed by taxpayers without filing Form 1116, Foreign Tax Credit. Foreign taxes withheld may also be deducted as a tax on Schedule A (see Chapter 5), but in almost all situations the credit will give a better tax benefit than the deduction.

Would You Believe?

On July 30, 2009, the *Wall Street Journal* ran a front page headline "Tax Evaders Flock to IRS to Confess Their Sins." The U.S. taxpayers in question were confessing the existence of Swiss bank accounts hiding investments which were illegally not reported on their tax returns, in hopes that criminal charges would not be brought against them. Since 2009, the IRS has collected billions of dollars in taxes from taxpayers with hidden offshore accounts, and is negotiating with countries around the world to obtain information-sharing agreements which will give them access to the names and accounts of numerous additional high-net-worth tax outlaws.

Self-Study Problem 6.6 *See Appendix E for Solutions to Self-Study Problems*

A taxpayer has income of $10,000 from Country A, which imposes a 20 percent income tax, and $20,000 from Country B, which imposes a 50 percent income tax. The taxpayer has U.S. taxable income, including income from Country A and Country B of $90,000, and U.S. tax liability before credits of $20,000. Calculate the amount of the foreign tax credit.

$____________

Learning Objective 6.7

Determine the proper use and calculation of the adoption credit.

ADOPTION EXPENSES

Taxpayers are allowed two tax breaks for adoption expenses. A tax credit is allowed for qualified adoption expenses paid by taxpayers, and an exclusion from W-2 income is allowed for qualified adoption expenses paid by taxpayers' employers.

Adoption Credit

Individuals are allowed an income tax credit for qualified adoption expenses (defined below). The total expense that can be taken as a credit for all tax years with respect to an adoption of a child is $13,190 for 2014. The credit is the total amount for each adoption and is not an annual amount (i.e., there is only one $13,190 credit per adopted child). The amount of the credit allowable for any tax year is reduced for taxpayers with AGI over $197,880 and is fully phased out when AGI reaches $237,880. The amount of the credit is reduced (but not below zero) by a factor equal to the excess of the taxpayer's AGI over $197,880 divided by $40,000. In some cases, beyond the scope of this text, AGI must be modified prior to calculating the adoption credit phase-out. For additional information on calculating modified adjusted gross income (MAGI), see the IRS website at **www.irs.gov**.

EXAMPLE Ben and Beverly pay $4,500 of qualified adoption expenses in 2014 to adopt a qualified child. Their AGI is $200,360 for 2014, which causes an adoption credit reduction for 2014 of $279 [$4,500 × ($200,360 − $197,880) / $40,000)]. Thus, Ben and Beverly's allowable adoption credit for 2014 is $4,221 ($4,500 − $279). ♦

For 2014, the credit is not refundable. To claim the credit, married individuals must file jointly, and the taxpayer must include (if known) the name, age, and taxpayer identification number (TIN) of the child on the return.

Domestic Multiyear Adoptions

In the case of the adoption of an eligible child who is a U.S. citizen or resident of the United States at the time the adoption commenced, the credit for qualified adoption expenses is allowed for the tax year that follows the year during which the expenses are paid or incurred, unless the expenses are paid or incurred in the tax year the adoption becomes final. If the expenses are paid or incurred during the tax year in which the adoption becomes final, the credit is allowed for that year. The $13,190 credit is allowed in special needs adoptions regardless of the amount of qualified adoption expenses paid.

EXAMPLE In connection with the adoption of an eligible child who is a U.S. citizen and is not a child with special needs, a taxpayer pays $6,000 of qualified adoption expenses in 2013 and $7,500 of qualified adoption expenses in 2014. The adoption is not finalized until 2015. The $6,000 of expenses paid or incurred in 2013 would be allowed in 2014, and $7,190 of the $7,500 paid or incurred in 2014 would be allowed in 2015. On the other hand, if the adoption were finalized in 2014, then $13,190 of qualified expenses would be allowed in 2014 (the maximum credit permitted as of 2014). ♦

Foreign Multiyear Adoptions

In the case of the adoption of a child who is *not* a U.S. citizen or resident of the United States, the credit for qualified adoption expenses is not available unless the adoption becomes final. Qualified adoption expenses paid or incurred before the tax year in which the adoption becomes final are taken into account for the credit as if the expenses were paid or incurred in the tax year in which the adoption becomes final. Therefore, the credit for qualified adoption expenses paid or incurred in the tax year in which the adoption becomes final, or in any earlier tax year, is allowed in the tax year the adoption becomes final.

EXAMPLE In 2013 and 2014, a taxpayer pays $3,000 and $6,000, respectively, of qualified adoption expenses in connection with the adoption of an eligible child who is not a U.S. citizen or resident of the United States. In 2015, the year the adoption becomes final, the taxpayer pays an additional $3,000 of qualified expenses. The taxpayer may claim a credit of $12,000 on his or her income tax return for 2015 (the year the adoption becomes final). Note: If a foreign adoption does not become final, then no credit is allowed. ♦

Employer-Provided Adoption Assistance

An employee may exclude from W-2 earnings amounts paid or expenses incurred by his or her employer for qualified adoption expenses connected with the adoption of a child by the employee, if the amounts are furnished under an adoption assistance program. The

total amount excludable per child is limited to $13,190. The excludable amount for any tax year is phased out for taxpayers with adjusted gross income over $197,880 and is fully eliminated when AGI reaches $237,880. The phase-out is calculated in the same manner as the phase-out for the adoption credit.

Coordination of Adoption Credit and Exclusion

An individual may claim both a credit and an exclusion in connection with the adoption of an eligible child, but may not claim both a credit and an exclusion for the same expense.

EXAMPLE In 2014, an unmarried individual pays $14,020 in qualified adoption expenses to an adoption agency for the final adoption of an eligible child who is not a child with special needs. In the same year, the individual's employer, under a qualified adoption assistance program, pays an additional $5,000 for other qualified adoption expenses to an attorney on behalf of the employee for the adoption of the child. Assuming the individual is not subject to the phase-out, the individual may claim a credit of $13,190 and may exclude $5,000 from gross income, because the credit and the exclusion are not for the same expenses. The remaining $830 may never be claimed as a credit or excluded from gross income. ♦

Qualified Adoption Expenses

Qualified adoption expenses are reasonable and necessary adoption fees, court costs, attorney fees, and other expenses directly related to, and of which the principal purpose is for, the taxpayer's legal adoption of an eligible child.

Would You Believe?

The following quotation is often attributed to Albert Einstein: "The hardest thing in the world to understand is the income tax."

Self-Study Problem 6.7 *See Appendix E for Solutions to Self-Study Problems*

Andrew and Amy Anderson finalized the adoption of their daughter Allison in October 2014. Allison is a U.S. citizen and is not a special needs child. Her Social Security number is 466-47-3311. In 2014, Andrew and Amy paid $17,000 in qualified adoption expenses. In addition, Amy's employer paid $4,000 directly to an adoption agency as an employer-provided adoption benefit. The Anderson's AGI for 2014 is $200,360 (assume adjusted gross income and modified adjusted gross income are the same for purposes of this problem). Use Form 8839 on Page 6-19 to calculate the Anderson's adoption credit and the amount of any employee adoption exclusion.

Learning Objective 6.8

Recognize the basic individual credits for energy efficiency.

ENERGY CREDITS

In 2014, two major energy credits are available to individual taxpayers to encourage the use of energy-efficient products. These include the credit for the purchase of plug-in electric vehicles and the 30 percent credit for the residential installation of solar, wind, and geothermal property.

Self-Study Problem 6.7

Form **8839**

Department of the Treasury
Internal Revenue Service (99)

Qualified Adoption Expenses

▶ Attach to Form 1040 or 1040NR.

▶ For information about Form 8839 and its separate instructions, see *www.irs.gov/form8839*.

OMB No. 1545-0074

2014

Attachment Sequence No. 38

Name(s) shown on return | Your social security number

DRAFT AS OF August 12, 2014 DO NOT FILE

Part I **Information About Your Eligible Child or Children**—You **must** complete this part. See instructions for details, including what to do if you need more space.

1	(a) Child's name First	Last	(b) Child's year of birth	Check if child was— (c) born **before** **1997** and disabled	(d) a child with special needs	(e) a foreign child	(f) Child's identifying number	(g) Check if adoption became final in 2014 or earlier
Child 1				☐	☐	☐		☐
Child 2				☐	☐	☐		☐
Child 3				☐	☐	☐		☐

Caution. If the child was a foreign child, see **Special rules** in the instructions for line 1, column (e) before you complete Part II or Part III. If you received **employer-provided adoption benefits,** complete Part III on the back next.

Part II **Adoption Credit**

			Child 1	Child 2	Child 3
2	Maximum adoption credit per child	2	$13,190 00	$13,190 00	$13,190 00
3	Did you file Form 8839 for a prior year for the same child? ☐ **No.** Enter -0-. ☐ **Yes.** See instructions for the amount to enter.	3			
4	Subtract line 3 from line 2	4			
5	**Qualified adoption expenses** (see instructions)	5			
	Caution. Your qualified adoption expenses may not be equal to the adoption expenses you paid in 2014.				
6	Enter the **smaller** of line 4 or line 5	6			

7 Enter modified adjusted gross income (see instructions) **7**

8 Is line 7 more than $197,880?
☐ **No.** Skip lines 8 and 9, and enter -0- on line 10.
☐ **Yes.** Subtract $197,880 from line 7 . . . . . . **8**

9 Divide line 8 by $40,000. Enter the result as a decimal (rounded to at least three places). Do not enter more than 1.000 . . . . . . **9** × .

			Child 1	Child 2	Child 3
10	Multiply each amount on line 6 by line 9	10			
11	Subtract line 10 from line 6	11			

12 Add the amounts on line 11 . . . . . . **12**

13 Credit carryforward, if any, from prior years. See your Adoption Credit Carryforward Worksheet in the 2013 Form 8839 instructions **13**

14 Add lines 12 and 13 . . . . . . **14**

15 Enter the amount from line 5 of the Credit Limit Worksheet in the instructions **15**

16 **Adoption Credit.** Enter the smaller of line 14 or line 15 here and on Form 1040, line 54, or Form 1040NR, line 51. Check box **c** on that line and enter **"8839"** in the space next to box **c**. If line 15 is smaller than line 14, you may have a credit carryforward (see instructions) **16**

Form 8839 (2014) Page **2**

Part III Employer-Provided Adoption Benefits

DRAFT AS OF August 12, 2014 DO NOT FILE

			Child 1	Child 2	Child 3		
17	Maximum exclusion per child	17	$13,190 00	$13,190 00	$13,190 00		
18	Did you receive employer-provided adoption benefits for a prior year for the same child? ☐ **No.** Enter -0-. ☐ **Yes.** See instructions for the amount to enter.	18					
19	Subtract line 18 from line 17	19					
20	Employer-provided adoption benefits you received in 2014. This amount should be shown in box 12 of your 2014 Form(s) W-2 with code **T**	20					
21	Add the amounts on line 20					21	
22	Enter the **smaller** of line 19 or line 20. But if the child was a child with special needs and the adoption became final in 2014, enter the amount from line 19	22					
23	Enter modified adjusted gross income (from the worksheet in the instructions)	23					
24	Is line 23 more than $197,880? ☐ **No.** Skip lines 24 and 25, and enter -0- on line 26. ☐ **Yes.** Subtract $197,880 from line 23	24					
25	Divide line 24 by $40,000. Enter the result as a decimal (rounded to at least three places). Do not enter more than 1.000	25	× .				
26	Multiply each amount on line 22 by line 25	26					
27	**Excluded benefits.** Subtract line 26 from line 22	27					
28	Add the amounts on line 27					28	
29	**Taxable benefits.** Is line 28 more than line 21? ☐ **No.** Subtract line 28 from line 21. Also, include this amount, if more than zero, on line 7 of Form 1040 or line 8 of Form 1040NR. On the dotted line next to line 7 of Form 1040 or line 8 of Form 1040NR, enter "AB." ☐ **Yes.** Subtract line 21 from line 28. Enter the result as a negative number. Reduce the total you would enter on line 7 of Form 1040 or line 8 of Form 1040NR by the amount on Form 8839, line 29. Enter the result on line 7 of Form 1040 or line 8 of Form 1040NR. Enter "SNE" on the dotted line next to the entry line. . .					29	

TIP

You may be able to claim the adoption credit in Part II on the front of this form if any of the following apply.

- You paid adoption expenses in 2013, those expenses were not fully reimbursed by your employer or otherwise, and the adoption was not final by the end of 2013.
- The total adoption expenses you paid in 2014 were not fully reimbursed by your employer or otherwise, and the adoption became final in 2014 or earlier.
- You adopted a child with special needs and the adoption became final in 2014.

Form **8839** (2014)

Plug-In Electric Vehicle Credits

Taxpayers are allowed a credit for the purchase of plug-in electric drive vehicles used for either business or personal purposes. The credit, which ranges between $2,500 and $7,500 for light-duty vehicles, varies depending on the weight of the vehicle and the kilowatt hour of traction battery capacity.

The Chevy Volt, Nissan Leaf, Tesla Model S, and numerous other new electric vehicles qualify for the full $7,500 credit. The Volt has both a plug-in electric engine and a gas engine but qualifies for the credit because it is powered to a significant extent by an electric motor. The credit phases out for each car manufacturer when they reach a total of 200,000 electric cars sold for use in the United States. More information on federal and state electric vehicle tax incentives may be found at **fueleconomy.gov**

Credits for Residential Energy-Efficient Property (REEP Credit)

In tax year 2014, taxpayers may claim a credit of 30 percent of the amount paid for qualified solar electric property (property which uses solar power to generate electricity in a home), qualified solar water-heating property, qualified small wind energy property, and qualified geothermal heat pump property, which uses ground or groundwater as a thermal energy source to heat or cool a residence. A different but significant credit is allowed for qualified fuel cell property to generate electricity for use in a residence.

The REEP credits described in the paragraph above may be claimed for both principal residences and vacation homes. No credit is allowed for installations used to heat swimming pools or hot tubs. The REEP credit is expected to significantly increase the number of solar and wind energy installations in coming years in addition to assisting the growing solar and wind energy industries.

EXAMPLE In 2014, Mary buys $30,000 of solar electric property for her second (vacation) home. The equipment is not used to heat her swimming pool or hot tub. She may claim a credit of $9,000 ($30,000 × 30%) for 2014. ♦

Self-Study Problem 6.8 ***See Appendix E for Solutions to Self-Study Problems***

Calculate the energy credit allowed for the following purchases:

a. Geoffrey purchases a Nissan Leaf in May of 2014.

Credit Allowed $______________

b. Betty purchases a solar system to heat her hot tub for $2,000 and a second, certified, energy-efficient solar system to heat her home for $10,000 in 2014.

Credit Allowed $______________

TAX BREAK

Numerous tax credits may be claimed by taxpayers in addition to the tax credits discussed in this text. Several of the more common credits not covered here include:

- **The Elderly or Disabled Credit** provides relief for low-income taxpayers who are not receiving substantial tax-free retirement benefits.
- **The Disabled Access Credit** is 50 percent of eligible access expenditures up to a maximum credit of $5,000, and is meant to encourage small businesses to become more accessible to disabled individuals.
- **The General Business Credit** is made up of a number of credits which are bundled into one for carryback and carryforward purposes, including the credit for **rehabilitation expenditures**, the **low-income housing credit**, and the credit for **employer-provided child care.**
- **The Small Employer Health Insurance Credit** provides small employers a credit for health insurance paid on behalf of workers who are not owners and who meet certain criteria.
- **The Research Activities Credit** is an incremental credit of 20 percent of expenditures in excess of a base amount, and is intended to encourage high-tech and energy research.
- **The Work Opportunity Credit** is limited to 40 percent of the first $6,000 of wages paid to each eligible employee. The purpose is to encourage employment of individuals in certain specified disadvantaged groups.

A large number of credits were allowed to expire at the end of 2013 and **as we go to press**, have not been extended by Congress. Many are likely to be extended retroactively for all of 2014. Be sure and check the Whittenburg companion website for updates.

Learning Objective 6.9

Understand the basic alternative minimum tax calculation.

THE INDIVIDUAL ALTERNATIVE MINIMUM TAX (AMT)

Many individual taxpayers are subject to two parallel tax calculations, the regular tax and the alternative minimum tax (AMT). The AMT was designed in the 1960s to ensure that wealthy taxpayers could not take advantage of special tax write-offs (tax preferences and other adjustments) to avoid paying tax. In general, taxpayers must pay the alternative minimum tax if their AMT tax liability is larger than their regular tax liability.

The AMT is calculated on Form 6251, using the following formula simplified for purposes of this text:

Regular taxable income (before exemptions and standard deduction)
± Plus or minus AMT preferences and adjustments
= Equals alternative minimum taxable income (AMTI)
− Less AMT exemption (phased out to zero as AMTI increases)
= Equals amount subject to AMT
× Multiplied by the AMT tax rate(s)
= Equals tentative minimum tax
− Less regular tax
= Equals amount of AMT due with tax return, if a positive amount

Common AMT Adjustments and Preferences

The terms "AMT adjustments" and "AMT preferences" are often used interchangeably, though they have slightly different meanings. In general, adjustments are *timing differences* that arise because of differences in the regular and AMT tax calculations

(e.g., depreciation timing differences), while preferences are special provisions for the regular tax that are not allowed for the AMT (e.g., state income taxes). Both terms refer to items which adjust regular taxable income to arrive at income which is subject to alternative minimum tax. There are over twenty different types of adjustments and preferences used in the calculation of AMT on Form 6251. Some of the common adjustments and preferences are as follows:

- The **standard deduction** allowed for regular tax is not allowed for AMT.
- **Personal and dependency exemptions** are not allowed as deductions for AMT.
- The deduction for AMT **medical expenses** must be limited to 10 percent of AGI rather than 7.5 percent as required by the regular tax for taxpayers age 65 and older.
- The deductions for **property tax, state income tax, and other taxes allowed as itemized deductions** for regular tax are not allowed for AMT.
- Only the deduction for home mortgage interest related to the purchase or improvement of a first or second residence is deductible for AMT, so **the interest deduction on home equity debt** of up to $100,000 used for personal purposes such as automobile purchases is not allowed for AMT.
- **Miscellaneous itemized deductions** are not allowed for AMT.
- **Depreciation** is generally calculated over a longer life for AMT, sometimes using a different method.
- **Net operating losses** are calculated differently for AMT and often result in an adjustment when they are present.
- **State income tax refunds** are not considered income for AMT since the state income tax deduction is not allowed for AMT.
- Interest from specified **private activity bonds** is not taxed for regular tax purposes, but is taxable for AMT.
- Other less commonly seen AMT differences include such items as the calculations related to **incentive stock options, oil and gas depletion, research and development expenses, gains on asset sales such as rental real estate, passive losses, and the gain exclusion for small business stock and other items.**

The actual details of the calculation of several of the AMT tax preferences and adjustments are complex and infrequently seen in practice. For further information, please consult the IRS website, a tax service, or an advanced tax textbook.

AMT Exemption Allowance

For 2014, the AMT exemption allowance is $82,100 for married taxpayers filing joint returns, $52,800 for single and head of household taxpayers, and $41,050 for married taxpayers filing separate returns. The exemption amount is phased out for high-income taxpayers. The amount of the exemption is reduced 25 cents for each dollar by which the taxpayer's alternative minimum taxable income exceeds certain threshold amounts, which are $156,500 for married taxpayers filing joint returns, $78,250 for married taxpayers filing separate returns, and $117,300 for single and head of household taxpayers.

EXAMPLE Abby, a single taxpayer, has AMTI of $124,000 in 2014. Her AMT exemption is $51,125, which is calculated as $52,800 − [25% × ($124,000 − $117,300)]. ♦

AMT Tax Rates

For 2014, the alternative minimum tax rates for calculating the tentative AMT are 26 percent of the first $182,500 ($91,250 for married taxpayers filing separately), plus 28 percent on amounts above $182,500. These rates are applied to the taxpayer's alternative minimum tax base from the formula above. The alternative minimum tax rate for capital gains and dividends is limited to the rate paid for regular tax purposes (e.g., capital gain or qualified dividends taxed at 15 percent for regular tax purposes will also be taxed at a 15 percent alternative minimum tax rate).

EXAMPLE Teddy has an alternative minimum taxable income after the exemption deduction of $270,000, none of which is from capital gains. His tentative AMT tax is $71,950, which is calculated as (26% × $182,500) + (28% × [$270,000 − $182,500]). ♦

The AMT has become a controversial tax in recent years. Many middle-class taxpayers now pay alternative minimum tax because the reduction in regular tax rates in recent years has not been matched by a reduction in AMT tax rates. Certain items not allowed as deductions for alternative minimum tax such as state income and property taxes, miscellaneous itemized deductions, including employee business expenses, and personal and dependency exemptions may cause a taxpayer to owe alternative minimum tax.

Would You Believe?

When legislation was introduced (and failed) to repeal the federal individual alternative minimum tax, Senator Baucus commented: "Now, the Darth Vader of the tax code is bearing down on millions of unsuspecting families. Repealing the AMT will protect millions of American families from this unfair and unexpected tax. It's time to put the AMT in a galaxy far, far away and erase it from the tax code" (Press release, Office of U.S. Senator Chuck Grassley).

An opposing opinion about the alternative minimum tax is that it represents a gradual implementation of a "flat tax" by accident rather than by design. As the regular tax rate schedule is indexed up every year and the AMT rate schedule stays the same, more and more people will be taxed using the AMT's nearly flat 26–28 percent rates and significantly limited deductions.

EXAMPLE Gram and Sally are married taxpayers who file a joint tax return. Their taxable income and regular tax for 2014 are calculated as follows:

Adjusted gross income		$ 200,000
Itemized deductions:		
State income tax	$18,000	
Home mortgage interest	20,000	
Contributions	2,000	
Other miscellaneous deductions (in excess of 2% of AGI)	22,000	
Total itemized deductions		(62,000)
Exemptions		(7,900)
Taxable income		$ 130,100
Tax from 2014 rate schedule		$ 24,238

If Gram and Sally have private activity bond interest of $30,000 which is taxable for AMT but not included in arriving at the amount of adjusted gross income shown on Page 6-24, the amount of their alternative minimum tax is computed as follows:

Adjusted gross income		$200,000
Add: tax preferences and adjustments		30,000
Total		230,000
Less: allowable itemized deductions:		
Home mortgage interest	$20,000	
Contributions	2,000	
Total deductions		(22,000)
Alternative minimum taxable income		208,000
The AMT exemption ($82,100 − ($208,000 − $156,500) × 25%)		(69,225)
Alternative minimum tax base		138,775
Tentative minimum tax (26% of $138,775)		$36,082

Since the gross alternative minimum tax is greater than the regular tax, the taxpayers must pay a net alternative minimum tax of $11,844 ($36,082 − $24,238).

Their alternative minimum taxable income may also be computed by starting with taxable income of $130,100, adding the $7,900 of personal and dependency exemptions, adding back any itemized deductions which are not allowed for AMT purposes (other miscellaneous deductions of $22,000 and state income tax of $18,000), and adding the $30,000 of tax preferences: $130,100 + $7,900 + $40,000 + $30,000 = $208,000. This method of calculation is similar to the one followed on Form 6251, Alternative Minimum Tax. ♦

TAX BREAK

Many taxpayers in states with high state income tax are finding themselves paying the alternative minimum tax for the sole reason that their state income taxes and property taxes are not allowed as a deduction in the AMT calculation. Careful timing of state income tax and property tax payments may result in significant tax savings for taxpayers in this situation.

Self-Study Problem 6.9 *See Appendix E for Solutions to Self-Study Problems*

Harold Brown, a single taxpayer, has adjusted gross income of $200,000. He has a deduction for home mortgage interest of $23,000, cash contributions of $11,000, property taxes of $10,000, state income taxes of $40,000, and miscellaneous itemized deductions (after the 2 percent limitation) of $10,000. Assuming Harold's regular tax liability is $21,750, use Form 6251 on Page 6-27 to calculate the amount of Harold's net alternative minimum tax. (Hint: First calculate taxable income before personal exemptions are taken, the starting point of Form 6251.)

© ILYA AKINSHIN/Shutterstock.com; © Zhukov Oleg/Shutterstock.com.

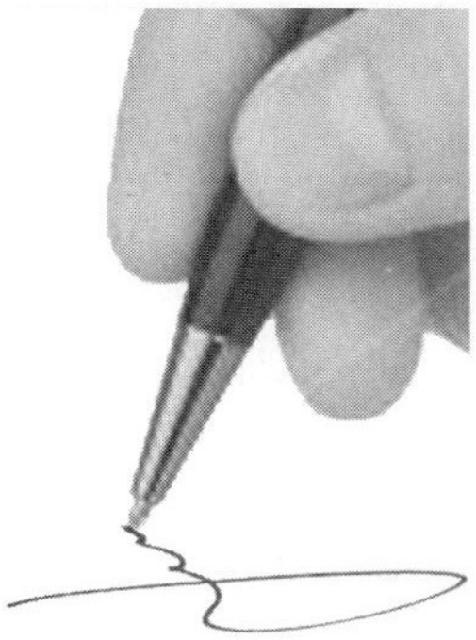

Would You Sign This Tax Return?

Paid Preparer Use Only	Print/Type preparer's name	Preparer's signature	Date	Check ☐ if self-employed	PTIN
	Firm's name ▶		Firm's EIN ▶		
	Firm's address ▶		Phone no.		

Your client, William Warrant, was hired for a management position at an Internet company planning to start a Web portal called "indulgedanimals.com" for dogs, cats, and other pets. When he was hired, William was given an incentive stock option (ISO) worth $500,000, which he exercised during the year. Exercise of the ISO creates a tax preference item for the alternative minimum tax (AMT) and causes him to have to pay substantial additional tax when combined with his other tax items for the year. He is livid about the extra tax and refuses to file the AMT Form 6251 with his tax return because the AMT tax is "unfair" and "un-American" according to him. Would you sign this tax return?

Learning Objective 6.10

Apply the rules for computing tax on the unearned income of minor children and certain students.

UNEARNED INCOME OF MINOR CHILDREN AND CERTAIN STUDENTS

Many parents have found it beneficial from a tax-planning standpoint to give income-earning assets, such as stocks, bonds, bank certificates of deposit, and mutual funds, to their minor children. Since the children are generally in a lower income tax bracket, the income from assets such as interest, dividends, and capital gains on stock sales has traditionally been taxed at a lower rate than the parents' rate. However, tax law contains provisions that limit the benefit of shifting income to certain dependent children. The net unearned income of dependent children may be taxed at their parents' rates. This parental tax rate applies to dependent children who are ages 18 or younger or students ages 19 through 23 at the end of the year, who have at least one living parent, and who have "net unearned income" for the year. Although there is no statutory definition for a parent, the term is generally considered to mean a parent or step-parent of the child.

For purposes of determining the child's (or young adult's) income subject to the parental tax rate, net unearned income is never considered to include wages or salary of a minor child and is computed as follows:

Unearned income	$xxxx.xx
Less the greater of:	
1. $1,000 (child's standard deduction), or	
2. The allowable itemized deductions directly connected with the production of the unearned income	(xxx.xx)
	xxxx.xx
Less statutory deduction	(1,000.00)
Net unearned income	$xxxx.xx

If the net unearned income is zero or less, the child's tax is calculated using the child's tax rate. However, if the net earned income amount is positive, the child's tax is calculated by applying the parents' tax rate, if higher, to that amount.

EXAMPLE Dyana and Mark have two children, Alex (age 1) and Nathan (age 7). Alex received $4,000 in interest income and Nathan received $3,000 in interest income during 2014. Alex and Nathan did not pay any investment expenses

Self-Study Problem 6.9

Form **6251**
Department of the Treasury
Internal Revenue Service (99)

Alternative Minimum Tax—Individuals

▶ **Information about Form 6251 and its separate instructions is at *www.irs.gov/form6251*.**
▶ **Attach to Form 1040 or Form 1040NR.**

OMB No. 1545-0074
2014
Attachment Sequence No. **32**

Name(s) shown on Form 1040 or Form 1040NR | **Your social security number**

DRAFT AS OF August 4, 2014 DO NOT FILE

Part I Alternative Minimum Taxable Income (See instructions for how to complete each line.)

1	If filing Schedule A (Form 1040), enter the amount from Form 1040, line 41, and go to line 2. Otherwise, enter the amount from Form 1040, line 38, and go to line 7. (If less than zero, enter as a negative amount.)	1	
2	Medical and dental. If you or your spouse was 65 or older, enter the **smaller** of Schedule A (Form 1040), line 4, **or** 2.5% (.025) of Form 1040, line 38. If zero or less, enter -0-	2	
3	Taxes from Schedule A (Form 1040), line 9	3	
4	Enter the home mortgage interest adjustment, if any, from line 6 of the worksheet in the instructions for this line	4	
5	Miscellaneous deductions from Schedule A (Form 1040), line 27	5	
6	If Form 1040, line 38, is $152,525 or less, enter -0-. Otherwise, see instructions	6	( )
7	Tax refund from Form 1040, line 10 or line 21	7	( )
8	Investment interest expense (difference between regular tax and AMT)	8	
9	Depletion (difference between regular tax and AMT)	9	
10	Net operating loss deduction from Form 1040, line 21. Enter as a positive amount	10	
11	Alternative tax net operating loss deduction	11	( )
12	Interest from specified private activity bonds exempt from the regular tax	12	
13	Qualified small business stock (7% of gain excluded under section 1202)	13	
14	Exercise of incentive stock options (excess of AMT income over regular tax income)	14	
15	Estates and trusts (amount from Schedule K-1 (Form 1041), box 12, code A)	15	
16	Electing large partnerships (amount from Schedule K-1 (Form 1065-B), box 6)	16	
17	Disposition of property (difference between AMT and regular tax gain or loss)	17	
18	Depreciation on assets placed in service after 1986 (difference between regular tax and AMT)	18	
19	Passive activities (difference between AMT and regular tax income or loss)	19	
20	Loss limitations (difference between AMT and regular tax income or loss)	20	
21	Circulation costs (difference between regular tax and AMT)	21	
22	Long-term contracts (difference between AMT and regular tax income)	22	
23	Mining costs (difference between regular tax and AMT)	23	
24	Research and experimental costs (difference between regular tax and AMT)	24	
25	Income from certain installment sales before January 1, 1987	25	( )
26	Intangible drilling costs preference	26	
27	Other adjustments, including income-based related adjustments	27	
28	**Alternative minimum taxable income.** Combine lines 1 through 27. (If married filing separately and line 28 is more than $242,450, see instructions.)	28	

Part II Alternative Minimum Tax (AMT)

29 Exemption. (If you were under age 24 at the end of 2014, see instructions.)

IF your filing status is . . .	**AND line 28 is not over . . .**	**THEN enter on line 29 . . .**
Single or head of household	$117,300	$52,800
Married filing jointly or qualifying widow(er)	156,500	82,100
Married filing separately	78,250	41,050

If line 28 is **over** the amount shown above for your filing status, see instructions. **29**

30	Subtract line 29 from line 28. If more than zero, go to line 31. If zero or less, enter -0- here and on lines 31, 33, and 35, and go to line 34	30	
31	• If you are filing Form 2555 or 2555-EZ, see instructions for the amount to enter. • If you reported capital gain distributions directly on Form 1040, line 13; you reported qualified dividends on Form 1040, line 9b; **or** you had a gain on both lines 15 and 16 of Schedule D (Form 1040) (as refigured for the AMT, if necessary), complete Part III on the back and enter the amount from line 64 here. • **All others:** If line 30 is $182,500 or less ($91,250 or less if married filing separately), multiply line 30 by 26% (.26). Otherwise, multiply line 30 by 28% (.28) and subtract $3,650 ($1,825 if married filing separately) from the result.	31	
32	Alternative minimum tax foreign tax credit (see instructions)	32	
33	Tentative minimum tax. Subtract line 32 from line 31	33	
34	Add Form 1040, line 44 (minus any tax from Form 4972), and Form 1040, line 46. Subtract from the result any foreign tax credit from Form 1040, line 48. If you used Schedule J to figure your tax on Form 1040, line 44, refigure that tax without using Schedule J before completing this line (see instructions)	34	
35	**AMT.** Subtract line 34 from line 33. If zero or less, enter -0-. Enter here and on Form 1040, line 45	35	

For Paperwork Reduction Act Notice, see your tax return instructions. Cat. No. 13600G Form **6251** (2014)

for the year. Dyana and Mark have taxable income for the year of $45,050. Alex and Nathan's 2014 income tax is calculated as follows:

Step 1: Calculate net unearned income	Alex	Nathan
Unearned income	$4,000	$ 3,000
Less the greater of:		
$1,000 (standard deduction), or investment expenses	(1,000)	(1,000)
	3,000	2,000
Less statutory deduction	(1,000)	(1,000)
Net unearned income	$2,000	$1,000

Step 2: Calculate the total parental tax	
Parents' taxable income	$45,050
Plus: the children's net unearned income ($2,000 + $1,000)	3,000
Revised taxable income	$48,050
Tax on revised income (from tax table)	$ 6,304
Tax on parents' regular income ($45,050)	(5,854)
Total parental tax	$ 450

Step 3: Allocate total parental tax

$$\text{Alex's parental tax } \frac{\$2{,}000}{(\$2{,}000 + \$1{,}000)} \times \$450 = \$300$$

$$\text{Nathan's parental tax } \frac{\$1{,}000}{(\$2{,}000 + \$1{,}000)} \times \$450 = \$150$$

Step 4: Calculate total tax	Alex	Nathan
Regular 10% tax on $1,000	$100	$100
Plus allocable parental tax	300	150
Total tax	$400	$250

Both Alex and Nathan must include a Form 8615, Tax for Certain Children Who Have Investment Income of More Than $2,000, with their individual income tax returns. ♦

If a child's parents are divorced, the taxable income of the parent with custody is used to calculate the parental tax. Also, if married parents file separate returns, the parent's return with the larger amount of taxable income is used in the calculation.

Election to Include a Child's Unearned Income on Parents' Return

If certain conditions are met, parents may elect to include a child's gross income on the parents' tax return. The election eliminates the child's return filing requirements and saves the parents the trouble of filing the special calculation Form 8615 for the "kiddie tax." To qualify for this election, the following conditions must be met:

1. The child's gross income is from interest and dividends only.
2. The gross income is more than $1,000 and less than $10,000.
3. No estimated tax has been paid in the name of the child and the child is not subject to backup withholding.

EXAMPLE Sam is 12 years old and has $2,300 of interest from a savings account set up for him by his grandparents. This is Sam's only income for the year. Instead of completing the "kiddie tax form" (Form 8615) and paying the tax on his $2,300 in income, Sam's parents may elect to include the $2,300 on their tax return thereby eliminating Sam's filing requirement. The election to include the income of a minor child on the parents' return is made on Form 8814, as illustrated on Page 6-31. ♦

Self-Study Problem 6.10 *See Appendix E for Solutions for Self-Study Problems*

Bill and Janet have one child, Robert, who is 9 years old. Robert has interest income of $3,000 for the year. Bill and Janet's taxable income for the year is $46,050. Calculate Robert's tax liability for 2014, assuming Bill and Janet do not make an election to include Robert's income on their tax return.

$____________

Learning Objective 6.11

Distinguish between the different rules for married taxpayers residing in community property states when filing separate returns.

COMMUNITY PROPERTY

When married couples file separate income tax returns, a special problem arises. Income derived from property held by a married couple, either jointly or separately, as well as wages and other income earned by a husband and wife, must be allocated between the spouses. State law becomes important in making this allocation.

The law in nine states is based on a community property system of marital law. In these states, the property rights of married couples differ from the property rights of married couples residing in the remaining common law states. The nine states that are community property states are:

Arizona	Louisiana	Texas
California	Nevada	Washington
Idaho	New Mexico	Wisconsin

Note: In Alaska, spouses may elect to treat income as community income.

Under the community property system, all property is deemed to be either separate property or community property. Separate property includes property acquired by a spouse before marriage or received after marriage as a gift or inheritance. All other property owned by a married couple is presumed to be community property. For federal income tax purposes, each spouse is automatically taxed on half of the income from community property.

The tax treatment of income from separate property depends on the taxpayer's state of residence. In Texas, Louisiana, Wisconsin, and Idaho, income from separate property produces community income. Thus, just as each spouse is taxed on half of the income from community property, each spouse is also taxed on half of the income from separate property. In the other five community property states, income on separate property is separate income and is reported in full on the tax return of the spouse who owns the property. Income such as nontaxable dividends or royalties from mineral interests assumes the classification of the asset from which the income is derived. Capital gains also retain their classification based on the classification of the property from which the gain arises.

Form **8814** | **Parents' Election To Report Child's Interest and Dividends** | OMB No. 1545-0074 **2014**

Department of the Treasury Internal Revenue Service (99)

► Information about Form 8814 and its instructions is at *www.irs.gov/form8814.*
► Attach to parents' Form 1040 or Form 1040NR.

Attachment Sequence No. 40

Name(s) shown on your return	Your social security number
Sam's Parents	

Caution. The federal income tax on your child's income, including qualified dividends and capital gain distributions, may be less if you file a separate tax return for the child instead of making this election. This is because you cannot take certain tax benefits that your child could take on his or her own return. For details, see **Tax benefits you cannot take** in the instructions.

DRAFT AS OF June 13, 2014 DO NOT FILE

A Child's name (first, initial, and last)	B Child's social security number
Sam	

C If more than one Form 8814 is attached, check here ► ☐

Part I Child's Interest and Dividends To Report on Your Return

1a	Enter your child's **taxable** interest. If this amount is different from the amounts shown on the child's Forms 1099-INT and 1099-OID, see the instructions			1a	2,300
b	Enter your child's **tax-exempt** interest. **Do not** include this amount on line 1a	1b			
2a	Enter your child's ordinary dividends, including any Alaska Permanent Fund dividends. If your child received any ordinary dividends as a nominee, see the instructions			2a	
b	Enter your child's qualified dividends included on line 2a. See the instructions	2b			
3	Enter your child's capital gain distributions. If your child received any capital gain distributions as a nominee, see the instructions			3	
4	Add lines 1a, 2a, and 3. If the total is $2,000 or less, skip lines 5 through 12 and go to line 13. If the total is $10,000 or more, **do not** file this form. Your child **must** file his or her own return to report the income			4	2,300
5	Base amount			5	2,000 00
6	Subtract line 5 from line 4			6	300
	If both lines 2b and 3 are zero or blank, skip lines 7 through 10, enter -0- on line 11, and go to line 12. Otherwise, go to line 7.				
7	Divide line 2b by line 4. Enter the result as a decimal (rounded to at least three places)	7	.		
8	Divide line 3 by line 4. Enter the result as a decimal (rounded to at least three places)	8	.		
9	Multiply line 6 by line 7. Enter the result here. See the instructions for where to report this amount on your return	9			
10	Multiply line 6 by line 8. Enter the result here. See the instructions for where to report this amount on your return	10			
11	Add lines 9 and 10			11	0
12	Subtract line 11 from line 6. Include this amount in the total on Form 1040, line 21, or Form 1040NR, line 21. In the space next to line 21, enter "Form 8814" and show the amount. If you checked the box on line C above, see the instructions. Go to line 13 below			12	300

Part II Tax on the First $2,000 of Child's Interest and Dividends

13	Amount not taxed	13	1,000 00
14	Subtract line 13 from line 4. If the result is zero or less, enter -0-	14	1,300
15	**Tax.** Is the amount on line 14 less than $1,000? ☑ **No.** Enter $100 here and see the **Note** below. ☐ **Yes.** Multiply line 14 by 10% (.10). Enter the result here and see the **Note** below.	15	100

Note. If you checked the box on line C above, see the instructions. Otherwise, include the amount from line 15 in the tax you enter on Form 1040, line 44, or Form 1040NR, line 42. Be sure to check box **a** on Form 1040, line 44, or Form 1040NR, line 42.

For Paperwork Reduction Act Notice, see your tax return instructions. Cat. No. 10750J Form **8814** (2014)

EXAMPLE John and Marsha are married and live in Texas. John owns, as his separate property, stock in AT&T Corporation. During the year, John receives dividends of $4,000. Assuming John and Marsha file separate returns, each of them must report $2,000 of the dividends. On the other hand, if John and Marsha lived in California, John would report the entire $4,000 of the dividends on his tax return and Marsha would not include any of the dividend income on her tax return. ♦

In all of the community property states, income from salary and wages is generally treated as having been earned one-half by each spouse.

EXAMPLE Robert and Linda are married but file separate tax returns. Robert receives a salary of $30,000 and has interest income of $500 from a savings account which is in his name. The savings account was established with salary earned by Robert since his marriage. Linda collects $20,000 in dividends on stock she inherited from her father. The amount of income which Linda must report on her separate income tax return depends on the state in which Robert and Linda reside. Three different assumptions are presented below:

	State of Residence		
Linda's Income:	***Texas***	***California***	***Common Law States***
Salary	$15,000	$15,000	$ 0
Dividends	10,000	20,000	20,000
Interest	250	250	0
Total	$25,250	$35,250	$20,000

♦

Spouses Living Apart

To simplify problems that could arise when married spouses residing in a community property state do not live together, the tax law contains an exception to the above community property rules. Under this special provision, a spouse will be taxed only on his or her actual earnings from personal services. For this provision to apply, the following conditions must be satisfied:

1. The individuals must live apart for the entire year,
2. They must not file a joint return, and
3. No portion of the earned income may be transferred between the spouses.

EXAMPLE Bill and Betty, both residents of Nevada, are married but live apart for the entire year. Bill has a salary of $30,000 and Betty has a salary of $35,000. Normally, Bill and Betty would each report $32,500. However, if the required conditions are met, Bill and Betty would each report their own salary. If Bill and Betty had any unearned income, such as dividends or interest, the income would be reported under the general community property rules. The special provision applies only to earned income of the spouses. ♦

Another provision addresses the problem of spouses who fail to qualify for the above special exception because they do not live apart for the entire year. In certain cases, a spouse who fails to include in income his or her share of community income, as required by the community property laws, may be relieved of any liability related to this income. To be granted relief, the taxpayer must not know of or have reason to know of the omitted community property income.

Same-Sex Couples

On June 26, 2013 the U.S. Supreme Court struck down the portion of the Defense of Marriage Act (DOMA) which denied federal benefits to married same-sex couples. Same-sex couples legally married under state law will now, for the first time, be not only allowed, but required, to file as married for federal tax purposes. Community property states that recognize same-sex marriage also accord community property rights to these unions. The rules discussed above related to the separate tax returns of married couples now apply equally to married same-sex couples.

Self-Study Problem 6.11 ***See Appendix E for Solutions to Self-Study Problems***

Tom and Rachel are married and living together in California. Their income is as follows:

Tom's salary	$40,000
Rachel's salary	30,000
Dividends (Tom's property)	5,000
Dividends (Rachel's property)	3,000
Interest (community property)	4,000
Total	$82,000

a. If Rachel files a separate tax return, she should report income of:

$____________

b. If Tom and Rachel lived in Texas, what should Rachel report as income?

$____________

KEY TERMS

child tax credit, 6-2
earned income credit (EIC), 6-2
"negative" income tax, 6-2
child and dependent care credit, 6-3
individual shared responsibility, 6-9
minimum essential coverage, 6-9
premium tax credit, 6-10
HOPE credit, 6-12
American Opportunity tax credit, 6-12
lifetime learning credit, 6-13
foreign tax credit, 6-15
adoption credit, 6-16
alternative minimum tax (AMT), 6-22
AMT adjustments, 6-22
AMT preferences, 6-22
AMT exemption allowance, 6-23
AMT tax rates, 6-24
parental tax rate, 6-26
"kiddie tax," 6-29
community property, 6-30
separate property, 6-30

KEY POINTS

Learning Objectives	Key Points
LO 6.1: Calculate the child tax credit.	• Credits are a direct reduction in tax liability instead of a deduction from income. • For 2014, the child tax credit is $1,000 per qualifying child. • The child tax credit begins phasing out when AGI reaches $110,000 for joint filers ($55,000 for married taxpayers filing separately) and $75,000 for single or head of household taxpayers.

LO 6.2: Determine the earned income credit (EIC).	• The earned income credit (EIC) is available to qualifying individuals with earned income and AGI below certain levels and is meant to assist the working poor. • The EIC formula for calculating the credit is based on the adjusted gross income of the taxpayer and the number of qualifying children of the taxpayer. • To compute the credit, the taxpayer must fill out a form calculating the credit from the tables based on earned income from wages, salaries, and self-employment income. • To be eligible for the credit with no qualifying children, a worker must be over 25 and under 65 years old and not be claimed as a dependent by another taxpayer.
LO 6.3: Compute the child and dependent care credit for an individual taxpayer.	• To be eligible for the child and dependent care credit, the dependent must either be under the age of 13 or be a dependent or spouse of any age who is incapable of self-care. • If a child's parents are divorced, the child need not be the dependent of the taxpayer claiming the credit, but the child must live with that parent more than he or she lives with the other parent. • The expenses that qualify for the credit include amounts paid to enable both the taxpayer and his or her spouse to be employed. • For taxpayers with AGI of less than $15,000, the child and dependent care credit is equal to 35 percent of the qualified expenses. For taxpayers with AGI of $15,000 or more, the credit gradually decreases from 35 percent to 20 percent for AGI over $43,000. • In determining the credit, the maximum amount of qualified expenses to which the applicable percentage is applied is $3,000 for one dependent and $6,000 for two or more dependents. • Full-time students with little or no income are deemed to have earned income of $250 per month for one dependent and $500 per month for two or more dependents for purposes of calculating this limitation.
LO 6.4: Describe minimum essential coverage, the individual shared responsibility provision, and calculate the premium tax credit available under the Affordable Care Act.	• Individual shared responsibility is a new tax in 2014 for taxpayers that do not have minimum essential coverage health care. • Most employer or government provided health care or health care purchased on an exchange meets minimum essential coverage standards. • There are exemptions from having to meet the minimum essential coverage requirements. • There is a cap on the individual shared responsibility amount. • Certain lower income taxpayers may be eligible for a premium tax credit to offset some or all of the cost of health care purchased through an exchange. • The credit can be paid in advance or at the time the tax return is filed. • The advanced credit and the actual credit are reconciled at the time the tax return is prepared. Repayments may be limited.
LO 6.5: Apply the special rules applicable to the American Opportunity tax credit and lifetime learning credit.	For 2014, the partially refundable American Opportunity tax credit is 100 percent of the first $2,000 of tuition, fees, books, and course materials paid and 25 percent of the next $2,000, for a total maximum annual credit of $2,500 per student. • The American Opportunity tax credit is available for the first 4 years of postsecondary education. • Taxpayers can elect a nonrefundable lifetime learning tax credit of 20 percent of tuition and fees up to $10,000 of qualified expenses in 2014.

	• The American Opportunity tax credit is phased out for joint filers with income between \$160,000 and \$180,000 and for single and head of household filers with income between \$80,000 and \$90,000. The lifetime learning credit is phased out between \$108,000 and \$128,000 for married taxpayers, and between \$54,000 and \$64,000 for those single or head of household taxpayers. • Taxpayers cannot take both the American Opportunity tax credit and the lifetime learning credit for the same student in the same tax year. • The credits cannot be used for expenses that are deducted from taxable income on a tax return for educational costs such as unreimbursed job-related educational expenses.
LO 6.6: Understand the operation of the foreign tax credit.	• U.S. taxpayers are allowed to claim a foreign tax credit on income earned in a foreign country and subject to income taxes in that country. • Taxpayers may make an annual election to claim a deduction instead of a credit for the foreign taxes, but most taxpayers receive a greater tax benefit by claiming the foreign tax credit. • Generally, the foreign tax credit is equal to the amount of the taxes paid to foreign governments; however, there is an "overall" limitation on the amount of the credit, which is calculated as the ratio of net foreign income to U.S. taxable income multiplied times the U.S. tax liability. • Unused foreign tax credits may be carried back 1 year and forward 10 years to reduce any tax liability in those years.
LO 6.7: Determine the proper use and calculation of the adoption credit.	• Individuals are allowed an income tax credit for qualified adoption expenses. The total expense that can be taken as a credit for all tax years with respect to an adoption of a child is \$13,190 for 2014.
LO 6.8: Recognize the basic individual credits for energy efficiency.	• A tax credit of up to \$7,500 for the purchase of new electric drive vehicles is available. • For 2014, taxpayers may claim a 30 percent credit of the amount paid for qualified solar, wind, or geothermal property.
LO 6.9: Understand the basic alternative minimum tax calculation.	• The AMT was designed in the 1960s to ensure that wealthy taxpayers could not take advantage of special tax write-offs (tax preferences and other adjustments) to avoid paying tax. • Adjustments are timing differences that arise because of differences in the regular and AMT tax calculations (e.g., depreciation timing differences), while preferences are special provisions for the regular tax that are not allowed for the AMT (e.g., state income taxes). • For 2014, the AMT exemption allowance is \$82,100 for married taxpayers filing joint returns, \$52,800 for single and head of household taxpayers, and \$41,050 for married taxpayers filing separate returns. The exemption allowance amount is phased out for high-income taxpayers. • For 2014, the alternative minimum tax rates for calculating the tentative AMT are 26 percent of the first \$182,500 (\$91,250 for married taxpayers filing separately), plus 28 percent on amounts above \$182,500 applied to the taxpayer's alternative minimum tax base.

LO 6.10: Apply the rules for computing tax on the unearned income of minor children and certain students.	• The tax law contains provisions that limit the benefit of shifting income to certain dependent children. • The net unearned income of dependent children may be taxed at their parents' rates. • This parental tax rate applies to dependent children who are age 18 or younger or are students ages 19 through 23 at the end of the year, who have at least one living parent, and who have "net unearned income" for the year. • If certain conditions are met, parents may elect to include a child's gross income on the parents' tax return. The election eliminates the child's return filing requirements and saves the parents the trouble of filing the special calculation Form 8615 for the "kiddie tax."
LO 6.11: Distinguish between the different rules for married taxpayers residing in community property states when filing separate returns.	• Income derived from community property held by a married couple, either jointly or separately, as well as wages and other income earned by a married couple, must be allocated between the spouses, if filing separately. • Nine states use a community property system of marital law. These states are Arizona, California, Idaho, Louisiana, Nevada, New Mexico, Texas, Washington, and Wisconsin. • In general, in a community property state, income is split one-half (50 percent) to each spouse. There are exceptions for certain separate property (e.g., property owned prior to marriage, etc.).

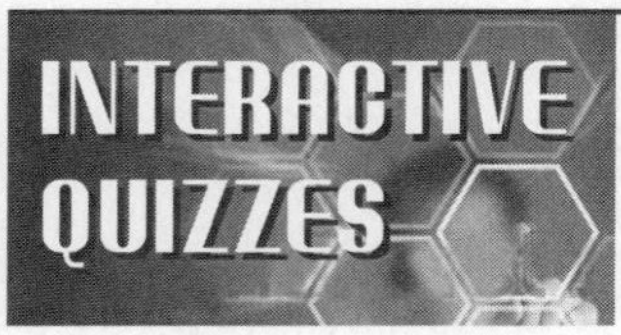

© Dusit/Shutterstock.com

Interactive quizzes are available as an optional online resource for Income Tax Fundamentals. Visit **www.cengagebrain.com** for more information.

QUESTIONS and PROBLEMS

GROUP 1: MULTIPLE CHOICE QUESTIONS

LO 6.1

1. Russ and Linda are married and file a joint tax return claiming their three children, ages 4, 7, and 18, as dependents. Their adjusted gross income for 2014 is $105,300. What is Russ and Linda's total child credit for 2014?
   a. $600
   b. $1,000
   c. $2,000
   d. $3,000
   e. Some other amount

LO 6.1

2. Jennifer is divorced and files a head of household tax return claiming her children, ages 4, 7, and 17, as dependents. Her adjusted gross income for 2014 is $81,300. What is Jennifer's total child credit for 2014?
   a. $850
   b. $1,200
   c. $1,650
   d. $2,000
   e. Some other amount

LO 6.2

3. Assuming they all meet the income requirements, which of the following taxpayers qualify for the earned income credit in 2014?
   a. A married taxpayer who files a separate tax return and has a dependent child
   b. A single taxpayer who waited on tables for 3 months of the tax year and is claimed as a dependent by her mother
   c. A single taxpayer who is self-employed and has a dependent child
   d. a and c above
   e. None of the above qualify for the earned income credit

LO 6.3

4. Which of the following payments does *not* qualify as a child care expense for purposes of the child and dependent care credit?
   a. Payments to a day care center
   b. Payments to the taxpayer's sister (21 years old) for daytime babysitting
   c. Payments to a housekeeper who also babysits the child
   d. Payments to the taxpayer's dependent brother (16 years old) for daytime babysitting
   e. All of the above qualify for the child and dependent care credit

LO 6.4

5. Which of the following taxpayers will require a payment for the individual shared responsibility?
   a. Jim's income was only $2,000 for the year, his employer did not provide health insurance, and the premiums for the cheapest plan on the exchange were $125 per month which he could not afford and thus did not purchase insurance.
   b. Peg changed jobs during the year and was without coverage for 2 months.
   c. Alice filed Form 8965 due to a hardship exemption.
   d. Bill, a self-employed architect, had a physical in January and was found to be in good health so he canceled his health insurance policy starting in February. His income for the year was about $110,000.
   e. All but c will be required to pay an individual shared responsibility amount.

LO 6.4

6. James did not have minimum essential coverage for any part of 2014. If James is single and has 2014 adjusted gross income of $46,000, what is his individual shared responsibility payment?
   a. $0
   b. $95
   c. $359
   d. $460

LO 6.5

7. The American Opportunity tax credit is 100 percent of the first ____ of tuition and fees paid and 25 percent of the next _____.
   a. $600; $1,200
   b. $1,100; $550
   c. $2,000; $2,000
   d. $1,100; $5,500
   e. None of the above

LO 6.5

8. Jane graduates from high school in June 2014. In the fall, she enrolls for six units at Big State University. Big State University considers students who take twelve or more units to be full-time. Jane's father pays her tuition and fees of $2,500 for the fall semester and in December prepays $2,500 for the spring semester. In 2014, the American Opportunity tax credit for Jane's tuition and fees before any AGI limitation is:
   a. $5,000
   b. $2,500

c. $2,200
d. $1,800
e. Some other amount

LO 6.5

9. In September 2014, Sam pays $2,200 to take a course to improve his job skills to qualify for a new position at work. Assuming there is no phase-out of the credit, his lifetime learning credit for 2014 is:
   a. $220
   b. $240
   c. $360
   d. $1,100
   e. Some other amount

LO 6.5

10. In November 2014, Simon pays $6,200 to take a course to improve his job skills to qualify for a new position at work. Simon's employer reimbursed him for the cost of the course. For 2014, Simon's lifetime learning credit is:
    a. $0
    b. $1,000
    c. $2,500
    d. $1,500
    e. Some other amount

LO 6.5

11. John, a single father, has AGI of $51,000 in 2014. In 2014, he pays $4,000 in qualified tuition for his dependent son, who just started attending Small University. What is John's American Opportunity tax credit for 2014?
    a. $0
    b. $800
    c. $2,500
    d. $4,000
    e. Some other amount

LO 6.5

12. Joan, a single mother, has AGI of $85,000 in 2014. In September 2014, she pays $5,000 in qualified tuition for her dependent son who just started at Big University. What is Joan's American Opportunity credit for 2014?
    a. $0
    b. $1,250
    c. $2,125
    d. $2,500
    e. Some other amount

LO 6.5

13. Becky, a college freshman, works part-time and pays $1,600 of her college tuition expenses. Although Becky files her own tax return, her parents claim her as a dependent on their tax return. Becky's parents have AGI of $50,000. What is the amount of American Opportunity tax credit her parents can claim on their tax return for the tuition Becky paid?
    a. $0
    b. $495
    c. $1,600
    d. $1,650
    e. Some other amount

______ 14. Taxpayer L has income of $55,000 from Norway, which imposes a 30 percent income tax, and income of $45,000 from France, which imposes a 40 percent income tax. L has taxable income from U.S. sources of $200,000 and U.S. tax liability before credits of $90,000. What is the amount of the foreign tax credit?

LO 6.6

a. $16,500
b. $34,500
c. $30,000
d. $100,000
e. $45,000

______ 15. John and Joan pay $16,500 of qualified adoption expenses in 2014 to finalize the adoption of a qualified child. Their AGI is $197,000 for 2014. What is their adoption credit for 2014?

LO 6.7

a. $0
b. $1,650
c. $12,970
d. $13,190

______ 16. In connection with the adoption of an eligible child who is a U.S. citizen and who is not a child with special needs, Sean pays $4,000 of qualified adoption expenses in 2013 and $3,000 of qualified adoption expenses in 2014. The adoption is finalized in 2014. There is no phase-out of the adoption credit. What are the adoption credits for both 2013 and 2014, respectively?

LO 6.7

a. $0; $7,000
b. $4,000; $1,000
c. $4,000; $3,000
d. $7,000; $0

______ 17. In 2014, Irene, an unmarried individual, pays $6,500 in qualified adoption expenses to an adoption agency for the final adoption of an eligible child who is not a child with special needs. In the same year, the individual's employer, under a qualified adoption assistance program, pays an additional $4,000 for other qualified adoption expenses to an attorney on behalf of Irene for the adoption of the child. Assuming Irene is not subject to the phase-out, she may exclude, from her personal income, how much of the $4,000 payment made by her employer?

LO 6.7

a. $6,500
b. $5,000
c. $4,000
d. $2,000

______ 18. If a taxpayer does not have enough tax liability to use all the available adoption credit, the unused portion may be carried forward for how many years?

LO 6.7

a. Two
b. Three
c. Five
d. There is no carryforward; for 2014, the credit is not refundable

______ 19. Which of the following is *not* a tax preference or adjustment item for the individual alternative minimum tax computation?

LO 6.9

a. Miscellaneous itemized deductions
b. State income taxes
c. State income tax refunds
d. Private activity bond interest
e. All of the above are adjustments or tax preference items

LO 6.11

________ 20. Dana and Larry are married and live in Texas. Dana earns a salary of $45,000 and Larry has $25,000 of rental income from his separate property. If Dana and Larry file separate tax returns, what amount of income must Larry report?

a. $0
b. $22,500
c. $25,000
d. $47,500
e. None of the above

LO 6.11

________ 21. Which of the following conditions need *not* be satisfied in order for a married taxpayer, residing in a community property state, to be taxed only on his or her separate salary?

a. The husband and wife must live apart for the entire year.
b. A minor child must be living with the spouse.
c. The husband and wife must not file a joint income tax return.
d. The husband and wife must not transfer earned income between themselves.
e. All of the above must be satisfied.

GROUP 2: PROBLEMS

LO 6.1

1. Calculate the child credit for the following taxpayers. Please show your work.
   a. Jeremy is a single (head of household) father with a dependent 8-year-old son and $79,600 of AGI:
   ____
   b. Jerry and Ann have two dependent preschool children and $100,000 of AGI:
   ____
   c. James and Apple have two dependent children (ages 7 and 10) and $120,400 of AGI:
   ____

LO 6.2

2. How does the earned income credit produce a "negative" income tax?
____
____
____

LO 6.2

3. Diane is a single taxpayer who qualifies for the earned income credit. Diane has two qualifying children who are 3 and 5 years old. During 2014, Diane's wages are $17,500 and she receives dividend income of $700. Calculate Diane's earned income credit using the EIC table in Appendix B.

$________

LO 6.2

4. Margaret and David Simmons are married and file a joint income tax return. They have two dependent children, Margo, 5 years old (Social Security number 316-31-4890), and Daniel, who was born during the year (Social Security number 316-31-7894). Margaret's wages are $3,000, and David has wages of $14,000. In addition, they receive interest income of $200 during the year. Margaret and David do not have any other items of income and do not have any deductions for adjusted gross income. Assuming the Simmons file Form 1040A for 2014, complete Schedule EIC and the Earned Income Credit Worksheet A, on Pages 6-45 and 6-46. (The EIC table is in Appendix B.)

LO 6.2

5. What is the maximum investment income a taxpayer is allowed to have and still be allowed to claim the earned income credit? Please speculate as to why there is an investment income limit in the tax law.

____

____

____

LO 6.3

6. Calculate the amount of the child and dependent care credit allowed for 2014 in each of the following cases, assuming the taxpayers had no income other than the stated amounts.
   a. William and Carla file a joint tax return. Carla earned $26,000 during the year, while William attended law school full-time for 9 months and earned no income. They paid $3,500 for the care of their 3-year-old child, Carl.

   $__________

   b. Raymond and Michele file a joint tax return. Raymond earned $32,500 during the year, while Michele earned $9,000 for the year from a part-time job. They paid $7,000 for the care of their two children under age 13.

   $__________

   c. Beth is a single taxpayer who has two dependent children under age 5. Beth earned $23,500 in wages during the year and paid $6,700 for the care of her children.

   $__________

LO 6.3

7. Clarita is a single taxpayer with two dependent children, ages 10 and 12. Clarita pays $3,000 in qualified child care expenses during the year. If her adjusted gross income (all from wages) for the year is $18,500, calculate Clarita's child and dependent care credit for 2014.

   $__________

LO 6.3

8. Go to the IRS website (**www.irs.gov**) and redo Problem 7 above using the most recent interactive Form 2441, Child and Dependent Care Expenses. Print out the *completed Form 2441*.

LO 6.3

9. Mary and John are married and have AGI of $100,000 and two young children. John doesn't work, and they pay $6,000 a year to day care providers so he can shop, clean, and read a little bit in peace. How much child and dependent care credit can Mary and John claim? Why?

LO 6.3

10. Martha has a 3-year-old child and pays $10,000 a year in day care costs. Her salary is $45,000. How much is her child and dependent care credit?

LO 6.3

11. Marty and Jean are married and have 4-year-old twins. Jean is going to school full-time for 9 months of the year, and Marty earns $45,000. The twins are in day care so Jean can go to school while Marty is at work. The cost of day care is $10,000. What is their child and dependent care credit? Please explain your calculation.

____

____

____

LO 6.4

12. Susan is a single taxpayer, 26 years of age, with AGI of $28,000 and no tax-exempt income. She did not have minimum essential coverage for 9 months in 2014. Compute Susan's individual shared responsibility payment for 2014.

LO 6.4 13. Susan and Stan Collins live in Iowa, are married and have two children ages 6 and 10. In 2014, Susan's adjusted gross income is $38,000 and Stan's is $12,000 and both are self-employed. They also have $500 in interest income from tax-exempt bonds. The Collins' enrolled in health insurance for all of 2014 through their state exchange but did not elect to have the credit paid in advance. The 2014 year-end Form 1095-A the Collins received from the exchange lists the following information:

Annual premiums	$9,800
Annual premium for the designated silver plan in the state	$10,800

Compute the Collins' premium tax credit for 2014.

LO 6.5 14. What is the reason there are education tax credits in the tax law?

LO 6.5 15. Please explain the difference between the types of education covered by the American Opportunity tax credit and the lifetime learning credit.

LO 6.5 16. Janie graduates from high school in 2014 and enrolls in college in the fall. Her parents pay $4,000 for her tuition and fees.

a. Assuming Janie's parents have AGI of $170,000, what is the American Opportunity tax credit they can claim for Janie?

b. Assuming Janie's parents have AGI of $75,000, what is the American Opportunity tax credit they can claim for Janie? ______

LO 6.5 17. Jasper is single and is a computer software consultant with a college degree. He feels that one of the reasons for his success is that he continually updates his knowledge by taking classes at the local college in various areas related to software design and information technology. This year he spent $2,000 on course tuition and fees.

a. Assuming Jasper has AGI of $92,000, how much lifetime learning credit can Jasper claim on his tax return? Would the answer be different if Jasper were married and supporting a wife who was not working?

b. Assuming Jasper has AGI of $45,000, how much lifetime learning credit can Jasper claim on his tax return?

LO 6.6

18. Martha and Lew are married taxpayers with $400 of foreign tax withholding from dividends in a mutual fund. They have enough foreign income from the mutual fund to claim the full $400 as a foreign tax credit. Their tax bracket is 25 percent and they itemize deductions. Should they claim the foreign tax credit or a deduction for foreign taxes on their Schedule A? Why?

____

____

____

LO 6.7

19. Carl and Jenny adopt a Russian orphan. The adoption takes 2 years and two trips to Russia and is finalized in 2014. They pay $6,000 in 2013 and $7,500 in 2014 of qualified adoption expenses. In 2014, Carl and Jenny have AGI of $150,000.
   a. What is the adoption credit Carl and Jenny can claim in 2014?

   $__________

   b. How much credit could they claim if the adoption falls through and is never finalized?

   ____

   c. How much credit could they claim if their AGI was $200,500?

   ____

LO 6.8

20. Mike bought a solar electric pump to heat his pool at a cost of $2,500 in 2014. What is Mike's credit?

   $__________

LO 6.8

21. In 2014, Jeff spends $6,000 on solar panels to heat water for his main home. What is Jeff's credit for his 2014 purchases?

   $__________

LO 6.9

22. Otto and Monica are married taxpayers who file a joint tax return. For the current tax year, they have AGI of $80,300. They have excess depreciation on real estate of $67,500, which must be added back to AGI to arrive at AMTI. The amount of their mortgage interest expense for the year was $25,000, and they made charitable contributions of $7,500. If Otto and Monica's taxable income for the current year is $40,000, determine the amount of their AMTI.

____

LO 6.9

23. List two common deductions which are allowed for regular tax purposes but are not deductible for AMT purposes.

____

____

LO 6.9

24. Although the AMT is meant to prevent high-income taxpayers from using tax shelters to avoid paying tax, why might married taxpayers with several children living in a state with high state income taxes and property taxes (e.g., California or New York) find themselves paying AMT?

____

____

____

LO 6.9

25. Why has the AMT become a controversial tax in recent years?

____

____

____

SCHEDULE EIC
(Form 1040A or 1040)

Department of the Treasury
Internal Revenue Service (99)

Earned Income Credit

Qualifying Child Information

▶ **Complete and attach to Form 1040A or 1040 only if you have a qualifying child.**

▶ **Information about Schedule EIC (Form 1040A or 1040) and its instructions is at *www.irs.gov/scheduleeic*.**

OMB No. 1545-0074

2014

Attachment Sequence No. **43**

Name(s) shown on return | **Your social security number**

DRAFT AS OF June 3, 2014 DO NOT FILE

Before you begin:

- See the instructions for Form 1040A, lines 42a and 42b, or Form 1040, lines 66a and 66b, to make sure that **(a)** you can take the EIC, and **(b)** you have a qualifying child.
- Be sure the child's name on line 1 and social security number (SSN) on line 2 agree with the child's social security card. Otherwise, at the time we process your return, we may reduce or disallow your EIC. If the name or SSN on the child's social security card is not correct, call the Social Security Administration at 1-800-772-1213.

CAUTION

- *If you take the EIC even though you are not eligible, you may not be allowed to take the credit for up to 10 years. See the instructions for details.*
- *It will take us longer to process your return and issue your refund if you do not fill in all lines that apply for each qualifying child.*

Qualifying Child Information	**Child 1**	**Child 2**	**Child 3**
1 Child's name If you have more than three qualifying children, you have to list only three to get the maximum credit.	First name / Last name	First name / Last name	First name / Last name
2 Child's SSN The child must have an SSN as defined in the instructions for Form 1040A, lines 42a and 42b, or Form 1040, lines 66a and 66b, unless the child was born and died in 2014. If your child was born and died in 2014 and did not have an SSN, enter "Died" on this line and attach a copy of the child's birth certificate, death certificate, or hospital medical records.			
3 Child's year of birth	Year ___ ___ ___ ___ *If born after 1995 **and** the child is younger than you (or your spouse, if filing jointly), skip lines 4a and 4b; go to line 5.*	Year ___ ___ ___ ___ *If born after 1995 **and** the child is younger than you (or your spouse, if filing jointly), skip lines 4a and 4b; go to line 5.*	Year ___ ___ ___ ___ *If born after 1995 **and** the child is younger than you (or your spouse, if filing jointly), skip lines 4a and 4b; go to line 5.*
4 a Was the child under age 24 at the end of 2014, a student, and younger than you (or your spouse, if filing jointly)?	☐ **Yes.** *Go to line 5.* ☐ **No.** *Go to line 4b.*	☐ **Yes.** *Go to line 5.* ☐ **No.** *Go to line 4b.*	☐ **Yes.** *Go to line 5.* ☐ **No.** *Go to line 4b.*
b Was the child permanently and totally disabled during any part of 2014?	☐ **Yes.** *Go to line 5.* ☐ **No.** The child is not a qualifying child.	☐ **Yes.** *Go to line 5.* ☐ **No.** The child is not a qualifying child.	☐ **Yes.** *Go to line 5.* ☐ **No.** The child is not a qualifying child.
5 Child's relationship to you (for example, son, daughter, grandchild, niece, nephew, foster child, etc.)			
6 Number of months child lived with you in the United States during 2014 • If the child lived with you for more than half of 2014 but less than 7 months, enter "7." • If the child was born or died in 2014 and your home was the child's home for more than half the time he or she was alive during 2014, enter "12."	______ months *Do not enter more than 12 months.*	______ months *Do not enter more than 12 months.*	______ months *Do not enter more than 12 months.*

For Paperwork Reduction Act Notice, see your tax return instructions. Cat. No. 13339M **Schedule EIC (Form 1040A or 1040) 2014**

Worksheet A—2014 EIC—Lines 66a and 66b

Keep for Your Records

Before you begin: √ Be sure you are using the correct worksheet. Use this worksheet only if you answered "No" to Step 5, question 2. Otherwise, use Worksheet B.

RAFT AS OF
ctober 8, 2014

Part 1

All Filers Using Worksheet A

1. Enter your earned income from Step 5. *(Wages, Salaries)* — **1** [ ]

2. Look up the amount on line 1 above in the EIC Table (right after Worksheet B) to find the credit. Be sure you use the correct column for your filing status and the number of children you have. Enter the credit here. — **2** [ ]

   If line 2 is zero, STOP You cannot take the credit. Enter "No" on the dotted line next to line 66a.

3. Enter the amount from Form 1040, line 38. *(Adjusted Gross Income)* — **3** [ ]

4. Are the amounts on lines 3 and 1 the same?

   ☐ **Yes.** Skip line 5; enter the amount from line 2 on line 6.

   ☐ **No.** Go to line 5.

Part 2

Filers Who Answered "No" on Line 4

5. If you have:
   - No qualifying children, is the amount on line 3 less than $8,150 ($13,550 if married filing jointly)?
   - 1 or more qualifying children, is the amount on line 3 less than $17,850 ($23,300 if married filing jointly)?

   ☐ **Yes.** Leave line 5 blank; enter the amount from line 2 on line 6.

   ☐ **No.** Look up the amount on line 3 in the EIC Table to find the credit. Be sure you use the correct column for your filing status and the number of children you have. Enter the credit here. — **5** [ ]
   Look at the amounts on lines 5 and 2.
   Then, enter the **smaller** amount on line 6.

Part 3

Your Earned Income Credit

6. **This is your earned income credit.** — **6** [ ]

   Enter this amount on Form 1040, line 66a.

Reminder—

√ If you have a qualifying child, complete and attach Schedule EIC.

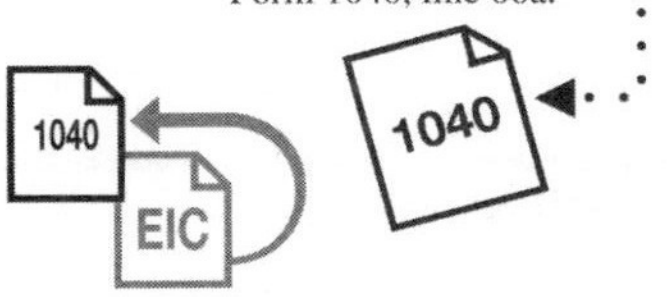

CAUTION — *If your EIC for a year after 1996 was reduced or disallowed, see* Form 8862, who must file, *earlier, to find out if you must file Form 8862 to take the credit for 2014.*

LO 6.9 26. What are the two tax rates which are used to calculate AMT, ignoring the special treatment of dividends and capital gains?

____

LO 6.9 27. Show the simplified formula for calculating AMT. Do not show tax rates or an exemption amount.

____

____

____

____

____

____

____

____

LO 6.10 28. Explain the purpose of the provision in the tax law that taxes unearned income of certain minor children at their parents' tax rates.

____

____

____

LO 6.10 29. Brian and Kim have a 12-year-old child, Stan. For 2014, Brian and Kim have taxable income of $52,000, and Stan has nonqualifying dividend income of $4,500 and investment expenses of $250. No election is made to include Stan's income on Brian and Kim's return.

a. For purposes of the parental tax, calculate Stan's net unearned income. $________

b. Calculate the amount of Stan's parental tax. $________

c. Calculate Stan's total tax for 2014. $________

LO 6.10 30. Nikkie and Jean have two children, Richard (age 4) and Roberta (age 3). For purposes of the parental tax, Richard has net unearned income of $6,000 and Roberta has net unearned income of $4,000. Assuming that their total parental tax for 2014 is $2,400, allocate the total parental tax to Richard and Roberta.

a. Richard's parental tax $________

b. Roberta's parental tax $________

LO 6.10 31. Explain the two different ways that the tax on unearned income of minor children, or "kiddie tax," can be reported.

____

____

____

LO 6.10 32. Does the tax on unearned income of minor children, or "kiddie tax," apply to wages earned by minors in summer and other jobs?

____

____

____

LO 6.11

33. Go to the IRS website (**www.irs.gov**) and determine which IRS publication addresses the topic of community property. Print out the page with the *Table of Contents of this IRS publication.*

LO 6.11

34. Cindy and Paul are married and live together in Arizona. During the year, Paul receives a salary of $45,000 and $4,000 of dividends from stock that is his separate property. Cindy receives a salary of $27,000. Cindy and Paul receive $1,500 in interest income from a savings account that was established with community funds.
    a. If Cindy and Paul file separate income tax returns, what amount of income must each report?

       Cindy $__________
       Paul $__________

    b. If Cindy and Paul lived in Louisiana instead of Arizona, what amount of income would each report on separate income tax returns?

       Cindy $__________
       Paul $__________

GROUP 3: WRITING ASSIGNMENT

RESEARCH

Your supervisor has asked you to research the following situation concerning Scott and Heather Moore. Scott and Heather are married and file a joint return. Scott works full-time as a wildlife biologist, and Heather is a full-time student enrolled at Online University. Scott's earned income for the year is $36,000. Heather does not have a job and concentrates solely on her schoolwork. The university she is enrolled in offers courses only through the Internet. Scott and Heather have one child, Elizabeth (age 8), and pay $3,000 for child care expenses during the year.

Required: Go to the IRS website **(www.irs.gov)**. Locate and review Publication 503. Write a file memorandum stating the amount of child and dependent care credit that Scott and Heather Moore can claim. (An example of a file memorandum is available at the website for this text located at **www.cengagebrain.com.**)

GROUP 4: COMPREHENSIVE PROBLEMS

1. David and Darlene Jasper have one child, Sam, who is 6 years old. The Jaspers reside at 4639 Honeysuckle Lane, Los Angeles, CA 90248. David's Social Security number is 577-11-3311, Darlene's is 477-98-4731, and Sam's is 589-22-1142. David and Darlene's earnings and withholdings for 2014 are:

David:	Earnings from Apple Company (office manager)	$25,000
	Federal income tax withheld	2,800
	State income tax withheld	1,050
Darlene:	Earnings from Rose Company (perfume tester)	$24,500
	Federal income tax withheld	2,650
	State income tax withheld	900

Their other income includes interest from Pine Tree Savings and Loan of $1,900. Other information and expenditures for 2014 are as follows:

Interest:	On home acquisition mortgage	$11,125
	Credit card	925
Taxes:	Property taxes on personal residence	1,515
	State income taxes paid in 2014 (for 2013)	315
Contribution (with written acknowledgement) to church		410
Medical insurance		475
Medical and dental expenses		2,800
Income tax return preparation fee paid in 2014		200
Payment of union dues		225
Child care for Sam		3,500

Required: Complete the Jaspers' federal tax return for 2014. Use Form 1040, Schedule A, Schedule B, and Form 2441, on Pages 6-53 through 6-57. Make realistic assumptions about any missing data.

2A. Steve Jackson (age 51) is a single taxpayer living at 3215 Pacific Dr., Del Mar, CA 92014. His Social Security number is 465-88-9415. In 2014, Steve's earnings and income tax withholding as the manager of a local hotel are:

Earnings from the Ocean View Hotel	$120,000
Federal income tax withheld	18,500
State income tax withheld	9,000

Steve's other income includes interest from General Electric bonds of $2,500 and interest on a savings account at Wells Fargo Bank of $3,190. Also, Steve received tax-exempt interest of $29,200 on private activity bonds that is subject to alternative minimum tax.

During the year, Steve paid the following amounts (all of which can be substantiated):

Home mortgage interest	$31,700
Credit card interest	1,760
Auto insurance	900
State income taxes paid in 2014 (for 2012 audit)	12,540
Property taxes on personal residence	6,200
Kaiser HMO premiums	4,800

Other medical expenses	790
CPA fees paid to handle 2012 state audit	7,000
Charitable contributions:	
Girl Scouts	800
San Diego State University (contribution)	10,000
Italian Red Cross	250

Required: Complete Steve's federal tax return for 2014. Use Form 1040, Schedule A, Schedule B, and Form 6251, on Pages 6-59 through 6-64. Make realistic assumptions about any missing data.

2B. Kent Pham, CPA, is a 45-year-old single taxpayer living at 169 Trendie Street, La Jolla, CA 92037. His Social Security number is 865-68-9635. In 2014, Kent's W-2 as the controller of a local corporation showed the following:

Earnings from the Gentry Corporation	$150,000
Federal income tax withheld	25,000
State income tax withheld	14,000

Kent's other income includes interest from GMAC bonds of $3,250 and interest on CDs at The Cove Bank of $4,145. Also, Kent received tax-exempt interest of $37,960 on private activity bonds that is subject to alternative minimum tax.

During the year, Kent paid the following amounts (all of which can be substantiated):

Home mortgage interest	$42,210
Home equity debt interest on loan used to purchase a Lexus	6,800
Credit card interest	2,280
California annual auto registration tax (deductible portion)	770
Auto insurance	1,170
State income taxes paid in 2014 (for 2013)	16,302
Property taxes on personal residence	8,060
Blue Cross premiums	2,340
Other medical expenses	1,025
CPA fees paid to handle 2010 IRS audit	9,100
Charitable contributions:	
Tree-huggers Historical Society (a qualified charity)	1,040
Campanile Educational (a qualified charity)	12,000
Tecaté Orphanage (a Mexican organization)	500

Required: Complete Kent's federal tax return for 2014. Use Form 1040, Schedule A, Schedule B, and Form 6251, on Pages 6-59 through 6-64. Make realistic assumptions about any missing data.

GROUP 5: CUMULATIVE SOFTWARE PROBLEM

The following additional information is available for the Dr. Ivan and Irene Incisor family from Chapters 1–5.

Ivan's grandfather died and left a portfolio of municipal bonds. In 2014, they pay Ivan $80,000 in tax-free interest. Since the bonds are private activity bonds, the $80,000 is a tax preference for purposes of the alternative minimum tax (AMT). Assume for Chapters 6, 7, and 8 that Ivan's federal income tax withholding from his wages is $12,000, not $6,000.

Required: Combine this new information about the Incisor family with the information from Chapters 1–5 and complete a revised 2014 tax return for Ivan and Irene. Be sure to save your data input files since this case will be expanded with more tax information in later chapters.

Please note: This problem requires the calculation of alternative minimum tax (AMT). The home equity interest of $900 on the purchase of an automobile is not deductible for AMT (see line 4 of Form 6251). Please also note that Page 2 of Form 6251 must be filled in to calculate the lower AMT amount on qualified dividends and that the Saver's Credit still applies.

Form **1040** Department of the Treasury—Internal Revenue Service (99)
U.S. Individual Income Tax Return **2014** OMB No. 1545-0074 IRS Use Only—Do not write or staple in this space.

For the year Jan. 1–Dec. 31, 2014, or other tax year beginning , 2014, ending , 20 See separate instructions.

Your first name and initial	Last name	**Your social security number**
If a joint return, spouse's first name and initial	Last name	**Spouse's social security number**
Home address (number and street). If you have a P.O. box, see instructions.	Apt. no.	▲ Make sure the SSN(s) above and on line 6c are correct.
City, town or post office, state, and ZIP code. If you have a foreign address, also complete spaces below (see instructions).		**Presidential Election Campaign** Check here if you, or your spouse if filing jointly, want $3 to go to this fund. Checking a box below will not change your tax or refund. ☐ You ☐ Spouse
Foreign country name	Foreign province/state/county / Foreign postal code	

Filing Status

Check only one box.

1 ☐ Single
2 ☐ Married filing jointly (even if only one had income)
3 ☐ Married filing separately. Enter spouse's SSN above and full name here. ▶
4 ☐ Head of household (with qualifying person). (See instructions.) If the qualifying person is a child but not your dependent, enter this child's name here. ▶
5 ☐ Qualifying widow(er) with dependent child

Exemptions

6a ☐ **Yourself.** If someone can claim you as a dependent, **do not** check box 6a
b ☐ **Spouse**
} Boxes checked on 6a and 6b

c **Dependents:**

(1) First name Last name	(2) Dependent's social security number	(3) Dependent's relationship to you	(4) ✓ if child under age 17 qualifying for child tax credit (see instructions)
			☐
			☐
			☐
			☐

If more than four dependents, see instructions and check here ▶ ☐

No. of children on 6c who:
• lived with you
• did not live with you due to divorce or separation (see instructions)
Dependents on 6c not entered above

d Total number of exemptions claimed

Add numbers on lines above ▶

Income

Attach Form(s) W-2 here. Also attach Forms W-2G and 1099-R if tax was withheld.

If you did not get a W-2, see instructions.

Line	Description		
7	Wages, salaries, tips, etc. Attach Form(s) W-2		7
8a	**Taxable** interest. Attach Schedule B if required		8a
b	**Tax-exempt** interest. **Do not** include on line 8a	8b	
9a	Ordinary dividends. Attach Schedule B if required		9a
b	Qualified dividends	9b	
10	Taxable refunds, credits, or offsets of state and local income taxes		10
11	Alimony received		11
12	Business income or (loss). Attach Schedule C or C-EZ		12
13	Capital gain or (loss). Attach Schedule D if required. If not required, check here ▶ ☐		13
14	Other gains or (losses). Attach Form 4797		14
15a	IRA distributions 15a	b Taxable amount	15b
16a	Pensions and annuities 16a	b Taxable amount	16b
17	Rental real estate, royalties, partnerships, S corporations, trusts, etc. Attach Schedule E		17
18	Farm income or (loss). Attach Schedule F		18
19	Unemployment compensation		19
20a	Social security benefits 20a	b Taxable amount	20b
21	Other income. List type and amount		21
22	Combine the amounts in the far right column for lines 7 through 21. This is your **total income** ▶		22

DRAFT AS OF August 28, 20 DO NOT FILE

Adjusted Gross Income

Line	Description		
23	Reserved	23	
24	Certain business expenses of reservists, performing artists, and fee-basis government officials. Attach Form 2106 or 2106-EZ	24	
25	Health savings account deduction. Attach Form 8889	25	
26	Moving expenses. Attach Form 3903	26	
27	Deductible part of self-employment tax. Attach Schedule SE	27	
28	Self-employed SEP, SIMPLE, and qualified plans	28	
29	Self-employed health insurance deduction	29	
30	Penalty on early withdrawal of savings	30	
31a	Alimony paid b Recipient's SSN ▶	31a	
32	IRA deduction	32	
33	Student loan interest deduction	33	
34	Reserved	34	
35	Domestic production activities deduction. Attach Form 8903	35	
36	Add lines 23 through 35		36
37	Subtract line 36 from line 22. This is your **adjusted gross income** ▶		37

For Disclosure, Privacy Act, and Paperwork Reduction Act Notice, see separate instructions. Cat. No. 11320B Form **1040** (2014)

Form 1040 (2014) Page **2**

Tax and Credits

Line	Description			Line	Amount
38	Amount from line 37 (adjusted gross income)			38	
39a	Check if: ☐ **You** were born before January 2, 1950, ☐ Blind. / ☐ **Spouse** was born before January 2, 1950, ☐ Blind. } **Total boxes checked ▶ 39a** ☐				
b	If your spouse itemizes on a separate return or you were a dual-status alien, check here ▶ **39b** ☐				
40	**Itemized deductions** (from Schedule A) **or** your **standard deduction** (see left margin)			40	
41	Subtract line 40 from line 38			41	
42	**Exemptions.** If line 38 is $152,525 or less, multiply $3,950 by the number on line 6d. Otherwise, see instructions			42	
43	**Taxable income.** Subtract line 42 from line 41. If line 42 is more than line 41, enter -0-			43	
44	**Tax** (see instructions). Check if any from: **a** ☐ Form(s) 8814 **b** ☐ Form 4972 **c** ☐			44	
45	**Alternative minimum tax** (see instructions). Attach Form 6251			45	
46	Excess advance premium tax credit repayment. Attach Form 8962			46	
47	Add lines 44, 45, and 46 ▶			47	
48	Foreign tax credit. Attach Form 1116 if required	48			
49	Credit for child and dependent care expenses. Attach Form 2441	49			
50	Education credits from Form 8863, line 19	50			
51	Retirement savings contributions credit. Attach Form 8880	51			
52	Child tax credit. Attach Schedule 8812, if required	52			
53	Residential energy credit. Attach Form 5695	53			
54	Other credits from Form: **a** ☐ 3800 **b** ☐ 8801 **c** ☐	54			
55	Add lines 48 through 54. These are your **total credits**			55	
56	Subtract line 55 from line 47. If line 55 is more than line 47, enter -0- ▶			56	

Standard Deduction for—
- People who check any box on line 39a or 39b **or** who can be claimed as a dependent, see instructions.
- All others:

Single or Married filing separately, $6,200

Married filing jointly or Qualifying widow(er), $12,400

Head of household, $9,100

Other Taxes

Line	Description			Line	Amount
57	Self-employment tax. Attach Schedule SE			57	
58	Unreported social security and Medicare tax from Form: **a** ☐ 4137 **b** ☐ 8919			58	
59	Additional tax on IRAs, other qualified retirement plans, etc. Attach Form 5329 if required			59	
60a	Household employment taxes from Schedule H			60a	
b	First-time homebuyer credit repayment. Attach Form 5405 if required			60b	
61	Health care: individual responsibility (see instructions) Full-year coverage ☐			61	
62	Taxes from: **a** ☐ Form 8959 **b** ☐ Form 8960 **c** ☐ Instructions; enter code(s)			62	
63	Add lines 56 through 62. This is your **total tax** ▶			63	

Payments

Line	Description			Line	Amount
64	Federal income tax withheld from Forms W-2 and 1099	64			
65	2014 estimated tax payments and amount applied from 2013 return	65			
66a	**Earned income credit (EIC)**	66a			
b	Nontaxable combat pay election **66b**				
67	Additional child tax credit. Attach Schedule 8812	67			
68	American opportunity credit from Form 8863, line 8	68			
69	Net premium tax credit. Attach Form 8962	69			
70	Amount paid with request for extension to file	70			
71	Excess social security and tier 1 RRTA tax withheld	71			
72	Credit for federal tax on fuels. Attach Form 4136	72			
73	Credits from Form: **a** ☐ 2439 **b** Reserved **c** Reserved **d** ☐	73			
74	Add lines 64, 65, 66a, and 67 through 73. These are your **total payments** ▶			74	

If you have a qualifying child, attach Schedule EIC.

Refund

Line	Description			Line	Amount
75	If line 74 is more than line 63, subtract line 63 from line 74. This is the amount you **overpaid**			75	
76a	Amount of line 75 you want **refunded to you.** If Form 8888 is attached, check here ▶ ☐			76a	
▶ b	Routing number ▶ **c** Type: ☐ Checking ☐ Savings				
▶ d	Account number				
77	Amount of line 75 you want **applied to your 2015 estimated tax** ▶	77			

Direct deposit? See instructions.

Amount You Owe

Line	Description			Line	Amount
78	**Amount you owe.** Subtract line 74 from line 63. For details on how to pay, see instructions ▶			78	
79	Estimated tax penalty (see instructions)	79			

Third Party Designee

Do you want to allow another person to discuss this return with the IRS (see instructions)? ☐ **Yes.** Complete below. ☐ **No**

Designee's name ▶ Phone no. ▶ Personal identification number (PIN) ▶

Sign Here

Under penalties of perjury, I declare that I have examined this return and accompanying schedules and statements, and to the best of my knowledge and belief, they are true, correct, and complete. Declaration of preparer (other than taxpayer) is based on all information of which preparer has any knowledge.

Joint return? See instructions. Keep a copy for your records.

Your signature	Date	Your occupation	Daytime phone number
Spouse's signature. If a joint return, **both** must sign.	Date	Spouse's occupation	If the IRS sent you an Identity Protection PIN, enter it here (see inst.)

Paid Preparer Use Only

Print/Type preparer's name	Preparer's signature	Date	Check ☐ if self-employed	PTIN
Firm's name ▶			Firm's EIN ▶	
Firm's address ▶			Phone no.	

www.irs.gov/form1040 Form **1040** (2014)

DRAFT AS OF August 28, 2014 DO NOT FILE

SCHEDULE A (Form 1040)

Department of the Treasury
Internal Revenue Service (99)

Itemized Deductions

▶ **Information about Schedule A and its separate instructions is at *www.irs.gov/schedulea*.**
▶ **Attach to Form 1040.**

OMB No. 1545-0074
2014
Attachment Sequence No. 07

Name(s) shown on Form 1040 | **Your social security number**

DRAFT AS OF August 15, 2014 DO NOT FILE

Section	Line	Description	Box	Amount	Box	Amount
Medical and Dental Expenses		**Caution.** Do not include expenses reimbursed or paid by others.				
	1	Medical and dental expenses (see instructions)	1			
	2	Enter amount from Form 1040, line 38 [2]				
	3	Multiply line 2 by 10% (.10). But if either you or your spouse was born before January 2, 1950, multiply line 2 by 7.5% (.075) instead	3			
	4	Subtract line 3 from line 1. If line 3 is more than line 1, enter -0-			4	
Taxes You Paid	5	State and local a ☐ Income taxes b ☐ RESERVED	5			
	6	Real estate taxes (see instructions)	6			
	7	Personal property taxes	7			
	8	Other taxes. List type and amount ▶	8			
	9	Add lines 5 through 8			9	
Interest You Paid	10	Home mortgage interest and points reported to you on Form 1098	10			
	11	Home mortgage interest not reported to you on Form 1098. If paid to the person from whom you bought the home, see instructions and show that person's name, identifying no., and address ▶	11			
Note. Your mortgage interest deduction may be limited (see instructions).	12	Points not reported to you on Form 1098. See instructions for special rules	12			
	13	RESERVED	13			
	14	Investment interest. Attach Form 4952 if required. (See instructions.)	14			
	15	Add lines 10 through 14			15	
Gifts to Charity	16	Gifts by cash or check. If you made any gift of $250 or more, see instructions	16			
If you made a gift and got a benefit for it, see instructions.	17	Other than by cash or check. If any gift of $250 or more, see instructions. You **must** attach Form 8283 if over $500	17			
	18	Carryover from prior year	18			
	19	Add lines 16 through 18			19	
Casualty and Theft Losses	20	Casualty or theft loss(es). Attach Form 4684. (See instructions.)			20	
Job Expenses and Certain Miscellaneous Deductions	21	Unreimbursed employee expenses—job travel, union dues, job education, etc. Attach Form 2106 or 2106-EZ if required. (See instructions.) ▶	21			
	22	Tax preparation fees	22			
	23	Other expenses—investment, safe deposit box, etc. List type and amount ▶	23			
	24	Add lines 21 through 23	24			
	25	Enter amount from Form 1040, line 38 [25]				
	26	Multiply line 25 by 2% (.02)	26			
	27	Subtract line 26 from line 24. If line 26 is more than line 24, enter -0-			27	
Other Miscellaneous Deductions	28	Other—from list in instructions. List type and amount ▶			28	
Total Itemized Deductions	29	Is Form 1040, line 38, over $152,525? ☐ **No.** Your deduction is not limited. Add the amounts in the far right column for lines 4 through 28. Also, enter this amount on Form 1040, line 40. ☐ **Yes.** Your deduction may be limited. See the Itemized Deductions Worksheet in the instructions to figure the amount to enter.			29	
	30	If you elect to itemize deductions even though they are less than your standard deduction, check here ▶ ☐				

For Paperwork Reduction Act Notice, see Form 1040 instructions. Cat. No. 17145C **Schedule A (Form 1040) 2014**

SCHEDULE B
(Form 1040A or 1040)

Department of the Treasury
Internal Revenue Service (99)

Interest and Ordinary Dividends

▶ Attach to Form 1040A or 1040.
▶ Information about Schedule B and its instructions is at *www.irs.gov/scheduleb*.

OMB No. 1545-0074

2014

Attachment Sequence No. **08**

Name(s) shown on return | **Your social security number**

DRAFT AS OF June 18, 2014 DO NOT FILE

Part I Interest

(See instructions on back and the instructions for Form 1040A, or Form 1040, line 8a.)

Note. If you received a Form 1099-INT, Form 1099-OID, or substitute statement from a brokerage firm, list the firm's name as the payer and enter the total interest shown on that form.

			Amount
1	List name of payer. If any interest is from a seller-financed mortgage and the buyer used the property as a personal residence, see instructions on back and list this interest first. Also, show that buyer's social security number and address ▶	1	
2	Add the amounts on line 1	2	
3	Excludable interest on series EE and I U.S. savings bonds issued after 1989. Attach Form 8815	3	
4	Subtract line 3 from line 2. Enter the result here and on Form 1040A, or Form 1040, line 8a . . . . ▶	4	

Note. If line 4 is over $1,500, you must complete Part III.

Part II Ordinary Dividends

(See instructions on back and the instructions for Form 1040A, or Form 1040, line 9a.)

Note. If you received a Form 1099-DIV or substitute statement from a brokerage firm, list the firm's name as the payer and enter the ordinary dividends shown on that form.

			Amount
5	List name of payer ▶	5	
6	Add the amounts on line 5. Enter the total here and on Form 1040A, or Form 1040, line 9a . . . . ▶	6	

Note. If line 6 is over $1,500, you must complete Part III.

Part III Foreign Accounts and Trusts

(See instructions on back.)

You must complete this part if you **(a)** had over $1,500 of taxable interest or ordinary dividends; **(b)** had a foreign account; or **(c)** received a distribution from, or were a grantor of, or a transferor to, a foreign trust.

		Yes	**No**
7a	At any time during 2014, did you have a financial interest in or signature authority over a financial account (such as a bank account, securities account, or brokerage account) located in a foreign country? See instructions		
	If "Yes," are you required to file FinCEN Form 114, Report of Foreign Bank and Financial Accounts (FBAR), to report that financial interest or signature authority? See FinCEN Form 114 and its instructions for filing requirements and exceptions to those requirements		
b	If you are required to file FinCEN Form 114, enter the name of the foreign country where the financial account is located ▶		
8	During 2014, did you receive a distribution from, or were you the grantor of, or transferor to, a foreign trust? If "Yes," you may have to file Form 3520. See instructions on back		

For Paperwork Reduction Act Notice, see your tax return instructions. Cat. No. 17146N **Schedule B (Form 1040A or 1040) 2014**

Form **2441** — Department of the Treasury, Internal Revenue Service (99)

Child and Dependent Care Expenses

▶ Attach to Form 1040, Form 1040A, or Form 1040NR.

▶ Information about Form 2441 and its separate instructions is at *www.irs.gov/form2441*.

1040 / 1040A / 1040NR — 2441

OMB No. 1545-0074 — 2014 — Attachment Sequence No. 21

Name(s) shown on return | **Your social security number**

DRAFT AS OF July 2, 2014 DO NOT FILE

Part I **Persons or Organizations Who Provided the Care—**You **must** complete this part. (If you have more than two care providers, see the instructions.)

1 (a) Care provider's name	(b) Address (number, street, apt. no., city, state, and ZIP code)	(c) Identifying number (SSN or EIN)	(d) Amount paid (see instructions)

Did you receive dependent care benefits? — **No** ▶ Complete only Part II below. — **Yes** ▶ Complete Part III on the back next.

Caution. If the care was provided in your home, you may owe employment taxes. If you do, you cannot file Form 1040A. For details, see the instructions for Form 1040, line 60a, or Form 1040NR, line 59a.

Part II **Credit for Child and Dependent Care Expenses**

2 Information about your **qualifying person(s).** If you have more than two qualifying persons, see the instructions.

(a) Qualifying person's name: First	Last	(b) Qualifying person's social security number	(c) **Qualified expenses** you incurred and paid in 2014 for the person listed in column (a)

3 Add the amounts in column (c) of line 2. **Do not** enter more than $3,000 for one qualifying person or $6,000 for two or more persons. If you completed Part III, enter the amount from line 31 . . . . . **3**

4 Enter your **earned income.** See instructions **4**

5 If married filing jointly, enter your spouse's earned income (if you or your spouse was a student or was disabled, see the instructions); **all others**, enter the amount from line 4 . **5**

6 Enter the **smallest** of line 3, 4, or 5 . . . . . **6**

7 Enter the amount from Form 1040, line 38; Form 1040A, line 22; or Form 1040NR, line 37. . . . . **7**

8 Enter on line 8 the decimal amount shown below that applies to the amount on line 7

If line 7 is: Over	But not over	Decimal amount is	If line 7 is: Over	But not over	Decimal amount is
$0	15,000	.35	$29,000	31,000	.27
15,000	17,000	.34	31,000	33,000	.26
17,000	19,000	.33	33,000	35,000	.25
19,000	21,000	.32	35,000	37,000	.24
21,000	23,000	.31	37,000	39,000	.23
23,000	25,000	.30	39,000	41,000	.22
25,000	27,000	.29	41,000	43,000	.21
27,000	29,000	.28	43,000	No limit	.20

8 X.

9 Multiply line 6 by the decimal amount on line 8. If you paid 2013 expenses in 2014, see the instructions **9**

10 Tax liability limit. Enter the amount from the Credit Limit Worksheet in the instructions. **10**

11 **Credit for child and dependent care expenses.** Enter the **smaller** of line 9 or line 10 here and on Form 1040, line 49; Form 1040A, line 31; or Form 1040NR, line 47 . . . . **11**

For Paperwork Reduction Act Notice, see your tax return instructions. Cat. No. 11862M Form **2441** (2014)

Form **1040** Department of the Treasury—Internal Revenue Service (99)
U.S. Individual Income Tax Return **2014** OMB No. 1545-0074 IRS Use Only—Do not write or staple in this space.

For the year Jan. 1–Dec. 31, 2014, or other tax year beginning , 2014, ending , 20 — See separate instructions.

Your first name and initial	Last name	**Your social security number**
If a joint return, spouse's first name and initial	Last name	**Spouse's social security number**
Home address (number and street). If you have a P.O. box, see instructions.	Apt. no.	▲ Make sure the SSN(s) above and on line 6c are correct.
City, town or post office, state, and ZIP code. If you have a foreign address, also complete spaces below (see instructions).		**Presidential Election Campaign** Check here if you, or your spouse if filing jointly, want $3 to go to this fund. Checking a box below will not change your tax or refund. ☐ You ☐ Spouse
Foreign country name	Foreign province/state/county	Foreign postal code

Filing Status

Check only one box.

1 ☐ Single
2 ☐ Married filing jointly (even if only one had income)
3 ☐ Married filing separately. Enter spouse's SSN above and full name here. ▶
4 ☐ Head of household (with qualifying person). (See instructions.) If the qualifying person is a child but not your dependent, enter this child's name here. ▶
5 ☐ Qualifying widow(er) with dependent child

Exemptions

6a ☐ **Yourself.** If someone can claim you as a dependent, **do not** check box 6a
b ☐ **Spouse**

Boxes checked on 6a and 6b

c **Dependents:**

(1) First name Last name	(2) Dependent's social security number	(3) Dependent's relationship to you	(4) ✓ if child under age 17 qualifying for child tax credit (see instructions)
			☐
			☐
			☐
			☐

If more than four dependents, see instructions and check here ▶ ☐

No. of children on 6c who:
• lived with you
• did not live with you due to divorce or separation (see instructions)
Dependents on 6c not entered above

d Total number of exemptions claimed — **Add numbers on lines above ▶**

Income

Attach Form(s) W-2 here. Also attach Forms W-2G and 1099-R if tax was withheld.

If you did not get a W-2, see instructions.

Line	Description		
7	Wages, salaries, tips, etc. Attach Form(s) W-2		7
8a	**Taxable** interest. Attach Schedule B if required		8a
b	**Tax-exempt** interest. **Do not** include on line 8a	8b	
9a	Ordinary dividends. Attach Schedule B if required		9a
b	Qualified dividends	9b	
10	Taxable refunds, credits, or offsets of state and local income taxes		10
11	Alimony received		11
12	Business income or (loss). Attach Schedule C or C-EZ		12
13	Capital gain or (loss). Attach Schedule D if required. If not required, check here ▶ ☐		13
14	Other gains or (losses). Attach Form 4797		14
15a	IRA distributions 15a	b Taxable amount	15b
16a	Pensions and annuities 16a	b Taxable amount	16b
17	Rental real estate, royalties, partnerships, S corporations, trusts, etc. Attach Schedule E		17
18	Farm income or (loss). Attach Schedule F		18
19	Unemployment compensation		19
20a	Social security benefits 20a	b Taxable amount	20b
21	Other income. List type and amount		21
22	Combine the amounts in the far right column for lines 7 through 21. This is your **total income** ▶		22

DRAFT AS OF August 28, 20[illegible] DO NOT FILE

Adjusted Gross Income

Line	Description		
23	Reserved	23	
24	Certain business expenses of reservists, performing artists, and fee-basis government officials. Attach Form 2106 or 2106-EZ	24	
25	Health savings account deduction. Attach Form 8889	25	
26	Moving expenses. Attach Form 3903	26	
27	Deductible part of self-employment tax. Attach Schedule SE	27	
28	Self-employed SEP, SIMPLE, and qualified plans	28	
29	Self-employed health insurance deduction	29	
30	Penalty on early withdrawal of savings	30	
31a	Alimony paid b Recipient's SSN ▶	31a	
32	IRA deduction	32	
33	Student loan interest deduction	33	
34	Reserved	34	
35	Domestic production activities deduction. Attach Form 8903	35	
36	Add lines 23 through 35		36
37	Subtract line 36 from line 22. This is your **adjusted gross income** ▶		37

For Disclosure, Privacy Act, and Paperwork Reduction Act Notice, see separate instructions. Cat. No. 11320B Form **1040** (2014)

Form 1040 (2014) Page **2**

Section	Line	Description	Box
	38	Amount from line 37 (adjusted gross income)	38
Tax and Credits	39a	Check if: ☐ **You** were born before January 2, 1950, ☐ Blind. ☐ **Spouse** was born before January 2, 1950, ☐ Blind. } **Total boxes checked ▶ 39a** ☐	
	b	If your spouse itemizes on a separate return or you were a dual-status alien, check here ▶ **39b** ☐	
Standard Deduction for—	40	**Itemized deductions** (from Schedule A) **or** your **standard deduction** (see left margin)	40
• People who check any box on line 39a or 39b **or** who can be claimed as a dependent, see instructions.	41	Subtract line 40 from line 38	41
• All others:	42	**Exemptions.** If line 38 is $152,525 or less, multiply $3,950 by the number on line 6d. Otherwise, see instructions	42
Single or Married filing separately, $6,200	43	**Taxable income.** Subtract line 42 from line 41. If line 42 is more than line 41, enter -0-	43
Married filing jointly or Qualifying widow(er), $12,400	44	**Tax** (see instructions). Check if any from: **a** ☐ Form(s) 8814 **b** ☐ Form 4972 **c** ☐ ______	44
Head of household, $9,100	45	**Alternative minimum tax** (see instructions). Attach Form 6251	45
	46	Excess advance premium tax credit repayment. Attach Form 8962	46
	47	Add lines 44, 45, and 46 ▶	47
	48	Foreign tax credit. Attach Form 1116 if required — 48	
	49	Credit for child and dependent care expenses. Attach Form 2441 — 49	
	50	Education credits from Form 8863, line 19 — 50	
	51	Retirement savings contributions credit. Attach Form 8880 — 51	
	52	Child tax credit. Attach Schedule 8812, if required — 52	
	53	Residential energy credit. Attach Form 5695 — 53	
	54	Other credits from Form: **a** ☐ 3800 **b** ☐ 8801 **c** ☐ — 54	
	55	Add lines 48 through 54. These are your **total credits**	55
	56	Subtract line 55 from line 47. If line 55 is more than line 47, enter -0- ▶	56
Other Taxes	57	Self-employment tax. Attach Schedule SE	57
	58	Unreported social security and Medicare tax from Form: **a** ☐ 4137 **b** ☐ 8919	58
	59	Additional tax on IRAs, other qualified retirement plans, etc. Attach Form 5329 if required	59
	60a	Household employment taxes from Schedule H	60a
	b	First-time homebuyer credit repayment. Attach Form 5405 if required	60b
	61	Health care: individual responsibility (see instructions) Full-year coverage ☐	61
	62	Taxes from: **a** ☐ Form 8959 **b** ☐ Form 8960 **c** ☐ Instructions; enter code(s)	62
	63	Add lines 56 through 62. This is your **total tax** ▶	63
Payments	64	Federal income tax withheld from Forms W-2 and 1099 — 64	
If you have a qualifying child, attach Schedule EIC.	65	2014 estimated tax payments and amount applied from 2013 return — 65	
	66a	**Earned income credit (EIC)** — 66a	
	b	Nontaxable combat pay election **66b**	
	67	Additional child tax credit. Attach Schedule 8812 — 67	
	68	American opportunity credit from Form 8863, line 8 — 68	
	69	Net premium tax credit. Attach Form 8962 — 69	
	70	Amount paid with request for extension to file — 70	
	71	Excess social security and tier 1 RRTA tax withheld — 71	
	72	Credit for federal tax on fuels. Attach Form 4136 — 72	
	73	Credits from Form: **a** ☐ 2439 **b** Reserved **c** Reserved **d** ☐ — 73	
	74	Add lines 64, 65, 66a, and 67 through 73. These are your **total payments** ▶	74
Refund	75	If line 74 is more than line 63, subtract line 63 from line 74. This is the amount you **overpaid**	75
	76a	Amount of line 75 you want **refunded to you.** If Form 8888 is attached, check here ▶ ☐	76a
Direct deposit? See instructions.	▶ b	Routing number ▶ **c** Type: ☐ Checking ☐ Savings	
	▶ d	Account number	
	77	Amount of line 75 you want **applied to your 2015 estimated tax** ▶ 77	
Amount You Owe	78	**Amount you owe.** Subtract line 74 from line 63. For details on how to pay, see instructions ▶	78
	79	Estimated tax penalty (see instructions) — 79	

Third Party Designee

Do you want to allow another person to discuss this return with the IRS (see instructions)? ☐ **Yes.** Complete below. ☐ **No**

Designee's name ▶ Phone no. ▶ Personal identification number (PIN) ▶

Sign Here

Under penalties of perjury, I declare that I have examined this return and accompanying schedules and statements, and to the best of my knowledge and belief, they are true, correct, and complete. Declaration of preparer (other than taxpayer) is based on all information of which preparer has any knowledge.

Joint return? See instructions. Keep a copy for your records.

Your signature	Date	Your occupation	Daytime phone number
Spouse's signature. If a joint return, **both** must sign.	Date	Spouse's occupation	If the IRS sent you an Identity Protection PIN, enter it here (see inst.)

Paid Preparer Use Only

Print/Type preparer's name	Preparer's signature	Date	Check ☐ if self-employed	PTIN
Firm's name ▶			Firm's EIN ▶	
Firm's address ▶			Phone no.	

www.irs.gov/form1040 Form **1040** (2014)

DRAFT AS OF August 28, 2014 DO NOT FILE

SCHEDULE A (Form 1040)

Department of the Treasury
Internal Revenue Service (99)

Itemized Deductions

▶ Information about Schedule A and its separate instructions is at *www.irs.gov/schedulea*.
▶ Attach to Form 1040.

OMB No. 1545-0074
2014
Attachment Sequence No. 07

Name(s) shown on Form 1040 | **Your social security number**

DRAFT AS OF August 15, 2014 DO NOT FILE

Section	Line	Description	Box	Amount
Medical and Dental Expenses		**Caution.** Do not include expenses reimbursed or paid by others.		
	1	Medical and dental expenses (see instructions)	1	
	2	Enter amount from Form 1040, line 38 [2]		
	3	Multiply line 2 by 10% (.10). But if either you or your spouse was born before January 2, 1950, multiply line 2 by 7.5% (.075) instead	3	
	4	Subtract line 3 from line 1. If line 3 is more than line 1, enter -0-		4
Taxes You Paid	5	State and local: a ☐ Income taxes; b ☐ RESERVED	5	
	6	Real estate taxes (see instructions)	6	
	7	Personal property taxes	7	
	8	Other taxes. List type and amount ▶	8	
	9	Add lines 5 through 8		9
Interest You Paid	10	Home mortgage interest and points reported to you on Form 1098	10	
Note. Your mortgage interest deduction may be limited (see instructions).	11	Home mortgage interest not reported to you on Form 1098. If paid to the person from whom you bought the home, see instructions and show that person's name, identifying no., and address ▶	11	
	12	Points not reported to you on Form 1098. See instructions for special rules	12	
	13	RESERVED	13	
	14	Investment interest. Attach Form 4952 if required. (See instructions.)	14	
	15	Add lines 10 through 14		15
Gifts to Charity	16	Gifts by cash or check. If you made any gift of $250 or more, see instructions	16	
If you made a gift and got a benefit for it, see instructions.	17	Other than by cash or check. If any gift of $250 or more, see instructions. You **must** attach Form 8283 if over $500	17	
	18	Carryover from prior year	18	
	19	Add lines 16 through 18		19
Casualty and Theft Losses	20	Casualty or theft loss(es). Attach Form 4684. (See instructions.)		20
Job Expenses and Certain Miscellaneous Deductions	21	Unreimbursed employee expenses—job travel, union dues, job education, etc. Attach Form 2106 or 2106-EZ if required. (See instructions.) ▶	21	
	22	Tax preparation fees	22	
	23	Other expenses—investment, safe deposit box, etc. List type and amount ▶	23	
	24	Add lines 21 through 23	24	
	25	Enter amount from Form 1040, line 38 [25]		
	26	Multiply line 25 by 2% (.02)	26	
	27	Subtract line 26 from line 24. If line 26 is more than line 24, enter -0-		27
Other Miscellaneous Deductions	28	Other—from list in instructions. List type and amount ▶		28
Total Itemized Deductions	29	Is Form 1040, line 38, over $152,525? ☐ **No.** Your deduction is not limited. Add the amounts in the far right column for lines 4 through 28. Also, enter this amount on Form 1040, line 40. ☐ **Yes.** Your deduction may be limited. See the Itemized Deductions Worksheet in the instructions to figure the amount to enter.		29
	30	If you elect to itemize deductions even though they are less than your standard deduction, check here ▶ ☐		

SCHEDULE B
(Form 1040A or 1040)

Department of the Treasury
Internal Revenue Service (99)

Interest and Ordinary Dividends

▶ **Attach to Form 1040A or 1040.**
▶ **Information about Schedule B and its instructions is at *www.irs.gov/scheduleb*.**

OMB No. 1545-0074
2014
Attachment Sequence No. **08**

Name(s) shown on return | **Your social security number**

DRAFT AS OF June 18, 2014 DO NOT FILE

Part I Interest

(See instructions on back and the instructions for Form 1040A, or Form 1040, line 8a.)

Note. If you received a Form 1099-INT, Form 1099-OID, or substitute statement from a brokerage firm, list the firm's name as the payer and enter the total interest shown on that form.

			Amount
1	List name of payer. If any interest is from a seller-financed mortgage and the buyer used the property as a personal residence, see instructions on back and list this interest first. Also, show that buyer's social security number and address ▶	1	
2	Add the amounts on line 1	2	
3	Excludable interest on series EE and I U.S. savings bonds issued after 1989. Attach Form 8815	3	
4	Subtract line 3 from line 2. Enter the result here and on Form 1040A, or Form 1040, line 8a ▶	4	

Note. If line 4 is over $1,500, you must complete Part III.

Part II Ordinary Dividends

(See instructions on back and the instructions for Form 1040A, or Form 1040, line 9a.)

Note. If you received a Form 1099-DIV or substitute statement from a brokerage firm, list the firm's name as the payer and enter the ordinary dividends shown on that form.

			Amount
5	List name of payer ▶	5	
6	Add the amounts on line 5. Enter the total here and on Form 1040A, or Form 1040, line 9a ▶	6	

Note. If line 6 is over $1,500, you must complete Part III.

Part III Foreign Accounts and Trusts

(See instructions on back.)

You must complete this part if you **(a)** had over $1,500 of taxable interest or ordinary dividends; **(b)** had a foreign account; or **(c)** received a distribution from, or were a grantor of, or a transferor to, a foreign trust.

		Yes	**No**
7a	At any time during 2014, did you have a financial interest in or signature authority over a financial account (such as a bank account, securities account, or brokerage account) located in a foreign country? See instructions		
	If "Yes," are you required to file FinCEN Form 114, Report of Foreign Bank and Financial Accounts (FBAR), to report that financial interest or signature authority? See FinCEN Form 114 and its instructions for filing requirements and exceptions to those requirements		
b	If you are required to file FinCEN Form 114, enter the name of the foreign country where the financial account is located ▶		
8	During 2014, did you receive a distribution from, or were you the grantor of, or transferor to, a foreign trust? If "Yes," you may have to file Form 3520. See instructions on back		

For Paperwork Reduction Act Notice, see your tax return instructions. Cat. No. 17146N **Schedule B (Form 1040A or 1040) 2014**

Form **6251** | **Alternative Minimum Tax—Individuals** | OMB No. 1545-0074

Department of the Treasury
Internal Revenue Service (99)

▶ Information about Form 6251 and its separate instructions is at *www.irs.gov/form6251*.
▶ Attach to Form 1040 or Form 1040NR.

2014
Attachment Sequence No. **32**

Name(s) shown on Form 1040 or Form 1040NR | **Your social security number**

DRAFT AS OF August 4, 2014 DO NOT FILE

Part I Alternative Minimum Taxable Income (See instructions for how to complete each line.)

1	If filing Schedule A (Form 1040), enter the amount from Form 1040, line 41, and go to line 2. Otherwise, enter the amount from Form 1040, line 38, and go to line 7. (If less than zero, enter as a negative amount.)	1	
2	Medical and dental. If you or your spouse was 65 or older, enter the **smaller** of Schedule A (Form 1040), line 4, **or** 2.5% (.025) of Form 1040, line 38. If zero or less, enter -0-	2	
3	Taxes from Schedule A (Form 1040), line 9	3	
4	Enter the home mortgage interest adjustment, if any, from line 6 of the worksheet in the instructions for this line	4	
5	Miscellaneous deductions from Schedule A (Form 1040), line 27	5	
6	If Form 1040, line 38, is $152,525 or less, enter -0-. Otherwise, see instructions	6	( )
7	Tax refund from Form 1040, line 10 or line 21	7	( )
8	Investment interest expense (difference between regular tax and AMT)	8	
9	Depletion (difference between regular tax and AMT)	9	
10	Net operating loss deduction from Form 1040, line 21. Enter as a positive amount	10	
11	Alternative tax net operating loss deduction	11	( )
12	Interest from specified private activity bonds exempt from the regular tax	12	
13	Qualified small business stock (7% of gain excluded under section 1202)	13	
14	Exercise of incentive stock options (excess of AMT income over regular tax income)	14	
15	Estates and trusts (amount from Schedule K-1 (Form 1041), box 12, code A)	15	
16	Electing large partnerships (amount from Schedule K-1 (Form 1065-B), box 6)	16	
17	Disposition of property (difference between AMT and regular tax gain or loss)	17	
18	Depreciation on assets placed in service after 1986 (difference between regular tax and AMT)	18	
19	Passive activities (difference between AMT and regular tax income or loss)	19	
20	Loss limitations (difference between AMT and regular tax income or loss)	20	
21	Circulation costs (difference between regular tax and AMT)	21	
22	Long-term contracts (difference between AMT and regular tax income)	22	
23	Mining costs (difference between regular tax and AMT)	23	
24	Research and experimental costs (difference between regular tax and AMT)	24	
25	Income from certain installment sales before January 1, 1987	25	( )
26	Intangible drilling costs preference	26	
27	Other adjustments, including income-based related adjustments	27	
28	**Alternative minimum taxable income.** Combine lines 1 through 27. (If married filing separately and line 28 is more than $242,450, see instructions.)	28	

Part II Alternative Minimum Tax (AMT)

29 Exemption. (If you were under age 24 at the end of 2014, see instructions.)

IF your filing status is . . .	**AND line 28 is not over . . .**	**THEN enter on line 29 . . .**
Single or head of household	$117,300	$52,800
Married filing jointly or qualifying widow(er)	156,500	82,100
Married filing separately	78,250	41,050

If line 28 is **over** the amount shown above for your filing status, see instructions. — **29**

30	Subtract line 29 from line 28. If more than zero, go to line 31. If zero or less, enter -0- here and on lines 31, 33, and 35, and go to line 34	30	
31	• If you are filing Form 2555 or 2555-EZ, see instructions for the amount to enter. • If you reported capital gain distributions directly on Form 1040, line 13; you reported qualified dividends on Form 1040, line 9b; **or** you had a gain on both lines 15 and 16 of Schedule D (Form 1040) (as refigured for the AMT, if necessary), complete Part III on the back and enter the amount from line 64 here. • **All others:** If line 30 is $182,500 or less ($91,250 or less if married filing separately), multiply line 30 by 26% (.26). Otherwise, multiply line 30 by 28% (.28) and subtract $3,650 ($1,825 if married filing separately) from the result.	31	
32	Alternative minimum tax foreign tax credit (see instructions)	32	
33	Tentative minimum tax. Subtract line 32 from line 31	33	
34	Add Form 1040, line 44 (minus any tax from Form 4972), and Form 1040, line 46. Subtract from the result any foreign tax credit from Form 1040, line 48. If you used Schedule J to figure your tax on Form 1040, line 44, refigure that tax without using Schedule J before completing this line (see instructions)	34	
35	**AMT.** Subtract line 34 from line 33. If zero or less, enter -0-. Enter here and on Form 1040, line 45	35	

For Paperwork Reduction Act Notice, see your tax return instructions. Cat. No. 13600G Form **6251** (2014)

Form 6251 (2014) Page **2**

Part III Tax Computation Using Maximum Capital Gains Rates

Complete Part III only if you are required to do so by line 31 or by the Foreign Earned Income Tax Worksheet in the instructions.

DRAFT AS OF August 4, 2014 DO NOT FILE

Line	Description	Box	Amount
36	Enter the amount from Form 6251, line 30. If you are filing Form 2555 or 2555-EZ, enter the amount from line 3 of the worksheet in the instructions for line 31	36	
37	Enter the amount from line 6 of the Qualified Dividends and Capital Gain Tax Worksheet in the instructions for Form 1040, line 44, or the amount from line 13 of the Schedule D Tax Worksheet in the instructions for Schedule D (Form 1040), whichever applies (as refigured for the AMT, if necessary) (see instructions). If you are filing Form 2555 or 2555-EZ, see instructions for the amount to enter	37	
38	Enter the amount from Schedule D (Form 1040), line 19 (as refigured for the AMT, if necessary) (see instructions). If you are filing Form 2555 or 2555-EZ, see instructions for the amount to enter	38	
39	If you did not complete a Schedule D Tax Worksheet for the regular tax or the AMT, enter the amount from line 37. Otherwise, add lines 37 and 38, and enter the **smaller** of that result or the amount from line 10 of the Schedule D Tax Worksheet (as refigured for the AMT, if necessary). If you are filing Form 2555 or 2555-EZ, see instructions for the amount to enter	39	
40	Enter the **smaller** of line 36 or line 39	40	
41	Subtract line 40 from line 36	41	
42	If line 41 is $182,500 or less ($91,250 or less if married filing separately), multiply line 41 by 26% (.26). Otherwise, multiply line 41 by 28% (.28) and subtract $3,650 ($1,825 if married filing separately) from the result ▶	42	
43	Enter: • $73,800 if married filing jointly or qualifying widow(er), • $36,900 if single or married filing separately, or • $49,400 if head of household.	43	
44	Enter the amount from line 7 of the Qualified Dividends and Capital Gain Tax Worksheet in the instructions for Form 1040, line 44, or the amount from line 14 of the Schedule D Tax Worksheet in the instructions for Schedule D (Form 1040), whichever applies (as figured for the regular tax). If you did not complete either worksheet for the regular tax, enter the amount from Form 1040, line 43; if zero or less, enter -0-. If you are filing Form 2555 or 2555-EZ, see instructions for the amount to enter	44	
45	Subtract line 44 from line 43. If zero or less, enter -0-	45	
46	Enter the **smaller** of line 36 or line 37	46	
47	Enter the **smaller** of line 45 or line 46. This amount is taxed at 0%	47	
48	Subtract line 47 from line 46	48	
49	Enter: • $406,750 if single • $228,800 if married filing separately • $457,600 if married filing jointly or qualifying widow(er) • $432,200 if head of household	49	
50	Enter the amount from line 45	50	
51	Enter the amount from line 7 of the Qualified Dividends and Capital Gain Tax Worksheet in the instructions for Form 1040, line 44, or the amount from line 19 of the Schedule D Tax Worksheet, whichever applies (as figured for the regular tax). If you did not complete either worksheet for the regular tax, enter the amount from Form 1040, line 43; if zero or less, enter -0-. If you are filing Form 2555 or Form 2555-EZ, see instructions for the amount to enter	51	
52	Add line 50 and line 51	52	
53	Subtract line 52 from line 49. If zero or less, enter -0-	53	
54	Enter the smaller of line 48 or line 53	54	
55	Multiply line 54 by 15% (.15) ▶	55	
56	Add lines 47 and 54	56	
	If lines 56 and 36 are the same, skip lines 57 through 61 and go to line 62. Otherwise, go to line 57.		
57	Subtract line 56 from line 46	57	
58	Multiply line 57 by 20% (.20) ▶	58	
	If line 38 is zero or blank, skip lines 59 through 61 and go to line 62. Otherwise, go to line 59.		
59	Add lines 41, 56, and 57	59	
60	Subtract line 59 from line 36	60	
61	Multiply line 60 by 25% (.25) ▶	61	
62	Add lines 42, 55, 58, and 61	62	
63	If line 36 is $182,500 or less ($91,250 or less if married filing separately), multiply line 36 by 26% (.26). Otherwise, multiply line 36 by 28% (.28) and subtract $3,650 ($1,825 if married filing separately) from the result	63	
64	Enter the **smaller** of line 62 or line 63 here and on line 31. If you are filing Form 2555 or 2555-EZ, do not enter this amount on line 31. Instead, enter it on line 4 of the worksheet in the instructions for line 31	64	

Form **6251** (2014)

Student Name ______________________

Class/Section ______________________

Date ______________________

KEY NUMBER TAX RETURN SUMMARY

CHAPTER 6

Comprehensive Problem 1

Adjusted Gross Income (Line 37) ____________

Taxable Income (Line 43) ____________

Credit for Child and Dependent Care (Line 49) ____________

Child Tax Credit (Line 52) ____________

Tax Overpaid (Line 75) ____________

Comprehensive Problem 2A

Adjusted Gross Income (Line 37) ____________

Itemized Deductions (Line 40) ____________

Alternative Minimum Tax (Line 45) ____________

Tax Liability (Line 63) ____________

Tax Overpaid (Line 75) ____________

Comprehensive Problem 2B

Adjusted Gross Income (Line 37) ____________

Itemized Deductions (Line 40) ____________

Alternative Minimum Tax (Line 45) ____________

Tax Liability (Line 63) ____________

Tax Overpaid (Line 75) ____________

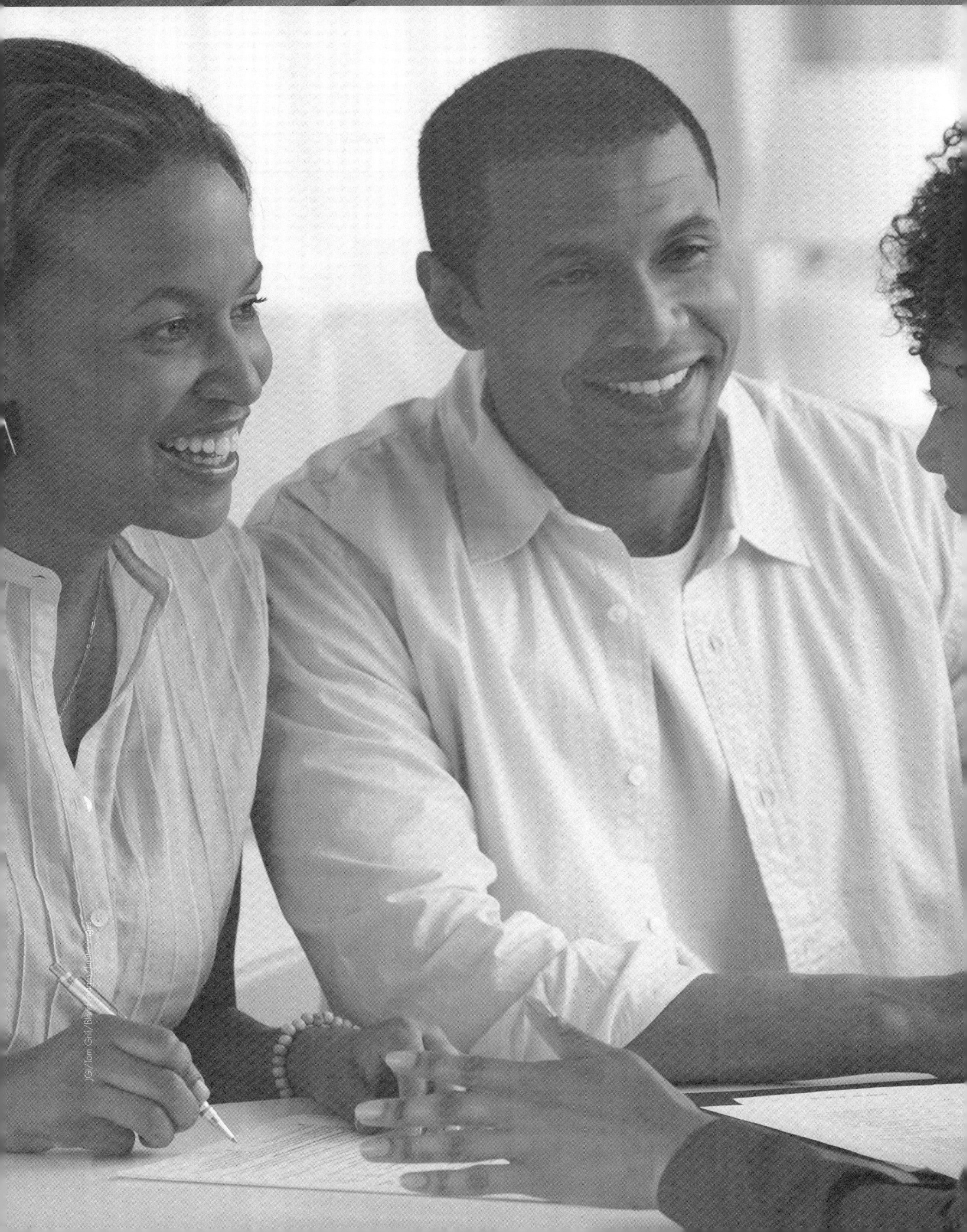
JGI/Tom Grill/Blend

CHAPTER 7

Accounting Periods and Methods and Depreciation

LEARNING OBJECTIVES

After completing this chapter, you should be able to:

LO 7.1 Determine the different accounting periods allowed for tax purposes.

LO 7.2 Determine the different accounting methods allowed for tax purposes.

LO 7.3 Understand the concept of depreciation.

LO 7.4 Understand the calculation of depreciation expense using the MACRS tables.

LO 7.5 Identify when a Section 179 election to expense the cost of property may be used.

LO 7.6 Apply the limitations placed on depreciation of "listed property."

LO 7.7 Apply the limitations on depreciation of "luxury automobiles."

LO 7.8 Understand the tax treatment for goodwill and certain other intangibles.

LO 7.9 Determine whether parties are considered related for tax purposes, and classify the tax treatment of certain related-party transactions.

OVERVIEW

Taxpayers operating a business, whether professional, rental, manufacturing, or another activity, should have an understanding of the accounting periods (calendar, fiscal, or short-period tax years) and accounting methods (cash, accrual, or hybrid methods) allowed. This chapter begins by addressing how and when individual, partnership, and corporate taxpayers should report taxable income.

The calculation of depreciation of business assets is also an important issue for most businesses. The Modified Accelerated Cost Recovery System (MACRS) is the tax depreciation method currently in use under U.S. tax law. There are many special depreciation provisions which are discussed in this chapter including bonus depreciation, the election to expense (Section 179), and the limitations on "listed property" and "luxury" automobiles.

The chapter covers the tax treatment of goodwill, going-concern value, covenants not to compete, franchises, trademarks, and other intangibles. Also covered is the limitation on the deduction of losses realized in certain related-party transactions.

Learning Objective 7.1

Determine the different accounting periods allowed for tax purposes.

ACCOUNTING PERIODS

Individual Tax Years

Almost all individuals file tax returns using a calendar-year accounting period. Individuals reporting tax income on a fiscal year other than a calendar year are extremely rare since the tax system is set up to accommodate calendar-year taxpayers. However, there are no restrictions on an individual taking a tax year other than a calendar year. The choice to file on a fiscal year basis must be made with an initial tax return, and books and records must be kept on that basis. An individual may also request IRS approval to change to a fiscal year if certain conditions are met.

Partnership and Corporation Tax Years

Many individual tax returns include the pass-through of income from partnerships, S corporations, and personal service corporations. The income or loss from partnerships and S corporations is passed through on Schedule K-1 to the owners and taxed in the owners' personal tax returns. Partnerships and S corporations are not taxable entities, only reporting entities. Similarly, wages are passed through to doctors, lawyers, accountants, actuaries, and other professionals from personal service corporations owned by them. Many individuals carry on businesses in partnership or corporate entities which comprise a large part of the income shown in their tax returns. Other individuals make investments, including the operation of real estate rental activities, in these entities. Because the pass-through of income and loss from partnerships and corporations plays such a large role in the taxation of many individuals, it is important to understand the rules governing the allowed accounting periods for these entities.

Partnerships and corporations had a great deal of freedom in selecting a tax year in the past. However, Congress decided that this freedom often resulted in an inappropriate deferral of taxable income. For example, if an individual taxpayer has a calendar tax year and receives income from a partnership with a tax year ending September 30, the taxpayer is able to defer 3 months of partnership income for an indefinite period of time. Therefore, the tax law was changed to include provisions that specify the required tax year for many partnerships and corporations, reducing the opportunities for deferring income.

Most partnerships, S corporations, and personal service corporations owned by individual taxpayers now conform to the same calendar-year reporting used by almost all individuals. These entities are allowed a September, October, or November year-end if the owners make an annual cash deposit on behalf of the entity or perform other required calculations to assure the IRS that they are not using the fiscal year to defer the payment of federal taxes. The details of the complex requirements which must be met by entities filing non-calendar tax years are beyond the scope of this text.

Short-Period Taxable Income

If taxpayers have a short year other than their first or last year of operations, they are required to annualize their taxable income to calculate the tax for the short period. The tax liability is calculated for the annualized period and allocated back to the short period.

EXAMPLE Omoto Corporation obtains permission to change from a calendar year to a tax year ending August 31. For the short period, January 1 through

August 31, 2014, the corporation's taxable income was $40,000. Omoto Corporation's tax for the short period is calculated as follows:

Step 1: Annualize the income	$40,000 × 12/8	=	$60,000
Step 2: Tax on annualized income	15% × $50,000	=	$ 7,500
	25% × $10,000	=	2,500
			$10,000
Step 3: Short period tax	$10,000 × 8/12	=	$ 6,667

♦

The calculation of short-year taxable income for individuals requires special adjustments. For example, deductions must be itemized for the short period, and the standard deduction is not allowed. Exemptions must also be prorated for the short period. As a general rule, individual taxpayers rarely change tax years.

Self-Study Problem 7.1 ***See Appendix E for Solutions to Self-Study Problems***

Juniper Corporation has taxable income of $48,000 for the short period ended on October 31, 2014. Calculate Juniper Corporation's short-period tax for the period January 1 through October 31, 2014. (The corporate tax rates are presented in Chapter 1.)

$______________

ACCOUNTING METHODS

Learning Objective 7.2

Determine the different accounting methods allowed for tax purposes.

The tax law requires taxpayers to report taxable income using the method of accounting regularly used by the taxpayer in keeping his or her books, provided the method clearly reflects the taxpayer's income. The cash receipts and disbursements (cash) method, the accrual method, and the hybrid method are accounting methods specifically recognized in the tax law.

The cash receipts and disbursements method of accounting is used by most individuals for their overall method of accounting. Generally, wages, interest and dividend income, capital gains, and personal deductions are accounted for on the cash basis for individuals. Individuals may choose to account for a particular business, such as a sole proprietorship reported on Schedule C, using the accrual or hybrid method of accounting. If a taxpayer has two businesses, a different method of accounting may be used for each. The choice of a tax accounting method is a general rule which will be overridden by tax laws for some items of income and expense. For example, individuals reporting on a cash basis may deduct IRAs or pension contributions which are paid in cash in the year following the deduction, the income from savings bonds may be included in taxable income even though it is not received in cash, and prepaid interest may not be allowed as a deduction in the year paid.

The cash receipts and disbursements method generally results in the recognition of income when it is actually or constructively received; deductions are recognized in the year of payment. Taxpayers on the accrual basis generally recognize income when it is earned, regardless of when it is received, and generally recognize deductions when they are incurred, regardless of when they are paid. Cash basis taxpayers may not use the cash method for all expenses. Tax provisions require cash basis taxpayers to always use the accrual basis for prepayments of interest. Other business expenses such as rent must also follow the accrual method if the prepayment extends substantially (generally 12 months) beyond the end of the tax year. Conversely, accrual basis taxpayers who receive certain types of prepaid income, such as rent in advance, must generally recognize the income on the cash basis.

EXAMPLE On December 1, 2014, Carol entered into a lease on a building for use in her business for $2,000 per month. Under the lease terms, Carol pays 18 months' rent ($36,000) in advance on December 1. Carol may deduct only 1 month's rent ($2,000) for the calendar year ended December 31, 2014 because the prepayment extends substantially beyond the end of the tax year, even though she is a cash basis taxpayer. The remainder of the prepaid rent is deducted at $2,000 per month in 2015 and 2016. The taxpayer receiving the rent must report all $36,000 as income even if he or she is an accrual basis taxpayer. ♦

The accrual method of accounting requires that income be recognized when (1) all events have occurred which fix the right to receive the income, and (2) the amount of income can be estimated with reasonable accuracy. An expense is deductible in the year in which all events have occurred that determine a liability exists and the amount can be estimated with reasonable accuracy. Also, "economic performance" must occur before an accrual basis deduction can be claimed. Economic performance means that all activities related to the incurrence of the liability have been performed. For example, economic performance occurs for the purchase of services when the taxpayer uses the services.

A hybrid method of accounting involves the use of both the cash and accrual methods of accounting. The tax law permits the use of a hybrid method, provided the taxpayer's income is clearly reflected by the method. An example of a hybrid method is the use of the accrual method for cost of products sold by the business and the use of the cash method for income and other expenses.

Taxpayers make an election to use an accounting method when they file an initial tax return and use that method. To change methods, taxpayers must obtain permission from the IRS.

TAX BREAK

The cash method allows a certain amount of flexibility in tax planning. Payment of business expenses may be accelerated before year-end to generate additional deductions, if desired. In addition, billings for services may be postponed at year-end so payment will not be received and included in income until the following year. Some itemized deductions such as property taxes, state income taxes, and charitable contributions may also be paid before year-end for an immediate deduction.

Self-Study Problem 7.2A *See Appendix E for Solutions to Self-Study Problems*

Melaleuca, Inc., is an accrual basis taxpayer with the following transactions during the calendar tax year:

Accrual business income (except rent and interest)	$63,000
Accrual business expenses (except rent)	42,000
Three months' rent received on a leased building on November 1 of this year	9,000
Prepaid interest for 1 year received on a note on July 1 of the current year	12,000
Six months' rent paid on December 1 for business property	7,200
Calculate Melaleuca, Inc.'s, net income for this year.	$________

Restrictions on the Use of the Cash Method

The tax law contains certain restrictions on use of the cash method of accounting. Regular corporations, partnerships that have a regular corporation as a partner, and tax-exempt

trusts with unrelated business income are generally prohibited from using the cash method. However, this requirement does not apply to farming businesses, qualified personal service corporations, and entities with average annual gross receipts of $5,000,000 or less.

EXAMPLE Orange Associates is a manufacturer of panty hose with gross receipts of $25,000,000. Orange is a partnership which has Lemon Corporation as one of its partners. Orange would not be allowed to use the cash method of accounting for tax purposes. ♦

Would You Believe?

The IRS will pay informants cash rewards based on the value of the information they furnish and the amount recovered from the target of the investigation. The official IRS form for snitching is Form 211, "Application for Reward for Original Information." Informants may receive up to 30 percent of what the IRS eventually collects as a result of the information provided. An Internet-based business at **http://taxsqueal.com** will forward tips to the IRS for people who wish to report on tax cheats but remain anonymous. In 2012, the IRS paid a former banker $104 million for providing insider information regarding secret offshore accounts. This award is believed to be the largest IRS whistle-blower award ever granted.

Self-Study Problem 7.2B *See Appendix E for Solutions to Self-Study Problems*

Indicate whether or not each of the following entities may use the cash method for tax purposes during 2014.

	Yes or No
1. A corporation engaged in orange farming.	________
2. A dentist with a personal service corporation.	________
3. A corporate car dealer with sales of $8,000,000 per year.	________
4. A corporation engaged in certified public accounting.	________

DEPRECIATION

Learning Objective 7.3
Understand the concept of depreciation.

Since many assets are used in the production of income over a number of years, income is not properly measured if the entire cost of these assets is deducted in the year the assets are purchased. Depreciation is the accounting process of allocating and deducting the cost of an asset over a period of years. The term *depreciation* does not necessarily mean physical deterioration or loss of value of the asset. In fact, in some cases the value of the asset may increase while it is being depreciated. Certain assets, such as land, cannot be depreciated for tax purposes. Under U.S. tax law, land is considered to be an asset that is not subject to obsolescence. These assets remain on the taxpayer's records at their original cost.

It is important to distinguish maintenance expenses from depreciation. Depreciation expense is the deduction of a portion of the original cost of the asset, whereas maintenance expenses are those expenditures incurred to keep the asset in good operating order. For example, a taxpayer who purchases a truck for use in his business depreciates the cost of the truck over a period of years. Maintenance costs such as tires and repairs are deducted in the year they are incurred.

The simplest method of depreciation is the straight-line method. Use of the straight-line method results in an equal portion of the cost being deducted in each period of the asset's life. Straight-line depreciation expense is calculated by dividing the cost by the asset's estimated useful life. The formula is:

$$\frac{\text{Cost}}{\text{Estimated useful life}} = \text{Depreciation for the period}$$

EXAMPLE Wilson purchases an asset for use in his business. The asset cost $14,400 on October 1, 20X1, and has a 3-year (36-month) useful life. Depreciation is calculated as follows:

$$\frac{\$14{,}400}{36 \text{ months}} = \$400 \text{ per month}$$

The depreciation for each year is displayed in the following table:

Year	***Months***	***Rate***	***Depreciation Deduction***
20X1	3	$400	$ 1,200
20X2	12	400	4,800
20X3	12	400	4,800
20X4	9	400	3,600
Total depreciation deduction			$14,400

At the end of 36 months, the asset has a basis of $0. ♦

The calculation of depreciation expense for tax purposes involves certain conventions and limitations which are not reflected in the previous example. The example is intended to illustrate the *concept* of depreciation expense as an allocation of the cost of an asset over the asset's estimated useful life. If more information is needed about depreciation, see any standard financial accounting textbook.

The regular straight-line depreciation method described above may be used for financial accounting purposes and for calculating tax depreciation expense on assets acquired before 1981. The tax depreciation rules for assets acquired after 1980 are described in the following sections.

Self-Study Problem 7.3 ***See Appendix E for Solutions to Self-Study Problems***

On March 1, 20X1, Jack purchases office equipment for use in his business. The equipment cost $3,500 and has a 5-year (60-month) estimated useful life. Calculate the depreciation expense for the following years, assuming the regular straight-line depreciation method (used for financial accounting purposes or for pre-1981 assets) is used.

Year	***Depreciation Deduction***
20X1	$________
20X2	$________
20X3	$________
20X4	$________
20X5	$________
20X6	$________
Total	$________

MODIFIED ACCELERATED COST RECOVERY SYSTEM (MACRS)

Learning Objective 7.4

Understand the calculation of depreciation expense using the MACRS tables.

For tax years after 1980, modifications in the tax law were made to encourage capital investment. As a major part of this tax law change, the Accelerated Cost Recovery System (ACRS) was enacted and later modified in 1986 to become the current tax depreciation system referred to as the Modified Accelerated Cost Recovery System (MACRS). The current MACRS

TABLE 7.1 RECOVERY PERIODS FOR ASSETS PLACED IN SERVICE AFTER 1986

Recovery Period	Recovery Method	Assets
3-year	200% declining balance	ADR midpoint life of 4 years or less, excluding cars and light trucks.
5-year	200% declining balance	ADR midpoint life of more than 4 years but less than 10 years, cars and light trucks, qualified technological equipment, certain energy property, R&D property, computers, and certain equipment.
7-year	200% declining balance	ADR midpoint life of 10 years or more but less than 16 years and property without an ADR life (e.g., most business furniture and certain equipment).
10-year	200% declining balance	ADR midpoint life of 16 years or more but less than 20 years,including trees and vines.
15-year	150% declining balance	ADR midpoint life of 20 years or more but less than 25 years, including treatment plants and land improvements (sidewalks, roads, fences, and landscaping).
20-year	150% declining balance	ADR midpoint life of 25 years or more, other than real property with an ADR life of 27.5 years or longer and municipal sewers.
27.5-year	Straight-line	Residential rental real estate, elevators, and escalators.
39-year	Straight-line	Other real property purchased generally on or after May 13,1993 (previously 31.5-year straight-line).

© Cengage Learning

system allows taxpayers who invest in capital assets to write off an asset's cost over a period designated in the tax law and to use an accelerated method for depreciation of assets other than real estate. The minimum number of years over which the cost of an asset may be deducted (the recovery period) depends on the type of the property and the year in which the property was acquired. The recovery periods are based on asset depreciation ranges (ADRs) as published by the IRS. A schedule of the recovery periods for assets acquired after 1986 is presented in Table 7.1. The recovery period classification for assets acquired after 1980, but before 1987, differs from the recovery period classification presented in Table 7.1.

Under MACRS, taxpayers calculate the depreciation of an asset using a table which contains a percentage rate for each year of the property's recovery period. The yearly rate is applied to the cost of the asset. The cost of the property to which the rate is applied is not reduced for prior years' depreciation. For personal property (all property except real estate) the percentages in Table 7.2 on the next page apply.

EXAMPLE Assume a taxpayer acquires an asset (5-year class property) in 2014 with a cost basis of $15,000 and uses accelerated depreciation under MACRS. The depreciation expense deduction for each year of the asset's life is calculated (using the percentages in Table 7.2) as follows:

Year	***Percent***		***Cost***		***Deduction***
2014	20.00	×	$15,000	=	$ 3,000
2015	32.00	×	15,000	=	4,800
2016	19.20	×	15,000	=	2,880
2017	11.52	×	15,000	=	1,728
2018	11.52	×	15,000	=	1,728
2019	5.76	×	15,000	=	864
Total	100.00%				$15,000

◆

In the above example, note that even though the asset is a 5-year class property, the cost is written off over a period of 6 tax years. This is due to the convention under MACRS which provides for 6 months of depreciation during the year the asset is first acquired and

TABLE 7.2

Accelerated Depreciation for Personal Property Assuming Half-Year Convention (For Property Placed in Service after December 31, 1986)

Recovery Year	3-Year (200% DB)	5-Year (200% DB)	7-Year (200% DB)	10-Year (200% DB)	15-Year (150% DB)	20-Year (150% DB)
1	33.33	20.00	14.29	10.00	5.00	3.750
2	44.45	32.00	24.49	18.00	9.50	7.219
3	14.81*	19.20	17.49	14.40	8.55	6.677
4	7.41	11.52*	12.49	11.52	7.70	6.177
5		11.52	8.93*	9.22	6.93	5.713
6		5.76	8.92	7.37	6.23	5.285
7			8.93	6.55*	5.90*	4.888
8			4.46	6.55	5.90	4.522
9				6.56	5.91	4.462*
10				6.55	5.90	4.461
11				3.28	5.91	4.462
12					5.90	4.461
13					5.91	4.462
14					5.90	4.461
15					5.91	4.462
16					2.95	4.461
17						4.462
18						4.461
19						4.462
20						4.461
21						2.231

© Cengage Learning

*Switch to straight-line depreciation.

6 months of depreciation during the year the asset is sold or disposed of. This convention is referred to as the *half-year convention* since only one-half of the year of depreciation is allowed in both the year of acquisition and the year of disposition, regardless of the actual acquisition and disposition dates. The half-year convention is built into the rates in Table 7.2.

For property (other than real estate), a taxpayer may elect to use straight-line depreciation instead of the accelerated depreciation rates under MACRS. The taxpayer must use the straight-line MACRS tables for assets for which a straight-line election has been made. The annual percentage rates to be applied to the cost of an asset for which a straight-line election under MACRS has been made are presented in Table 7.3.

EXAMPLE On April 1, 2014, Lori purchased and placed in service a computer for use in her business. The computer cost $18,000 and Lori elects to use straight-line depreciation over 5 years instead of accelerated depreciation under MACRS. The annual deduction for depreciation over the life of the computer is calculated below (the percentages are taken from Table 7.3).

Year	***Percent***		***Cost***		***Deduction***
2014	10.00	×	$18,000	=	$ 1,800
2015	20.00	×	18,000	=	3,600
2016	20.00	×	18,000	=	3,600
2017	20.00	×	18,000	=	3,600
2018	20.00	×	18,000	=	3,600
2019	10.00	×	18,000	=	1,800
Total	100.00%				$18,000

TABLE 7.3

Straight-Line Depreciation for Personal Property, Assuming Half-Year Convention* (For Property Placed in Service after December 31, 1986)

ACRS Class	% First Recovery Year	Other Recovery Years: Years	Other Recovery Years: %	Last Recovery Years: Year	Last Recovery Years: %
3-year	16.67	2–3	33.33	4	16.67
5-year	10.00	2–5	20.00	6	10.00
7-year	7.14	2–7	14.29	8	7.14
10-year	5.00	2–10	10.00	11	5.00
15-year	3.33	2–15	6.67	16	3.33
20-year	2.50	2–20	5.00	21	2.50

© Cengage Learning

*The official table contains a separate row for each year. For ease of presentation, certain years are grouped together in this table. In some instances, this will cause a difference of .01 percent for the last digit when compared with the official table.

Note that Lori receives a deduction based on 6 months in the year of purchase, even though the asset was put into service on April 1. On the other hand, if the asset had been placed into service on September 1, Lori still would have received a deduction for 6 months of depreciation. ♦

Under MACRS, the same method of depreciation (accelerated or straight-line) must be used for all property in a given class placed in service during that year.

Mid-Quarter Convention

When a taxpayer acquires a significant amount of assets during the last quarter of the tax year, the half-year convention, referred to in the above examples, may be replaced with a mid-quarter convention. The mid-quarter convention must be applied if more than 40 percent of the total cost of a taxpayer's property acquired during the year, other than real property, is placed in service during the last 3 months of the tax year. The mid-quarter convention treats all property placed in service during any quarter of the tax year as being placed in service on the midpoint of the quarter. The mid-quarter convention, if applied in the year the asset is acquired, also applies upon the disposition of the asset. Assets placed in service and disposed of during the same tax year are not considered in determining whether the taxpayer meets the 40-percent test. Special tables are available which must be used when the mid-quarter convention applies. These tables may be found at any of the major tax services (such as Commerce Clearing House or Research Institute of America).

EXAMPLE Jane, a calendar-year taxpayer, purchases the following property during 2014 for use in her business:

March 2, 2014	Office furniture	$ 3,000
July 31, 2014	Apartment building	200,000
November 1, 2014	Automobile	18,000

The cost of the automobile acquired during the last 3 months of the year represents 86 percent of the total cost of assets, other than real property, acquired during the tax year. Since more than 40 percent of Jane's purchases, other than real property, were made during the last 3 months of the tax year, the mid-quarter convention would apply and the special tables must be used to calculate depreciation expense for both the office furniture and the automobile acquired during 2014. ♦

Bonus Depreciation for Certain Property—2001 through 2013 Tax Law

Bonus depreciation has been a part of the tax law on and off since September 11, 2001. The bonus depreciation rules have allowed taxpayers purchasing new or original-use property with a MACRS recovery period of 20 years or less (see Table 7.1), water utility property, computer software, and certain leasehold improvements to directly write off between 30 percent and 100 percent of the cost of the assets in the year of purchase. Taxpayers may take 50 percent of the purchase price of the described new property as a deduction for 2013.

Taxpayers are allowed to elect to take a 50-percent bonus depreciation deduction for any specific class of equipment placed in service in 2013, and are also allowed to elect out of bonus depreciation entirely, rather than claim the 50 percent bonus depreciation deduction. A taxpayer might choose to elect out of using bonus depreciation if they have a net operating loss about to expire or anticipate using larger depreciation deductions during higher tax bracket years in the future.

EXAMPLE Mary places a new 5-year MACRS-class machine costing $20,000 into service on March 1, 2013. She elects 50 percent bonus depreciation on the machine. The bonus depreciation on the machine for 2013 is $10,000 ($20,000 × 50%). The MACRS depreciation on the machine is ($20,000 − $10,000) × 20% = $2,000 for total depreciation in 2013 of $10,000 + $2,000 = $12,000. ♦

Note: The first bonus depreciation provisions were signed into law in the aftermath of the September 11, 2001 terrorist attacks, and were designed to help businesses and to stimulate the economy. Between September 11, 2001 and December 31, 2004, taxpayers were allowed to elect first-year bonus depreciation of 30 percent. Alternatively, additional first-year bonus depreciation of 50 percent for qualified assets purchased after May 5, 2003 and by December 31, 2004 could be elected as a deduction. No bonus depreciation was allowed in 2005, 2006, and 2007. Bonus depreciation of 50 percent was allowed for the period beginning in 2008 and ending September 8, 2010. From September 9, 2010 through the end of 2011, the maximum rate was 100 percent. For 2012 and 2013 the rate is 50 percent. At the time we go to print, no bonus depreciation provisions have been extended into 2014. Given the current state of the U.S. economy, it is not likely that Congress will extend these provisions. The law in effect during these prior years is mentioned for reference only since many assets still in service were placed in service during this time period using the bonus depreciation rules.

Real Estate

For real estate acquired before 1981, the annual depreciation expense deduction is calculated under a regular depreciation method, such as the straight-line method discussed in LO 7.3. For real estate acquired after 1980 and before 1987, ACRS deductions were calculated based on class lives of 15, 18, or 19 years depending on the date the property was placed in service. For a complete description of the accelerated ACRS method, as well as the optional straight-line method, in use for real estate acquired after 1980 but before 1987, the taxpayer should refer to any standard tax service (such as CCH IntelliConnect or Thomson Reuters Checkpoint).

For real estate acquired after 1986, MACRS requires the property to be depreciated using the straight-line method. The straight-line MACRS realty tables for residential realty (e.g., an apartment building) provide for depreciation over 27.5 years. Nonresidential realty (e.g., an office building) is depreciated over 39 years (31.5 years for realty acquired generally before May 13, 1993). The annual depreciation percentages for real estate under MACRS are shown in Table 7.4.

TABLE 7.4

Straight-Line Depreciation for Real Property Assuming Mid-Month Convention*

27.5-Year Residential Real Property

The applicable annual percentage is (use the column for the month in the first year the property is placed in service):

Recovery Year(s)	1	2	3	4	5	6	7	8	9	10	11	12
1	3.485	3.182	2.879	2.576	2.273	1.970	1.667	1.364	1.061	0.758	0.455	0.152
2–18	3.636	3.636	3.636	3.636	3.636	3.636	3.636	3.636	3.636	3.636	3.636	3.636
19–27	3.637	3.637	3.637	3.637	3.637	3.637	3.637	3.637	3.637	3.637	3.637	3.637
28	1.970	2.273	2.576	2.879	3.182	3.485	3.636	3.636	3.636	3.636	3.636	3.636
29	0.000	0.000	0.000	0.000	0.000	0.000	0.152	0.455	0.758	1.061	1.364	1.667

39-Year Nonresidential Real Property

The applicable annual percentage is (use the column for the month in the first year the property is placed in service):

Recovery Year(s)	1	2	3	4	5	6	7	8	9	10	11	12
1	2.461	2.247	2.033	1.819	1.605	1.391	1.177	0.963	0.749	0.535	0.321	0.107
2–39	2.564	2.564	2.564	2.564	2.564	2.564	2.564	2.564	2.564	2.564	2.564	2.564
40	0.107	0.321	0.535	0.749	0.963	1.177	1.391	1.605	1.819	2.033	2.247	2.461

© Cengage Learning

*The official tables contain a separate row for each year. For ease of presentation, certain years are grouped together in these two tables. In some instances, this will produce a difference of .001 percent when compared with the official tables.

EXAMPLE Carlos purchases a rental house on September 3, 2014, for $90,000 (the land is accounted for separately). The house is already rented to a tenant. The annual depreciation expense deduction under MACRS for each of the first 4 years is illustrated below (the percentages are taken from Table 7.4, 27.5-Year Residential Real Property).

Year	***Percent***		***Cost***		***Deduction***
2014	1.061	×	$90,000	=	$ 955
2015	3.636	×	90,000	=	3,272
2016	3.636	×	90,000	=	3,272
2017	3.636	×	90,000	=	3,272

Note that the percentages are taken from Table 7.4 under column 9, because the month of acquisition (September) is the ninth month of the year. ♦

Mid-Month Convention

For the depreciation of real property under MACRS, a mid-month convention replaces the half-year convention. Real estate is treated as placed in service in the middle of the month of acquisition. Likewise, a disposition during a month is treated as occurring on the midpoint of such month. For example, under the mid-month convention, an asset purchased and placed in service on April 2 is treated as being placed in service on April 15. The mid-month convention is built into the first year's rates in Table 7.4.

Reporting Depreciation Expense

Depreciation expense is reported on Form 4562, Depreciation and Amortization. Individual taxpayers who have no current year asset additions and who are not reporting depreciation on listed property (see LO 7.6) are not required to file Form 4562 with their return.

TAX BREAK

In 2013, the IRS revised the regulations that help business taxpayers decide whether an item must be capitalized and depreciated or expensed as an ordinary and necessary business expense. As a result of the revision certain "safeharbors" were created to permit taxpayers to expense certain items that may not be material. Non-inventory supplies and materials costing less than $200 may be expensed. In addition, if a small business taxpayer ordinarily expenses tangible goods on their books and records, costing up to $500, the same expense recognition may be adopted for tax purposes. Small businesses may find these an attractive alternative to tracking the purchase and depreciation of insignificant costs.

Self-Study Problem 7.4 ***See Appendix E for Solutions to Self-Study Problems***

During 2014, Mary Moser purchases the following items for use in her business:

Manufacturing equipment (7-year property, purchased August 1)	$ 12,000
Office furniture (7-year property, purchased December 15)	2,000
Office building, land is accounted for separately (purchased March 30)	175,000

Assume that Mary uses the accelerated depreciation method under MACRS.

a. Use Form 4562 on Page 7-15 to report Mary's depreciation deduction for 2014.
b. Calculate Mary's depreciation deduction on the assets for 2015 (Year 2).

	Depreciation Deduction
7-year property	$__________
Office building	$__________

Learning Objective 7.5

Identify when a Section 179 election to expense the cost of property may be used.

ELECTION TO EXPENSE

The Section 179 expense limit and phase-out thresholds had been raised considerably in previous years in an effort to stimulate the economy. For example, the 2013 expense limit was $500,000 and the phase-out started at $2,000,000. As we go to press, there is a high likelihood that Congress will authorize an increase in the Section 179 limits for 2014. Please check the Whittenburg companion website for updates.

Under Internal Revenue Code Section 179, taxpayers may elect to expense a limited amount of the acquisition cost of certain property. This cost would otherwise have to be deducted over a period of time using the regular cost recovery depreciation rules. The Section 179 deduction applies to both new and used property. To qualify for this limited expensing election, the property must be personal property (property other than real estate or assets used in residential real estate rental activities unless certain qualified real estate property, the treatment of which is beyond the scope of this text) placed in service during the year and used in a trade or business. The maximum cost that may be expensed in the year of acquisition is $25,000 for 2014. The $25,000 maximum amount available in 2014 under the election to expense is subject to two limitations. First, the $25,000 maximum is reduced dollar for dollar by the cost of qualifying property placed in service during the year in excess of $200,000. Second, the amount that may be expensed is limited to the taxpayer's

taxable income, before considering any amount expensed under this election, from any trade or business of the taxpayer. Any amount which is limited due to the taxable income limitation may be carried over to succeeding tax years. Due to a return to a relatively low level of expensing permitted under Section 179 in 2014 (see note above), fewer taxpayers are likely to be limited under the income limitation than in recent years.

EXAMPLE During 2014, Bob buys used equipment costing $30,000 for his factory. The first $25,000 of the cost may be expensed in 2014, and the remaining $5,000 may be depreciated over the equipment's recovery period. ♦

EXAMPLE During 2014, Joe purchases used manufacturing equipment for use in his business. The machinery cost is $45,000. Joe has taxable income (after considering any MACRS depreciation) from his business of $22,000. The $25,000 annual maximum may be expensed in 2014. However, the maximum amount that can be expensed is further limited to Joe's income of $22,000. The remaining $3,000 (the $25,000 amount allowable before considering the taxable income limitation, less the $22,000 amount actually allowable) is carried over to succeeding tax years. ♦

A taxpayer who has made the election to expense must reduce the basis of the asset by the amount expensed before calculating regular MACRS depreciation on the remaining cost of the asset. Even if the taxpayer is not able to deduct the full amount expensed in the current year due to the taxable income limitation, the basis must be reduced by the full amount of the expense election.

EXAMPLE On August 1, 2014, Joan purchases a used machine for her business. The machine cost $30,000 and qualifies as 5-year MACRS property. Her business income is $32,000. Joan first claims the full $25,000 deduction under Section 179. Joan then claims regular MACRS depreciation on the machine of $1,000 ($30,000 − $25,000 = $5,000 × 20% = $1,000). Joan's total first-year Section 179 and depreciation deductions related to her $30,000 purchase are $25,000 + $1,000, for a total of $26,000. ♦

When calculating depreciation on an asset, if an election to expense only part of the asset has been made, the amount of the Section 179 election to expense must be decided first. When a taxpayer decides to take only a portion of the cost of the asset as a Section 179 deduction, the rest of the cost of the asset must be depreciated. The depreciation must be deducted from taxable income to determine the income limitation for the Section 179 deduction.

EXAMPLE Scott has taxable income of $24,000 from his sole proprietorship before depreciation. A $50,000 machine was purchased during the year. He elects to expense $20,000 of the machine under Section 179. The remaining $30,000 cost of the machine is depreciated over a 5-year life. The depreciation is $30,000 × 20%, or $6,000. Scott's taxable income after depreciation is $24,000 − $6,000, or $18,000. Only $18,000 of the election to expense can be used in the current year, bringing Scott's income down to zero, and $2,000 will be carried forward to the next year, subject again to the income limitation. Scott will also be able to depreciate the $30,000 not elected as expense under Section 179 for the second year and following years until the $30,000 is fully depreciated. ♦

TAX BREAK

Small-business owners may wish to consider the optimal amount to elect to expense under Section 179 if subject to the income limitation. Consider the example above. If Scott is concerned about his ability to use the carryforward next year, he can elect to expense only $17,500 leaving $32,500 to depreciate over 5 years or $6,500 in the first year. Thus Scott's total cost recovery is $24,000 (same as in example) with no carryforward. Since tax returns are often extended, taxpayers can generally develop a good estimate of next year's income prior to making the 179 expensing election.

Self-Study Problem 7.5 *See Appendix E for Solutions to Self-Study Problems*

On June 15, 2014, Chang purchases used equipment (7-year property) for use in his business. He pays $37,500 for the equipment. For 2014, Chang has $29,000 of taxable income from his business. Calculate the total amount of Chang's depreciation deduction (including both regular depreciation and any deduction allowable under the election to expense) for 2014 for the equipment, assuming he makes the election to expense and his goal is to maximize 2014 deductions.

$__________

Learning Objective 7.6

Apply the limitations placed on depreciation of "listed property."

LISTED PROPERTY

Congress felt some taxpayers were using the favorable tax incentives of the accelerated cost recovery system and the limited expensing election to claim depreciation deductions on assets used for personal purposes. To curtail this perceived abuse of the tax system, Congress enacted special rules which apply to the depreciation of "listed property." "Listed property" includes those types of assets which lend themselves to personal use, including the following:

1. Passenger automobiles, defined to include any four-wheeled vehicle manufactured primarily for use on public streets, roads, and highways, rated at 6,000 pounds or less unloaded gross vehicle weight. Specifically excluded from the definition of passenger automobiles are vehicles used directly in the trade or business of transporting persons or property, ambulances and hearses used in a trade or business, and certain trucks and vans not likely to be used more than a de minimus amount for personal purposes, including vehicles which display the company name or advertising.
2. Other property used as a means of transportation (trucks, buses, boats, airplanes, and motorcycles), except vehicles which are not likely to be used for personal purposes, such as marked police cars, school buses, and tractors, or vehicles used for transporting persons or cargo for compensation.
3. Property generally used for entertainment, recreation, or amusement (video recording equipment, communication equipment, etc.).
4. Computer or peripheral equipment, unless used exclusively at a regular business establishment. This includes computer equipment used at home for partly personal or investment purposes.

If "listed property" is used 50 percent or less in a qualified business use, any depreciation deduction must be calculated using the straight-line method of depreciation over an alternate recovery period, and the special election to expense is not allowed.

Qualified business use does not include investment use or the use of property by an employee in performing services as an employee, unless the use meets the convenience-of-employer and condition-of-employment tests. In addition, the excess depreciation allowed by reason of the property meeting the more-than-50-percent-use test must be included in income if property which meets the test in one year subsequently fails to meet the more-than-50-percent-use test in a succeeding year.

Self-Study Problem 7.4

Form **4562** | **Depreciation and Amortization** (Including Information on Listed Property) | OMB No. 1545-0172

Department of the Treasury Internal Revenue Service (99)

▶ Attach to your tax return.

▶ Information about Form 4562 and its separate instructions is at *www.irs.gov/form4562.*

2014 Attachment Sequence No. **179**

Name(s) shown on return	Business or activity to which this form relates	Identifying number

DRAFT AS OF June 10, 2014 DO NOT FILE

Part I Election To Expense Certain Property Under Section 179

Note: *If you have any listed property, complete Part V before you complete Part I.*

1	Maximum amount (see instructions)	1	
2	Total cost of section 179 property placed in service (see instructions)	2	
3	Threshold cost of section 179 property before reduction in limitation (see instructions)	3	
4	Reduction in limitation. Subtract line 3 from line 2. If zero or less, enter -0-	4	
5	Dollar limitation for tax year. Subtract line 4 from line 1. If zero or less, enter -0-. If married filing separately, see instructions	5	

6	(a) Description of property	(b) Cost (business use only)	(c) Elected cost

7	Listed property. Enter the amount from line 29	7	
8	Total elected cost of section 179 property. Add amounts in column (c), lines 6 and 7	8	
9	Tentative deduction. Enter the **smaller** of line 5 or line 8	9	
10	Carryover of disallowed deduction from line 13 of your 2013 Form 4562	10	
11	Business income limitation. Enter the smaller of business income (not less than zero) or line 5 (see instructions)	11	
12	Section 179 expense deduction. Add lines 9 and 10, but do not enter more than line 11	12	
13	Carryover of disallowed deduction to 2015. Add lines 9 and 10, less line 12 ▶	13	

Note: *Do not use Part II or Part III below for listed property. Instead, use Part V.*

Part II Special Depreciation Allowance and Other Depreciation (Do not include listed property.) (See instructions.)

14	Special depreciation allowance for qualified property (other than listed property) placed in service during the tax year (see instructions)	14	
15	Property subject to section 168(f)(1) election	15	
16	Other depreciation (including ACRS)	16	

Part III MACRS Depreciation (Do not include listed property.) (See instructions.)

Section A

17	MACRS deductions for assets placed in service in tax years beginning before 2014	17	
18	If you are electing to group any assets placed in service during the tax year into one or more general asset accounts, check here ▶ ☐		

Section B—Assets Placed in Service During 2014 Tax Year Using the General Depreciation System

(a) Classification of property	(b) Month and year placed in service	(c) Basis for depreciation (business/investment use only—see instructions)	(d) Recovery period	(e) Convention	(f) Method	(g) Depreciation deduction
19a 3-year property						
b 5-year property						
c 7-year property						
d 10-year property						
e 15-year property						
f 20-year property						
g 25-year property			25 yrs.		S/L	
h Residential rental property			27.5 yrs.	MM	S/L	
			27.5 yrs.	MM	S/L	
i Nonresidential real property			39 yrs.	MM	S/L	
				MM	S/L	

Section C—Assets Placed in Service During 2014 Tax Year Using the Alternative Depreciation System

20a Class life					S/L	
b 12-year			12 yrs.		S/L	
c 40-year			40 yrs.	MM	S/L	

Part IV Summary (See instructions.)

21	Listed property. Enter amount from line 28	21	
22	**Total.** Add amounts from line 12, lines 14 through 17, lines 19 and 20 in column (g), and line 21. Enter here and on the appropriate lines of your return. Partnerships and S corporations—see instructions	22	
23	For assets shown above and placed in service during the current year, enter the portion of the basis attributable to section 263A costs	23	

For Paperwork Reduction Act Notice, see separate instructions. Cat. No. 12906N Form **4562** (2014)

Form 4562 (2014) Page **2**

Part V **Listed Property** (Include automobiles, certain other vehicles, certain aircraft, certain computers, and property used for entertainment, recreation, or amusement.)

Note: *For any vehicle for which you are using the standard mileage rate or deducting lease expense, complete* ***only*** *24a, 24b, columns (a) through (c) of Section A, all of Section B, and Section C if applicable.*

DRAFT AS OF June 10, 2014 DO NOT FILE

Section A—Depreciation and Other Information (Caution: *See the instructions for limits for passenger automobiles.***)**

24a Do you have evidence to support the business/investment use claimed? ☐ **Yes** ☐ **No** **24b** If "Yes," is the evidence written? ☐ **Yes** ☐ **No**

(a) Type of property (list vehicles first)	(b) Date placed in service	(c) Business/ investment use percentage	(d) Cost or other basis	(e) Basis for depreciation (business/investment use only)	(f) Recovery period	(g) Method/ Convention	(h) Depreciation deduction	(i) Elected section 179 cost
25 Special depreciation allowance for qualified listed property placed in service during the tax year and used more than 50% in a qualified business use (see instructions) .						**25**		
26 Property used more than 50% in a qualified business use:								
		%						
		%						
		%						
27 Property used 50% or less in a qualified business use:								
		%				S/L –		
		%				S/L –		
		%				S/L –		
28 Add amounts in column (h), lines 25 through 27. Enter here and on line 21, page 1 .						**28**		
29 Add amounts in column (i), line 26. Enter here and on line 7, page 1							**29**	

Section B—Information on Use of Vehicles

Complete this section for vehicles used by a sole proprietor, partner, or other "more than 5% owner," or related person. If you provided vehicles to your employees, first answer the questions in Section C to see if you meet an exception to completing this section for those vehicles.

	(a) Vehicle 1		(b) Vehicle 2		(c) Vehicle 3		(d) Vehicle 4		(e) Vehicle 5		(f) Vehicle 6	
30 Total business/investment miles driven during the year (**do not** include commuting miles) .												
31 Total commuting miles driven during the year												
32 Total other personal (noncommuting) miles driven												
33 Total miles driven during the year. Add lines 30 through 32												
	Yes	**No**	**Yes**	**No**	**Yes**	**No**	**Yes**	**No**	**Yes**	**No**	**Yes**	**No**
34 Was the vehicle available for personal use during off-duty hours?												
35 Was the vehicle used primarily by a more than 5% owner or related person? . .												
36 Is another vehicle available for personal use?												

Section C—Questions for Employers Who Provide Vehicles for Use by Their Employees

Answer these questions to determine if you meet an exception to completing Section B for vehicles used by employees who **are not** more than 5% owners or related persons (see instructions).

	Yes	**No**
37 Do you maintain a written policy statement that prohibits all personal use of vehicles, including commuting, by your employees?		
38 Do you maintain a written policy statement that prohibits personal use of vehicles, except commuting, by your employees? See the instructions for vehicles used by corporate officers, directors, or 1% or more owners . .		
39 Do you treat all use of vehicles by employees as personal use?		
40 Do you provide more than five vehicles to your employees, obtain information from your employees about the use of the vehicles, and retain the information received?		
41 Do you meet the requirements concerning qualified automobile demonstration use? (See instructions.) . . .		

Note: *If your answer to 37, 38, 39, 40, or 41 is "Yes," do not complete Section B for the covered vehicles.*

Part VI **Amortization**

(a) Description of costs	(b) Date amortization begins	(c) Amortizable amount	(d) Code section	(e) Amortization period or percentage	(f) Amortization for this year
42 Amortization of costs that begins during your 2014 tax year (see instructions):					
43 Amortization of costs that began before your 2014 tax year				**43**	
44 **Total.** Add amounts in column (f). See the instructions for where to report				**44**	

Form **4562** (2014)

EXAMPLE Ellen uses a personal computer in her home to manage her investments. The computer is listed property. Depreciation must be calculated using the straight-line method over an alternate recovery period. ♦

EXAMPLE Oscar has a personal computer at his home which he uses 30 percent of the time to manage his investments and 65 percent of the time in his accounting business. Since Oscar's business-use percentage of 65 percent exceeds 50 percent, Oscar is not required to use the straight-line method in calculating depreciation. The accelerated depreciation method and the election to expense may be used by Oscar. In determining his total depreciation expense for the year, Oscar will consider the combined business and investment use of 95 percent. ♦

Self-Study Problem 7.6 ***See Appendix E for Solutions to Self-Study Problems***

For each of the following independent situations, indicate with a Y (yes) or an N (no) whether or not the taxpayer is required to depreciate the property using the straight-line method over the alternate recovery period:

	Straight-Line Required?
1. Alvarez has a laptop computer which he purchased so he could contact his stockbroker from anywhere and manage his investments more efficiently.	________
2. Laura has a personal computer at her home which she uses 40 percent of the time to account for her real estate investments, 5 percent of the time for personal letters, and 55 percent of the time in her accounting business.	________
3. For her own convenience, Vicky, an employee of an investment firm, purchased a personal computer for her home to enable her to work at home in the evening on various projects for her employer.	________

LIMITATION ON DEPRECIATION OF LUXURY AUTOMOBILES

Learning Objective 7.7

Apply the limitations on depreciation of "luxury automobiles."

In addition to the limitations on the depreciation of passenger automobiles imposed by the listed property rules discussed in the preceding section, the depreciation of passenger automobiles is subject to an additional limitation, commonly referred to as the luxury automobile limitation. Regardless of the method of depreciation used by the taxpayer, accelerated or straight-line, or the election to expense, the amount of depreciation expense that may be claimed on a passenger automobile is subject to an annual dollar limitation. The annual dollar limitations that apply to passenger automobiles acquired in 2014 are listed below. Any automobile which would have actual MACRS depreciation exceeding the limits below is considered a "luxury" automobile by the IRS for purposes of the depreciation limitation rules.

ANNUAL AUTOMOBILE DEPRECIATION LIMITATIONS—AUTOMOBILES ACQUIRED IN 2014

2014	*Auto Depreciation*
Year 1*	$3,160
Year 2	$5,100
Year 3	$3,050
Year 4 (and subsequent years until fully depreciated)	$1,875

*In recent years, Congress has approved $8,000 of additional bonus depreciation in the first year on autos. At the time we go to press, it is not known whether Congress will extend this form of bonus depreciation in 2014. Please check the Whittenburg companion website for updates.

Separate higher depreciation limits apply for certain trucks and vans and also for electric automobiles.

Some sport utility vehicles fall outside of the definition of passenger automobiles and can be depreciated or expensed under Section 179 or the bonus depreciation rules without regard to the automobile depreciation limits. To qualify for the exception, the sport utility vehicle must have a gross vehicle weight rating above 6,000 pounds. Due to the increase in Section 179 expensing limits, some commentators called this a "Hummer-sized loophole." On October 22, 2004, legislation was enacted to reduce the election to expense to $25,000 for large sport utility vehicles purchased after enactment of the legislation. However, new large sport utility vehicles may still be depreciated using 5-year MACRS percentages rather than using the restricted depreciation for automobiles.

The annual limitations must be reduced to reflect the actual business-use percentage where business use is less than 100 percent.

EXAMPLE Sally purchased a new car for $60,000 in September 2014 which she uses 75 percent for business. Depreciation on the automobile is calculated as follows:

MACRS depreciation (half-year convention)	$60,000 × 20% =	$12,000
		× .75
Depreciation limited to business-use percentage		$ 9,000
Depreciation further limited to maximum luxury automobile depreciation allowed	$3,160 × 75% =	$ 2,370

♦

EXAMPLE Rob purchased a used car for $14,000 in August 2014, which he uses 90 percent for business. Depreciation on the automobile is calculated as follows:

MACRS depreciation (half-year convention)	$14,000 × 20% =	$ 2,800
		× .90
Depreciation limited to business-use percentage		$ 2,520
Depreciation further limited to maximum luxury automobile depreciation allowed	$3,160 × 90% =	$ 2,844

Because the luxury automobile limitation is larger than the actual depreciation calculated, Rob's depreciation deduction is $2,520, his actual depreciation on the car. Rob's $14,000 automobile is not considered a luxury automobile for purposes of the depreciation limitation rules. ♦

EXAMPLE In August 2014, Mary purchased a passenger automobile at a cost of $30,000. The auto is used 40 percent for business and 60 percent for personal purposes. Since the greater-than-50-percent test is not met, Mary must use straight-line depreciation over the alternate recovery period. In addition, depreciation expense cannot exceed the annual dollar limitation multiplied by the business-use percentage, $3,160 × 40% = $1,264. ♦

EXAMPLE In September 2014, Joan purchased a passenger automobile which cost $32,610. The automobile is used 100 percent for business purposes. If

there were no annual limitation, the MACRS depreciation (using the half-year convention) on the automobile would be calculated as follows:

	Five-Year MACRS	***Annual Limit***
Year 1	$ 6,522	$3,160
Year 2	10,435	5,100
Year 3	6,261	3,050
Year 4	3,757	1,875
Year 5	3,757	1,875
Year 6	1,878	1,875
Years 7–14		1,875
Year 15		675

Note that, although the automobile is a 5-year property, it will take 15 years to recover the entire cost of the asset because of the annual dollar limits, assuming no election to expense under Section 179 or bonus depreciation. ♦

TAX BREAK

Taxpayers hoping to get around the luxury auto depreciation limits by leasing an auto should be aware that there is a rule designed to put them in the same economic position as if they had purchased the auto. The IRS issued tables for computation of an "income inclusion" which must be used to reduce the lease expense deduction for leased autos.

Self-Study Problem 7.7

See Appendix E for Solutions to Self-Study Problems

On June 17, 2014, Donald purchased a passenger automobile at a cost of $26,000. The automobile is used 90 percent for qualified business use and 10 percent for personal purposes. Calculate the depreciation expense for the automobile for 2014, assuming half-year convention.

$_______________

Paid Preparer Use Only	Print/Type preparer's name	Preparer's signature	Date	Check ☐ if self-employed	PTIN
	Firm's name ▶		Firm's EIN ▶		
	Firm's address ▶		Phone no.		

Duncan Devious (age 52) is a self-employed attorney. Duncan has issues with self-esteem and, therefore, he drives a 7,000-pound, military-type, crossover SUV, the only vehicle he owns. When you are preparing his tax return, you notice that he claims 90 percent of his total auto expenses as a business deduction on his Schedule C and 10 percent as personal use, with total miles driven in 2014 as 10,000. You note from his home and office addresses on his tax return that he lives approximately 15 miles from his office. The total of the expenses (i.e., gas, oil, maintenance, depreciation) he claims is $31,200. He does not have a mileage log to substantiate the business use of the SUV. Would you sign the Paid Preparer's declaration (see example above) on this return? Why or why not?

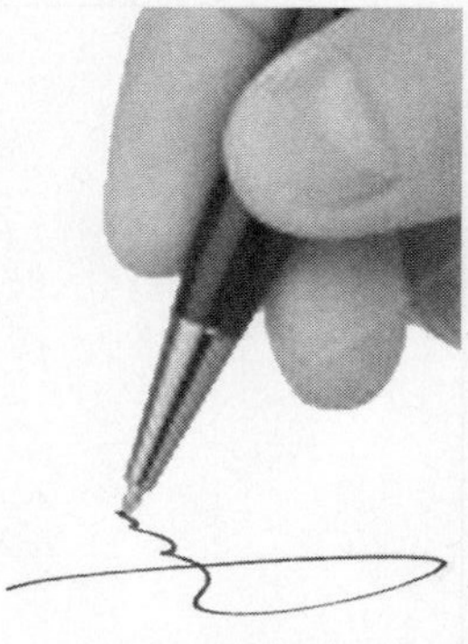

Would You Sign This Tax Return?

©ILYA AKINSHIN/Shutterstock.com; ©Zhukov Oleg/Shutterstock.com.

Learning Objective 7.8

Understand the tax treatment for goodwill and certain other intangibles.

INTANGIBLES

The current tax guidance provides for two main categories of intangibles: (1) Section 197 intangibles and (2) non-Section 197 intangibles. Section 197 intangibles are those acquired by a taxpayer as part of the acquisition of a trade or business. Section 197 intangibles are amortized over a 15-year period, beginning with the month of acquisition. Amortization is a cost recovery method similar to depreciation in that it spreads the cost recovery over a fixed period of years. It differs from depreciation in that it is applied to intangible assets rather than tangible personal or real property and does not include the half-year or mid-quarter conventions. The 15-year life applies despite the actual estimated useful life of the intangible asset. No other amortization or depreciation method may be claimed on Section 197 assets. When acquired as part of a trade or business, the following are defined as qualified Section 197 intangibles:

- Goodwill
- Going-concern value
- Workforce in place
- Information bases including business books and records and operating systems
- Know-how
- Any customer-based intangible
- Any license, permit, or right granted by a governmental unit
- Any covenant not to compete
- Any franchise, trademark, or trade name

EXAMPLE In March 2014, Mary purchases a business from Bill for $250,000. Section 197 goodwill of $36,000 is included in the $250,000 purchase price. Mary amortizes the goodwill over a 15-year period at the rate of $200 per month, starting with the month of purchase. ♦

Exclusions

Many intangible assets are specifically excluded from the definition of Section 197 intangibles. Examples of these Section 197 exclusions include items which are not generally amortizable:

- Interests in a corporation, partnership, trust, or estate
- Interests in land

Section 197 exclusions that are generally amortizable:

- Computer software readily available for purchase by the general public
- Interests in films, sound recordings, video recordings, and similar property
- Self-created intangible assets

Non-Section 197 intangibles that are separately acquired are generally amortized over their remaining useful life using the straight-line method. For example, a patent could be acquired as part of the purchase of a business (Section 197 intangible) or a patent could be acquired separately (non-Section 197 intangible). A franchise, trademark, or tradename, is treated as a Section 197 intangible whether acquired as part of a business or not.

EXAMPLE Sam purchases computer software sold to the general public for $20,000. The $20,000 is not a Section 197 intangible and therefore the amount would be amortized under regular amortization rules (typically 3 years). ♦

Self-Study Problem 7.8 *See Appendix E for Solutions to Self-Study Problems*

Indicate by check marks whether the following items are generally amortizable over 15 years, amortized over their useful life, or not amortized.

	15-Year Amortization	*Useful Life*	*Not Amortizable*
1. Patent acquired as part of a business	________	________	________
2. Separately acquired film rights	________	________	________
3. Computer software sold at an office supply store	________	________	________
4. Goodwill	________	________	________
5. Franchise	________	________	________
6. Land	________	________	________
7. Trademark	________	________	________
8. Interest in a corporation	________	________	________

RELATED PARTIES (SECTION 267)

Learning Objective 7.9

Determine whether parties are considered related for tax purposes, and classify the tax treatment of certain related-party transactions.

When taxpayers who are not independent of each other engage in transactions, there is potential for abuse of the tax system. To prevent this abuse, the tax law contains provisions that govern related-party transactions. Under these rules, related parties who undertake certain types of transactions may find their tax benefits limited.

There are two types of transactions between related parties restricted by Section 267 of the tax law. These transactions are:

1. Sales of property at a loss
2. Unpaid expenses and interest

Losses

Under the tax law "losses from sale or exchange of property . . . directly or indirectly" are disallowed between related parties. When the property is later sold to an unrelated party, any disallowed loss may be used to offset gain on that transaction.

EXAMPLE Mary sells IBM stock with a basis of $10,000 to her son, Steve, for $8,000, resulting in a disallowed loss of $2,000. Three years later, Steve sells the stock to Kim, an unrelated party, for $13,000. Steve has a gain on the sale of $5,000 ($13,000 − $8,000). However, only $3,000 ($5,000 − $2,000) of the gain is taxable to Steve since the previous disallowed loss can reduce his gain. ♦

EXAMPLE Assume the same facts as in the example above, except the IBM stock is sold for $9,500 (instead of $13,000). None of the gain of $1,500 ($9,500 − $8,000) would be taxable, because the disallowed loss would absorb it. $500 of Mary's disallowed loss is not available to her son. ♦

EXAMPLE Assume the same facts as in the example above, except Steve sells the IBM stock 3 years later for $7,000 (instead of $9,500). Steve now has a $1,000 realized loss, which can be deducted subject to any capital loss limitations. Because there is no gain on this transaction, the tax benefit of Mary's $2,000 disallowed loss is not available to her son. ♦

Unpaid Expenses and Interest

Under Section 267, related taxpayers are prevented from engaging in tax avoidance schemes in which one taxpayer uses the cash method of accounting and the other taxpayer uses the accrual method.

EXAMPLE Ficus Corporation, an accrual basis taxpayer, is owned by Bill, an individual who uses the cash method of accounting for tax purposes. On December 31, Ficus Corporation accrues interest expense of $10,000 on a loan from Bill, but the interest is not paid to him. Ficus Corporation may not deduct the $10,000 until the tax year in which it is actually paid to Bill. This rule also applies to other expenses such as salaries and bonuses. ♦

Relationships

Section 267 has a complex set of rules to define who is a related party for disallowance purposes. The common related parties under Section 267 would include the following:

1. Family members. A taxpayer's family includes brothers and sisters (whole or half), a spouse, ancestors (parents, grandparents, etc.), and lineal descendants (children, grandchildren, etc.).
2. A corporation and an individual who directly or indirectly owns more than 50 percent of the corporation.
3. Two corporations that are members of the same controlled group.
4. Trusts, corporations, and certain charitable organizations. They are subject to a complex set of relationship rules.

EXAMPLE Kalmia Corporation is owned 70 percent by Jim and 30 percent by Kathy. Jim and Kathy are unrelated to each other. Since Jim owns over 50 percent of the corporation, he is deemed to be a related party to the corporation. As a result, if Jim sells property to the corporation at a loss, the loss will be disallowed. ♦

Related-party rules also consider constructive ownership in determining whether parties are related to each other. Under these rules, taxpayers are deemed to own stock owned by certain relatives and related entities. The common constructive ownership rules are as follows:

1. A taxpayer is deemed to own all the stock owned by his or her spouse, brothers and sisters (whole or half), ancestors, and lineal descendants.
2. A taxpayer is deemed to own his or her proportionate share of stock owned by any partnership, corporation, trust, or estate in which he or she is a partner, shareholder, or beneficiary.
3. A taxpayer is deemed to own any stock owned directly or indirectly by a partner.

EXAMPLE ABC Corporation is owned 40 percent by Andy, 30 percent by Betty, and 30 percent by Chee. Betty and Chee are married to each other. For purposes of related-party rules, Andy is not a related party to the corporation since he does not own more than 50 percent of the corporation. Betty is a related party because she is a 60 percent shareholder (30 percent directly and 30 percent from her husband, Chee). Using the same rule, Chee is also a related party since he also owns 60 percent (30 percent directly and 30 percent from his wife, Betty). ♦

EXAMPLE Robert owns 40 percent of R Corporation and 40 percent of T Corporation. T Corporation owns 60 percent of R Corporation. Since Robert is deemed to own 64 percent of R Corporation, he is a related party to R Corp. The 64 percent is calculated as 40 percent direct ownership and 24 percent (40% × 60%) constructive ownership. ♦

There are other sets of related-party and constructive ownership rules in the tax law, which differ from the related-party rules discussed in this section and should not be confused with the Section 267 related-party provisions.

TAX BREAK

Commentators are calling the current tax law a "temporary tax code." Before 2000, there were very few temporary provisions in the tax code. In the intervening years, the number of temporary provisions has grown to well over 100. The rules with respect to bonus depreciation and the Section 179 deduction are excellent examples of laws that have phased in and out and changed in nature nearly every year. Tax return preparers must be careful to check the expiration dates of tax law provisions when preparing tax returns or doing tax planning in the current legislative environment.

Self-Study Problem 7.9

See Appendix E for Solutions to Self-Study Problems

EFG Corporation is owned 40 percent by Ed, 20 percent by Frank, 20 percent by Gene, and 20 percent by X Corporation. X Corporation is owned 80 percent by Ed and 20 percent by an unrelated party. Frank and Gene are brothers. Answer each of the following questions about EFG under the constructive ownership rules of Section 267.

1. What is Ed's percentage ownership? ____________%
2. What is Frank's percentage ownership? ____________%
3. What is Gene's percentage ownership? ____________%
4. If EFG sells property to Ed for a $15,000 loss, what amount of that loss can be recognized for tax purposes?

$____________

KEY TERMS

accounting periods, 7-2
fiscal year, 7-2
short-period taxable income, 7-2
annualized period, 7-2
accounting methods, 7-3,
depreciation, 7-5
straight-line depreciation, 7-5
accelerated cost recovery system (ACRS) 7-6
modified accelerated cost recovery system (MACRS), 7-6
conventions, 7-6
asset depreciation ranges (ADRs), 7-7
accelerated depreciation, 7-7
bonus depreciation, 7-10
Code Section 179, 7-12
listed property, 7-14
intangible assets, 7-20
Section 197 intangibles, 7-20
goodwill and going-concern values, 7-20
related parties, 7-21
Section 267, 7-21

KEY POINTS

Learning Objectives	Key Points
LO 7.1: Determine the different accounting periods allowed for tax purposes.	• Almost all individuals file tax returns using a calendar-year accounting period. • Partnerships and corporations had a great deal of freedom in selecting a tax year in the past. However, Congress set limits on this freedom when it resulted in an inappropriate deferral of taxable income. • A personal service corporation is a corporation whose shareholder-employees provide personal services (e.g., medical, legal, accounting, actuarial, or consulting services) for the corporation's patients or clients. Personal service corporations generally must adopt a calendar year-end. • If taxpayers have a short year other than their first or last year of operations, they are required to annualize their taxable income to calculate the tax for the short period.
LO 7.2: Determine the different accounting methods allowed for tax purposes.	• The tax law requires taxpayers to report taxable income using the method of accounting regularly used by the taxpayer in keeping his or her books, provided the method clearly reflects the taxpayer's income. • The cash receipts and disbursements (cash) method, the accrual method, and the hybrid method are accounting methods specifically recognized in the tax law.
LO 7.3: Understand the concept of depreciation.	• Depreciation is the accounting process of allocating and deducting the cost of an asset over a period of years and does not necessarily mean physical deterioration or loss of value of the asset. • The simplest method of depreciation is the straight-line method, which results in an equal portion of the cost of an asset being deducted in each period of the asset's life.
LO 7.4: Understand the calculation of depreciation expense using the MACRS tables.	• The Modified Accelerated Cost Recovery System (MACRS) allows taxpayers who invest in capital assets to write off an asset's cost over a period designated in the tax law and to use an accelerated method for depreciation of assets other than real estate. • The minimum number of years over which the cost of an asset may be deducted (the recovery period) depends on the type of property and the year in which the property was acquired. • Under MACRS, taxpayers calculate the depreciation of an asset using a table, which contains a percentage rate for each year of the property's recovery period and includes the half-year convention for personal property and mid-month convention for real property. • The mid-quarter convention must be applied if more than 40 percent of the total cost of a taxpayer's tangible property acquired during the year, other than real property, is placed in service during the last quarter of the tax year. • For post-1986 acquired real estate, MACRS uses the straight-line method over 27.5 years for residential realty and 39 years for nonresidential realty (31.5 years for realty acquired generally before May 13, 1993).
LO 7.5: Identify when a Section 179 election to expense the cost of property may be used.	• Qualified Section 179 property is personal property (property other than real estate or assets used in residential real estate rental activities) placed in service during the year and used in a trade or business. • The maximum cost that may be expensed in the year of acquisition under Section 179 is $25,000 for 2014. The property may be new or used.

	• The $25,000 maximum is reduced dollar for dollar by the cost of qualifying property placed in service during the year in excess of $200,000. • The amount that may be expensed is limited to the taxpayer's taxable income, before considering any amount expensed under this election, from any trade or business of the taxpayer. • Section 179 expensed amounts reduce the basis of the asset before calculating any regular MACRS depreciation on the remaining cost of the asset.
LO 7.6: Apply the limitations placed on depreciation of "listed property."	• Special rules apply to the depreciation of "listed property." • "Listed property" includes those types of assets which lend themselves to personal use. • Listed property includes automobiles, certain other vehicles, certain computers, and property used for entertainment, recreation, or amusement. • If "listed property" is used 50 percent or less in a qualified business use, any depreciation deduction must be calculated using the straight-line method of depreciation over an alternate recovery period, and the special election to expense is not allowed.
LO 7.7: Apply the limitations on depreciation of "luxury automobiles."	• The depreciation of passenger automobiles is subject to a limitation, commonly referred to as the luxury automobile limitation. • For automobiles acquired in 2014, the maximum depreciation is $3,160 (Year 1), $5,100 (Year 2), $3,050 (Year 3), and $1,875 (Year 4 and subsequent years until fully depreciated).
LO 7.8: Understand the tax treatment for goodwill and certain other intangibles.	• Section 197 intangibles are amortized over a 15-year period, beginning with the month of acquisition. • Qualified Section 197 intangibles include goodwill, going-concern value, workforce in place, information bases, know-how, customer-based intangibles, licenses, permits, rights granted by a governmental unit, covenants not to compete, franchises, trademarks, and trade names. • Examples of Section 197 exclusions are interests in a corporation, partnership, trust, or estate; interests in land; computer software readily available for purchase by the general public; interests in films, sound recordings, and video recordings; and self-created intangible assets.
LO 7.9: Determine whether parties are considered related for tax purposes, and classify the tax treatment of certain related-party transactions.	• Transactions between related parties are restricted by Section 267 of the tax law. • The two types of restricted related-party transactions are (1) sales of property at a loss and (2) unpaid expenses and interest. • The common related parties under Section 267 include brothers and sisters (whether by whole or half), a spouse, ancestors (parents, grandparents, etc.), lineal descendants (children, grandchildren, etc.), and a corporation and an individual shareholder who directly or indirectly owns more than 50 percent of the corporation. • Related-party rules also consider constructive ownership in determining whether parties are related to each other (e.g., taxpayers are deemed to own stock owned by certain relatives and related entities).

INTERACTIVE QUIZZES

© Dusit/Shutterstock.com

Interactive quizzes are available as an optional online resource for Income Tax Fundamentals. Visit **www.cengagebrain.com** for more information.

QUESTIONS and PROBLEMS

GROUP 1: MULTIPLE CHOICE QUESTIONS

LO 7.1

1. E Corporation is a subchapter S corporation owned by three individuals with calendar year-ends. The corporation sells a sports drink as its principal product and has similar sales each month. What options does E Corporation have in choosing a tax year?
   a. E Corporation may choose any month end as its tax year.
   b. Because the owners of E Corporation have tax years ending in December, E Corporation must also choose a December year-end.
   c. E Corporation may choose an October, November, or December tax year-end.
   d. E Corporation may choose a tax year ending in September, October, or November, but only if the corporation also makes an annual cash deposit and adjusts the amount every year depending on the income deferred.

LO 7.1

2. Income and loss from which of the following entities is passed through and taxed on the individual's personal tax returns?
   a. S corporation
   b. Partnership
   c. Each of the above
   d. Neither of the above

LO 7.2

3. Which of the following is an acceptable method of accounting under the tax law?
   a. The accrual method
   b. The hybrid method
   c. The cash method
   d. All of the above are acceptable
   e. None of the above

LO 7.2

4. Which of the following entities is required to report on the accrual basis?
   a. An accounting firm operating as a Personal Service Corporation.
   b. A manufacturing business with $15 million of gross receipts operating as a regular C corporation.
   c. A corporation engaged in tropical fruit farming in Southern California.
   d. All of the above corporations must report on the accrual basis.

LO 7.4

5. Alice purchases a rental house on August 22, 2014, for a cost of $174,000. Of this amount, $100,000 is considered to be allocable to the cost of the home, with the remaining $74,000 allocable to the cost of the land. What is Alice's maximum depreciation deduction for 2014 using MACRS?
   a. $2,373
   b. $2,071
   c. $1,364
   d. $1,190
   e. $1,009

LO 7.4

6. An asset (not an automobile) put in service in June 2014 has a depreciable basis of $35,000 and a recovery period of 5 years. Assuming half-year convention and

no election to expense is made, what is the maximum amount of cost that can be deducted in 2014?

a. $3,500
b. $5,833
c. $7,000
d. $35,000
e. None of the above

LO 7.4

7. James purchased office equipment for his business. The equipment has a depreciable basis of $14,000 and was put in service on June 1, 2014. James decides to elect straight-line depreciation under MACRS for the asset over the minimum number of years (7 years), and does not make the election to expense. What is the amount of his depreciation deduction for the equipment for the 2014 tax year?
   a. $2,000
   b. $1,000
   c. $500
   d. $0
   e. None of the above

LO 7.4

8. Which of the following statements with respect to the depreciation of property under MACRS is *incorrect?*
   a. Under the half-year convention, one-half year of depreciation is allowed in the year the property is placed in service.
   b. If a taxpayer elects to use the straight-line method of depreciation for property in the 5-year class, all other 5-year class property acquired during the year must also be depreciated using the straight-line method.
   c. In some cases, when a taxpayer places a significant amount of property in service during the last quarter of the year, real property must be depreciated using a mid-quarter convention.
   d. Real property acquired after 1986 must be depreciated using the straight-line method.
   e. The cost of property to which the MACRS rate is applied is not reduced for estimated salvage value.

LO 7.4

9. Which of the following is *not* true about the MACRS depreciation system:
   a. A salvage value must be determined before depreciation percentages are applied to depreciable real estate.
   b. Residential rental buildings are depreciated over 27.5 years straight-line.
   c. Commercial real estate buildings are depreciated over 39 years straight-line.
   d. No matter when during the month depreciable real estate is purchased, it is considered to have been purchased at mid-month for MACRS depreciation purposes.

LO 7.4
LO 7.6

10. Assume that a taxpayer purchases a computer in 2014 that has an estimated useful life of 10 years. If the computer is used 100 percent for business and no election to expense was made, what is the MACRS recovery period that must be used for cost recovery on the taxpayer's tax return?
    a. 5 years
    b. 7 years
    c. 8 years
    d. 10 years
    e. 1 year

LO 7.5

11. On July 20, 2014, Kelli purchases office equipment at a cost of $12,000. Kelli makes the election to expense for 2014. She is self-employed as an attorney, and, in 2014, her business has a net income of $6,000 before considering this election to expense. Kelli has no other income or expenses for the year. What is the maximum amount that Kelli may deduct for 2014 under the election to expense, assuming she elects to expense the entire $12,000 purchase?
    a. $24,000
    b. $12,000
    c. $6,000
    d. $3,000
    e. $1,000

LO 7.6

12. Which of the following is not considered listed property for purposes of determining the taxpayer's depreciation deduction?
    a. A computer used exclusively by the taxpayer in managing his investment portfolio
    b. An automobile used 40 percent by an employee in providing services to his employer
    c. A computer used by a bank executive, on the bank premises, in performing services as an employee
    d. A computer used by a taxpayer 40 percent in managing her investment portfolio and 20 percent in her business as an accountant
    e. None of the above

LO 7.8

13. The amortization period for Section 197 intangibles is:
    a. 5 years
    b. 7 years
    c. 10 years
    d. 15 years
    e. 40 years

LO 7.8

14. Which of the following intangibles is defined as a Section 197 intangible asset?
    a. An interest in land
    b. A partnership interest
    c. An interest in a corporation
    d. A covenant not to compete acquired as part of a business
    e. A separately acquired sound recording

LO 7.9

15. Pekoe sold stock to Rose for $13,000, its fair market value. The stock cost Pekoe $16,000 5 years ago. Also, Pekoe sold Earl (an unrelated party) stock for $6,500 that cost $7,500 3 years ago. Rose and Pekoe are brother and sister. What is Pekoe's recognized loss?
    a. $6,500
    b. $4,000
    c. $3,000
    d. $1,000
    e. $0

LO 7.2
LO 7.9

16. B Corporation, an accrual basis taxpayer, is owned 75 percent by Bonnie, a cash basis taxpayer. On December 31, 20X1, the corporation accrues interest of $4,000 on a loan from Bonnie and also accrues a $15,000 bonus to Bonnie. The bonus is

paid to Bonnie on March 1, 20X2; the interest is not paid until 20X3. How much can B Corporation deduct on its 20X1 tax return?

a. $0
b. $4,000
c. $15,000
d. $19,000
e. $12,000

LO 7.2
LO 7.9

_____ 17. Using the same facts as in Question 16, how much can B Corporation deduct on its 20X2 tax return?

a. $0
b. $4,000
c. $15,000
d. $19,000
e. $12,000

LO 7.9

_____ 18. BJT Corporation is owned 40 percent by Bill, 35 percent by Jack, and 25 percent by Teresa. Bill and Jack are father and son. What is Jack's total direct and indirect ownership under Section 267?

a. 65 percent
b. 40 percent
c. 75 percent
d. 35 percent
e. None of the above

GROUP 2: PROBLEMS

LO 7.1

1. The Au Natural Clothing Factory has changed its year-end from a calendar year-end to March 31, with permission from the IRS. The income for its short period from January 1 to March 31 is $21,000. Calculate the tax for this short period.

$_____________

LO 7.2

2. Yolanda is a cash basis taxpayer with the following transactions during the year:

Cash received from sales of products	$65,000
Cash paid for expenses (except rent and interest)	40,000
Rent paid on a leased building for 18 months beginning December 1	36,000
Prepaid interest on a bank loan, paid on December 31 for the next 3 months	5,000

Calculate Yolanda's income from her business for this calendar year.

Sales income	$_____________
Expenses:	
Other than rent and interest	$_____________
Rent	$_____________
Interest	$_____________
Net income	$_____________

LO 7.2

3. Geraldine is an accrual basis taxpayer who has the following transactions during the current calendar tax year:

Accrued business income (except rent)	$220,000
Accrued business expenses (except rent)	170,000
Rental income on a building lease for the next 6 months, received on December 1	21,000
Prepaid rent expense for 6 months, paid on December 1	12,000

Calculate Geraldine's net income from her business for the current year.

Income:	
Other than rental	$__________
Rental	$__________
Expenses:	
Other than rental	$__________
Rental	$__________
Net income	$__________

LO 7.2

4. Amy is a calendar-year taxpayer reporting on the cash basis. Please indicate how she should treat the following items for 2014:
   a. She makes a deductible contribution to an IRA on April 15, 2015.
   ____
   b. She has made an election to accrue the increase in value of savings bonds even though the increase is not received in cash.
   ____
   c. She prepays half a year of interest in advance on her mortgage on the last day of 2014. ________________________
   d. She pays all of her outstanding invoices for standard business expenses in the last week of December. ________________________
   e. She sends out a big bill to a customer on January 1, 2015, even though she did all of the work in December of 2014. ____________________

LO 7.3

5. Is land allowed to be depreciated? Why or why not?

____

____

____

LO 7.3

6. Is it possible to depreciate a residential rental building when it is actually increasing in value? Why?

____

____

LO 7.4

7. Mike purchases a heavy-duty truck (5-year class recovery property) for his delivery service on April 30, 2014. The truck is not considered a passenger automobile for purposes of the listed property and luxury automobile limitations. The truck has a depreciable basis of $39,080 and an estimated useful life of 5 years. Assume half-year convention for tax and no election to expense is made.
   a. Calculate the amount of depreciation for 2014 using financial accounting straight-line depreciation (not the straight-line MACRS election) over the truck's estimated useful life.

   $__________

b. Calculate the amount of depreciation for 2014 using the straight-line depreciation election, using MACRS tables over the minimum number of years.

$__________

c. Calculate the amount of accelerated depreciation for 2014 that Mike could deduct using the MACRS tables.

$__________

LO 7.4

8. On August 8, 2014, Holly purchased a residential apartment building. The cost basis assigned to the building is $800,000. Holly also owns another residential apartment building that she purchased on June 15, 2014, with a cost basis of $500,000.

a. Calculate Holly's total depreciation deduction for the apartments for 2014 using MACRS.

$__________

b. Calculate Holly's total depreciation deduction for the apartments for 2015 using MACRS.

$__________

LO 7.4

9. Give the MACRS depreciation life of the following assets:

a. An automobile __________
b. Business furniture __________
c. A computer __________
d. Residential real estate __________
e. Commercial real estate __________
f. Land __________

LO 7.4

10. Explain the use of the mid-quarter convention for MACRS depreciation:

____
____
____
____

LO 7.4

11. Calculate the following:

a. The first year of depreciation on a residential rental building costing $200,000 purchased May 2, 2014.

$__________

b. The second year of depreciation on a computer costing $3,000 purchased in May 2013, using the half-year convention and accelerated depreciation.

$__________

c. The first year of depreciation on a computer costing $4,000 purchased in May 2014, using the half-year convention and straight-line depreciation.

$__________

d. The third year of depreciation on business furniture costing $10,000 purchased in March 2012, using the half-year convention and accelerated depreciation.

$__________

LO 7.4
LO 7.5
LO 7.6
LO 7.7

12. During 2014, William purchases the following capital assets for use in his catering business:

New passenger automobile (September 30)	$21,500
Baking equipment (June 30)	6,500

Assume that William decides to use the election to expense on the baking equipment (and has adequate taxable income to cover the deduction) but not on the automobile, and he also uses the MACRS accelerated method to calculate depreciation. Calculate William's maximum depreciation deduction for 2014, assuming he uses the automobile 100 percent in his business.

$__________

LO 7.4
LO 7.6

13. On February 2, 2014, Alexandra purchases a personal computer for her home. The computer cost $3,000. Alexandra uses the computer 80 percent of the time in her accounting business, and the remaining 20 percent of the time for various personal uses. Calculate Alexandra's maximum depreciation deduction for 2014 for the computer, assuming half-year convention and she does not make the election to expense.

$__________

LO 7.4
LO 7.6
LO 7.7

14. On September 14, 2014, Jay purchased a passenger automobile that is used 75 percent in his accounting business. The automobile has a basis for depreciation purposes of $35,000, and Jay uses the accelerated method under MACRS. Jay does not elect to expense.
   a. Calculate Jay's depreciation deduction for 2014.

   $__________

   b. Assuming the same business percentage (75 percent) in 2015, calculate Jay's depreciation deduction for 2015.

   $__________

LO 7.4
LO 7.6
LO 7.7

15. During 2014, Palo Fiero purchases the following property for use in his calendar year-end manufacturing business:

Item	*Date Acquired*	*Cost*
Manufacturing equipment	June 2	$ 35,000
Office furniture	November 15	4,500
Office computer	September 18	3,500
Passenger automobile (used 90 percent for business)	May 31	35,000
Warehouse	March 23	
Building		165,000
Land		135,000

Palo uses the accelerated depreciation method under MACRS, if available, and does not make the election to expense or take bonus depreciation. Use Form 4562 on Pages 7-37 and 7-38 to report Palo's depreciation expense for 2014.

LO 7.4
LO 7.6
LO 7.7

16. Go to the IRS website (**www.irs.gov**) and redo Problem 15, using the most recent interactive Form 4562, Depreciation and Amortization. Print out the *completed Form 4562.*

LO 7.5 17. Tom has a successful business with $100,000 of income in 2014. He purchases one new asset in 2014, a new machine which is 7-year MACRS property and costs $25,000. If you are Tom's tax advisor, how would you advise Tom to treat the purchase for tax purposes in 2014? Why?

____

____

LO 7.4
LO 7.7 18. Deborah purchases a new $30,000 car in 2014 to use exclusively in her business. If Deborah does not elect to expense in 2014 and holds the car until it is fully depreciated, how many years will this take? Please show your calculation:

____

____

____

LO 7.8 19. Derek purchases a small business from Art on September 1, 2014. He paid the following amounts for the business:

Fixed assets	$220,000
Goodwill	40,000
Covenant not to compete	45,000
Total	$305,000

a. How much of the $305,000 purchase price is for Section 197 intangible assets?

$______________

b. What amount can Derek deduct on his 2014 tax return as Section 197 intangible amortization?

$______________

LO 7.8 20. Annie develops a successful tax practice. She sells the practice to her friend Carol for $54,000 and moves to Florida to retire. The tax practice has no assets except intangible benefits such as the goodwill and going-concern value Annie has developed over the years. How should Carol treat the $54,000 cost of the tax practice she has purchased?

LO 7.9 21. JBC Corporation is owned 20 percent by John, 30 percent by Brian, 30 percent by Charlie, and 20 percent by Z Corporation. Z Corporation is owned 80 percent by John and 20 percent by an unrelated party. Brian and Charlie are brothers. Answer each of the following questions about JBC under the constructive ownership rules of Section 267:

a. What is John's percentage ownership? ______________%

b. What is Brian's percentage ownership? ______________%

c. What is Charlie's percentage ownership? ______________%

d. If Brian sells property to JBC for a $6,000 loss, what amount of that loss can be recognized for tax purposes (before any annual limitations)?

$______________

LO 7.9 22. You have a problem and need a full-text copy of the Related Party Code Section 267. Go to the U.S. House of Representatives' website (**www.house.gov**) and enter "U.S. Code" in the Search box at the top of the page. The Internal Revenue Code is Title 26. Use the search field to find Section 267 and print out a *copy of Section 267(a)*.

GROUP 3:
WRITING ASSIGNMENT

ETHICS

Charlie's Green Lawn Care is a cash basis taxpayer. Charlie Adame, the sole proprietor, is considering delaying some of his December 2014 customer billings for lawn care into the next year. In addition, he is thinking about paying some of the bills in late December 2014, which he would ordinarily pay in January 2015. This way, Charlie claims, he will have "less income and more expenses, thereby paying less tax!" Is Charlie's way of thinking all right?

GROUP 4:
COMPREHENSIVE PROBLEMS

1. Sherry Hopson owns a retail family clothing store. Her store is located at 4321 Circle Drive, Houston, TX 77001. Her employer identification number is 95-1234321 and her Social Security number is 123-45-6789. Sherry keeps her books on an accrual basis. The income and expenses for the year are:

Gross sales		$350,000
Returns and allowances		(4,500)
Net sales		$345,500
Expenses:		
Beginning inventory (at cost)	$ 82,500	
Add: purchases	210,000	
Cost of goods available for sale	292,500	
Less: ending inventory (at cost)	(71,000)	
Cost of goods sold		$221,500
Rent		9,000
Insurance		1,500
Legal and accounting fees		900
Payroll		38,000
Payroll taxes		2,600
Utilities		1,850
Office supplies		750
Advertising		2,100

On June 1 of this year, Sherry purchased the following new assets for the store:

	Depreciable Basis	*Recovery Period*
Heavy-duty truck	$31,000	5 years
Desk and file cabinets	2,000	7 years
Computer	6,000	5 years

The truck is not considered a passenger automobile for purposes of the luxury automobile limitations.

Required: Assuming that all other assets are fully depreciated and Sherry does not make the election to expense, complete her 2014 Schedule C and Form 4562 on Pages 7-39 to 7-42. Make realistic assumptions about any missing data.

2. Larry and Lisa Williams, both 33 years old, have been married for 9 years. They live at 638 Arctic Way, Fairbanks, AK 99701. Lisa's Social Security number is 445-81-1423 and Larry's is 798-09-8526. Larry is the president of Arctic Birch Corporation located in Fairbanks. The Arctic Birch stock is owned 40 percent by Larry, 40 percent by Lisa, and 20 percent by Larry's father. Larry's Arctic Birch wages and income tax withholding for 2014 are:

Earnings from Arctic Birch	$152,000
Federal tax withheld	10,000
State tax withheld	0

The Williams' other income includes interest on a savings account at Alaska National Bank of $500. In April, Larry canceled a small certificate of deposit at Alaska National Bank and had to pay a $360 penalty on this early withdrawal of savings.

During the year, Larry and Lisa paid the following amounts (all of which can be substantiated):

Home mortgage interest	$35,000
Real estate taxes on personal residence	5,600
Auto loan interest	4,800
Medical insurance	3,400
Other medical expenses	3,600
Income tax preparation fee	750
Charitable contributions:	
A painting to the Fairbanks Museum of Arts for exhibition (fair market value established by qualified appraisal)	40,000
Church	2,000
Tree Huggers Foundation (a qualified charity)	3,000
University of Alaska, Fairbanks	5,000
Safe-deposit box	300

The tax basis for the donated painting is $25,000 and the painting has been owned by Larry and Lisa for 5 years.

During the year, Larry sold land to Arctic Birch Corporation for $75,000. He acquired the land 5 years ago for $160,000. No Form 1099-B was filed for this transaction.

Arctic Birch Corporation does not have a qualified pension plan or Section 401(k) plan for its employees. Therefore, Larry deposited $11,000 ($5,500 each) into traditional IRA accounts for Lisa and himself.

Required: Complete the Williams' federal tax return for 2014. Use Form 1040, Schedule A, Schedule B, Schedule D, and Form 8949 from Pages 7-43 through 7-50 to complete this tax return. Make realistic assumptions about any missing data and ignore any alternative minimum tax. Do not complete Form 8283, which is used when large noncash donations are made to charity.

GROUP 5: CUMULATIVE SOFTWARE PROBLEM

The following additional information is available for the Dr. Ivan and Irene Incisor family from Chapters 1–6.

On December 12, Irene purchased the building where her store is located. She paid $240,000 for the building and $100,000 for the land it is located on. Irene's store is the only business in the building.

Ivan owned 1,000 shares of Behemoth Airline stock with a basis of $30 per share. The stock was purchased 6 years ago on June 10. Ivan sells 500 shares of Behemoth stock to his uncle Seth and 500 of the shares to his sister Sara for $5 per share on December 31, 2014.

Assume for purposes of the continuation of this problem and the problem in Chapter 8 that the Incisors do not have $80,000 in private activity bond interest income. As a result, no AMT will be due.

Required: Combine this new information about the Incisor family with the information from Chapters 1–6 and complete a revised 2014 tax return for Ivan and Irene. Be sure to save your data input files since this case will be expanded with more tax information in the next chapter.

Form **4562** | **Depreciation and Amortization** **(Including Information on Listed Property)** ▶ Attach to your tax return. ▶ Information about Form 4562 and its separate instructions is at *www.irs.gov/form4562.* | OMB No. 1545-0172 **2014** Attachment Sequence No. **179**

Department of the Treasury
Internal Revenue Service (99)

Name(s) shown on return	Business or activity to which this form relates	Identifying number

DRAFT AS OF June 10, 2014 DO NOT FILE

Part I Election To Expense Certain Property Under Section 179
Note: *If you have any listed property, complete Part V before you complete Part I.*

1	Maximum amount (see instructions)	1	
2	Total cost of section 179 property placed in service (see instructions)	2	
3	Threshold cost of section 179 property before reduction in limitation (see instructions)	3	
4	Reduction in limitation. Subtract line 3 from line 2. If zero or less, enter -0-	4	
5	Dollar limitation for tax year. Subtract line 4 from line 1. If zero or less, enter -0-. If married filing separately, see instructions	5	

6	(a) Description of property	(b) Cost (business use only)	(c) Elected cost

7	Listed property. Enter the amount from line 29 . . . 7		
8	Total elected cost of section 179 property. Add amounts in column (c), lines 6 and 7	8	
9	Tentative deduction. Enter the **smaller** of line 5 or line 8	9	
10	Carryover of disallowed deduction from line 13 of your 2013 Form 4562	10	
11	Business income limitation. Enter the smaller of business income (not less than zero) or line 5 (see instructions)	11	
12	Section 179 expense deduction. Add lines 9 and 10, but do not enter more than line 11	12	
13	Carryover of disallowed deduction to 2015. Add lines 9 and 10, less line 12 ▶ 13		

Note: *Do not use Part II or Part III below for listed property. Instead, use Part V.*

Part II Special Depreciation Allowance and Other Depreciation (Do not include listed property.) (See instructions.)

14	Special depreciation allowance for qualified property (other than listed property) placed in service during the tax year (see instructions)	14	
15	Property subject to section 168(f)(1) election	15	
16	Other depreciation (including ACRS)	16	

Part III MACRS Depreciation (Do not include listed property.) (See instructions.)

Section A

17	MACRS deductions for assets placed in service in tax years beginning before 2014	17	
18	If you are electing to group any assets placed in service during the tax year into one or more general asset accounts, check here ▶ ☐		

Section B—Assets Placed in Service During 2014 Tax Year Using the General Depreciation System

(a) Classification of property	(b) Month and year placed in service	(c) Basis for depreciation (business/investment use only—see instructions)	(d) Recovery period	(e) Convention	(f) Method	(g) Depreciation deduction
19a 3-year property						
b 5-year property						
c 7-year property						
d 10-year property						
e 15-year property						
f 20-year property						
g 25-year property			25 yrs.		S/L	
h Residential rental property			27.5 yrs.	MM	S/L	
			27.5 yrs.	MM	S/L	
i Nonresidential real property			39 yrs.	MM	S/L	
				MM	S/L	

Section C—Assets Placed in Service During 2014 Tax Year Using the Alternative Depreciation System

20a Class life					S/L	
b 12-year			12 yrs.		S/L	
c 40-year			40 yrs.	MM	S/L	

Part IV Summary (See instructions.)

21	Listed property. Enter amount from line 28	21	
22	**Total.** Add amounts from line 12, lines 14 through 17, lines 19 and 20 in column (g), and line 21. Enter here and on the appropriate lines of your return. Partnerships and S corporations—see instructions	22	
23	For assets shown above and placed in service during the current year, enter the portion of the basis attributable to section 263A costs . . . 23		

For Paperwork Reduction Act Notice, see separate instructions. Cat. No. 12906N Form **4562** (2014)

Form 4562 (2014) Page **2**

Part V **Listed Property** (Include automobiles, certain other vehicles, certain aircraft, certain computers, and property used for entertainment, recreation, or amusement.)

Note: *For any vehicle for which you are using the standard mileage rate or deducting lease expense, complete* ***only*** *24a, 24b, columns (a) through (c) of Section A, all of Section B, and Section C if applicable.*

DRAFT AS OF June 10, 2014 DO NOT FILE

Section A—Depreciation and Other Information (Caution: *See the instructions for limits for passenger automobiles.***)**

24a Do you have evidence to support the business/investment use claimed? ☐ **Yes** ☐ **No** **24b** If "Yes," is the evidence written? ☐ **Yes** ☐ **No**

(a) Type of property (list vehicles first)	(b) Date placed in service	(c) Business/ investment use percentage	(d) Cost or other basis	(e) Basis for depreciation (business/investment use only)	(f) Recovery period	(g) Method/ Convention	(h) Depreciation deduction	(i) Elected section 179 cost
25 Special depreciation allowance for qualified listed property placed in service during the tax year and used more than 50% in a qualified business use (see instructions) .						**25**		
26 Property used more than 50% in a qualified business use:								
		%						
		%						
		%						
27 Property used 50% or less in a qualified business use:								
		%				S/L –		
		%				S/L –		
		%				S/L –		
28 Add amounts in column (h), lines 25 through 27. Enter here and on line 21, page 1 .						**28**		
29 Add amounts in column (i), line 26. Enter here and on line 7, page 1							**29**	

Section B—Information on Use of Vehicles

Complete this section for vehicles used by a sole proprietor, partner, or other "more than 5% owner," or related person. If you provided vehicles to your employees, first answer the questions in Section C to see if you meet an exception to completing this section for those vehicles.

	(a) Vehicle 1		(b) Vehicle 2		(c) Vehicle 3		(d) Vehicle 4		(e) Vehicle 5		(f) Vehicle 6	
30 Total business/investment miles driven during the year (**do not** include commuting miles) .												
31 Total commuting miles driven during the year												
32 Total other personal (noncommuting) miles driven												
33 Total miles driven during the year. Add lines 30 through 32												
	Yes	**No**	**Yes**	**No**	**Yes**	**No**	**Yes**	**No**	**Yes**	**No**	**Yes**	**No**
34 Was the vehicle available for personal use during off-duty hours?												
35 Was the vehicle used primarily by a more than 5% owner or related person? . .												
36 Is another vehicle available for personal use?												

Section C—Questions for Employers Who Provide Vehicles for Use by Their Employees

Answer these questions to determine if you meet an exception to completing Section B for vehicles used by employees who **are not** more than 5% owners or related persons (see instructions).

	Yes	**No**
37 Do you maintain a written policy statement that prohibits all personal use of vehicles, including commuting, by your employees?		
38 Do you maintain a written policy statement that prohibits personal use of vehicles, except commuting, by your employees? See the instructions for vehicles used by corporate officers, directors, or 1% or more owners . .		
39 Do you treat all use of vehicles by employees as personal use?		
40 Do you provide more than five vehicles to your employees, obtain information from your employees about the use of the vehicles, and retain the information received?		
41 Do you meet the requirements concerning qualified automobile demonstration use? (See instructions.) . . .		
Note: *If your answer to 37, 38, 39, 40, or 41 is "Yes," do not complete Section B for the covered vehicles.*		

Part VI **Amortization**

(a) Description of costs	(b) Date amortization begins	(c) Amortizable amount	(d) Code section	(e) Amortization period or percentage	(f) Amortization for this year
42 Amortization of costs that begins during your 2014 tax year (see instructions):					
43 Amortization of costs that began before your 2014 tax year				**43**	
44 **Total.** Add amounts in column (f). See the instructions for where to report				**44**	

Form **4562** (2014)

SCHEDULE C (Form 1040)

Department of the Treasury Internal Revenue Service (99)

Profit or Loss From Business
(Sole Proprietorship)

▶ Information about Schedule C and its separate instructions is at *www.irs.gov/schedulec*.
▶ Attach to Form 1040, 1040NR, or 1041; partnerships generally must file Form 1065.

OMB No. 1545-0074
2014
Attachment Sequence No. 09

DRAFT AS OF June 19, 2014 DO NOT FILE

Name of proprietor | **Social security number (SSN)**

A Principal business or profession, including product or service (see instructions) | **B Enter code from instructions** ▶

C Business name. If no separate business name, leave blank. | **D Employer ID number (EIN),** (see instr.)

E Business address (including suite or room no.) ▶
City, town or post office, state, and ZIP code

F Accounting method: **(1)** ☐ Cash **(2)** ☐ Accrual **(3)** ☐ Other (specify) ▶

G Did you "materially participate" in the operation of this business during 2014? If "No," see instructions for limit on losses ☐ Yes ☐ No

H If you started or acquired this business during 2014, check here ▶ ☐

I Did you make any payments in 2014 that would require you to file Form(s) 1099? (see instructions) ☐ Yes ☐ No

J If "Yes," did you or will you file required Forms 1099? ☐ Yes ☐ No

Part I Income

1	Gross receipts or sales. See instructions for line 1 and check the box if this income was reported to you on Form W-2 and the "Statutory employee" box on that form was checked ▶ ☐	1	
2	Returns and allowances	2	
3	Subtract line 2 from line 1	3	
4	Cost of goods sold (from line 42)	4	
5	**Gross profit.** Subtract line 4 from line 3	5	
6	Other income, including federal and state gasoline or fuel tax credit or refund (see instructions)	6	
7	**Gross income.** Add lines 5 and 6 ▶	7	

Part II Expenses. Enter expenses for business use of your home **only** on line 30.

8	Advertising	8		18	Office expense (see instructions)	18	
9	Car and truck expenses (see instructions)	9		19	Pension and profit-sharing plans	19	
10	Commissions and fees	10		20	Rent or lease (see instructions):		
11	Contract labor (see instructions)	11		a	Vehicles, machinery, and equipment	20a	
12	Depletion	12		b	Other business property	20b	
13	Depreciation and section 179 expense deduction (not included in Part III) (see instructions)	13		21	Repairs and maintenance	21	
				22	Supplies (not included in Part III)	22	
				23	Taxes and licenses	23	
				24	Travel, meals, and entertainment:		
14	Employee benefit programs (other than on line 19)	14		a	Travel	24a	
15	Insurance (other than health)	15		b	Deductible meals and entertainment (see instructions)	24b	
16	Interest:			25	Utilities	25	
a	Mortgage (paid to banks, etc.)	16a		26	Wages (less employment credits)	26	
b	Other	16b		27a	Other expenses (from line 48)	27a	
17	Legal and professional services	17		b	**Reserved for future use**	27b	

28	**Total expenses** before expenses for business use of home. Add lines 8 through 27a ▶	28	
29	Tentative profit or (loss). Subtract line 28 from line 7	29	
30	Expenses for business use of your home. Do not report these expenses elsewhere. Attach Form 8829 unless using the simplified method (see instructions). **Simplified method filers only:** enter the total square footage of: (a) your home: ________ and (b) the part of your home used for business: ________ . Use the Simplified Method Worksheet in the instructions to figure the amount to enter on line 30	30	
31	**Net profit or (loss).** Subtract line 30 from line 29. • If a profit, enter on both **Form 1040, line 12** (or **Form 1040NR, line 13**) and on **Schedule SE, line 2.** (If you checked the box on line 1, see instructions). Estates and trusts, enter on **Form 1041, line 3.** • If a loss, you **must** go to line 32.	31	

32 If you have a loss, check the box that describes your investment in this activity (see instructions).
- If you checked 32a, enter the loss on both **Form 1040, line 12,** (or **Form 1040NR, line 13**) and on **Schedule SE, line 2.** (If you checked the box on line 1, see the line 31 instructions). Estates and trusts, enter on **Form 1041, line 3.**
- If you checked 32b, you **must** attach **Form 6198.** Your loss may be limited.

32a ☐ All investment is at risk.
32b ☐ Some investment is not at risk.

Schedule C (Form 1040) 2014 Page **2**

Part III **Cost of Goods Sold** (see instructions)

DRAFT AS OF June 19, 2014 DO NOT FILE

33 Method(s) used to value closing inventory: **a** ☐ Cost **b** ☐ Lower of cost or market **c** ☐ Other (attach explanation)

34 Was there any change in determining quantities, costs, or valuations between opening and closing inventory? If "Yes," attach explanation . . . ☐ **Yes** ☐ **No**

35 Inventory at beginning of year. If different from last year's closing inventory, attach explanation . . .	35	
36 Purchases less cost of items withdrawn for personal use . . .	36	
37 Cost of labor. Do not include any amounts paid to yourself . . .	37	
38 Materials and supplies . . .	38	
39 Other costs . . .	39	
40 Add lines 35 through 39 . . .	40	
41 Inventory at end of year . . .	41	
42 **Cost of goods sold.** Subtract line 41 from line 40. Enter the result here and on line 4 . . .	42	

Part IV **Information on Your Vehicle.** Complete this part **only** if you are claiming car or truck expenses on line 9 and are not required to file Form 4562 for this business. See the instructions for line 13 to find out if you must file Form 4562.

43 When did you place your vehicle in service for business purposes? (month, day, year) ► ____ / ____ / ____

44 Of the total number of miles you drove your vehicle during 2014, enter the number of miles you used your vehicle for:

a Business ____________ **b** Commuting (see instructions) ____________ **c** Other ____________

45 Was your vehicle available for personal use during off-duty hours? . . . ☐ **Yes** ☐ **No**

46 Do you (or your spouse) have another vehicle available for personal use?. . . ☐ **Yes** ☐ **No**

47a Do you have evidence to support your deduction? . . . ☐ **Yes** ☐ **No**

b If "Yes," is the evidence written? . . . ☐ **Yes** ☐ **No**

Part V **Other Expenses.** List below business expenses not included on lines 8–26 or line 30.

48 **Total other expenses.** Enter here and on line 27a . . .	48	

Schedule C (Form 1040) 2014

Form **4562** | **Depreciation and Amortization** (Including Information on Listed Property) | OMB No. 1545-0172 2014

Department of the Treasury Internal Revenue Service (99)

► Attach to your tax return.
► Information about Form 4562 and its separate instructions is at *www.irs.gov/form4562.*

Attachment Sequence No. 179

Name(s) shown on return	Business or activity to which this form relates	Identifying number

DRAFT AS OF June 10, 2014 DO NOT FILE

Part I Election To Expense Certain Property Under Section 179
Note: *If you have any listed property, complete Part V before you complete Part I.*

1	Maximum amount (see instructions)	1	
2	Total cost of section 179 property placed in service (see instructions)	2	
3	Threshold cost of section 179 property before reduction in limitation (see instructions)	3	
4	Reduction in limitation. Subtract line 3 from line 2. If zero or less, enter -0-	4	
5	Dollar limitation for tax year. Subtract line 4 from line 1. If zero or less, enter -0-. If married filing separately, see instructions	5	

6	(a) Description of property	(b) Cost (business use only)	(c) Elected cost

7	Listed property. Enter the amount from line 29	7	
8	Total elected cost of section 179 property. Add amounts in column (c), lines 6 and 7	8	
9	Tentative deduction. Enter the **smaller** of line 5 or line 8	9	
10	Carryover of disallowed deduction from line 13 of your 2013 Form 4562	10	
11	Business income limitation. Enter the smaller of business income (not less than zero) or line 5 (see instructions)	11	
12	Section 179 expense deduction. Add lines 9 and 10, but do not enter more than line 11	12	
13	Carryover of disallowed deduction to 2015. Add lines 9 and 10, less line 12 ►	13	

Note: *Do not use Part II or Part III below for listed property. Instead, use Part V.*

Part II Special Depreciation Allowance and Other Depreciation (Do not include listed property.) (See instructions.)

14	Special depreciation allowance for qualified property (other than listed property) placed in service during the tax year (see instructions)	14	
15	Property subject to section 168(f)(1) election	15	
16	Other depreciation (including ACRS)	16	

Part III MACRS Depreciation (Do not include listed property.) (See instructions.)

Section A

17	MACRS deductions for assets placed in service in tax years beginning before 2014	17	
18	If you are electing to group any assets placed in service during the tax year into one or more general asset accounts, check here ► ☐		

Section B—Assets Placed in Service During 2014 Tax Year Using the General Depreciation System

(a) Classification of property	(b) Month and year placed in service	(c) Basis for depreciation (business/investment use only—see instructions)	(d) Recovery period	(e) Convention	(f) Method	(g) Depreciation deduction
19a 3-year property						
b 5-year property						
c 7-year property						
d 10-year property						
e 15-year property						
f 20-year property						
g 25-year property			25 yrs.		S/L	
h Residential rental property			27.5 yrs.	MM	S/L	
			27.5 yrs.	MM	S/L	
i Nonresidential real property			39 yrs.	MM	S/L	
				MM	S/L	

Section C—Assets Placed in Service During 2014 Tax Year Using the Alternative Depreciation System

20a Class life					S/L	
b 12-year			12 yrs.		S/L	
c 40-year			40 yrs.	MM	S/L	

Part IV Summary (See instructions.)

21	Listed property. Enter amount from line 28	21	
22	**Total.** Add amounts from line 12, lines 14 through 17, lines 19 and 20 in column (g), and line 21. Enter here and on the appropriate lines of your return. Partnerships and S corporations—see instructions	22	
23	For assets shown above and placed in service during the current year, enter the portion of the basis attributable to section 263A costs	23	

For Paperwork Reduction Act Notice, see separate instructions. Cat. No. 12906N Form **4562** (2014)

Form 4562 (2014) Page **2**

Part V **Listed Property** (Include automobiles, certain other vehicles, certain aircraft, certain computers, and property used for entertainment, recreation, or amusement.)

Note: *For any vehicle for which you are using the standard mileage rate or deducting lease expense, complete* ***only*** *24a, 24b, columns (a) through (c) of Section A, all of Section B, and Section C if applicable.*

Section A—Depreciation and Other Information (Caution: *See the instructions for limits for passenger automobiles.***)**

24a Do you have evidence to support the business/investment use claimed? ☐ **Yes** ☐ **No** **24b** If "Yes," is the evidence written? ☐ **Yes** ☐ **No**

(a) Type of property (list vehicles first)	(b) Date placed in service	(c) Business/ investment use percentage	(d) Cost or other basis	(e) Basis for depreciation (business/investment use only)	(f) Recovery period	(g) Method/ Convention	(h) Depreciation deduction	(i) Elected section 179 cost
25 Special depreciation allowance for qualified listed property placed in service during the tax year and used more than 50% in a qualified business use (see instructions) .						**25**		
26 Property used more than 50% in a qualified business use:								
		%						
		%						
		%						
27 Property used 50% or less in a qualified business use:								
		%				S/L –		
		%				S/L –		
		%				S/L –		
28 Add amounts in column (h), lines 25 through 27. Enter here and on line 21, page 1 .						**28**		
29 Add amounts in column (i), line 26. Enter here and on line 7, page 1							**29**	

DRAFT AS OF June 10, 2014 DO NOT FILE

Section B—Information on Use of Vehicles

Complete this section for vehicles used by a sole proprietor, partner, or other "more than 5% owner," or related person. If you provided vehicles to your employees, first answer the questions in Section C to see if you meet an exception to completing this section for those vehicles.

	(a) Vehicle 1		(b) Vehicle 2		(c) Vehicle 3		(d) Vehicle 4		(e) Vehicle 5		(f) Vehicle 6	
30 Total business/investment miles driven during the year (**do not** include commuting miles) .												
31 Total commuting miles driven during the year												
32 Total other personal (noncommuting) miles driven												
33 Total miles driven during the year. Add lines 30 through 32												
	Yes	**No**	**Yes**	**No**	**Yes**	**No**	**Yes**	**No**	**Yes**	**No**	**Yes**	**No**
34 Was the vehicle available for personal use during off-duty hours?												
35 Was the vehicle used primarily by a more than 5% owner or related person? . .												
36 Is another vehicle available for personal use?												

Section C—Questions for Employers Who Provide Vehicles for Use by Their Employees

Answer these questions to determine if you meet an exception to completing Section B for vehicles used by employees who **are not** more than 5% owners or related persons (see instructions).

	Yes	No
37 Do you maintain a written policy statement that prohibits all personal use of vehicles, including commuting, by your employees?		
38 Do you maintain a written policy statement that prohibits personal use of vehicles, except commuting, by your employees? See the instructions for vehicles used by corporate officers, directors, or 1% or more owners . .		
39 Do you treat all use of vehicles by employees as personal use?		
40 Do you provide more than five vehicles to your employees, obtain information from your employees about the use of the vehicles, and retain the information received?		
41 Do you meet the requirements concerning qualified automobile demonstration use? (See instructions.) . . .		
Note: *If your answer to 37, 38, 39, 40, or 41 is "Yes," do not complete Section B for the covered vehicles.*		

Part VI **Amortization**

(a) Description of costs	(b) Date amortization begins	(c) Amortizable amount	(d) Code section	(e) Amortization period or percentage	(f) Amortization for this year
42 Amortization of costs that begins during your 2014 tax year (see instructions):					
43 Amortization of costs that began before your 2014 tax year				**43**	
44 **Total.** Add amounts in column (f). See the instructions for where to report				**44**	

Form **4562** (2014)

Form **1040** Department of the Treasury—Internal Revenue Service (99)
U.S. Individual Income Tax Return **2014** OMB No. 1545-0074 IRS Use Only—Do not write or staple in this space.

For the year Jan. 1–Dec. 31, 2014, or other tax year beginning , 2014, ending , 20 See separate instructions.

Your first name and initial	Last name	Your social security number
If a joint return, spouse's first name and initial	Last name	Spouse's social security number
Home address (number and street). If you have a P.O. box, see instructions.	Apt. no.	▲ Make sure the SSN(s) above and on line 6c are correct.
City, town or post office, state, and ZIP code. If you have a foreign address, also complete spaces below (see instructions).		**Presidential Election Campaign** Check here if you, or your spouse if filing jointly, want $3 to go to this fund. Checking a box below will not change your tax or refund. ☐ You ☐ Spouse
Foreign country name	Foreign province/state/county	Foreign postal code

Filing Status

Check only one box.

1 ☐ Single
2 ☐ Married filing jointly (even if only one had income)
3 ☐ Married filing separately. Enter spouse's SSN above and full name here. ▶
4 ☐ Head of household (with qualifying person). (See instructions.) If the qualifying person is a child but not your dependent, enter this child's name here. ▶
5 ☐ Qualifying widow(er) with dependent child

Exemptions

6a ☐ **Yourself.** If someone can claim you as a dependent, **do not** check box 6a
b ☐ **Spouse**

Boxes checked on 6a and 6b

No. of children on 6c who:
• lived with you
• did not live with you due to divorce or separation (see instructions)

Dependents on 6c not entered above

c **Dependents:**

(1) First name Last name	(2) Dependent's social security number	(3) Dependent's relationship to you	(4) ✓ if child under age 17 qualifying for child tax credit (see instructions)
			☐
			☐
			☐
			☐

If more than four dependents, see instructions and check here ▶ ☐

d Total number of exemptions claimed

Add numbers on lines above ▶

Income

Attach Form(s) W-2 here. Also attach Forms W-2G and 1099-R if tax was withheld.

If you did not get a W-2, see instructions.

DRAFT AS OF August 28, 20 DO NOT FILE

7	Wages, salaries, tips, etc. Attach Form(s) W-2		7
8a	**Taxable** interest. Attach Schedule B if required		8a
b	**Tax-exempt** interest. **Do not** include on line 8a	8b	
9a	Ordinary dividends. Attach Schedule B if required		9a
b	Qualified dividends	9b	
10	Taxable refunds, credits, or offsets of state and local income taxes		10
11	Alimony received		11
12	Business income or (loss). Attach Schedule C or C-EZ		12
13	Capital gain or (loss). Attach Schedule D if required. If not required, check here ▶ ☐		13
14	Other gains or (losses). Attach Form 4797		14
15a	IRA distributions 15a	b Taxable amount	15b
16a	Pensions and annuities 16a	b Taxable amount	16b
17	Rental real estate, royalties, partnerships, S corporations, trusts, etc. Attach Schedule E		17
18	Farm income or (loss). Attach Schedule F		18
19	Unemployment compensation		19
20a	Social security benefits 20a	b Taxable amount	20b
21	Other income. List type and amount		21
22	Combine the amounts in the far right column for lines 7 through 21. This is your **total income** ▶		22

Adjusted Gross Income

23	Reserved	23	
24	Certain business expenses of reservists, performing artists, and fee-basis government officials. Attach Form 2106 or 2106-EZ	24	
25	Health savings account deduction. Attach Form 8889	25	
26	Moving expenses. Attach Form 3903	26	
27	Deductible part of self-employment tax. Attach Schedule SE	27	
28	Self-employed SEP, SIMPLE, and qualified plans	28	
29	Self-employed health insurance deduction	29	
30	Penalty on early withdrawal of savings	30	
31a	Alimony paid b Recipient's SSN ▶	31a	
32	IRA deduction	32	
33	Student loan interest deduction	33	
34	Reserved	34	
35	Domestic production activities deduction. Attach Form 8903	35	
36	Add lines 23 through 35		36
37	Subtract line 36 from line 22. This is your **adjusted gross income** ▶		37

For Disclosure, Privacy Act, and Paperwork Reduction Act Notice, see separate instructions. Cat. No. 11320B Form **1040** (2014)

Form 1040 (2014) Page **2**

Section	Line	Description	Box
Tax and Credits	38	Amount from line 37 (adjusted gross income)	38
	39a	Check if: ☐ **You** were born before January 2, 1950, ☐ Blind. ☐ **Spouse** was born before January 2, 1950, ☐ Blind. } **Total boxes checked ▶ 39a** ☐	
	b	If your spouse itemizes on a separate return or you were a dual-status alien, check here ▶ **39b** ☐	
	40	**Itemized deductions** (from Schedule A) **or** your **standard deduction** (see left margin)	40
	41	Subtract line 40 from line 38	41
	42	**Exemptions.** If line 38 is $152,525 or less, multiply $3,950 by the number on line 6d. Otherwise, see instructions	42
	43	**Taxable income.** Subtract line 42 from line 41. If line 42 is more than line 41, enter -0-	43
	44	**Tax** (see instructions). Check if any from: **a** ☐ Form(s) 8814 **b** ☐ Form 4972 **c** ☐	44
	45	**Alternative minimum tax** (see instructions). Attach Form 6251	45
	46	Excess advance premium tax credit repayment. Attach Form 8962	46
	47	Add lines 44, 45, and 46 ▶	47
	48	Foreign tax credit. Attach Form 1116 if required — 48	
	49	Credit for child and dependent care expenses. Attach Form 2441 — 49	
	50	Education credits from Form 8863, line 19 — 50	
	51	Retirement savings contributions credit. Attach Form 8880 — 51	
	52	Child tax credit. Attach Schedule 8812, if required — 52	
	53	Residential energy credit. Attach Form 5695 — 53	
	54	Other credits from Form: **a** ☐ 3800 **b** ☐ 8801 **c** ☐ — 54	
	55	Add lines 48 through 54. These are your **total credits**	55
	56	Subtract line 55 from line 47. If line 55 is more than line 47, enter -0- ▶	56
Other Taxes	57	Self-employment tax. Attach Schedule SE	57
	58	Unreported social security and Medicare tax from Form: **a** ☐ 4137 **b** ☐ 8919	58
	59	Additional tax on IRAs, other qualified retirement plans, etc. Attach Form 5329 if required	59
	60a	Household employment taxes from Schedule H	60a
	b	First-time homebuyer credit repayment. Attach Form 5405 if required	60b
	61	Health care: individual responsibility (see instructions) Full-year coverage ☐	61
	62	Taxes from: **a** ☐ Form 8959 **b** ☐ Form 8960 **c** ☐ Instructions; enter code(s)	62
	63	Add lines 56 through 62. This is your **total tax** ▶	63
Payments	64	Federal income tax withheld from Forms W-2 and 1099 — 64	
	65	2014 estimated tax payments and amount applied from 2013 return — 65	
	66a	**Earned income credit (EIC)** — 66a	
	b	Nontaxable combat pay election — 66b	
	67	Additional child tax credit. Attach Schedule 8812 — 67	
	68	American opportunity credit from Form 8863, line 8 — 68	
	69	Net premium tax credit. Attach Form 8962 — 69	
	70	Amount paid with request for extension to file — 70	
	71	Excess social security and tier 1 RRTA tax withheld — 71	
	72	Credit for federal tax on fuels. Attach Form 4136 — 72	
	73	Credits from Form: **a** ☐ 2439 **b** ☐ Reserved **c** ☐ Reserved **d** ☐ — 73	
	74	Add lines 64, 65, 66a, and 67 through 73. These are your **total payments** ▶	74
Refund	75	If line 74 is more than line 63, subtract line 63 from line 74. This is the amount you **overpaid**	75
	76a	Amount of line 75 you want **refunded to you.** If Form 8888 is attached, check here ▶ ☐	76a
Direct deposit? See instructions.	▶ b	Routing number ▶ **c** Type: ☐ Checking ☐ Savings	
	▶ d	Account number	
	77	Amount of line 75 you want **applied to your 2015 estimated tax** ▶ — 77	
Amount You Owe	78	**Amount you owe.** Subtract line 74 from line 63. For details on how to pay, see instructions ▶	78
	79	Estimated tax penalty (see instructions) — 79	

Standard Deduction for—
- People who check any box on line 39a or 39b **or** who can be claimed as a dependent, see instructions.
- All others:

Single or Married filing separately, $6,200

Married filing jointly or Qualifying widow(er), $12,400

Head of household, $9,100

If you have a qualifying child, attach Schedule EIC.

Third Party Designee — Do you want to allow another person to discuss this return with the IRS (see instructions)? ☐ **Yes.** Complete below. ☐ **No**

Designee's name ▶ Phone no. ▶ Personal identification number (PIN) ▶

Sign Here — Under penalties of perjury, I declare that I have examined this return and accompanying schedules and statements, and to the best of my knowledge and belief they are true, correct, and complete. Declaration of preparer (other than taxpayer) is based on all information of which preparer has any knowledge.

Joint return? See instructions. Keep a copy for your records.

Your signature	Date	Your occupation	Daytime phone number
Spouse's signature. If a joint return, **both** must sign.	Date	Spouse's occupation	If the IRS sent you an Identity Protection PIN, enter it here (see inst.)

Paid Preparer Use Only

Print/Type preparer's name	Preparer's signature	Date	Check ☐ if self-employed	PTIN
Firm's name ▶			Firm's EIN ▶	
Firm's address ▶			Phone no.	

www.irs.gov/form1040 Form **1040** (2014)

DRAFT AS OF August 28, 2014 DO NOT FILE

SCHEDULE A (Form 1040)

Department of the Treasury
Internal Revenue Service (99)

Itemized Deductions

▶ Information about Schedule A and its separate instructions is at *www.irs.gov/schedulea*.
▶ Attach to Form 1040.

OMB No. 1545-0074
2014
Attachment Sequence No. 07

Name(s) shown on Form 1040 | **Your social security number**

DRAFT AS OF August 15, 2014 DO NOT FILE

Medical and Dental Expenses		**Caution.** Do not include expenses reimbursed or paid by others.			
	1	Medical and dental expenses (see instructions)	1		
	2	Enter amount from Form 1040, line 38 [2]			
	3	Multiply line 2 by 10% (.10). But if either you or your spouse was born before January 2, 1950, multiply line 2 by 7.5% (.075) instead	3		
	4	Subtract line 3 from line 1. If line 3 is more than line 1, enter -0-		4	
Taxes You Paid	5	State and local a ☐ Income taxes b ☐ RESERVED	5		
	6	Real estate taxes (see instructions)	6		
	7	Personal property taxes	7		
	8	Other taxes. List type and amount ▶	8		
	9	Add lines 5 through 8		9	
Interest You Paid	10	Home mortgage interest and points reported to you on Form 1098	10		
Note. Your mortgage interest deduction may be limited (see instructions).	11	Home mortgage interest not reported to you on Form 1098. If paid to the person from whom you bought the home, see instructions and show that person's name, identifying no., and address ▶	11		
	12	Points not reported to you on Form 1098. See instructions for special rules	12		
	13	RESERVED	13		
	14	Investment interest. Attach Form 4952 if required. (See instructions.)	14		
	15	Add lines 10 through 14		15	
Gifts to Charity	16	Gifts by cash or check. If you made any gift of $250 or more, see instructions	16		
If you made a gift and got a benefit for it, see instructions.	17	Other than by cash or check. If any gift of $250 or more, see instructions. You **must** attach Form 8283 if over $500	17		
	18	Carryover from prior year	18		
	19	Add lines 16 through 18		19	
Casualty and Theft Losses	20	Casualty or theft loss(es). Attach Form 4684. (See instructions.)		20	
Job Expenses and Certain Miscellaneous Deductions	21	Unreimbursed employee expenses—job travel, union dues, job education, etc. Attach Form 2106 or 2106-EZ if required. (See instructions.) ▶	21		
	22	Tax preparation fees	22		
	23	Other expenses—investment, safe deposit box, etc. List type and amount ▶	23		
	24	Add lines 21 through 23	24		
	25	Enter amount from Form 1040, line 38 [25]			
	26	Multiply line 25 by 2% (.02)	26		
	27	Subtract line 26 from line 24. If line 26 is more than line 24, enter -0-		27	
Other Miscellaneous Deductions	28	Other—from list in instructions. List type and amount ▶		28	
Total Itemized Deductions	29	Is Form 1040, line 38, over $152,525? ☐ **No.** Your deduction is not limited. Add the amounts in the far right column for lines 4 through 28. Also, enter this amount on Form 1040, line 40. ☐ **Yes.** Your deduction may be limited. See the Itemized Deductions Worksheet in the instructions to figure the amount to enter.		29	
	30	If you elect to itemize deductions even though they are less than your standard deduction, check here ▶ ☐			

For Paperwork Reduction Act Notice, see Form 1040 instructions. Cat. No. 17145C **Schedule A (Form 1040) 2014**

SCHEDULE B
(Form 1040A or 1040)

Department of the Treasury
Internal Revenue Service (99)

Interest and Ordinary Dividends

▶ Attach to Form 1040A or 1040.
▶ Information about Schedule B and its instructions is at *www.irs.gov/scheduleb*.

OMB No. 1545-0074
2014
Attachment Sequence No. 08

Name(s) shown on return | **Your social security number**

DRAFT AS OF June 18, 2014 DO NOT FILE

Part I Interest

(See instructions on back and the instructions for Form 1040A, or Form 1040, line 8a.)

Note. If you received a Form 1099-INT, Form 1099-OID, or substitute statement from a brokerage firm, list the firm's name as the payer and enter the total interest shown on that form.

			Amount
1	List name of payer. If any interest is from a seller-financed mortgage and the buyer used the property as a personal residence, see instructions on back and list this interest first. Also, show that buyer's social security number and address ▶	1	
2	Add the amounts on line 1	2	
3	Excludable interest on series EE and I U.S. savings bonds issued after 1989. Attach Form 8815	3	
4	Subtract line 3 from line 2. Enter the result here and on Form 1040A, or Form 1040, line 8a . . . . ▶	4	

Note. If line 4 is over $1,500, you must complete Part III.

Part II Ordinary Dividends

(See instructions on back and the instructions for Form 1040A, or Form 1040, line 9a.)

Note. If you received a Form 1099-DIV or substitute statement from a brokerage firm, list the firm's name as the payer and enter the ordinary dividends shown on that form.

			Amount
5	List name of payer ▶	5	
6	Add the amounts on line 5. Enter the total here and on Form 1040A, or Form 1040, line 9a . . . . ▶	6	

Note. If line 6 is over $1,500, you must complete Part III.

Part III Foreign Accounts and Trusts

(See instructions on back.)

You must complete this part if you **(a)** had over $1,500 of taxable interest or ordinary dividends; **(b)** had a foreign account; or **(c)** received a distribution from, or were a grantor of, or a transferor to, a foreign trust.

		Yes	**No**
7a	At any time during 2014, did you have a financial interest in or signature authority over a financial account (such as a bank account, securities account, or brokerage account) located in a foreign country? See instructions		
	If "Yes," are you required to file FinCEN Form 114, Report of Foreign Bank and Financial Accounts (FBAR), to report that financial interest or signature authority? See FinCEN Form 114 and its instructions for filing requirements and exceptions to those requirements		
b	If you are required to file FinCEN Form 114, enter the name of the foreign country where the financial account is located ▶		
8	During 2014, did you receive a distribution from, or were you the grantor of, or transferor to, a foreign trust? If "Yes," you may have to file Form 3520. See instructions on back		

SCHEDULE D (Form 1040)

Department of the Treasury
Internal Revenue Service (99)

Capital Gains and Losses

► Attach to Form 1040 or Form 1040NR.
► Information about Schedule D and its separate instructions is at *www.irs.gov/scheduled*.
► Use Form 8949 to list your transactions for lines 1b, 2, 3, 8b, 9, and 10.

OMB No. 1545-0074
2014
Attachment Sequence No. 12

Name(s) shown on return | **Your social security number**

DRAFT AS OF June 9, 2014 DO NOT FILE

Part I Short-Term Capital Gains and Losses—Assets Held One Year or Less

See instructions for how to figure the amounts to enter on the lines below. This form may be easier to complete if you round off cents to whole dollars.	(d) Proceeds (sales price)	(e) Cost (or other basis)	(g) Adjustments to gain or loss from Form(s) 8949, Part I, line 2, column (g)	(h) Gain or (loss) Subtract column (e) from column (d) and combine the result with column (g)
1a Totals for all short-term transactions reported on Form 1099-B for which basis was reported to the IRS and for which you have no adjustments (see instructions). However, if you choose to report all these transactions on Form 8949, leave this line blank and go to line 1b				
1b Totals for all transactions reported on Form(s) 8949 with **Box A** checked				
2 Totals for all transactions reported on Form(s) 8949 with **Box B** checked				
3 Totals for all transactions reported on Form(s) 8949 with **Box C** checked				

4 Short-term gain from Form 6252 and short-term gain or (loss) from Forms 4684, 6781, and 8824	4	
5 Net short-term gain or (loss) from partnerships, S corporations, estates, and trusts from Schedule(s) K-1	5	
6 Short-term capital loss carryover. Enter the amount, if any, from line 8 of your **Capital Loss Carryover Worksheet** in the instructions	6	( )
7 **Net short-term capital gain or (loss).** Combine lines 1a through 6 in column (h). If you have any long-term capital gains or losses, go to Part II below. Otherwise, go to Part III on the back	7	

Part II Long-Term Capital Gains and Losses—Assets Held More Than One Year

See instructions for how to figure the amounts to enter on the lines below. This form may be easier to complete if you round off cents to whole dollars.	(d) Proceeds (sales price)	(e) Cost (or other basis)	(g) Adjustments to gain or loss from Form(s) 8949, Part II, line 2, column (g)	(h) Gain or (loss) Subtract column (e) from column (d) and combine the result with column (g)
8a Totals for all long-term transactions reported on Form 1099-B for which basis was reported to the IRS and for which you have no adjustments (see instructions). However, if you choose to report all these transactions on Form 8949, leave this line blank and go to line 8b				
8b Totals for all transactions reported on Form(s) 8949 with **Box D** checked				
9 Totals for all transactions reported on Form(s) 8949 with **Box E** checked				
10 Totals for all transactions reported on Form(s) 8949 with **Box F** checked				

11 Gain from Form 4797, Part I; long-term gain from Forms 2439 and 6252; and long-term gain or (loss) from Forms 4684, 6781, and 8824	11	
12 Net long-term gain or (loss) from partnerships, S corporations, estates, and trusts from Schedule(s) K-1	12	
13 Capital gain distributions. See the instructions	13	
14 Long-term capital loss carryover. Enter the amount, if any, from line 13 of your **Capital Loss Carryover Worksheet** in the instructions	14	( )
15 **Net long-term capital gain or (loss).** Combine lines 8a through 14 in column (h). Then go to Part III on the back	15	

For Paperwork Reduction Act Notice, see your tax return instructions. Cat. No. 11338H **Schedule D (Form 1040) 2014**

Schedule D (Form 1040) 2014 Page **2**

Part III **Summary**

DRAFT AS OF June 9, 2014 DO NOT FILE

16 Combine lines 7 and 15 and enter the result **16**

• If line 16 is a **gain,** enter the amount from line 16 on Form 1040, line 13, or Form 1040NR, line 14. Then go to line 17 below.

• If line 16 is a **loss,** skip lines 17 through 20 below. Then go to line 21. Also be sure to complete line 22.

• If line 16 is **zero,** skip lines 17 through 21 below and enter -0- on Form 1040, line 13, or Form 1040NR, line 14. Then go to line 22.

17 Are lines 15 and 16 **both** gains?

☐ **Yes.** Go to line 18.

☐ **No.** Skip lines 18 through 21, and go to line 22.

18 Enter the amount, if any, from line 7 of the **28% Rate Gain Worksheet** in the instructions . . ▶ **18**

19 Enter the amount, if any, from line 18 of the **Unrecaptured Section 1250 Gain Worksheet** in the instructions . . . . ▶ **19**

20 Are lines 18 and 19 **both** zero or blank?

☐ **Yes.** Complete the **Qualified Dividends and Capital Gain Tax Worksheet** in the instructions for Form 1040, line 44 (or in the instructions for Form 1040NR, line 42). **Do not** complete lines 21 and 22 below.

☐ **No.** Complete the **Schedule D Tax Worksheet** in the instructions. **Do not** complete lines 21 and 22 below.

21 If line 16 is a loss, enter here and on Form 1040, line 13, or Form 1040NR, line 14, the **smaller** of:

• The loss on line 16 or
• ($3,000), or if married filing separately, ($1,500) } . . . . **21** (   )

Note. When figuring which amount is smaller, treat both amounts as positive numbers.

22 Do you have qualified dividends on Form 1040, line 9b, or Form 1040NR, line 10b?

☐ **Yes.** Complete the **Qualified Dividends and Capital Gain Tax Worksheet** in the instructions for Form 1040, line 44 (or in the instructions for Form 1040NR, line 42).

☐ **No.** Complete the rest of Form 1040 or Form 1040NR.

Schedule D (Form 1040) 2014

Form **8949**

Department of the Treasury
Internal Revenue Service

Sales and Other Dispositions of Capital Assets

▶ **Information about Form 8949 and its separate instructions is at *www.irs.gov/form8949*.**

▶ **File with your Schedule D to list your transactions for lines 1b, 2, 3, 8b, 9, and 10 of Schedule D.**

OMB No. 1545-0123

2014

Attachment Sequence No. **12A**

Name(s) shown on return	**Social security number or taxpayer identification number**

Before you check Box A, B, or C below, see whether you received any Form(s) 1099-B or substitute statement(s) from your broker. A substitute statement will have the same information as Form 1099-B. Either may show your basis (usually your cost) even if your broker did not report it to the IRS. Brokers must report basis to the IRS for most stock you bought in 2011 or later (and for certain debt instruments you bought in 2014 or later).

DRAFT AS OF June 12, 2014 DO NOT FILE

Part I **Short-Term.** Transactions involving capital assets you held 1 year or less are short term. For long-term transactions, see page 2.

Note. You may aggregate all short-term transactions reported on Form(s) 1099-B showing basis was reported to the IRS and for which no adjustments or codes are required. Enter the total directly on Schedule D, line 1a; you are not required to report these transactions on Form 8949 (see instructions).

You *must* check Box A, B, *or* C below. Check only one box. If more than one box applies for your short-term transactions, complete a separate Form 8949, page 1, for each applicable box. If you have more short-term transactions than will fit on this page for one or more of the boxes, complete as many forms with the same box checked as you need.

☐ **(A)** Short-term transactions reported on Form(s) 1099-B showing basis was reported to the IRS (see **Note** above)

☐ **(B)** Short-term transactions reported on Form(s) 1099-B showing basis was **not** reported to the IRS

☐ **(C)** Short-term transactions not reported to you on Form 1099-B

1 (a) Description of property (Example: 100 sh. XYZ Co.)	(b) Date acquired (Mo., day, yr.)	(c) Date sold or disposed (Mo., day, yr.)	(d) Proceeds (sales price) (see instructions)	(e) Cost or other basis. See the **Note** below and see *Column (e)* in the separate instructions	Adjustment, if any, to gain or loss. If you enter an amount in column (g), enter a code in column (f). See the separate instructions. (f) Code(s) from instructions	(g) Amount of adjustment	(h) Gain or (loss). Subtract column (e) from column (d) and combine the result with column (g)
2 Totals. Add the amounts in columns (d), (e), (g), and (h) (subtract negative amounts). Enter each total here and include on your Schedule D, **line 1b** (if **Box A** above is checked), **line 2** (if **Box B** above is checked), or **line 3** (if **Box C** above is checked) ▶							

Note. If you checked Box A above but the basis reported to the IRS was incorrect, enter in column (e) the basis as reported to the IRS, and enter an adjustment in column (g) to correct the basis. See *Column (g)* in the separate instructions for how to figure the amount of the adjustment.

For Paperwork Reduction Act Notice, see instructions. Cat. No. 37768Z Form **8949** (2014)

Form 8949 (2014) Attachment Sequence No. **12A** Page **2**

Name(s) shown on return. Name and SSN or taxpayer identification no. not required if shown on other side	**Social security number or taxpayer identification number**

Before you check Box D, E, or F below, see whether you received any Form(s) 1099-B or substitute statement(s) from your broker. A substitute statement will have the same information as Form 1099-B. Either may show your basis (usually your cost) even if your broker did not report it to the IRS. Brokers must report basis to the IRS for most stock you bought in 2011 or later (and for certain debt instruments you bought in 2014 or later).

Part II **Long-Term.** Transactions involving capital assets you held more than 1 year are long term. For short-term transactions, see page 1.

Note. You may aggregate all long-term transactions reported on Form(s) 1099-B showing basis was reported to the IRS and for which no adjustments or codes are required. Enter the total directly on Schedule D, line 8a; you are not required to report these transactions on Form 8949 (see instructions).

DRAFT AS OF June 12, 2014 DO NOT FILE

You *must* check Box D, E, *or* F below. Check only one box. If more than one box applies for your long-term transactions, complete a separate Form 8949, page 2, for each applicable box. If you have more long-term transactions than will fit on this page for one or more of the boxes, complete as many forms with the same box checked as you need.

- ☐ **(D)** Long-term transactions reported on Form(s) 1099-B showing basis was reported to the IRS (see **Note** above)
- ☐ **(E)** Long-term transactions reported on Form(s) 1099-B showing basis was **not** reported to the IRS
- ☐ **(F)** Long-term transactions not reported to you on Form 1099-B

1 (a) Description of property (Example: 100 sh. XYZ Co.)	(b) Date acquired (Mo., day, yr.)	(c) Date sold or disposed (Mo., day, yr.)	(d) Proceeds (sales price) (see instructions)	(e) Cost or other basis. See the **Note** below and see *Column (e)* in the separate instructions	Adjustment, if any, to gain or loss. If you enter an amount in column (g), enter a code in column (f). **See the separate instructions.** (f) Code(s) from instructions	(g) Amount of adjustment	(h) Gain or (loss). Subtract column (e) from column (d) and combine the result with column (g)
2 Totals. Add the amounts in columns (d), (e), (g), and (h) (subtract negative amounts). Enter each total here and include on your Schedule D, **line 8b** (if **Box D** above is checked), **line 9** (if **Box E** above is checked), or **line 10** (if **Box F** above is checked) ▶							

Note. If you checked Box D above but the basis reported to the IRS was incorrect, enter in column (e) the basis as reported to the IRS, and enter an adjustment in column (g) to correct the basis. See *Column (g)* in the separate instructions for how to figure the amount of the adjustment.

Form **8949** (2014)

Student Name ______________________

Class/Section ______________________

Date ______________________

KEY NUMBER TAX RETURN SUMMARY

CHAPTER 7

Comprehensive Problem 1

Schedule C, Gross Income (Line 7) ____________

Form 4562, Depreciation on 7-year Property (Line 19c) ____________

Schedule C, Depreciation (Line 13) ____________

Schedule C, Total Expenses (Line 28) ____________

Schedule C, Net Profit or Loss (Line 31) ____________

Comprehensive Problem 2

Adjusted Gross Income (Line 37) ____________

Itemized Deductions (Line 40) ____________

Exemptions (Line 42) ____________

Tax Liability (Line 63) ____________

Tax Overpaid (Line 75) ____________

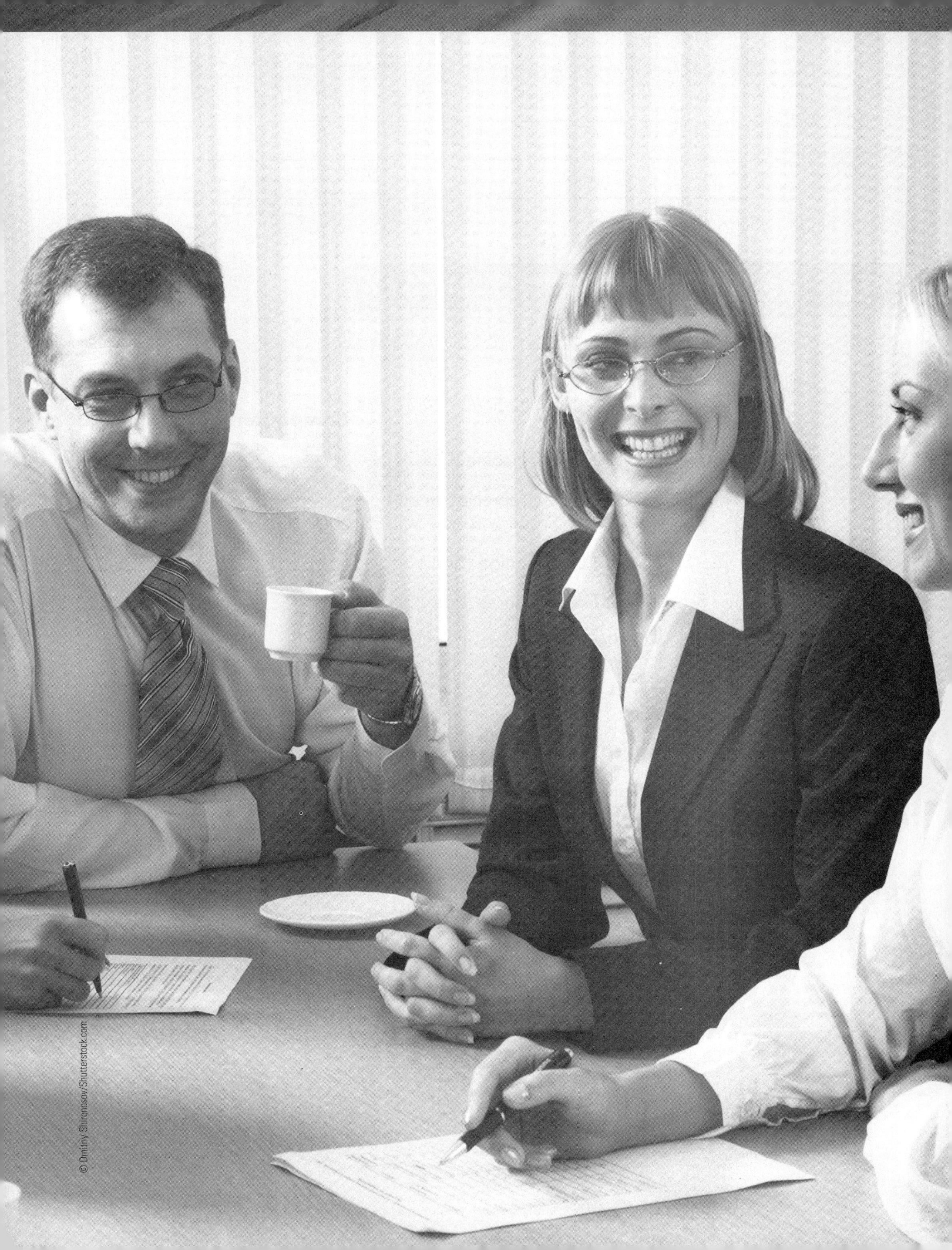

© Dmitriy Shironosov/Shutterstock.com

CHAPTER 8

Capital Gains and Losses

LEARNING OBJECTIVES

After completing this chapter, you should be able to:

LO 8.1	Define the term "capital asset."
LO 8.2	Know the holding period for long-term and short-term capital gains.
LO 8.3	Calculate the gain or loss on the disposition of an asset.
LO 8.4	Compute the tax on capital gains.
LO 8.5	Understand the treatment of capital losses.
LO 8.6	Understand the treatment of Section 1231 assets.
LO 8.7	Describe the depreciation recapture rules.
LO 8.8	Know the general treatment of casualty losses for both personal and business purposes.
LO 8.9	Understand the provisions allowing deferral of gain on installment sales.
LO 8.10	Know the general treatment of like-kind exchanges.
LO 8.11	Understand the basic tax treatment of involuntary conversions.
LO 8.12	Know the rules governing the exclusion on gain from personal residence sales.

OVERVIEW

This chapter covers the reporting and taxability of gains and losses from the sale of capital and noncapital assets. Different tax rates apply to different gains depending on the type of asset sold and the tax bracket of the taxpayer. Some gains may be deferred into future years or even excluded from income. Losses may be fully deductible, partly deductible, or nondeductible depending on the type of transaction.

In general, gains and losses realized are recognized for tax purposes unless there is a tax provision that specifically allows for a different treatment. Transactions covered in this chapter include:

1. Section 1231 (business) gains and losses
2. Capital loss netting and carryovers
3. Depreciation recapture on business assets
4. Casualty gains and losses
5. Installment sales
6. Like-kind exchanges

7. Involuntary conversions
8. Sales of personal residences

Capital gains and losses are generally reported on Schedule D, many business asset sale transactions are reported on Form 4797, and installment sales are reported on Form 6252.

Learning Objective 8.1

Define the term "capital asset."

WHAT IS A CAPITAL ASSET?

When taxpayers dispose of property, they must calculate any gain or loss on the transaction and report the gain or loss on their tax returns. The gain or loss realized is equal to the difference between the amount realized on the sale or exchange of the property and the taxpayer's adjusted basis in the property. How gains and losses are reported is dependent on the nature of the property and the length of time the property has been owned. Gains and losses on the sale of capital assets are known as capital gains and losses and are classified as either short-term or long-term. For a gain on the sale of a capital asset to be classified as a long-term capital gain, the taxpayer must have held the asset for the required holding period.

The tax law defines a capital asset as any property, whether or not used in a trade or business, other than:

1. Stock in trade, inventory, or property held primarily for sale to customers in the ordinary course of a trade or business;
2. Depreciable property or real property used in a trade or business (Section 1231 assets);
3. Copyrights, literary, musical, or artistic compositions, letters or memorandums, or similar property if the property is created by the taxpayer;
4. Accounts or notes receivable; and
5. Certain U.S. government publications.

The definition of a capital asset is a definition by exception. All property owned by a taxpayer, other than property specifically noted as an exception, is a capital asset. Depreciable property and real estate used in a trade or business are referred to as Section 1231 assets and will be discussed later in this chapter since special rules apply to such assets.

Self-Study Problem 8.1

See Appendix E for Solutions to Self-Study Problems

Indicate, by circling your answer, whether each of the following properties is or is not a capital asset.

Property	*Capital Asset?*	
1. Shoes held by a shoe store	Yes	No
2. A taxpayer's personal residence	Yes	No
3. A painting held by the artist	Yes	No
4. Accounts receivable of a dentist	Yes	No
5. A copyright purchased from a company	Yes	No
6. A truck used in the taxpayer's business	Yes	No
7. IBM stock owned by an investor	Yes	No
8. AT&T bonds owned by an investor	Yes	No
9. Land held as an investment	Yes	No
10. A taxpayer's television	Yes	No
11. Automobiles for sale owned by a car dealer	Yes	No
12. A taxpayer's sailboat	Yes	No

HOLDING PERIOD

Learning Objective 8.2

Know the holding period for long-term and short-term capital gains.

Assets must be held for more than 1 year for the gain or loss to be considered long-term. A capital asset sold before it is owned for the required holding period results in a short-term capital gain or loss. A net short-term capital gain is treated as ordinary income for tax purposes. In calculating the holding period, the taxpayer excludes the date of acquisition and includes the date of disposition.

EXAMPLE Glen purchased stock as an investment on March 27, 2014. The first day the stock may be sold for long-term capital gain treatment is March 28, 2015. ♦

To satisfy the long-term holding period requirement, a capital asset acquired on the last day of a month must not be disposed of before the first day of the thirteenth month following the month of purchase.

EXAMPLE If Elwood purchases a painting on March 31, 2014, the first day the painting may be sold for long-term capital gain treatment is April 1, 2015. ♦

Self-Study Problem 8.2 ***See Appendix E for Solutions to Self-Study Problems***

Indicate whether a gain or loss realized in each of the following situations would be long-term or short-term by putting an "X" in the appropriate blank.

Date Acquired	*Date Sold*	*Long-Term*	*Short-Term*
1. October 16, 2013	May 30, 2014	________	________
2. May 2, 2013	October 12, 2014	________	________
3. July 18, 2013	July 18, 2014	________	________
4. August 31, 2012	March 1, 2014	________	________

CALCULATION OF GAIN OR LOSS

Learning Objective 8.3

Calculate the gain or loss on the disposition of an asset.

A taxpayer must calculate his or her amount realized and the adjusted basis of property sold or exchanged to arrive at the amount of the gain or loss realized on the disposition. The taxpayer's gain or loss is calculated using the following formula:

Amount realized − Adjusted basis = Gain or loss realized

Sale or Exchange

The realization of a gain or loss requires the "sale or exchange" of an asset. The term "sale or exchange" is not defined in the tax law, but a sale generally requires the receipt of money or the relief from liabilities in exchange for property, and an exchange is the transfer of ownership of one property for another property.

EXAMPLE Maggie sells stock for $8,500 that she purchased 2 years ago for $6,000. Maggie's adjusted basis in the stock is its cost, $6,000; therefore, she realizes a long-term capital gain of $2,500 ($8,500 − $6,000) on the sale. ♦

EXAMPLE Art owns a home which has increased in value during 2014. If Art does not sell the home, there is no realized gain in 2014. ♦

Amount Realized

The amount realized from a sale or other disposition of property is equal to the sum of the money received, plus the fair market value of other property received, less the costs paid to transfer the property. If the taxpayer is relieved of a liability, the amount of the liability is added to the amount realized.

EXAMPLE In 2014, Ted sells real estate held as an investment for $75,000 in cash, and the buyer assumes the mortgage on the property of $120,000. Ted pays real estate commissions and other transfer costs of $11,000. The amount realized on the sale is calculated as:

Cash received	$ 75,000
Liabilities transferred	120,000
Total sales price	195,000
Less: transfer costs	(11,000)
Amount realized	$ 184,000

♦

Adjusted Basis

The adjusted basis of property is equal to the original basis adjusted by adding capital (major) improvements and deducting depreciation allowed or allowable, as illustrated by the following formula:

Adjusted basis = Original basis + Capital improvements − Accumulated depreciation

The original basis is usually the cost of the property at the date of acquisition, plus any costs incidental to the purchase, such as title insurance, escrow fees, and inspection fees. Capital improvements are major expenditures for permanent improvements to or restoration of the taxpayer's property. These expenditures include amounts which result in an increase in the value of the taxpayer's property or substantially increase the useful life of the property, as well as amounts which are spent to adapt property to a new use. For example, architect fees paid to plan an addition to a building, as well as the cost of the addition, must be added to the original basis of the asset as capital improvements. Ordinary repairs and maintenance expenditures are not capital expenditures.

EXAMPLE James and his wife purchased a house on September 19, 2014. Their closing statement for the purchase is illustrated on Page 8-5. Their original tax basis in the house is equal to the purchase price of $100,000 plus the incidental costs of title insurance, inspection fee, escrow fee, appraisal fee, tax service, credit report, notary fee, recording fee, and pest control inspection fee. Therefore, their original basis is $101,381 ($100,000 + $550 + $35 + $255 + $250 + $56 + $50 + $10 + $25 + $150). The loan origination fee represents "points" on the mortgage loan. If the house is their principal residence, the points are deductible as interest in the year of payment. The prorated interest and taxes affect their deductions for interest and taxes, as described in Chapter 5. The insurance is a nondeductible personal expense, assuming the house is their personal residence. ♦

BUYER'S CLOSING COSTS

Based on Purchase price of $ 100,000 and proration date of: 9-19-14

Prepared by: Freda Jones Date: 8-28-14

Office: Sunset Realtors Phone: 245-7896

Prepared for: Mr. & Mrs. James Green

Property Address: 3454 Westwood Dr., Emporia, KS 66801

(IF NOT APPLICABLE, FILL IN "NONE." DO NOT LEAVE BLANK SPACES!)

ESTIMATED NON-RECURRING COSTS:

Title Insurance	$ 550.00	
	$ NONE	
ALTA Inspection Fee	$ 35.00	
FHA — Mortgage Insurance Premium	$ NONE	
Escrow Fee	$ 255.00	
Legal Fee	$ NONE	
Loan Origination Fee 2%	$ 1,600.00	
Loan Assumption or Transfer Fee	$ NONE	
Loan Document Charges	$ NONE	
Appraisal Fee	$ 250.00	
Tax Service	$ 56.00	
Credit Report	$ 50.00	
Notary Fee	$ 10.00	
Recording Fee	$ 25.00	
Pest Control Inspection Fee	$ 150.00	
ESTIMATED RECURRING COSTS:		
Hazard Insurance (1 year premium)	$ 350.00	
Trust Fund or Import Account	$ NONE	
Prorated Taxes (if beyond proration date)	$ NONE	
Prorated Special Taxes (if paid beyond proration date)	$ NONE	
Prorated Interest to end of month	$ 235.67	
Private Mortgage Insurance Premium	$ NONE	
	$ NONE	
	$ NONE	
TOTAL COSTS		$ 3,566.67
CREDITS:		
Prorated Taxes (if not paid to proration date)	$ 254.89	
Prorated Special Taxes (if not paid to proration date)	$ NONE	
Prorated Rents	$ NONE	
Security Deposits and Prepaid Rents on hand	$ NONE	
Damage and Cleaning Deposits on hand	$ NONE	
	$ NONE	
	$ NONE	
LESS: TOTAL CREDITS		$ 254.89
TOTAL ESTIMATED BUYER'S COSTS		$ 3,311.78
DOWN PAYMENT:		$ 20,000.00
TOTAL ESTIMATED CASH REQUIRED		$ 23,311.78

EXAMPLE Paul acquired a rental house 4 years ago for $91,000. Depreciation claimed on the house for the 4 years totals $14,000. Paul installed a new roof at a cost of $2,500. The adjusted basis of the house is $79,500, as calculated below:

Adjusted basis = Original basis + Capital improvements − Accumulated depreciation
= $91,000 + $2,500 − $14,000
= $79,500 ♦

If property is received from a decedent (as an inheritance), the original basis is generally equal to the fair market value at the decedent's date of death. For property acquired as a gift, the amount of the donee's basis depends on whether the property is sold for a gain or a loss by the donee. If a gain results from the disposition of the property, the donee's basis is equal to the donor's basis. If the disposition of the property results in a loss, the donee's basis is equal to the lesser of the donor's basis or the fair market value of the property on the date of the gift. When property acquired by gift is disposed of at an amount between the basis for gain and the basis for loss, no gain or loss is recognized. Note that the basis for gain and the basis for loss will be different only where the gifted property has a fair market value, on the date of the gift, that is less than the donor's adjusted basis in the property.

EXAMPLE Ron received AT&T stock upon the death of his grandfather. The stock cost his grandfather $6,000 40 years ago and was worth $97,000 on the date of his grandfather's death. Ron's basis in the stock is $97,000. ♦

EXAMPLE Jane received a gift of stock from her mother. The stock cost her mother $9,000 5 years ago and was worth $6,500 on the date of the gift. If the stock is sold by Jane for $12,000, her gain would be $3,000 ($12,000 − $9,000). However, if the stock is sold for $5,000, the loss would be only $1,500 ($5,000 − $6,500). If the stock is sold for an amount between $6,500 and $9,000, no gain or loss is recognized on the sale. ♦

Self-Study Problem 8.3

See Appendix E for Solutions to Self-Study Problems

Supply the missing information in the following blanks:

	Original Cost	Accumulated Depreciation	Capital Improvements	Adjusted Basis
1.	$15,000	$5,000	$1,000	$______
2.	15,000	8,000	______	9,000
3.	30,000	______	2,000	17,000
4.	______	9,000	4,000	18,000

NET CAPITAL GAINS

Learning Objective 8.4

Compute the tax on capital gains.

In recent years, the tax rates on long-term and short-term capital gains have become complex. Short-term capital gains are taxed as ordinary income, while there are various different preferential long-term capital gains tax rates. The 2014 capital gains tax rates are as follows:

Ordinary Tax Rate	*Short-Term Capital Gains*	*Typical Long-Term Capital Gains*	*Long-Term Unrecaptured Section 1250 Gain (See LO 8.7)*	*Long-Term Collectibles Gains (Art, Gems, Coins, Stamps, etc.)*
10% to 15%	10% to 15%	0%	10% to 15%	10% to 15%
25% to 35%	25% to 35%	Capped at 15%	Capped at 25%	Capped at 28%
39.6%	39.6%	Capped at 20%	Capped at 25%	Capped at 28%
3.8% ACA Medicare Surtax*	3.8% added for "high-income" taxpayers	3.8% added for "high-income" taxpayers	3.8% added for "high-income" taxpayers	3.8% added for "high-income" taxpayers
Top Total Rate	43.4%	23.8%	28.8%	31.8%

*The 3.8 percent Medicare surtax on net investment income, including qualifying dividends, applies to high-income taxpayers with income over certain thresholds. Please see Chapter 1, LO 1.9, for further details.

EXAMPLE In 2014, Pedro and Paula's (married, filing jointly) only long-term capital gain is $30,000 from the sale of stock. Their noncapital ordinary income (salary, interest, etc.) is $82,000, putting them in the 25 percent ordinary tax bracket. Pedro and Paula would pay the tax shown in the tax tables on the $82,000. The $30,000 would be taxed at the 15 percent preferential long-term capital gain rate. Thus, the tax on the gain from the stock would be $4,500 (15% × $30,000). ♦

EXAMPLE In October 2014, Frank and Fran (married, filing jointly) have a long-term capital gain of $30,000 on the sale of stock. They have no other capital gains or losses for the year. Their ordinary income after the standard deduction and exemptions for the year is $13,000, making their total taxable income for the year $43,000 ($13,000 + $30,000). In 2014, taxpayers who are married and file jointly pay 10 percent on taxable income up to $18,150 and 15 percent on taxable income from $18,150 up to $73,800. The capital gains rate used for Frank and Fran would be selected based on their income in the 10 percent to 15 percent ordinary income brackets; that is, a 0 percent long-term capital gains rate would apply.

For purposes of illustration, their total tax liability would be calculated as follows:

Tax on ordinary income	$13,000 × 10% =	$1,300
Tax on capital gains	$30,000 × 0% =	0
Total tax		$1,300

Tax on ordinary income up to $100,000 is taken from the tax tables, and in the tables, amounts are calculated based on the midpoint of ranges, not exact numbers. The tax table shows $1,303 as tax on $13,000, slightly different from the example. In practice, the amounts from the tax tables would be used. ♦

Ordering Rules for Capital Gains

Since there are multiple kinds of capital gains on which to calculate tax, an ordering system is necessary to know which capital gains to tax at what rates. The various kinds of gains are included in taxable income in the following order:

1. Short-term capital gains
2. Unrecaptured Section 1250 gains on real estate
3. Gains on collectibles
4. Long-term capital gains

If taxpayers (or tax practitioners) have several different types of capital gains that interact with each other, the calculation may become very complex. A good tax preparation computer program will provide the calculation along with supporting worksheets for further review. The rules for the taxation of capital gains are exceptionally complex, and a complete discussion of them is beyond the scope of this text.

Calculation of a Net Capital Position

If a taxpayer has a "net capital gain" (net long-term capital gain in excess of net short-term capital loss), the gain is subject to a preferential tax rate as discussed above. Thus, a taxpayer has to net all of the long-term and short-term capital transactions that take place during a year to calculate tax liability. In calculating a taxpayer's net capital gain or net capital loss, the following procedure is followed:

1. Capital gains and losses are classified into two groups, long-term and short-term.
2. Long-term capital gains are offset by long-term capital losses, resulting in either a net long-term capital gain or a net long-term capital loss.
3. Short-term capital gains are offset by short-term capital losses, resulting in a net short-term capital gain or a net short-term capital loss.
4. If Step 2 above results in a net long-term capital gain, it is offset by any net short-term capital loss (Step 3), resulting in either a net capital gain (net long-term capital gain exceeds net short-term capital loss) or a net short-term capital loss (net short-term capital loss exceeds net long-term capital gain). If Step 2 above results in a net long-term capital loss, it is offset against any net short-term capital gain (Step 3), resulting in either a net long-term capital loss (net long-term capital loss exceeds net short-term capital gain) or ordinary income (net short-term capital gain exceeds net long-term capital loss).

The net capital gain computation is illustrated with the following examples:

Example	*Net LT Capital Gain or (Loss)*	*Net ST Capital Gain or (Loss)*	*Net Capital Position*	*Taxable LT Gain*	*Taxable ST Gain*
a.	$10,000	$ 0	$ 10,000	$10,000	$ 0
b.	10,000	(4,000)	6,000	6,000	0
c.	0	20,000	20,000	0	20,000
d.	0	(20,000)	(20,000)	0	0
e.	10,000	8,000	18,000	10,000	8,000
f.	(8,000)	12,000	4,000	0	4,000
g.	(8,000)	(6,000)	(14,000)	0	0

Self-Study Problem 8.4 ***See Appendix E for Solutions to Self-Study Problems***

In October 2014, Jack, a single taxpayer, sold IBM stock for $12,000, which he purchased 4 years ago for $4,000. He also sold GM stock for $14,000, which cost $17,500 3 years ago,and he had a short-term capital loss of $1,800 on the sale of land. If Jack's other taxable income (salary) is $75,000, what is the amount of Jack's tax on these capital transactions?

$__________

NET CAPITAL LOSSES

Learning Objective 8.5

Understand the treatment of capital losses.

Calculation of Net Capital Losses

The computation of an individual taxpayer's net capital loss is accomplished in a manner similar to the computation of a net capital gain. A net capital loss is incurred when the total capital losses for the period exceed the total capital gains for the period.

EXAMPLE Connie has net long-term capital gains of $6,500 and a short-term capital loss of $8,000. The net (short-term) capital loss is $1,500 ($6,500 – $8,000). ♦

EXAMPLE Delvin has net long-term capital losses of $8,000 and a short-term capital gain of $4,500. The net (long-term) capital loss is $3,500 ($4,500 – $8,000). ♦

Treatment of Net Capital Losses

Individual taxpayers may deduct net capital losses against ordinary income in amounts up to $3,000 per year. Unused capital losses in a particular year may be carried forward indefinitely. Capital losses and capital loss carryovers first offset capital gains using the ordering rules discussed on the next page. Any remaining net capital loss may be used to offset ordinary income, subject to the $3,000 annual limitation.

EXAMPLE In 2014, Carter has a net long-term capital loss of $15,000 and other taxable income for the year of $25,000. He may deduct $3,000 of the loss against the $25,000 of other taxable income. The remaining capital loss of $12,000 ($15,000 − $3,000) is carried forward to future years. ♦

When unused capital losses are carried forward, they maintain their character as either long-term or short-term. If a taxpayer has both net long-term losses and net short-term losses in the same year, the net short-term losses are deducted first.

EXAMPLE Frances has a long-term capital loss of $7,000 and a $2,000 short-term capital loss in 2014. For that year, Frances may deduct $3,000 in capital losses, the $2,000 short-term capital loss, and $1,000 of the long-term capital loss. Her carryforward would be a $6,000 long-term capital loss. If Frances has no capital gains or losses in 2015, she would deduct $3,000 in long-term capital losses and carry forward $3,000 ($6,000 − $3,000) to 2016. Assuming she has no other capital gains and losses, the deduction of losses by year can be summarized as follows:

	2014	***2015***	***2016***
Long-term capital loss	$7,000	$6,000	$3,000
Short-term capital loss	2,000	0	0
Deduction	3,000	3,000	3,000
Long-term capital loss used	1,000	3,000	3,000
Carryforward, long-term capital loss	6,000	3,000	0 ♦

TAX BREAK

Taxpayers who have recognized a large capital loss during the year may wish to sell stock or other property to generate enough capital gains prior to year-end to use up all but $3,000 of the capital loss. This way, the capital loss in excess of $3,000 will be used in the current period rather than carried forward, and the capital gains will be fully sheltered from tax.

Personal Capital Losses

Losses from the sale of personal capital assets are not allowed for tax purposes. For instance, the sale of a personal automobile at a loss or the sale of a personal residence at a loss does not generate a tax-deductible capital loss for individual taxpayers.

EXAMPLE Rose moved to a nursing home in 2014 and sold both her personal auto and her principal residence. She originally purchased her auto for $20,000 and sold it for $10,000. She originally purchased her residence for $125,000 and sold it for $100,000. The losses on these sales are not tax deductible to Rose because the assets were personal-use assets. ♦

Ordering Rules for Capital Losses

When a taxpayer ends up with net capital losses, the losses offset capital gains using the following ordering rules:

- Net short-term capital losses first reduce 28 percent gains, then 25 percent gains, then regular long-term capital gains.
- Net long-term capital losses first reduce 28 percent gains, then 25 percent gains, then any short-term capital gains.

As with the ordering rules for capital gains, the ordering calculation may become quite complex when different classes of capital assets are present. A detailed discussion is beyond the scope of this text.

Self-Study Problem 8.5 ***See Appendix E for Solutions to Self-Study Problems***

During 2014, Gerry Appel, who is single, received a Form 1099-B showing the following information:

Description	***Date Acquired***	***Date Sold***	***Selling Price***	***Cost Basis***
Purple stock	06/21/05	08/15/14	$18,000	$12,500
Rose stock	04/18/14	12/07/14	12,000	19,200
Blue stock	12/18/06	10/02/14	25,000	21,000

His taxable income is $59,000. Calculate Gerry's net capital gain or loss and tax liability using Schedule D of Form 1040, Parts I, II, and III; Form 8949, Parts I and II; and the qualified dividends and capital gains tax worksheet on Pages 8-13 to 8-17.

SECTION 1231 GAINS AND LOSSES

Learning Objective 8.6

Understand the treatment of Section 1231 assets.

Section 1231 assets are not capital assets (see LO 8.1), but they are given special tax treatment. Gains on Section 1231 assets may be treated as long-term capital gains, while losses in some cases may be deducted as ordinary losses. Section 1231 assets include:

1. Depreciable or real property used in a trade or business;
2. Timber, coal, or domestic iron ore;
3. Livestock (not including poultry) held for draft, breeding, dairy, or sporting purposes; and
4. Unharvested crops on land used in a trade or business.

Any property held 1 year or less, inventory and property held for sale to customers, and copyrights, paintings, government publications, etc., are not Section 1231 property.

The calculation of net Section 1231 gains and losses is summarized as follows:

Combine all Section 1231 gains and losses to compute net Section 1231 gains or losses. If the gains exceed the losses, the excess is a long-term capital gain. When the losses exceed the gains, all gains are treated as ordinary income, and all losses are fully deductible as ordinary losses.

EXAMPLE Frank Harper had the following gains and losses during August of 2014:

Gain on the sale of land used in his business	$ 9,500
Loss on the sale of a truck used in his business	(2,100)

Assuming that all of the property was owned for more than 12 months, Frank's gains and losses would be calculated as follows:

Gain on land	$ 9,500
Loss on truck	(2,100)
Net Section 1231 gain	$ 7,400

The $7,400 gain would be treated as a long-term capital gain and would be reported on Schedule D of Form 1040. ♦

Self-Study Problem 8.6 *See Appendix E for Solutions to Self-Study Problems*

Gary Farmer had the following Section 1231 gains and losses during the 2014 tax year:

1. Sold land acquired on December 3, 2003, at a cost of $24,000, for $37,000 on January 5, 2014. The cost of selling the land was $500, and there was no depreciation allowable or capital improvements made to the asset over the life of the asset.
2. Sold a business computer with an adjusted basis of $20,700 that was acquired on April 5, 2011. The original cost was $25,875, and accumulated depreciation was $5,175. The computer was sold on May 2, 2014, for $14,000, resulting in a $6,700 loss.

Gary's employer identification number is 74-8976432. Use Form 4797 on Pages 8-19 and 8-20 to report the above gains and losses.

Learning Objective 8.7

Describe the depreciation recapture rules.

DEPRECIATION RECAPTURE

Since long-term capital gains traditionally have been taxed at a lower rate than ordinary income, taxpayers have attempted to maximize the amount of income treated as capital gain. Congress enacted depreciation recapture provisions to prevent taxpayers from converting ordinary income into capital gains by claiming maximum depreciation deductions over the life of the asset and then selling the asset and receiving capital gain treatment on the resulting gain at sale. There are three major depreciation recapture provisions: (1) Section 1245, which generally applies to personal property, (2) Section 1250, which applies to real estate, and (3) "unrecaptured depreciation" previously taken on real estate. The depreciation recapture provisions are extremely complex. Only a brief overview of the general provisions contained in the law is presented here.

Section 1245 Recapture

Under the provisions of Section 1245, any gain recognized on the disposition of a Section 1245 asset will be classified as ordinary income up to an amount equal to the depreciation claimed. Any gain in excess of depreciation taken is classified as a Section 1231 gain. Section 1245 property is:

- Depreciable personal property such as furniture, machines, computers, and automobiles
- Livestock
- Amortizable personal property such as patents, copyrights, leaseholds, and professional sports contracts
- Elevators and escalators
- Pollution control facilities, railroad grading and tunnel-boring equipment, on-the-job training, and child care facilities
- Nonresidential real property (e.g., office buildings) acquired after 1980 but before 1987, on which accelerated ACRS depreciation was claimed

Section 1245 recapture potential is defined as the total depreciation claimed on Section 1245 property. The amount of ordinary income recognized upon the sale of an asset under Section 1245 is equal to the lesser of (1) the recomputed basis less the adjusted basis, or (2) the amount realized less the adjusted basis. The recomputed basis of an asset is the

Self-Study Problem 8.5

SCHEDULE D (Form 1040)

Department of the Treasury Internal Revenue Service (99)

Capital Gains and Losses

► Attach to Form 1040 or Form 1040NR.
► **Information about Schedule D and its separate instructions is at *www.irs.gov/scheduled*.**
► **Use Form 8949 to list your transactions for lines 1b, 2, 3, 8b, 9, and 10.**

OMB No. 1545-0074

2014

Attachment Sequence No. **12**

Name(s) shown on return | **Your social security number**

DRAFT AS OF June 9, 2014 DO NOT FILE

Part I Short-Term Capital Gains and Losses—Assets Held One Year or Less

See instructions for how to figure the amounts to enter on the lines below. This form may be easier to complete if you round off cents to whole dollars.	**(d)** Proceeds (sales price)	**(e)** Cost (or other basis)	**(g)** Adjustments to gain or loss from Form(s) 8949, Part I, line 2, column (g)	**(h) Gain or (loss)** Subtract column (e) from column (d) and combine the result with column (g)
1a Totals for all short-term transactions reported on Form 1099-B for which basis was reported to the IRS and for which you have no adjustments (see instructions). However, if you choose to report all these transactions on Form 8949, leave this line blank and go to line 1b .				
1b Totals for all transactions reported on Form(s) 8949 with **Box A** checked				
2 Totals for all transactions reported on Form(s) 8949 with **Box B** checked				
3 Totals for all transactions reported on Form(s) 8949 with **Box C** checked				

4 Short-term gain from Form 6252 and short-term gain or (loss) from Forms 4684, 6781, and 8824 .	4	
5 Net short-term gain or (loss) from partnerships, S corporations, estates, and trusts from Schedule(s) K-1	5	
6 Short-term capital loss carryover. Enter the amount, if any, from line 8 of your **Capital Loss Carryover Worksheet** in the instructions	6	( )
7 **Net short-term capital gain or (loss).** Combine lines 1a through 6 in column (h). If you have any long-term capital gains or losses, go to Part II below. Otherwise, go to Part III on the back	7	

Part II Long-Term Capital Gains and Losses—Assets Held More Than One Year

See instructions for how to figure the amounts to enter on the lines below. This form may be easier to complete if you round off cents to whole dollars.	**(d)** Proceeds (sales price)	**(e)** Cost (or other basis)	**(g)** Adjustments to gain or loss from Form(s) 8949, Part II, line 2, column (g)	**(h) Gain or (loss)** Subtract column (e) from column (d) and combine the result with column (g)
8a Totals for all long-term transactions reported on Form 1099-B for which basis was reported to the IRS and for which you have no adjustments (see instructions). However, if you choose to report all these transactions on Form 8949, leave this line blank and go to line 8b .				
8b Totals for all transactions reported on Form(s) 8949 with **Box D** checked				
9 Totals for all transactions reported on Form(s) 8949 with **Box E** checked				
10 Totals for all transactions reported on Form(s) 8949 with **Box F** checked.				

11 Gain from Form 4797, Part I; long-term gain from Forms 2439 and 6252; and long-term gain or (loss) from Forms 4684, 6781, and 8824	11	
12 Net long-term gain or (loss) from partnerships, S corporations, estates, and trusts from Schedule(s) K-1	12	
13 Capital gain distributions. See the instructions	13	
14 Long-term capital loss carryover. Enter the amount, if any, from line 13 of your **Capital Loss Carryover Worksheet** in the instructions	14	( )
15 **Net long-term capital gain or (loss).** Combine lines 8a through 14 in column (h). Then go to Part III on the back	15	

Schedule D (Form 1040) 2014 Page **2**

Part III **Summary**

16 Combine lines 7 and 15 and enter the result **16**

- If line 16 is a **gain,** enter the amount from line 16 on Form 1040, line 13, or Form 1040NR, line 14. Then go to line 17 below.
- If line 16 is a **loss,** skip lines 17 through 20 below. Then go to line 21. Also be sure to complete line 22.
- If line 16 is **zero,** skip lines 17 through 21 below and enter -0- on Form 1040, line 13, or Form 1040NR, line 14. Then go to line 22.

17 Are lines 15 and 16 **both** gains?
☐ **Yes.** Go to line 18.
☐ **No.** Skip lines 18 through 21, and go to line 22.

18 Enter the amount, if any, from line 7 of the **28% Rate Gain Worksheet** in the instructions . . ▶ **18**

19 Enter the amount, if any, from line 18 of the **Unrecaptured Section 1250 Gain Worksheet** in the instructions . . . . ▶ **19**

20 Are lines 18 and 19 **both** zero or blank?
☐ **Yes.** Complete the **Qualified Dividends and Capital Gain Tax Worksheet** in the instructions for Form 1040, line 44 (or in the instructions for Form 1040NR, line 42). **Do not** complete lines 21 and 22 below.

☐ **No.** Complete the **Schedule D Tax Worksheet** in the instructions. **Do not** complete lines 21 and 22 below.

21 If line 16 is a loss, enter here and on Form 1040, line 13, or Form 1040NR, line 14, the **smaller** of:

- The loss on line 16 or
- ($3,000), or if married filing separately, ($1,500) } . . . . **21** (   )

Note. When figuring which amount is smaller, treat both amounts as positive numbers.

22 Do you have qualified dividends on Form 1040, line 9b, or Form 1040NR, line 10b?

☐ **Yes.** Complete the **Qualified Dividends and Capital Gain Tax Worksheet** in the instructions for Form 1040, line 44 (or in the instructions for Form 1040NR, line 42).

☐ **No.** Complete the rest of Form 1040 or Form 1040NR.

Schedule D (Form 1040) 2014

DRAFT AS OF June 9, 2014 DO NOT FILE

Self-Study Problem 8.5

Form **8949** Department of the Treasury Internal Revenue Service

Sales and Other Dispositions of Capital Assets

▶ Information about Form 8949 and its separate instructions is at *www.irs.gov/form8949.*
▶ File with your Schedule D to list your transactions for lines 1b, 2, 3, 8b, 9, and 10 of Schedule D.

OMB No. 1545-0123 **2014** Attachment Sequence No. **12A**

Name(s) shown on return	**Social security number or taxpayer identification number**

Before you check Box A, B, or C below, see whether you received any Form(s) 1099-B or substitute statement(s) from your broker. A substitute statement will have the same information as Form 1099-B. Either may show your basis (usually your cost) even if your broker did not report it to the IRS. Brokers must report basis to the IRS for most stock you bought in 2011 or later (and for certain debt instruments you bought in 2014 or later).

DRAFT AS OF June 12, 2014 DO NOT FILE

Part I **Short-Term.** Transactions involving capital assets you held 1 year or less are short term. For long-term transactions, see page 2.

Note. You may aggregate all short-term transactions reported on Form(s) 1099-B showing basis was reported to the IRS and for which no adjustments or codes are required. Enter the total directly on Schedule D, line 1a; you are not required to report these transactions on Form 8949 (see instructions).

You *must* check Box A, B, *or* C below. Check only one box. If more than one box applies for your short-term transactions, complete a separate Form 8949, page 1, for each applicable box. If you have more short-term transactions than will fit on this page for one or more of the boxes, complete as many forms with the same box checked as you need.

☐ **(A)** Short-term transactions reported on Form(s) 1099-B showing basis was reported to the IRS (see **Note** above)
☐ **(B)** Short-term transactions reported on Form(s) 1099-B showing basis was **not** reported to the IRS
☐ **(C)** Short-term transactions not reported to you on Form 1099-B

1 (a) Description of property (Example: 100 sh. XYZ Co.)	(b) Date acquired (Mo., day, yr.)	(c) Date sold or disposed (Mo., day, yr.)	(d) Proceeds (sales price) (see instructions)	(e) Cost or other basis. See the **Note** below and see *Column (e)* in the separate instructions	Adjustment, if any, to gain or loss. If you enter an amount in column (g), enter a code in column (f). See the separate instructions. (f) Code(s) from instructions	(g) Amount of adjustment	(h) **Gain or (loss).** Subtract column (e) from column (d) and combine the result with column (g)
2 Totals. Add the amounts in columns (d), (e), (g), and (h) (subtract negative amounts). Enter each total here and include on your Schedule D, **line 1b** (if **Box A** above is checked), **line 2** (if **Box B** above is checked), or **line 3** (if **Box C** above is checked) ▶							

Note. If you checked Box A above but the basis reported to the IRS was incorrect, enter in column (e) the basis as reported to the IRS, and enter an adjustment in column (g) to correct the basis. See *Column (g)* in the separate instructions for how to figure the amount of the adjustment.

Form 8949 (2014) Attachment Sequence No. **12A** Page **2**

Name(s) shown on return. Name and SSN or taxpayer identification no. not required if shown on other side	**Social security number or taxpayer identification number**

Before you check Box D, E, or F below, see whether you received any Form(s) 1099-B or substitute statement(s) from your broker. A substitute statement will have the same information as Form 1099-B. Either may show your basis (usually your cost) even if your broker did not report it to the IRS. Brokers must report basis to the IRS for most stock you bought in 2011 or later (and for certain debt instruments you bought in 2014 or later).

Part II **Long-Term.** Transactions involving capital assets you held more than 1 year are long term. For short-term transactions, see page 1.

Note. You may aggregate all long-term transactions reported on Form(s) 1099-B showing basis was reported to the IRS and for which no adjustments or codes are required. Enter the total directly on Schedule D, line 8a; you are not required to report these transactions on Form 8949 (see instructions).

DRAFT AS OF June 12, 2014 DO NOT FILE

You *must* check Box D, E, *or* F below. Check only one box. If more than one box applies for your long-term transactions, complete a separate Form 8949, page 2, for each applicable box. If you have more long-term transactions than will fit on this page for one or more of the boxes, complete as many forms with the same box checked as you need.

☐ **(D)** Long-term transactions reported on Form(s) 1099-B showing basis was reported to the IRS (see **Note** above)

☐ **(E)** Long-term transactions reported on Form(s) 1099-B showing basis was **not** reported to the IRS

☐ **(F)** Long-term transactions not reported to you on Form 1099-B

1 (a) Description of property (Example: 100 sh. XYZ Co.)	(b) Date acquired (Mo., day, yr.)	(c) Date sold or disposed (Mo., day, yr.)	(d) Proceeds (sales price) (see instructions)	(e) Cost or other basis. See the **Note** below and see *Column (e)* in the separate instructions	Adjustment, if any, to gain or loss. If you enter an amount in column (g), enter a code in column (f). **See the separate instructions.** (f) Code(s) from instructions	(g) Amount of adjustment	(h) **Gain or (loss).** Subtract column (e) from column (d) and combine the result with column (g)
2 Totals. Add the amounts in columns (d), (e), (g), and (h) (subtract negative amounts). Enter each total here and include on your Schedule D, **line 8b** (if **Box D** above is checked), **line 9** (if **Box E** above is checked), or **line 10** (if **Box F** above is checked) ►							

Note. If you checked Box D above but the basis reported to the IRS was incorrect, enter in column (e) the basis as reported to the IRS, and enter an adjustment in column (g) to correct the basis. See *Column (g)* in the separate instructions for how to figure the amount of the adjustment.

Self-Study Problem 8.5

Qualified Dividends and Capital Gain Tax Worksheet—Line 44

Keep for Your Records

Before you begin:
- ✓ See the earlier instructions for line 44 to see if you can use this worksheet to figure your tax.
- ✓ Before completing this worksheet, complete Form 1040 through line 43.
- ✓ If you do not have to file Schedule D and you received capital gain distributions, be sure you checked the box on line 13 of Form 1040.

1. Enter the amount from Form 1040, line 43. However, if you are filing Form 2555 or 2555-EZ (relating to foreign earned income), enter the amount from line 3 of the Foreign Earned Income Tax Worksheet . . . . . **1.** ________

2. Enter the amount from Form 1040, line 9b* . . . . . **2.** ________

3. Are you filing Schedule D?*
- ☐ **Yes.** Enter the **smaller** of line 15 or 16 of Schedule D. If either line 15 or line 16 is blank or a loss, enter -0-
- ☐ **No.** Enter the amount from Form 1040, line 13

3. ________

4. Add lines 2 and 3 . . . . . **4.** ________

5. If filing Form 4952 (used to figure investment interest expense deduction), enter any amount from line 4g of that form. Otherwise, enter -0- . . . . . **5.** ________

6. Subtract line 5 from line 4. If zero or less, enter -0- . . . . . **6.** ________

7. Subtract line 6 from line 1. If zero or less, enter -0- . . . . . **7.** ________

8. Enter:
$36,900 if single or married filing separately,
$73,800 if married filing jointly or qualifying widow(er),
$49,400 if head of household. . . . . . **8.** ________

9. Enter the smaller of line 1 or line 8 . . . . . **9.** ________

10. Enter the smaller of line 7 or line 9 . . . . . **10.** ________

11. Subtract line 10 from line 9. This amount is taxed at 0% . . . . . **11.** ________

12. Enter the smaller of line 1 or line 6 . . . . . **12.** ________

13. Enter the amount from line 11 . . . . . **13.** ________

14. Subtract line 13 from line 12 . . . . . **14.** ________

15. Enter:
$406,750 if single,
$228,800 if married filing separately,
$457,600 if married filing jointly or qualifying widow(er),
$432,200 if head of household. . . . . . **15.** ________

16. Enter the smaller of line 1 or line 15 . . . . . **16.** ________

17. Add lines 7 and 11 . . . . . **17.** ________

18. Subtract line 17 from line 16. If zero or less, enter -0- . . . . . **18.** ________

19. Enter the smaller of line 14 or line 18 . . . . . **19.** ________

20. Multiply line 19 by 15% (.15) . . . . . **20.** ________

21. Add lines 11 and 19 . . . . . **21.** ________

22. Subtract line 21 from line 12 . . . . . **22.** ________

23. Multiply line 22 by 20% (.20) . . . . . **23.** ________

24. Figure the tax on the amount on line 7. If the amount on line 7 is less than $100,000, use the Tax Table to figure the tax. If the amount on line 7 is $100,000 or more, use the Tax Computation Worksheet . . . . . **24.** ________

25. Add lines 20, 23, and 24 . . . . . **25.** ________

26. Figure the tax on the amount on line 1. If the amount on line 1 is less than $100,000, use the Tax Table to figure the tax. If the amount on line 1 is $100,000 or more, use the Tax Computation Worksheet . . . . . **26.** ________

27. **Tax on all taxable income.** Enter the **smaller** of line 25 or line 26. Also include this amount on Form 1040, line 44. If you are filing Form 2555 or 2555-EZ, do not enter this amount on Form 1040, line 44. Instead, enter it on line 4 of the Foreign Earned Income Tax Worksheet . . . . . **27.** ________

**If you are filing Form 2555 or 2555-EZ, see the footnote in the Foreign Earned Income Tax Worksheet before completing this line.*

Self-Study Problem 8.6

Form **4797**

Department of the Treasury
Internal Revenue Service

Sales of Business Property

(Also Involuntary Conversions and Recapture Amounts Under Sections 179 and 280F(b)(2))

► **Attach to your tax return.**
► **Information about Form 4797 and its separate instructions is at *www.irs.gov/form4797.***

OMB No. 1545-0184
2014
Attachment Sequence No. **27**

DRAFT AS OF
June 13, 2014
DO NOT FILE

Name(s) shown on return	**Identifying number**

1	Enter the gross proceeds from sales or exchanges reported to you for 2014 on Form(s) 1099-B or 1099-S (or substitute statement) that you are including on line 2, 10, or 20 (see instructions)	1	

Part I **Sales or Exchanges of Property Used in a Trade or Business and Involuntary Conversions From Other Than Casualty or Theft—Most Property Held More Than 1 Year** (see instructions)

2 (a) Description of property	(b) Date acquired (mo., day, yr.)	(c) Date sold (mo., day, yr.)	(d) Gross sales price	(e) Depreciation allowed or allowable since acquisition	(f) Cost or other basis, plus improvements and expense of sale	(g) Gain or (loss) Subtract (f) from the sum of (d) and (e)

3	Gain, if any, from Form 4684, line 39	3	
4	Section 1231 gain from installment sales from Form 6252, line 26 or 37	4	
5	Section 1231 gain or (loss) from like-kind exchanges from Form 8824	5	
6	Gain, if any, from line 32, from other than casualty or theft	6	
7	Combine lines 2 through 6. Enter the gain or (loss) here and on the appropriate line as follows:	7	
	Partnerships (except electing large partnerships) and S corporations. Report the gain or (loss) following the instructions for Form 1065, Schedule K, line 10, or Form 1120S, Schedule K, line 9. Skip lines 8, 9, 11, and 12 below. **Individuals, partners, S corporation shareholders, and all others.** If line 7 is zero or a loss, enter the amount from line 7 on line 11 below and skip lines 8 and 9. If line 7 is a gain and you did not have any prior year section 1231 losses, or they were recaptured in an earlier year, enter the gain from line 7 as a long-term capital gain on the Schedule D filed with your return and skip lines 8, 9, 11, and 12 below.		
8	Nonrecaptured net section 1231 losses from prior years (see instructions)	8	
9	Subtract line 8 from line 7. If zero or less, enter -0-. If line 9 is zero, enter the gain from line 7 on line 12 below. If line 9 is more than zero, enter the amount from line 8 on line 12 below and enter the gain from line 9 as a long-term capital gain on the Schedule D filed with your return (see instructions)	9	

Part II **Ordinary Gains and Losses** (see instructions)

10 Ordinary gains and losses not included on lines 11 through 16 (include property held 1 year or less):

11	Loss, if any, from line 7	11	( )
12	Gain, if any, from line 7 or amount from line 8, if applicable	12	
13	Gain, if any, from line 31	13	
14	Net gain or (loss) from Form 4684, lines 31 and 38a	14	
15	Ordinary gain from installment sales from Form 6252, line 25 or 36	15	
16	Ordinary gain or (loss) from like-kind exchanges from Form 8824	16	
17	Combine lines 10 through 16	17	
18	For all except individual returns, enter the amount from line 17 on the appropriate line of your return and skip lines a and b below. For individual returns, complete lines a and b below:		
a	If the loss on line 11 includes a loss from Form 4684, line 35, column (b)(ii), enter that part of the loss here. Enter the part of the loss from income-producing property on Schedule A (Form 1040), line 28, and the part of the loss from property used as an employee on Schedule A (Form 1040), line 23. Identify as from "Form 4797, line 18a." See instructions	18a	
b	Redetermine the gain or (loss) on line 17 excluding the loss, if any, on line 18a. Enter here and on Form 1040, line 14	18b	

For Paperwork Reduction Act Notice, see separate instructions. Cat. No. 13086I Form **4797** (2014)

Form 4797 (2014) Page **2**

Part III Gain From Disposition of Property Under Sections 1245, 1250, 1252, 1254, and 1255 (see instructions)

19 (a) Description of section 1245, 1250, 1252, 1254, or 1255 property:	(b) Date acquired (mo., day, yr.)	(c) Date sold (mo., day, yr.)
A		
B		
C		
D		

DRAFT AS OF June 13, 2014 DO NOT FILE

These columns relate to the properties on lines 19A through 19D. ▶		Property A	Property B	Property C	Property D
20 Gross sales price (**Note:** *See line 1 before completing.*)	20				
21 Cost or other basis plus expense of sale	21				
22 Depreciation (or depletion) allowed or allowable	22				
23 Adjusted basis. Subtract line 22 from line 21	23				
24 Total gain. Subtract line 23 from line 20	24				
25 **If section 1245 property:**					
a Depreciation allowed or allowable from line 22	25a				
b Enter the **smaller** of line 24 or 25a	25b				
26 **If section 1250 property:** If straight line depreciation was used, enter -0- on line 26g, except for a corporation subject to section 291.					
a Additional depreciation after 1975 (see instructions)	26a				
b Applicable percentage multiplied by the **smaller** of line 24 or line 26a (see instructions)	26b				
c Subtract line 26a from line 24. If residential rental property **or** line 24 is not more than line 26a, skip lines 26d and 26e	26c				
d Additional depreciation after 1969 and before 1976	26d				
e Enter the **smaller** of line 26c or 26d	26e				
f Section 291 amount (corporations only)	26f				
g Add lines 26b, 26e, and 26f	26g				
27 **If section 1252 property:** Skip this section if you did not dispose of farmland or if this form is being completed for a partnership (other than an electing large partnership).					
a Soil, water, and land clearing expenses	27a				
b Line 27a multiplied by applicable percentage (see instructions)	27b				
c Enter the **smaller** of line 24 or 27b	27c				
28 **If section 1254 property:**					
a Intangible drilling and development costs, expenditures for development of mines and other natural deposits, mining exploration costs, and depletion (see instructions)	28a				
b Enter the **smaller** of line 24 or 28a	28b				
29 **If section 1255 property:**					
a Applicable percentage of payments excluded from income under section 126 (see instructions)	29a				
b Enter the **smaller** of line 24 or 29a (see instructions)	29b				

Summary of Part III Gains. Complete property columns A through D through line 29b before going to line 30.

30 Total gains for all properties. Add property columns A through D, line 24	30	
31 Add property columns A through D, lines 25b, 26g, 27c, 28b, and 29b. Enter here and on line 13	31	
32 Subtract line 31 from line 30. Enter the portion from casualty or theft on Form 4684, line 33. Enter the portion from other than casualty or theft on Form 4797, line 6	32	

Part IV Recapture Amounts Under Sections 179 and 280F(b)(2) When Business Use Drops to 50% or Less (see instructions)

		(a) Section 179	(b) Section 280F(b)(2)
33 Section 179 expense deduction or depreciation allowable in prior years	33		
34 Recomputed depreciation (see instructions)	34		
35 Recapture amount. Subtract line 34 from line 33. See the instructions for where to report	35		

Form **4797** (2014)

adjusted basis of the property plus Section 1245 recapture potential. Any gain recognized in excess of the amount of ordinary income is a Section 1231 gain.

EXAMPLE On March 1, 2014, Melvin sells Section 1245 property, which was purchased for $6,000, 4 years ago. Melvin had claimed depreciation on the property of $2,500, and sold the property for $5,000. The recapture under Section 1245 is calculated below:

Section 1245 recapture potential	$2,500
Adjusted basis ($6,000 − $2,500)	3,500
Recomputed basis ($3,500 + $2,500)	6,000
Gain realized ($5,000 − $3,500)	1,500

The ordinary income is equal to the lesser of (1) $2,500, the recomputed basis ($6,000) less the adjusted basis ($3,500), or (2) $1,500, the amount realized ($5,000) less the adjusted basis ($3,500). The entire gain of $1,500 is ordinary income instead of a Section 1231 gain. ♦

EXAMPLE Assume the same facts as in the previous example, except that the property is sold for $7,800. The recapture under Section 1245 is calculated below:

Section 1245 recapture potential	$2,500
Adjusted basis ($6,000 − $2,500)	3,500
Recomputed basis ($3,500 + $2,500)	6,000
Gain realized ($7,800 − $3,500)	4,300

The portion classified as ordinary income is equal to the lesser of (1) $2,500, the recomputed basis ($6,000) less the adjusted basis ($3,500), or (2) $4,300, the amount realized ($7,800) less the adjusted basis ($3,500). Of the $4,300 total gain, $2,500 is classified as ordinary income and the remaining $1,800 ($4,300 − $2,500) is a Section 1231 gain. ♦

Section 1250 Recapture

Section 1250 applies to the gain on the sale of real property, other than real property included in the definition of Section 1245 property. The amount of Section 1250 recapture potential is equal to the excess of depreciation expense claimed over the life of the asset under an accelerated method of depreciation over the amount of depreciation that would have been allowed if the straight-line method of depreciation had been used. However, for commercial real property depreciated under accelerated methods under pre-1987 law, 100 percent of depreciation taken may be subject to recapture. If property is depreciated using the straight-line method, there is no Section 1250 recapture potential. Since the use of the straight-line method is required for real property acquired after 1986, there will be no Section 1250 recapture on the disposition of such property. In practice, Section 1250 recapture is rarely seen.

"Unrecaptured Depreciation" on Real Estate—25 or 28.8 Percent Rate

A special 25 or 28.8 percent tax rate applies to real property gains attributable to depreciation previously taken and not already recaptured under the Section 1250 or Section 1245 rules discussed above. Any remaining gain attributable to "unrecaptured depreciation" previously taken, including straight-line depreciation, is taxed at 25 percent rather than the

long-term capital gain rate of 15 percent. When the taxpayer's ordinary tax rate is only 10 or 15 percent, the depreciation recapture will be taxed at 10 or 15 percent to the extent of the remaining amount in the 10 or 15 percent bracket and then at 25 percent. The application of the 25 percent rate for "unrecaptured depreciation" is frequently seen in practice because it applies to every rental property which is first depreciated and then sold at a gain. If the Medicare surtax discussed in LO 1.9 and LO 8.4 applies, the 25 percent rate will be increased to 28.8 percent and the 15 percent rate will be increased to 18.8 percent.

EXAMPLE Lew acquires an apartment building in 2004 for $300,000, and he sells it in October 2014 for $500,000. The accumulated straight-line depreciation on the building at the time of the sale is $50,000. Lew is in the 35 percent tax bracket for ordinary income. Lew's gain on the sale of the property is $250,000 ($500,000 less adjusted basis of $250,000). $50,000 of the gain is attributable to unrecaptured depreciation and is taxed at 25 percent, while the remaining $200,000 gain is taxed at the 15 percent long-term capital gain rate. Lew may also be subject to the 3.8 percent Medicare surtax which is discussed in LO 1.9 and LO 8.4. If this is the case, his tax rates will increase to 28.8 percent and 18.8 percent, respectively. ♦

Self-Study Problem 8.7 *See Appendix E for Solutions to Self-Study Problems*

A taxpayer acquired Section 1245 property at a cost of $12,000. The asset was sold 10 years later for $6,000, and depreciation claimed on the asset was $7,000. Calculate the following amounts:

1. Adjusted basis $________
2. Recomputed basis $________
3. Recomputed basis less the adjusted basis $________
4. Amount realized less adjusted basis (gain realized) $________
5. Ordinary income under Section 1245 $________
6. Section 1231 gain $________

Learning Objective 8.8

Know the general treatment of casualty losses for both personal and business purposes.

CAPITAL GAINS AND CASUALTY GAINS AND LOSSES

The treatment of casualty gains and losses differs depending on whether the property involved is personal-use, business, or investment property. Therefore, a taxpayer's business and investment casualty gains and losses are computed separately from personal casualty gains and losses.

Personal-Use Property Casualty Gains and Losses

In Chapter 5, the deduction of personal casualty losses as itemized deductions was discussed. Occasionally, taxpayers may have a gain from a casualty as a result of receiving an insurance reimbursement in an amount in excess of the basis of the property. In such a case, the taxpayer must first determine the total casualty gains and total casualty losses, after applying a $100 floor, but before the 10 percent of adjusted gross income limitation for the year. The total gains and losses are then netted. If losses exceed gains, the excess loss is treated as an itemized deduction on Schedule A, subject to the 10 percent of adjusted gross income limitation. If, however, the casualty gains exceed the casualty losses, the taxpayer must follow the general rules applicable to capital gains and losses. That is, all short-term

casualty gains and losses are netted, all long-term casualty gains and losses are netted, and the resulting amounts are included with the taxpayer's other capital gains or losses in determining the taxpayer's net capital gain or loss. When casualty gains exceed casualty losses for the year, none of the casualty losses are subject to the 10 percent of adjusted gross income limitation.

EXAMPLE During 2014, Emily has the following casualties on personal-use property.

	Decrease in Fair Market Value Due to Casualty	***Adjusted Basis***	***Insurance Reimbursement***	***Holding Period***
Automobile	$5,000	$12,000	$4,000	2 years
Jewelry	7,000	3,000	7,000	9 years
Furniture	1,500	3,000	0	6 months

The properties were damaged as a result of separate casualties.

Step 1: Compute separate casualty gains and losses

		Casualty Gain or (Loss)
Automobile	$5,000, lesser of adjusted basis or decrease in fair market value, less $4,000 insurance reimbursement, less $100 floor	$ (900)
Jewelry	$7,000 insurance reimbursement, less $3,000 adjusted basis	4,000
Furniture	$1,500, lesser of adjusted basis or decrease in fair market value, less $100 floor	(1,400)

Step 2: Net all personal casualty gains and losses

$(900) + $4,000 + $(1,400) = $1,700 net casualty gain

Step 3: Determine treatment of casualty gains and losses

Since an overall gain results, the gain or loss on each item is treated as a capital gain or loss as follows:

Automobile—Long-term capital loss	$ (900)
Jewelry—Long-term capital gain	4,000
Furniture—Short-term capital loss	(1,400)

The capital gains and losses are combined with Emily's other capital gains and losses for the year. Since casualty gains exceeded casualty losses for the year, the casualty losses recognized on the automobile and the furniture are not subject to the 10 percent of adjusted gross income limitation. ♦

Would You Believe?

The Ninth Circuit Court decided that a man's payment to a woman to keep her from revealing their extramarital affair was not a deductible casualty loss.

Casualty Gains and Losses from Business or Investment Property

Gains and losses arising from a casualty or theft of property used in a trade or business or held for investment are treated differently from gains and losses arising from a casualty or theft of personal-use property. Business and investment property must be identified as a capital asset, trade or business property subject to an allowance for depreciation, or ordinary income property. The following rules apply to the treatment of business or investment property:

1. Property held for 1 year or less—Gains from trade or business property (including property used in the production of rental or royalty income) and gains from investment property are netted against losses from trade or business property, and the resulting net gain or loss is treated as ordinary income or loss. Losses from investment property are considered separately.
2. Property held over 1 year—Gains and losses from trade or business property and investment property are netted.
   a. Net gain—If the result is a net gain, the net gain is included in the calculation of the net Section 1231 gain or loss (the gains and losses are treated as Section 1231 gains and losses).
   b. Net loss—If the result is a net loss, the gains and losses from business and investment property are excluded from Section 1231 treatment. The tax treatment of the gains and losses depends on whether the property was used in the taxpayer's trade or business or held for investment. Gains and losses from business-use assets are treated as ordinary income and ordinary losses, respectively.

If the taxpayer recognizes a gain as a result of a casualty, and the property involved is depreciable property, the depreciation recapture provisions may cause all or a part of the gain to be treated as ordinary income. A casualty involving business property is included in the definition of an involuntary conversion, so that gain realized may be eligible for deferral under the special involuntary conversion provisions discussed in LO 8.11 of this chapter. The interaction of Section 1231 and casualty gains and losses from business or investment property is complex. Taxpayers should follow the instructions included with Form 4684 and Form 4797. See the IRS website (**www.irs.gov**) for samples of these forms and instructions.

EXAMPLE Two pieces of manufacturing equipment used by Robert in his business are completely destroyed by fire. One of the pieces of equipment had an adjusted basis of $5,000 ($11,000 original basis less $6,000 accumulated depreciation) and a fair market value of $3,000 on the date of the fire. The other piece of equipment had an adjusted basis of $7,000 ($18,000 original basis less $11,000 of accumulated depreciation) and a fair market value of $10,000. Robert receives $3,000 from his insurance company to compensate him for the loss of the first piece of equipment, and he receives $8,000 for the second piece of equipment. As a result of the casualty, Robert's casualty gain or loss is calculated as follows:

	Item 1	***Item 2***
Insurance proceeds	$ 3,000	$ 8,000
Basis of property	(5,000)	(7,000)
(Loss) gain	$(2,000)	$ 1,000

The netting of the business casualty gains and losses results in a net loss; thus, the gains and losses are excluded from Section 1231 treatment. Since the loss on Item 1 represents a loss arising from an asset used in the taxpayer's business (not an asset held for investment), the loss is considered an ordinary loss. The $1,000 gain from Item 2 is treated as ordinary income, Section 1245 recapture. ♦

Self-Study Problem 8.8 ***See Appendix E for Solutions to Self-Study Problems***

Jonathan has the following separate casualties during the year:

	Decrease in Fair Market Value	***Adjusted Basis***	***Insurance Reimbursement***	***Holding Period***
Personal furniture	$ 2,000	$ 3,000	$ 1,600	3 months
Personal jewelry	3,000	1,800	2,500	8 years
Business machinery	15,000	14,000	10,000	3 years

Calculate the amount and nature of Jonathan's gains and losses as a result of these casualities.

INSTALLMENT SALES

Learning Objective 8.9

Understand the provisions allowing deferral of gain on installment sales.

Some taxpayers sell property and do not receive payment immediately. Instead, they take a note from the purchaser and receive payments over an extended period of time. It would be a financial hardship to require those taxpayers to pay tax on all of the gain on the sale of the property in the year of sale when they may not have received enough cash to cover the taxes. To provide equity in such situations, Congress passed the installment sale provision. The installment sale provision allows cash basis taxpayers to spread the gain over the tax years in which payments are received. On an installment sale, the taxable gain reported each year is determined as follows:

$$\text{Taxable gain} = \frac{\text{Total gain realized on the sale}}{\text{Contract price}} \times \text{Cash collections during the year}$$

Taxpayers who receive payments over a period of time automatically report gain on the installment method, unless they elect to report all the gain in the year of the sale. An election to report all the gain in the year of sale is made by including all the gain in income for the year of the sale. Taxpayers use Form 6252, Installment Sale Income, to report the installment sale gain on their income tax returns.

EXAMPLE Howard Scripp sells land with an adjusted basis of $20,000 for $50,000. He receives $10,000 in the year of sale, and the balance is payable at $8,000 per year for 5 years, plus a reasonable amount of interest. If Howard elects not to report under the installment method, the gain in the year of sale would be calculated in the following manner:

Cash	$ 10,000
Note at fair market value	40,000
Amount realized	$ 50,000
Less: the land's basis	(20,000)
Taxable gain	$ 30,000

♦

EXAMPLE If, instead, Howard reports the gain on the installment method, the amount of the taxable gain in the year of sale is \$6,000, which is calculated below.

$$\text{Taxable gain} = \frac{\text{Total gain}}{\text{Contract price}} \times \text{Cash collections}$$

$$\text{Taxable gain} = \frac{\$30{,}000}{\$50{,}000} \times \$10{,}000 = \$6{,}000$$

Howard must complete Form 6252 as illustrated on Page 8-27.

If \$8,000 is collected in the first year after the year of sale, the gain in that year would be \$4,800, as illustrated below.

$$\text{Taxable gain} = \frac{\$30{,}000}{\$50{,}000} \times \$8{,}000 = \$4{,}800$$

Of course, any interest income received on the note is also included in income as ordinary income. ♦

Complex installment sale rules apply to taxpayers who regularly sell real or personal property and to taxpayers who sell certain business or rental real property. For example, any recapture under Section 1245 or Section 1250 must be reported in full in the year of sale, regardless of the taxpayer's use of the installment method. Any remaining gain may be reported under the installment method. In addition, certain limitations apply where there is an installment sale between related parties.

The Contract Price

The contract price used in calculating the taxable gain is the amount the seller will ultimately collect from the purchaser (other than interest). This amount is usually the sale price of the property. However, the purchaser will occasionally assume the seller's liability on the property, in which case the contract price is computed by subtracting from the selling price any mortgage or notes assumed by the buyer. If the mortgage or notes assumed by the buyer exceed the adjusted basis of the property, the excess is treated as a cash payment received in the year of sale and must be included in the contract price.

EXAMPLE Roger receives the following for an installment sale of real estate:

Cash	\$ 3,000
Roger's mortgage assumed by the purchaser	9,000
Note payable to Roger from the purchaser	39,000
Selling price	\$ 51,000

Roger's total gain is computed as follows:

Selling price	\$ 51,000
Less: selling expenses	(1,500)
Amount realized	49,500
Less: Roger's basis in the property	(30,000)
Total gain	\$ 19,500

The contract price is \$42,000 (\$51,000 − \$9,000), and assuming the \$3,000 is the only cash received in the year of sale, the taxable gain in the year of sale is \$1,393 as shown below:

$$\text{Taxable gain} = \frac{\$19{,}500}{\$42{,}000} \times \$3{,}000 = \$1{,}393$$ ♦

Form **6252**

Department of the Treasury
Internal Revenue Service

Installment Sale Income

▶ Attach to your tax return.
▶ Use a separate form for each sale or other disposition of property on the installment method.
▶ Information about Form 6252 and its instructions is at *www.irs.gov/form6252.*

OMB No. 1545-0228
2014
Attachment Sequence No. 79

DRAFT AS OF June 30, 2014 DO NOT FILE

Name(s) shown on return: **Howard Scripp** | **Identifying number**

1	Description of property ▶ **Land**		
2a	Date acquired (mm/dd/yyyy) ▶	**b** Date sold (mm/dd/yyyy) ▶	
3	Was the property sold to a related party (see instructions) after May 14, 1980? If "No," skip line 4		☐ Yes ☑ No
4	Was the property you sold to a related party a marketable security? If "Yes," complete Part III. If "No," complete Part III for the year of sale and the 2 years after the year of sale		☐ Yes ☐ No

Part I Gross Profit and Contract Price. Complete this part for the year of sale only.

5	Selling price including mortgages and other debts. **Do not** include interest, whether stated or unstated			5	50,000
6	Mortgages, debts, and other liabilities the buyer assumed or took the property subject to (see instructions)	6	0		
7	Subtract line 6 from line 5	7	50,000		
8	Cost or other basis of property sold	8	20,000		
9	Depreciation allowed or allowable	9	0		
10	Adjusted basis. Subtract line 9 from line 8	10	20,000		
11	Commissions and other expenses of sale	11			
12	Income recapture from Form 4797, Part III (see instructions)	12			
13	Add lines 10, 11, and 12			13	20,000
14	Subtract line 13 from line 5. If zero or less, **do not** complete the rest of this form (see instructions)			14	30,000
15	If the property described on line 1 above was your main home, enter the amount of your excluded gain (see instructions). Otherwise, enter -0-			15	0
16	**Gross profit.** Subtract line 15 from line 14			16	30,000
17	Subtract line 13 from line 6. If zero or less, enter -0-			17	
18	**Contract price.** Add line 7 and line 17			18	50,000

Part II Installment Sale Income. Complete this part for the year of sale **and** any year you receive a payment or have certain debts you must treat as a payment on installment obligations.

June 12, 2014

19	Gross profit percentage (expressed as a decimal amount). Divide line 16 by line 18. For years after the year of sale, see instructions			19	.60
20	If this is the year of sale, enter the amount from line 17. Otherwise, enter -0-			20	0
21	Payments received during year (see instructions). **Do not** include interest, whether stated or unstated			21	10,000
22	Add lines 20 and 21			22	10,000
23	Payments received in prior years (see instructions). **Do not** include interest, whether stated or unstated	23	0		
24	**Installment sale income.** Multiply line 22 by line 19			24	6,000
25	Enter the part of line 24 that is ordinary income under the recapture rules (see instructions)			25	0
26	Subtract line 25 from line 24. Enter here and on Schedule D or Form 4797 (see instructions)			26	6,000

Part III Related Party Installment Sale Income. Do not complete if you received the final payment this tax year.

27 Name, address, and taxpayer identifying number of related party

28 Did the related party resell or dispose of the property ("second disposition") during this tax year? ☐ Yes ☐ No

29 **If the answer to question 28 is "Yes," complete lines 30 through 37 below unless one of the following conditions is met. Check the box that applies.**

- **a** ☐ The second disposition was more than 2 years after the first disposition (other than dispositions of marketable securities). If this box is checked, enter the date of disposition (mm/dd/yyyy) ▶
- **b** ☐ The first disposition was a sale or exchange of stock to the issuing corporation.
- **c** ☐ The second disposition was an involuntary conversion and the threat of conversion occurred after the first disposition.
- **d** ☐ The second disposition occurred after the death of the original seller or buyer.
- **e** ☐ It can be established to the satisfaction of the IRS that tax avoidance was not a principal purpose for either of the dispositions. If this box is checked, attach an explanation (see instructions).

30	Selling price of property sold by related party (see instructions)	30	
31	Enter contract price from line 18 for year of first sale	31	
32	Enter the **smaller** of line 30 or line 31	32	
33	Total payments received by the end of your 2014 tax year (see instructions)	33	
34	Subtract line 33 from line 32. If zero or less, enter -0-	34	
35	Multiply line 34 by the gross profit percentage on line 19 for year of first sale	35	
36	Enter the part of line 35 that is ordinary income under the recapture rules (see instructions)	36	
37	Subtract line 36 from line 35. Enter here and on Schedule D or Form 4797 (see instructions)	37	

For Paperwork Reduction Act Notice, see page 4. Cat. No. 13601R Form **6252** (2014)

Self-Study Problem 8.9 *See Appendix E for Solutions to Self-Study Problems*

Brian acquired a rental house in 1999 for a cost of $80,000. Straight-line depreciation on the property of $26,000 has been claimed by Brian. In January 2014, he sells the property for $120,000, receiving $20,000 cash on March 1 and the buyer's note for $100,000 at 10 percent interest. The note is payable at $10,000 per year for 10 years, with the first payment to be received 1 year after the date of sale. Calculate his taxable gain under the installment method for the year of sale of the rental house.

Gain reportable in 2014 $____________

TAX BREAK

Taxpayers may wish to elect out of the installment treatment for a sale which could qualify, and instead recognize all of the gain in the year of sale when they have low income and expect that the gain would be taxed at a higher rate if deferred to later years.

LIKE-KIND EXCHANGES

Learning Objective 8.10

Know the general treatment of like-kind exchanges.

Although a taxpayer realizes a gain or loss on the sale or exchange of property, the recognition of the gain or loss may be deferred for tax purposes. One example of such a situation arises when a taxpayer exchanges property for other property of a like kind. Under certain circumstances, the transaction may be nontaxable. To qualify as a nontaxable exchange, the property exchanged must be held for productive use in a trade or business or for investment. Property held for personal purposes, such as a taxpayer's residence, will not qualify for a like-kind exchange. When the exchange involves only qualified like-kind property, no gain or loss is recognized. However, some exchanges include cash or other property in addition to the like-kind property. Even when the exchange is not solely for like-kind assets, the nontaxable treatment usually is not completely lost. Gain is recognized in an amount equal to the lesser of (1) the gain realized or (2) the "boot" received. Boot is money or the fair market value of other property received in addition to the like-kind property. Relief from a liability is the same as receiving cash and is treated as boot.

The basis of other property received as boot in an exchange is its fair market value on the date of the exchange. The basis of the like-kind property received is:

The basis of the like-kind property given up
\+ Any boot paid
− Any boot received
\+ Any gain recognized
Basis of property received

The holding period for property acquired in a like-kind exchange includes the holding period of the property exchanged. For example, if long-term capital gain property is exchanged today, the new property may be sold immediately, and the gain recognized would be long-term capital gain.

Taxpayers must file Form 8824, Like-Kind Exchanges, to report the exchange of property. This form must be completed even if no gain is recognized.

EXAMPLE Janis and Kevin exchange real estate held as an investment. Janis gives up property with an adjusted basis of $350,000 and a fair market value of $560,000. The property is subject to a mortgage of $105,000 which is assumed by Kevin. In return for this property, Janis receives from Kevin property with a fair market value of $420,000 and cash of $35,000. Kevin's adjusted basis in the property he exchanges is $280,000.

1. Janis recognizes a gain of $140,000, equal to the lesser of the gain realized or the boot received as calculated below.

Calculation of gain realized:	
Fair market value of property received	$ 420,000
Cash received	35,000
Liability assumed by Kevin	105,000
Total amount realized	$ 560,000
Less: the adjusted basis of the property given up	(350,000)
Gain realized	$ 210,000
Calculation of boot received:	
Cash received	$ 35,000
Liability assumed by Kevin	105,000
Total boot received	$ 140,000
Gain: Lesser of gain realized or boot received	$ 140,000

2. The basis of Janis's property is calculated below.

Basis of the property given up	$ 350,000
+ Boot paid	0
− Boot received	(140,000)
+ Gain recognized	140,000
Basis of the like-kind property received	$ 350,000

3. Kevin's recognized gain is equal to the lesser of the gain realized or the boot received. Since he received no boot, the recognized gain is zero.

Calculation of gain realized:	
Fair market value of the property received	$ 560,000
Less: boot paid ($105,000 + $35,000)	(140,000)
Less: adjusted basis of property given up	(280,000)
Gain realized	$ 140,000
Boot received	$ 0

4. The basis of Kevin's new property is calculated below.

Basis of the property given up	$ 280,000
+ Boot paid	140,000
− Boot received	0
+ Gain recognized	0
Basis of the property received	$ 420,000

♦

Like-Kind Property

The term "like-kind property" does not include inventory, stocks, bonds, or other securities. A like-kind exchange must involve real estate for real estate, or personal property for personal property of a like kind or class. Examples of different classes of personal property

are office furniture and equipment, airplanes, computers and peripheral equipment, trucks, and automobiles. The exchange of office furniture for a computer, for instance, will not qualify as a like-kind exchange. The like-kind exchange provision is not elective. Taxpayers must use the provision if a transaction qualifies as a like-kind exchange, regardless of whether the transaction results in a realized gain or a realized loss.

TAX BREAK

Tax planning for the sale of business automobiles can sometimes save significant tax dollars. The luxury auto depreciation rules covered in Chapter 7 allow only small amounts of depreciation on business autos, so the tax basis of business automobiles may be much larger than the trade-in or direct sale value, especially for expensive cars. The direct sale of a business auto will therefore often generate a deductible loss. An auto trade-in is generally treated as a mandatory like-kind exchange, so the potential tax-deductible loss must be added to the basis of the new vehicle and may not be deducted. Taxpayers should consider selling business autos instead of trading them in when the sale results in a large tax deduction.

Self-Study Problem 8.10 *See Appendix E for Solutions to Self-Study Problems*

During the current year, Daniel James exchanges a truck used in his business for a new truck. Daniel's basis in the truck is $18,000, and the truck is subject to a liability of $8,000, which is assumed by the other party to the exchange. Daniel receives a new truck that is worth $22,000. Calculate Daniel's recognized gain on the exchange and his basis in the new truck.

Recognized gain	$ ________
Basis in the new truck	$ ________

INVOLUNTARY CONVERSIONS

Learning Objective 8.11

Understand the basic tax treatment of involuntary conversions.

Occasionally, taxpayers are forced to dispose of property as a result of circumstances beyond their control. At the election of the taxpayer, and provided certain conditions are met, the gain on an involuntary conversion of property may be deferred. The provisions require that the property must be replaced and the basis of the replacement property reduced by the amount of the gain deferred. An involuntary conversion is defined as the destruction of the taxpayer's property in whole or in part, or loss of the property by theft, seizure, requisition, or condemnation. Also, property sold pursuant to reclamation laws, and livestock destroyed by disease or drought, are subject to the involuntary conversion rules. To qualify for nonrecognition of gain, the taxpayer must obtain qualified replacement property. The replacement property must be "similar or related in service or use." This definition is narrower than the like-kind rule; the property must be very similar to the property converted. Generally, a taxpayer has 2 years after the close of the tax year in which a gain was realized to obtain replacement property.

A realized gain on the involuntary conversion of property occurs when the taxpayer receives insurance proceeds or other payments in excess of his or her adjusted basis in the converted property. Taxpayers need not recognize any gain if they completely reinvest the proceeds or payments in qualified replacement property within the required time period. If they do not reinvest the total amount of the payments received, they must recognize a gain equal to the amount of the payment not reinvested (but limited to the gain realized). The basis of the replacement property is equal to the cost of the replacement property reduced by any gain not recognized on the transaction. The holding period of the replacement property includes the period the original property was held.

EXAMPLE Tammy's building, which has an adjusted basis of $50,000, is destroyed by fire in 2014. In the same year, Tammy receives $100,000 of insurance proceeds for the loss. She has until December 31, 2016 (2 years after the end of the taxable year in which the gain is realized), to acquire a replacement building. In 2015, Tammy replaces the building with a new building costing $80,000. Her realized gain on the involuntary conversion is $50,000 ($100,000 − $50,000), and the gain recognized is $20,000, which is the $100,000 of cash received less the amount reinvested ($80,000). The basis of the new building is $50,000 ($80,000 − $30,000), the cost of the new building less the portion of the gain not recognized. ♦

The involuntary conversion provision applies only to gains, not to losses. The provision must be elected by the taxpayer. In contrast, the like-kind exchange provision discussed previously applies to both gains and losses and is not elective.

Self-Study Problem 8.11 *See Appendix E for Solutions to Self-Study Problems*

Sam's store is destroyed in 2014 as a result of a flood. The store has an adjusted basis of $70,000, and Sam receives insurance proceeds of $150,000 on the loss. Sam invests $135,000 in a replacement store in 2015.

1. Calculate Sam's recognized gain, assuming an election under the involuntary conversion provision is made. $__________
2. Calculate Sam's basis in the replacement store. $__________

Learning Objective 8.12

Know the rules governing the exclusion on gain from personal residence sales.

SALE OF A PERSONAL RESIDENCE

Sales After May 6, 1997

For sales of a principal residence after May 6, 1997, the long-standing rollover rule (see below) and the $125,000 exclusion for taxpayers over 55 years old were replaced by a new general exclusion. For gains on the sale of a personal residence after May 6, 1997, a seller of any age who has owned and used a home as a principal residence for at least 2 of the last 5 years before the sale can exclude from income up to $250,000 of gain ($500,000 for joint return filers). In general, this exclusion can be used only once every 2 years. As under prior law, a personal residence includes single-family homes, mobile homes, houseboats, condominiums, cooperative apartments, duplexes, or row houses.

EXAMPLE Joe, a single taxpayer, bought his home 22 years ago for $25,000. He has lived in the home continuously since he purchased it. In November 2014, he sells his home for $300,000. Therefore, his realized gain on the sale of his personal residence is $275,000 ($300,000 − $25,000). Joe's taxable gain on this sale is $25,000, which is his total gain of $275,000 less the exclusion of $250,000. ♦

A seller otherwise qualified to exclude gain on a principal residence who fails to satisfy the 2-year ownership and use requirements may calculate the amount of excluded gain by prorating the exclusion amount if the residence sale is due to an employment-related move, health, or unforeseen circumstances. Unforeseen circumstances include death, divorce or separation, a change in employment that leaves the taxpayer unable to pay the mortgage,

multiple births from the same pregnancy, and becoming eligible for unemployment compensation. The $250,000 or $500,000 exclusion amount is prorated by multiplying the exclusion amount by the length of time the taxpayer owned and used the home divided by 2 years.

EXAMPLE John is a single taxpayer who owns and uses his principal residence for 1 year. He then sells the residence due to an employment-related move at a $100,000 gain. Because he may exclude up to one-half (1 year divided by 2 years) of the $250,000 exclusion amount, or $125,000, none of his gain is taxable. ♦

Married Taxpayers

Taxpayers who are married and file a joint return for the year of sale may exclude up to $500,000 of gain realized on the sale of a personal residence. The full $500,000 for a married couple can be excluded if:

1. Either spouse owned the home for at least 2 of the 5 years before the sale,
2. Both spouses used the home as a principal residence for at least 2 of the last 5 years, and
3. Neither spouse has used the exclusion during the prior 2 years.

EXAMPLE Don and Dolly have been married for 20 years. At the time they were married, they purchased a home for $200,000 and have lived in the home since their marriage. Don and Dolly sell their home for $800,000 and retire to Arizona. Their realized gain on the sale is $600,000 ($800,000 − $200,000), of which only $100,000 is taxable because of the $500,000 exclusion. ♦

The $500,000 exclusion for married taxpayers has been extended to spouses who sell the residence within 2 years of their spouse's death, for sales after December 31, 2007.

Beginning in 2009, Congress closed a loophole in the residence gain exclusion laws, which was used effectively by some owners of multiple rental properties. Under the residence gain exclusion laws in operation prior to 2009, taxpayers with multiple rental properties could move into a previously rented property every 2 years, reside in the property for the required 2-year period, and then sell the property using the $250,000 or $500,000 gain exclusion. Over a period of 10 years, a married couple could theoretically exclude $2.5 million of taxable gain on five separate properties. Beginning in 2009, taxpayers who rent their residence prior to their 2 years of personal use are generally limited to an exclusion smaller than the full $250,000 or $500,000 amounts. For details, examples, and exceptions to the law, visit **www.irs.gov.**

Sales Before May 7, 1997

Please note: The law below no longer applies to sales of principal residences. However, because many taxpayers still own residences with "rollover" basis determined under this law, it is important to understand how the law operated.

For sales of a personal residence before May 7, 1997, taxpayers did not have to recognize gain on the sale if they rolled the gain into a new house with a cost as high as the adjusted sales price of the old residence. The adjusted sales price was the amount realized on the sale less any qualified fixing-up expenses. Fixing-up expenses must have been incurred within 90 days prior to the date of sale and paid within 30 days after the date of sale. In addition, the purchase of the new residence had to be within 2 years of the date of sale of the old residence to qualify for nonrecognition of the gain. The adjusted basis of the new residence was reduced by any gain not recognized on the sale of the old residence.

EXAMPLE Mary sold her personal residence for $60,000 in 1994 and paid selling expenses of $3,600. Mary had fixing-up expenses of $1,400, and the basis of her old residence was $40,000. If Mary purchased a new residence within 2 years for $85,000, her recognized gain and the basis of the new residence was calculated as follows:

1. Sales price	$ 60,000
Less: selling expenses	(3,600)
Amount realized	$ 56,400
Adjusted basis of the old residence	(40,000)
Gain realized on the sale	$ 16,400
2. Amount realized	$ 56,400
Less: fixing-up expenses	(1,400)
Adjusted sales price	$ 55,000
Less: cost of the new residence	(85,000)
Gain recognized	$ 0
3. Gain realized	$ 16,400
Less: gain recognized	(0)
Gain not recognized (deferred)	$ 16,400
4. Cost of the new residence	$ 85,000
Less: gain deferred	(16,400)
Basis of the new residence	$ 68,600

♦

EXAMPLE Assume instead that Mary paid only $50,000 for a new residence. The gain and basis of the new residence are calculated as follows:

1. Adjusted sales price (from above)	$ 55,000
Less: cost of new residence	(50,000)
Gain recognized	$ 5,000
2. Gain realized (from above example)	$ 16,400
Less: gain recognized	(5,000)
Gain not recognized (deferred)	$ 11,400
3. Cost of the new residence	$ 50,000
Less: gain deferred	(11,400)
Basis of the new residence	$ 38,600

♦

The above calculations show that a taxpayer who sold one or more principal residences over a period of years and has a "rollover" basis under the old law may have a principal residence basis that is far lower than the cost of the taxpayer's residence. Because the current law does not require rollover treatment, taxpayers receive a fresh basis in a newly purchased residence which is equal to the purchase price.

Would You Believe?

The IRS has ruled that, in certain cases, a yacht may qualify as a taxpayer's principal residence.

Self-Study Problem 8.12

See Appendix E for Solutions to Self-Study Problems

Mike, a single taxpayer, purchased a house 20 years ago for $30,000. He sells the house in December 2014 for $350,000. He has always lived in the house.

a. How much taxable gain does Mike have from the sale of his personal residence?

$ ___________

b. Assume Mike married Mary 3 years ago and she has lived in the house since their marriage. If they sell the house in December 2014 for $350,000, what is their taxable gain on a joint tax return?

$ ___________

c. Assume Mike is not married and purchased the house only 1 year ago for $200,000, and he sells the house for $350,000 due to an employment-related move. What is Mike's taxable gain?

$ ___________

Paid Preparer Use Only	Print/Type preparer's name	Preparer's signature	Date	Check ☐ if self-employed	PTIN
	Firm's name ▶		Firm's EIN ▶		
	Firm's address ▶		Phone no.		

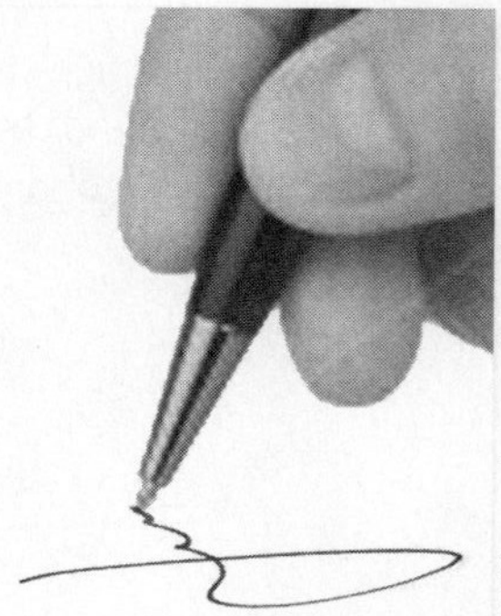

© ILYA AKINSHIN/Shutterstock.com; © Zhukov Oleg/Shutterstock.com.

Would You Sign This Tax Return?

Ivy Tower (age 45), a history professor at Coastal State University, recently purchased a house near the beach. In the current year, she accepted an offer from a buyer who wants to make the house into a B&B. She sold her personal residence for a $100,000 gain. She owned the house 11 months as of the date of sale. After the sale closed, she discovered that the $100,000 is taxable as a short-term taxable gain (i.e., ordinary income) because she had not lived there the 2 years required for exclusion of gain on the sale of a residence. She is upset that she will have to pay substantial tax on the sale. Her best friend's husband is an M.D. who signed a letter that Ivy had to move due to the dampness and humidity at the beach. She is not a regular patient of the doctor and Ivy has no history of respiratory problems. Ivy claims she meets the medical extraordinary circumstances exception and therefore refuses to report the gain on her Form 1040. If Ivy were your tax client, would you sign the Paid Preparer's declaration (see example above) on her return? Why or why not?

KEY TERMS

capital asset, 8-2
holding period, 8-3
short-term capital gain or loss, 8-3
"sale or exchange," 8-3
adjusted basis, 8-4
net capital gain, 8-7
net capital loss, 8-9
capital loss carryovers, 8-9
personal capital assets, 8-10
section 1231 assets, 8-11
depreciation recapture, 8-12
section 1245 recapture, 8-12
section 1250 recapture, 8-21
installment sale, 8-25
like-kind exchange, 8-29
"boot," 8-29
like-kind property, 8-30
involuntary conversion, 8-31
replacement property, 8-31
personal residence exclusion, 8-32

KEY POINTS

Learning Objectives	Key Points
LO 8.1: Define the term "capital asset."	• A capital asset is any property, whether or not used in a trade or business, except: (1) inventory, (2) depreciable property or real property used in a trade or business, (3) certain copyrights, literary, musical, or artistic compositions, letters or memorandums, (4) accounts or notes receivable, and (5) certain U.S. government publications. • Assets excluded from the definition of a capital asset generate ordinary income or loss on their disposition.
LO 8.2: Know the holding period for long-term and short-term capital gains.	• Assets must be held for more than 1 year for the gain or loss to be considered long-term. • A capital asset held 1 year or less results in a short-term capital gain or loss. • In calculating the holding period, the taxpayer excludes the date of acquisition and includes the date of disposition.
LO 8.3: Calculate the gain or loss on the disposition of an asset.	• The taxpayer's gain or loss is calculated using the following formula: amount realized − adjusted basis = gain or loss realized. • The amount realized from a sale or other disposition of property is equal to the sum of the money received, plus the fair market value of other property received, less the costs paid to transfer the property. • The adjusted basis of property = the original basis + capital improvements − accumulated depreciation. • In most cases, the original basis is the cost of the property at the date of acquisition, plus any costs incidental to the purchase, such as title insurance, escrow fees, and inspection fees. • Capital improvements are major expenditures for permanent improvements to or restoration of the taxpayer's property.
LO 8.4: Compute the tax on capital gains.	• Short-term capital gains are taxed as ordinary income, while there are various different preferential long-term capital gains tax rates. • For 2014, net long-term capital gains may be subject to rates ranging from 0 percent to 31.8 percent. • Special rates apply to gains on collectibles (e.g., art, stamps, gems, coins, etc.) and depreciation recapture on the disposition of certain Section 1250 assets.
LO 8.5: Understand the treatment of capital losses.	• Individual taxpayers may deduct net capital losses against ordinary income in amounts up to $3,000 per year with any unused capital losses carried forward indefinitely. • When a taxpayer ends up with net capital losses, the losses offset capital gains as follows: 1) net short-term capital losses first reduce 28 percent gains, then 25 percent gains, then regular long-term capital gains, and 2) net long-term capital losses first reduce 28 percent gains, then 25 percent gains, then any short-term capital gains.
LO 8.6: Understand the treatment of Section 1231 assets.	• Section 1231 assets include (1) depreciable or real property used in a trade or business, (2) timber, coal, or domestic iron ore, (3) livestock (not including poultry) held for draft, breeding, dairy, or sporting purposes, and (4) unharvested crops on land used in a trade or business. • If net Section 1231 gains exceed the losses, the excess is a long-term capital gain. When the net Section 1231 losses exceed the gains, all gains are treated as ordinary income, and all losses are fully deductible as ordinary losses.

LO 8.7: Describe the depreciation recapture rules.	• Depreciation recapture provisions are meant to prevent taxpayers from converting ordinary income into capital gains by claiming maximum depreciation deductions over the life of the asset and then selling the asset and receiving capital gain treatment on the resulting gain at sale. • Under Section 1245, any gain recognized on the disposition of a Section 1245 asset (generally personal property) will be classified as ordinary income up to an amount equal to the depreciation claimed. Any gain in excess of depreciation taken is classified as a Section 1231 gain. • Section 1250 real property recapture is the excess of depreciation expense claimed, using an accelerated method of depreciation, over what would have been allowed if the straight-line method were used. Under pre-1987 law, 100 percent of depreciation taken for commercial property may be subject to recapture. • Since the straight-line method is required for real property acquired after 1986, there will be no Section 1250 recapture on the disposition of real property unless it was acquired more than 28 years ago. • A special 25 percent tax rate applies to real property gains attributable to depreciation previously taken and not already recaptured under Section 1250 or Section 1245.
LO 8.8: Know the general treatment of casualty gains and losses for both personal and business purposes.	• Taxpayers may have a gain from a casualty due to receipt of an insurance reimbursement in an amount in excess of the basis of the property. • The taxpayer must first determine net personal casualty gains and losses, after applying the $100 floor, but before the 10 percent of adjusted gross income limitation, for the year. • The total casualty gains and losses are then netted, and if losses exceed gains, the excess loss is treated as an itemized deduction on Schedule A, subject to the 10 percent of AGI limitation. • If the casualty gains exceed the casualty losses, the taxpayer must follow the general rules applicable to capital gains and losses. • Gains and losses arising from a casualty or theft of property used in a trade or business or held for investment are treated differently than gains and losses from a casualty or theft of personal-use property.
LO 8.9: Understand the provisions allowing deferral of gain on installment sales.	• On an installment sale, the taxable gain reported each year is determined as follows: taxable gain equals total gain realized on the sale, divided by the contract price, and multiplied by the cash collections during the year.
LO 8.10: Know the general treatment of like-kind exchanges.	• To qualify as a nontaxable like-kind exchange, the property exchanged must be held for use in a trade or business or for investment, and exchanged for property of a like kind. • Like-kind gain is recognized in an amount equal to the lesser of (1) the gain realized or (2) the "boot" received. Boot is money or the fair market value of other property received in addition to the like-kind property. • If a transaction qualifies as a like-kind exchange, the like-kind exchange provisions must be followed.
LO 8.11: Understand the basic tax treatment of involuntary conversions.	• A realized gain on the involuntary conversion of property occurs when the taxpayer receives proceeds in excess of his or her adjusted basis. • Involuntary conversion gain is not recognized if the proceeds or payments are reinvested in qualified replacement property within the required time period and the taxpayer makes the proper election.
LO 8.12: Know the rules governing the exclusion on gain from personal residence sales.	• Taxpayers who have owned their personal residence and used it for at least 2 of the 5 years before the sale can exclude up to $250,000 of gain ($500,000 for joint return filers).

© Dusit/Shutterstock.com

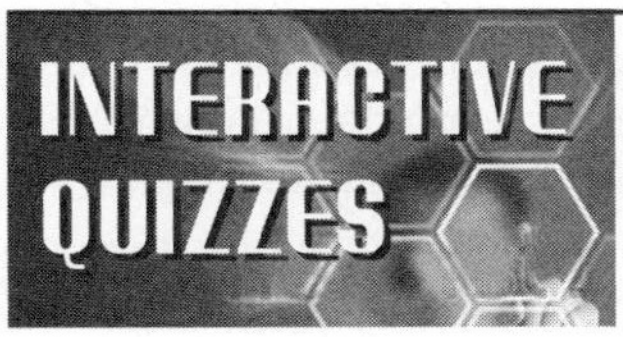

Interactive quizzes are available as an optional online resource for Income Tax Fundamentals. Visit **www.cengagebrain.com** for more information.

QUESTIONS and PROBLEMS

GROUP 1: MULTIPLE CHOICE QUESTIONS

____

LO 8.1

1. All of the following assets are capital assets, except:
   a. A personal automobile
   b. IBM stock
   c. Business inventory
   d. Personal furniture
   e. An individual's stamp collection

____

LO 8.1

2. Which of the following is a capital asset?
   a. Account receivable
   b. Copyright created by the taxpayer
   c. Copyright (held by the writer)
   d. Business inventory
   e. A taxpayer's residence

____

LO 8.3

3. Bob sells a stock investment for $45,000 cash, and the purchaser assumes Bob's $32,500 debt on the investment. The basis of Bob's stock investment is $55,000. What is the gain or loss realized on the sale?
   a. $10,000 loss
   b. $10,000 gain
   c. $12,500 gain
   d. $22,500 loss
   e. $22,500 gain

____

LO 8.4

4. In 2014, the top tax rates are ______ percent on individual long-term capital gains on sale of stock, and ______ percent on capital gains on sales of collectible items, assuming the ACA Medicare surtax does not apply.
   a. 10; 20
   b. 15; 25
   c. 20; 28
   d. 25; 28

____

LO 8.4

5. In November 2014, Ben and Betty (married, filing jointly) have a long-term capital gain of $50,000 on the sale of stock. They have no other capital gains and losses for the year. Their ordinary income for the year after the standard deduction and personal exemptions is $72,500, making their total taxable income for the year $122,500 ($72,500 + $50,000). In 2014, married taxpayers pay 10 percent on taxable income up to $18,150, 15 percent on the next $55,650, and 25 percent on the next $75,050 of taxable income. What will be their 2014 total tax liability assuming a tax of $9,971 on the $72,500 of ordinary income?

a. $9,971
b. $18,375
c. $17,471
d. $22,338

LO 8.4

6. Harold and Wanda (married filing jointly) have $30,000 ordinary income after the standard deduction and personal exemptions, and $50,000 in unrecaptured depreciation on the sale of rental property, for total taxable income of $80,000. For 2014, the 10 percent tax bracket for married taxpayers filing jointly ends at $18,150, the next $55,650 in taxable income is taxed at 15 percent, and 25 percent applies to the next $75,050. What is Harold and Wanda's tax? (Please use the percentages given in this problem to calculate your answer.)
   a. $7,500
   b. $11,093
   c. $11,713
   d. $16,093

LO 8.4

7. In 2014, Tim, a single taxpayer, has ordinary income of $30,000. In addition, he has $2,000 in short-term capital gains, long-term capital losses of $5,000, and long-term capital gains of $4,000. What is Tim's AGI for 2014?
   a. $28,000
   b. $30,000
   c. $31,000
   d. $32,000

LO 8.6

8. Which of the following is Section 1231 property?
   a. A building used in a trade or business
   b. Poultry used for egg production
   c. Accounts receivable
   d. Inventory
   e. Paintings owned by the artist

LO 8.6
LO 8.7

9. In 2014, Mary sells for $15,000 a machine used in her business. The property was purchased on May 1, 2012, at a cost of $12,500. Mary has claimed depreciation on the machine of $4,750. What is the amount and nature of Mary's gain as a result of the sale of the machine?
   a. $7,250 Section 1231 gain
   b. $7,250 ordinary income under Section 1245
   c. $2,500 ordinary income and $4,750 Section 1231 gain
   d. $2,500 Section 1231 gain and $4,750 ordinary income under Section 1245
   e. None of the above

LO 8.6
LO 8.7

10. During 2014, Paul sells residential rental property for $300,000, which he acquired in 1994 for $150,000. Paul has claimed straight-line depreciation on the building of $57,525. What is the amount and nature of Paul's gain on the sale of the rental property?
   a. $207,525 Section 1231 gain
   b. $150,000 Section 1231 gain, $57,525 "unrecaptured depreciation"
   c. $167,400 Section 1231 gain, $57,525 ordinary income
   d. $190,125 Section 1231 gain, $17,400 "unrecaptured depreciation"
   e. None of the above

LO 8.7

11. Jeanie acquires an apartment building in 2003 for $260,000 and sells it for $500,000 in 2014. At the time of sale there is $78,000 of accumulated straight-line depreciation

on the apartment building. Assuming Jeanie is in the highest tax bracket for ordinary income and the Medicare surtax applies, how much of her gain is taxed at 28.8 percent?

a. None
b. $240,000
c. $318,000
d. $162,000
e. $78,000

LO 8.8

12. Virginia has a casualty gain of $5,000 and a casualty loss of $2,500, before reduction by the $100 floor. The gain and loss were the result of two separate casualties, and both properties were personal-use assets. What is Virginia's gain or loss as a result of these casualties?

a. $5,000 capital gain and $2,500 capital loss
b. $5,000 capital gain and $2,400 itemized deduction, subject to the 10 percent of adjusted gross income limitation
c. $5,000 capital gain and $2,500 itemized deduction, subject to the 10 percent of adjusted gross income limitation
d. $5,000 capital gain and $2,400 capital loss
e. None of the above

LO 8.9

13. Pat sells real estate for $30,000 cash and a $120,000 5-year note. If her basis in the property is $90,000 and she receives only the $30,000 down payment in the year of sale, how much is Pat's taxable gain in the year of sale using the installment sales method?

a. $60,000
b. $30,000
c. $15,000
d. $12,000
e. $0

LO 8.10

14. Fred and Sarajane exchanged equipment in a qualifying like-kind exchange. Fred gives up equipment with an adjusted basis of $14,000 (fair market value of $15,000) in exchange for Sarajane's equipment with a fair market value of $12,000 plus $3,000 cash. How much gain should Fred recognize on the exchange?

a. $3,000
b. $2,000
c. $1,000
d. $0
e. None of the above

LO 8.10

15. What is Sarajane's basis in the equipment received in the exchange described in Question 14, assuming her basis in the equipment given up was $12,000?

a. $0
b. $12,000
c. $14,000
d. $15,000
e. None of the above

LO 8.12

16. Oscar, a single taxpayer, sells his residence of the last 10 years in January of 2014 for $190,000. Oscar's basis in the residence is $45,000, and his selling expenses are $11,000. If Oscar does not buy a new residence, what is the taxable gain on the sale of his residence?

a. $145,000
b. $134,000
c. $45,000

d. $9,000
e. $0

LO 8.12

17. Jim, a single taxpayer, bought his home 20 years ago for $25,000. He has lived in the home continuously since he purchased it. In 2014, he sells his home for $200,000. What is Jim's taxable gain on the sale?
a. $0
b. $50,000
c. $125,000
d. $175,000

LO 8.12

18. Susan, a single taxpayer, bought her home 25 years ago for $30,000. She has lived in the home continuously since she purchased it. In 2014, she sells her home for $300,000. What is Susan's taxable gain on the sale?
a. $0
b. $20,000
c. $250,000
d. $270,000

LO 8.12

19. Kevin purchased a house 20 years ago for $100,000 and he has always lived in the house. Three years ago Kevin married Karen, and she has lived in the house since their marriage. If they sell Kevin's house in December 2014 for $425,000, what is their taxable gain on a joint tax return?
a. $0
b. $75,000
c. $125,000
d. $250,000

LO 8.12

20. Gene, a single taxpayer, purchased a house 18 months ago for $350,000. If Gene sells his house due to unforeseen circumstances for $550,000 after living in it for a full 18 months, what is his taxable gain?
a. $0
b. $12,500
c. $50,000
d. $200,000

GROUP 2: PROBLEMS

LO 8.1
LO 8.2
LO 8.3

1. Martin sells a stock investment for $25,000 on August 2, 2014. Martin's adjusted basis in the stock is $14,000.
   a. If Martin acquired the stock on November 15, 2013, calculate the amount and the nature of the gain or loss.

   $ ____________

   b. If Martin had acquired the stock on September 11, 2012, calculate the amount and nature of the gain or loss.

   $ ____________

LO 8.1
LO 8.2
LO 8.3

2. During 2014, Tom sold Sears stock for $10,000. The stock was purchased 4 years ago for $13,000. Tom also sold Ford Motor Company bonds for $35,000. The bonds were purchased 2 months ago for $30,000. Home Depot stock, purchased 2 years ago for

$1,000, was sold by Tom for $1,500. Calculate Tom's net gain or loss, and indicate the nature of the gain or loss.

$ __________

LO 8.1
LO 8.2
LO 8.3
LO 8.5

3. Karim Depak received a Form 1099-B showing the following stock transactions and basis during 2014:

Stock	*Date Purchased*	*Date Sold*	*Sales Price*	*Cost Basis*
4,000 shares Green Co.	06/04/03	08/05/14	$12,000	$ 4,000
500 shares Gold Co.	02/12/14	09/05/14	54,000	58,000
5,000 shares Blue Co.	02/04/04	10/08/14	18,000	22,000

None of the stock is qualified small business stock. Calculate Karim's net capital gain or loss using Schedule D and Form 8949 on Pages 8-43 through 8-46.

LO 8.3

4. Jocasta owns an apartment complex that she purchased 6 years ago for $750,000. Jocasta has made $40,000 of capital improvements on the complex, and her depreciation claimed on the building to date is $150,000. Calculate Jocasta's adjusted basis in the building.

$ __________

LO 8.3

5. Chrissy receives 200 shares of Chevron Texaco stock as a gift from her father. The stock cost her father $8,500 10 years ago and is worth $10,000 at the date of the gift.
   a. If the stock is sold for $12,500, calculate the amount of the gain or loss on the sale.

   $ __________

   b. If the stock is sold for $4,600, calculate the amount of the gain or loss on the sale.

   $ __________

LO 8.3
LO 8.6

6. Frank Willingham has the following transactions during the year:

   Sale of office equipment on March 15 that cost $20,000 when purchased on July 1, 2012. Frank has claimed $5,000 in depreciation and sells the asset for $13,000 with no selling costs.

   Sale of land on April 19 for $120,000. The land cost $130,000 when purchased on February 1, 2003. Frank's selling costs are $5,000.

   Assume there were no capital improvements on either business asset sold. Frank's Social Security number is 924-56-5783. Complete Form 4797 on Pages 8-47 and 8-48 to report the above gains or losses.

LO 8.3
LO 8.9

7. Steve Drake sells a rental house on January 1, 2014, and receives $130,000 cash and a note for $55,000 at 10 percent interest. The purchaser also assumes the mortgage on the property of $45,000. Steve's adjusted basis in the house on the date of sale is $152,500, and he collects only the $130,000 down payment in the year of sale.
   a. If Steve elects to recognize the total gain on the property in the year of sale, calculate the taxable gain.

   $ __________

   b. Assuming Steve uses the installment sale method, complete Form 6252 on Page 8-49 for the year of the sale.
   c. Assuming Steve collects $5,000 (not including interest) of the note principal in the year following the year of sale, calculate the amount of income recognized under the installment sale method.

   $ __________

SCHEDULE D (Form 1040)

Department of the Treasury Internal Revenue Service (99)

Capital Gains and Losses

► Attach to Form 1040 or Form 1040NR.
► Information about Schedule D and its separate instructions is at *www.irs.gov/scheduled*.
► Use Form 8949 to list your transactions for lines 1b, 2, 3, 8b, 9, and 10.

OMB No. 1545-0074

2014

Attachment Sequence No. 12

Name(s) shown on return | **Your social security number**

DRAFT AS OF June 9, 2014 DO NOT FILE

Part I Short-Term Capital Gains and Losses—Assets Held One Year or Less

See instructions for how to figure the amounts to enter on the lines below. This form may be easier to complete if you round off cents to whole dollars.	(d) Proceeds (sales price)	(e) Cost (or other basis)	(g) Adjustments to gain or loss from Form(s) 8949, Part I, line 2, column (g)	(h) Gain or (loss) Subtract column (e) from column (d) and combine the result with column (g)
1a Totals for all short-term transactions reported on Form 1099-B for which basis was reported to the IRS and for which you have no adjustments (see instructions). However, if you choose to report all these transactions on Form 8949, leave this line blank and go to line 1b				
1b Totals for all transactions reported on Form(s) 8949 with **Box A** checked				
2 Totals for all transactions reported on Form(s) 8949 with **Box B** checked				
3 Totals for all transactions reported on Form(s) 8949 with **Box C** checked				

4 Short-term gain from Form 6252 and short-term gain or (loss) from Forms 4684, 6781, and 8824	**4**	
5 Net short-term gain or (loss) from partnerships, S corporations, estates, and trusts from Schedule(s) K-1	**5**	
6 Short-term capital loss carryover. Enter the amount, if any, from line 8 of your **Capital Loss Carryover Worksheet** in the instructions	**6**	( )
7 **Net short-term capital gain or (loss).** Combine lines 1a through 6 in column (h). If you have any long-term capital gains or losses, go to Part II below. Otherwise, go to Part III on the back	**7**	

Part II Long-Term Capital Gains and Losses—Assets Held More Than One Year

See instructions for how to figure the amounts to enter on the lines below. This form may be easier to complete if you round off cents to whole dollars.	(d) Proceeds (sales price)	(e) Cost (or other basis)	(g) Adjustments to gain or loss from Form(s) 8949, Part II, line 2, column (g)	(h) Gain or (loss) Subtract column (e) from column (d) and combine the result with column (g)
8a Totals for all long-term transactions reported on Form 1099-B for which basis was reported to the IRS and for which you have no adjustments (see instructions). However, if you choose to report all these transactions on Form 8949, leave this line blank and go to line 8b				
8b Totals for all transactions reported on Form(s) 8949 with **Box D** checked				
9 Totals for all transactions reported on Form(s) 8949 with **Box E** checked				
10 Totals for all transactions reported on Form(s) 8949 with **Box F** checked				

11 Gain from Form 4797, Part I; long-term gain from Forms 2439 and 6252; and long-term gain or (loss) from Forms 4684, 6781, and 8824	**11**	
12 Net long-term gain or (loss) from partnerships, S corporations, estates, and trusts from Schedule(s) K-1	**12**	
13 Capital gain distributions. See the instructions	**13**	
14 Long-term capital loss carryover. Enter the amount, if any, from line 13 of your **Capital Loss Carryover Worksheet** in the instructions	**14**	( )
15 **Net long-term capital gain or (loss).** Combine lines 8a through 14 in column (h). Then go to Part III on the back	**15**	

For Paperwork Reduction Act Notice, see your tax return instructions. Cat. No. 11338H **Schedule D (Form 1040) 2014**

Schedule D (Form 1040) 2014 Page **2**

Part III **Summary**

DRAFT AS OF June 9, 2014 DO NOT FILE

16 Combine lines 7 and 15 and enter the result **16**

- If line 16 is a **gain,** enter the amount from line 16 on Form 1040, line 13, or Form 1040NR, line 14. Then go to line 17 below.
- If line 16 is a **loss,** skip lines 17 through 20 below. Then go to line 21. Also be sure to complete line 22.
- If line 16 is **zero,** skip lines 17 through 21 below and enter -0- on Form 1040, line 13, or Form 1040NR, line 14. Then go to line 22.

17 Are lines 15 and 16 **both** gains?

☐ **Yes.** Go to line 18.

☐ **No.** Skip lines 18 through 21, and go to line 22.

18 Enter the amount, if any, from line 7 of the **28% Rate Gain Worksheet** in the instructions . . ▶ **18**

19 Enter the amount, if any, from line 18 of the **Unrecaptured Section 1250 Gain Worksheet** in the instructions . . . . ▶ **19**

20 Are lines 18 and 19 **both** zero or blank?

☐ **Yes.** Complete the **Qualified Dividends and Capital Gain Tax Worksheet** in the instructions for Form 1040, line 44 (or in the instructions for Form 1040NR, line 42). **Do not** complete lines 21 and 22 below.

☐ **No.** Complete the **Schedule D Tax Worksheet** in the instructions. **Do not** complete lines 21 and 22 below.

21 If line 16 is a loss, enter here and on Form 1040, line 13, or Form 1040NR, line 14, the **smaller** of:

- The loss on line 16 or
- ($3,000), or if married filing separately, ($1,500)

} . . . . **21** ( )

Note. When figuring which amount is smaller, treat both amounts as positive numbers.

22 Do you have qualified dividends on Form 1040, line 9b, or Form 1040NR, line 10b?

☐ **Yes.** Complete the **Qualified Dividends and Capital Gain Tax Worksheet** in the instructions for Form 1040, line 44 (or in the instructions for Form 1040NR, line 42).

☐ **No.** Complete the rest of Form 1040 or Form 1040NR.

Schedule D (Form 1040) 2014

Form **8949**

Department of the Treasury
Internal Revenue Service

Sales and Other Dispositions of Capital Assets

▶ Information about Form 8949 and its separate instructions is at *www.irs.gov/form8949.*

▶ File with your Schedule D to list your transactions for lines 1b, 2, 3, 8b, 9, and 10 of Schedule D.

OMB No. 1545-0123

2014

Attachment Sequence No. **12A**

Name(s) shown on return | **Social security number or taxpayer identification number**

Before you check Box A, B, or C below, see whether you received any Form(s) 1099-B or substitute statement(s) from your broker. A substitute statement will have the same information as Form 1099-B. Either may show your basis (usually your cost) even if your broker did not report it to the IRS. Brokers must report basis to the IRS for most stock you bought in 2011 or later (and for certain debt instruments you bought in 2014 or later).

DRAFT AS OF June 12, 2014 DO NOT FILE

Part I **Short-Term.** Transactions involving capital assets you held 1 year or less are short term. For long-term transactions, see page 2.

Note. You may aggregate all short-term transactions reported on Form(s) 1099-B showing basis was reported to the IRS and for which no adjustments or codes are required. Enter the total directly on Schedule D, line 1a; you are not required to report these transactions on Form 8949 (see instructions).

You *must* check Box A, B, *or* C below. Check only one box. If more than one box applies for your short-term transactions, complete a separate Form 8949, page 1, for each applicable box. If you have more short-term transactions than will fit on this page for one or more of the boxes, complete as many forms with the same box checked as you need.

☐ **(A)** Short-term transactions reported on Form(s) 1099-B showing basis was reported to the IRS (see **Note** above)

☐ **(B)** Short-term transactions reported on Form(s) 1099-B showing basis was **not** reported to the IRS

☐ **(C)** Short-term transactions not reported to you on Form 1099-B

1 (a) Description of property (Example: 100 sh. XYZ Co.)	(b) Date acquired (Mo., day, yr.)	(c) Date sold or disposed (Mo., day, yr.)	(d) Proceeds (sales price) (see instructions)	(e) Cost or other basis. See the **Note** below and see *Column (e)* in the separate instructions	**Adjustment, if any, to gain or loss.** If you enter an amount in column (g), enter a code in column (f). **See the separate instructions.** (f) Code(s) from instructions	(g) Amount of adjustment	(h) **Gain or (loss).** Subtract column (e) from column (d) and combine the result with column (g)
2 Totals. Add the amounts in columns (d), (e), (g), and (h) (subtract negative amounts). Enter each total here and include on your Schedule D, **line 1b** (if **Box A** above is checked), **line 2** (if **Box B** above is checked), or **line 3** (if **Box C** above is checked) ▶							

Note. If you checked Box A above but the basis reported to the IRS was incorrect, enter in column (e) the basis as reported to the IRS, and enter an adjustment in column (g) to correct the basis. See *Column (g)* in the separate instructions for how to figure the amount of the adjustment.

For Paperwork Reduction Act Notice, see instructions. Cat. No. 37768Z Form **8949** (2014)

Form 8949 (2014) Attachment Sequence No. **12A** Page **2**

Name(s) shown on return. Name and SSN or taxpayer identification no. not required if shown on other side	**Social security number or taxpayer identification number**

Before you check Box D, E, or F below, see whether you received any Form(s) 1099-B or substitute statement(s) from your broker. A substitute statement will have the same information as Form 1099-B. Either may show your basis (usually your cost) even if your broker did not report it to the IRS. Brokers must report basis to the IRS for most stock you bought in 2011 or later (and for certain debt instruments you bought in 2014 or later).

Part II **Long-Term.** Transactions involving capital assets you held more than 1 year are long term. For short-term transactions, see page 1.

Note. You may aggregate all long-term transactions reported on Form(s) 1099-B showing basis was reported to the IRS and for which no adjustments or codes are required. Enter the total directly on Schedule D, line 8a; you are not required to report these transactions on Form 8949 (see instructions).

DRAFT AS OF June 12, 2014 DO NOT FILE

You *must* check Box D, E, *or* F below. Check only one box. If more than one box applies for your long-term transactions, complete a separate Form 8949, page 2, for each applicable box. If you have more long-term transactions than will fit on this page for one or more of the boxes, complete as many forms with the same box checked as you need.

☐ **(D)** Long-term transactions reported on Form(s) 1099-B showing basis was reported to the IRS (see **Note** above)
☐ **(E)** Long-term transactions reported on Form(s) 1099-B showing basis was **not** reported to the IRS
☐ **(F)** Long-term transactions not reported to you on Form 1099-B

1 (a) Description of property (Example: 100 sh. XYZ Co.)	(b) Date acquired (Mo., day, yr.)	(c) Date sold or disposed (Mo., day, yr.)	(d) Proceeds (sales price) (see instructions)	(e) Cost or other basis. See the **Note** below and see *Column (e)* in the separate instructions	Adjustment, if any, to gain or loss. If you enter an amount in column (g), enter a code in column (f). **See the separate instructions.** (f) Code(s) from instructions	(g) Amount of adjustment	(h) **Gain or (loss).** Subtract column (e) from column (d) and combine the result with column (g)
2 Totals. Add the amounts in columns (d), (e), (g), and (h) (subtract negative amounts). Enter each total here and include on your Schedule D, **line 8b** (if **Box D** above is checked), **line 9** (if **Box E** above is checked), or **line 10** (if **Box F** above is checked) ▶							

Note. If you checked Box D above but the basis reported to the IRS was incorrect, enter in column (e) the basis as reported to the IRS, and enter an adjustment in column (g) to correct the basis. See *Column (g)* in the separate instructions for how to figure the amount of the adjustment.

Form **8949** (2014)

Form **4797** | **Sales of Business Property** | OMB No. 1545-0184

(Also Involuntary Conversions and Recapture Amounts Under Sections 179 and 280F(b)(2))

2014

Department of the Treasury
Internal Revenue Service

▶ **Attach to your tax return.**
▶ **Information about Form 4797 and its separate instructions is at *www.irs.gov/form4797*.**

Attachment Sequence No. **27**

Name(s) shown on return | **Identifying number**

DRAFT AS OF June 13, 2014 DO NOT FILE

1 Enter the gross proceeds from sales or exchanges reported to you for 2014 on Form(s) 1099-B or 1099-S (or substitute statement) that you are including on line 2, 10, or 20 (see instructions) **1**

Part I **Sales or Exchanges of Property Used in a Trade or Business and Involuntary Conversions From Other Than Casualty or Theft—Most Property Held More Than 1 Year** (see instructions)

2	(a) Description of property	(b) Date acquired (mo., day, yr.)	(c) Date sold (mo., day, yr.)	(d) Gross sales price	(e) Depreciation allowed or allowable since acquisition	(f) Cost or other basis, plus improvements and expense of sale	(g) Gain or (loss) Subtract (f) from the sum of (d) and (e)

3 Gain, if any, from Form 4684, line 39 . . . . **3**

4 Section 1231 gain from installment sales from Form 6252, line 26 or 37 . . . . **4**

5 Section 1231 gain or (loss) from like-kind exchanges from Form 8824 . . . . **5**

6 Gain, if any, from line 32, from other than casualty or theft. **6**

7 Combine lines 2 through 6. Enter the gain or (loss) here and on the appropriate line as follows: **7**

Partnerships (except electing large partnerships) and S corporations. Report the gain or (loss) following the instructions for Form 1065, Schedule K, line 10, or Form 1120S, Schedule K, line 9. Skip lines 8, 9, 11, and 12 below.

Individuals, partners, S corporation shareholders, and all others. If line 7 is zero or a loss, enter the amount from line 7 on line 11 below and skip lines 8 and 9. If line 7 is a gain and you did not have any prior year section 1231 losses, or they were recaptured in an earlier year, enter the gain from line 7 as a long-term capital gain on the Schedule D filed with your return and skip lines 8, 9, 11, and 12 below.

8 Nonrecaptured net section 1231 losses from prior years (see instructions) **8**

9 Subtract line 8 from line 7. If zero or less, enter -0-. If line 9 is zero, enter the gain from line 7 on line 12 below. If line 9 is more than zero, enter the amount from line 8 on line 12 below and enter the gain from line 9 as a long-term capital gain on the Schedule D filed with your return (see instructions) **9**

Part II **Ordinary Gains and Losses** (see instructions)

10 Ordinary gains and losses not included on lines 11 through 16 (include property held 1 year or less):

11 Loss, if any, from line 7 . . . . **11** ( )

12 Gain, if any, from line 7 or amount from line 8, if applicable **12**

13 Gain, if any, from line 31 . . . . **13**

14 Net gain or (loss) from Form 4684, lines 31 and 38a **14**

15 Ordinary gain from installment sales from Form 6252, line 25 or 36 . . . . **15**

16 Ordinary gain or (loss) from like-kind exchanges from Form 8824. . . . . . . **16**

17 Combine lines 10 through 16 . . . . **17**

18 For all except individual returns, enter the amount from line 17 on the appropriate line of your return and skip lines a and b below. For individual returns, complete lines a and b below:

a If the loss on line 11 includes a loss from Form 4684, line 35, column (b)(ii), enter that part of the loss here. Enter the part of the loss from income-producing property on Schedule A (Form 1040), line 28, and the part of the loss from property used as an employee on Schedule A (Form 1040), line 23. Identify as from "Form 4797, line 18a." See instructions . . **18a**

b Redetermine the gain or (loss) on line 17 excluding the loss, if any, on line 18a. Enter here and on Form 1040, line 14 **18b**

For Paperwork Reduction Act Notice, see separate instructions. Cat. No. 13086I Form **4797** (2014)

Form 4797 (2014) Page **2**

Part III Gain From Disposition of Property Under Sections 1245, 1250, 1252, 1254, and 1255 (see instructions)

DRAFT AS OF June 13, 2014 DO NOT FILE

19	(a) Description of section 1245, 1250, 1252, 1254, or 1255 property:	(b) Date acquired (mo., day, yr.)	(c) Date sold (mo., day, yr.)
A			
B			
C			
D			

	These columns relate to the properties on lines 19A through 19D. ▶		Property A	Property B	Property C	Property D
20	Gross sales price (**Note:** *See line 1 before completing.*)	20				
21	Cost or other basis plus expense of sale	21				
22	Depreciation (or depletion) allowed or allowable	22				
23	Adjusted basis. Subtract line 22 from line 21	23				
24	Total gain. Subtract line 23 from line 20	24				
25	**If section 1245 property:**					
a	Depreciation allowed or allowable from line 22	25a				
b	Enter the **smaller** of line 24 or 25a	25b				
26	**If section 1250 property:** If straight line depreciation was used, enter -0- on line 26g, except for a corporation subject to section 291.					
a	Additional depreciation after 1975 (see instructions)	26a				
b	Applicable percentage multiplied by the **smaller** of line 24 or line 26a (see instructions)	26b				
c	Subtract line 26a from line 24. If residential rental property **or** line 24 is not more than line 26a, skip lines 26d and 26e	26c				
d	Additional depreciation after 1969 and before 1976	26d				
e	Enter the **smaller** of line 26c or 26d	26e				
f	Section 291 amount (corporations only)	26f				
g	Add lines 26b, 26e, and 26f	26g				
27	**If section 1252 property:** Skip this section if you did not dispose of farmland or if this form is being completed for a partnership (other than an electing large partnership).					
a	Soil, water, and land clearing expenses	27a				
b	Line 27a multiplied by applicable percentage (see instructions)	27b				
c	Enter the **smaller** of line 24 or 27b	27c				
28	**If section 1254 property:**					
a	Intangible drilling and development costs, expenditures for development of mines and other natural deposits, mining exploration costs, and depletion (see instructions)	28a				
b	Enter the **smaller** of line 24 or 28a	28b				
29	**If section 1255 property:**					
a	Applicable percentage of payments excluded from income under section 126 (see instructions)	29a				
b	Enter the **smaller** of line 24 or 29a (see instructions)	29b				

Summary of Part III Gains. Complete property columns A through D through line 29b before going to line 30.

30	Total gains for all properties. Add property columns A through D, line 24	30	
31	Add property columns A through D, lines 25b, 26g, 27c, 28b, and 29b. Enter here and on line 13	31	
32	Subtract line 31 from line 30. Enter the portion from casualty or theft on Form 4684, line 33. Enter the portion from other than casualty or theft on Form 4797, line 6	32	

Part IV Recapture Amounts Under Sections 179 and 280F(b)(2) When Business Use Drops to 50% or Less (see instructions)

			(a) Section 179	(b) Section 280F(b)(2)
33	Section 179 expense deduction or depreciation allowable in prior years	33		
34	Recomputed depreciation (see instructions)	34		
35	Recapture amount. Subtract line 34 from line 33. See the instructions for where to report	35		

Form **4797** (2014)

Form **6252**

Department of the Treasury
Internal Revenue Service

Installment Sale Income

▶ Attach to your tax return.
▶ Use a separate form for each sale or other disposition of property on the installment method.
▶ Information about Form 6252 and its instructions is at *www.irs.gov/form6252.*

OMB No. 1545-0228
2014
Attachment Sequence No. 79

Name(s) shown on return | **Identifying number**

DRAFT AS OF June 30, 2014 DO NOT FILE

1	Description of property ▶		
2a	Date acquired (mm/dd/yyyy) ▶ **b** Date sold (mm/dd/yyyy) ▶		
3	Was the property sold to a related party (see instructions) after May 14, 1980? If "No," skip line 4	☐ Yes ☐ No	
4	Was the property you sold to a related party a marketable security? If "Yes," complete Part III. If "No," complete Part III for the year of sale and the 2 years after the year of sale	☐ Yes ☐ No	

Part I Gross Profit and Contract Price. Complete this part for the year of sale only.

5	Selling price including mortgages and other debts. **Do not** include interest, whether stated or unstated	5	
6	Mortgages, debts, and other liabilities the buyer assumed or took the property subject to (see instructions)	6	
7	Subtract line 6 from line 5	7	
8	Cost or other basis of property sold	8	
9	Depreciation allowed or allowable	9	
10	Adjusted basis. Subtract line 9 from line 8	10	
11	Commissions and other expenses of sale	11	
12	Income recapture from Form 4797, Part III (see instructions)	12	
13	Add lines 10, 11, and 12	13	
14	Subtract line 13 from line 5. If zero or less, **do not** complete the rest of this form (see instructions)	14	
15	If the property described on line 1 above was your main home, enter the amount of your excluded gain (see instructions). Otherwise, enter -0-	15	
16	**Gross profit.** Subtract line 15 from line 14	16	
17	Subtract line 13 from line 6. If zero or less, enter -0-	17	
18	**Contract price.** Add line 7 and line 17	18	

Part II Installment Sale Income. Complete this part for the year of sale **and** any year you receive a payment or have certain debts you must treat as a payment on installment obligations.

June 12, 2014

19	Gross profit percentage (expressed as a decimal amount). Divide line 16 by line 18. For years after the year of sale, see instructions	19	
20	If this is the year of sale, enter the amount from line 17. Otherwise, enter -0-	20	
21	Payments received during year (see instructions). **Do not** include interest, whether stated or unstated	21	
22	Add lines 20 and 21	22	
23	Payments received in prior years (see instructions). **Do not** include interest, whether stated or unstated	23	
24	**Installment sale income.** Multiply line 22 by line 19	24	
25	Enter the part of line 24 that is ordinary income under the recapture rules (see instructions)	25	
26	Subtract line 25 from line 24. Enter here and on Schedule D or Form 4797 (see instructions)	26	

Part III Related Party Installment Sale Income. Do not complete if you received the final payment this tax year.

27 Name, address, and taxpayer identifying number of related party

28 Did the related party resell or dispose of the property ("second disposition") during this tax year? ☐ Yes ☐ No

29 **If the answer to question 28 is "Yes," complete lines 30 through 37 below unless one of the following conditions is met. Check the box that applies.**

- **a** ☐ The second disposition was more than 2 years after the first disposition (other than dispositions of marketable securities). If this box is checked, enter the date of disposition (mm/dd/yyyy) ▶
- **b** ☐ The first disposition was a sale or exchange of stock to the issuing corporation.
- **c** ☐ The second disposition was an involuntary conversion and the threat of conversion occurred after the first disposition.
- **d** ☐ The second disposition occurred after the death of the original seller or buyer.
- **e** ☐ It can be established to the satisfaction of the IRS that tax avoidance was not a principal purpose for either of the dispositions. If this box is checked, attach an explanation (see instructions).

30	Selling price of property sold by related party (see instructions)	30	
31	Enter contract price from line 18 for year of first sale	31	
32	Enter the **smaller** of line 30 or line 31	32	
33	Total payments received by the end of your 2014 tax year (see instructions)	33	
34	Subtract line 33 from line 32. If zero or less, enter -0-	34	
35	Multiply line 34 by the gross profit percentage on line 19 for year of first sale	35	
36	Enter the part of line 35 that is ordinary income under the recapture rules (see instructions)	36	
37	Subtract line 36 from line 35. Enter here and on Schedule D or Form 4797 (see instructions)	37	

For Paperwork Reduction Act Notice, see page 4. Cat. No. 13601R Form **6252** (2014)

LO 8.3
LO 8.12

8. Elvin, 45 years of age, sells his residence in 2014. He receives $30,000 in cash, and the buyer assumes his $105,000 mortgage. Elvin also pays $6,500 in commissions and transfer costs.
   a. Calculate the amount realized on the sale. $ __________
   b. If the residence was acquired in 1986, and its adjusted basis is $75,000, calculate the amount and nature of the taxable gain on the sale (assuming he does not purchase a new residence). $ __________

LO 8.5

9. In 2014, Michael has net short-term capital losses of $2,000, a net long-term capital loss of $45,000, and other ordinary taxable income of $45,000.
   a. Calculate the amount of Michael's deduction for capital losses for 2014. $ __________
   b. Calculate the amount and nature of his capital loss carryforward. $ __________
   c. For how long may Michael carry forward the unused loss? __________

LO 8.7

10. William sold Section 1245 property for $25,000 in 2014. The property cost $35,000 when it was purchased 5 years ago. The depreciation claimed on the property was $16,000.
   a. Calculate the adjusted basis of the property. $ __________
   b. Calculate the recomputed basis of the property. $ __________
   c. Calculate the amount of ordinary income under Section 1245. $ __________
   d. Calculate the Section 1231 gain. $ __________

LO 8.8

11. An office machine used by Josie in her accounting business was completely destroyed by fire. The adjusted basis of the machine was $7,500 (original basis of $12,500 less accumulated depreciation of $5,000). The machine was not insured. Calculate the amount and nature of Josie's gain or loss as a result of this casualty.

    Amount of gain or loss $ __________
    Nature __________

LO 8.8

12. Rebecca has a $6,400 casualty loss, before any limitations, as a result of the complete destruction of personal-use property. She also receives $1,200 of insurance proceeds for the destruction of a second item of personal-use property which was damaged in a separate casualty. The damaged property had a fair market value before the casualty of $2,000 and after the casualty of $700. The adjusted basis of the property was $500. Determine the amount and nature of Rebecca's gain or loss as a result of these casualties.

    Amount of gain or loss $ __________
    Nature __________

LO 8.10

13. Carey exchanges real estate for other real estate in a qualifying like-kind exchange. Carey's basis in the real estate given up is $110,000, and the property has a fair market value of $170,000. In exchange for her property, Carey receives real estate with a fair market value of $100,000 and cash of $20,000. In addition, the other party to the exchange assumes a mortgage loan on Carey's property of $50,000.

a. Calculate Carey's recognized gain, if any, on the exchange. $ __________
b. Calculate Carey's basis in the property received. $ __________

LO 8.11

14. Teresa's manufacturing plant is destroyed by fire. The plant has an adjusted basis of $260,000, and Teresa receives insurance proceeds of $400,000 for the loss. Teresa reinvests $425,000 in a replacement plant.

a. Calculate Teresa's recognized gain if she elects to utilize the involuntary conversion provision. $ __________
b. Calculate Teresa's basis in the new plant. $ __________

LO 8.12

15. Larry Gaines, age 42, sells his personal residence on November 12, 2014, for $144,000. He lived in the house for 7 years. The expenses of the sale are $10,500, and he has made capital improvements of $5,500. Larry's cost basis in his residence is $84,000. On November 30, 2014, Larry purchases and occupies a new residence at a cost of $148,000. Calculate Larry's realized gain, recognized gain, and the adjusted basis of his new residence.

a. Realized gain $ __________
b. Recognized gain $ __________
c. Adjusted basis of new residence $ __________

LO 8.12

16. On July 1, 2014, Ted, age 73 and single, sells his personal residence of the last 30 years for $365,000. Ted's basis in his residence is $35,000. The expenses associated with the sale of his home total $20,000. On December 15, 2014, Ted purchases and occupies a new residence at a cost of $175,000. Calculate Ted's realized gain, recognized gain, and the adjusted basis of his new residence.

a. Realized gain $ __________
b. Recognized gain $ __________
c. Adjusted basis of the new residence $ __________

17. You have a problem and need a full-text copy of Code Section 1033. Go to the U.S. House of Representatives' website (**www.house.gov**) and search for the "United States Code." The Internal Revenue Code is "Title 26." Use the search function to find Section 1033 and print out a *copy of Section 1033(a)*, "*General Rule*." Do not print the entire Section 1033.

18. Go to the IRS website (**www.irs.gov**) and redo Problem 7 using the most recent interactive Form 6252, Installment Sale Income. Print out the *completed Form 6252*.

GROUP 3: WRITING ASSIGNMENT

RESEARCH

1. Your supervisor has asked you to research the following situation concerning Owen and Lisa Cordoncillo. Owen and Lisa are brother and sister. In May 2014, Owen and Lisa exchange business pickup trucks. Lisa gives up a blue pickup truck with an adjusted basis of $2,000 and a fair market value of $6,000. In return for this property, Lisa receives from Owen a red pickup truck with a fair market value of $5,500 and cash of $500. Owen's adjusted basis in the truck he exchanges is $2,500. In March 2015, Owen sells the blue pickup truck to a third party for $5,800.

Required: Go to the IRS website (**www.irs.gov**). Locate and review Publication 544, Chapter 1, Nontaxable Exchanges. Write a file memorandum stating the amount of Owen and Lisa's gain recognition for 2014. Also determine the effect, if any, of the subsequent sale in 2015. (An example of a file memorandum is available at the website for this text located at **www.cengagebrain.com.**)

ETHICS

2. Lisa Sizemore, a taxpayer in the 10–15 percent tax bracket, purchased stock as an investment on July 11, 2013. She sold the stock on July 9, 2014, 2 days before qualifying for the long-term holding period. If Lisa had waited until July 12, 2014 to sell the stock, she would have qualified for the 0 percent tax rate. Instead, the sale will now be taxed at ordinary income rates. Upon realizing this, Lisa has told you that she will "fudge" the sale date to July 12. She says to you, "What's the big deal? It's just 2 days." What would you say to Lisa?

GROUP 4: COMPREHENSIVE PROBLEMS

1. Robert Ramos (age 36) is a single taxpayer, living at 8765 Bay Dr., Monterey, CA 93940. His Social Security number is 976-23-5132. Robert's earnings and income tax withholding as the manager of a local supermarket store for 2014 are:

Earnings	$68,000
Federal income tax withheld	14,800
State income tax withheld	2,300

Robert's other income includes qualifying dividends on Arizona Public Service stock of $3,600 and interest on a long-term certificate of deposits at Bank of America of $5,885.

During the year, Robert paid the following amounts (all of which can be substantiated):

Home mortgage interest	$10,500
Credit card interest	550
Auto loan interest	1,700
Life insurance (universal policy)	750
Property taxes on personal residence	1,350
Blue Cross medical insurance premiums	650
Other medical expenses	790
Income tax preparation fee	250
Charitable contributions (in cash)	550

In his spare time, Robert trades stocks and bonds. During the year, he sold several stocks and received a Form 1099-B, which showed the following:

Stock	*Acquired*	*Sold*	*Price*	*Basis*
Red Co.	02/01/04	10/05/14	$6,000	$2,500
Green Co.	06/11/14	08/03/14	4,000	4,500
Blue Co.	03/12/14	09/22/14	6,000	5,200
White Co.	05/12/03	10/15/14	8,000	5,000
Black Co.	09/15/03	11/01/14	6,000	7,000

Required: Complete Robert's federal tax return for 2014. Use Form 1040, Schedule A, Schedule B, Schedule D, Form 8949, and the Qualified Dividends and Capital Gain Tax Worksheet on Pages 8-57 to 8-65 to complete this tax return. Make realistic assumptions about any missing data.

2. Kathy Kennedy (age 44) is a single taxpayer and she lives at 212 North Pine Way, Payson, AZ 85541. Her Social Security number is 467-98-9784. Kathy's earnings and income tax withholding as the principal of the local high school for 2014 are:

Earnings	$55,000
Federal income tax withheld	8,800
State income tax withheld	700

Kathy's other income includes qualifying dividends on New Mexico Public Service stock of $4,000 and interest on a certificate of deposit at Payson National Bank of $275. In April 2014, Kathy paid $450 due on her 2013 Arizona state income tax.

During the year, Kathy paid the following amounts (all of which can be substantiated):

Home mortgage interest	$9,300
MasterCard interest	550
Life insurance (whole life policy)	750
Property taxes on personal residence	1,350
Blue Cross medical insurance premiums	250
Other medical expenses	560
Income tax preparation fee	300
Charitable contributions (in cash)	750

Kathy had one stock transaction in 2014. Kathy received the following Form 1099-B from her sale of Gold Company stock. All stock sales must be reported both to taxpayers and to the IRS on Form 1099-B so the proceeds can be matched by the IRS to each tax return. Kathy purchased the stock on August 31, 2013, for $42,800 before the stock plummeted in the last months of 2013.

7979 ☐ VOID ☐ CORRECTED

PAYER'S name, street address, city or town, state or province, country, ZIP or foreign postal code, and telephone no. *Big Brokerage Company* *123 Wall Street* *New York, NY 10014*	Applicable check box on Form 8949 / OMB No. 1545-0715 / **2014** / Form **1099-B** **1a** Description of property (Example 100 sh. XYZ Co.) *100 shares Gold Company Stock* **1b** Date acquired / **1c** Date sold or disposed *2-15-14*	**Proceeds From Broker and Barter Exchange Transactions**
PAYER'S federal identification number *XX-XXXXXXX* / RECIPIENT'S identification number *467-98-9784*	**1d** Proceeds $ *17,000* / **1e** Cost or other basis $ **1f** Code, if any / **1g** Adjustments $	**Copy A** **For Internal Revenue Service Center** **File with Form 1096.**
RECIPIENT'S name *Kathy Kennedy*	**2** Type of gain or loss: Short-term ☐ Long-term ☐ / **3** Check if basis reported to IRS ☐	
Street address (including apt. no.) *212 North Pine Way*	**4** Federal income tax withheld $ / **5** Check if noncovered security ☐	
City or town, state or province, country, and ZIP or foreign postal code *Payson, AZ 85541*	**6** Reported to IRS: Gross proceeds ☒ Net proceeds ☐ / **7** Check if loss is not allowed based on amount in 1d ☐	For Privacy Act and Paperwork Reduction Act Notice, see the **2014 General Instructions for Certain Information Returns.**
Account number (see instructions) / 2nd TIN not. ☐	**8** Profit or (loss) realized in 2014 on closed contracts $ / **9** Unrealized profit or (loss) on open contracts—12/31/2013 $	
CUSIP number	**10** Unrealized profit or (loss) on open contracts—12/31/2014 $ / **11** Aggregate profit or (loss) on contracts $	
14 State name / **15** State identification no. / **16** State tax withheld $ $	**12** / **13** Bartering $	

Form **1099-B** Cat. No. 14411V www.irs.gov/form1099b Department of the Treasury - Internal Revenue Service

Do Not Cut or Separate Forms on This Page — Do Not Cut or Separate Forms on This Page

On January 28, 2014, Kathy sold raw land for $150,000 (basis to Kathy of $90,000). The land was purchased 6 years ago. She received $30,000 as a down payment and the buyer's 10-year note for $120,000. The note is payable at the rate of $12,000 per year plus 8 percent interest. On January 28, 2015, the first of the ten principal and interest payments is due.

Required: Complete Kathy's federal tax return for 2014. Use Form 1040, Schedule A, Schedule B, Schedule D, Form 8949, the Qualified Dividends and Capital Gain Tax Worksheet, and Form 6252 on Pages 8-67 to 8-77 to complete this tax return. Make realistic assumptions about any missing data.

GROUP 5: CUMULATIVE SOFTWARE PROBLEM

The following additional information is available for the Dr. Ivan and Irene Incisor family from Chapters 1–7.

Ivan sold the following securities during the year and received a Form 1099-B that showed the following information:

Security	*Description*	*Date Acquired*	*Date Sold*	*Selling Price*	*Adjusted Basis*
Orange, Inc.	100 Shares Common	02/11/96	04/16/14	$ 3,000	$ 2,150
Banana, Inc.	100 Shares Common	07/17/00	07/31/14	1,950	4,210
Grape, Corp.	100 Shares Preferred	12/08/13	09/25/14	9,975	10,430
Plum, Inc.	5 Bonds due 4/2015	12/30/04	01/02/14	5,130	5,320
Peach Mutual Fund	5,010.150 Shares	05/30/05	10/22/14	60,120	56,480

The selling price given is net of sales commissions. In addition to the above amounts, the Mango mutual fund distributed a long-term capital gain of $750 on December 30, 2014.

Ivan purchased 5 acres of raw land in Reno, NV, 10 years ago. His basis in the land was $50,000. On August 1, 2014, he sold the land for $150,000 on the installment method. Ivan received $30,000 in the year of sale, and the balance was payable at $12,000 per year for the next 10 years, plus a market rate of interest.

On May 15, 2014, Ivan and Irene sold their personal residence for $585,000 and purchased a new house for $725,000. They had owned the old house for 20 years and it had an adjusted basis of $35,000. The house had been their personal residence for all the years they were married. They moved into the new house on May 18, 2014.

Required: Combine this new information about the Incisor family with the information from Chapters 1–7 and complete a revised 2014 tax return for Ivan and Irene. No AMT is payable. This completes the Group 5 multichapter case.

Form **1040** Department of the Treasury—Internal Revenue Service (99)
U.S. Individual Income Tax Return **2014** OMB No. 1545-0074 IRS Use Only—Do not write or staple in this space.

For the year Jan. 1–Dec. 31, 2014, or other tax year beginning , 2014, ending , 20 See separate instructions.

Your first name and initial	Last name	**Your social security number**
If a joint return, spouse's first name and initial	Last name	**Spouse's social security number**
Home address (number and street). If you have a P.O. box, see instructions.	Apt. no.	▲ Make sure the SSN(s) above and on line 6c are correct.
City, town or post office, state, and ZIP code. If you have a foreign address, also complete spaces below (see instructions).		**Presidential Election Campaign** Check here if you, or your spouse if filing jointly, want $3 to go to this fund. Checking a box below will not change your tax or refund. ☐ You ☐ Spouse
Foreign country name	Foreign province/state/county	Foreign postal code

Filing Status

Check only one box.

1 ☐ Single
2 ☐ Married filing jointly (even if only one had income)
3 ☐ Married filing separately. Enter spouse's SSN above and full name here. ▶
4 ☐ Head of household (with qualifying person). (See instructions.) If the qualifying person is a child but not your dependent, enter this child's name here. ▶
5 ☐ Qualifying widow(er) with dependent child

Exemptions

6a ☐ **Yourself.** If someone can claim you as a dependent, **do not** check box 6a
b ☐ **Spouse**

Boxes checked on 6a and 6b

c **Dependents:**

(1) First name Last name	(2) Dependent's social security number	(3) Dependent's relationship to you	(4) ✓ if child under age 17 qualifying for child tax credit (see instructions)
			☐
			☐
			☐
			☐

If more than four dependents, see instructions and check here ▶ ☐

No. of children on 6c who:
• lived with you
• did not live with you due to divorce or separation (see instructions)
Dependents on 6c not entered above
Add numbers on lines above ▶

d Total number of exemptions claimed

Income

Attach Form(s) W-2 here. Also attach Forms W-2G and 1099-R if tax was withheld.

If you did not get a W-2, see instructions.

Line	Description		Line
7	Wages, salaries, tips, etc. Attach Form(s) W-2		7
8a	**Taxable** interest. Attach Schedule B if required		8a
b	**Tax-exempt** interest. **Do not** include on line 8a	8b	
9a	Ordinary dividends. Attach Schedule B if required		9a
b	Qualified dividends	9b	
10	Taxable refunds, credits, or offsets of state and local income taxes		10
11	Alimony received		11
12	Business income or (loss). Attach Schedule C or C-EZ		12
13	Capital gain or (loss). Attach Schedule D if required. If not required, check here ▶ ☐		13
14	Other gains or (losses). Attach Form 4797		14
15a	IRA distributions 15a	b Taxable amount	15b
16a	Pensions and annuities 16a	b Taxable amount	16b
17	Rental real estate, royalties, partnerships, S corporations, trusts, etc. Attach Schedule E		17
18	Farm income or (loss). Attach Schedule F		18
19	Unemployment compensation		19
20a	Social security benefits 20a	b Taxable amount	20b
21	Other income. List type and amount		21
22	Combine the amounts in the far right column for lines 7 through 21. This is your **total income** ▶		22

DRAFT AS OF August 28, 20[illegible] DO NOT FILE

Adjusted Gross Income

Line	Description		Line
23	Reserved	23	
24	Certain business expenses of reservists, performing artists, and fee-basis government officials. Attach Form 2106 or 2106-EZ	24	
25	Health savings account deduction. Attach Form 8889	25	
26	Moving expenses. Attach Form 3903	26	
27	Deductible part of self-employment tax. Attach Schedule SE	27	
28	Self-employed SEP, SIMPLE, and qualified plans	28	
29	Self-employed health insurance deduction	29	
30	Penalty on early withdrawal of savings	30	
31a	Alimony paid b Recipient's SSN ▶	31a	
32	IRA deduction	32	
33	Student loan interest deduction	33	
34	Reserved	34	
35	Domestic production activities deduction. Attach Form 8903	35	
36	Add lines 23 through 35		36
37	Subtract line 36 from line 22. This is your **adjusted gross income** ▶		37

For Disclosure, Privacy Act, and Paperwork Reduction Act Notice, see separate instructions. Cat. No. 11320B Form **1040** (2014)

Form 1040 (2014) Page **2**

Tax and Credits

Line	Description	Box
38	Amount from line 37 (adjusted gross income)	38
39a	Check if: ☐ **You** were born before January 2, 1950, ☐ Blind. ☐ **Spouse** was born before January 2, 1950, ☐ Blind. } **Total boxes checked ▶ 39a** ☐	
b	If your spouse itemizes on a separate return or you were a dual-status alien, check here ▶ 39b ☐	
40	**Itemized deductions** (from Schedule A) **or** your **standard deduction** (see left margin)	40
41	Subtract line 40 from line 38	41
42	**Exemptions.** If line 38 is $152,525 or less, multiply $3,950 by the number on line 6d. Otherwise, see instructions	42
43	**Taxable income.** Subtract line 42 from line 41. If line 42 is more than line 41, enter -0-	43
44	**Tax** (see instructions). Check if any from: **a** ☐ Form(s) 8814 **b** ☐ Form 4972 **c** ☐ ______	44
45	**Alternative minimum tax** (see instructions). Attach Form 6251	45
46	Excess advance premium tax credit repayment. Attach Form 8962	46
47	Add lines 44, 45, and 46 ▶	47
48	Foreign tax credit. Attach Form 1116 if required	48
49	Credit for child and dependent care expenses. Attach Form 2441	49
50	Education credits from Form 8863, line 19	50
51	Retirement savings contributions credit. Attach Form 8880	51
52	Child tax credit. Attach Schedule 8812, if required	52
53	Residential energy credit. Attach Form 5695	53
54	Other credits from Form: **a** ☐ 3800 **b** ☐ 8801 **c** ☐ ______	54
55	Add lines 48 through 54. These are your **total credits**	55
56	Subtract line 55 from line 47. If line 55 is more than line 47, enter -0- ▶	56

Standard Deduction for—
- People who check any box on line 39a or 39b **or** who can be claimed as a dependent, see instructions.
- All others:

Single or Married filing separately, $6,200

Married filing jointly or Qualifying widow(er), $12,400

Head of household, $9,100

Other Taxes

Line	Description	Box
57	Self-employment tax. Attach Schedule SE	57
58	Unreported social security and Medicare tax from Form: **a** ☐ 4137 **b** ☐ 8919	58
59	Additional tax on IRAs, other qualified retirement plans, etc. Attach Form 5329 if required	59
60a	Household employment taxes from Schedule H	60a
b	First-time homebuyer credit repayment. Attach Form 5405 if required	60b
61	Health care: individual responsibility (see instructions) Full-year coverage ☐	61
62	Taxes from: **a** ☐ Form 8959 **b** ☐ Form 8960 **c** ☐ Instructions; enter code(s) ______	62
63	Add lines 56 through 62. This is your **total tax** ▶	63

Payments

If you have a qualifying child, attach Schedule EIC.

Line	Description	Box
64	Federal income tax withheld from Forms W-2 and 1099	64
65	2014 estimated tax payments and amount applied from 2013 return	65
66a	**Earned income credit (EIC)**	66a
b	Nontaxable combat pay election **66b**	
67	Additional child tax credit. Attach Schedule 8812	67
68	American opportunity credit from Form 8863, line 8	68
69	Net premium tax credit. Attach Form 8962	69
70	Amount paid with request for extension to file	70
71	Excess social security and tier 1 RRTA tax withheld	71
72	Credit for federal tax on fuels. Attach Form 4136	72
73	Credits from Form: **a** ☐ 2439 **b** ☐ Reserved **c** ☐ Reserved **d** ☐ ______	73
74	Add lines 64, 65, 66a, and 67 through 73. These are your **total payments** ▶	74

Refund

Direct deposit? See instructions.

Line	Description	Box
75	If line 74 is more than line 63, subtract line 63 from line 74. This is the amount you **overpaid**	75
76a	Amount of line 75 you want **refunded to you.** If Form 8888 is attached, check here ▶ ☐	76a
▶ b	Routing number ▶ **c** Type: ☐ Checking ☐ Savings	
▶ d	Account number	
77	Amount of line 75 you want **applied to your 2015 estimated tax** ▶	77

Amount You Owe

Line	Description	Box
78	**Amount you owe.** Subtract line 74 from line 63. For details on how to pay, see instructions ▶	78
79	Estimated tax penalty (see instructions)	79

Third Party Designee

Do you want to allow another person to discuss this return with the IRS (see instructions)? ☐ **Yes.** Complete below. ☐ **No**

Designee's name ▶ Phone no. ▶ Personal identification number (PIN) ▶

Sign Here

Joint return? See instructions. Keep a copy for your records.

Under penalties of perjury, I declare that I have examined this return and accompanying schedules and statements, and to the best of my knowledge and belief, they are true, correct, and complete. Declaration of preparer (other than taxpayer) is based on all information of which preparer has any knowledge.

Your signature	Date	Your occupation	Daytime phone number
Spouse's signature. If a joint return, **both** must sign.	Date	Spouse's occupation	If the IRS sent you an Identity Protection PIN, enter it here (see inst.)

Paid Preparer Use Only

Print/Type preparer's name	Preparer's signature	Date	Check ☐ if self-employed	PTIN
Firm's name ▶			Firm's EIN ▶	
Firm's address ▶			Phone no.	

DRAFT AS OF August 28, 2014 DO NOT FILE

SCHEDULE A (Form 1040)

Department of the Treasury
Internal Revenue Service (99)

Itemized Deductions

► Information about Schedule A and its separate instructions is at *www.irs.gov/schedulea*.
► Attach to Form 1040.

OMB No. 1545-0074
2014
Attachment Sequence No. 07

Name(s) shown on Form 1040 | **Your social security number**

DRAFT AS OF
August 15, 2014
DO NOT FILE

Section	Line	Description	Box	Amount
Medical and Dental Expenses		**Caution.** Do not include expenses reimbursed or paid by others.		
	1	Medical and dental expenses (see instructions)	1	
	2	Enter amount from Form 1040, line 38 [2]		
	3	Multiply line 2 by 10% (.10). But if either you or your spouse was born before January 2, 1950, multiply line 2 by 7.5% (.075) instead	3	
	4	Subtract line 3 from line 1. If line 3 is more than line 1, enter -0-	4	
Taxes You Paid	5	State and local a ☐ Income taxes b ☐ RESERVED	5	
	6	Real estate taxes (see instructions)	6	
	7	Personal property taxes	7	
	8	Other taxes. List type and amount ►	8	
	9	Add lines 5 through 8	9	
Interest You Paid	10	Home mortgage interest and points reported to you on Form 1098	10	
Note. Your mortgage interest deduction may be limited (see instructions).	11	Home mortgage interest not reported to you on Form 1098. If paid to the person from whom you bought the home, see instructions and show that person's name, identifying no., and address ►	11	
	12	Points not reported to you on Form 1098. See instructions for special rules	12	
	13	RESERVED	13	
	14	Investment interest. Attach Form 4952 if required. (See instructions.)	14	
	15	Add lines 10 through 14	15	
Gifts to Charity	16	Gifts by cash or check. If you made any gift of $250 or more, see instructions	16	
If you made a gift and got a benefit for it, see instructions.	17	Other than by cash or check. If any gift of $250 or more, see instructions. You **must** attach Form 8283 if over $500	17	
	18	Carryover from prior year	18	
	19	Add lines 16 through 18	19	
Casualty and Theft Losses	20	Casualty or theft loss(es). Attach Form 4684. (See instructions.)	20	
Job Expenses and Certain Miscellaneous Deductions	21	Unreimbursed employee expenses—job travel, union dues, job education, etc. Attach Form 2106 or 2106-EZ if required. (See instructions.) ►	21	
	22	Tax preparation fees	22	
	23	Other expenses—investment, safe deposit box, etc. List type and amount ►	23	
	24	Add lines 21 through 23	24	
	25	Enter amount from Form 1040, line 38 [25]		
	26	Multiply line 25 by 2% (.02)	26	
	27	Subtract line 26 from line 24. If line 26 is more than line 24, enter -0-	27	
Other Miscellaneous Deductions	28	Other—from list in instructions. List type and amount ►	28	
Total Itemized Deductions	29	Is Form 1040, line 38, over $152,525? ☐ **No.** Your deduction is not limited. Add the amounts in the far right column for lines 4 through 28. Also, enter this amount on Form 1040, line 40. ☐ **Yes.** Your deduction may be limited. See the Itemized Deductions Worksheet in the instructions to figure the amount to enter.	29	
	30	If you elect to itemize deductions even though they are less than your standard deduction, check here ► ☐		

For Paperwork Reduction Act Notice, see Form 1040 instructions. Cat. No. 17145C **Schedule A (Form 1040) 2014**

SCHEDULE B
(Form 1040A or 1040)

Department of the Treasury
Internal Revenue Service (99)

Interest and Ordinary Dividends

► Attach to Form 1040A or 1040.
► Information about Schedule B and its instructions is at *www.irs.gov/scheduleb.*

OMB No. 1545-0074
2014
Attachment Sequence No. 08

Name(s) shown on return | Your social security number

DRAFT AS OF June 18, 2014 DO NOT FILE

Part I Interest

(See instructions on back and the instructions for Form 1040A, or Form 1040, line 8a.)

Note. If you received a Form 1099-INT, Form 1099-OID, or substitute statement from a brokerage firm, list the firm's name as the payer and enter the total interest shown on that form.

			Amount
1	List name of payer. If any interest is from a seller-financed mortgage and the buyer used the property as a personal residence, see instructions on back and list this interest first. Also, show that buyer's social security number and address ►	1	
2	Add the amounts on line 1	2	
3	Excludable interest on series EE and I U.S. savings bonds issued after 1989. Attach Form 8815	3	
4	Subtract line 3 from line 2. Enter the result here and on Form 1040A, or Form 1040, line 8a . . . . ►	4	

Note. If line 4 is over $1,500, you must complete Part III.

Part II Ordinary Dividends

(See instructions on back and the instructions for Form 1040A, or Form 1040, line 9a.)

Note. If you received a Form 1099-DIV or substitute statement from a brokerage firm, list the firm's name as the payer and enter the ordinary dividends shown on that form.

			Amount
5	List name of payer ►	5	
6	Add the amounts on line 5. Enter the total here and on Form 1040A, or Form 1040, line 9a . . . . ►	6	

Note. If line 6 is over $1,500, you must complete Part III.

Part III Foreign Accounts and Trusts

(See instructions on back.)

You must complete this part if you **(a)** had over $1,500 of taxable interest or ordinary dividends; **(b)** had a foreign account; or **(c)** received a distribution from, or were a grantor of, or a transferor to, a foreign trust.

		Yes	No
7a	At any time during 2014, did you have a financial interest in or signature authority over a financial account (such as a bank account, securities account, or brokerage account) located in a foreign country? See instructions		
	If "Yes," are you required to file FinCEN Form 114, Report of Foreign Bank and Financial Accounts (FBAR), to report that financial interest or signature authority? See FinCEN Form 114 and its instructions for filing requirements and exceptions to those requirements		
b	If you are required to file FinCEN Form 114, enter the name of the foreign country where the financial account is located ►		
8	During 2014, did you receive a distribution from, or were you the grantor of, or transferor to, a foreign trust? If "Yes," you may have to file Form 3520. See instructions on back		

SCHEDULE D (Form 1040)

Department of the Treasury
Internal Revenue Service (99)

Capital Gains and Losses

► Attach to Form 1040 or Form 1040NR.
► Information about Schedule D and its separate instructions is at *www.irs.gov/scheduled*.
► Use Form 8949 to list your transactions for lines 1b, 2, 3, 8b, 9, and 10.

OMB No. 1545-0074
2014
Attachment Sequence No. 12

Name(s) shown on return | **Your social security number**

DRAFT AS OF June 9, 2014 DO NOT FILE

Part I Short-Term Capital Gains and Losses—Assets Held One Year or Less

See instructions for how to figure the amounts to enter on the lines below. This form may be easier to complete if you round off cents to whole dollars.	(d) Proceeds (sales price)	(e) Cost (or other basis)	(g) Adjustments to gain or loss from Form(s) 8949, Part I, line 2, column (g)	(h) Gain or (loss) Subtract column (e) from column (d) and combine the result with column (g)
1a Totals for all short-term transactions reported on Form 1099-B for which basis was reported to the IRS and for which you have no adjustments (see instructions). However, if you choose to report all these transactions on Form 8949, leave this line blank and go to line 1b .				
1b Totals for all transactions reported on Form(s) 8949 with **Box A** checked				
2 Totals for all transactions reported on Form(s) 8949 with **Box B** checked				
3 Totals for all transactions reported on Form(s) 8949 with **Box C** checked				

4 Short-term gain from Form 6252 and short-term gain or (loss) from Forms 4684, 6781, and 8824 .	4	
5 Net short-term gain or (loss) from partnerships, S corporations, estates, and trusts from Schedule(s) K-1	5	
6 Short-term capital loss carryover. Enter the amount, if any, from line 8 of your **Capital Loss Carryover Worksheet** in the instructions	6	( )
7 **Net short-term capital gain or (loss).** Combine lines 1a through 6 in column (h). If you have any long-term capital gains or losses, go to Part II below. Otherwise, go to Part III on the back	7	

Part II Long-Term Capital Gains and Losses—Assets Held More Than One Year

See instructions for how to figure the amounts to enter on the lines below. This form may be easier to complete if you round off cents to whole dollars.	(d) Proceeds (sales price)	(e) Cost (or other basis)	(g) Adjustments to gain or loss from Form(s) 8949, Part II, line 2, column (g)	(h) Gain or (loss) Subtract column (e) from column (d) and combine the result with column (g)
8a Totals for all long-term transactions reported on Form 1099-B for which basis was reported to the IRS and for which you have no adjustments (see instructions). However, if you choose to report all these transactions on Form 8949, leave this line blank and go to line 8b .				
8b Totals for all transactions reported on Form(s) 8949 with **Box D** checked				
9 Totals for all transactions reported on Form(s) 8949 with **Box E** checked				
10 Totals for all transactions reported on Form(s) 8949 with **Box F** checked.				

11 Gain from Form 4797, Part I; long-term gain from Forms 2439 and 6252; and long-term gain or (loss) from Forms 4684, 6781, and 8824	11	
12 Net long-term gain or (loss) from partnerships, S corporations, estates, and trusts from Schedule(s) K-1	12	
13 Capital gain distributions. See the instructions	13	
14 Long-term capital loss carryover. Enter the amount, if any, from line 13 of your **Capital Loss Carryover Worksheet** in the instructions	14	( )
15 **Net long-term capital gain or (loss).** Combine lines 8a through 14 in column (h). Then go to Part III on the back	15	

Schedule D (Form 1040) 2014 Page **2**

Part III Summary

16 Combine lines 7 and 15 and enter the result **16**

- If line 16 is a **gain,** enter the amount from line 16 on Form 1040, line 13, or Form 1040NR, line 14. Then go to line 17 below.
- If line 16 is a **loss,** skip lines 17 through 20 below. Then go to line 21. Also be sure to complete line 22.
- If line 16 is **zero,** skip lines 17 through 21 below and enter -0- on Form 1040, line 13, or Form 1040NR, line 14. Then go to line 22.

17 Are lines 15 and 16 **both** gains?

☐ **Yes.** Go to line 18.

☐ **No.** Skip lines 18 through 21, and go to line 22.

18 Enter the amount, if any, from line 7 of the **28% Rate Gain Worksheet** in the instructions . . ▶ **18**

19 Enter the amount, if any, from line 18 of the **Unrecaptured Section 1250 Gain Worksheet** in the instructions . . . . ▶ **19**

20 Are lines 18 and 19 **both** zero or blank?

☐ **Yes.** Complete the **Qualified Dividends and Capital Gain Tax Worksheet** in the instructions for Form 1040, line 44 (or in the instructions for Form 1040NR, line 42). **Do not** complete lines 21 and 22 below.

☐ **No.** Complete the **Schedule D Tax Worksheet** in the instructions. **Do not** complete lines 21 and 22 below.

21 If line 16 is a loss, enter here and on Form 1040, line 13, or Form 1040NR, line 14, the **smaller** of:

- The loss on line 16 or
- ($3,000), or if married filing separately, ($1,500)

} . . . . **21** (   )

Note. When figuring which amount is smaller, treat both amounts as positive numbers.

22 Do you have qualified dividends on Form 1040, line 9b, or Form 1040NR, line 10b?

☐ **Yes.** Complete the **Qualified Dividends and Capital Gain Tax Worksheet** in the instructions for Form 1040, line 44 (or in the instructions for Form 1040NR, line 42).

☐ **No.** Complete the rest of Form 1040 or Form 1040NR.

Schedule D (Form 1040) 2014

DRAFT AS OF June 9, 2014 DO NOT FILE

Form **8949**

Department of the Treasury
Internal Revenue Service

Sales and Other Dispositions of Capital Assets

▶ Information about Form 8949 and its separate instructions is at *www.irs.gov/form8949.*

▶ File with your Schedule D to list your transactions for lines 1b, 2, 3, 8b, 9, and 10 of Schedule D.

OMB No. 1545-0123

2014

Attachment Sequence No. 12A

Name(s) shown on return	Social security number or taxpayer identification number

Before you check Box A, B, or C below, see whether you received any Form(s) 1099-B or substitute statement(s) from your broker. A substitute statement will have the same information as Form 1099-B. Either may show your basis (usually your cost) even if your broker did not report it to the IRS. Brokers must report basis to the IRS for most stock you bought in 2011 or later (and for certain debt instruments you bought in 2014 or later).

Part I **Short-Term.** Transactions involving capital assets you held 1 year or less are short term. For long-term transactions, see page 2.

Note. You may aggregate all short-term transactions reported on Form(s) 1099-B showing basis was reported to the IRS and for which no adjustments or codes are required. Enter the total directly on Schedule D, line 1a; you are not required to report these transactions on Form 8949 (see instructions).

You *must* check Box A, B, *or* C below. Check only one box. If more than one box applies for your short-term transactions, complete a separate Form 8949, page 1, for each applicable box. If you have more short-term transactions than will fit on this page for one or more of the boxes, complete as many forms with the same box checked as you need.

☐ **(A)** Short-term transactions reported on Form(s) 1099-B showing basis was reported to the IRS (see **Note** above)

☐ **(B)** Short-term transactions reported on Form(s) 1099-B showing basis was **not** reported to the IRS

☐ **(C)** Short-term transactions not reported to you on Form 1099-B

DRAFT AS OF June 12, 2014 DO NOT FILE

1 (a) Description of property (Example: 100 sh. XYZ Co.)	(b) Date acquired (Mo., day, yr.)	(c) Date sold or disposed (Mo., day, yr.)	(d) Proceeds (sales price) (see instructions)	(e) Cost or other basis. See the **Note** below and see *Column (e)* in the separate instructions	Adjustment, if any, to gain or loss. If you enter an amount in column (g), enter a code in column (f). See the separate instructions. (f) Code(s) from instructions	(g) Amount of adjustment	(h) Gain or (loss). Subtract column (e) from column (d) and combine the result with column (g)
2 Totals. Add the amounts in columns (d), (e), (g), and (h) (subtract negative amounts). Enter each total here and include on your Schedule D, **line 1b** (if **Box A** above is checked), **line 2** (if **Box B** above is checked), or **line 3** (if **Box C** above is checked) ▶							

Note. If you checked Box A above but the basis reported to the IRS was incorrect, enter in column (e) the basis as reported to the IRS, and enter an adjustment in column (g) to correct the basis. See *Column (g)* in the separate instructions for how to figure the amount of the adjustment.

For Paperwork Reduction Act Notice, see instructions. Cat. No. 37768Z Form **8949** (2014)

Form 8949 (2014) Attachment Sequence No. **12A** Page **2**

Name(s) shown on return. Name and SSN or taxpayer identification no. not required if shown on other side	**Social security number or taxpayer identification number**

Before you check Box D, E, or F below, see whether you received any Form(s) 1099-B or substitute statement(s) from your broker. A substitute statement will have the same information as Form 1099-B. Either may show your basis (usually your cost) even if your broker did not report it to the IRS. Brokers must report basis to the IRS for most stock you bought in 2011 or later (and for certain debt instruments you bought in 2014 or later).

Part II **Long-Term.** Transactions involving capital assets you held more than 1 year are long term. For short-term transactions, see page 1.

Note. You may aggregate all long-term transactions reported on Form(s) 1099-B showing basis was reported to the IRS and for which no adjustments or codes are required. Enter the total directly on Schedule D, line 8a; you are not required to report these transactions on Form 8949 (see instructions).

DRAFT AS OF June 12, 2014 DO NOT FILE

You *must* check Box D, E, *or* F below. Check only one box. If more than one box applies for your long-term transactions, complete a separate Form 8949, page 2, for each applicable box. If you have more long-term transactions than will fit on this page for one or more of the boxes, complete as many forms with the same box checked as you need.

☐ **(D)** Long-term transactions reported on Form(s) 1099-B showing basis was reported to the IRS (see **Note** above)
☐ **(E)** Long-term transactions reported on Form(s) 1099-B showing basis was **not** reported to the IRS
☐ **(F)** Long-term transactions not reported to you on Form 1099-B

1 **(a)** Description of property (Example: 100 sh. XYZ Co.)	**(b)** Date acquired (Mo., day, yr.)	**(c)** Date sold or disposed (Mo., day, yr.)	**(d)** Proceeds (sales price) (see instructions)	**(e)** Cost or other basis. See the **Note** below and see *Column (e)* in the separate instructions	Adjustment, if any, to gain or loss. If you enter an amount in column (g), enter a code in column (f). **See the separate instructions.** **(f)** Code(s) from instructions	**(g)** Amount of adjustment	**(h)** **Gain or (loss).** Subtract column (e) from column (d) and combine the result with column (g)
2 Totals. Add the amounts in columns (d), (e), (g), and (h) (subtract negative amounts). Enter each total here and include on your Schedule D, **line 8b** (if **Box D** above is checked), **line 9** (if **Box E** above is checked), or **line 10** (if **Box F** above is checked) ▶							

Note. If you checked Box D above but the basis reported to the IRS was incorrect, enter in column (e) the basis as reported to the IRS, and enter an adjustment in column (g) to correct the basis. See *Column (g)* in the separate instructions for how to figure the amount of the adjustment.

Form **8949** (2014)

Qualified Dividends and Capital Gain Tax Worksheet—Line 44

Keep for Your Records

Before you begin:
- ✓ See the earlier instructions for line 44 to see if you can use this worksheet to figure your tax.
- ✓ Before completing this worksheet, complete Form 1040 through line 43.
- ✓ If you do not have to file Schedule D and you received capital gain distributions, be sure you checked the box on line 13 of Form 1040.

1. Enter the amount from Form 1040, line 43. However, if you are filing Form 2555 or 2555-EZ (relating to foreign earned income), enter the amount from line 3 of the Foreign Earned Income Tax Worksheet . . . . . . **1.** ________

2. Enter the amount from Form 1040, line 9b* . . . . **2.** ________

3. Are you filing Schedule D?*
- ☐ **Yes.** Enter the **smaller** of line 15 or 16 of Schedule D. If either line 15 or line 16 is blank or a loss, enter -0-
- ☐ **No.** Enter the amount from Form 1040, line 13

3. ________

4. Add lines 2 and 3 . . . . **4.** ________

5. If filing Form 4952 (used to figure investment interest expense deduction), enter any amount from line 4g of that form. Otherwise, enter -0- . . . . **5.** ________

6. Subtract line 5 from line 4. If zero or less, enter -0- . . . . . . **6.** ________

7. Subtract line 6 from line 1. If zero or less, enter -0- . . . . . . **7.** ________

8. Enter:
$36,900 if single or married filing separately,
$73,800 if married filing jointly or qualifying widow(er),
$49,400 if head of household. . . . . **8.** ________

9. Enter the smaller of line 1 or line 8 . . . . **9.** ________

10. Enter the smaller of line 7 or line 9 . . . . **10.** ________

11. Subtract line 10 from line 9. This amount is taxed at 0% . . . . . . **11.** ________

12. Enter the smaller of line 1 or line 6 . . . . **12.** ________

13. Enter the amount from line 11 . . . . **13.** ________

14. Subtract line 13 from line 12 . . . . **14.** ________

15. Enter:
$406,750 if single,
$228,800 if married filing separately,
$457,600 if married filing jointly or qualifying widow(er),
$432,200 if head of household. . . . . **15.** ________

16. Enter the smaller of line 1 or line 15 . . . . **16.** ________

17. Add lines 7 and 11 . . . . **17.** ________

18. Subtract line 17 from line 16. If zero or less, enter -0- . . . . . . **18.** ________

19. Enter the smaller of line 14 or line 18 . . . . **19.** ________

20. Multiply line 19 by 15% (.15) . . . . **20.** ________

21. Add lines 11 and 19 . . . . **21.** ________

22. Subtract line 21 from line 12 . . . . **22.** ________

23. Multiply line 22 by 20% (.20) . . . . **23.** ________

24. Figure the tax on the amount on line 7. If the amount on line 7 is less than $100,000, use the Tax Table to figure the tax. If the amount on line 7 is $100,000 or more, use the Tax Computation Worksheet . . . . **24.** ________

25. Add lines 20, 23, and 24 . . . . **25.** ________

26. Figure the tax on the amount on line 1. If the amount on line 1 is less than $100,000, use the Tax Table to figure the tax. If the amount on line 1 is $100,000 or more, use the Tax Computation Worksheet . . . . **26.** ________

27. **Tax on all taxable income.** Enter the **smaller** of line 25 or line 26. Also include this amount on Form 1040, line 44. If you are filing Form 2555 or 2555-EZ, do not enter this amount on Form 1040, line 44. Instead, enter it on line 4 of the Foreign Earned Income Tax Worksheet . . . . **27.** ________

**If you are filing Form 2555 or 2555-EZ, see the footnote in the Foreign Earned Income Tax Worksheet before completing this line.*

Form **1040** Department of the Treasury—Internal Revenue Service (99)
U.S. Individual Income Tax Return **2014** OMB No. 1545-0074 IRS Use Only—Do not write or staple in this space.

For the year Jan. 1–Dec. 31, 2014, or other tax year beginning , 2014, ending , 20 See separate instructions.

Your first name and initial	Last name	**Your social security number**
If a joint return, spouse's first name and initial	Last name	**Spouse's social security number**
Home address (number and street). If you have a P.O. box, see instructions.	Apt. no.	▲ Make sure the SSN(s) above and on line 6c are correct.
City, town or post office, state, and ZIP code. If you have a foreign address, also complete spaces below (see instructions).		**Presidential Election Campaign** Check here if you, or your spouse if filing jointly, want $3 to go to this fund. Checking a box below will not change your tax or refund. ☐ You ☐ Spouse
Foreign country name	Foreign province/state/county / Foreign postal code	

Filing Status

Check only one box.

1 ☐ Single
2 ☐ Married filing jointly (even if only one had income)
3 ☐ Married filing separately. Enter spouse's SSN above and full name here. ▶
4 ☐ Head of household (with qualifying person). (See instructions.) If the qualifying person is a child but not your dependent, enter this child's name here. ▶
5 ☐ Qualifying widow(er) with dependent child

Exemptions

6a ☐ **Yourself.** If someone can claim you as a dependent, **do not** check box 6a . . . . .
b ☐ **Spouse** . . . . .

Boxes checked on 6a and 6b

c **Dependents:**

(1) First name Last name	(2) Dependent's social security number	(3) Dependent's relationship to you	(4) ✓ if child under age 17 qualifying for child tax credit (see instructions)
			☐
			☐
			☐
			☐

If more than four dependents, see instructions and check here ▶ ☐

No. of children on 6c who:
• lived with you
• did not live with you due to divorce or separation (see instructions)
Dependents on 6c not entered above

d Total number of exemptions claimed . . . . . **Add numbers on lines above ▶**

Income

Attach Form(s) W-2 here. Also attach Forms W-2G and 1099-R if tax was withheld.

If you did not get a W-2, see instructions.

Line	Description		
7	Wages, salaries, tips, etc. Attach Form(s) W-2		7
8a	**Taxable** interest. Attach Schedule B if required		8a
b	**Tax-exempt** interest. **Do not** include on line 8a	8b	
9a	Ordinary dividends. Attach Schedule B if required		9a
b	Qualified dividends	9b	
10	Taxable refunds, credits, or offsets of state and local income taxes		10
11	Alimony received		11
12	Business income or (loss). Attach Schedule C or C-EZ		12
13	Capital gain or (loss). Attach Schedule D if required. If not required, check here ▶ ☐		13
14	Other gains or (losses). Attach Form 4797		14
15a	IRA distributions 15a	b Taxable amount	15b
16a	Pensions and annuities 16a	b Taxable amount	16b
17	Rental real estate, royalties, partnerships, S corporations, trusts, etc. Attach Schedule E		17
18	Farm income or (loss). Attach Schedule F		18
19	Unemployment compensation		19
20a	Social security benefits 20a	b Taxable amount	20b
21	Other income. List type and amount		21
22	Combine the amounts in the far right column for lines 7 through 21. This is your **total income** ▶		22

DRAFT AS OF August 28, 2014 DO NOT FILE

Adjusted Gross Income

Line	Description		
23	Reserved	23	
24	Certain business expenses of reservists, performing artists, and fee-basis government officials. Attach Form 2106 or 2106-EZ	24	
25	Health savings account deduction. Attach Form 8889	25	
26	Moving expenses. Attach Form 3903	26	
27	Deductible part of self-employment tax. Attach Schedule SE	27	
28	Self-employed SEP, SIMPLE, and qualified plans	28	
29	Self-employed health insurance deduction	29	
30	Penalty on early withdrawal of savings	30	
31a	Alimony paid b Recipient's SSN ▶	31a	
32	IRA deduction	32	
33	Student loan interest deduction	33	
34	Reserved	34	
35	Domestic production activities deduction. Attach Form 8903	35	
36	Add lines 23 through 35		36
37	Subtract line 36 from line 22. This is your **adjusted gross income** ▶		37

For Disclosure, Privacy Act, and Paperwork Reduction Act Notice, see separate instructions. Cat. No. 11320B Form **1040** (2014)

Form 1040 (2014) Page **2**

Section	Line	Description			Line	Amount
	38	Amount from line 37 (adjusted gross income)			38	
Tax and Credits	39a	Check if: ☐ **You** were born before January 2, 1950, ☐ Blind. ☐ **Spouse** was born before January 2, 1950, ☐ Blind. } **Total boxes checked ▶ 39a** ☐				
	b	If your spouse itemizes on a separate return or you were a dual-status alien, check here ▶ 39b ☐				
Standard Deduction for— • People who check any box on line 39a or 39b **or** who can be claimed as a dependent, see instructions. • All others: Single or Married filing separately, $6,200 Married filing jointly or Qualifying widow(er), $12,400 Head of household, $9,100	40	**Itemized deductions** (from Schedule A) **or** your **standard deduction** (see left margin)			40	
	41	Subtract line 40 from line 38			41	
	42	**Exemptions.** If line 38 is $152,525 or less, multiply $3,950 by the number on line 6d. Otherwise, see instructions			42	
	43	**Taxable income.** Subtract line 42 from line 41. If line 42 is more than line 41, enter -0-			43	
	44	**Tax** (see instructions). Check if any from: **a** ☐ Form(s) 8814 **b** ☐ Form 4972 **c** ☐			44	
	45	**Alternative minimum tax** (see instructions). Attach Form 6251			45	
	46	Excess advance premium tax credit repayment. Attach Form 8962			46	
	47	Add lines 44, 45, and 46 ▶			47	
	48	Foreign tax credit. Attach Form 1116 if required	48			
	49	Credit for child and dependent care expenses. Attach Form 2441	49			
	50	Education credits from Form 8863, line 19	50			
	51	Retirement savings contributions credit. Attach Form 8880	51			
	52	Child tax credit. Attach Schedule 8812, if required	52			
	53	Residential energy credit. Attach Form 5695	53			
	54	Other credits from Form: **a** ☐ 3800 **b** ☐ 8801 **c** ☐	54			
	55	Add lines 48 through 54. These are your **total credits**			55	
	56	Subtract line 55 from line 47. If line 55 is more than line 47, enter -0- ▶			56	
Other Taxes	57	Self-employment tax. Attach Schedule SE			57	
	58	Unreported social security and Medicare tax from Form: **a** ☐ 4137 **b** ☐ 8919			58	
	59	Additional tax on IRAs, other qualified retirement plans, etc. Attach Form 5329 if required			59	
	60a	Household employment taxes from Schedule H			60a	
	b	First-time homebuyer credit repayment. Attach Form 5405 if required			60b	
	61	Health care: individual responsibility (see instructions) Full-year coverage ☐			61	
	62	Taxes from: **a** ☐ Form 8959 **b** ☐ Form 8960 **c** ☐ Instructions; enter code(s)			62	
	63	Add lines 56 through 62. This is your **total tax** ▶			63	
Payments	64	Federal income tax withheld from Forms W-2 and 1099	64			
If you have a qualifying child, attach Schedule EIC.	65	2014 estimated tax payments and amount applied from 2013 return	65			
	66a	**Earned income credit (EIC)**	66a			
	b	Nontaxable combat pay election 66b				
	67	Additional child tax credit. Attach Schedule 8812	67			
	68	American opportunity credit from Form 8863, line 8	68			
	69	Net premium tax credit. Attach Form 8962	69			
	70	Amount paid with request for extension to file	70			
	71	Excess social security and tier 1 RRTA tax withheld	71			
	72	Credit for federal tax on fuels. Attach Form 4136	72			
	73	Credits from Form: **a** ☐ 2439 **b** Reserved **c** Reserved **d** ☐	73			
	74	Add lines 64, 65, 66a, and 67 through 73. These are your **total payments** ▶			74	
Refund	75	If line 74 is more than line 63, subtract line 63 from line 74. This is the amount you **overpaid**			75	
	76a	Amount of line 75 you want **refunded to you.** If Form 8888 is attached, check here ▶ ☐			76a	
Direct deposit? See instructions.	▶ b	Routing number ▶ **c** Type: ☐ Checking ☐ Savings				
	▶ d	Account number				
	77	Amount of line 75 you want **applied to your 2015 estimated tax** ▶	77			
Amount You Owe	78	**Amount you owe.** Subtract line 74 from line 63. For details on how to pay, see instructions ▶			78	
	79	Estimated tax penalty (see instructions)	79			

Third Party Designee

Do you want to allow another person to discuss this return with the IRS (see instructions)? ☐ **Yes.** Complete below. ☐ **No**

Designee's name ▶ Phone no. ▶ Personal identification number (PIN) ▶

Sign Here

Joint return? See instructions. Keep a copy for your records.

Under penalties of perjury, I declare that I have examined this return and accompanying schedules and statements, and to the best of my knowledge and belief, they are true, correct, and complete. Declaration of preparer (other than taxpayer) is based on all information of which preparer has any knowledge.

Your signature	Date	Your occupation	Daytime phone number
Spouse's signature. If a joint return, **both** must sign.	Date	Spouse's occupation	If the IRS sent you an Identity Protection PIN, enter it here (see inst.)

Paid Preparer Use Only

Print/Type preparer's name	Preparer's signature	Date	Check ☐ if self-employed	PTIN
Firm's name ▶			Firm's EIN ▶	
Firm's address ▶			Phone no.	

DRAFT AS OF August 28, 2014 DO NOT FILE

SCHEDULE A (Form 1040)

Department of the Treasury
Internal Revenue Service (99)

Itemized Deductions

▶ **Information about Schedule A and its separate instructions is at *www.irs.gov/schedulea*.**
▶ **Attach to Form 1040.**

OMB No. 1545-0074
2014
Attachment Sequence No. **07**

DRAFT AS OF August 15, 2014 DO NOT FILE

Name(s) shown on Form 1040 | **Your social security number**

Section	Line	Description	Box	Amount	Line	Total
		Caution. Do not include expenses reimbursed or paid by others.				
Medical and Dental Expenses	1	Medical and dental expenses (see instructions)	1			
	2	Enter amount from Form 1040, line 38 [2]				
	3	Multiply line 2 by 10% (.10). But if either you or your spouse was born before January 2, 1950, multiply line 2 by 7.5% (.075) instead	3			
	4	Subtract line 3 from line 1. If line 3 is more than line 1, enter -0-			4	
Taxes You Paid	5	State and local a ☐ Income taxes b ☐ RESERVED	5			
	6	Real estate taxes (see instructions)	6			
	7	Personal property taxes	7			
	8	Other taxes. List type and amount ▶	8			
	9	Add lines 5 through 8			9	
Interest You Paid	10	Home mortgage interest and points reported to you on Form 1098	10			
Note. Your mortgage interest deduction may be limited (see instructions).	11	Home mortgage interest not reported to you on Form 1098. If paid to the person from whom you bought the home, see instructions and show that person's name, identifying no., and address ▶	11			
	12	Points not reported to you on Form 1098. See instructions for special rules	12			
	13	RESERVED	13			
	14	Investment interest. Attach Form 4952 if required. (See instructions.)	14			
	15	Add lines 10 through 14			15	
Gifts to Charity	16	Gifts by cash or check. If you made any gift of $250 or more, see instructions	16			
If you made a gift and got a benefit for it, see instructions.	17	Other than by cash or check. If any gift of $250 or more, see instructions. You **must** attach Form 8283 if over $500	17			
	18	Carryover from prior year	18			
	19	Add lines 16 through 18			19	
Casualty and Theft Losses	20	Casualty or theft loss(es). Attach Form 4684. (See instructions.)			20	
Job Expenses and Certain Miscellaneous Deductions	21	Unreimbursed employee expenses—job travel, union dues, job education, etc. Attach Form 2106 or 2106-EZ if required. (See instructions.) ▶	21			
	22	Tax preparation fees	22			
	23	Other expenses—investment, safe deposit box, etc. List type and amount ▶	23			
	24	Add lines 21 through 23	24			
	25	Enter amount from Form 1040, line 38 [25]				
	26	Multiply line 25 by 2% (.02)	26			
	27	Subtract line 26 from line 24. If line 26 is more than line 24, enter -0-			27	
Other Miscellaneous Deductions	28	Other—from list in instructions. List type and amount ▶			28	
Total Itemized Deductions	29	Is Form 1040, line 38, over $152,525? ☐ **No.** Your deduction is not limited. Add the amounts in the far right column for lines 4 through 28. Also, enter this amount on Form 1040, line 40. ☐ **Yes.** Your deduction may be limited. See the Itemized Deductions Worksheet in the instructions to figure the amount to enter.			29	
	30	If you elect to itemize deductions even though they are less than your standard deduction, check here ▶ ☐				

For Paperwork Reduction Act Notice, see Form 1040 instructions. Cat. No. 17145C **Schedule A (Form 1040) 2014**

SCHEDULE B
(Form 1040A or 1040)

Department of the Treasury
Internal Revenue Service (99)

Interest and Ordinary Dividends

▶ Attach to Form 1040A or 1040.
▶ Information about Schedule B and its instructions is at *www.irs.gov/scheduleb*.

OMB No. 1545-0074

2014

Attachment Sequence No. **08**

Name(s) shown on return | **Your social security number**

DRAFT AS OF
June 18, 2014
DO NOT FILE

Part I Interest

(See instructions on back and the instructions for Form 1040A, or Form 1040, line 8a.)

Note. If you received a Form 1099-INT, Form 1099-OID, or substitute statement from a brokerage firm, list the firm's name as the payer and enter the total interest shown on that form.

			Amount
1	List name of payer. If any interest is from a seller-financed mortgage and the buyer used the property as a personal residence, see instructions on back and list this interest first. Also, show that buyer's social security number and address ▶	1	
2	Add the amounts on line 1	2	
3	Excludable interest on series EE and I U.S. savings bonds issued after 1989. Attach Form 8815	3	
4	Subtract line 3 from line 2. Enter the result here and on Form 1040A, or Form 1040, line 8a . . . . ▶	4	

Note. If line 4 is over $1,500, you must complete Part III.

Part II Ordinary Dividends

(See instructions on back and the instructions for Form 1040A, or Form 1040, line 9a.)

Note. If you received a Form 1099-DIV or substitute statement from a brokerage firm, list the firm's name as the payer and enter the ordinary dividends shown on that form.

			Amount
5	List name of payer ▶	5	
6	Add the amounts on line 5. Enter the total here and on Form 1040A, or Form 1040, line 9a . . . . ▶	6	

Note. If line 6 is over $1,500, you must complete Part III.

Part III Foreign Accounts and Trusts

(See instructions on back.)

You must complete this part if you **(a)** had over $1,500 of taxable interest or ordinary dividends; **(b)** had a foreign account; or **(c)** received a distribution from, or were a grantor of, or a transferor to, a foreign trust.

		Yes	**No**
7a	At any time during 2014, did you have a financial interest in or signature authority over a financial account (such as a bank account, securities account, or brokerage account) located in a foreign country? See instructions		
	If "Yes," are you required to file FinCEN Form 114, Report of Foreign Bank and Financial Accounts (FBAR), to report that financial interest or signature authority? See FinCEN Form 114 and its instructions for filing requirements and exceptions to those requirements		
b	If you are required to file FinCEN Form 114, enter the name of the foreign country where the financial account is located ▶		
8	During 2014, did you receive a distribution from, or were you the grantor of, or transferor to, a foreign trust? If "Yes," you may have to file Form 3520. See instructions on back		

SCHEDULE D (Form 1040)

Department of the Treasury
Internal Revenue Service (99)

Capital Gains and Losses

▶ Attach to Form 1040 or Form 1040NR.
▶ Information about Schedule D and its separate instructions is at *www.irs.gov/scheduled*.
▶ Use Form 8949 to list your transactions for lines 1b, 2, 3, 8b, 9, and 10.

OMB No. 1545-0074
2014
Attachment Sequence No. 12

Name(s) shown on return | **Your social security number**

DRAFT AS OF June 9, 2014 DO NOT FILE

Part I Short-Term Capital Gains and Losses—Assets Held One Year or Less

See instructions for how to figure the amounts to enter on the lines below. This form may be easier to complete if you round off cents to whole dollars.	(d) Proceeds (sales price)	(e) Cost (or other basis)	(g) Adjustments to gain or loss from Form(s) 8949, Part I, line 2, column (g)	(h) Gain or (loss) Subtract column (e) from column (d) and combine the result with column (g)
1a Totals for all short-term transactions reported on Form 1099-B for which basis was reported to the IRS and for which you have no adjustments (see instructions). However, if you choose to report all these transactions on Form 8949, leave this line blank and go to line 1b .				
1b Totals for all transactions reported on Form(s) 8949 with **Box A** checked				
2 Totals for all transactions reported on Form(s) 8949 with **Box B** checked				
3 Totals for all transactions reported on Form(s) 8949 with **Box C** checked				

4 Short-term gain from Form 6252 and short-term gain or (loss) from Forms 4684, 6781, and 8824 .	4	
5 Net short-term gain or (loss) from partnerships, S corporations, estates, and trusts from Schedule(s) K-1	5	
6 Short-term capital loss carryover. Enter the amount, if any, from line 8 of your **Capital Loss Carryover Worksheet** in the instructions	6	( )
7 **Net short-term capital gain or (loss).** Combine lines 1a through 6 in column (h). If you have any long-term capital gains or losses, go to Part II below. Otherwise, go to Part III on the back	7	

Part II Long-Term Capital Gains and Losses—Assets Held More Than One Year

See instructions for how to figure the amounts to enter on the lines below. This form may be easier to complete if you round off cents to whole dollars.	(d) Proceeds (sales price)	(e) Cost (or other basis)	(g) Adjustments to gain or loss from Form(s) 8949, Part II, line 2, column (g)	(h) Gain or (loss) Subtract column (e) from column (d) and combine the result with column (g)
8a Totals for all long-term transactions reported on Form 1099-B for which basis was reported to the IRS and for which you have no adjustments (see instructions). However, if you choose to report all these transactions on Form 8949, leave this line blank and go to line 8b .				
8b Totals for all transactions reported on Form(s) 8949 with **Box D** checked				
9 Totals for all transactions reported on Form(s) 8949 with **Box E** checked				
10 Totals for all transactions reported on Form(s) 8949 with **Box F** checked.				

11 Gain from Form 4797, Part I; long-term gain from Forms 2439 and 6252; and long-term gain or (loss) from Forms 4684, 6781, and 8824	11	
12 Net long-term gain or (loss) from partnerships, S corporations, estates, and trusts from Schedule(s) K-1	12	
13 Capital gain distributions. See the instructions	13	
14 Long-term capital loss carryover. Enter the amount, if any, from line 13 of your **Capital Loss Carryover Worksheet** in the instructions	14	( )
15 **Net long-term capital gain or (loss).** Combine lines 8a through 14 in column (h). Then go to Part III on the back	15	

For Paperwork Reduction Act Notice, see your tax return instructions. Cat. No. 11338H **Schedule D (Form 1040) 2014**

Schedule D (Form 1040) 2014 Page **2**

Part III **Summary**

DRAFT AS OF June 9, 2014 DO NOT FILE

16 Combine lines 7 and 15 and enter the result 16

- If line 16 is a **gain,** enter the amount from line 16 on Form 1040, line 13, or Form 1040NR, line 14. Then go to line 17 below.
- If line 16 is a **loss,** skip lines 17 through 20 below. Then go to line 21. Also be sure to complete line 22.
- If line 16 is **zero,** skip lines 17 through 21 below and enter -0- on Form 1040, line 13, or Form 1040NR, line 14. Then go to line 22.

17 Are lines 15 and 16 **both** gains?
☐ **Yes.** Go to line 18.
☐ **No.** Skip lines 18 through 21, and go to line 22.

18 Enter the amount, if any, from line 7 of the **28% Rate Gain Worksheet** in the instructions . . ▶ 18

19 Enter the amount, if any, from line 18 of the **Unrecaptured Section 1250 Gain Worksheet** in the instructions . . . . ▶ 19

20 Are lines 18 and 19 **both** zero or blank?
☐ **Yes.** Complete the **Qualified Dividends and Capital Gain Tax Worksheet** in the instructions for Form 1040, line 44 (or in the instructions for Form 1040NR, line 42). **Do not** complete lines 21 and 22 below.

☐ **No.** Complete the **Schedule D Tax Worksheet** in the instructions. **Do not** complete lines 21 and 22 below.

21 If line 16 is a loss, enter here and on Form 1040, line 13, or Form 1040NR, line 14, the **smaller** of:

- The loss on line 16 or
- ($3,000), or if married filing separately, ($1,500)

} . . . . 21 (   )

Note. When figuring which amount is smaller, treat both amounts as positive numbers.

22 Do you have qualified dividends on Form 1040, line 9b, or Form 1040NR, line 10b?

☐ **Yes.** Complete the **Qualified Dividends and Capital Gain Tax Worksheet** in the instructions for Form 1040, line 44 (or in the instructions for Form 1040NR, line 42).

☐ **No.** Complete the rest of Form 1040 or Form 1040NR.

Form **8949**

Department of the Treasury
Internal Revenue Service

Sales and Other Dispositions of Capital Assets

▶ **Information about Form 8949 and its separate instructions is at *www.irs.gov/form8949*.**

▶ **File with your Schedule D to list your transactions for lines 1b, 2, 3, 8b, 9, and 10 of Schedule D.**

OMB No. 1545-0123

2014

Attachment Sequence No. **12A**

Name(s) shown on return	**Social security number or taxpayer identification number**

Before you check Box A, B, or C below, see whether you received any Form(s) 1099-B or substitute statement(s) from your broker. A substitute statement will have the same information as Form 1099-B. Either may show your basis (usually your cost) even if your broker did not report it to the IRS. Brokers must report basis to the IRS for most stock you bought in 2011 or later (and for certain debt instruments you bought in 2014 or later).

DRAFT AS OF June 12, 2014 DO NOT FILE

Part I **Short-Term.** Transactions involving capital assets you held 1 year or less are short term. For long-term transactions, see page 2.

Note. You may aggregate all short-term transactions reported on Form(s) 1099-B showing basis was reported to the IRS and for which no adjustments or codes are required. Enter the total directly on Schedule D, line 1a; you are not required to report these transactions on Form 8949 (see instructions).

You *must* check Box A, B, *or* C below. Check only one box. If more than one box applies for your short-term transactions, complete a separate Form 8949, page 1, for each applicable box. If you have more short-term transactions than will fit on this page for one or more of the boxes, complete as many forms with the same box checked as you need.

☐ **(A)** Short-term transactions reported on Form(s) 1099-B showing basis was reported to the IRS (see **Note** above)

☐ **(B)** Short-term transactions reported on Form(s) 1099-B showing basis was **not** reported to the IRS

☐ **(C)** Short-term transactions not reported to you on Form 1099-B

1 **(a)** Description of property (Example: 100 sh. XYZ Co.)	**(b)** Date acquired (Mo., day, yr.)	**(c)** Date sold or disposed (Mo., day, yr.)	**(d)** Proceeds (sales price) (see instructions)	**(e)** Cost or other basis. See the **Note** below and see *Column (e)* in the separate instructions	**Adjustment, if any, to gain or loss.** If you enter an amount in column (g), enter a code in column (f). **See the separate instructions.** **(f)** Code(s) from instructions	**(g)** Amount of adjustment	**(h)** **Gain or (loss).** Subtract column (e) from column (d) and combine the result with column (g)
2 Totals. Add the amounts in columns (d), (e), (g), and (h) (subtract negative amounts). Enter each total here and include on your Schedule D, **line 1b** (if **Box A** above is checked), **line 2** (if **Box B** above is checked), or **line 3** (if **Box C** above is checked) ▶							

Note. If you checked Box A above but the basis reported to the IRS was incorrect, enter in column (e) the basis as reported to the IRS, and enter an adjustment in column (g) to correct the basis. See *Column (g)* in the separate instructions for how to figure the amount of the adjustment.

Form 8949 (2014) Attachment Sequence No. **12A** Page **2**

Name(s) shown on return. Name and SSN or taxpayer identification no. not required if shown on other side	**Social security number or taxpayer identification number**

Before you check Box D, E, or F below, see whether you received any Form(s) 1099-B or substitute statement(s) from your broker. A substitute statement will have the same information as Form 1099-B. Either may show your basis (usually your cost) even if your broker did not report it to the IRS. Brokers must report basis to the IRS for most stock you bought in 2011 or later (and for certain debt instruments you bought in 2014 or later).

Part II **Long-Term.** Transactions involving capital assets you held more than 1 year are long term. For short-term transactions, see page 1.

Note. You may aggregate all long-term transactions reported on Form(s) 1099-B showing basis was reported to the IRS and for which no adjustments or codes are required. Enter the total directly on Schedule D, line 8a; you are not required to report these transactions on Form 8949 (see instructions).

DRAFT AS OF June 12, 2014 DO NOT FILE

You *must* check Box D, E, *or* F below. Check only one box. If more than one box applies for your long-term transactions, complete a separate Form 8949, page 2, for each applicable box. If you have more long-term transactions than will fit on this page for one or more of the boxes, complete as many forms with the same box checked as you need.

☐ **(D)** Long-term transactions reported on Form(s) 1099-B showing basis was reported to the IRS (see **Note** above)
☐ **(E)** Long-term transactions reported on Form(s) 1099-B showing basis was **not** reported to the IRS
☐ **(F)** Long-term transactions not reported to you on Form 1099-B

1 **(a)** Description of property (Example: 100 sh. XYZ Co.)	**(b)** Date acquired (Mo., day, yr.)	**(c)** Date sold or disposed (Mo., day, yr.)	**(d)** Proceeds (sales price) (see instructions)	**(e)** Cost or other basis. See the **Note** below and see *Column (e)* in the separate instructions	**Adjustment, if any, to gain or loss.** If you enter an amount in column (g), enter a code in column (f). **See the separate instructions.** **(f)** Code(s) from instructions	**(g)** Amount of adjustment	**(h)** **Gain or (loss).** Subtract column (e) from column (d) and combine the result with column (g)
2 Totals. Add the amounts in columns (d), (e), (g), and (h) (subtract negative amounts). Enter each total here and include on your Schedule D, **line 8b** (if **Box D** above is checked), **line 9** (if **Box E** above is checked), or **line 10** (if **Box F** above is checked) ▶							

Note. If you checked Box D above but the basis reported to the IRS was incorrect, enter in column (e) the basis as reported to the IRS, and enter an adjustment in column (g) to correct the basis. See *Column (g)* in the separate instructions for how to figure the amount of the adjustment.

Form **8949** (2014)

Qualified Dividends and Capital Gain Tax Worksheet—Line 44

Keep for Your Records

Before you begin:
- ✓ See the earlier instructions for line 44 to see if you can use this worksheet to figure your tax.
- ✓ Before completing this worksheet, complete Form 1040 through line 43.
- ✓ If you do not have to file Schedule D and you received capital gain distributions, be sure you checked the box on line 13 of Form 1040.

1. Enter the amount from Form 1040, line 43. However, if you are filing Form 2555 or 2555-EZ (relating to foreign earned income), enter the amount from line 3 of the Foreign Earned Income Tax Worksheet . . . . . **1.** ______

2. Enter the amount from Form 1040, line 9b* . . . . . **2.** ______

3. Are you filing Schedule D?*
- ☐ **Yes.** Enter the **smaller** of line 15 or 16 of Schedule D. If either line 15 or line 16 is blank or a loss, enter -0-
- ☐ **No.** Enter the amount from Form 1040, line 13

3. ______

4. Add lines 2 and 3 . . . . . **4.** ______

5. If filing Form 4952 (used to figure investment interest expense deduction), enter any amount from line 4g of that form. Otherwise, enter -0- . . . . . **5.** ______

6. Subtract line 5 from line 4. If zero or less, enter -0- . . . . . **6.** ______

7. Subtract line 6 from line 1. If zero or less, enter -0- . . . . . **7.** ______

8. Enter:
$36,900 if single or married filing separately,
$73,800 if married filing jointly or qualifying widow(er),
$49,400 if head of household. . . . . . **8.** ______

9. Enter the smaller of line 1 or line 8 . . . . . **9.** ______

10. Enter the smaller of line 7 or line 9 . . . . . **10.** ______

11. Subtract line 10 from line 9. This amount is taxed at 0% . . . . . **11.** ______

12. Enter the smaller of line 1 or line 6 . . . . . **12.** ______

13. Enter the amount from line 11 . . . . . **13.** ______

14. Subtract line 13 from line 12 . . . . . **14.** ______

15. Enter:
$406,750 if single,
$228,800 if married filing separately,
$457,600 if married filing jointly or qualifying widow(er),
$432,200 if head of household. . . . . . **15.** ______

16. Enter the smaller of line 1 or line 15 . . . . . **16.** ______

17. Add lines 7 and 11 . . . . . **17.** ______

18. Subtract line 17 from line 16. If zero or less, enter -0- . . . . . **18.** ______

19. Enter the smaller of line 14 or line 18 . . . . . **19.** ______

20. Multiply line 19 by 15% (.15) . . . . . **20.** ______

21. Add lines 11 and 19 . . . . . **21.** ______

22. Subtract line 21 from line 12 . . . . . **22.** ______

23. Multiply line 22 by 20% (.20) . . . . . **23.** ______

24. Figure the tax on the amount on line 7. If the amount on line 7 is less than $100,000, use the Tax Table to figure the tax. If the amount on line 7 is $100,000 or more, use the Tax Computation Worksheet . . . . . **24.** ______

25. Add lines 20, 23, and 24 . . . . . **25.** ______

26. Figure the tax on the amount on line 1. If the amount on line 1 is less than $100,000, use the Tax Table to figure the tax. If the amount on line 1 is $100,000 or more, use the Tax Computation Worksheet . . . . . **26.** ______

27. **Tax on all taxable income.** Enter the **smaller** of line 25 or line 26. Also include this amount on Form 1040, line 44. If you are filing Form 2555 or 2555-EZ, do not enter this amount on Form 1040, line 44. Instead, enter it on line 4 of the Foreign Earned Income Tax Worksheet . . . . . **27.** ______

**If you are filing Form 2555 or 2555-EZ, see the footnote in the Foreign Earned Income Tax Worksheet before completing this line.*

Form **6252** | **Installment Sale Income** | OMB No. 1545-0228

Department of the Treasury
Internal Revenue Service

▶ Attach to your tax return.
▶ Use a separate form for each sale or other disposition of property on the installment method.
▶ Information about Form 6252 and its instructions is at *www.irs.gov/form6252.*

2014
Attachment Sequence No. **79**

Name(s) shown on return | **Identifying number**

DRAFT AS OF June 30, 2014 DO NOT FILE

1 Description of property ▶

2a Date acquired (mm/dd/yyyy) ▶ **b** Date sold (mm/dd/yyyy) ▶

3 Was the property sold to a related party (see instructions) after May 14, 1980? If "No," skip line 4 . . . ☐ Yes ☐ No

4 Was the property you sold to a related party a marketable security? If "Yes," complete Part III. If "No," complete Part III for the year of sale and the 2 years after the year of sale . . . ☐ Yes ☐ No

Part I Gross Profit and Contract Price. Complete this part for the year of sale only.

5	Selling price including mortgages and other debts. **Do not** include interest, whether stated or unstated		5	
6	Mortgages, debts, and other liabilities the buyer assumed or took the property subject to (see instructions)	6		
7	Subtract line 6 from line 5	7		
8	Cost or other basis of property sold	8		
9	Depreciation allowed or allowable	9		
10	Adjusted basis. Subtract line 9 from line 8	10		
11	Commissions and other expenses of sale	11		
12	Income recapture from Form 4797, Part III (see instructions)	12		
13	Add lines 10, 11, and 12		13	
14	Subtract line 13 from line 5. If zero or less, **do not** complete the rest of this form (see instructions)		14	
15	If the property described on line 1 above was your main home, enter the amount of your excluded gain (see instructions). Otherwise, enter -0-		15	
16	**Gross profit.** Subtract line 15 from line 14		16	
17	Subtract line 13 from line 6. If zero or less, enter -0-		17	
18	**Contract price.** Add line 7 and line 17		18	

Part II Installment Sale Income. Complete this part for the year of sale **and** any year you receive a payment or have certain debts you must treat as a payment on installment obligations.

June 12, 2014

19	Gross profit percentage (expressed as a decimal amount). Divide line 16 by line 18. For years after the year of sale, see instructions		19	
20	If this is the year of sale, enter the amount from line 17. Otherwise, enter -0-		20	
21	Payments received during year (see instructions). **Do not** include interest, whether stated or unstated		21	
22	Add lines 20 and 21		22	
23	Payments received in prior years (see instructions). **Do not** include interest, whether stated or unstated	23		
24	**Installment sale income.** Multiply line 22 by line 19		24	
25	Enter the part of line 24 that is ordinary income under the recapture rules (see instructions)		25	
26	Subtract line 25 from line 24. Enter here and on Schedule D or Form 4797 (see instructions)		26	

Part III Related Party Installment Sale Income. Do not complete if you received the final payment this tax year.

27 Name, address, and taxpayer identifying number of related party

28 Did the related party resell or dispose of the property ("second disposition") during this tax year? . . . ☐ Yes ☐ No

29 **If the answer to question 28 is "Yes," complete lines 30 through 37 below unless one of the following conditions is met. Check the box that applies.**

a ☐ The second disposition was more than 2 years after the first disposition (other than dispositions of marketable securities). If this box is checked, enter the date of disposition (mm/dd/yyyy) ▶

b ☐ The first disposition was a sale or exchange of stock to the issuing corporation.

c ☐ The second disposition was an involuntary conversion and the threat of conversion occurred after the first disposition.

d ☐ The second disposition occurred after the death of the original seller or buyer.

e ☐ It can be established to the satisfaction of the IRS that tax avoidance was not a principal purpose for either of the dispositions. If this box is checked, attach an explanation (see instructions).

30	Selling price of property sold by related party (see instructions)	30	
31	Enter contract price from line 18 for year of first sale	31	
32	Enter the **smaller** of line 30 or line 31	32	
33	Total payments received by the end of your 2014 tax year (see instructions)	33	
34	Subtract line 33 from line 32. If zero or less, enter -0-	34	
35	Multiply line 34 by the gross profit percentage on line 19 for year of first sale	35	
36	Enter the part of line 35 that is ordinary income under the recapture rules (see instructions)	36	
37	Subtract line 36 from line 35. Enter here and on Schedule D or Form 4797 (see instructions)	37	

For Paperwork Reduction Act Notice, see page 4. Cat. No. 13601R Form **6252** (2014)

Student Name ______________________

Class/Section ______________________

Date ______________________

KEY NUMBER TAX RETURN SUMMARY

CHAPTER 8

Comprehensive Problem 1

Adjusted Gross Income (Line 37) ______________

Schedule D, Net Short-Term Capital Gain or (Loss) (Line 7) ______________

Schedule D, Net Long-Term Capital Gain or (Loss) (Line 15) ______________

Taxable Income (Line 43) ______________

Tax Overpaid (Line 75) ______________

Comprehensive Problem 2

Adjusted Gross Income (Line 37) ______________

Schedule D, Net Short-Term Capital Gain or (Loss) (Line 7) ______________

Schedule D, Net Long-Term Capital Gain or (Loss) (Line 15) ______________

Form 6252, Installment Sale Income (Line 26) ______________

Tax Overpaid (Line 75) ______________

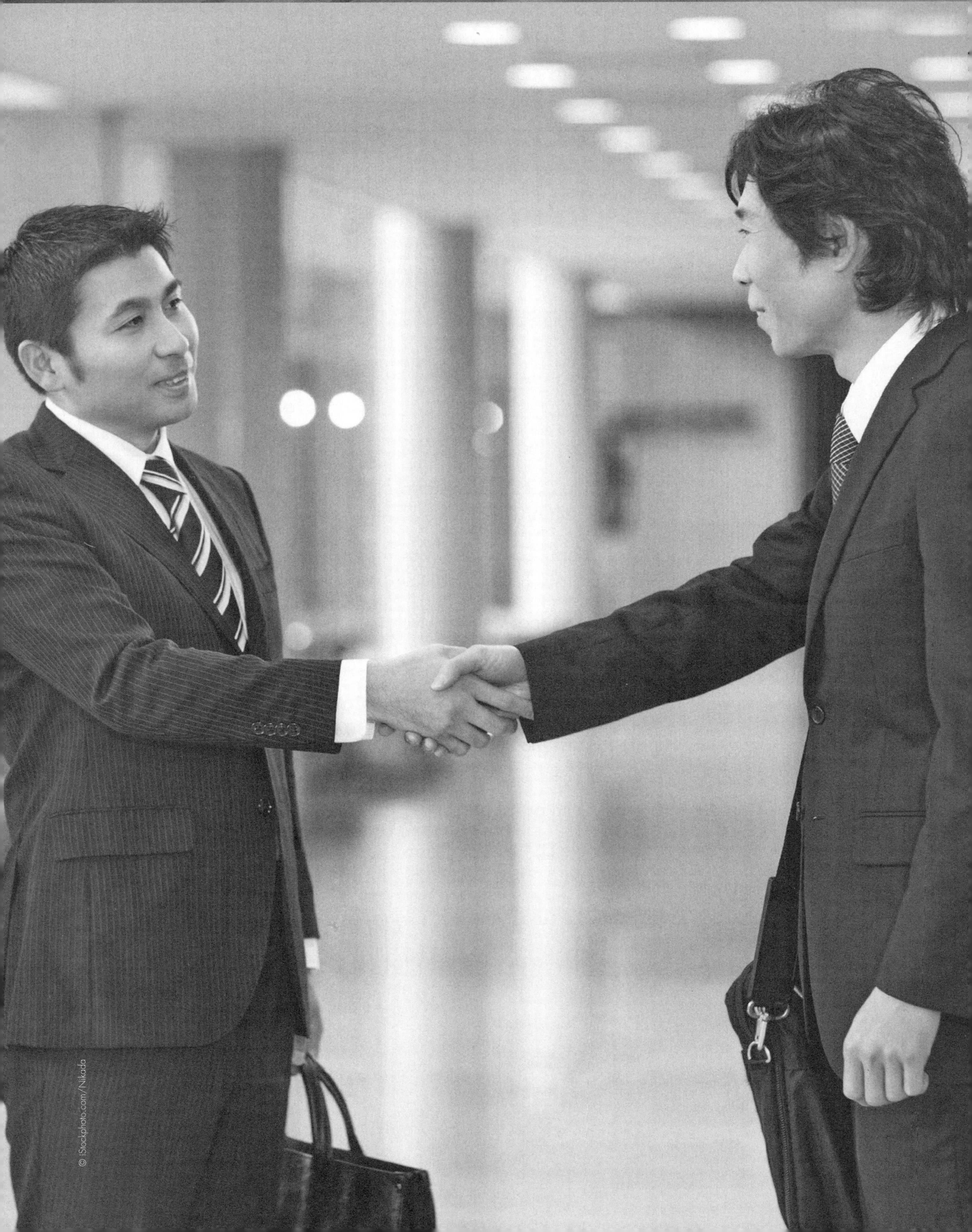

© iStockphoto.com/Nikada

CHAPTER 9

Withholding, Estimated Payments, and Payroll Taxes

LEARNING OBJECTIVES

After completing this chapter, you should be able to:

- **LO 9.1** Compute the income tax withholding from employee wages.
- **LO 9.2** Determine taxpayers' quarterly estimated payments.
- **LO 9.3** Understand the FICA tax.
- **LO 9.4** Understand the federal deposit system.
- **LO 9.5** Understand employer payroll reporting.
- **LO 9.6** Calculate the self-employment tax (both Social Security and Medicare portions) for self-employed taxpayers.
- **LO 9.7** Compute the amount of FUTA tax for an employer.
- **LO 9.8** Apply the special tax and reporting requirements for household employees (the nanny tax).
- **LO 9.9** Calculate the 0.9 percent Medicare surtax on the earned income of high-income taxpayers.

OVERVIEW

This chapter focuses on the payment and reporting of income and other taxes by employers, employees, and self-employed taxpayers. Payroll and other tax topics covered include withholding methods for employees, estimated payments, the FICA tax (Social Security and Medicare taxes), the federal tax deposit system, and employer reporting requirements. In addition, related taxes such as the self-employment (SE) tax, the Federal Unemployment Tax Act (FUTA) tax, the nanny tax, and the Medicare surtax on high-income taxpayers are covered.

The FICA tax is a combined Social Security (6.2% up to the annual wage limit, $117,000 in 2014) and Medicare tax (1.45% with no limit) that is paid by both employees and employers. The tax is withheld from each employee's paycheck, then the tax is matched by the employer, and the total amount is remitted to the IRS.

The FUTA tax is unemployment insurance with a joint state and federal payment plan to provide benefits for taxpayers when they become unemployed. The FUTA tax is paid only by employers, not employees.

Self-employed taxpayers do not have an employer to match their Social Security and Medicare taxes, so they have to pay the full amount of the SE tax (15.3% for 2014 up to the $117,000 earnings limit and then 2.9% on all earnings over $117,000). In many cases, the SE tax exceeds a self-employed individual's income tax. Beginning in 2013, the Affordable Care Act (sometimes referred to as "Obamacare") imposes a 0.9 percent Medicare surtax on the earned income of certain high-income taxpayers.

The nanny tax is a reporting system for wages paid to household employees such as babysitters, caretakers, cooks, drivers, gardeners, housekeepers, and maids who earn more than an annual threshold amount.

Every working individual, whether an employee or self-employed, is affected by the rules covered in this chapter.

Learning Objective 9.1

Compute the income tax withholding from employee wages.

WITHHOLDING METHODS

Employers are required to withhold taxes from amounts paid to employees for wages, including salaries, fees, bonuses, commissions, vacation and retirement pay. Form W-4, showing the filing status and the number of withholding allowances an employee is claiming, is furnished to the employer by the employee. Form W-4 is the key to the amount of the employee's withholding for federal income taxes. Usually, employees claim the same number of allowances on Form W-4 as the number of exemptions claimed on their federal tax returns. Employees with alimony payments, a large amount of itemized deductions, or tax credits may claim additional withholding allowances. Each additional withholding allowance reduces annual income tax withholding by the value of one exemption. Form W-4 includes a worksheet for calculating the number of allowances an employee should claim.

Some employees want extra tax withheld from their wages; this may be authorized on Form W-4. Also, exemption from withholding may be claimed on Form W-4 by employees who anticipate no federal tax liability for the current year. To be exempt from withholding, the employee must also have had no tax liability for the prior year. If an employee does not complete Form W-4, the employer is required to withhold as if the employee is single with no exemptions.

Single employees with only one job may claim one "special withholding allowance." Married employees may also claim a "special withholding allowance" if one of the following conditions exists:

1. The employee has only one job and his or her spouse does not work, or
2. Wages earned from the employee's second job, or wages earned by his or her spouse, or the total of both are $1,500 or less.

Employees with two or more jobs or employees with a spouse who also is employed must complete the "Two Earners/Multiple Jobs Worksheet" on Page 2 of Form W-4.

Employees do not have to provide proof to their employers that they are entitled to the number of allowances claimed on their Form W-4s. Employers must submit copies of W-4s to the IRS only when directed to do so by written notice. Where there is significant under-withholding for a particular employee, the IRS may require the employer to withhold income tax at a higher rate. Employees are given the right to contest the IRS determination.

EXAMPLE Tom Barry earns $50,000 per year and his wife does not work. All of Tom's salary is from one job, and the Barrys have two dependent children under 17. The Barrys estimate their itemized deductions to be $12,800 for the year. Tom should claim nine withholding allowances as illustrated on Form W-4 on Pages 9-3 and 9-4. ♦

Form W-4 (2014)

Purpose. Complete Form W-4 so that your employer can withhold the correct federal income tax from your pay. Consider completing a new Form W-4 each year and when your personal or financial situation changes.

Exemption from withholding. If you are exempt, complete **only** lines 1, 2, 3, 4, and 7 and sign the form to validate it. Your exemption for 2014 expires February 17, 2015. See Pub. 505, Tax Withholding and Estimated Tax.

Note. If another person can claim you as a dependent on his or her tax return, you cannot claim exemption from withholding if your income exceeds $1,000 and includes more than $350 of unearned income (for example, interest and dividends).

Exceptions. An employee may be able to claim exemption from withholding even if the employee is a dependent, if the employee:

- Is age 65 or older,
- Is blind, or
- Will claim adjustments to income; tax credits; or itemized deductions, on his or her tax return.

The exceptions do not apply to supplemental wages greater than $1,000,000.

Basic instructions. If you are not exempt, complete the **Personal Allowances Worksheet** below. The worksheets on page 2 further adjust your withholding allowances based on itemized deductions, certain credits, adjustments to income, or two-earners/multiple jobs situations.

Complete all worksheets that apply. However, you may claim fewer (or zero) allowances. For regular wages, withholding must be based on allowances you claimed and may not be a flat amount or percentage of wages.

Head of household. Generally, you can claim head of household filing status on your tax return only if you are unmarried and pay more than 50% of the costs of keeping up a home for yourself and your dependent(s) or other qualifying individuals. See Pub. 501, Exemptions, Standard Deduction, and Filing Information, for information.

Tax credits. You can take projected tax credits into account in figuring your allowable number of withholding allowances. Credits for child or dependent care expenses and the child tax credit may be claimed using the **Personal Allowances Worksheet** below. See Pub. 505 for information on converting your other credits into withholding allowances.

Nonwage income. If you have a large amount of nonwage income, such as interest or dividends, consider making estimated tax payments using Form 1040-ES, Estimated Tax for Individuals. Otherwise, you may owe additional tax. If you have pension or annuity iincome, see Pub. 505 to find out if you should adjust your withholding on Form W-4 or W-4P.

Two earners or multiple jobs. If you have a working spouse or more than one job, figure the total number of allowances you are entitled to claim on all jobs using worksheets from only one Form W-4. Your withholding usually will be most accurate when all allowances are claimed on the Form W-4 for the highest paying job and zero allowances are claimed on the others. See Pub. 505 for details.

Nonresident alien. If you are a nonresident alien, see Notice 1392, Supplemental Form W-4 Instructions for Nonresident Aliens, before completing this form.

Check your withholding. After your Form W-4 takes effect, use Pub. 505 to see how the amount you are having withheld compares to your projected total tax for 2014. See Pub. 505, especially if your earnings exceed $130,000 (Single) or $180,000 (Married).

Future developments. Information about any future developments affecting Form W-4 (such as legislation enacted after we release it) will be posted at *www.irs.gov/w4*.

Personal Allowances Worksheet (Keep for your records.)

A Enter "1" for **yourself** if no one else can claim you as a dependent . . . . . **A** 1

B Enter "1" if:
- You are single and have only one job; or
- You are married, have only one job, and your spouse does not work; or
- Your wages from a second job or your spouse's wages (or the total of both) are $1,500 or less.

. . . **B** 1

C Enter "1" for your **spouse.** But, you may choose to enter "-0-" if you are married and have either a working spouse or more than one job. (Entering "-0-" may help you avoid having too little tax withheld.) . . . . . **C** 1

D Enter number of **dependents** (other than your spouse or yourself) you will claim on your tax return . . . . **D** 2

E Enter "1" if you will file as **head of household** on your tax return (see conditions under **Head of household** above) . . **E** ____

F Enter "1" if you have at least $2,000 of **child or dependent care expenses** for which you plan to claim a credit . . . **F** ____

(**Note.** Do **not** include child support payments. See Pub. 503, Child and Dependent Care Expenses, for details.)

G **Child Tax Credit** (including additional child tax credit). See Pub. 972, Child Tax Credit, for more information.
- If your total income will be less than $65,000 ($95,000 if married), enter "2" for each eligible child; then **less** "1" if you have three to six eligible children or **less** "2" if you have seven or more eligible children.
- If your total income will be between $65,000 and $84,000 ($95,000 and $119,000 if married), enter "1" for each eligible child . . . **G** 4

H Add lines A through G and enter total here. (**Note.** This may be different from the number of exemptions you claim on your tax return.) ▶ **H** 9

For accuracy, **complete all worksheets that apply.**
- If you plan to **itemize** or **claim adjustments to income** and want to reduce your withholding, see the **Deductions and Adjustments Worksheet** on page 2.
- If you are **single and have more than one job** or are **married and you and your spouse both work** and the combined earnings from all jobs exceed $50,000 ($20,000 if married), see the **Two-Earners/Multiple Jobs Worksheet** on page 2 to avoid having too little tax withheld.
- If **neither** of the above situations applies, **stop here** and enter the number from line H on line 5 of Form W-4 below.

---------- **Separate here and give Form W-4 to your employer. Keep the top part for your records.** ----------

Form **W-4** | Department of the Treasury, Internal Revenue Service

Employee's Withholding Allowance Certificate

▶ **Whether you are entitled to claim a certain number of allowances or exemption from withholding is subject to review by the IRS. Your employer may be required to send a copy of this form to the IRS.**

OMB No. 1545-0074 | **2014**

1 Your first name and middle initial Tom	Last name Barry	2 **Your social security number**
Home address (number and street or rural route)	3 ☐ Single ☑ Married ☐ Married, but withhold at higher Single rate. **Note.** If married, but legally separated, or spouse is a nonresident alien, check the "Single" box.	
City or town, state, and ZIP code	4 **If your last name differs from that shown on your social security card, check here. You must call 1-800-772-1213 for a replacement card.** ▶ ☐	

5	Total number of allowances you are claiming (from line **H** above **or** from the applicable worksheet on page 2)	5	9
6	Additional amount, if any, you want withheld from each paycheck	6	$
7	I claim exemption from withholding for 2014, and I certify that I meet **both** of the following conditions for exemption. • Last year I had a right to a refund of **all** federal income tax withheld because I had **no** tax liability, **and** • This year I expect a refund of **all** federal income tax withheld because I expect to have **no** tax liability. If you meet both conditions, write "Exempt" here . . . . . ▶ 7		

Under penalties of perjury, I declare that I have examined this certificate and, to the best of my knowledge and belief, it is true, correct, and complete.

Employee's signature
(This form is not valid unless you sign it.) ▶ **Date** ▶

8 Employer's name and address (Employer: Complete lines 8 and 10 only if sending to the IRS.)	9 Office code (optional)	10 Employer identification number (EIN)

For Privacy Act and Paperwork Reduction Act Notice, see page 2. Cat. No. 10220Q Form **W-4** (2014)

Form W-4 (2014) Page **2**

Deductions and Adjustments Worksheet

Note. Use this worksheet *only* if you plan to itemize deductions or claim certain credits or adjustments to income.

1	Enter an estimate of your 2014 itemized deductions. These include qualifying home mortgage interest, charitable contributions, state and local taxes, medical expenses in excess of 10% (7.5% if either you or your spouse was born before January 2, 1950) of your income, and miscellaneous deductions. For 2014, you may have to reduce your itemized deductions if your income is over $305,050 and you are married filing jointly or are a qualifying widow(er); $279,650 if you are head of household; $254,200 if you are single and not head of household or a qualifying widow(er); or $152,525 if you are married filing separately. See Pub. 505 for details	1	$ 12,800
2	Enter: { $12,400 if married filing jointly or qualifying widow(er); $9,100 if head of household; $6,200 if single or married filing separately }	2	$ 12,400
3	**Subtract** line 2 from line 1. If zero or less, enter "-0-"	3	$ 400
4	Enter an estimate of your 2014 adjustments to income and any additional standard deduction (see Pub. 505)	4	$
5	**Add** lines 3 and 4 and enter the total. (Include any amount for credits from the *Converting Credits to Withholding Allowances for 2014 Form W-4* worksheet in Pub. 505.)	5	$ 400
6	Enter an estimate of your 2014 nonwage income (such as dividends or interest)	6	$
7	**Subtract** line 6 from line 5. If zero or less, enter "-0-"	7	$ 400
8	**Divide** the amount on line 7 by $3,950 and enter the result here. Drop any fraction	8	0
9	Enter the number from the **Personal Allowances Worksheet,** line H, page 1	9	9
10	**Add** lines 8 and 9 and enter the total here. If you plan to use the **Two-Earners/Multiple Jobs Worksheet,** also enter this total on line 1 below. Otherwise, **stop here** and enter this total on Form W-4, line 5, page 1	10	9

Two-Earners/Multiple Jobs Worksheet (See *Two earners or multiple jobs* on page 1.)

Note. Use this worksheet *only* if the instructions under line H on page 1 direct you here.

1	Enter the number from line H, page 1 (or from line 10 above if you used the **Deductions and Adjustments Worksheet**)	1	
2	Find the number in **Table 1** below that applies to the **LOWEST** paying job and enter it here. **However,** if you are married filing jointly and wages from the highest paying job are $65,000 or less, do not enter more than "3"	2	
3	If line 1 is **more than or equal to** line 2, subtract line 2 from line 1. Enter the result here (if zero, enter "-0-") and on Form W-4, line 5, page 1. **Do not** use the rest of this worksheet	3	

Note. If line 1 is **less than** line 2, enter "-0-" on Form W-4, line 5, page 1. Complete lines 4 through 9 below to figure the additional withholding amount necessary to avoid a year-end tax bill.

4	Enter the number from line 2 of this worksheet . . . 4 ______		
5	Enter the number from line 1 of this worksheet . . . 5 ______		
6	**Subtract** line 5 from line 4	6	
7	Find the amount in **Table 2** below that applies to the **HIGHEST** paying job and enter it here	7	$
8	**Multiply** line 7 by line 6 and enter the result here. This is the additional annual withholding needed	8	$
9	Divide line 8 by the number of pay periods remaining in 2014. For example, divide by 25 if you are paid every two weeks and you complete this form on a date in January when there are 25 pay periods remaining in 2014. Enter the result here and on Form W-4, line 6, page 1. This is the additional amount to be withheld from each paycheck	9	$

Table 1

Married Filing Jointly		All Others	
If wages from **LOWEST** paying job are—	Enter on line 2 above	If wages from **LOWEST** paying job are—	Enter on line 2 above
$0 - $6,000	0	$0 - $6,000	0
6,001 - 13,000	1	6,001 - 16,000	1
13,001 - 24,000	2	16,001 - 25,000	2
24,001 - 26,000	3	25,001 - 34,000	3
26,001 - 33,000	4	34,001 - 43,000	4
33,001 - 43,000	5	43,001 - 70,000	5
43,001 - 49,000	6	70,001 - 85,000	6
49,001 - 60,000	7	85,001 - 110,000	7
60,001 - 75,000	8	110,001 - 125,000	8
75,001 - 80,000	9	125,001 - 140,000	9
80,001 - 100,000	10	140,001 and over	10
100,001 - 115,000	11		
115,001 - 130,000	12		
130,001 - 140,000	13		
140,001 - 150,000	14		
150,001 and over	15		

Table 2

Married Filing Jointly		All Others	
If wages from **HIGHEST** paying job are—	Enter on line 7 above	If wages from **HIGHEST** paying job are—	Enter on line 7 above
$0 - $74,000	$590	$0 - $37,000	$590
74,001 - 130,000	990	37,001 - 80,000	990
130,001 - 200,000	1,110	80,001 - 175,000	1,110
200,001 - 355,000	1,300	175,001 - 385,000	1,300
355,001 - 400,000	1,380	385,001 and over	1,560
400,001 and over	1,560		

Privacy Act and Paperwork Reduction Act Notice. We ask for the information on this form to carry out the Internal Revenue laws of the United States. Internal Revenue Code sections 3402(f)(2) and 6109 and their regulations require you to provide this information; your employer uses it to determine your federal income tax withholding. Failure to provide a properly completed form will result in your being treated as a single person who claims no withholding allowances; providing fraudulent information may subject you to penalties. Routine uses of this information include giving it to the Department of Justice for civil and criminal litigation; to cities, states, the District of Columbia, and U.S. commonwealths and possessions for use in administering their tax laws; and to the Department of Health and Human Services for use in the National Directory of New Hires. We may also disclose this information to other countries under a tax treaty, to federal and state agencies to enforce federal nontax criminal laws, or to federal law enforcement and intelligence agencies to combat terrorism.

You are not required to provide the information requested on a form that is subject to the Paperwork Reduction Act unless the form displays a valid OMB control number. Books or records relating to a form or its instructions must be retained as long as their contents may become material in the administration of any Internal Revenue law. Generally, tax returns and return information are confidential, as required by Code section 6103.

The average time and expenses required to complete and file this form will vary depending on individual circumstances. For estimated averages, see the instructions for your income tax return.

If you have suggestions for making this form simpler, we would be happy to hear from you. See the instructions for your income tax return.

Would You Believe?

A former president of Sprint Corporation claimed approximately 300,000 exemptions connected to a complex tax shelter that eventually cost him his job, according to the *Wall Street Journal*.

TAX BREAK

It pays to fill in Form W-4 correctly. When taxpayers have too much tax withheld, they are giving the government an interest-free loan of the extra income tax withholding until their tax return is filed and a refund is obtained. When taxpayers have too little income tax withheld, they are subject to penalties for underpayment of taxes (see LO 9.2).

Computing Withholding

The amount to be withheld by the employer is based on gross wages before deducting Social Security taxes, pension payments, union dues, insurance, and other deductions. An employer may elect to use any of several methods to determine the amount of the withholding for each individual employee. Most commonly, withholding amounts are determined by use of the percentage method or by use of wage bracket tables. To compute the withholding amount under the percentage method, the employer should:

1. Multiply the number of allowances claimed by the employee (from Form W-4) by the allowance amount;
2. Subtract that amount from the employee's gross wages for the pay period; and
3. Multiply the result in Step 2 by the percentage obtained from the tables in Appendix C for the appropriate marital status.

The allowance amounts used in Step 1 for 2014 for various pay periods are from IRS Publication 15, "Circular E, Employer's Tax Guide." All are based on the fact that in 2014, one allowance is $3,950.

Pay Period	*2014 Allowance Amount*
Weekly	$ 76.00
Biweekly	151.90
Semimonthly	164.60
Monthly	329.20
Quarterly	987.50
Semiannually	1,975.00
Annually	3,950.00

EXAMPLE Sharon is married, and her pay is $2,250 per month. On her Form W-4, Sharon claims married with a total of two allowances. The amount of withholding for Sharon is calculated as follows:

1. Allowances amount (monthly)	$ 329.20
Number of allowances claimed	× 2
Total	$ 658.40
2. Gross wages	$2,250.00
Less: amount from above	(658.40)
Withholding income	$1,591.60

3. Withholding from percentage tables in Appendix C:
($1,591.60 − $704.00) × 10% = $88.76 ♦

Under the second method of determining withholding, wage bracket tables are provided for weekly, biweekly, semimonthly, monthly, and daily payroll periods for both married and single taxpayers. The amount of withholding is obtained from the table for the appropriate payroll period and marital status, and is based on the total wages and the number of withholding allowances claimed. The monthly tables for married taxpayers are reproduced in Appendix C.

EXAMPLE Sharon's withholding from the previous example may also be obtained from the wage bracket tables in Appendix C. For a wage payment of $2,250 with two allowances, on the married person's monthly payroll period table, the amount of the withholding is found to be $90. ♦

Pension and Deferred Income

Withholding is also required on pension and other deferred income payments based on Form W-4P, Withholding Certificate for Pension or Annuity Payments, as completed and signed by the taxpayer. Financial institutions and corporations must withhold on the taxable part of pension, profit sharing, stock bonus, and individual retirement account payments. The rates used for withholding vary depending on the nature of the payment, as described below:

1. Periodic payments (such as annuities): Rates are based on the taxpayer's withholding certificate as if the payments were additional wages.
2. Nonperiodic payments: The withholding is deducted at a flat 10 percent rate, except for certain distributions from qualified retirement plans, which have a required 20 percent withholding tax rate. See Chapter 4 for a discussion of withholding on rollover distributions.

EXAMPLE Adam is a retired college professor and receives a pension of $775 per month. The payor should withhold on the pension, based on Adam's signed W-4P, in the same manner as if it were Adam's salary. ♦

Tip Reporting

The receipt of tips is part of the vast economy of cash transactions which are underreported or simply ignored as income by many taxpayers. To combat widespread underreporting of tips in the food and beverage industry, the IRS developed requirements for employees and employers. Employees are generally required to report tips to their employers. Then employers are generally required to report the amount of gross food and beverage sales (other than carryout) to the IRS. If total reported tips are less than 8 percent of sales, the employer must allocate among the employees the excess of 8 percent of gross sales over the amount of tips reported to the employer by the employees. The employer is not required to withhold income, Social Security, or Medicare tax on allocated tips, but is required to collect those taxes on tips reported by employees.

The allocation of tip income can be accomplished in one of three ways. The employer may allocate the amount based on (1) gross receipts per employee, (2) hours worked by each employee (available only to employers having fewer than the equivalent of twenty-five full-time employees), or (3) a good faith agreement as explained on Form 8027, Employer's Annual Information Return of Tip Income and Allocated Tips. For a detailed explanation of the allocation process, see the instructions for Form 8027. For more information on tip reporting in general, see the IRS website or a tax research service.

Starting in 2014, compulsory and fixed charges included in a customer's bill are no longer considered "tips" under federal tax law. Restaurants and similar businesses must include the service charges as wages. For example, a required 18-percent service charge for a party of eight or more must be treated as additional wages to the restaurant's employees.

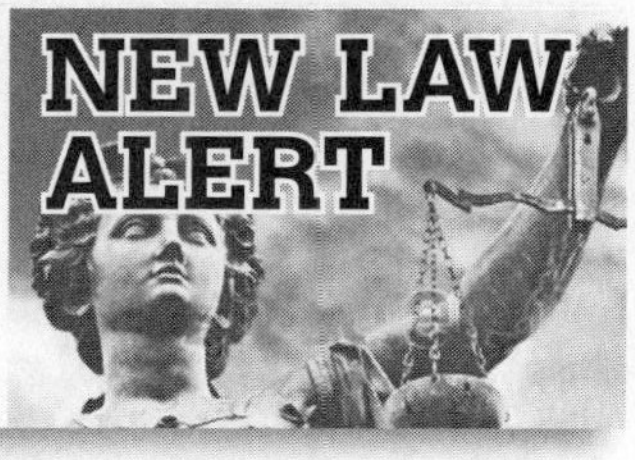

© ER_09/Shutterstock.com

Would You Believe?

For years employers were required to send the IRS any Form W-4s for employees claiming more than 10 allowances. In 2005, the IRS ended this practice. Now the IRS identifies under-withholding in different ways and when appropriate sends a "lock-in letter" to employers specifying the number of allowances an employee may use.

Backup Withholding

In some situations, individuals may be subject to backup withholding on payments such as interest and dividends. The purpose of backup withholding is to ensure that income tax is paid on income reported on Form 1099. If backup withholding applies, the payor (i.e., bank or insurance company) must withhold 28 percent of the amount paid to the taxpayer. Payors are required to use backup withholding in the following cases:

1. The taxpayer does not give the payor his or her taxpayer identification number (e.g., Social Security number),
2. The taxpayer fails to certify that he or she is not subject to backup withholding,
3. The IRS informs the payor that the taxpayer gave an incorrect identification number, or
4. The IRS informs the payor to start withholding because the taxpayer has not reported the income on his or her tax return.

EXAMPLE Barbra earned $2,000 in interest income from Cactus Savings Bank. Barbra failed to certify that she was not subject to backup withholding. As a result, the bank must withhold taxes of $560 (28 percent of $2,000) from the interest payments to Barbra. ♦

Taxpayers who give false information to avoid backup withholding are subject to a $500 civil penalty and a criminal penalty of up to $1,000 or up to 1 year of imprisonment, or both.

Would You Believe?

Despite IRS efforts, tax cheating is on the rise. The Treasury Department estimated that unreported income and other forms of cheating cost the government $300 billion or more a year. Other studies have estimated a "tax-gap" as high as $600 billion. Although there is disagreement about the actual amount of tax cheating, experts agree it is a significant problem.

Self-Study Problem 9.1 ***See Appendix E for Solutions to Self-Study Problems***

For 2014, John earns $3,000 per month and has three dependent children. He is divorced and claims five allowances on his Form W-4. Calculate John's withholding using:

1. The percentage method $__________
2. The wage bracket method $__________

Learning Objective 9.2

Determine taxpayers' quarterly estimated payments.

ESTIMATED PAYMENTS

Self-employed taxpayers are not subject to withholding; however, they must make quarterly estimated tax payments. Taxpayers with large amounts of interest, dividends, and other income not subject to withholding are also generally required to make estimated payments. Payments are made in four installments on April 15, June 15, and September 15 of the tax year, and January 15 of the following year, based on the taxpayer's estimate of the amount of the tax liability for the year. A taxpayer with self-employment income must begin making the payments when he or she first meets the filing requirements.

TAX BREAK

Never write out a check to the "IRS." The IRS issues this warning every year, because "IRS" may be easily changed to "MRS" plus an individual's name if the check falls into the wrong hands. Checks must be made payable to the U.S. Treasury, as a reminder that the IRS is merely the collector of revenue for the federal government.

Any individual taxpayer who has estimated tax for the year of $1,000 or more, after subtracting withholding, and whose withholding does not equal or exceed the "required annual payment," must make quarterly estimated payments. The required annual payment is the smallest of the following amounts:

1. Ninety percent of the tax shown on the current year's return,
2. One hundred percent of the tax shown on the preceding year's return (such return must cover a full 12 months), or
3. Ninety percent of the current-year tax determined by placing taxable income, alternative minimum taxable income, and adjusted self-employment income on an annualized basis for each quarter.

A special rule applies to individuals with adjusted gross income in excess of $150,000 for the previous year. These high-income taxpayers must pay 110 percent of the amount of tax shown on the prior year tax return for the current year estimated payments, instead of 100 percent, to meet the requirements in the second exception above.

Estimated payments need not be paid if the estimated tax, after subtracting withholding, can reasonably be expected to be less than $1,000. Therefore, employees who also have self-employment income may avoid making estimated payments by filing a new Form W-4 and increasing the amount of their withholding on their regular salary.

The IRS imposes a nondeductible penalty on the amounts of any underpayments of estimated tax. The penalty applies when any installment is less than the required annual payment divided by the number of installments that should have been made, which is usually four. Form 2210, Underpayment of Estimated Tax by Individuals and Fiduciaries, is used for the calculation of the penalty associated with the underpayment of estimated tax.

Good tax planning dictates that a taxpayer postpone payment of taxes as long as no penalty is imposed. Unpaid taxes are equivalent to an interest-free loan from the government. Therefore, taxpayers should base their estimated payments on the method which results in the lowest amount of required quarterly or annual payment. For example, a taxpayer who expects his tax liability to increase might base his estimated payments this year on the amount of the tax liability for the prior year.

Self-Study Problem 9.2 *See Appendix E for Solutions to Self-Study Problems*

Ray Adams (Social Security number 466-47-1131) estimates his required annual payment for 2014 to be $7,560. He has a $510 overpayment of last year's taxes that he wishes to apply to the first quarter estimated tax payment for 2014. Complete the first quarter voucher below for Ray for 2014 by assuming any additional information, such as Ray's address.

Form **1040-ES** Department of the Treasury Internal Revenue Service | **2014 Estimated Tax** | **Payment Voucher 1** | OMB No. 1545-0074

File only if you are making a payment of estimated tax by check or money order. Mail this voucher with your check or money order payable to **"United States Treasury."** Write your social security number and "2014 Form 1040-ES" on your check or money order. Do not send cash. Enclose, but do not staple or attach, your payment with this voucher.

Calendar year—Due April 15, 2014

Amount of estimated tax you are paying by check or money order. | Dollars | Cents |

Print or type

Your first name and initial	Your last name	Your social security number
If joint payment, complete for spouse		
Spouse's first name and initial	Spouse's last name	Spouse's social security number
Address (number, street, and apt. no.)		
City, state, and ZIP code. (If a foreign address, enter city, also complete spaces below.)		
Foreign country name	Foreign province/county	Foreign postal code

For Privacy Act and Paperwork Reduction Act Notice, see instructions. **Form 1040-ES (2014)**

THE FICA TAX

Learning Objective 9.3

Understand the FICA tax.

The Federal Insurance Contributions Act (FICA) imposes Social Security taxes. It was passed by Congress in 1935 to provide benefits for qualified retired and disabled workers. If a worker should die, it would also provide the family of the worker with benefits. The Medicare program for the elderly is also funded by FICA taxes.

FICA taxes have two parts, Social Security (Old Age, Survivors, and Disability Insurance [OASDI]) and Medicare. Employees and their employers are both required to pay FICA taxes. Employers withhold a specified percentage of each employee's wages up to a maximum base amount, match the amount withheld with an equal amount, and pay the total to the Social Security Administration.

The Social Security (OASDI) tax rate is 6.2 percent and the Medicare tax rate is 1.45 percent each for employees and employers. The maximum wage subject to the Social Security portion of the FICA tax is $117,000, and all wages are subject to the Medicare portion of the FICA tax. The maximum wages to which the rates apply have increased over the years, the most recent being the 0.9% Medicare surtax added in 2013.

Year	*Employee %*	*Employer %*	*Maximum Base*
2010	6.20	6.20	$106,800 (Social Security)
	1.45	1.45	Unlimited (Medicare)
2011	4.20	6.20	$106,800 (Social Security)
	1.45	1.45	Unlimited (Medicare)
2012	4.20	6.20	$110,100 (Social Security)
	1.45	1.45	Unlimited (Medicare)
2013	6.20	6.20	$113,700 (Social Security)
	1.45	1.45	Unlimited (Medicare)
2014	6.20	6.20	$117,000 (Social Security)
	1.45	1.45	Up to $200,000 (single and head of household) or $250,000 (MFJ)
	2.35	1.45	Above $200,000 (single and head of household) and $250,000 (MFJ)

The original FICA tax in 1935 was 1 percent of the first $3,000 in earnings.

TAX BREAK

Taxpayers age 18 and older may request an online statement of Social Security benefits including estimates of projected retirement, survivors', and disability benefits. The statement also shows the taxpayer's Social Security earnings history, giving the taxpayer an opportunity to correct any errors or omissions. The personalized online statement is available at **www.socialsecurity.gov/mystatement**. In some cases, the Social Security Administration will provide a paper version of this statement by mail.

EXAMPLE Katherine earns $21,500 for 2014. The FICA tax on her wages is calculated as follows:

Katherine:	Soc. Sec. – 6.2% × $21,500	$1,333.00
	Medicare – 1.45% × $21,500	311.75
	Total employee FICA tax	$1,644.75
Katherine's employer:	Soc. Sec. – 6.2% × $21,500	$1,333.00
	Medicare – 1.45% × $21,500	311.75
	Total employer FICA tax	$1,644.75
Total FICA tax		$3,289.50

♦

EXAMPLE Sam is an employee of Serissa Company. His salary for 2014 is $132,000. Sam's portion of the FICA tax is calculated as follows:

Soc. Sec. – 6.2% × $117,000	$7,254.00
Medicare – 1.45% × $132,000	1,914.00
Total employee FICA tax	$9,168.00

The total combined FICA tax (employee's and employer's share) is $18,336.00. ♦

Would You Believe?

According to the Tax Policy Center (www.taxpolicycenrer.org), over three quarters of households pay more in payroll taxes (including the employer's share) than income taxes.

Overpayment of FICA Taxes

Taxpayers who work for more than one employer during the same tax year may pay more than the maximum amount of FICA taxes. This occurs when the taxpayer's total wages are more than the maximum base amount for the year. When this happens, the taxpayer should compute the excess taxes paid, and report the excess on Form 1040 as an additional payment against his or her tax liability.

EXAMPLE Jerry worked for two employers during 2014. The first employer withheld and paid FICA taxes on $70,000 of salary paid to Jerry, and the second employer withheld and paid FICA taxes on $50,000 of salary paid to Jerry. The amount of Jerry's excess FICA taxes paid for 2014 is computed as follows: 6.2% (Social Security rate) × [$70,000 + $50,000 − $117,000 (maximum for Social Security portion of FICA tax)] = $186. Jerry receives credit against his 2014 income tax liability equal to the excess Social Security taxes of $186. No excess Medicare tax has been paid, as there is no upper limit on Medicare wages. ♦

Self-Study Problem 9.3 ***See Appendix E for Solutions to Self-Study Problems***

Debbie earns $125,000 in 2014. Calculate the total FICA tax that must be paid by:

Debbie:	Soc. Sec.	$__________
	Medicare	$__________
Debbie's employer:	Soc. Sec.	$__________
	Medicare	$__________
Total FICA tax		$__________

FEDERAL TAX DEPOSIT SYSTEM

Learning Objective 9.4

Understand the federal deposit system.

Employers must make periodic deposits of the taxes that are withheld from employees' wages. The frequency of the deposits depends on the total income tax withheld and the total FICA taxes for all employees. Employers are either monthly depositors or semiweekly depositors, depending on the total income taxes withheld from wages and FICA taxes attributable to wages. Prior to the beginning of each calendar year, taxpayers are required to determine which of the two deposit schedules they are required to use. If withholding and FICA taxes of $100,000 or more are accumulated at any time during the year, the depositor is subject to a special one-day deposit rule.

Monthly or semiweekly deposit status is determined by using a lookback period, consisting of the four quarters beginning July 1 of the second preceding year and ending June 30 of the prior year. If the total income tax withheld from wages and FICA attributable to wages for the four quarters in the lookback period is $50,000 or less, employers are monthly depositors for the current year. Monthly depositors must make deposits of employment taxes and taxes withheld by the fifteenth day of the month following the month of withholding. New employers are automatically monthly depositors.

If the total income tax withheld from wages and FICA attributable to wages for the four quarters in the lookback period is more than $50,000, the employer is a semiweekly depositor for the current year. Taxes on payments made on Wednesday, Thursday, or Friday must be deposited by the following Wednesday; taxes on payments made on the other days

of the week must be deposited by the following Friday. If a deposit is scheduled for a day that is not a banking day, the deposit is considered to be made timely if it is made by the close of the next banking day.

EXAMPLE Tom runs a small business with ten employees. During the lookback period for the current year, the total withholding and FICA taxes amounted to $40,000. Since this is less than $50,000, Tom is a monthly depositor. His payroll tax deposits must be made by the fifteenth day of the month following the month of withholding. ♦

Tax payments (monthly, semiweekly, or daily for large depositors) must be made by EFTPS (Electronic Federal Tax Payment System), or by another electronic transfer method. Generally, employers must file Form 941, Employer's Quarterly Federal Tax Return, which reports the federal income taxes withheld from wages and the total FICA taxes attributable to wages paid during each quarter. Form 941 must be accompanied by any payroll taxes not yet deposited for the quarter. A special deposit rule allows small employers who accumulate less than $2,500 tax liability during a quarter to skip monthly payments and pay the entire amount of their payroll taxes with their quarterly Form 941. Form 941 must be filed by the last day of the month following the end of the quarter. For example, the first quarter Form 941, covering the months of January through March, must be filed by April 30. The Form 941 e-file program allows a taxpayer to electronically file Form 941 or Form 944.

Nearly a million very small employers with employment tax liability of $1,000 or less per year are allowed to file employment tax returns just once a year, instead of quarterly; for example, by January 31 of 2015 for 2014 employment taxes. Qualifying small employers receive written notification from the IRS that they should file using a Form 944 instead of the standard Form 941 used by most employers. The Form 944 is due annually, at the end of the month, following the taxpayer's year end.

IRS Publication 15, "Circular E, Employers Tax Guide," covers the rules regarding the calculation and deposit of payroll taxes in detail and is an indispensable resource for those working in this complex area.

Self-Study Problem 9.4

See Appendix E for Solutions to Self-Study Problems

For the first quarter of 2014, Rita O'Miya has two employees. The payroll information for these two employees for the first quarter is as follows:

	Mary			***Chris***		
	January	***February***	***March***	***January***	***February***	***March***
Gross wages	$2,000	$2,000	$2,100	$1,000	$1,000	$1,500
Federal income tax withheld	230	230	235	60	60	180
FICA tax withheld	153	153	161	77	77	115

Rita deposited $750 on February 15, $750 on March 15, and $967 on April 15. Using this information, complete page 1 of Rita's Form 941, on Page 9-13, for the first quarter of 2014.

Self-Study Problem 9.4

Form **941 for 2014: Employer's QUARTERLY Federal Tax Return** 950114
(Rev. January 2014) Department of the Treasury — Internal Revenue Service OMB No. 1545-0029

Employer identification number (EIN) ☐☐ – ☐☐☐☐☐☐☐

Name *(not your trade name)* Rita O'Miya

Trade name *(if any)*

Address
Number Street Suite or room number
City State ZIP code
Foreign country name Foreign province/county Foreign postal code

Report for this Quarter of 2014
(Check one.)
☐ **1:** January, February, March
☐ **2:** April, May, June
☐ **3:** July, August, September
☐ **4:** October, November, December

Instructions and prior year forms are available at *www.irs.gov/form941.*

Read the separate instructions before you complete Form 941. Type or print within the boxes.

Part 1: Answer these questions for this quarter.

1 **Number of employees who received wages, tips, or other compensation for the pay period including:** ***Mar. 12*** **(Quarter 1),** ***June 12*** **(Quarter 2),** ***Sept. 12*** **(Quarter 3), or** ***Dec. 12*** **(Quarter 4)** 1 ____

2 **Wages, tips, and other compensation** 2 ____ .

3 **Federal income tax withheld from wages, tips, and other compensation** 3 ____ .

4 **If no wages, tips, and other compensation are subject to social security or Medicare tax** ☐ **Check and go to line 6.**

		Column 1		Column 2
5a	Taxable social security wages	.	× .124 =	.
5b	Taxable social security tips	.	× .124 =	.
5c	Taxable Medicare wages & tips	.	× .029 =	.
5d	Taxable wages & tips subject to Additional Medicare Tax withholding	.	× .009 =	.

5e **Add Column 2 from lines 5a, 5b, 5c, and 5d** 5e ____ .

5f **Section 3121(q) Notice and Demand—Tax due on unreported tips** (see instructions) 5f ____ .

6 **Total taxes before adjustments.** Add lines 3, 5e, and 5f 6 ____ .

7 **Current quarter's adjustment for fractions of cents** 7 ____ .

8 **Current quarter's adjustment for sick pay** 8 ____ .

9 **Current quarter's adjustments for tips and group-term life insurance** 9 ____ .

10 **Total taxes after adjustments.** Combine lines 6 through 9 10 ____ .

11 **Total deposits for this quarter, including overpayment applied from a prior quarter and overpayments applied from Form 941-X, 941-X (PR), 944-X, 944-X (PR), or 944-X (SP) filed in the current quarter** 11 ____ .

12 **Balance due.** If line 10 is more than line 11, enter the difference and see instructions 12 ____ .

13 **Overpayment.** If line 11 is more than line 10, enter the difference ____ . Check one: ☐ Apply to next return. ☐ Send a refund.

► **You MUST complete both pages of Form 941 and SIGN it.** Next ►

For Privacy Act and Paperwork Reduction Act Notice, see the back of the Payment Voucher. Cat. No. 17001Z Form **941** (Rev. 1-2014)

950214

Name *(not your trade name)* | **Employer identification number (EIN)**

Part 2: **Tell us about your deposit schedule and tax liability for this quarter.**

If you are unsure about whether you are a monthly schedule depositor or a semiweekly schedule depositor, see Pub. 15 (Circular E), section 11.

14 Check one: ☐ **Line 10 on this return is less than $2,500 or line 10 on the return for the prior quarter was less than $2,500, and you did not incur a $100,000 next-day deposit obligation during the current quarter.** If line 10 for the prior quarter was less than $2,500 but line 10 on this return is $100,000 or more, you must provide a record of your federal tax liability. If you are a monthly schedule depositor, complete the deposit schedule below; if you are a semiweekly schedule depositor, attach Schedule B (Form 941). Go to Part 3.

☐ **You were a monthly schedule depositor for the entire quarter.** Enter your tax liability for each month and total liability for the quarter, then go to Part 3.

Tax liability: **Month 1** ______ .

Month 2 ______ .

Month 3 ______ .

Total liability for quarter ______ . **Total must equal line 10.**

☐ **You were a semiweekly schedule depositor for any part of this quarter.** Complete Schedule B (Form 941), Report of Tax Liability for Semiweekly Schedule Depositors, and attach it to Form 941.

Part 3: **Tell us about your business. If a question does NOT apply to your business, leave it blank.**

15 If your business has closed or you stopped paying wages . . . . ☐ Check here, and

enter the final date you paid wages ___ / ___ / ___ .

16 If you are a seasonal employer and you do not have to file a return for every quarter of the year . . ☐ Check here.

Part 4: **May we speak with your third-party designee?**

Do you want to allow an employee, a paid tax preparer, or another person to discuss this return with the IRS? See the instructions for details.

☐ Yes. Designee's name and phone number ______ ______

Select a 5-digit Personal Identification Number (PIN) to use when talking to the IRS. ☐☐☐☐☐

☐ No.

Part 5: **Sign here. You MUST complete both pages of Form 941 and SIGN it.**

Under penalties of perjury, I declare that I have examined this return, including accompanying schedules and statements, and to the best of my knowledge and belief, it is true, correct, and complete. Declaration of preparer (other than taxpayer) is based on all information of which preparer has any knowledge.

X **Sign your name here** ______

Print your name here ______

Print your title here ______

Date ___ / ___ / ___

Best daytime phone ______

Paid Preparer Use Only

Check if you are self-employed . . . ☐

Preparer's name		PTIN	
Preparer's signature		Date	/ /
Firm's name (or yours if self-employed)		EIN	
Address		Phone	
City	State	ZIP code	

EMPLOYER REPORTING REQUIREMENTS

Learning Objective 9.5

Understand employer payroll reporting.

On or before January 31 of the year following the calendar year of payment, an employer must furnish to each employee two copies of the employee's Wage and Tax Statement, Form W-2, for the previous calendar year. If employment is terminated before the end of the year and the employee requests a Form W-2, the employer must furnish the Form W-2 within 30 days after the last wage payment is made or after the employee request, whichever is later. Otherwise the general rule requiring the W-2 to be furnished to the employee by January 31 applies. The original copy (Copy A) of all W-2 forms and Form W-3 (Transmittal of Income and Tax Statements) must be filed with the Social Security Administration by February 28 of the year following the calendar year of payment. Copy B of Form W-2 is filed with the employee's federal tax return. Employers retain Copy D of Form W-2 for their records. Extra copies of Form W-2 are prepared for the employee to use when filing state and local tax returns.

Form W-2 is used to report wages, tips, and other compensation paid to an employee. Not all of the amounts included on a taxpayer's Form W-2 are subject to income tax withholding. Among the items which must be reported on the employee's Form W-2 are reimbursements for nonqualified moving expenses (a nonqualified moving expense is an expense the employee cannot deduct for tax purposes), excess group-term life insurance premiums, the value of noncash prizes and awards presented to individuals normally paid on a commission basis, and certain reimbursements of travel and other ordinary and necessary expenses. Special rules apply to the reimbursement of travel and other ordinary and necessary employee business expenses.

If an employee is reimbursed for travel and other ordinary and necessary business expenses, income and employment tax withholding may be required. If a reimbursement payment is considered to have been made under an accountable plan, as discussed in Chapter 5, the amount is excluded from the employee's gross income and consequently is not required to be included on Form W-2, and no withholding is required. Alternatively, reimbursements of travel and other employee business expenses made under a nonaccountable plan must be included as wages on Form W-2, and the amounts are subject to withholding. Payments are considered made under a nonaccountable plan in the following circumstances: (1) the employee receives a reimbursement for expenses under an arrangement which does not require the employee to account adequately to the employer, or the employee receives advances under an arrangement which does not require the employee to return amounts in excess of substantiated expenses; or (2) the employee receives amounts under an arrangement that requires the employee to substantiate reimbursed expenses, but the amounts are not substantiated within a reasonable period of time, or the employee receives amounts under a plan which requires excess reimbursements to be returned to the employer, but the employee does not return such excess amounts within a reasonable period of time. In the first case, the entire amount paid under the expense account plan is considered wages subject to withholding, whereas under the circumstances described in the second situation, only the amounts in excess of the substantiated expenses are subject to withholding.

Every year the IRS releases a list of twelve scams, called by some the "we've already seen it, so don't try it" list, or "The Dirty Dozen." The list includes offshore financial account misuse and frivolous arguments including "wages are not income" and "paying taxes is voluntary." Filling in a corrected wage form (Form 4852, Substitute Form W-2) to change taxable wages to zero is a creative additional item on the list, as is impersonating a charitable organization. Actor Wesley Snipes was sentenced to 3 years in prison after failing to file taxes and using a frivolous tax protester argument as his excuse.

Would You Believe?

TABLE 9.1 1099 FORMS

Form	Used For
1099-B	Payments of proceeds from brokers
1099-DIV	Dividend payments
1099-INT	Interest payments
1099-K	Merchant card and third-party network payments
1099-MISC	Miscellaneous payments
1099-R	Pension, annuity, profit sharing, retirement plan, IRA, insurance contracts, etc.
1099-S	Proceeds from real estate transactions

© Cengage Learning

Other W-2 Forms

Gambling winnings are reported by the gambling establishment on Form W-2G. Amounts that must be reported include certain winnings on horse and dog racing, jai alai, lotteries, state-conducted lotteries, sweepstakes, wagering pools, bingo, keno, and slot machines. In certain cases, withholding of income taxes is required. Forms W-2G must be transmitted to the taxpayer not later than January 31 of the year following the calendar year of payment, and to the IRS along with Form 1096 by February 28 of the year following the calendar year of payment.

Information Returns

Taxpayers engaged in a trade or business are required to file Form 1099 for each recipient of certain payments made in the course of their trade or business. Where applicable, federal income tax withheld with respect to the payment is also reported on Form 1099. The common types of payments and the related Form 1099 are summarized in Table 9.1.

Forms 1099 must be mailed to the recipients by January 31 of the year following the calendar year of payment. However, payors are allowed until February 15 of the year following the calendar year of payment to provide Forms 1099-B, 1099-S, and certain 1099-MISC forms. A separate Form 1096 must be used to transmit each type of 1099 to the appropriate IRS Campus Processing Site by February 28 of the year following the calendar year of payment.

Would You Believe?

Court clerks must report to the IRS cash payments of bail exceeding $10,000 when it is posted in narcotics, racketeering, or money-laundering cases. The payors of large cash bail amounts must also be given a statement similar to a 1099 form at year-end.

Self-Study Problem 9.5 *See Appendix E for Solutions to Self-Study Problems*

Big Bank (P.O. Box 12344, San Diego, CA 92101; E.I.N. 95-1234567; California ID 800 4039 250 092) paid an employee, Mary Jones (6431 Gary Street, San Diego, CA 92115), wages of $16,150 for 2014. The federal income tax withholding for the year amounted to $2,422, and FICA withheld was $1,235.48 ($1,001.30 for Social Security tax and $234.18 for Medicare tax). State income tax withheld was $969.00. Mary's FICA wages were the same as her total wages, and her Social Security number is 464-74-1132.

Self-Study Problem 9.5 (*continued*)

a. Complete the following Form W-2 for Mary Jones from Big Bank.

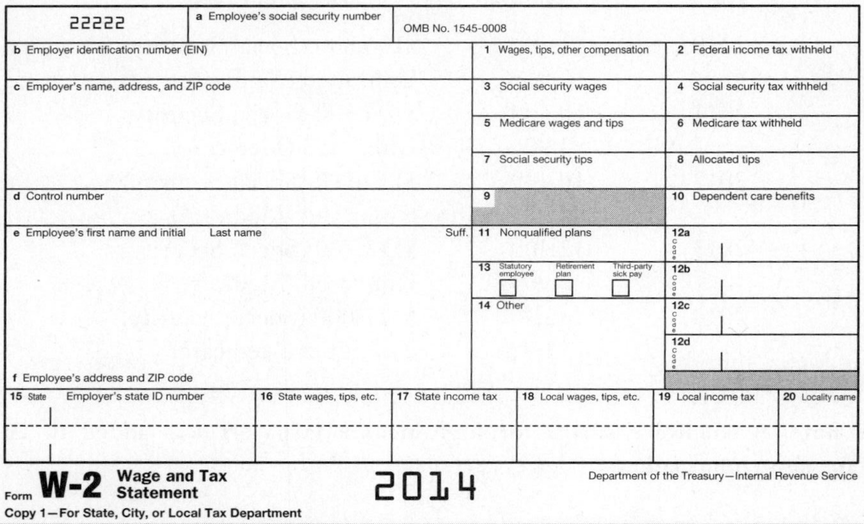
22222
a Employee's social security number
OMB No. 1545-0008
b Employer identification number (EIN)
1 Wages, tips, other compensation
2 Federal income tax withheld
c Employer's name, address, and ZIP code
3 Social security wages
4 Social security tax withheld
5 Medicare wages and tips
6 Medicare tax withheld
7 Social security tips
8 Allocated tips
d Control number
9
10 Dependent care benefits
e Employee's first name and initial Last name Suff.
11 Nonqualified plans
12a
13 Statutory employee Retirement plan Third-party sick pay
12b
14 Other
12c
12d
f Employee's address and ZIP code
15 State Employer's state ID number
16 State wages, tips, etc.
17 State income tax
18 Local wages, tips, etc.
19 Local income tax
20 Locality name
Form W-2 Wage and Tax Statement 2014
Department of the Treasury—Internal Revenue Service
Copy 1—For State, City, or Local Tax Department

b. Mary also has a savings account at Big Bank, which paid her interest for 2014 of $461. Complete the following Form 1099-INT for Mary's interest income.

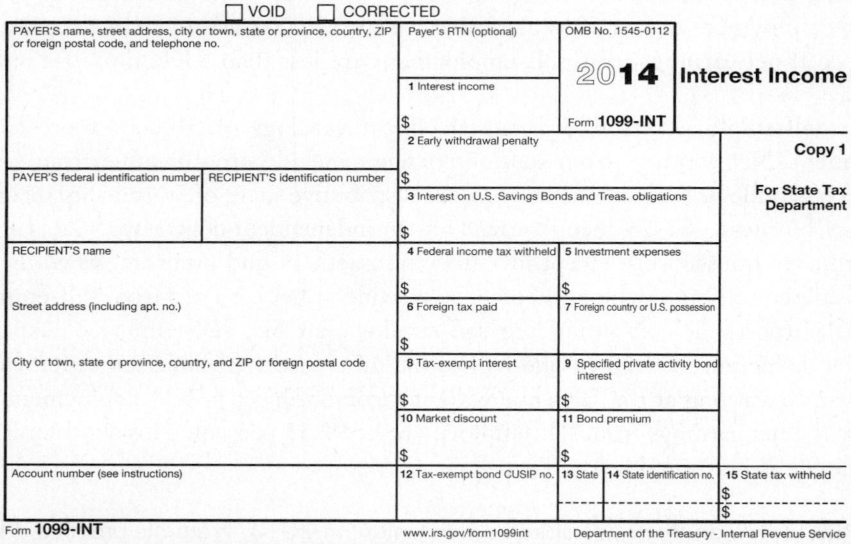
VOID CORRECTED
PAYER'S name, street address, city or town, state or province, country, ZIP or foreign postal code, and telephone no.
Payer's RTN (optional)
OMB No. 1545-0112
2014 Interest Income
1 Interest income $
Form 1099-INT
2 Early withdrawal penalty $
Copy 1
For State Tax Department
PAYER'S federal identification number
RECIPIENT'S identification number
3 Interest on U.S. Savings Bonds and Treas. obligations $
RECIPIENT'S name
4 Federal income tax withheld $
5 Investment expenses $
Street address (including apt. no.)
6 Foreign tax paid $
7 Foreign country or U.S. possession
City or town, state or province, country, and ZIP or foreign postal code
8 Tax-exempt interest $
9 Specified private activity bond interest $
10 Market discount $
11 Bond premium $
Account number (see instructions)
12 Tax-exempt bond CUSIP no.
13 State
14 State identification no.
15 State tax withheld $ $
Form 1099-INT
www.irs.gov/form1099int
Department of the Treasury - Internal Revenue Service

SELF-EMPLOYMENT TAX

Learning Objective 9.6

Calculate the self-employment tax (both Social Security and Medicare portions) for self-employed taxpayers.

Self-employed individuals pay self-employment taxes instead of FICA taxes. Since these individuals have no employers, the entire tax is paid by the self-employed individuals. Like the FICA taxes to which employees and their employers are subject, the self-employment tax consists of two parts, Social Security (Old Age, Survivors, and Disability Insurance [OASDI]) and Medicare. The maximum base amount of earnings subject to the Social Security portion of the FICA tax is $117,000 in 2014. All earnings are subject to the

Medicare portion of the FICA tax. The Social Security tax rate is 12.40 percent and the Medicare rate is 2.9 percent. The self-employment tax rates and the maximum base amounts for 5 years are illustrated in the following table*:

Year	*Percentage*	*Maximum Base*
2010	12.40%	$106,800 (Social Security)
	2.90%	Unlimited (Medicare)
2011	10.40%	$106,800 (Social Security)
	2.90%	Unlimited (Medicare)
2012	10.40%	$110,100 (Social Security)
	2.90%	Unlimited (Medicare)
2013	12.40%	$113,700 (Social Security)
	2.90%	Unlimited (Medicare)
2014	12.4%	$117,000 (Social Security)
	2.9%	Unlimited (Medicare)

***Please note: A Medicare surtax for high-income taxpayers was added in 2013. See LO 9.9 for more information.**

If an individual, subject to self-employment taxes, also receives wages subject to FICA taxes during a tax year, the individual's maximum base amount for self-employment taxes is reduced by the amount of wages as both employee and employer have already paid FICA taxes on the wages. Therefore, the total amount of earnings subject to both FICA and self-employment tax for 2014 cannot exceed $117,000 for the Social Security portion of the tax. If net earnings from self-employment are less than $400, no self-employment tax is payable.

The self-employment tax is imposed on net earnings of $400 or more from self-employment. Net earnings from self-employment include gross income from a trade or business less trade or business deductions, the distributive share of partnership income from a trade or business, and net income earned as an independent contractor. Gains and losses from property transactions, except inventory transactions, and other unearned income are not considered self-employment income. In arriving at net earnings from self-employment only for purposes of computing the self-employment tax, self-employed taxpayers are allowed a deduction for AGI of one-half of the otherwise applicable self-employment tax. A shortcut to arriving at the self-employment income subject to self-employment tax is to multiply the net earnings from self-employment by 92.35 percent. This shortcut is used on Schedule SE as illustrated below.

EXAMPLE Norman is a self-employed accountant in 2014. From his practice, Norman earns $130,000, and has wages subject to FICA from a part-time job of $9,100. Norman's self-employment tax is calculated as follows:

Step 1:

Net earnings from self-employment, before the self-employment tax deduction	$130,000
	× 92.35%
Tentative net earnings from self-employment after deduction for self-employment tax	$120,055

Step 2:

	Social Security	Medicare
Maximum base for 2014	$117,000	Unlimited
Less: FICA wages	(9,100)	Not Applicable
Maximum self-employment tax base	$107,900	Unlimited
Lesser of net earnings from self-employment after deduction for self-employment tax or maximum base	$107,900	$120,055
Self-employment tax rate	12.4%	2.9%
Self-employment tax for 2014	$ 13,380	$ 3,482

Norman's total self-employment tax for 2014 is $16,862 ($13,380 + $3,482). On his 2014 income tax return, Norman will report net earnings from self-employment of $130,000, a deduction for adjusted gross income of $8,431 (50% × $16,862), and a self-employment tax liability of $16,862. ♦

The calculation summarized here is done on Page 2 of Schedule SE, Part I, and must be included with a taxpayer's Form 1040. See Pages 9-21 and 9-22 which show the same calculation on Schedule SE.

Self-Study Problem 9.6 ***See Appendix E for Solutions to Self-Study Problems***

Robert Boyd is self-employed in 2014. His Schedule C net income is $27,450 for the year, and Robert also had a part-time job and earned $4,400 that was subject to FICA tax. Robert received taxable dividends of $1,110 during the year, and he had a capital gain on the sale of stock of $9,100. Calculate Robert's self-employment tax using Schedule SE of Form 1040 on Pages 9-23 and 9-24.

THE FUTA TAX

Learning Objective 9.7

Compute the amount of FUTA tax for an employer.

Please note: Employers in states that have not repaid money borrowed from the federal government for unemployment benefits will have a higher FUTA tax than the 0.6 percent illustrated below. For purposes of the problems and examples in this text, assume that the employer does not reside in one of the states where a higher FUTA tax applies.

The Federal Unemployment Tax Act (FUTA) instituted a tax that is not withheld from employees' wages, but instead is paid in full by employers. The federal tax rate is 6 percent of an employee's wages up to $7,000. A credit is allowed for state unemployment taxes of 5.4 percent. Therefore, the effective federal tax rate is only 0.6 percent if the state also assesses an unemployment tax.

EXAMPLE Karen has two employees in 2014, John, who earned $12,500 this year, and Sue, who earned $15,000. The FUTA tax is calculated as follows:

John's wages, $12,500 (maximum $7,000)	$ 7,000
Sue's wages, $15,000 (maximum $7,000)	$ 7,000
Total FUTA wages	$14,000
FUTA tax at 0.6%	$ 84

◆

Employers report their Federal Unemployment Tax liability for the year on Form 940, Employer's Annual Federal Unemployment (FUTA) Tax Return. Like federal income tax withholding and FICA taxes, federal unemployment taxes must be deposited by electronic funds transfer. A deposit is required when the FUTA taxes for the quarter, plus any amount not yet deposited for the prior quarter(s), exceed $500. If required, the deposit must be made by the last day of the first month after the end of each quarter.

EXAMPLE Ti Corporation's federal unemployment tax liability for the first quarter of 2014, after reduction by the credit for state unemployment taxes, is $255; for the second quarter, $200; for the third quarter, $75; and for the fourth quarter, $25. Ti Corporation must deposit $530, the sum of the first, second, and third quarters' liability, by October 31, 2014. The remaining $25 may be either deposited or paid with Form 940. ◆

Employers make the largest portion of unemployment tax payments to state governments that administer the federal-state program. Employers must pay all state unemployment taxes for the year by the due date of the federal Form 940 to get full credit for the state taxes against FUTA.

Would You Believe?

When a state runs out of funds to pay unemployment benefits, it may borrow from the Federal government. If a state has outstanding loan balances for two consecutive years, and does not repay its loans by November of the second year, the FUTA credit rate for employers in that state will be reduced until the loan is repaid. Because the state unemployment (SUTA) generally stays the same, the result is a net increase in unemployment taxes. As we go to press 11 states (including California, Connecticut, Kentucky, New York, Ohio, and both Carolinas) are facing a credit reduction for 2014.

Self-Study Problem 9.7

See Appendix E for Solutions to Self-Study Problems

The Rhus Company's payroll information for 2014 is summarized as follows:

	Quarter 1	***Quarter 2***	***Quarter 3***	***Quarter 4***
Gross earnings of employees	$25,000	$30,000	$26,000	$32,000
Individual employee earnings in excess of $7,000	None	$ 4,000	$15,000	$20,000

Rhus Company (E.I.N. 94-0001112) pays California state unemployment tax. The company makes the required deposits of both federal and state unemployment taxes on a timely basis. Complete the Rhus Company's 2014 Form 940 on Pages 9-29 and 9-30, using the above information.

SCHEDULE SE (Form 1040)

Department of the Treasury
Internal Revenue Service (99)

Self-Employment Tax

▶ Information about Schedule SE and its separate instructions is at *www.irs.gov/schedulese*.
▶ Attach to Form 1040 or Form 1040NR.

OMB No. 1545-0074
2014
Attachment Sequence No. **17**

Name of person with **self-employment** income (as shown on Form 1040 or Form 1040NR) | Social security number of person with **self-employment** income ▶

Before you begin: To determine if you must file Schedule SE, see the instructions.

May I Use Short Schedule SE or Must I Use Long Schedule SE?

DRAFT AS OF May 14, 2014 DO NOT FILE

Note. Use this flowchart **only if** you must file Schedule SE. If unsure, see *Who Must File Schedule SE* in the instructions.

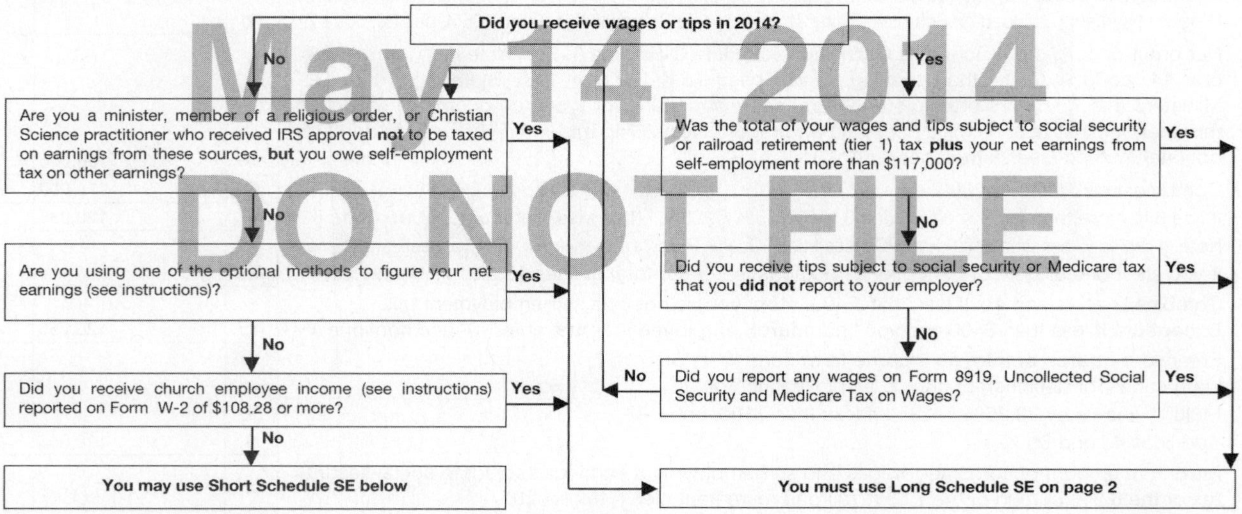

Section A—Short Schedule SE. Caution. Read above to see if you can use Short Schedule SE.

1a Net farm profit or (loss) from Schedule F, line 34, and farm partnerships, Schedule K-1 (Form 1065), box 14, code A **1a**

b If you received social security retirement or disability benefits, enter the amount of Conservation Reserve Program payments included on Schedule F, line 4b, or listed on Schedule K-1 (Form 1065), box 20, code Z **1b** ( )

2 Net profit or (loss) from Schedule C, line 31; Schedule C-EZ, line 3; Schedule K-1 (Form 1065), box 14, code A (other than farming); and Schedule K-1 (Form 1065-B), box 9, code J1. Ministers and members of religious orders, see instructions for types of income to report on this line. See instructions for other income to report **2**

3 Combine lines 1a, 1b, and 2 . . . . . **3**

4 Multiply line 3 by 92.35% (.9235). If less than $400, you do not owe self-employment tax; **do not** file this schedule unless you have an amount on line 1b . . . . . ▶ **4**

Note. If line 4 is less than $400 due to Conservation Reserve Program payments on line 1b, see instructions.

5 **Self-employment tax.** If the amount on line 4 is:

- $117,000 or less, multiply line 4 by 15.3% (.153). Enter the result here and on **Form 1040, line 57,** or **Form 1040NR, line 55**
- More than $117,000, multiply line 4 by 2.9% (.029). Then, add $14,508 to the result.

Enter the total here and on **Form 1040, line 57,** or **Form 1040NR, line 55** **5**

6 **Deduction for one-half of self-employment tax.** Multiply line 5 by 50% (.50). Enter the result here and on **Form 1040, line 27,** or **Form 1040NR, line 27** **6**

For Paperwork Reduction Act Notice, see your tax return instructions. Cat. No. 11358Z **Schedule SE (Form 1040) 2014**

Schedule SE (Form 1040) 2014 Attachment Sequence No. **17** Page **2**

Name of person with **self-employment** income (as shown on Form 1040 or Form 1040NR): Norman

Social security number of person with **self-employment** income ▶

Section B—Long Schedule SE

Part I Self-Employment Tax

Note. If your only income subject to self-employment tax is **church employee income,** see instructions. Also see instructions for the definition of church employee income.

DRAFT AS OF May 14, 2014 DO NOT FILE

Line	Description	Box	Amount	Cents
A	If you are a minister, member of a religious order, or Christian Science practitioner **and** you filed Form 4361, but you had $400 or more of **other** net earnings from self-employment, check here and continue with Part I . . . . ▶ ☐			
1a	Net farm profit or (loss) from Schedule F, line 34, and farm partnerships, Schedule K-1 (Form 1065), box 14, code A. **Note.** Skip lines 1a and 1b if you use the farm optional method (see instructions)	1a		
b	If you received social security retirement or disability benefits, enter the amount of Conservation Reserve Program payments included on Schedule F, line 4b, or listed on Schedule K-1 (Form 1065), box 20, code Z	1b	( )	
2	Net profit or (loss) from Schedule C, line 31; Schedule C-EZ, line 3; Schedule K-1 (Form 1065), box 14, code A (other than farming); and Schedule K-1 (Form 1065-B), box 9, code J1. Ministers and members of religious orders, see instructions for types of income to report on this line. See instructions for other income to report. **Note.** Skip this line if you use the nonfarm optional method (see instructions)	2	130,000	
3	Combine lines 1a, 1b, and 2	3	130,000	
4a	If line 3 is more than zero, multiply line 3 by 92.35% (.9235). Otherwise, enter amount from line 3. **Note.** If line 4a is less than $400 due to Conservation Reserve Program payments on line 1b, see instructions.	4a	120,055	
b	If you elect one or both of the optional methods, enter the total of lines 15 and 17 here . .	4b		
c	Combine lines 4a and 4b. If less than $400, **stop**; you do not owe self-employment tax. **Exception.** If less than $400 and you had **church employee income,** enter -0- and continue ▶	4c	120,055	
5a	Enter your **church employee income** from Form W-2. See instructions for definition of church employee income . . . | 5a |			
b	Multiply line 5a by 92.35% (.9235). If less than $100, enter -0-	5b		
6	Add lines 4c and 5b	6	120,055	
7	Maximum amount of combined wages and self-employment earnings subject to social security tax or the 6.2% portion of the 7.65% railroad retirement (tier 1) tax for 2014	7	117,000	00
8a	Total social security wages and tips (total of boxes 3 and 7 on Form(s) W-2) and railroad retirement (tier 1) compensation. If $117,000 or more, skip lines 8b through 10, and go to line 11 | 8a | 9,100			
b	Unreported tips subject to social security tax (from Form 4137, line 10) | 8b |			
c	Wages subject to social security tax (from Form 8919, line 10) | 8c |			
d	Add lines 8a, 8b, and 8c	8d	9,100	
9	Subtract line 8d from line 7. If zero or less, enter -0- here and on line 10 and go to line 11 . ▶	9	107,900	
10	Multiply the **smaller** of line 6 or line 9 by 12.4% (.124)	10	13,380	
11	Multiply line 6 by 2.9% (.029)	11	3,482	
12	**Self-employment tax.** Add lines 10 and 11. Enter here and on **Form 1040, line 57,** or **Form 1040NR, line 55**	12	16,862	
13	**Deduction for one-half of self-employment tax.** Multiply line 12 by 50% (.50). Enter the result here and on **Form 1040, line 27,** or **Form 1040NR, line 27** . . . . . | 13 | 8,431			

Part II Optional Methods To Figure Net Earnings (see instructions)

Farm Optional Method. You may use this method **only** if **(a)** your gross farm income[1] was not more than $7,200, **or (b)** your net farm profits[2] were less than $5,198.

Line	Description	Box	Amount	Cents
14	Maximum income for optional methods	14	4,800	00
15	Enter the **smaller** of: two-thirds (2/3) of gross farm income[1] (not less than zero) **or** $4,800. Also include this amount on line 4b above	15		

Nonfarm Optional Method. You may use this method **only** if **(a)** your net nonfarm profits[3] were less than $5,198 and also less than 72.189% of your gross nonfarm income,[4] **and (b)** you had net earnings from self-employment of at least $400 in 2 of the prior 3 years. **Caution.** You may use this method no more than five times.

Line	Description	Box	Amount	Cents
16	Subtract line 15 from line 14	16		
17	Enter the **smaller** of: two-thirds (2/3) of gross nonfarm income[4] (not less than zero) **or** the amount on line 16. Also include this amount on line 4b above	17		

[1] From Sch. F, line 9, and Sch. K-1 (Form 1065), box 14, code B.

[2] From Sch. F, line 34, and Sch. K-1 (Form 1065), box 14, code A—minus the amount you would have entered on line 1b had you not used the optional method.

[3] From Sch. C, line 31; Sch. C-EZ, line 3; Sch. K-1 (Form 1065), box 14, code A; and Sch. K-1 (Form 1065-B), box 9, code J1.

[4] From Sch. C, line 7; Sch. C-EZ, line 1; Sch. K-1 (Form 1065), box 14, code C; and Sch. K-1 (Form 1065-B), box 9, code J2.

Schedule SE (Form 1040) 2014

Self-Study Problem 9.6

SCHEDULE SE (Form 1040)

Department of the Treasury Internal Revenue Service (99)

Self-Employment Tax

▶ **Information about Schedule SE and its separate instructions is at *www.irs.gov/schedulese*.**

▶ **Attach to Form 1040 or Form 1040NR.**

OMB No. 1545-0074

2014

Attachment Sequence No. **17**

Name of person with **self-employment** income (as shown on Form 1040 or Form 1040NR)	Social security number of person with **self-employment** income ▶	

Before you begin: To determine if you must file Schedule SE, see the instructions.

DRAFT AS OF
May 14, 2014
DO NOT FILE

May I Use Short Schedule SE or Must I Use Long Schedule SE?

Note. Use this flowchart **only if** you must file Schedule SE. If unsure, see *Who Must File Schedule SE* in the instructions.

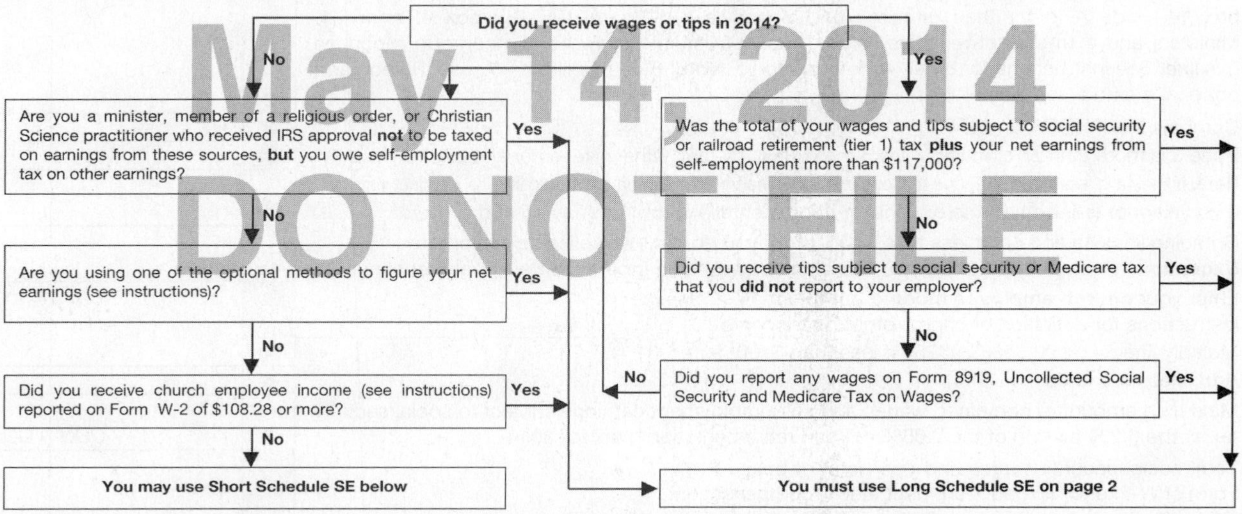

Section A—Short Schedule SE. Caution. Read above to see if you can use Short Schedule SE.

1a	Net farm profit or (loss) from Schedule F, line 34, and farm partnerships, Schedule K-1 (Form 1065), box 14, code A	**1a**	
b	If you received social security retirement or disability benefits, enter the amount of Conservation Reserve Program payments included on Schedule F, line 4b, or listed on Schedule K-1 (Form 1065), box 20, code Z	**1b**	( )
2	Net profit or (loss) from Schedule C, line 31; Schedule C-EZ, line 3; Schedule K-1 (Form 1065), box 14, code A (other than farming); and Schedule K-1 (Form 1065-B), box 9, code J1. Ministers and members of religious orders, see instructions for types of income to report on this line. See instructions for other income to report	**2**	
3	Combine lines 1a, 1b, and 2	**3**	
4	Multiply line 3 by 92.35% (.9235). If less than $400, you do not owe self-employment tax; **do not** file this schedule unless you have an amount on line 1b . . . . ▶	**4**	
	Note. If line 4 is less than $400 due to Conservation Reserve Program payments on line 1b, see instructions.		
5	**Self-employment tax.** If the amount on line 4 is: • $117,000 or less, multiply line 4 by 15.3% (.153). Enter the result here and on **Form 1040, line 57,** or **Form 1040NR, line 55** • More than $117,000, multiply line 4 by 2.9% (.029). Then, add $14,508 to the result. Enter the total here and on **Form 1040, line 57,** or **Form 1040NR, line 55**	**5**	
6	**Deduction for one-half of self-employment tax.** Multiply line 5 by 50% (.50). Enter the result here and on **Form 1040, line 27,** or **Form 1040NR, line 27** **6**		

Schedule SE (Form 1040) 2014 Attachment Sequence No. **17** Page **2**

Name of person with **self-employment** income (as shown on Form 1040 or Form 1040NR) | Social security number of person with **self-employment** income ▶

Section B—Long Schedule SE

Part I Self-Employment Tax

Note. If your only income subject to self-employment tax is **church employee income,** see instructions. Also see instructions for the definition of church employee income.

DRAFT AS OF May 14, 2014 DO NOT FILE

A	If you are a minister, member of a religious order, or Christian Science practitioner **and** you filed Form 4361, but you had $400 or more of **other** net earnings from self-employment, check here and continue with Part I . . . . . . ▶ ☐		
1a	Net farm profit or (loss) from Schedule F, line 34, and farm partnerships, Schedule K-1 (Form 1065), box 14, code A. **Note.** Skip lines 1a and 1b if you use the farm optional method (see instructions)	**1a**	
b	If you received social security retirement or disability benefits, enter the amount of Conservation Reserve Program payments included on Schedule F, line 4b, or listed on Schedule K-1 (Form 1065), box 20, code Z	**1b**	( )
2	Net profit or (loss) from Schedule C, line 31; Schedule C-EZ, line 3; Schedule K-1 (Form 1065), box 14, code A (other than farming); and Schedule K-1 (Form 1065-B), box 9, code J1. Ministers and members of religious orders, see instructions for types of income to report on this line. See instructions for other income to report. **Note.** Skip this line if you use the nonfarm optional method (see instructions) . . .	**2**	
3	Combine lines 1a, 1b, and 2 . . .	**3**	
4a	If line 3 is more than zero, multiply line 3 by 92.35% (.9235). Otherwise, enter amount from line 3 **Note.** If line 4a is less than $400 due to Conservation Reserve Program payments on line 1b, see instructions.	**4a**	
b	If you elect one or both of the optional methods, enter the total of lines 15 and 17 here . .	**4b**	
c	Combine lines 4a and 4b. If less than $400, **stop**; you do not owe self-employment tax. **Exception.** If less than $400 and you had **church employee income,** enter -0- and continue ▶	**4c**	
5a	Enter your **church employee income** from Form W-2. See instructions for definition of church employee income . . . **5a**		
b	Multiply line 5a by 92.35% (.9235). If less than $100, enter -0- . . .	**5b**	
6	Add lines 4c and 5b . . .	**6**	
7	Maximum amount of combined wages and self-employment earnings subject to social security tax or the 6.2% portion of the 7.65% railroad retirement (tier 1) tax for 2014 . . .	**7**	117,000 00
8a	Total social security wages and tips (total of boxes 3 and 7 on Form(s) W-2) and railroad retirement (tier 1) compensation. If $117,000 or more, skip lines 8b through 10, and go to line 11 **8a**		
b	Unreported tips subject to social security tax (from Form 4137, line 10) **8b**		
c	Wages subject to social security tax (from Form 8919, line 10) **8c**		
d	Add lines 8a, 8b, and 8c . . .	**8d**	
9	Subtract line 8d from line 7. If zero or less, enter -0- here and on line 10 and go to line 11 . ▶	**9**	
10	Multiply the **smaller** of line 6 or line 9 by 12.4% (.124) . . .	**10**	
11	Multiply line 6 by 2.9% (.029) . . .	**11**	
12	**Self-employment tax.** Add lines 10 and 11. Enter here and on **Form 1040, line 57,** or **Form 1040NR, line 55**	**12**	
13	**Deduction for one-half of self-employment tax.** Multiply line 12 by 50% (.50). Enter the result here and on **Form 1040, line 27,** or **Form 1040NR, line 27** . . . **13**		

Part II Optional Methods To Figure Net Earnings (see instructions)

Farm Optional Method. You may use this method **only** if **(a)** your gross farm income[1] was not more than $7,200, **or (b)** your net farm profits[2] were less than $5,198.

14	Maximum income for optional methods . . .	**14**	4,800 00
15	Enter the **smaller** of: two-thirds (2/3) of gross farm income[1] (not less than zero) **or** $4,800. Also include this amount on line 4b above . . .	**15**	

Nonfarm Optional Method. You may use this method **only** if **(a)** your net nonfarm profits[3] were less than $5,198 and also less than 72.189% of your gross nonfarm income,[4] **and (b)** you had net earnings from self-employment of at least $400 in 2 of the prior 3 years. **Caution.** You may use this method no more than five times.

16	Subtract line 15 from line 14 . . .	**16**	
17	Enter the **smaller** of: two-thirds (2/3) of gross nonfarm income[4] (not less than zero) **or** the amount on line 16. Also include this amount on line 4b above . . .	**17**	

[1] From Sch. F, line 9, and Sch. K-1 (Form 1065), box 14, code B.

[2] From Sch. F, line 34, and Sch. K-1 (Form 1065), box 14, code A—minus the amount you would have entered on line 1b had you not used the optional method.

[3] From Sch. C, line 31; Sch. C-EZ, line 3; Sch. K-1 (Form 1065), box 14, code A; and Sch. K-1 (Form 1065-B), box 9, code J1.

[4] From Sch. C, line 7; Sch. C-EZ, line 1; Sch. K-1 (Form 1065), box 14, code C; and Sch. K-1 (Form 1065-B), box 9, code J2.

THE NANNY TAX

Learning Objective 9.8

Apply the special tax and reporting requirements for household employees (the "nanny tax").

Over the years, the taxation and reporting of household employees' wages has caused many problems for taxpayers and the IRS. The threshold for filing was low ($50 per quarter of wages), and the tax forms to be completed were complex. As a result, many taxpayers ignored the reporting of household workers' wages and taxes. Congress addressed this problem by enacting what are commonly referred to as the "nanny tax" provisions. These provisions simplified the reporting process for employers of domestic household workers.

Household employers are not required to pay FICA taxes on cash payments of less than $1,900 paid to any household employee in a calendar year. If the cash payment to any household employee is $1,900 or more in a calendar year, all the cash payments (including the first $1,900) are subject to FICA taxes (see LO 9.3). The $1,900 threshold is indexed each year. Household employers must also withhold income taxes if requested by the employee and are required to pay FUTA tax (see LO 9.7) if more than $1,000 in cash wages are paid to household employees during any calendar quarter.

A taxpayer is a household employer if he or she hires workers to perform household services, in or around the taxpayer's home, that are subject to the "will and control" of the taxpayer. Examples of household workers include:

- Babysitters
- Caretakers
- Cooks
- Drivers
- Gardeners
- Housekeepers
- Maids

If the household worker has an employee-employer relationship with the taxpayer, it does not matter if the worker is called something else, such as "independent contractor." Also, it does not matter if the worker works full-time or part-time. The household employer is responsible for the proper reporting, withholding, and payment of any taxes due.

The following workers are not subject to FICA and Medicare taxes on wages paid for *work in the home*:

- The taxpayer's spouse
- The taxpayer's father or mother
- The taxpayer's children under 21 years of age
- Anyone who is under age 18 during the year, unless providing household services is his or her principal occupation (being a student is considered an occupation for purposes of this requirement)

EXAMPLE Allison is a 17-year-old high school student. During the year, she earns $1,700 by babysitting for a neighbor with four children. Any amount she earns is exempt from FICA requirements. However, if Allison is not a student and works full-time as a nanny, any amount she earns will be subject to the general FICA withholding requirements. ♦

Under the nanny tax provisions, household employers only have to report FICA, federal income tax withholding, and FUTA tax once a year. The taxpayer completes Schedule H and files it with his or her individual Form 1040. Taxpayers who have nonhousehold worker(s) in addition to household worker(s) can elect to report any FICA taxes and withholding on

Forms 941 and 940 with their regular employees. Also, at the close of a tax year, taxpayers must file Form W-2 (Copy A) and Form W-3 with the Social Security Administration for each household employee who earned more than $1,900 in cash wages subject to FICA tax. For complete details on reporting the wages of household employees, see IRS Publication 926.

Would You Believe?

While no one knows how many people should be filing Schedule H, some estimates indicate that fewer than one in thirteen are complying with the law.

Self-Study Problem 9.8 *See Appendix E for Solutions to Self-Study Problems*

Susan Green hires Helen in February 2014 to clean her house for $50 per week. Susan does not withhold income taxes from Helen's wages. Helen's quarterly wages are as follows:

1st quarter	$ 300	($50 × 6 weeks)
2nd quarter	650	($50 × 13 weeks)
3rd quarter	650	($50 × 13 weeks)
4th quarter	650	($50 × 13 weeks)
Total	$2,250	

Complete Susan's 2014 Schedule H (Form 1040) on Pages 9-31 and 9-32, using the above information.

Learning Objective 9.9

Calculate the 0.9 percent Medicare surtax on the earned income of high-income taxpayers.

COMPUTING THE 0.9 PERCENT MEDICARE SURTAX FOR HIGH-INCOME TAXPAYERS

Beginning in 2013, the Affordable Care Act (ACA), also referred to as "Obamacare," imposed a 0.9 percent Medicare surtax on earned income such as salaries, wages, and self-employment income. The 0.9 percent surtax applies to high-income taxpayers defined as taxpayers with earned income from wages, compensation, and self-employment income over the following thresholds:

a. $250,000 for joint filers
b. $125,000 if married filing separately
c. $200,000 for single filers (including head of household filers and qualifying widow(er)s)

The ordinary Medicare tax is 2.9 percent of earned income with no upper limitation. Employees split the cost of this tax with employers, with the employee paying 1.45 percent through withholding, and the employer paying 1.45 percent directly. Self-employed individuals pay the full 2.9 percent as calculated on Schedule SE with their Form 1040 income tax return.

Employees

Under the new law, the 0.9 percent surtax must be withheld from each employee with a salary in excess of $200,000, whether single or married. Unlike the ordinary Medicare tax, employers do not share in paying the surtax. Married couples must combine their earned income and compare the total with the $250,000 threshold for married taxpayers to determine if they owe the 0.9 percent Medicare surtax. Depending on the income of each spouse, the couple may owe more Medicare surtax when computing the actual surtax on their

Form 1040 to make up for amounts not fully withheld, or they may receive a refund. The withholding is reported on each individual's Form W-2 along with other Medicare withholding.

EXAMPLE Will and Karen are married. Will earns $225,000 in 2014 and Karen does not work. They have no other income in 2014. Will's employer must withhold $225 (0.9% × ($225,000 − $200,000)), from his wages. Because Will and Karen do not have earned income in their joint return in excess of the $250,000 threshold for joint filers, the $225 withholding will be refunded when they file their Form 1040 income tax return for 2014. ♦

EXAMPLE Fran and Steve are married and each has wages of $150,000. Because they each earn less than $200,000, their employers are not required to withhold the 0.9 percent Medicare surtax. However, when they file their 2014 Form 1040, they will be required to pay $450 (0.9% × $50,000) with their tax return since their $300,000 in joint earnings exceeds the $250,000 threshold for married taxpayers filing jointly. ♦

EXAMPLE Johnny is single and changes jobs during 2014. His wages are $175,000 from each job for a total of $350,000 of wage income. Johnny's employers are not required to withhold any Medicare surtax from his wages since he does not reach the $200,000 threshold in either job. Johnny must pay $1,350 (0.9% × $150,000, the excess of $350,000 over the $200,000 single threshold amount) with his tax return for 2014. ♦

Self-Employed Taxpayers

Self-employed taxpayers generally report earnings on Schedule C, Schedule F, and Schedule E in the case of earned royalty income and partnership income passed through on Schedule K-1. The 0.9 percent Medicare surtax for self-employed taxpayers must be paid with Form 1040. The following additional rules apply to high-income, self-employed taxpayers:

a. The additional 0.9 percent Medicare surtax is not allowed as part of the computation of the deductible self-employment tax adjustment for AGI shown on the front page of Form 1040.

b. A loss from self-employment may offset gains from another self-employment enterprise by the same individual. In the case of married individuals, a loss incurred by one spouse may offset the income earned by the other self-employed spouse for purposes of the 0.9 percent surtax. This is not true for the 2.9 percent Medicare tax on self-employment income because the 2.9 percent Medicare tax of each spouse is required to be computed separately.

c. Losses from self-employment are not allowed to offset salary or wages for purposes of the 0.9 percent Medicare surtax.

EXAMPLE Barry is single and earns $500,000 from his construction business, and has a loss of $100,000 from his commercial nursery business. Both businesses are reported on Schedule C in his income tax return. His net self-employment earnings of $400,000 exceed the single individual threshold by $200,000. He must pay $1,800 with his 2014 Form 1040 (0.9% × $200,000) to cover his Medicare surtax. None of the $1,800 is allowed as part of the computation of the self-employment tax adjustment included with his deductions for AGI. ♦

Self-Study Problem 9.9

See Appendix E for Solutions to Self-Study Problems

Scott and Marcia are married. Scott earns $250,000. Marcia is a homemaker and has no earnings.

a. How much Medicare surtax must Scott's employer withhold from his pay? ________

b. What is the additional payment or refund of the Medicare surtax that Scott and Marcia will owe or receive when they file their joint income tax return for 2014? ______________

Self-Study Problem 9.7

Form **940 for 2014: Employer's Annual Federal Unemployment (FUTA) Tax Return** 850113

Department of the Treasury — Internal Revenue Service OMB No. 1545-0028

DRAFT AS July 9, 2014 DO NOT FILE

Employer identification number (EIN) [ ][ ] – [ ][ ][ ][ ][ ][ ][ ]

Name *(not your trade name)* ____________

Trade name *(if any)* ____________

Address ____________
Number Street Suite or room number

City State ZIP code

Foreign country name Foreign province/county Foreign postal code

Type of Return
(Check all that apply.)

- ☐ **a.** Amended
- ☐ **b.** Successor employer
- ☐ **c.** No payments to employees in 2014
- ☐ **d.** Final: Business closed or stopped paying wages

Instructions and prior-year forms are available at *www.irs.gov/form940.*

Read the separate instructions before you complete this form. Please type or print within the boxes.

Part 1: Tell us about your return. If any line does NOT apply, leave it blank.

1a **If you had to pay state unemployment tax in one state only, enter the state abbreviation** . 1a [ ][ ]

1b **If you had to pay state unemployment tax in more than one state, you are a multi-state employer** . . . . . 1b ☐ Check here. Complete Schedule A (Form 940).

2 **If you paid wages in a state that is subject to CREDIT REDUCTION** . . . . . 2 ☐ Check here. Complete Schedule A (Form 940).

Part 2: Determine your FUTA tax before adjustments for 2014. If any line does NOT apply, leave it blank.

3 **Total payments to all employees** . . . . . 3 ______ .

4 **Payments exempt from FUTA tax** . . . . . 4 ______ .

Check all that apply: 4a ☐ Fringe benefits 4c ☐ Retirement/Pension 4e ☐ Other
4b ☐ Group-term life insurance 4d ☐ Dependent care

5 **Total of payments made to each employee in excess of $7,000** . . . . . 5 ______ .

6 **Subtotal** (line 4 + line 5 = line 6) . . . . . 6 ______ .

7 **Total taxable FUTA wages** (line 3 – line 6 = line 7) (see instructions) . . . . . 7 ______ .

8 **FUTA tax before adjustments** (line 7 x .006 = line 8) . . . . . 8 ______ .

Part 3: Determine your adjustments. If any line does NOT apply, leave it blank.

9 **If ALL of the taxable FUTA wages you paid were excluded from state unemployment tax, multiply line 7 by .054** (line 7 × .054 = line 9). Go to line 12 . . . . . 9 ______ .

10 **If SOME of the taxable FUTA wages you paid were excluded from state unemployment tax, OR you paid ANY state unemployment tax late** (after the due date for filing Form 940), complete the worksheet in the instructions. Enter the amount from line 7 of the worksheet . . 10 ______ .

11 **If credit reduction applies,** enter the total from Schedule A (Form 940) . . . . . 11 ______ .

Part 4: Determine your FUTA tax and balance due or overpayment for 2014. If any line does NOT apply, leave it blank.

12 **Total FUTA tax after adjustments** (lines 8 + 9 + 10 + 11 = line 12) . . . . . 12 ______ .

13 **FUTA tax deposited for the year, including any overpayment applied from a prior year** . 13 ______ .

14 **Balance due** (If line 12 is more than line 13, enter the excess on line 14.)
- If line 14 is more than $500, you must deposit your tax.
- If line 14 is $500 or less, you may pay with this return. (see instructions) . . . . . 14 ______ .

15 **Overpayment** (If line 13 is more than line 12, enter the excess on line 15 and check a box below.) . . . . . 15 ______ .

► You **MUST** complete both pages of this form and **SIGN** it. Check one: ☐ Apply to next return. ☐ Send a refund.

Next ►

For Privacy Act and Paperwork Reduction Act Notice, see the back of Form 940-V, Payment Voucher. Cat. No. 11234O Form **940** (2014)

850212

Name *(not your trade name)* | **Employer identification number (EIN)**

Part 5: Report your FUTA tax liability by quarter only if line 12 is more than $500. If not, go to Part 6.

16 **Report the amount of your FUTA tax liability for each quarter; do NOT enter the amount you deposited. If you had no liability for a quarter, leave the line blank.**

16a	**1st quarter** (January 1 – March 31)	16a	.
16b	**2nd quarter** (April 1 – June 30)	16b	.
16c	**3rd quarter** (July 1 – September 30)	16c	.
16d	**4th quarter** (October 1 – December 31)	16d	.

17 **Total tax liability for the year** (lines 16a + 16b + 16c + 16d = line 17) **17** . **Total must equal line 12.**

DRAFT AS OF July 9, 2014 DO NOT FILE

Part 6: May we speak with your third-party designee?

Do you want to allow an employee, a paid tax preparer, or another person to discuss this return with the IRS? See the instructions for details.

☐ **Yes.** Designee's name and phone number

Select a 5-digit Personal Identification Number (PIN) to use when talking to IRS

☐ **No.**

Part 7: Sign here. You MUST complete both pages of this form and SIGN it.

Under penalties of perjury, I declare that I have examined this return, including accompanying schedules and statements, and to the best of my knowledge and belief, it is true, correct, and complete, and that no part of any payment made to a state unemployment fund claimed as a credit was, or is to be, deducted from the payments made to employees. Declaration of preparer (other than taxpayer) is based on all information of which preparer has any knowledge.

✗ Sign your name here

Print your name here

Print your title here

Date / /

Best daytime phone

Paid Preparer Use Only

Check if you are self-employed . ☐

Preparer's name		PTIN	
Preparer's signature		Date	/ /
Firm's name (or yours if self-employed)		EIN	
Address		Phone	
City	State	ZIP code	

Self-Study Problem 9.8

SCHEDULE H (Form 1040)
Department of the Treasury Internal Revenue Service (99)

Household Employment Taxes

(For Social Security, Medicare, Withheld Income, and Federal Unemployment (FUTA) Taxes)

▶ **Attach to Form 1040, 1040NR, 1040-SS, or 1041.**

▶ **Information about Schedule H and its separate instructions is at *www.irs.gov/scheduleh.***

OMB No. 1545-1971
2014
Attachment Sequence No. **44**

Name of employer | **Social security number** | **Employer identification number**

DRAFT AS OF June 13, 2014 DO NOT FILE

Calendar year taxpayers having no household employees in 2014 do not have to complete this form for 2014.

A Did you pay **any one** household employee cash wages of $1,900 or more in 2014? (If any household employee was your spouse, your child under age 21, your parent, or anyone under age 18, see the line A instructions before you answer this question.)

☐ **Yes.** Skip lines B and C and go to line 1.
☐ **No.** Go to line B.

B Did you withhold federal income tax during 2014 for any household employee?

☐ **Yes.** Skip line C and go to line 7.
☐ **No.** Go to line C.

C Did you pay **total** cash wages of $1,000 or more in **any** calendar **quarter** of 2013 or 2014 to **all** household employees? (**Do not** count cash wages paid in 2013 or 2014 to your spouse, your child under age 21, or your parent.)

☐ **No. Stop.** Do not file this schedule.
☐ **Yes.** Skip lines 1-9 and go to line 10.

Part I Social Security, Medicare, and Federal Income Taxes

1	Total cash wages subject to social security tax	1		
2	Social security tax. Multiply line 1 by 12.4% (.124)		2	
3	Total cash wages subject to Medicare tax	3		
4	Medicare tax. Multiply line 3 by 2.9% (.029)		4	
5	Total cash wages subject to Additional Medicare Tax withholding	5		
6	Additional Medicare Tax withholding. Multiply line 5 by 0.9% (.009)		6	
7	Federal income tax withheld, if any		7	
8	**Total social security, Medicare, and federal income taxes.** Add lines 2, 4, 6, and 7		8	

9 Did you pay **total** cash wages of $1,000 or more in **any** calendar **quarter** of 2013 or 2014 to **all** household employees? (**Do not** count cash wages paid in 2013 or 2014 to your spouse, your child under age 21, or your parent.)

☐ **No. Stop.** Include the amount from line 8 above on Form 1040, line 60a. If you are not required to file Form 1040, see the line 9 instructions.

☐ **Yes.** Go to line 10.

For Privacy Act and Paperwork Reduction Act Notice, see the instructions. Cat. No. 12187K **Schedule H (Form 1040) 2014**

Schedule H (Form 1040) 2014 Page **2**

Part II Federal Unemployment (FUTA) Tax

			Yes	No
10	Did you pay unemployment contributions to only one state? (If you paid contributions to a credit reduction state, see instructions and check "No.")	10		
11	Did you pay all state unemployment contributions for 2014 by April 15, 2015? Fiscal year filers see instructions	11		
12	Were all wages that are taxable for FUTA tax also taxable for your state's unemployment tax?	12		

DRAFT AS OF June 13, 2014 DO NOT FILE

Next: If you checked the **"Yes"** box on **all** the lines above, complete Section A.
If you checked the **"No"** box on **any** of the lines above, skip Section A and complete Section B.

Section A

13 Name of the state where you paid unemployment contributions ▶ ____________

14 Contributions paid to your state unemployment fund 14

15 Total cash wages subject to FUTA tax . . . 15

16 **FUTA tax.** Multiply line 15 by .6% (.006). Enter the result here, skip Section B, and go to line 25 16

Section B

17 Complete all columns below that apply (if you need more space, see instructions):

(a) Name of state	(b) Taxable wages (as defined in state act)	(c) State experience rate period From	To	(d) State experience rate	(e) Multiply col. (b) by .054	(f) Multiply col. (b) by col. (d)	(g) Subtract col. (f) from col. (e). If zero or less, enter -0-.	(h) Contributions paid to state unemployment fund

18 Totals . . . 18

19 Add columns (g) and (h) of line 18 . . . 19

20 Total cash wages subject to FUTA tax (see the line 15 instructions) . . . 20

21 Multiply line 20 by 6.0% (.060) . . . 21

22 Multiply line 20 by 5.4% (.054) . . . 22

23 Enter the **smaller** of line 19 or line 22
(Employers in a credit reduction state must use the worksheet on page H-7 and check here) . ☐ 23

24 **FUTA tax.** Subtract line 23 from line 21. Enter the result here and go to line 25 . . . 24

Part III Total Household Employment Taxes

25 Enter the amount from line 8. If you checked the "Yes" box on line C of page 1, enter -0- . . . 25

26 Add line 16 (or line 24) and line 25 . . . 26

27 Are you required to file Form 1040?

☐ **Yes. Stop.** Include the amount from line 26 above on Form 1040, line 60a. **Do not** complete Part IV below.

☐ **No.** You may have to complete Part IV. See instructions for details.

Part IV Address and Signature— Complete this part **only** if required. See the line 27 instructions.

Address (number and street) or P.O. box if mail is not delivered to street address | Apt., room, or suite no.

City, town or post office, state, and ZIP code

Under penalties of perjury, I declare that I have examined this schedule, including accompanying statements, and to the best of my knowledge and belief, it is true, correct, and complete. No part of any payment made to a state unemployment fund claimed as a credit was, or is to be, deducted from the payments to employees. Declaration of preparer (other than taxpayer) is based on all information of which preparer has any knowledge.

▶ Employer's signature ▶ Date

Paid Preparer Use Only	Print/Type preparer's name	Preparer's signature	Date	Check ☐ if self-employed	PTIN
	Firm's name ▶			Firm's EIN ▶	
	Firm's address ▶			Phone no.	

Schedule H (Form 1040) 2014

KEY POINTS

Learning Objectives	Key Points
LO 9.1: Compute the income tax withholding from employee wages.	• Employers are required to withhold taxes from amounts paid to employees for wages, including salaries, fees, bonuses, commissions, and vacation and retirement pay. • Form W-4, showing the filing status and the number of withholding allowances an employee is claiming, must be furnished to the employer by the employee. • When using the percentage withholding method, an employer (1) multiplies the number of allowances by a specified allowance amount, (2) subtracts that amount from the employee's gross wages for the pay period, and (3) multiplies the result by the percentage obtained from the withholding tables. • Under the wage bracket method, the amount of withholding is obtained from the tables based on the total wages and the number of withholding allowances claimed for the appropriate payroll period and marital status. • Tip income must be reported using one of several methods. An employer is not required to withhold income, Social Security, or Medicare tax on allocated tips.
LO 9.2: Determine taxpayers' quarterly estimated payments.	• Self-employed taxpayers are not subject to withholding; however, they must make quarterly estimated tax payments. • Payments are made in four installments on April 15, June 15, and September 15 of the tax year, and January 15 of the following year. • Any individual taxpayer who has estimated tax for the year of $1,000 or more, after subtracting withholding, and whose withholding does not equal or exceed the "required annual payment," must make quarterly estimated payments. • The required annual payment is the smallest of three amounts: (1) 90 percent of the tax shown on the current year's return, (2) 100 percent (or 110 percent at certain income levels) of the tax shown on the preceding year's return, or (3) 90 percent of the current-year tax determined each quarter on an annualized basis.
LO 9.3: Understand the FICA tax.	• For 2014, the Social Security (OASDI) tax rate is 6.2 percent and the Medicare tax rate is 1.45 percent for employers and employees. The maximum wage subject to the Social Security portion of the FICA tax is $117,000, and all wages are subject to the Medicare portion of the FICA tax. • Taxpayers working for more than one employer during the same tax year may pay more than the maximum amount of FICA taxes. If this happens, the taxpayer should compute the excess taxes paid, and report the excess on Form 1040 as a payment against his or her income tax liability.
LO 9.4: Understand the federal deposit system.	• Employers must make periodic deposits of the taxes that are withheld from employees' wages. Deposits must be made electronically. • Employers are either monthly depositors or semiweekly depositors, depending on the total income taxes withheld from wages and FICA taxes attributable to wages. However, if withholding and FICA taxes of $100,000 or more are accumulated at any time during the year, the depositor is subject to a special 1-day deposit rule.
LO 9.5: Understand employer payroll reporting.	• On or before January 31 of the year following the calendar year of payment, an employer must furnish to each employee two copies of the employee's Wage and Tax Statement, Form W-2, for the previous calendar year. • The original copy (Copy A) of all W-2 forms and Form W-3 (Transmittal of Income and Tax Statements) must be filed with the Social Security Administration by February 28 of the year following the calendar year of payment. • Forms 1099 must be mailed to the recipients by January 31 of the year following the calendar year of payment.

LO 9.6: Calculate the self-employment tax (both Social Security and Medicare portions) for self-employed taxpayers.	• Self-employed individuals pay self-employment taxes instead of FICA taxes and, since these individuals have no employers, the entire tax is paid by the self-employed individuals. • For 2014, the Social Security (OASDI) tax rate is 12.4 percent and the Medicare tax rate is 2.9 percent with a maximum base amount of earnings subject to the Social Security portion of $117,000 (all earnings are subject to the Medicare portion). • If an individual, subject to self-employment (SE) taxes, also receives wages subject to FICA taxes during a tax year, the individual's maximum base amount for SE taxes is reduced by the amount of the wages, when calculating the SE taxes. • Net earnings from self-employment include gross income from a trade or business, less trade or business deductions, the distributive share of partnership income from a trade or business, and net income earned as an independent contractor. • Self-employed taxpayers are allowed a deduction for AGI of one-half of the self-employment tax.
LO 9.7: Compute the amount of FUTA tax for an employer.	• The FUTA (Federal Unemployment Tax Act) tax is not withheld from employees' wages, but instead is paid in full by employers. • The federal tax rate is 6.0 percent of an employee's wages up to $7,000, but a credit of up to 5.4 percent is allowed if state unemployment taxes are paid, for an effective federal tax rate of only 0.6 percent. • Employers make the largest portion of unemployment tax payments to state governments that administer the federal-state program.
LO 9.8: Apply the special tax and reporting requirements for household employees (the "nanny tax").	• The "nanny tax" provisions provide a simplified reporting process for employers of domestic household workers. • Household employers are not required to pay FICA taxes on cash payments of less than $1,900 paid to any household employee in a calendar year. • If the cash payment to any household employee is $1,900 or more in a calendar year, all the cash payments (including the first $1,900) are subject to Social Security and Medicare taxes. • If more than $1,000 in cash wages are paid to household employees during any calender quarter, employers are required to pay FUTA. • A taxpayer is a household employer if he or she hires workers to perform household services, in or around the taxpayer's home, that are subject to the "will and control" of the taxpayer (e.g., babysitters, caretakers, cooks, drivers, gardeners, housekeepers, and maids). • Certain workers are not subject to Social Security and Medicare taxes on wages paid for work in the home. These workers include the taxpayer's spouse, the taxpayer's father or mother, the taxpayer's children under 21 years of age, and anyone who is under age 18 during the year, unless providing household services is his or her principal occupation. • Under the nanny tax provisions, a household employer only has to report Social Security and Medicare, federal income tax withholding, and FUTA tax once a year by filing Schedule H with his or her individual Form 1040.
LO 9.9 Calculate the 0.9 percent Medicare surtax on the earned income of high-income taxpayers.	• The 0.9 percent Medicare surtax is imposed on earned income from salaries, wages, and self-employment income of single taxpayers with earned income over $200,000 and joint filers with income over $250,000. • Employers are required to withhold the 0.9 percent tax when a taxpayer's salary reaches $200,000. • Self-employed taxpayers must pay the tax with their individual income tax returns.

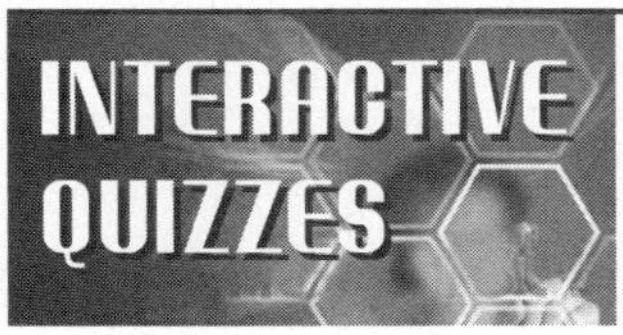

© Dusit/Shutterstock.com

Interactive quizzes are available as an optional online resource for Income Tax Fundamentals. Visit **www.cengagebrain.com** for more information.

QUESTIONS and PROBLEMS

GROUP 1:
MULTIPLE CHOICE QUESTIONS

LO 9.1

1. Which of the following amounts paid by an employer to an employee is not subject to withholding?
   a. Salary
   b. Bonus
   c. Commissions
   d. Reimbursement of expenses under an accountable plan
   e. All of the above are subject to withholding

LO 9.1

2. Abbe, age 56, is married and has three dependent children over age 17. Abbe has one job, and her husband, age 58, is not employed. How many allowances should Abbe claim on her Form W-4 for 2014?
   a. 3
   b. 4
   c. 5
   d. 6
   e. 7

LO 9.1

3. Michele is single with no dependents and earns $23,000 this year. Michele claims sixteen allowances on her Form W-4 for 2014. Which of the following is correct concerning her Form W-4?
   a. Michele may not under any circumstances claim sixteen allowances.
   b. Michele's employer will require her to verify her right to claim sixteen allowances.
   c. Michele's employer will disregard her Form W-4 and withhold as single with no allowances.
   d. Michele's employer will submit a copy of her W-4 to the IRS if directed to do so by written notice.
   e. None of the above is correct.

LO 9.2

4. Estimated payments for individual taxpayers are due on the following dates:
   a. Twice a year on April 15 and September 15
   b. Four times a year on April 15, June 15, September 15, and January 15 of the next year
   c. Four times a year on April 15, July 15, September 15, and December 15
   d. Twice a year on June 15 and December 15

LO 9.3

5. Which of the following is not true about FICA taxes?
   a. The FICA tax has two parts, Social Security (Old Age, Survivors, and Disability Insurance) and Medicare (hospital insurance).
   b. In 2014, the maximum wage base for Social Security tax withholding is $117,000.
   c. In 2014, there is no maximum wage base for Medicare tax withholding.
   d. When employees work for more than one employer and exceed the maximum wage base for Social Security tax withholding in total, they are not allowed a refund of excess tax withheld.

______ 6. Employers must file a quarterly tax return showing the amount of wages paid and the amount of income tax and FICA tax withholding due. This tax return is filed on:

LO 9.4

a. Form 944 or Form 945
b. Schedule H
c. Schedule SE
d. Form 941

______ 7. Which of the following forms would a lottery winner receive for her winnings?

LO 9.5

a. Form W-4
b. Form W-2G
c. Form 1099-DIV
d. Form 1099-R
e. Form 1099-MISC

______ 8. For 2014, Roberta is a self-employed truck driver with earnings of $43,000 from her business. During the year, Roberta received $2,500 in interest income and dividends of $500. She also sold investment property and recognized a $1,500 gain. What is the amount of Roberta's self-employment tax (Social Security and Medicare taxes) liability for 2014?

LO 9.6

a. $3,038
b. $3,290
c. $6,076
d. $6,579
e. None of the above

______ 9. Which of the following is not subject to self-employment tax?

LO 9.6

a. Net earnings of the owner of a shoe store
b. Net earnings of a self-employed lawyer
c. Distributive share of earnings of a partnership
d. Gain on the sale of real estate held for investment
e. Net earnings of the owner of a dry cleaner

______ 10. The FUTA tax is:

LO 9.7

a. An unemployment tax with a rate of 2.9 percent up to $117,000 of salary per employee.
b. A disability tax with a rate of 2.9 percent up to $7,000 of salary per employee.
c. An unemployment tax with a rate as low as 0.6 percent up to $7,000 of salary per employee.
d. A disability tax with a rate of 0.6 percent up to $117,000 of salary per employee.

______ 11. Bob employs a maid to clean his house. He pays her $1,900 during the current year. What is the proper tax treatment of the FICA and Medicare tax for the maid?

LO 9.8

a. None of the $1,900 is subject to FICA or Medicare tax.
b. The $1,900 is subject to the Medicare tax, but not the FICA tax.
c. $500 is subject to the FICA and Medicare tax.
d. The entire $1,900 is subject to the FICA and Medicare tax.

______ 12. Which of the following employees would not be exempt from the FICA and Medicare taxes on wages paid for household work?

LO 9.8

a. The taxpayer's 20-year-old sister
b. The taxpayer's wife
c. The taxpayer's 16-year-old daughter
d. The 14-year-old babysitter from down the street

Form W-4 (2014)

Purpose. Complete Form W-4 so that your employer can withhold the correct federal income tax from your pay. Consider completing a new Form W-4 each year and when your personal or financial situation changes.

Exemption from withholding. If you are exempt, complete **only** lines 1, 2, 3, 4, and 7 and sign the form to validate it. Your exemption for 2014 expires February 17, 2015. See Pub. 505, Tax Withholding and Estimated Tax.

Note. If another person can claim you as a dependent on his or her tax return, you cannot claim exemption from withholding if your income exceeds $1,000 and includes more than $350 of unearned income (for example, interest and dividends).

Exceptions. An employee may be able to claim exemption from withholding even if the employee is a dependent, if the employee:

- Is age 65 or older,
- Is blind, or
- Will claim adjustments to income; tax credits; or itemized deductions, on his or her tax return.

The exceptions do not apply to supplemental wages greater than $1,000,000.

Basic instructions. If you are not exempt, complete the **Personal Allowances Worksheet** below. The worksheets on page 2 further adjust your withholding allowances based on itemized deductions, certain credits, adjustments to income, or two-earners/multiple jobs situations.

Complete all worksheets that apply. However, you may claim fewer (or zero) allowances. For regular wages, withholding must be based on allowances you claimed and may not be a flat amount or percentage of wages.

Head of household. Generally, you can claim head of household filing status on your tax return only if you are unmarried and pay more than 50% of the costs of keeping up a home for yourself and your dependent(s) or other qualifying individuals. See Pub. 501, Exemptions, Standard Deduction, and Filing Information, for information.

Tax credits. You can take projected tax credits into account in figuring your allowable number of withholding allowances. Credits for child or dependent care expenses and the child tax credit may be claimed using the **Personal Allowances Worksheet** below. See Pub. 505 for information on converting your other credits into withholding allowances.

Nonwage income. If you have a large amount of nonwage income, such as interest or dividends, consider making estimated tax payments using Form 1040-ES, Estimated Tax for Individuals. Otherwise, you may owe additional tax. If you have pension or annuity iincome, see Pub. 505 to find out if you should adjust your withholding on Form W-4 or W-4P.

Two earners or multiple jobs. If you have a working spouse or more than one job, figure the total number of allowances you are entitled to claim on all jobs using worksheets from only one Form W-4. Your withholding usually will be most accurate when all allowances are claimed on the Form W-4 for the highest paying job and zero allowances are claimed on the others. See Pub. 505 for details.

Nonresident alien. If you are a nonresident alien, see Notice 1392, Supplemental Form W-4 Instructions for Nonresident Aliens, before completing this form.

Check your withholding. After your Form W-4 takes effect, use Pub. 505 to see how the amount you are having withheld compares to your projected total tax for 2014. See Pub. 505, especially if your earnings exceed $130,000 (Single) or $180,000 (Married).

Future developments. Information about any future developments affecting Form W-4 (such as legislation enacted after we release it) will be posted at *www.irs.gov/w4*.

Personal Allowances Worksheet (Keep for your records.)

A Enter "1" for **yourself** if no one else can claim you as a dependent . . . . A ______

B Enter "1" if:
- You are single and have only one job; or
- You are married, have only one job, and your spouse does not work; or
- Your wages from a second job or your spouse's wages (or the total of both) are $1,500 or less.

. . . B ______

C Enter "1" for your **spouse.** But, you may choose to enter "-0-" if you are married and have either a working spouse or more than one job. (Entering "-0-" may help you avoid having too little tax withheld.) . . . . C ______

D Enter number of **dependents** (other than your spouse or yourself) you will claim on your tax return . . . . D ______

E Enter "1" if you will file as **head of household** on your tax return (see conditions under **Head of household** above) . . E ______

F Enter "1" if you have at least $2,000 of **child or dependent care expenses** for which you plan to claim a credit . . . F ______
(**Note.** Do **not** include child support payments. See Pub. 503, Child and Dependent Care Expenses, for details.)

G **Child Tax Credit** (including additional child tax credit). See Pub. 972, Child Tax Credit, for more information.
- If your total income will be less than $65,000 ($95,000 if married), enter "2" for each eligible child; then **less** "1" if you have three to six eligible children or **less** "2" if you have seven or more eligible children.
- If your total income will be between $65,000 and $84,000 ($95,000 and $119,000 if married), enter "1" for each eligible child . . G ______

H Add lines A through G and enter total here. (**Note.** This may be different from the number of exemptions you claim on your tax return.) ► H ______

For accuracy, **complete all worksheets that apply.**
- If you plan to **itemize** or **claim adjustments to income** and want to reduce your withholding, see the **Deductions and Adjustments Worksheet** on page 2.
- If you are **single and have more than one job** or are **married and you and your spouse both work** and the combined earnings from all jobs exceed $50,000 ($20,000 if married), see the **Two-Earners/Multiple Jobs Worksheet** on page 2 to avoid having too little tax withheld.
- If **neither** of the above situations applies, **stop here** and enter the number from line H on line 5 of Form W-4 below.

Separate here and give Form W-4 to your employer. Keep the top part for your records.

Form **W-4** | **Employee's Withholding Allowance Certificate** | OMB No. 1545-0074

Department of the Treasury
Internal Revenue Service

► **Whether you are entitled to claim a certain number of allowances or exemption from withholding is subject to review by the IRS. Your employer may be required to send a copy of this form to the IRS.**

2014

1 Your first name and middle initial	Last name	2 **Your social security number**
Home address (number and street or rural route)	3 ☐ Single ☐ Married ☐ Married, but withhold at higher Single rate. **Note.** If married, but legally separated, or spouse is a nonresident alien, check the "Single" box.	
City or town, state, and ZIP code	4 **If your last name differs from that shown on your social security card, check here. You must call 1-800-772-1213 for a replacement card.** ► ☐	

5 Total number of allowances you are claiming (from line **H** above **or** from the applicable worksheet on page 2) | 5 |

6 Additional amount, if any, you want withheld from each paycheck . . . . | 6 | $

7 I claim exemption from withholding for 2014, and I certify that I meet **both** of the following conditions for exemption.
- Last year I had a right to a refund of **all** federal income tax withheld because I had **no** tax liability, **and**
- This year I expect a refund of **all** federal income tax withheld because I expect to have **no** tax liability.

If you meet both conditions, write "Exempt" here . . . . ► | 7 |

Under penalties of perjury, I declare that I have examined this certificate and, to the best of my knowledge and belief, it is true, correct, and complete.

Employee's signature
(This form is not valid unless you sign it.) ► **Date** ►

8 Employer's name and address (Employer: Complete lines 8 and 10 only if sending to the IRS.)	9 Office code (optional)	10 Employer identification number (EIN)

For Privacy Act and Paperwork Reduction Act Notice, see page 2. Cat. No. 10220Q Form **W-4** (2014)

Form W-4 (2014) Page **2**

Deductions and Adjustments Worksheet

Note. Use this worksheet *only* if you plan to itemize deductions or claim certain credits or adjustments to income.

1 Enter an estimate of your 2014 itemized deductions. These include qualifying home mortgage interest, charitable contributions, state and local taxes, medical expenses in excess of 10% (7.5% if either you or your spouse was born before January 2, 1950) of your income, and miscellaneous deductions. For 2014, you may have to reduce your itemized deductions if your income is over $305,050 and you are married filing jointly or are a qualifying widow(er); $279,650 if you are head of household; $254,200 if you are single and not head of household or a qualifying widow(er); or $152,525 if you are married filing separately. See Pub. 505 for details . . . . **1** $ ________

2 Enter: { $12,400 if married filing jointly or qualifying widow(er); $9,100 if head of household; $6,200 if single or married filing separately } . . . . **2** $ ________

3 **Subtract** line 2 from line 1. If zero or less, enter "-0-" . . . . **3** $ ________

4 Enter an estimate of your 2014 adjustments to income and any additional standard deduction (see Pub. 505) **4** $ ________

5 **Add** lines 3 and 4 and enter the total. (Include any amount for credits from the *Converting Credits to Withholding Allowances for 2014 Form W-4* worksheet in Pub. 505.) . . . . **5** $ ________

6 Enter an estimate of your 2014 nonwage income (such as dividends or interest) . . . . **6** $ ________

7 **Subtract** line 6 from line 5. If zero or less, enter "-0-" . . . . **7** $ ________

8 **Divide** the amount on line 7 by $3,950 and enter the result here. Drop any fraction . . . . **8** ________

9 Enter the number from the **Personal Allowances Worksheet,** line H, page 1 . . . . **9** ________

10 **Add** lines 8 and 9 and enter the total here. If you plan to use the **Two-Earners/Multiple Jobs Worksheet,** also enter this total on line 1 below. Otherwise, **stop here** and enter this total on Form W-4, line 5, page 1 **10** ________

Two-Earners/Multiple Jobs Worksheet (See *Two earners or multiple jobs* on page 1.)

Note. Use this worksheet *only* if the instructions under line H on page 1 direct you here.

1 Enter the number from line H, page 1 (or from line 10 above if you used the **Deductions and Adjustments Worksheet**) **1** ________

2 Find the number in **Table 1** below that applies to the **LOWEST** paying job and enter it here. **However,** if you are married filing jointly and wages from the highest paying job are $65,000 or less, do not enter more than "3" . . . . **2** ________

3 If line 1 is **more than or equal to** line 2, subtract line 2 from line 1. Enter the result here (if zero, enter "-0-") and on Form W-4, line 5, page 1. **Do not** use the rest of this worksheet . . . . **3** ________

Note. If line 1 is **less than** line 2, enter "-0-" on Form W-4, line 5, page 1. Complete lines 4 through 9 below to figure the additional withholding amount necessary to avoid a year-end tax bill.

4 Enter the number from line 2 of this worksheet . . . . **4** ________

5 Enter the number from line 1 of this worksheet . . . . **5** ________

6 **Subtract** line 5 from line 4 . . . . **6** ________

7 Find the amount in **Table 2** below that applies to the **HIGHEST** paying job and enter it here . . . . **7** $ ________

8 **Multiply** line 7 by line 6 and enter the result here. This is the additional annual withholding needed . . **8** $ ________

9 Divide line 8 by the number of pay periods remaining in 2014. For example, divide by 25 if you are paid every two weeks and you complete this form on a date in January when there are 25 pay periods remaining in 2014. Enter the result here and on Form W-4, line 6, page 1. This is the additional amount to be withheld from each paycheck **9** $ ________

Table 1

Married Filing Jointly		All Others	
If wages from **LOWEST** paying job are—	Enter on line 2 above	If wages from **LOWEST** paying job are—	Enter on line 2 above
$0 - $6,000	0	$0 - $6,000	0
6,001 - 13,000	1	6,001 - 16,000	1
13,001 - 24,000	2	16,001 - 25,000	2
24,001 - 26,000	3	25,001 - 34,000	3
26,001 - 33,000	4	34,001 - 43,000	4
33,001 - 43,000	5	43,001 - 70,000	5
43,001 - 49,000	6	70,001 - 85,000	6
49,001 - 60,000	7	85,001 - 110,000	7
60,001 - 75,000	8	110,001 - 125,000	8
75,001 - 80,000	9	125,001 - 140,000	9
80,001 - 100,000	10	140,001 and over	10
100,001 - 115,000	11		
115,001 - 130,000	12		
130,001 - 140,000	13		
140,001 - 150,000	14		
150,001 and over	15		

Table 2

Married Filing Jointly		All Others	
If wages from **HIGHEST** paying job are—	Enter on line 7 above	If wages from **HIGHEST** paying job are—	Enter on line 7 above
$0 - $74,000	$590	$0 - $37,000	$590
74,001 - 130,000	990	37,001 - 80,000	990
130,001 - 200,000	1,110	80,001 - 175,000	1,110
200,001 - 355,000	1,300	175,001 - 385,000	1,300
355,001 - 400,000	1,380	385,001 and over	1,560
400,001 and over	1,560		

Privacy Act and Paperwork Reduction Act Notice. We ask for the information on this form to carry out the Internal Revenue laws of the United States. Internal Revenue Code sections 3402(f)(2) and 6109 and their regulations require you to provide this information; your employer uses it to determine your federal income tax withholding. Failure to provide a properly completed form will result in your being treated as a single person who claims no withholding allowances; providing fraudulent information may subject you to penalties. Routine uses of this information include giving it to the Department of Justice for civil and criminal litigation; to cities, states, the District of Columbia, and U.S. commonwealths and possessions for use in administering their tax laws; and to the Department of Health and Human Services for use in the National Directory of New Hires. We may also disclose this information to other countries under a tax treaty, to federal and state agencies to enforce federal nontax criminal laws, or to federal law enforcement and intelligence agencies to combat terrorism.

You are not required to provide the information requested on a form that is subject to the Paperwork Reduction Act unless the form displays a valid OMB control number. Books or records relating to a form or its instructions must be retained as long as their contents may become material in the administration of any Internal Revenue law. Generally, tax returns and return information are confidential, as required by Code section 6103.

The average time and expenses required to complete and file this form will vary depending on individual circumstances. For estimated averages, see the instructions for your income tax return.

If you have suggestions for making this form simpler, we would be happy to hear from you. See the instructions for your income tax return.

Form W-4 (2014)

Purpose. Complete Form W-4 so that your employer can withhold the correct federal income tax from your pay. Consider completing a new Form W-4 each year and when your personal or financial situation changes.

Exemption from withholding. If you are exempt, complete **only** lines 1, 2, 3, 4, and 7 and sign the form to validate it. Your exemption for 2014 expires February 17, 2015. See Pub. 505, Tax Withholding and Estimated Tax.

Note. If another person can claim you as a dependent on his or her tax return, you cannot claim exemption from withholding if your income exceeds $1,000 and includes more than $350 of unearned income (for example, interest and dividends).

Exceptions. An employee may be able to claim exemption from withholding even if the employee is a dependent, if the employee:

- Is age 65 or older,
- Is blind, or
- Will claim adjustments to income; tax credits; or itemized deductions, on his or her tax return.

The exceptions do not apply to supplemental wages greater than $1,000,000.

Basic instructions. If you are not exempt, complete the **Personal Allowances Worksheet** below. The worksheets on page 2 further adjust your withholding allowances based on itemized deductions, certain credits, adjustments to income, or two-earners/multiple jobs situations.

Complete all worksheets that apply. However, you may claim fewer (or zero) allowances. For regular wages, withholding must be based on allowances you claimed and may not be a flat amount or percentage of wages.

Head of household. Generally, you can claim head of household filing status on your tax return only if you are unmarried and pay more than 50% of the costs of keeping up a home for yourself and your dependent(s) or other qualifying individuals. See Pub. 501, Exemptions, Standard Deduction, and Filing Information, for information.

Tax credits. You can take projected tax credits into account in figuring your allowable number of withholding allowances. Credits for child or dependent care expenses and the child tax credit may be claimed using the **Personal Allowances Worksheet** below. See Pub. 505 for information on converting your other credits into withholding allowances.

Nonwage income. If you have a large amount of nonwage income, such as interest or dividends, consider making estimated tax payments using Form 1040-ES, Estimated Tax for Individuals. Otherwise, you may owe additional tax. If you have pension or annuity iincome, see Pub. 505 to find out if you should adjust your withholding on Form W-4 or W-4P.

Two earners or multiple jobs. If you have a working spouse or more than one job, figure the total number of allowances you are entitled to claim on all jobs using worksheets from only one Form W-4. Your withholding usually will be most accurate when all allowances are claimed on the Form W-4 for the highest paying job and zero allowances are claimed on the others. See Pub. 505 for details.

Nonresident alien. If you are a nonresident alien, see Notice 1392, Supplemental Form W-4 Instructions for Nonresident Aliens, before completing this form.

Check your withholding. After your Form W-4 takes effect, use Pub. 505 to see how the amount you are having withheld compares to your projected total tax for 2014. See Pub. 505, especially if your earnings exceed $130,000 (Single) or $180,000 (Married).

Future developments. Information about any future developments affecting Form W-4 (such as legislation enacted after we release it) will be posted at *www.irs.gov/w4*.

Personal Allowances Worksheet (Keep for your records.)

A Enter "1" for **yourself** if no one else can claim you as a dependent . . . . **A** ____

B Enter "1" if:
- You are single and have only one job; or
- You are married, have only one job, and your spouse does not work; or
- Your wages from a second job or your spouse's wages (or the total of both) are $1,500 or less.

. . . **B** ____

C Enter "1" for your **spouse.** But, you may choose to enter "-0-" if you are married and have either a working spouse or more than one job. (Entering "-0-" may help you avoid having too little tax withheld.) . . . . **C** ____

D Enter number of **dependents** (other than your spouse or yourself) you will claim on your tax return . . . . . . **D** ____

E Enter "1" if you will file as **head of household** on your tax return (see conditions under **Head of household** above) . . **E** ____

F Enter "1" if you have at least $2,000 of **child or dependent care expenses** for which you plan to claim a credit . . . **F** ____

(**Note.** Do **not** include child support payments. See Pub. 503, Child and Dependent Care Expenses, for details.)

G **Child Tax Credit** (including additional child tax credit). See Pub. 972, Child Tax Credit, for more information.

- If your total income will be less than $65,000 ($95,000 if married), enter "2" for each eligible child; then **less** "1" if you have three to six eligible children or **less** "2" if you have seven or more eligible children.
- If your total income will be between $65,000 and $84,000 ($95,000 and $119,000 if married), enter "1" for each eligible child . . . **G** ____

H Add lines A through G and enter total here. (**Note.** This may be different from the number of exemptions you claim on your tax return.) ▶ **H** ____

For accuracy, **complete all worksheets that apply.**
- If you plan to **itemize** or **claim adjustments to income** and want to reduce your withholding, see the **Deductions and Adjustments Worksheet** on page 2.
- If you are **single and have more than one job** or are **married and you and your spouse both work** and the combined earnings from all jobs exceed $50,000 ($20,000 if married), see the **Two-Earners/Multiple Jobs Worksheet** on page 2 to avoid having too little tax withheld.
- If **neither** of the above situations applies, **stop here** and enter the number from line H on line 5 of Form W-4 below.

---------- **Separate here and give Form W-4 to your employer. Keep the top part for your records.** ----------

Form **W-4**
Department of the Treasury
Internal Revenue Service

Employee's Withholding Allowance Certificate

▶ **Whether you are entitled to claim a certain number of allowances or exemption from withholding is subject to review by the IRS. Your employer may be required to send a copy of this form to the IRS.**

OMB No. 1545-0074
2014

1 Your first name and middle initial	Last name	2 **Your social security number**
Home address (number and street or rural route)		3 ☐ Single ☐ Married ☐ Married, but withhold at higher Single rate. **Note.** If married, but legally separated, or spouse is a nonresident alien, check the "Single" box.
City or town, state, and ZIP code		4 **If your last name differs from that shown on your social security card, check here. You must call 1-800-772-1213 for a replacement card.** ▶ ☐

5 Total number of allowances you are claiming (from line **H** above **or** from the applicable worksheet on page 2) **5** ____

6 Additional amount, if any, you want withheld from each paycheck . . . . **6** $ ____

7 I claim exemption from withholding for 2014, and I certify that I meet **both** of the following conditions for exemption.
- Last year I had a right to a refund of **all** federal income tax withheld because I had **no** tax liability, **and**
- This year I expect a refund of **all** federal income tax withheld because I expect to have **no** tax liability.

If you meet both conditions, write "Exempt" here . . . . ▶ **7** ____

Under penalties of perjury, I declare that I have examined this certificate and, to the best of my knowledge and belief, it is true, correct, and complete.

Employee's signature
(This form is not valid unless you sign it.) ▶ **Date** ▶

8 Employer's name and address (Employer: Complete lines 8 and 10 only if sending to the IRS.)	9 Office code (optional)	10 Employer identification number (EIN)

For Privacy Act and Paperwork Reduction Act Notice, see page 2. Cat. No. 10220Q Form **W-4** (2014)

Form W-4 (2014) Page **2**

Deductions and Adjustments Worksheet

Note. Use this worksheet *only* if you plan to itemize deductions or claim certain credits or adjustments to income.

1	Enter an estimate of your 2014 itemized deductions. These include qualifying home mortgage interest, charitable contributions, state and local taxes, medical expenses in excess of 10% (7.5% if either you or your spouse was born before January 2, 1950) of your income, and miscellaneous deductions. For 2014, you may have to reduce your itemized deductions if your income is over $305,050 and you are married filing jointly or are a qualifying widow(er); $279,650 if you are head of household; $254,200 if you are single and not head of household or a qualifying widow(er); or $152,525 if you are married filing separately. See Pub. 505 for details	1	$
2	Enter: $12,400 if married filing jointly or qualifying widow(er); $9,100 if head of household; $6,200 if single or married filing separately	2	$
3	**Subtract** line 2 from line 1. If zero or less, enter "-0-"	3	$
4	Enter an estimate of your 2014 adjustments to income and any additional standard deduction (see Pub. 505)	4	$
5	**Add** lines 3 and 4 and enter the total. (Include any amount for credits from the *Converting Credits to Withholding Allowances for 2014 Form W-4* worksheet in Pub. 505.)	5	$
6	Enter an estimate of your 2014 nonwage income (such as dividends or interest)	6	$
7	**Subtract** line 6 from line 5. If zero or less, enter "-0-"	7	$
8	**Divide** the amount on line 7 by $3,950 and enter the result here. Drop any fraction	8	
9	Enter the number from the **Personal Allowances Worksheet,** line H, page 1	9	
10	**Add** lines 8 and 9 and enter the total here. If you plan to use the **Two-Earners/Multiple Jobs Worksheet,** also enter this total on line 1 below. Otherwise, **stop here** and enter this total on Form W-4, line 5, page 1	10	

Two-Earners/Multiple Jobs Worksheet (See *Two earners or multiple jobs* on page 1.)

Note. Use this worksheet *only* if the instructions under line H on page 1 direct you here.

1	Enter the number from line H, page 1 (or from line 10 above if you used the **Deductions and Adjustments Worksheet**)	1	
2	Find the number in **Table 1** below that applies to the **LOWEST** paying job and enter it here. **However,** if you are married filing jointly and wages from the highest paying job are $65,000 or less, do not enter more than "3"	2	
3	If line 1 is **more than or equal to** line 2, subtract line 2 from line 1. Enter the result here (if zero, enter "-0-") and on Form W-4, line 5, page 1. **Do not** use the rest of this worksheet	3	

Note. If line 1 is **less than** line 2, enter "-0-" on Form W-4, line 5, page 1. Complete lines 4 through 9 below to figure the additional withholding amount necessary to avoid a year-end tax bill.

4	Enter the number from line 2 of this worksheet . . . 4 ______		
5	Enter the number from line 1 of this worksheet . . . 5 ______		
6	**Subtract** line 5 from line 4	6	
7	Find the amount in **Table 2** below that applies to the **HIGHEST** paying job and enter it here	7	$
8	**Multiply** line 7 by line 6 and enter the result here. This is the additional annual withholding needed	8	$
9	Divide line 8 by the number of pay periods remaining in 2014. For example, divide by 25 if you are paid every two weeks and you complete this form on a date in January when there are 25 pay periods remaining in 2014. Enter the result here and on Form W-4, line 6, page 1. This is the additional amount to be withheld from each paycheck	9	$

Table 1

Married Filing Jointly		All Others	
If wages from **LOWEST** paying job are—	Enter on line 2 above	If wages from **LOWEST** paying job are—	Enter on line 2 above
$0 - $6,000	0	$0 - $6,000	0
6,001 - 13,000	1	6,001 - 16,000	1
13,001 - 24,000	2	16,001 - 25,000	2
24,001 - 26,000	3	25,001 - 34,000	3
26,001 - 33,000	4	34,001 - 43,000	4
33,001 - 43,000	5	43,001 - 70,000	5
43,001 - 49,000	6	70,001 - 85,000	6
49,001 - 60,000	7	85,001 - 110,000	7
60,001 - 75,000	8	110,001 - 125,000	8
75,001 - 80,000	9	125,001 - 140,000	9
80,001 - 100,000	10	140,001 and over	10
100,001 - 115,000	11		
115,001 - 130,000	12		
130,001 - 140,000	13		
140,001 - 150,000	14		
150,001 and over	15		

Table 2

Married Filing Jointly		All Others	
If wages from **HIGHEST** paying job are—	Enter on line 7 above	If wages from **HIGHEST** paying job are—	Enter on line 7 above
$0 - $74,000	$590	$0 - $37,000	$590
74,001 - 130,000	990	37,001 - 80,000	990
130,001 - 200,000	1,110	80,001 - 175,000	1,110
200,001 - 355,000	1,300	175,001 - 385,000	1,300
355,001 - 400,000	1,380	385,001 and over	1,560
400,001 and over	1,560		

Privacy Act and Paperwork Reduction Act Notice. We ask for the information on this form to carry out the Internal Revenue laws of the United States. Internal Revenue Code sections 3402(f)(2) and 6109 and their regulations require you to provide this information; your employer uses it to determine your federal income tax withholding. Failure to provide a properly completed form will result in your being treated as a single person who claims no withholding allowances; providing fraudulent information may subject you to penalties. Routine uses of this information include giving it to the Department of Justice for civil and criminal litigation; to cities, states, the District of Columbia, and U.S. commonwealths and possessions for use in administering their tax laws; and to the Department of Health and Human Services for use in the National Directory of New Hires. We may also disclose this information to other countries under a tax treaty, to federal and state agencies to enforce federal nontax criminal laws, or to federal law enforcement and intelligence agencies to combat terrorism.

You are not required to provide the information requested on a form that is subject to the Paperwork Reduction Act unless the form displays a valid OMB control number. Books or records relating to a form or its instructions must be retained as long as their contents may become material in the administration of any Internal Revenue law. Generally, tax returns and return information are confidential, as required by Code section 6103.

The average time and expenses required to complete and file this form will vary depending on individual circumstances. For estimated averages, see the instructions for your income tax return.

If you have suggestions for making this form simpler, we would be happy to hear from you. See the instructions for your income tax return.

LO 9.8

_____ 13. Individual taxpayers may pay withholding taxes due with their individual income tax returns using Schedule H for each of the following workers except:
   a. a nanny hired to watch their children.
   b. a maid hired to clean house and cook every day.
   c. an attorney with her own business, hired to handle a legal dispute with the taxpayers' neighbor.
   d. an unlicensed caregiver for a disabled spouse.

LO 9.9

_____ 14. Skylar is single and earns $400,000 in salary during 2014. What is the amount of Medicare surtax for high-income taxpayers that his employer must withhold from his wages?
   a. $3,600
   b. $1,800
   c. $1,350
   d. $900

LO 9.9

_____ 15. Christine and Doug are married. In 2014, Christine earns a salary of $250,000 and Doug earns a salary of $50,000. They have no other income and work for the same employers for all of 2014. How much Medicare surtax for high-income taxpayers will Christine and Doug have to pay with their 2014 income tax return?
   a. $450
   b. $900
   c. $2,700
   d. None

GROUP 2: PROBLEMS

LO 9.1

1. Phan Mai is a single taxpayer with two dependent children under age 17. Phan estimates her wages for the year will be $36,000 and her itemized deductions will be $11,000. Assuming Phan files as head of household, use Form W-4 on Pages 9-37 and 9-38 to determine the number of withholding allowances Phan should claim.

LO 9.1

2. Ralph and Kathy Gump are married with one 20-year-old dependent child. Ralph earns a total of $39,000 and estimates their itemized deductions to be $16,000 for the year. Kathy is not employed. Use Form W-4 on Pages 9-39 and 9-40 to determine the number of withholding allowances that Ralph should claim.

LO 9.1

3. Sophie is a single taxpayer. For the first payroll period in October 2014, she is paid wages of $3,250 monthly. Sophie claims three allowances on her Form W-4.
   a. Use the percentage method to calculate the amount of Sophie's withholding for a monthly pay period.

   $ __________

   b. Use the withholding tables to determine the amount of Sophie's withholding for the same period.

   $ __________

LO 9.1

4. Big Bull restaurant employs twenty-three employees who receive tips. During the current year, Big Bull has $410,000 in gross revenues, and its employees do not report any tip income. In what ways may the restaurant allocate the tip income to the employees?

LO 9.2

5. Harold Conners (Social Security number 785-23-9873) lives at 13234 DeMilo Drive, Houston, TX 77052, and is self-employed for 2014. He estimates his required annual estimated tax payment for 2014 to be $6,544. He had a $674 overpayment of last year's taxes, which he will apply against his first quarter estimated payment. Complete the first quarter voucher below for Harold for 2014.

Form **1040-ES** Department of the Treasury Internal Revenue Service | **2014 Estimated Tax** | **Payment Voucher 1** | OMB No. 1545-0074

File only if you are making a payment of estimated tax by check or money order. Mail this voucher with your check or money order payable to **"United States Treasury."** Write your social security number and "2014 Form 1040-ES" on your check or money order. Do not send cash. Enclose, but do not staple or attach, your payment with this voucher.	**Calendar year—Due April 15, 2014** Amount of estimated tax you are paying by check or money order. Dollars / Cents

Print or type

Your first name and initial	Your last name	Your social security number
If joint payment, complete for spouse		
Spouse's first name and initial	Spouse's last name	Spouse's social security number
Address (number, street, and apt. no.)		
City, state, and ZIP code. (If a foreign address, enter city, also complete spaces below.)		
Foreign country name	Foreign province/county	Foreign postal code

For Privacy Act and Paperwork Reduction Act Notice, see instructions. **Form 1040-ES (2014)**

LO 9.2

6. Go to the IRS website **(www.irs.gov)** and redo Problem 5 using the most recent interactive Form 1040-ES. Print out the *completed Form 1040-ES.*

LO 9.3

7. Jenny earns $34,500 in 2014. Calculate the FICA tax that must be paid by:

Jenny:	Soc. Sec.	$________
	Medicare	$________
Jenny's Employer:	Soc. Sec.	$________
	Medicare	$________
Total FICA Tax		$________

LO 9.3

8. Yolanda earns $119,000 in 2014. Calculate the FICA tax that must be paid by:

Yolanda:	Soc. Sec.	$________
	Medicare	$________
Yolanda's Employer:	Soc. Sec.	$________
	Medicare	$________
Total FICA Tax		$________

LO 9.3

9. Jan has two jobs during 2014. One employer withheld and paid FICA taxes on $70,000 of Jan's salary, and the other employer withheld and paid FICA taxes on $47,700 in salary paid to Jan. Calculate the amount of Jan's overpayment of FICA taxes that she should claim on her 2014 Form 1040.

$____________

LO 9.4

10. Locate IRS Publication 15, "Circular E, Employer's Tax Guide" at the IRS website **(www.irs.gov)**, and review the table of contents on page one of the publication. Familiarize yourself with the items covered in the publication and print the first page of the section titled "Depositing Taxes."

LO 9.5

11. For each of the following payments, indicate the form that should be used to report the payment:
    a. Interest of $400 paid by a bank ____________
    b. Payment of $400 in dividends by a corporation to a shareholder ____________
    c. Periodic payments from a retirement plan ____________
    d. Salary as president of the company ____________
    e. Las Vegas keno winnings of $25,000 ____________

LO 9.5

12. General Corporation (P.O. Box 4563, Houston, TX 77003; EIN 12-3456789) paid Louise Bryant, an employee who lives at 5471 DeMilo Street, Houston, TX 77052, wages of $24,554 in 2014. The withholding tax for the year amounted to $6,050.40, and the FICA tax withheld was $1,878.38 ($1,522.35 for Social Security and $356.03 for Medicare). Louise's FICA wages were the same as her total wages. Her Social Security number is 545-64-7745.
    a. Complete the following Form W-2 for Louise Bryant from General Corporation.
    b. General Corporation also paid $900 to William Russel for presenting a management seminar. William lives at 1455 Cullen Boulevard, Houston, TX 77008, and his Social Security number is 475-45-3226. Complete the following Form 1099-MISC for the payment to William from General Corporation.

22222	a Employee's social security number	OMB No. 1545-0008	
b Employer identification number (EIN)		1 Wages, tips, other compensation	2 Federal income tax withheld
c Employer's name, address, and ZIP code		3 Social security wages	4 Social security tax withheld
		5 Medicare wages and tips	6 Medicare tax withheld
		7 Social security tips	8 Allocated tips
d Control number		9	10 Dependent care benefits
e Employee's first name and initial Last name Suff.		11 Nonqualified plans	12a Code
		13 Statutory employee / Retirement plan / Third-party sick pay	12b Code
		14 Other	12c Code
			12d Code
f Employee's address and ZIP code			

15 State Employer's state ID number	16 State wages, tips, etc.	17 State income tax	18 Local wages, tips, etc.	19 Local income tax	20 Locality name

Form **W-2** Wage and Tax Statement 2014

Department of the Treasury—Internal Revenue Service

Copy 1—For State, City, or Local Tax Department

☐ VOID ☐ CORRECTED

PAYER'S name, street address, city or town, state or province, country, ZIP or foreign postal code, and telephone no.		1 Rents $ 2 Royalties $	OMB No. 1545-0115 **2014** Form **1099-MISC**	**Miscellaneous Income**
		3 Other income $	4 Federal income tax withheld $	**Copy 1**
PAYER'S federal identification number	RECIPIENT'S identification number	5 Fishing boat proceeds $	6 Medical and health care payments $	**For State Tax Department**
RECIPIENT'S name Street address (including apt. no.)		7 Nonemployee compensation $	8 Substitute payments in lieu of dividends or interest $	
City or town, state or province, country, and ZIP or foreign postal code		9 Payer made direct sales of $5,000 or more of consumer products to a buyer (recipient) for resale ► ☐	10 Crop insurance proceeds $	
		11	12	
Account number (see instructions)		13 Excess golden parachute payments $	14 Gross proceeds paid to an attorney $	
15a Section 409A deferrals $	15b Section 409A income $	16 State tax withheld $ $	17 State/Payer's state no.	18 State income $ $

Form **1099-MISC** www.irs.gov/form1099misc Department of the Treasury - Internal Revenue Service

LO 9.5 13. Fly-By-Night (P.O. Box 1234, Dallas, TX 75221, EIN 12-9876543) paid George Smith, an employee who lives at 432 Second Street, Garland, TX 75040, wages of $24,300. The income tax withholding amounted to $5,320 and the FICA tax was $1,858.95 ($1,506.60 for Social Security and $352.35 for Medicare). George's FICA wages were the same as the total wages, and his Social Security number is 466-47-3313. Fly-By-Night's owner, a shady character, took off to South America with all the firm's funds, and did not file the required W-2s, etc., for George (and other employees). The above numbers are taken from the year-to-date section of George's last pay stub.

Go to the IRS website **(www.irs.gov)** and complete a Substitute W-2 using the most recent interactive Form 4852. Print out the *completed Form 4852.*

LO 9.6 14. Stew is a self-employed surfboard-maker in 2014. His Schedule C net income is $104,000 for the year. He also has a part-time job and earns $8,500 in wages subject to FICA taxes. Calculate Stew's self-employment tax for 2014 using Schedule SE on Pages 9-47 and 9-48.

LO 9.7 15. Thomas is an employer with one employee, Sarah. Sarah's wages are $19,450, and the state unemployment tax rate is 5.4 percent. Calculate the following amounts for Thomas:

a. FUTA tax before the state tax credit $ ____________

b. State unemployment tax $ ____________

c. FUTA tax after the state tax credit $ ____________

LO 9.8 16. Sally hires a maid to work in her home for $250 per month. The maid is 25 years old and not related to Sally. During 2014, the maid worked 10 months for Sally.

a. What is the amount of Social Security tax Sally must pay as the maid's employer?

$ ____________

b. What is the amount of Medicare tax Sally must pay as the maid's employer?

$ ____________

c. What is the amount of Social Security and Medicare tax which must be withheld from the maid's wages?

$ ____________

LO 9.8

17. Ann hires a nanny to watch her two children while she works at a local hospital. She pays the 19-year-old nanny $125 per week for 48 weeks during the current year.
    a. What is the employer's portion of Social Security and Medicare tax for the nanny that Ann should pay when she files her Form 1040 for 2014?
    $____________
    b. What is the nanny's portion of the FICA and Medicare tax?
    $____________

LO 9.9

18. Married taxpayers Otto and Ruth are both self-employed. Otto earns $350,000 of self-employment income and Ruth has a self-employment loss of $10,000. How much Medicare surtax for high-income taxpayers will Otto and Ruth have to pay with their 2014 income tax return?

GROUP 3: WRITING ASSIGNMENT

ETHICS

Rocky Jackson, a friend of yours, just started a new job. He is attempting to fill out Form W-4 and has asked for your help. He would like to receive a large refund when he files his return and would therefore like to claim as few allowances as possible. Even though he is married and has four children, he is planning on claiming no allowances. What would you tell Rocky?

GROUP 4: COMPREHENSIVE PROBLEM

Dr. Carol Harris, CPA, is a single taxpayer and she lives at 674 Yankee Street, Durham, NC 27409. Her Social Security number is 793-52-4335. Carol is an Associate Professor of Accounting at a local college. Carol's earnings and withholding from the college for 2014 are:

Earnings	$54,000
Federal income tax withheld	8,800
State income tax withheld	2,500

FICA tax of $3,348 and Medicare tax of $783 were also withheld from Carol's earnings. Carol's other income includes interest of $145 from a savings account at New England Bank and $450 of qualified dividends from Microsoft.

During the year, Carol paid the following amounts (all of which can be substantiated):

Home mortgage interest	$6,300
Visa card interest	350
Auto insurance	750
Property taxes on personal residence	2,650
Other medical expenses	810
Charitable contributions (in cash)	1,000

Carol had the following stock market transactions, all of which were reported on Form 1099-B, along with the basis of the stock sold:

Stock	*Acquired*	*Sold*	*Price*	*Basis*
Trout Co.	04/05/04	10/15/14	$6,000	$3,600
Bass Co.	02/01/14	08/03/14	$7,000	$5,500
Shark Co.	09/12/05	10/15/14	$7,000	$8,500

In addition to being a professor at the local college, Carol maintains a CPA practice. Income and expenses from this activity are:

Fees from CPA practice (all paid by check)	$38,800
Office rent	3,600
Supplies	750
Computer tax service	1,200
Mileage (4,107 miles)	2,300
Client meals and entertainment	2,740
Telephone	975
Other expenses	1,400

Carol drove her car (placed in service on January 1, 2012) 20,000 miles in total, of which 5,000 miles were for commuting. Carol made 2014 estimated tax payments to the U.S. Treasury of $3,000 for each quarter.

Required: Complete Carol's federal tax return for 2014. Use Form 1040, Schedule A, Schedule C, Schedule D, Form 8949, Schedule SE, and the worksheet on Pages 9-49 through 9-61 to complete this tax return. Make realistic assumptions about any missing data.

SCHEDULE SE (Form 1040)

Department of the Treasury
Internal Revenue Service (99)

Self-Employment Tax

▶ Information about Schedule SE and its separate instructions is at *www.irs.gov/schedulese*.

▶ Attach to Form 1040 or Form 1040NR.

OMB No. 1545-0074

2014

Attachment Sequence No. **17**

Name of person with **self-employment** income (as shown on Form 1040 or Form 1040NR)	Social security number of person with **self-employment** income ▶

Before you begin: To determine if you must file Schedule SE, see the instructions.

DRAFT AS OF May 14, 2014 DO NOT FILE

May I Use Short Schedule SE or Must I Use Long Schedule SE?

Note. Use this flowchart **only if** you must file Schedule SE. If unsure, see *Who Must File Schedule SE* in the instructions.

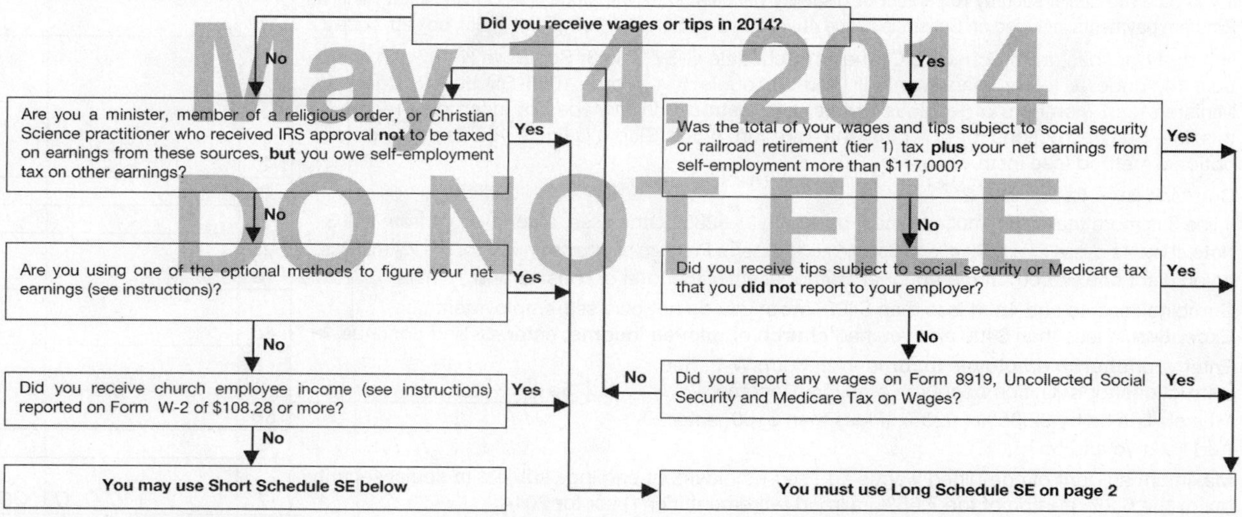

Section A—Short Schedule SE. Caution. Read above to see if you can use Short Schedule SE.

1a	Net farm profit or (loss) from Schedule F, line 34, and farm partnerships, Schedule K-1 (Form 1065), box 14, code A	**1a**	
b	If you received social security retirement or disability benefits, enter the amount of Conservation Reserve Program payments included on Schedule F, line 4b, or listed on Schedule K-1 (Form 1065), box 20, code Z	**1b**	( )
2	Net profit or (loss) from Schedule C, line 31; Schedule C-EZ, line 3; Schedule K-1 (Form 1065), box 14, code A (other than farming); and Schedule K-1 (Form 1065-B), box 9, code J1. Ministers and members of religious orders, see instructions for types of income to report on this line. See instructions for other income to report	**2**	
3	Combine lines 1a, 1b, and 2	**3**	
4	Multiply line 3 by 92.35% (.9235). If less than $400, you do not owe self-employment tax; **do not** file this schedule unless you have an amount on line 1b . . . . . ▶	**4**	
	Note. If line 4 is less than $400 due to Conservation Reserve Program payments on line 1b, see instructions.		
5	**Self-employment tax.** If the amount on line 4 is: • $117,000 or less, multiply line 4 by 15.3% (.153). Enter the result here and on **Form 1040, line 57,** or **Form 1040NR, line 55** • More than $117,000, multiply line 4 by 2.9% (.029). Then, add $14,508 to the result. Enter the total here and on **Form 1040, line 57,** or **Form 1040NR, line 55**	**5**	
6	**Deduction for one-half of self-employment tax.** Multiply line 5 by 50% (.50). Enter the result here and on **Form 1040, line 27,** or **Form 1040NR, line 27** **6**		

For Paperwork Reduction Act Notice, see your tax return instructions. Cat. No. 11358Z **Schedule SE (Form 1040) 2014**

Schedule SE (Form 1040) 2014 — Attachment Sequence No. **17** — Page **2**

Name of person with **self-employment** income (as shown on Form 1040 or Form 1040NR)	Social security number of person with **self-employment** income ▶

Section B—Long Schedule SE

Part I Self-Employment Tax

Note. If your only income subject to self-employment tax is **church employee income,** see instructions. Also see instructions for the definition of church employee income.

Line	Description	Box	Amount
A	If you are a minister, member of a religious order, or Christian Science practitioner **and** you filed Form 4361, but you had $400 or more of **other** net earnings from self-employment, check here and continue with Part I . . . . . . ▶ ☐		
1a	Net farm profit or (loss) from Schedule F, line 34, and farm partnerships, Schedule K-1 (Form 1065), box 14, code A. **Note.** Skip lines 1a and 1b if you use the farm optional method (see instructions)	1a	
b	If you received social security retirement or disability benefits, enter the amount of Conservation Reserve Program payments included on Schedule F, line 4b, or listed on Schedule K-1 (Form 1065), box 20, code Z	1b	( )
2	Net profit or (loss) from Schedule C, line 31; Schedule C-EZ, line 3; Schedule K-1 (Form 1065), box 14, code A (other than farming); and Schedule K-1 (Form 1065-B), box 9, code J1. Ministers and members of religious orders, see instructions for types of income to report on this line. See instructions for other income to report. **Note.** Skip this line if you use the nonfarm optional method (see instructions)	2	
3	Combine lines 1a, 1b, and 2	3	
4a	If line 3 is more than zero, multiply line 3 by 92.35% (.9235). Otherwise, enter amount from line 3. **Note.** If line 4a is less than $400 due to Conservation Reserve Program payments on line 1b, see instructions.	4a	
b	If you elect one or both of the optional methods, enter the total of lines 15 and 17 here . .	4b	
c	Combine lines 4a and 4b. If less than $400, **stop**; you do not owe self-employment tax. **Exception.** If less than $400 and you had **church employee income,** enter -0- and continue ▶	4c	
5a	Enter your **church employee income** from Form W-2. See instructions for definition of church employee income . . . **5a**		
b	Multiply line 5a by 92.35% (.9235). If less than $100, enter -0-	5b	
6	Add lines 4c and 5b	6	
7	Maximum amount of combined wages and self-employment earnings subject to social security tax or the 6.2% portion of the 7.65% railroad retirement (tier 1) tax for 2014	7	117,000 00
8a	Total social security wages and tips (total of boxes 3 and 7 on Form(s) W-2) and railroad retirement (tier 1) compensation. If $117,000 or more, skip lines 8b through 10, and go to line 11 **8a**		
b	Unreported tips subject to social security tax (from Form 4137, line 10) **8b**		
c	Wages subject to social security tax (from Form 8919, line 10) **8c**		
d	Add lines 8a, 8b, and 8c	8d	
9	Subtract line 8d from line 7. If zero or less, enter -0- here and on line 10 and go to line 11 . ▶	9	
10	Multiply the **smaller** of line 6 or line 9 by 12.4% (.124)	10	
11	Multiply line 6 by 2.9% (.029)	11	
12	**Self-employment tax.** Add lines 10 and 11. Enter here and on **Form 1040, line 57,** or **Form 1040NR, line 55**	12	
13	**Deduction for one-half of self-employment tax.** Multiply line 12 by 50% (.50). Enter the result here and on **Form 1040, line 27,** or **Form 1040NR, line 27** **13**		

Part II Optional Methods To Figure Net Earnings (see instructions)

Farm Optional Method. You may use this method **only** if **(a)** your gross farm income[1] was not more than $7,200, **or (b)** your net farm profits[2] were less than $5,198.

Line	Description	Box	Amount
14	Maximum income for optional methods	14	4,800 00
15	Enter the **smaller** of: two-thirds (2/3) of gross farm income[1] (not less than zero) **or** $4,800. Also include this amount on line 4b above	15	

Nonfarm Optional Method. You may use this method **only** if **(a)** your net nonfarm profits[3] were less than $5,198 and also less than 72.189% of your gross nonfarm income,[4] **and (b)** you had net earnings from self-employment of at least $400 in 2 of the prior 3 years. **Caution.** You may use this method no more than five times.

Line	Description	Box	Amount
16	Subtract line 15 from line 14	16	
17	Enter the **smaller** of: two-thirds (2/3) of gross nonfarm income[4] (not less than zero) **or** the amount on line 16. Also include this amount on line 4b above	17	

[1] From Sch. F, line 9, and Sch. K-1 (Form 1065), box 14, code B.

[2] From Sch. F, line 34, and Sch. K-1 (Form 1065), box 14, code A—minus the amount you would have entered on line 1b had you not used the optional method.

[3] From Sch. C, line 31; Sch. C-EZ, line 3; Sch. K-1 (Form 1065), box 14, code A; and Sch. K-1 (Form 1065-B), box 9, code J1.

[4] From Sch. C, line 7; Sch. C-EZ, line 1; Sch. K-1 (Form 1065), box 14, code C; and Sch. K-1 (Form 1065-B), box 9, code J2.

Schedule SE (Form 1040) 2014

DRAFT AS OF May 14, 2014 DO NOT FILE

Form **1040** Department of the Treasury—Internal Revenue Service (99)
U.S. Individual Income Tax Return **2014** OMB No. 1545-0074 IRS Use Only—Do not write or staple in this space.

For the year Jan. 1–Dec. 31, 2014, or other tax year beginning , 2014, ending , 20 See separate instructions.

Your first name and initial	Last name	**Your social security number**
If a joint return, spouse's first name and initial	Last name	**Spouse's social security number**
Home address (number and street). If you have a P.O. box, see instructions.	Apt. no.	▲ Make sure the SSN(s) above and on line 6c are correct.
City, town or post office, state, and ZIP code. If you have a foreign address, also complete spaces below (see instructions).		**Presidential Election Campaign** Check here if you, or your spouse if filing jointly, want $3 to go to this fund. Checking a box below will not change your tax or refund. ☐ You ☐ Spouse
Foreign country name	Foreign province/state/county	Foreign postal code

Filing Status

Check only one box.

1 ☐ Single
2 ☐ Married filing jointly (even if only one had income)
3 ☐ Married filing separately. Enter spouse's SSN above and full name here. ▶
4 ☐ Head of household (with qualifying person). (See instructions.) If the qualifying person is a child but not your dependent, enter this child's name here. ▶
5 ☐ Qualifying widow(er) with dependent child

Exemptions

6a ☐ **Yourself.** If someone can claim you as a dependent, **do not** check box 6a
b ☐ **Spouse**
c **Dependents:**

(1) First name Last name	(2) Dependent's social security number	(3) Dependent's relationship to you	(4) ✓ if child under age 17 qualifying for child tax credit (see instructions)
			☐
			☐
			☐
			☐

If more than four dependents, see instructions and check here ▶ ☐

d Total number of exemptions claimed

Boxes checked on 6a and 6b
No. of children on 6c who:
• lived with you
• did not live with you due to divorce or separation (see instructions)
Dependents on 6c not entered above
Add numbers on lines above ▶

Income

Attach Form(s) W-2 here. Also attach Forms W-2G and 1099-R if tax was withheld.

If you did not get a W-2, see instructions.

7 Wages, salaries, tips, etc. Attach Form(s) W-2 — 7
8a **Taxable** interest. Attach Schedule B if required — 8a
b **Tax-exempt** interest. **Do not** include on line 8a — 8b
9a Ordinary dividends. Attach Schedule B if required — 9a
b Qualified dividends — 9b
10 Taxable refunds, credits, or offsets of state and local income taxes — 10
11 Alimony received — 11
12 Business income or (loss). Attach Schedule C or C-EZ — 12
13 Capital gain or (loss). Attach Schedule D if required. If not required, check here ▶ ☐ — 13
14 Other gains or (losses). Attach Form 4797 — 14
15a IRA distributions 15a — b Taxable amount — 15b
16a Pensions and annuities 16a — b Taxable amount — 16b
17 Rental real estate, royalties, partnerships, S corporations, trusts, etc. Attach Schedule E — 17
18 Farm income or (loss). Attach Schedule F — 18
19 Unemployment compensation — 19
20a Social security benefits 20a — b Taxable amount — 20b
21 Other income. List type and amount — 21
22 Combine the amounts in the far right column for lines 7 through 21. This is your **total income** ▶ — 22

Adjusted Gross Income

23 Reserved — 23
24 Certain business expenses of reservists, performing artists, and fee-basis government officials. Attach Form 2106 or 2106-EZ — 24
25 Health savings account deduction. Attach Form 8889 — 25
26 Moving expenses. Attach Form 3903 — 26
27 Deductible part of self-employment tax. Attach Schedule SE — 27
28 Self-employed SEP, SIMPLE, and qualified plans — 28
29 Self-employed health insurance deduction — 29
30 Penalty on early withdrawal of savings — 30
31a Alimony paid b Recipient's SSN ▶ — 31a
32 IRA deduction — 32
33 Student loan interest deduction — 33
34 Reserved — 34
35 Domestic production activities deduction. Attach Form 8903 — 35
36 Add lines 23 through 35 — 36
37 Subtract line 36 from line 22. This is your **adjusted gross income** ▶ — 37

DRAFT AS OF August 28, 20 DO NOT FIL

For Disclosure, Privacy Act, and Paperwork Reduction Act Notice, see separate instructions. Cat. No. 11320B Form **1040** (2014)

Form 1040 (2014) Page **2**

Tax and Credits	38	Amount from line 37 (adjusted gross income)		38
	39a	Check if: ☐ **You** were born before January 2, 1950, ☐ Blind. ☐ **Spouse** was born before January 2, 1950, ☐ Blind. **Total boxes checked ▶ 39a**		
	b	If your spouse itemizes on a separate return or you were a dual-status alien, check here ▶ 39b☐		
	40	**Itemized deductions** (from Schedule A) **or** your **standard deduction** (see left margin)		40
	41	Subtract line 40 from line 38		41
	42	**Exemptions.** If line 38 is $152,525 or less, multiply $3,950 by the number on line 6d. Otherwise, see instructions		42
	43	**Taxable income.** Subtract line 42 from line 41. If line 42 is more than line 41, enter -0-		43
	44	**Tax** (see instructions). Check if any from: **a** ☐ Form(s) 8814 **b** ☐ Form 4972 **c** ☐		44
	45	**Alternative minimum tax** (see instructions). Attach Form 6251		45
	46	Excess advance premium tax credit repayment. Attach Form 8962		46
	47	Add lines 44, 45, and 46 ▶		47
	48	Foreign tax credit. Attach Form 1116 if required	48	
	49	Credit for child and dependent care expenses. Attach Form 2441	49	
	50	Education credits from Form 8863, line 19	50	
	51	Retirement savings contributions credit. Attach Form 8880	51	
	52	Child tax credit. Attach Schedule 8812, if required	52	
	53	Residential energy credit. Attach Form 5695	53	
	54	Other credits from Form: **a** ☐ 3800 **b** ☐ 8801 **c** ☐	54	
	55	Add lines 48 through 54. These are your **total credits**		55
	56	Subtract line 55 from line 47. If line 55 is more than line 47, enter -0- ▶		56
Other Taxes	57	Self-employment tax. Attach Schedule SE		57
	58	Unreported social security and Medicare tax from Form: **a** ☐ 4137 **b** ☐ 8919		58
	59	Additional tax on IRAs, other qualified retirement plans, etc. Attach Form 5329 if required		59
	60a	Household employment taxes from Schedule H		60a
	b	First-time homebuyer credit repayment. Attach Form 5405 if required		60b
	61	Health care: individual responsibility (see instructions) Full-year coverage ☐		61
	62	Taxes from: **a** ☐ Form 8959 **b** ☐ Form 8960 **c** ☐ Instructions; enter code(s)		62
	63	Add lines 56 through 62. This is your **total tax** ▶		63
Payments	64	Federal income tax withheld from Forms W-2 and 1099	64	
	65	2014 estimated tax payments and amount applied from 2013 return	65	
	66a	**Earned income credit (EIC)**	66a	
	b	Nontaxable combat pay election 66b		
	67	Additional child tax credit. Attach Schedule 8812	67	
	68	American opportunity credit from Form 8863, line 8	68	
	69	Net premium tax credit. Attach Form 8962	69	
	70	Amount paid with request for extension to file	70	
	71	Excess social security and tier 1 RRTA tax withheld	71	
	72	Credit for federal tax on fuels. Attach Form 4136	72	
	73	Credits from Form: **a** ☐ 2439 **b** ☐ Reserved **c** ☐ Reserved **d** ☐	73	
	74	Add lines 64, 65, 66a, and 67 through 73. These are your **total payments** ▶		74
Refund	75	If line 74 is more than line 63, subtract line 63 from line 74. This is the amount you **overpaid**		75
	76a	Amount of line 75 you want **refunded to you.** If Form 8888 is attached, check here ▶ ☐		76a
Direct deposit? See instructions.	▶ b	Routing number ▶ **c** Type: ☐ Checking ☐ Savings		
	▶ d	Account number		
	77	Amount of line 75 you want **applied to your 2015 estimated tax** ▶	77	
Amount You Owe	78	**Amount you owe.** Subtract line 74 from line 63. For details on how to pay, see instructions ▶		78
	79	Estimated tax penalty (see instructions)	79	

Standard Deduction for—
- People who check any box on line 39a or 39b **or** who can be claimed as a dependent, see instructions.
- All others:

Single or Married filing separately, $6,200

Married filing jointly or Qualifying widow(er), $12,400

Head of household, $9,100

If you have a qualifying child, attach Schedule EIC.

Third Party Designee

Do you want to allow another person to discuss this return with the IRS (see instructions)? ☐ **Yes.** Complete below. ☐ **No**

Designee's name ▶ Phone no. ▶ Personal identification number (PIN) ▶

Sign Here

Joint return? See instructions. Keep a copy for your records.

Under penalties of perjury, I declare that I have examined this return and accompanying schedules and statements, and to the best of my knowledge and belief, they are true, correct, and complete. Declaration of preparer (other than taxpayer) is based on all information of which preparer has any knowledge.

Your signature	Date	Your occupation	Daytime phone number
Spouse's signature. If a joint return, **both** must sign.	Date	Spouse's occupation	If the IRS sent you an Identity Protection PIN, enter it here (see inst.)

Paid Preparer Use Only

Print/Type preparer's name	Preparer's signature	Date	Check ☐ if self-employed	PTIN
Firm's name ▶			Firm's EIN ▶	
Firm's address ▶			Phone no.	

www.irs.gov/form1040 Form **1040** (2014)

DRAFT AS OF August 28, 2014 DO NOT FILE

SCHEDULE A (Form 1040)

Department of the Treasury
Internal Revenue Service (99)

Itemized Deductions

▶ Information about Schedule A and its separate instructions is at *www.irs.gov/schedulea*.
▶ Attach to Form 1040.

OMB No. 1545-0074
2014
Attachment Sequence No. 07

Name(s) shown on Form 1040 | **Your social security number**

DRAFT AS OF August 15, 2014 DO NOT FILE

Section	Line	Description		
Medical and Dental Expenses		**Caution.** Do not include expenses reimbursed or paid by others.		
	1	Medical and dental expenses (see instructions)	1	
	2	Enter amount from Form 1040, line 38 [2]		
	3	Multiply line 2 by 10% (.10). But if either you or your spouse was born before January 2, 1950, multiply line 2 by 7.5% (.075) instead	3	
	4	Subtract line 3 from line 1. If line 3 is more than line 1, enter -0-		4
Taxes You Paid	5	State and local		
		a ☐ Income taxes / b ☐ RESERVED	5	
	6	Real estate taxes (see instructions)	6	
	7	Personal property taxes	7	
	8	Other taxes. List type and amount ▶	8	
	9	Add lines 5 through 8		9
Interest You Paid	10	Home mortgage interest and points reported to you on Form 1098	10	
Note. Your mortgage interest deduction may be limited (see instructions).	11	Home mortgage interest not reported to you on Form 1098. If paid to the person from whom you bought the home, see instructions and show that person's name, identifying no., and address ▶	11	
	12	Points not reported to you on Form 1098. See instructions for special rules	12	
	13	RESERVED	13	
	14	Investment interest. Attach Form 4952 if required. (See instructions.)	14	
	15	Add lines 10 through 14		15
Gifts to Charity	16	Gifts by cash or check. If you made any gift of $250 or more, see instructions	16	
If you made a gift and got a benefit for it, see instructions.	17	Other than by cash or check. If any gift of $250 or more, see instructions. You **must** attach Form 8283 if over $500	17	
	18	Carryover from prior year	18	
	19	Add lines 16 through 18		19
Casualty and Theft Losses	20	Casualty or theft loss(es). Attach Form 4684. (See instructions.)		20
Job Expenses and Certain Miscellaneous Deductions	21	Unreimbursed employee expenses—job travel, union dues, job education, etc. Attach Form 2106 or 2106-EZ if required. (See instructions.) ▶	21	
	22	Tax preparation fees	22	
	23	Other expenses—investment, safe deposit box, etc. List type and amount ▶	23	
	24	Add lines 21 through 23	24	
	25	Enter amount from Form 1040, line 38 [25]		
	26	Multiply line 25 by 2% (.02)	26	
	27	Subtract line 26 from line 24. If line 26 is more than line 24, enter -0-		27
Other Miscellaneous Deductions	28	Other—from list in instructions. List type and amount ▶		28
Total Itemized Deductions	29	Is Form 1040, line 38, over $152,525? ☐ **No.** Your deduction is not limited. Add the amounts in the far right column for lines 4 through 28. Also, enter this amount on Form 1040, line 40. ☐ **Yes.** Your deduction may be limited. See the Itemized Deductions Worksheet in the instructions to figure the amount to enter.		29
	30	If you elect to itemize deductions even though they are less than your standard deduction, check here ▶ ☐		

For Paperwork Reduction Act Notice, see Form 1040 instructions. Cat. No. 17145C **Schedule A (Form 1040) 2014**

SCHEDULE C (Form 1040)
Department of the Treasury
Internal Revenue Service (99)

Profit or Loss From Business
(Sole Proprietorship)

▶ Information about Schedule C and its separate instructions is at *www.irs.gov/schedulec*.
▶ Attach to Form 1040, 1040NR, or 1041; partnerships generally must file Form 1065.

OMB No. 1545-0074
2014
Attachment Sequence No. 09

DRAFT AS OF
June 19, 2014
DO NOT FILE

Name of proprietor | **Social security number (SSN)**

A Principal business or profession, including product or service (see instructions) | **B Enter code from instructions** ▶

C Business name. If no separate business name, leave blank. | **D Employer ID number (EIN),** (see instr.)

E Business address (including suite or room no.) ▶
City, town or post office, state, and ZIP code

F Accounting method: **(1)** ☐ Cash **(2)** ☐ Accrual **(3)** ☐ Other (specify) ▶

G Did you "materially participate" in the operation of this business during 2014? If "No," see instructions for limit on losses ☐ Yes ☐ No

H If you started or acquired this business during 2014, check here ▶ ☐

I Did you make any payments in 2014 that would require you to file Form(s) 1099? (see instructions) ☐ Yes ☐ No

J If "Yes," did you or will you file required Forms 1099? ☐ Yes ☐ No

Part I Income

1	Gross receipts or sales. See instructions for line 1 and check the box if this income was reported to you on Form W-2 and the "Statutory employee" box on that form was checked ▶ ☐	1	
2	Returns and allowances	2	
3	Subtract line 2 from line 1	3	
4	Cost of goods sold (from line 42)	4	
5	**Gross profit.** Subtract line 4 from line 3	5	
6	Other income, including federal and state gasoline or fuel tax credit or refund (see instructions)	6	
7	**Gross income.** Add lines 5 and 6 ▶	7	

Part II Expenses. Enter expenses for business use of your home **only** on line 30.

8	Advertising	8		18	Office expense (see instructions)	18	
9	Car and truck expenses (see instructions)	9		19	Pension and profit-sharing plans	19	
10	Commissions and fees	10		20	Rent or lease (see instructions):		
11	Contract labor (see instructions)	11		a	Vehicles, machinery, and equipment	20a	
12	Depletion	12		b	Other business property	20b	
13	Depreciation and section 179 expense deduction (not included in Part III) (see instructions)	13		21	Repairs and maintenance	21	
				22	Supplies (not included in Part III)	22	
				23	Taxes and licenses	23	
				24	Travel, meals, and entertainment:		
14	Employee benefit programs (other than on line 19)	14		a	Travel	24a	
15	Insurance (other than health)	15		b	Deductible meals and entertainment (see instructions)	24b	
16	Interest:			25	Utilities	25	
a	Mortgage (paid to banks, etc.)	16a		26	Wages (less employment credits)	26	
b	Other	16b		27a	Other expenses (from line 48)	27a	
17	Legal and professional services	17		b	**Reserved for future use**	27b	

28	**Total expenses** before expenses for business use of home. Add lines 8 through 27a ▶	28	
29	Tentative profit or (loss). Subtract line 28 from line 7	29	
30	Expenses for business use of your home. Do not report these expenses elsewhere. Attach Form 8829 unless using the simplified method (see instructions). **Simplified method filers only:** enter the total square footage of: (a) your home: ________ and (b) the part of your home used for business: ________ . Use the Simplified Method Worksheet in the instructions to figure the amount to enter on line 30	30	
31	**Net profit or (loss).** Subtract line 30 from line 29. • If a profit, enter on both **Form 1040, line 12** (or **Form 1040NR, line 13**) and on **Schedule SE, line 2.** (If you checked the box on line 1, see instructions). Estates and trusts, enter on **Form 1041, line 3.** • If a loss, you **must** go to line 32.	31	

32 If you have a loss, check the box that describes your investment in this activity (see instructions).

- If you checked 32a, enter the loss on both **Form 1040, line 12,** (or **Form 1040NR, line 13**) and on **Schedule SE, line 2.** (If you checked the box on line 1, see the line 31 instructions). Estates and trusts, enter on **Form 1041, line 3.**
- If you checked 32b, you **must** attach **Form 6198.** Your loss may be limited.

32a ☐ All investment is at risk.
32b ☐ Some investment is not at risk.

For Paperwork Reduction Act Notice, see the separate instructions. Cat. No. 11334P **Schedule C (Form 1040) 2014**

Schedule C (Form 1040) 2014 Page **2**

Part III Cost of Goods Sold (see instructions)

33 Method(s) used to value closing inventory: a ☐ Cost b ☐ Lower of cost or market c ☐ Other (attach explanation)

34 Was there any change in determining quantities, costs, or valuations between opening and closing inventory? If "Yes," attach explanation . . . ☐ Yes ☐ No

DRAFT AS OF June 19, 2014 DO NOT FILE

35	Inventory at beginning of year. If different from last year's closing inventory, attach explanation	35	
36	Purchases less cost of items withdrawn for personal use	36	
37	Cost of labor. Do not include any amounts paid to yourself	37	
38	Materials and supplies	38	
39	Other costs	39	
40	Add lines 35 through 39	40	
41	Inventory at end of year	41	
42	**Cost of goods sold.** Subtract line 41 from line 40. Enter the result here and on line 4	42	

Part IV Information on Your Vehicle. Complete this part only if you are claiming car or truck expenses on line 9 and are not required to file Form 4562 for this business. See the instructions for line 13 to find out if you must file Form 4562.

43 When did you place your vehicle in service for business purposes? (month, day, year) ▶ / /

44 Of the total number of miles you drove your vehicle during 2014, enter the number of miles you used your vehicle for:

a Business ________ b Commuting (see instructions) ________ c Other ________

45 Was your vehicle available for personal use during off-duty hours? . . . ☐ Yes ☐ No

46 Do you (or your spouse) have another vehicle available for personal use? . . . ☐ Yes ☐ No

47a Do you have evidence to support your deduction? . . . ☐ Yes ☐ No

b If "Yes," is the evidence written? . . . ☐ Yes ☐ No

Part V Other Expenses. List below business expenses not included on lines 8–26 or line 30.

48 **Total other expenses.** Enter here and on line 27a	48	

SCHEDULE D (Form 1040)

Department of the Treasury
Internal Revenue Service (99)

Capital Gains and Losses

▶ Attach to Form 1040 or Form 1040NR.
▶ Information about Schedule D and its separate instructions is at *www.irs.gov/scheduled*.
▶ Use Form 8949 to list your transactions for lines 1b, 2, 3, 8b, 9, and 10.

OMB No. 1545-0074
2014
Attachment Sequence No. **12**

Name(s) shown on return | **Your social security number**

DRAFT AS OF June 9, 2014 DO NOT FILE

Part I Short-Term Capital Gains and Losses—Assets Held One Year or Less

See instructions for how to figure the amounts to enter on the lines below. This form may be easier to complete if you round off cents to whole dollars.	(d) Proceeds (sales price)	(e) Cost (or other basis)	(g) Adjustments to gain or loss from Form(s) 8949, Part I, line 2, column (g)	(h) Gain or (loss) Subtract column (e) from column (d) and combine the result with column (g)
1a Totals for all short-term transactions reported on Form 1099-B for which basis was reported to the IRS and for which you have no adjustments (see instructions). However, if you choose to report all these transactions on Form 8949, leave this line blank and go to line 1b				
1b Totals for all transactions reported on Form(s) 8949 with **Box A** checked				
2 Totals for all transactions reported on Form(s) 8949 with **Box B** checked				
3 Totals for all transactions reported on Form(s) 8949 with **Box C** checked				

4 Short-term gain from Form 6252 and short-term gain or (loss) from Forms 4684, 6781, and 8824	4	
5 Net short-term gain or (loss) from partnerships, S corporations, estates, and trusts from Schedule(s) K-1	5	
6 Short-term capital loss carryover. Enter the amount, if any, from line 8 of your **Capital Loss Carryover Worksheet** in the instructions	6	( )
7 **Net short-term capital gain or (loss).** Combine lines 1a through 6 in column (h). If you have any long-term capital gains or losses, go to Part II below. Otherwise, go to Part III on the back	7	

Part II Long-Term Capital Gains and Losses—Assets Held More Than One Year

See instructions for how to figure the amounts to enter on the lines below. This form may be easier to complete if you round off cents to whole dollars.	(d) Proceeds (sales price)	(e) Cost (or other basis)	(g) Adjustments to gain or loss from Form(s) 8949, Part II, line 2, column (g)	(h) Gain or (loss) Subtract column (e) from column (d) and combine the result with column (g)
8a Totals for all long-term transactions reported on Form 1099-B for which basis was reported to the IRS and for which you have no adjustments (see instructions). However, if you choose to report all these transactions on Form 8949, leave this line blank and go to line 8b				
8b Totals for all transactions reported on Form(s) 8949 with **Box D** checked				
9 Totals for all transactions reported on Form(s) 8949 with **Box E** checked				
10 Totals for all transactions reported on Form(s) 8949 with **Box F** checked				

11 Gain from Form 4797, Part I; long-term gain from Forms 2439 and 6252; and long-term gain or (loss) from Forms 4684, 6781, and 8824	11	
12 Net long-term gain or (loss) from partnerships, S corporations, estates, and trusts from Schedule(s) K-1	12	
13 Capital gain distributions. See the instructions	13	
14 Long-term capital loss carryover. Enter the amount, if any, from line 13 of your **Capital Loss Carryover Worksheet** in the instructions	14	( )
15 **Net long-term capital gain or (loss).** Combine lines 8a through 14 in column (h). Then go to Part III on the back	15	

For Paperwork Reduction Act Notice, see your tax return instructions. Cat. No. 11338H **Schedule D (Form 1040) 2014**

Schedule D (Form 1040) 2014 Page **2**

Part III **Summary**

16 Combine lines 7 and 15 and enter the result . . . . | 16 |

- If line 16 is a **gain,** enter the amount from line 16 on Form 1040, line 13, or Form 1040NR, line 14. Then go to line 17 below.
- If line 16 is a **loss,** skip lines 17 through 20 below. Then go to line 21. Also be sure to complete line 22.
- If line 16 is **zero,** skip lines 17 through 21 below and enter -0- on Form 1040, line 13, or Form 1040NR, line 14. Then go to line 22.

17 Are lines 15 and 16 **both** gains?

☐ **Yes.** Go to line 18.

☐ **No.** Skip lines 18 through 21, and go to line 22.

18 Enter the amount, if any, from line 7 of the **28% Rate Gain Worksheet** in the instructions . . ▶ | 18 |

19 Enter the amount, if any, from line 18 of the **Unrecaptured Section 1250 Gain Worksheet** in the instructions . . . . ▶ | 19 |

20 Are lines 18 and 19 **both** zero or blank?

☐ **Yes.** Complete the **Qualified Dividends and Capital Gain Tax Worksheet** in the instructions for Form 1040, line 44 (or in the instructions for Form 1040NR, line 42). **Do not** complete lines 21 and 22 below.

☐ **No.** Complete the **Schedule D Tax Worksheet** in the instructions. **Do not** complete lines 21 and 22 below.

21 If line 16 is a loss, enter here and on Form 1040, line 13, or Form 1040NR, line 14, the **smaller** of:

- The loss on line 16 or
- ($3,000), or if married filing separately, ($1,500)

} . . . . | 21 | ( )

Note. When figuring which amount is smaller, treat both amounts as positive numbers.

22 Do you have qualified dividends on Form 1040, line 9b, or Form 1040NR, line 10b?

☐ **Yes.** Complete the **Qualified Dividends and Capital Gain Tax Worksheet** in the instructions for Form 1040, line 44 (or in the instructions for Form 1040NR, line 42).

☐ **No.** Complete the rest of Form 1040 or Form 1040NR.

Schedule D (Form 1040) 2014

DRAFT AS OF June 9, 2014 DO NOT FILE

Form **8949** Department of the Treasury Internal Revenue Service

Sales and Other Dispositions of Capital Assets

► Information about Form 8949 and its separate instructions is at *www.irs.gov/form8949.*

► File with your Schedule D to list your transactions for lines 1b, 2, 3, 8b, 9, and 10 of Schedule D.

OMB No. 1545-0123

2014

Attachment Sequence No. **12A**

Name(s) shown on return	**Social security number or taxpayer identification number**

Before you check Box A, B, or C below, see whether you received any Form(s) 1099-B or substitute statement(s) from your broker. A substitute statement will have the same information as Form 1099-B. Either may show your basis (usually your cost) even if your broker did not report it to the IRS. Brokers must report basis to the IRS for most stock you bought in 2011 or later (and for certain debt instruments you bought in 2014 or later).

DRAFT AS OF June 12, 2014 DO NOT FILE

Part I **Short-Term.** Transactions involving capital assets you held 1 year or less are short term. For long-term transactions, see page 2.

Note. You may aggregate all short-term transactions reported on Form(s) 1099-B showing basis was reported to the IRS and for which no adjustments or codes are required. Enter the total directly on Schedule D, line 1a; you are not required to report these transactions on Form 8949 (see instructions).

You *must* check Box A, B, *or* C below. Check only one box. If more than one box applies for your short-term transactions, complete a separate Form 8949, page 1, for each applicable box. If you have more short-term transactions than will fit on this page for one or more of the boxes, complete as many forms with the same box checked as you need.

☐ **(A)** Short-term transactions reported on Form(s) 1099-B showing basis was reported to the IRS (see **Note** above)

☐ **(B)** Short-term transactions reported on Form(s) 1099-B showing basis was **not** reported to the IRS

☐ **(C)** Short-term transactions not reported to you on Form 1099-B

1 (a) Description of property (Example: 100 sh. XYZ Co.)	(b) Date acquired (Mo., day, yr.)	(c) Date sold or disposed (Mo., day, yr.)	(d) Proceeds (sales price) (see instructions)	(e) Cost or other basis. See the **Note** below and see *Column (e)* in the separate instructions	**Adjustment, if any, to gain or loss.** If you enter an amount in column (g), enter a code in column (f). **See the separate instructions.** (f) Code(s) from instructions	(g) Amount of adjustment	(h) **Gain or (loss).** Subtract column (e) from column (d) and combine the result with column (g)
2 Totals. Add the amounts in columns (d), (e), (g), and (h) (subtract negative amounts). Enter each total here and include on your Schedule D, **line 1b** (if **Box A** above is checked), **line 2** (if **Box B** above is checked), or **line 3** (if **Box C** above is checked) ►							

Note. If you checked Box A above but the basis reported to the IRS was incorrect, enter in column (e) the basis as reported to the IRS, and enter an adjustment in column (g) to correct the basis. See *Column (g)* in the separate instructions for how to figure the amount of the adjustment.

Form 8949 (2014) Attachment Sequence No. **12A** Page **2**

Name(s) shown on return. Name and SSN or taxpayer identification no. not required if shown on other side	**Social security number or taxpayer identification number**

Before you check Box D, E, or F below, see whether you received any Form(s) 1099-B or substitute statement(s) from your broker. A substitute statement will have the same information as Form 1099-B. Either may show your basis (usually your cost) even if your broker did not report it to the IRS. Brokers must report basis to the IRS for most stock you bought in 2011 or later (and for certain debt instruments you bought in 2014 or later).

Part II **Long-Term.** Transactions involving capital assets you held more than 1 year are long term. For short-term transactions, see page 1.

Note. You may aggregate all long-term transactions reported on Form(s) 1099-B showing basis was reported to the IRS and for which no adjustments or codes are required. Enter the total directly on Schedule D, line 8a; you are not required to report these transactions on Form 8949 (see instructions).

DRAFT AS OF June 12, 2014 DO NOT FILE

You *must* check Box D, E, *or* F below. Check only one box. If more than one box applies for your long-term transactions, complete a separate Form 8949, page 2, for each applicable box. If you have more long-term transactions than will fit on this page for one or more of the boxes, complete as many forms with the same box checked as you need.

☐ **(D)** Long-term transactions reported on Form(s) 1099-B showing basis was reported to the IRS (see **Note** above)
☐ **(E)** Long-term transactions reported on Form(s) 1099-B showing basis was **not** reported to the IRS
☐ **(F)** Long-term transactions not reported to you on Form 1099-B

1 **(a)** Description of property (Example: 100 sh. XYZ Co.)	**(b)** Date acquired (Mo., day, yr.)	**(c)** Date sold or disposed (Mo., day, yr.)	**(d)** Proceeds (sales price) (see instructions)	**(e)** Cost or other basis. See the **Note** below and see *Column (e)* in the separate instructions	Adjustment, if any, to gain or loss. If you enter an amount in column (g), enter a code in column (f). **See the separate instructions.** **(f)** Code(s) from instructions	**(g)** Amount of adjustment	**(h)** **Gain or (loss).** Subtract column (e) from column (d) and combine the result with column (g)
2 **Totals.** Add the amounts in columns (d), (e), (g), and (h) (subtract negative amounts). Enter each total here and include on your Schedule D, **line 8b** (if **Box D** above is checked), **line 9** (if **Box E** above is checked), or **line 10** (if **Box F** above is checked) ►							

Note. If you checked Box D above but the basis reported to the IRS was incorrect, enter in column (e) the basis as reported to the IRS, and enter an adjustment in column (g) to correct the basis. See *Column (g)* in the separate instructions for how to figure the amount of the adjustment.

Form **8949** (2014)

SCHEDULE SE (Form 1040)

Department of the Treasury
Internal Revenue Service (99)

Self-Employment Tax

▶ **Information about Schedule SE and its separate instructions is at *www.irs.gov/schedulese*.**

▶ **Attach to Form 1040 or Form 1040NR.**

OMB No. 1545-0074

2014

Attachment Sequence No. **17**

Name of person with **self-employment** income (as shown on Form 1040 or Form 1040NR)	Social security number of person with **self-employment** income ▶

Before you begin: To determine if you must file Schedule SE, see the instructions.

DRAFT AS OF May 14, 2014 DO NOT FILE

May I Use Short Schedule SE or Must I Use Long Schedule SE?

Note. Use this flowchart **only if** you must file Schedule SE. If unsure, see *Who Must File Schedule SE* in the instructions.

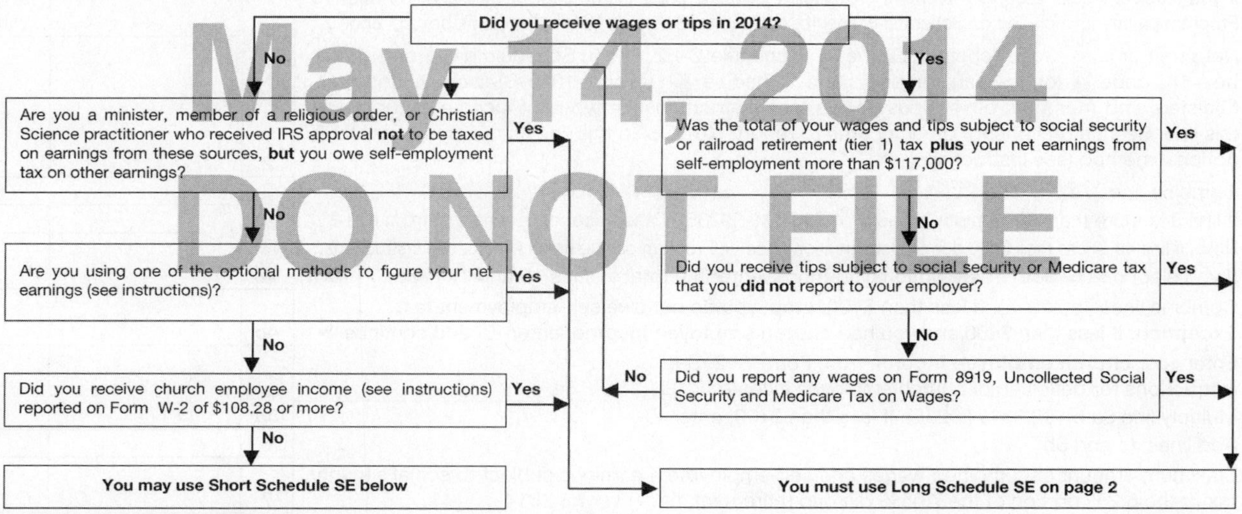

Section A—Short Schedule SE. Caution. Read above to see if you can use Short Schedule SE.

1a	Net farm profit or (loss) from Schedule F, line 34, and farm partnerships, Schedule K-1 (Form 1065), box 14, code A	**1a**	
b	If you received social security retirement or disability benefits, enter the amount of Conservation Reserve Program payments included on Schedule F, line 4b, or listed on Schedule K-1 (Form 1065), box 20, code Z	**1b**	( )
2	Net profit or (loss) from Schedule C, line 31; Schedule C-EZ, line 3; Schedule K-1 (Form 1065), box 14, code A (other than farming); and Schedule K-1 (Form 1065-B), box 9, code J1. Ministers and members of religious orders, see instructions for types of income to report on this line. See instructions for other income to report	**2**	
3	Combine lines 1a, 1b, and 2	**3**	
4	Multiply line 3 by 92.35% (.9235). If less than $400, you do not owe self-employment tax; **do not** file this schedule unless you have an amount on line 1b . . . . . ▶	**4**	
	Note. If line 4 is less than $400 due to Conservation Reserve Program payments on line 1b, see instructions.		
5	**Self-employment tax.** If the amount on line 4 is: • $117,000 or less, multiply line 4 by 15.3% (.153). Enter the result here and on **Form 1040, line 57,** or **Form 1040NR, line 55** • More than $117,000, multiply line 4 by 2.9% (.029). Then, add $14,508 to the result. Enter the total here and on **Form 1040, line 57,** or **Form 1040NR, line 55**	**5**	
6	**Deduction for one-half of self-employment tax.** Multiply line 5 by 50% (.50). Enter the result here and on **Form 1040, line 27,** or **Form 1040NR, line 27** **6**		

For Paperwork Reduction Act Notice, see your tax return instructions. Cat. No. 11358Z **Schedule SE (Form 1040) 2014**

Schedule SE (Form 1040) 2014 Attachment Sequence No. **17** Page **2**

Name of person with **self-employment** income (as shown on Form 1040 or Form 1040NR) | Social security number of person with **self-employment** income ▶

DRAFT AS OF May 14, 2014 DO NOT FILE

Section B—Long Schedule SE

Part I Self-Employment Tax

Note. If your only income subject to self-employment tax is **church employee income,** see instructions. Also see instructions for the definition of church employee income.

Line	Description	Box	Amount	
A	If you are a minister, member of a religious order, or Christian Science practitioner **and** you filed Form 4361, but you had $400 or more of **other** net earnings from self-employment, check here and continue with Part I ▶ ☐			
1a	Net farm profit or (loss) from Schedule F, line 34, and farm partnerships, Schedule K-1 (Form 1065), box 14, code A. **Note.** Skip lines 1a and 1b if you use the farm optional method (see instructions)	1a		
b	If you received social security retirement or disability benefits, enter the amount of Conservation Reserve Program payments included on Schedule F, line 4b, or listed on Schedule K-1 (Form 1065), box 20, code Z	1b	(	)
2	Net profit or (loss) from Schedule C, line 31; Schedule C-EZ, line 3; Schedule K-1 (Form 1065), box 14, code A (other than farming); and Schedule K-1 (Form 1065-B), box 9, code J1. Ministers and members of religious orders, see instructions for types of income to report on this line. See instructions for other income to report. **Note.** Skip this line if you use the nonfarm optional method (see instructions)	2		
3	Combine lines 1a, 1b, and 2	3		
4a	If line 3 is more than zero, multiply line 3 by 92.35% (.9235). Otherwise, enter amount from line 3. **Note.** If line 4a is less than $400 due to Conservation Reserve Program payments on line 1b, see instructions.	4a		
b	If you elect one or both of the optional methods, enter the total of lines 15 and 17 here	4b		
c	Combine lines 4a and 4b. If less than $400, **stop**; you do not owe self-employment tax. **Exception.** If less than $400 and you had **church employee income,** enter -0- and continue ▶	4c		
5a	Enter your **church employee income** from Form W-2. See instructions for definition of church employee income — 5a			
b	Multiply line 5a by 92.35% (.9235). If less than $100, enter -0-	5b		
6	Add lines 4c and 5b	6		
7	Maximum amount of combined wages and self-employment earnings subject to social security tax or the 6.2% portion of the 7.65% railroad retirement (tier 1) tax for 2014	7	117,000	00
8a	Total social security wages and tips (total of boxes 3 and 7 on Form(s) W-2) and railroad retirement (tier 1) compensation. If $117,000 or more, skip lines 8b through 10, and go to line 11 — 8a			
b	Unreported tips subject to social security tax (from Form 4137, line 10) — 8b			
c	Wages subject to social security tax (from Form 8919, line 10) — 8c			
d	Add lines 8a, 8b, and 8c	8d		
9	Subtract line 8d from line 7. If zero or less, enter -0- here and on line 10 and go to line 11 ▶	9		
10	Multiply the **smaller** of line 6 or line 9 by 12.4% (.124)	10		
11	Multiply line 6 by 2.9% (.029)	11		
12	**Self-employment tax.** Add lines 10 and 11. Enter here and on **Form 1040, line 57,** or **Form 1040NR, line 55**	12		
13	**Deduction for one-half of self-employment tax.** Multiply line 12 by 50% (.50). Enter the result here and on **Form 1040, line 27,** or **Form 1040NR, line 27** — 13			

Part II Optional Methods To Figure Net Earnings (see instructions)

Farm Optional Method. You may use this method **only** if **(a)** your gross farm income[1] was not more than $7,200, **or (b)** your net farm profits[2] were less than $5,198.

Line	Description	Box	Amount	
14	Maximum income for optional methods	14	4,800	00
15	Enter the **smaller** of: two-thirds (2/3) of gross farm income[1] (not less than zero) **or** $4,800. Also include this amount on line 4b above	15		

Nonfarm Optional Method. You may use this method **only** if **(a)** your net nonfarm profits[3] were less than $5,198 and also less than 72.189% of your gross nonfarm income,[4] **and (b)** you had net earnings from self-employment of at least $400 in 2 of the prior 3 years. **Caution.** You may use this method no more than five times.

Line	Description	Box	Amount	
16	Subtract line 15 from line 14	16		
17	Enter the **smaller** of: two-thirds (2/3) of gross nonfarm income[4] (not less than zero) **or** the amount on line 16. Also include this amount on line 4b above	17		

[1] From Sch. F, line 9, and Sch. K-1 (Form 1065), box 14, code B.

[2] From Sch. F, line 34, and Sch. K-1 (Form 1065), box 14, code A—minus the amount you would have entered on line 1b had you not used the optional method.

[3] From Sch. C, line 31; Sch. C-EZ, line 3; Sch. K-1 (Form 1065), box 14, code A; and Sch. K-1 (Form 1065-B), box 9, code J1.

[4] From Sch. C, line 7; Sch. C-EZ, line 1; Sch. K-1 (Form 1065), box 14, code C; and Sch. K-1 (Form 1065-B), box 9, code J2.

Schedule SE (Form 1040) 2014

Qualified Dividends and Capital Gain Tax Worksheet—Line 44

Keep for Your Records

Before you begin:
- √ See the earlier instructions for line 44 to see if you can use this worksheet to figure your tax.
- √ Before completing this worksheet, complete Form 1040 through line 43.
- √ If you do not have to file Schedule D and you received capital gain distributions, be sure you checked the box on line 13 of Form 1040.

1. Enter the amount from Form 1040, line 43. However, if you are filing Form 2555 or 2555-EZ (relating to foreign earned income), enter the amount from line 3 of the Foreign Earned Income Tax Worksheet . . . . . 1. ______
2. Enter the amount from Form 1040, line 9b* . . . . . 2. ______
3. Are you filing Schedule D?*
   ☐ **Yes.** Enter the **smaller** of line 15 or 16 of Schedule D. If either line 15 or line 16 is blank or a loss, enter -0-
   ☐ **No.** Enter the amount from Form 1040, line 13 . . . . . 3. ______
4. Add lines 2 and 3 . . . . . 4. ______
5. If filing Form 4952 (used to figure investment interest expense deduction), enter any amount from line 4g of that form. Otherwise, enter -0- . . . . . 5. ______
6. Subtract line 5 from line 4. If zero or less, enter -0- . . . . . 6. ______
7. Subtract line 6 from line 1. If zero or less, enter -0- . . . . . 7. ______
8. Enter:
   $36,900 if single or married filing separately,
   $73,800 if married filing jointly or qualifying widow(er),
   $49,400 if head of household. . . . . . 8. ______
9. Enter the smaller of line 1 or line 8 . . . . . 9. ______
10. Enter the smaller of line 7 or line 9 . . . . . 10. ______
11. Subtract line 10 from line 9. This amount is taxed at 0% . . . . . 11. ______
12. Enter the smaller of line 1 or line 6 . . . . . 12. ______
13. Enter the amount from line 11 . . . . . 13. ______
14. Subtract line 13 from line 12 . . . . . 14. ______
15. Enter:
    $406,750 if single,
    $228,800 if married filing separately,
    $457,600 if married filing jointly or qualifying widow(er),
    $432,200 if head of household. . . . . . 15. ______
16. Enter the smaller of line 1 or line 15 . . . . . 16. ______
17. Add lines 7 and 11 . . . . . 17. ______
18. Subtract line 17 from line 16. If zero or less, enter -0- . . . . . 18. ______
19. Enter the smaller of line 14 or line 18 . . . . . 19. ______
20. Multiply line 19 by 15% (.15) . . . . . 20. ______
21. Add lines 11 and 19 . . . . . 21. ______
22. Subtract line 21 from line 12 . . . . . 22. ______
23. Multiply line 22 by 20% (.20) . . . . . 23. ______
24. Figure the tax on the amount on line 7. If the amount on line 7 is less than $100,000, use the Tax Table to figure the tax. If the amount on line 7 is $100,000 or more, use the Tax Computation Worksheet . . . . . 24. ______
25. Add lines 20, 23, and 24 . . . . . 25. ______
26. Figure the tax on the amount on line 1. If the amount on line 1 is less than $100,000, use the Tax Table to figure the tax. If the amount on line 1 is $100,000 or more, use the Tax Computation Worksheet . . . . . 26. ______
27. **Tax on all taxable income.** Enter the **smaller** of line 25 or line 26. Also include this amount on Form 1040, line 44. If you are filing Form 2555 or 2555-EZ, do not enter this amount on Form 1040, line 44. Instead, enter it on line 4 of the Foreign Earned Income Tax Worksheet . . . . . 27. ______

**If you are filing Form 2555 or 2555-EZ, see the footnote in the Foreign Earned Income Tax Worksheet before completing this line.*

Student Name ______________________

Class/Section ______________________

Date ______________________

KEY NUMBER TAX RETURN SUMMARY

CHAPTER 9

Comprehensive Problem

Adjusted Gross Income (Line 37) ______________

Profit or Loss from Business (Line 12, Form 1040) ______________

Total Self-Employment Tax, Schedule SE (Line 5) ______________

Tax Liability (Line 63) ______________

Tax Overpaid (Line 75) ______________

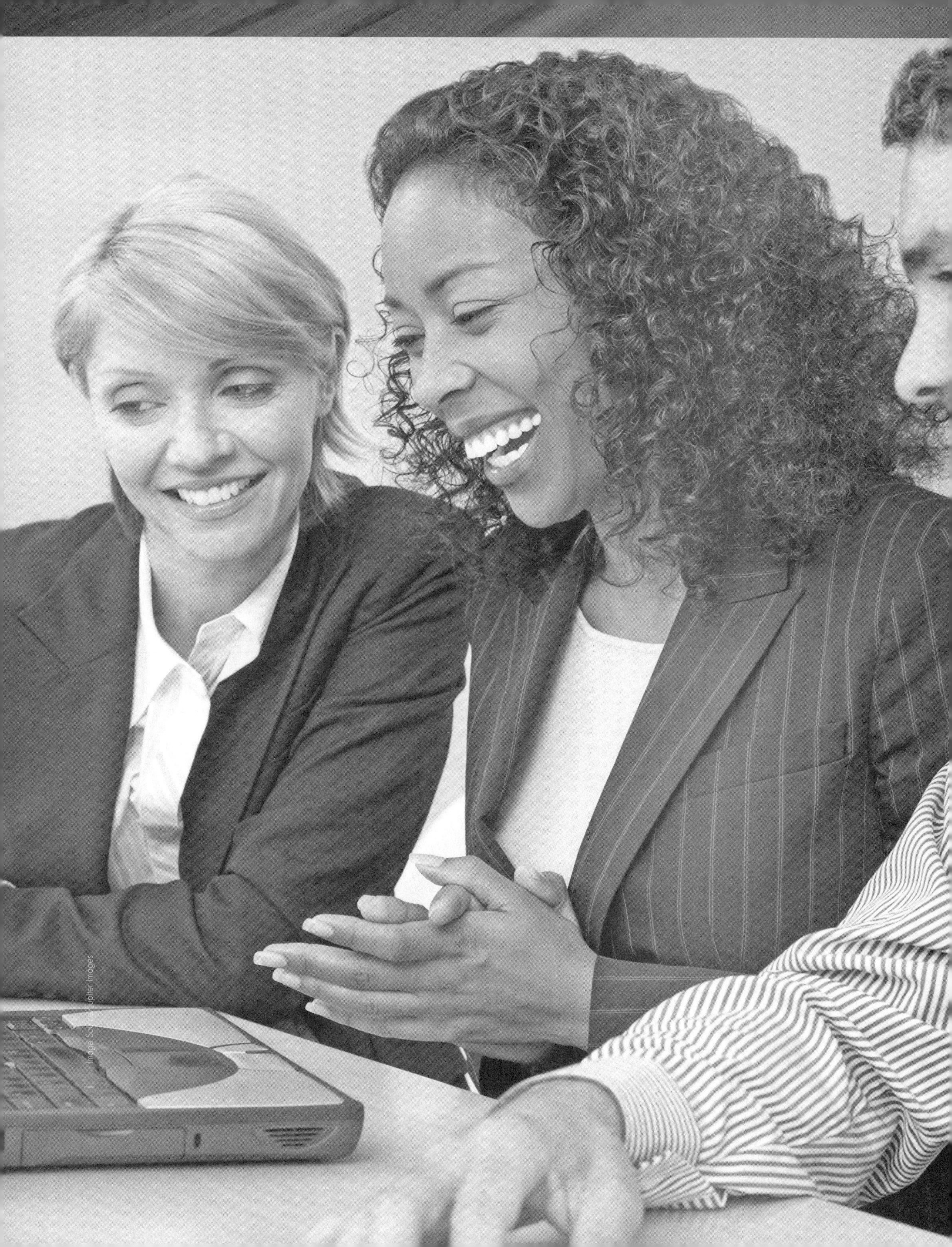

Image Source/Jupiter Images

CHAPTER 10

Partnership Taxation

LEARNING OBJECTIVES

After completing this chapter, you should be able to:

LO 10.1 Define a partnership for tax purposes.

LO 10.2 Understand the basic tax rules for partnership formation and operation.

LO 10.3 Summarize the rules for partnership income reporting.

LO 10.4 Describe the tax treatment of partnership distributions.

LO 10.5 Determine partnership tax years.

LO 10.6 Identify the tax treatment of transactions between partners and their partnerships.

LO 10.7 Understand the application of the at-risk rule to partnerships.

LO 10.8 Analyze the advantages and disadvantages of limited liability companies (LLCs).

OVERVIEW

In recent years, partnerships have been used increasingly as an organizational form. The partnership form allows taxpayers considerable flexibility in terms of contributions, income and loss allocations, and distributions. One of the primary benefits of the partnership is that partnership income is only taxed at the partner level. Corporate taxpayers (other than S corporations) pay tax at the corporate level and often again at the shareholder level (see Chapter 11), which results in corporate double taxation. Since a partnership's income passes through to the partners, there is no tax at the entity level, only at the partner level.

One of the disadvantages of partnerships over corporations has been the lack of limited liability for partners while corporate shareholders enjoy protection from liability to third parties (e.g., creditors of the corporation). In recent years, however, the advent of the limited liability company (LLC) and the limited liability partnership (LLP) has provided partners this important legal benefit. Because LLCs and LLPs are taxed like partnerships, they are included in this chapter on partnership taxation.

This chapter will provide an understanding of the tax treatment of partnerships and the tax forms (Form 1065 and Schedule K-1) related to reporting partnership income or loss.

Learning Objective 10.1

Define a partnership for tax purposes.

NATURE OF PARTNERSHIP TAXATION

Partnership tax returns are information returns only. Returns show the amount of income by type and the allocation of the income to the partners. Partnership income and other items are passed through to the partners, and each partner is taxed on his or her distributive share of partnership income. Partnership income is taxable to the partner even if he or she does not actually receive it in cash.

Even though the return is only informational, partnerships do have to make various elections and select accounting methods and periods. For example, partnerships must select depreciation and inventory methods. In addition, partnerships are legal entities under civil law, and in most states have rights under the Uniform Partnership Act.

What Is a Partnership?

The tax law defines a partnership as a syndicate, group, pool, joint venture, or other unincorporated organization through or by means of which any business, financial operation, or venture is carried on, and which is not classified as a corporation, trust, or estate. The mere co-ownership of property does not constitute a partnership; the partners must engage in some type of business or financial activity.

Ordinary partnerships, or general partnerships as they are often called, may be formed by a simple verbal agreement or "handshake" between partners. In contrast, the formation of corporations, limited partnerships, limited liability companies (LLCs), and limited liability partnerships (LLPs) must be documented in writing and the entity must be legally registered in the state in which it is formed. Even though general partnerships may be formed by verbal agreement between partners, partners usually document their agreement in writing with the help of lawyers in case disagreements arise during the course of operations. General partners usually take on the risk of legal liability for certain actions of the partnership or debts of the partnership, as specified under state law. To limit some of the liability exposure of operating a joint business, many partnerships are created formally as limited partnerships, LLCs, or LLPs for licensed professionals such as attorneys and accountants.

Entities generally treated as partnerships for tax law purposes include limited partnerships, LLCs, and LLPs. Limited partnerships have one or more general partners and one or more limited partners. General partners participate in management and have unlimited liability for partnership obligations. Limited partners may not participate in management and have no liability for partnership obligations beyond their capital contributions. Many partnerships are formed as limited partnerships because the limited liability helps to attract passive investors. LLCs and LLPs are relatively new legal entities which combine the limited liability of corporations with the tax treatment of partnerships. LLCs and LLPs are discussed later in this chapter.

EXAMPLE Avery and Roberta buy a rental house which they hold jointly. The house is rented and they share the income and expenses for the year. Avery and Roberta have not formed a partnership. However, if they had bought and operated a store together, a partnership would have been formed. Although the ownership of real estate may not rise to the level of a business requiring a partnership return, co-owners of real estate frequently do choose to operate in a partnership, limited partnership, or LLC form. ♦

Self-Study Problem 10.1 *See Appendix E for Solutions to Self-Study Problems*

Indicate, by placing a check in the appropriate blank, whether each of the following is or is not required to file a partnership return.

	Yes	No
1. Duncan and Clyde purchase and operate a plumbing business together.	______	______
2. Ellen and Walter form a corporation to operate a plumbing business.	______	______
3. George and Marty buy a duplex to hold as rental property, which is not considered an active business.	______	______
4. Howard and Sally form a joint venture to drill for and sell oil.	______	______
5. Ted and Joyce purchase and operate a candy store.	______	______

PARTNERSHIP FORMATION

Learning Objective 10.2

Understand the basic tax rules for partnership formation and operation.

Generally, there is no gain or loss recognized by a partnership or any of its partners when property is contributed to a partnership in exchange for an interest in the partnership. This rule applies to the formation of a partnership as well as any subsequent contributions to the partnership. However, there are exceptions to the nonrecognition rule. On formation, income may be recognized when a partnership interest is received in exchange for services performed by the partner for the partnership or when a partner transfers to a partnership, property subject to a liability exceeding that partner's basis in the property transferred. In this situation, gain is recognized to the extent that the portion of the liability allocable to the other partners exceeds the basis of the property contributed. If a partner receives money or other property from the partnership, in addition to an interest in the partnership, the transaction may be considered in part a sale or exchange, and a gain or loss may be recognized.

EXAMPLE Dunn and Church form the Dunn & Church Partnership. Dunn contributes a building with a fair market value of $90,000 and an adjusted basis of $55,000 for a 50 percent interest in the partnership. Dunn does not recognize a gain on the transfer of the building to the partnership. Church performs services for the partnership for his 50 percent interest which is worth $90,000. Church must report $90,000 in ordinary income for the receipt of an interest in the partnership in exchange for services provided to the partnership. ♦

EXAMPLE Ann and Keith form the A&K Partnership. Ann contributes a building with a fair market value of $200,000 and an adjusted basis of $45,000 for a 50 percent interest in the partnership. The building is subject to a liability of $130,000. Keith contributes cash of $70,000 for a 50 percent interest in the partnership. Ann must recognize a gain on the transfer of the building to the partnership equal to $20,000, the amount by which the liability allocable to Keith, $65,000 (50% × $130,000), exceeds the basis of the building, $45,000. Keith does not recognize a gain on the contribution of cash to the partnership. ♦

A partner's original basis in a partnership interest is equal to the basis of the property transferred plus cash contributed to the partnership. If gain is recognized on the transfer, the partner's basis in the partnership interest is increased by the gain recognized. In addition, the basis is reduced by any liabilities of the contributing partner assumed by the other partners through the partnership. For example, if a one-third partner is relieved of a $90,000 liability by the partnership, he or she would reduce by $60,000 (⅔ of $90,000) his or her partnership interest basis. After the original basis in the partnership interest is established, the basis is adjusted for future earnings, losses, and distributions from the partnership.

EXAMPLE Prentice contributes cash of $50,000 and property with a fair market value of $110,000 (adjusted basis of $30,000) to the P&H Partnership. Prentice's basis in the partnership interest is $80,000 ($50,000 + $30,000). ♦

EXAMPLE Assume that Prentice, in the example above, also received a partnership interest worth $15,000 for services provided to the partnership. She must recognize $15,000 in ordinary income, and her basis in the partnership interest is $95,000 ($80,000 + $15,000). ♦

EXAMPLE Darnell contributes property with a fair market value of $110,000 and an adjusted basis of $30,000, subject to a liability of $20,000, to a partnership in exchange for a 25 percent interest in the partnership. Darnell's basis in his partnership interest is $15,000 [$30,000 − ($20,000 × 75%)]. ♦

The basis of a partner's interest in a partnership changes due to partnership activities. A partner's basis in his or her partnership interest is increased by the partner's share of (1) additional contributions to the partnership, (2) net ordinary taxable income of the partnership, and (3) capital gains and other income of the partnership. Alternatively, a partner's basis is reduced (but not below zero) by the partner's share of (1) distributions of partnership property, (2) losses from operations of the partnership, and (3) capital losses and other deductions of the partnership. In addition, changes in partnership liabilities will affect the basis of a partner's partnership interest.

EXAMPLE Reid has a 50 percent interest in the Reid Partnership. Her basis in her partnership interest at the beginning of 2014 is $12,000. For 2014, the partnership reports ordinary income of $15,000, a capital gain of $3,000, and charitable contributions of $700. The basis of Reid's partnership interest, after considering the above items, would be $20,650 ($12,000 beginning basis + $7,500 share of partnership ordinary income + $1,500 share of partnership capital gain − $350 share of partnership charitable contributions). ♦

The partnership's basis in property contributed by a partner is equal to the partner's adjusted basis in the property at the time of the contribution plus any gain recognized by the partner. The transfer of liabilities to the partnership by the partner does not impact the basis of the property to the partnership. The partnership's holding period for the property contributed to the partnership includes the partner's holding period. For example, long-term capital gain property may be transferred to a partnership by a partner and sold immediately, and any gain would be long-term, assuming the property is a capital asset to the partnership.

EXAMPLE Clark contributes property to the Rose Partnership in exchange for a partnership interest. The property contributed has an adjusted basis to Clark of $45,000 and a fair market value of $75,000 on the date of the contribution. The partnership's basis in the property is $45,000. ♦

Self-Study Problem 10.2 ***See Appendix E for Solutions to Self-Study Problems***

John and Linda form the J&L Partnership. John contributes cash of $36,000 for a 40 percent interest in the partnership. Linda contributes equipment worth $54,000 with an adjusted basis of $17,500 for a 60 percent partnership interest.

1. What is John's recognized gain or loss on the contribution? $__________
2. What is John's basis in his partnership interest? $__________
3. What is Linda's recognized gain or loss on the contribution? $__________
4. What is Linda's basis in her partnership interest? $__________
5. What is J&L Partnership's basis in the equipment received from Linda? $__________

PARTNERSHIP INCOME REPORTING

Learning Objective 10.3

Summarize the rules for partnership income reporting.

A partnership is required to report its income and other items on Form 1065, U.S. Partnership Return of Income, even though the partnership entity does not pay federal income tax. The tax return is due on the fifteenth day of the fourth month following the close of the partnership's tax year. When reporting partnership taxable income, certain transactions must be separated rather than being reported as part of ordinary income. The primary items that must be reported separately are capital gains and losses, Section 1231 gains and losses, dividends, interest income, casualty gains and losses, tax-exempt income, retirement contributions, charitable contributions, and most credits. These items are listed as separate income or expenses, since they are subject to special calculations or limitations on the tax returns of the partners.

After the special items are separated, the partnership reports the remainder of its ordinary income or loss. The ordinary income or loss of a partnership is calculated in the same manner as that of an individual, except the partnership is not allowed to deduct the standard deduction, amounts for exemptions, foreign taxes paid, charitable contributions, net operating losses, or personal itemized deductions. Schedule K-1 of Form 1065 presents the allocation of ordinary income or loss, special income and deductions, and gains and losses to each partner. The partners report the amounts from their Schedules K-1 on their own tax returns.

A partner's deductible loss from a partnership is limited to the basis of the partner's partnership interest at the end of the year in which the loss was incurred. The partner's partnership basis cannot be reduced below zero. Any unused losses may be carried forward and reported in a future year when there is partnership basis available to be reduced by the loss.

Form 1099-K Reporting Merchant Card and Third-Party Payments

Since 2011, banks and online payment networks ("payment settlement entities"), such as PayPal, are required to use Form 1099-K to report credit card sales and other reportable sales transactions to the IRS and to the businesses making reportable sales. The reporting requirement is triggered for an entity when the total dollar amount of transactions for a particular merchant exceeds $20,000 and the total number of transactions exceeds 200. Form 1099-K is a potentially powerful IRS enforcement tool for matching business income to sellers' tax returns and, thereby, assuring business income is reported. Estimates show that as little as 50 percent of income is correctly reported when information reporting is not required.

Self-Study Problem 10.3 *See Appendix E for Solutions to Self-Study Problems*

Robert Conrad and Jan Springs are equal partners in the Malus Valley Partnership. During 2014, the partnership began operations and had the following income and expenses:

Gross income from operations	$255,600
Deductions:	
Salaries to employees	$168,000
Rent	12,000
Payroll taxes	6,100
Depreciation	9,250
Charitable contributions (to 50 percent organizations)	1,500
Cash withdrawals ($25,000 for each partner)	50,000

The partnership's balance sheet is as follows:

Malus Valley Balance Sheet as of December 31, 2014

Assets:		
Cash		$ 27,000
Accounts receivable		10,000
Land		115,000
Building	$115,000	
Less: accumulated depreciation	(9,250)	105,750
Total Assets		$257,750
Liabilities and Partners' Capital:		
Accounts payable		$ 29,750
Mortgage payable		187,750
Partners' capital ($31,500 contributed, $15,750 by each partner)		40,250
Total Liabilities and Partners' Capital		$257,750

Complete Form 1065, Page 1, and Schedules K, L, M-1, and M-2 on Pages 10-7 to 10-11 for Malus Valley. Also, complete Schedule K-1 on Pages 10-13 and 10-14 for Robert.

Self-Study Problem 10.3

Form **1065** | **U.S. Return of Partnership Income** | OMB No. 1545-0123

Department of the Treasury
Internal Revenue Service

For calendar year 2014, or tax year beginning ________, 2014, ending ________, 20 ____.
► Information about Form 1065 and its separate instructions is at *www.irs.gov/form1065*.

2014

A Principal business activity	Name of partnership	D Employer identification number
B Principal product or service	Type or Print — Number, street, and room or suite no. If a P.O. box, see the instructions.	E Date business started
C Business code number	City or town, state or province, country, and ZIP or foreign postal code	F Total assets (see the instructions) $

DRAFT AS OF
August 4, 2014
DO NOT FILE

G Check applicable boxes: (1) ☐ Initial return (2) ☐ Final return (3) ☐ Name change (4) ☐ Address change (5) ☐ Amended return
(6) ☐ Technical termination - also check (1) or (2)

H Check accounting method: (1) ☐ Cash (2) ☐ Accrual (3) ☐ Other (specify) ►

I Number of Schedules K-1. Attach one for each person who was a partner at any time during the tax year ►

J Check if Schedules C and M-3 are attached . . . ☐

Caution. *Include **only** trade or business income and expenses on lines 1a through 22 below. See the instructions for more information.*

Income	1a	Gross receipts or sales	1a			
	b	Returns and allowances	1b			
	c	Balance. Subtract line 1b from line 1a			1c	
	2	Cost of goods sold (attach Form 1125-A)			2	
	3	Gross profit. Subtract line 2 from line 1c			3	
	4	Ordinary income (loss) from other partnerships, estates, and trusts (attach statement)			4	
	5	Net farm profit (loss) (attach Schedule F (Form 1040))			5	
	6	Net gain (loss) from Form 4797, Part II, line 17 (attach Form 4797)			6	
	7	Other income (loss) (attach statement)			7	
	8	**Total income (loss).** Combine lines 3 through 7			8	
Deductions (see the instructions for limitations)	9	Salaries and wages (other than to partners) (less employment credits)			9	
	10	Guaranteed payments to partners			10	
	11	Repairs and maintenance			11	
	12	Bad debts			12	
	13	Rent			13	
	14	Taxes and licenses			14	
	15	Interest			15	
	16a	Depreciation (if required, attach Form 4562)	16a			
	b	Less depreciation reported on Form 1125-A and elsewhere on return	16b		16c	
	17	Depletion **(Do not deduct oil and gas depletion.)**			17	
	18	Retirement plans, etc.			18	
	19	Employee benefit programs			19	
	20	Other deductions (attach statement)			20	
	21	**Total deductions.** Add the amounts shown in the far right column for lines 9 through 20			21	
	22	**Ordinary business income (loss).** Subtract line 21 from line 8			22	

Sign Here

Under penalties of perjury, I declare that I have examined this return, including accompanying schedules and statements, and to the best of my knowledge and belief, it is true, correct, and complete. Declaration of preparer (other than general partner or limited liability company member manager) is based on all information of which preparer has any knowledge.

▶ Signature of general partner or limited liability company member manager ▶ Date

May the IRS discuss this return with the preparer shown below (see instructions)? ☐ Yes ☐ No

Paid Preparer Use Only

Print/Type preparer's name	Preparer's signature	Date	Check ☐ if self-employed	PTIN
Firm's name ►			Firm's EIN ►	
Firm's address ►			Phone no.	

Form 1065 (2014) Page **2**

Schedule B **Other Information**

		Yes	No
1	What type of entity is filing this return? Check the applicable box: **a** ☐ Domestic general partnership **b** ☐ Domestic limited partnership **c** ☐ Domestic limited liability company **d** ☐ Domestic limited liability partnership **e** ☐ Foreign partnership **f** ☐ Other ▶		
2	At any time during the tax year, was any partner in the partnership a disregarded entity, a partnership (including an entity treated as a partnership), a trust, an S corporation, an estate (other than an estate of a deceased partner), or a nominee or similar person?		
3	At the end of the tax year:		
a	Did any foreign or domestic corporation, partnership (including any entity treated as a partnership), trust, or tax-exempt organization, or any foreign government own, directly or indirectly, an interest of 50% or more in the profit, loss, or capital of the partnership? For rules of constructive ownership, see instructions. If "Yes," attach Schedule B-1, Information on Partners Owning 50% or More of the Partnership		
b	Did any individual or estate own, directly or indirectly, an interest of 50% or more in the profit, loss, or capital of the partnership? For rules of constructive ownership, see instructions. If "Yes," attach Schedule B-1, Information on Partners Owning 50% or More of the Partnership		
4	At the end of the tax year, did the partnership:		
a	Own directly 20% or more, or own, directly or indirectly, 50% or more of the total voting power of all classes of stock entitled to vote of any foreign or domestic corporation? For rules of constructive ownership, see instructions. If "Yes," complete (i) through (iv) below		

(i) Name of Corporation	**(ii)** Employer Identification Number (if any)	**(iii)** Country of Incorporation	**(iv)** Percentage Owned in Voting Stock

		Yes	No
b	Own directly an interest of 20% or more, or own, directly or indirectly, an interest of 50% or more in the profit, loss, or capital in any foreign or domestic partnership (including an entity treated as a partnership) or in the beneficial interest of a trust? For rules of constructive ownership, see instructions. If "Yes," complete (i) through (v) below		

(i) Name of Entity	**(ii)** Employer Identification Number (if any)	**(iii)** Type of Entity	**(iv)** Country of Organization	**(v)** Maximum Percentage Owned in Profit, Loss, or Capital

		Yes	No
5	Did the partnership file Form 8893, Election of Partnership Level Tax Treatment, or an election statement under section 6231(a)(1)(B)(ii) for partnership-level tax treatment, that is in effect for this tax year? See Form 8893 for more details		
6	Does the partnership satisfy **all four** of the following conditions?		
a	The partnership's total receipts for the tax year were less than $250,000.		
b	The partnership's total assets at the end of the tax year were less than $1 million.		
c	Schedules K-1 are filed with the return and furnished to the partners on or before the due date (including extensions) for the partnership return.		
d	The partnership is not filing and is not required to file Schedule M-3 If "Yes," the partnership is not required to complete Schedules L, M-1, and M-2; Item F on page 1 of Form 1065; or Item L on Schedule K-1.		
7	Is this partnership a publicly traded partnership as defined in section 469(k)(2)?		
8	During the tax year, did the partnership have any debt that was cancelled, was forgiven, or had the terms modified so as to reduce the principal amount of the debt?		
9	Has this partnership filed, or is it required to file, Form 8918, Material Advisor Disclosure Statement, to provide information on any reportable transaction?		
10	At any time during calendar year 2014, did the partnership have an interest in or a signature or other authority over a financial account in a foreign country (such as a bank account, securities account, or other financial account)? See the instructions for exceptions and filing requirements for FinCEN Form 114, Report of Foreign Bank and Financial Accounts (FBAR). If "Yes," enter the name of the foreign country. ▶		

Form **1065** (2014)

DRAFT AS OF August 4, 2014 DO NOT FILE

Form 1065 (2014) Page 3

Schedule B Other Information *(continued)*

		Yes	No
11	At any time during the tax year, did the partnership receive a distribution from, or was it the grantor of, or transferor to, a foreign trust? If "Yes," the partnership may have to file Form 3520, Annual Return To Report Transactions With Foreign Trusts and Receipt of Certain Foreign Gifts. See instructions		
12a	Is the partnership making, or had it previously made (and not revoked), a section 754 election? . . . . . . See instructions for details regarding a section 754 election.		
b	Did the partnership make for this tax year an optional basis adjustment under section 743(b) or 734(b)? If "Yes," attach a statement showing the computation and allocation of the basis adjustment. See instructions		
c	Is the partnership required to adjust the basis of partnership assets under section 743(b) or 734(b) because of a substantial built-in loss (as defined under section 743(d)) or substantial basis reduction (as defined under section 734(d))? If "Yes," attach a statement showing the computation and allocation of the basis adjustment. See instructions		
13	Check this box if, during the current or prior tax year, the partnership distributed any property received in a like-kind exchange or contributed such property to another entity (other than disregarded entities wholly owned by the partnership throughout the tax year) . . . . ▶ ☐		
14	At any time during the tax year, did the partnership distribute to any partner a tenancy-in-common or other undivided interest in partnership property?		
15	If the partnership is required to file Form 8858, Information Return of U.S. Persons With Respect To Foreign Disregarded Entities, enter the number of Forms 8858 attached. See instructions ▶		
16	Does the partnership have any foreign partners? If "Yes," enter the number of Forms 8805, Foreign Partner's Information Statement of Section 1446 Withholding Tax, filed for this partnership. ▶		
17	Enter the number of Forms 8865, Return of U.S. Persons With Respect to Certain Foreign Partnerships, attached to this return. ▶		
18a	Did you make any payments in 2014 that would require you to file Form(s) 1099? See instructions		
b	If "Yes," did you or will you file required Form(s) 1099?		
19	Enter the number of Form(s) 5471, Information Return of U.S. Persons With Respect To Certain Foreign Corporations, attached to this return. ▶		
20	Enter the number of partners that are foreign governments under section 892. ▶		

Designation of Tax Matters Partner (see instructions)

Enter below the general partner or member-manager designated as the tax matters partner (TMP) for the tax year of this return:

Name of designated TMP ▶		Identifying number of TMP ▶	
If the TMP is an entity, name of TMP representative ▶		Phone number of TMP ▶	
Address of designated TMP ▶			

Form **1065** (2014)

DRAFT AS OF
August 4, 2014
DO NOT FILE

Self-Study Problem 10.3

Form 1065 (2014) Page **4**

DRAFT AS OF August 4, 2014 DO NOT FILE

Schedule K		Partners' Distributive Share Items		Total amount
Income (Loss)	1	Ordinary business income (loss) (page 1, line 22)	1	
	2	Net rental real estate income (loss) (attach Form 8825)	2	
	3a	Other gross rental income (loss) — 3a		
	b	Expenses from other rental activities (attach statement) — 3b		
	c	Other net rental income (loss). Subtract line 3b from line 3a	3c	
	4	Guaranteed payments	4	
	5	Interest income	5	
	6	Dividends: a Ordinary dividends	6a	
		b Qualified dividends — 6b		
	7	Royalties	7	
	8	Net short-term capital gain (loss) (attach Schedule D (Form 1065))	8	
	9a	Net long-term capital gain (loss) (attach Schedule D (Form 1065))	9a	
	b	Collectibles (28%) gain (loss) — 9b		
	c	Unrecaptured section 1250 gain (attach statement) — 9c		
	10	Net section 1231 gain (loss) (attach Form 4797)	10	
	11	Other income (loss) (see instructions) Type ▶	11	
Deductions	12	Section 179 deduction (attach Form 4562)	12	
	13a	Contributions	13a	
	b	Investment interest expense	13b	
	c	Section 59(e)(2) expenditures: (1) Type ▶ (2) Amount ▶	13c(2)	
	d	Other deductions (see instructions) Type ▶	13d	
Self-Employment	14a	Net earnings (loss) from self-employment	14a	
	b	Gross farming or fishing income	14b	
	c	Gross nonfarm income	14c	
Credits	15a	Low-income housing credit (section 42(j)(5))	15a	
	b	Low-income housing credit (other)	15b	
	c	Qualified rehabilitation expenditures (rental real estate) (attach Form 3468, if applicable)	15c	
	d	Other rental real estate credits (see instructions) Type ▶	15d	
	e	Other rental credits (see instructions) Type ▶	15e	
	f	Other credits (see instructions) Type ▶	15f	
Foreign Transactions	16a	Name of country or U.S. possession ▶		
	b	Gross income from all sources	16b	
	c	Gross income sourced at partner level	16c	
		Foreign gross income sourced at partnership level		
	d	Passive category ▶ e General category ▶ f Other ▶	16f	
		Deductions allocated and apportioned at partner level		
	g	Interest expense ▶ h Other ▶	16h	
		Deductions allocated and apportioned at partnership level to foreign source income		
	i	Passive category ▶ j General category ▶ k Other ▶	16k	
	l	Total foreign taxes (check one): ▶ Paid ☐ Accrued ☐	16l	
	m	Reduction in taxes available for credit (attach statement)	16m	
	n	Other foreign tax information (attach statement)		
Alternative Minimum Tax (AMT) Items	17a	Post-1986 depreciation adjustment	17a	
	b	Adjusted gain or loss	17b	
	c	Depletion (other than oil and gas)	17c	
	d	Oil, gas, and geothermal properties—gross income	17d	
	e	Oil, gas, and geothermal properties—deductions	17e	
	f	Other AMT items (attach statement)	17f	
Other Information	18a	Tax-exempt interest income	18a	
	b	Other tax-exempt income	18b	
	c	Nondeductible expenses	18c	
	19a	Distributions of cash and marketable securities	19a	
	b	Distributions of other property	19b	
	20a	Investment income	20a	
	b	Investment expenses	20b	
	c	Other items and amounts (attach statement)		

Form **1065** (2014)

Form 1065 (2014) Page **5**

Analysis of Net Income (Loss)

1	Net income (loss). Combine Schedule K, lines 1 through 11. From the result, subtract the sum of Schedule K, lines 12 through 13d, and 16l	1	

2	Analysis by partner type:	(i) Corporate	(ii) Individual (active)	(iii) Individual (passive)	(iv) Partnership	(v) Exempt Organization	(vi) Nominee/Other
a	General partners						
b	Limited partners						

DRAFT AS OF August 1, 2014 DO NOT FILE

Schedule L Balance Sheets per Books

	Assets	Beginning of tax year (a)	(b)	End of tax year (c)	(d)
1	Cash				
2a	Trade notes and accounts receivable				
b	Less allowance for bad debts				
3	Inventories				
4	U.S. government obligations				
5	Tax-exempt securities				
6	Other current assets (attach statement)				
7a	Loans to partners (or persons related to partners)				
b	Mortgage and real estate loans				
8	Other investments (attach statement)				
9a	Buildings and other depreciable assets				
b	Less accumulated depreciation				
10a	Depletable assets				
b	Less accumulated depletion				
11	Land (net of any amortization)				
12a	Intangible assets (amortizable only)				
b	Less accumulated amortization				
13	Other assets (attach statement)				
14	Total assets				
	Liabilities and Capital				
15	Accounts payable				
16	Mortgages, notes, bonds payable in less than 1 year				
17	Other current liabilities (attach statement)				
18	All nonrecourse loans				
19a	Loans from partners (or persons related to partners)				
b	Mortgages, notes, bonds payable in 1 year or more				
20	Other liabilities (attach statement)				
21	Partners' capital accounts				
22	Total liabilities and capital				

Schedule M-1 Reconciliation of Income (Loss) per Books With Income (Loss) per Return

Note. The partnership may be required to file Schedule M-3 (see instructions).

1	Net income (loss) per books		6	Income recorded on books this year not included on Schedule K, lines 1 through 11 (itemize):	
2	Income included on Schedule K, lines 1, 2, 3c, 5, 6a, 7, 8, 9a, 10, and 11, not recorded on books this year (itemize):		a	Tax-exempt interest $	
3	Guaranteed payments (other than health insurance)		7	Deductions included on Schedule K, lines 1 through 13d, and 16l, not charged against book income this year (itemize):	
4	Expenses recorded on books this year not included on Schedule K, lines 1 through 13d, and 16l (itemize):		a	Depreciation $	
a	Depreciation $				
b	Travel and entertainment $		8	Add lines 6 and 7	
5	Add lines 1 through 4		9	Income (loss) (Analysis of Net Income (Loss), line 1). Subtract line 8 from line 5	

Schedule M-2 Analysis of Partners' Capital Accounts

1	Balance at beginning of year		6	Distributions: a Cash	
2	Capital contributed: a Cash			b Property	
	b Property		7	Other decreases (itemize):	
3	Net income (loss) per books				
4	Other increases (itemize):		8	Add lines 6 and 7	
5	Add lines 1 through 4		9	Balance at end of year. Subtract line 8 from line 5	

Form **1065** (2014)

651113

☐ Final K-1 ☐ Amended K-1

OMB No. 1545-0123

Schedule K-1 (Form 1065) 2014

Department of the Treasury
Internal Revenue Service

For calendar year 2014, or tax year beginning ________, 2014 ending ________, 20____

Partner's Share of Income, Deductions, Credits, etc. ▶ See back of form and separate instructions.

DRAFT AS OF July 11, 2014 DO NOT FILE

Part I Information About the Partnership

A Partnership's employer identification number

B Partnership's name, address, city, state, and ZIP code

C IRS Center where partnership filed return

D ☐ Check if this is a publicly traded partnership (PTP)

Part II Information About the Partner

E Partner's identifying number

F Partner's name, address, city, state, and ZIP code

G ☐ General partner or LLC member-manager ☐ Limited partner or other LLC member

H ☐ Domestic partner ☐ Foreign partner

I1 What type of entity is this partner? ________

I2 If this partner is a retirement plan (IRA/SEP/Keogh/etc.), check here . . . ☐

J Partner's share of profit, loss, and capital (see instructions):

	Beginning	Ending
Profit	%	%
Loss	%	%
Capital	%	%

K Partner's share of liabilities at year end:

Nonrecourse . . . . $ ________
Qualified nonrecourse financing . $ ________
Recourse . . . . $ ________

L Partner's capital account analysis:

Beginning capital account . . . $ ________
Capital contributed during the year $ ________
Current year increase (decrease) . $ ________
Withdrawals & distributions . . $ (________)
Ending capital account . . . . $ ________

☐ Tax basis ☐ GAAP ☐ Section 704(b) book
☐ Other (explain)

M Did the partner contribute property with a built-in gain or loss?
☐ **Yes** ☐ **No**
If "Yes," attach statement (see instructions)

Part III Partner's Share of Current Year Income, Deductions, Credits, and Other Items

1	Ordinary business income (loss)	15	Credits
2	Net rental real estate income (loss)		
3	Other net rental income (loss)	16	Foreign transactions
4	Guaranteed payments		
5	Interest income		
6a	Ordinary dividends		
6b	Qualified dividends		
7	Royalties		
8	Net short-term capital gain (loss)		
9a	Net long-term capital gain (loss)	17	Alternative minimum tax (AMT) items
9b	Collectibles (28%) gain (loss)		
9c	Unrecaptured section 1250 gain		
10	Net section 1231 gain (loss)	18	Tax-exempt income and nondeductible expenses
11	Other income (loss)		
		19	Distributions
12	Section 179 deduction		
13	Other deductions	20	Other information
14	Self-employment earnings (loss)		

*See attached statement for additional information.

For IRS Use Only

For Paperwork Reduction Act Notice, see Instructions for Form 1065. IRS.gov/form1065 Cat. No. 11394R **Schedule K-1 (Form 1065) 2014**

Schedule K-1 (Form 1065) 2014 Page **2**

This list identifies the codes used on Schedule K-1 for all partners and provides summarized reporting information for partners who file Form 1040. For detailed reporting and filing information, see the separate Partner's Instructions for Schedule K-1 and the instructions for your income tax return.

DRAFT AS OF July 11, 2014 DO NOT FILE

1. Ordinary business income (loss). Determine whether the income (loss) is passive or nonpassive and enter on your return as follows.

	Report on
Passive loss	See the Partner's Instructions
Passive income	Schedule E, line 28, column (g)
Nonpassive loss	Schedule E, line 28, column (h)
Nonpassive income	Schedule E, line 28, column (j)
2. Net rental real estate income (loss)	See the Partner's Instructions
3. Other net rental income (loss)	
Net income	Schedule E, line 28, column (g)
Net loss	See the Partner's Instructions
4. Guaranteed payments	Schedule E, line 28, column (j)
5. Interest income	Form 1040, line 8a
6a. Ordinary dividends	Form 1040, line 9a
6b. Qualified dividends	Form 1040, line 9b
7. Royalties	Schedule E, line 4
8. Net short-term capital gain (loss)	Schedule D, line 5
9a. Net long-term capital gain (loss)	Schedule D, line 12
9b. Collectibles (28%) gain (loss)	28% Rate Gain Worksheet, line 4 (Schedule D instructions)
9c. Unrecaptured section 1250 gain	See the Partner's Instructions
10. Net section 1231 gain (loss)	See the Partner's Instructions
11. Other income (loss)	
Code	
A Other portfolio income (loss)	See the Partner's Instructions
B Involuntary conversions	See the Partner's Instructions
C Sec. 1256 contracts & straddles	Form 6781, line 1
D Mining exploration costs recapture	See Pub. 535
E Cancellation of debt	Form 1040, line 21 or Form 982
F Other income (loss)	See the Partner's Instructions
12. Section 179 deduction	See the Partner's Instructions
13. Other deductions	
A Cash contributions (50%)	See the Partner's Instructions (A–G)
B Cash contributions (30%)	
C Noncash contributions (50%)	
D Noncash contributions (30%)	
E Capital gain property to a 50% organization (30%)	
F Capital gain property (20%)	
G Contributions (100%)	
H Investment interest expense	Form 4952, line 1
I Deductions—royalty income	Schedule E, line 19
J Section 59(e)(2) expenditures	See the Partner's Instructions
K Deductions—portfolio (2% floor)	Schedule A, line 23
L Deductions—portfolio (other)	Schedule A, line 28
M Amounts paid for medical insurance	Schedule A, line 1 or Form 1040, line 29
N Educational assistance benefits	See the Partner's Instructions
O Dependent care benefits	Form 2441, line 12
P Preproductive period expenses	See the Partner's Instructions
Q Commercial revitalization deduction from rental real estate activities	See Form 8582 instructions
R Pensions and IRAs	See the Partner's Instructions
S Reforestation expense deduction	See the Partner's Instructions
T Domestic production activities information	See Form 8903 instructions
U Qualified production activities income	Form 8903, line 7b
V Employer's Form W-2 wages	Form 8903, line 17
W Other deductions	See the Partner's Instructions
14. Self-employment earnings (loss)	

Note. *If you have a section 179 deduction or any partner-level deductions, see the Partner's Instructions before completing Schedule SE.*

A Net earnings (loss) from self-employment	Schedule SE, Section A or B
B Gross farming or fishing income	See the Partner's Instructions
C Gross non-farm income	See the Partner's Instructions
15. Credits	
A Low-income housing credit (section 42(j)(5)) from pre-2008 buildings	See the Partner's Instructions (A–G)
B Low-income housing credit (other) from pre-2008 buildings	
C Low-income housing credit (section 42(j)(5)) from post-2007 buildings	
D Low-income housing credit (other) from post-2007 buildings	
E Qualified rehabilitation expenditures (rental real estate)	
F Other rental real estate credits	
G Other rental credits	
H Undistributed capital gains credit	Form 1040, line 73; check box a
I Biofuel producer credit	See the Partner's Instructions (I–K)
J Work opportunity credit	
K Disabled access credit	

Code	*Report on*
L Empowerment zone employment credit	See the Partner's Instructions (L–P)
M Credit for increasing research activities	
N Credit for employer social security and Medicare taxes	
O Backup withholding	
P Other credits	
16. Foreign transactions	
A Name of country or U.S. possession	Form 1116, Part I (A–C)
B Gross income from all sources	
C Gross income sourced at partner level	
Foreign gross income sourced at partnership level	
D Passive category	Form 1116, Part I (D–F)
E General category	
F Other	
Deductions allocated and apportioned at partner level	
G Interest expense	Form 1116, Part I
H Other	Form 1116, Part I
Deductions allocated and apportioned at partnership level to foreign source income	
I Passive category	Form 1116, Part I (I–K)
J General category	
K Other	
Other information	
L Total foreign taxes paid	Form 1116, Part II
M Total foreign taxes accrued	Form 1116, Part II
N Reduction in taxes available for credit	Form 1116, line 12
O Foreign trading gross receipts	Form 8873
P Extraterritorial income exclusion	Form 8873
Q Other foreign transactions	See the Partner's Instructions
17. Alternative minimum tax (AMT) items	
A Post-1986 depreciation adjustment	See the Partner's Instructions and the Instructions for Form 6251 (A–F)
B Adjusted gain or loss	
C Depletion (other than oil & gas)	
D Oil, gas, & geothermal—gross income	
E Oil, gas, & geothermal—deductions	
F Other AMT items	
18. Tax-exempt income and nondeductible expenses	
A Tax-exempt interest income	Form 1040, line 8b
B Other tax-exempt income	See the Partner's Instructions
C Nondeductible expenses	See the Partner's Instructions
19. Distributions	
A Cash and marketable securities	See the Partner's Instructions (A–C)
B Distribution subject to section 737	
C Other property	
20. Other information	
A Investment income	Form 4952, line 4a
B Investment expenses	Form 4952, line 5
C Fuel tax credit information	Form 4136
D Qualified rehabilitation expenditures (other than rental real estate)	See the Partner's Instructions
E Basis of energy property	See the Partner's Instructions
F Recapture of low-income housing credit (section 42(j)(5))	Form 8611, line 8
G Recapture of low-income housing credit (other)	Form 8611, line 8
H Recapture of investment credit	See Form 4255
I Recapture of other credits	See the Partner's Instructions
J Look-back interest—completed long-term contracts	See Form 8697
K Look-back interest—income forecast method	See Form 8866
L Dispositions of property with section 179 deductions	See the Partner's Instructions (L–Z)
M Recapture of section 179 deduction	
N Interest expense for corporate partners	
O Section 453(l)(3) information	
P Section 453A(c) information	
Q Section 1260(b) information	
R Interest allocable to production expenditures	
S CCF nonqualified withdrawals	
T Depletion information—oil and gas	
U Reserved	
V Unrelated business taxable income	
W Precontribution gain (loss)	
X Section 108(i) information	
Y Net investment income	
Z Other information	

CURRENT DISTRIBUTIONS AND GUARANTEED PAYMENTS

Learning Objective 10.4

Describe the tax treatment of partnership distributions.

A partnership may make distributions of money or other property to the partners. A current distribution is defined as one which does not result in the complete termination of the partner's interest in the partnership.

In a current distribution, no gain is recognized by the partner receiving the distribution unless the partner's basis in the partnership has reached zero. In such a case, gain is recognized only to the extent that a distribution of money exceeds the partner's basis in his or her partnership interest.

The distribution of money or other property reduces the partner's basis in his or her partnership interest, but not below zero.

EXAMPLE Calvin is a partner in K&G Interests, and his basis in his partnership interest is $75,000. In 2014, Calvin receives a $45,000 cash distribution from the partnership. He does not recognize a gain or loss on the distribution, but his basis in his partnership interest is reduced to $30,000 ($75,000 − $45,000). If the distribution of cash were $80,000 instead of $45,000, Calvin would have a taxable gain of $5,000 ($80,000 − $75,000), and his basis in the partnership interest would be reduced to zero ($75,000 − $80,000 + $5,000). ♦

The basis of property received by a partner in a current distribution will generally be the same as the basis of the property to the partnership immediately prior to the distribution. An overall limitation is imposed which states that the basis of the assets distributed cannot exceed the partner's basis in his partnership interest, reduced by any money distributed. In some cases, this overall limitation may require that the partner's basis in the partnership interest be allocated among the assets received in the distribution.

Guaranteed Payments

Payments made to a partner for services rendered or for use of the partner's capital that are made without regard to the income of the partnership are termed *guaranteed payments*. Such payments are treated by the partnership in the same manner as payments made to a person who is not a partner. The payments are ordinary income to the partner and deductible by the partnership.

EXAMPLE Alexander and Bryant operate the A&B Partnership. Alexander, a 50 percent partner, receives guaranteed payments of $15,000 for the year. If A&B has net ordinary income (after guaranteed payments) of $53,000, Alexander's total income from A&B is $41,500 ($15,000 + 50% of $53,000). ♦

A partnership may show a loss after deducting guaranteed payments. In that case, the partner reports the guaranteed payments as income and reports his or her share of the partnership loss.

Self-Study Problem 10.4 ***See Appendix E for Solutions to Self-Study Problems***

Jim and Jack are equal partners in J&J Interests, which has ordinary income for the year of $32,000 before guaranteed payments. Jim receives guaranteed payments of $36,000 during the year. Calculate the total amount of income or loss from the partnership that should be reported by Jim and by Jack.

1. Jim should report total income (loss) of $__________
2. Jack should report total income (loss) of $__________

Learning Objective 10.5

Determine partnership tax years.

TAX YEARS

The tax law requires that each partner include in gross income for a particular tax year, his or her distributive share of income, including guaranteed payments, from a partnership whose tax year ends with or within that tax year. For example, a calendar-year individual partner should report his or her income from a partnership with a tax year ending June 30, 2014, on his or her 2014 tax return. Since a partner reports only income reported by a partnership whose year ends with or within his or her tax year, it is possible to delay the reporting of partnership income and guaranteed payments for almost an entire year. This would happen, for example, if the partnership's year-end is January 31, and the partner's tax year is a calendar year. To prevent this deferral of income, rigid rules have been established regarding partnership tax years. Under these rules, unless a partnership can establish a business purpose for a fiscal year-end or meet certain tests it must adopt the same taxable year as that of the majority partners. If such partners do not have the same tax year, then the partnership is required to adopt the tax year of all its principal partners. If neither of these rules can be met, the partnership must adopt a year based on the least aggregate deferral method (see IRS Publication 538 for more information).

Once established, a partnership will not close its tax year early unless the partnership is terminated. The tax year does not generally close upon the entry of a new partner, or the liquidation, sale, or exchange of an existing partnership interest. A partnership is terminated, and will close its tax year, if business activity by the partnership ceases or if, within a 12-month period, there is a sale or exchange of 50 percent or more of the total interests in the partnership.

EXAMPLE Wells is a 60 percent partner in Wells Associates, a partnership. On August 15, 2014, Wells sells her interest to Howard. The partnership is terminated for tax purposes on that date, and the tax year closes. ♦

Self-Study Problem 10.5 *See Appendix E for Solutions to Self-Study Problems*

R&S Associates is a partnership with a tax year that ends on August 31, 2014. During the partnership's tax year, Robert, a partner, received $1,000 per month as a guaranteed payment, and his share of partnership income after guaranteed payments was $21,000. For September through December of 2014, Robert's guaranteed payment was increased to $1,500 per month. Calculate the amount of income from the partnership that Robert should report for his 2014 calendar tax year.

$____________

Learning Objective 10.6

Identify the tax treatment of transactions between partners and their partnerships.

TRANSACTIONS BETWEEN PARTNERS AND THE PARTNERSHIP

When engaging in a transaction with a partnership, a partner is generally regarded as an outside party, and the transaction is reported as it would be if the two parties were unrelated. However, it is recognized that occasionally transactions may lack substance because one party to the transaction exercises significant influence over the other party. Therefore, losses are disallowed for (1) transactions between a partnership and a partner who has a direct or indirect capital or profit interest in the partnership of more than 50 percent, and (2) transactions between two partnerships owned more than 50 percent by the same partners. When a loss is disallowed, the purchaser may reduce a future gain on the disposition of the property by the amount of the disallowed loss.

EXAMPLE Kyle owns 55 percent of Willow Interests, a partnership. During the current year, Kyle sells property to the partnership for $60,000. Kyle's adjusted basis in the property is $75,000. The $15,000 loss is disallowed, since Kyle is a more than 50 percent partner. If later the partnership sells the property for $80,000, realizing a $20,000 gain ($80,000 − $60,000), only $5,000 of the gain is recognized, since the partnership can use Kyle's disallowed loss to offset $15,000 of the gain. ♦

In a transaction between a partner and a partnership, a gain will be taxed as ordinary income if the partner has more than a 50 percent interest in the partnership and the property sold or transferred is not a capital asset to the transferee. The interest may be owned directly or indirectly. For example, a taxpayer indirectly owns the interests owned by his or her spouse, brothers, sisters, ancestors, and lineal descendants.

EXAMPLE Amy is a 50 percent partner in the A&B Partnership, and her brother, Ben, is the other 50 percent partner. Amy sells for $65,000 a building (with a basis of $50,000) to the partnership for use in its business. The property qualifies as a long-term capital asset to Amy. The gain of $15,000 ($65,000 − $50,000), however, is ordinary income, since Amy is considered a 100 percent partner (50 percent directly and 50 percent indirectly) and the building is a Section 1231 asset to the partnership. ♦

Self-Study Problem 10.6 ***See Appendix E for Solutions to Self-Study Problems***

Maxwell is a 50 percent partner in M&P Associates. Pam, Maxwell's daughter, owns the other 50 percent interest in the partnership. During 2014, Maxwell sells ordinary income property to M&P Associates for $70,000. The property's basis to Maxwell is $75,000. Also, Pam sells her personal Mercedes-Benz, with a basis of $25,000, for $40,000 to M&P Associates for use in the partnership's business.

1. What is the amount of Maxwell's recognized gain or loss on his transaction, and what is the nature of the gain or loss?

   $____________

2. What is the amount and nature of Pam's gain or loss on her transaction with the partnership?

   $____________

THE AT-RISK RULE

Learning Objective 10.7

Understand the application of the at-risk rule to partnerships.

The at-risk rule is designed to prevent taxpayers from deducting losses from activities in excess of their investment in those activities. Although the at-risk rule applies to most taxpayers, it is discussed here because the rule is a common problem related to investments in partnerships. In general, the at-risk rule limits the losses from a taxpayer's business activities to "amounts at risk" (AAR) in the activity.

To understand the at-risk rule, it is necessary to understand two related terms, "nonrecourse liabilities" and "encumbered property." A nonrecourse liability is a debt for which the borrower is not personally liable. If the debt is not paid, the lender generally can only repossess the property pledged as collateral on the loan. Encumbered property (also referred to as "collateral") is property pledged for the liability. The property is said to be encumbered in

the amount of the liability. Taxpayers are at risk in amounts equal to their cash and property contributions to the activities, borrowed amounts to the extent of the property pledged, liabilities for which the taxpayers are personally liable, and retained profits of the activity. For contributions of unencumbered property, the amount considered at risk is the adjusted basis of the property contributed to the activity. For encumbered property, the amount at risk is also the adjusted basis of the property to the taxpayer if he or she is personally liable for repayment of the debt. If there is no personal liability for the debt, the amount at risk is the difference between the adjusted basis of the property and the amount of the nonrecourse debt on the property.

EXAMPLE A taxpayer contributes property with an adjusted basis of $100,000, subject to a recourse liability of $25,000 and a nonrecourse liability of $40,000. His AAR is the basis of the property less the amount of the nonrecourse liability, or $60,000 ($100,000 − $40,000). ♦

Under the at-risk rule, taxpayers are allowed a deduction for losses allocable to a business activity to the extent of (1) income received or accrued from the activity without regard to the amount at risk, or (2) the taxpayer's amount at risk at the end of the tax year. Any losses not allowed in the current year may be treated as deductions in succeeding years, with no limit on the number of years the losses may be carried forward. Remember that passive loss rules (discussed in Chapter 4) may also limit the taxpayer's ability to deduct certain losses.

EXAMPLE A taxpayer contributes $100,000 to an activity. Her amount at risk is $100,000. In the current year, the activity incurs losses of $250,000. For the current year, the taxpayer is allowed a loss of $100,000, the amount at risk. ♦

While real estate acquired before 1987 is not subject to the at-risk rules, the at-risk rules do apply to real estate acquired after 1986. For real estate acquired after 1986, "qualified nonrecourse financing" on real estate is still considered to be an amount at risk. Qualified nonrecourse financing is debt that is secured by the real estate and loaned or guaranteed by a governmental agency or borrowed from any person who actively and regularly engages in the lending of money, such as a bank, savings and loan, or insurance company. A taxpayer is not considered at risk for financing obtained from sellers or promoters, including loans from parties related to the sellers or promoters.

EXAMPLE In 2014, Donna buys a real estate investment for a $20,000 cash down payment and she borrows $80,000 from a savings and loan company secured by a mortgage on the property. Donna has $100,000 at risk in this investment. If the mortgage were obtained from the seller, her amount at risk would be limited to her down payment of $20,000. ♦

Self-Study Problem 10.7

See Appendix E for Solutions to Self-Study Problems

During 2014, Joe is a partner in a plumbing business. His amount at risk at the beginning of 2014 is $45,000. During the year, Joe's share of loss is $60,000.

1. What is the amount of the loss that Joe may deduct for 2014? $__________
2. If Joe has a profit of $31,000 in 2015, how much is taxable? $__________

LIMITED LIABILITY COMPANIES

Learning Objective 10.8

Analyze the advantages and disadvantages of limited liability companies (LLCs).

A limited liability company (LLC) is a hybrid form of business organization having some attributes of a partnership and other attributes of a corporation. Each owner of an LLC has limited liability, which may be similar to a stockholder in a corporation. However, an LLC is generally treated as a partnership for tax purposes. Because of this tax treatment, owners of LLCs can have the tax advantages of a partnership and still have limited liability similar to a corporation. LLCs are recognized legal entities in all states. Licensed professionals such as attorneys and accountants must generally use limited liability partnerships (LLPs) if they wish to operate in a partnership form with legal liability protection similar to LLCs.

Advantages

Besides limited liability, there are tax and nontax advantages to an LLC. Some of these are:

1. Taxable income and losses pass through to owners, thereby either avoiding the corporate tax or allowing the owner to use the losses. An LLC may elect to be taxed like a corporation rather than a partnership, but very few do.
2. There is no general partner requirement as in a limited partnership. In a limited partnership there has to be at least one general partner who does not have limited liability.
3. Limited partners in a limited partnership cannot normally participate in management. This is not true of LLCs. Owners of LLCs can participate in the management of the business.
4. For security law purposes, an ownership interest in an LLC is not necessarily a security. This could help avoid many accounting and reporting legal requirements.
5. Tax attributes of an LLC transaction pass through to owners. Items such as capital gains and charitable contributions keep their character on pass-through.
6. LLCs offer greater tax flexibility than S corporations. Single member LLCs are common, and there is no limit on the number or kind of owners who may have an interest in an LLC.

Disadvantages

There are also disadvantages to a limited liability company. The major disadvantage is that there is a limited body of court cases dealing with LLCs. Over the years, the courts will issue many rulings that will guide taxpayers using LLCs. Another disadvantage is that the states are not uniform in their treatment of LLCs. Since aspects of LLC legal liability and operating requirements are governed by state law, this may cause confusion for LLCs operating in more than one state.

A limited liability company is a relatively new legal form that is yet to be fully defined and understood. In the future, many questions about LLCs will be addressed. The LLC is fast becoming a major form of business organization in the United States.

Self-Study Problem 10.8 ***See Appendix E for Solutions to Self-Study Problems***

Indicate whether the following statements are true or false by circling the appropriate letter.

T F 1. A limited liability company is treated like a corporation for federal income tax purposes.

T F 2. A general partner is required for a limited liability company.

T F 3. Tax attributes of an LLC transaction pass through to the owners of an LLC.

T F 4. Owners of an LLC can participate in the management of the LLC business.

T F 5. Limited liability companies have more flexibility for tax purposes than S corporations.

KEY POINTS

Learning Objectives	Key Points
LO 10.1: Define a partnership for tax purposes.	• A partnership is a syndicate, group, pool, joint venture, or other unincorporated organization through or by means of which any business, financial operation, or venture is carried on, and which is not classified as a corporation, trust, or estate. • Partnership tax returns are information returns only, which show the amount of income by type and the allocation of the income to the partners. • Partnership income is taxable to the partner even if he or she does not actually receive it in cash. • Co-ownership of property does not constitute a partnership (e.g., owning investment property); the partners must engage in some type of business or financial activity. • Limited partnerships, limited liability partnerships (LLPs), and limited liability companies (LLCs) are generally treated as partnerships for tax law purposes.
LO 10.2: Understand the basic tax rules for partnership formation and operation.	• Normally, there is no gain or loss recognized by a partnership or any of its partners when property is contributed to a partnership in exchange for an interest in the partnership. • When a partner receives a partnership interest in exchange for providing services to the partnership, income is recognized by the partner. • When a partner transfers property to a partnership in exchange for a partnership interest and that property is subject to a liability exceeding the partner's basis, income may be recognized by the partner.
LO 10.3: Summarize the rules for partnership income reporting.	• A partnership is required to report its income and other items on Form 1065, U.S. Partnership Return of Income, even though the partnership does not pay federal income tax. • When reporting partnership taxable income, certain transactions must be separated rather than being reported as part of ordinary income. Separately reported items include capital gains and losses, Section 1231 gains and losses, dividends, interest income, casualty gains and losses, tax-exempt income, retirement contributions, charitable contributions, and most credits. • Schedule K-1 of Form 1065 presents the allocation of ordinary income or loss, special income and deductions, and gains and losses to each partner. The partners report the K-1 amounts on their own tax returns.
LO 10.4: Describe the tax treatment of partnership distributions.	• No gain is recognized by the partner receiving a current distribution unless the partner's basis in the partnership has reached zero, in which case, gain is recognized to the extent that a distribution of money exceeds the partner's basis in his or her partnership interest. • Payments made to a partner for services rendered or for use of the partner's capital that are made without regard to the income of the partnership are termed *guaranteed payments*. • Guaranteed payments are treated by the partnership in the same manner as payments made to a person who is not a partner. • Guaranteed payments are ordinary income to the partner and deductible by the partnership. • A partnership may show a loss after deducting guaranteed payments, in which case, the partner reports the guaranteed payments as income and reports his or her share of the partnership loss.
LO 10.5: Determine partnership tax years.	• Each partner includes in gross income for a particular tax year his or her distributive share of income, including guaranteed payments, from a partnership whose tax year ends with or within that tax year. • Unless a partnership can establish a business purpose for a fiscal year-end or meet certain tests, it must adopt the same taxable year as that of the majority partners.

	• If the majority partners do not have the same tax year, then the partnership is required to adopt the tax year of all its principal partners; otherwise, the partnership must adopt a year based on the least aggregate deferral method. • The tax year does not generally close upon the entry of a new partner or upon the liquidation, sale, or exchange of an existing partnership interest. • A partnership will not close its tax year early unless the partnership is terminated. • A partnership is terminated and will close its tax year if business activity by the partnership ceases or if, within a 12-month period, there is a sale or exchange of 50 percent or more of the total interests in the partnership.
LO 10.6: Identify the tax treatment of transactions between partners and their partnerships.	• Generally, in a transaction with a partnership, a partner is regarded as an outside party, and the transaction is reported as it would be if the two parties were unrelated. • Losses, however, are disallowed for (1) transactions between a partnership and a partner who has a direct or indirect capital or profit interest in the partnership of more than 50 percent, and (2) transactions between two partnerships owned more than 50 percent by the same partners. • When a loss is disallowed, the purchaser may reduce a future gain on the disposition of the property by the amount of the disallowed loss. • A gain in a transaction between a partner and a partnership will be taxed as ordinary income if the partner has more than a 50 percent interest in the partnership and the property sold or transferred is not a capital asset to the transferee.
LO 10.7: Understand the application of the at-risk rule to partnerships.	• In general, the at-risk rule limits the losses from a taxpayer's business activities to "amounts at risk" in the activity. • Taxpayers are at risk in amounts equal to their cash and property contributions to the activities, borrowed amounts to the extent of the property pledged, liabilities for which the taxpayers are personally liable, and retained profits of the activity. • Under the at-risk rule, taxpayers are allowed a deduction for losses allocable to a business activity to the extent of (1) income received or accrued from the activity without regard to the amount at risk, or (2) the taxpayer's amount at risk at the end of the tax year. • Any losses not allowed in the current year may be treated as deductions in succeeding years, with no limit on the number of years the losses may be carried forward.
LO 10.8: Analyze the advantages and disadvantages of limited liability companies (LLCs).	• A limited liability company (LLC) is a hybrid form of business organization having some attributes of a partnership and other attributes of a corporation. • Each owner of an LLC has limited liability similar to that of a stockholder in a corporation and at the same time has the tax advantages of a partnership (e.g., no tax at the entity level, loss pass-through, etc.). • Licensed professionals, such as attorneys and accountants, generally use limited liability partnerships (LLPs), which are similar in many respects to LLCs. • LLCs offer greater tax flexibility than S corporations (e.g., there is no limit on the number or the kind of owners who may have an interest in an LLC).

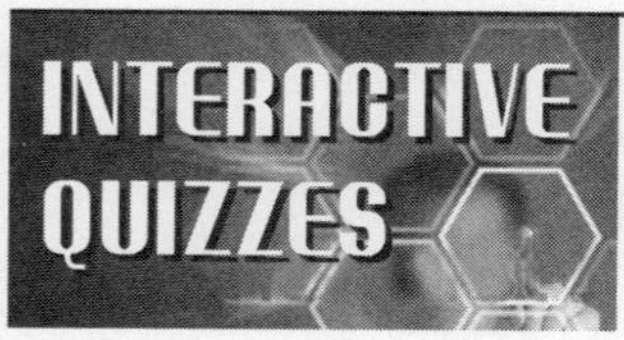

© Dusit/Shutterstock.com

Interactive quizzes are available as an optional online resource for Income Tax Fundamentals. Visit **www.cengagebrain.com** for more information.

QUESTIONS and PROBLEMS

GROUP 1: MULTIPLE CHOICE QUESTIONS

LO 10.1

1. Which of the following is *not* a partnership for tax purposes?
   a. Willis and James purchase and operate a shoe store.
   b. Sharon and Gary operate an accounting practice together.
   c. Lillian and Don purchase real estate together as an investment, not as a business.
   d. Carlos and Michael purchase and operate a hardware store.
   e. All of the above are partnerships.

LO 10.1

2. Which of the following is a partnership for tax purposes?
   a. Jackson and Wilson purchase and operate a shoe store as a corporation.
   b. Linda and Bill purchase an automobile and operate a limousine service.
   c. Carey and Gene purchase a condominium and hold it as rental property.
   d. Laura purchases a drug store and hires Miles to manage it.
   e. None of the above.

LO 10.2

3. A partner's interest in a partnership is decreased by:
   a. Capital gains of the partnership
   b. Distributions from the partnership
   c. Taxable income of the partnership
   d. Additional contributions by the partner
   e. None of the above

LO 10.2

4. Olson contributes property with an adjusted basis of $75,000 and a fair market value of $100,000 to O&W Associates, a partnership, in exchange for a 75 percent interest in the partnership. What is the partnership's basis in the property contributed?
   a. $50,000
   b. $75,000
   c. $100,000
   d. $125,000
   e. None of the above

LO 10.2

5. Linda and Ellen form an equal partnership. Linda contributes cash of $20,000 in exchange for a 50 percent partnership interest. Ellen contributes property with a fair market value of $30,000 (adjusted basis of $18,000) and subject to a liability of $10,000 in exchange for her 50 percent interest in the partnership. What amount of gain must Ellen recognize as a result of her transfer of property to the partnership?
   a. $7,000
   b. $14,000
   c. $20,000
   d. $0
   e. None of the above

LO 10.3

6. Which of the following items do *not* have to be reported separately on a partnership return?
   a. Miscellaneous income
   b. Casualty gains and losses
   c. Tax-exempt income
   d. Capital gains and losses
   e. Charitable contributions

LO 10.3

7. When calculating ordinary income, partnerships are *not* allowed which of the following deductions?
   a. Miscellaneous expenses
   b. Wages and salaries
   c. Depreciation
   d. Cost of goods sold
   e. Personal exemptions

LO 10.4

8. Trevor is a 50-percent partner in the Dalmatian Partnership. His basis in his partnership interest is $30,000 at the end of 2014. The partnership gives Trevor a cash distribution of $15,000. What is Trevor's recognized income due to the $15,000 distribution, and what is his partnership basis after the distribution?
   a. $15,000 income; $15,000 basis
   b. $15,000 income; $30,000 basis
   c. No income; $15,000 basis
   d. No income; $30,000 basis

LO 10.5

9. Which of the following circumstances will *not* cause a partnership to close its tax year early?
   a. The partnership terminates by agreement of the partners.
   b. The business activity of the partnership permanently ceases.
   c. 50 percent or more of the total interests in the partnership are sold or exchanged in a 12-month period.
   d. A new partner enters the partnership.

LO 10.6

10. Kendra is an attorney and owns 60 percent of a law partnership. Kendra sells land to the partnership for $50,000 in 2014. She bought the land for $100,000 in 2007 when real estate prices were at their peak. How much gain or loss must Kendra recognize on the land sale to the partnership?
    a. No gain or loss
    b. $30,000 loss
    c. $50,000 loss
    d. $50,000 short-term capital loss, limited to $3,000 allowed per year

LO 10.6

11. A loss from the sale or exchange of property will be disallowed in which of the following situations?
    a. A transaction between a partnership and a partner who owns 40 percent of the partnership capital
    b. A transaction between a partnership and a partner who has a 40 percent profit interest in the partnership
    c. A transaction between two partnerships owned 40 percent by the same partners
    d. A transaction between two partners with investments in the same partnership
    e. None of the above

______________ 12. Mike purchases a rental property for $200,000 and takes out a loan from a lending institution to finance half of the purchase, or $100,000. The loan is considered to be qualified nonrecourse financing. What is Mike's at-risk amount?

LO 10.7

a. $300,000
b. $200,000
c. $100,000
d. $0

______________ 13. Which of the following is considered to be a disadvantage of an LLC?

LO 10.8

a. There is no limit on the numbers or kinds of owners who may have an interest in an LLC.
b. LLCs are relatively new legal entities compared to partnerships and corporations.
c. An LLC may elect to be taxed like a partnership while retaining legal liability protection that is more like a corporation.
d. Unlike a partnership, an LLC can operate with only one member.

GROUP 2: PROBLEMS

LO 10.1

1. Debbie and Alan open a Web-based bookstore together. They have been friends for so long that they start their business on a handshake after discussing how they will share both work and profits or losses from the business. Have Debbie and Alan formed a real partnership given that they have signed no written partnership agreement?

____

____

LO 10.2

2. Hal, Steve, and Lew form a partnership to operate a grocery store. For each of the following contributions by the partners, indicate (1) the amount of income or gain recognized, if any, by the partner, and (2) the partner's basis in the partnership interest immediately after the contribution.

a. Hal contributes property with a basis of $45,000 and subject to a $75,000 liability to the partnership for a one-third partnership interest worth $105,000. The partnership assumes the liability.

Income or gain recognized $______________
His basis in the partnership interest $______________

b. Steve contributes property with a basis of $25,000 and a fair market value of $105,000 to the partnership for a one-third partnership interest.

Income or gain recognized $______________
His basis in the partnership interest $______________

c. Lew performs services valued at $105,000 for the partnership for his one-third interest in the partnership.

Income or gain recognized $______________
His basis in the partnership interest $______________

LO 10.2

3. Nan contributes property with an adjusted basis of $75,000 to a partnership. The property has a fair market value of $120,000 on the date of the contribution. What is the partnership's basis in the property contributed by Nan?

$______________

LO 10.2

4. Elaine's original basis in the Hornbeam Partnership was $25,000. Her share of the taxable income from the partnership since she purchased the interest has been $100,000, and Elaine has received $75,000 in cash distributions from the

partnership. Elaine did not recognize any gains as a result of the distributions. Calculate Elaine's current basis in her partnership interest.

$__________

LO 10.2

5. Larry and Jessica form the L&J Partnership. Larry contributes property with an adjusted basis of $70,000, a fair market value of $200,000, and subject to a liability of $80,000 in exchange for a 40 percent interest in the partnership. Jessica receives a 60 percent interest in the partnership in exchange for services performed for the partnership, valued at $10,000, and cash of $170,000.
   a. What amount of gain or loss must Larry recognize as a result of his transfer of the property to the partnership?

      $__________

   b. What is Larry's basis in his partnership interest immediately after the formation of the partnership?

      $__________

   c. What is the partnership's basis in the property contributed by Larry?

      $__________

   d. What is Jessica's basis in her partnership interest immediately after the formation of the partnership?

      $__________

LO 10.2

6. Jay contributes property with a fair market value of $14,000 and an adjusted basis of $4,000 to a partnership in exchange for an 8 percent partnership interest.
   a. Calculate the amount of gain recognized by Jay as a result of the transfer of the property to the partnership.

      $__________

   b. Calculate Jay's basis in his partnership interest immediately following the contribution to the partnership.

      $__________

LO 10.2
LO 10.4

7. Wilson has a 40 percent interest in the assets and income of the CC&W Partnership, and the basis in his partnership interest is $45,000 at the beginning of 2014. During 2014, the partnership's net loss is $60,000 and Wilson's share of the loss is $24,000. Also, Wilson receives a cash distribution from the partnership of $12,000 on June 30, 2014.
   a. Indicate the amount of income or loss from the partnership that should be reported by Wilson on his 2014 individual income tax return.

      $__________

   b. Calculate Wilson's basis in his partnership interest at the end of 2014.

      $__________

LO 10.3

8. Go to the IRS website (**www.irs.gov**) and print Pages 1 and 2 of Schedule K-1 (Form 1065), Partner's Share of Income, Deductions, Credits, etc. Review the different elements of income which must be passed through to each partner and be reported as separately stated items. Review the numerous codes on Page 2 of Schedule K-1 which identify additional items that are required to be separately stated.

LO 10.4

9. L&J Interests is a partnership with two equal partners, Linda and Joanne. The partnership has income of $67,000 for the year before guaranteed payments. Guaranteed payments of $42,000 are paid to Linda during the year. Calculate the amount of income that should be reported by Linda and Joanne from the partnership for the year.

   Linda should report income of $__________
   Joanne should report income of $__________

LO 10.4

10. Walter receives cash of $18,000 and land with a fair market value of $75,000 (adjusted basis of $50,000) in a current distribution. His basis in his partnership is $16,000.
    a. What amount of gain must Walter recognize as a result of the current distribution?

    $____________

    b. What amount of gain must the partnership recognize as a result of the distribution?

    $____________

    c. What is Walter's basis in his partnership interest immediately after the distribution?

    $____________

LO 10.5

11. Quince Interests is a partnership with a tax year that ends on September 30, 2014. During that year, Potter, a partner, received $3,000 per month as a guaranteed payment, and his share of partnership income after guaranteed payments was $23,000. For October through December of 2014, Potter received guaranteed payments of $4,000 per month. Calculate the amount of income from the partnership that Potter should report for his tax year ending December 31, 2014.

    $____________

LO 10.6

12. Louise owns 45 percent of a partnership, and her brother owns the remaining 55 percent interest. During the current tax year, Louise sold a building to the partnership for $160,000 to be used for the partnership's office. She had held the building for 3 years, and it had an adjusted basis of $120,000 at the time of the sale. What is the amount and nature of Louise's gain on this transaction?

    $____________

LO 10.7

13. Van makes an investment in a partnership in 2014. Van's capital contributions to the partnership consisted of $30,000 cash and a building with an adjusted basis of $70,000, subject to a nonrecourse liability of (seller financing) $20,000.
    a. Calculate the amount that Van has at risk in the activity immediately after making the capital contributions.

    $____________

    b. If Van's share of the loss from the partnership is $100,000 in 2014, and assuming that Van has sufficient amounts of passive income, how much of the loss may he deduct in 2014?

    $____________

    c. What may be done with the nondeductible part of the loss in Part b?

    ____

    ____

LO 10.8

14. Describe one advantage and one disadvantage of doing business as an LLC.

    ____

    ____

15. Go to the IRS website (**www.irs.gov**) and determine which IRS publication addresses the topic of partnership taxation. Print out the page with the *Table of Contents* of this IRS publication.

16. Go to the IRS website (**www.irs.gov**) and print out a copy of the most recent *Schedule D of Form 1065*.

line 22 (figure) 208,500

GROUP 3: COMPREHENSIVE PROBLEM

Emily Jackson (Social Security number 765-12-4326) and James Stewart (Social Security number 466-74-9932) are partners in a partnership that owns and operates a barber shop. The partnership's first year of operation is 2014. Emily and James divide income and expenses equally. The partnership name is J&S Barbers, it is located at 1023 Broadway, New York, NY 10004, and its Federal ID number is 95-6767676. The 2014 financial statements for the partnership are presented below.

J&S Barbers Income Statement
for the Year Ending December 31, 2014

Gross income from operations	$371,600
Deductions:	
Salaries to employees	94,000
Payroll taxes	10,000
Supplies	9,000
Rent	45,000
Depreciation	5,100
Short-term capital loss	2,000
Charitable contributions	500
Net income	$206,000
Partners' withdrawals (each partner)	$ 80,000

J&S Barbers Balance Sheet
as of December 31, 2014

Assets:		
Cash		$100,850
Accounts receivable		10,000
Equipment	$32,000	
Accum. depreciation	(5,100)	26,900
		$137,750
Liabilities and Capital:		
Accounts payable		$ 29,750
Notes payable		22,000
Partners' capital ($20,000 contributed by each partner)		86,000
		$137,750

Emily lives at 456 E. 70th Street, New York, NY 10006, and James lives at 436 E. 63rd Street, New York, NY 10012.

Required: Complete J&S Barbers' Form 1065 and Emily and James' Schedule K-1s on Pages 10-29 to 10-38. Do not fill in Schedule D for the capital loss, Form 4562 for depreciation, or Schedule B-1 related to ownership of the partnership. Make realistic assumptions about any missing data.

Form **1065** | Department of the Treasury, Internal Revenue Service

U.S. Return of Partnership Income

For calendar year 2014, or tax year beginning ________, 2014, ending ________, 20 ____.

▶ Information about Form 1065 and its separate instructions is at *www.irs.gov/form1065*.

OMB No. 1545-0123 | **2014**

DRAFT AS OF August 4, 2014 DO NOT FILE

A Principal business activity: Barbershop	Name of partnership: J+S Barbers	D Employer identification number: 95-6767676
B Principal product or service: Barbering	Type or Print — Number, street, and room or suite no. If a P.O. box, see the instructions.: 1023 Broadway	E Date business started: 1/2/2014
C Business code number: 812111	City or town, state or province, country, and ZIP or foreign postal code: New York NY 10004	F Total assets (see the instructions): $ 137750 00

G Check applicable boxes: (1) ☑ Initial return (2) ☐ Final return (3) ☐ Name change (4) ☐ Address change (5) ☐ Amended return
(6) ☐ Technical termination - also check (1) or (2)

H Check accounting method: (1) ☑ Cash (2) ☐ Accrual (3) ☐ Other (specify) ▶

I Number of Schedules K-1. Attach one for each person who was a partner at any time during the tax year ▶ 2

J Check if Schedules C and M-3 are attached . . . ☐

Caution. *Include **only** trade or business income and expenses on lines 1a through 22 below. See the instructions for more information.*

Section	Line	Description			Line	Amount
Income	1a	Gross receipts or sales	1a	371,600		
	b	Returns and allowances	1b	0		
	c	Balance. Subtract line 1b from line 1a			1c	371,600 00
	2	Cost of goods sold (attach Form 1125-A)			2	
	3	Gross profit. Subtract line 2 from line 1c			3	371,600 —
	4	Ordinary income (loss) from other partnerships, estates, and trusts (attach statement)			4	
	5	Net farm profit (loss) (attach Schedule F (Form 1040))			5	
	6	Net gain (loss) from Form 4797, Part II, line 17 (attach Form 4797)			6	
	7	Other income (loss) (attach statement)			7	
	8	**Total income (loss).** Combine lines 3 through 7			8	371,600 —
Deductions (see the instructions for limitations)	9	Salaries and wages (other than to partners) (less employment credits)			9	94,000
	10	Guaranteed payments to partners			10	
	11	Repairs and maintenance			11	
	12	Bad debts			12	
	13	Rent			13	45,000
	14	Taxes and licenses			14	10,000
	15	Interest			15	
	16a	Depreciation (if required, attach Form 4562)	16a			
	b	Less depreciation reported on Form 1125-A and elsewhere on return	16b		16c	5100
	17	Depletion **(Do not deduct oil and gas depletion.)**			17	
	18	Retirement plans, etc.			18	
	19	Employee benefit programs			19	
	20	Other deductions (attach statement)			20	9000
	21	**Total deductions.** Add the amounts shown in the far right column for lines 9 through 20			21	
	22	**Ordinary business income (loss).** Subtract line 21 from line 8			22	208,500 00

Sign Here

Under penalties of perjury, I declare that I have examined this return, including accompanying schedules and statements, and to the best of my knowledge and belief, it is true, correct, and complete. Declaration of preparer (other than general partner or limited liability company member manager) is based on all information of which preparer has any knowledge.

▶ Signature of general partner or limited liability company member manager ▶ Date

May the IRS discuss this return with the preparer shown below (see instructions)? ☐ Yes ☐ No

Paid Preparer Use Only

Print/Type preparer's name	Preparer's signature	Date	Check ☐ if self-employed	PTIN
Firm's name ▶			Firm's EIN ▶	
Firm's address ▶			Phone no.	

For Paperwork Reduction Act Notice, see separate instructions. Cat. No. 11390Z Form **1065** (2014)

Form 1065 (2014) Page **2**

DRAFT AS OF August 4, 2014 DO NOT FILE

Schedule B Other Information

		Yes	No
1	What type of entity is filing this return? Check the applicable box: **a** ☒ Domestic general partnership **b** ☐ Domestic limited partnership **c** ☐ Domestic limited liability company **d** ☐ Domestic limited liability partnership **e** ☐ Foreign partnership **f** ☐ Other ▶		
2	At any time during the tax year, was any partner in the partnership a disregarded entity, a partnership (including an entity treated as a partnership), a trust, an S corporation, an estate (other than an estate of a deceased partner), or a nominee or similar person?		✓
3	At the end of the tax year:		
a	Did any foreign or domestic corporation, partnership (including any entity treated as a partnership), trust, or tax-exempt organization, or any foreign government own, directly or indirectly, an interest of 50% or more in the profit, loss, or capital of the partnership? For rules of constructive ownership, see instructions. If "Yes," attach Schedule B-1, Information on Partners Owning 50% or More of the Partnership		✓
b	Did any individual or estate own, directly or indirectly, an interest of 50% or more in the profit, loss, or capital of the partnership? For rules of constructive ownership, see instructions. If "Yes," attach Schedule B-1, Information on Partners Owning 50% or More of the Partnership	✓	
4	At the end of the tax year, did the partnership:		
a	Own directly 20% or more, or own, directly or indirectly, 50% or more of the total voting power of all classes of stock entitled to vote of any foreign or domestic corporation? For rules of constructive ownership, see instructions. If "Yes," complete (i) through (iv) below		✓

(i) Name of Corporation	**(ii)** Employer Identification Number (if any)	**(iii)** Country of Incorporation	**(iv)** Percentage Owned in Voting Stock

		Yes	No
b	Own directly an interest of 20% or more, or own, directly or indirectly, an interest of 50% or more in the profit, loss, or capital in any foreign or domestic partnership (including an entity treated as a partnership) or in the beneficial interest of a trust? For rules of constructive ownership, see instructions. If "Yes," complete (i) through (v) below		

(i) Name of Entity	**(ii)** Employer Identification Number (if any)	**(iii)** Type of Entity	**(iv)** Country of Organization	**(v)** Maximum Percentage Owned in Profit, Loss, or Capital

		Yes	No
5	Did the partnership file Form 8893, Election of Partnership Level Tax Treatment, or an election statement under section 6231(a)(1)(B)(ii) for partnership-level tax treatment, that is in effect for this tax year? See Form 8893 for more details		
6	Does the partnership satisfy **all four** of the following conditions? **a** The partnership's total receipts for the tax year were less than $250,000. **b** The partnership's total assets at the end of the tax year were less than $1 million. **c** Schedules K-1 are filed with the return and furnished to the partners on or before the due date (including extensions) for the partnership return. **d** The partnership is not filing and is not required to file Schedule M-3		✓
	If "Yes," the partnership is not required to complete Schedules L, M-1, and M-2; Item F on page 1 of Form 1065; or Item L on Schedule K-1.		
7	Is this partnership a publicly traded partnership as defined in section 469(k)(2)?		✓
8	During the tax year, did the partnership have any debt that was cancelled, was forgiven, or had the terms modified so as to reduce the principal amount of the debt?		✓
9	Has this partnership filed, or is it required to file, Form 8918, Material Advisor Disclosure Statement, to provide information on any reportable transaction?		✓
10	At any time during calendar year 2014, did the partnership have an interest in or a signature or other authority over a financial account in a foreign country (such as a bank account, securities account, or other financial account)? See the instructions for exceptions and filing requirements for FinCEN Form 114, Report of Foreign Bank and Financial Accounts (FBAR). If "Yes," enter the name of the foreign country. ▶		✓

Form **1065** (2014)

Form 1065 (2014) Page **3**

Schedule B **Other Information *(continued)***

		Yes	No
11	At any time during the tax year, did the partnership receive a distribution from, or was it the grantor of, or transferor to, a foreign trust? If "Yes," the partnership may have to file Form 3520, Annual Return To Report Transactions With Foreign Trusts and Receipt of Certain Foreign Gifts. See instructions		✓
12a	Is the partnership making, or had it previously made (and not revoked), a section 754 election? . . . . . . See instructions for details regarding a section 754 election.		
b	Did the partnership make for this tax year an optional basis adjustment under section 743(b) or 734(b)? If "Yes," attach a statement showing the computation and allocation of the basis adjustment. See instructions		✓
c	Is the partnership required to adjust the basis of partnership assets under section 743(b) or 734(b) because of a substantial built-in loss (as defined under section 743(d)) or substantial basis reduction (as defined under section 734(d))? If "Yes," attach a statement showing the computation and allocation of the basis adjustment. See instructions		✓
13	Check this box if, during the current or prior tax year, the partnership distributed any property received in a like-kind exchange or contributed such property to another entity (other than disregarded entities wholly owned by the partnership throughout the tax year) . . . . ▶ ☐		
14	At any time during the tax year, did the partnership distribute to any partner a tenancy-in-common or other undivided interest in partnership property?		✓
15	If the partnership is required to file Form 8858, Information Return of U.S. Persons With Respect To Foreign Disregarded Entities, enter the number of Forms 8858 attached. See instructions ▶		
16	Does the partnership have any foreign partners? If "Yes," enter the number of Forms 8805, Foreign Partner's Information Statement of Section 1446 Withholding Tax, filed for this partnership. ▶		✓
17	Enter the number of Forms 8865, Return of U.S. Persons With Respect to Certain Foreign Partnerships, attached to this return. ▶		
18a	Did you make any payments in 2014 that would require you to file Form(s) 1099? See instructions		✓
b	If "Yes," did you or will you file required Form(s) 1099?		
19	Enter the number of Form(s) 5471, Information Return of U.S. Persons With Respect To Certain Foreign Corporations, attached to this return. ▶		
20	Enter the number of partners that are foreign governments under section 892. ▶		

DRAFT AS OF August 4, 2014 DO NOT FILE

Designation of Tax Matters Partner (see instructions)

Enter below the general partner or member-manager designated as the tax matters partner (TMP) for the tax year of this return:

Name of designated TMP ▶		Identifying number of TMP ▶	
If the TMP is an entity, name of TMP representative ▶		Phone number of TMP ▶	
Address of designated TMP ▶			

Form **1065** (2014)

Form 1065 (2014) Page **4**

DRAFT AS OF August 4, 2014 DO NOT FILE

Schedule K		Partners' Distributive Share Items			Total amount
Income (Loss)	1	Ordinary business income (loss) (page 1, line 22)		1	208500
	2	Net rental real estate income (loss) (attach Form 8825)		2	
	3a	Other gross rental income (loss)	3a		
	b	Expenses from other rental activities (attach statement)	3b		
	c	Other net rental income (loss). Subtract line 3b from line 3a		3c	
	4	Guaranteed payments		4	
	5	Interest income		5	
	6	Dividends: a Ordinary dividends		6a	
		b Qualified dividends	6b		
	7	Royalties		7	
	8	Net short-term capital gain (loss) (attach Schedule D (Form 1065))		8	<2000> →
	9a	Net long-term capital gain (loss) (attach Schedule D (Form 1065))		9a	
	b	Collectibles (28%) gain (loss)	9b		
	c	Unrecaptured section 1250 gain (attach statement)	9c		
	10	Net section 1231 gain (loss) (attach Form 4797)		10	
	11	Other income (loss) (see instructions) Type ▶		11	
Deductions	12	Section 179 deduction (attach Form 4562)		12	
	13a	Contributions		13a	500
	b	Investment interest expense		13b	
	c	Section 59(e)(2) expenditures: (1) Type ▶ (2) Amount ▶		13c(2)	
	d	Other deductions (see instructions) Type ▶		13d	
Self-Employment	14a	Net earnings (loss) from self-employment		14a	
	b	Gross farming or fishing income		14b	
	c	Gross nonfarm income		14c	
Credits	15a	Low-income housing credit (section 42(j)(5))		15a	
	b	Low-income housing credit (other)		15b	
	c	Qualified rehabilitation expenditures (rental real estate) (attach Form 3468, if applicable)		15c	
	d	Other rental real estate credits (see instructions) Type ▶		15d	
	e	Other rental credits (see instructions) Type ▶		15e	
	f	Other credits (see instructions) Type ▶		15f	
Foreign Transactions	16a	Name of country or U.S. possession ▶			
	b	Gross income from all sources		16b	
	c	Gross income sourced at partner level		16c	
		Foreign gross income sourced at partnership level			
	d	Passive category ▶ e General category ▶ f Other ▶		16f	
		Deductions allocated and apportioned at partner level			
	g	Interest expense ▶ h Other ▶		16h	
		Deductions allocated and apportioned at partnership level to foreign source income			
	i	Passive category ▶ j General category ▶ k Other ▶		16k	
	l	Total foreign taxes (check one): ▶ Paid ☐ Accrued ☐		16l	
	m	Reduction in taxes available for credit (attach statement)		16m	
	n	Other foreign tax information (attach statement)			
Alternative Minimum Tax (AMT) Items	17a	Post-1986 depreciation adjustment		17a	
	b	Adjusted gain or loss		17b	
	c	Depletion (other than oil and gas)		17c	
	d	Oil, gas, and geothermal properties—gross income		17d	
	e	Oil, gas, and geothermal properties—deductions		17e	
	f	Other AMT items (attach statement)		17f	
Other Information	18a	Tax-exempt interest income		18a	
	b	Other tax-exempt income		18b	
	c	Nondeductible expenses		18c	
	19a	Distributions of cash and marketable securities		19a	
	b	Distributions of other property		19b	
	20a	Investment income		20a	
	b	Investment expenses		20b	
	c	Other items and amounts (attach statement)			

Form **1065** (2014)

Form 1065 (2014) Page **5**

Analysis of Net Income (Loss)

1	Net income (loss). Combine Schedule K, lines 1 through 11. From the result, subtract the sum of Schedule K, lines 12 through 13d, and 16l	1	206000 —

2 Analysis by partner type:	(i) Corporate	(ii) Individual (active)	(iii) Individual (passive)	(iv) Partnership	(v) Exempt Organization	(vi) Nominee/Other
a General partners				✓		
b Limited partners						

DRAFT AS OF August 1, 2014 DO NOT FILE

Schedule L **Balance Sheets per Books**

Assets	Beginning of tax year (a)	(b)	End of tax year (c)	(d)
1 Cash		∅		100 850
2a Trade notes and accounts receivable	∅		10,000	
b Less allowance for bad debts				
3 Inventories				
4 U.S. government obligations				
5 Tax-exempt securities				
6 Other current assets (attach statement)				
7a Loans to partners (or persons related to partners)				
b Mortgage and real estate loans				
8 Other investments (attach statement)				
9a Buildings and other depreciable assets				
b Less accumulated depreciation				
10a Depletable assets	∅		32,000	
b Less accumulated depletion			(5,100)	
11 Land (net of any amortization)				
12a Intangible assets (amortizable only)				
b Less accumulated amortization				
13 Other assets (attach statement)		∅		137,750
14 Total assets				
Liabilities and Capital				
15 Accounts payable		∅		29,750
16 Mortgages, notes, bonds payable in less than 1 year				
17 Other current liabilities (attach statement)				
18 All nonrecourse loans				
19a Loans from partners (or persons related to partners)				
b Mortgages, notes, bonds payable in 1 year or more		∅		22000
20 Other liabilities (attach statement)				
21 Partners' capital accounts		∅		86000
22 Total liabilities and capital		∅		137 750

Schedule M-1 **Reconciliation of Income (Loss) per Books With Income (Loss) per Return**

Note. The partnership may be required to file Schedule M-3 (see instructions).

1	Net income (loss) per books	206 000	6	Income recorded on books this year not included on Schedule K, lines 1 through 11 (itemize):	
2	Income included on Schedule K, lines 1, 2, 3c, 5, 6a, 7, 8, 9a, 10, and 11, not recorded on books this year (itemize):		a	Tax-exempt interest $	
3	Guaranteed payments (other than health insurance)		7	Deductions included on Schedule K, lines 1 through 13d, and 16l, not charged against book income this year (itemize):	
4	Expenses recorded on books this year not included on Schedule K, lines 1 through 13d, and 16l (itemize):		a	Depreciation $	
a	Depreciation $		8	Add lines 6 and 7	
b	Travel and entertainment $		9	Income (loss) (Analysis of Net Income (Loss), line 1). Subtract line 8 from line 5	
5	Add lines 1 through 4	206060			

Schedule M-2 **Analysis of Partners' Capital Accounts**

1	Balance at beginning of year	∅	6	Distributions: **a** Cash	160,000
2	Capital contributed: **a** Cash	40,000		**b** Property	
	b Property		7	Other decreases (itemize):	
3	Net income (loss) per books	206000			
4	Other increases (itemize):		8	Add lines 6 and 7	
5	Add lines 1 through 4	246 000	9	Balance at end of year. Subtract line 8 from line 5	86 000

Form **1065** (2014)

651113

☐ Final K-1 ☐ Amended K-1 OMB No. 1545-0123

Schedule K-1 (Form 1065) **2014**

Department of the Treasury
Internal Revenue Service

For calendar year 2014, or tax year beginning 1/1, 2014 ending 12/31, 20 14

Partner's Share of Income, Deductions, Credits, etc.

▶ See back of form and separate instructions.

DRAFT AS OF July 11, 2014 DO NOT FILE

Part I Information About the Partnership

A Partnership's employer identification number
95-6767676

B Partnership's name, address, city, state, and ZIP code
J+S Barbers
1023 Broadway
NewYork, NY 10004

C IRS Center where partnership filed return
NYC

D ☐ Check if this is a publicly traded partnership (PTP)

Part II Information About the Partner

E Partner's identifying number
765-12-4326

F Partner's name, address, city, state, and ZIP code
Emily Jackson
456 E 70th St
NewYork, NY 10006

G ☑ General partner or LLC member-manager ☐ Limited partner or other LLC member

H ☐ Domestic partner ☐ Foreign partner

I1 What type of entity is this partner? General partner

I2 If this partner is a retirement plan (IRA/SEP/Keogh/etc.), check here ☐

J Partner's share of profit, loss, and capital (see instructions):

	Beginning	Ending
Profit	50 %	50 %
Loss	50 %	50 %
Capital	50 %	50 %

K Partner's share of liabilities at year end:

Nonrecourse	$ 0
Qualified nonrecourse financing	$ 0
Recourse	$ 25,875

L Partner's capital account analysis:

Beginning capital account	$ 0
Capital contributed during the year	$ 20,000
Current year increase (decrease)	$ 103,000
Withdrawals & distributions	$ (80,000)
Ending capital account	$ 43,000

☐ Tax basis ☐ GAAP ☐ Section 704(b) book
☐ Other (explain)

M Did the partner contribute property with a built-in gain or loss?
☐ Yes ☑ No
If "Yes," attach statement (see instructions)

Part III Partner's Share of Current Year Income, Deductions, Credits, and Other Items

1	Ordinary business income (loss): 104,3250	15	Credits
2	Net rental real estate income (loss)		
3	Other net rental income (loss)	16	Foreign transactions
4	Guaranteed payments		
5	Interest income		
6a	Ordinary dividends		
6b	Qualified dividends		
7	Royalties		
8	Net short-term capital gain (loss): 1000		
9a	Net long-term capital gain (loss)	17	Alternative minimum tax (AMT) items
9b	Collectibles (28%) gain (loss)		
9c	Unrecaptured section 1250 gain		
10	Net section 1231 gain (loss)	18	Tax-exempt income and nondeductible expenses
11	Other income (loss)		
		19	Distributions
12	Section 179 deduction		
13	Other deductions: 250	20	Other information
14	Self-employment earnings (loss)		

*See attached statement for additional information.

For IRS Use Only

Schedule K-1 (Form 1065) 2014 Page **2**

This list identifies the codes used on Schedule K-1 for all partners and provides summarized reporting information for partners who file Form 1040. For detailed reporting and filing information, see the separate Partner's Instructions for Schedule K-1 and the instructions for your income tax return.

DRAFT AS OF July 11, 2014 DO NOT FILE

1. Ordinary business income (loss). Determine whether the income (loss) is passive or nonpassive and enter on your return as follows.

	Report on
Passive loss	See the Partner's Instructions
Passive income	Schedule E, line 28, column (g)
Nonpassive loss	Schedule E, line 28, column (h)
Nonpassive income	Schedule E, line 28, column (j)
2. Net rental real estate income (loss)	See the Partner's Instructions
3. Other net rental income (loss)	
Net income	Schedule E, line 28, column (g)
Net loss	See the Partner's Instructions
4. Guaranteed payments	Schedule E, line 28, column (j)
5. Interest income	Form 1040, line 8a
6a. Ordinary dividends	Form 1040, line 9a
6b. Qualified dividends	Form 1040, line 9b
7. Royalties	Schedule E, line 4
8. Net short-term capital gain (loss)	Schedule D, line 5
9a. Net long-term capital gain (loss)	Schedule D, line 12
9b. Collectibles (28%) gain (loss)	28% Rate Gain Worksheet, line 4 (Schedule D instructions)
9c. Unrecaptured section 1250 gain	See the Partner's Instructions
10. Net section 1231 gain (loss)	See the Partner's Instructions
11. Other income (loss)	
Code	
A Other portfolio income (loss)	See the Partner's Instructions
B Involuntary conversions	See the Partner's Instructions
C Sec. 1256 contracts & straddles	Form 6781, line 1
D Mining exploration costs recapture	See Pub. 535
E Cancellation of debt	Form 1040, line 21 or Form 982
F Other income (loss)	See the Partner's Instructions
12. Section 179 deduction	See the Partner's Instructions
13. Other deductions	
A Cash contributions (50%)	See the Partner's Instructions
B Cash contributions (30%)	See the Partner's Instructions
C Noncash contributions (50%)	See the Partner's Instructions
D Noncash contributions (30%)	See the Partner's Instructions
E Capital gain property to a 50% organization (30%)	See the Partner's Instructions
F Capital gain property (20%)	See the Partner's Instructions
G Contributions (100%)	See the Partner's Instructions
H Investment interest expense	Form 4952, line 1
I Deductions—royalty income	Schedule E, line 19
J Section 59(e)(2) expenditures	See the Partner's Instructions
K Deductions—portfolio (2% floor)	Schedule A, line 23
L Deductions—portfolio (other)	Schedule A, line 28
M Amounts paid for medical insurance	Schedule A, line 1 or Form 1040, line 29
N Educational assistance benefits	See the Partner's Instructions
O Dependent care benefits	Form 2441, line 12
P Preproductive period expenses	See the Partner's Instructions
Q Commercial revitalization deduction from rental real estate activities	See Form 8582 instructions
R Pensions and IRAs	See the Partner's Instructions
S Reforestation expense deduction	See the Partner's Instructions
T Domestic production activities information	See Form 8903 instructions
U Qualified production activities income	Form 8903, line 7b
V Employer's Form W-2 wages	Form 8903, line 17
W Other deductions	See the Partner's Instructions
14. Self-employment earnings (loss)	

Note. *If you have a section 179 deduction or any partner-level deductions, see the Partner's Instructions before completing Schedule SE.*

A Net earnings (loss) from self-employment	Schedule SE, Section A or B
B Gross farming or fishing income	See the Partner's Instructions
C Gross non-farm income	See the Partner's Instructions
15. Credits	
A Low-income housing credit (section 42(j)(5)) from pre-2008 buildings	See the Partner's Instructions
B Low-income housing credit (other) from pre-2008 buildings	See the Partner's Instructions
C Low-income housing credit (section 42(j)(5)) from post-2007 buildings	See the Partner's Instructions
D Low-income housing credit (other) from post-2007 buildings	See the Partner's Instructions
E Qualified rehabilitation expenditures (rental real estate)	See the Partner's Instructions
F Other rental real estate credits	See the Partner's Instructions
G Other rental credits	See the Partner's Instructions
H Undistributed capital gains credit	Form 1040, line 73; check box a
I Biofuel producer credit	See the Partner's Instructions
J Work opportunity credit	See the Partner's Instructions
K Disabled access credit	See the Partner's Instructions

Code	*Report on*
L Empowerment zone employment credit	See the Partner's Instructions
M Credit for increasing research activities	See the Partner's Instructions
N Credit for employer social security and Medicare taxes	See the Partner's Instructions
O Backup withholding	See the Partner's Instructions
P Other credits	See the Partner's Instructions
16. Foreign transactions	
A Name of country or U.S. possession	Form 1116, Part I
B Gross income from all sources	Form 1116, Part I
C Gross income sourced at partner level	Form 1116, Part I
Foreign gross income sourced at partnership level	
D Passive category	Form 1116, Part I
E General category	Form 1116, Part I
F Other	Form 1116, Part I
Deductions allocated and apportioned at partner level	
G Interest expense	Form 1116, Part I
H Other	Form 1116, Part I
Deductions allocated and apportioned at partnership level to foreign source income	
I Passive category	Form 1116, Part I
J General category	Form 1116, Part I
K Other	Form 1116, Part I
Other information	
L Total foreign taxes paid	Form 1116, Part II
M Total foreign taxes accrued	Form 1116, Part II
N Reduction in taxes available for credit	Form 1116, line 12
O Foreign trading gross receipts	Form 8873
P Extraterritorial income exclusion	Form 8873
Q Other foreign transactions	See the Partner's Instructions
17. Alternative minimum tax (AMT) items	
A Post-1986 depreciation adjustment	See the Partner's Instructions and the Instructions for Form 6251
B Adjusted gain or loss	See the Partner's Instructions and the Instructions for Form 6251
C Depletion (other than oil & gas)	See the Partner's Instructions and the Instructions for Form 6251
D Oil, gas, & geothermal—gross income	See the Partner's Instructions and the Instructions for Form 6251
E Oil, gas, & geothermal—deductions	See the Partner's Instructions and the Instructions for Form 6251
F Other AMT items	See the Partner's Instructions and the Instructions for Form 6251
18. Tax-exempt income and nondeductible expenses	
A Tax-exempt interest income	Form 1040, line 8b
B Other tax-exempt income	See the Partner's Instructions
C Nondeductible expenses	See the Partner's Instructions
19. Distributions	
A Cash and marketable securities	See the Partner's Instructions
B Distribution subject to section 737	See the Partner's Instructions
C Other property	See the Partner's Instructions
20. Other information	
A Investment income	Form 4952, line 4a
B Investment expenses	Form 4952, line 5
C Fuel tax credit information	Form 4136
D Qualified rehabilitation expenditures (other than rental real estate)	See the Partner's Instructions
E Basis of energy property	See the Partner's Instructions
F Recapture of low-income housing credit (section 42(j)(5))	Form 8611, line 8
G Recapture of low-income housing credit (other)	Form 8611, line 8
H Recapture of investment credit	See Form 4255
I Recapture of other credits	See the Partner's Instructions
J Look-back interest—completed long-term contracts	See Form 8697
K Look-back interest—income forecast method	See Form 8866
L Dispositions of property with section 179 deductions	See the Partner's Instructions
M Recapture of section 179 deduction	See the Partner's Instructions
N Interest expense for corporate partners	See the Partner's Instructions
O Section 453(l)(3) information	See the Partner's Instructions
P Section 453A(c) information	See the Partner's Instructions
Q Section 1260(b) information	See the Partner's Instructions
R Interest allocable to production expenditures	See the Partner's Instructions
S CCF nonqualified withdrawals	See the Partner's Instructions
T Depletion information—oil and gas	See the Partner's Instructions
U Reserved	See the Partner's Instructions
V Unrelated business taxable income	See the Partner's Instructions
W Precontribution gain (loss)	See the Partner's Instructions
X Section 108(i) information	See the Partner's Instructions
Y Net investment income	See the Partner's Instructions
Z Other information	See the Partner's Instructions

651113

☐ Final K-1 ☐ Amended K-1

OMB No. 1545-0123

Schedule K-1 (Form 1065) **2014**

Department of the Treasury
Internal Revenue Service

For calendar year 2014, or tax year beginning 1/1, 2014 ending 12/31, 20 14

Partner's Share of Income, Deductions, Credits, etc.

► See back of form and separate instructions.

DRAFT AS OF July 11, 2014 DO NOT FILE

Part I Information About the Partnership

A Partnership's employer identification number
466 74 9932

B Partnership's name, address, city, state, and ZIP code
James Stewart
436 E 63rd
New York NY 10012

C IRS Center where partnership filed return

D ☐ Check if this is a publicly traded partnership (PTP)

Part II Information About the Partner

E Partner's identifying number

F Partner's name, address, city, state, and ZIP code

G ☐ General partner or LLC member-manager ☐ Limited partner or other LLC member

H ☐ Domestic partner ☐ Foreign partner

I1 What type of entity is this partner? ______

I2 If this partner is a retirement plan (IRA/SEP/Keogh/etc.), check here . . . ☐

J Partner's share of profit, loss, and capital (see instructions):

	Beginning	Ending
Profit	%	%
Loss	%	%
Capital	%	%

K Partner's share of liabilities at year end:

Nonrecourse . . . . $ ______
Qualified nonrecourse financing . $ ______
Recourse . . . . $ ______

L Partner's capital account analysis:

Beginning capital account . . . $ ______
Capital contributed during the year $ ______
Current year increase (decrease) . $ ______
Withdrawals & distributions . . $ (______)
Ending capital account . . . . $ ______

☐ Tax basis ☐ GAAP ☐ Section 704(b) book
☐ Other (explain)

M Did the partner contribute property with a built-in gain or loss?
☐ Yes ☐ No
If "Yes," attach statement (see instructions)

Part III Partner's Share of Current Year Income, Deductions, Credits, and Other Items

1	Ordinary business income (loss)	15	Credits
2	Net rental real estate income (loss)		
3	Other net rental income (loss)	16	Foreign transactions
4	Guaranteed payments		
5	Interest income		
6a	Ordinary dividends		
6b	Qualified dividends		
7	Royalties		
8	Net short-term capital gain (loss)		
9a	Net long-term capital gain (loss)	17	Alternative minimum tax (AMT) items
9b	Collectibles (28%) gain (loss)		
9c	Unrecaptured section 1250 gain		
10	Net section 1231 gain (loss)	18	Tax-exempt income and nondeductible expenses
11	Other income (loss)		
		19	Distributions
12	Section 179 deduction		
13	Other deductions		
		20	Other information
14	Self-employment earnings (loss)		

*See attached statement for additional information.

For IRS Use Only

Schedule K-1 (Form 1065) 2014 Page **2**

This list identifies the codes used on Schedule K-1 for all partners and provides summarized reporting information for partners who file Form 1040. For detailed reporting and filing information, see the separate Partner's Instructions for Schedule K-1 and the instructions for your income tax return.

DRAFT AS OF July 11, 2014 DO NOT FILE

1. Ordinary business income (loss). Determine whether the income (loss) is passive or nonpassive and enter on your return as follows.

	Report on
Passive loss	See the Partner's Instructions
Passive income	Schedule E, line 28, column (g)
Nonpassive loss	Schedule E, line 28, column (h)
Nonpassive income	Schedule E, line 28, column (j)
2. Net rental real estate income (loss)	See the Partner's Instructions
3. Other net rental income (loss)	
Net income	Schedule E, line 28, column (g)
Net loss	See the Partner's Instructions
4. Guaranteed payments	Schedule E, line 28, column (j)
5. Interest income	Form 1040, line 8a
6a. Ordinary dividends	Form 1040, line 9a
6b. Qualified dividends	Form 1040, line 9b
7. Royalties	Schedule E, line 4
8. Net short-term capital gain (loss)	Schedule D, line 5
9a. Net long-term capital gain (loss)	Schedule D, line 12
9b. Collectibles (28%) gain (loss)	28% Rate Gain Worksheet, line 4 (Schedule D instructions)
9c. Unrecaptured section 1250 gain	See the Partner's Instructions
10. Net section 1231 gain (loss)	See the Partner's Instructions
11. Other income (loss)	
Code	
A Other portfolio income (loss)	See the Partner's Instructions
B Involuntary conversions	See the Partner's Instructions
C Sec. 1256 contracts & straddles	Form 6781, line 1
D Mining exploration costs recapture	See Pub. 535
E Cancellation of debt	Form 1040, line 21 or Form 982
F Other income (loss)	See the Partner's Instructions
12. Section 179 deduction	See the Partner's Instructions
13. Other deductions	
A Cash contributions (50%)	See the Partner's Instructions (A–G)
B Cash contributions (30%)	
C Noncash contributions (50%)	
D Noncash contributions (30%)	
E Capital gain property to a 50% organization (30%)	
F Capital gain property (20%)	
G Contributions (100%)	
H Investment interest expense	Form 4952, line 1
I Deductions—royalty income	Schedule E, line 19
J Section 59(e)(2) expenditures	See the Partner's Instructions
K Deductions—portfolio (2% floor)	Schedule A, line 23
L Deductions—portfolio (other)	Schedule A, line 28
M Amounts paid for medical insurance	Schedule A, line 1 or Form 1040, line 29
N Educational assistance benefits	See the Partner's Instructions
O Dependent care benefits	Form 2441, line 12
P Preproductive period expenses	See the Partner's Instructions
Q Commercial revitalization deduction from rental real estate activities	See Form 8582 instructions
R Pensions and IRAs	See the Partner's Instructions
S Reforestation expense deduction	See the Partner's Instructions
T Domestic production activities information	See Form 8903 instructions
U Qualified production activities income	Form 8903, line 7b
V Employer's Form W-2 wages	Form 8903, line 17
W Other deductions	See the Partner's Instructions
14. Self-employment earnings (loss)	

Note. *If you have a section 179 deduction or any partner-level deductions, see the Partner's Instructions before completing Schedule SE.*

A Net earnings (loss) from self-employment	Schedule SE, Section A or B
B Gross farming or fishing income	See the Partner's Instructions
C Gross non-farm income	See the Partner's Instructions
15. Credits	
A Low-income housing credit (section 42(j)(5)) from pre-2008 buildings	See the Partner's Instructions (A–G)
B Low-income housing credit (other) from pre-2008 buildings	
C Low-income housing credit (section 42(j)(5)) from post-2007 buildings	
D Low-income housing credit (other) from post-2007 buildings	
E Qualified rehabilitation expenditures (rental real estate)	
F Other rental real estate credits	
G Other rental credits	
H Undistributed capital gains credit	Form 1040, line 73; check box a
I Biofuel producer credit	See the Partner's Instructions (I–K)
J Work opportunity credit	
K Disabled access credit	

Code	*Report on*
L Empowerment zone employment credit	See the Partner's Instructions (L–P)
M Credit for increasing research activities	
N Credit for employer social security and Medicare taxes	
O Backup withholding	
P Other credits	
16. Foreign transactions	
A Name of country or U.S. possession	Form 1116, Part I (A–C)
B Gross income from all sources	
C Gross income sourced at partner level	
Foreign gross income sourced at partnership level	
D Passive category	Form 1116, Part I (D–F)
E General category	
F Other	
Deductions allocated and apportioned at partner level	
G Interest expense	Form 1116, Part I
H Other	Form 1116, Part I
Deductions allocated and apportioned at partnership level to foreign source income	
I Passive category	Form 1116, Part I (I–K)
J General category	
K Other	
Other information	
L Total foreign taxes paid	Form 1116, Part II
M Total foreign taxes accrued	Form 1116, Part II
N Reduction in taxes available for credit	Form 1116, line 12
O Foreign trading gross receipts	Form 8873
P Extraterritorial income exclusion	Form 8873
Q Other foreign transactions	See the Partner's Instructions
17. Alternative minimum tax (AMT) items	
A Post-1986 depreciation adjustment	See the Partner's Instructions and the Instructions for Form 6251 (A–F)
B Adjusted gain or loss	
C Depletion (other than oil & gas)	
D Oil, gas, & geothermal—gross income	
E Oil, gas, & geothermal—deductions	
F Other AMT items	
18. Tax-exempt income and nondeductible expenses	
A Tax-exempt interest income	Form 1040, line 8b
B Other tax-exempt income	See the Partner's Instructions
C Nondeductible expenses	See the Partner's Instructions
19. Distributions	
A Cash and marketable securities	See the Partner's Instructions (A–C)
B Distribution subject to section 737	
C Other property	
20. Other information	
A Investment income	Form 4952, line 4a
B Investment expenses	Form 4952, line 5
C Fuel tax credit information	Form 4136
D Qualified rehabilitation expenditures (other than rental real estate)	See the Partner's Instructions
E Basis of energy property	See the Partner's Instructions
F Recapture of low-income housing credit (section 42(j)(5))	Form 8611, line 8
G Recapture of low-income housing credit (other)	Form 8611, line 8
H Recapture of investment credit	See Form 4255
I Recapture of other credits	See the Partner's Instructions
J Look-back interest—completed long-term contracts	See Form 8697
K Look-back interest—income forecast method	See Form 8866
L Dispositions of property with section 179 deductions	See the Partner's Instructions (L–Z)
M Recapture of section 179 deduction	
N Interest expense for corporate partners	
O Section 453(l)(3) information	
P Section 453A(c) information	
Q Section 1260(b) information	
R Interest allocable to production expenditures	
S CCF nonqualified withdrawals	
T Depletion information—oil and gas	
U Reserved	
V Unrelated business taxable income	
W Precontribution gain (loss)	
X Section 108(i) information	
Y Net investment income	
Z Other information	

Student Name ______________________________

Class/Section ______________________________

Date ______________________________

KEY NUMBER TAX RETURN SUMMARY

CHAPTER 10

Comprehensive Problem

Ordinary Income (Line 22) ______________________________

Net Income (Page 5, Line 1) ______________________________

Short-Term Capital Loss (Page 4, Line 8) ______________________________

Contributions (Page 4, Line 13a) ______________________________

Net Income per Books (Schedule M-2, Line 3) ______________________________

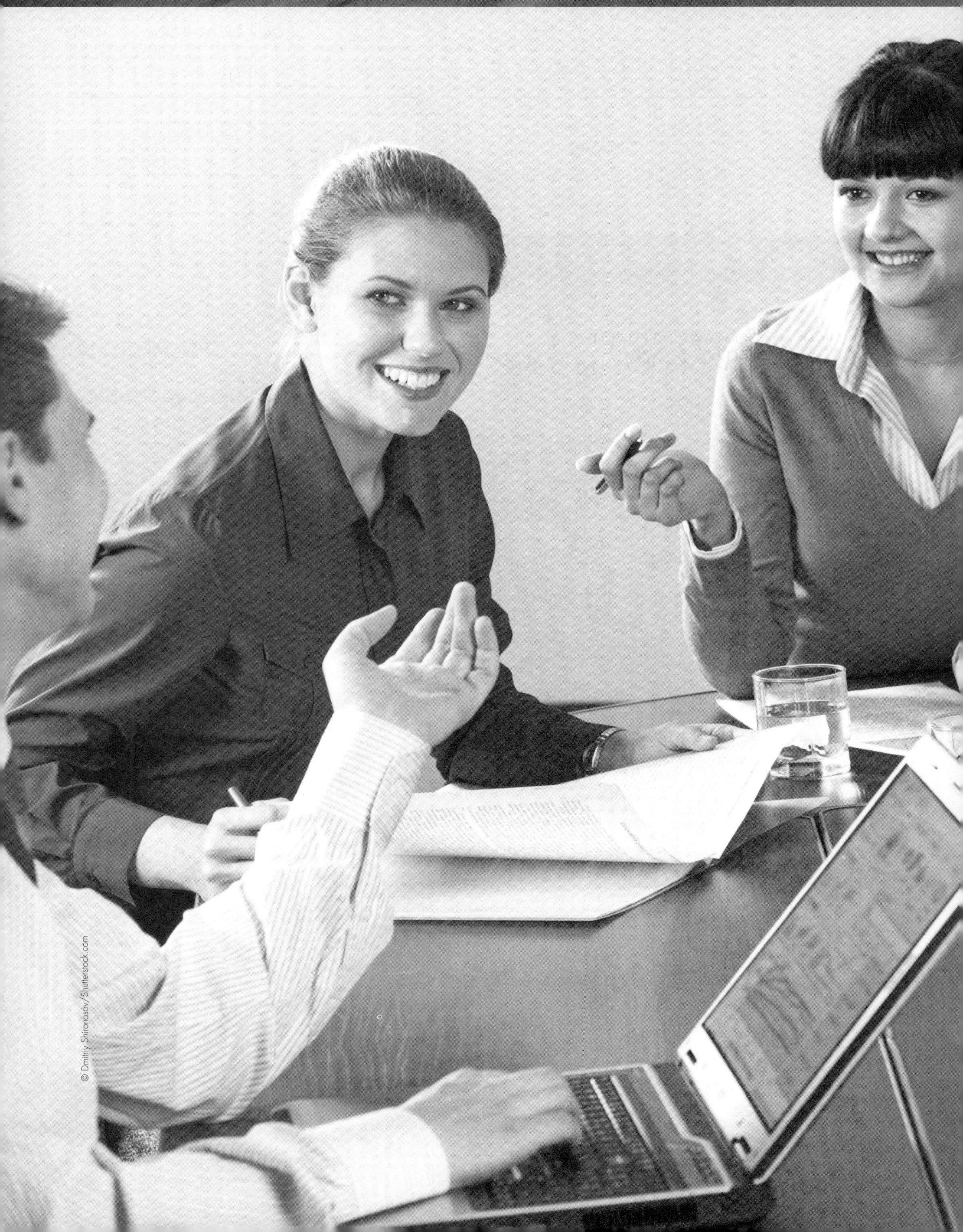

© Dmitriy Shironosov/Shutterstock.com

CHAPTER 11

The Corporate Income Tax

LEARNING OBJECTIVES

After completing this chapter, you should be able to:

LO 11.1 Employ the corporate tax rates to calculate corporate tax liability.

LO 11.2 Compute basic capital gains and losses for corporations.

LO 11.3 Ascertain how special deductions may affect corporate taxable income.

LO 11.4 Identify the components of Schedule M-1 and how they are reported to the IRS.

LO 11.5 Know the corporate tax return filing and estimated tax payment requirements.

LO 11.6 Understand, in general, how an S corporation is taxed and operates.

LO 11.7 Understand the basic tax rules for the formation of a corporation.

LO 11.8 Describe the rules for the accumulated earnings tax and the personal holding company tax.

LO 11.9 Define the elements of the corporate alternative minimum tax (AMT) calculation.

OVERVIEW

There are many forms of organization which may be used by individual taxpayers to operate a business. These include the sole proprietorship (Form 1040, Schedule C, covered in Chapter 3); the partnership, LLC, and LLP (Form 1065 covered in Chapter 10); and the regular C corporation and S corporation (covered in this chapter). Regular C corporations are taxed as separate legal taxpaying entities, and S corporations are taxed as flow-through entities similar to partnerships.

This chapter covers corporate tax rates, capital gains and losses, special deductions, the Schedule M-1, filing requirements, corporate formations, accumulations, and the corporate AMT. Additionally, basic coverage of the S corporation election and operating requirements are presented in this chapter.

This chapter provides a summary of corporate taxation and the tax forms (Form 1120, Form 1120S, and related schedules) related to reporting C or S corporation income or loss.

Learning Objective 11.1

Employ the corporate tax rates to calculate corporate tax liability.

CORPORATE TAX RATES

The U.S. corporate tax rate structure has eight tax brackets with marginal tax rates ranging from 15 percent to 39 percent. The situations where the marginal rate increases then decreases (e.g., from 34 percent to 39 percent and back to 34 percent and from 35 percent to 38 percent and back to 35 percent) are called "bubbles." These bubbles occur when the tax rate schedule recaptures the tax savings from the prior tax bracket's progressive marginal rates. For taxable income over $335,000 and less than or equal to $10,000,000, the corporate tax rate is a flat 34 percent. For large corporations with taxable income over $18,333,333, the corporate tax rate is a flat 35 percent. Table 11.1 contains the tax rates which currently apply to U.S. corporations.

TABLE 11.1

Corporate Tax Rates

Taxable Income Over	But Not Over	The Tax Is	Of the Amount Over
$ 0	$ 50,000	15%	$ 0
50,000	75,000	$ 7,500 + 25%	50,000
75,000	100,000	13,750 + 34%	75,000
100,000	335,000	22,250 + 39%	100,000
335,000	10,000,000	113,900 + 34%	335,000
10,000,000	15,000,000	3,400,000 + 35%	10,000,000
15,000,000	18,333,333	5,150,000 + 38%	15,000,000
18,333,333	—	6,416,667 + 35%	18,333,333

© Cengage Learning

EXAMPLE Jasmine Corporation has taxable income of $175,000 for its tax year ending December 31, 2014. The corporation's tax liability for the year is calculated as follows:

Taxable income	$ 175,000
Amount from table	(100,000)
Excess	$ 75,000
Rate on excess	× 39%
Tax on excess	$ 29,250
Tax table amount on $100,000	22,250
Tax liability	$ 51,500

♦

Qualified personal service corporations are taxed at a flat 35 percent tax rate on all taxable income. Thus, they do not receive any benefit from the progressive corporate tax rates shown in Table 11.1. A qualified personal service corporation is substantially employee-owned and engages in one of the following activities:

- Health
- Law
- Engineering
- Architecture
- Accounting
- Actuarial science
- Performing arts
- Consulting

EXAMPLE Elm & Ash, Inc., is a professional service corporation of CPAs. For 2014, the corporation has taxable income of $175,000. Because Elm & Ash, Inc., is a personal service corporation, its tax liability is $61,250 (35% × $175,000). The corporate tax liability would be only $51,500 if Elm & Ash, Inc., were a regular corporation. ♦

Self-Study Problem 11.1 *See Appendix E for Solutions to Self-Study Problems*

Maple Corporation has taxable income of $275,000 for its tax year ending December 31, 2014. Calculate the corporation's tax liability for 2014, before tax credits.

Tax liability $____________

CORPORATE CAPITAL GAINS AND LOSSES

Learning Objective 11.2

Compute basic capital gains and losses for corporations.

Corporations with net long-term capital gains can choose from two alternative tax treatments. The net long-term capital gain can be included in ordinary income and the tax is computed at the regular rates, or the corporation can elect to pay an alternative tax on the net long-term capital gain. For 2014, the alternative tax rate is 35 percent, the same as the maximum regular corporate tax. Thus, Congress intends the ordinary income and capital gains rates to be the same for corporations, so there will be no benefit to having long-term capital gains in a corporation. Net short-term capital gains of a corporation are taxed as ordinary income.

Capital Losses

Corporations are not allowed to deduct capital losses against ordinary income. Capital losses may be used only to offset capital gains. If capital losses cannot be used in the year they occur, they may be carried back 3 years and forward 5 years to offset capital gains in those years. When a long-term capital loss is carried to another year, it is treated as a short-term capital loss, and may be offset against either long-term or short-term capital gains.

EXAMPLE In 2014, Eucalyptus Corporation incurs a long-term capital loss of $8,000, none of which may be deducted in that year. The loss is carried back to tax years 2011, 2012, and 2013, in that order. If the loss is not entirely used to offset capital gains in those years, it may be carried forward to 2015, 2016, 2017, 2018, and 2019, in that order. When the long-term loss is carried to another year, it is considered to be short-term, and may offset either long-term or short-term capital gains. ♦

Self-Study Problem 11.2 *See Appendix E for Solutions to Self-Study Problems*

During 2014, Taxus Corporation has ordinary income of $110,000, a long-term capital loss of $20,000, and a short-term capital loss of $5,000. Calculate Taxus Corporation's tax liability.

$____________

SPECIAL DEDUCTIONS AND LIMITATIONS

Learning Objective 11.3

Ascertain how special deductions may affect corporate taxable income.

Corporations are allowed certain "special deductions," including the dividends received deduction and the deduction for organizational expenditures. In addition, corporations are subject to limitations on the deduction of charitable contributions.

Dividends Received Deduction

When a corporation owns stock in another corporation, income earned by the first corporation could be taxed at least three times in the absence of a special provision. The income would be taxed to the first corporation when earned by the first corporation. Then it would be taxed to the corporation owning the stock in the first corporation when the income is distributed as dividend income. Finally, the income would be taxed to the shareholders of the second corporation when that corporation in turn distributes the earnings to its stockholders as dividends. To mitigate this potential for triple taxation of corporate earnings, corporations are allowed a deduction for all or a portion of dividends received from domestic corporations. Corporations are entitled to a dividends received deduction based on their percentage of ownership in the corporation paying the dividend. The deduction percentages are described below:

Percent Ownership	*Dividends Received Deduction Percentage*
Less than 20%	70%
20% or more, but less than 80%	80%
80% or more	100%

The dividends received deduction is limited to the applicable deduction percentage times the corporation's taxable income calculated before the dividends received deduction, the net operating loss deduction, and capital loss carrybacks. This taxable income limitation, however, does not apply if the receiving corporation has a net operating loss after reducing taxable income by the dividends received deduction. In other words, there is no taxable income limit if the dividends received deduction creates or increases a net operating loss.

EXAMPLE During 2014, Hackberry Corporation has the following income and expenses:

Gross income from operations	$240,000
Expenses from operations	200,000
Dividend received from a 30 percent-owned domestic corporation	100,000

The dividends received deduction is equal to the lesser of $80,000 (80% × $100,000) or 80 percent of taxable income before the dividends received deduction. Since taxable income (for computing this limitation) is $140,000 ($240,000 − $200,000 + $100,000) and 80 percent of $140,000 is $112,000, the full $80,000 is allowed as a deduction. ♦

EXAMPLE Assume the same facts as in the previous example, except Hackberry Corporation's gross income from operations is $190,000 (instead of $240,000). The dividends received deduction is equal to the lesser of $80,000 or 80 percent of $90,000 ($190,000 − $200,000 + $100,000), $72,000. Therefore, the dividends received deduction is limited to $72,000. Note that deducting the potential $80,000 dividends received deduction from taxable income does not generate a net operating loss. Accordingly, the taxable income limit is not avoided. ♦

Organizational Expenditures and Start-Up Costs

New businesses may incur organizational expenditures or start-up costs, or both, prior to starting a business. Organizational expenditures are incurred by partnerships, LLCs, and

corporations in the process of forming an entity in which to operate a business. Start-up costs may be incurred by any business, including sole proprietorships reported on Schedule C, as well as the entities listed above.

Corporations amortize qualifying *organizational costs* over 180 months, and there is no upper limit to the amount of qualifying costs that can be amortized. Corporations can elect to deduct up to $5,000 of organizational costs in the year they begin business. The $5,000 amount is reduced by each dollar of organizational expenses exceeding $50,000. Costs not expensed as part of the first-year election to expense are amortized ratably over the 180-month period beginning with the month the corporation begins business. Generally, organizational expenditures that qualify for amortization include legal and accounting services incident to organization, expenses of temporary directors and organizational meetings, and fees paid to the state for incorporation. Expenses such as the cost of transferring assets to the corporation and expenses connected with selling the corporation's stock are not organizational expenditures and, therefore, are not subject to amortization.

EXAMPLE Coco Bola Corporation, an accrual-basis, calendar-year taxpayer, incurred $500 in fees to the state for incorporation, legal and accounting fees incident to the incorporation of $1,000, and temporary directors' expenses of $300. Assuming the corporation does not make an election to expense in the first year, the total $1,800 ($500 + $1,000 + $300) may be amortized over 15 years at a rate of $10 per month ($1,800/180 months). If the corporation began operations on June 1, 2014, $70 ($10 per month × 7 months) may be deducted for organizational expenditures for 2014. Alternatively, the corporation could elect to deduct the full $1,800 of organization costs in the first year of business. ♦

In 2014, the *start-up costs* of a new business are given the same tax treatment as organization costs, as illustrated in the previous paragraph and example. Start-up costs include both investigatory expenses and preopening costs. Investigatory expenses are expenses to investigate the potential success of a new business before the decision is made to actually pursue the business. Preopening costs are incurred after the taxpayer decides to start a new business but prior to the date the business actually begins. These expenses may include the training of new employees, advertising, and fees paid to consultants and professionals for advisory services.

Charitable Contributions

Corporations are allowed a deduction for contributions to qualified charitable organizations. Generally, a deduction is allowed in the year in which a payment is made. If, however, the directors of a corporation which maintains its books on the accrual basis make a pledge before year-end and the payment is made on or before the fifteenth day of the third month after the close of the tax year, the deduction may be claimed in the year of the pledge.

A corporation's charitable contribution deduction is limited to 10 percent of taxable income, computed before the deduction for charitable contributions, net operating loss carrybacks, capital loss carrybacks, and the dividends received deduction. Any excess contributions may be carried forward to the 5 succeeding tax years, but carryforward amounts are subject to the 10 percent annual limitation in the carryover years, with the current year's contributions deducted first.

EXAMPLE Zircote Corporation had net operating income of $40,000 for 2014 and made a charitable contribution of $6,000 (not included in the above amount). Also not included in the above operating income were dividends received of $10,000. The corporation's charitable contribution deduction is limited to 10 percent of $50,000 ($40,000 + $10,000), or $5,000. Note that the dividends received deduction is not used in calculating taxable income for purposes of determining the limitation on the charitable contribution deduction. The $1,000 ($6,000 − $5,000) of the charitable contribution that is disallowed is carried forward for up to 5 years. ♦

Self-Study Problem 11.3 *See Appendix E for Solutions to Self-Study Problems*

During 2014, Fraxinia Corporation has the following income and expenses:

Gross income from operations, excluding dividends	$ 90,000
Expenses from operations	100,000
Dividends received from a 25 percent-owned domestic corporation	70,000

Calculate the amount of Fraxinia Corporation's dividends received deduction.

$__________

Learning Objective 11.4

Identify the components of Schedule M-1 and how they are reported to the IRS.

SCHEDULE M-1

Because of various provisions in the tax law, a corporation's taxable income seldom is the same as its accounting income (commonly referred to as "book income"). The purpose of Schedule M-1 of the corporate tax return is to reconcile a corporation's book income to its taxable income, computed before the net operating loss and special deductions such as the dividends received deduction. On the left side of Schedule M-1 are adjustments that must be added to book income, and on the right side of the schedule are adjustments that must be subtracted from book income to arrive at the amount of taxable income. The amounts that must be added to book income include the amount of federal income tax expense, net capital losses deducted for book purposes, income recorded on the tax return but not on the books, and expenses recorded on the books but not deducted on the tax return. Alternatively, the amounts that must be deducted from book income are income recorded on the books but not included on the tax return, and deductions on the return not deducted on the books.

EXAMPLE For 2014, Wisteria Corporation, an accrual basis taxpayer, has net income from its books of $40,000. Included in this figure are the following items:

Net capital loss	$ 5,000
Interest income on tax-exempt bonds	9,000
Federal income tax expense	16,000
Depreciation deducted on the tax return, not deducted on the books	3,500
Interest deducted on the books, not deductible for tax purposes	4,000

Wisteria Corporation's Schedule M-1, Form 1120, is illustrated below.

Schedule M-1 **Reconciliation of Income (Loss) per Books With Income per Return**
Note: The corporation may be required to file Schedule M-3 (see instructions).

1	Net income (loss) per books	40,000	7	Income recorded on books this year not included on this return (itemize):	
2	Federal income tax per books	16,000			
3	Excess of capital losses over capital gains	5,000		Tax-exempt interest $ 9,000	
4	Income subject to tax not recorded on books this year (itemize):				9,000
5	Expenses recorded on books this year not deducted on this return (itemize):		8	Deductions on this return not charged against book income this year (itemize):	
a	Depreciation $		a	Depreciation $ 3,500	
b	Charitable contributions $		b	Charitable contributions $	
c	Travel and entertainment $				3,500
	interest	4,000	9	Add lines 7 and 8	12,500
6	Add lines 1 through 5	65,000	10	Income (page 1, line 28)—line 6 less line 9	52,500

◆

Self-Study Problem 11.4

See Appendix E for Solutions to Self-Study Problems

Redwood Corporation has net income from its books of $104,000. For the current year, the corporation had federal income tax expense of $41,000, a net capital loss of $9,100, and tax-exempt interest income of $4,700. The company deducted depreciation of $17,000 on its tax return and $13,000 on its books. Using Schedule M-1 below, calculate Redwood Corporation's taxable income, before any net operating loss or special deductions, for the current year.

Schedule M-1 **Reconciliation of Income (Loss) per Books With Income per Return**
Note: The corporation may be required to file Schedule M-3 (see instructions).

1	Net income (loss) per books		7	Income recorded on books this year not included on this return (itemize):	
2	Federal income tax per books				
3	Excess of capital losses over capital gains			Tax-exempt interest $	
4	Income subject to tax not recorded on books this year (itemize):				
5	Expenses recorded on books this year not deducted on this return (itemize):		8	Deductions on this return not charged against book income this year (itemize):	
a	Depreciation $		a	Depreciation $	
b	Charitable contributions $		b	Charitable contributions $	
c	Travel and entertainment $				
			9	Add lines 7 and 8	
6	Add lines 1 through 5		10	Income (page 1, line 28)—line 6 less line 9	

Would You Believe?

Beginning in 2010, a new tax form is required for certain large corporations: Schedule UTP, Uncertain Tax Position Statement. This form has rattled the accounting world, since it requires corporations to disclose the uncertain tax positions taken on corporate tax returns directly to the IRS. The IRS is expected to use Schedule UTP to make audits of corporations more pointed and efficient and to generate more tax revenue. However, corporations will likely fight back through the courts, and they may win the right to keep "privileged" information private. Only time will tell how Schedule UTP will affect IRS audits of large corporations.

FILING REQUIREMENTS AND ESTIMATED TAX

Learning Objective 11.5

Know the corporate tax return filing and estimated tax payment requirements.

The tax return form for a regular corporation is Form 1120; for an S corporation, the tax return form is Form 1120S. Corporate tax returns are due on or before the fifteenth day of the third month following the close of the corporation's tax year, but corporations may receive an automatic 6-month extension by filing Form 7004. A corporation must pay any tax liability by the original due date of the return.*

*When an IRS due date falls on a weekend or a holiday, the actual due date is considered to be the next business day.

Corporations must make estimated tax payments in a manner similar to those made by self-employed individual taxpayers. The payments are made in four installments due on the fifteenth day of the fourth, sixth, ninth, and twelfth months of the corporation's tax year.

TAX BREAK

Small corporations with less than $250,000 in gross receipts and less than $250,000 in assets do not have to complete Schedule L (Balance Sheet) or Schedules M-1 and M-2. The rule applies to both S and C corporations, and allows small businesses to keep records based on their checkbook or cash receipts and disbursements journal. This makes the reporting requirements for a small corporation similar to the reporting requirements for a Schedule C sole proprietorship.

Self-Study Problem 11.5 *See Appendix E for Solutions to Self-Study Problems*

Aspen Corporation was formed and began operations on January 1, 2014.

Aspen Corporation
Income Statement
for the Year Ended December 31, 2014

Gross income from operations		$ 285,000
Qualified dividends received from a 10 percent-owned domestic corporation		10,000
Total gross income		$ 295,000
Cost of goods sold		(80,000)
Total income		$ 215,000
Other expenses:		
Compensation of officers	$90,000	
Salaries and wages	82,000	
Repairs	8,000	
Depreciation expense	5,000	
Payroll taxes	11,000	
Total other expenses		(196,000)
Net income (before federal income tax expense)		$ 19,000

Aspen Corporation
Balance Sheet
as of December 31, 2014

Assets:		
Cash	$ 35,000	
Accounts receivable	10,000	
Land	18,000	
Building	125,000	
Less: accumulated depreciation	(5,000)	
Total assets		$ 183,000
Liabilities and owners' equity:		
Accounts payable	$ 25,800	
Common stock	140,000	
Retained earnings	17,200	
Total liabilities and owners' equity		$ 183,000

Aspen Corporation made estimated tax payments of $2,000.

Based on the above information, complete Form 1120 on Pages 11-9 through 11-13. Assume the corporation's federal income tax expense is equal to its 2014 federal income tax liability and that any tax overpayment is to be applied to the next year's estimated tax. Schedule UTP, Form 4562, Form 1125-A, and Form 1125-E are not required. Make reasonable assumptions for any missing data.

Self-Study Problem 11.5

Form **1120** — Department of the Treasury, Internal Revenue Service

U.S. Corporation Income Tax Return

For calendar year 2014 or tax year beginning ________, 2014, ending ________, 20 ____

▶ Information about Form 1120 and its separate instructions is at *www.irs.gov/form1120.*

OMB No. 1545-0123 — **2014**

DRAFT AS OF June 25, 2014 DO NOT FILE

A Check if:
- 1a Consolidated return (attach Form 851) ☐
- b Life/nonlife consolidated return ☐
- 2 Personal holding co. (attach Sch. PH) ☐
- 3 Personal service corp. (see instructions) ☐
- 4 Schedule M-3 attached ☐

TYPE OR PRINT — Name; Number, street, and room or suite no. If a P.O. box, see instructions.; City or town, state, or province, country and ZIP or foreign postal code

B Employer identification number
C Date incorporated
D Total assets (see instructions) $

E Check if: (1) ☐ Initial return (2) ☐ Final return (3) ☐ Name change (4) ☐ Address change

Section	Line	Description			Line	Amount
Income	1a	Gross receipts or sales	1a			
	b	Returns and allowances	1b			
	c	Balance. Subtract line 1b from line 1a			1c	
	2	Cost of goods sold (attach Form 1125-A)			2	
	3	Gross profit. Subtract line 2 from line 1c			3	
	4	Dividends (Schedule C, line 19)			4	
	5	Interest			5	
	6	Gross rents			6	
	7	Gross royalties			7	
	8	Capital gain net income (attach Schedule D (Form 1120))			8	
	9	Net gain or (loss) from Form 4797, Part II, line 17 (attach Form 4797)			9	
	10	Other income (see instructions—attach statement)			10	
	11	**Total income.** Add lines 3 through 10 ▶			11	
Deductions (See instructions for limitations on deductions.)	12	Compensation of officers (see instructions—attach Form 1125-E) ▶			12	
	13	Salaries and wages (less employment credits)			13	
	14	Repairs and maintenance			14	
	15	Bad debts			15	
	16	Rents			16	
	17	Taxes and licenses			17	
	18	Interest			18	
	19	Charitable contributions			19	
	20	Depreciation from Form 4562 not claimed on Form 1125-A or elsewhere on return (attach Form 4562)			20	
	21	Depletion			21	
	22	Advertising			22	
	23	Pension, profit-sharing, etc., plans			23	
	24	Employee benefit programs			24	
	25	Domestic production activities deduction (attach Form 8903)			25	
	26	Other deductions (attach statement)			26	
	27	**Total deductions.** Add lines 12 through 26 ▶			27	
	28	Taxable income before net operating loss deduction and special deductions. Subtract line 27 from line 11.			28	
	29a	Net operating loss deduction (see instructions)	29a			
	b	Special deductions (Schedule C, line 20)	29b			
	c	Add lines 29a and 29b			29c	
Tax, Refundable Credits, and Payments	30	**Taxable income.** Subtract line 29c from line 28 (see instructions)			30	
	31	Total tax (Schedule J, Part I, line 11)			31	
	32	Total payments and refundable credits (Schedule J, Part II, line 21)			32	
	33	Estimated tax penalty (see instructions). Check if Form 2220 is attached ▶ ☐			33	
	34	**Amount owed.** If line 32 is smaller than the total of lines 31 and 33, enter amount owed			34	
	35	**Overpayment.** If line 32 is larger than the total of lines 31 and 33, enter amount overpaid			35	
	36	Enter amount from line 35 you want: **Credited to 2015 estimated tax** ▶		Refunded ▶	36	

Sign Here — Under penalties of perjury, I declare that I have examined this return, including accompanying schedules and statements, and to the best of my knowledge and belief, it is true, correct, and complete. Declaration of preparer (other than taxpayer) is based on all information of which preparer has any knowledge.

▶ Signature of officer — Date — ▶ Title

May the IRS discuss this return with the preparer shown below (see instructions)? ☐ Yes ☐ No

Paid Preparer Use Only

Print/Type preparer's name	Preparer's signature	Date	Check ☐ if self-employed	PTIN
Firm's name ▶			Firm's EIN ▶	
Firm's address ▶			Phone no.	

For Paperwork Reduction Act Notice, see separate instructions. Cat. No. 11450Q Form **1120** (2014)

Form 1120 (2014) Page **2**

Schedule C	**Dividends and Special Deductions** (see instructions)	**(a)** Dividends received	**(b)** %	**(c)** Special deductions **(a)** × **(b)**
1	Dividends from less-than-20%-owned domestic corporations (other than debt-financed stock)		70	
2	Dividends from 20%-or-more-owned domestic corporations (other than debt-financed stock)		80	
3	Dividends on debt-financed stock of domestic and foreign corporations		see instructions	
4	Dividends on certain preferred stock of less-than-20%-owned public utilities		42	
5	Dividends on certain preferred stock of 20%-or-more-owned public utilities		48	
6	Dividends from less-than-20%-owned foreign corporations and certain FSCs		70	
7	Dividends from 20%-or-more-owned foreign corporations and certain FSCs		80	
8	Dividends from wholly owned foreign subsidiaries		100	
9	**Total.** Add lines 1 through 8. See instructions for limitation			
10	Dividends from domestic corporations received by a small business investment company operating under the Small Business Investment Act of 1958		100	
11	Dividends from affiliated group members		100	
12	Dividends from certain FSCs		100	
13	Dividends from foreign corporations not included on lines 3, 6, 7, 8, 11, or 12			
14	Income from controlled foreign corporations under subpart F (attach Form(s) 5471)			
15	Foreign dividend gross-up			
16	IC-DISC and former DISC dividends not included on lines 1, 2, or 3			
17	Other dividends			
18	Deduction for dividends paid on certain preferred stock of public utilities			
19	**Total dividends.** Add lines 1 through 17. Enter here and on page 1, line 4 ▶			
20	**Total special deductions.** Add lines 9, 10, 11, 12, and 18. Enter here and on page 1, line 29b ▶			

DRAFT AS OF June 25, 2014 DO NOT FILE

Form **1120** (2014)

Form 1120 (2014) Page **3**

DRAFT AS OF June 25, 2014 DO NOT FILE

Schedule J Tax Computation and Payment (see instructions)

Part I–Tax Computation

1	Check if the corporation is a member of a controlled group (attach Schedule O (Form 1120)) ▶ ☐				
2	Income tax. Check if a qualified personal service corporation (see instructions) ▶ ☐			2	
3	Alternative minimum tax (attach Form 4626)			3	
4	Add lines 2 and 3			4	
5a	Foreign tax credit (attach Form 1118)	5a			
b	Credit from Form 8834 (see instructions)	5b			
c	General business credit (attach Form 3800)	5c			
d	Credit for prior year minimum tax (attach Form 8827)	5d			
e	Bond credits from Form 8912	5e			
6	**Total credits.** Add lines 5a through 5e			6	
7	Subtract line 6 from line 4			7	
8	Personal holding company tax (attach Schedule PH (Form 1120))			8	
9a	Recapture of investment credit (attach Form 4255)	9a			
b	Recapture of low-income housing credit (attach Form 8611)	9b			
c	Interest due under the look-back method—completed long-term contracts (attach Form 8697)	9c			
d	Interest due under the look-back method—income forecast method (attach Form 8866)	9d			
e	Alternative tax on qualifying shipping activities (attach Form 8902)	9e			
f	Other (see instructions—attach statement)	9f			
10	**Total.** Add lines 9a through 9f			10	
11	**Total tax.** Add lines 7, 8, and 10. Enter here and on page 1, line 31			11	

Part II–Payments and Refundable Credits

12	2013 overpayment credited to 2014			12	
13	2014 estimated tax payments			13	
14	2014 refund applied for on Form 4466			14	( )
15	Combine lines 12, 13, and 14			15	
16	Tax deposited with Form 7004			16	
17	Withholding (see instructions)			17	
18	**Total payments.** Add lines 15, 16, and 17			18	
19	Refundable credits from:				
a	Form 2439	19a			
b	Form 4136	19b			
c	Form 8827, line 8c	19c			
d	Other (attach statement—see instructions)	19d			
20	**Total credits.** Add lines 19a through 19d			20	
21	**Total payments and credits.** Add lines 18 and 20. Enter here and on page 1, line 32			21	

Schedule K Other Information (see instructions)

		Yes	No
1	Check accounting method: **a** ☐ Cash **b** ☐ Accrual **c** ☐ Other (specify) ▶		
2	See the instructions and enter the:		
a	Business activity code no. ▶		
b	Business activity ▶		
c	Product or service ▶		
3	Is the corporation a subsidiary in an affiliated group or a parent-subsidiary controlled group? If "Yes," enter name and EIN of the parent corporation ▶		
4	At the end of the tax year:		
a	Did any foreign or domestic corporation, partnership (including any entity treated as a partnership), trust, or tax-exempt organization own directly 20% or more, or own, directly or indirectly, 50% or more of the total voting power of all classes of the corporation's stock entitled to vote? If "Yes," complete Part I of Schedule G (Form 1120) (attach Schedule G)		
b	Did any individual or estate own directly 20% or more, or own, directly or indirectly, 50% or more of the total voting power of all classes of the corporation's stock entitled to vote? If "Yes," complete Part II of Schedule G (Form 1120) (attach Schedule G)		

Form **1120** (2014)

Form 1120 (2014) Page **4**

Schedule K **Other Information** *continued* (see instructions)

DRAFT AS OF June 25, 2014 DO NOT FILE

		Yes	No
5	At the end of the tax year, did the corporation:		
a	Own directly 20% or more, or own, directly or indirectly, 50% or more of the total voting power of all classes of stock entitled to vote of any foreign or domestic corporation not included on **Form 851,** Affiliations Schedule? For rules of constructive ownership, see instructions. If "Yes," complete (i) through (iv) below.		

(i) Name of Corporation	**(ii)** Employer Identification Number (if any)	**(iii)** Country of Incorporation	**(iv)** Percentage Owned in Voting Stock

		Yes	No
b	Own directly an interest of 20% or more, or own, directly or indirectly, an interest of 50% or more in any foreign or domestic partnership (including an entity treated as a partnership) or in the beneficial interest of a trust? For rules of constructive ownership, see instructions. If "Yes," complete (i) through (iv) below.		

(i) Name of Entity	**(ii)** Employer Identification Number (if any)	**(iii)** Country of Organization	**(iv)** Maximum Percentage Owned in Profit, Loss, or Capital

		Yes	No
6	During this tax year, did the corporation pay dividends (other than stock dividends and distributions in exchange for stock) in excess of the corporation's current and accumulated earnings and profits? (See sections 301 and 316.) . . . . If "Yes," file **Form 5452,** Corporate Report of Nondividend Distributions. If this is a consolidated return, answer here for the parent corporation and on Form 851 for each subsidiary.		
7	At any time during the tax year, did one foreign person own, directly or indirectly, at least 25% of **(a)** the total voting power of all classes of the corporation's stock entitled to vote or **(b)** the total value of all classes of the corporation's stock? . . . . For rules of attribution, see section 318. If "Yes," enter: **(i)** Percentage owned ▶ ________ and **(ii)** Owner's country ▶ ________ **(c)** The corporation may have to file **Form 5472,** Information Return of a 25% Foreign-Owned U.S. Corporation or a Foreign Corporation Engaged in a U.S. Trade or Business. Enter the number of Forms 5472 attached ▶ ________		
8	Check this box if the corporation issued publicly offered debt instruments with original issue discount . . . . ▶ ☐ If checked, the corporation may have to file **Form 8281,** Information Return for Publicly Offered Original Issue Discount Instruments.		
9	Enter the amount of tax-exempt interest received or accrued during the tax year ▶ $ ________		
10	Enter the number of shareholders at the end of the tax year (if 100 or fewer) ▶ ________		
11	If the corporation has an NOL for the tax year and is electing to forego the carryback period, check here . . . . . . ▶ ☐ If the corporation is filing a consolidated return, the statement required by Regulations section 1.1502-21(b)(3) must be attached or the election will not be valid.		
12	Enter the available NOL carryover from prior tax years (do not reduce it by any deduction on line 29a.) ▶ $ ________		
13	Are the corporation's total receipts (page 1, line 1a, plus lines 4 through 10) for the tax year **and** its total assets at the end of the tax year less than $250,000? . . . . If "Yes," the corporation is not required to complete Schedules L, M-1, and M-2. Instead, enter the total amount of cash distributions and the book value of property distributions (other than cash) made during the tax year ▶ $ ________		
14	Is the corporation required to file Schedule UTP (Form 1120), Uncertain Tax Position Statement (see instructions)? . . . . If "Yes," complete and attach Schedule UTP.		
15a	Did the corporation make any payments in 2014 that would require it to file Form(s) 1099?		
b	If "Yes," did or will the corporation file required Forms 1099?		
16	During this tax year, did the corporation have an 80% or more change in ownership, including a change due to redemption of its own stock?		
17	During or subsequent to this tax year, but before the filing of this return, did the corporation dispose of more than 65% (by value) of its assets in a taxable, non-taxable, or tax deferred transaction?		
18	Did the corporation receive assets in a section 351 transfer in which any of the transferred assets had a fair market basis or fair market value of more than $1 million?		

Form **1120** (2014)

Form 1120 (2014) Page 5

Schedule L	Balance Sheets per Books	Beginning of tax year		End of tax year	
	Assets	(a)	(b)	(c)	(d)
1	Cash				
2a	Trade notes and accounts receivable				
b	Less allowance for bad debts	( )		( )	
3	Inventories				
4	U.S. government obligations				
5	Tax-exempt securities (see instructions)				
6	Other current assets (attach statement)				
7	Loans to shareholders				
8	Mortgage and real estate loans				
9	Other investments (attach statement)				
10a	Buildings and other depreciable assets				
b	Less accumulated depreciation	( )		( )	
11a	Depletable assets				
b	Less accumulated depletion	( )		( )	
12	Land (net of any amortization)				
13a	Intangible assets (amortizable only)				
b	Less accumulated amortization	( )		( )	
14	Other assets (attach statement)				
15	Total assets				
	Liabilities and Shareholders' Equity				
16	Accounts payable				
17	Mortgages, notes, bonds payable in less than 1 year				
18	Other current liabilities (attach statement)				
19	Loans from shareholders				
20	Mortgages, notes, bonds payable in 1 year or more				
21	Other liabilities (attach statement)				
22	Capital stock: a Preferred stock				
	b Common stock				
23	Additional paid-in capital				
24	Retained earnings—Appropriated (attach statement)				
25	Retained earnings—Unappropriated				
26	Adjustments to shareholders' equity (attach statement)				
27	Less cost of treasury stock		( )		( )
28	Total liabilities and shareholders' equity				

DRAFT AS OF June 25, 2014 DO NOT FILE

Schedule M-1 Reconciliation of Income (Loss) per Books With Income per Return

Note: The corporation may be required to file Schedule M-3 (see instructions).

1	Net income (loss) per books		7	Income recorded on books this year not included on this return (itemize): Tax-exempt interest $	
2	Federal income tax per books				
3	Excess of capital losses over capital gains				
4	Income subject to tax not recorded on books this year (itemize):		8	Deductions on this return not charged against book income this year (itemize):	
5	Expenses recorded on books this year not deducted on this return (itemize):		a	Depreciation $	
a	Depreciation $		b	Charitable contributions $	
b	Charitable contributions $				
c	Travel and entertainment $				
			9	Add lines 7 and 8	
6	Add lines 1 through 5		10	Income (page 1, line 28)—line 6 less line 9	

Schedule M-2 Analysis of Unappropriated Retained Earnings per Books (Line 25, Schedule L)

1	Balance at beginning of year		5	Distributions: a Cash	
2	Net income (loss) per books			b Stock	
3	Other increases (itemize):			c Property	
			6	Other decreases (itemize):	
			7	Add lines 5 and 6	
4	Add lines 1, 2, and 3		8	Balance at end of year (line 4 less line 7)	

Form **1120** (2014)

S CORPORATIONS

Learning Objective 11.6

Understand, in general, how an S corporation is taxed and operates.

Qualified corporations may elect to be taxed under Subchapter S of the Internal Revenue Code in a manner similar to partnerships. An S corporation does not generally pay tax, and each shareholder reports his or her share of corporate income. The S corporation election is designed to relieve corporations of certain corporate tax disadvantages, such as the double taxation of income.

To elect S corporation status, a corporation must have the following characteristics:

1. The corporation must be a domestic corporation;
2. The corporation must have 100 or fewer shareholders who are all either individuals, estates, certain trusts, certain financial institutions, or certain exempt organizations;
3. The corporation must have only one class of stock; and
4. All shareholders must be U.S. citizens or resident aliens.

The S corporation election must be made during the prior year or the first two and one-half months of the current tax year to obtain the status for the current year. Relief provisions may apply for elections which are filed late.

EXAMPLE Laurel Corporation is a calendar-year corporation that makes an S corporation election on November 2, 2014. The corporation does not qualify for any of the relief provisions for late S corporation elections for the 2014 tax year. The corporation is not an S corporation until the 2015 tax year; it is a regular C corporation for 2014. ♦

After electing S corporation status, the corporation retains the status until the election is voluntarily revoked or statutorily terminated. If the corporation ceases to qualify as an S corporation (e.g., it has 102 shareholders in 2014), the election is statutorily terminated. Also, the election is terminated when a corporation receives 25 percent or more of its gross income from passive investments for 3 consecutive tax years and the corporation has accumulated earnings and profits at the end of each of those years. If a corporation experiences an involuntary termination of S corporation status, the election is terminated on the day the status changes. For example, the loss of S corporation status on June 1, 2014, causes the corporation to be a regular corporation from that day on.

Upon consent of shareholders owning a majority of the voting stock, an S corporation election can be voluntarily revoked. If the consent to revoke the election is made during the first two and one-half months of the tax year, the S corporation status will be considered voluntarily terminated effective at the beginning of that year. Shareholders may specify a date on or after the date of the revocation as the effective date for the voluntary termination of the S corporation election. If a prospective revocation date is not specified, and the consent to revoke the election is made after the fifteenth day of the third month of the tax year, the earliest that the S corporation status can be terminated is the first day of the following tax year.

EXAMPLE On January 20, 2014, Juniper Corporation, a calendar-year corporation, files a consent to revoke its S corporation election. No date is specified in the consent as the effective date of the revocation. The corporation is no longer an S corporation effective January 1, 2014. If the election were made after March 15, the corporation would not become a regular corporation until the 2015 tax year. ♦

Reporting Income

Each shareholder of an S corporation reports his or her share of corporate income based on his or her stock ownership during the year. The taxable income of an S corporation is computed in the same manner as for a partnership.

Each shareholder of an S corporation takes into account separately his or her share of items of income, deductions, and credits on a per share per day basis. Schedule K-1 of Form 1120S is used to report the allocation of ordinary income or loss, plus all separately stated items of income or loss, to each of the shareholders. Each shareholder's share of these items is included in the shareholder's computation of taxable income for the tax year during which the corporation's year ends. In the case of the death of a shareholder, the shareholder's portion of S corporation items will be taken into account on the shareholder's final tax return.

EXAMPLE Freda is the sole shareholder of the Freda Corporation, which has an S corporation election in effect. During calendar year 2014, the corporation has ordinary taxable income of $100,000. Freda must report $100,000 on her individual income tax return for 2014 as income from the Freda Corporation. ♦

S Corporation Losses

Losses from an S corporation also pass through to the shareholders. However, the amount of loss from an S corporation that a shareholder may report is limited to his or her adjusted basis in the corporation's stock plus the amount of any loans from the shareholder to the corporation. Any loss in excess of the shareholder's basis in the stock of the corporation plus loans is disallowed and becomes a carryforward loss. If a shareholder was not a shareholder for the entire tax year, losses must be allocated to the shareholder on a daily basis (the seller gets credit for the date of sale). This prevents a shareholder from selling losses late in the year to another taxpayer by selling the stock of an S corporation.

EXAMPLE Lawson and Mary are equal shareholders in L&M Corporation, an S corporation. On December 1, 20XX, Mary sells her interest to Connley for $15,000. Lawson's basis in his L&M Corporation stock is $10,000. For the 20XX tax year, the corporation has a loss of $24,000. Lawson can deduct only $10,000 of his half of the loss ($12,000), since that is the amount of his stock basis. Even though she is not a shareholder at year end, Mary may deduct $11,014 of the loss, which is 335/365 of $12,000, assuming her basis was at least that amount. Connley may deduct $986, 30/365 of $12,000. In leap years, the amounts would be $11,016 (336/366 × $12,000) and $984 (30/366 × $12,000) for Mary and Connley, respectively. ♦

Pass-Through Items

Certain items pass through from an S corporation to the shareholders and retain their tax attributes on the shareholders' tax returns. The following are examples of pass-through items:

- Capital gains and losses
- Section 1231 gains and losses
- Dividend income
- Charitable contributions
- Tax-exempt interest
- Most credits

Special Taxes

S corporations are not subject to the corporate income tax on their regular taxable income. Under certain circumstances, an S corporation may be liable for tax at the corporate level. An S corporation may be subject to a tax on gains attributable to appreciation in the value of assets held by the corporation prior to the S corporation election, the built-in gains tax. In addition, a tax may be imposed on certain S corporations that have large amounts of passive investment income, such as income from dividends and interest. The rules for the application of these taxes are complex.

Self-Study Problem 11.6 *See Appendix E for Solutions to Self-Study Problems*

Assume that Aspen Corporation in Self-Study Problem 11.5 is owned by Janet Nall, who is a 100 percent shareholder. Also, assume that the corporation has a valid S corporation election in effect for 2014 and is not subject to any special taxes. Using the relevant information given and assuming the corporation's retained earnings are $19,000, instead of $17,200, accounts payable are $24,000, rather than $25,800, and no estimated tax payments are made, complete Form 1120S on Pages 11-19 through 11-22 for Aspen Corporation, and complete Schedule K-1 on Pages 11-23 and 11-24 for Janet. Assume there were no cash distributions to Janet during the year.

CORPORATE FORMATION

Learning Objective 11.7

Understand the basic tax rules for the formation of a corporation.

When a taxpayer incorporates a business, he or she often transfers high-value, low-basis property to the corporation in exchange for corporate stock. Thus, a substantial gain is realized when the corporation is formed. Favorable tax treatment is available in certain cases which allows many taxpayers to defer the gain realized in the year of formation. To defer the gain, the taxpayer must meet certain requirements, including:

1. The taxpayer must transfer property or money to the corporation,
2. The transfer must be solely in exchange for stock of the corporation, and
3. The shareholder(s) qualifying for nonrecognition must own at least 80 percent of the corporation's stock after the transfer.

When the above requirements are met, losses as well as gains are not recognized on the formation of the corporation.

The shareholder must transfer property or cash to the corporation; performing services for corporate stock does not qualify for nonrecognition treatment. The shareholder performing services must recognize income in an amount equal to the value of the stock received. If the shareholder receives other property (boot) in addition to stock of the corporation in exchange for the transfer of cash or other property, the transaction may still qualify for partial nonrecognition treatment, provided the control requirement is met. However, realized gain must be recognized to the extent of the boot received.

Liabilities

As a general rule, the assumption of shareholder liabilities by the corporation is not considered to be boot. For example, if a shareholder transfers land to the corporation for stock and the land is subject to a liability that is assumed by the corporation, no gain would normally be recognized on the transfer. However, if there is no business purpose for transfer of the liability, or tax avoidance appears to be involved, the recognition of any realized gain is required. Also, when the total liabilities transferred to the corporation by a shareholder exceed the total basis of the property transferred by the shareholder, the excess amount is a gain that must be recognized without regard to whether gain is realized.

EXAMPLE Robusta Corporation is formed by Max, who contributes property with a basis of $12,000 in exchange for 100 percent of the company's stock. On the date of the contribution, the property contributed has a fair market value of $120,000 and is subject to a liability of $20,000. Max must recognize a gain of $8,000 on the transfer of the property to the corporation since the liability transferred to the corporation exceeds his basis in the property transferred. ♦

Shareholder's Stock Basis

After the transfer, the shareholder's basis in his or her stock is determined by the following formula:

Basis of the property transferred	$ xxxx
Less: boot received	(xxxx)
Plus: gain recognized	xxxx
Less: liabilities transferred	(xxxx)
Basis in the stock	$ xxxx

Corporation's Basis in Property Contributed

The corporation's basis in the property received from a shareholder in a transaction to which nonrecognition treatment applies is the same as the basis of the property to the shareholder, increased by any gain recognized by the shareholder on the transfer.

EXAMPLE A, B, and C form Hornbeam Corporation. A contributes property with a basis of $25,000 in exchange for 40 shares of stock worth $40,000. B performs services for the corporation in exchange for 10 shares of stock worth $10,000. C contributes property with a basis of $10,000 in exchange for 45 shares of stock worth $45,000 plus $5,000 cash. The stock described above is all of the outstanding stock of the corporation. A and C qualify for complete or partial nonrecognition treatment, since together they own 89 percent (85 of 95 shares) of the stock after the transfer. B's stock is not considered because it was received in exchange for services.

1. A has a realized gain of $15,000 ($40,000 − $25,000), but no recognized gain since he received no boot.
2. B's recognized income is $10,000, since he performed services in exchange for the stock, and stock received for services does not fall within the nonrecognition provisions.
3. C's realized gain is $40,000 ($45,000 + $5,000 − $10,000), but his recognized gain is $5,000, the amount of boot received.
4. A's basis in the stock is $25,000 ($25,000 − $0 + $0 − $0), B's basis in the stock is $10,000 ($0 − $0 + $10,000 − $0), and C's basis in the stock is $10,000 ($10,000 − $5,000 + $5,000 − $0).
5. Hornbeam Corporation's basis in the property contributed by A is $25,000 ($25,000 + $0). The corporation's basis in the property contributed by C is $15,000 ($10,000 + $5,000 gain recognized). ♦

Self-Study Problem 11.7

See Appendix E for Solutions to Self-Study Problems

Tammy has a business which she decides to incorporate. She transfers to the new corporation real estate with a basis of $75,000 and subject to a $34,000 mortgage in exchange for all of its stock. The stock is worth $125,000.

What is Tammy's realized gain? $________

What is Tammy's recognized gain? $________

What is Tammy's basis in her stock? $________

What is the corporation's basis in the real estate? $________

Self-Study Problem 11.6

Form **1120S**

Department of the Treasury
Internal Revenue Service

U.S. Income Tax Return for an S Corporation

▶ **Do not file this form unless the corporation has filed or is attaching Form 2553 to elect to be an S corporation.**
▶ **Information about Form 1120S and its separate instructions is at *www.irs.gov/form1120s*.**

OMB No. 1545-0123

2014

For calendar year 2014 or tax year beginning , 2014, ending , 20

DRAFT AS OF August 1, 2014 DO NOT FILE

A S election effective date	TYPE OR PRINT	Name	**D Employer identification number**
B Business activity code number (see instructions)		Number, street, and room or suite no. If a P.O. box, see instructions.	**E** Date incorporated
C Check if Sch. M-3 attached ☐		City or town, state or province, country, and ZIP or foreign postal code	**F** Total assets (see instructions) $

G Is the corporation electing to be an S corporation beginning with this tax year? ☐ Yes ☐ No If "Yes," attach Form 2553 if not already filed

H Check if: **(1)** ☐ Final return **(2)** ☐ Name change **(3)** ☐ Address change **(4)** ☐ Amended return **(5)** ☐ S election termination or revocation

I Enter the number of shareholders who were shareholders during any part of the tax year . . . . . . ▶

Caution. Include **only** trade or business income and expenses on lines 1a through 21. See the instructions for more information.

Section	Line	Description	Box		Line	Amount
Income	1a	Gross receipts or sales	1a			
	b	Returns and allowances	1b			
	c	Balance. Subtract line 1b from line 1a			1c	
	2	Cost of goods sold (attach Form 1125-A)			2	
	3	Gross profit. Subtract line 2 from line 1c			3	
	4	Net gain (loss) from Form 4797, line 17 (attach Form 4797)			4	
	5	Other income (loss) (see instructions—attach statement)			5	
	6	**Total income (loss).** Add lines 3 through 5 ▶			6	
Deductions (see instructions for limitations)	7	Compensation of officers (see instructions—attach Form 1125-E)			7	
	8	Salaries and wages (less employment credits)			8	
	9	Repairs and maintenance			9	
	10	Bad debts			10	
	11	Rents			11	
	12	Taxes and licenses			12	
	13	Interest			13	
	14	Depreciation not claimed on Form 1125-A or elsewhere on return (attach Form 4562)			14	
	15	Depletion **(Do not deduct oil and gas depletion.)**			15	
	16	Advertising			16	
	17	Pension, profit-sharing, etc., plans			17	
	18	Employee benefit programs			18	
	19	Other deductions (attach statement)			19	
	20	**Total deductions.** Add lines 7 through 19 ▶			20	
	21	**Ordinary business income (loss).** Subtract line 20 from line 6			21	
Tax and Payments	22a	Excess net passive income or LIFO recapture tax (see instructions)	22a			
	b	Tax from Schedule D (Form 1120S)	22b			
	c	Add lines 22a and 22b (see instructions for additional taxes)			22c	
	23a	2014 estimated tax payments and 2013 overpayment credited to 2014	23a			
	b	Tax deposited with Form 7004	23b			
	c	Credit for federal tax paid on fuels (attach Form 4136)	23c			
	d	Add lines 23a through 23c			23d	
	24	Estimated tax penalty (see instructions). Check if Form 2220 is attached ▶ ☐			24	
	25	**Amount owed.** If line 23d is smaller than the total of lines 22c and 24, enter amount owed			25	
	26	**Overpayment.** If line 23d is larger than the total of lines 22c and 24, enter amount overpaid			26	
	27	Enter amount from line 26 **Credited to 2015 estimated tax** ▶	**Refunded** ▶		27	

Sign Here

Under penalties of perjury, I declare that I have examined this return, including accompanying schedules and statements, and to the best of my knowledge and belief, it is true, correct, and complete. Declaration of preparer (other than taxpayer) is based on all information of which preparer has any knowledge.

▶ Signature of officer | Date | ▶ Title

May the IRS discuss this return with the preparer shown below (see instructions)? ☐ Yes ☐ No

Paid Preparer Use Only

Print/Type preparer's name	Preparer's signature	Date	Check ☐ if self-employed	PTIN
Firm's name ▶			Firm's EIN ▶	
Firm's address ▶			Phone no.	

For Paperwork Reduction Act Notice, see separate instructions. Cat. No. 11510H Form **1120S** (2014)

Form 1120S (2014) Page **2**

Schedule B **Other Information** (see instructions)

		Yes	No
1	Check accounting method: **a** ☐ Cash **b** ☐ Accrual **c** ☐ Other (specify) ▶		
2	See the instructions and enter the: **a** Business activity ▶ **b** Product or service ▶		
3	At any time during the tax year, was any shareholder of the corporation a disregarded entity, a trust, an estate, or a nominee or similar person? If "Yes," attach Schedule B-1, Information on Certain Shareholders of an S Corporation . .		
4	At the end of the tax year, did the corporation:		
a	Own directly 20% or more, or own, directly or indirectly, 50% or more of the total stock issued and outstanding of any foreign or domestic corporation? For rules of constructive ownership, see instructions. If "Yes," complete (i) through (v) below		

(i) Name of Corporation	**(ii)** Employer Identification Number (if any)	**(iii)** Country of Incorporation	**(iv)** Percentage of Stock Owned	**(v)** If Percentage in (iv) is 100%, Enter the Date (if any) a Qualified Subchapter S Subsidiary Election Was Made

DRAFT AS OF August 1, 2014 DO NOT FILE

		Yes	No
b	Own directly an interest of 20% or more, or own, directly or indirectly, an interest of 50% or more in the profit, loss, or capital in any foreign or domestic partnership (including an entity treated as a partnership) or in the beneficial interest of a trust? For rules of constructive ownership, see instructions. If "Yes," complete (i) through (v) below		

(i) Name of Entity	**(ii)** Employer Identification Number (if any)	**(iii)** Type of Entity	**(iv)** Country of Organization	**(v)** Maximum Percentage Owned in Profit, Loss, or Capital

		Yes	No
5 a	At the end of the tax year, did the corporation have any outstanding shares of restricted stock? If "Yes," complete lines (i) and (ii) below. **(i)** Total shares of restricted stock ▶ **(ii)** Total shares of non-restricted stock ▶		
b	At the end of the tax year, did the corporation have any outstanding stock options, warrants, or similar instruments? If "Yes," complete lines (i) and (ii) below. **(i)** Total shares of stock outstanding at the end of the tax year ▶ **(ii)** Total shares of stock outstanding if all instruments were executed ▶		
6	Has this corporation filed, or is it required to file, **Form 8918,** Material Advisor Disclosure Statement, to provide information on any reportable transaction?		
7	Check this box if the corporation issued publicly offered debt instruments with original issue discount . . . . ▶ ☐ If checked, the corporation may have to file **Form 8281,** Information Return for Publicly Offered Original Issue Discount Instruments.		
8	If the corporation: **(a)** was a C corporation before it elected to be an S corporation **or** the corporation acquired an asset with a basis determined by reference to the basis of the asset (or the basis of any other property) in the hands of a C corporation **and (b)** has net unrealized built-in gain in excess of the net recognized built-in gain from prior years, enter the net unrealized built-in gain reduced by net recognized built-in gain from prior years (see instructions) ▶ $		
9	Enter the accumulated earnings and profits of the corporation at the end of the tax year. $		
10	Does the corporation satisfy **both** of the following conditions?		
a	The corporation's total receipts (see instructions) for the tax year were less than $250,000		
b	The corporation's total assets at the end of the tax year were less than $250,000 If "Yes," the corporation is not required to complete Schedules L and M-1.		
11	During the tax year, did the corporation have any non-shareholder debt that was canceled, was forgiven, or had the terms modified so as to reduce the principal amount of the debt? If "Yes," enter the amount of principal reduction $		
12	During the tax year, was a qualified subchapter S subsidiary election terminated or revoked? If "Yes," see instructions		
13a	Did the corporation make any payments in 2014 that would require it to file Form(s) 1099?		
b	If "Yes," did the corporation file or will it file required Forms 1099?		

Form **1120S** (2014)

Form 1120S (2014) Page 3

Schedule K **Shareholders' Pro Rata Share Items**

DRAFT AS OF August 1, 2014 DO NOT FILE

Section	Line	Description		Line no.	Total amount
Income (Loss)	1	Ordinary business income (loss) (page 1, line 21)		1	
	2	Net rental real estate income (loss) (attach Form 8825)		2	
	3a	Other gross rental income (loss)	3a		
	b	Expenses from other rental activities (attach statement)	3b		
	c	Other net rental income (loss). Subtract line 3b from line 3a		3c	
	4	Interest income		4	
	5	Dividends: **a** Ordinary dividends		5a	
		b Qualified dividends	5b		
	6	Royalties		6	
	7	Net short-term capital gain (loss) (attach Schedule D (Form 1120S))		7	
	8a	Net long-term capital gain (loss) (attach Schedule D (Form 1120S))		8a	
	b	Collectibles (28%) gain (loss)	8b		
	c	Unrecaptured section 1250 gain (attach statement)	8c		
	9	Net section 1231 gain (loss) (attach Form 4797)		9	
	10	Other income (loss) (see instructions) Type ▶		10	
Deductions	11	Section 179 deduction (attach Form 4562)		11	
	12a	Charitable contributions		12a	
	b	Investment interest expense		12b	
	c	Section 59(e)(2) expenditures **(1)** Type ▶ **(2)** Amount ▶		12c(2)	
	d	Other deductions (see instructions) Type ▶		12d	
Credits	13a	Low-income housing credit (section 42(j)(5))		13a	
	b	Low-income housing credit (other)		13b	
	c	Qualified rehabilitation expenditures (rental real estate) (attach Form 3468, if applicable)		13c	
	d	Other rental real estate credits (see instructions) Type ▶		13d	
	e	Other rental credits (see instructions) Type ▶		13e	
	f	Biofuel producer credit (attach Form 6478)		13f	
	g	Other credits (see instructions) Type ▶		13g	
Foreign Transactions	14a	Name of country or U.S. possession ▶			
	b	Gross income from all sources		14b	
	c	Gross income sourced at shareholder level		14c	
		Foreign gross income sourced at corporate level			
	d	Passive category		14d	
	e	General category		14e	
	f	Other (attach statement)		14f	
		Deductions allocated and apportioned at shareholder level			
	g	Interest expense		14g	
	h	Other		14h	
		Deductions allocated and apportioned at corporate level to foreign source income			
	i	Passive category		14i	
	j	General category		14j	
	k	Other (attach statement)		14k	
		Other information			
	l	Total foreign taxes (check one): ▶ ☐ Paid ☐ Accrued		14l	
	m	Reduction in taxes available for credit (attach statement)		14m	
	n	Other foreign tax information (attach statement)			
Alternative Minimum Tax (AMT) Items	15a	Post-1986 depreciation adjustment		15a	
	b	Adjusted gain or loss		15b	
	c	Depletion (other than oil and gas)		15c	
	d	Oil, gas, and geothermal properties—gross income		15d	
	e	Oil, gas, and geothermal properties—deductions		15e	
	f	Other AMT items (attach statement)		15f	
Items Affecting Shareholder Basis	16a	Tax-exempt interest income		16a	
	b	Other tax-exempt income		16b	
	c	Nondeductible expenses		16c	
	d	Distributions (attach statement if required) (see instructions)		16d	
	e	Repayment of loans from shareholders		16e	

Form **1120S** (2014)

Form 1120S (2014) Page **4**

Schedule K **Shareholders' Pro Rata Share Items** (continued)

				Total amount
Other Information	17a	Investment income	17a	
	b	Investment expenses	17b	
	c	Dividend distributions paid from accumulated earnings and profits	17c	
	d	Other items and amounts (attach statement)		
Reconciliation	18	**Income/loss reconciliation.** Combine the amounts on lines 1 through 10 in the far right column. From the result, subtract the sum of the amounts on lines 11 through 12d and 14l	18	

Schedule L **Balance Sheets per Books**

	Beginning of tax year		End of tax year	
Assets	(a)	(b)	(c)	(d)
1 Cash				
2a Trade notes and accounts receivable				
b Less allowance for bad debts	( )		( )	
3 Inventories				
4 U.S. government obligations				
5 Tax-exempt securities (see instructions)				
6 Other current assets (attach statement)				
7 Loans to shareholders				
8 Mortgage and real estate loans				
9 Other investments (attach statement)				
10a Buildings and other depreciable assets				
b Less accumulated depreciation	( )		( )	
11a Depletable assets				
b Less accumulated depletion	( )		( )	
12 Land (net of any amortization)				
13a Intangible assets (amortizable only)				
b Less accumulated amortization	( )		( )	
14 Other assets (attach statement)				
15 Total assets				
Liabilities and Shareholders' Equity				
16 Accounts payable				
17 Mortgages, notes, bonds payable in less than 1 year				
18 Other current liabilities (attach statement)				
19 Loans from shareholders				
20 Mortgages, notes, bonds payable in 1 year or more				
21 Other liabilities (attach statement)				
22 Capital stock				
23 Additional paid-in capital				
24 Retained earnings				
25 Adjustments to shareholders' equity (attach statement)				
26 Less cost of treasury stock		( )		( )
27 Total liabilities and shareholders' equity				

Form **1120S** (2014)

DRAFT AS OF August 1, 2014 DO NOT FILE

Form 1120S (2014) Page **5**

Schedule M-1 **Reconciliation of Income (Loss) per Books With Income (Loss) per Return**
Note. The corporation may be required to file Schedule M-3 (see instructions)

1 Net income (loss) per books		5 Income recorded on books this year not included on Schedule K, lines 1 through 10 (itemize): a Tax-exempt interest $	
2 Income included on Schedule K, lines 1, 2, 3c, 4, 5a, 6, 7, 8a, 9, and 10, not recorded on books this year (itemize)			
3 Expenses recorded on books this year not included on Schedule K, lines 1 through 12 and 14l (itemize): a Depreciation $ b Travel and entertainment $		6 Deductions included on Schedule K, lines 1 through 12 and 14l, not charged against book income this year (itemize): a Depreciation $	
		7 Add lines 5 and 6	
4 Add lines 1 through 3		8 Income (loss) (Schedule K, line 18). Line 4 less line 7	

Schedule M-2 **Analysis of Accumulated Adjustments Account, Other Adjustments Account, and Shareholders' Undistributed Taxable Income Previously Taxed** (see instructions)

	(a) Accumulated adjustments account	(b) Other adjustments account	(c) Shareholders' undistributed taxable income previously taxed
1 Balance at beginning of tax year			
2 Ordinary income from page 1, line 21			
3 Other additions			
4 Loss from page 1, line 21	( )		
5 Other reductions	( )	( )	
6 Combine lines 1 through 5			
7 Distributions other than dividend distributions			
8 Balance at end of tax year. Subtract line 7 from line 6			

Form **1120S** (2014)

DRAFT AS OF August 1, 2014 DO NOT FILE

Self-Study Problem 11.6

671113

☐ Final K-1 ☐ Amended K-1 OMB No. 1545-0123

Schedule K-1 (Form 1120S) **2014**

Department of the Treasury
Internal Revenue Service

For calendar year 2014, or tax year beginning ________, 2014 ending ________, 20____

Shareholder's Share of Income, Deductions, Credits, etc. ► See back of form and separate instructions.

DRAFT AS OF July 8, 2014 DO NOT FILE

Part I Information About the Corporation

A Corporation's employer identification number

B Corporation's name, address, city, state, and ZIP code

C IRS Center where corporation filed return

Part II Information About the Shareholder

D Shareholder's identifying number

E Shareholder's name, address, city, state, and ZIP code

F Shareholder's percentage of stock ownership for tax year . . . . ________ %

For IRS Use Only

Part III Shareholder's Share of Current Year Income, Deductions, Credits, and Other Items

1	Ordinary business income (loss)	13	Credits
2	Net rental real estate income (loss)		
3	Other net rental income (loss)		
4	Interest income		
5a	Ordinary dividends		
5b	Qualified dividends	14	Foreign transactions
6	Royalties		
7	Net short-term capital gain (loss)		
8a	Net long-term capital gain (loss)		
8b	Collectibles (28%) gain (loss)		
8c	Unrecaptured section 1250 gain		
9	Net section 1231 gain (loss)		
10	Other income (loss)	15	Alternative minimum tax (AMT) items
11	Section 179 deduction	16	Items affecting shareholder basis
12	Other deductions		
		17	Other information

* See attached statement for additional information.

For Paperwork Reduction Act Notice, see Instructions for Form 1120S. IRS.gov/form1120s Cat. No. 11520D **Schedule K-1 (Form 1120S) 2014**

Schedule K-1 (Form 1120S) 2014 — Page **2**

This list identifies the codes used on Schedule K-1 for all shareholders and provides summarized reporting information for shareholders who file Form 1040. For detailed reporting and filing information, see the separate Shareholder's Instructions for Schedule K-1 and the instructions for your income tax return.

DRAFT AS OF July 8, 2014 DO NOT FILE

1. Ordinary business income (loss). Determine whether the income (loss) is passive or nonpassive and enter on your return as follows:

	Report on
Passive loss	See the Shareholder's Instructions
Passive income	Schedule E, line 28, column (g)
Nonpassive loss	Schedule E, line 28, column (h)
Nonpassive income	Schedule E, line 28, column (j)
2. Net rental real estate income (loss)	See the Shareholder's Instructions
3. Other net rental income (loss)	
Net income	Schedule E, line 28, column (g)
Net loss	See the Shareholder's Instructions
4. Interest income	Form 1040, line 8a
5a. Ordinary dividends	Form 1040, line 9a
5b. Qualified dividends	Form 1040, line 9b
6. Royalties	Schedule E, line 4
7. Net short-term capital gain (loss)	Schedule D, line 5
8a. Net long-term capital gain (loss)	Schedule D, line 12
8b. Collectibles (28%) gain (loss)	28% Rate Gain Worksheet, line 4 (Schedule D instructions)
8c. Unrecaptured section 1250 gain	See the Shareholder's Instructions
9. Net section 1231 gain (loss)	See the Shareholder's Instructions

10. Other income (loss)

Code		
A	Other portfolio income (loss)	See the Shareholder's Instructions
B	Involuntary conversions	See the Shareholder's Instructions
C	Sec. 1256 contracts & straddles	Form 6781, line 1
D	Mining exploration costs recapture	See Pub. 535
E	Other income (loss)	See the Shareholder's Instructions

11. Section 179 deduction — See the Shareholder's Instructions

12. Other deductions

Code		
A	Cash contributions (50%)	See the Shareholder's Instructions
B	Cash contributions (30%)	See the Shareholder's Instructions
C	Noncash contributions (50%)	See the Shareholder's Instructions
D	Noncash contributions (30%)	See the Shareholder's Instructions
E	Capital gain property to a 50% organization (30%)	See the Shareholder's Instructions
F	Capital gain property (20%)	See the Shareholder's Instructions
G	Contributions (100%)	See the Shareholder's Instructions
H	Investment interest expense	Form 4952, line 1
I	Deductions—royalty income	Schedule E, line 19
J	Section 59(e)(2) expenditures	See the Shareholder's Instructions
K	Deductions—portfolio (2% floor)	Schedule A, line 23
L	Deductions—portfolio (other)	Schedule A, line 28
M	Preproductive period expenses	See the Shareholder's Instructions
N	Commercial revitalization deduction from rental real estate activities	See Form 8582 instructions
O	Reforestation expense deduction	See the Shareholder's Instructions
P	Domestic production activities information	See Form 8903 instructions
Q	Qualified production activities income	Form 8903, line 7b
R	Employer's Form W-2 wages	Form 8903, line 17
S	Other deductions	See the Shareholder's Instructions

13. Credits

Code		
A	Low-income housing credit (section 42(j)(5)) from pre-2008 buildings	See the Shareholder's Instructions
B	Low-income housing credit (other) from pre-2008 buildings	See the Shareholder's Instructions
C	Low-income housing credit (section 42(j)(5)) from post-2007 buildings	See the Shareholder's Instructions
D	Low-income housing credit (other) from post-2007 buildings	See the Shareholder's Instructions
E	Qualified rehabilitation expenditures (rental real estate)	See the Shareholder's Instructions
F	Other rental real estate credits	See the Shareholder's Instructions
G	Other rental credits	See the Shareholder's Instructions
H	Undistributed capital gains credit	Form 1040, line 73, box a
I	Biofuel producer credit	See the Shareholder's Instructions
J	Work opportunity credit	See the Shareholder's Instructions
K	Disabled access credit	See the Shareholder's Instructions
L	Empowerment zone employment credit	See the Shareholder's Instructions
M	Credit for increasing research activities	See the Shareholder's Instructions
N	Credit for employer social security and Medicare taxes	See the Shareholder's Instructions
O	Backup withholding	See the Shareholder's Instructions
P	Other credits	See the Shareholder's Instructions

14. Foreign transactions

Code		Report on
A	Name of country or U.S. possession	Form 1116, Part I
B	Gross income from all sources	Form 1116, Part I
C	Gross income sourced at shareholder level	Form 1116, Part I
	Foreign gross income sourced at corporate level	
D	Passive category	Form 1116, Part I
E	General category	Form 1116, Part I
F	Other	Form 1116, Part I
	Deductions allocated and apportioned at shareholder level	
G	Interest expense	Form 1116, Part I
H	Other	Form 1116, Part I
	Deductions allocated and apportioned at corporate level to foreign source income	
I	Passive category	Form 1116, Part I
J	General category	Form 1116, Part I
K	Other	Form 1116, Part I
	Other information	
L	Total foreign taxes paid	Form 1116, Part II
M	Total foreign taxes accrued	Form 1116, Part II
N	Reduction in taxes available for credit	Form 1116, line 12
O	Foreign trading gross receipts	Form 8873
P	Extraterritorial income exclusion	Form 8873
Q	Other foreign transactions	See the Shareholder's Instructions

15. Alternative minimum tax (AMT) items

Code		
A	Post-1986 depreciation adjustment	See the Shareholder's Instructions and the Instructions for Form 6251
B	Adjusted gain or loss	See the Shareholder's Instructions and the Instructions for Form 6251
C	Depletion (other than oil & gas)	See the Shareholder's Instructions and the Instructions for Form 6251
D	Oil, gas, & geothermal—gross income	See the Shareholder's Instructions and the Instructions for Form 6251
E	Oil, gas, & geothermal—deductions	See the Shareholder's Instructions and the Instructions for Form 6251
F	Other AMT items	See the Shareholder's Instructions and the Instructions for Form 6251

16. Items affecting shareholder basis

Code		
A	Tax-exempt interest income	Form 1040, line 8b
B	Other tax-exempt income	See the Shareholder's Instructions
C	Nondeductible expenses	See the Shareholder's Instructions
D	Distributions	See the Shareholder's Instructions
E	Repayment of loans from shareholders	See the Shareholder's Instructions

17. Other information

Code		
A	Investment income	Form 4952, line 4a
B	Investment expenses	Form 4952, line 5
C	Qualified rehabilitation expenditures (other than rental real estate)	See the Shareholder's Instructions
D	Basis of energy property	See the Shareholder's Instructions
E	Recapture of low-income housing credit (section 42(j)(5))	Form 8611, line 8
F	Recapture of low-income housing credit (other)	Form 8611, line 8
G	Recapture of investment credit	See Form 4255
H	Recapture of other credits	See the Shareholder's Instructions
I	Look-back interest—completed long-term contracts	See Form 8697
J	Look-back interest—income forecast method	See Form 8866
K	Dispositions of property with section 179 deductions	See the Shareholder's Instructions
L	Recapture of section 179 deduction	See the Shareholder's Instructions
M	Section 453(l)(3) information	See the Shareholder's Instructions
N	Section 453A(c) information	See the Shareholder's Instructions
O	Section 1260(b) information	See the Shareholder's Instructions
P	Interest allocable to production expenditures	See the Shareholder's Instructions
Q	CCF nonqualified withdrawals	See the Shareholder's Instructions
R	Depletion information—oil and gas	See the Shareholder's Instructions
S	Reserved	See the Shareholder's Instructions
T	Section 108(i) information	See the Shareholder's Instructions
U	Net investment income	See the Shareholder's Instructions
V	Other information	See the Shareholder's Instructions

CORPORATE ACCUMULATIONS

Learning Objective 11.8

Describe the rules for the accumulated earnings tax and the personal holding company tax.

In many cases, taxpayers have established corporations to avoid paying individual income taxes by allowing earnings to be accumulated by the corporations. To prevent that practice, Congress has enacted two special taxes which may be applied to certain corporations; the accumulated earnings tax and the personal holding company tax.

Accumulated Earnings Tax

The accumulated earnings tax is designed to prevent the shareholders of a corporation from avoiding tax at the shareholder level by retaining earnings in the corporation. The tax is a penalty tax imposed in addition to the regular corporate income tax. The tax is imposed at a rate of 15 percent on amounts that are deemed to be unreasonable accumulations of earnings. For all corporations except service corporations, such as accounting, law, and health care corporations, the first $250,000 in accumulated earnings is exempt from tax. Service corporations will not be taxed on their first $150,000 of accumulated earnings. Even if the accumulated earnings of a corporation exceed the exemption amount, the tax will not be imposed on accumulations that can be shown to be necessary to meet the reasonable needs of the business.

EXAMPLE Alder Corporation is a manufacturing corporation that has accumulated earnings of $625,000. The corporation can establish reasonable needs for $450,000 of this accumulation. Alder Corporation would be subject to the accumulated earnings tax on $175,000 ($625,000 − $450,000). The amount of the accumulated earnings tax is $26,250 (15% of $175,000). ♦

Personal Holding Company Tax

Personal holding companies, which are corporations with few shareholders and with income primarily from investments, are subject to a 15 percent tax on their undistributed earnings. The tax is imposed in addition to the regular corporate income tax; however, a corporation cannot be subject to both the accumulated earnings tax and the personal holding company tax in the same year. If both taxes are imposed, the taxpayer pays only the personal holding company tax. The rules for the personal holding company tax are very complex.

Self-Study Problem 11.8 *See Appendix E for Solutions to Self-Study Problems*

Sugarbush Corporation, an accounting corporation, has accumulated earnings of $340,000,and the corporation cannot establish a reasonable need for any of that amount. Calculate the amount of accumulated earnings tax (if any) that will be imposed on Sugarbush Corporation.

$__________

THE CORPORATE ALTERNATIVE MINIMUM TAX

Learning Objective 11.9

Define the elements of the corporate alternative minimum tax (AMT) calculation.

For tax years beginning after 1997, the corporate alternative minimum tax does not apply to small corporations. A "small corporation" is one with average annual gross receipts of less than $5 million for the corporation's first 3-year period beginning after December 31, 1994. Thereafter, average annual gross receipts for all 3-year periods beginning after 1993 must not exceed $7.5 million.

The corporate alternative minimum tax is calculated in a manner similar to the individual alternative minimum tax. The tax is imposed at a rate of 20 percent on the alternative minimum tax base. The alternative minimum tax base is equal to the corporation's regular taxable income increased or decreased for certain adjustments, increased by tax preference items, and decreased by the exemption amount. Corporations with alternative minimum taxable income of $150,000 or less receive an exemption of $40,000. The exemption is phased out at a rate of 25 cents for every $1.00 by which the corporation's alternative minimum taxable income exceeds $150,000. Therefore, corporations with alternative minimum taxable income of $310,000 or more receive no exemption.

EXAMPLE Yew Corporation has regular taxable income of $75,000 and a regular tax liability of $13,750 during 2014. Yew Corporation is not a "small corporation." The company has tax preferences of $45,000. Yew's alternative minimum tax would be calculated as follows:

Regular taxable income	$ 75,000
Corporate tax preferences	45,000
Alternative minimum taxable income	$120,000
Less: exemption	(40,000)
Alternative minimum tax base	$ 80,000
Tax rate	20%
Gross alternative minimum tax	$ 16,000
Less: regular corporate tax	(13,750)
Alternative minimum tax due	$ 2,250

◆

Tax Preferences and Adjustments

The tax law defines adjustment and tax preference items for the corporate alternative minimum tax. The more common corporate tax adjustments and preferences include:

1. Accelerated depreciation on real estate,
2. Accelerated depreciation on personal property,
3. Certain tax-exempt bond interest,
4. Percentage depletion in excess of the property's adjusted basis, and
5. Seventy-five percent of the difference between adjusted current earnings and alternative minimum taxable income determined before this adjustment and the alternative tax net operating loss deduction.

Self-Study Problem 11.9 *See Appendix E for Solutions to Self-Study Problems*

In 2014, Plum Corporation has regular taxable income of $70,000 and a regular tax liability of $12,500. The corporation also has $55,000 of tax preference items. Calculate Plum Corporation's alternative minimum tax liability. Assume Plum Corporation is not a "small corporation."

$__________

KEY POINTS

Learning Objectives	Key Points
LO 11.1: Employ the corporate tax rates to calculate corporate tax liability.	• The U.S. corporate tax rate rate structure has eight tax brackets with marginal tax rates ranging from 15 percent to 39 percent. • "Bubbles" occur where the marginal corporate rate increases then decreases (e.g., from 34 percent to 39 percent and back and from 35 percent to 38 percent and back). Such bubbles recapture the tax savings from the prior tax bracket's progressive marginal rates. • For taxable income over $335,000 and less than or equal to $10,000,000, the corporate tax rate is a flat 34 percent. • For large corporations with taxable income over $18,333,333, the corporate tax rate is a flat 35 percent. • Qualified personal service corporations (health, law, engineering, architecture, accounting, actuarial science, performing arts, and consulting) are taxed at a flat 35 percent tax rate on all taxable income.
LO 11.2: Compute basic capital gains and losses for corporations.	• Corporate ordinary income and capital gains rates are the same, so there is no benefit to having long-term capital gains in a corporation. • Net short-term capital gains of a corporation are taxed as ordinary income. • Corporations are not allowed to deduct capital losses against ordinary income. • Capital losses may be used only to offset capital gains. • If capital losses cannot be used in the year they occur, they may be carried back 3 years and forward 5 years to offset capital gains in those years. • When a long-term capital loss is carried to another year, it is treated as a short-term capital loss and may be offset against either long-term or short-term capital gains.
LO 11.3: Ascertain how special deductions may affect corporate taxable income.	• Corporations are allowed a dividend received deduction based on their percentage of ownership in the corporation paying the dividend. • The deduction percentage is 70 percent (for ownership less than 20 percent), 80 percent (for ownership of 20 percent or more, but less than 80 percent), or 100 percent (for ownership of 80 percent or more). • Corporations amortize qualifying organizational costs over 180 months, and there is no upper limit to the amount of qualifying costs that can be amortized. • Corporations can elect to deduct up to $5,000 of organizational costs and $5,000 of start-up costs in the year they begin business (the $5,000 amount is reduced by each dollar of organizational expenses exceeding $50,000). • A corporation's charitable contribution deduction is limited to 10 percent of taxable income, computed before the deduction for charitable contributions, net operating loss carrybacks, capital loss carrybacks, and the dividends received deduction. • Excess charitable contributions are carried forward to the 5 succeeding tax years, subject to the 10 percent annual limitation in the carryover years, with the current year's contributions deducted first.
LO 11.4: Identify the components of Schedule M-1 and how they are reported to the IRS.	• The purpose of Schedule M-1 of the corporate tax return is to reconcile a corporation's accounting "book" income to its taxable income. • On the left side of Schedule M-1 are adjustments that must be added to book income, and on the right side of the schedule are adjustments that must be subtracted from book income to arrive at the amount of taxable income. • The additions to book income include the amount of federal income tax expense, net capital losses deducted for book purposes, income recorded on the tax return but not on the books, and expenses recorded on the books but not deducted on the tax return.

	• The amounts that must be deducted from book income include income recorded on the books but not included on the tax return, and deductions included on the return but not deducted on the books.
LO 11.5: Know the corporate tax return filing and estimated tax payment requirements.	• Corporate tax returns are due on or before the fifteenth day of the third month following the close of the corporation's tax year, but corporations may receive an automatic 6-month extension by filing Form 7004. • A corporation must pay any tax liability by the original due date of the return. • Corporations must make estimated tax payments similar to those made by self-employed individual taxpayers. The payments are due on the fifteenth day of the fourth, sixth, ninth, and twelfth months of the corporation's tax year.
LO 11.6: Understand, in general, how an S corporation is taxed and operates.	• Certain qualified corporations (S corporations) may elect to be taxed under Subchapter S of the Internal Revenue Code in a manner similar to partnerships. • To elect S corporation status, a corporation must have the following characteristics: (1) be a domestic corporation; (2) have 100 or fewer shareholders who are all either individuals, estates, certain trusts, certain financial institutions, or certain exempt organizations; (3) have only one class of stock; and (4) all shareholders must be U.S. citizens or resident aliens. • Each shareholder of an S corporation reports his or her share of corporate income based on his or her stock ownership during the year. • Schedule K-1 of Form 1120S is used to report the allocation of ordinary income or loss, and all separately stated items of income or loss, to each of the shareholders. • Losses from an S corporation pass through to the shareholders, but the loss deduction is limited to the shareholders' adjusted basis in the corporation's stock plus the amount of any loans from the shareholder to the corporation.
LO 11.7: Understand the basic tax rules for the formation of a corporation.	• If property is exchanged for stock in a corporation and the shareholders are in "control" of the corporation after the transfer, gain on the transfer is not recognized. • Realized gain is recognized to the extent that the shareholder receives boot. • The basis of the stock received by the shareholder is equal to the basis of the property transferred plus any gain recognized by the shareholder, less the fair market value of any boot received by the shareholder, less liabilities assumed by the corporation. • The basis of property received by the corporation is equal to the basis in the hands of the transferor plus any gain recognized by the transferor.
LO 11.8: Describe the rules for the accumulated earnings tax and the personal holding company tax.	• The accumulated earnings tax is a penalty tax, imposed in addition to the regular corporate income tax, at a rate of 15 percent on amounts that are deemed to be unreasonable accumulations of earnings. • For all corporations, except personal service corporations such as accounting, law, and health care corporations, the first $250,000 in accumulated earnings is exempt from tax. The amount is $150,000 for personal service corporations. • Personal holding companies, which are corporations with few shareholders and income primarily from investments, are subject to an extra 15 percent tax on undistributed earnings.
LO 11.9: Define the elements of the corporate alternative minimum tax (AMT) calculation.	• The corporate alternative minimum tax is similar to the individual AMT. • The tax preferences that apply to the calculation of the alternative minimum tax for individual taxpayers generally apply to corporations. • Corporations, however, have certain adjustments which differ from those that apply to individuals. • The AMT rate for corporations is 20 percent instead of the individual rate of 26 percent or 28 percent. • The corporate alternative minimum tax does not apply to small corporations as defined in the tax law.

© Dusit/Shutterstock.com

INTERACTIVE QUIZZES

Interactive quizzes are available as an optional online resource for Income Tax Fundamentals. Visit **www.cengagebrain.com** for more information.

QUESTIONS and PROBLEMS

GROUP 1: MULTIPLE CHOICE QUESTIONS

LO 11.1

1. Ironwood Corporation has ordinary taxable income of $40,000 for calendar-year 2014, and a long-term capital loss of $20,000. What is the corporation's tax liability for 2014?
   a. $4,500
   b. $6,000
   c. $7,500
   d. $10,000
   e. None of the above

LO 11.2

2. Which of the following statements is false regarding corporate capital losses?
   a. Corporations are not allowed to deduct capital losses against ordinary income.
   b. Corporations may carry capital losses back 3 years and forward 5 years to offset capital gains in those years.
   c. Corporations may deduct $3,000 of net capital loss each year until the loss is used up.
   d. A long-term capital loss carried to another year is treated as a short-term capital loss.

LO 11.3

3. Walnut Corporation owns 60 percent of Teak Corporation, a domestic corporation. During 2014, Walnut Corporation received $20,000 in dividends from Teak Corporation. Assuming that Walnut's taxable income for 2014 before the dividends received deduction is $500,000, what is the amount of Walnut's dividends received deduction for 2014?
   a. $0
   b. $14,000
   c. $16,000
   d. $20,000
   e. None of the above

LO 11.3

4. Which of the following is *not* a corporate organizational expenditure that may be amortized?
   a. The cost of organizational meetings
   b. Fees paid to the state for incorporation
   c. Accounting fees incident to organization
   d. Legal fees incident to organization
   e. All of the above are organizational expenditures

LO 11.4

5. The purpose of Schedule M-1 on the corporate tax return is to:
   a. Reconcile accounting (book) income to taxable income.
   b. Summarize the dividends received deduction calculation.
   c. List the officers of the corporation and their compensation.
   d. Calculate the net operating loss deduction.

LO 11.5

6. Which of the following statements is false regarding corporate tax return due dates?
   a. Corporate tax returns for calendar-year corporations are due March 15.
   b. Corporate tax returns may receive an automatic 6-month extension with the filing of a Form 7004.
   c. Corporate taxes due must be paid by March 15 if the corporation reports on a calendar-year basis.
   d. When an IRS due date falls on a weekend, the due date is considered to be the Friday preceding the weekend.

LO 11.6

7. Which of the following is *not* required for a corporation to be eligible to make an S corporation election in 2014?
   a. The corporation must have 100 or fewer shareholders.
   b. The corporation must be a domestic corporation.
   c. The corporation must have both common and preferred stock.
   d. The shareholders of the corporation must not be nonresident aliens.
   e. All shareholders must be either individuals, estates, certain trusts, or financial institutions.

LO 11.6

8. Which of the following items retains its character when passed through to shareholders of an S corporation?
   a. Wages paid
   b. Accelerated depreciation
   c. Net long-term capital gains
   d. Advertising expense
   e. All of the above retain their character when passed through

LO 11.6

9. Which of the following is true about S corporations?
   a. S corporations pay corporate taxes like other corporations.
   b. S corporations pay the alternative minimum tax for all income.
   c. S corporations cannot issue corporate stock.
   d. The S corporation status may be elected by stockholders only for corporations that meet certain qualifications.
   e. None of the above.

LO 11.7

10. Travis transfers land with a fair market value of $125,000 and basis of $25,000, to a corporation in exchange for 100 percent of the corporation's stock. What amount of gain must Travis recognize as a result of this transaction?
   a. $0
   b. $25,000
   c. $100,000
   d. $125,000
   e. None of the above

LO 11.7

11. Carl transfers land with a fair market value of $120,000 and basis of $30,000, to a new corporation in exchange for 85 percent of the corporation's stock. The land is subject to a $40,000 liability, which the corporation assumes. What amount of gain must Carl recognize as a result of this transaction?

a. $0
b. $40,000
c. $30,000
d. $10,000
e. None of the above

LO 11.7

12. What is the shareholder's basis in stock of a corporation received as a result of the transfer of property to the corporation and as a result of which gain was recognized by the stockholder?
    a. The shareholder's basis is equal to the basis of the property transferred less the gain.
    b. The shareholder's basis is equal to the fair market value of the stock received, less any liabilities transferred by the stockholder.
    c. The shareholder's basis is equal to the basis of the property transferred to the corporation, minus any liabilities transferred by the shareholder, plus the gain.
    d. The shareholder's basis is equal to the basis of the property transferred to the corporation, plus any liabilities transferred by the shareholder.
    e. None of the above.

LO 11.8

13. Which of the following statements regarding personal holding companies is false?
    a. A personal holding company is one which has few shareholders.
    b. A personal holding company has income primarily from investments.
    c. A personal holding company operates a business which is a hobby for its owners.
    d. Personal holding companies are subject to an extra 15 percent tax on income that is left undistributed.

LO 11.9

14. Which of the following statements is true about the corporate alternative minimum tax?
    a. The corporate alternative minimum tax only applies to small corporations.
    b. The corporate alternative minimum tax preferences and adjustments are exactly the same as those for individuals.
    c. The corporate alternative minimum tax rate is a flat 28 percent.
    d. Corporations with alternative minimum taxable income greater than $310,000 receive no exemption.

GROUP 2: PROBLEMS

LO 11.1

1. Quince Corporation has taxable income of $450,000 for its 2014 calendar tax year. Calculate the corporation's income tax liability for 2014 before tax credits.

$ ____________

LO 11.1

2. Ulmus Corporation has $1,230,000 in taxable income for 2014. Calculate the corporation's income tax liability for 2014.

$ ____________

LO 11.1
LO 11.2

3. For its 2014 tax year, Ilex Corporation has ordinary income of $240,000, a short-term capital loss of $60,000, and a long-term capital gain of $20,000. Calculate Ilex Corporation's tax liability for 2014.

$ ____________

LO 11.3

4. Fisafolia Corporation has gross income from operations of $220,000 and operating expenses of $160,000 for 2014. The corporation also has $20,000 in dividends from publicly traded domestic corporations (ownership in all corporations was less than 20 percent).
   a. Calculate the corporation's dividends received deduction for 2014.

   $____________

   b. Assume that instead of $220,000, Fisafolia Corporation has gross income from operations of $135,000. Calculate the corporation's dividends received deduction for 2014.

   $____________

LO 11.3

5. Beech Corporation, an accrual basis taxpayer, was organized and began business on July 1, 2014. During 2014, the corporation incurred the following expenses:

State fees for incorporation	$ 500
Legal and accounting fees incident to organization	1,800
Expenses for the sale of stock	2,100
Organizational meeting expenses	750

Assuming that Beech Corporation does not elect to expense but chooses to amortize organizational expenditures over 15 years, calculate the corporation's deduction for its calendar tax year 2014.

$____________

LO 11.3

6. Citradoria Corporation is a regular corporation that contributes $35,000 cash to qualified charitable organizations during 2014. The corporation has net operating income of $140,000, before deducting the contributions, and dividends received from domestic corporations (ownership in all corporations is less than 20 percent) in the amount of $20,000.
   a. What is the amount of Citradoria Corporation's allowable deduction for charitable contributions for the current year?

   $____________

   b. What may the corporation do with any excess amount of contributions?

   ____
   ____
   ____
   ____
   ____

LO 11.4

7. The Loquat Corporation has book net income of $50,000 for 2014. Included in this figure are the following items, which are reported on the corporation's Schedule M-1, Reconciliation of Income (Loss) per Books with Income per Return.

Federal income tax expense	$ 7,500
Depreciation deducted on the books which is not deductible for tax purposes	10,000
Deduction for 50 percent of meals and entertainment expense which is not allowed for tax purposes	4,500
Deduction for a tax penalty not allowed for tax purposes	2,000
Tax-exempt interest income included in book income but not in tax income	3,000

Calculate Loquat Corporation's taxable income for 2014 based on the information given. Show your calculations.

$____________

LO 11.5

8. Mallory Corporation has a calendar year-end. The corporation has paid estimated payments of $10,000 during 2014 but still owes an additional $5,000 for its 2014 tax year.
   a. When is the 2014 tax return due?

   ____

   b. If an automatic extension of time to file is requested, when is the 2014 tax return due?

   ____

   c. If an extension of time to file is requested, when is the additional $5,000 of tax for 2014 due?

   ____

LO 11.6

9. Cedar Corporation has an S corporation election in effect. During the 2014 calendar tax year, the corporation had ordinary taxable income of $200,000, and on January 15, 2014, the corporation paid dividends to shareholders in the amount of $120,000. How much taxable income, in total, must the shareholders of the corporation report on their 2014 tax returns?

   $__________

   Explain your answer ______________________________

   ____

LO 11.6

10. Bill and Guilda each own 50 percent of the stock of Radiata Corporation, an S corporation. Guilda's basis in her stock is $25,000. On July 31, 2014, Bill sells his stock, with a basis of $40,000, to Loraine for $50,000. For the 2014 tax year, Radiata Corporation has a loss of $100,375.
    a. Calculate the amount of the corporation's loss that may be deducted by Bill on his 2014 tax return.

    $__________

    b. Calculate the amount of the corporation's loss that may be deducted by Guilda on her 2014 tax return.

    $__________

    c. Calculate the amount of the corporation's loss that may be deducted by Loraine on her 2014 tax return.

    $__________

LO 11.7

11. Karen, in forming a new corporation, transfers land to the corporation in exchange for 100 percent of the stock of the corporation. Karen's basis in the land is $275,000, and the corporation assumes a liability on the property in the amount of $300,000. The stock received by Karen has a fair market value of $550,000.
    a. What is the amount of gain or loss that must be recognized by Karen on this transfer?

    $__________

    b. What is the amount of Karen's basis in the corporation's stock?

    $__________

    c. What is the amount of the corporation's basis in the land?

    $__________

LO 11.8

12. Grevilla Corporation is a manufacturing company. The corporation has accumulated earnings of $950,000, and it can establish reasonable needs for $400,000 of that amount. Calculate the amount of the accumulated earnings tax (if any) that Grevilla Corporation is subject to for this year.

$__________

LO 11.9

13. Cypress Corporation has regular taxable income of $170,000 (assume annual gross receipts are greater than $5 million) and a regular tax liability of $49,550 for 2014. The corporation also has tax preference items amounting to $105,000. Calculate Cypress Corporation's alternative minimum tax liability. Assume Cypress Corporation is not a "small corporation" for AMT purposes.

$__________

14. Go to the IRS website **(www.irs.gov)** and determine which IRS publication addresses the topic of corporate taxation. Print out the page with the *Table of Contents* of this IRS publication.

15. Go to the IRS website **(www.irs.gov)** and print out a copy of the most recent *Schedule K-1 of Form 1120S.*

GROUP 3:
COMPREHENSIVE PROBLEMS

1. Olive Corporation was formed and began operations on January 1, 2014. The corporation's income statement for the year and the balance sheet at year-end are presented below.

The Olive Corporation Income Statement
for the Year Ended December 31, 2014

Gross income from operations		$ 260,000
Qualified dividends received from a 10 percent-owned domestic corporation		20,000
Total gross income		$ 280,000
Cost of goods sold		(105,000)
Total income		$ 175,000
Other expenses:		
Compensation of officers	$75,000	
Salaries and wages	30,000	
Bad debts (direct charge-offs)	7,000	
Repairs	3,000	
Depreciation	10,000	
Advertising	5,000	
Payroll taxes	10,000	
Total other expenses		(140,000)
Net income (before federal income tax expense)		$ 35,000

The Olive Corporation Balance Sheet
as of December 31, 2014

Assets:		
Cash	$ 30,000	
Accounts receivable	20,000	
Inventory (at cost)	80,000	
Equipment	90,000	
Less: accumulated depreciation	(10,000)	
Total assets		$210,000
Liabilities and owners' equity:		
Accounts payable	$ 13,150	
Note payable (due in 10 years)	85,000	
Common stock	80,000	
Retained earnings	31,850	
Total liabilities and owners' equity		$210,000

The corporation made estimated tax payments of $4,000 and the corporation's federal income tax expense is equal to the federal tax liability. Complete Form 1120 for Olive Corporation on Pages 11-37 through 11-41.

2. Assume that Olive Corporation, in Comprehensive Problem 1, is an S corporation owned 50 percent by Linda Holiday and 50 percent by Ralph Winston. The corporation is not subject to any special taxes. Using the relevant information given in Comprehensive Problem 1 and assuming the corporation's retained earnings are $35,000 instead of $31,850, accounts payable are $10,000 instead of $13,150, and no estimated tax payments are made, complete Form 1120S for Olive Corporation and Schedule K-1 for Linda on Pages 11-43 through 11-48. Assume there were no cash distributions during the year.

Form **1120** Department of the Treasury Internal Revenue Service

U.S. Corporation Income Tax Return

For calendar year 2014 or tax year beginning ______, 2014, ending ______, 20 ___

▶ Information about Form 1120 and its separate instructions is at *www.irs.gov/form1120.*

OMB No. 1545-0123 **2014**

DRAFT AS OF June 25, 2014 DO NOT FILE

A Check if:
1a Consolidated return (attach Form 851) ☐
b Life/nonlife consolidated return ☐
2 Personal holding co. (attach Sch. PH) ☐
3 Personal service corp. (see instructions) ☐
4 Schedule M-3 attached ☐

TYPE OR PRINT
Name: Olive Corporation
Number, street, and room or suite no. If a P.O. box, see instructions.
City or town, state, or province, country and ZIP or foreign postal code

B Employer identification number
C Date incorporated
D Total assets (see instructions) $

E Check if: (1) ☑ Initial return (2) ☐ Final return (3) ☐ Name change (4) ☐ Address change

Section	Line	Description	Sub-line	Sub-amount	Line	Amount
Income	1a	Gross receipts or sales	1a	280,000		
	b	Returns and allowances	1b			
	c	Balance. Subtract line 1b from line 1a			1c	280,000
	2	Cost of goods sold (attach Form 1125-A)			2	105,000
	3	Gross profit. Subtract line 2 from line 1c			3	155,000
	4	Dividends (Schedule C, line 19)			4	20,000
	5	Interest			5	
	6	Gross rents			6	
	7	Gross royalties			7	
	8	Capital gain net income (attach Schedule D (Form 1120))			8	
	9	Net gain or (loss) from Form 4797, Part II, line 17 (attach Form 4797)			9	
	10	Other income (see instructions—attach statement)			10	
	11	**Total income.** Add lines 3 through 10 ▶			11	175,000
Deductions (See instructions for limitations on deductions.)	12	Compensation of officers (see instructions—attach Form 1125-E) ▶			12	75,000
	13	Salaries and wages (less employment credits)			13	30,000
	14	Repairs and maintenance			14	3,000
	15	Bad debts			15	7000
	16	Rents			16	
	17	Taxes and licenses			17	10,000
	18	Interest			18	
	19	Charitable contributions			19	
	20	Depreciation from Form 4562 not claimed on Form 1125-A or elsewhere on return (attach Form 4562)			20	10,000
	21	Depletion			21	
	22	Advertising			22	5,000
	23	Pension, profit-sharing, etc., plans			23	
	24	Employee benefit programs			24	
	25	Domestic production activities deduction (attach Form 8903)			25	
	26	Other deductions (attach statement)			26	
	27	**Total deductions.** Add lines 12 through 26 ▶			27	140,000
	28	Taxable income before net operating loss deduction and special deductions. Subtract line 27 from line 11			28	35,000
	29a	Net operating loss deduction (see instructions)	29a	∅		
	b	Special deductions (Schedule C, line 20)	29b	14,000		
	c	Add lines 29a and 29b			29c	14,000
Tax, Refundable Credits, and Payments	30	**Taxable income.** Subtract line 29c from line 28 (see instructions)			30	21,000
	31	Total tax (Schedule J, Part I, line 11)			31	3,150
	32	Total payments and refundable credits (Schedule J, Part II, line 21)			32	4,000
	33	Estimated tax penalty (see instructions). Check if Form 2220 is attached ▶ ☐			33	
	34	**Amount owed.** If line 32 is smaller than the total of lines 31 and 33, enter amount owed			34	
	35	**Overpayment.** If line 32 is larger than the total of lines 31 and 33, enter amount overpaid			35	850
	36	Enter amount from line 35 you want: **Credited to 2015 estimated tax** ▶		**Refunded** ▶	36	

Sign Here

Under penalties of perjury, I declare that I have examined this return, including accompanying schedules and statements, and to the best of my knowledge and belief, it is true, correct, and complete. Declaration of preparer (other than taxpayer) is based on all information of which preparer has any knowledge.

▶ Signature of officer | Date | ▶ Title

May the IRS discuss this return with the preparer shown below (see instructions)? ☐ Yes ☐ No

Paid Preparer Use Only

Print/Type preparer's name	Preparer's signature	Date	Check ☐ if self-employed	PTIN
Firm's name ▶			Firm's EIN ▶	
Firm's address ▶			Phone no.	

Form 1120 (2014) Page **2**

Schedule C	**Dividends and Special Deductions** (see instructions)	**(a)** Dividends received	**(b)** %	**(c)** Special deductions **(a)** × **(b)**
1	Dividends from less-than-20%-owned domestic corporations (other than debt-financed stock)	20,000	70	14,000
2	Dividends from 20%-or-more-owned domestic corporations (other than debt-financed stock)		80	
3	Dividends on debt-financed stock of domestic and foreign corporations		see instructions	
4	Dividends on certain preferred stock of less-than-20%-owned public utilities		42	
5	Dividends on certain preferred stock of 20%-or-more-owned public utilities		48	
6	Dividends from less-than-20%-owned foreign corporations and certain FSCs		70	
7	Dividends from 20%-or-more-owned foreign corporations and certain FSCs		80	
8	Dividends from wholly owned foreign subsidiaries		100	
9	**Total.** Add lines 1 through 8. See instructions for limitation			14,000
10	Dividends from domestic corporations received by a small business investment company operating under the Small Business Investment Act of 1958		100	
11	Dividends from affiliated group members		100	
12	Dividends from certain FSCs		100	
13	Dividends from foreign corporations not included on lines 3, 6, 7, 8, 11, or 12			
14	Income from controlled foreign corporations under subpart F (attach Form(s) 5471)			
15	Foreign dividend gross-up			
16	IC-DISC and former DISC dividends not included on lines 1, 2, or 3			
17	Other dividends			
18	Deduction for dividends paid on certain preferred stock of public utilities			
19	**Total dividends.** Add lines 1 through 17. Enter here and on page 1, line 4 ▶			
20	**Total special deductions.** Add lines 9, 10, 11, 12, and 18. Enter here and on page 1, line 29b ▶			14,000

Form **1120** (2014)

DRAFT AS OF June 25, 2014 DO NOT FILE

Form 1120 (2014) Page **3**

Schedule J Tax Computation and Payment (see instructions)

Part I–Tax Computation

1	Check if the corporation is a member of a controlled group (attach Schedule O (Form 1120)) ▶ ☐				
2	Income tax. Check if a qualified personal service corporation (see instructions) ▶ ☐			2	3150
3	Alternative minimum tax (attach Form 4626)			3	
4	Add lines 2 and 3			4	3150
5a	Foreign tax credit (attach Form 1118)	5a			
b	Credit from Form 8834 (see instructions)	5b			
c	General business credit (attach Form 3800)	5c			
d	Credit for prior year minimum tax (attach Form 8827)	5d			
e	Bond credits from Form 8912	5e			
6	**Total credits.** Add lines 5a through 5e			6	
7	Subtract line 6 from line 4			7	3150
8	Personal holding company tax (attach Schedule PH (Form 1120))			8	
9a	Recapture of investment credit (attach Form 4255)	9a			
b	Recapture of low-income housing credit (attach Form 8611)	9b			
c	Interest due under the look-back method—completed long-term contracts (attach Form 8697)	9c			
d	Interest due under the look-back method—income forecast method (attach Form 8866)	9d			
e	Alternative tax on qualifying shipping activities (attach Form 8902)	9e			
f	Other (see instructions—attach statement)	9f			
10	**Total.** Add lines 9a through 9f			10	
11	**Total tax.** Add lines 7, 8, and 10. Enter here and on page 1, line 31			11	3150

15%

Part II–Payments and Refundable Credits

12	2013 overpayment credited to 2014			12	
13	2014 estimated tax payments			13	4000
14	2014 refund applied for on Form 4466			14	( )
15	Combine lines 12, 13, and 14			15	
16	Tax deposited with Form 7004			16	
17	Withholding (see instructions)			17	
18	**Total payments.** Add lines 15, 16, and 17			18	4000
19	Refundable credits from:				
a	Form 2439	19a			
b	Form 4136	19b			
c	Form 8827, line 8c	19c			
d	Other (attach statement—see instructions)	19d			
20	**Total credits.** Add lines 19a through 19d			20	∅
21	**Total payments and credits.** Add lines 18 and 20. Enter here and on page 1, line 32			21	4000

Schedule K Other Information (see instructions)

		Yes	No
1	Check accounting method: a ☑ Cash b ☐ Accrual c ☐ Other (specify) ▶		
2	See the instructions and enter the:		
a	Business activity code no. ▶		
b	Business activity ▶		
c	Product or service ▶		
3	Is the corporation a subsidiary in an affiliated group or a parent-subsidiary controlled group? If "Yes," enter name and EIN of the parent corporation ▶		
4	At the end of the tax year:		
a	Did any foreign or domestic corporation, partnership (including any entity treated as a partnership), trust, or tax-exempt organization own directly 20% or more, or own, directly or indirectly, 50% or more of the total voting power of all classes of the corporation's stock entitled to vote? If "Yes," complete Part I of Schedule G (Form 1120) (attach Schedule G)		
b	Did any individual or estate own directly 20% or more, or own, directly or indirectly, 50% or more of the total voting power of all classes of the corporation's stock entitled to vote? If "Yes," complete Part II of Schedule G (Form 1120) (attach Schedule G)		

Form **1120** (2014)

DRAFT AS OF June 25, 2014 DO NOT FILE

Form 1120 (2014) Page **4**

Schedule K **Other Information** *continued* (see instructions)

		Yes	No
5	At the end of the tax year, did the corporation:		
a	Own directly 20% or more, or own, directly or indirectly, 50% or more of the total voting power of all classes of stock entitled to vote of any foreign or domestic corporation not included on **Form 851,** Affiliations Schedule? For rules of constructive ownership, see instructions. If "Yes," complete (i) through (iv) below.		

(i) Name of Corporation	**(ii)** Employer Identification Number (if any)	**(iii)** Country of Incorporation	**(iv)** Percentage Owned in Voting Stock

DRAFT AS OF June 25, 2014 DO NOT FILE

		Yes	No
b	Own directly an interest of 20% or more, or own, directly or indirectly, an interest of 50% or more in any foreign or domestic partnership (including an entity treated as a partnership) or in the beneficial interest of a trust? For rules of constructive ownership, see instructions. If "Yes," complete (i) through (iv) below.		

(i) Name of Entity	**(ii)** Employer Identification Number (if any)	**(iii)** Country of Organization	**(iv)** Maximum Percentage Owned in Profit, Loss, or Capital

6 During this tax year, did the corporation pay dividends (other than stock dividends and distributions in exchange for stock) in excess of the corporation's current and accumulated earnings and profits? (See sections 301 and 316.) . . . .
If "Yes," file **Form 5452,** Corporate Report of Nondividend Distributions.
If this is a consolidated return, answer here for the parent corporation and on Form 851 for each subsidiary.

7 At any time during the tax year, did one foreign person own, directly or indirectly, at least 25% of **(a)** the total voting power of all classes of the corporation's stock entitled to vote or **(b)** the total value of all classes of the corporation's stock? . . . .
For rules of attribution, see section 318. If "Yes," enter:
(i) Percentage owned ▶ ________ and **(ii)** Owner's country ▶ ________
(c) The corporation may have to file **Form 5472,** Information Return of a 25% Foreign-Owned U.S. Corporation or a Foreign Corporation Engaged in a U.S. Trade or Business. Enter the number of Forms 5472 attached ▶ ________

8 Check this box if the corporation issued publicly offered debt instruments with original issue discount . . . . ▶ ☐
If checked, the corporation may have to file **Form 8281,** Information Return for Publicly Offered Original Issue Discount Instruments.

9 Enter the amount of tax-exempt interest received or accrued during the tax year ▶ $ ________

10 Enter the number of shareholders at the end of the tax year (if 100 or fewer) ▶ ________

11 If the corporation has an NOL for the tax year and is electing to forego the carryback period, check here . . . . . . ▶ ☐
If the corporation is filing a consolidated return, the statement required by Regulations section 1.1502-21(b)(3) must be attached or the election will not be valid.

12 Enter the available NOL carryover from prior tax years (do not reduce it by any deduction on line 29a.) ▶ $ ________

13 Are the corporation's total receipts (page 1, line 1a, plus lines 4 through 10) for the tax year **and** its total assets at the end of the tax year less than $250,000? . . . .
If "Yes," the corporation is not required to complete Schedules L, M-1, and M-2. Instead, enter the total amount of cash distributions and the book value of property distributions (other than cash) made during the tax year ▶ $ ________

14 Is the corporation required to file Schedule UTP (Form 1120), Uncertain Tax Position Statement (see instructions)? . . . .
If "Yes," complete and attach Schedule UTP.

15a Did the corporation make any payments in 2014 that would require it to file Form(s) 1099? . . . .

b If "Yes," did or will the corporation file required Forms 1099? . . . .

16 During this tax year, did the corporation have an 80% or more change in ownership, including a change due to redemption of its own stock? . . . .

17 During or subsequent to this tax year, but before the filing of this return, did the corporation dispose of more than 65% (by value) of its assets in a taxable, non-taxable, or tax deferred transaction? . . . .

18 Did the corporation receive assets in a section 351 transfer in which any of the transferred assets had a fair market basis or fair market value of more than $1 million? . . . .

Form **1120** (2014)

Form 1120 (2014) Page 5

DRAFT AS OF June 25, 2014 DO NOT FILE

Schedule L — Balance Sheets per Books

	Assets	Beginning of tax year (a)	Beginning of tax year (b)	End of tax year (c)	End of tax year (d)
1	Cash		∅		30,000
2a	Trade notes and accounts receivable	∅		20,000	
b	Less allowance for bad debts	( )		( )	20,000
3	Inventories		∅		80,000
4	U.S. government obligations				
5	Tax-exempt securities (see instructions)				
6	Other current assets (attach statement)				
7	Loans to shareholders				
8	Mortgage and real estate loans				
9	Other investments (attach statement)				
10a	Buildings and other depreciable assets	∅		90,000	
b	Less accumulated depreciation	(∅)		(10,000)	80,000
11a	Depletable assets				
b	Less accumulated depletion	( )		( )	
12	Land (net of any amortization)				
13a	Intangible assets (amortizable only)				
b	Less accumulated amortization	( )		( )	
14	Other assets (attach statement)				
15	Total assets		∅		210,000
	Liabilities and Shareholders' Equity				
16	Accounts payable		∅		13,150
17	Mortgages, notes, bonds payable in less than 1 year				
18	Other current liabilities (attach statement)				
19	Loans from shareholders				
20	Mortgages, notes, bonds payable in 1 year or more		∅		85,000
21	Other liabilities (attach statement)				
22	Capital stock: a Preferred stock				
	b Common stock		∅	80,000	80,000
23	Additional paid-in capital				
24	Retained earnings—Appropriated (attach statement)		∅		31,850
25	Retained earnings—Unappropriated				
26	Adjustments to shareholders' equity (attach statement)				
27	Less cost of treasury stock		( )		( )
28	Total liabilities and shareholders' equity		∅		210,000

Schedule M-1 — Reconciliation of Income (Loss) per Books With Income per Return

Note: The corporation may be required to file Schedule M-3 (see instructions).

1	Net income (loss) per books	35,000	7	Income recorded on books this year not included on this return (itemize): Tax-exempt interest $	
2	Federal income tax per books	3150			
3	Excess of capital losses over capital gains				
4	Income subject to tax not recorded on books this year (itemize):		8	Deductions on this return not charged against book income this year (itemize):	
5	Expenses recorded on books this year not deducted on this return (itemize):		a	Depreciation $ 10,000	
a	Depreciation $		b	Charitable contributions $	
b	Charitable contributions $				
c	Travel and entertainment $				
			9	Add lines 7 and 8	10,000
6	Add lines 1 through 5	38150	10	Income (page 1, line 28)—line 6 less line 9	35,000

Schedule M-2 — Analysis of Unappropriated Retained Earnings per Books (Line 25, Schedule L)

1	Balance at beginning of year	∅	5	Distributions: a Cash	
2	Net income (loss) per books	35,000		b Stock	
3	Other increases (itemize):			c Property	
			6	Other decreases (itemize):	
			7	Add lines 5 and 6	
4	Add lines 1, 2, and 3	35,000	8	Balance at end of year (line 4 less line 7)	35,000

Form **1120** (2014)

Form **1120S**
Department of the Treasury
Internal Revenue Service

U.S. Income Tax Return for an S Corporation

▶ **Do not file this form unless the corporation has filed or is attaching Form 2553 to elect to be an S corporation.**
▶ **Information about Form 1120S and its separate instructions is at *www.irs.gov/form1120s.***

OMB No. 1545-0123
2014

DRAFT AS OF
August 1, 2014
DO NOT FILE

For calendar year 2014 or tax year beginning , 2014, ending , 20

A S election effective date	TYPE OR PRINT — Name	**D Employer identification number**
B Business activity code number (see instructions)	Number, street, and room or suite no. If a P.O. box, see instructions.	**E** Date incorporated
C Check if Sch. M-3 attached ☐	City or town, state or province, country, and ZIP or foreign postal code	**F** Total assets (see instructions) $

G Is the corporation electing to be an S corporation beginning with this tax year? ☐ Yes ☐ No If "Yes," attach Form 2553 if not already filed

H Check if: **(1)** ☐ Final return **(2)** ☐ Name change **(3)** ☐ Address change **(4)** ☐ Amended return **(5)** ☐ S election termination or revocation

I Enter the number of shareholders who were shareholders during any part of the tax year . . . . . . ▶

Caution. Include **only** trade or business income and expenses on lines 1a through 21. See the instructions for more information.

Section	Line	Description	Sub-line	Line	Amount
Income	1a	Gross receipts or sales	1a		
	b	Returns and allowances	1b		
	c	Balance. Subtract line 1b from line 1a		1c	
	2	Cost of goods sold (attach Form 1125-A)		2	
	3	Gross profit. Subtract line 2 from line 1c		3	
	4	Net gain (loss) from Form 4797, line 17 (attach Form 4797)		4	
	5	Other income (loss) (see instructions—attach statement)		5	
	6	**Total income (loss).** Add lines 3 through 5 ▶		6	
Deductions (see instructions for limitations)	7	Compensation of officers (see instructions—attach Form 1125-E)		7	
	8	Salaries and wages (less employment credits)		8	
	9	Repairs and maintenance		9	
	10	Bad debts		10	
	11	Rents		11	
	12	Taxes and licenses		12	
	13	Interest		13	
	14	Depreciation not claimed on Form 1125-A or elsewhere on return (attach Form 4562)		14	
	15	Depletion **(Do not deduct oil and gas depletion.)**		15	
	16	Advertising		16	
	17	Pension, profit-sharing, etc., plans		17	
	18	Employee benefit programs		18	
	19	Other deductions (attach statement)		19	
	20	**Total deductions.** Add lines 7 through 19 ▶		20	
	21	**Ordinary business income (loss).** Subtract line 20 from line 6		21	
Tax and Payments	22a	Excess net passive income or LIFO recapture tax (see instructions)	22a		
	b	Tax from Schedule D (Form 1120S)	22b		
	c	Add lines 22a and 22b (see instructions for additional taxes)		22c	
	23a	2014 estimated tax payments and 2013 overpayment credited to 2014	23a		
	b	Tax deposited with Form 7004	23b		
	c	Credit for federal tax paid on fuels (attach Form 4136)	23c		
	d	Add lines 23a through 23c		23d	
	24	Estimated tax penalty (see instructions). Check if Form 2220 is attached ▶ ☐		24	
	25	**Amount owed.** If line 23d is smaller than the total of lines 22c and 24, enter amount owed		25	
	26	**Overpayment.** If line 23d is larger than the total of lines 22c and 24, enter amount overpaid		26	
	27	Enter amount from line 26 **Credited to 2015 estimated tax** ▶	**Refunded** ▶	27	

Sign Here

Under penalties of perjury, I declare that I have examined this return, including accompanying schedules and statements, and to the best of my knowledge and belief, it is true, correct, and complete. Declaration of preparer (other than taxpayer) is based on all information of which preparer has any knowledge.

▶ Signature of officer   Date   ▶ Title

May the IRS discuss this return with the preparer shown below (see instructions)? ☐ Yes ☐ No

Paid Preparer Use Only

Print/Type preparer's name	Preparer's signature	Date	Check ☐ if self-employed	PTIN
Firm's name ▶			Firm's EIN ▶	
Firm's address ▶			Phone no.	

For Paperwork Reduction Act Notice, see separate instructions. Cat. No. 11510H Form **1120S** (2014)

Form 1120S (2014) Page **2**

Schedule B Other Information (see instructions)

DRAFT AS OF August 1, 2014 DO NOT FILE

		Yes	No
1	Check accounting method: **a** ☐ Cash **b** ☐ Accrual **c** ☐ Other (specify) ▶		
2	See the instructions and enter the: **a** Business activity ▶ **b** Product or service ▶		
3	At any time during the tax year, was any shareholder of the corporation a disregarded entity, a trust, an estate, or a nominee or similar person? If "Yes," attach Schedule B-1, Information on Certain Shareholders of an S Corporation		
4	At the end of the tax year, did the corporation:		
a	Own directly 20% or more, or own, directly or indirectly, 50% or more of the total stock issued and outstanding of any foreign or domestic corporation? For rules of constructive ownership, see instructions. If "Yes," complete (i) through (v) below		

(i) Name of Corporation	(ii) Employer Identification Number (if any)	(iii) Country of Incorporation	(iv) Percentage of Stock Owned	(v) If Percentage in (iv) is 100%, Enter the Date (if any) a Qualified Subchapter S Subsidiary Election Was Made

		Yes	No
b	Own directly an interest of 20% or more, or own, directly or indirectly, an interest of 50% or more in the profit, loss, or capital in any foreign or domestic partnership (including an entity treated as a partnership) or in the beneficial interest of a trust? For rules of constructive ownership, see instructions. If "Yes," complete (i) through (v) below		

(i) Name of Entity	(ii) Employer Identification Number (if any)	(iii) Type of Entity	(iv) Country of Organization	(v) Maximum Percentage Owned in Profit, Loss, or Capital

		Yes	No
5 a	At the end of the tax year, did the corporation have any outstanding shares of restricted stock?		
	If "Yes," complete lines (i) and (ii) below.		
	(i) Total shares of restricted stock ▶		
	(ii) Total shares of non-restricted stock ▶		
b	At the end of the tax year, did the corporation have any outstanding stock options, warrants, or similar instruments?		
	If "Yes," complete lines (i) and (ii) below.		
	(i) Total shares of stock outstanding at the end of the tax year ▶		
	(ii) Total shares of stock outstanding if all instruments were executed ▶		
6	Has this corporation filed, or is it required to file, **Form 8918,** Material Advisor Disclosure Statement, to provide information on any reportable transaction?		
7	Check this box if the corporation issued publicly offered debt instruments with original issue discount ▶ ☐		
	If checked, the corporation may have to file **Form 8281,** Information Return for Publicly Offered Original Issue Discount Instruments.		
8	If the corporation: **(a)** was a C corporation before it elected to be an S corporation **or** the corporation acquired an asset with a basis determined by reference to the basis of the asset (or the basis of any other property) in the hands of a C corporation **and (b)** has net unrealized built-in gain in excess of the net recognized built-in gain from prior years, enter the net unrealized built-in gain reduced by net recognized built-in gain from prior years (see instructions) ▶ $		
9	Enter the accumulated earnings and profits of the corporation at the end of the tax year. $		
10	Does the corporation satisfy **both** of the following conditions?		
a	The corporation's total receipts (see instructions) for the tax year were less than $250,000		
b	The corporation's total assets at the end of the tax year were less than $250,000		
	If "Yes," the corporation is not required to complete Schedules L and M-1.		
11	During the tax year, did the corporation have any non-shareholder debt that was canceled, was forgiven, or had the terms modified so as to reduce the principal amount of the debt?		
	If "Yes," enter the amount of principal reduction $		
12	During the tax year, was a qualified subchapter S subsidiary election terminated or revoked? If "Yes," see instructions		
13a	Did the corporation make any payments in 2014 that would require it to file Form(s) 1099?		
b	If "Yes," did the corporation file or will it file required Forms 1099?		

Form 1120S (2014) Page 3

DRAFT AS OF August 1, 2014 DO NOT FILE

Schedule K		Shareholders' Pro Rata Share Items		Total amount
Income (Loss)	1	Ordinary business income (loss) (page 1, line 21)	1	
	2	Net rental real estate income (loss) (attach Form 8825)	2	
	3a	Other gross rental income (loss) — 3a		
	b	Expenses from other rental activities (attach statement) — 3b		
	c	Other net rental income (loss). Subtract line 3b from line 3a	3c	
	4	Interest income	4	
	5	Dividends: **a** Ordinary dividends	5a	
		b Qualified dividends — 5b		
	6	Royalties	6	
	7	Net short-term capital gain (loss) (attach Schedule D (Form 1120S))	7	
	8a	Net long-term capital gain (loss) (attach Schedule D (Form 1120S))	8a	
	b	Collectibles (28%) gain (loss) — 8b		
	c	Unrecaptured section 1250 gain (attach statement) — 8c		
	9	Net section 1231 gain (loss) (attach Form 4797)	9	
	10	Other income (loss) (see instructions) Type ▶	10	
Deductions	11	Section 179 deduction (attach Form 4562)	11	
	12a	Charitable contributions	12a	
	b	Investment interest expense	12b	
	c	Section 59(e)(2) expenditures **(1)** Type ▶ **(2)** Amount ▶	12c(2)	
	d	Other deductions (see instructions) Type ▶	12d	
Credits	13a	Low-income housing credit (section 42(j)(5))	13a	
	b	Low-income housing credit (other)	13b	
	c	Qualified rehabilitation expenditures (rental real estate) (attach Form 3468, if applicable)	13c	
	d	Other rental real estate credits (see instructions) Type ▶	13d	
	e	Other rental credits (see instructions) Type ▶	13e	
	f	Biofuel producer credit (attach Form 6478)	13f	
	g	Other credits (see instructions) Type ▶	13g	
Foreign Transactions	14a	Name of country or U.S. possession ▶		
	b	Gross income from all sources	14b	
	c	Gross income sourced at shareholder level	14c	
		Foreign gross income sourced at corporate level		
	d	Passive category	14d	
	e	General category	14e	
	f	Other (attach statement)	14f	
		Deductions allocated and apportioned at shareholder level		
	g	Interest expense	14g	
	h	Other	14h	
		Deductions allocated and apportioned at corporate level to foreign source income		
	i	Passive category	14i	
	j	General category	14j	
	k	Other (attach statement)	14k	
		Other information		
	l	Total foreign taxes (check one): ▶ ☐ Paid ☐ Accrued	14l	
	m	Reduction in taxes available for credit (attach statement)	14m	
	n	Other foreign tax information (attach statement)		
Alternative Minimum Tax (AMT) Items	15a	Post-1986 depreciation adjustment	15a	
	b	Adjusted gain or loss	15b	
	c	Depletion (other than oil and gas)	15c	
	d	Oil, gas, and geothermal properties—gross income	15d	
	e	Oil, gas, and geothermal properties—deductions	15e	
	f	Other AMT items (attach statement)	15f	
Items Affecting Shareholder Basis	16a	Tax-exempt interest income	16a	
	b	Other tax-exempt income	16b	
	c	Nondeductible expenses	16c	
	d	Distributions (attach statement if required) (see instructions)	16d	
	e	Repayment of loans from shareholders	16e	

Form **1120S** (2014)

Form 1120S (2014) Page **4**

Schedule K **Shareholders' Pro Rata Share Items** (continued)

				Total amount
Other Information	17a	Investment income	17a	
	b	Investment expenses	17b	
	c	Dividend distributions paid from accumulated earnings and profits	17c	
	d	Other items and amounts (attach statement)		
Recon-ciliation	18	**Income/loss reconciliation.** Combine the amounts on lines 1 through 10 in the far right column. From the result, subtract the sum of the amounts on lines 11 through 12d and 14l	18	

Schedule L **Balance Sheets per Books**

		Beginning of tax year		End of tax year	
	Assets	(a)	(b)	(c)	(d)
1	Cash				
2a	Trade notes and accounts receivable				
b	Less allowance for bad debts	( )		( )	
3	Inventories				
4	U.S. government obligations				
5	Tax-exempt securities (see instructions)				
6	Other current assets (attach statement)				
7	Loans to shareholders				
8	Mortgage and real estate loans				
9	Other investments (attach statement)				
10a	Buildings and other depreciable assets				
b	Less accumulated depreciation	( )		( )	
11a	Depletable assets				
b	Less accumulated depletion	( )		( )	
12	Land (net of any amortization)				
13a	Intangible assets (amortizable only)				
b	Less accumulated amortization	( )		( )	
14	Other assets (attach statement)				
15	Total assets				
	Liabilities and Shareholders' Equity				
16	Accounts payable				
17	Mortgages, notes, bonds payable in less than 1 year				
18	Other current liabilities (attach statement)				
19	Loans from shareholders				
20	Mortgages, notes, bonds payable in 1 year or more				
21	Other liabilities (attach statement)				
22	Capital stock				
23	Additional paid-in capital				
24	Retained earnings				
25	Adjustments to shareholders' equity (attach statement)				
26	Less cost of treasury stock		( )		( )
27	Total liabilities and shareholders' equity				

Form **1120S** (2014)

DRAFT AS OF August 1, 2014 DO NOT FILE

Form 1120S (2014) Page **5**

Schedule M-1 **Reconciliation of Income (Loss) per Books With Income (Loss) per Return**
Note. The corporation may be required to file Schedule M-3 (see instructions)

1	Net income (loss) per books		5	Income recorded on books this year not included on Schedule K, lines 1 through 10 (itemize): a Tax-exempt interest $	
2	Income included on Schedule K, lines 1, 2, 3c, 4, 5a, 6, 7, 8a, 9, and 10, not recorded on books this year (itemize)				
3	Expenses recorded on books this year not included on Schedule K, lines 1 through 12 and 14l (itemize): a Depreciation $ b Travel and entertainment $		6	Deductions included on Schedule K, lines 1 through 12 and 14l, not charged against book income this year (itemize): a Depreciation $	
			7	Add lines 5 and 6	
4	Add lines 1 through 3		8	Income (loss) (Schedule K, line 18). Line 4 less line 7	

Schedule M-2 **Analysis of Accumulated Adjustments Account, Other Adjustments Account, and Shareholders' Undistributed Taxable Income Previously Taxed** (see instructions)

		(a) Accumulated adjustments account	(b) Other adjustments account	(c) Shareholders' undistributed taxable income previously taxed
1	Balance at beginning of tax year			
2	Ordinary income from page 1, line 21			
3	Other additions			
4	Loss from page 1, line 21	( )		
5	Other reductions	( )	( )	
6	Combine lines 1 through 5			
7	Distributions other than dividend distributions			
8	Balance at end of tax year. Subtract line 7 from line 6			

Form **1120S** (2014)

DRAFT AS OF August 1, 2014 DO NOT FILE

671113

☐ Final K-1 ☐ Amended K-1 OMB No. 1545-0123

Schedule K-1 (Form 1120S) **2014**
Department of the Treasury
Internal Revenue Service

For calendar year 2014, or tax year beginning ________, 2014 ending ________, 20____

Shareholder's Share of Income, Deductions, Credits, etc.

▶ See back of form and separate instructions.

DRAFT AS OF July 8, 2014 DO NOT FILE

Part I Information About the Corporation

A Corporation's employer identification number

B Corporation's name, address, city, state, and ZIP code

C IRS Center where corporation filed return

Part II Information About the Shareholder

D Shareholder's identifying number

E Shareholder's name, address, city, state, and ZIP code

F Shareholder's percentage of stock ownership for tax year . . . . ________ %

For IRS Use Only

Part III Shareholder's Share of Current Year Income, Deductions, Credits, and Other Items

1	Ordinary business income (loss)	13	Credits
2	Net rental real estate income (loss)		
3	Other net rental income (loss)		
4	Interest income		
5a	Ordinary dividends		
5b	Qualified dividends	14	Foreign transactions
6	Royalties		
7	Net short-term capital gain (loss)		
8a	Net long-term capital gain (loss)		
8b	Collectibles (28%) gain (loss)		
8c	Unrecaptured section 1250 gain		
9	Net section 1231 gain (loss)		
10	Other income (loss)	15	Alternative minimum tax (AMT) items
11	Section 179 deduction	16	Items affecting shareholder basis
12	Other deductions		
		17	Other information

* See attached statement for additional information.

Schedule K-1 (Form 1120S) 2014 Page **2**

This list identifies the codes used on Schedule K-1 for all shareholders and provides summarized reporting information for shareholders who file Form 1040. For detailed reporting and filing information, see the separate Shareholder's Instructions for Schedule K-1 and the instructions for your income tax return.

DRAFT AS OF July 8, 2014 DO NOT FILE

1. Ordinary business income (loss). Determine whether the income (loss) is passive or nonpassive and enter on your return as follows:

	Report on
Passive loss	See the Shareholder's Instructions
Passive income	Schedule E, line 28, column (g)
Nonpassive loss	Schedule E, line 28, column (h)
Nonpassive income	Schedule E, line 28, column (j)
2. Net rental real estate income (loss)	See the Shareholder's Instructions
3. Other net rental income (loss)	
Net income	Schedule E, line 28, column (g)
Net loss	See the Shareholder's Instructions
4. Interest income	Form 1040, line 8a
5a. Ordinary dividends	Form 1040, line 9a
5b. Qualified dividends	Form 1040, line 9b
6. Royalties	Schedule E, line 4
7. Net short-term capital gain (loss)	Schedule D, line 5
8a. Net long-term capital gain (loss)	Schedule D, line 12
8b. Collectibles (28%) gain (loss)	28% Rate Gain Worksheet, line 4 (Schedule D instructions)
8c. Unrecaptured section 1250 gain	See the Shareholder's Instructions
9. Net section 1231 gain (loss)	See the Shareholder's Instructions

10. Other income (loss)

Code		
A	Other portfolio income (loss)	See the Shareholder's Instructions
B	Involuntary conversions	See the Shareholder's Instructions
C	Sec. 1256 contracts & straddles	Form 6781, line 1
D	Mining exploration costs recapture	See Pub. 535
E	Other income (loss)	See the Shareholder's Instructions

11. Section 179 deduction — See the Shareholder's Instructions

12. Other deductions

A	Cash contributions (50%)	See the Shareholder's Instructions (A–G)
B	Cash contributions (30%)	
C	Noncash contributions (50%)	
D	Noncash contributions (30%)	
E	Capital gain property to a 50% organization (30%)	
F	Capital gain property (20%)	
G	Contributions (100%)	
H	Investment interest expense	Form 4952, line 1
I	Deductions—royalty income	Schedule E, line 19
J	Section 59(e)(2) expenditures	See the Shareholder's Instructions
K	Deductions—portfolio (2% floor)	Schedule A, line 23
L	Deductions—portfolio (other)	Schedule A, line 28
M	Preproductive period expenses	See the Shareholder's Instructions
N	Commercial revitalization deduction from rental real estate activities	See Form 8582 instructions
O	Reforestation expense deduction	See the Shareholder's Instructions
P	Domestic production activities information	See Form 8903 instructions
Q	Qualified production activities income	Form 8903, line 7b
R	Employer's Form W-2 wages	Form 8903, line 17
S	Other deductions	See the Shareholder's Instructions

13. Credits

A	Low-income housing credit (section 42(j)(5)) from pre-2008 buildings	See the Shareholder's Instructions (A–G)
B	Low-income housing credit (other) from pre-2008 buildings	
C	Low-income housing credit (section 42(j)(5)) from post-2007 buildings	
D	Low-income housing credit (other) from post-2007 buildings	
E	Qualified rehabilitation expenditures (rental real estate)	
F	Other rental real estate credits	
G	Other rental credits	
H	Undistributed capital gains credit	Form 1040, line 73, box a
I	Biofuel producer credit	See the Shareholder's Instructions (I–P)
J	Work opportunity credit	
K	Disabled access credit	
L	Empowerment zone employment credit	
M	Credit for increasing research activities	
N	Credit for employer social security and Medicare taxes	
O	Backup withholding	
P	Other credits	

14. Foreign transactions

Code		*Report on*
A	Name of country or U.S. possession	Form 1116, Part I (A–C)
B	Gross income from all sources	
C	Gross income sourced at shareholder level	
	Foreign gross income sourced at corporate level	
D	Passive category	Form 1116, Part I (D–F)
E	General category	
F	Other	
	Deductions allocated and apportioned at shareholder level	
G	Interest expense	Form 1116, Part I
H	Other	Form 1116, Part I
	Deductions allocated and apportioned at corporate level to foreign source income	
I	Passive category	Form 1116, Part I (I–K)
J	General category	
K	Other	
	Other information	
L	Total foreign taxes paid	Form 1116, Part II
M	Total foreign taxes accrued	Form 1116, Part II
N	Reduction in taxes available for credit	Form 1116, line 12
O	Foreign trading gross receipts	Form 8873
P	Extraterritorial income exclusion	Form 8873
Q	Other foreign transactions	See the Shareholder's Instructions

15. Alternative minimum tax (AMT) items

A	Post-1986 depreciation adjustment	See the Shareholder's Instructions and the Instructions for Form 6251 (A–F)
B	Adjusted gain or loss	
C	Depletion (other than oil & gas)	
D	Oil, gas, & geothermal—gross income	
E	Oil, gas, & geothermal—deductions	
F	Other AMT items	

16. Items affecting shareholder basis

A	Tax-exempt interest income	Form 1040, line 8b
B	Other tax-exempt income	See the Shareholder's Instructions (B–E)
C	Nondeductible expenses	
D	Distributions	
E	Repayment of loans from shareholders	

17. Other information

A	Investment income	Form 4952, line 4a
B	Investment expenses	Form 4952, line 5
C	Qualified rehabilitation expenditures (other than rental real estate)	See the Shareholder's Instructions
D	Basis of energy property	See the Shareholder's Instructions
E	Recapture of low-income housing credit (section 42(j)(5))	Form 8611, line 8
F	Recapture of low-income housing credit (other)	Form 8611, line 8
G	Recapture of investment credit	See Form 4255
H	Recapture of other credits	See the Shareholder's Instructions
I	Look-back interest—completed long-term contracts	See Form 8697
J	Look-back interest—income forecast method	See Form 8866
K	Dispositions of property with section 179 deductions	See the Shareholder's Instructions (K–V)
L	Recapture of section 179 deduction	
M	Section 453(l)(3) information	
N	Section 453A(c) information	
O	Section 1260(b) information	
P	Interest allocable to production expenditures	
Q	CCF nonqualified withdrawals	
R	Depletion information—oil and gas	
S	Reserved	
T	Section 108(i) information	
U	Net investment income	
V	Other information	

Student Name ____________________

Class/Section ____________________

Date ____________________

KEY NUMBER TAX RETURN SUMMARY

CHAPTER 11

Comprehensive Problem 1

Total Income (Line 11) ____________

Dividends Received Deduction (Line 29c) ____________

Taxable Income (Line 30) ____________

Tax Liability (Line 31) ____________

Tax Overpaid (Line 35) ____________

Comprehensive Problem 2

Cost of Goods Sold (Line 2) ____________

Total Income (Line 6) ____________

Ordinary Business Income (Line 21) ____________

Tax Liability (Line 25) ____________

Qualified Dividends (Schedule K-1, Line 5b) ____________

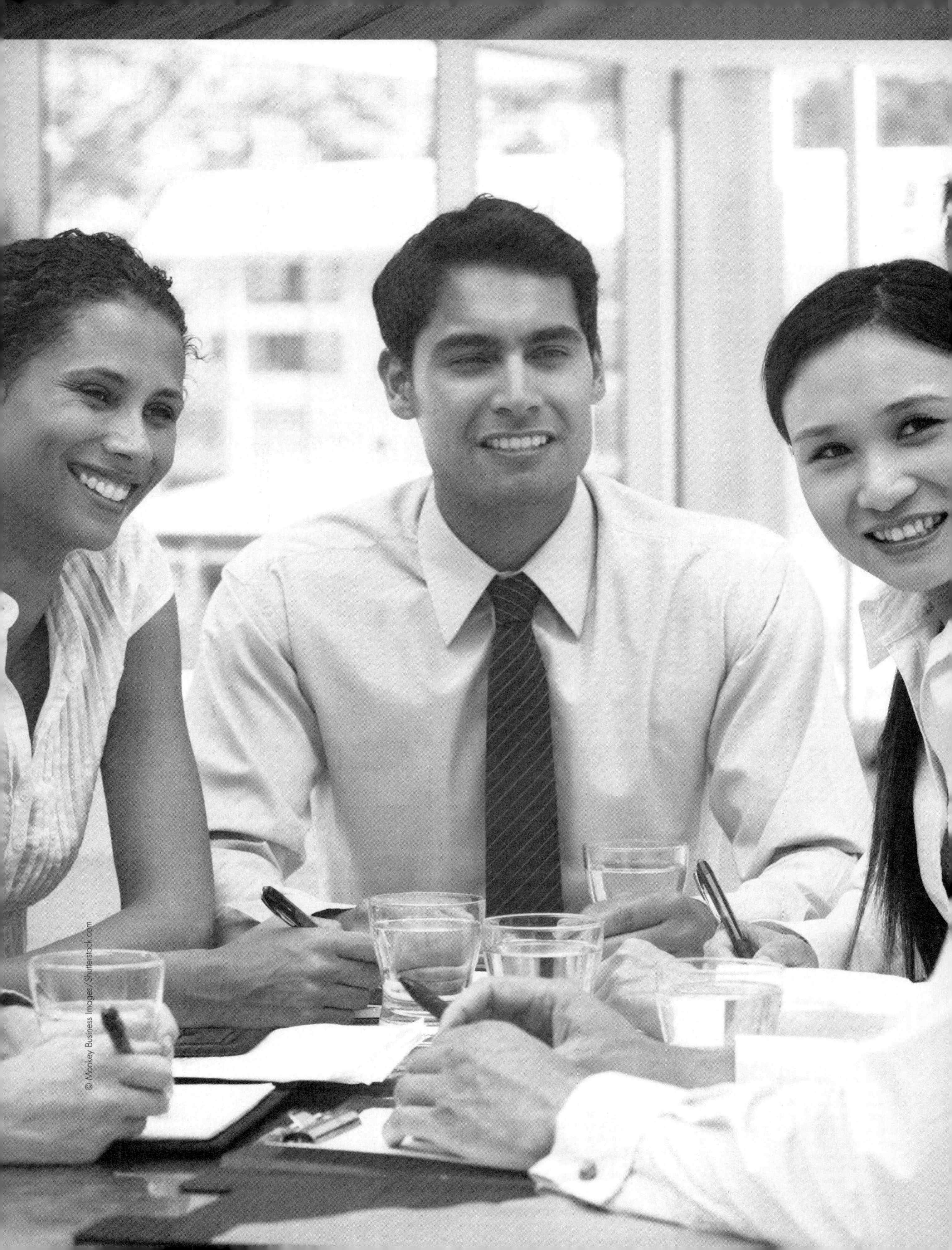
© Monkey Business Images/Shutterstock.com

CHAPTER 12

Tax Administration and Tax Planning

LEARNING OBJECTIVES

After completing this chapter, you should be able to:

LO 12.1	Identify the organizational structure of the IRS.
LO 12.2	Understand the IRS audit process.
LO 12.3	Define the common penalties for taxpayers and be able to apply them to specific situations.
LO 12.4	Apply the general rule for the statute of limitations on tax returns and the important exceptions to the general rule.
LO 12.5	Describe the rules and penalties that apply to tax practitioners.
LO 12.6	Describe the Taxpayer Bill of Rights.
LO 12.7	Understand the basic concepts of tax planning.

OVERVIEW

Knowing how the IRS operates, and how and why the IRS audits certain returns, is extremely important to tax practitioners. This chapter covers these topics as well as tax penalties that apply to taxpayers and tax preparers, the statute of limitations on tax liabilities, and rules applicable to tax practitioners (i.e., Circular 230). The taxpayer "Bill of Rights," also covered in this chapter, provides taxpayers with significant rights when dealing with the IRS, such as the ability to record an IRS interview.

Arranging one's financial affairs in order to minimize tax liability is referred to as tax planning. This chapter includes a discussion of basic tax-planning techniques that may be used by individual taxpayers. This final chapter is intended to give an appreciation for the process of dealing with the IRS and several of the many issues involved in conducting a tax practice.

Learning Objective 12.1

Identify the organizational structure of the IRS.

THE INTERNAL REVENUE SERVICE

The tax laws of the United States are administered by the Internal Revenue Service (IRS). In administering the tax law, the IRS has the responsibility for determining, assessing, and collecting internal revenue taxes and enforcing other provisions of the tax law. The IRS is a division of the Treasury Department.

The IRS organization currently consists of a national office in Washington, D.C., IRS Campus Processing Sites, and various operational offices throughout the United States. The national office is the headquarters of the commissioner of internal revenue and various deputy and associate commissioners. The commissioner of internal revenue is appointed by the president of the United States with the advice and consent of the Senate. The responsibilities of the commissioner are to establish policy, to supervise the activities of the organization, and to act in an advisory capacity to the Treasury Department on legislative matters. In addition, the commissioner is responsible for the collection of income tax, auditing of tax returns, intelligence operations, and appellate procedures.

IRS Campus Processing Sites

In addition to the various operational offices discussed below, the IRS currently maintains IRS Campus Processing Sites. At these processing sites, the IRS computers process the information from tax documents such as tax returns, payroll tax forms, Form 1099s, and withholding forms. Processing sites are located in the following cities:

Austin, TX
Andover, MA
Cincinnati, OH
Fresno, CA
Kansas City, MO
Ogden, UT
Philadelphia, PA

Paper returns for individuals are processed at only the Austin, Fresno, and Kansas City offices while e-filings are still processed at many of the sites. The IRS also maintains a national computer center in Martinsburg, West Virginia, where information from various processing sites is matched with records from other processing sites. This cross-matching of records helps to assure that taxpayers report all their income and do not file multiple refund claims.

Would You Believe?

"April 15 is lurking around the corner, so if you have yet to file your federal tax return, it's time to set aside a few hours, gather together your financial records, and flee the country."
– Dave Barry

The IRS Organizational Structure

The Internal Revenue Service was completely reorganized under the 1998 IRS Restructuring Act (RRA 98), which resulted in the structure as shown in Figure 12.1.

FIGURE 12.1

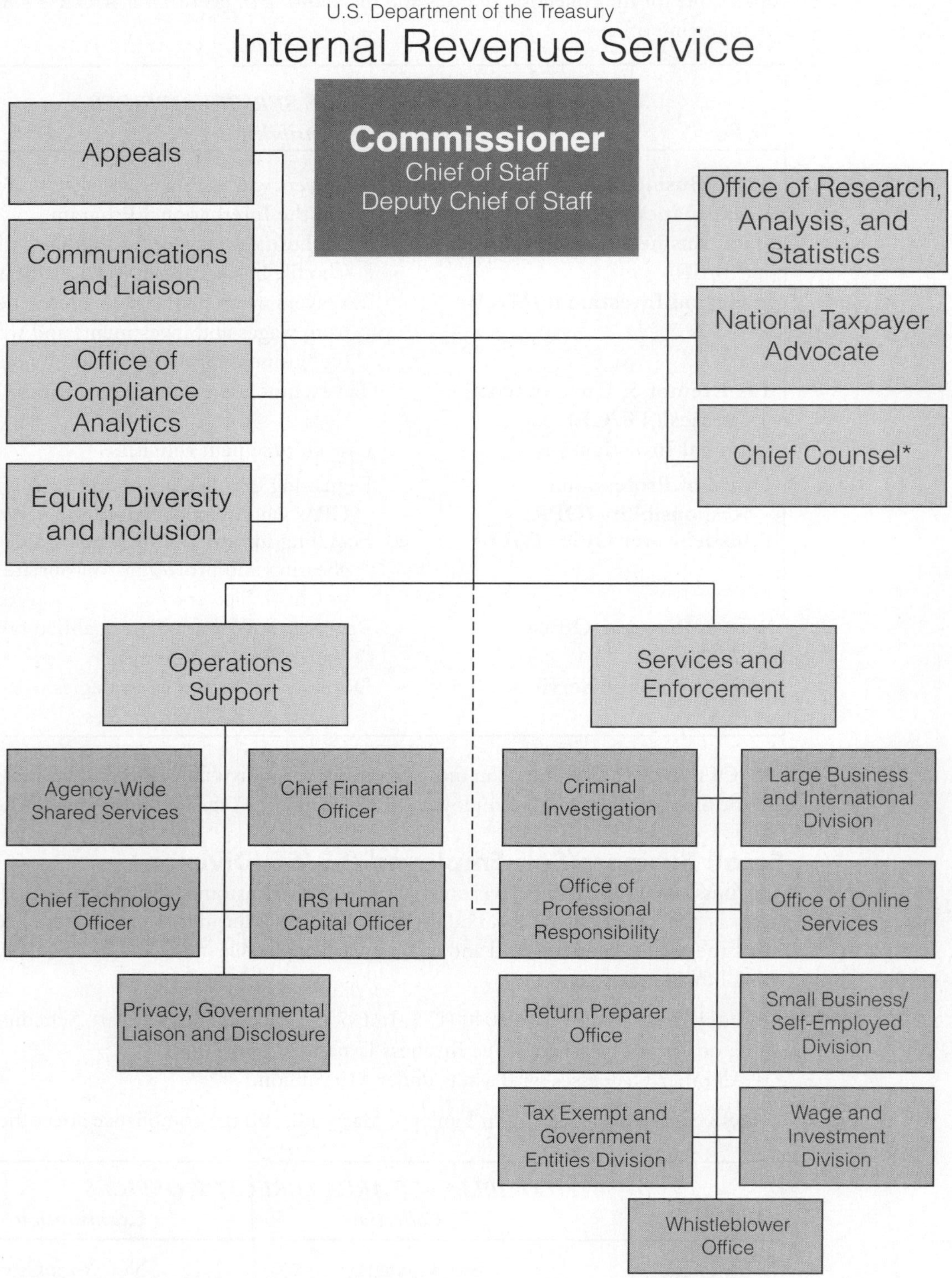

* With respect to tax litigation and the legal interpretation of tax law, the Chief Counsel also reports to the General Counsel of the Treasury Department. On matters solely related to tax policy, the Chief Counsel reports to the Treasury General Counsel.

www.irs.gov

Note: In addition to Figure 12.1 above, more extensive information about the IRS organizational structure is available to the public at **www.irs.gov.**

The Services and Enforcement arm of the IRS, as shown in Figure 12.1, is now responsible for the collection of taxes and the auditing of tax returns, which is done through the following offices:

INTERNAL REVENUE SERVICE OFFICES	
Office	*Responsibility*
Large Business and International (LB&I)	Taxpayers with assets of $10 million or more and the International Program
Small Business/Self-Employed (SB/SE)	Small business taxpayers including individuals who file business forms with their tax returns
Wage and Investment (W&I)	Taxpayers whose primary income is derived from wages and investments and who do not file business forms with their tax returns
Tax Exempt & Government Entities (TE/GE)	Tax exempt and government entities
Criminal Investigation	Law enforcement activities
Office of Professional Responsibility (OPR)	Regulating enrolled agents, attorneys, and CPAs who practice before the Service
Whistleblower Office (WO)	Handling information that helps uncover tax cheating and providing appropriate rewards to whistleblowers
Return Preparer Office	Registers and promotes a qualified tax professional community
Office of Online Services	Develops and executes strategies to update and integrate IRS Web services

Of these IRS divisions, the most significant to individual and small business taxpayers are the Small Business/Self-Employed (SB/SE) and the Wage and Investment (W&I) offices.

Small Business/Self-Employed (SB/SE) Division

The mission of the SB/SE Division is to serve SB/SE customers by educating and informing them of their tax obligations. The division develops educational products and services and helps the public to understand and comply with applicable laws. The SB/SE Division serves the following taxpayers:

- Individuals filing Form 1040 (U.S. Individual Income Tax Return), Schedules C, E, or F, or Form 2106 (Employee Business Expenses), and
- All other businesses with assets under $10 million.

The SB/SE headquarters are in Lanham, Maryland, and the compliance area offices are:

COMPLIANCE AREA DIRECTOR OFFICES		
Area	*Collection*	*Examination*
North Atlantic	Manhattan	New York City
South Atlantic	Plantation, FL	Jacksonville
Central	Cincinnati	Nashville
Midwest	Chicago	Downers Grove, IL
Gulf States	Austin	Dallas
Western	Salt Lake City	Denver
California	Los Angeles	Los Angeles

The SB/SE Division serves this taxpayer segment through five organizations:

- Collection (specializing in delinquent taxes and tax returns)
- Compliance Services Campus Operations
- Examination (specializing in office and field audits)
- Specialty Taxes (employment taxes, excise taxes, estate and gift taxes, and international taxes)
- Communications and Stakeholder Outreach (CSO)

Wage and Investment (W&I) Division

The mission of the W&I Division is to help taxpayers understand and comply with applicable tax laws and to protect the public interest by applying the tax law with integrity and fairness. The headquarters of the W&I office is in Atlanta, Georgia. The taxpayer profile of W&I is as follows:

- Most pay taxes through withholdings,
- More than half prepare their own returns,
- Most interact with the IRS once a year, and
- Most receive refunds.

Organizationally, the W&I Division is broken down into several operational administrative centers (offices). The key operations of the W&I offices include:

- The Customer Assistance, Relationships, and Education (CARE) office
- The Customer Account Services (CAS) office
- The Compliance office
- The Return Integrity and Correspondence Services (RICS) office

Note: Extensive additional information about the IRS organizational structure is available to the public at www.irs.gov.

Examination of Records

Federal tax law gives the IRS authority to examine a taxpayer's books and records to determine the correct amount of tax due. The IRS also has the right to summon taxpayers and to make them appear before the IRS and produce necessary accounting records. Taxpayers are required by law to maintain accounting records to facilitate an IRS audit.

The IRS may also issue a summons for taxpayer records from third parties such as banks, brokers, and CPAs. The IRS must notify the taxpayer within 3 days of serving a third-party summons to allow the taxpayer to intervene in any proceeding involving the summons. If a taxpayer receives notice that the IRS is summoning records from a third party, he or she should seek immediate professional tax advice.

Would You Believe?

The IRS has always had a problem with snoops in its ranks. The IRS opens numerous employee "browsing" investigations every year. Apparently, a small number of employees are willing to risk their careers and prosecution in exchange for a peek at the tax information of a range of friends, enemies, relatives, neighbors, ex-spouses, and celebrities. The IRS works vigilantly as an organization to deter snooping and to protect the legal confidentiality of taxpayer information.

Collections

Taxpayers have several options when they are unable to pay the money they owe to the IRS. The IRS wants to help taxpayers move their issues toward resolution, and it has tools to help delinquent taxpayers pay the taxes they owe. Taxpayers may ask the IRS for a short-term administrative extension of time and then borrow money or sell assets to pay

their tax debt. They may also enter into an installment agreement with the IRS, if their debt is below certain limits, and pay the debt within a 2-year or 3-year time frame. Another option for certain taxpayers is an *offer in compromise* where the IRS accepts a settlement less than the total amount of tax due. Generally, taxpayers who qualify for an offer in compromise are unlikely to ever be able to pay the amount they owe. Alternatively, sometimes the IRS will accept an offer in compromise when the tax liability is disputed, or to avert a costly and time-consuming legal battle.

If a taxpayer does not pay taxes that are due, ignores notices and demands for payment, and fails to make arrangements to pay the amount owed, the IRS will generally start a collection process. This process may include a tax levy that allows the IRS to take a portion of a taxpayer's wages or to seize property such as the taxpayer's house, car, bank account, or other financial accounts. The IRS may also put a tax lien on the taxpayer's property, which is a legal claim to the property. Liens will not be filed unless a taxpayer owes more than $10,000 in taxes. The IRS also has the power to assess significant penalties, some of which are covered later in this chapter.

Self-Study Problem 12.1 *See Appendix E for Solutions to Self-Study Problems*

Indicate whether the following statements are true or false in the current year by circling the appropriate letter.

T F 1. The IRS has seventeen major services and enforcement offices.
T F 2. Tax returns are processed at IRS Campus Processing Sites.
T F 3. The commissioner of internal revenue is an elected position.
T F 4. The IRS is part of the Justice Department.
T F 5. The IRS has the right to summon a taxpayer's tax records.

Learning Objective 12.2

Understand the IRS audit process.

THE AUDIT PROCESS

A primary function of the IRS is to audit taxpayers' tax returns. After the service centers have checked the returns for accuracy, some returns are selected for audit. When a return is selected for examination, it may be subject to an "office audit" or a "field audit." An audit may also be conducted through the mail in what is called a "correspondence audit."

Correspondence audits now account for about 80 percent of the IRS examinations of individual returns each year. Correspondence audits are generally handled entirely by mail. The audit begins when the IRS sends a letter to a taxpayer requesting specific information about their tax return. Usually, the areas covered in correspondence audits relate to questions about W-2s or 1099s that do not agree with the tax return, requests for information supporting employee business expenses and charitable contributions, and information related to eligibility for claimed earned income credits.

The office audit is conducted in an IRS office and is typically used for individual taxpayers with little or no business activities. In an office audit, the taxpayer takes his or her records to the IRS office where they are reviewed by a revenue agent. The taxpayer is simply required to substantiate deductions, credits, or income items that appear on his or her tax return.

In a field audit, the IRS agent reviews a taxpayer's books and records at the taxpayer's place of business or at the office of the taxpayer's accountant. This type of audit is generally used when the accounting records are too extensive to take to the IRS office. Field audits are usually used for taxpayers with substantial trade or business activities. If a taxpayer can present a valid reason, he or she may have an office audit changed to a field audit.

Selection of Returns for Audits

The IRS uses a computerized statistical sampling technique to select tax returns for most audits. The process used in selecting returns is called the Discriminant Function System (DIF). Under this system, the IRS uses mathematical formulas to assign a DIF score to each return. The DIF score represents the potential for discovery of improper treatment of items on the tax return. The higher the DIF score, the more likely the tax return is to be audited.

The DIF score is designed to identify tax returns likely to contain errors because they contain amounts of income, deductions, or tax credits that fall outside "normal" ranges. For example, a tax return that contains a large casualty loss claimed as a deduction will be assigned a high DIF score, and the chances of it being selected for audit are greater.

In 2007, the IRS announced a special research program to update their audit selection process. Nearly 13,000 randomly selected 2006 tax returns were audited beginning in October of 2007, and similar samples have been audited in subsequent years. The taxpayers were audited in special audits to determine the areas on which the IRS should best concentrate when targeting taxpayers for audit. The results of the IRS research program have been used to update the DIF system. The IRS reports that the "recalibration" of the audit formulas has resulted in fewer no-change audits and a larger average additional tax assessment. Over a decade ago, the IRS suspended Taxpayer Compliance Measurement Program (TCMP) audits due to protests from both taxpayers and lawmakers. These audits were extremely detailed and time-consuming and required the taxpayer to verify most or all of the items on their tax return. Some commentators have referred to the audits which began in 2007 as "Son of TCMP."

Would You Believe?

The old TCMP audits were sometimes so time-consuming and intrusive that one taxpayer referred to them as "an autopsy without the benefit of dying," according to a *Wall Street Journal's* "Tax Report" column.

Other tax returns are audited that are not selected by the DIF system. These returns are selected using information from other sources such as informants, other governmental agencies, news items, and associated tax returns.

The Appeals Process

After a return is selected for examination, an agent is assigned to perform the audit. There are three possible results arising from the agent's audit. First, the tax return may be found to require no adjustment, in which case the findings are reviewed and the tax return is sent to storage. A second possible outcome of the audit is an agreement between the agent and the taxpayer on a needed change in the tax liability on the tax return. Then, the tax is collected or the refund is paid, and after a review the return is stored.

The final possible outcome of the audit is a disagreement between the agent and the taxpayer on the amount of the required adjustment to the tax return. In this situation, the appeals procedure begins with the IRS inviting the taxpayer to an informal conference with an appellate agent. If an agreement cannot be reached at the appeals level, then the matter is taken into the federal court system. The Federal Tax Court is open to the public. For tax professionals and tax students, watching the Tax Court in action can be an educational experience. Any group planning a court visit should contact the judge's chambers in advance since the courts are often small and cannot accommodate many spectators. Figures 12.2 and 12.3 on Pages 12-8 and 12-9, respectively, illustrate the audit process, beginning with the selection of a tax return for audit and ending with a decision of the federal courts.

FIGURE 12.2

INCOME TAX AUDIT PROCEDURE OF THE INTERNAL REVENUE SERVICE

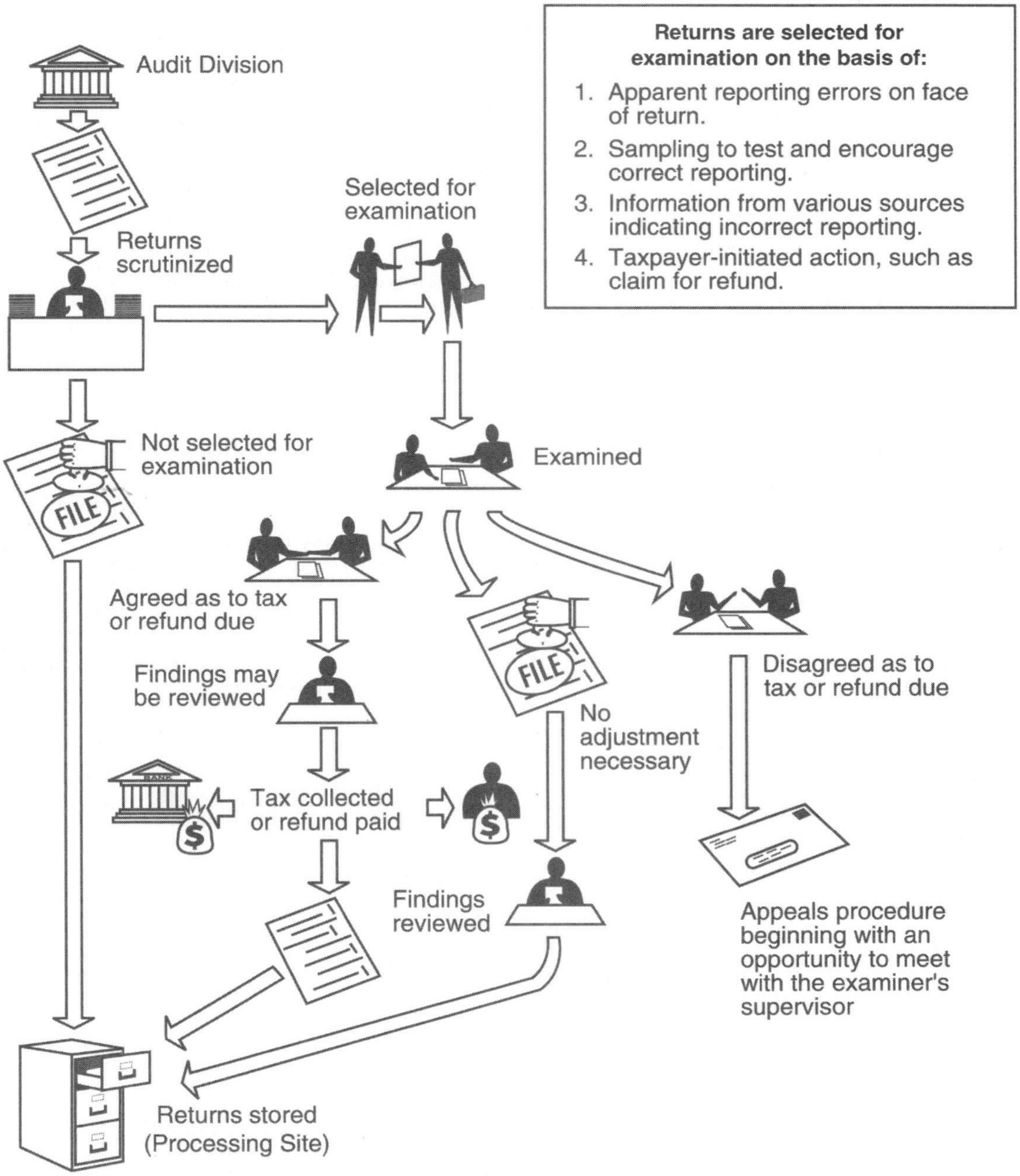

© Cengage Learning

FIGURE 12.3

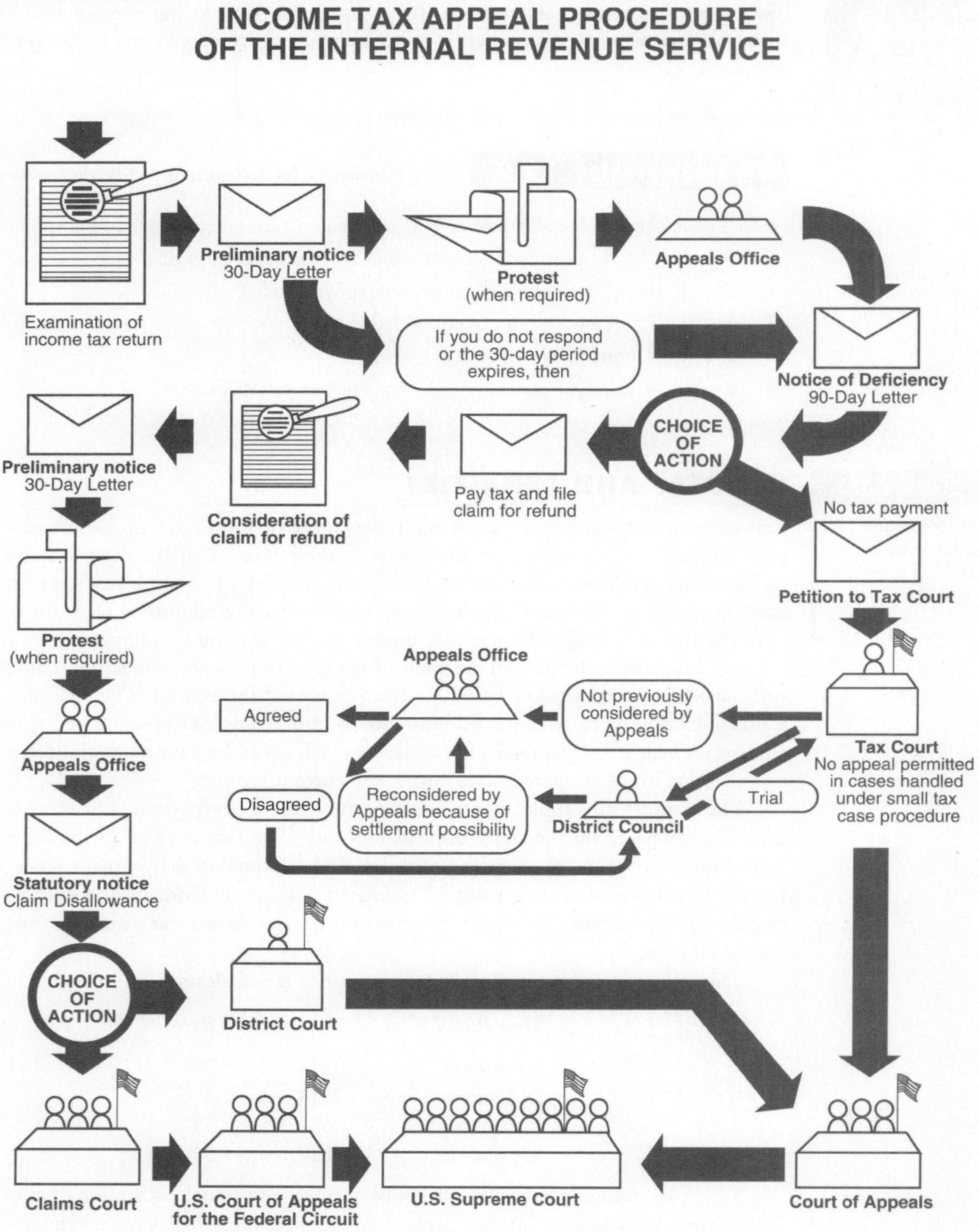

At any stage of procedure:

- You can agree and arrange to pay.
- You can ask the IRS to issue you a notice of deficiency so you can file a petition with the Tax Court.
- You can pay the tax and file a claim for a refund.

© Cengage Learning

TAX BREAK

Taxpayers selected for audit should consider hiring professionals to represent them. Lawyers say taxpayers confronted by IRS agents often tend to get nervous and talk too much, blurting out unnecessary details or becoming overly emotional and arousing needless suspicions.

Self-Study Problem 12.2 *See Appendix E for Solutions to Self-Study Problems*

Indicate whether the following statements are true or false by circling the appropriate letter.

T F 1. The IRS uses computers to select tax returns for most audits.
T F 2. An office audit is done at the taxpayer's office.
T F 3. TCMP audits are not performed currently.
T F 4. An audit may result in a refund.
T F 5. A taxpayer cannot appeal the results of an IRS audit.

Learning Objective 12.3

Define the common penalties for taxpayers and be able to apply them to specific situations.

INTEREST AND PENALTIES

Taxpayers are charged interest on underpayments of taxes, and in some cases the IRS pays interest to taxpayers when they overpay their taxes. Usually, these interest charges or payments result from the settlement of a tax liability for a prior year's tax return. For example, when an IRS audit results in the taxpayer paying additional taxes for a prior tax year, the IRS will charge the taxpayer interest on the amount of additional taxes from the original due date to the date of payment of the tax. If the audit results in a refund, interest will be paid to the taxpayer based on the amount of the refund. The IRS also imposes a nondeductible penalty based on amounts of underpayments of estimated taxes for the current tax year (see Chapter 9), but a taxpayer is not paid interest on a refund arising from an overpayment of estimated taxes during the current tax year.

The interest rate applicable to underpayments and overpayments of taxes is adjusted each quarter based on the short-term federal rate. The rate is equal to the federal short-term rate plus 3 percentage points. Interest is compounded daily except when calculating the penalty for underpayment of estimated taxes by individuals and corporations. In calculating the penalty for underpayment of estimated taxes, the penalty is calculated as simple interest.

The rate of interest for selected recent periods is as follows:

Time Period		*Rate*
1st quarter	2014	3%
2nd quarter	2014	3%
3rd quarter	2014	3%
4th quarter	2014	3%

Tables are available from the IRS for performing the actual calculation of interest owed from or due to taxpayers. Interest paid on an underpayment of tax is considered consumer interest and, therefore, no deduction is allowed (see Chapter 5). The penalty for underpayment of estimated tax is calculated as interest but is a nondeductible penalty. Interest received on an overpayment is income in the year the payment is received.

EXAMPLE James pays $2,000 of interest in 2014 for an underpayment of taxes on his 2011 tax return. The $2,000 is not deductible since no deduction is allowed for consumer interest. ♦

EXAMPLE John receives $700 of interest income on the overpayment of his taxes resulting from an IRS audit on his 2011 tax return. The $700 interest is income in the year it is received by John. ♦

The tax law contains various penalties to ensure taxpayers accurately report and pay their taxes. Penalty payments are considered an addition to the amount of the taxes and, therefore, are not deductible. Several of the major taxpayer penalties are described in the following paragraphs.

The Failure-to-File and Failure-to-Pay Penalties

If a taxpayer does not file a tax return on the due date (including extensions), he or she is subject to a penalty equal to 5 percent of the tax due with the return for every month or portion of a month the return is late. The amount of the penalty for failure to file, however, is limited to a maximum of 25 percent of the amount of taxes due with the tax return. In the event the failure to file is fraudulent, the penalty is increased from 5 percent for each month or portion thereof to 15 percent, and the maximum penalty is increased from 25 percent to 75 percent. Also, if the taxpayer fails to file the return within 60 days of its due date, the minimum failure-to-file penalty is the lesser of $135 or the total amount of the taxes due with the tax return. The failure-to-file penalty will not be assessed if the taxpayer can demonstrate that he or she had "reasonable cause" for failing to file the tax return on time.

Taxpayers are also subject to a penalty for failure to pay the amount of the taxes due on the due date of their tax return. The penalty for failure to pay is ½ of 1 percent of the amount of taxes due for every month or portion of a month that the payment is late, up to a maximum of 25 percent of the amount of taxes due. The penalty increases to 1 percent per month beginning 10 days after a notice of levy has been given to the taxpayer. If both the failure-to-file and the failure-to-pay penalties apply, the failure-to-file penalty is reduced by the amount of the failure-to-pay penalty. Both the failure-to-file and the failure-to-pay penalties are zero if there is no tax due or if a refund is due from the IRS on the late tax return.

EXAMPLE Nancy filed her tax return 3½ months after the due date, and she had not requested an extension of time to file. The failure to file was not due to fraud. She included with her late return a check for $2,000, which was the balance of the tax she owed. Disregarding interest, her penalties are calculated as follows:

Failure-to-pay penalty (0.5% × $2,000) × 4 months		$ 40
Plus:		
Failure-to-file penalty (5% × $2,000) × 4 months	$400	
Less: Failure-to-pay penalty	(40)	
Net failure-to-file penalty		360
Total penalties		$400

Note that in general, the maximum total penalty possible in this example is 25 percent of $2,000, or $500. ♦

TAX BREAK

In 2001, the IRS created a first-time penalty abatement program which was meant to allow taxpayers who were assessed penalties for the first time to request a one-time penalty amnesty. The program applies to the failure-to-file and failure-to-pay penalties as well as several others, and can save taxpayers significant amounts of money in certain cases. The penalty abatement waiver must be requested by the taxpayer, but few taxpayers who qualify for the waiver request it or even know the program exists.

Accuracy-Related Penalty

The tax law imposes a penalty of 20 percent of the applicable underpayment due to (1) negligence of or disregard for rules or regulations, (2) a substantial understatement of income tax, or (3) a substantial valuation overstatement, as well as certain other understatements of income tax. Negligence includes the failure to make a reasonable attempt to comply with the tax law. For example, the penalty could be imposed on a taxpayer who deducts a personal expenditure as a business expense. A substantial understatement of income tax occurs where the required amount of tax exceeds the tax shown on the taxpayer's return by the greater of 10 percent of the amount of tax that should be shown on the return or $5,000 ($10,000 for corporate taxpayers other than S corporations). A substantial valuation overstatement occurs when the value of property is 150 percent or more of the correct valuation. For example, a taxpayer who inflates the value of depreciable property to generate additional depreciation deductions may be subject to this penalty. The accuracy-related penalty applies only if the taxpayer has filed a return. In addition, if the taxpayer can demonstrate that he or she has reasonable cause for the understatement of tax and that he or she acted in good faith, the penalty will not be assessed.

EXAMPLE Kim underpaid her taxes for the current year by $15,000 due to negligence. Kim's penalty for negligence under the accuracy-related penalty is calculated as follows:

Negligence penalty (20% × $15,000)	$3,000 ♦

Fraud Penalty

The tax law also contains provisions for penalties for filing fraudulent tax returns. The fraud penalty is equal to 75 percent of the amount of underpayment of taxes attributable to fraud.

For the IRS to impose the fraud penalty, it must be shown by a "preponderance of evidence" that the taxpayer had an intent to evade taxes; however, once the IRS establishes that any portion of an underpayment of taxes is due to fraud, the entire underpayment is assumed to be attributable to fraud unless the taxpayer establishes otherwise. The tax law does not provide clear rules for what constitutes fraud; however, what is clearly mere negligence by a taxpayer will not cause this penalty to be imposed. When the fraud penalty is applicable, the accuracy-related penalty cannot be imposed. The fraud penalty will be applied only where the taxpayer has actually filed a return. Like the accuracy-related penalty, the fraud penalty will not be assessed if the taxpayer can demonstrate reasonable cause for the underpayment of tax and the taxpayer acted in good faith.

EXAMPLE Jeff has a $20,000 tax deficiency because of civil fraud. Interest on this underpayment amounts to $8,000. Jeff's total amount due on this underpayment is

calculated as follows:

Tax deficiency	$20,000
Fraud penalty (75% × $20,000)	15,000
Interest	8,000
Total due	$43,000

The interest is not deductible due to the disallowance of deductions for consumer interest. The fraud penalty is also not deductible. ♦

According to an IRS poll, 17 percent of Americans feel cheating on taxes is acceptable. Experts agree that tax cheating is a significant problem for the IRS, which must enforce the laws, and for honest taxpayers who pay more in taxes than they would otherwise have to. It is generally believed that tax evasion and noncompliance are costing the government more than $300 billion dollars in lost revenue each year.

Paid Preparer Use Only	Print/Type preparer's name	Preparer's signature	Date	Check ☐ if self-employed / PTIN
	Firm's name ▶		Firm's EIN ▶	
	Firm's address ▶		Phone no.	

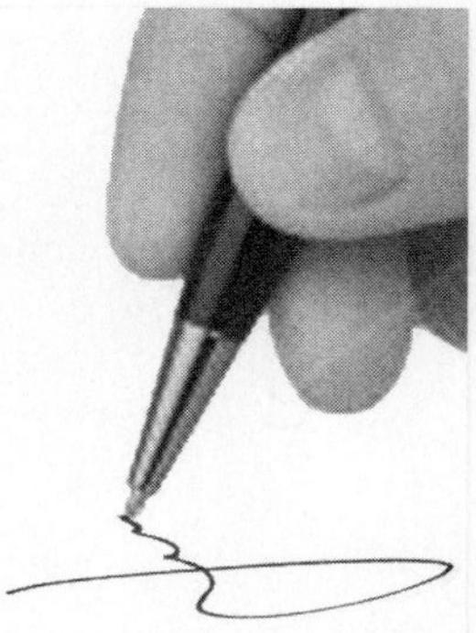

Would You Sign This Tax Return?

© ILYA AKINSHIN/Shutterstock.com; © Zhukov Oleg/Shutterstock.com.

Tim Trying, who is single, purchased a house on the beach in sunny Southern California 35 years ago. He is now retiring and moving to Hawaii for his golden years. Tim sold his house for $1,200,000 this year. Tim has been a client of yours for the past decade. He became a client when he was referred to you by your parents, who lived two houses away from Tim. When asked what his tax basis is in the house, Tim says it is $975,000. Your parents bought their house at about the same time, and you know they paid $100,000 for it. You have seen Tim's house many times and, although the house is well-maintained, you know it does not have any major improvements or betterments. You are reasonably certain that Tim is overstating his tax basis by hundreds of thousands of dollars in order to avoid reporting a taxable gain on the sale. Would you sign the Paid Preparer's declaration (see example above) on this return? Why or why not?

Miscellaneous Penalties

The tax law contains many other penalties applicable to taxpayers. The following are examples of such penalties:

- A civil penalty of $500 and a criminal penalty of $1,000 are imposed for filing false withholding information.
- An immediate $5,000 penalty can be assessed against a taxpayer who files a "frivolous" tax return (or document) as a tax protest.
- A tiered penalty system dependent on the timeliness of correction and filing of information returns is imposed for failing to file correct information returns. The penalty is assessed at up to $100 per return, $1,500,000 ($500,000 for small business) annual maximum. If the failure to file is corrected, the penalties may be reduced.
- A $100 penalty per occurrence (annual maximum of $1,500,000) is imposed for failing to provide timely payee information returns. Exceptions to the information return penalties may be made for reasonable cause.
- Employers are subject to a penalty of 2, 5, or 10 percent of the amount of payroll taxes not deposited on time, depending on the number of days the taxes remain undeposited. A 15 percent penalty may apply where taxes remain undeposited after a delinquency notice has been presented to the taxpayer.

- Taxpayers are subject to a penalty for failure to pay estimated taxes. The penalty is calculated using the interest rates for the period of underpayment (but it is not deductible as interest).
- Taxpayers are subject to a penalty for issuing a "bad" check, unless the taxpayer can demonstrate that the check was issued in good faith. The penalty is equal to 2 percent of the amount of the check. If the check is less than $1,250, then the penalty is the lesser of $25 or the amount of the check.

Would You Believe?

According to the human rights group, Amnesty International, until recently, tax fraud in China was a crime that could carry the death penalty.

Self-Study Problem 12.3 *See Appendix E for Solutions to Self-Study Problems*

Part a

Linda filed her tax return 2 months late. The tax paid with the return amounts to $3,000. What is Linda's total penalty for failure to file and failure to pay, assuming the failure to file is not fraudulent?

$__________

Part b

Kim underpaid her taxes by $10,000 due to negligence. What is Kim's penalty for negligence?

$__________

Part c

Using the same information as in Part b, what is the amount of the penalty if the underpayment were determined to be due to civil fraud?

$__________

Learning Objective 12.4

Apply the general rule for the statute of limitations on tax returns and the important exceptions to the general rule.

STATUTE OF LIMITATIONS

The statute of limitations is the time period within which an action may be taken by the IRS on a tax return. After the statute of limitations has run out on a given tax return, the government cannot assess additional taxes and the taxpayer cannot amend the return to request a refund. In general, the statute of limitations for a tax return runs for 3 years from the date the tax return was filed or the return due date, whichever is later. If a valid extension is filed, the due date is the extended due date.

EXAMPLE Norm files his 2014 tax return on March 20, 2015. Unless an exception discussed below applies, the IRS has until April 15, 2018, to assess any additional taxes. ♦

Exceptions

The tax law contains several exceptions to the general rule of a 3-year statute of limitations. Several of these special rules are summarized below:

- If a fraudulent tax return is filed or no return is filed, there is no statute of limitations. The IRS may assess a tax deficiency at any time in the future.
- If a taxpayer omits an amount of gross income in excess of 25 percent of the gross income shown on the return, then the statute of limitations is increased to 6 years. For example, if a tax return with gross income of $40,000 contains an omission of over $10,000 (25 percent of $40,000) of gross income, the statute of limitations is increased to 6 years.

- The statute of limitations for the deduction of a bad debt or worthless securities is 7 years. This limitation applies only to the bad debt deduction or the worthless security deduction; all other items on the tax return would normally close out after 3 years.

Besides these exceptions, the statute of limitations may be extended by mutual consent of the IRS and the taxpayer. This extension is for a specific time period and is made by signing the appropriate form in the Form 872 series. An extension is generally used when the statute of limitations is about to lapse and an audit has not been completed.

If a tax deficiency has been assessed by the IRS within the period of the statute of limitations, then the government has 10 years from the date of assessment to collect the tax due.

Would You Believe?

An IRS study shows that many taxpayers lose refunds because they fail to file their returns within the statute of limitations for claiming a refund, which can be either 2 or 3 years depending on the circumstances. The IRS denies millions of dollars in refunds each year which were claimed in delinquent returns.

Self-Study Problem 12.4 *See Appendix E for Solutions to Self-Study Problems*

Indicate whether the following statements are true or false by circling the appropriate letter.

T F 1. The general statute of limitations for a tax return is 3 years.

T F 2. The statute of limitations for a bad debt deduction on a tax return is 6 years.

T F 3. The statute of limitations for a fraudulent tax return is 7 years.

T F 4. The special statute of limitations for a tax return that omits income greater than 25 percent of gross income is 6 years.

T F 5. For the deduction of worthless securities, the statute of limitations is 7 years.

PREPARERS, PROOF, AND PRIVILEGE

Learning Objective 12.5

Describe the rules and penalties that apply to tax practitioners.

Tax Practitioners

Many taxpayers find it desirable or necessary to have their tax returns prepared by a tax practitioner. Tax practitioners include commercial preparers, enrolled agents, attorneys, and certified public accountants (CPAs). Commercial preparers generally prepare noncomplex returns of individuals, small corporations, and partnerships. Enrolled agents are individuals who have passed an IRS exam and are allowed to represent clients at IRS proceedings, as well as prepare tax returns. Attorneys and CPAs are individuals who have met education, examination, and experience requirements and are licensed to practice in their respective professions. CPAs and attorneys normally work with complex tax returns of individuals, corporations, partnerships, estates, and trusts. They also provide tax-planning advice to aid their clients in minimizing the amount of their taxes. Preparers that are enrolled agents, CPAs, and attorneys are sometimes referred to as enrolled preparers while other non-credentialed preparers are known as unenrolled preparers.

Would You Believe?

The IRS operates a program for taxpayers that failed to report offshore income known as the offshore voluntary disclosure program (OVDP). The Taxpayer Advocate's Office examined taxpayers that participated in the OVDP and found that those with the largest offshore accounts ($4.2 million or more) paid penalties of about three times the unpaid taxes. However, those with the smallest accounts (about $87,000 of less) paid nearly six times the unpaid tax.

Annual Filing Season Program

In 2011, the IRS attempted to regulate the national tax preparation industry by implementing the Registered Tax Return Preparer (RTRP) system which required all unenrolled tax preparers to obtain a preparer tax identification number (PTIN), pass a background check, and pass a competency exam. In 2013, the RTRP program was put on hold as a result of a court decision and finally the program was disbanded after the IRS exhausted its appeals of the case. Unless Congress takes legislative action, the RTRP program is dead. One important part of the RTRP program that did remain is the PTIN requirement. All paid tax return preparers must sign up with the IRS, pay a registration fee, and obtain a PTIN. Every year, paid tax preparers must sign up or refresh their PTIN online.

In 2014, the IRS introduced the Annual Filing Season Program (AFSP), a new voluntary tax return preparer program designed to encourage preparers to participate in continuing education courses to help stay abreast of changes in tax law and help reduce the risk of using a preparer without professional credentials. The AFSP requires unenrolled preparers to obtain 18 hours of continuing education from an approved provider including at least 6 hours of an Annual Federal Tax Refresher (AFTR) course focused on filing season issues and tax updates. The AFTR must include a knowledge-based exam administered at the end of the course by the course provider. Because the program was introduced during 2014, the requirements for the 2015 filing season have been reduced to 11 hours of education including the 6 hour AFTR plus 3 hours of federal tax law and 2 hours of ethics.

In addition to being better prepared for the upcoming filing season, a list of tax preparers meeting the AFSP requirements will be published at **www.irs.gov** to permit taxpayers to search for qualified tax return preparers. For additional information on the Annual Filing Season Program requirements, see the IRS website **(www.irs.gov)**.

Would You Believe?

According to the IRS, more than 60 percent of returns filed in the last several years have been prepared and signed by professional preparers. Many tax lawmakers in Congress also hire professional preparers rather than wrestle with the laws they have written.

Preparer Penalties

Under the tax law, any person who prepares a tax return, including nonincome tax returns (e.g., excise tax returns), for compensation is a "tax return preparer." The tax law has various penalty provisions applicable to tax return preparers. These penalties are designed to help the IRS regulate the preparation of tax returns; the more significant ones are described below:

- $50 for failing to sign a tax return or failing to furnish the preparer's identifying number, $25,000 annual maximum

- $50 for each failure to keep a copy of the prepared return or include the return on a list of taxpayers for whom returns have been prepared, $25,000 annual maximum
- $50 for failing to provide a taxpayer a copy of the tax return prepared, $25,000 annual maximum
- $500 for endorsing or cashing a refund check issued to a taxpayer
- Greater of $1,000 or 50 percent of the income derived (or to be derived) by the tax return preparer for an undisclosed unrealistic position on a return which does not meet a "substantial authority" standard, and which the preparer knew or reasonably should have known about
- Greater of $5,000 or 50 percent of the income derived (or to be derived) by the tax return preparer for each return in which the preparer willfully attempts to understate the amount of the taxpayer's tax liability, or each return in which an understatement is due to the preparer's reckless or intentional disregard of rules or regulations, reduced by the amount of the $1,000 (or 50 percent) penalty for unrealistic positions (discussed above)
- $1,000 ($10,000 for corporate returns) for each return or document filed in aiding or abetting a taxpayer in understating a tax liability
- For each separate activity (sale of an interest, organization of an entity, etc.), the lesser of $1,000 or 100 percent of the gross income derived by the promoter from promoting an "abusive tax shelter"

Burden of Proof

In most litigation, the party initiating the case has the burden of convincing the court that he or she is correct with respect to the issue. Historically, however, in most civil tax cases, the Internal Revenue Code placed the burden of proof on the taxpayer, whether or not he or she initiated the case, except in cases involving such items as hobby losses, fraud with intent to evade tax, and the accumulated earnings tax.

In the IRS Restructuring and Reform Act of 1998, the tax law was changed to shift the burden of proof to the IRS in many situations. The IRS now has the burden of proof in any court proceeding on an income, gift, estate, or generation-skipping tax liability with respect to factual issues, provided the taxpayer (1) introduces credible evidence of the factual issue, (2) maintains records and substantiates items as presently required under the Code and Regulations, and (3) cooperates with reasonable IRS requests for meetings, interviews, witnesses, information, and documents. For corporations, trusts, and partnerships with net worth exceeding $7 million, the burden of proof remains on the taxpayer.

The burden of proof also automatically shifts to the IRS in two situations:

1. If the IRS uses statistics to reconstruct an individual's income, or
2. If the court proceeding against an individual taxpayer involves a penalty or addition to tax.

Tax Confidentiality Privilege

The 1998 Act also extended the existing attorney-client privilege of confidentiality in tax matters to nonattorneys authorized to practice before the IRS (e.g., CPAs and enrolled agents). The nonattorney-client privilege may be asserted only in a *noncriminal tax* proceeding before the IRS or federal courts. Also, the nonattorney-client privilege does not

extend to written communications between a tax practitioner and a corporation in connection with the promotion of any tax shelter.

CPAs and enrolled agents need to understand the rules regarding tax confidentiality as they have been applied to lawyers to be aware of the tax privilege limits. For example, tax privileged communication usually does not apply to the preparation of tax returns, the giving of accounting or business advice, or to tax accrual workpapers. Also, unlike the general attorney-client privilege, the nonattorney-client privilege does not automatically apply to state tax situations.

Self-Study Problem 12.5 *See Appendix E for Solutions to Self-Study Problems*

Indicate whether the following statements are true or false by circling the appropriate letter.

T F 1. Only certified public accountants may represent taxpayers before the IRS.
T F 2. A college degree is required to prepare tax returns for compensation.
T F 3. Only attorneys may prepare corporate tax returns.
T F 4. The tax preparer penalty for filing a document aiding and abetting an individual taxpayer in the understatement of a tax liability is $1,000.
T F 5. The tax preparer penalty for endorsing a taxpayer's refund check is $500.
T F 6. The tax preparer penalty for failing to provide a copy of a tax return to a taxpayer is $50.
T F 7. For audits after 1998, if the IRS uses statistics to reconstruct an individual taxpayer's income, the burden of proof is on the taxpayer.
T F 8. For corporations, trusts, and partnerships with net worth over $7 million, the burden of proof is on the IRS in civil tax matters.
T F 9. CPAs and enrolled agents have tax privileged communication only in noncriminal proceedings before the IRS or federal courts.
T F 10. If an individual taxpayer does not cooperate with reasonable IRS requests for meetings, interviews, witnesses, information, and documents, the burden of proof in a tax matter is on the taxpayer.
T F 11. Commercial tax preparers must have a PTIN.

Learning Objective 12.6

Describe the Taxpayer Bill of Rights.

THE TAXPAYER BILL OF RIGHTS

Over the years, the news media carried many horror stories about taxpayers who claimed they had been abused by the IRS. As a result of this publicity, in 1988 Congress passed a set of provisions referred to as the Taxpayer Bill of Rights. The Taxpayer Bill of Rights has been amended several times since it was originally passed by Congress. This set of provisions requires the IRS to inform taxpayers of their rights in dealing with the IRS, and expands taxpayers' rights and remedies when they are involved in disputes with the IRS. The provisions of the Taxpayer Bill of Rights are summarized in IRS Publication 1, which is reproduced on Pages 12-19 and 12-20. Also note, Publication 1 directs taxpayers to other IRS publications with more details on specific taxpayer rights.

The first part of this publication explains some of your most important rights as a taxpayer. The second part explains the examination, appeal, collection, and refund processes.

IRS Your Rights as a Taxpayer

Publication 1

This publication explains your rights as a taxpayer and the processes for examination, appeal, collection, and refunds. Also available in Spanish.

The Taxpayer Bill of Rights

1. The Right to Be Informed

Taxpayers have the right to know what they need to do to comply with the tax laws. They are entitled to clear explanations of the laws and IRS procedures in all tax forms, instructions, publications, notices, and correspondence. They have the right to be informed of IRS decisions about their tax accounts and to receive clear explanations of the outcomes.

2. The Right to Quality Service

Taxpayers have the right to receive prompt, courteous, and professional assistance in their dealings with the IRS, to be spoken to in a way they can easily understand, to receive clear and easily understandable communications from the IRS, and to speak to a supervisor about inadequate service.

3. The Right to Pay No More than the Correct Amount of Tax

Taxpayers have the right to pay only the amount of tax legally due, including interest and penalties, and to have the IRS apply all tax payments properly.

4. The Right to Challenge the IRS's Position and Be Heard

Taxpayers have the right to raise objections and provide additional documentation in response to formal IRS actions or proposed actions, to expect that the IRS will consider their timely objections and documentation promptly and fairly, and to receive a response if the IRS does not agree with their position.

5. The Right to Appeal an IRS Decision in an Independent Forum

Taxpayers are entitled to a fair and impartial administrative appeal of most IRS decisions, including many penalties, and have the right to receive a written response regarding the Office of Appeals' decision. Taxpayers generally have the right to take their cases to court.

6. The Right to Finality

Taxpayers have the right to know the maximum amount of time they have to challenge the IRS's position as well as the maximum amount of time the IRS has to audit a particular tax year or collect a tax debt. Taxpayers have the right to know when the IRS has finished an audit.

7. The Right to Privacy

Taxpayers have the right to expect that any IRS inquiry, examination, or enforcement action will comply with the law and be no more intrusive than necessary, and will respect all due process rights, including search and seizure protections and will provide, where applicable, a collection due process hearing.

8. The Right to Confidentiality

Taxpayers have the right to expect that any information they provide to the IRS will not be disclosed unless authorized by the taxpayer or by law. Taxpayers have the right to expect appropriate action will be taken against employees, return preparers, and others who wrongfully use or disclose taxpayer return information.

9. The Right to Retain Representation

Taxpayers have the right to retain an authorized representative of their choice to represent them in their dealings with the IRS. Taxpayers have the right to seek assistance from a Low Income Taxpayer Clinic if they cannot afford representation.

10. The Right to a Fair and Just Tax System

Taxpayers have the right to expect the tax system to consider facts and circumstances that might affect their underlying liabilities, ability to pay, or ability to provide information timely. Taxpayers have the right to receive assistance from the Taxpayer Advocate Service if they are experiencing financial difficulty or if the IRS has not resolved their tax issues properly and timely through its normal channels.

The IRS Mission | Provide America's taxpayers top-quality service by helping them understand and meet their tax responsibilities and enforce the law with integrity and fairness to all.

Publication 1 (Rev. 6-2014) Catalog Number 64731W Department of the Treasury **Internal Revenue Service** www.irs.gov

Examinations, Appeals, Collections, and Refunds

Examinations (Audits)

We accept most taxpayers' returns as filed. If we inquire about your return or select it for examination, it does not suggest that you are dishonest. The inquiry or examination may or may not result in more tax. We may close your case without change; or, you may receive a refund.

The process of selecting a return for examination usually begins in one of two ways. First, we use computer programs to identify returns that may have incorrect amounts. These programs may be based on information returns, such as Forms 1099 and W-2, on studies of past examinations, or on certain issues identified by compliance projects. Second, we use information from outside sources that indicates that a return may have incorrect amounts. These sources may include newspapers, public records, and individuals. If we determine that the information is accurate and reliable, we may use it to select a return for examination.

Publication 556, Examination of Returns, Appeal Rights, and Claims for Refund, explains the rules and procedures that we follow in examinations. The following sections give an overview of how we conduct examinations.

By Mail

We handle many examinations and inquiries by mail. We will send you a letter with either a request for more information or a reason why we believe a change to your return may be needed. You can respond by mail or you can request a personal interview with an examiner. If you mail us the requested information or provide an explanation, we may or may not agree with you, and we will explain the reasons for any changes. Please do not hesitate to write to us about anything you do not understand.

By Interview

If we notify you that we will conduct your examination through a personal interview, or you request such an interview, you have the right to ask that the examination take place at a reasonable time and place that is convenient for both you and the IRS. If our examiner proposes any changes to your return, he or she will explain the reasons for the changes. If you do not agree with these changes, you can meet with the examiner's supervisor.

Repeat Examinations

If we examined your return for the same items in either of the 2 previous years and proposed no change to your tax liability, please contact us as soon as possible so we can see if we should discontinue the examination.

Appeals

If you do not agree with the examiner's proposed changes, you can appeal them to the Appeals Office of IRS. Most differences can be settled without expensive and time-consuming court trials. Your appeal rights are explained in detail in both Publication 5, Your Appeal Rights and How To Prepare a Protest If You Don't Agree, and Publication 556, Examination of Returns, Appeal Rights, and Claims for Refund.

If you do not wish to use the Appeals Office or disagree with its findings, you may be able to take your case to the U.S. Tax Court, U.S. Court of Federal Claims, or the U.S. District Court where you live. If you take your case to court, the IRS will have the burden of proving certain facts if you kept adequate records to show your tax liability, cooperated with the IRS, and meet certain other conditions. If the court agrees with you on most issues in your case and finds that our position was largely unjustified, you may be able to recover some of your administrative and litigation costs. You will not be eligible to recover these costs unless you tried to resolve your case administratively, including going through the appeals system, and you gave us the information necessary to resolve the case.

Collections

Publication 594, The IRS Collection Process, explains your rights and responsibilities regarding payment of federal taxes. It describes:

- What to do when you owe taxes. It describes what to do if you get a tax bill and what to do if you think your bill is wrong. It also covers making installment payments, delaying collection action, and submitting an offer in compromise.
- IRS collection actions. It covers liens, releasing a lien, levies, releasing a levy, seizures and sales, and release of property.

Your collection appeal rights are explained in detail in Publication 1660, Collection Appeal Rights.

Innocent Spouse Relief

Generally, both you and your spouse are each responsible for paying the full amount of tax, interest, and penalties due on your joint return. However, if you qualify for innocent spouse relief, you may be relieved of part or all of the joint liability. To request relief, you must file Form 8857, Request for Innocent Spouse Relief. For more information on innocent spouse relief, see Publication 971, Innocent Spouse Relief, and Form 8857.

Potential Third Party Contacts

Generally, the IRS will deal directly with you or your duly authorized representative. However, we sometimes talk with other persons if we need information that you have been unable to provide, or to verify information we have received. If we do contact other persons, such as a neighbor, bank, employer, or employees, we will generally need to tell them limited information, such as your name. The law prohibits us from disclosing any more information than is necessary to obtain or verify the information we are seeking. Our need to contact other persons may continue as long as there is activity in your case. If we do contact other persons, you have a right to request a list of those contacted.

Refunds

You may file a claim for refund if you think you paid too much tax. You must generally file the claim within 3 years from the date you filed your original return or 2 years from the date you paid the tax, whichever is later. The law generally provides for interest on your refund if it is not paid within 45 days of the date you filed your return or claim for refund. Publication 556, Examination of Returns, Appeal Rights, and Claims for Refund, has more information on refunds.

If you were due a refund but you did not file a return, you generally must file your return within 3 years from the date the return was due (including extensions) to get that refund.

Tax Information

The IRS provides the following sources for forms, publications, and additional information.

- ***Tax Questions:*** 1-800-829-1040 (1-800-829-4059 for TTY/TDD)
- ***Forms and Publications:*** 1-800-829-3676 (1-800-829-4059 for TTY/TDD)
- ***Internet:*** *www.irs.gov*
- ***Small Business Ombudsman:*** A small business entity can participate in the regulatory process and comment on enforcement actions of IRS by calling 1-888-REG-FAIR.
- ***Treasury Inspector General for Tax Administration:*** You can confidentially report misconduct, waste, fraud, or abuse by an IRS employee by calling 1-800-366-4484 (1-800-877-8339 for TTY/TDD). You can remain anonymous.

Self-Study Problem 12.6 *See Appendix E for Solutions to Self-Study Problems*

Indicate whether the following statements are true or false by circling the appropriate letter.

T F 1. Taxpayers have the right to represent themselves or, with proper written authorization, have someone else represent them.

T F 2. The IRS will waive penalties when allowed by law if taxpayers can show they acted reasonably in good faith or relied on incorrect advice from an IRS employee.

T F 3. IRS Publication 594 explains a taxpayer's rights and responsibilities regarding payment of federal taxes.

T F 4. If a taxpayer is audited in the current year for an item that was audited in either of the 2 previous years and the IRS proposed no change to the tax liability, the taxpayer should contact the IRS as soon as possible to attempt to stop the repeat audit.

T F 5. Generally, both a taxpayer and his or her spouse are responsible, jointly and individually, for the tax and any interest or penalty due on a joint return.

T F 6. Taxpayers must file a claim for refund within 3 years of the date they filed their return or 2 years from the date they paid the tax if they think they paid too much tax.

TAX PLANNING

Learning Objective 12.7

Understand the basic concepts of tax planning.

The process of arranging one's financial affairs to minimize one's overall tax liability is often referred to as tax planning. There is nothing wrong with tax planning to avoid tax, provided legal methods are used. Judge Learned Hand best stated the doctrine of tax planning in 1947 when he wrote:

"Over and over again, courts have said there is nothing sinister in so arranging one's affairs as to keep taxes as low as possible. Everybody does so, rich or poor, and all do right, for nobody owes any public duty to pay more than the law demands: taxes are enforced extractions, not voluntary contributions." *Commissioner v. Newman*, 159 F.2d 848 (CA-2, 1947).

When illegal methods are used to reduce tax liability, the process can no longer be considered tax planning, but instead becomes tax evasion. Tax evasion can subject the taxpayer and tax practitioner to fines, penalties, or incarceration. Illegal acts are outside the realm of tax-planning services offered by a professional tax practitioner.

Tax planning covers two basic categories of transactions, the "open transaction" and the "closed transaction." In an open transaction, all the events have not yet been completed; therefore, the taxpayer has some degree of control over the tax consequences. In a closed transaction, all material parts of the transaction have been completed. As a result, tax planning involving a closed transaction is limited to presentation of the facts to the IRS in the most favorable, legally acceptable manner possible.

EXAMPLE Annie enters into an agreement with Erik to exchange real estate held as an investment. Escrow has not closed and the title of the property has not passed between the parties. Since all significant events (title passing) are not complete, the transaction is considered an open transaction. Once the title to the real estate passes, the tax planning involves a closed transaction. ♦

Tax planning cannot be considered in a void. Any tax-planning advice must consider the business goals of the taxpayer. Tax planning for a transaction should not override sound business judgment.

Tax Rate Terminology

Important to any tax-planning situation is an evaluation of the tax savings arising from increasing deductions or the tax cost of generating additional income. The tax consequences are dependent on the taxpayer's tax rate. The taxpayer's tax rate may be defined in several ways. For tax-planning purposes, the taxpayer needs to understand the difference between the "average" tax rate and the "marginal" tax rate. The average tax rate merely represents the average rate of tax applicable to the taxpayer's income and is calculated as the total tax paid divided by the total income of the taxpayer. The marginal tax rate represents the rate at which tax is imposed on the "next" dollar of income.

EXAMPLE Becky, a single taxpayer, has income of $40,000 during the current year on which she pays tax of $5,863. Her average tax rate is 14.66 percent ($5,863 / $40,000). If Becky's income increases to $50,000, her tax liability will be $8,363. Thus, Becky's marginal rate is 25 percent [($8,363 − $5,863) / ($50,000 − $40,000)]. ♦

When making tax-planning decisions, the taxpayer's marginal tax rate is the most important tax rate. For example, Jason has a 30 percent marginal tax rate and a 20 percent average tax rate and is considering making a tax-deductible investment of $2,000. His after-tax cost of the investment is calculated using his marginal tax rate, not his average tax rate. Jason's after-tax cost of the investment would be $1,400, calculated as follows: [$2,000 − ($2,000 × 30 percent)]. On the other hand, if Jason is to receive any additional income, he knows that he will pay tax at a rate of 30 percent on the next dollar of income.

Examples of Tax Planning

Tax planning opportunities can be classified into four categories: (1) timing, (2) jurisdiction, (3) entity, and (4) character. Most tax planning techniques employ at least one of these characteristics in an attempt to save taxpayers money.

Timing

In its simplest form, timing implies deferring the payment of taxes to a future year and is generally achieved by either deferring income recognition or accelerating expense deduction.

EXAMPLE Karen operates a small cash basis, calendar year-end business. In order to lower her current year's income, Karen may prepay January's rent in December. She could also delay invoicing her customers in an attempt to defer the recognition of income. ♦

Most simple timing techniques work best when tax rates are not expected to change. If tax rates are expected to change across the periods in which the timing is being changed, a more thorough analysis is going to be required.

EXAMPLE If in the previous example Karen expects her tax rate to increase from 25 percent in the current year to 35 percent next year, she may want to consider accelerating the recognition of income into the current year at the lower rate and deferring the deduction of expenses until next year increasing the value of the deduction. ♦

One disadvantage of using the timing technique is that tax recognition frequently occurs simultaneously with cash transactions. For example, one way to defer income recognition might be to earn no income; however, that generally spells the end of the business as well.

Jurisdiction

Using jurisdiction for tax planning involves exploiting differences in tax rates or tax systems to lower tax liabilities.

EXAMPLE Mark worked for the Lake Tahoe office of the state of California Department of Motor Vehicles for 35 years. In the current year, he starts his well-deserved retirement. Realizing that the individual tax rate in California can be over 10 percent, he moves 10 miles east to Reno, Nevada knowing that Nevada has no state income tax on individuals. He continues to collect his pension without paying state income tax. ♦

Jurisdiction, although simple in concept, can be difficult to implement for many taxpayers. Most individuals do not have the luxury to simply move to a new state to lower the state income tax rate. Larger business may have more flexibility than individuals or small businesses to implement a jurisdictional tax plan.

Entity

Entity-based tax planning involves making a choice about the type of entity a taxpayer chooses to operate as.

EXAMPLE Raquel is starting a new small business and expects to operate at a loss for the first few years. In an attempt to take advantage of using the losses to offset her other forms of income, she establishes her new business as a flow-through entity such as an LLC in hopes of passing those losses through to her individual tax return. ♦

Character

Using character for tax planning often requires a deeper understanding of tax law than the other tax planning techniques. Using character means the transaction will be designed to take advantage of the tax law or a taxpayer's current situation.

EXAMPLE Axel owns stock purchased 11 months ago and has now doubled in value. Although Axel thinks the stock's value has peaked, he wishes to wait one additional month before selling to convert the short-term capital gain taxed at ordinary tax rates into a long-term capital gain taxed at preferential rates. Although this might also feel like a timing-based plan, the one month deferral of taxes is not likely to be significant. ♦

EXAMPLE Beck needs to purchase a new auto. His loan options include dealer financing at a 4 percent interest rate or a home equity loan at 5 percent interest. Home equity loans generally result in tax deductible interest (see Chapter 5), whereas interest on personal auto loans is not deductible. The after-tax rate of interest on the home equity loan will be lower if Beck's tax rate is greater than 20 percent ($5\% \times (1 - 0.20 \text{ tax rate}) = 4\%$). ♦

Self-Study Problem 12.7 *See Appendix E for Solutions to Self-Study Problems*

During the current year, K's taxable income is $89,000 and he pays income tax of $18,113. K is single, has no dependents, and does not itemize his deductions. J, who files in *exactly* the same manner as K, has taxable income of $90,000 and pays income tax of $18,383.

1. What is K's average tax rate? __________
2. What is J's average tax rate? __________
3. What is J's marginal tax rate? __________

KEY POINTS

Learning Objectives	Key Points
LO 12.1: Identify the organizational structure of the IRS.	• The national IRS office is the headquarters of the commissioner of internal revenue. The commissioner of internal revenue is appointed by the president of the United States with the advice and consent of the Senate. • The IRS maintains Campus Processing Sites where the IRS computers process the information from tax documents such as tax returns, payroll tax forms, Forms 1099s, and withholding forms. • The IRS maintains a national computer center in Martinsburg, West Virginia, where information from various processing sites is matched with records from other processing sites. • The IRS has the authority to examine a taxpayer's books and records to determine the correct amount of tax due, and the IRS also has the right to summon taxpayers to appear before the IRS and produce necessary accounting records.
LO 12.2: Understand the IRS audit process.	• A primary function of the IRS is to audit taxpayers' tax returns. • Correspondence audits are generally handled entirely by mail and account for about 80 percent of the individual returns examined each year. • The office audit is conducted in an IRS office and is typically used for individual taxpayers with little or no business activities. • In a field audit, the IRS agent reviews a taxpayer's books and records at the taxpayer's place of business or at the office of the taxpayer's accountant. • The IRS uses a computerized statistical sampling technique called the Discriminant Function System (DIF) to select tax returns for most audits. • Under the DIF system, the IRS uses mathematical formulas to assign a DIF score to each return, which represents the potential for discovery of improper treatment of items on the tax return. • The IRS also selects returns for audit using information from other sources such as informants, other governmental agencies, news items, and associated tax returns. • If an audit results in a disagreement between the agent and the taxpayer, the appeals procedure begins with the IRS inviting the taxpayer to an informal conference with an appellate agent.
LO 12.3: Define the common penalties for taxpayers and be able to apply them to specific situations.	• Taxpayers are charged interest on underpayments of taxes, and in some cases, the IRS pays interest to taxpayers when they overpay their taxes. • The interest rate applicable to underpayments and overpayments of taxes is adjusted each quarter and is equal to the federal short-term rate plus three percentage points. • The failure to file is subject to a penalty equal to 5 percent of the tax due with the return, for every month or portion of a month the return is late (up to a maximum of 25 percent). • The penalty for failure to pay is ½ of 1 percent of the amount of taxes due for every month or portion of a month that the payment is late (up to a maximum of 25 percent).

	• The accuracy-related penalty is 20 percent of the applicable underpayment due to (1) negligence of or disregard for rules or regulations, (2) a substantial understatement of income tax, or (3) a substantial valuation overstatement, as well as certain other understatements of income tax. • When a taxpayer files a fraudulent tax return, there is a fraud penalty equal to 75 percent of the amount of underpayment of taxes attributable to fraud. • The tax law contains many other penalties applicable to taxpayers, including but not limited to a civil penalty of $500 and a criminal penalty of $1,000 are imposed for filing false withholding information, and there is an immediate $5,000 penalty for filing a "frivolous" tax return (or document) as a tax protest.
LO 12.4: Apply the general rule for the statute of limitations on tax returns and the important exceptions to the general rule.	• In general, the statute of limitations for a tax return runs for 3 years from the date the tax return was filed or the return due date, whichever is later. • If a fraudulent tax return is filed or no return is filed, there is no statute of limitations. • If a taxpayer omits an amount of gross income in excess of 25 percent of the gross income shown on the return, then the statute of limitations is increased to 6 years. • The statute of limitations for the deduction of a bad debt or worthless securities is 7 years (all other items on the tax return would normally be considered closed after 3 years). • The statute of limitations may be extended by mutual consent of the IRS and the taxpayer.
LO 12.5: Describe the rules and penalties that apply to tax practitioners.	• Tax practitioners include commercial preparers, enrolled agents, attorneys, and certified public accountants (CPAs). • Unenrolled preparers can currently participate in the Annual Filing Season Program, a voluntary program to distinguish preparers with a recognizable record of completion. • Tax return preparer penalties include but are not limited to (1) $50 for failing to sign a tax return or failing to furnish the preparer's identifying number, (2) $50 for each failure to keep a copy of the prepared return or include the return on a list of taxpayers for whom returns have been prepared, or (3) $50 for failing to provide a taxpayer with a copy of the tax return prepared. • The IRS has the burden of proof in any court proceeding with respect to factual issues, provided the taxpayer (1) introduces credible evidence of the factual issue, (2) maintains records and substantiates items, and (3) cooperates with reasonable IRS requests for meetings, interviews, witnesses, information, and documents. • The tax law extends the attorney-client privilege of confidentiality in tax matters to nonattorneys authorized to practice before the IRS (e.g., CPAs and enrolled agents).
LO 12.6: Describe the Taxpayer Bill of Rights.	• The Taxpayer Bill of Rights (IRS Publication 1) requires the IRS (the "Service") to inform taxpayers of their rights in dealing with the Service, and expands taxpayers' rights and remedies when they are involved in disputes with the IRS.
LO 12.7: Understand the basic concepts of tax planning.	• Tax planning is the process of arranging one's financial affairs to minimize one's overall tax liability. • When illegal methods are used to reduce tax liability, the process can no longer be considered tax planning, but instead becomes tax evasion. • For making tax-planning decisions, the taxpayer's marginal tax rate is the most important tax rate to consider.

© Dusit/Shutterstock.com

INTERACTIVE QUIZZES

Interactive quizzes are available as an optional online resource for Income Tax Fundamentals. Visit **www.cengagebrain.com** for more information.

QUESTIONS and PROBLEMS

GROUP 1: MULTIPLE CHOICE QUESTIONS

LO 12.1

1. Which of the following is a responsibility of a local office of the IRS?
   a. Advising the Treasury Department on legislation
   b. Intelligence operations
   c. Appellate procedures
   d. Developing IRS rules and regulations
   e. None of the above

LO 12.2

2. Which of the following is the most common type of audit for an individual taxpayer who conducts no significant business activities?
   a. Office audit
   b. Correspondence audit
   c. Telephone audit
   d. Field audit
   e. Service center audit

LO 12.2

3. In which of the following ways are tax returns selected for most audits?
   a. Through the Discriminant Function System
   b. Through informants
   c. Through news sources
   d. Through information from other government agencies

LO 12.3

4. Which of the following is *not* a penalty that may be imposed by the IRS?
   a. Failure-to-file penalty
   b. Failure-to-pay penalty
   c. Penalty for negligence
   d. Fraud penalty
   e. All of the above may be imposed by the IRS

LO 12.4

5. If a taxpayer's 2014 individual income tax return was filed on February 1, 2015, the statute of limitations would normally run out on:
   a. April 15, 2018
   b. February 1, 2016
   c. February 1, 2017
   d. February 1, 2018
   e. None of the above

LO 12.4

6. Which of the following deductions has a 6-year statute of limitations?
   a. Depreciation
   b. Salaries
   c. Travel and entertainment
   d. A return in which the taxpayer omitted gross income in excess of 25 percent of the gross income shown on the return
   e. Worthless securities

LO 12.5

7. Which of the following tax preparers may *not* represent their clients in all IRS proceedings?
   a. An enrolled agent
   b. A certified public accountant
   c. An attorney
   d. All of the above may represent their clients in IRS proceedings

LO 12.5

8. After the 2015 filing season, of the following is not required to participate in the Annual Filing Season Program?
   a. 18 total hours of continuing education from an approved provider
   b. An annual federal tax refresher course lasting at least 6 hours
   c. A comprehensive oral exam administered by the IRS that tests preparer knowledge
   d. A PTIN if the preparer wishes to prepare and file tax returns.
   e. All of the above are required

LO 12.5

9. The Registered Tax Return Preparer program:
   a. Has been abandoned for the time being barring any legislative action
   b. Remains in force for the 2015 filing season
   c. Is continuing to be litigated by the IRS
   d. Required all types of preparers, including CPAs and attorneys, to comply with its requirements
   e. All of the above are true with respect to the RTRP

LO 12.5

10. In which of the following situations does the burden of proof in a tax matter not automatically shift to the IRS?
    a. The IRS uses statistics to reconstruct an individual's income.
    b. A court proceeding against an individual taxpayer involves a penalty or addition to tax.
    c. A taxpayer who did not maintain records.
    d. a and b are correct.
    e. a, b, and c are correct.

LO 12.5

11. Which of the following have privileged communication with a client in a noncriminal tax matter?
    a. CPAs
    b. Enrolled agents
    c. Attorneys
    d. a and c
    e. a, b, and c

LO 12.5

12. The burden of proof remains on the taxpayer for corporations, trusts, and partnerships with net worth exceeding:
    a. $1 million
    b. $3 million
    c. $5 million
    d. $7 million
    e. Some other amount

______ 13. The IRS does *not* have to furnish the taxpayer with information concerning which of the following items?
LO 12.6
a. The way the taxpayer's return was selected for audit
b. The procedures for appealing an IRS ruling
c. The refund claims process
d. The IRS collection process
e. All of the above must be provided to the taxpayer

______ 14. Both spouses are responsible, jointly and individually, for paying the full amount of any tax, interest, or penalties due on a joint return.
LO 12.6
a. This does not apply to spouses who have divorced after the return was filed.
b. Spouses are responsible jointly but not individually.
c. Spouses are responsible individually but not jointly.
d. Innocent spouses may be relieved of the liability for tax, interest, and penalties.
e. None of the above.

______ 15. A taxpayer's rights are explained in:
LO 12.6
a. Publication 5
b. Publication 17
c. Publication 556
d. Publication 1
e. None of the above

______ 16. Taxpayers have the right to have an IRS examination take place at:
LO 12.6
a. The IRS office
b. Any city of the taxpayer's choosing
c. A neutral site
d. A reasonable time and place
e. None of the above

______ 17. If a U.S. Tax Court agrees with the taxpayer on appeal that the IRS position was largely unjustified, which of the following is correct?
LO 12.6
a. The taxpayer must still pay administrative and litigation costs.
b. The taxpayer may recover administrative but not litigation costs.
c. The taxpayer may recover litigation but not administrative costs.
d. To be eligible to recover some of the administrative and litigation costs, the taxpayer must have tried to resolve the case administratively, including going through the appeals process, and must have given the IRS the information necessary to resolve the case.
e. None of the above.

______ 18. If the IRS owes a taxpayer a refund, the law generally provides that the IRS must pay interest on the refund if it is not paid within ______ days of the date the taxpayer filed his or her tax return or claim for refund.
LO 12.6
a. 30
b. 45
c. 60
d. 90
e. None of the above

LO 12.7

19. Glen's taxable income is $50,000 and he pays income tax of $8,375. If his income were $60,000, he would pay taxes of $10,875. What is Glen's marginal tax rate?
    a. 18.23%
    b. 17.87%
    c. 15.00%
    d. 25.00%
    e. Some other amount

LO 12.7

20. Melodie's taxable income is $40,000 and she pays income tax of $5,863. If Melodie's taxable income increases to $41,000, she would pay income taxes of $6,113. What is Melodie's marginal tax rate?
    a. 14.66%
    b. 25.00%
    c. 14.91%
    d. 15.00%
    e. Some other amount

LO 12.7

21. Jim has a house payment of $2,000 per month of which $1,800 is interest and real estate taxes with the remaining $200 representing a repayment of the principal balance of the note. Jim's marginal tax rate is 30 percent. What is Jim's after-tax cost of his home mortgage payment?
    a. $600
    b. $540
    c. $1,400
    d. $1,460
    e. Some other amount

GROUP 2: PROBLEMS

LO 12.1
LO 12.2

1. Indicate which of the following statements are true or false:

    ____ The IRS is a division of the Treasury Department.
    ____ The IRS has four major divisions.
    ____ The IRS local offices process most individual tax returns.
    ____ IRS Campus Processing Sites are the locations that taxpayers should call to obtain tax information.
    ____ Taxpayers should have their CPAs keep their tax records to prevent the IRS from being able to summon their records.
    ____ Most IRS audits are conducted through the mail.

LO 12.2
LO 12.3

2. Indicate whether the following statements are true or false:

    ____ A field audit by the IRS is an audit conducted at the IRS field office.
    ____ A low Discriminant Function System score for a tax return increases the possibility that the return will be selected for audit.
    ____ The IRS charges interest on underpayments of taxes, but never pays interest on amounts of overpayments of taxes.
    ____ If a taxpayer fails to file a tax return on its due date, he or she may be subject to a failure-to-file penalty.
    ____ The tax law includes a penalty for preparing a tax return in a negligent manner.
    ____ If a taxpayer fails to file a tax return, the IRS may impose both the failure-to-file penalty and the fraud penalty.

LO 12.3

3. a. Wilson filed his individual tax return on the original due date, but failed to pay $700 in taxes that were due with the return. If Wilson pays the taxes exactly 2 months late, calculate the amount of his failure-to-pay penalty.

   $ ____________

   b. Joan filed her individual income tax return 4½ months after it was due. She did not request an extension of time for filing. Along with her return, Joan remitted a check for $750, which was the balance of the taxes she owed with her return. Disregarding interest, calculate the total penalty that Joan will be required to pay, assuming the failure to file was not fraudulent.

   $ ____________

   c. Jack filed his tax return 2 months and 3 days late and did not request an extension of time for filing. Jack's return indicated that he is to receive a $50 refund in taxes. Calculate the amount of Jack's penalty for failure to file his tax return on time, assuming the failure to file was not fraudulent.

   $ ____________

LO 12.3

4. In the 2014 tax year, Michelle paid the following amounts relating to her 2012 tax return:

Tax deficiency	$5,000
Negligence penalty	1,000
Interest	500
Underpayment of estimated tax penalty	350

   What amount of the above items may be deducted on Michelle's 2014 individual income tax return?

   $ ____________

   Explain ____

   ____

LO 12.3

5. Linda underpaid her taxes for 2014 by $4,000 due to negligence.
   a. Calculate Linda's accuracy-related penalty for negligence.

   $ ____________

   b. Assume that the underpayment of taxes by Linda was determined to be fraudulent, and calculate the total amount of Linda's fraud penalty.

   $ ____________

LO 12.3

6. For each of the following situations, indicate the nature and amount of the penalty that could be imposed.

	Description of the Penalty	*Penalty Amount*
a. Larry is a tax protester and files his tax return in the name of "Mickey Mouse."	____________	$ ____________
b. Anne writes a check for $900 in payment of her taxes that she knows will not clear the bank due to insufficient funds in her account.	____________	$ ____________
c. Gerald understated his tax liability by $10,000. The total amount of tax that should have been shown on his return was $70,000.	____________	$ ____________

LO 12.3
LO 12.4
LO 12.5
LO 12.6

7. Indicate whether the following statements are true or false:

    ____ The tax law includes a penalty for writing a "bad" check in payment of the taxpayer's tax liability.
    ____ The statute of limitations for a tax return is normally 4 years.
    ____ If a fraudulent tax return is filed, the IRS may assess a deficiency at any time in the future.
    ____ Enrolled agents work for the IRS.
    ____ A commercial tax preparer may represent tax clients in any proceeding with the IRS.
    ____ The IRS is entitled to choose a place and time for an audit, without regard to the inconvenience to the taxpayer or the reasonableness of the request.

LO 12.4

8. Indicate the date that the statute of limitations would run out on each of the following individual tax returns:

    a. A fraudulent 2014 tax return that was filed April 15, 2015. ____________
    b. A 2014 tax return that was filed May 19, 2015. ____________
    c. A 2014 tax return that was filed February 12, 2015. ____________
    d. A 2014 tax return that was filed March 1, 2015, and omitted $15,000 in income. The total gross income shown on the tax return was $50,000. ____________

LO 12.5

9. For each of the following situations, indicate the amount of the penalty that could be imposed on the tax return preparer:

    a. A tax return preparer understates the taxpayer's tax liability with a frivolous position and does not disclose the position. $____________
    b. A tax return preparer fails to furnish his identifying number. $____________
    c. A tax return preparer aids a taxpayer in understating a tax liability. $____________
    d. A tax return preparer endorses and cashes a client's tax refund check. $____________

LO 12.7

10. Indicate whether the following statements are true or false:

    ____ Decreasing one's tax liability through legal methods is called tax avoidance, while illegally reducing taxes is called tax evasion.
    ____ In a "closed" transaction, all tax-significant events have been completed.
    ____ The marginal tax rate is computed as the total tax paid divided by the total income of the taxpayer.
    ____ The marginal tax rate is the most important rate for decision making in tax-planning situations.
    ____ The timing tax planning technique takes advantage of deferring the payment of tax until a later year.

11. Go to the IRS website (**www.irs.gov**) and answer the following questions:
    a. Who is the commissioner of the IRS?
    b. When did he or she take office?
    c. What was his or her background before becoming commissioner of the IRS?

12. The IRS maintains a section called "Tax Pro News and Events." Locate this website and print out the first page of the first item appearing on "Tax Pro News and Events."

APPENDIX A

Tax Rate Schedules and Tax Tables

CONTENTS

2014 Tax Rate Schedules A-2

2014 Tax Tables A-4

2014 Tax Rate Schedules

Schedule X—Use if your 2014 filing status is **Single**

The tax is:

Over—	But not over—			Of the excess over—
$0	$9,075	-----------	+ 10%	$0
9,075	36,900	$907.50	+ 15%	9,075
36,900	89,350	5,081.25	+ 25%	36,900
89,350	186,350	18,193.75	+ 28%	89,350
186,350	405,100	45,353.75	+ 33%	186,350
405,100	406,750	117,541.25	+ 35%	405,100
406,750	-----------	118,118.75	+ 39.6%	406,750

Schedule Z—Use if your 2014 filing status is **Head of Household**

The tax is:

Over—	But not over—			Of the excess over—
$0	$12,950	--------------	+ 10%	$0
12,950	49,400	$1,295.00	+ 15%	12,950
49,400	127,550	6,762.50	+ 25%	49,400
127,550	206,600	26,300.00	+ 28%	127,550
206,600	405,100	48,434.00	+ 33%	206,600
405,100	432,200	113,939.00	+ 35%	405,100
432,200	-----------	123,424.00	+ 39.6%	432,200

Schedule Y-1—Use if your 2014 filing status is **Married filing jointly or Qualifying widow(er)**

The tax is:

Over—	But not over—			Of the excess over—
$0	$18,150	-------------	+ 10%	$0
18,150	73,800	$1,815.00	+ 15%	18,150
73,800	148,850	10,162.50	+ 25%	73,800
148,850	226,850	28,925.00	+ 28%	148,850
226,850	405,100	50,765.00	+ 33%	226,850
405,100	457,600	109,587.50	+ 35%	405,100
457,600	-----------	127,962.50	+ 39.6%	457,600

Schedule Y-2—Use if your 2014 filing status is **Married filing separately**

The tax is:

Over—	But not over—			Of the excess over—
$0	$9,075	-------------	+ 10%	$0
9,075	36,900	$907.50	+ 15%	9,075
36,900	74,425	5,081.25	+ 25%	36,900
74,425	113,425	14,462.50	+ 28%	74,425
113,425	202,550	25,382.50	+ 33%	113,425
202,550	228,800	54,793.75	+ 35%	202,550
228,800	-----------	63,981.25	+ 39.6%	228,800

Note: Just before going to press, the IRS released new 2014 Tax Rate Schedules in a slightly different format. Because we were unable to revise the text to present examples and solutions using the new format, we are presenting the previous format here and the new format on page A-3 of Appendix A. Both formats will compute the same tax amounts for taxable income of at least $100,000.

2014 Tax Computation Worksheet—Line 44

CAUTION *See the instructions for line 44 to see if you must use the worksheet below to figure your tax.*

Note. If you are required to use this worksheet to figure the tax on an amount from another form or worksheet, such as the Qualified Dividends and Capital Gain Tax Worksheet, the Schedule D Tax Worksheet, Schedule J, Form 8615, or the Foreign Earned Income Tax Worksheet, enter the amount from that form or worksheet in column (a) of the row that applies to the amount you are looking up. Enter the result on the appropriate line of the form or worksheet that you are completing.

Section A—Use if your filing status is **Single.** Complete the row below that applies to you.

Taxable income. If line 43 is—	**(a)** Enter the amount from line 43	**(b)** Multiplication amount	**(c)** Multiply (a) by (b)	**(d)** Subtraction amount	**Tax.** Subtract (d) from (c). Enter the result here and on Form 1040, line 44
At least $100,000 but not over $186,350	$	× 28% (.28)	$	$ 6,824.25	$
Over $186,350 but not over $405,100	$	× 33% (.33)	$	$ 16,141.75	$
Over $405,100 but not over $406,750	$	× 35% (.35)	$	$ 24,243.75	$
Over $406,750	$	× 39.6% (.396)	$	$ 42,954.25	$

Section B—Use if your filing status is **Married filing jointly** or **Qualifying widow(er).** Complete the row below that applies to you.

Taxable income. If line 43 is—	**(a)** Enter the amount from line 43	**(b)** Multiplication amount	**(c)** Multiply (a) by (b)	**(d)** Subtraction amount	**Tax.** Subtract (d) from (c). Enter the result here and on Form 1040, line 44
At least $100,000 but not over $148,850	$	× 25% (.25)	$	$ 8,287.50	$
Over $148,850 but not over $226,850	$	× 28% (.28)	$	$ 12,753.00	$
Over $226,850 but not over $405,100	$	× 33% (.33)	$	$ 24,095.50	$
Over $405,100 but not over $457,600	$	× 35% (.35)	$	$ 32,197.50	$
Over $457,600	$	× 39.6% (.396)	$	$ 53,247.10	$

Section C—Use if your filing status is **Married filing separately.** Complete the row below that applies to you.

Taxable income. If line 43 is—	**(a)** Enter the amount from line 43	**(b)** Multiplication amount	**(c)** Multiply (a) by (b)	**(d)** Subtraction amount	**Tax.** Subtract (d) from (c). Enter the result here and on Form 1040, line 44
At least $100,000 but not over $113,425	$	× 28% (.28)	$	$ 6,376.50	$
Over $113,425 but not over $202,550	$	× 33% (.33)	$	$ 12,047.75	$
Over $202,550 but not over $228,800	$	× 35% (.35)	$	$ 16,098.75	$
Over $228,800	$	× 39.6% (.396)	$	$ 26,623.55	$

Section D—Use if your filing status is **Head of household.** Complete the row below that applies to you.

Taxable income. If line 43 is—	**(a)** Enter the amount from line 43	**(b)** Multiplication amount	**(c)** Multiply (a) by (b)	**(d)** Subtraction amount	**Tax.** Subtract (d) from (c). Enter the result here and on Form 1040, line 44
At least $100,000 but not over $127,550	$	× 25% (.25)	$	$ 5,587.50	$
Over $127,550 but not over $206,600	$	× 28% (.28)	$	$ 9,414.00	$
Over $206,600 but not over $405,100	$	× 33% (.33)	$	$ 19,744.00	$
Over $405,100 but not over $432,200	$	× 35% (.35)	$	$ 27,846.00	$
Over $432,200	$	× 39.6% (.396)	$	$ 47,727.20	$

2014 Tax Table

CAUTION

See the instructions for line 44 to see if you must use the Tax Table below to figure your tax.

Example. Mr. and Mrs. Brown are filing a joint return. Their taxable income on Form 1040, line 43, is $25,300. First, they find the $25,300-25,350 taxable income line. Next, they find the column for married filing jointly and read down the column. The amount shown where the taxable income line and filing status column meet is $2,891. This is the tax amount they should enter on Form 1040, line 44.

Sample Table

At Least	But Less Than	Single	Married filing jointly*	Married filing sepa-rately	Head of a house-hold
		Your tax is—			
25,200	**25,250**	3,330	2,876	3,330	3,136
25,250	**25,300**	3,338	2,884	3,338	3,144
25,300	**25,350**	3,345	(2,891)	3,345	3,151
25,350	**25,400**	3,353	2,899	3,353	3,159

DRAFT AS OF October 8, 2014

If line 43 (taxable income) is—		And you are—			
At least	But less than	Single	Married filing jointly *	Married filing sepa-rately	Head of a house-hold
		Your tax is—			
0	5	0	0	0	0
5	15	1	1	1	1
15	25	2	2	2	2
25	50	4	4	4	4
50	75	6	6	6	6
75	100	9	9	9	9
100	125	11	11	11	11
125	150	14	14	14	14
150	175	16	16	16	16
175	200	19	19	19	19
200	225	21	21	21	21
225	250	24	24	24	24
250	275	26	26	26	26
275	300	29	29	29	29
300	325	31	31	31	31
325	350	34	34	34	34
350	375	36	36	36	36
375	400	39	39	39	39
400	425	41	41	41	41
425	450	44	44	44	44
450	475	46	46	46	46
475	500	49	49	49	49
500	525	51	51	51	51
525	550	54	54	54	54
550	575	56	56	56	56
575	600	59	59	59	59
600	625	61	61	61	61
625	650	64	64	64	64
650	675	66	66	66	66
675	700	69	69	69	69
700	725	71	71	71	71
725	750	74	74	74	74
750	775	76	76	76	76
775	800	79	79	79	79
800	825	81	81	81	81
825	850	84	84	84	84
850	875	86	86	86	86
875	900	89	89	89	89
900	925	91	91	91	91
925	950	94	94	94	94
950	975	96	96	96	96
975	1,000	99	99	99	99

If line 43 (taxable income) is—		And you are—			
At least	But less than	Single	Married filing jointly *	Married filing sepa-rately	Head of a house-hold
		Your tax is—			
1,000					
1,000	1,025	101	101	101	101
1,025	1,050	104	104	104	104
1,050	1,075	106	106	106	106
1,075	1,100	109	109	109	109
1,100	1,125	111	111	111	111
1,125	1,150	114	114	114	114
1,150	1,175	116	116	116	116
1,175	1,200	119	119	119	119
1,200	1,225	121	121	121	121
1,225	1,250	124	124	124	124
1,250	1,275	126	126	126	126
1,275	1,300	129	129	129	129
1,300	1,325	131	131	131	131
1,325	1,350	134	134	134	134
1,350	1,375	136	136	136	136
1,375	1,400	139	139	139	139
1,400	1,425	141	141	141	141
1,425	1,450	144	144	144	144
1,450	1,475	146	146	146	146
1,475	1,500	149	149	149	149
1,500	1,525	151	151	151	151
1,525	1,550	154	154	154	154
1,550	1,575	156	156	156	156
1,575	1,600	159	159	159	159
1,600	1,625	161	161	161	161
1,625	1,650	164	164	164	164
1,650	1,675	166	166	166	166
1,675	1,700	169	169	169	169
1,700	1,725	171	171	171	171
1,725	1,750	174	174	174	174
1,750	1,775	176	176	176	176
1,775	1,800	179	179	179	179
1,800	1,825	181	181	181	181
1,825	1,850	184	184	184	184
1,850	1,875	186	186	186	186
1,875	1,900	189	189	189	189
1,900	1,925	191	191	191	191
1,925	1,950	194	194	194	194
1,950	1,975	196	196	196	196
1,975	2,000	199	199	199	199

If line 43 (taxable income) is—		And you are—			
At least	But less than	Single	Married filing jointly *	Married filing sepa-rately	Head of a house-hold
		Your tax is—			
2,000					
2,000	2,025	201	201	201	201
2,025	2,050	204	204	204	204
2,050	2,075	206	206	206	206
2,075	2,100	209	209	209	209
2,100	2,125	211	211	211	211
2,125	2,150	214	214	214	214
2,150	2,175	216	216	216	216
2,175	2,200	219	219	219	219
2,200	2,225	221	221	221	221
2,225	2,250	224	224	224	224
2,250	2,275	226	226	226	226
2,275	2,300	229	229	229	229
2,300	2,325	231	231	231	231
2,325	2,350	234	234	234	234
2,350	2,375	236	236	236	236
2,375	2,400	239	239	239	239
2,400	2,425	241	241	241	241
2,425	2,450	244	244	244	244
2,450	2,475	246	246	246	246
2,475	2,500	249	249	249	249
2,500	2,525	251	251	251	251
2,525	2,550	254	254	254	254
2,550	2,575	256	256	256	256
2,575	2,600	259	259	259	259
2,600	2,625	261	261	261	261
2,625	2,650	264	264	264	264
2,650	2,675	266	266	266	266
2,675	2,700	269	269	269	269
2,700	2,725	271	271	271	271
2,725	2,750	274	274	274	274
2,750	2,775	276	276	276	276
2,775	2,800	279	279	279	279
2,800	2,825	281	281	281	281
2,825	2,850	284	284	284	284
2,850	2,875	286	286	286	286
2,875	2,900	289	289	289	289
2,900	2,925	291	291	291	291
2,925	2,950	294	294	294	294
2,950	2,975	296	296	296	296
2,975	3,000	299	299	299	299

(Continued)

* This column must also be used by a qualifying widow(er).

2014 Tax Table — *Continued*

If line 43 (taxable income) is— At least	But less than	And you are— Single	Married filing jointly *	Married filing sepa-rately	Head of a house-hold
		Your tax is—			
3,000					
3,000	3,050	303	303	303	303
3,050	3,100	308	308	308	308
3,100	3,150	313	313	313	313
3,150	3,200	318	318	318	318
3,200	3,250	323	323	323	323
3,250	3,300	328	328	328	328
3,300	3,350	333	333	333	333
3,350	3,400	338	338	338	338
3,400	3,450	343	343	343	343
3,450	3,500	348	348	348	348
3,500	3,550	353	353	353	353
3,550	3,600	358	358	358	358
3,600	3,650	363	363	363	363
3,650	3,700	368	368	368	368
3,700	3,750	373	373	373	373
3,750	3,800	378	378	378	378
3,800	3,850	383	383	383	383
3,850	3,900	388	388	388	388
3,900	3,950	393	393	393	393
3,950	4,000	398	398	398	398
4,000					
4,000	4,050	403	403	403	403
4,050	4,100	408	408	408	408
4,100	4,150	413	413	413	413
4,150	4,200	418	418	418	418
4,200	4,250	423	423	423	423
4,250	4,300	428	428	428	428
4,300	4,350	433	433	433	433
4,350	4,400	438	438	438	438
4,400	4,450	443	443	443	443
4,450	4,500	448	448	448	448
4,500	4,550	453	453	453	453
4,550	4,600	458	458	458	458
4,600	4,650	463	463	463	463
4,650	4,700	468	468	468	468
4,700	4,750	473	473	473	473
4,750	4,800	478	478	478	478
4,800	4,850	483	483	483	483
4,850	4,900	488	488	488	488
4,900	4,950	493	493	493	493
4,950	5,000	498	498	498	498
5,000					
5,000	5,050	503	503	503	503
5,050	5,100	508	508	508	508
5,100	5,150	513	513	513	513
5,150	5,200	518	518	518	518
5,200	5,250	523	523	523	523
5,250	5,300	528	528	528	528
5,300	5,350	533	533	533	533
5,350	5,400	538	538	538	538
5,400	5,450	543	543	543	543
5,450	5,500	548	548	548	548
5,500	5,550	553	553	553	553
5,550	5,600	558	558	558	558
5,600	5,650	563	563	563	563
5,650	5,700	568	568	568	568
5,700	5,750	573	573	573	573
5,750	5,800	578	578	578	578
5,800	5,850	583	583	583	583
5,850	5,900	588	588	588	588
5,900	5,950	593	593	593	593
5,950	6,000	598	598	598	598

If line 43 (taxable income) is— At least	But less than	And you are— Single	Married filing jointly *	Married filing sepa-rately	Head of a house-hold
		Your tax is—			
6,000					
6,000	6,050	603	603	603	603
6,050	6,100	608	608	608	608
6,100	6,150	613	613	613	613
6,150	6,200	618	618	618	618
6,200	6,250	623	623	623	623
6,250	6,300	628	628	628	628
6,300	6,350	633	633	633	633
6,350	6,400	638	638	638	638
6,400	6,450	643	643	643	643
6,450	6,500	648	648	648	648
6,500	6,550	653	653	653	653
6,550	6,600	658	658	658	658
6,600	6,650	663	663	663	663
6,650	6,700	668	668	668	668
6,700	6,750	673	673	673	673
6,750	6,800	678	678	678	678
6,800	6,850	683	683	683	683
6,850	6,900	688	688	688	688
6,900	6,950	693	693	693	693
6,950	7,000	698	698	698	698
7,000					
7,000	7,050	703	703	703	703
7,050	7,100	708	708	708	708
7,100	7,150	713	713	713	713
7,150	7,200	718	718	718	718
7,200	7,250	723	723	723	723
7,250	7,300	728	728	728	728
7,300	7,350	733	733	733	733
7,350	7,400	738	738	738	738
7,400	7,450	743	743	743	743
7,450	7,500	748	748	748	748
7,500	7,550	753	753	753	753
7,550	7,600	758	758	758	758
7,600	7,650	763	763	763	763
7,650	7,700	768	768	768	768
7,700	7,750	773	773	773	773
7,750	7,800	778	778	778	778
7,800	7,850	783	783	783	783
7,850	7,900	788	788	788	788
7,900	7,950	793	793	793	793
7,950	8,000	798	798	798	798
8,000					
8,000	8,050	803	803	803	803
8,050	8,100	808	808	808	808
8,100	8,150	813	813	813	813
8,150	8,200	818	818	818	818
8,200	8,250	823	823	823	823
8,250	8,300	828	828	828	828
8,300	8,350	833	833	833	833
8,350	8,400	838	838	838	838
8,400	8,450	843	843	843	843
8,450	8,500	848	848	848	848
8,500	8,550	853	853	853	853
8,550	8,600	858	858	858	858
8,600	8,650	863	863	863	863
8,650	8,700	868	868	868	868
8,700	8,750	873	873	873	873
8,750	8,800	878	878	878	878
8,800	8,850	883	883	883	883
8,850	8,900	888	888	888	888
8,900	8,950	893	893	893	893
8,950	9,000	898	898	898	898

If line 43 (taxable income) is— At least	But less than	And you are— Single	Married filing jointly *	Married filing sepa-rately	Head of a house-hold
		Your tax is—			
9,000					
9,000	9,050	903	903	903	903
9,050	9,100	908	908	908	908
9,100	9,150	915	913	915	913
9,150	9,200	923	918	923	918
9,200	9,250	930	923	930	923
9,250	9,300	938	928	938	928
9,300	9,350	945	933	945	933
9,350	9,400	953	938	953	938
9,400	9,450	960	943	960	943
9,450	9,500	968	948	968	948
9,500	9,550	975	953	975	953
9,550	9,600	983	958	983	958
9,600	9,650	990	963	990	963
9,650	9,700	998	968	998	968
9,700	9,750	1,005	973	1,005	973
9,750	9,800	1,013	978	1,013	978
9,800	9,850	1,020	983	1,020	983
9,850	9,900	1,028	988	1,028	988
9,900	9,950	1,035	993	1,035	993
9,950	10,000	1,043	998	1,043	998
10,000					
10,000	10,050	1,050	1,003	1,050	1,003
10,050	10,100	1,058	1,008	1,058	1,008
10,100	10,150	1,065	1,013	1,065	1,013
10,150	10,200	1,073	1,018	1,073	1,018
10,200	10,250	1,080	1,023	1,080	1,023
10,250	10,300	1,088	1,028	1,088	1,028
10,300	10,350	1,095	1,033	1,095	1,033
10,350	10,400	1,103	1,038	1,103	1,038
10,400	10,450	1,110	1,043	1,110	1,043
10,450	10,500	1,118	1,048	1,118	1,048
10,500	10,550	1,125	1,053	1,125	1,053
10,550	10,600	1,133	1,058	1,133	1,058
10,600	10,650	1,140	1,063	1,140	1,063
10,650	10,700	1,148	1,068	1,148	1,068
10,700	10,750	1,155	1,073	1,155	1,073
10,750	10,800	1,163	1,078	1,163	1,078
10,800	10,850	1,170	1,083	1,170	1,083
10,850	10,900	1,178	1,088	1,178	1,088
10,900	10,950	1,185	1,093	1,185	1,093
10,950	11,000	1,193	1,098	1,193	1,098
11,000					
11,000	11,050	1,200	1,103	1,200	1,103
11,050	11,100	1,208	1,108	1,208	1,108
11,100	11,150	1,215	1,113	1,215	1,113
11,150	11,200	1,223	1,118	1,223	1,118
11,200	11,250	1,230	1,123	1,230	1,123
11,250	11,300	1,238	1,128	1,238	1,128
11,300	11,350	1,245	1,133	1,245	1,133
11,350	11,400	1,253	1,138	1,253	1,138
11,400	11,450	1,260	1,143	1,260	1,143
11,450	11,500	1,268	1,148	1,268	1,148
11,500	11,550	1,275	1,153	1,275	1,153
11,550	11,600	1,283	1,158	1,283	1,158
11,600	11,650	1,290	1,163	1,290	1,163
11,650	11,700	1,298	1,168	1,298	1,168
11,700	11,750	1,305	1,173	1,305	1,173
11,750	11,800	1,313	1,178	1,313	1,178
11,800	11,850	1,320	1,183	1,320	1,183
11,850	11,900	1,328	1,188	1,328	1,188
11,900	11,950	1,335	1,193	1,335	1,193
11,950	12,000	1,343	1,198	1,343	1,198

* This column must also be used by a qualifying widow(er).

(Continued)

2014 Tax Table — *Continued*

DRAFT AS OF October 8, 2014

If line 43 (taxable income) is—		And you are—			
At least	But less than	Single	Married filing jointly *	Married filing sepa-rately	Head of a house-hold
		Your tax is—			
12,000					
12,000	**12,050**	1,350	1,203	1,350	1,203
12,050	**12,100**	1,358	1,208	1,358	1,208
12,100	**12,150**	1,365	1,213	1,365	1,213
12,150	**12,200**	1,373	1,218	1,373	1,218
12,200	**12,250**	1,380	1,223	1,380	1,223
12,250	**12,300**	1,388	1,228	1,388	1,228
12,300	**12,350**	1,395	1,233	1,395	1,233
12,350	**12,400**	1,403	1,238	1,403	1,238
12,400	**12,450**	1,410	1,243	1,410	1,243
12,450	**12,500**	1,418	1,248	1,418	1,248
12,500	**12,550**	1,425	1,253	1,425	1,253
12,550	**12,600**	1,433	1,258	1,433	1,258
12,600	**12,650**	1,440	1,263	1,440	1,263
12,650	**12,700**	1,448	1,268	1,448	1,268
12,700	**12,750**	1,455	1,273	1,455	1,273
12,750	**12,800**	1,463	1,278	1,463	1,278
12,800	**12,850**	1,470	1,283	1,470	1,283
12,850	**12,900**	1,478	1,288	1,478	1,288
12,900	**12,950**	1,485	1,293	1,485	1,293
12,950	**13,000**	1,493	1,298	1,493	1,299
13,000					
13,000	**13,050**	1,500	1,303	1,500	1,306
13,050	**13,100**	1,508	1,308	1,508	1,314
13,100	**13,150**	1,515	1,313	1,515	1,321
13,150	**13,200**	1,523	1,318	1,523	1,329
13,200	**13,250**	1,530	1,323	1,530	1,336
13,250	**13,300**	1,538	1,328	1,538	1,344
13,300	**13,350**	1,545	1,333	1,545	1,351
13,350	**13,400**	1,553	1,338	1,553	1,359
13,400	**13,450**	1,560	1,343	1,560	1,366
13,450	**13,500**	1,568	1,348	1,568	1,374
13,500	**13,550**	1,575	1,353	1,575	1,381
13,550	**13,600**	1,583	1,358	1,583	1,389
13,600	**13,650**	1,590	1,363	1,590	1,396
13,650	**13,700**	1,598	1,368	1,598	1,404
13,700	**13,750**	1,605	1,373	1,605	1,411
13,750	**13,800**	1,613	1,378	1,613	1,419
13,800	**13,850**	1,620	1,383	1,620	1,426
13,850	**13,900**	1,628	1,388	1,628	1,434
13,900	**13,950**	1,635	1,393	1,635	1,441
13,950	**14,000**	1,643	1,398	1,643	1,449
14,000					
14,000	**14,050**	1,650	1,403	1,650	1,456
14,050	**14,100**	1,658	1,408	1,658	1,464
14,100	**14,150**	1,665	1,413	1,665	1,471
14,150	**14,200**	1,673	1,418	1,673	1,479
14,200	**14,250**	1,680	1,423	1,680	1,486
14,250	**14,300**	1,688	1,428	1,688	1,494
14,300	**14,350**	1,695	1,433	1,695	1,501
14,350	**14,400**	1,703	1,438	1,703	1,509
14,400	**14,450**	1,710	1,443	1,710	1,516
14,450	**14,500**	1,718	1,448	1,718	1,524
14,500	**14,550**	1,725	1,453	1,725	1,531
14,550	**14,600**	1,733	1,458	1,733	1,539
14,600	**14,650**	1,740	1,463	1,740	1,546
14,650	**14,700**	1,748	1,468	1,748	1,554
14,700	**14,750**	1,755	1,473	1,755	1,561
14,750	**14,800**	1,763	1,478	1,763	1,569
14,800	**14,850**	1,770	1,483	1,770	1,576
14,850	**14,900**	1,778	1,488	1,778	1,584
14,900	**14,950**	1,785	1,493	1,785	1,591
14,950	**15,000**	1,793	1,498	1,793	1,599
15,000					
15,000	**15,050**	1,800	1,503	1,800	1,606
15,050	**15,100**	1,808	1,508	1,808	1,614
15,100	**15,150**	1,815	1,513	1,815	1,621
15,150	**15,200**	1,823	1,518	1,823	1,629
15,200	**15,250**	1,830	1,523	1,830	1,636
15,250	**15,300**	1,838	1,528	1,838	1,644
15,300	**15,350**	1,845	1,533	1,845	1,651
15,350	**15,400**	1,853	1,538	1,853	1,659
15,400	**15,450**	1,860	1,543	1,860	1,666
15,450	**15,500**	1,868	1,548	1,868	1,674
15,500	**15,550**	1,875	1,553	1,875	1,681
15,550	**15,600**	1,883	1,558	1,883	1,689
15,600	**15,650**	1,890	1,563	1,890	1,696
15,650	**15,700**	1,898	1,568	1,898	1,704
15,700	**15,750**	1,905	1,573	1,905	1,711
15,750	**15,800**	1,913	1,578	1,913	1,719
15,800	**15,850**	1,920	1,583	1,920	1,726
15,850	**15,900**	1,928	1,588	1,928	1,734
15,900	**15,950**	1,935	1,593	1,935	1,741
15,950	**16,000**	1,943	1,598	1,943	1,749
16,000					
16,000	**16,050**	1,950	1,603	1,950	1,756
16,050	**16,100**	1,958	1,608	1,958	1,764
16,100	**16,150**	1,965	1,613	1,965	1,771
16,150	**16,200**	1,973	1,618	1,973	1,779
16,200	**16,250**	1,980	1,623	1,980	1,786
16,250	**16,300**	1,988	1,628	1,988	1,794
16,300	**16,350**	1,995	1,633	1,995	1,801
16,350	**16,400**	2,003	1,638	2,003	1,809
16,400	**16,450**	2,010	1,643	2,010	1,816
16,450	**16,500**	2,018	1,648	2,018	1,824
16,500	**16,550**	2,025	1,653	2,025	1,831
16,550	**16,600**	2,033	1,658	2,033	1,839
16,600	**16,650**	2,040	1,663	2,040	1,846
16,650	**16,700**	2,048	1,668	2,048	1,854
16,700	**16,750**	2,055	1,673	2,055	1,861
16,750	**16,800**	2,063	1,678	2,063	1,869
16,800	**16,850**	2,070	1,683	2,070	1,876
16,850	**16,900**	2,078	1,688	2,078	1,884
16,900	**16,950**	2,085	1,693	2,085	1,891
16,950	**17,000**	2,093	1,698	2,093	1,899
17,000					
17,000	**17,050**	2,100	1,703	2,100	1,906
17,050	**17,100**	2,108	1,708	2,108	1,914
17,100	**17,150**	2,115	1,713	2,115	1,921
17,150	**17,200**	2,123	1,718	2,123	1,929
17,200	**17,250**	2,130	1,723	2,130	1,936
17,250	**17,300**	2,138	1,728	2,138	1,944
17,300	**17,350**	2,145	1,733	2,145	1,951
17,350	**17,400**	2,153	1,738	2,153	1,959
17,400	**17,450**	2,160	1,743	2,160	1,966
17,450	**17,500**	2,168	1,748	2,168	1,974
17,500	**17,550**	2,175	1,753	2,175	1,981
17,550	**17,600**	2,183	1,758	2,183	1,989
17,600	**17,650**	2,190	1,763	2,190	1,996
17,650	**17,700**	2,198	1,768	2,198	2,004
17,700	**17,750**	2,205	1,773	2,205	2,011
17,750	**17,800**	2,213	1,778	2,213	2,019
17,800	**17,850**	2,220	1,783	2,220	2,026
17,850	**17,900**	2,228	1,788	2,228	2,034
17,900	**17,950**	2,235	1,793	2,235	2,041
17,950	**18,000**	2,243	1,798	2,243	2,049
18,000					
18,000	**18,050**	2,250	1,803	2,250	2,056
18,050	**18,100**	2,258	1,808	2,258	2,064
18,100	**18,150**	2,265	1,813	2,265	2,071
18,150	**18,200**	2,273	1,819	2,273	2,079
18,200	**18,250**	2,280	1,826	2,280	2,086
18,250	**18,300**	2,288	1,834	2,288	2,094
18,300	**18,350**	2,295	1,841	2,295	2,101
18,350	**18,400**	2,303	1,849	2,303	2,109
18,400	**18,450**	2,310	1,856	2,310	2,116
18,450	**18,500**	2,318	1,864	2,318	2,124
18,500	**18,550**	2,325	1,871	2,325	2,131
18,550	**18,600**	2,333	1,879	2,333	2,139
18,600	**18,650**	2,340	1,886	2,340	2,146
18,650	**18,700**	2,348	1,894	2,348	2,154
18,700	**18,750**	2,355	1,901	2,355	2,161
18,750	**18,800**	2,363	1,909	2,363	2,169
18,800	**18,850**	2,370	1,916	2,370	2,176
18,850	**18,900**	2,378	1,924	2,378	2,184
18,900	**18,950**	2,385	1,931	2,385	2,191
18,950	**19,000**	2,393	1,939	2,393	2,199
19,000					
19,000	**19,050**	2,400	1,946	2,400	2,206
19,050	**19,100**	2,408	1,954	2,408	2,214
19,100	**19,150**	2,415	1,961	2,415	2,221
19,150	**19,200**	2,423	1,969	2,423	2,229
19,200	**19,250**	2,430	1,976	2,430	2,236
19,250	**19,300**	2,438	1,984	2,438	2,244
19,300	**19,350**	2,445	1,991	2,445	2,251
19,350	**19,400**	2,453	1,999	2,453	2,259
19,400	**19,450**	2,460	2,006	2,460	2,266
19,450	**19,500**	2,468	2,014	2,468	2,274
19,500	**19,550**	2,475	2,021	2,475	2,281
19,550	**19,600**	2,483	2,029	2,483	2,289
19,600	**19,650**	2,490	2,036	2,490	2,296
19,650	**19,700**	2,498	2,044	2,498	2,304
19,700	**19,750**	2,505	2,051	2,505	2,311
19,750	**19,800**	2,513	2,059	2,513	2,319
19,800	**19,850**	2,520	2,066	2,520	2,326
19,850	**19,900**	2,528	2,074	2,528	2,334
19,900	**19,950**	2,535	2,081	2,535	2,341
19,950	**20,000**	2,543	2,089	2,543	2,349
20,000					
20,000	**20,050**	2,550	2,096	2,550	2,356
20,050	**20,100**	2,558	2,104	2,558	2,364
20,100	**20,150**	2,565	2,111	2,565	2,371
20,150	**20,200**	2,573	2,119	2,573	2,379
20,200	**20,250**	2,580	2,126	2,580	2,386
20,250	**20,300**	2,588	2,134	2,588	2,394
20,300	**20,350**	2,595	2,141	2,595	2,401
20,350	**20,400**	2,603	2,149	2,603	2,409
20,400	**20,450**	2,610	2,156	2,610	2,416
20,450	**20,500**	2,618	2,164	2,618	2,424
20,500	**20,550**	2,625	2,171	2,625	2,431
20,550	**20,600**	2,633	2,179	2,633	2,439
20,600	**20,650**	2,640	2,186	2,640	2,446
20,650	**20,700**	2,648	2,194	2,648	2,454
20,700	**20,750**	2,655	2,201	2,655	2,461
20,750	**20,800**	2,663	2,209	2,663	2,469
20,800	**20,850**	2,670	2,216	2,670	2,476
20,850	**20,900**	2,678	2,224	2,678	2,484
20,900	**20,950**	2,685	2,231	2,685	2,491
20,950	**21,000**	2,693	2,239	2,693	2,499

(Continued)

* This column must also be used by a qualifying widow(er).

2014 Tax Table — *Continued*

DRAFT AS OF October 8, 2014

If line 43 (taxable income) is— At least	But less than	And you are— Single	Married filing jointly *	Married filing separately	Head of a household
		Your tax is—			
21,000					
21,000	21,050	2,700	2,246	2,700	2,506
21,050	21,100	2,708	2,254	2,708	2,514
21,100	21,150	2,715	2,261	2,715	2,521
21,150	21,200	2,723	2,269	2,723	2,529
21,200	21,250	2,730	2,276	2,730	2,536
21,250	21,300	2,738	2,284	2,738	2,544
21,300	21,350	2,745	2,291	2,745	2,551
21,350	21,400	2,753	2,299	2,753	2,559
21,400	21,450	2,760	2,306	2,760	2,566
21,450	21,500	2,768	2,314	2,768	2,574
21,500	21,550	2,775	2,321	2,775	2,581
21,550	21,600	2,783	2,329	2,783	2,589
21,600	21,650	2,790	2,336	2,790	2,596
21,650	21,700	2,798	2,344	2,798	2,604
21,700	21,750	2,805	2,351	2,805	2,611
21,750	21,800	2,813	2,359	2,813	2,619
21,800	21,850	2,820	2,366	2,820	2,626
21,850	21,900	2,828	2,374	2,828	2,634
21,900	21,950	2,835	2,381	2,835	2,641
21,950	22,000	2,843	2,389	2,843	2,649
22,000					
22,000	22,050	2,850	2,396	2,850	2,656
22,050	22,100	2,858	2,404	2,858	2,664
22,100	22,150	2,865	2,411	2,865	2,671
22,150	22,200	2,873	2,419	2,873	2,679
22,200	22,250	2,880	2,426	2,880	2,686
22,250	22,300	2,888	2,434	2,888	2,694
22,300	22,350	2,895	2,441	2,895	2,701
22,350	22,400	2,903	2,449	2,903	2,709
22,400	22,450	2,910	2,456	2,910	2,716
22,450	22,500	2,918	2,464	2,918	2,724
22,500	22,550	2,925	2,471	2,925	2,731
22,550	22,600	2,933	2,479	2,933	2,739
22,600	22,650	2,940	2,486	2,940	2,746
22,650	22,700	2,948	2,494	2,948	2,754
22,700	22,750	2,955	2,501	2,955	2,761
22,750	22,800	2,963	2,509	2,963	2,769
22,800	22,850	2,970	2,516	2,970	2,776
22,850	22,900	2,978	2,524	2,978	2,784
22,900	22,950	2,985	2,531	2,985	2,791
22,950	23,000	2,993	2,539	2,993	2,799
23,000					
23,000	23,050	3,000	2,546	3,000	2,806
23,050	23,100	3,008	2,554	3,008	2,814
23,100	23,150	3,015	2,561	3,015	2,821
23,150	23,200	3,023	2,569	3,023	2,829
23,200	23,250	3,030	2,576	3,030	2,836
23,250	23,300	3,038	2,584	3,038	2,844
23,300	23,350	3,045	2,591	3,045	2,851
23,350	23,400	3,053	2,599	3,053	2,859
23,400	23,450	3,060	2,606	3,060	2,866
23,450	23,500	3,068	2,614	3,068	2,874
23,500	23,550	3,075	2,621	3,075	2,881
23,550	23,600	3,083	2,629	3,083	2,889
23,600	23,650	3,090	2,636	3,090	2,896
23,650	23,700	3,098	2,644	3,098	2,904
23,700	23,750	3,105	2,651	3,105	2,911
23,750	23,800	3,113	2,659	3,113	2,919
23,800	23,850	3,120	2,666	3,120	2,926
23,850	23,900	3,128	2,674	3,128	2,934
23,900	23,950	3,135	2,681	3,135	2,941
23,950	24,000	3,143	2,689	3,143	2,949

If line 43 (taxable income) is— At least	But less than	And you are— Single	Married filing jointly *	Married filing separately	Head of a household
		Your tax is—			
24,000					
24,000	24,050	3,150	2,696	3,150	2,956
24,050	24,100	3,158	2,704	3,158	2,964
24,100	24,150	3,165	2,711	3,165	2,971
24,150	24,200	3,173	2,719	3,173	2,979
24,200	24,250	3,180	2,726	3,180	2,986
24,250	24,300	3,188	2,734	3,188	2,994
24,300	24,350	3,195	2,741	3,195	3,001
24,350	24,400	3,203	2,749	3,203	3,009
24,400	24,450	3,210	2,756	3,210	3,016
24,450	24,500	3,218	2,764	3,218	3,024
24,500	24,550	3,225	2,771	3,225	3,031
24,550	24,600	3,233	2,779	3,233	3,039
24,600	24,650	3,240	2,786	3,240	3,046
24,650	24,700	3,248	2,794	3,248	3,054
24,700	24,750	3,255	2,801	3,255	3,061
24,750	24,800	3,263	2,809	3,263	3,069
24,800	24,850	3,270	2,816	3,270	3,076
24,850	24,900	3,278	2,824	3,278	3,084
24,900	24,950	3,285	2,831	3,285	3,091
24,950	25,000	3,293	2,839	3,293	3,099
25,000					
25,000	25,050	3,300	2,846	3,300	3,106
25,050	25,100	3,308	2,854	3,308	3,114
25,100	25,150	3,315	2,861	3,315	3,121
25,150	25,200	3,323	2,869	3,323	3,129
25,200	25,250	3,330	2,876	3,330	3,136
25,250	25,300	3,338	2,884	3,338	3,144
25,300	25,350	3,345	2,891	3,345	3,151
25,350	25,400	3,353	2,899	3,353	3,159
25,400	25,450	3,360	2,906	3,360	3,166
25,450	25,500	3,368	2,914	3,368	3,174
25,500	25,550	3,375	2,921	3,375	3,181
25,550	25,600	3,383	2,929	3,383	3,189
25,600	25,650	3,390	2,936	3,390	3,196
25,650	25,700	3,398	2,944	3,398	3,204
25,700	25,750	3,405	2,951	3,405	3,211
25,750	25,800	3,413	2,959	3,413	3,219
25,800	25,850	3,420	2,966	3,420	3,226
25,850	25,900	3,428	2,974	3,428	3,234
25,900	25,950	3,435	2,981	3,435	3,241
25,950	26,000	3,443	2,989	3,443	3,249
26,000					
26,000	26,050	3,450	2,996	3,450	3,256
26,050	26,100	3,458	3,004	3,458	3,264
26,100	26,150	3,465	3,011	3,465	3,271
26,150	26,200	3,473	3,019	3,473	3,279
26,200	26,250	3,480	3,026	3,480	3,286
26,250	26,300	3,488	3,034	3,488	3,294
26,300	26,350	3,495	3,041	3,495	3,301
26,350	26,400	3,503	3,049	3,503	3,309
26,400	26,450	3,510	3,056	3,510	3,316
26,450	26,500	3,518	3,064	3,518	3,324
26,500	26,550	3,525	3,071	3,525	3,331
26,550	26,600	3,533	3,079	3,533	3,339
26,600	26,650	3,540	3,086	3,540	3,346
26,650	26,700	3,548	3,094	3,548	3,354
26,700	26,750	3,555	3,101	3,555	3,361
26,750	26,800	3,563	3,109	3,563	3,369
26,800	26,850	3,570	3,116	3,570	3,376
26,850	26,900	3,578	3,124	3,578	3,384
26,900	26,950	3,585	3,131	3,585	3,391
26,950	27,000	3,593	3,139	3,593	3,399

If line 43 (taxable income) is— At least	But less than	And you are— Single	Married filing jointly *	Married filing separately	Head of a household
		Your tax is—			
27,000					
27,000	27,050	3,600	3,146	3,600	3,406
27,050	27,100	3,608	3,154	3,608	3,414
27,100	27,150	3,615	3,161	3,615	3,421
27,150	27,200	3,623	3,169	3,623	3,429
27,200	27,250	3,630	3,176	3,630	3,436
27,250	27,300	3,638	3,184	3,638	3,444
27,300	27,350	3,645	3,191	3,645	3,451
27,350	27,400	3,653	3,199	3,653	3,459
27,400	27,450	3,660	3,206	3,660	3,466
27,450	27,500	3,668	3,214	3,668	3,474
27,500	27,550	3,675	3,221	3,675	3,481
27,550	27,600	3,683	3,229	3,683	3,489
27,600	27,650	3,690	3,236	3,690	3,496
27,650	27,700	3,698	3,244	3,698	3,504
27,700	27,750	3,705	3,251	3,705	3,511
27,750	27,800	3,713	3,259	3,713	3,519
27,800	27,850	3,720	3,266	3,720	3,526
27,850	27,900	3,728	3,274	3,728	3,534
27,900	27,950	3,735	3,281	3,735	3,541
27,950	28,000	3,743	3,289	3,743	3,549
28,000					
28,000	28,050	3,750	3,296	3,750	3,556
28,050	28,100	3,758	3,304	3,758	3,564
28,100	28,150	3,765	3,311	3,765	3,571
28,150	28,200	3,773	3,319	3,773	3,579
28,200	28,250	3,780	3,326	3,780	3,586
28,250	28,300	3,788	3,334	3,788	3,594
28,300	28,350	3,795	3,341	3,795	3,601
28,350	28,400	3,803	3,349	3,803	3,609
28,400	28,450	3,810	3,356	3,810	3,616
28,450	28,500	3,818	3,364	3,818	3,624
28,500	28,550	3,825	3,371	3,825	3,631
28,550	28,600	3,833	3,379	3,833	3,639
28,600	28,650	3,840	3,386	3,840	3,646
28,650	28,700	3,848	3,394	3,848	3,654
28,700	28,750	3,855	3,401	3,855	3,661
28,750	28,800	3,863	3,409	3,863	3,669
28,800	28,850	3,870	3,416	3,870	3,676
28,850	28,900	3,878	3,424	3,878	3,684
28,900	28,950	3,885	3,431	3,885	3,691
28,950	29,000	3,893	3,439	3,893	3,699
29,000					
29,000	29,050	3,900	3,446	3,900	3,706
29,050	29,100	3,908	3,454	3,908	3,714
29,100	29,150	3,915	3,461	3,915	3,721
29,150	29,200	3,923	3,469	3,923	3,729
29,200	29,250	3,930	3,476	3,930	3,736
29,250	29,300	3,938	3,484	3,938	3,744
29,300	29,350	3,945	3,491	3,945	3,751
29,350	29,400	3,953	3,499	3,953	3,759
29,400	29,450	3,960	3,506	3,960	3,766
29,450	29,500	3,968	3,514	3,968	3,774
29,500	29,550	3,975	3,521	3,975	3,781
29,550	29,600	3,983	3,529	3,983	3,789
29,600	29,650	3,990	3,536	3,990	3,796
29,650	29,700	3,998	3,544	3,998	3,804
29,700	29,750	4,005	3,551	4,005	3,811
29,750	29,800	4,013	3,559	4,013	3,819
29,800	29,850	4,020	3,566	4,020	3,826
29,850	29,900	4,028	3,574	4,028	3,834
29,900	29,950	4,035	3,581	4,035	3,841
29,950	30,000	4,043	3,589	4,043	3,849

* This column must also be used by a qualifying widow(er).

(Continued)

DRAFT AS OF October 8, 2014

2014 Tax Table — *Continued*

If line 43 (taxable income) is— At least	But less than	And you are— Single	Married filing jointly *	Married filing separately	Head of a household
		Your tax is—			
30,000					
30,000	30,050	4,050	3,596	4,050	3,856
30,050	30,100	4,058	3,604	4,058	3,864
30,100	30,150	4,065	3,611	4,065	3,871
30,150	30,200	4,073	3,619	4,073	3,879
30,200	30,250	4,080	3,626	4,080	3,886
30,250	30,300	4,088	3,634	4,088	3,894
30,300	30,350	4,095	3,641	4,095	3,901
30,350	30,400	4,103	3,649	4,103	3,909
30,400	30,450	4,110	3,656	4,110	3,916
30,450	30,500	4,118	3,664	4,118	3,924
30,500	30,550	4,125	3,671	4,125	3,931
30,550	30,600	4,133	3,679	4,133	3,939
30,600	30,650	4,140	3,686	4,140	3,946
30,650	30,700	4,148	3,694	4,148	3,954
30,700	30,750	4,155	3,701	4,155	3,961
30,750	30,800	4,163	3,709	4,163	3,969
30,800	30,850	4,170	3,716	4,170	3,976
30,850	30,900	4,178	3,724	4,178	3,984
30,900	30,950	4,185	3,731	4,185	3,991
30,950	31,000	4,193	3,739	4,193	3,999
31,000					
31,000	31,050	4,200	3,746	4,200	4,006
31,050	31,100	4,208	3,754	4,208	4,014
31,100	31,150	4,215	3,761	4,215	4,021
31,150	31,200	4,223	3,769	4,223	4,029
31,200	31,250	4,230	3,776	4,230	4,036
31,250	31,300	4,238	3,784	4,238	4,044
31,300	31,350	4,245	3,791	4,245	4,051
31,350	31,400	4,253	3,799	4,253	4,059
31,400	31,450	4,260	3,806	4,260	4,066
31,450	31,500	4,268	3,814	4,268	4,074
31,500	31,550	4,275	3,821	4,275	4,081
31,550	31,600	4,283	3,829	4,283	4,089
31,600	31,650	4,290	3,836	4,290	4,096
31,650	31,700	4,298	3,844	4,298	4,104
31,700	31,750	4,305	3,851	4,305	4,111
31,750	31,800	4,313	3,859	4,313	4,119
31,800	31,850	4,320	3,866	4,320	4,126
31,850	31,900	4,328	3,874	4,328	4,134
31,900	31,950	4,335	3,881	4,335	4,141
31,950	32,000	4,343	3,889	4,343	4,149
32,000					
32,000	32,050	4,350	3,896	4,350	4,156
32,050	32,100	4,358	3,904	4,358	4,164
32,100	32,150	4,365	3,911	4,365	4,171
32,150	32,200	4,373	3,919	4,373	4,179
32,200	32,250	4,380	3,926	4,380	4,186
32,250	32,300	4,388	3,934	4,388	4,194
32,300	32,350	4,395	3,941	4,395	4,201
32,350	32,400	4,403	3,949	4,403	4,209
32,400	32,450	4,410	3,956	4,410	4,216
32,450	32,500	4,418	3,964	4,418	4,224
32,500	32,550	4,425	3,971	4,425	4,231
32,550	32,600	4,433	3,979	4,433	4,239
32,600	32,650	4,440	3,986	4,440	4,246
32,650	32,700	4,448	3,994	4,448	4,254
32,700	32,750	4,455	4,001	4,455	4,261
32,750	32,800	4,463	4,009	4,463	4,269
32,800	32,850	4,470	4,016	4,470	4,276
32,850	32,900	4,478	4,024	4,478	4,284
32,900	32,950	4,485	4,031	4,485	4,291
32,950	33,000	4,493	4,039	4,493	4,299

If line 43 (taxable income) is— At least	But less than	And you are— Single	Married filing jointly *	Married filing separately	Head of a household
		Your tax is—			
33,000					
33,000	33,050	4,500	4,046	4,500	4,306
33,050	33,100	4,508	4,054	4,508	4,314
33,100	33,150	4,515	4,061	4,515	4,321
33,150	33,200	4,523	4,069	4,523	4,329
33,200	33,250	4,530	4,076	4,530	4,336
33,250	33,300	4,538	4,084	4,538	4,344
33,300	33,350	4,545	4,091	4,545	4,351
33,350	33,400	4,553	4,099	4,553	4,359
33,400	33,450	4,560	4,106	4,560	4,366
33,450	33,500	4,568	4,114	4,568	4,374
33,500	33,550	4,575	4,121	4,575	4,381
33,550	33,600	4,583	4,129	4,583	4,389
33,600	33,650	4,590	4,136	4,590	4,396
33,650	33,700	4,598	4,144	4,598	4,404
33,700	33,750	4,605	4,151	4,605	4,411
33,750	33,800	4,613	4,159	4,613	4,419
33,800	33,850	4,620	4,166	4,620	4,426
33,850	33,900	4,628	4,174	4,628	4,434
33,900	33,950	4,635	4,181	4,635	4,441
33,950	34,000	4,643	4,189	4,643	4,449
34,000					
34,000	34,050	4,650	4,196	4,650	4,456
34,050	34,100	4,658	4,204	4,658	4,464
34,100	34,150	4,665	4,211	4,665	4,471
34,150	34,200	4,673	4,219	4,673	4,479
34,200	34,250	4,680	4,226	4,680	4,486
34,250	34,300	4,688	4,234	4,688	4,494
34,300	34,350	4,695	4,241	4,695	4,501
34,350	34,400	4,703	4,249	4,703	4,509
34,400	34,450	4,710	4,256	4,710	4,516
34,450	34,500	4,718	4,264	4,718	4,524
34,500	34,550	4,725	4,271	4,725	4,531
34,550	34,600	4,733	4,279	4,733	4,539
34,600	34,650	4,740	4,286	4,740	4,546
34,650	34,700	4,748	4,294	4,748	4,554
34,700	34,750	4,755	4,301	4,755	4,561
34,750	34,800	4,763	4,309	4,763	4,569
34,800	34,850	4,770	4,316	4,770	4,576
34,850	34,900	4,778	4,324	4,778	4,584
34,900	34,950	4,785	4,331	4,785	4,591
34,950	35,000	4,793	4,339	4,793	4,599
35,000					
35,000	35,050	4,800	4,346	4,800	4,606
35,050	35,100	4,808	4,354	4,808	4,614
35,100	35,150	4,815	4,361	4,815	4,621
35,150	35,200	4,823	4,369	4,823	4,629
35,200	35,250	4,830	4,376	4,830	4,636
35,250	35,300	4,838	4,384	4,838	4,644
35,300	35,350	4,845	4,391	4,845	4,651
35,350	35,400	4,853	4,399	4,853	4,659
35,400	35,450	4,860	4,406	4,860	4,666
35,450	35,500	4,868	4,414	4,868	4,674
35,500	35,550	4,875	4,421	4,875	4,681
35,550	35,600	4,883	4,429	4,883	4,689
35,600	35,650	4,890	4,436	4,890	4,696
35,650	35,700	4,898	4,444	4,898	4,704
35,700	35,750	4,905	4,451	4,905	4,711
35,750	35,800	4,913	4,459	4,913	4,719
35,800	35,850	4,920	4,466	4,920	4,726
35,850	35,900	4,928	4,474	4,928	4,734
35,900	35,950	4,935	4,481	4,935	4,741
35,950	36,000	4,943	4,489	4,943	4,749

If line 43 (taxable income) is— At least	But less than	And you are— Single	Married filing jointly *	Married filing separately	Head of a household
		Your tax is—			
36,000					
36,000	36,050	4,950	4,496	4,950	4,756
36,050	36,100	4,958	4,504	4,958	4,764
36,100	36,150	4,965	4,511	4,965	4,771
36,150	36,200	4,973	4,519	4,973	4,779
36,200	36,250	4,980	4,526	4,980	4,786
36,250	36,300	4,988	4,534	4,988	4,794
36,300	36,350	4,995	4,541	4,995	4,801
36,350	36,400	5,003	4,549	5,003	4,809
36,400	36,450	5,010	4,556	5,010	4,816
36,450	36,500	5,018	4,564	5,018	4,824
36,500	36,550	5,025	4,571	5,025	4,831
36,550	36,600	5,033	4,579	5,033	4,839
36,600	36,650	5,040	4,586	5,040	4,846
36,650	36,700	5,048	4,594	5,048	4,854
36,700	36,750	5,055	4,601	5,055	4,861
36,750	36,800	5,063	4,609	5,063	4,869
36,800	36,850	5,070	4,616	5,070	4,876
36,850	36,900	5,078	4,624	5,078	4,884
36,900	36,950	5,088	4,631	5,088	4,891
36,950	37,000	5,100	4,639	5,100	4,899
37,000					
37,000	37,050	5,113	4,646	5,113	4,906
37,050	37,100	5,125	4,654	5,125	4,914
37,100	37,150	5,138	4,661	5,138	4,921
37,150	37,200	5,150	4,669	5,150	4,929
37,200	37,250	5,163	4,676	5,163	4,936
37,250	37,300	5,175	4,684	5,175	4,944
37,300	37,350	5,188	4,691	5,188	4,951
37,350	37,400	5,200	4,699	5,200	4,959
37,400	37,450	5,213	4,706	5,213	4,966
37,450	37,500	5,225	4,714	5,225	4,974
37,500	37,550	5,238	4,721	5,238	4,981
37,550	37,600	5,250	4,729	5,250	4,989
37,600	37,650	5,263	4,736	5,263	4,996
37,650	37,700	5,275	4,744	5,275	5,004
37,700	37,750	5,288	4,751	5,288	5,011
37,750	37,800	5,300	4,759	5,300	5,019
37,800	37,850	5,313	4,766	5,313	5,026
37,850	37,900	5,325	4,774	5,325	5,034
37,900	37,950	5,338	4,781	5,338	5,041
37,950	38,000	5,350	4,789	5,350	5,049
38,000					
38,000	38,050	5,363	4,796	5,363	5,056
38,050	38,100	5,375	4,804	5,375	5,064
38,100	38,150	5,388	4,811	5,388	5,071
38,150	38,200	5,400	4,819	5,400	5,079
38,200	38,250	5,413	4,826	5,413	5,086
38,250	38,300	5,425	4,834	5,425	5,094
38,300	38,350	5,438	4,841	5,438	5,101
38,350	38,400	5,450	4,849	5,450	5,109
38,400	38,450	5,463	4,856	5,463	5,116
38,450	38,500	5,475	4,864	5,475	5,124
38,500	38,550	5,488	4,871	5,488	5,131
38,550	38,600	5,500	4,879	5,500	5,139
38,600	38,650	5,513	4,886	5,513	5,146
38,650	38,700	5,525	4,894	5,525	5,154
38,700	38,750	5,538	4,901	5,538	5,161
38,750	38,800	5,550	4,909	5,550	5,169
38,800	38,850	5,563	4,916	5,563	5,176
38,850	38,900	5,575	4,924	5,575	5,184
38,900	38,950	5,588	4,931	5,588	5,191
38,950	39,000	5,600	4,939	5,600	5,199

(Continued)

* This column must also be used by a qualifying widow(er).

2014 Tax Table — *Continued*

DRAFT AS OF October 8 2014

If line 43 (taxable income) is—		And you are—			
At least	But less than	Single	Married filing jointly *	Married filing sepa-rately	Head of a house-hold
		Your tax is—			
39,000					
39,000	39,050	5,613	4,946	5,613	5,206
39,050	39,100	5,625	4,954	5,625	5,214
39,100	39,150	5,638	4,961	5,638	5,221
39,150	39,200	5,650	4,969	5,650	5,229
39,200	39,250	5,663	4,976	5,663	5,236
39,250	39,300	5,675	4,984	5,675	5,244
39,300	39,350	5,688	4,991	5,688	5,251
39,350	39,400	5,700	4,999	5,700	5,259
39,400	39,450	5,713	5,006	5,713	5,266
39,450	39,500	5,725	5,014	5,725	5,274
39,500	39,550	5,738	5,021	5,738	5,281
39,550	39,600	5,750	5,029	5,750	5,289
39,600	39,650	5,763	5,036	5,763	5,296
39,650	39,700	5,775	5,044	5,775	5,304
39,700	39,750	5,788	5,051	5,788	5,311
39,750	39,800	5,800	5,059	5,800	5,319
39,800	39,850	5,813	5,066	5,813	5,326
39,850	39,900	5,825	5,074	5,825	5,334
39,900	39,950	5,838	5,081	5,838	5,341
39,950	40,000	5,850	5,089	5,850	5,349
40,000					
40,000	40,050	5,863	5,096	5,863	5,356
40,050	40,100	5,875	5,104	5,875	5,364
40,100	40,150	5,888	5,111	5,888	5,371
40,150	40,200	5,900	5,119	5,900	5,379
40,200	40,250	5,913	5,126	5,913	5,386
40,250	40,300	5,925	5,134	5,925	5,394
40,300	40,350	5,938	5,141	5,938	5,401
40,350	40,400	5,950	5,149	5,950	5,409
40,400	40,450	5,963	5,156	5,963	5,416
40,450	40,500	5,975	5,164	5,975	5,424
40,500	40,550	5,988	5,171	5,988	5,431
40,550	40,600	6,000	5,179	6,000	5,439
40,600	40,650	6,013	5,186	6,013	5,446
40,650	40,700	6,025	5,194	6,025	5,454
40,700	40,750	6,038	5,201	6,038	5,461
40,750	40,800	6,050	5,209	6,050	5,469
40,800	40,850	6,063	5,216	6,063	5,476
40,850	40,900	6,075	5,224	6,075	5,484
40,900	40,950	6,088	5,231	6,088	5,491
40,950	41,000	6,100	5,239	6,100	5,499
41,000					
41,000	41,050	6,113	5,246	6,113	5,506
41,050	41,100	6,125	5,254	6,125	5,514
41,100	41,150	6,138	5,261	6,138	5,521
41,150	41,200	6,150	5,269	6,150	5,529
41,200	41,250	6,163	5,276	6,163	5,536
41,250	41,300	6,175	5,284	6,175	5,544
41,300	41,350	6,188	5,291	6,188	5,551
41,350	41,400	6,200	5,299	6,200	5,559
41,400	41,450	6,213	5,306	6,213	5,566
41,450	41,500	6,225	5,314	6,225	5,574
41,500	41,550	6,238	5,321	6,238	5,581
41,550	41,600	6,250	5,329	6,250	5,589
41,600	41,650	6,263	5,336	6,263	5,596
41,650	41,700	6,275	5,344	6,275	5,604
41,700	41,750	6,288	5,351	6,288	5,611
41,750	41,800	6,300	5,359	6,300	5,619
41,800	41,850	6,313	5,366	6,313	5,626
41,850	41,900	6,325	5,374	6,325	5,634
41,900	41,950	6,338	5,381	6,338	5,641
41,950	42,000	6,350	5,389	6,350	5,649

If line 43 (taxable income) is—		And you are—			
At least	But less than	Single	Married filing jointly *	Married filing sepa-rately	Head of a house-hold
		Your tax is—			
42,000					
42,000	42,050	6,363	5,396	6,363	5,656
42,050	42,100	6,375	5,404	6,375	5,664
42,100	42,150	6,388	5,411	6,388	5,671
42,150	42,200	6,400	5,419	6,400	5,679
42,200	42,250	6,413	5,426	6,413	5,686
42,250	42,300	6,425	5,434	6,425	5,694
42,300	42,350	6,438	5,441	6,438	5,701
42,350	42,400	6,450	5,449	6,450	5,709
42,400	42,450	6,463	5,456	6,463	5,716
42,450	42,500	6,475	5,464	6,475	5,724
42,500	42,550	6,488	5,471	6,488	5,731
42,550	42,600	6,500	5,479	6,500	5,739
42,600	42,650	6,513	5,486	6,513	5,746
42,650	42,700	6,525	5,494	6,525	5,754
42,700	42,750	6,538	5,501	6,538	5,761
42,750	42,800	6,550	5,509	6,550	5,769
42,800	42,850	6,563	5,516	6,563	5,776
42,850	42,900	6,575	5,524	6,575	5,784
42,900	42,950	6,588	5,531	6,588	5,791
42,950	43,000	6,600	5,539	6,600	5,799
43,000					
43,000	43,050	6,613	5,546	6,613	5,806
43,050	43,100	6,625	5,554	6,625	5,814
43,100	43,150	6,638	5,561	6,638	5,821
43,150	43,200	6,650	5,569	6,650	5,829
43,200	43,250	6,663	5,576	6,663	5,836
43,250	43,300	6,675	5,584	6,675	5,844
43,300	43,350	6,688	5,591	6,688	5,851
43,350	43,400	6,700	5,599	6,700	5,859
43,400	43,450	6,713	5,606	6,713	5,866
43,450	43,500	6,725	5,614	6,725	5,874
43,500	43,550	6,738	5,621	6,738	5,881
43,550	43,600	6,750	5,629	6,750	5,889
43,600	43,650	6,763	5,636	6,763	5,896
43,650	43,700	6,775	5,644	6,775	5,904
43,700	43,750	6,788	5,651	6,788	5,911
43,750	43,800	6,800	5,659	6,800	5,919
43,800	43,850	6,813	5,666	6,813	5,926
43,850	43,900	6,825	5,674	6,825	5,934
43,900	43,950	6,838	5,681	6,838	5,941
43,950	44,000	6,850	5,689	6,850	5,949
44,000					
44,000	44,050	6,863	5,696	6,863	5,956
44,050	44,100	6,875	5,704	6,875	5,964
44,100	44,150	6,888	5,711	6,888	5,971
44,150	44,200	6,900	5,719	6,900	5,979
44,200	44,250	6,913	5,726	6,913	5,986
44,250	44,300	6,925	5,734	6,925	5,994
44,300	44,350	6,938	5,741	6,938	6,001
44,350	44,400	6,950	5,749	6,950	6,009
44,400	44,450	6,963	5,756	6,963	6,016
44,450	44,500	6,975	5,764	6,975	6,024
44,500	44,550	6,988	5,771	6,988	6,031
44,550	44,600	7,000	5,779	7,000	6,039
44,600	44,650	7,013	5,786	7,013	6,046
44,650	44,700	7,025	5,794	7,025	6,054
44,700	44,750	7,038	5,801	7,038	6,061
44,750	44,800	7,050	5,809	7,050	6,069
44,800	44,850	7,063	5,816	7,063	6,076
44,850	44,900	7,075	5,824	7,075	6,084
44,900	44,950	7,088	5,831	7,088	6,091
44,950	45,000	7,100	5,839	7,100	6,099

If line 43 (taxable income) is—		And you are—			
At least	But less than	Single	Married filing jointly *	Married filing sepa-rately	Head of a house-hold
		Your tax is—			
45,000					
45,000	45,050	7,113	5,846	7,113	6,106
45,050	45,100	7,125	5,854	7,125	6,114
45,100	45,150	7,138	5,861	7,138	6,121
45,150	45,200	7,150	5,869	7,150	6,129
45,200	45,250	7,163	5,876	7,163	6,136
45,250	45,300	7,175	5,884	7,175	6,144
45,300	45,350	7,188	5,891	7,188	6,151
45,350	45,400	7,200	5,899	7,200	6,159
45,400	45,450	7,213	5,906	7,213	6,166
45,450	45,500	7,225	5,914	7,225	6,174
45,500	45,550	7,238	5,921	7,238	6,181
45,550	45,600	7,250	5,929	7,250	6,189
45,600	45,650	7,263	5,936	7,263	6,196
45,650	45,700	7,275	5,944	7,275	6,204
45,700	45,750	7,288	5,951	7,288	6,211
45,750	45,800	7,300	5,959	7,300	6,219
45,800	45,850	7,313	5,966	7,313	6,226
45,850	45,900	7,325	5,974	7,325	6,234
45,900	45,950	7,338	5,981	7,338	6,241
45,950	46,000	7,350	5,989	7,350	6,249
46,000					
46,000	46,050	7,363	5,996	7,363	6,256
46,050	46,100	7,375	6,004	7,375	6,264
46,100	46,150	7,388	6,011	7,388	6,271
46,150	46,200	7,400	6,019	7,400	6,279
46,200	46,250	7,413	6,026	7,413	6,286
46,250	46,300	7,425	6,034	7,425	6,294
46,300	46,350	7,438	6,041	7,438	6,301
46,350	46,400	7,450	6,049	7,450	6,309
46,400	46,450	7,463	6,056	7,463	6,316
46,450	46,500	7,475	6,064	7,475	6,324
46,500	46,550	7,488	6,071	7,488	6,331
46,550	46,600	7,500	6,079	7,500	6,339
46,600	46,650	7,513	6,086	7,513	6,346
46,650	46,700	7,525	6,094	7,525	6,354
46,700	46,750	7,538	6,101	7,538	6,361
46,750	46,800	7,550	6,109	7,550	6,369
46,800	46,850	7,563	6,116	7,563	6,376
46,850	46,900	7,575	6,124	7,575	6,384
46,900	46,950	7,588	6,131	7,588	6,391
46,950	47,000	7,600	6,139	7,600	6,399
47,000					
47,000	47,050	7,613	6,146	7,613	6,406
47,050	47,100	7,625	6,154	7,625	6,414
47,100	47,150	7,638	6,161	7,638	6,421
47,150	47,200	7,650	6,169	7,650	6,429
47,200	47,250	7,663	6,176	7,663	6,436
47,250	47,300	7,675	6,184	7,675	6,444
47,300	47,350	7,688	6,191	7,688	6,451
47,350	47,400	7,700	6,199	7,700	6,459
47,400	47,450	7,713	6,206	7,713	6,466
47,450	47,500	7,725	6,214	7,725	6,474
47,500	47,550	7,738	6,221	7,738	6,481
47,550	47,600	7,750	6,229	7,750	6,489
47,600	47,650	7,763	6,236	7,763	6,496
47,650	47,700	7,775	6,244	7,775	6,504
47,700	47,750	7,788	6,251	7,788	6,511
47,750	47,800	7,800	6,259	7,800	6,519
47,800	47,850	7,813	6,266	7,813	6,526
47,850	47,900	7,825	6,274	7,825	6,534
47,900	47,950	7,838	6,281	7,838	6,541
47,950	48,000	7,850	6,289	7,850	6,549

(Continued)

* This column must also be used by a qualifying widow(er).

2014 Tax Table — *Continued*

DRAFT AS OF October 8, 2014

If line 43 (taxable income) is— At least	But less than	And you are— Single	Married filing jointly *	Married filing separately	Head of a household
		Your tax is—			
48,000					
48,000	48,050	7,863	6,296	7,863	6,556
48,050	48,100	7,875	6,304	7,875	6,564
48,100	48,150	7,888	6,311	7,888	6,571
48,150	48,200	7,900	6,319	7,900	6,579
48,200	48,250	7,913	6,326	7,913	6,586
48,250	48,300	7,925	6,334	7,925	6,594
48,300	48,350	7,938	6,341	7,938	6,601
48,350	48,400	7,950	6,349	7,950	6,609
48,400	48,450	7,963	6,356	7,963	6,616
48,450	48,500	7,975	6,364	7,975	6,624
48,500	48,550	7,988	6,371	7,988	6,631
48,550	48,600	8,000	6,379	8,000	6,639
48,600	48,650	8,013	6,386	8,013	6,646
48,650	48,700	8,025	6,394	8,025	6,654
48,700	48,750	8,038	6,401	8,038	6,661
48,750	48,800	8,050	6,409	8,050	6,669
48,800	48,850	8,063	6,416	8,063	6,676
48,850	48,900	8,075	6,424	8,075	6,684
48,900	48,950	8,088	6,431	8,088	6,691
48,950	49,000	8,100	6,439	8,100	6,699
49,000					
49,000	49,050	8,113	6,446	8,113	6,706
49,050	49,100	8,125	6,454	8,125	6,714
49,100	49,150	8,138	6,461	8,138	6,721
49,150	49,200	8,150	6,469	8,150	6,729
49,200	49,250	8,163	6,476	8,163	6,736
49,250	49,300	8,175	6,484	8,175	6,744
49,300	49,350	8,188	6,491	8,188	6,751
49,350	49,400	8,200	6,499	8,200	6,759
49,400	49,450	8,213	6,506	8,213	6,769
49,450	49,500	8,225	6,514	8,225	6,781
49,500	49,550	8,238	6,521	8,238	6,794
49,550	49,600	8,250	6,529	8,250	6,806
49,600	49,650	8,263	6,536	8,263	6,819
49,650	49,700	8,275	6,544	8,275	6,831
49,700	49,750	8,288	6,551	8,288	6,844
49,750	49,800	8,300	6,559	8,300	6,856
49,800	49,850	8,313	6,566	8,313	6,869
49,850	49,900	8,325	6,574	8,325	6,881
49,900	49,950	8,338	6,581	8,338	6,894
49,950	50,000	8,350	6,589	8,350	6,906
50,000					
50,000	50,050	8,363	6,596	8,363	6,919
50,050	50,100	8,375	6,604	8,375	6,931
50,100	50,150	8,388	6,611	8,388	6,944
50,150	50,200	8,400	6,619	8,400	6,956
50,200	50,250	8,413	6,626	8,413	6,969
50,250	50,300	8,425	6,634	8,425	6,981
50,300	50,350	8,438	6,641	8,438	6,994
50,350	50,400	8,450	6,649	8,450	7,006
50,400	50,450	8,463	6,656	8,463	7,019
50,450	50,500	8,475	6,664	8,475	7,031
50,500	50,550	8,488	6,671	8,488	7,044
50,550	50,600	8,500	6,679	8,500	7,056
50,600	50,650	8,513	6,686	8,513	7,069
50,650	50,700	8,525	6,694	8,525	7,081
50,700	50,750	8,538	6,701	8,538	7,094
50,750	50,800	8,550	6,709	8,550	7,106
50,800	50,850	8,563	6,716	8,563	7,119
50,850	50,900	8,575	6,724	8,575	7,131
50,900	50,950	8,588	6,731	8,588	7,144
50,950	51,000	8,600	6,739	8,600	7,156

If line 43 (taxable income) is— At least	But less than	And you are— Single	Married filing jointly *	Married filing separately	Head of a household
		Your tax is—			
51,000					
51,000	51,050	8,613	6,746	8,613	7,169
51,050	51,100	8,625	6,754	8,625	7,181
51,100	51,150	8,638	6,761	8,638	7,194
51,150	51,200	8,650	6,769	8,650	7,206
51,200	51,250	8,663	6,776	8,663	7,219
51,250	51,300	8,675	6,784	8,675	7,231
51,300	51,350	8,688	6,791	8,688	7,244
51,350	51,400	8,700	6,799	8,700	7,256
51,400	51,450	8,713	6,806	8,713	7,269
51,450	51,500	8,725	6,814	8,725	7,281
51,500	51,550	8,738	6,821	8,738	7,294
51,550	51,600	8,750	6,829	8,750	7,306
51,600	51,650	8,763	6,836	8,763	7,319
51,650	51,700	8,775	6,844	8,775	7,331
51,700	51,750	8,788	6,851	8,788	7,344
51,750	51,800	8,800	6,859	8,800	7,356
51,800	51,850	8,813	6,866	8,813	7,369
51,850	51,900	8,825	6,874	8,825	7,381
51,900	51,950	8,838	6,881	8,838	7,394
51,950	52,000	8,850	6,889	8,850	7,406
52,000					
52,000	52,050	8,863	6,896	8,863	7,419
52,050	52,100	8,875	6,904	8,875	7,431
52,100	52,150	8,888	6,911	8,888	7,444
52,150	52,200	8,900	6,919	8,900	7,456
52,200	52,250	8,913	6,926	8,913	7,469
52,250	52,300	8,925	6,934	8,925	7,481
52,300	52,350	8,938	6,941	8,938	7,494
52,350	52,400	8,950	6,949	8,950	7,506
52,400	52,450	8,963	6,956	8,963	7,519
52,450	52,500	8,975	6,964	8,975	7,531
52,500	52,550	8,988	6,971	8,988	7,544
52,550	52,600	9,000	6,979	9,000	7,556
52,600	52,650	9,013	6,986	9,013	7,569
52,650	52,700	9,025	6,994	9,025	7,581
52,700	52,750	9,038	7,001	9,038	7,594
52,750	52,800	9,050	7,009	9,050	7,606
52,800	52,850	9,063	7,016	9,063	7,619
52,850	52,900	9,075	7,024	9,075	7,631
52,900	52,950	9,088	7,031	9,088	7,644
52,950	53,000	9,100	7,039	9,100	7,656
53,000					
53,000	53,050	9,113	7,046	9,113	7,669
53,050	53,100	9,125	7,054	9,125	7,681
53,100	53,150	9,138	7,061	9,138	7,694
53,150	53,200	9,150	7,069	9,150	7,706
53,200	53,250	9,163	7,076	9,163	7,719
53,250	53,300	9,175	7,084	9,175	7,731
53,300	53,350	9,188	7,091	9,188	7,744
53,350	53,400	9,200	7,099	9,200	7,756
53,400	53,450	9,213	7,106	9,213	7,769
53,450	53,500	9,225	7,114	9,225	7,781
53,500	53,550	9,238	7,121	9,238	7,794
53,550	53,600	9,250	7,129	9,250	7,806
53,600	53,650	9,263	7,136	9,263	7,819
53,650	53,700	9,275	7,144	9,275	7,831
53,700	53,750	9,288	7,151	9,288	7,844
53,750	53,800	9,300	7,159	9,300	7,856
53,800	53,850	9,313	7,166	9,313	7,869
53,850	53,900	9,325	7,174	9,325	7,881
53,900	53,950	9,338	7,181	9,338	7,894
53,950	54,000	9,350	7,189	9,350	7,906

If line 43 (taxable income) is— At least	But less than	And you are— Single	Married filing jointly *	Married filing separately	Head of a household
		Your tax is—			
54,000					
54,000	54,050	9,363	7,196	9,363	7,919
54,050	54,100	9,375	7,204	9,375	7,931
54,100	54,150	9,388	7,211	9,388	7,944
54,150	54,200	9,400	7,219	9,400	7,956
54,200	54,250	9,413	7,226	9,413	7,969
54,250	54,300	9,425	7,234	9,425	7,981
54,300	54,350	9,438	7,241	9,438	7,994
54,350	54,400	9,450	7,249	9,450	8,006
54,400	54,450	9,463	7,256	9,463	8,019
54,450	54,500	9,475	7,264	9,475	8,031
54,500	54,550	9,488	7,271	9,488	8,044
54,550	54,600	9,500	7,279	9,500	8,056
54,600	54,650	9,513	7,286	9,513	8,069
54,650	54,700	9,525	7,294	9,525	8,081
54,700	54,750	9,538	7,301	9,538	8,094
54,750	54,800	9,550	7,309	9,550	8,106
54,800	54,850	9,563	7,316	9,563	8,119
54,850	54,900	9,575	7,324	9,575	8,131
54,900	54,950	9,588	7,331	9,588	8,144
54,950	55,000	9,600	7,339	9,600	8,156
55,000					
55,000	55,050	9,613	7,346	9,613	8,169
55,050	55,100	9,625	7,354	9,625	8,181
55,100	55,150	9,638	7,361	9,638	8,194
55,150	55,200	9,650	7,369	9,650	8,206
55,200	55,250	9,663	7,376	9,663	8,219
55,250	55,300	9,675	7,384	9,675	8,231
55,300	55,350	9,688	7,391	9,688	8,244
55,350	55,400	9,700	7,399	9,700	8,256
55,400	55,450	9,713	7,406	9,713	8,269
55,450	55,500	9,725	7,414	9,725	8,281
55,500	55,550	9,738	7,421	9,738	8,294
55,550	55,600	9,750	7,429	9,750	8,306
55,600	55,650	9,763	7,436	9,763	8,319
55,650	55,700	9,775	7,444	9,775	8,331
55,700	55,750	9,788	7,451	9,788	8,344
55,750	55,800	9,800	7,459	9,800	8,356
55,800	55,850	9,813	7,466	9,813	8,369
55,850	55,900	9,825	7,474	9,825	8,381
55,900	55,950	9,838	7,481	9,838	8,394
55,950	56,000	9,850	7,489	9,850	8,406
56,000					
56,000	56,050	9,863	7,496	9,863	8,419
56,050	56,100	9,875	7,504	9,875	8,431
56,100	56,150	9,888	7,511	9,888	8,444
56,150	56,200	9,900	7,519	9,900	8,456
56,200	56,250	9,913	7,526	9,913	8,469
56,250	56,300	9,925	7,534	9,925	8,481
56,300	56,350	9,938	7,541	9,938	8,494
56,350	56,400	9,950	7,549	9,950	8,506
56,400	56,450	9,963	7,556	9,963	8,519
56,450	56,500	9,975	7,564	9,975	8,531
56,500	56,550	9,988	7,571	9,988	8,544
56,550	56,600	10,000	7,579	10,000	8,556
56,600	56,650	10,013	7,586	10,013	8,569
56,650	56,700	10,025	7,594	10,025	8,581
56,700	56,750	10,038	7,601	10,038	8,594
56,750	56,800	10,050	7,609	10,050	8,606
56,800	56,850	10,063	7,616	10,063	8,619
56,850	56,900	10,075	7,624	10,075	8,631
56,900	56,950	10,088	7,631	10,088	8,644
56,950	57,000	10,100	7,639	10,100	8,656

(Continued)

* This column must also be used by a qualifying widow(er).

2014 Tax Table — *Continued*

DRAFT AS OF October 8, 2014

If line 43 (taxable income) is—		And you are—			
At least	But less than	Single	Married filing jointly *	Married filing separately	Head of a household
		Your tax is—			
57,000					
57,000	57,050	10,113	7,646	10,113	8,669
57,050	57,100	10,125	7,654	10,125	8,681
57,100	57,150	10,138	7,661	10,138	8,694
57,150	57,200	10,150	7,669	10,150	8,706
57,200	57,250	10,163	7,676	10,163	8,719
57,250	57,300	10,175	7,684	10,175	8,731
57,300	57,350	10,188	7,691	10,188	8,744
57,350	57,400	10,200	7,699	10,200	8,756
57,400	57,450	10,213	7,706	10,213	8,769
57,450	57,500	10,225	7,714	10,225	8,781
57,500	57,550	10,238	7,721	10,238	8,794
57,550	57,600	10,250	7,729	10,250	8,806
57,600	57,650	10,263	7,736	10,263	8,819
57,650	57,700	10,275	7,744	10,275	8,831
57,700	57,750	10,288	7,751	10,288	8,844
57,750	57,800	10,300	7,759	10,300	8,856
57,800	57,850	10,313	7,766	10,313	8,869
57,850	57,900	10,325	7,774	10,325	8,881
57,900	57,950	10,338	7,781	10,338	8,894
57,950	58,000	10,350	7,789	10,350	8,906
58,000					
58,000	58,050	10,363	7,796	10,363	8,919
58,050	58,100	10,375	7,804	10,375	8,931
58,100	58,150	10,388	7,811	10,388	8,944
58,150	58,200	10,400	7,819	10,400	8,956
58,200	58,250	10,413	7,826	10,413	8,969
58,250	58,300	10,425	7,834	10,425	8,981
58,300	58,350	10,438	7,841	10,438	8,994
58,350	58,400	10,450	7,849	10,450	9,006
58,400	58,450	10,463	7,856	10,463	9,019
58,450	58,500	10,475	7,864	10,475	9,031
58,500	58,550	10,488	7,871	10,488	9,044
58,550	58,600	10,500	7,879	10,500	9,056
58,600	58,650	10,513	7,886	10,513	9,069
58,650	58,700	10,525	7,894	10,525	9,081
58,700	58,750	10,538	7,901	10,538	9,094
58,750	58,800	10,550	7,909	10,550	9,106
58,800	58,850	10,563	7,916	10,563	9,119
58,850	58,900	10,575	7,924	10,575	9,131
58,900	58,950	10,588	7,931	10,588	9,144
58,950	59,000	10,600	7,939	10,600	9,156
59,000					
59,000	59,050	10,613	7,946	10,613	9,169
59,050	59,100	10,625	7,954	10,625	9,181
59,100	59,150	10,638	7,961	10,638	9,194
59,150	59,200	10,650	7,969	10,650	9,206
59,200	59,250	10,663	7,976	10,663	9,219
59,250	59,300	10,675	7,984	10,675	9,231
59,300	59,350	10,688	7,991	10,688	9,244
59,350	59,400	10,700	7,999	10,700	9,256
59,400	59,450	10,713	8,006	10,713	9,269
59,450	59,500	10,725	8,014	10,725	9,281
59,500	59,550	10,738	8,021	10,738	9,294
59,550	59,600	10,750	8,029	10,750	9,306
59,600	59,650	10,763	8,036	10,763	9,319
59,650	59,700	10,775	8,044	10,775	9,331
59,700	59,750	10,788	8,051	10,788	9,344
59,750	59,800	10,800	8,059	10,800	9,356
59,800	59,850	10,813	8,066	10,813	9,369
59,850	59,900	10,825	8,074	10,825	9,381
59,900	59,950	10,838	8,081	10,838	9,394
59,950	60,000	10,850	8,089	10,850	9,406

If line 43 (taxable income) is—		And you are—			
At least	But less than	Single	Married filing jointly *	Married filing separately	Head of a household
		Your tax is—			
60,000					
60,000	60,050	10,863	8,096	10,863	9,419
60,050	60,100	10,875	8,104	10,875	9,431
60,100	60,150	10,888	8,111	10,888	9,444
60,150	60,200	10,900	8,119	10,900	9,456
60,200	60,250	10,913	8,126	10,913	9,469
60,250	60,300	10,925	8,134	10,925	9,481
60,300	60,350	10,938	8,141	10,938	9,494
60,350	60,400	10,950	8,149	10,950	9,506
60,400	60,450	10,963	8,156	10,963	9,519
60,450	60,500	10,975	8,164	10,975	9,531
60,500	60,550	10,988	8,171	10,988	9,544
60,550	60,600	11,000	8,179	11,000	9,556
60,600	60,650	11,013	8,186	11,013	9,569
60,650	60,700	11,025	8,194	11,025	9,581
60,700	60,750	11,038	8,201	11,038	9,594
60,750	60,800	11,050	8,209	11,050	9,606
60,800	60,850	11,063	8,216	11,063	9,619
60,850	60,900	11,075	8,224	11,075	9,631
60,900	60,950	11,088	8,231	11,088	9,644
60,950	61,000	11,100	8,239	11,100	9,656
61,000					
61,000	61,050	11,113	8,246	11,113	9,669
61,050	61,100	11,125	8,254	11,125	9,681
61,100	61,150	11,138	8,261	11,138	9,694
61,150	61,200	11,150	8,269	11,150	9,706
61,200	61,250	11,163	8,276	11,163	9,719
61,250	61,300	11,175	8,284	11,175	9,731
61,300	61,350	11,188	8,291	11,188	9,744
61,350	61,400	11,200	8,299	11,200	9,756
61,400	61,450	11,213	8,306	11,213	9,769
61,450	61,500	11,225	8,314	11,225	9,781
61,500	61,550	11,238	8,321	11,238	9,794
61,550	61,600	11,250	8,329	11,250	9,806
61,600	61,650	11,263	8,336	11,263	9,819
61,650	61,700	11,275	8,344	11,275	9,831
61,700	61,750	11,288	8,351	11,288	9,844
61,750	61,800	11,300	8,359	11,300	9,856
61,800	61,850	11,313	8,366	11,313	9,869
61,850	61,900	11,325	8,374	11,325	9,881
61,900	61,950	11,338	8,381	11,338	9,894
61,950	62,000	11,350	8,389	11,350	9,906
62,000					
62,000	62,050	11,363	8,396	11,363	9,919
62,050	62,100	11,375	8,404	11,375	9,931
62,100	62,150	11,388	8,411	11,388	9,944
62,150	62,200	11,400	8,419	11,400	9,956
62,200	62,250	11,413	8,426	11,413	9,969
62,250	62,300	11,425	8,434	11,425	9,981
62,300	62,350	11,438	8,441	11,438	9,994
62,350	62,400	11,450	8,449	11,450	10,006
62,400	62,450	11,463	8,456	11,463	10,019
62,450	62,500	11,475	8,464	11,475	10,031
62,500	62,550	11,488	8,471	11,488	10,044
62,550	62,600	11,500	8,479	11,500	10,056
62,600	62,650	11,513	8,486	11,513	10,069
62,650	62,700	11,525	8,494	11,525	10,081
62,700	62,750	11,538	8,501	11,538	10,094
62,750	62,800	11,550	8,509	11,550	10,106
62,800	62,850	11,563	8,516	11,563	10,119
62,850	62,900	11,575	8,524	11,575	10,131
62,900	62,950	11,588	8,531	11,588	10,144
62,950	63,000	11,600	8,539	11,600	10,156

If line 43 (taxable income) is—		And you are—			
At least	But less than	Single	Married filing jointly *	Married filing separately	Head of a household
		Your tax is—			
63,000					
63,000	63,050	11,613	8,546	11,613	10,169
63,050	63,100	11,625	8,554	11,625	10,181
63,100	63,150	11,638	8,561	11,638	10,194
63,150	63,200	11,650	8,569	11,650	10,206
63,200	63,250	11,663	8,576	11,663	10,219
63,250	63,300	11,675	8,584	11,675	10,231
63,300	63,350	11,688	8,591	11,688	10,244
63,350	63,400	11,700	8,599	11,700	10,256
63,400	63,450	11,713	8,606	11,713	10,269
63,450	63,500	11,725	8,614	11,725	10,281
63,500	63,550	11,738	8,621	11,738	10,294
63,550	63,600	11,750	8,629	11,750	10,306
63,600	63,650	11,763	8,636	11,763	10,319
63,650	63,700	11,775	8,644	11,775	10,331
63,700	63,750	11,788	8,651	11,788	10,344
63,750	63,800	11,800	8,659	11,800	10,356
63,800	63,850	11,813	8,666	11,813	10,369
63,850	63,900	11,825	8,674	11,825	10,381
63,900	63,950	11,838	8,681	11,838	10,394
63,950	64,000	11,850	8,689	11,850	10,406
64,000					
64,000	64,050	11,863	8,696	11,863	10,419
64,050	64,100	11,875	8,704	11,875	10,431
64,100	64,150	11,888	8,711	11,888	10,444
64,150	64,200	11,900	8,719	11,900	10,456
64,200	64,250	11,913	8,726	11,913	10,469
64,250	64,300	11,925	8,734	11,925	10,481
64,300	64,350	11,938	8,741	11,938	10,494
64,350	64,400	11,950	8,749	11,950	10,506
64,400	64,450	11,963	8,756	11,963	10,519
64,450	64,500	11,975	8,764	11,975	10,531
64,500	64,550	11,988	8,771	11,988	10,544
64,550	64,600	12,000	8,779	12,000	10,556
64,600	64,650	12,013	8,786	12,013	10,569
64,650	64,700	12,025	8,794	12,025	10,581
64,700	64,750	12,038	8,801	12,038	10,594
64,750	64,800	12,050	8,809	12,050	10,606
64,800	64,850	12,063	8,816	12,063	10,619
64,850	64,900	12,075	8,824	12,075	10,631
64,900	64,950	12,088	8,831	12,088	10,644
64,950	65,000	12,100	8,839	12,100	10,656
65,000					
65,000	65,050	12,113	8,846	12,113	10,669
65,050	65,100	12,125	8,854	12,125	10,681
65,100	65,150	12,138	8,861	12,138	10,694
65,150	65,200	12,150	8,869	12,150	10,706
65,200	65,250	12,163	8,876	12,163	10,719
65,250	65,300	12,175	8,884	12,175	10,731
65,300	65,350	12,188	8,891	12,188	10,744
65,350	65,400	12,200	8,899	12,200	10,756
65,400	65,450	12,213	8,906	12,213	10,769
65,450	65,500	12,225	8,914	12,225	10,781
65,500	65,550	12,238	8,921	12,238	10,794
65,550	65,600	12,250	8,929	12,250	10,806
65,600	65,650	12,263	8,936	12,263	10,819
65,650	65,700	12,275	8,944	12,275	10,831
65,700	65,750	12,288	8,951	12,288	10,844
65,750	65,800	12,300	8,959	12,300	10,856
65,800	65,850	12,313	8,966	12,313	10,869
65,850	65,900	12,325	8,974	12,325	10,881
65,900	65,950	12,338	8,981	12,338	10,894
65,950	66,000	12,350	8,989	12,350	10,906

(Continued)

* This column must also be used by a qualifying widow(er).

2014 Tax Table — *Continued*

DRAFT AS OF October 8, 2014

If line 43 (taxable income) is—		And you are—			
At least	But less than	Single	Married filing jointly *	Married filing separately	Head of a household
		Your tax is—			
66,000					
66,000	66,050	12,363	8,996	12,363	10,919
66,050	66,100	12,375	9,004	12,375	10,931
66,100	66,150	12,388	9,011	12,388	10,944
66,150	66,200	12,400	9,019	12,400	10,956
66,200	66,250	12,413	9,026	12,413	10,969
66,250	66,300	12,425	9,034	12,425	10,981
66,300	66,350	12,438	9,041	12,438	10,994
66,350	66,400	12,450	9,049	12,450	11,006
66,400	66,450	12,463	9,056	12,463	11,019
66,450	66,500	12,475	9,064	12,475	11,031
66,500	66,550	12,488	9,071	12,488	11,044
66,550	66,600	12,500	9,079	12,500	11,056
66,600	66,650	12,513	9,086	12,513	11,069
66,650	66,700	12,525	9,094	12,525	11,081
66,700	66,750	12,538	9,101	12,538	11,094
66,750	66,800	12,550	9,109	12,550	11,106
66,800	66,850	12,563	9,116	12,563	11,119
66,850	66,900	12,575	9,124	12,575	11,131
66,900	66,950	12,588	9,131	12,588	11,144
66,950	67,000	12,600	9,139	12,600	11,156
67,000					
67,000	67,050	12,613	9,146	12,613	11,169
67,050	67,100	12,625	9,154	12,625	11,181
67,100	67,150	12,638	9,161	12,638	11,194
67,150	67,200	12,650	9,169	12,650	11,206
67,200	67,250	12,663	9,176	12,663	11,219
67,250	67,300	12,675	9,184	12,675	11,231
67,300	67,350	12,688	9,191	12,688	11,244
67,350	67,400	12,700	9,199	12,700	11,256
67,400	67,450	12,713	9,206	12,713	11,269
67,450	67,500	12,725	9,214	12,725	11,281
67,500	67,550	12,738	9,221	12,738	11,294
67,550	67,600	12,750	9,229	12,750	11,306
67,600	67,650	12,763	9,236	12,763	11,319
67,650	67,700	12,775	9,244	12,775	11,331
67,700	67,750	12,788	9,251	12,788	11,344
67,750	67,800	12,800	9,259	12,800	11,356
67,800	67,850	12,813	9,266	12,813	11,369
67,850	67,900	12,825	9,274	12,825	11,381
67,900	67,950	12,838	9,281	12,838	11,394
67,950	68,000	12,850	9,289	12,850	11,406
68,000					
68,000	68,050	12,863	9,296	12,863	11,419
68,050	68,100	12,875	9,304	12,875	11,431
68,100	68,150	12,888	9,311	12,888	11,444
68,150	68,200	12,900	9,319	12,900	11,456
68,200	68,250	12,913	9,326	12,913	11,469
68,250	68,300	12,925	9,334	12,925	11,481
68,300	68,350	12,938	9,341	12,938	11,494
68,350	68,400	12,950	9,349	12,950	11,506
68,400	68,450	12,963	9,356	12,963	11,519
68,450	68,500	12,975	9,364	12,975	11,531
68,500	68,550	12,988	9,371	12,988	11,544
68,550	68,600	13,000	9,379	13,000	11,556
68,600	68,650	13,013	9,386	13,013	11,569
68,650	68,700	13,025	9,394	13,025	11,581
68,700	68,750	13,038	9,401	13,038	11,594
68,750	68,800	13,050	9,409	13,050	11,606
68,800	68,850	13,063	9,416	13,063	11,619
68,850	68,900	13,075	9,424	13,075	11,631
68,900	68,950	13,088	9,431	13,088	11,644
68,950	69,000	13,100	9,439	13,100	11,656
69,000					
69,000	69,050	13,113	9,446	13,113	11,669
69,050	69,100	13,125	9,454	13,125	11,681
69,100	69,150	13,138	9,461	13,138	11,694
69,150	69,200	13,150	9,469	13,150	11,706
69,200	69,250	13,163	9,476	13,163	11,719
69,250	69,300	13,175	9,484	13,175	11,731
69,300	69,350	13,188	9,491	13,188	11,744
69,350	69,400	13,200	9,499	13,200	11,756
69,400	69,450	13,213	9,506	13,213	11,769
69,450	69,500	13,225	9,514	13,225	11,781
69,500	69,550	13,238	9,521	13,238	11,794
69,550	69,600	13,250	9,529	13,250	11,806
69,600	69,650	13,263	9,536	13,263	11,819
69,650	69,700	13,275	9,544	13,275	11,831
69,700	69,750	13,288	9,551	13,288	11,844
69,750	69,800	13,300	9,559	13,300	11,856
69,800	69,850	13,313	9,566	13,313	11,869
69,850	69,900	13,325	9,574	13,325	11,881
69,900	69,950	13,338	9,581	13,338	11,894
69,950	70,000	13,350	9,589	13,350	11,906
70,000					
70,000	70,050	13,363	9,596	13,363	11,919
70,050	70,100	13,375	9,604	13,375	11,931
70,100	70,150	13,388	9,611	13,388	11,944
70,150	70,200	13,400	9,619	13,400	11,956
70,200	70,250	13,413	9,626	13,413	11,969
70,250	70,300	13,425	9,634	13,425	11,981
70,300	70,350	13,438	9,641	13,438	11,994
70,350	70,400	13,450	9,649	13,450	12,006
70,400	70,450	13,463	9,656	13,463	12,019
70,450	70,500	13,475	9,664	13,475	12,031
70,500	70,550	13,488	9,671	13,488	12,044
70,550	70,600	13,500	9,679	13,500	12,056
70,600	70,650	13,513	9,686	13,513	12,069
70,650	70,700	13,525	9,694	13,525	12,081
70,700	70,750	13,538	9,701	13,538	12,094
70,750	70,800	13,550	9,709	13,550	12,106
70,800	70,850	13,563	9,716	13,563	12,119
70,850	70,900	13,575	9,724	13,575	12,131
70,900	70,950	13,588	9,731	13,588	12,144
70,950	71,000	13,600	9,739	13,600	12,156
71,000					
71,000	71,050	13,613	9,746	13,613	12,169
71,050	71,100	13,625	9,754	13,625	12,181
71,100	71,150	13,638	9,761	13,638	12,194
71,150	71,200	13,650	9,769	13,650	12,206
71,200	71,250	13,663	9,776	13,663	12,219
71,250	71,300	13,675	9,784	13,675	12,231
71,300	71,350	13,688	9,791	13,688	12,244
71,350	71,400	13,700	9,799	13,700	12,256
71,400	71,450	13,713	9,806	13,713	12,269
71,450	71,500	13,725	9,814	13,725	12,281
71,500	71,550	13,738	9,821	13,738	12,294
71,550	71,600	13,750	9,829	13,750	12,306
71,600	71,650	13,763	9,836	13,763	12,319
71,650	71,700	13,775	9,844	13,775	12,331
71,700	71,750	13,788	9,851	13,788	12,344
71,750	71,800	13,800	9,859	13,800	12,356
71,800	71,850	13,813	9,866	13,813	12,369
71,850	71,900	13,825	9,874	13,825	12,381
71,900	71,950	13,838	9,881	13,838	12,394
71,950	72,000	13,850	9,889	13,850	12,406
72,000					
72,000	72,050	13,863	9,896	13,863	12,419
72,050	72,100	13,875	9,904	13,875	12,431
72,100	72,150	13,888	9,911	13,888	12,444
72,150	72,200	13,900	9,919	13,900	12,456
72,200	72,250	13,913	9,926	13,913	12,469
72,250	72,300	13,925	9,934	13,925	12,481
72,300	72,350	13,938	9,941	13,938	12,494
72,350	72,400	13,950	9,949	13,950	12,506
72,400	72,450	13,963	9,956	13,963	12,519
72,450	72,500	13,975	9,964	13,975	12,531
72,500	72,550	13,988	9,971	13,988	12,544
72,550	72,600	14,000	9,979	14,000	12,556
72,600	72,650	14,013	9,986	14,013	12,569
72,650	72,700	14,025	9,994	14,025	12,581
72,700	72,750	14,038	10,001	14,038	12,594
72,750	72,800	14,050	10,009	14,050	12,606
72,800	72,850	14,063	10,016	14,063	12,619
72,850	72,900	14,075	10,024	14,075	12,631
72,900	72,950	14,088	10,031	14,088	12,644
72,950	73,000	14,100	10,039	14,100	12,656
73,000					
73,000	73,050	14,113	10,046	14,113	12,669
73,050	73,100	14,125	10,054	14,125	12,681
73,100	73,150	14,138	10,061	14,138	12,694
73,150	73,200	14,150	10,069	14,150	12,706
73,200	73,250	14,163	10,076	14,163	12,719
73,250	73,300	14,175	10,084	14,175	12,731
73,300	73,350	14,188	10,091	14,188	12,744
73,350	73,400	14,200	10,099	14,200	12,756
73,400	73,450	14,213	10,106	14,213	12,769
73,450	73,500	14,225	10,114	14,225	12,781
73,500	73,550	14,238	10,121	14,238	12,794
73,550	73,600	14,250	10,129	14,250	12,806
73,600	73,650	14,263	10,136	14,263	12,819
73,650	73,700	14,275	10,144	14,275	12,831
73,700	73,750	14,288	10,151	14,288	12,844
73,750	73,800	14,300	10,159	14,300	12,856
73,800	73,850	14,313	10,169	14,313	12,869
73,850	73,900	14,325	10,181	14,325	12,881
73,900	73,950	14,338	10,194	14,338	12,894
73,950	74,000	14,350	10,206	14,350	12,906
74,000					
74,000	74,050	14,363	10,219	14,363	12,919
74,050	74,100	14,375	10,231	14,375	12,931
74,100	74,150	14,388	10,244	14,388	12,944
74,150	74,200	14,400	10,256	14,400	12,956
74,200	74,250	14,413	10,269	14,413	12,969
74,250	74,300	14,425	10,281	14,425	12,981
74,300	74,350	14,438	10,294	14,438	12,994
74,350	74,400	14,450	10,306	14,450	13,006
74,400	74,450	14,463	10,319	14,463	13,019
74,450	74,500	14,475	10,331	14,477	13,031
74,500	74,550	14,488	10,344	14,491	13,044
74,550	74,600	14,500	10,356	14,505	13,056
74,600	74,650	14,513	10,369	14,519	13,069
74,650	74,700	14,525	10,381	14,533	13,081
74,700	74,750	14,538	10,394	14,547	13,094
74,750	74,800	14,550	10,406	14,561	13,106
74,800	74,850	14,563	10,419	14,575	13,119
74,850	74,900	14,575	10,431	14,589	13,131
74,900	74,950	14,588	10,444	14,603	13,144
74,950	75,000	14,600	10,456	14,617	13,156

(Continued)

* This column must also be used by a qualifying widow(er).

2014 Tax Table — *Continued*

DRAFT AS OF October 8 2014

If line 43 (taxable income) is—		And you are—			
At least	But less than	Single	Married filing jointly *	Married filing separately	Head of a household
		Your tax is—			
75,000					
75,000	75,050	14,613	10,469	14,631	13,169
75,050	75,100	14,625	10,481	14,645	13,181
75,100	75,150	14,638	10,494	14,659	13,194
75,150	75,200	14,650	10,506	14,673	13,206
75,200	75,250	14,663	10,519	14,687	13,219
75,250	75,300	14,675	10,531	14,701	13,231
75,300	75,350	14,688	10,544	14,715	13,244
75,350	75,400	14,700	10,556	14,729	13,256
75,400	75,450	14,713	10,569	14,743	13,269
75,450	75,500	14,725	10,581	14,757	13,281
75,500	75,550	14,738	10,594	14,771	13,294
75,550	75,600	14,750	10,606	14,785	13,306
75,600	75,650	14,763	10,619	14,799	13,319
75,650	75,700	14,775	10,631	14,813	13,331
75,700	75,750	14,788	10,644	14,827	13,344
75,750	75,800	14,800	10,656	14,841	13,356
75,800	75,850	14,813	10,669	14,855	13,369
75,850	75,900	14,825	10,681	14,869	13,381
75,900	75,950	14,838	10,694	14,883	13,394
75,950	76,000	14,850	10,706	14,897	13,406
76,000					
76,000	76,050	14,863	10,719	14,911	13,419
76,050	76,100	14,875	10,731	14,925	13,431
76,100	76,150	14,888	10,744	14,939	13,444
76,150	76,200	14,900	10,756	14,953	13,456
76,200	76,250	14,913	10,769	14,967	13,469
76,250	76,300	14,925	10,781	14,981	13,481
76,300	76,350	14,938	10,794	14,995	13,494
76,350	76,400	14,950	10,806	15,009	13,506
76,400	76,450	14,963	10,819	15,023	13,519
76,450	76,500	14,975	10,831	15,037	13,531
76,500	76,550	14,988	10,844	15,051	13,544
76,550	76,600	15,000	10,856	15,065	13,556
76,600	76,650	15,013	10,869	15,079	13,569
76,650	76,700	15,025	10,881	15,093	13,581
76,700	76,750	15,038	10,894	15,107	13,594
76,750	76,800	15,050	10,906	15,121	13,606
76,800	76,850	15,063	10,919	15,135	13,619
76,850	76,900	15,075	10,931	15,149	13,631
76,900	76,950	15,088	10,944	15,163	13,644
76,950	77,000	15,100	10,956	15,177	13,656
77,000					
77,000	77,050	15,113	10,969	15,191	13,669
77,050	77,100	15,125	10,981	15,205	13,681
77,100	77,150	15,138	10,994	15,219	13,694
77,150	77,200	15,150	11,006	15,233	13,706
77,200	77,250	15,163	11,019	15,247	13,719
77,250	77,300	15,175	11,031	15,261	13,731
77,300	77,350	15,188	11,044	15,275	13,744
77,350	77,400	15,200	11,056	15,289	13,756
77,400	77,450	15,213	11,069	15,303	13,769
77,450	77,500	15,225	11,081	15,317	13,781
77,500	77,550	15,238	11,094	15,331	13,794
77,550	77,600	15,250	11,106	15,345	13,806
77,600	77,650	15,263	11,119	15,359	13,819
77,650	77,700	15,275	11,131	15,373	13,831
77,700	77,750	15,288	11,144	15,387	13,844
77,750	77,800	15,300	11,156	15,401	13,856
77,800	77,850	15,313	11,169	15,415	13,869
77,850	77,900	15,325	11,181	15,429	13,881
77,900	77,950	15,338	11,194	15,443	13,894
77,950	78,000	15,350	11,206	15,457	13,906
78,000					
78,000	78,050	15,363	11,219	15,471	13,919
78,050	78,100	15,375	11,231	15,485	13,931
78,100	78,150	15,388	11,244	15,499	13,944
78,150	78,200	15,400	11,256	15,513	13,956
78,200	78,250	15,413	11,269	15,527	13,969
78,250	78,300	15,425	11,281	15,541	13,981
78,300	78,350	15,438	11,294	15,555	13,994
78,350	78,400	15,450	11,306	15,569	14,006
78,400	78,450	15,463	11,319	15,583	14,019
78,450	78,500	15,475	11,331	15,597	14,031
78,500	78,550	15,488	11,344	15,611	14,044
78,550	78,600	15,500	11,356	15,625	14,056
78,600	78,650	15,513	11,369	15,639	14,069
78,650	78,700	15,525	11,381	15,653	14,081
78,700	78,750	15,538	11,394	15,667	14,094
78,750	78,800	15,550	11,406	15,681	14,106
78,800	78,850	15,563	11,419	15,695	14,119
78,850	78,900	15,575	11,431	15,709	14,131
78,900	78,950	15,588	11,444	15,723	14,144
78,950	79,000	15,600	11,456	15,737	14,156
79,000					
79,000	79,050	15,613	11,469	15,751	14,169
79,050	79,100	15,625	11,481	15,765	14,181
79,100	79,150	15,638	11,494	15,779	14,194
79,150	79,200	15,650	11,506	15,793	14,206
79,200	79,250	15,663	11,519	15,807	14,219
79,250	79,300	15,675	11,531	15,821	14,231
79,300	79,350	15,688	11,544	15,835	14,244
79,350	79,400	15,700	11,556	15,849	14,256
79,400	79,450	15,713	11,569	15,863	14,269
79,450	79,500	15,725	11,581	15,877	14,281
79,500	79,550	15,738	11,594	15,891	14,294
79,550	79,600	15,750	11,606	15,905	14,306
79,600	79,650	15,763	11,619	15,919	14,319
79,650	79,700	15,775	11,631	15,933	14,331
79,700	79,750	15,788	11,644	15,947	14,344
79,750	79,800	15,800	11,656	15,961	14,356
79,800	79,850	15,813	11,669	15,975	14,369
79,850	79,900	15,825	11,681	15,989	14,381
79,900	79,950	15,838	11,694	16,003	14,394
79,950	80,000	15,850	11,706	16,017	14,406
80,000					
80,000	80,050	15,863	11,719	16,031	14,419
80,050	80,100	15,875	11,731	16,045	14,431
80,100	80,150	15,888	11,744	16,059	14,444
80,150	80,200	15,900	11,756	16,073	14,456
80,200	80,250	15,913	11,769	16,087	14,469
80,250	80,300	15,925	11,781	16,101	14,481
80,300	80,350	15,938	11,794	16,115	14,494
80,350	80,400	15,950	11,806	16,129	14,506
80,400	80,450	15,963	11,819	16,143	14,519
80,450	80,500	15,975	11,831	16,157	14,531
80,500	80,550	15,988	11,844	16,171	14,544
80,550	80,600	16,000	11,856	16,185	14,556
80,600	80,650	16,013	11,869	16,199	14,569
80,650	80,700	16,025	11,881	16,213	14,581
80,700	80,750	16,038	11,894	16,227	14,594
80,750	80,800	16,050	11,906	16,241	14,606
80,800	80,850	16,063	11,919	16,255	14,619
80,850	80,900	16,075	11,931	16,269	14,631
80,900	80,950	16,088	11,944	16,283	14,644
80,950	81,000	16,100	11,956	16,297	14,656
81,000					
81,000	81,050	16,113	11,969	16,311	14,669
81,050	81,100	16,125	11,981	16,325	14,681
81,100	81,150	16,138	11,994	16,339	14,694
81,150	81,200	16,150	12,006	16,353	14,706
81,200	81,250	16,163	12,019	16,367	14,719
81,250	81,300	16,175	12,031	16,381	14,731
81,300	81,350	16,188	12,044	16,395	14,744
81,350	81,400	16,200	12,056	16,409	14,756
81,400	81,450	16,213	12,069	16,423	14,769
81,450	81,500	16,225	12,081	16,437	14,781
81,500	81,550	16,238	12,094	16,451	14,794
81,550	81,600	16,250	12,106	16,465	14,806
81,600	81,650	16,263	12,119	16,479	14,819
81,650	81,700	16,275	12,131	16,493	14,831
81,700	81,750	16,288	12,144	16,507	14,844
81,750	81,800	16,300	12,156	16,521	14,856
81,800	81,850	16,313	12,169	16,535	14,869
81,850	81,900	16,325	12,181	16,549	14,881
81,900	81,950	16,338	12,194	16,563	14,894
81,950	82,000	16,350	12,206	16,577	14,906
82,000					
82,000	82,050	16,363	12,219	16,591	14,919
82,050	82,100	16,375	12,231	16,605	14,931
82,100	82,150	16,388	12,244	16,619	14,944
82,150	82,200	16,400	12,256	16,633	14,956
82,200	82,250	16,413	12,269	16,647	14,969
82,250	82,300	16,425	12,281	16,661	14,981
82,300	82,350	16,438	12,294	16,675	14,994
82,350	82,400	16,450	12,306	16,689	15,006
82,400	82,450	16,463	12,319	16,703	15,019
82,450	82,500	16,475	12,331	16,717	15,031
82,500	82,550	16,488	12,344	16,731	15,044
82,550	82,600	16,500	12,356	16,745	15,056
82,600	82,650	16,513	12,369	16,759	15,069
82,650	82,700	16,525	12,381	16,773	15,081
82,700	82,750	16,538	12,394	16,787	15,094
82,750	82,800	16,550	12,406	16,801	15,106
82,800	82,850	16,563	12,419	16,815	15,119
82,850	82,900	16,575	12,431	16,829	15,131
82,900	82,950	16,588	12,444	16,843	15,144
82,950	83,000	16,600	12,456	16,857	15,156
83,000					
83,000	83,050	16,613	12,469	16,871	15,169
83,050	83,100	16,625	12,481	16,885	15,181
83,100	83,150	16,638	12,494	16,899	15,194
83,150	83,200	16,650	12,506	16,913	15,206
83,200	83,250	16,663	12,519	16,927	15,219
83,250	83,300	16,675	12,531	16,941	15,231
83,300	83,350	16,688	12,544	16,955	15,244
83,350	83,400	16,700	12,556	16,969	15,256
83,400	83,450	16,713	12,569	16,983	15,269
83,450	83,500	16,725	12,581	16,997	15,281
83,500	83,550	16,738	12,594	17,011	15,294
83,550	83,600	16,750	12,606	17,025	15,306
83,600	83,650	16,763	12,619	17,039	15,319
83,650	83,700	16,775	12,631	17,053	15,331
83,700	83,750	16,788	12,644	17,067	15,344
83,750	83,800	16,800	12,656	17,081	15,356
83,800	83,850	16,813	12,669	17,095	15,369
83,850	83,900	16,825	12,681	17,109	15,381
83,900	83,950	16,838	12,694	17,123	15,394
83,950	84,000	16,850	12,706	17,137	15,406

(Continued)

* This column must also be used by a qualifying widow(er).

2014 Tax Table — *Continued*

DRAFT AS OF October 8, 2014

If line 43 (taxable income) is—		And you are—			
At least	But less than	Single	Married filing jointly *	Married filing separately	Head of a household
		Your tax is—			
84,000					
84,000	84,050	16,863	12,719	17,151	15,419
84,050	84,100	16,875	12,731	17,165	15,431
84,100	84,150	16,888	12,744	17,179	15,444
84,150	84,200	16,900	12,756	17,193	15,456
84,200	84,250	16,913	12,769	17,207	15,469
84,250	84,300	16,925	12,781	17,221	15,481
84,300	84,350	16,938	12,794	17,235	15,494
84,350	84,400	16,950	12,806	17,249	15,506
84,400	84,450	16,963	12,819	17,263	15,519
84,450	84,500	16,975	12,831	17,277	15,531
84,500	84,550	16,988	12,844	17,291	15,544
84,550	84,600	17,000	12,856	17,305	15,556
84,600	84,650	17,013	12,869	17,319	15,569
84,650	84,700	17,025	12,881	17,333	15,581
84,700	84,750	17,038	12,894	17,347	15,594
84,750	84,800	17,050	12,906	17,361	15,606
84,800	84,850	17,063	12,919	17,375	15,619
84,850	84,900	17,075	12,931	17,389	15,631
84,900	84,950	17,088	12,944	17,403	15,644
84,950	85,000	17,100	12,956	17,417	15,656
85,000					
85,000	85,050	17,113	12,969	17,431	15,669
85,050	85,100	17,125	12,981	17,445	15,681
85,100	85,150	17,138	12,994	17,459	15,694
85,150	85,200	17,150	13,006	17,473	15,706
85,200	85,250	17,163	13,019	17,487	15,719
85,250	85,300	17,175	13,031	17,501	15,731
85,300	85,350	17,188	13,044	17,515	15,744
85,350	85,400	17,200	13,056	17,529	15,756
85,400	85,450	17,213	13,069	17,543	15,769
85,450	85,500	17,225	13,081	17,557	15,781
85,500	85,550	17,238	13,094	17,571	15,794
85,550	85,600	17,250	13,106	17,585	15,806
85,600	85,650	17,263	13,119	17,599	15,819
85,650	85,700	17,275	13,131	17,613	15,831
85,700	85,750	17,288	13,144	17,627	15,844
85,750	85,800	17,300	13,156	17,641	15,856
85,800	85,850	17,313	13,169	17,655	15,869
85,850	85,900	17,325	13,181	17,669	15,881
85,900	85,950	17,338	13,194	17,683	15,894
85,950	86,000	17,350	13,206	17,697	15,906
86,000					
86,000	86,050	17,363	13,219	17,711	15,919
86,050	86,100	17,375	13,231	17,725	15,931
86,100	86,150	17,388	13,244	17,739	15,944
86,150	86,200	17,400	13,256	17,753	15,956
86,200	86,250	17,413	13,269	17,767	15,969
86,250	86,300	17,425	13,281	17,781	15,981
86,300	86,350	17,438	13,294	17,795	15,994
86,350	86,400	17,450	13,306	17,809	16,006
86,400	86,450	17,463	13,319	17,823	16,019
86,450	86,500	17,475	13,331	17,837	16,031
86,500	86,550	17,488	13,344	17,851	16,044
86,550	86,600	17,500	13,356	17,865	16,056
86,600	86,650	17,513	13,369	17,879	16,069
86,650	86,700	17,525	13,381	17,893	16,081
86,700	86,750	17,538	13,394	17,907	16,094
86,750	86,800	17,550	13,406	17,921	16,106
86,800	86,850	17,563	13,419	17,935	16,119
86,850	86,900	17,575	13,431	17,949	16,131
86,900	86,950	17,588	13,444	17,963	16,144
86,950	87,000	17,600	13,456	17,977	16,156

If line 43 (taxable income) is—		And you are—			
At least	But less than	Single	Married filing jointly *	Married filing separately	Head of a household
		Your tax is—			
87,000					
87,000	87,050	17,613	13,469	17,991	16,169
87,050	87,100	17,625	13,481	18,005	16,181
87,100	87,150	17,638	13,494	18,019	16,194
87,150	87,200	17,650	13,506	18,033	16,206
87,200	87,250	17,663	13,519	18,047	16,219
87,250	87,300	17,675	13,531	18,061	16,231
87,300	87,350	17,688	13,544	18,075	16,244
87,350	87,400	17,700	13,556	18,089	16,256
87,400	87,450	17,713	13,569	18,103	16,269
87,450	87,500	17,725	13,581	18,117	16,281
87,500	87,550	17,738	13,594	18,131	16,294
87,550	87,600	17,750	13,606	18,145	16,306
87,600	87,650	17,763	13,619	18,159	16,319
87,650	87,700	17,775	13,631	18,173	16,331
87,700	87,750	17,788	13,644	18,187	16,344
87,750	87,800	17,800	13,656	18,201	16,356
87,800	87,850	17,813	13,669	18,215	16,369
87,850	87,900	17,825	13,681	18,229	16,381
87,900	87,950	17,838	13,694	18,243	16,394
87,950	88,000	17,850	13,706	18,257	16,406
88,000					
88,000	88,050	17,863	13,719	18,271	16,419
88,050	88,100	17,875	13,731	18,285	16,431
88,100	88,150	17,888	13,744	18,299	16,444
88,150	88,200	17,900	13,756	18,313	16,456
88,200	88,250	17,913	13,769	18,327	16,469
88,250	88,300	17,925	13,781	18,341	16,481
88,300	88,350	17,938	13,794	18,355	16,494
88,350	88,400	17,950	13,806	18,369	16,506
88,400	88,450	17,963	13,819	18,383	16,519
88,450	88,500	17,975	13,831	18,397	16,531
88,500	88,550	17,988	13,844	18,411	16,544
88,550	88,600	18,000	13,856	18,425	16,556
88,600	88,650	18,013	13,869	18,439	16,569
88,650	88,700	18,025	13,881	18,453	16,581
88,700	88,750	18,038	13,894	18,467	16,594
88,750	88,800	18,050	13,906	18,481	16,606
88,800	88,850	18,063	13,919	18,495	16,619
88,850	88,900	18,075	13,931	18,509	16,631
88,900	88,950	18,088	13,944	18,523	16,644
88,950	89,000	18,100	13,956	18,537	16,656
89,000					
89,000	89,050	18,113	13,969	18,551	16,669
89,050	89,100	18,125	13,981	18,565	16,681
89,100	89,150	18,138	13,994	18,579	16,694
89,150	89,200	18,150	14,006	18,593	16,706
89,200	89,250	18,163	14,019	18,607	16,719
89,250	89,300	18,175	14,031	18,621	16,731
89,300	89,350	18,188	14,044	18,635	16,744
89,350	89,400	18,201	14,056	18,649	16,756
89,400	89,450	18,215	14,069	18,663	16,769
89,450	89,500	18,229	14,081	18,677	16,781
89,500	89,550	18,243	14,094	18,691	16,794
89,550	89,600	18,257	14,106	18,705	16,806
89,600	89,650	18,271	14,119	18,719	16,819
89,650	89,700	18,285	14,131	18,733	16,831
89,700	89,750	18,299	14,144	18,747	16,844
89,750	89,800	18,313	14,156	18,761	16,856
89,800	89,850	18,327	14,169	18,775	16,869
89,850	89,900	18,341	14,181	18,789	16,881
89,900	89,950	18,355	14,194	18,803	16,894
89,950	90,000	18,369	14,206	18,817	16,906

If line 43 (taxable income) is—		And you are—			
At least	But less than	Single	Married filing jointly *	Married filing separately	Head of a household
		Your tax is—			
90,000					
90,000	90,050	18,383	14,219	18,831	16,919
90,050	90,100	18,397	14,231	18,845	16,931
90,100	90,150	18,411	14,244	18,859	16,944
90,150	90,200	18,425	14,256	18,873	16,956
90,200	90,250	18,439	14,269	18,887	16,969
90,250	90,300	18,453	14,281	18,901	16,981
90,300	90,350	18,467	14,294	18,915	16,994
90,350	90,400	18,481	14,306	18,929	17,006
90,400	90,450	18,495	14,319	18,943	17,019
90,450	90,500	18,509	14,331	18,957	17,031
90,500	90,550	18,523	14,344	18,971	17,044
90,550	90,600	18,537	14,356	18,985	17,056
90,600	90,650	18,551	14,369	18,999	17,069
90,650	90,700	18,565	14,381	19,013	17,081
90,700	90,750	18,579	14,394	19,027	17,094
90,750	90,800	18,593	14,406	19,041	17,106
90,800	90,850	18,607	14,419	19,055	17,119
90,850	90,900	18,621	14,431	19,069	17,131
90,900	90,950	18,635	14,444	19,083	17,144
90,950	91,000	18,649	14,456	19,097	17,156
91,000					
91,000	91,050	18,663	14,469	19,111	17,169
91,050	91,100	18,677	14,481	19,125	17,181
91,100	91,150	18,691	14,494	19,139	17,194
91,150	91,200	18,705	14,506	19,153	17,206
91,200	91,250	18,719	14,519	19,167	17,219
91,250	91,300	18,733	14,531	19,181	17,231
91,300	91,350	18,747	14,544	19,195	17,244
91,350	91,400	18,761	14,556	19,209	17,256
91,400	91,450	18,775	14,569	19,223	17,269
91,450	91,500	18,789	14,581	19,237	17,281
91,500	91,550	18,803	14,594	19,251	17,294
91,550	91,600	18,817	14,606	19,265	17,306
91,600	91,650	18,831	14,619	19,279	17,319
91,650	91,700	18,845	14,631	19,293	17,331
91,700	91,750	18,859	14,644	19,307	17,344
91,750	91,800	18,873	14,656	19,321	17,356
91,800	91,850	18,887	14,669	19,335	17,369
91,850	91,900	18,901	14,681	19,349	17,381
91,900	91,950	18,915	14,694	19,363	17,394
91,950	92,000	18,929	14,706	19,377	17,406
92,000					
92,000	92,050	18,943	14,719	19,391	17,419
92,050	92,100	18,957	14,731	19,405	17,431
92,100	92,150	18,971	14,744	19,419	17,444
92,150	92,200	18,985	14,756	19,433	17,456
92,200	92,250	18,999	14,769	19,447	17,469
92,250	92,300	19,013	14,781	19,461	17,481
92,300	92,350	19,027	14,794	19,475	17,494
92,350	92,400	19,041	14,806	19,489	17,506
92,400	92,450	19,055	14,819	19,503	17,519
92,450	92,500	19,069	14,831	19,517	17,531
92,500	92,550	19,083	14,844	19,531	17,544
92,550	92,600	19,097	14,856	19,545	17,556
92,600	92,650	19,111	14,869	19,559	17,569
92,650	92,700	19,125	14,881	19,573	17,581
92,700	92,750	19,139	14,894	19,587	17,594
92,750	92,800	19,153	14,906	19,601	17,606
92,800	92,850	19,167	14,919	19,615	17,619
92,850	92,900	19,181	14,931	19,629	17,631
92,900	92,950	19,195	14,944	19,643	17,644
92,950	93,000	19,209	14,956	19,657	17,656

(Continued)

* This column must also be used by a qualifying widow(er).

2014 Tax Table — *Continued*

DRAFT AS OF October 8, 2014

If line 43 (taxable income) is—		And you are—			
At least	But less than	Single	Married filing jointly *	Married filing separately	Head of a household
		Your tax is—			
93,000					
93,000	93,050	19,223	14,969	19,671	17,669
93,050	93,100	19,237	14,981	19,685	17,681
93,100	93,150	19,251	14,994	19,699	17,694
93,150	93,200	19,265	15,006	19,713	17,706
93,200	93,250	19,279	15,019	19,727	17,719
93,250	93,300	19,293	15,031	19,741	17,731
93,300	93,350	19,307	15,044	19,755	17,744
93,350	93,400	19,321	15,056	19,769	17,756
93,400	93,450	19,335	15,069	19,783	17,769
93,450	93,500	19,349	15,081	19,797	17,781
93,500	93,550	19,363	15,094	19,811	17,794
93,550	93,600	19,377	15,106	19,825	17,806
93,600	93,650	19,391	15,119	19,839	17,819
93,650	93,700	19,405	15,131	19,853	17,831
93,700	93,750	19,419	15,144	19,867	17,844
93,750	93,800	19,433	15,156	19,881	17,856
93,800	93,850	19,447	15,169	19,895	17,869
93,850	93,900	19,461	15,181	19,909	17,881
93,900	93,950	19,475	15,194	19,923	17,894
93,950	94,000	19,489	15,206	19,937	17,906
94,000					
94,000	94,050	19,503	15,219	19,951	17,919
94,050	94,100	19,517	15,231	19,965	17,931
94,100	94,150	19,531	15,244	19,979	17,944
94,150	94,200	19,545	15,256	19,993	17,956
94,200	94,250	19,559	15,269	20,007	17,969
94,250	94,300	19,573	15,281	20,021	17,981
94,300	94,350	19,587	15,294	20,035	17,994
94,350	94,400	19,601	15,306	20,049	18,006
94,400	94,450	19,615	15,319	20,063	18,019
94,450	94,500	19,629	15,331	20,077	18,031
94,500	94,550	19,643	15,344	20,091	18,044
94,550	94,600	19,657	15,356	20,105	18,056
94,600	94,650	19,671	15,369	20,119	18,069
94,650	94,700	19,685	15,381	20,133	18,081
94,700	94,750	19,699	15,394	20,147	18,094
94,750	94,800	19,713	15,406	20,161	18,106
94,800	94,850	19,727	15,419	20,175	18,119
94,850	94,900	19,741	15,431	20,189	18,131
94,900	94,950	19,755	15,444	20,203	18,144
94,950	95,000	19,769	15,456	20,217	18,156
95,000					
95,000	95,050	19,783	15,469	20,231	18,169
95,050	95,100	19,797	15,481	20,245	18,181
95,100	95,150	19,811	15,494	20,259	18,194
95,150	95,200	19,825	15,506	20,273	18,206
95,200	95,250	19,839	15,519	20,287	18,219
95,250	95,300	19,853	15,531	20,301	18,231
95,300	95,350	19,867	15,544	20,315	18,244
95,350	95,400	19,881	15,556	20,329	18,256
95,400	95,450	19,895	15,569	20,343	18,269
95,450	95,500	19,909	15,581	20,357	18,281
95,500	95,550	19,923	15,594	20,371	18,294
95,550	95,600	19,937	15,606	20,385	18,306
95,600	95,650	19,951	15,619	20,399	18,319
95,650	95,700	19,965	15,631	20,413	18,331
95,700	95,750	19,979	15,644	20,427	18,344
95,750	95,800	19,993	15,656	20,441	18,356
95,800	95,850	20,007	15,669	20,455	18,369
95,850	95,900	20,021	15,681	20,469	18,381
95,900	95,950	20,035	15,694	20,483	18,394
95,950	96,000	20,049	15,706	20,497	18,406
96,000					
96,000	96,050	20,063	15,719	20,511	18,419
96,050	96,100	20,077	15,731	20,525	18,431
96,100	96,150	20,091	15,744	20,539	18,444
96,150	96,200	20,105	15,756	20,553	18,456
96,200	96,250	20,119	15,769	20,567	18,469
96,250	96,300	20,133	15,781	20,581	18,481
96,300	96,350	20,147	15,794	20,595	18,494
96,350	96,400	20,161	15,806	20,609	18,506
96,400	96,450	20,175	15,819	20,623	18,519
96,450	96,500	20,189	15,831	20,637	18,531
96,500	96,550	20,203	15,844	20,651	18,544
96,550	96,600	20,217	15,856	20,665	18,556
96,600	96,650	20,231	15,869	20,679	18,569
96,650	96,700	20,245	15,881	20,693	18,581
96,700	96,750	20,259	15,894	20,707	18,594
96,750	96,800	20,273	15,906	20,721	18,606
96,800	96,850	20,287	15,919	20,735	18,619
96,850	96,900	20,301	15,931	20,749	18,631
96,900	96,950	20,315	15,944	20,763	18,644
96,950	97,000	20,329	15,956	20,777	18,656
97,000					
97,000	97,050	20,343	15,969	20,791	18,669
97,050	97,100	20,357	15,981	20,805	18,681
97,100	97,150	20,371	15,994	20,819	18,694
97,150	97,200	20,385	16,006	20,833	18,706
97,200	97,250	20,399	16,019	20,847	18,719
97,250	97,300	20,413	16,031	20,861	18,731
97,300	97,350	20,427	16,044	20,875	18,744
97,350	97,400	20,441	16,056	20,889	18,756
97,400	97,450	20,455	16,069	20,903	18,769
97,450	97,500	20,469	16,081	20,917	18,781
97,500	97,550	20,483	16,094	20,931	18,794
97,550	97,600	20,497	16,106	20,945	18,806
97,600	97,650	20,511	16,119	20,959	18,819
97,650	97,700	20,525	16,131	20,973	18,831
97,700	97,750	20,539	16,144	20,987	18,844
97,750	97,800	20,553	16,156	21,001	18,856
97,800	97,850	20,567	16,169	21,015	18,869
97,850	97,900	20,581	16,181	21,029	18,881
97,900	97,950	20,595	16,194	21,043	18,894
97,950	98,000	20,609	16,206	21,057	18,906
98,000					
98,000	98,050	20,623	16,219	21,071	18,919
98,050	98,100	20,637	16,231	21,085	18,931
98,100	98,150	20,651	16,244	21,099	18,944
98,150	98,200	20,665	16,256	21,113	18,956
98,200	98,250	20,679	16,269	21,127	18,969
98,250	98,300	20,693	16,281	21,141	18,981
98,300	98,350	20,707	16,294	21,155	18,994
98,350	98,400	20,721	16,306	21,169	19,006
98,400	98,450	20,735	16,319	21,183	19,019
98,450	98,500	20,749	16,331	21,197	19,031
98,500	98,550	20,763	16,344	21,211	19,044
98,550	98,600	20,777	16,356	21,225	19,056
98,600	98,650	20,791	16,369	21,239	19,069
98,650	98,700	20,805	16,381	21,253	19,081
98,700	98,750	20,819	16,394	21,267	19,094
98,750	98,800	20,833	16,406	21,281	19,106
98,800	98,850	20,847	16,419	21,295	19,119
98,850	98,900	20,861	16,431	21,309	19,131
98,900	98,950	20,875	16,444	21,323	19,144
98,950	99,000	20,889	16,456	21,337	19,156
99,000					
99,000	99,050	20,903	16,469	21,351	19,169
99,050	99,100	20,917	16,481	21,365	19,181
99,100	99,150	20,931	16,494	21,379	19,194
99,150	99,200	20,945	16,506	21,393	19,206
99,200	99,250	20,959	16,519	21,407	19,219
99,250	99,300	20,973	16,531	21,421	19,231
99,300	99,350	20,987	16,544	21,435	19,244
99,350	99,400	21,001	16,556	21,449	19,256
99,400	99,450	21,015	16,569	21,463	19,269
99,450	99,500	21,029	16,581	21,477	19,281
99,500	99,550	21,043	16,594	21,491	19,294
99,550	99,600	21,057	16,606	21,505	19,306
99,600	99,650	21,071	16,619	21,519	19,319
99,650	99,700	21,085	16,631	21,533	19,331
99,700	99,750	21,099	16,644	21,547	19,344
99,750	99,800	21,113	16,656	21,561	19,356
99,800	99,850	21,127	16,669	21,575	19,369
99,850	99,900	21,141	16,681	21,589	19,381
99,900	99,950	21,155	16,694	21,603	19,394
99,950	100,000	21,169	16,706	21,617	19,406

$100,000 or over use the Tax Computation Worksheet

* This column must also be used by a qualifying widow(er).

APPENDIX B

Earned Income Credit Table

CONTENTS

2014 Earned Income Credit Worksheet B-2

2014 Earned Income Credit Table B-3

Worksheet A—2014 EIC—Lines 66a and 66b

Keep for Your Records

Before you begin: √ Be sure you are using the correct worksheet. Use this worksheet only if you answered "No" to Step 5, question 2. Otherwise, use Worksheet B.

RAFT AS OF ctober 8, 2014

Part 1

All Filers Using Worksheet A

1. Enter your earned income from Step 5. **1** ______

Wages, Salaries

2. Look up the amount on line 1 above in the EIC Table (right after Worksheet B) to find the credit. Be sure you use the correct column for your filing status and the number of children you have. Enter the credit here. **2** ______

If line 2 is zero, STOP You cannot take the credit. Enter "No" on the dotted line next to line 66a.

3. Enter the amount from Form 1040, line 38. **3** ______

Adjusted Gross Income

4. Are the amounts on lines 3 and 1 the same?

☐ **Yes.** Skip line 5; enter the amount from line 2 on line 6.

☐ **No.** Go to line 5.

Part 2

Filers Who Answered "No" on Line 4

5. If you have:

- No qualifying children, is the amount on line 3 less than $8,150 ($13,550 if married filing jointly)?
- 1 or more qualifying children, is the amount on line 3 less than $17,850 ($23,300 if married filing jointly)?

☐ **Yes.** Leave line 5 blank; enter the amount from line 2 on line 6.

☐ **No.** Look up the amount on line 3 in the EIC Table to find the credit. Be sure you use the correct column for your filing status and the number of children you have. Enter the credit here. **5** ______
Look at the amounts on lines 5 and 2.
Then, enter the **smaller** amount on line 6.

Part 3

Your Earned Income Credit

6. This is your earned income credit. **6** ______

Enter this amount on Form 1040, line 66a.

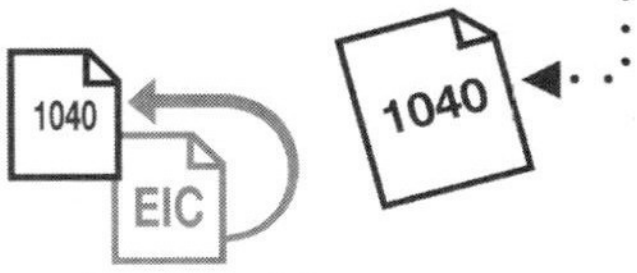

Reminder—

√ If you have a qualifying child, complete and attach Schedule EIC.

CAUTION *If your EIC for a year after 1996 was reduced or disallowed, see* Form 8862, who must file, *earlier, to find out if you must file Form 8862 to take the credit for 2014.*

2014 Earned Income Credit (EIC) Table

Caution. This is **not** a tax table.

1. To find your credit, read down the "At least - But less than" columns and find the line that includes the amount you were told to look up from your EIC Worksheet.

2. Then, go to the column that includes your filing status and the number of qualifying children you have. Enter the credit from that column on your EIC Worksheet.

Example. If your filing status is single, you have one qualifying child, and the amount you are looking up from your EIC Worksheet is $2,455, you would enter $842.

If the amount you are looking up from the worksheet is—		And your filing status is— Single, head of household, or qualifying widow(er) and the number of children you have is—			
		0	1	2	3
At least	But less than	Your credit is—			
2,400	2,450	186	825	970	1,091
2,450	2,500	189	842	990	1,114

DRAFT AS OF

If the amount you are looking up from the worksheet is–		And your filing status is– Single, head of household, or qualifying widow(er) and the number of children you have is–				Married filing jointly and the number of children you have is–			
		0	1	2	3	0	1	2	3
At least	But less than	Your credit is–				Your credit is–			
$1	$50	$2	$9	$10	$11	$2	$9	$10	$11
50	100	6	26	30	34	6	26	30	34
100	150	10	43	50	56	10	43	50	56
150	200	13	60	70	79	13	60	70	79
200	250	17	77	90	101	17	77	90	101
250	300	21	94	110	124	21	94	110	124
300	350	25	111	130	146	25	111	130	146
350	400	29	128	150	169	29	128	150	169
400	450	33	145	170	191	33	145	170	191
450	500	36	162	190	214	36	162	190	214
500	550	40	179	210	236	40	179	210	236
550	600	44	196	230	259	44	196	230	259
600	650	48	213	250	281	48	213	250	281
650	700	52	230	270	304	52	230	270	304
700	750	55	247	290	326	55	247	290	326
750	800	59	264	310	349	59	264	310	349
800	850	63	281	330	371	63	281	330	371
850	900	67	298	350	394	67	298	350	394
900	950	71	315	370	416	71	315	370	416
950	1,000	75	332	390	439	75	332	390	439
1,000	1,050	78	349	410	461	78	349	410	461
1,050	1,100	82	366	430	484	82	366	430	484
1,100	1,150	86	383	450	506	86	383	450	506
1,150	1,200	90	400	470	529	90	400	470	529
1,200	1,250	94	417	490	551	94	417	490	551
1,250	1,300	98	434	510	574	98	434	510	574
1,300	1,350	101	451	530	596	101	451	530	596
1,350	1,400	105	468	550	619	105	468	550	619
1,400	1,450	109	485	570	641	109	485	570	641
1,450	1,500	113	502	590	664	113	502	590	664
1,500	1,550	117	519	610	686	117	519	610	686
1,550	1,600	120	536	630	709	120	536	630	709
1,600	1,650	124	553	650	731	124	553	650	731
1,650	1,700	128	570	670	754	128	570	670	754
1,700	1,750	132	587	690	776	132	587	690	776
1,750	1,800	136	604	710	799	136	604	710	799
1,800	1,850	140	621	730	821	140	621	730	821
1,850	1,900	143	638	750	844	143	638	750	844
1,900	1,950	147	655	770	866	147	655	770	866
1,950	2,000	151	672	790	889	151	672	790	889
2,000	2,050	155	689	810	911	155	689	810	911
2,050	2,100	159	706	830	934	159	706	830	934
2,100	2,150	163	723	850	956	163	723	850	956
2,150	2,200	166	740	870	979	166	740	870	979
2,200	2,250	170	757	890	1,001	170	757	890	1,001
2,250	2,300	174	774	910	1,024	174	774	910	1,024
2,300	2,350	178	791	930	1,046	178	791	930	1,046
2,350	2,400	182	808	950	1,069	182	808	950	1,069
2,400	2,450	186	825	970	1,091	186	825	970	1,091
2,450	2,500	189	842	990	1,114	189	842	990	1,114
2,500	2,550	193	859	1,010	1,136	193	859	1,010	1,136
2,550	2,600	197	876	1,030	1,159	197	876	1,030	1,159
2,600	2,650	201	893	1,050	1,181	201	893	1,050	1,181
2,650	2,700	205	910	1,070	1,204	205	910	1,070	1,204
2,700	2,750	208	927	1,090	1,226	208	927	1,090	1,226
2,750	2,800	212	944	1,110	1,249	212	944	1,110	1,249

If the amount you are looking up from the worksheet is–		And your filing status is– Single, head of household, or qualifying widow(er) and the number of children you have is–				Married filing jointly and the number of children you have is–			
		0	1	2	3	0	1	2	3
At least	But less than	Your credit is–				Your credit is–			
2,800	2,850	216	961	1,130	1,271	216	961	1,130	1,271
2,850	2,900	220	978	1,150	1,294	220	978	1,150	1,294
2,900	2,950	224	995	1,170	1,316	224	995	1,170	1,316
2,950	3,000	228	1,012	1,190	1,339	228	1,012	1,190	1,339
3,000	3,050	231	1,029	1,210	1,361	231	1,029	1,210	1,361
3,050	3,100	235	1,046	1,230	1,384	235	1,046	1,230	1,384
3,100	3,150	239	1,063	1,250	1,406	239	1,063	1,250	1,406
3,150	3,200	243	1,080	1,270	1,429	243	1,080	1,270	1,429
3,200	3,250	247	1,097	1,290	1,451	247	1,097	1,290	1,451
3,250	3,300	251	1,114	1,310	1,474	251	1,114	1,310	1,474
3,300	3,350	254	1,131	1,330	1,496	254	1,131	1,330	1,496
3,350	3,400	258	1,148	1,350	1,519	258	1,148	1,350	1,519
3,400	3,450	262	1,165	1,370	1,541	262	1,165	1,370	1,541
3,450	3,500	266	1,182	1,390	1,564	266	1,182	1,390	1,564
3,500	3,550	270	1,199	1,410	1,586	270	1,199	1,410	1,586
3,550	3,600	273	1,216	1,430	1,609	273	1,216	1,430	1,609
3,600	3,650	277	1,233	1,450	1,631	277	1,233	1,450	1,631
3,650	3,700	281	1,250	1,470	1,654	281	1,250	1,470	1,654
3,700	3,750	285	1,267	1,490	1,676	285	1,267	1,490	1,676
3,750	3,800	289	1,284	1,510	1,699	289	1,284	1,510	1,699
3,800	3,850	293	1,301	1,530	1,721	293	1,301	1,530	1,721
3,850	3,900	296	1,318	1,550	1,744	296	1,318	1,550	1,744
3,900	3,950	300	1,335	1,570	1,766	300	1,335	1,570	1,766
3,950	4,000	304	1,352	1,590	1,789	304	1,352	1,590	1,789
4,000	4,050	308	1,369	1,610	1,811	308	1,369	1,610	1,811
4,050	4,100	312	1,386	1,630	1,834	312	1,386	1,630	1,834
4,100	4,150	316	1,403	1,650	1,856	316	1,403	1,650	1,856
4,150	4,200	319	1,420	1,670	1,879	319	1,420	1,670	1,879
4,200	4,250	323	1,437	1,690	1,901	323	1,437	1,690	1,901
4,250	4,300	327	1,454	1,710	1,924	327	1,454	1,710	1,924
4,300	4,350	331	1,471	1,730	1,946	331	1,471	1,730	1,946
4,350	4,400	335	1,488	1,750	1,969	335	1,488	1,750	1,969
4,400	4,450	339	1,505	1,770	1,991	339	1,505	1,770	1,991
4,450	4,500	342	1,522	1,790	2,014	342	1,522	1,790	2,014
4,500	4,550	346	1,539	1,810	2,036	346	1,539	1,810	2,036
4,550	4,600	350	1,556	1,830	2,059	350	1,556	1,830	2,059
4,600	4,650	354	1,573	1,850	2,081	354	1,573	1,850	2,081
4,650	4,700	358	1,590	1,870	2,104	358	1,590	1,870	2,104
4,700	4,750	361	1,607	1,890	2,126	361	1,607	1,890	2,126
4,750	4,800	365	1,624	1,910	2,149	365	1,624	1,910	2,149
4,800	4,850	369	1,641	1,930	2,171	369	1,641	1,930	2,171
4,850	4,900	373	1,658	1,950	2,194	373	1,658	1,950	2,194
4,900	4,950	377	1,675	1,970	2,216	377	1,675	1,970	2,216
4,950	5,000	381	1,692	1,990	2,239	381	1,692	1,990	2,239
5,000	5,050	384	1,709	2,010	2,261	384	1,709	2,010	2,261
5,050	5,100	388	1,726	2,030	2,284	388	1,726	2,030	2,284
5,100	5,150	392	1,743	2,050	2,306	392	1,743	2,050	2,306
5,150	5,200	396	1,760	2,070	2,329	396	1,760	2,070	2,329
5,200	5,250	400	1,777	2,090	2,351	400	1,777	2,090	2,351
5,250	5,300	404	1,794	2,110	2,374	404	1,794	2,110	2,374
5,300	5,350	407	1,811	2,130	2,396	407	1,811	2,130	2,396
5,350	5,400	411	1,828	2,150	2,419	411	1,828	2,150	2,419
5,400	5,450	415	1,845	2,170	2,441	415	1,845	2,170	2,441
5,450	5,500	419	1,862	2,190	2,464	419	1,862	2,190	2,464
5,500	5,550	423	1,879	2,210	2,486	423	1,879	2,210	2,486
5,550	5,600	426	1,896	2,230	2,509	426	1,896	2,230	2,509

(Continued)

Earned Income Credit (EIC) Table - *Continued* **(Caution.** This is **not** a tax table.)

DRAFT AS OF October 6, 2014

If the amount you are looking up from the worksheet is–		And your filing status is– Single, head of household, or qualifying widow(er) and the number of children you have is–				Married filing jointly and the number of children you have is–			
At least	But less than	0	1	2	3	0	1	2	3
		Your credit is–				Your credit is–			
5,600	5,650	430	1,913	2,250	2,531	430	1,913	2,250	2,531
5,650	5,700	434	1,930	2,270	2,554	434	1,930	2,270	2,554
5,700	5,750	438	1,947	2,290	2,576	438	1,947	2,290	2,576
5,750	5,800	442	1,964	2,310	2,599	442	1,964	2,310	2,599
5,800	5,850	446	1,981	2,330	2,621	446	1,981	2,330	2,621
5,850	5,900	449	1,998	2,350	2,644	449	1,998	2,350	2,644
5,900	5,950	453	2,015	2,370	2,666	453	2,015	2,370	2,666
5,950	6,000	457	2,032	2,390	2,689	457	2,032	2,390	2,689
6,000	6,050	461	2,049	2,410	2,711	461	2,049	2,410	2,711
6,050	6,100	465	2,066	2,430	2,734	465	2,066	2,430	2,734
6,100	6,150	469	2,083	2,450	2,756	469	2,083	2,450	2,756
6,150	6,200	472	2,100	2,470	2,779	472	2,100	2,470	2,779
6,200	6,250	476	2,117	2,490	2,801	476	2,117	2,490	2,801
6,250	6,300	480	2,134	2,510	2,824	480	2,134	2,510	2,824
6,300	6,350	484	2,151	2,530	2,846	484	2,151	2,530	2,846
6,350	6,400	488	2,168	2,550	2,869	488	2,168	2,550	2,869
6,400	6,450	492	2,185	2,570	2,891	492	2,185	2,570	2,891
6,450	6,500	496	2,202	2,590	2,914	496	2,202	2,590	2,914
6,500	6,550	496	2,219	2,610	2,936	496	2,219	2,610	2,936
6,550	6,600	496	2,236	2,630	2,959	496	2,236	2,630	2,959
6,600	6,650	496	2,253	2,650	2,981	496	2,253	2,650	2,981
6,650	6,700	496	2,270	2,670	3,004	496	2,270	2,670	3,004
6,700	6,750	496	2,287	2,690	3,026	496	2,287	2,690	3,026
6,750	6,800	496	2,304	2,710	3,049	496	2,304	2,710	3,049
6,800	6,850	496	2,321	2,730	3,071	496	2,321	2,730	3,071
6,850	6,900	496	2,338	2,750	3,094	496	2,338	2,750	3,094
6,900	6,950	496	2,355	2,770	3,116	496	2,355	2,770	3,116
6,950	7,000	496	2,372	2,790	3,139	496	2,372	2,790	3,139
7,000	7,050	496	2,389	2,810	3,161	496	2,389	2,810	3,161
7,050	7,100	496	2,406	2,830	3,184	496	2,406	2,830	3,184
7,100	7,150	496	2,423	2,850	3,206	496	2,423	2,850	3,206
7,150	7,200	496	2,440	2,870	3,229	496	2,440	2,870	3,229
7,200	7,250	496	2,457	2,890	3,251	496	2,457	2,890	3,251
7,250	7,300	496	2,474	2,910	3,274	496	2,474	2,910	3,274
7,300	7,350	496	2,491	2,930	3,296	496	2,491	2,930	3,296
7,350	7,400	496	2,508	2,950	3,319	496	2,508	2,950	3,319
7,400	7,450	496	2,525	2,970	3,341	496	2,525	2,970	3,341
7,450	7,500	496	2,542	2,990	3,364	496	2,542	2,990	3,364
7,500	7,550	496	2,559	3,010	3,386	496	2,559	3,010	3,386
7,550	7,600	496	2,576	3,030	3,409	496	2,576	3,030	3,409
7,600	7,650	496	2,593	3,050	3,431	496	2,593	3,050	3,431
7,650	7,700	496	2,610	3,070	3,454	496	2,610	3,070	3,454
7,700	7,750	496	2,627	3,090	3,476	496	2,627	3,090	3,476
7,750	7,800	496	2,644	3,110	3,499	496	2,644	3,110	3,499
7,800	7,850	496	2,661	3,130	3,521	496	2,661	3,130	3,521
7,850	7,900	496	2,678	3,150	3,544	496	2,678	3,150	3,544
7,900	7,950	496	2,695	3,170	3,566	496	2,695	3,170	3,566
7,950	8,000	496	2,712	3,190	3,589	496	2,712	3,190	3,589
8,000	8,050	496	2,729	3,210	3,611	496	2,729	3,210	3,611
8,050	8,100	496	2,746	3,230	3,634	496	2,746	3,230	3,634
8,100	8,150	496	2,763	3,250	3,656	496	2,763	3,250	3,656
8,150	8,200	491	2,780	3,270	3,679	496	2,780	3,270	3,679
8,200	8,250	487	2,797	3,290	3,701	496	2,797	3,290	3,701
8,250	8,300	483	2,814	3,310	3,724	496	2,814	3,310	3,724
8,300	8,350	479	2,831	3,330	3,746	496	2,831	3,330	3,746
8,350	8,400	475	2,848	3,350	3,769	496	2,848	3,350	3,769
8,400	8,450	472	2,865	3,370	3,791	496	2,865	3,370	3,791
8,450	8,500	468	2,882	3,390	3,814	496	2,882	3,390	3,814
8,500	8,550	464	2,899	3,410	3,836	496	2,899	3,410	3,836
8,550	8,600	460	2,916	3,430	3,859	496	2,916	3,430	3,859
8,600	8,650	456	2,933	3,450	3,881	496	2,933	3,450	3,881
8,650	8,700	452	2,950	3,470	3,904	496	2,950	3,470	3,904
8,700	8,750	449	2,967	3,490	3,926	496	2,967	3,490	3,926
8,750	8,800	445	2,984	3,510	3,949	496	2,984	3,510	3,949
8,800	8,850	441	3,001	3,530	3,971	496	3,001	3,530	3,971
8,850	8,900	437	3,018	3,550	3,994	496	3,018	3,550	3,994
8,900	8,950	433	3,035	3,570	4,016	496	3,035	3,570	4,016
8,950	9,000	430	3,052	3,590	4,039	496	3,052	3,590	4,039
9,000	9,050	426	3,069	3,610	4,061	496	3,069	3,610	4,061
9,050	9,100	422	3,086	3,630	4,084	496	3,086	3,630	4,084
9,100	9,150	418	3,103	3,650	4,106	496	3,103	3,650	4,106
9,150	9,200	414	3,120	3,670	4,129	496	3,120	3,670	4,129
9,200	9,250	410	3,137	3,690	4,151	496	3,137	3,690	4,151
9,250	9,300	407	3,154	3,710	4,174	496	3,154	3,710	4,174
9,300	9,350	403	3,171	3,730	4,196	496	3,171	3,730	4,196
9,350	9,400	399	3,188	3,750	4,219	496	3,188	3,750	4,219
9,400	9,450	395	3,205	3,770	4,241	496	3,205	3,770	4,241
9,450	9,500	391	3,222	3,790	4,264	496	3,222	3,790	4,264
9,500	9,550	387	3,239	3,810	4,286	496	3,239	3,810	4,286
9,550	9,600	384	3,256	3,830	4,309	496	3,256	3,830	4,309
9,600	9,650	380	3,273	3,850	4,331	496	3,273	3,850	4,331
9,650	9,700	376	3,290	3,870	4,354	496	3,290	3,870	4,354
9,700	9,750	372	3,305	3,890	4,376	496	3,305	3,890	4,376
9,750	9,800	368	3,305	3,910	4,399	496	3,305	3,910	4,399
9,800	9,850	365	3,305	3,930	4,421	496	3,305	3,930	4,421
9,850	9,900	361	3,305	3,950	4,444	496	3,305	3,950	4,444
9,900	9,950	357	3,305	3,970	4,466	496	3,305	3,970	4,466
9,950	10,000	353	3,305	3,990	4,489	496	3,305	3,990	4,489
10,000	10,050	349	3,305	4,010	4,511	496	3,305	4,010	4,511
10,050	10,100	345	3,305	4,030	4,534	496	3,305	4,030	4,534
10,100	10,150	342	3,305	4,050	4,556	496	3,305	4,050	4,556
10,150	10,200	338	3,305	4,070	4,579	496	3,305	4,070	4,579
10,200	10,250	334	3,305	4,090	4,601	496	3,305	4,090	4,601
10,250	10,300	330	3,305	4,110	4,624	496	3,305	4,110	4,624
10,300	10,350	326	3,305	4,130	4,646	496	3,305	4,130	4,646
10,350	10,400	322	3,305	4,150	4,669	496	3,305	4,150	4,669
10,400	10,450	319	3,305	4,170	4,691	496	3,305	4,170	4,691
10,450	10,500	315	3,305	4,190	4,714	496	3,305	4,190	4,714
10,500	10,550	311	3,305	4,210	4,736	496	3,305	4,210	4,736
10,550	10,600	307	3,305	4,230	4,759	496	3,305	4,230	4,759
10,600	10,650	303	3,305	4,250	4,781	496	3,305	4,250	4,781
10,650	10,700	299	3,305	4,270	4,804	496	3,305	4,270	4,804
10,700	10,750	296	3,305	4,290	4,826	496	3,305	4,290	4,826
10,750	10,800	292	3,305	4,310	4,849	496	3,305	4,310	4,849
10,800	10,850	288	3,305	4,330	4,871	496	3,305	4,330	4,871
10,850	10,900	284	3,305	4,350	4,894	496	3,305	4,350	4,894
10,900	10,950	280	3,305	4,370	4,916	496	3,305	4,370	4,916
10,950	11,000	277	3,305	4,390	4,939	496	3,305	4,390	4,939
11,000	11,050	273	3,305	4,410	4,961	496	3,305	4,410	4,961
11,050	11,100	269	3,305	4,430	4,984	496	3,305	4,430	4,984
11,100	11,150	265	3,305	4,450	5,006	496	3,305	4,450	5,006
11,150	11,200	261	3,305	4,470	5,029	496	3,305	4,470	5,029
11,200	11,250	257	3,305	4,490	5,051	496	3,305	4,490	5,051
11,250	11,300	254	3,305	4,510	5,074	496	3,305	4,510	5,074
11,300	11,350	250	3,305	4,530	5,096	496	3,305	4,530	5,096
11,350	11,400	246	3,305	4,550	5,119	496	3,305	4,550	5,119
11,400	11,450	242	3,305	4,570	5,141	496	3,305	4,570	5,141
11,450	11,500	238	3,305	4,590	5,164	496	3,305	4,590	5,164
11,500	11,550	234	3,305	4,610	5,186	496	3,305	4,610	5,186
11,550	11,600	231	3,305	4,630	5,209	496	3,305	4,630	5,209
11,600	11,650	227	3,305	4,650	5,231	496	3,305	4,650	5,231
11,650	11,700	223	3,305	4,670	5,254	496	3,305	4,670	5,254
11,700	11,750	219	3,305	4,690	5,276	496	3,305	4,690	5,276
11,750	11,800	215	3,305	4,710	5,299	496	3,305	4,710	5,299
11,800	11,850	212	3,305	4,730	5,321	496	3,305	4,730	5,321
11,850	11,900	208	3,305	4,750	5,344	496	3,305	4,750	5,344
11,900	11,950	204	3,305	4,770	5,366	496	3,305	4,770	5,366
11,950	12,000	200	3,305	4,790	5,389	496	3,305	4,790	5,389
12,000	12,050	196	3,305	4,810	5,411	496	3,305	4,810	5,411
12,050	12,100	192	3,305	4,830	5,434	496	3,305	4,830	5,434
12,100	12,150	189	3,305	4,850	5,456	496	3,305	4,850	5,456
12,150	12,200	185	3,305	4,870	5,479	496	3,305	4,870	5,479
12,200	12,250	181	3,305	4,890	5,501	496	3,305	4,890	5,501
12,250	12,300	177	3,305	4,910	5,524	496	3,305	4,910	5,524
12,300	12,350	173	3,305	4,930	5,546	496	3,305	4,930	5,546
12,350	12,400	169	3,305	4,950	5,569	496	3,305	4,950	5,569
12,400	12,450	166	3,305	4,970	5,591	496	3,305	4,970	5,591
12,450	12,500	162	3,305	4,990	5,614	496	3,305	4,990	5,614
12,500	12,550	158	3,305	5,010	5,636	496	3,305	5,010	5,636
12,550	12,600	154	3,305	5,030	5,659	496	3,305	5,030	5,659
12,600	12,650	150	3,305	5,050	5,681	496	3,305	5,050	5,681
12,650	12,700	146	3,305	5,070	5,704	496	3,305	5,070	5,704
12,700	12,750	143	3,305	5,090	5,726	496	3,305	5,090	5,726
12,750	12,800	139	3,305	5,110	5,749	496	3,305	5,110	5,749

(Continued)

DRAFT AS OF October 8 2014

Earned Income Credit (EIC) Table - *Continued*

(Caution. This is **not** a tax table.)

If the amount you are looking up from the worksheet is–		And your filing status is– Single, head of household, or qualifying widow(er) and the number of children you have is–				Married filing jointly and the number of children you have is–			
		0	1	2	3	0	1	2	3
At least	But less than	Your credit is–				Your credit is–			
12,800	12,850	135	3,305	5,130	5,771	496	3,305	5,130	5,771
12,850	12,900	131	3,305	5,150	5,794	496	3,305	5,150	5,794
12,900	12,950	127	3,305	5,170	5,816	496	3,305	5,170	5,816
12,950	13,000	124	3,305	5,190	5,839	496	3,305	5,190	5,839
13,000	13,050	120	3,305	5,210	5,861	496	3,305	5,210	5,861
13,050	13,100	116	3,305	5,230	5,884	496	3,305	5,230	5,884
13,100	13,150	112	3,305	5,250	5,906	496	3,305	5,250	5,906
13,150	13,200	108	3,305	5,270	5,929	496	3,305	5,270	5,929
13,200	13,250	104	3,305	5,290	5,951	496	3,305	5,290	5,951
13,250	13,300	101	3,305	5,310	5,974	496	3,305	5,310	5,974
13,300	13,350	97	3,305	5,330	5,996	496	3,305	5,330	5,996
13,350	13,400	93	3,305	5,350	6,019	496	3,305	5,350	6,019
13,400	13,450	89	3,305	5,370	6,041	496	3,305	5,370	6,041
13,450	13,500	85	3,305	5,390	6,064	496	3,305	5,390	6,064
13,500	13,550	81	3,305	5,410	6,086	496	3,305	5,410	6,086
13,550	13,600	78	3,305	5,430	6,109	493	3,305	5,430	6,109
13,600	13,650	74	3,305	5,450	6,131	489	3,305	5,450	6,131
13,650	13,700	70	3,305	5,460	6,143	485	3,305	5,460	6,143
13,700	13,750	66	3,305	5,460	6,143	482	3,305	5,460	6,143
13,750	13,800	62	3,305	5,460	6,143	478	3,305	5,460	6,143
13,800	13,850	59	3,305	5,460	6,143	474	3,305	5,460	6,143
13,850	13,900	55	3,305	5,460	6,143	470	3,305	5,460	6,143
13,900	13,950	51	3,305	5,460	6,143	466	3,305	5,460	6,143
13,950	14,000	47	3,305	5,460	6,143	462	3,305	5,460	6,143
14,000	14,050	43	3,305	5,460	6,143	459	3,305	5,460	6,143
14,050	14,100	39	3,305	5,460	6,143	455	3,305	5,460	6,143
14,100	14,150	36	3,305	5,460	6,143	451	3,305	5,460	6,143
14,150	14,200	32	3,305	5,460	6,143	447	3,305	5,460	6,143
14,200	14,250	28	3,305	5,460	6,143	443	3,305	5,460	6,143
14,250	14,300	24	3,305	5,460	6,143	439	3,305	5,460	6,143
14,300	14,350	20	3,305	5,460	6,143	436	3,305	5,460	6,143
14,350	14,400	16	3,305	5,460	6,143	432	3,305	5,460	6,143
14,400	14,450	13	3,305	5,460	6,143	428	3,305	5,460	6,143
14,450	14,500	9	3,305	5,460	6,143	424	3,305	5,460	6,143
14,500	14,550	5	3,305	5,460	6,143	420	3,305	5,460	6,143
14,550	14,600	*	3,305	5,460	6,143	417	3,305	5,460	6,143
14,600	14,650	0	3,305	5,460	6,143	413	3,305	5,460	6,143
14,650	14,700	0	3,305	5,460	6,143	409	3,305	5,460	6,143
14,700	14,750	0	3,305	5,460	6,143	405	3,305	5,460	6,143
14,750	14,800	0	3,305	5,460	6,143	401	3,305	5,460	6,143
14,800	14,850	0	3,305	5,460	6,143	397	3,305	5,460	6,143
14,850	14,900	0	3,305	5,460	6,143	394	3,305	5,460	6,143
14,900	14,950	0	3,305	5,460	6,143	390	3,305	5,460	6,143
14,950	15,000	0	3,305	5,460	6,143	386	3,305	5,460	6,143
15,000	15,050	0	3,305	5,460	6,143	382	3,305	5,460	6,143
15,050	15,100	0	3,305	5,460	6,143	378	3,305	5,460	6,143
15,100	15,150	0	3,305	5,460	6,143	374	3,305	5,460	6,143
15,150	15,200	0	3,305	5,460	6,143	371	3,305	5,460	6,143
15,200	15,250	0	3,305	5,460	6,143	367	3,305	5,460	6,143
15,250	15,300	0	3,305	5,460	6,143	363	3,305	5,460	6,143
15,300	15,350	0	3,305	5,460	6,143	359	3,305	5,460	6,143
15,350	15,400	0	3,305	5,460	6,143	355	3,305	5,460	6,143
15,400	15,450	0	3,305	5,460	6,143	352	3,305	5,460	6,143
15,450	15,500	0	3,305	5,460	6,143	348	3,305	5,460	6,143
15,500	15,550	0	3,305	5,460	6,143	344	3,305	5,460	6,143
15,550	15,600	0	3,305	5,460	6,143	340	3,305	5,460	6,143
15,600	15,650	0	3,305	5,460	6,143	336	3,305	5,460	6,143
15,650	15,700	0	3,305	5,460	6,143	332	3,305	5,460	6,143
15,700	15,750	0	3,305	5,460	6,143	329	3,305	5,460	6,143
15,750	15,800	0	3,305	5,460	6,143	325	3,305	5,460	6,143
15,800	15,850	0	3,305	5,460	6,143	321	3,305	5,460	6,143
15,850	15,900	0	3,305	5,460	6,143	317	3,305	5,460	6,143
15,900	15,950	0	3,305	5,460	6,143	313	3,305	5,460	6,143
15,950	16,000	0	3,305	5,460	6,143	309	3,305	5,460	6,143

If the amount you are looking up from the worksheet is–		And your filing status is– Single, head of household, or qualifying widow(er) and the number of children you have is–				Married filing jointly and the number of children you have is–			
		0	1	2	3	0	1	2	3
At least	But less than	Your credit is–				Your credit is–			
16,000	16,050	0	3,305	5,460	6,143	306	3,305	5,460	6,143
16,050	16,100	0	3,305	5,460	6,143	302	3,305	5,460	6,143
16,100	16,150	0	3,305	5,460	6,143	298	3,305	5,460	6,143
16,150	16,200	0	3,305	5,460	6,143	294	3,305	5,460	6,143
16,200	16,250	0	3,305	5,460	6,143	290	3,305	5,460	6,143
16,250	16,300	0	3,305	5,460	6,143	286	3,305	5,460	6,143
16,300	16,350	0	3,305	5,460	6,143	283	3,305	5,460	6,143
16,350	16,400	0	3,305	5,460	6,143	279	3,305	5,460	6,143
16,400	16,450	0	3,305	5,460	6,143	275	3,305	5,460	6,143
16,450	16,500	0	3,305	5,460	6,143	271	3,305	5,460	6,143
16,500	16,550	0	3,305	5,460	6,143	267	3,305	5,460	6,143
16,550	16,600	0	3,305	5,460	6,143	264	3,305	5,460	6,143
16,600	16,650	0	3,305	5,460	6,143	260	3,305	5,460	6,143
16,650	16,700	0	3,305	5,460	6,143	256	3,305	5,460	6,143
16,700	16,750	0	3,305	5,460	6,143	252	3,305	5,460	6,143
16,750	16,800	0	3,305	5,460	6,143	248	3,305	5,460	6,143
16,800	16,850	0	3,305	5,460	6,143	244	3,305	5,460	6,143
16,850	16,900	0	3,305	5,460	6,143	241	3,305	5,460	6,143
16,900	16,950	0	3,305	5,460	6,143	237	3,305	5,460	6,143
16,950	17,000	0	3,305	5,460	6,143	233	3,305	5,460	6,143
17,000	17,050	0	3,305	5,460	6,143	229	3,305	5,460	6,143
17,050	17,100	0	3,305	5,460	6,143	225	3,305	5,460	6,143
17,100	17,150	0	3,305	5,460	6,143	221	3,305	5,460	6,143
17,150	17,200	0	3,305	5,460	6,143	218	3,305	5,460	6,143
17,200	17,250	0	3,305	5,460	6,143	214	3,305	5,460	6,143
17,250	17,300	0	3,305	5,460	6,143	210	3,305	5,460	6,143
17,300	17,350	0	3,305	5,460	6,143	206	3,305	5,460	6,143
17,350	17,400	0	3,305	5,460	6,143	202	3,305	5,460	6,143
17,400	17,450	0	3,305	5,460	6,143	199	3,305	5,460	6,143
17,450	17,500	0	3,305	5,460	6,143	195	3,305	5,460	6,143
17,500	17,550	0	3,305	5,460	6,143	191	3,305	5,460	6,143
17,550	17,600	0	3,305	5,460	6,143	187	3,305	5,460	6,143
17,600	17,650	0	3,305	5,460	6,143	183	3,305	5,460	6,143
17,650	17,700	0	3,305	5,460	6,143	179	3,305	5,460	6,143
17,700	17,750	0	3,305	5,460	6,143	176	3,305	5,460	6,143
17,750	17,800	0	3,305	5,460	6,143	172	3,305	5,460	6,143
17,800	17,850	0	3,305	5,460	6,143	168	3,305	5,460	6,143
17,850	17,900	0	3,298	5,451	6,133	164	3,305	5,460	6,143
17,900	17,950	0	3,290	5,440	6,122	160	3,305	5,460	6,143
17,950	18,000	0	3,282	5,429	6,112	156	3,305	5,460	6,143
18,000	18,050	0	3,274	5,419	6,101	153	3,305	5,460	6,143
18,050	18,100	0	3,266	5,408	6,091	149	3,305	5,460	6,143
18,100	18,150	0	3,258	5,398	6,080	145	3,305	5,460	6,143
18,150	18,200	0	3,250	5,387	6,070	141	3,305	5,460	6,143
18,200	18,250	0	3,242	5,377	6,059	137	3,305	5,460	6,143
18,250	18,300	0	3,234	5,366	6,049	133	3,305	5,460	6,143
18,300	18,350	0	3,226	5,356	6,038	130	3,305	5,460	6,143
18,350	18,400	0	3,218	5,345	6,028	126	3,305	5,460	6,143
18,400	18,450	0	3,210	5,335	6,017	122	3,305	5,460	6,143
18,450	18,500	0	3,202	5,324	6,007	118	3,305	5,460	6,143
18,500	18,550	0	3,194	5,314	5,996	114	3,305	5,460	6,143
18,550	18,600	0	3,186	5,303	5,986	111	3,305	5,460	6,143
18,600	18,650	0	3,178	5,293	5,975	107	3,305	5,460	6,143
18,650	18,700	0	3,170	5,282	5,965	103	3,305	5,460	6,143
18,700	18,750	0	3,162	5,272	5,954	99	3,305	5,460	6,143
18,750	18,800	0	3,154	5,261	5,943	95	3,305	5,460	6,143
18,800	18,850	0	3,146	5,250	5,933	91	3,305	5,460	6,143
18,850	18,900	0	3,138	5,240	5,922	88	3,305	5,460	6,143
18,900	18,950	0	3,130	5,229	5,912	84	3,305	5,460	6,143
18,950	19,000	0	3,122	5,219	5,901	80	3,305	5,460	6,143
19,000	19,050	0	3,114	5,208	5,891	76	3,305	5,460	6,143
19,050	19,100	0	3,106	5,198	5,880	72	3,305	5,460	6,143
19,100	19,150	0	3,098	5,187	5,870	68	3,305	5,460	6,143
19,150	19,200	0	3,090	5,177	5,859	65	3,305	5,460	6,143

* If the amount you are looking up from the worksheet is at least $14,550 but less than $14,590, and you have no qualifying children, your credit is $2. If the amount you are looking up from the worksheet is $14,590 or more, and you have no qualifying children, you cannot take the credit.

(Continued)

Earned Income Credit (EIC) Table - *Continued*

(**Caution.** This is **not** a tax table.)

If the amount you are looking up from the worksheet is–		And your filing status is– Single, head of household, or qualifying widow(er) and the number of children you have is–				Married filing jointly and the number of children you have is–			
At least	But less than	0	1	2	3	0	1	2	3
		Your credit is–				Your credit is–			
19,200	19,250	0	3,082	5,166	5,849	61	3,305	5,460	6,143
19,250	19,300	0	3,074	5,156	5,838	57	3,305	5,460	6,143
19,300	19,350	0	3,066	5,145	5,828	53	3,305	5,460	6,143
19,350	19,400	0	3,058	5,135	5,817	49	3,305	5,460	6,143
19,400	19,450	0	3,050	5,124	5,807	46	3,305	5,460	6,143
19,450	19,500	0	3,042	5,114	5,796	42	3,305	5,460	6,143
19,500	19,550	0	3,034	5,103	5,786	38	3,305	5,460	6,143
19,550	19,600	0	3,026	5,093	5,775	34	3,305	5,460	6,143
19,600	19,650	0	3,018	5,082	5,764	30	3,305	5,460	6,143
19,650	19,700	0	3,010	5,071	5,754	26	3,305	5,460	6,143
19,700	19,750	0	3,002	5,061	5,743	23	3,305	5,460	6,143
19,750	19,800	0	2,994	5,050	5,733	19	3,305	5,460	6,143
19,800	19,850	0	2,986	5,040	5,722	15	3,305	5,460	6,143
19,850	19,900	0	2,978	5,029	5,712	11	3,305	5,460	6,143
19,900	19,950	0	2,970	5,019	5,701	7	3,305	5,460	6,143
19,950	20,000	0	2,962	5,008	5,691	3	3,305	5,460	6,143
20,000	20,050	0	2,954	4,998	5,680	*	3,305	5,460	6,143
20,050	20,100	0	2,946	4,987	5,670	0	3,305	5,460	6,143
20,100	20,150	0	2,938	4,977	5,659	0	3,305	5,460	6,143
20,150	20,200	0	2,930	4,966	5,649	0	3,305	5,460	6,143
20,200	20,250	0	2,922	4,956	5,638	0	3,305	5,460	6,143
20,250	20,300	0	2,914	4,945	5,628	0	3,305	5,460	6,143
20,300	20,350	0	2,906	4,935	5,617	0	3,305	5,460	6,143
20,350	20,400	0	2,898	4,924	5,607	0	3,305	5,460	6,143
20,400	20,450	0	2,890	4,913	5,596	0	3,305	5,460	6,143
20,450	20,500	0	2,882	4,903	5,585	0	3,305	5,460	6,143
20,500	20,550	0	2,874	4,892	5,575	0	3,305	5,460	6,143
20,550	20,600	0	2,866	4,882	5,564	0	3,305	5,460	6,143
20,600	20,650	0	2,858	4,871	5,554	0	3,305	5,460	6,143
20,650	20,700	0	2,850	4,861	5,543	0	3,305	5,460	6,143
20,700	20,750	0	2,842	4,850	5,533	0	3,305	5,460	6,143
20,750	20,800	0	2,834	4,840	5,522	0	3,305	5,460	6,143
20,800	20,850	0	2,826	4,829	5,512	0	3,305	5,460	6,143
20,850	20,900	0	2,818	4,819	5,501	0	3,305	5,460	6,143
20,900	20,950	0	2,810	4,808	5,491	0	3,305	5,460	6,143
20,950	21,000	0	2,802	4,798	5,480	0	3,305	5,460	6,143
21,000	21,050	0	2,794	4,787	5,470	0	3,305	5,460	6,143
21,050	21,100	0	2,786	4,777	5,459	0	3,305	5,460	6,143
21,100	21,150	0	2,778	4,766	5,449	0	3,305	5,460	6,143
21,150	21,200	0	2,770	4,756	5,438	0	3,305	5,460	6,143
21,200	21,250	0	2,762	4,745	5,428	0	3,305	5,460	6,143
21,250	21,300	0	2,754	4,734	5,417	0	3,305	5,460	6,143
21,300	21,350	0	2,746	4,724	5,406	0	3,305	5,460	6,143
21,350	21,400	0	2,738	4,713	5,396	0	3,305	5,460	6,143
21,400	21,450	0	2,730	4,703	5,385	0	3,305	5,460	6,143
21,450	21,500	0	2,722	4,692	5,375	0	3,305	5,460	6,143
21,500	21,550	0	2,714	4,682	5,364	0	3,305	5,460	6,143
21,550	21,600	0	2,706	4,671	5,354	0	3,305	5,460	6,143
21,600	21,650	0	2,698	4,661	5,343	0	3,305	5,460	6,143
21,650	21,700	0	2,690	4,650	5,333	0	3,305	5,460	6,143
21,700	21,750	0	2,682	4,640	5,322	0	3,305	5,460	6,143
21,750	21,800	0	2,674	4,629	5,312	0	3,305	5,460	6,143
21,800	21,850	0	2,666	4,619	5,301	0	3,305	5,460	6,143
21,850	21,900	0	2,658	4,608	5,291	0	3,305	5,460	6,143
21,900	21,950	0	2,650	4,598	5,280	0	3,305	5,460	6,143
21,950	22,000	0	2,642	4,587	5,270	0	3,305	5,460	6,143
22,000	22,050	0	2,634	4,577	5,259	0	3,305	5,460	6,143
22,050	22,100	0	2,626	4,566	5,249	0	3,305	5,460	6,143
22,100	22,150	0	2,618	4,555	5,238	0	3,305	5,460	6,143
22,150	22,200	0	2,610	4,545	5,227	0	3,305	5,460	6,143
22,200	22,250	0	2,602	4,534	5,217	0	3,305	5,460	6,143
22,250	22,300	0	2,594	4,524	5,206	0	3,305	5,460	6,143
22,300	22,350	0	2,586	4,513	5,196	0	3,305	5,460	6,143
22,350	22,400	0	2,579	4,503	5,185	0	3,305	5,460	6,143

If the amount you are looking up from the worksheet is–		And your filing status is– Single, head of household, or qualifying widow(er) and the number of children you have is–				Married filing jointly and the number of children you have is–			
At least	But less than	0	1	2	3	0	1	2	3
		Your credit is–				Your credit is–			
22,400	22,450	0	2,571	4,492	5,175	0	3,305	5,460	6,143
22,450	22,500	0	2,563	4,482	5,164	0	3,305	5,460	6,143
22,500	22,550	0	2,555	4,471	5,154	0	3,305	5,460	6,143
22,550	22,600	0	2,547	4,461	5,143	0	3,305	5,460	6,143
22,600	22,650	0	2,539	4,450	5,133	0	3,305	5,460	6,143
22,650	22,700	0	2,531	4,440	5,122	0	3,305	5,460	6,143
22,700	22,750	0	2,523	4,429	5,112	0	3,305	5,460	6,143
22,750	22,800	0	2,515	4,419	5,101	0	3,305	5,460	6,143
22,800	22,850	0	2,507	4,408	5,091	0	3,305	5,460	6,143
22,850	22,900	0	2,499	4,398	5,080	0	3,305	5,460	6,143
22,900	22,950	0	2,491	4,387	5,069	0	3,305	5,460	6,143
22,950	23,000	0	2,483	4,376	5,059	0	3,305	5,460	6,143
23,000	23,050	0	2,475	4,366	5,048	0	3,305	5,460	6,143
23,050	23,100	0	2,467	4,355	5,038	0	3,305	5,460	6,143
23,100	23,150	0	2,459	4,345	5,027	0	3,305	5,460	6,143
23,150	23,200	0	2,451	4,334	5,017	0	3,305	5,460	6,143
23,200	23,250	0	2,443	4,324	5,006	0	3,305	5,460	6,143
23,250	23,300	0	2,435	4,313	4,996	0	3,305	5,460	6,143
23,300	23,350	0	2,427	4,303	4,985	0	3,294	5,446	6,129
23,350	23,400	0	2,419	4,292	4,975	0	3,286	5,436	6,118
23,400	23,450	0	2,411	4,282	4,964	0	3,278	5,425	6,108
23,450	23,500	0	2,403	4,271	4,954	0	3,270	5,415	6,097
23,500	23,550	0	2,395	4,261	4,943	0	3,262	5,404	6,087
23,550	23,600	0	2,387	4,250	4,933	0	3,254	5,394	6,076
23,600	23,650	0	2,379	4,240	4,922	0	3,246	5,383	6,066
23,650	23,700	0	2,371	4,229	4,912	0	3,238	5,373	6,055
23,700	23,750	0	2,363	4,219	4,901	0	3,230	5,362	6,045
23,750	23,800	0	2,355	4,208	4,890	0	3,223	5,352	6,034
23,800	23,850	0	2,347	4,197	4,880	0	3,215	5,341	6,024
23,850	23,900	0	2,339	4,187	4,869	0	3,207	5,330	6,013
23,900	23,950	0	2,331	4,176	4,859	0	3,199	5,320	6,002
23,950	24,000	0	2,323	4,166	4,848	0	3,191	5,309	5,992
24,000	24,050	0	2,315	4,155	4,838	0	3,183	5,299	5,981
24,050	24,100	0	2,307	4,145	4,827	0	3,175	5,288	5,971
24,100	24,150	0	2,299	4,134	4,817	0	3,167	5,278	5,960
24,150	24,200	0	2,291	4,124	4,806	0	3,159	5,267	5,950
24,200	24,250	0	2,283	4,113	4,796	0	3,151	5,257	5,939
24,250	24,300	0	2,275	4,103	4,785	0	3,143	5,246	5,929
24,300	24,350	0	2,267	4,092	4,775	0	3,135	5,236	5,918
24,350	24,400	0	2,259	4,082	4,764	0	3,127	5,225	5,908
24,400	24,450	0	2,251	4,071	4,754	0	3,119	5,215	5,897
24,450	24,500	0	2,243	4,061	4,743	0	3,111	5,204	5,887
24,500	24,550	0	2,235	4,050	4,733	0	3,103	5,194	5,876
24,550	24,600	0	2,227	4,040	4,722	0	3,095	5,183	5,866
24,600	24,650	0	2,219	4,029	4,711	0	3,087	5,173	5,855
24,650	24,700	0	2,211	4,018	4,701	0	3,079	5,162	5,845
24,700	24,750	0	2,203	4,008	4,690	0	3,071	5,151	5,834
24,750	24,800	0	2,195	3,997	4,680	0	3,063	5,141	5,823
24,800	24,850	0	2,187	3,987	4,669	0	3,055	5,130	5,813
24,850	24,900	0	2,179	3,976	4,659	0	3,047	5,120	5,802
24,900	24,950	0	2,171	3,966	4,648	0	3,039	5,109	5,792
24,950	25,000	0	2,163	3,955	4,638	0	3,031	5,099	5,781
25,000	25,050	0	2,155	3,945	4,627	0	3,023	5,088	5,771
25,050	25,100	0	2,147	3,934	4,617	0	3,015	5,078	5,760
25,100	25,150	0	2,139	3,924	4,606	0	3,007	5,067	5,750
25,150	25,200	0	2,131	3,913	4,596	0	2,999	5,057	5,739
25,200	25,250	0	2,123	3,903	4,585	0	2,991	5,046	5,729
25,250	25,300	0	2,115	3,892	4,575	0	2,983	5,036	5,718
25,300	25,350	0	2,107	3,882	4,564	0	2,975	5,025	5,708
25,350	25,400	0	2,099	3,871	4,554	0	2,967	5,015	5,697
25,400	25,450	0	2,091	3,860	4,543	0	2,959	5,004	5,687
25,450	25,500	0	2,083	3,850	4,532	0	2,951	4,994	5,676
25,500	25,550	0	2,075	3,839	4,522	0	2,943	4,983	5,665
25,550	25,600	0	2,067	3,829	4,511	0	2,935	4,972	5,655

DRAFT AS OF October 6, 2014

* If the amount you are looking up from the worksheet is at least $20,000 but less than $20,020, and you have no qualifying children, your credit is $1. If the amount you are looking up from the worksheet is $20,020 or more, and you have no qualifying children, you cannot take the credit.

(Continued)

DRAFT AS OF October 8, 2014

Earned Income Credit (EIC) Table - *Continued* (**Caution.** This is **not** a tax table.)

If the amount you are looking up from the worksheet is–		And your filing status is– Single, head of household, or qualifying widow(er) and the number of children you have is–				Married filing jointly and the number of children you have is–			
		0	1	2	3	0	1	2	3
At least	But less than	Your credit is–				Your credit is–			
25,600	25,650	0	2,059	3,818	4,501	0	2,927	4,962	5,644
25,650	25,700	0	2,051	3,808	4,490	0	2,919	4,951	5,634
25,700	25,750	0	2,043	3,797	4,480	0	2,911	4,941	5,623
25,750	25,800	0	2,035	3,787	4,469	0	2,903	4,930	5,613
25,800	25,850	0	2,027	3,776	4,459	0	2,895	4,920	5,602
25,850	25,900	0	2,019	3,766	4,448	0	2,887	4,909	5,592
25,900	25,950	0	2,011	3,755	4,438	0	2,879	4,899	5,581
25,950	26,000	0	2,003	3,745	4,427	0	2,871	4,888	5,571
26,000	26,050	0	1,995	3,734	4,417	0	2,863	4,878	5,560
26,050	26,100	0	1,987	3,724	4,406	0	2,855	4,867	5,550
26,100	26,150	0	1,979	3,713	4,396	0	2,847	4,857	5,539
26,150	26,200	0	1,971	3,703	4,385	0	2,839	4,846	5,529
26,200	26,250	0	1,963	3,692	4,375	0	2,831	4,836	5,518
26,250	26,300	0	1,955	3,681	4,364	0	2,823	4,825	5,508
26,300	26,350	0	1,947	3,671	4,353	0	2,815	4,815	5,497
26,350	26,400	0	1,939	3,660	4,343	0	2,807	4,804	5,486
26,400	26,450	0	1,931	3,650	4,332	0	2,799	4,793	5,476
26,450	26,500	0	1,923	3,639	4,322	0	2,791	4,783	5,465
26,500	26,550	0	1,915	3,629	4,311	0	2,783	4,772	5,455
26,550	26,600	0	1,907	3,618	4,301	0	2,775	4,762	5,444
26,600	26,650	0	1,899	3,608	4,290	0	2,767	4,751	5,434
26,650	26,700	0	1,891	3,597	4,280	0	2,759	4,741	5,423
26,700	26,750	0	1,883	3,587	4,269	0	2,751	4,730	5,413
26,750	26,800	0	1,875	3,576	4,259	0	2,743	4,720	5,402
26,800	26,850	0	1,867	3,566	4,248	0	2,735	4,709	5,392
26,850	26,900	0	1,859	3,555	4,238	0	2,727	4,699	5,381
26,900	26,950	0	1,851	3,545	4,227	0	2,719	4,688	5,371
26,950	27,000	0	1,843	3,534	4,217	0	2,711	4,678	5,360
27,000	27,050	0	1,835	3,524	4,206	0	2,703	4,667	5,350
27,050	27,100	0	1,827	3,513	4,196	0	2,695	4,657	5,339
27,100	27,150	0	1,819	3,502	4,185	0	2,687	4,646	5,329
27,150	27,200	0	1,811	3,492	4,174	0	2,679	4,636	5,318
27,200	27,250	0	1,803	3,481	4,164	0	2,671	4,625	5,307
27,250	27,300	0	1,795	3,471	4,153	0	2,663	4,614	5,297
27,300	27,350	0	1,787	3,460	4,143	0	2,655	4,604	5,286
27,350	27,400	0	1,780	3,450	4,132	0	2,647	4,593	5,276
27,400	27,450	0	1,772	3,439	4,122	0	2,639	4,583	5,265
27,450	27,500	0	1,764	3,429	4,111	0	2,631	4,572	5,255
27,500	27,550	0	1,756	3,418	4,101	0	2,623	4,562	5,244
27,550	27,600	0	1,748	3,408	4,090	0	2,615	4,551	5,234
27,600	27,650	0	1,740	3,397	4,080	0	2,607	4,541	5,223
27,650	27,700	0	1,732	3,387	4,069	0	2,599	4,530	5,213
27,700	27,750	0	1,724	3,376	4,059	0	2,591	4,520	5,202
27,750	27,800	0	1,716	3,366	4,048	0	2,583	4,509	5,192
27,800	27,850	0	1,708	3,355	4,038	0	2,575	4,499	5,181
27,850	27,900	0	1,700	3,345	4,027	0	2,567	4,488	5,171
27,900	27,950	0	1,692	3,334	4,016	0	2,559	4,478	5,160
27,950	28,000	0	1,684	3,323	4,006	0	2,551	4,467	5,150
28,000	28,050	0	1,676	3,313	3,995	0	2,543	4,456	5,139
28,050	28,100	0	1,668	3,302	3,985	0	2,535	4,446	5,128
28,100	28,150	0	1,660	3,292	3,974	0	2,527	4,435	5,118
28,150	28,200	0	1,652	3,281	3,964	0	2,519	4,425	5,107
28,200	28,250	0	1,644	3,271	3,953	0	2,511	4,414	5,097
28,250	28,300	0	1,636	3,260	3,943	0	2,503	4,404	5,086
28,300	28,350	0	1,628	3,250	3,932	0	2,495	4,393	5,076
28,350	28,400	0	1,620	3,239	3,922	0	2,487	4,383	5,065
28,400	28,450	0	1,612	3,229	3,911	0	2,479	4,372	5,055
28,450	28,500	0	1,604	3,218	3,901	0	2,471	4,362	5,044
28,500	28,550	0	1,596	3,208	3,890	0	2,463	4,351	5,034
28,550	28,600	0	1,588	3,197	3,880	0	2,455	4,341	5,023
28,600	28,650	0	1,580	3,187	3,869	0	2,447	4,330	5,013
28,650	28,700	0	1,572	3,176	3,859	0	2,439	4,320	5,002
28,700	28,750	0	1,564	3,166	3,848	0	2,431	4,309	4,992
28,750	28,800	0	1,556	3,155	3,837	0	2,424	4,299	4,981
28,800	28,850	0	1,548	3,144	3,827	0	2,416	4,288	4,971
28,850	28,900	0	1,540	3,134	3,816	0	2,408	4,277	4,960
28,900	28,950	0	1,532	3,123	3,806	0	2,400	4,267	4,949
28,950	29,000	0	1,524	3,113	3,795	0	2,392	4,256	4,939
29,000	29,050	0	1,516	3,102	3,785	0	2,384	4,246	4,928
29,050	29,100	0	1,508	3,092	3,774	0	2,376	4,235	4,918
29,100	29,150	0	1,500	3,081	3,764	0	2,368	4,225	4,907
29,150	29,200	0	1,492	3,071	3,753	0	2,360	4,214	4,897

If the amount you are looking up from the worksheet is–		And your filing status is– Single, head of household, or qualifying widow(er) and the number of children you have is–				Married filing jointly and the number of children you have is–			
		0	1	2	3	0	1	2	3
At least	But less than	Your credit is–				Your credit is–			
29,200	29,250	0	1,484	3,060	3,743	0	2,352	4,204	4,886
29,250	29,300	0	1,476	3,050	3,732	0	2,344	4,193	4,876
29,300	29,350	0	1,468	3,039	3,722	0	2,336	4,183	4,865
29,350	29,400	0	1,460	3,029	3,711	0	2,328	4,172	4,855
29,400	29,450	0	1,452	3,018	3,701	0	2,320	4,162	4,844
29,450	29,500	0	1,444	3,008	3,690	0	2,312	4,151	4,834
29,500	29,550	0	1,436	2,997	3,680	0	2,304	4,141	4,823
29,550	29,600	0	1,428	2,987	3,669	0	2,296	4,130	4,813
29,600	29,650	0	1,420	2,976	3,658	0	2,288	4,120	4,802
29,650	29,700	0	1,412	2,965	3,648	0	2,280	4,109	4,792
29,700	29,750	0	1,404	2,955	3,637	0	2,272	4,098	4,781
29,750	29,800	0	1,396	2,944	3,627	0	2,264	4,088	4,770
29,800	29,850	0	1,388	2,934	3,616	0	2,256	4,077	4,760
29,850	29,900	0	1,380	2,923	3,606	0	2,248	4,067	4,749
29,900	29,950	0	1,372	2,913	3,595	0	2,240	4,056	4,739
29,950	30,000	0	1,364	2,902	3,585	0	2,232	4,046	4,728
30,000	30,050	0	1,356	2,892	3,574	0	2,224	4,035	4,718
30,050	30,100	0	1,348	2,881	3,564	0	2,216	4,025	4,707
30,100	30,150	0	1,340	2,871	3,553	0	2,208	4,014	4,697
30,150	30,200	0	1,332	2,860	3,543	0	2,200	4,004	4,686
30,200	30,250	0	1,324	2,850	3,532	0	2,192	3,993	4,676
30,250	30,300	0	1,316	2,839	3,522	0	2,184	3,983	4,665
30,300	30,350	0	1,308	2,829	3,511	0	2,176	3,972	4,655
30,350	30,400	0	1,300	2,818	3,501	0	2,168	3,962	4,644
30,400	30,450	0	1,292	2,807	3,490	0	2,160	3,951	4,634
30,450	30,500	0	1,284	2,797	3,479	0	2,152	3,941	4,623
30,500	30,550	0	1,276	2,786	3,469	0	2,144	3,930	4,612
30,550	30,600	0	1,268	2,776	3,458	0	2,136	3,919	4,602
30,600	30,650	0	1,260	2,765	3,448	0	2,128	3,909	4,591
30,650	30,700	0	1,252	2,755	3,437	0	2,120	3,898	4,581
30,700	30,750	0	1,244	2,744	3,427	0	2,112	3,888	4,570
30,750	30,800	0	1,236	2,734	3,416	0	2,104	3,877	4,560
30,800	30,850	0	1,228	2,723	3,406	0	2,096	3,867	4,549
30,850	30,900	0	1,220	2,713	3,395	0	2,088	3,856	4,539
30,900	30,950	0	1,212	2,702	3,385	0	2,080	3,846	4,528
30,950	31,000	0	1,204	2,692	3,374	0	2,072	3,835	4,518
31,000	31,050	0	1,196	2,681	3,364	0	2,064	3,825	4,507
31,050	31,100	0	1,188	2,671	3,353	0	2,056	3,814	4,497
31,100	31,150	0	1,180	2,660	3,343	0	2,048	3,804	4,486
31,150	31,200	0	1,172	2,650	3,332	0	2,040	3,793	4,476
31,200	31,250	0	1,164	2,639	3,322	0	2,032	3,783	4,465
31,250	31,300	0	1,156	2,628	3,311	0	2,024	3,772	4,455
31,300	31,350	0	1,148	2,618	3,300	0	2,016	3,762	4,444
31,350	31,400	0	1,140	2,607	3,290	0	2,008	3,751	4,433
31,400	31,450	0	1,132	2,597	3,279	0	2,000	3,740	4,423
31,450	31,500	0	1,124	2,586	3,269	0	1,992	3,730	4,412
31,500	31,550	0	1,116	2,576	3,258	0	1,984	3,719	4,402
31,550	31,600	0	1,108	2,565	3,248	0	1,976	3,709	4,391
31,600	31,650	0	1,100	2,555	3,237	0	1,968	3,698	4,381
31,650	31,700	0	1,092	2,544	3,227	0	1,960	3,688	4,370
31,700	31,750	0	1,084	2,534	3,216	0	1,952	3,677	4,360
31,750	31,800	0	1,076	2,523	3,206	0	1,944	3,667	4,349
31,800	31,850	0	1,068	2,513	3,195	0	1,936	3,656	4,339
31,850	31,900	0	1,060	2,502	3,185	0	1,928	3,646	4,328
31,900	31,950	0	1,052	2,492	3,174	0	1,920	3,635	4,318
31,950	32,000	0	1,044	2,481	3,164	0	1,912	3,625	4,307
32,000	32,050	0	1,036	2,471	3,153	0	1,904	3,614	4,297
32,050	32,100	0	1,028	2,460	3,143	0	1,896	3,604	4,286
32,100	32,150	0	1,020	2,449	3,132	0	1,888	3,593	4,276
32,150	32,200	0	1,012	2,439	3,121	0	1,880	3,583	4,265
32,200	32,250	0	1,004	2,428	3,111	0	1,872	3,572	4,254
32,250	32,300	0	996	2,418	3,100	0	1,864	3,561	4,244
32,300	32,350	0	988	2,407	3,090	0	1,856	3,551	4,233
32,350	32,400	0	981	2,397	3,079	0	1,848	3,540	4,223
32,400	32,450	0	973	2,386	3,069	0	1,840	3,530	4,212
32,450	32,500	0	965	2,376	3,058	0	1,832	3,519	4,202
32,500	32,550	0	957	2,365	3,048	0	1,824	3,509	4,191
32,550	32,600	0	949	2,355	3,037	0	1,816	3,498	4,181
32,600	32,650	0	941	2,344	3,027	0	1,808	3,488	4,170
32,650	32,700	0	933	2,334	3,016	0	1,800	3,477	4,160
32,700	32,750	0	925	2,323	3,006	0	1,792	3,467	4,149
32,750	32,800	0	917	2,313	2,995	0	1,784	3,456	4,139

(Continued)

Earned Income Credit (EIC) Table - *Continued* **(Caution.** This is **not** a tax table.)

If the amount you are looking up from the worksheet is–		And your filing status is– Single, head of household, or qualifying widow(er) and the number of children you have is–				Married filing jointly and the number of children you have is–			
At least	But less than	0	1	2	3	0	1	2	3
		Your credit is–				Your credit is–			
32,800	32,850	0	909	2,302	2,985	0	1,776	3,446	4,128
32,850	32,900	0	901	2,292	2,974	0	1,768	3,435	4,118
32,900	32,950	0	893	2,281	2,963	0	1,760	3,425	4,107
32,950	33,000	0	885	2,270	2,953	0	1,752	3,414	4,097
33,000	33,050	0	877	2,260	2,942	0	1,744	3,403	4,086
33,050	33,100	0	869	2,249	2,932	0	1,736	3,393	4,075
33,100	33,150	0	861	2,239	2,921	0	1,728	3,382	4,065
33,150	33,200	0	853	2,228	2,911	0	1,720	3,372	4,054
33,200	33,250	0	845	2,218	2,900	0	1,712	3,361	4,044
33,250	33,300	0	837	2,207	2,890	0	1,704	3,351	4,033
33,300	33,350	0	829	2,197	2,879	0	1,696	3,340	4,023
33,350	33,400	0	821	2,186	2,869	0	1,688	3,330	4,012
33,400	33,450	0	813	2,176	2,858	0	1,680	3,319	4,002
33,450	33,500	0	805	2,165	2,848	0	1,672	3,309	3,991
33,500	33,550	0	797	2,155	2,837	0	1,664	3,298	3,981
33,550	33,600	0	789	2,144	2,827	0	1,656	3,288	3,970
33,600	33,650	0	781	2,134	2,816	0	1,648	3,277	3,960
33,650	33,700	0	773	2,123	2,806	0	1,640	3,267	3,949
33,700	33,750	0	765	2,113	2,795	0	1,632	3,256	3,939
33,750	33,800	0	757	2,102	2,784	0	1,625	3,246	3,928
33,800	33,850	0	749	2,091	2,774	0	1,617	3,235	3,918
33,850	33,900	0	741	2,081	2,763	0	1,609	3,224	3,907
33,900	33,950	0	733	2,070	2,753	0	1,601	3,214	3,896
33,950	34,000	0	725	2,060	2,742	0	1,593	3,203	3,886
34,000	34,050	0	717	2,049	2,732	0	1,585	3,193	3,875
34,050	34,100	0	709	2,039	2,721	0	1,577	3,182	3,865
34,100	34,150	0	701	2,028	2,711	0	1,569	3,172	3,854
34,150	34,200	0	693	2,018	2,700	0	1,561	3,161	3,844
34,200	34,250	0	685	2,007	2,690	0	1,553	3,151	3,833
34,250	34,300	0	677	1,997	2,679	0	1,545	3,140	3,823
34,300	34,350	0	669	1,986	2,669	0	1,537	3,130	3,812
34,350	34,400	0	661	1,976	2,658	0	1,529	3,119	3,802
34,400	34,450	0	653	1,965	2,648	0	1,521	3,109	3,791
34,450	34,500	0	645	1,955	2,637	0	1,513	3,098	3,781
34,500	34,550	0	637	1,944	2,627	0	1,505	3,088	3,770
34,550	34,600	0	629	1,934	2,616	0	1,497	3,077	3,760
34,600	34,650	0	621	1,923	2,605	0	1,489	3,067	3,749
34,650	34,700	0	613	1,912	2,595	0	1,481	3,056	3,739
34,700	34,750	0	605	1,902	2,584	0	1,473	3,045	3,728
34,750	34,800	0	597	1,891	2,574	0	1,465	3,035	3,717
34,800	34,850	0	589	1,881	2,563	0	1,457	3,024	3,707
34,850	34,900	0	581	1,870	2,553	0	1,449	3,014	3,696
34,900	34,950	0	573	1,860	2,542	0	1,441	3,003	3,686
34,950	35,000	0	565	1,849	2,532	0	1,433	2,993	3,675
35,000	35,050	0	557	1,839	2,521	0	1,425	2,982	3,665
35,050	35,100	0	549	1,828	2,511	0	1,417	2,972	3,654
35,100	35,150	0	541	1,818	2,500	0	1,409	2,961	3,644
35,150	35,200	0	533	1,807	2,490	0	1,401	2,951	3,633
35,200	35,250	0	525	1,797	2,479	0	1,393	2,940	3,623
35,250	35,300	0	517	1,786	2,469	0	1,385	2,930	3,612
35,300	35,350	0	509	1,776	2,458	0	1,377	2,919	3,602
35,350	35,400	0	501	1,765	2,448	0	1,369	2,909	3,591
35,400	35,450	0	493	1,754	2,437	0	1,361	2,898	3,581
35,450	35,500	0	485	1,744	2,426	0	1,353	2,888	3,570
35,500	35,550	0	477	1,733	2,416	0	1,345	2,877	3,559
35,550	35,600	0	469	1,723	2,405	0	1,337	2,866	3,549
35,600	35,650	0	461	1,712	2,395	0	1,329	2,856	3,538
35,650	35,700	0	453	1,702	2,384	0	1,321	2,845	3,528
35,700	35,750	0	445	1,691	2,374	0	1,313	2,835	3,517
35,750	35,800	0	437	1,681	2,363	0	1,305	2,824	3,507
35,800	35,850	0	429	1,670	2,353	0	1,297	2,814	3,496
35,850	35,900	0	421	1,660	2,342	0	1,289	2,803	3,486
35,900	35,950	0	413	1,649	2,332	0	1,281	2,793	3,475
35,950	36,000	0	405	1,639	2,321	0	1,273	2,782	3,465

If the amount you are looking up from the worksheet is–		And your filing status is– Single, head of household, or qualifying widow(er) and the number of children you have is–				Married filing jointly and the number of children you have is–			
At least	But less than	0	1	2	3	0	1	2	3
		Your credit is–				Your credit is–			
36,000	36,050	0	397	1,628	2,311	0	1,265	2,772	3,454
36,050	36,100	0	389	1,618	2,300	0	1,257	2,761	3,444
36,100	36,150	0	381	1,607	2,290	0	1,249	2,751	3,433
36,150	36,200	0	373	1,597	2,279	0	1,241	2,740	3,423
36,200	36,250	0	365	1,586	2,269	0	1,233	2,730	3,412
36,250	36,300	0	357	1,575	2,258	0	1,225	2,719	3,402
36,300	36,350	0	349	1,565	2,247	0	1,217	2,709	3,391
36,350	36,400	0	341	1,554	2,237	0	1,209	2,698	3,380
36,400	36,450	0	333	1,544	2,226	0	1,201	2,687	3,370
36,450	36,500	0	325	1,533	2,216	0	1,193	2,677	3,359
36,500	36,550	0	317	1,523	2,205	0	1,185	2,666	3,349
36,550	36,600	0	309	1,512	2,195	0	1,177	2,656	3,338
36,600	36,650	0	301	1,502	2,184	0	1,169	2,645	3,328
36,650	36,700	0	293	1,491	2,174	0	1,161	2,635	3,317
36,700	36,750	0	285	1,481	2,163	0	1,153	2,624	3,307
36,750	36,800	0	277	1,470	2,153	0	1,145	2,614	3,296
36,800	36,850	0	269	1,460	2,142	0	1,137	2,603	3,286
36,850	36,900	0	261	1,449	2,132	0	1,129	2,593	3,275
36,900	36,950	0	253	1,439	2,121	0	1,121	2,582	3,265
36,950	37,000	0	245	1,428	2,111	0	1,113	2,572	3,254
37,000	37,050	0	237	1,418	2,100	0	1,105	2,561	3,244
37,050	37,100	0	229	1,407	2,090	0	1,097	2,551	3,233
37,100	37,150	0	221	1,396	2,079	0	1,089	2,540	3,223
37,150	37,200	0	213	1,386	2,068	0	1,081	2,530	3,212
37,200	37,250	0	205	1,375	2,058	0	1,073	2,519	3,201
37,250	37,300	0	197	1,365	2,047	0	1,065	2,508	3,191
37,300	37,350	0	189	1,354	2,037	0	1,057	2,498	3,180
37,350	37,400	0	182	1,344	2,026	0	1,049	2,487	3,170
37,400	37,450	0	174	1,333	2,016	0	1,041	2,477	3,159
37,450	37,500	0	166	1,323	2,005	0	1,033	2,466	3,149
37,500	37,550	0	158	1,312	1,995	0	1,025	2,456	3,138
37,550	37,600	0	150	1,302	1,984	0	1,017	2,445	3,128
37,600	37,650	0	142	1,291	1,974	0	1,009	2,435	3,117
37,650	37,700	0	134	1,281	1,963	0	1,001	2,424	3,107
37,700	37,750	0	126	1,270	1,953	0	993	2,414	3,096
37,750	37,800	0	118	1,260	1,942	0	985	2,403	3,086
37,800	37,850	0	110	1,249	1,932	0	977	2,393	3,075
37,850	37,900	0	102	1,239	1,921	0	969	2,382	3,065
37,900	37,950	0	94	1,228	1,910	0	961	2,372	3,054
37,950	38,000	0	86	1,217	1,900	0	953	2,361	3,044
38,000	38,050	0	78	1,207	1,889	0	945	2,350	3,033
38,050	38,100	0	70	1,196	1,879	0	937	2,340	3,022
38,100	38,150	0	62	1,186	1,868	0	929	2,329	3,012
38,150	38,200	0	54	1,175	1,858	0	921	2,319	3,001
38,200	38,250	0	46	1,165	1,847	0	913	2,308	2,991
38,250	38,300	0	38	1,154	1,837	0	905	2,298	2,980
38,300	38,350	0	30	1,144	1,826	0	897	2,287	2,970
38,350	38,400	0	22	1,133	1,816	0	889	2,277	2,959
38,400	38,450	0	14	1,123	1,805	0	881	2,266	2,949
38,450	38,500	0	6	1,112	1,795	0	873	2,256	2,938
38,500	38,550	0	*	1,102	1,784	0	865	2,245	2,928
38,550	38,600	0	0	1,091	1,774	0	857	2,235	2,917
38,600	38,650	0	0	1,081	1,763	0	849	2,224	2,907
38,650	38,700	0	0	1,070	1,753	0	841	2,214	2,896
38,700	38,750	0	0	1,060	1,742	0	833	2,203	2,886
38,750	38,800	0	0	1,049	1,731	0	826	2,193	2,875
38,800	38,850	0	0	1,038	1,721	0	818	2,182	2,865
38,850	38,900	0	0	1,028	1,710	0	810	2,171	2,854
38,900	38,950	0	0	1,017	1,700	0	802	2,161	2,843
38,950	39,000	0	0	1,007	1,689	0	794	2,150	2,833
39,000	39,050	0	0	996	1,679	0	786	2,140	2,822
39,050	39,100	0	0	986	1,668	0	778	2,129	2,812
39,100	39,150	0	0	975	1,658	0	770	2,119	2,801
39,150	39,200	0	0	965	1,647	0	762	2,108	2,791

* If the amount you are looking up from the worksheet is at least $38,500 but less than $38,511, and you have one qualifying child, your credit is $1.
If the amount you are looking up from the worksheet is $38,511 or more, and you have one qualifying child, you cannot take the credit.

(Continued)

Earned Income Credit (EIC) Table - *Continued* (**Caution.** This is **not** a tax table.)

If the amount you are looking up from the worksheet is–		And your filing status is–							
		Single, head of household, or qualifying widow(er) and the number of children you have is–				Married filing jointly and the number of children you have is–			
		0	1	2	3	0	1	2	3
At least	But less than	Your credit is–				Your credit is–			
39,200	39,250	0	0	954	1,637	0	754	2,098	2,780
39,250	39,300	0	0	944	1,626	0	746	2,087	2,770
39,300	39,350	0	0	933	1,616	0	738	2,077	2,759
39,350	39,400	0	0	923	1,605	0	730	2,066	2,749
39,400	39,450	0	0	912	1,595	0	722	2,056	2,738
39,450	39,500	0	0	902	1,584	0	714	2,045	2,728
39,500	39,550	0	0	891	1,574	0	706	2,035	2,717
39,550	39,600	0	0	881	1,563	0	698	2,024	2,707
39,600	39,650	0	0	870	1,552	0	690	2,014	2,696
39,650	39,700	0	0	859	1,542	0	682	2,003	2,686
39,700	39,750	0	0	849	1,531	0	674	1,992	2,675
39,750	39,800	0	0	838	1,521	0	666	1,982	2,664
39,800	39,850	0	0	828	1,510	0	658	1,971	2,654
39,850	39,900	0	0	817	1,500	0	650	1,961	2,643
39,900	39,950	0	0	807	1,489	0	642	1,950	2,633
39,950	40,000	0	0	796	1,479	0	634	1,940	2,622
40,000	40,050	0	0	786	1,468	0	626	1,929	2,612
40,050	40,100	0	0	775	1,458	0	618	1,919	2,601
40,100	40,150	0	0	765	1,447	0	610	1,908	2,591
40,150	40,200	0	0	754	1,437	0	602	1,898	2,580
40,200	40,250	0	0	744	1,426	0	594	1,887	2,570
40,250	40,300	0	0	733	1,416	0	586	1,877	2,559
40,300	40,350	0	0	723	1,405	0	578	1,866	2,549
40,350	40,400	0	0	712	1,395	0	570	1,856	2,538
40,400	40,450	0	0	701	1,384	0	562	1,845	2,528
40,450	40,500	0	0	691	1,373	0	554	1,835	2,517
40,500	40,550	0	0	680	1,363	0	546	1,824	2,506
40,550	40,600	0	0	670	1,352	0	538	1,813	2,496
40,600	40,650	0	0	659	1,342	0	530	1,803	2,485
40,650	40,700	0	0	649	1,331	0	522	1,792	2,475
40,700	40,750	0	0	638	1,321	0	514	1,782	2,464
40,750	40,800	0	0	628	1,310	0	506	1,771	2,454
40,800	40,850	0	0	617	1,300	0	498	1,761	2,443
40,850	40,900	0	0	607	1,289	0	490	1,750	2,433
40,900	40,950	0	0	596	1,279	0	482	1,740	2,422
40,950	41,000	0	0	586	1,268	0	474	1,729	2,412
41,000	41,050	0	0	575	1,258	0	466	1,719	2,401
41,050	41,100	0	0	565	1,247	0	458	1,708	2,391
41,100	41,150	0	0	554	1,237	0	450	1,698	2,380
41,150	41,200	0	0	544	1,226	0	442	1,687	2,370
41,200	41,250	0	0	533	1,216	0	434	1,677	2,359
41,250	41,300	0	0	522	1,205	0	426	1,666	2,349
41,300	41,350	0	0	512	1,194	0	418	1,656	2,338
41,350	41,400	0	0	501	1,184	0	410	1,645	2,327
41,400	41,450	0	0	491	1,173	0	402	1,634	2,317
41,450	41,500	0	0	480	1,163	0	394	1,624	2,306
41,500	41,550	0	0	470	1,152	0	386	1,613	2,296
41,550	41,600	0	0	459	1,142	0	378	1,603	2,285
41,600	41,650	0	0	449	1,131	0	370	1,592	2,275
41,650	41,700	0	0	438	1,121	0	362	1,582	2,264
41,700	41,750	0	0	428	1,110	0	354	1,571	2,254
41,750	41,800	0	0	417	1,100	0	346	1,561	2,243
41,800	41,850	0	0	407	1,089	0	338	1,550	2,233
41,850	41,900	0	0	396	1,079	0	330	1,540	2,222
41,900	41,950	0	0	386	1,068	0	322	1,529	2,212
41,950	42,000	0	0	375	1,058	0	314	1,519	2,201
42,000	42,050	0	0	365	1,047	0	306	1,508	2,191
42,050	42,100	0	0	354	1,037	0	298	1,498	2,180
42,100	42,150	0	0	343	1,026	0	290	1,487	2,170
42,150	42,200	0	0	333	1,015	0	282	1,477	2,159
42,200	42,250	0	0	322	1,005	0	274	1,466	2,148
42,250	42,300	0	0	312	994	0	266	1,455	2,138
42,300	42,350	0	0	301	984	0	258	1,445	2,127
42,350	42,400	0	0	291	973	0	250	1,434	2,117

If the amount you are looking up from the worksheet is–		And your filing status is–							
		Single, head of household, or qualifying widow(er) and the number of children you have is–				Married filing jointly and the number of children you have is–			
		0	1	2	3	0	1	2	3
At least	But less than	Your credit is–				Your credit is–			
42,400	42,450	0	0	280	963	0	242	1,424	2,106
42,450	42,500	0	0	270	952	0	234	1,413	2,096
42,500	42,550	0	0	259	942	0	226	1,403	2,085
42,550	42,600	0	0	249	931	0	218	1,392	2,075
42,600	42,650	0	0	238	921	0	210	1,382	2,064
42,650	42,700	0	0	228	910	0	202	1,371	2,054
42,700	42,750	0	0	217	900	0	194	1,361	2,043
42,750	42,800	0	0	207	889	0	186	1,350	2,033
42,800	42,850	0	0	196	879	0	178	1,340	2,022
42,850	42,900	0	0	186	868	0	170	1,329	2,012
42,900	42,950	0	0	175	857	0	162	1,319	2,001
42,950	43,000	0	0	164	847	0	154	1,308	1,991
43,000	43,050	0	0	154	836	0	146	1,297	1,980
43,050	43,100	0	0	143	826	0	138	1,287	1,969
43,100	43,150	0	0	133	815	0	130	1,276	1,959
43,150	43,200	0	0	122	805	0	122	1,266	1,948
43,200	43,250	0	0	112	794	0	114	1,255	1,938
43,250	43,300	0	0	101	784	0	106	1,245	1,927
43,300	43,350	0	0	91	773	0	98	1,234	1,917
43,350	43,400	0	0	80	763	0	90	1,224	1,906
43,400	43,450	0	0	70	752	0	82	1,213	1,896
43,450	43,500	0	0	59	742	0	74	1,203	1,885
43,500	43,550	0	0	49	731	0	66	1,192	1,875
43,550	43,600	0	0	38	721	0	58	1,182	1,864
43,600	43,650	0	0	28	710	0	50	1,171	1,854
43,650	43,700	0	0	17	700	0	42	1,161	1,843
43,700	43,750	0	0	7	689	0	34	1,150	1,833
43,750	43,800	0	0	*	678	0	27	1,140	1,822
43,800	43,850	0	0	0	668	0	19	1,129	1,812
43,850	43,900	0	0	0	657	0	11	1,118	1,801
43,900	43,950	0	0	0	647	0	**	1,108	1,790
43,950	44,000	0	0	0	636	0	0	1,097	1,780
44,000	44,050	0	0	0	626	0	0	1,087	1,769
44,050	44,100	0	0	0	615	0	0	1,076	1,759
44,100	44,150	0	0	0	605	0	0	1,066	1,748
44,150	44,200	0	0	0	594	0	0	1,055	1,738
44,200	44,250	0	0	0	584	0	0	1,045	1,727
44,250	44,300	0	0	0	573	0	0	1,034	1,717
44,300	44,350	0	0	0	563	0	0	1,024	1,706
44,350	44,400	0	0	0	552	0	0	1,013	1,696
44,400	44,450	0	0	0	542	0	0	1,003	1,685
44,450	44,500	0	0	0	531	0	0	992	1,675
44,500	44,550	0	0	0	521	0	0	982	1,664
44,550	44,600	0	0	0	510	0	0	971	1,654
44,600	44,650	0	0	0	499	0	0	961	1,643
44,650	44,700	0	0	0	489	0	0	950	1,633
44,700	44,750	0	0	0	478	0	0	939	1,622
44,750	44,800	0	0	0	468	0	0	929	1,611
44,800	44,850	0	0	0	457	0	0	918	1,601
44,850	44,900	0	0	0	447	0	0	908	1,590
44,900	44,950	0	0	0	436	0	0	897	1,580
44,950	45,000	0	0	0	426	0	0	887	1,569
45,000	45,050	0	0	0	415	0	0	876	1,559
45,050	45,100	0	0	0	405	0	0	866	1,548
45,100	45,150	0	0	0	394	0	0	855	1,538
45,150	45,200	0	0	0	384	0	0	845	1,527
45,200	45,250	0	0	0	373	0	0	834	1,517
45,250	45,300	0	0	0	363	0	0	824	1,506
45,300	45,350	0	0	0	352	0	0	813	1,496
45,350	45,400	0	0	0	342	0	0	803	1,485
45,400	45,450	0	0	0	331	0	0	792	1,475
45,450	45,500	0	0	0	320	0	0	782	1,464
45,500	45,550	0	0	0	310	0	0	771	1,453
45,550	45,600	0	0	0	299	0	0	760	1,443

* If the amount you are looking up from the worksheet is at least $43,750 but less than $43,756, and you have two qualifying children, your credit is $1. If the amount you are looking up from the worksheet is $43,756 or more, and you have two qualifying children, you cannot take the credit.

** If the amount you are looking up from the worksheet is at least $43,900 but less than $43,941, and you have one qualifying child, your credit is $3. If the amount you are looking up from the worksheet is $43,941 or more, and you have one qualifying child, you cannot take the credit.

(Continued)

Earned Income Credit (EIC) Table - *Continued*

(**Caution.** This is **not** a tax table.)

DRAFT AS OF October 8 2014

If the amount you are looking up from the worksheet is–		And your filing status is– Single, head of household, or qualifying widow(er) and the number of children you have is–				Married filing jointly and the number of children you have is–			
At least	But less than	0	1	2	3	0	1	2	3
		Your credit is–				Your credit is–			
45,600	45,650	0	0	0	289	0	0	750	1,432
45,650	45,700	0	0	0	278	0	0	739	1,422
45,700	45,750	0	0	0	268	0	0	729	1,411
45,750	45,800	0	0	0	257	0	0	718	1,401
45,800	45,850	0	0	0	247	0	0	708	1,390
45,850	45,900	0	0	0	236	0	0	697	1,380
45,900	45,950	0	0	0	226	0	0	687	1,369
45,950	46,000	0	0	0	215	0	0	676	1,359
46,000	46,050	0	0	0	205	0	0	666	1,348
46,050	46,100	0	0	0	194	0	0	655	1,338
46,100	46,150	0	0	0	184	0	0	645	1,327
46,150	46,200	0	0	0	173	0	0	634	1,317
46,200	46,250	0	0	0	163	0	0	624	1,306
46,250	46,300	0	0	0	152	0	0	613	1,296
46,300	46,350	0	0	0	141	0	0	603	1,285
46,350	46,400	0	0	0	131	0	0	592	1,274
46,400	46,450	0	0	0	120	0	0	581	1,264
46,450	46,500	0	0	0	110	0	0	571	1,253
46,500	46,550	0	0	0	99	0	0	560	1,243
46,550	46,600	0	0	0	89	0	0	550	1,232
46,600	46,650	0	0	0	78	0	0	539	1,222
46,650	46,700	0	0	0	68	0	0	529	1,211
46,700	46,750	0	0	0	57	0	0	518	1,201
46,750	46,800	0	0	0	47	0	0	508	1,190
46,800	46,850	0	0	0	36	0	0	497	1,180
46,850	46,900	0	0	0	26	0	0	487	1,169
46,900	46,950	0	0	0	15	0	0	476	1,159
46,950	47,000	0	0	0	*	0	0	466	1,148
47,000	47,050	0	0	0	0	0	0	455	1,138
47,050	47,100	0	0	0	0	0	0	445	1,127
47,100	47,150	0	0	0	0	0	0	434	1,117
47,150	47,200	0	0	0	0	0	0	424	1,106
47,200	47,250	0	0	0	0	0	0	413	1,095
47,250	47,300	0	0	0	0	0	0	402	1,085
47,300	47,350	0	0	0	0	0	0	392	1,074
47,350	47,400	0	0	0	0	0	0	381	1,064
47,400	47,450	0	0	0	0	0	0	371	1,053
47,450	47,500	0	0	0	0	0	0	360	1,043
47,500	47,550	0	0	0	0	0	0	350	1,032
47,550	47,600	0	0	0	0	0	0	339	1,022
47,600	47,650	0	0	0	0	0	0	329	1,011
47,650	47,700	0	0	0	0	0	0	318	1,001
47,700	47,750	0	0	0	0	0	0	308	990
47,750	47,800	0	0	0	0	0	0	297	980
47,800	47,850	0	0	0	0	0	0	287	969
47,850	47,900	0	0	0	0	0	0	276	959
47,900	47,950	0	0	0	0	0	0	266	948
47,950	48,000	0	0	0	0	0	0	255	938
48,000	48,050	0	0	0	0	0	0	244	927
48,050	48,100	0	0	0	0	0	0	234	916
48,100	48,150	0	0	0	0	0	0	223	906
48,150	48,200	0	0	0	0	0	0	213	895
48,200	48,250	0	0	0	0	0	0	202	885
48,250	48,300	0	0	0	0	0	0	192	874
48,300	48,350	0	0	0	0	0	0	181	864
48,350	48,400	0	0	0	0	0	0	171	853
48,400	48,450	0	0	0	0	0	0	160	843
48,450	48,500	0	0	0	0	0	0	150	832
48,500	48,550	0	0	0	0	0	0	139	822
48,550	48,600	0	0	0	0	0	0	129	811
48,600	48,650	0	0	0	0	0	0	118	801
48,650	48,700	0	0	0	0	0	0	108	790
48,700	48,750	0	0	0	0	0	0	97	780
48,750	48,800	0	0	0	0	0	0	87	769
48,800	48,850	0	0	0	0	0	0	76	759
48,850	48,900	0	0	0	0	0	0	65	748
48,900	48,950	0	0	0	0	0	0	55	737
48,950	49,000	0	0	0	0	0	0	44	727
49,000	49,050	0	0	0	0	0	0	34	716
49,050	49,100	0	0	0	0	0	0	23	706
49,100	49,150	0	0	0	0	0	0	13	695
49,150	49,200	0	0	0	0	0	0	**	685
49,200	49,250	0	0	0	0	0	0	0	674
49,250	49,300	0	0	0	0	0	0	0	664
49,300	49,350	0	0	0	0	0	0	0	653
49,350	49,400	0	0	0	0	0	0	0	643
49,400	49,450	0	0	0	0	0	0	0	632
49,450	49,500	0	0	0	0	0	0	0	622
49,500	49,550	0	0	0	0	0	0	0	611
49,550	49,600	0	0	0	0	0	0	0	601
49,600	49,650	0	0	0	0	0	0	0	590
49,650	49,700	0	0	0	0	0	0	0	580
49,700	49,750	0	0	0	0	0	0	0	569
49,750	49,800	0	0	0	0	0	0	0	558
49,800	49,850	0	0	0	0	0	0	0	548
49,850	49,900	0	0	0	0	0	0	0	537
49,900	49,950	0	0	0	0	0	0	0	527
49,950	50,000	0	0	0	0	0	0	0	516
50,000	50,050	0	0	0	0	0	0	0	506
50,050	50,100	0	0	0	0	0	0	0	495
50,100	50,150	0	0	0	0	0	0	0	485
50,150	50,200	0	0	0	0	0	0	0	474
50,200	50,250	0	0	0	0	0	0	0	464
50,250	50,300	0	0	0	0	0	0	0	453
50,300	50,350	0	0	0	0	0	0	0	443
50,350	50,400	0	0	0	0	0	0	0	432
50,400	50,450	0	0	0	0	0	0	0	422
50,450	50,500	0	0	0	0	0	0	0	411
50,500	50,550	0	0	0	0	0	0	0	400
50,550	50,600	0	0	0	0	0	0	0	390
50,600	50,650	0	0	0	0	0	0	0	379
50,650	50,700	0	0	0	0	0	0	0	369
50,700	50,750	0	0	0	0	0	0	0	358
50,750	50,800	0	0	0	0	0	0	0	348
50,800	50,850	0	0	0	0	0	0	0	337
50,850	50,900	0	0	0	0	0	0	0	327
50,900	50,950	0	0	0	0	0	0	0	316
50,950	51,000	0	0	0	0	0	0	0	306
51,000	51,050	0	0	0	0	0	0	0	295
51,050	51,100	0	0	0	0	0	0	0	285
51,100	51,150	0	0	0	0	0	0	0	274
51,150	51,200	0	0	0	0	0	0	0	264
51,200	51,250	0	0	0	0	0	0	0	253
51,250	51,300	0	0	0	0	0	0	0	243
51,300	51,350	0	0	0	0	0	0	0	232
51,350	51,400	0	0	0	0	0	0	0	221
51,400	51,450	0	0	0	0	0	0	0	211
51,450	51,500	0	0	0	0	0	0	0	200
51,500	51,550	0	0	0	0	0	0	0	190
51,550	51,600	0	0	0	0	0	0	0	179
51,600	51,650	0	0	0	0	0	0	0	169
51,650	51,700	0	0	0	0	0	0	0	158
51,700	51,750	0	0	0	0	0	0	0	148
51,750	51,800	0	0	0	0	0	0	0	137
51,800	51,850	0	0	0	0	0	0	0	127
51,850	51,900	0	0	0	0	0	0	0	116
51,900	51,950	0	0	0	0	0	0	0	106
51,950	52,000	0	0	0	0	0	0	0	95

* If the amount you are looking up from the worksheet is at least $46,950 but less than $46,997, and you have three qualifying children, your credit is $5.
If the amount you are looking up from the worksheet is $46,997 or more, and you have three qualifying children, you cannot take the credit.

** If the amount you are looking up from the worksheet is at least $49,150 but less than $49,186, and you have two qualifying children, your credit is $4.
If the amount you are looking up from the worksheet is $49,186 or more, and you have two qualifying children, you cannot take the credit.

(Continued)

Earned Income Credit (EIC) Table - *Continued* (**Caution.** This is **not** a tax table.)

If the amount you are looking up from the worksheet is–		And your filing status is–							
		Single, head of household, or qualifying widow(er) and the number of children you have is–				**Married filing jointly** and the number of children you have is–			
At least	But less than	0	1	2	3	0	1	2	3
		Your credit is–				Your credit is–			
52,000	52,050	0	0	0	0	0	0	0	85
52,050	52,100	0	0	0	0	0	0	0	74
52,100	52,150	0	0	0	0	0	0	0	64
52,150	52,200	0	0	0	0	0	0	0	53
52,200	52,250	0	0	0	0	0	0	0	42
52,250	52,300	0	0	0	0	0	0	0	32
52,300	52,350	0	0	0	0	0	0	0	21
52,350	52,400	0	0	0	0	0	0	0	11
52,400	52,427	0	0	0	0	0	0	0	3

DRAFT AS OF
October 8, 2014

APPENDIX C

Withholding Tables

CONTENTS

Tables for Percentage Method of Withholding C-2
Single Persons: Monthly Payroll Period C-4
Married Persons: Monthly Payroll Period C-6

Percentage Method Tables for Income Tax Withholding

(For Wages Paid in 2014)

TABLE 1—WEEKLY Payroll Period

(a) SINGLE person (including head of household)—

If the amount of wages (after subtracting withholding allowances) is: Not over $43 . . . . The amount of income tax to withhold is: $0

Over—	But not over—		of excess over—
$43	—$218	$0.00 plus 10%	—$43
$218	—$753	$17.50 plus 15%	—$218
$753	—$1,762	$97.75 plus 25%	—$753
$1,762	—$3,627	$350.00 plus 28%	—$1,762
$3,627	—$7,834	$872.20 plus 33%	—$3,627
$7,834	—$7,865	$2,260.51 plus 35%	—$7,834
$7,865	. . . .	$2,271.36 plus 39.6%	—$7,865

(b) MARRIED person—

If the amount of wages (after subtracting withholding allowances) is: Not over $163 . . . . The amount of income tax to withhold is: $0

Over—	But not over—		of excess over—
$163	—$512	$0.00 plus 10%	—$163
$512	—$1,582	$34.90 plus 15%	—$512
$1,582	—$3,025	$195.40 plus 25%	—$1,582
$3,025	—$4,525	$556.15 plus 28%	—$3,025
$4,525	—$7,953	$976.15 plus 33%	—$4,525
$7,953	—$8,963	$2,107.39 plus 35%	—$7,953
$8,963	. . . .	$2,460.89 plus 39.6%	—$8,963

TABLE 2—BIWEEKLY Payroll Period

(a) SINGLE person (including head of household)—

If the amount of wages (after subtracting withholding allowances) is: Not over $87 . . . . The amount of income tax to withhold is: $0

Over—	But not over—		of excess over—
$87	—$436	$0.00 plus 10%	—$87
$436	—$1,506	$34.90 plus 15%	—$436
$1,506	—$3,523	$195.40 plus 25%	—$1,506
$3,523	—$7,254	$699.65 plus 28%	—$3,523
$7,254	—$15,667	$1,744.33 plus 33%	—$7,254
$15,667	—$15,731	$4,520.62 plus 35%	—$15,667
$15,731	. . . .	$4,543.02 plus 39.6%	—$15,731

(b) MARRIED person—

If the amount of wages (after subtracting withholding allowances) is: Not over $325 . . . . The amount of income tax to withhold is: $0

Over—	But not over—		of excess over—
$325	—$1,023	$0.00 plus 10%	—$325
$1,023	—$3,163	$69.80 plus 15%	—$1,023
$3,163	—$6,050	$390.80 plus 25%	—$3,163
$6,050	—$9,050	$1,112.55 plus 28%	—$6,050
$9,050	—$15,906	$1,952.55 plus 33%	—$9,050
$15,906	—$17,925	$4,215.03 plus 35%	—$15,906
$17,925	. . . .	$4,921.68 plus 39.6%	—$17,925

TABLE 3—SEMIMONTHLY Payroll Period

(a) SINGLE person (including head of household)—

If the amount of wages (after subtracting withholding allowances) is: Not over $94 . . . . The amount of income tax to withhold is: $0

Over—	But not over—		of excess over—
$94	—$472	$0.00 plus 10%	—$94
$472	—$1,631	$37.80 plus 15%	—$472
$1,631	—$3,817	$211.65 plus 25%	—$1,631
$3,817	—$7,858	$758.15 plus 28%	—$3,817
$7,858	—$16,973	$1,889.63 plus 33%	—$7,858
$16,973	—$17,042	$4,897.58 plus 35%	—$16,973
$17,042	. . . .	$4,921.73 plus 39.6%	—$17,042

(b) MARRIED person—

If the amount of wages (after subtracting withholding allowances) is: Not over $352 . . . . The amount of income tax to withhold is: $0

Over—	But not over—		of excess over—
$352	—$1,108	$0.00 plus 10%	—$352
$1,108	—$3,427	$75.60 plus 15%	—$1,108
$3,427	—$6,554	$423.45 plus 25%	—$3,427
$6,554	—$9,804	$1,205.20 plus 28%	—$6,554
$9,804	—$17,231	$2,115.20 plus 33%	—$9,804
$17,231	—$19,419	$4,566.11 plus 35%	—$17,231
$19,419	. . . .	$5,331.91 plus 39.6%	—$19,419

TABLE 4—MONTHLY Payroll Period

(a) SINGLE person (including head of household)—

If the amount of wages (after subtracting withholding allowances) is: Not over $188 . . . . The amount of income tax to withhold is: $0

Over—	But not over—		of excess over—
$188	—$944	$0.00 plus 10%	—$188
$944	—$3,263	$75.60 plus 15%	—$944
$3,263	—$7,633	$423.45 plus 25%	—$3,263
$7,633	—$15,717	$1,515.95 plus 28%	—$7,633
$15,717	—$33,946	$3,779.47 plus 33%	—$15,717
$33,946	—$34,083	$9,795.04 plus 35%	—$33,946
$34,083	. . . .	$9,842.99 plus 39.6%	—$34,083

(b) MARRIED person—

If the amount of wages (after subtracting withholding allowances) is: Not over $704 . . . . The amount of income tax to withhold is: $0

Over—	But not over—		of excess over—
$704	—$2,217	$0.00 plus 10%	—$704
$2,217	—$6,854	$151.30 plus 15%	—$2,217
$6,854	—$13,108	$846.85 plus 25%	—$6,854
$13,108	—$19,608	$2,410.35 plus 28%	—$13,108
$19,608	—$34,463	$4,230.35 plus 33%	—$19,608
$34,463	—$38,838	$9,132.50 plus 35%	—$34,463
$38,838	. . . .	$10,663.75 plus 39.6%	—$38,838

Percentage Method Tables for Income Tax Withholding (continued)

(For Wages Paid in 2014)

TABLE 5—QUARTERLY Payroll Period

(a) SINGLE person (including head of household)—

If the amount of wages (after subtracting withholding allowances) is: Not over $563 — The amount of income tax to withhold is: $0

Over—	But not over—		of excess over—
$563	—$2,831	$0.00 plus 10%	—$563
$2,831	—$9,788	$226.80 plus 15%	—$2,831
$9,788	—$22,900	$1,270.35 plus 25%	—$9,788
$22,900	—$47,150	$4,548.35 plus 28%	—$22,900
$47,150	—$101,838	$11,338.35 plus 33%	—$47,150
$101,838	—$102,250	$29,385.39 plus 35%	—$101,838
$102,250		$29,529.59 plus 39.6%	—$102,250

(b) MARRIED person—

If the amount of wages (after subtracting withholding allowances) is: Not over $2,113 — The amount of income tax to withhold is: $0

Over—	But not over—		of excess over—
$2,113	—$6,650	$0.00 plus 10%	—$2,113
$6,650	—$20,563	$453.70 plus 15%	—$6,650
$20,563	—$39,325	$2,540.65 plus 25%	—$20,563
$39,325	—$58,825	$7,231.15 plus 28%	—$39,325
$58,825	—$103,388	$12,691.15 plus 33%	—$58,825
$103,388	—$116,513	$27,396.94 plus 35%	—$103,388
$116,513		$31,990.69 plus 39.6%	—$116,513

TABLE 6—SEMIANNUAL Payroll Period

(a) SINGLE person (including head of household)—

If the amount of wages (after subtracting withholding allowances) is: Not over $1,125 — The amount of income tax to withhold is: $0

Over—	But not over—		of excess over—
$1,125	—$5,663	$0.00 plus 10%	—$1,125
$5,663	—$19,575	$453.80 plus 15%	—$5,663
$19,575	—$45,800	$2,540.60 plus 25%	—$19,575
$45,800	—$94,300	$9,096.85 plus 28%	—$45,800
$94,300	—$203,675	$22,676.85 plus 33%	—$94,300
$203,675	—$204,500	$58,770.60 plus 35%	—$203,675
$204,500		$59,059.35 plus 39.6%	—$204,500

(b) MARRIED person—

If the amount of wages (after subtracting withholding allowances) is: Not over $4,225 — The amount of income tax to withhold is: $0

Over—	But not over—		of excess over—
$4,225	—$13,300	$0.00 plus 10%	—$4,225
$13,300	—$41,125	$907.50 plus 15%	—$13,300
$41,125	—$78,650	$5,081.25 plus 25%	—$41,125
$78,650	—$117,650	$14,462.50 plus 28%	—$78,650
$117,650	—$206,775	$25,382.50 plus 33%	—$117,650
$206,775	—$233,025	$54,793.75 plus 35%	—$206,775
$233,025		$63,981.25 plus 39.6%	—$233,025

TABLE 7—ANNUAL Payroll Period

(a) SINGLE person (including head of household)—

If the amount of wages (after subtracting withholding allowances) is: Not over $2,250 — The amount of income tax to withhold is: $0

Over—	But not over—		of excess over—
$2,250	—$11,325	$0.00 plus 10%	—$2,250
$11,325	—$39,150	$907.50 plus 15%	—$11,325
$39,150	—$91,600	$5,081.25 plus 25%	—$39,150
$91,600	—$188,600	$18,193.75 plus 28%	—$91,600
$188,600	—$407,350	$45,353.75 plus 33%	—$188,600
$407,350	—$409,000	$117,541.25 plus 35%	—$407,350
$409,000		$118,118.75 plus 39.6%	—$409,000

(b) MARRIED person—

If the amount of wages (after subtracting withholding allowances) is: Not over $8,450 — The amount of income tax to withhold is: $0

Over—	But not over—		of excess over—
$8,450	—$26,600	$0.00 plus 10%	—$8,450
$26,600	—$82,250	$1,815.00 plus 15%	—$26,600
$82,250	—$157,300	$10,162.50 plus 25%	—$82,250
$157,300	—$235,300	$28,925.00 plus 28%	—$157,300
$235,300	—$413,550	$50,765.00 plus 33%	—$235,300
$413,550	—$466,050	$109,587.50 plus 35%	—$413,550
$466,050		$127,962.50 plus 39.6%	—$466,050

TABLE 8—DAILY or MISCELLANEOUS Payroll Period

(a) SINGLE person (including head of household)—

If the amount of wages (after subtracting withholding allowances) divided by the number of days in the payroll period is: Not over $8.70 — The amount of income tax to withhold per day is: $0

Over—	But not over—		of excess over—
$8.70	—$43.60	$0.00 plus 10%	—$8.70
$43.60	—$150.60	$3.49 plus 15%	—$43.60
$150.60	—$352.30	$19.54 plus 25%	—$150.60
$352.30	—$725.40	$69.97 plus 28%	—$352.30
$725.40	—$1,566.70	$174.44 plus 33%	—$725.40
$1,566.70	—$1,573.10	$452.07 plus 35%	—$1,566.70
$1,573.10		$454.31 plus 39.6%	—$1,573.10

(b) MARRIED person—

If the amount of wages (after subtracting withholding allowances) divided by the number of days in the payroll period is: Not over $32.50 — The amount of income tax to withhold per day is: $0

Over—	But not over—		of excess over—
$32.50	—$102.30	$0.00 plus 10%	—$32.50
$102.30	—$316.30	$6.98 plus 15%	—$102.30
$316.30	—$605.00	$39.08 plus 25%	—$316.30
$605.00	—$905.00	$111.26 plus 28%	—$605.00
$905.00	—$1,590.60	$195.26 plus 33%	—$905.00
$1,590.60	—$1,792.50	$421.51 plus 35%	—$1,590.60
$1,792.50		$492.18 plus 39.6%	—$1,792.50

SINGLE Persons—**MONTHLY** Payroll Period

(For Wages Paid through December 2014)

And the wages are–		And the number of withholding allowances claimed is—										
At least	But less than	0	1	2	3	4	5	6	7	8	9	10
		The amount of income tax to be withheld is—										
$ 0	$220	$0	$0	$0	$0	$0	$0	$0	$0	$0	$0	$0
220	230	4	0	0	0	0	0	0	0	0	0	0
230	240	5	0	0	0	0	0	0	0	0	0	0
240	250	6	0	0	0	0	0	0	0	0	0	0
250	260	7	0	0	0	0	0	0	0	0	0	0
260	270	8	0	0	0	0	0	0	0	0	0	0
270	280	9	0	0	0	0	0	0	0	0	0	0
280	290	10	0	0	0	0	0	0	0	0	0	0
290	300	11	0	0	0	0	0	0	0	0	0	0
300	320	12	0	0	0	0	0	0	0	0	0	0
320	340	14	0	0	0	0	0	0	0	0	0	0
340	360	16	0	0	0	0	0	0	0	0	0	0
360	380	18	0	0	0	0	0	0	0	0	0	0
380	400	20	0	0	0	0	0	0	0	0	0	0
400	420	22	0	0	0	0	0	0	0	0	0	0
420	440	24	0	0	0	0	0	0	0	0	0	0
440	460	26	0	0	0	0	0	0	0	0	0	0
460	480	28	0	0	0	0	0	0	0	0	0	0
480	500	30	0	0	0	0	0	0	0	0	0	0
500	520	32	0	0	0	0	0	0	0	0	0	0
520	540	34	1	0	0	0	0	0	0	0	0	0
540	560	36	3	0	0	0	0	0	0	0	0	0
560	580	38	5	0	0	0	0	0	0	0	0	0
580	600	40	7	0	0	0	0	0	0	0	0	0
600	640	43	10	0	0	0	0	0	0	0	0	0
640	680	47	14	0	0	0	0	0	0	0	0	0
680	720	51	18	0	0	0	0	0	0	0	0	0
720	760	55	22	0	0	0	0	0	0	0	0	0
760	800	59	26	0	0	0	0	0	0	0	0	0
800	840	63	30	0	0	0	0	0	0	0	0	0
840	880	67	34	1	0	0	0	0	0	0	0	0
880	920	71	38	5	0	0	0	0	0	0	0	0
920	960	75	42	9	0	0	0	0	0	0	0	0
960	1,000	81	46	13	0	0	0	0	0	0	0	0
1,000	1,040	87	50	17	0	0	0	0	0	0	0	0
1,040	1,080	93	54	21	0	0	0	0	0	0	0	0
1,080	1,120	99	58	25	0	0	0	0	0	0	0	0
1,120	1,160	105	62	29	0	0	0	0	0	0	0	0
1,160	1,200	111	66	33	1	0	0	0	0	0	0	0
1,200	1,240	117	70	37	5	0	0	0	0	0	0	0
1,240	1,280	123	74	41	9	0	0	0	0	0	0	0
1,280	1,320	129	80	45	13	0	0	0	0	0	0	0
1,320	1,360	135	86	49	17	0	0	0	0	0	0	0
1,360	1,400	141	92	53	21	0	0	0	0	0	0	0
1,400	1,440	147	98	57	25	0	0	0	0	0	0	0
1,440	1,480	153	104	61	29	0	0	0	0	0	0	0
1,480	1,520	159	110	65	33	0	0	0	0	0	0	0
1,520	1,560	165	116	69	37	4	0	0	0	0	0	0
1,560	1,600	171	122	73	41	8	0	0	0	0	0	0
1,600	1,640	177	128	78	45	12	0	0	0	0	0	0
1,640	1,680	183	134	84	49	16	0	0	0	0	0	0
1,680	1,720	189	140	90	53	20	0	0	0	0	0	0
1,720	1,760	195	146	96	57	24	0	0	0	0	0	0
1,760	1,800	201	152	102	61	28	0	0	0	0	0	0
1,800	1,840	207	158	108	65	32	0	0	0	0	0	0
1,840	1,880	213	164	114	69	36	3	0	0	0	0	0
1,880	1,920	219	170	120	73	40	7	0	0	0	0	0
1,920	1,960	225	176	126	77	44	11	0	0	0	0	0
1,960	2,000	231	182	132	83	48	15	0	0	0	0	0
2,000	2,040	237	188	138	89	52	19	0	0	0	0	0
2,040	2,080	243	194	144	95	56	23	0	0	0	0	0
2,080	2,120	249	200	150	101	60	27	0	0	0	0	0
2,120	2,160	255	206	156	107	64	31	0	0	0	0	0
2,160	2,200	261	212	162	113	68	35	2	0	0	0	0
2,200	2,240	267	218	168	119	72	39	6	0	0	0	0
2,240	2,280	273	224	174	125	76	43	10	0	0	0	0
2,280	2,320	279	230	180	131	82	47	14	0	0	0	0
2,320	2,360	285	236	186	137	88	51	18	0	0	0	0
2,360	2,400	291	242	192	143	94	55	22	0	0	0	0

SINGLE Persons—MONTHLY Payroll Period

(For Wages Paid through December 2014)

And the wages are–		And the number of withholding allowances claimed is—										
At least	But less than	0	1	2	3	4	5	6	7	8	9	10
		The amount of income tax to be withheld is—										
$2,400	$2,440	$297	$248	$198	$149	$100	$59	$26	$0	$0	$0	$0
2,440	2,480	303	254	204	155	106	63	30	0	0	0	0
2,480	2,520	309	260	210	161	112	67	34	1	0	0	0
2,520	2,560	315	266	216	167	118	71	38	5	0	0	0
2,560	2,600	321	272	222	173	124	75	42	9	0	0	0
2,600	2,640	327	278	228	179	130	80	46	13	0	0	0
2,640	2,680	333	284	234	185	136	86	50	17	0	0	0
2,680	2,720	339	290	240	191	142	92	54	21	0	0	0
2,720	2,760	345	296	246	197	148	98	58	25	0	0	0
2,760	2,800	351	302	252	203	154	104	62	29	0	0	0
2,800	2,840	357	308	258	209	160	110	66	33	0	0	0
2,840	2,880	363	314	264	215	166	116	70	37	4	0	0
2,880	2,920	369	320	270	221	172	122	74	41	8	0	0
2,920	2,960	375	326	276	227	178	128	79	45	12	0	0
2,960	3,000	381	332	282	233	184	134	85	49	16	0	0
3,000	3,040	387	338	288	239	190	140	91	53	20	0	0
3,040	3,080	393	344	294	245	196	146	97	57	24	0	0
3,080	3,120	399	350	300	251	202	152	103	61	28	0	0
3,120	3,160	405	356	306	257	208	158	109	65	32	0	0
3,160	3,200	411	362	312	263	214	164	115	69	36	3	0
3,200	3,240	417	368	318	269	220	170	121	73	40	7	0
3,240	3,280	423	374	324	275	226	176	127	77	44	11	0
3,280	3,320	433	380	330	281	232	182	133	83	48	15	0
3,320	3,360	443	386	336	287	238	188	139	89	52	19	0
3,360	3,400	453	392	342	293	244	194	145	95	56	23	0
3,400	3,440	463	398	348	299	250	200	151	101	60	27	0
3,440	3,480	473	404	354	305	256	206	157	107	64	31	0
3,480	3,520	483	410	360	311	262	212	163	113	68	35	2
3,520	3,560	493	416	366	317	268	218	169	119	72	39	6
3,560	3,600	503	422	372	323	274	224	175	125	76	43	10
3,600	3,640	513	431	378	329	280	230	181	131	82	47	14
3,640	3,680	523	441	384	335	286	236	187	137	88	51	18
3,680	3,720	533	451	390	341	292	242	193	143	94	55	22
3,720	3,760	543	461	396	347	298	248	199	149	100	59	26
3,760	3,800	553	471	402	353	304	254	205	155	106	63	30
3,800	3,840	563	481	408	359	310	260	211	161	112	67	34
3,840	3,880	573	491	414	365	316	266	217	167	118	71	38
3,880	3,920	583	501	420	371	322	272	223	173	124	75	42
3,920	3,960	593	511	428	377	328	278	229	179	130	81	46
3,960	4,000	603	521	438	383	334	284	235	185	136	87	50
4,000	4,040	613	531	448	389	340	290	241	191	142	93	54
4,040	4,080	623	541	458	395	346	296	247	197	148	99	58
4,080	4,120	633	551	468	401	352	302	253	203	154	105	62
4,120	4,160	643	561	478	407	358	308	259	209	160	111	66
4,160	4,200	653	571	488	413	364	314	265	215	166	117	70
4,200	4,240	663	581	498	419	370	320	271	221	172	123	74
4,240	4,280	673	591	508	426	376	326	277	227	178	129	79
4,280	4,320	683	601	518	436	382	332	283	233	184	135	85
4,320	4,360	693	611	528	446	388	338	289	239	190	141	91
4,360	4,400	703	621	538	456	394	344	295	245	196	147	97
4,400	4,440	713	631	548	466	400	350	301	251	202	153	103
4,440	4,480	723	641	558	476	406	356	307	257	208	159	109
4,480	4,520	733	651	568	486	412	362	313	263	214	165	115
4,520	4,560	743	661	578	496	418	368	319	269	220	171	121
4,560	4,600	753	671	588	506	424	374	325	275	226	177	127
4,600	4,640	763	681	598	516	434	380	331	281	232	183	133
4,640	4,680	773	691	608	526	444	386	337	287	238	189	139
4,680	4,720	783	701	618	536	454	392	343	293	244	195	145
4,720	4,760	793	711	628	546	464	398	349	299	250	201	151
4,760	4,800	803	721	638	556	474	404	355	305	256	207	157
4,800	4,840	813	731	648	566	484	410	361	311	262	213	163
4,840	4,880	823	741	658	576	494	416	367	317	268	219	169
4,880	4,920	833	751	668	586	504	422	373	323	274	225	175
4,920	4,960	843	761	678	596	514	431	379	329	280	231	181
4,960	5,000	853	771	688	606	524	441	385	335	286	237	187
5,000	5,040	863	781	698	616	534	451	391	341	292	243	193
5,040	5,080	873	791	708	626	544	461	397	347	298	249	199

$5,080 and over — Use Table 4(a) for a **SINGLE person** on page 43. Also see the instructions on page 41.

MARRIED Persons—**MONTHLY** Payroll Period

(For Wages Paid through December 2014)

And the wages are–		And the number of withholding allowances claimed is—										
At least	But less than	0	1	2	3	4	5	6	7	8	9	10
		The amount of income tax to be withheld is—										
$ 0	$720	$0	$0	$0	$0	$0	$0	$0	$0	$0	$0	$0
720	760	4	0	0	0	0	0	0	0	0	0	0
760	800	8	0	0	0	0	0	0	0	0	0	0
800	840	12	0	0	0	0	0	0	0	0	0	0
840	880	16	0	0	0	0	0	0	0	0	0	0
880	920	20	0	0	0	0	0	0	0	0	0	0
920	960	24	0	0	0	0	0	0	0	0	0	0
960	1,000	28	0	0	0	0	0	0	0	0	0	0
1,000	1,040	32	0	0	0	0	0	0	0	0	0	0
1,040	1,080	36	3	0	0	0	0	0	0	0	0	0
1,080	1,120	40	7	0	0	0	0	0	0	0	0	0
1,120	1,160	44	11	0	0	0	0	0	0	0	0	0
1,160	1,200	48	15	0	0	0	0	0	0	0	0	0
1,200	1,240	52	19	0	0	0	0	0	0	0	0	0
1,240	1,280	56	23	0	0	0	0	0	0	0	0	0
1,280	1,320	60	27	0	0	0	0	0	0	0	0	0
1,320	1,360	64	31	0	0	0	0	0	0	0	0	0
1,360	1,400	68	35	2	0	0	0	0	0	0	0	0
1,400	1,440	72	39	6	0	0	0	0	0	0	0	0
1,440	1,480	76	43	10	0	0	0	0	0	0	0	0
1,480	1,520	80	47	14	0	0	0	0	0	0	0	0
1,520	1,560	84	51	18	0	0	0	0	0	0	0	0
1,560	1,600	88	55	22	0	0	0	0	0	0	0	0
1,600	1,640	92	59	26	0	0	0	0	0	0	0	0
1,640	1,680	96	63	30	0	0	0	0	0	0	0	0
1,680	1,720	100	67	34	1	0	0	0	0	0	0	0
1,720	1,760	104	71	38	5	0	0	0	0	0	0	0
1,760	1,800	108	75	42	9	0	0	0	0	0	0	0
1,800	1,840	112	79	46	13	0	0	0	0	0	0	0
1,840	1,880	116	83	50	17	0	0	0	0	0	0	0
1,880	1,920	120	87	54	21	0	0	0	0	0	0	0
1,920	1,960	124	91	58	25	0	0	0	0	0	0	0
1,960	2,000	128	95	62	29	0	0	0	0	0	0	0
2,000	2,040	132	99	66	33	0	0	0	0	0	0	0
2,040	2,080	136	103	70	37	4	0	0	0	0	0	0
2,080	2,120	140	107	74	41	8	0	0	0	0	0	0
2,120	2,160	144	111	78	45	12	0	0	0	0	0	0
2,160	2,200	148	115	82	49	16	0	0	0	0	0	0
2,200	2,240	152	119	86	53	20	0	0	0	0	0	0
2,240	2,280	158	123	90	57	24	0	0	0	0	0	0
2,280	2,320	164	127	94	61	28	0	0	0	0	0	0
2,320	2,360	170	131	98	65	32	0	0	0	0	0	0
2,360	2,400	176	135	102	69	36	3	0	0	0	0	0
2,400	2,440	182	139	106	73	40	7	0	0	0	0	0
2,440	2,480	188	143	110	77	44	11	0	0	0	0	0
2,480	2,520	194	147	114	81	48	15	0	0	0	0	0
2,520	2,560	200	151	118	85	52	19	0	0	0	0	0
2,560	2,600	206	156	122	89	56	23	0	0	0	0	0
2,600	2,640	212	162	126	93	60	27	0	0	0	0	0
2,640	2,680	218	168	130	97	64	31	0	0	0	0	0
2,680	2,720	224	174	134	101	68	35	2	0	0	0	0
2,720	2,760	230	180	138	105	72	39	6	0	0	0	0
2,760	2,800	236	186	142	109	76	43	10	0	0	0	0
2,800	2,840	242	192	146	113	80	47	14	0	0	0	0
2,840	2,880	248	198	150	117	84	51	18	0	0	0	0
2,880	2,920	254	204	155	121	88	55	22	0	0	0	0
2,920	2,960	260	210	161	125	92	59	26	0	0	0	0
2,960	3,000	266	216	167	129	96	63	30	0	0	0	0
3,000	3,040	272	222	173	133	100	67	34	1	0	0	0
3,040	3,080	278	228	179	137	104	71	38	5	0	0	0
3,080	3,120	284	234	185	141	108	75	42	9	0	0	0
3,120	3,160	290	240	191	145	112	79	46	13	0	0	0
3,160	3,200	296	246	197	149	116	83	50	17	0	0	0
3,200	3,240	302	252	203	154	120	87	54	21	0	0	0
3,240	3,280	308	258	209	160	124	91	58	25	0	0	0
3,280	3,320	314	264	215	166	128	95	62	29	0	0	0
3,320	3,360	320	270	221	172	132	99	66	33	0	0	0
3,360	3,400	326	276	227	178	136	103	70	37	4	0	0

MARRIED Persons—MONTHLY Payroll Period

(For Wages Paid through December 2014)

And the wages are–		And the number of withholding allowances claimed is—										
At least	But less than	0	1	2	3	4	5	6	7	8	9	10
		The amount of income tax to be withheld is—										
$3,400	**$3,440**	$332	$282	$233	$184	$140	$107	$74	$41	$8	$0	$0
3,440	**3,480**	338	288	239	190	144	111	78	45	12	0	0
3,480	**3,520**	344	294	245	196	148	115	82	49	16	0	0
3,520	**3,560**	350	300	251	202	152	119	86	53	20	0	0
3,560	**3,600**	356	306	257	208	158	123	90	57	24	0	0
3,600	**3,640**	362	312	263	214	164	127	94	61	28	0	0
3,640	**3,680**	368	318	269	220	170	131	98	65	32	0	0
3,680	**3,720**	374	324	275	226	176	135	102	69	36	3	0
3,720	**3,760**	380	330	281	232	182	139	106	73	40	7	0
3,760	**3,800**	386	336	287	238	188	143	110	77	44	11	0
3,800	**3,840**	392	342	293	244	194	147	114	81	48	15	0
3,840	**3,880**	398	348	299	250	200	151	118	85	52	19	0
3,880	**3,920**	404	354	305	256	206	157	122	89	56	23	0
3,920	**3,960**	410	360	311	262	212	163	126	93	60	27	0
3,960	**4,000**	416	366	317	268	218	169	130	97	64	31	0
4,000	**4,040**	422	372	323	274	224	175	134	101	68	35	2
4,040	**4,080**	428	378	329	280	230	181	138	105	72	39	6
4,080	**4,120**	434	384	335	286	236	187	142	109	76	43	10
4,120	**4,160**	440	390	341	292	242	193	146	113	80	47	14
4,160	**4,200**	446	396	347	298	248	199	150	117	84	51	18
4,200	**4,240**	452	402	353	304	254	205	156	121	88	55	22
4,240	**4,280**	458	408	359	310	260	211	162	125	92	59	26
4,280	**4,320**	464	414	365	316	266	217	168	129	96	63	30
4,320	**4,360**	470	420	371	322	272	223	174	133	100	67	34
4,360	**4,400**	476	426	377	328	278	229	180	137	104	71	38
4,400	**4,440**	482	432	383	334	284	235	186	141	108	75	42
4,440	**4,480**	488	438	389	340	290	241	192	145	112	79	46
4,480	**4,520**	494	444	395	346	296	247	198	149	116	83	50
4,520	**4,560**	500	450	401	352	302	253	204	154	120	87	54
4,560	**4,600**	506	456	407	358	308	259	210	160	124	91	58
4,600	**4,640**	512	462	413	364	314	265	216	166	128	95	62
4,640	**4,680**	518	468	419	370	320	271	222	172	132	99	66
4,680	**4,720**	524	474	425	376	326	277	228	178	136	103	70
4,720	**4,760**	530	480	431	382	332	283	234	184	140	107	74
4,760	**4,800**	536	486	437	388	338	289	240	190	144	111	78
4,800	**4,840**	542	492	443	394	344	295	246	196	148	115	82
4,840	**4,880**	548	498	449	400	350	301	252	202	153	119	86
4,880	**4,920**	554	504	455	406	356	307	258	208	159	123	90
4,920	**4,960**	560	510	461	412	362	313	264	214	165	127	94
4,960	**5,000**	566	516	467	418	368	319	270	220	171	131	98
5,000	**5,040**	572	522	473	424	374	325	276	226	177	135	102
5,040	**5,080**	578	528	479	430	380	331	282	232	183	139	106
5,080	**5,120**	584	534	485	436	386	337	288	238	189	143	110
5,120	**5,160**	590	540	491	442	392	343	294	244	195	147	114
5,160	**5,200**	596	546	497	448	398	349	300	250	201	151	118
5,200	**5,240**	602	552	503	454	404	355	306	256	207	157	122
5,240	**5,280**	608	558	509	460	410	361	312	262	213	163	126
5,280	**5,320**	614	564	515	466	416	367	318	268	219	169	130
5,320	**5,360**	620	570	521	472	422	373	324	274	225	175	134
5,360	**5,400**	626	576	527	478	428	379	330	280	231	181	138
5,400	**5,440**	632	582	533	484	434	385	336	286	237	187	142
5,440	**5,480**	638	588	539	490	440	391	342	292	243	193	146
5,480	**5,520**	644	594	545	496	446	397	348	298	249	199	150
5,520	**5,560**	650	600	551	502	452	403	354	304	255	205	156
5,560	**5,600**	656	606	557	508	458	409	360	310	261	211	162
5,600	**5,640**	662	612	563	514	464	415	366	316	267	217	168
5,640	**5,680**	668	618	569	520	470	421	372	322	273	223	174
5,680	**5,720**	674	624	575	526	476	427	378	328	279	229	180
5,720	**5,760**	680	630	581	532	482	433	384	334	285	235	186
5,760	**5,800**	686	636	587	538	488	439	390	340	291	241	192
5,800	**5,840**	692	642	593	544	494	445	396	346	297	247	198
5,840	**5,880**	698	648	599	550	500	451	402	352	303	253	204
5,880	**5,920**	704	654	605	556	506	457	408	358	309	259	210
5,920	**5,960**	710	660	611	562	512	463	414	364	315	265	216
5,960	**6,000**	716	666	617	568	518	469	420	370	321	271	222
6,000	**6,040**	722	672	623	574	524	475	426	376	327	277	228
6,040	**6,080**	728	678	629	580	530	481	432	382	333	283	234
6,080	**6,120**	734	684	635	586	536	487	438	388	339	289	240

$6,120 and over Use Table 4(b) for a **MARRIED person** on page 43. Also see the instructions on page 41.

APPENDIX D

Additional Comprehensive Tax Return Problems

CONTENTS

Comprehensive Problem One: Noah and Joan Arc's Tax Return D-2

Comprehensive Problem Two: Gregory and Lulu Clifden's Tax Return D-6

Forms for Comprehensive Problems One and Two* D-11

***Please note**: Additional forms can be printed by going to the IRS website at **www.irs.gov** but are not required to complete these problems.

√figure Refund 9189

Comprehensive Problem One

Noah and Joan Arc's Tax Return

Noah and Joan Arc live with their family at 4342 Josie Jo, Santee, CA 92071. Noah's Social Security number is 434-11-3311; Joan's is 456-87-5432. Both are in their mid-30s and enjoy good health and eyesight. Noah owns and operates a pet store and Joan is a firefighter for the city.

1. The Arcs have two children, a son named Billie Bob (Social Security number 598-01-2345), who is 7 years old, and a daughter named Mary Sue (Social Security number 554-33-2411), who is 4 years old. The Arcs paid $2,800 to the Roundup Day Care Center to take care of Mary Sue while they worked. Because Joan is a firefighter, she was home in the afternoon to care for Billie Bob after school.

2. For the current year, Joan's W-2 from the city fire department is located on Page D-4. Noah made estimated federal income tax payments of $12,000 and estimated state income tax payments of $1,000 during the current year.

3. Noah's pet store is located at 18542 Mission Road, Santee, CA 92071. The name of the store is "The Arc," and its taxpayer ID number is 95-9876556. The beginning inventories and ending inventories are both $10,000. The revenue and expenses for the year are as follows:

Sales revenue (merchant card sales)		$ 144,000
Expenses:		
Cost of sales	$62,000	
Insurance	750	
Accounting fees	1,800	
Wages	25,000	
Payroll taxes	2,250	
Utilities	2,700	
Rental expense	7,200	
Total expenses		(101,700)
Net income		$ 42,300

4. Noah and Joan paid the following amounts during the year (all by check):

Political contributions	$ 250
Church donations (for which a written acknowledgment was received)	2300
Real estate taxes on their home	1,200
Mortgage interest for purchase of home	See Form 1098 (Page D-5)
Tax return preparation fees	350
Credit card interest	220
Automobile insurance premiums	600
Uniforms for Joan	125

5. Noah likes to invest in the stock market. His Form 1099-B showed the following information for Noah's stock sales:

Stock	*Date Acquired*	*Date Sold*	*Sales Price*	*Cost Basis*
Blue Co.	02/11/04	08/15/14	$ 4,500	$2,300
Yellow Co.	01/31/14	06/05/14	6,000	5,000
Red Co.	10/02/05	10/07/14	12,000	1,600

The expenses of sale are included in the cost basis. Noah has a long-term capital loss carryover from last year of $2,300.

6. During the year, Noah and Joan received the following qualifying dividends:

Exxon	$320
Texas Utilities	220
Coca-Cola	See 1099-DIV (Page D-4)

All stocks, bonds, and savings accounts were purchased or established with community property.

7. Noah and Joan own rental property located at 6431 Gary Ct., San Diego, CA 92115. The revenue and expenses for the year are as follows:

Rent income	See 1099-MISC (Page D-5)
Insurance	$ 550
Interest expense	7,000
Property taxes	1,000
Miscellaneous expenses	600
Depreciation (the house was acquired in 1990)	3,000

Required: Although Noah and Joan do not believe their tax return will be unduly complicated, they do realize their limitations and come to you for assistance. You are to prepare their federal income tax return in good form, signing the return as the preparer. Do not complete a California state income tax return. Noah and Joan have completed a tax organizer and have also given you several IRS forms (see Pages D-4 and D-5) that they were not sure what to do with. Make realistic assumptions about any missing data (addresses, etc.) that you may need. The following forms and schedules are required:

Form 1040	Schedule E
Schedule A	Schedule SE
Schedule B	Form 2441
Schedule C	Form 8949
Schedule D	Qualified Dividends and Capital Gain Tax Worksheet

Note: The forms included in Appendix D are provided for the student to work on only one of the two comprehensive problems. If desired, additional forms may be obtained from the IRS website at **www.irs.gov.**

a Employee's social security number: 456-87-5432	OMB No. 1545-0008	Safe, accurate, FAST! Use IRS e-file. Visit the IRS website at www.irs.gov/efile
b Employer identification number (EIN): 33-4382966	1 Wages, tips, other compensation: 27,000.00	2 Federal income tax withheld: 5,050.00
c Employer's name, address, and ZIP code: Santee Fire Department, Santee, CA 92071	3 Social security wages: 27,000.00	4 Social security tax withheld: 1,674.00
	5 Medicare wages and tips: 27,000.00	6 Medicare tax withheld: 391.50
	7 Social security tips	8 Allocated tips
d Control number	9	10 Dependent care benefits
e Employee's first name and initial / Last name / Suff.: Joan Arc, 4342 Josie Jo, Santee, CA 92071	11 Nonqualified plans	12a See instructions for box 12
	13 Statutory employee / Retirement plan / Third-party sick pay	12b
	14 Other	12c
f Employee's address and ZIP code		12d

15 State	Employer's state ID number	16 State wages, tips, etc.	17 State income tax	18 Local wages, tips, etc.	19 Local income tax	20 Locality name
CA	1126-87021	27,000.00	1,200.00			

Form **W-2** Wage and Tax Statement **2014** Department of the Treasury—Internal Revenue Service

Copy B—To Be Filed With Employee's FEDERAL Tax Return.
This information is being furnished to the Internal Revenue Service.

☐ CORRECTED (if checked)

PAYER'S name, street address, city or town, state or province, country, ZIP or foreign postal code, and telephone no.: Coca-Cola, 1296 Peachtree Road, Atlanta, GA 14628	1a Total ordinary dividends: $ 268.00	OMB No. 1545-0110 **2014** Form 1099-DIV	**Dividends and Distributions**
	1b Qualified dividends: $ 268.00		
	2a Total capital gain distr. $	2b Unrecap. Sec. 1250 gain $	**Copy B For Recipient**
PAYER'S federal identification number: 33-0042111 / RECIPIENT'S identification number: 434-11-3311	2c Section 1202 gain $	2d Collectibles (28%) gain $	
RECIPIENT'S name: Noah Arc	3 Nondividend distributions $	4 Federal income tax withheld $	This is important tax information and is being furnished to the Internal Revenue Service. If you are required to file a return, a negligence penalty or other sanction may be imposed on you if this income is taxable and the IRS determines that it has not been reported.
Street address (including apt. no.): 4342 Josie Jo		5 Investment expenses $	
	6 Foreign tax paid $	7 Foreign country or U.S. possession	
City or town, state or province, country, and ZIP or foreign postal code: Santee, CA 92071	8 Cash liquidation distributions $	9 Noncash liquidation distributions $	
	10 Exempt-interest dividends $	11 Specified private activity bond interest dividends $	
Account number (see instructions)	12 State / 13 State identification no.	14 State tax withheld $ $	

Form **1099-DIV** (keep for your records) www.irs.gov/form1099div Department of the Treasury - Internal Revenue Service

☐ CORRECTED (if checked)

PAYER'S name, street address, city or town, state or province, country, ZIP or foreign postal code, and telephone no. **Santee Property Mgmt.** **1234 Main Street** **Santee, CA 92078**	1 Rents $ **14,000.00** 2 Royalties $	OMB No. 1545-0115 **2014** Form **1099-MISC**	**Miscellaneous Income**
	3 Other income $	4 Federal income tax withheld $	**Copy B** **For Recipient**
PAYER'S federal identification number **33-6295014** / RECIPIENT'S identification number **434-11-3311**	5 Fishing boat proceeds $	6 Medical and health care payments $	
RECIPIENT'S name **Noah Arc**	7 Nonemployee compensation $	8 Substitute payments in lieu of dividends or interest $	This is important tax information and is being furnished to the Internal Revenue Service. If you are required to file a return, a negligence penalty or other sanction may be imposed on you if this income is taxable and the IRS determines that it has not been reported.
Street address (including apt. no.) **4342 Josie Jo** City or town, state or province, country, and ZIP or foreign postal code **Santee, CA 92071**	9 Payer made direct sales of $5,000 or more of consumer products to a buyer (recipient) for resale ▶ ☐	10 Crop insurance proceeds $	
	11	12	
Account number (see instructions)	13 Excess golden parachute payments $	14 Gross proceeds paid to an attorney $	
15a Section 409A deferrals $ / 15b Section 409A income $	16 State tax withheld $ $	17 State/Payer's state no.	18 State income $ $

Form **1099-MISC** (keep for your records) www.irs.gov/form1099misc Department of the Treasury - Internal Revenue Service

☐ CORRECTED (if checked)

RECIPIENT'S/LENDER'S name, street address, city or town, state or province, country, ZIP or foreign postal code, and telephone number **Chase Mortgage**	* **Caution:** *The amount shown may not be fully deductible by you. Limits based on the loan amount and the cost and value of the secured property may apply. Also, you may only deduct interest to the extent it was incurred by you, actually paid by you, and not reimbursed by another person.*	OMB No. 1545-0901 **2014** Form **1098**	**Mortgage Interest Statement**
RECIPIENT'S federal identification no. **13-4296127** / PAYER'S social security number **434-11-3311**	1 Mortgage interest received from payer(s)/borrower(s)* $ **12,000.00**		**Copy B** **For Payer/Borrower**
PAYER'S/BORROWER'S name **Noah and Joan Arc**	2 Points paid on purchase of principal residence $		The information in boxes 1, 2, 3, and 4 is important tax information and is being furnished to the Internal Revenue Service. If you are required to file a return, a negligence penalty or other sanction may be imposed on you if the IRS determines that an underpayment of tax results because you overstated a deduction for this mortgage interest or for these points or because you did not report this refund of interest on your return.
Street address (including apt. no.) **4342 Josie Jo**	3 Refund of overpaid interest $		
City or town, state or province, country, and ZIP or foreign postal code **Santee, CA 92071**	4		
Account number (see instructions)	5		

Form **1098** (keep for your records) www.irs.gov/form1098 Department of the Treasury - Internal Revenue Service

Comprehensive Problem Two

Gregory and Lulu Clifden's Tax Return

Gregory R. and Lulu B. Clifden live with their family at the Rock Glen House Bed & Breakfast, which Gregory operates. The Bed & Breakfast (B&B) is located at 33333 Fume Blanc Way, Temecula, CA 92591. Gregory's Social Security number is 543-88-9756 and Lulu's is 256-43-8819. Both are in their mid-40s and enjoy good health and eyesight.

1. The Clifdens have three sons, Gerald A. (SS# 466-74-1131), Gary T. (SS# 465-76-8375), and Glenn E. (SS# 475-23-1426). Gerald is 17 years old, Gary is 12 years old, and Glenn is 10 years old.

2. The Rock Glen House Bed & Breakfast is operated as a sole proprietorship and had the following income and expenses for the year:

Room rental income	$164,250
Vending machine income	2,325
Advertising expense	4,720
Depreciation	18,180
Mortgage interest on the B&B	32,940
Wages of maid	15,450
Taxes and licenses	6,420
Supplies	8,930
Business insurance	6,300
Laundry expenses	4,290
Accounting fees	1,850
Office expenses	2,380
Utilities	6,350

   All of the above amounts relate to the business portion of the Bed & Breakfast; the personal portion is accounted for separately. The Rock Glen House Bed & Breakfast uses the cash method of accounting and has no inventory. The employer tax ID number is 95-1234567.

3. The Clifdens made estimated federal income tax payments of $16,000 and estimated state income tax payments of $6,000 (all made during 2014).

4. Lulu is a substitute schoolteacher with the local school district. For the current year, Lulu's Form W-2 from the school district showed the following:

Wages	$10,200
Federal income tax withheld	1,650
State income tax withheld	380
FICA (OASDI & Medicare)	780

5. Gregory is retired from the U.S. Navy. His annual statement from the Navy, Form 1099-R, is on Page D-9.

6. Gregory and Lulu paid (and can substantiate) the following amounts during the year:

Mastercard interest	$1,480
Dental expenses	2,600
California state income tax (for 2013)	450
Charitable contributions	1,875
Mortgage interest on home purchase (personal portion)	6,400
Real estate taxes (personal portion)	820
Life insurance premiums	845
Investment interest	4,300
Automobile registration fees (deductible portion)	450
Tax return preparation fee	475
Contributions to George Clinton's reelection campaign	1,000

None of the investment interest is related to amounts borrowed to purchase the City of Atlanta tax-exempt bonds.

7. During the year, Gregory and Lulu received the following qualifying dividends and interest:

Interest:	
Bob's Big Bank	$ 360
Bank of Ireland	220
City of Atlanta Tax Exempt Bonds	1,490
Vintage Bank	See 1099-INT (Page D-9)
Qualified dividends:	
Southwest Airlines	$ 110
Heinz Foods	216

Also, Lulu owns Series EE U.S. savings bonds. During the year, the bond redemption value increased by $1,300. Lulu has not elected the accrual method for these bonds. There were no Irish taxes paid on the interest from the Bank of Ireland. All the above stocks, bonds, and bank accounts are community property.

8. Lulu has a stock portfolio. During the year she sold the following stock, shown on her Forms 1099-B as follows:

	Orange Co.	*Gold Co.*	*Green Co.*
Sales price	$8,200	See	$7,500
Basis	3,800	Form	1,450
Date acquired	02/11/04	1099-B	10/31/04
Date sold	06/19/14	(Page D-9)	10/23/14

9. Lulu paid her ex-husband $6,000 alimony in the current year, as required under the divorce decree. Her ex-husband's name is Hector Leach and his Social Security number is 566-23-5431.

10. Gregory does all the significant work in the Bed & Breakfast and therefore he pays self-employment tax on 100 percent of the earnings from the B&B.

11. During the year, Gregory's uncle Martin died. Martin had a $50,000 life insurance policy that named Gregory as the beneficiary. Gregory received the check for the benefits payable under the policy on November 30 of the current year. Martin also left Gregory a small nonoperating farm with an appraised value of $120,000.

12. Two years ago, Gary won a contest and received a cash prize. The money is in a savings account in Gary's name. His interest on the savings account in the current year is $3,400. Instead of having Gary fill out a tax return and pay the "kiddie tax," Gregory and Lulu elect to report the interest income on their joint tax return.

Required: Gregory and Lulu have come to you to prepare their 2014 federal income tax return. Do not complete a California state income tax return. Gregory and Lulu have completed a tax organizer and have also given you several IRS forms (see Page D-9) that they were not sure what to do with. Make realistic assumptions about any missing data (addresses, etc.) that you need. Do not file a federal Form 4562, Form 4952, or Form 8829 for the Clifdens. The following is a list of the forms and schedules that you will need to complete the tax return:

Form 1040	Schedule SE
Schedule A	Form 8814
Schedule B	Form 8849
Schedule C	Qualified Dividends and Capital Gain Tax Worksheet
Schedule D	

Note: The forms included in Appendix D are provided for the student to work on only one of the two comprehensive problems. If desired, additional forms may be obtained from the IRS website at **www.irs.gov.**

☐ CORRECTED (if checked)

Distributions From Pensions, Annuities, Retirement or Profit-Sharing Plans, IRAs, Insurance Contracts, etc. — OMB No. 1545-0119 — 2014 — Form 1099-R

Field	Value
PAYER'S name, street address, city or town, state or province, country, and ZIP or foreign postal code	*U.S. Navy, Retired Benefits Center, Cleveland, OH 43267*
1 Gross distribution	$ *9,400.00*
2a Taxable amount	$ *9,400.00*
2b Taxable amount not determined	☐
Total distribution	☐
PAYER'S federal identification number	*11-4662891*
RECIPIENT'S identification number	*543-88-9756*
3 Capital gain (included in box 2a)	$
4 Federal income tax withheld	$ *1,200.00*
RECIPIENT'S name	*Gregory R. Clifden*
5 Employee contributions /Designated Roth contributions or insurance premiums	$
6 Net unrealized appreciation in employer's securities	$
Street address (including apt. no.)	*33333 Fume Blanc Way*
7 Distribution code(s)	
IRA/SEP/SIMPLE	☐
8 Other	$ %
City or town, state or province, country, and ZIP or foreign postal code	*Temecula, CA 92591*
9a Your percentage of total distribution	%
9b Total employee contributions	$
10 Amount allocable to IRR within 5 years	$
11 1st year of desig. Roth contrib.	
12 State tax withheld	$ *290.00* / $
13 State/Payer's state no.	*CA*
14 State distribution	$ *9,400.00* / $
Account number (see instructions)	
15 Local tax withheld	$ / $
16 Name of locality	
17 Local distribution	$ / $

Copy B Report this income on your federal tax return. If this form shows federal income tax withheld in box 4, attach this copy to your return.

This information is being furnished to the Internal Revenue Service.

Form **1099-R** www.irs.gov/form1099r Department of the Treasury - Internal Revenue Service

☐ CORRECTED (if checked)

Proceeds From Broker and Barter Exchange Transactions — OMB No. 1545-0715 — 2014 — Form 1099-B

Field	Value
PAYER'S name, street address, city or town, state or province, country, ZIP or foreign postal code, and telephone no.	*Morgan Stanley, 269 Wall Street, New York, NY 10001*
Applicable check box on Form 8949	*A*
1a Description of property (Example 100 sh. XYZ Co.)	*Gold Company Stock*
1b Date acquired	*03/27/2014*
1c Date sold or disposed	*09/18/2014*
PAYER'S federal identification number	*11-4396782*
RECIPIENT'S identification number	*256-43-8819*
1d Proceeds	$ *12,100.00*
1e Cost or other basis	$ *14,200.00*
1f Code, if any	
1g Adjustments	$
RECIPIENT'S name	*Lulu B. Clifden*
2 Type of gain or loss: Short-term	☒
Long-term	☐
3 If checked, basis reported to IRS	☐
Street address (including apt. no.)	*33333 Fume Blanc Way*
4 Federal income tax withheld	$
5 If checked, noncovered security	☐
City or town, state or province, country, and ZIP or foreign postal code	*Temecula, CA 92591*
6 Reported to IRS: Gross proceeds	☐
Net proceeds	☐
7 If checked, loss is not allowed based on amount in 1d	☐
Account number (see instructions)	
8 Profit or (loss) realized in 2014 on closed contracts	$
9 Unrealized profit or (loss) on open contracts—12/31/2013	$
CUSIP number	
10 Unrealized profit or (loss) on open contracts—12/31/2014	$
11 Aggregate profit or (loss) on contracts	$
14 State name	
15 State identification no	
16 State tax withheld	$ / $
12	
13 Bartering	$

Copy B For Recipient

This is important tax information and is being furnished to the Internal Revenue Service. If you are required to file a return, a negligence penalty or other sanction may be imposed on you if this income is taxable and the IRS determines that it has not been reported.

Form **1099-B** www.irs.gov/form1099b Department of the Treasury - Internal Revenue Service

☐ CORRECTED (if checked)

Interest Income — OMB No. 1545-0112 — 2014 — Form 1099-INT

Field	Value
PAYER'S name, street address, city or town, state or province, country, ZIP or foreign postal code, and telephone no.	*Vintage Bank, 6792 Main Street, Temecula, CA 92591*
Payer's RTN (optional)	
1 Interest income	$ *3,375.00*
2 Early withdrawal penalty	$
PAYER'S federal identification number	*96-8724390*
RECIPIENT'S identification number	*256-43-8819*
3 Interest on U.S. Savings Bonds and Treas. obligations	$
RECIPIENT'S name	*Gregory R. Clifden*
4 Federal income tax withheld	$
5 Investment expenses	$
Street address (including apt. no.)	*33333 Fume Blanc Way*
6 Foreign tax paid	$
7 Foreign country or U.S. possession	
City or town, state or province, country, and ZIP or foreign postal code	*Temecula, CA 92591*
8 Tax-exempt interest	$
9 Specified private activity bond interest	$
10 Market discount	$
11 Bond premium	$
Account number (see instructions)	
12 Tax-exempt bond CUSIP no.	
13 State	
14 State identification no.	
15 State tax withheld	$ / $

Copy B For Recipient

This is important tax information and is being furnished to the Internal Revenue Service. If you are required to file a return, a negligence penalty or other sanction may be imposed on you if this income is taxable and the IRS determines that it has not been reported.

Form **1099-INT** (keep for your records) www.irs.gov/form1099int Department of the Treasury - Internal Revenue Service

Form **1040** Department of the Treasury—Internal Revenue Service (99)
U.S. Individual Income Tax Return **2014** OMB No. 1545-0074 IRS Use Only—Do not write or staple in this space.

For the year Jan. 1–Dec. 31, 2014, or other tax year beginning , 2014, ending , 20 — See separate instructions.

Your first name and initial	Last name	**Your social security number**
If a joint return, spouse's first name and initial	Last name	**Spouse's social security number**
Home address (number and street). If you have a P.O. box, see instructions.	Apt. no.	▲ Make sure the SSN(s) above and on line 6c are correct.
City, town or post office, state, and ZIP code. If you have a foreign address, also complete spaces below (see instructions).		**Presidential Election Campaign** Check here if you, or your spouse if filing jointly, want $3 to go to this fund. Checking a box below will not change your tax or refund. ☐ You ☐ Spouse
Foreign country name	Foreign province/state/county	Foreign postal code

Filing Status

Check only one box.

1 ☐ Single
2 ☐ Married filing jointly (even if only one had income)
3 ☐ Married filing separately. Enter spouse's SSN above and full name here. ▶
4 ☐ Head of household (with qualifying person). (See instructions.) If the qualifying person is a child but not your dependent, enter this child's name here. ▶
5 ☐ Qualifying widow(er) with dependent child

Exemptions

6a ☐ **Yourself.** If someone can claim you as a dependent, **do not** check box 6a . . . . . .
b ☐ **Spouse** . . . . .

Boxes checked on 6a and 6b

c **Dependents:**

(1) First name Last name	(2) Dependent's social security number	(3) Dependent's relationship to you	(4) ✓ if child under age 17 qualifying for child tax credit (see instructions)
			☐
			☐
			☐
			☐

If more than four dependents, see instructions and check here ▶ ☐

No. of children on 6c who:
• lived with you
• did not live with you due to divorce or separation (see instructions)
Dependents on 6c not entered above

d Total number of exemptions claimed . . . . . — **Add numbers on lines above ▶**

Income

Attach Form(s) W-2 here. Also attach Forms W-2G and 1099-R if tax was withheld.

If you did not get a W-2, see instructions.

Line	Description		Amount
7	Wages, salaries, tips, etc. Attach Form(s) W-2		7
8a	**Taxable** interest. Attach Schedule B if required		8a
b	**Tax-exempt** interest. **Do not** include on line 8a	8b	
9a	Ordinary dividends. Attach Schedule B if required		9a
b	Qualified dividends	9b	
10	Taxable refunds, credits, or offsets of state and local income taxes		10
11	Alimony received		11
12	Business income or (loss). Attach Schedule C or C-EZ		12
13	Capital gain or (loss). Attach Schedule D if required. If not required, check here ▶ ☐		13
14	Other gains or (losses). Attach Form 4797		14
15a	IRA distributions	15a	b Taxable amount 15b
16a	Pensions and annuities	16a	b Taxable amount 16b
17	Rental real estate, royalties, partnerships, S corporations, trusts, etc. Attach Schedule E		17
18	Farm income or (loss). Attach Schedule F		18
19	Unemployment compensation		19
20a	Social security benefits	20a	b Taxable amount 20b
21	Other income. List type and amount		21
22	Combine the amounts in the far right column for lines 7 through 21. This is your **total income** ▶		22

DRAFT AS OF August 28, 201 DO NOT FIL

Adjusted Gross Income

Line	Description		Amount
23	Reserved	23	
24	Certain business expenses of reservists, performing artists, and fee-basis government officials. Attach Form 2106 or 2106-EZ	24	
25	Health savings account deduction. Attach Form 8889	25	
26	Moving expenses. Attach Form 3903	26	
27	Deductible part of self-employment tax. Attach Schedule SE	27	
28	Self-employed SEP, SIMPLE, and qualified plans	28	
29	Self-employed health insurance deduction	29	
30	Penalty on early withdrawal of savings	30	
31a	Alimony paid b Recipient's SSN ▶	31a	
32	IRA deduction	32	
33	Student loan interest deduction	33	
34	Reserved	34	
35	Domestic production activities deduction. Attach Form 8903	35	
36	Add lines 23 through 35		36
37	Subtract line 36 from line 22. This is your **adjusted gross income** ▶		37

For Disclosure, Privacy Act, and Paperwork Reduction Act Notice, see separate instructions. Cat. No. 11320B Form **1040** (2014)

Form 1040 (2014) Page **2**

DRAFT AS OF August 28, 2014 DO NOT FILE

Tax and Credits

38	Amount from line 37 (adjusted gross income)	38	
39a	Check if: { ☐ **You** were born before January 2, 1950, ☐ Blind. / ☐ **Spouse** was born before January 2, 1950, ☐ Blind. } **Total boxes checked** ▶ 39a ☐		
b	If your spouse itemizes on a separate return or you were a dual-status alien, check here ▶ 39b ☐		
40	**Itemized deductions** (from Schedule A) **or** your **standard deduction** (see left margin)	40	
41	Subtract line 40 from line 38	41	
42	**Exemptions.** If line 38 is $152,525 or less, multiply $3,950 by the number on line 6d. Otherwise, see instructions	42	
43	**Taxable income.** Subtract line 42 from line 41. If line 42 is more than line 41, enter -0-	43	
44	**Tax** (see instructions). Check if any from: **a** ☐ Form(s) 8814 **b** ☐ Form 4972 **c** ☐ ______	44	
45	**Alternative minimum tax** (see instructions). Attach Form 6251	45	
46	Excess advance premium tax credit repayment. Attach Form 8962	46	
47	Add lines 44, 45, and 46 ▶	47	
48	Foreign tax credit. Attach Form 1116 if required	48	
49	Credit for child and dependent care expenses. Attach Form 2441	49	
50	Education credits from Form 8863, line 19	50	
51	Retirement savings contributions credit. Attach Form 8880	51	
52	Child tax credit. Attach Schedule 8812, if required	52	
53	Residential energy credit. Attach Form 5695	53	
54	Other credits from Form: **a** ☐ 3800 **b** ☐ 8801 **c** ☐	54	
55	Add lines 48 through 54. These are your **total credits**	55	
56	Subtract line 55 from line 47. If line 55 is more than line 47, enter -0- ▶	56	

Standard Deduction for—
- People who check any box on line 39a or 39b **or** who can be claimed as a dependent, see instructions.
- All others:

Single or Married filing separately, $6,200

Married filing jointly or Qualifying widow(er), $12,400

Head of household, $9,100

Other Taxes

57	Self-employment tax. Attach Schedule SE	57	
58	Unreported social security and Medicare tax from Form: **a** ☐ 4137 **b** ☐ 8919	58	
59	Additional tax on IRAs, other qualified retirement plans, etc. Attach Form 5329 if required	59	
60a	Household employment taxes from Schedule H	60a	
b	First-time homebuyer credit repayment. Attach Form 5405 if required	60b	
61	Health care: individual responsibility (see instructions) Full-year coverage ☐	61	
62	Taxes from: **a** ☐ Form 8959 **b** ☐ Form 8960 **c** ☐ Instructions; enter code(s) ______	62	
63	Add lines 56 through 62. This is your **total tax** ▶	63	

Payments

If you have a qualifying child, attach Schedule EIC.

64	Federal income tax withheld from Forms W-2 and 1099	64	
65	2014 estimated tax payments and amount applied from 2013 return	65	
66a	**Earned income credit (EIC)**	66a	
b	Nontaxable combat pay election 66b		
67	Additional child tax credit. Attach Schedule 8812	67	
68	American opportunity credit from Form 8863, line 8	68	
69	Net premium tax credit. Attach Form 8962	69	
70	Amount paid with request for extension to file	70	
71	Excess social security and tier 1 RRTA tax withheld	71	
72	Credit for federal tax on fuels. Attach Form 4136	72	
73	Credits from Form: **a** ☐ 2439 **b** Reserved **c** Reserved **d** ☐ ______	73	
74	Add lines 64, 65, 66a, and 67 through 73. These are your **total payments** ▶	74	

Refund

75	If line 74 is more than line 63, subtract line 63 from line 74. This is the amount you **overpaid**	75	
76a	Amount of line 75 you want **refunded to you.** If Form 8888 is attached, check here ▶ ☐	76a	
▶ b	Routing number ▶ **c** Type: ☐ Checking ☐ Savings		
▶ d	Account number		
77	Amount of line 75 you want **applied to your 2015 estimated tax** ▶ 77		

Direct deposit? See instructions.

Amount You Owe

78	**Amount you owe.** Subtract line 74 from line 63. For details on how to pay, see instructions ▶	78	
79	Estimated tax penalty (see instructions) 79		

Third Party Designee

Do you want to allow another person to discuss this return with the IRS (see instructions)? ☐ **Yes.** Complete below. ☐ **No**

Designee's name ▶ Phone no. ▶ Personal identification number (PIN) ▶

Sign Here

Under penalties of perjury, I declare that I have examined this return and accompanying schedules and statements, and to the best of my knowledge and belief, they are true, correct, and complete. Declaration of preparer (other than taxpayer) is based on all information of which preparer has any knowledge.

Joint return? See instructions. Keep a copy for your records.

Your signature	Date	Your occupation	Daytime phone number
Spouse's signature. If a joint return, **both** must sign.	Date	Spouse's occupation	If the IRS sent you an Identity Protection PIN, enter it here (see inst.)

Paid Preparer Use Only

Print/Type preparer's name	Preparer's signature	Date	Check ☐ if self-employed	PTIN
Firm's name ▶			Firm's EIN ▶	
Firm's address ▶			Phone no.	

www.irs.gov/form1040 Form **1040** (2014)

SCHEDULE A (Form 1040)

Department of the Treasury
Internal Revenue Service (99)

Itemized Deductions

▶ Information about Schedule A and its separate instructions is at *www.irs.gov/schedulea*.

▶ Attach to Form 1040.

OMB No. 1545-0074

2014

Attachment Sequence No. 07

Name(s) shown on Form 1040 | Your social security number

DRAFT AS OF August 15, 2014 DO NOT FILE

Section	Line	Description	Box	Total box
Medical and Dental Expenses		**Caution.** Do not include expenses reimbursed or paid by others.		
	1	Medical and dental expenses (see instructions)	1	
	2	Enter amount from Form 1040, line 38 [2]		
	3	Multiply line 2 by 10% (.10). But if either you or your spouse was born before January 2, 1950, multiply line 2 by 7.5% (.075) instead	3	
	4	Subtract line 3 from line 1. If line 3 is more than line 1, enter -0-		4
Taxes You Paid	5	State and local		
		a ☐ Income taxes / b ☐ RESERVED	5	
	6	Real estate taxes (see instructions)	6	
	7	Personal property taxes	7	
	8	Other taxes. List type and amount ▶	8	
	9	Add lines 5 through 8		9
Interest You Paid	10	Home mortgage interest and points reported to you on Form 1098	10	
Note. Your mortgage interest deduction may be limited (see instructions).	11	Home mortgage interest not reported to you on Form 1098. If paid to the person from whom you bought the home, see instructions and show that person's name, identifying no., and address ▶	11	
	12	Points not reported to you on Form 1098. See instructions for special rules	12	
	13	RESERVED	13	
	14	Investment interest. Attach Form 4952 if required. (See instructions.)	14	
	15	Add lines 10 through 14		15
Gifts to Charity	16	Gifts by cash or check. If you made any gift of $250 or more, see instructions	16	
If you made a gift and got a benefit for it, see instructions.	17	Other than by cash or check. If any gift of $250 or more, see instructions. You **must** attach Form 8283 if over $500	17	
	18	Carryover from prior year	18	
	19	Add lines 16 through 18		19
Casualty and Theft Losses	20	Casualty or theft loss(es). Attach Form 4684. (See instructions.)		20
Job Expenses and Certain Miscellaneous Deductions	21	Unreimbursed employee expenses—job travel, union dues, job education, etc. Attach Form 2106 or 2106-EZ if required. (See instructions.) ▶	21	
	22	Tax preparation fees	22	
	23	Other expenses—investment, safe deposit box, etc. List type and amount ▶	23	
	24	Add lines 21 through 23	24	
	25	Enter amount from Form 1040, line 38 [25]		
	26	Multiply line 25 by 2% (.02)	26	
	27	Subtract line 26 from line 24. If line 26 is more than line 24, enter -0-		27
Other Miscellaneous Deductions	28	Other—from list in instructions. List type and amount ▶		28
Total Itemized Deductions	29	Is Form 1040, line 38, over $152,525? ☐ **No.** Your deduction is not limited. Add the amounts in the far right column for lines 4 through 28. Also, enter this amount on Form 1040, line 40. ☐ **Yes.** Your deduction may be limited. See the Itemized Deductions Worksheet in the instructions to figure the amount to enter.		29
	30	If you elect to itemize deductions even though they are less than your standard deduction, check here ▶ ☐		

SCHEDULE B
(Form 1040A or 1040)

Department of the Treasury
Internal Revenue Service (99)

Interest and Ordinary Dividends

► Attach to Form 1040A or 1040.
► Information about Schedule B and its instructions is at *www.irs.gov/scheduleb*.

OMB No. 1545-0074
2014
Attachment Sequence No. 08

Name(s) shown on return | **Your social security number**

DRAFT AS OF June 18, 2014 DO NOT FILE

Part I Interest

(See instructions on back and the instructions for Form 1040A, or Form 1040, line 8a.)

Note. If you received a Form 1099-INT, Form 1099-OID, or substitute statement from a brokerage firm, list the firm's name as the payer and enter the total interest shown on that form.

			Amount
1	List name of payer. If any interest is from a seller-financed mortgage and the buyer used the property as a personal residence, see instructions on back and list this interest first. Also, show that buyer's social security number and address ►	1	
2	Add the amounts on line 1	2	
3	Excludable interest on series EE and I U.S. savings bonds issued after 1989. Attach Form 8815	3	
4	Subtract line 3 from line 2. Enter the result here and on Form 1040A, or Form 1040, line 8a ►	4	

Note. If line 4 is over $1,500, you must complete Part III.

Part II Ordinary Dividends

(See instructions on back and the instructions for Form 1040A, or Form 1040, line 9a.)

Note. If you received a Form 1099-DIV or substitute statement from a brokerage firm, list the firm's name as the payer and enter the ordinary dividends shown on that form.

			Amount
5	List name of payer ►	5	
6	Add the amounts on line 5. Enter the total here and on Form 1040A, or Form 1040, line 9a ►	6	

Note. If line 6 is over $1,500, you must complete Part III.

Part III Foreign Accounts and Trusts

(See instructions on back.)

You must complete this part if you **(a)** had over $1,500 of taxable interest or ordinary dividends; **(b)** had a foreign account; or **(c)** received a distribution from, or were a grantor of, or a transferor to, a foreign trust.

		Yes	No
7a	At any time during 2014, did you have a financial interest in or signature authority over a financial account (such as a bank account, securities account, or brokerage account) located in a foreign country? See instructions		
	If "Yes," are you required to file FinCEN Form 114, Report of Foreign Bank and Financial Accounts (FBAR), to report that financial interest or signature authority? See FinCEN Form 114 and its instructions for filing requirements and exceptions to those requirements		
b	If you are required to file FinCEN Form 114, enter the name of the foreign country where the financial account is located ►		
8	During 2014, did you receive a distribution from, or were you the grantor of, or transferor to, a foreign trust? If "Yes," you may have to file Form 3520. See instructions on back		

For Paperwork Reduction Act Notice, see your tax return instructions. Cat. No. 17146N **Schedule B (Form 1040A or 1040) 2014**

SCHEDULE C (Form 1040)

Department of the Treasury
Internal Revenue Service (99)

Profit or Loss From Business
(Sole Proprietorship)

▶ **Information about Schedule C and its separate instructions is at *www.irs.gov/schedulec.***
▶ **Attach to Form 1040, 1040NR, or 1041; partnerships generally must file Form 1065.**

OMB No. 1545-0074
2014
Attachment Sequence No. **09**

DRAFT AS OF June 19, 2014 DO NOT FILE

Name of proprietor: **Gregory Clifden** | **Social security number (SSN)**

A Principal business or profession, including product or service (see instructions)
Bed & Breakfast

B Enter code from instructions ▶

C Business name. If no separate business name, leave blank.
Rock Glen House Bed & Breakfast

D Employer ID number (EIN), (see instr.)

E Business address (including suite or room no.) ▶
City, town or post office, state, and ZIP code

F Accounting method: **(1)** ☑ Cash **(2)** ☐ Accrual **(3)** ☐ Other (specify) ▶

G Did you "materially participate" in the operation of this business during 2014? If "No," see instructions for limit on losses ☑ **Yes** ☐ **No**

H If you started or acquired this business during 2014, check here ▶ ☐

I Did you make any payments in 2014 that would require you to file Form(s) 1099? (see instructions) ☑ **Yes** ☐ **No**

J If "Yes," did you or will you file required Forms 1099? ☑ **Yes** ☐ **No**

Part I Income

1	Gross receipts or sales. See instructions for line 1 and check the box if this income was reported to you on Form W-2 and the "Statutory employee" box on that form was checked ▶ ☐	1	
2	Returns and allowances	2	
3	Subtract line 2 from line 1	3	
4	Cost of goods sold (from line 42)	4	
5	**Gross profit.** Subtract line 4 from line 3	5	
6	Other income, including federal and state gasoline or fuel tax credit or refund (see instructions)	6	
7	**Gross income.** Add lines 5 and 6 ▶	7	

Part II Expenses. Enter expenses for business use of your home **only** on line 30.

8	Advertising	8		18	Office expense (see instructions)	18	
9	Car and truck expenses (see instructions)	9		19	Pension and profit-sharing plans	19	
10	Commissions and fees	10		20	Rent or lease (see instructions):		
11	Contract labor (see instructions)	11		a	Vehicles, machinery, and equipment	20a	
12	Depletion	12		b	Other business property	20b	
13	Depreciation and section 179 expense deduction (not included in Part III) (see instructions)	13		21	Repairs and maintenance	21	
				22	Supplies (not included in Part III)	22	
				23	Taxes and licenses	23	
				24	Travel, meals, and entertainment:		
14	Employee benefit programs (other than on line 19)	14		a	Travel	24a	
15	Insurance (other than health)	15		b	Deductible meals and entertainment (see instructions)	24b	
16	Interest:			25	Utilities	25	
a	Mortgage (paid to banks, etc.)	16a		26	Wages (less employment credits)	26	
b	Other	16b		27a	Other expenses (from line 48)	27a	
17	Legal and professional services	17		b	**Reserved for future use**	27b	

28	**Total expenses** before expenses for business use of home. Add lines 8 through 27a ▶	28	
29	Tentative profit or (loss). Subtract line 28 from line 7	29	
30	Expenses for business use of your home. Do not report these expenses elsewhere. Attach Form 8829 unless using the simplified method (see instructions). **Simplified method filers only:** enter the total square footage of: (a) your home: ______ and (b) the part of your home used for business: ______. Use the Simplified Method Worksheet in the instructions to figure the amount to enter on line 30	30	
31	**Net profit or (loss).** Subtract line 30 from line 29. • If a profit, enter on both **Form 1040, line 12** (or **Form 1040NR, line 13**) and on **Schedule SE, line 2.** (If you checked the box on line 1, see instructions). Estates and trusts, enter on **Form 1041, line 3.** • If a loss, you **must** go to line 32.	31	

32 If you have a loss, check the box that describes your investment in this activity (see instructions).

- If you checked 32a, enter the loss on both **Form 1040, line 12,** (or **Form 1040NR, line 13**) and on **Schedule SE, line 2.** (If you checked the box on line 1, see the line 31 instructions). Estates and trusts, enter on **Form 1041, line 3.**
- If you checked 32b, you **must** attach **Form 6198.** Your loss may be limited.

32a ☐ All investment is at risk.
32b ☐ Some investment is not at risk.

Schedule C (Form 1040) 2014 Page **2**

Part III Cost of Goods Sold (see instructions)

DRAFT AS OF June 19, 2014 DO NOT FILE

33 Method(s) used to value closing inventory: a ☐ Cost b ☐ Lower of cost or market c ☐ Other (attach explanation)

34 Was there any change in determining quantities, costs, or valuations between opening and closing inventory? If "Yes," attach explanation . . . ☐ Yes ☐ No

35	Inventory at beginning of year. If different from last year's closing inventory, attach explanation	35	
36	Purchases less cost of items withdrawn for personal use	36	
37	Cost of labor. Do not include any amounts paid to yourself	37	
38	Materials and supplies	38	
39	Other costs	39	
40	Add lines 35 through 39	40	
41	Inventory at end of year	41	
42	**Cost of goods sold.** Subtract line 41 from line 40. Enter the result here and on line 4	42	

Part IV Information on Your Vehicle.

Complete this part **only** if you are claiming car or truck expenses on line 9 and are not required to file Form 4562 for this business. See the instructions for line 13 to find out if you must file Form 4562.

43 When did you place your vehicle in service for business purposes? (month, day, year) ▶ ____ / ____ / ____

44 Of the total number of miles you drove your vehicle during 2014, enter the number of miles you used your vehicle for:

a Business ______________ b Commuting (see instructions) ______________ c Other ______________

45 Was your vehicle available for personal use during off-duty hours? . . . ☐ Yes ☐ No

46 Do you (or your spouse) have another vehicle available for personal use?. . . ☐ Yes ☐ No

47a Do you have evidence to support your deduction? . . . ☐ Yes ☐ No

b If "Yes," is the evidence written? . . . ☐ Yes ☐ No

Part V Other Expenses.

List below business expenses not included on lines 8–26 or line 30.

48 **Total other expenses.** Enter here and on line 27a	48	

Schedule C (Form 1040) 2014

SCHEDULE D (Form 1040)

Department of the Treasury Internal Revenue Service (99)

Capital Gains and Losses

▶ Attach to Form 1040 or Form 1040NR.
▶ Information about Schedule D and its separate instructions is at *www.irs.gov/scheduled*.
▶ Use Form 8949 to list your transactions for lines 1b, 2, 3, 8b, 9, and 10.

OMB No. 1545-0074

2014

Attachment Sequence No. **12**

Name(s) shown on return: **Gregory and Lulu Clifden**

Your social security number

DRAFT AS OF June 9, 2014 DO NOT FILE

Part I Short-Term Capital Gains and Losses—Assets Held One Year or Less

See instructions for how to figure the amounts to enter on the lines below. This form may be easier to complete if you round off cents to whole dollars.	(d) Proceeds (sales price)	(e) Cost (or other basis)	(g) Adjustments to gain or loss from Form(s) 8949, Part I, line 2, column (g)	(h) Gain or (loss) Subtract column (e) from column (d) and combine the result with column (g)
1a Totals for all short-term transactions reported on Form 1099-B for which basis was reported to the IRS and for which you have no adjustments (see instructions). However, if you choose to report all these transactions on Form 8949, leave this line blank and go to line 1b				
1b Totals for all transactions reported on Form(s) 8949 with **Box A** checked				
2 Totals for all transactions reported on Form(s) 8949 with **Box B** checked				
3 Totals for all transactions reported on Form(s) 8949 with **Box C** checked				

4 Short-term gain from Form 6252 and short-term gain or (loss) from Forms 4684, 6781, and 8824	4	
5 Net short-term gain or (loss) from partnerships, S corporations, estates, and trusts from Schedule(s) K-1	5	
6 Short-term capital loss carryover. Enter the amount, if any, from line 8 of your **Capital Loss Carryover Worksheet** in the instructions	6	( )
7 **Net short-term capital gain or (loss).** Combine lines 1a through 6 in column (h). If you have any long-term capital gains or losses, go to Part II below. Otherwise, go to Part III on the back	7	

Part II Long-Term Capital Gains and Losses—Assets Held More Than One Year

See instructions for how to figure the amounts to enter on the lines below. This form may be easier to complete if you round off cents to whole dollars.	(d) Proceeds (sales price)	(e) Cost (or other basis)	(g) Adjustments to gain or loss from Form(s) 8949, Part II, line 2, column (g)	(h) Gain or (loss) Subtract column (e) from column (d) and combine the result with column (g)
8a Totals for all long-term transactions reported on Form 1099-B for which basis was reported to the IRS and for which you have no adjustments (see instructions). However, if you choose to report all these transactions on Form 8949, leave this line blank and go to line 8b				
8b Totals for all transactions reported on Form(s) 8949 with **Box D** checked				
9 Totals for all transactions reported on Form(s) 8949 with **Box E** checked				
10 Totals for all transactions reported on Form(s) 8949 with **Box F** checked				

11 Gain from Form 4797, Part I; long-term gain from Forms 2439 and 6252; and long-term gain or (loss) from Forms 4684, 6781, and 8824	11	
12 Net long-term gain or (loss) from partnerships, S corporations, estates, and trusts from Schedule(s) K-1	12	
13 Capital gain distributions. See the instructions	13	
14 Long-term capital loss carryover. Enter the amount, if any, from line 13 of your **Capital Loss Carryover Worksheet** in the instructions	14	( )
15 **Net long-term capital gain or (loss).** Combine lines 8a through 14 in column (h). Then go to Part III on the back	15	

Schedule D (Form 1040) 2014 Page **2**

Part III **Summary**

16 Combine lines 7 and 15 and enter the result . . . . **16** ____

- If line 16 is a **gain,** enter the amount from line 16 on Form 1040, line 13, or Form 1040NR, line 14. Then go to line 17 below.
- If line 16 is a **loss,** skip lines 17 through 20 below. Then go to line 21. Also be sure to complete line 22.
- If line 16 is **zero,** skip lines 17 through 21 below and enter -0- on Form 1040, line 13, or Form 1040NR, line 14. Then go to line 22.

17 Are lines 15 and 16 **both** gains?

☑ **Yes.** Go to line 18.

☐ **No.** Skip lines 18 through 21, and go to line 22.

18 Enter the amount, if any, from line 7 of the **28% Rate Gain Worksheet** in the instructions . . ▶ **18** ____

19 Enter the amount, if any, from line 18 of the **Unrecaptured Section 1250 Gain Worksheet** in the instructions . . . . ▶ **19** ____

20 Are lines 18 and 19 **both** zero or blank?

☑ **Yes.** Complete the **Qualified Dividends and Capital Gain Tax Worksheet** in the instructions for Form 1040, line 44 (or in the instructions for Form 1040NR, line 42). **Do not** complete lines 21 and 22 below.

☐ **No.** Complete the **Schedule D Tax Worksheet** in the instructions. **Do not** complete lines 21 and 22 below.

21 If line 16 is a loss, enter here and on Form 1040, line 13, or Form 1040NR, line 14, the **smaller** of:

- The loss on line 16 or
- ($3,000), or if married filing separately, ($1,500)

. . . . **21** (   )

Note. When figuring which amount is smaller, treat both amounts as positive numbers.

22 Do you have qualified dividends on Form 1040, line 9b, or Form 1040NR, line 10b?

☑ **Yes.** Complete the **Qualified Dividends and Capital Gain Tax Worksheet** in the instructions for Form 1040, line 44 (or in the instructions for Form 1040NR, line 42).

☐ **No.** Complete the rest of Form 1040 or Form 1040NR.

Schedule D (Form 1040) 2014

DRAFT AS OF June 9, 2014 DO NOT FILE

Form **8949**

Department of the Treasury
Internal Revenue Service

Sales and Other Dispositions of Capital Assets

▶ **Information about Form 8949 and its separate instructions is at *www.irs.gov/form8949*.**
▶ **File with your Schedule D to list your transactions for lines 1b, 2, 3, 8b, 9, and 10 of Schedule D.**

OMB No. 1545-0123
2014
Attachment Sequence No. **12A**

Name(s) shown on return	**Social security number or taxpayer identification number**
Noah and Joan Arc	

Before you check Box A, B, or C below, see whether you received any Form(s) 1099-B or substitute statement(s) from your broker. A substitute statement will have the same information as Form 1099-B. Either may show your basis (usually your cost) even if your broker did not report it to the IRS. Brokers must report basis to the IRS for most stock you bought in 2011 or later (and for certain debt instruments you bought in 2014 or later).

Part I **Short-Term.** Transactions involving capital assets you held 1 year or less are short term. For long-term transactions, see page 2.

Note. You may aggregate all short-term transactions reported on Form(s) 1099-B showing basis was reported to the IRS and for which no adjustments or codes are required. Enter the total directly on Schedule D, line 1a; you are not required to report these transactions on Form 8949 (see instructions).

DRAFT AS OF June 12, 2014 DO NOT FILE

You *must* check Box A, B, *or* C below. Check only one box. If more than one box applies for your short-term transactions, complete a separate Form 8949, page 1, for each applicable box. If you have more short-term transactions than will fit on this page for one or more of the boxes, complete as many forms with the same box checked as you need.

☑ **(A)** Short-term transactions reported on Form(s) 1099-B showing basis was reported to the IRS (see **Note** above)
☐ **(B)** Short-term transactions reported on Form(s) 1099-B showing basis was **not** reported to the IRS
☐ **(C)** Short-term transactions not reported to you on Form 1099-B

1 (a) Description of property (Example: 100 sh. XYZ Co.)	(b) Date acquired (Mo., day, yr.)	(c) Date sold or disposed (Mo., day, yr.)	(d) Proceeds (sales price) (see instructions)	(e) Cost or other basis. See the **Note** below and see *Column (e)* in the separate instructions	**Adjustment, if any, to gain or loss.** If you enter an amount in column (g), enter a code in column (f). **See the separate instructions.** (f) Code(s) from instructions	(g) Amount of adjustment	(h) **Gain or (loss).** Subtract column (e) from column (d) and combine the result with column (g)
2 Totals. Add the amounts in columns (d), (e), (g), and (h) (subtract negative amounts). Enter each total here and include on your Schedule D, **line 1b** (if **Box A** above is checked), **line 2** (if **Box B** above is checked), or **line 3** (if **Box C** above is checked) ▶							

Note. If you checked Box A above but the basis reported to the IRS was incorrect, enter in column (e) the basis as reported to the IRS, and enter an adjustment in column (g) to correct the basis. See *Column (g)* in the separate instructions for how to figure the amount of the adjustment.

Form 8949 (2014) Attachment Sequence No. **12A** Page **2**

Name(s) shown on return. Name and SSN or taxpayer identification no. not required if shown on other side	**Social security number or taxpayer identification number**

Before you check Box D, E, or F below, see whether you received any Form(s) 1099-B or substitute statement(s) from your broker. A substitute statement will have the same information as Form 1099-B. Either may show your basis (usually your cost) even if your broker did not report it to the IRS. Brokers must report basis to the IRS for most stock you bought in 2011 or later (and for certain debt instruments you bought in 2014 or later).

Part II **Long-Term.** Transactions involving capital assets you held more than 1 year are long term. For short-term transactions, see page 1.

Note. You may aggregate all long-term transactions reported on Form(s) 1099-B showing basis was reported to the IRS and for which no adjustments or codes are required. Enter the total directly on Schedule D, line 8a; you are not required to report these transactions on Form 8949 (see instructions).

DRAFT AS OF June 12, 2014 DO NOT FILE

You *must* check Box D, E, *or* F below. Check only one box. If more than one box applies for your long-term transactions, complete a separate Form 8949, page 2, for each applicable box. If you have more long-term transactions than will fit on this page for one or more of the boxes, complete as many forms with the same box checked as you need.

- ☑ **(D)** Long-term transactions reported on Form(s) 1099-B showing basis was reported to the IRS (see **Note** above)
- ☐ **(E)** Long-term transactions reported on Form(s) 1099-B showing basis was **not** reported to the IRS
- ☐ **(F)** Long-term transactions not reported to you on Form 1099-B

1 (a) Description of property (Example: 100 sh. XYZ Co.)	(b) Date acquired (Mo., day, yr.)	(c) Date sold or disposed (Mo., day, yr.)	(d) Proceeds (sales price) (see instructions)	(e) Cost or other basis. See the **Note** below and see *Column (e)* in the separate instructions	**Adjustment, if any, to gain or loss.** If you enter an amount in column (g), enter a code in column (f). **See the separate instructions.** (f) Code(s) from instructions	(g) Amount of adjustment	(h) **Gain or (loss).** Subtract column (e) from column (d) and combine the result with column (g)
2 Totals. Add the amounts in columns (d), (e), (g), and (h) (subtract negative amounts). Enter each total here and include on your Schedule D, **line 8b** (if **Box D** above is checked), **line 9** (if **Box E** above is checked), or **line 10** (if **Box F** above is checked) ▶							

Note. If you checked Box D above but the basis reported to the IRS was incorrect, enter in column (e) the basis as reported to the IRS, and enter an adjustment in column (g) to correct the basis. See *Column (g)* in the separate instructions for how to figure the amount of the adjustment.

SCHEDULE SE (Form 1040)
Department of the Treasury
Internal Revenue Service (99)

Self-Employment Tax

▶ **Information about Schedule SE and its separate instructions is at *www.irs.gov/schedulese*.**
▶ **Attach to Form 1040 or Form 1040NR.**

OMB No. 1545-0074
2014
Attachment Sequence No. **17**

Name of person with **self-employment** income (as shown on Form 1040 or Form 1040NR)	Social security number of person with **self-employment** income ▶	

Before you begin: To determine if you must file Schedule SE, see the instructions.

DRAFT AS OF May 14, 2014 DO NOT FILE

May I Use Short Schedule SE or Must I Use Long Schedule SE?

Note. Use this flowchart **only if** you must file Schedule SE. If unsure, see *Who Must File Schedule SE* in the instructions.

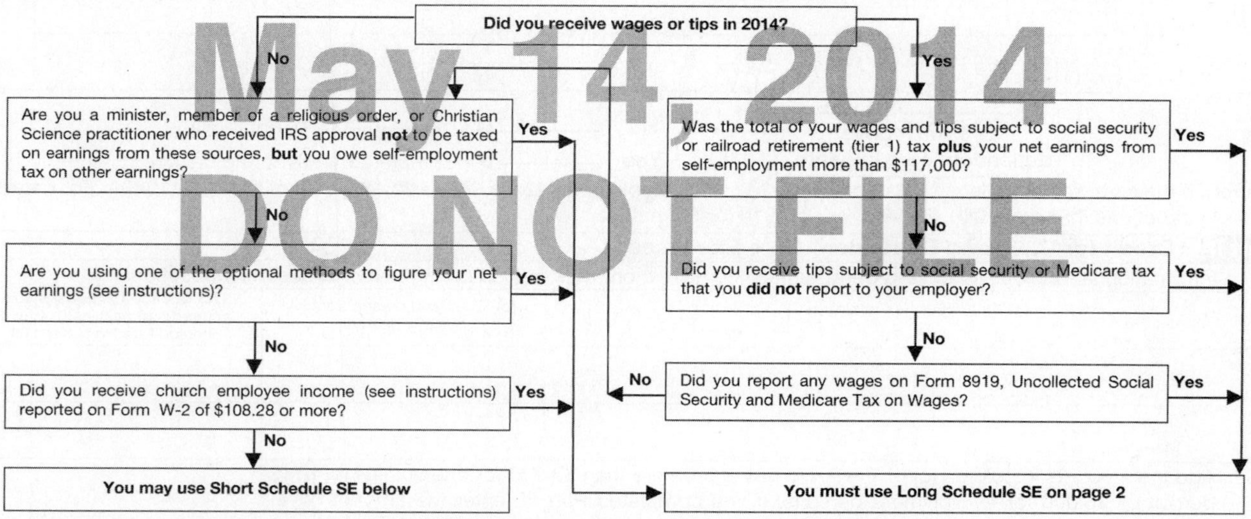

Section A—Short Schedule SE. Caution. Read above to see if you can use Short Schedule SE.

1a	Net farm profit or (loss) from Schedule F, line 34, and farm partnerships, Schedule K-1 (Form 1065), box 14, code A	**1a**	
b	If you received social security retirement or disability benefits, enter the amount of Conservation Reserve Program payments included on Schedule F, line 4b, or listed on Schedule K-1 (Form 1065), box 20, code Z	**1b**	( )
2	Net profit or (loss) from Schedule C, line 31; Schedule C-EZ, line 3; Schedule K-1 (Form 1065), box 14, code A (other than farming); and Schedule K-1 (Form 1065-B), box 9, code J1. Ministers and members of religious orders, see instructions for types of income to report on this line. See instructions for other income to report	**2**	
3	Combine lines 1a, 1b, and 2	**3**	
4	Multiply line 3 by 92.35% (.9235). If less than $400, you do not owe self-employment tax; **do not** file this schedule unless you have an amount on line 1b . . . . ▶	**4**	
	Note. If line 4 is less than $400 due to Conservation Reserve Program payments on line 1b, see instructions.		
5	**Self-employment tax.** If the amount on line 4 is: • $117,000 or less, multiply line 4 by 15.3% (.153). Enter the result here and on **Form 1040, line 57,** or **Form 1040NR, line 55** • More than $117,000, multiply line 4 by 2.9% (.029). Then, add $14,508 to the result. Enter the total here and on **Form 1040, line 57,** or **Form 1040NR, line 55**	**5**	
6	**Deduction for one-half of self-employment tax.** Multiply line 5 by 50% (.50). Enter the result here and on **Form 1040, line 27,** or **Form 1040NR, line 27** **6**		

For Paperwork Reduction Act Notice, see your tax return instructions. Cat. No. 11358Z **Schedule SE (Form 1040) 2014**

Form **2441**

Department of the Treasury
Internal Revenue Service (99)

Child and Dependent Care Expenses

▶ Attach to Form 1040, Form 1040A, or Form 1040NR.

▶ Information about Form 2441 and its separate instructions is at *www.irs.gov/form2441.*

1040 / 1040A / 1040NR / 2441

OMB No. 1545-0074

2014

Attachment Sequence No. **21**

Name(s) shown on return | **Your social security number**

DRAFT AS OF July 2, 2014 DO NOT FILE

Part I **Persons or Organizations Who Provided the Care**—You **must** complete this part.
(If you have more than two care providers, see the instructions.)

1 **(a)** Care provider's name	**(b)** Address (number, street, apt. no., city, state, and ZIP code)	**(c)** Identifying number (SSN or EIN)	**(d)** Amount paid (see instructions)

Did you receive **dependent care benefits?** — **No** ▶ Complete only Part II below. — **Yes** ▶ Complete Part III on the back next.

Caution. If the care was provided in your home, you may owe employment taxes. If you do, you cannot file Form 1040A. For details, see the instructions for Form 1040, line 60a, or Form 1040NR, line 59a.

Part II **Credit for Child and Dependent Care Expenses**

2 Information about your **qualifying person(s).** If you have more than two qualifying persons, see the instructions.

(a) Qualifying person's name — First	Last	**(b)** Qualifying person's social security number	**(c) Qualified expenses** you incurred and paid in 2014 for the person listed in column (a)

3 Add the amounts in column (c) of line 2. **Do not** enter more than $3,000 for one qualifying person or $6,000 for two or more persons. If you completed Part III, enter the amount from line 31 . . . . . **3**

4 Enter your **earned income.** See instructions **4**

5 If married filing jointly, enter your spouse's earned income (if you or your spouse was a student or was disabled, see the instructions); **all others,** enter the amount from line 4 . **5**

6 Enter the **smallest** of line 3, 4, or 5 . . . . . **6**

7 Enter the amount from Form 1040, line 38; Form 1040A, line 22; or Form 1040NR, line 37. . . . . **7** 80,270

8 Enter on line 8 the decimal amount shown below that applies to the amount on line 7

If line 7 is: Over	But not over	Decimal amount is	If line 7 is: Over	But not over	Decimal amount is
$0	15,000	.35	$29,000	31,000	.27
15,000	17,000	.34	31,000	33,000	.26
17,000	19,000	.33	33,000	35,000	.25
19,000	21,000	.32	35,000	37,000	.24
21,000	23,000	.31	37,000	39,000	.23
23,000	25,000	.30	39,000	41,000	.22
25,000	27,000	.29	41,000	43,000	.21
27,000	29,000	.28	43,000	No limit	.20

8 X.

9 Multiply line 6 by the decimal amount on line 8. If you paid 2013 expenses in 2014, see the instructions **9**

10 Tax liability limit. Enter the amount from the Credit Limit Worksheet in the instructions. . . . . **10** n/a*

11 **Credit for child and dependent care expenses.** Enter the **smaller** of line 9 or line 10 here and on Form 1040, line 49; Form 1040A, line 31; or Form 1040NR, line 47 . . . . **11**

For Paperwork Reduction Act Notice, see your tax return instructions. Cat. No. 11862M Form **2441** (2014)

Form **8814**

Department of the Treasury
Internal Revenue Service (99)

Parents' Election To Report Child's Interest and Dividends

▶ **Information about Form 8814 and its instructions is at *www.irs.gov/form8814*.**
▶ **Attach to parents' Form 1040 or Form 1040NR.**

OMB No. 1545-0074
2014
Attachment Sequence No. **40**

DRAFT AS OF June 13, 2014 DO NOT FILE

Name(s) shown on your return	**Your social security number**

Caution. The federal income tax on your child's income, including qualified dividends and capital gain distributions, may be less if you file a separate tax return for the child instead of making this election. This is because you cannot take certain tax benefits that your child could take on his or her own return. For details, see **Tax benefits you cannot take** in the instructions.

A Child's name (first, initial, and last)	**B Child's social security number**

C If more than one Form 8814 is attached, check here . . . . . ▶ ☐

Part I **Child's Interest and Dividends To Report on Your Return**

1a	Enter your child's **taxable** interest. If this amount is different from the amounts shown on the child's Forms 1099-INT and 1099-OID, see the instructions			**1a**	
b	Enter your child's **tax-exempt** interest. **Do not** include this amount on line 1a	**1b**			
2a	Enter your child's ordinary dividends, including any Alaska Permanent Fund dividends. If your child received any ordinary dividends as a nominee, see the instructions			**2a**	
b	Enter your child's qualified dividends included on line 2a. See the instructions	**2b**			
3	Enter your child's capital gain distributions. If your child received any capital gain distributions as a nominee, see the instructions			**3**	
4	Add lines 1a, 2a, and 3. If the total is $2,000 or less, skip lines 5 through 12 and go to line 13. If the total is $10,000 or more, **do not** file this form. Your child **must** file his or her own return to report the income			**4**	
5	Base amount			**5**	2,000 00
6	Subtract line 5 from line 4			**6**	
	If both lines 2b and 3 are zero or blank, skip lines 7 through 10, enter -0- on line 11, and go to line 12. Otherwise, go to line 7.				
7	Divide line 2b by line 4. Enter the result as a decimal (rounded to at least three places)	**7**	.		
8	Divide line 3 by line 4. Enter the result as a decimal (rounded to at least three places)	**8**	.		
9	Multiply line 6 by line 7. Enter the result here. See the instructions for where to report this amount on your return	**9**			
10	Multiply line 6 by line 8. Enter the result here. See the instructions for where to report this amount on your return	**10**			
11	Add lines 9 and 10			**11**	
12	Subtract line 11 from line 6. Include this amount in the total on Form 1040, line 21, or Form 1040NR, line 21. In the space next to line 21, enter "Form 8814" and show the amount. If you checked the box on line C above, see the instructions. Go to line 13 below			**12**	

Part II **Tax on the First $2,000 of Child's Interest and Dividends**

13	Amount not taxed	**13**	1,000 00
14	Subtract line 13 from line 4. If the result is zero or less, enter -0-	**14**	
15	**Tax.** Is the amount on line 14 less than $1,000? ☐ **No.** Enter $100 here and see the **Note** below. ☐ **Yes.** Multiply line 14 by 10% (.10). Enter the result here and see the **Note** below.	**15**	.

Note. If you checked the box on line C above, see the instructions. Otherwise, include the amount from line 15 in the tax you enter on Form 1040, line 44, or Form 1040NR, line 42. Be sure to check box **a** on Form 1040, line 44, or Form 1040NR, line 42.

Solutions to Self-Study Problems

CHAPTER 1 THE INDIVIDUAL INCOME TAX RETURN

Self-Study Problem 1.1

Answer is d. Answers a, b, and c are goals of the U.S. income tax system.

Self-Study Problem 1.2

1. Schedule B, Form 1040
2. Schedule D, Form 1040
3. Schedule F, Form 1040
4. Form 1041
5. Schedule K-1, Form 1065
6. Form 1040
7. Schedule C, Form 1040
8. Schedule E, Form 1040
9. Schedule B, Form 1040
10. Form 1120
11. Form 1065
12. Schedule A, Form 1040
13. Form 1040EZ

Self-Study Problem 1.3

1. Gross income = $28,500 + $1,500 = $30,000
2. Adjusted gross income = $30,000 − $2,100 = $27,900
3. Itemized deductions = $6,400
4. Taxable income = $27,900 − $6,400 − $3,950 = $17,550

Self-Study Problem 1.4

Refer to Figures 1.1, 1.2, and 1.3 in Chapter 1.

1. No Income is below single under 65 threshold. See Fig. 1.1
2. No Income is below MFJ with one spouse 65 or older limit. See Fig. 1.1
3. Yes Earned income above threshold for single dependent. See Fig. 1.2
4. Yes Self-employment income greater than $400. See Fig. 1.3
5. No Income is below MFJ threshold; however, the taxpayers should file to obtain a refund (See Fig. 1.1).
6. Yes Social Security taxes are due (See Fig. 1.3).
7. Yes Income is above threshold for qualifying widow for under 65 with dependent. (See Fig. 1.1).

Self-Study Problem 1.5

1. B or C
2. D
3. A
4. C
5. D
6. E The taxpayer is a "qualifying widower."

Self-Study Problem 1.6

1. 2 Two personal exemptions. Although age and blindness affect the standard deduction, they do not affect exemptions.
2. 4 Two personal and two dependency exemptions.
3. 1 One personal exemption; the brother fails to meet the gross income test to be a qualifying relative. The fact that the brother is a student is irrelevant since he is older than 24.
4. 2 One personal exemption and one dependency exemption for the mother.
5. 3 One personal and two dependency exemptions.
6. 2 One personal and one dependency exemption since the scholarship is not considered support.
7. 2 One personal and one dependency exemption.

Self-Study Problem 1.7

1. $6,200
2. $13,600 = $12,400 + $1,200
3. $9,300 = $6,200 + $1,550 + $1,550
4. $9,100
5. $1,000
6. $12,400

Self-Study Problem 1.8

1. $12,600 = $12,800 − $200
2. $8,750
3. $3,850 = $12,800 − $200 − $8,750
4. $3,850 = $12,800 − $200 − $8,750
5. Because the stock has been held for more than a year, the gain is a long-term capital gain. The long-term capital gain will be taxed at 0 percent for taxpayers in the 10 or 15 percent tax brackets or 15 percent for most other taxpayers and 20% for high-income taxpayers. A net investment income tax of 3.8% may also apply.

Self-Study Problem 1.9

See page E-3 to E-4.

Self-Study Problem 1.10

1. True
2. True
3. True

Self-Study Problem 1.11

1. True
2. False
3. True
4. False

Self-Study Problem 1.9

Form **8960** — **Net Investment Income Tax—Individuals, Estates, and Trusts**

Department of the Treasury
Internal Revenue Service (99)

▶ Attach to Form 1040 or Form 1041.
▶ Information about Form 8960 and its separate instructions is at *www.irs.gov/form8960*.

OMB No. 1545-2227
2013*
Attachment Sequence No. 72

Name(s) shown on Form 1040 or Form 1041: *Ronald Trunk* | Your social security number or EIN:

Part I Investment Income ☐ Section 6013(g) election (see instructions)
☐ Regulations section 1.1411-10(g) election (see instructions)

1	Taxable interest (Form 1040, line 8a; or Form 1041, line 1)			1	*450,000*
2	Ordinary dividends (Form 1040, line 9a; or Form 1041, line 2a)			2	
3	Annuities from nonqualified plans (see instructions)			3	
4a	Rental real estate, royalties, partnerships, S corporations, trusts, etc. (Form 1040, line 17; or Form 1041, line 5)	4a			
b	Adjustment for net income or loss derived in the ordinary course of a non-section 1411 trade or business (see instructions)	4b			
c	Combine lines 4a and 4b			4c	
5a	Net gain or loss from disposition of property from Form 1040, combine lines 13 and 14; or from Form 1041, combine lines 4 and 7	5a			
b	Net gain or loss from disposition of property that is not subject to net investment income tax (see instructions)	5b			
c	Adjustment from disposition of partnership interest or S corporation stock (see instructions)	5c			
d	Combine lines 5a through 5c			5d	
6	Changes to investment income for certain CFCs and PFICs (see instructions)			6	
7	Other modifications to investment income (see instructions)			7	
8	Total investment income. Combine lines 1, 2, 3, 4c, 5d, 6, and 7			8	*450,000*

Part II Investment Expenses Allocable to Investment Income and Modifications

9a	Investment interest expenses (see instructions)	9a			
b	State income tax (see instructions)	9b			
c	Miscellaneous investment expenses (see instructions)	9c			
d	Add lines 9a, 9b, and 9c			9d	
10	Additional modifications (see instructions)			10	
11	Total deductions and modifications. Add lines 9d and 10			11	

Part III Tax Computation

12	Net investment income. Subtract Part II, line 11 from Part I, line 8. Individuals complete lines 13–17. Estates and trusts complete lines 18a–21. If zero or less, enter -0-			12	*450,000*
	Individuals:				
13	Modified adjusted gross income (see instructions)	13	*450,000*		
14	Threshold based on filing status (see instructions)	14	*200,000*		
15	Subtract line 14 from line 13. If zero or less, enter -0-	15	*250,000*		
16	Enter the smaller of line 12 or line 15			16	*250,000*
17	Net investment income tax for individuals. Multiply line 16 by 3.8% (.038). Enter here and on Form 1040, line 60			17	*9,500*
	Estates and Trusts:				
18a	Net investment income (line 12 above)	18a			
b	Deductions for distributions of net investment income and deductions under section 642(c) (see instructions)	18b			
c	Undistributed net investment income. Subtract line 18b from 18a (see instructions)	18c			
19a	Adjusted gross income (see instructions)	19a			
b	Highest tax bracket for estates and trusts for the year (see instructions)	19b			
c	Subtract line 19b from line 19a. If zero or less, enter -0-	19c			
20	Enter the smaller of line 18c or line 19c			20	
21	Net investment income tax for estates and trusts. Multiply line 20 by 3.8% (.038). Enter here and on Form 1041, Schedule G, line 4			21	

For Paperwork Reduction Act Notice, see your tax return instructions. Cat. No. 59474M Form **8960** (2013)

***The 2014 version of this form was not available as we went to press. Please check the IRS website (www.irs.gov) for updates.**

Self-Study Problem 1.9

Form **8959**	**Additional Medicare Tax**	OMB No. 1545-0074
Department of the Treasury Internal Revenue Service	► If any line does not apply to you, leave it blank. See separate instructions. ► Attach to Form 1040, 1040NR, 1040-PR, or 1040-SS. ► Information about Form 8959 and its instructions is at *www.irs.gov/form8959*.	**2014** Attachment Sequence No. **71**

Name(s) shown on return: *Marcie and Scott Chang*

Your social security number

DRAFT AS OF October 6, 2014 DO NOT FILE

Part I Additional Medicare Tax on Medicare Wages

Line	Description	Box	Amount	Box	Amount
1	Medicare wages and tips from Form W-2, box 5. If you have more than one Form W-2, enter the total of the amounts from box 5	1			
2	Unreported tips from Form 4137, line 6	2			
3	Wages from Form 8919, line 6	3			
4	Add lines 1 through 3	4			
5	Enter the following amount for your filing status: Married filing jointly . . . $250,000 Married filing separately . . . $125,000 Single, Head of household, or Qualifying widow(er) $200,000	5			
6	Subtract line 5 from line 4. If zero or less, enter -0-			6	
7	Additional Medicare Tax on Medicare wages. Multiply line 6 by 0.9% (.009). Enter here and go to Part II			7	

Part II Additional Medicare Tax on Self-Employment Income

Line	Description	Box	Amount	Box	Amount
8	Self-employment income from Schedule SE (Form 1040), Section A, line 4, or Section B, line 6. If you had a loss, enter -0- (Form 1040-PR and Form 1040-SS filers, see instructions.)	8	*330,000*		
9	Enter the following amount for your filing status: Married filing jointly . . . $250,000 Married filing separately . . . $125,000 Single, Head of household, or Qualifying widow(er) $200,000	9	*250,000*		
10	Enter the amount from line 4	10	*0*		
11	Subtract line 10 from line 9. If zero or less, enter -0-	11	*250,000*		
12	Subtract line 11 from line 8. If zero or less, enter -0-			12	*80,000*
13	Additional Medicare Tax on self-employment income. Multiply line 12 by 0.9% (.009). Enter here and go to Part III			13	*720*

Part III Additional Medicare Tax on Railroad Retirement Tax Act (RRTA) Compensation

Line	Description	Box	Amount	Box	Amount
14	Railroad retirement (RRTA) compensation and tips from Form(s) W-2, box 14 (see instructions)	14			
15	Enter the following amount for your filing status: Married filing jointly . . . $250,000 Married filing separately . . . $125,000 Single, Head of household, or Qualifying widow(er) $200,000	15			
16	Subtract line 15 from line 14. If zero or less, enter -0-			16	
17	Additional Medicare Tax on railroad retirement (RRTA) compensation. Multiply line 16 by 0.9% (.009). Enter here and go to Part IV			17	

Part IV Total Additional Medicare Tax

Line	Description	Box	Amount
18	Add lines 7, 13, and 17. Also include this amount on Form 1040, line 62, (Form 1040NR, 1040-PR, and 1040-SS filers, see instructions) and go to Part V	18	*720*

Part V Withholding Reconciliation

Line	Description	Box	Amount	Box	Amount
19	Medicare tax withheld from Form W-2, box 6. If you have more than one Form W-2, enter the total of the amounts from box 6	19			
20	Enter the amount from line 1	20			
21	Multiply line 20 by 1.45% (.0145). This is your regular Medicare tax withholding on Medicare wages	21			
22	Subtract line 21 from line 19. If zero or less, enter -0-. This is your Additional Medicare Tax withholding on Medicare wages			22	
23	Additional Medicare Tax withholding on railroad retirement (RRTA) compensation from Form W-2, box 14 (see instructions)			23	
24	**Total Additional Medicare Tax withholding.** Add lines 22 and 23. Also include this amount with federal income tax withholding on Form 1040, line 64 (Form 1040NR, 1040-PR, and 1040-SS filers, see instructions)			24	

CHAPTER 2 GROSS INCOME AND EXCLUSIONS

Self-Study Problem 2.1

1. Included	11. Excluded
2. Included	12. Included
3. Excluded	13. Included
4. Included	14. Included
5. Included	15. Excluded
6. Excluded	16. Excluded
7. Excluded	17. Included
8. Excluded	18. Included
9. Included	19. Excluded
10. Included	

Self-Study Problem 2.2

See Pages E-7 and E-8.

Self-Study Problem 2.3

1. None	For divorce agreements executed after 1984, an alimony payment is defined as a payment in cash.
2. $1,200/month	The remainder, $800 ($2,000 − $1,200), is treated as child support.
3. None	Transfers of property in settlement of a marital obligation are not taxable. The husband is likely to take the ex-wife's $20,000 basis.

Self-Study Problem 2.4

1. $2,000
2. $10,000
3. $2,500
4. $5,000
5. $0. A service award less than $400 may be excluded from income.

Self-Study Problem 2.5

Part a

$14,645 The amount excluded from income will be $16,500 × [$42,500/($1,500 × 12 months × 21 years)] = $1,855. Therefore, Phil will have taxable income of $14,645 ($16,500 − $1,855).

Part b

SIMPLIFIED METHOD WORKSHEET

1. Enter total amount received this year.	1. $16,500.00
2. Enter cost in the plan at the annuity starting date.	2. $42,500.00

3. Age at annuity starting date:

	Enter		
55 and under	360		
56–60	310		
61–65	260	3.	260
66–70	210		
71 and older	160		

4. Divide line 2 by line 3.	4.	$ 163.46
5. Multiply line 4 by the number of monthly payments this year. If the annuity starting date was before 1987, also enter this amount on line 8; and skip lines 6 and 7. Otherwise, go to line 6.	5.	$ 1,798.06
6. Enter the amount, if any, recovered tax free in prior years.	6.	0.00
7. Subtract line 6 from line 2.	7.	$ 42,500.00
8. Enter the smaller of line 5 or 7.	8.	$ 1,798.06
9. Taxable amount this year: Subtract line 8 from line 1. Do not enter less than 0.	9.	$ 14,701.94

Self-Study Problem 2.6

Amount received	$ 13,250
Less: 1/10 of $100,000	(10,000)
Taxable interest	$ 3,250

Self-Study Problem 2.7

$40,000 This problem is similar to the facts of a court case in which the Supreme Court held that the value of the automobile was income, even where there was no legal obligation to make the gift.

Self-Study Problem 2.8

1. Excluded
2. Included
3. Included
4. Included
5. Included
6. Included

Self-Study Problem 2.9

None. Neither the premiums nor the reimbursement are included in gross income.

Self-Study Problem 2.10

1. Excluded
2. Included
3. Excluded
4. Included
5. Excluded
6. Excluded

Self-Study Problem 2.11

1. $\frac{7\%}{1 - .28} = 9.72\%$

2. $\frac{6.5\%}{1 - .33} = 9.70\%$

Self-Study Problem 2.2

SCHEDULE B (Form 1040A or 1040)
Department of the Treasury
Internal Revenue Service (99)

Interest and Ordinary Dividends

▶ Attach to Form 1040A or 1040.
▶ Information about Schedule B and its instructions is at *www.irs.gov/scheduleb*.

OMB No. 1545-0074
2014
Attachment Sequence No. **08**

DRAFT AS OF June 18, 2014 DO NOT FILE

Name(s) shown on return: *Bill and Betty Brown* | **Your social security number**

Part I Interest

(See instructions on back and the instructions for Form 1040A, or Form 1040, line 8a.)

Note. If you received a Form 1099-INT, Form 1099-OID, or substitute statement from a brokerage firm, list the firm's name as the payer and enter the total interest shown on that form.

Line	Description		Amount
1	List name of payer. If any interest is from a seller-financed mortgage and the buyer used the property as a personal residence, see instructions on back and list this interest first. Also, show that buyer's social security number and address ▶	1	
	Ford Bonds		*425*
	Big Savings and Loan		*2,150*
	U.S. Bonds		*175*
2	Add the amounts on line 1	2	*2,750*
3	Excludable interest on series EE and I U.S. savings bonds issued after 1989. Attach Form 8815	3	
4	Subtract line 3 from line 2. Enter the result here and on Form 1040A, or Form 1040, line 8a ▶	4	*2,750*

Note. If line 4 is over $1,500, you must complete Part III.

Part II Ordinary Dividends

(See instructions on back and the instructions for Form 1040A, or Form 1040, line 9a.)

Note. If you received a Form 1099-DIV or substitute statement from a brokerage firm, list the firm's name as the payer and enter the ordinary dividends shown on that form.

Line	Description		Amount
5	List name of payer ▶	5	
	IBM		*275*
	IBM		*175*
	GM		*450*
	AT & T		*300*
	AT & T		*450*
6	Add the amounts on line 5. Enter the total here and on Form 1040A, or Form 1040, line 9a ▶	6	*1,650*

Note. If line 6 is over $1,500, you must complete Part III.

Part III Foreign Accounts and Trusts

(See instructions on back.)

You must complete this part if you **(a)** had over $1,500 of taxable interest or ordinary dividends; **(b)** had a foreign account; or **(c)** received a distribution from, or were a grantor of, or a transferor to, a foreign trust.

Line	Question	Yes	No
7a	At any time during 2014, did you have a financial interest in or signature authority over a financial account (such as a bank account, securities account, or brokerage account) located in a foreign country? See instructions		✓
	If "Yes," are you required to file FinCEN Form 114, Report of Foreign Bank and Financial Accounts (FBAR), to report that financial interest or signature authority? See FinCEN Form 114 and its instructions for filing requirements and exceptions to those requirements		
b	If you are required to file FinCEN Form 114, enter the name of the foreign country where the financial account is located ▶		
8	During 2014, did you receive a distribution from, or were you the grantor of, or transferor to, a foreign trust? If "Yes," you may have to file Form 3520. See instructions on back		✓

For Paperwork Reduction Act Notice, see your tax return instructions. Cat. No. 17146N **Schedule B (Form 1040A or 1040) 2014**

Self-Study Problem 2.2

Qualified Dividends and Capital Gain Tax Worksheet—Line 44

Keep for Your Records

Before you begin:
- ✓ See the earlier instructions for line 44 to see if you can use this worksheet to figure your tax.
- ✓ Before completing this worksheet, complete Form 1040 through line 43.
- ✓ If you do not have to file Schedule D and you received capital gain distributions, be sure you checked the box on line 13 of Form 1040.

Line	Description			
1.	Enter the amount from Form 1040, line 43. However, if you are filing Form 2555 or 2555-EZ (relating to foreign earned income), enter the amount from line 3 of the Foreign Earned Income Tax Worksheet . *(Taxable income)* . . . . . . 1.		*40,000*	
2.	Enter the amount from Form 1040, line 9b* *Qualified dividends* . . . . 2.	*1,650*		
3.	Are you filing Schedule D?* ☐ **Yes.** Enter the **smaller** of line 15 or 16 of Schedule D. If either line 15 or line 16 is blank or a loss, enter -0- ☒ **No.** Enter the amount from Form 1040, line 13 . . . 3.	*0*		
4.	Add lines 2 and 3 . . . 4.	*1,650*		
5.	If filing Form 4952 (used to figure investment interest expense deduction), enter any amount from line 4g of that form. Otherwise, enter -0- . . . 5.	*0*		
6.	Subtract line 5 from line 4. If zero or less, enter -0- . . . 6.		*1,650*	
7.	Subtract line 6 from line 1. If zero or less, enter -0- . . . 7.		*38,350*	
8.	Enter: $36,900 if single or married filing separately, $73,800 if married filing jointly or qualifying widow(er), $49,400 if head of household. . . . 8.		*73,800*	
9.	Enter the smaller of line 1 or line 8 . . . 9.		*40,000*	
10.	Enter the smaller of line 7 or line 9 . . . 10.		*38,350*	
11.	Subtract line 10 from line 9. This amount is taxed at 0% . . . 11.		*1,650*	
12.	Enter the smaller of line 1 or line 6 . . . 12.		*1,650*	
13.	Enter the amount from line 11 . . . 13.		*1,650*	
14.	Subtract line 13 from line 12 . . . 14.		*0*	
15.	Enter: $406,750 if single, $228,800 if married filing separately, $457,600 if married filing jointly or qualifying widow(er), $432,200 if head of household. . . . 15.		*457,600*	
16.	Enter the smaller of line 1 or line 15 . . . 16.		*40,000*	
17.	Add lines 7 and 11 . . . 17.		*40,000*	
18.	Subtract line 17 from line 16. If zero or less, enter -0- . . . 18.		*0*	
19.	Enter the smaller of line 14 or line 18 . . . 19.		*0*	
20.	Multiply line 19 by 15% (.15) . . . 20.			*0*
21.	Add lines 11 and 19 . . . 21.		*1,650*	
22.	Subtract line 21 from line 12 . . . 22.		*0*	
23.	Multiply line 22 by 20% (.20) . . . 23.			*0*
24.	Figure the tax on the amount on line 7. If the amount on line 7 is less than $100,000, use the Tax Table to figure the tax. If the amount on line 7 is $100,000 or more, use the Tax Computation Worksheet . . . 24.			*4,849*
25.	Add lines 20, 23, and 24 . . . 25.			*4,849*
26.	Figure the tax on the amount on line 1. If the amount on line 1 is less than $100,000, use the Tax Table to figure the tax. If the amount on line 1 is $100,000 or more, use the Tax Computation Worksheet . . . 26.			*5,096*
27.	**Tax on all taxable income.** Enter the **smaller** of line 25 or line 26. Also include this amount on Form 1040, line 44. If you are filing Form 2555 or 2555-EZ, do not enter this amount on Form 1040, line 44. Instead, enter it on line 4 of the Foreign Earned Income Tax Worksheet . . . 27.			*4,849*

**If you are filing Form 2555 or 2555-EZ, see the footnote in the Foreign Earned Income Tax Worksheet before completing this line.*

Self-Study Problem 2.12

$3,000 Unemployment compensation is fully taxable.

Self-Study Problem 2.13

1. Excluded
2. Included
3. Excluded
4. Excluded
5. Included
6. Included
7. Excluded

Self-Study Problem 2.14

Simplified Taxable Social Security Worksheet (for most people)

1.	Enter the total amount of Social Security income.	1. 13,000
2.	Enter one-half of line 1.	2. 6,500
3.	Enter the total of taxable income items on Form 1040 except Social Security income.	3. 20,000
4.	Enter the amount of tax-exempt interest income.	4. 30,000
5.	Add lines 2, 3, and 4.	5. 56,500
6.	Enter all adjustments for AGI except for student loan interest, the domestic production activities deduction, and the tuition and fees deduction.	6. 0
7.	Subtract line 6 from line 5. If 0 or less, stop here, none of the Social Security benefits are taxable.	7. 56,500
8.	Enter $25,000 ($32,000 if married filing jointly; $0 if married filing separately and living with spouse at any time during the year).	8. 32,000
9.	Subtract line 8 from line 7. If 0 or less, enter -0-.	9. 24,500
	Note: *If line 9 is 0 or less, stop here; none of your benefits are taxable. Otherwise, go on to line 10.*	
10.	Enter $9,000 ($12,000 if married filing jointly; $0 if married filing separately and living with spouse at any time during the year).	10. 12,000
11.	Subtract line 10 from line 9. If 0 or less, enter -0-.	11. 12,500
12.	Enter the **smaller of line 9 or line 10.**	12. 12,000
13.	Enter one-half of line 12.	13. 6,000
14.	Enter the **smaller of line 2 or line 13.**	14. 6,000
15.	Multiply line 11 by 85% (.85). If line 11 is 0, enter -0-.	15. 10,625
16.	Add lines 14 and 15.	16. 16,625
17.	Multiply line 1 by 85% (.85).	17. 11,050
18.	**Taxable benefits. Enter the smaller of line 16 or line 17.**	18. 11,050

CHAPTER 3 BUSINESS INCOME AND EXPENSES, PART I

Self-Study Problem 3.1

See Schedule C on Pages E-11 and E-12.

Self-Study Problem 3.2

Part III **Cost of Goods Sold** (see instructions)

33 Method(s) used to value closing inventory: a ☑ Cost b ☐ Lower of cost or market c ☐ Other (attach explanation)

34 Was there any change in determining quantities, costs, or valuations between opening and closing inventory? If "Yes," attach explanation . . . ☐ Yes ☑ No

35	Inventory at beginning of year. If different from last year's closing inventory, attach explanation	35	62,500
36	Purchases less cost of items withdrawn for personal use	36	170,500
37	Cost of labor. Do not include any amounts paid to yourself	37	
38	Materials and supplies	38	
39	Other costs	39	
40	Add lines 35 through 39	40	233,000
41	Inventory at end of year	41	57,200
42	**Cost of goods sold.** Subtract line 41 from line 40. Enter the result here and on line 4	42	175,800

DRAFT AS OF June 19, 2014 DO NOT FILE

Self-Study Problem 3.3

Marc's transportation deduction is the greater of his actual costs or his deduction using the standard mileage method.

Actual Cost Calculation:

Cash Outlays	$ 6,040
Depreciation	2,800
	$ 8,840
Business percentage (17,944/23,925)	×75%
Subtotal	$ 6,630
Tolls & Fees	316
Actual Costs	$ 6,946

Standard Mileage Calculation:

17,944 miles @ 56¢	$ 10,049
Tolls & Fees	316
Marc's deduction for 2014 is	$10,365

Self-Study Problem 3.4

Deductible expenses:

Airfare	$190	
Hotel while working on the audit	325	
Meals while working on the audit	68	(50% of $136)
Laundry	22	
Taxi	72	
Total travel deduction	$677	

Self-Study Problem 3.5

Business meals $1,700 × 50% = $850 Dues and personal expenses are not generally deductible.

Self-Study Problem 3.1

SCHEDULE C (Form 1040)
Department of the Treasury Internal Revenue Service (99)

Profit or Loss From Business
(Sole Proprietorship)

► **Information about Schedule C and its separate instructions is at *www.irs.gov/schedulec*.**
► **Attach to Form 1040, 1040NR, or 1041; partnerships generally must file Form 1065.**

OMB No. 1545-0074
2014
Attachment Sequence No. **09**

DRAFT AS OF June 19, 2014 DO NOT FILE

Name of proprietor: *Teri Kataoka*
Social security number (SSN): *466 47 8833*

A Principal business or profession, including product or service (see instructions): *Golf Teacher*
B Enter code from instructions ► *8 1 2 9 9 0*

C Business name. If no separate business name, leave blank.
D Employer ID number (EIN), (see instr.)

E Business address (including suite or room no.) ► *1234 Golfcrest Drive*
City, town or post office, state, and ZIP code: *Palm Springs, CA 92262*

F Accounting method: **(1)** ☑ Cash **(2)** ☐ Accrual **(3)** ☐ Other (specify) ►

G Did you "materially participate" in the operation of this business during 2014? If "No," see instructions for limit on losses . ☑ Yes ☐ No

H If you started or acquired this business during 2014, check here ► ☐

I Did you make any payments in 2014 that would require you to file Form(s) 1099? (see instructions) ☐ Yes ☑ No

J If "Yes," did you or will you file required Forms 1099? ☐ Yes ☐ No

Part I Income

Line	Description	Box	Amount
1	Gross receipts or sales. See instructions for line 1 and check the box if this income was reported to you on Form W-2 and the "Statutory employee" box on that form was checked ► ☐	1	39,250
2	Returns and allowances	2	
3	Subtract line 2 from line 1	3	39,250
4	Cost of goods sold (from line 42)	4	
5	**Gross profit.** Subtract line 4 from line 3	5	39,250
6	Other income, including federal and state gasoline or fuel tax credit or refund (see instructions)	6	
7	**Gross income.** Add lines 5 and 6 ►	7	39,250

Part II Expenses. Enter expenses for business use of your home **only** on line 30.

Line	Description	Box	Amount	Line	Description	Box	Amount
8	Advertising	8		18	Office expense (see instructions)	18	640
9	Car and truck expenses (see instructions)	9	3,028	19	Pension and profit-sharing plans	19	
10	Commissions and fees	10		20	Rent or lease (see instructions):		
11	Contract labor (see instructions)	11		a	Vehicles, machinery, and equipment	20a	
12	Depletion	12		b	Other business property	20b	2,700
13	Depreciation and section 179 expense deduction (not included in Part III) (see instructions)	13		21	Repairs and maintenance	21	
14	Employee benefit programs (other than on line 19)	14		22	Supplies (not included in Part III)	22	
15	Insurance (other than health)	15	450	23	Taxes and licenses	23	250
16	Interest:			24	Travel, meals, and entertainment:		
a	Mortgage (paid to banks, etc.)	16a		a	Travel	24a	3,100
b	Other	16b		b	Deductible meals and entertainment (see instructions)	24b	895
17	Legal and professional services	17		25	Utilities	25	975
				26	Wages (less employment credits)	26	
				27a	Other expenses (from line 48)	27a	
				b	**Reserved for future use**	27b	

Line	Description	Box	Amount
28	**Total expenses** before expenses for business use of home. Add lines 8 through 27a ►	28	12,038
29	Tentative profit or (loss). Subtract line 28 from line 7	29	27,212
30	Expenses for business use of your home. Do not report these expenses elsewhere. Attach Form 8829 unless using the simplified method (see instructions). **Simplified method filers only:** enter the total square footage of: (a) your home: ______ and (b) the part of your home used for business: ______ . Use the Simplified Method Worksheet in the instructions to figure the amount to enter on line 30	30	
31	**Net profit or (loss).** Subtract line 30 from line 29. • If a profit, enter on both **Form 1040, line 12** (or **Form 1040NR, line 13**) and on **Schedule SE, line 2.** (If you checked the box on line 1, see instructions). Estates and trusts, enter on **Form 1041, line 3.** • If a loss, you **must** go to line 32.	31	27,212

32 If you have a loss, check the box that describes your investment in this activity (see instructions).
- If you checked 32a, enter the loss on both **Form 1040, line 12,** (or **Form 1040NR, line 13**) and on **Schedule SE, line 2.** (If you checked the box on line 1, see the line 31 instructions). Estates and trusts, enter on **Form 1041, line 3.**
- If you checked 32b, you **must** attach **Form 6198.** Your loss may be limited.

32a ☐ All investment is at risk.
32b ☐ Some investment is not at risk.

For Paperwork Reduction Act Notice, see the separate instructions. Cat. No. 11334P **Schedule C (Form 1040) 2014**

Self-Study Problem 3.1

Schedule C (Form 1040) 2014 Page **2**

Part III **Cost of Goods Sold** (see instructions)

33 Method(s) used to value closing inventory: a ☐ Cost b ☐ Lower of cost or market c ☐ Other (attach explanation)

34 Was there any change in determining quantities, costs, or valuations between opening and closing inventory? If "Yes," attach explanation . . . ☐ Yes ☐ No

35 Inventory at beginning of year. If different from last year's closing inventory, attach explanation	35	
36 Purchases less cost of items withdrawn for personal use	36	
37 Cost of labor. Do not include any amounts paid to yourself	37	
38 Materials and supplies	38	
39 Other costs	39	
40 Add lines 35 through 39	40	
41 Inventory at end of year	41	
42 **Cost of goods sold.** Subtract line 41 from line 40. Enter the result here and on line 4	42	

DRAFT AS OF June 19, 2014 DO NOT FILE

Part IV **Information on Your Vehicle.** Complete this part **only** if you are claiming car or truck expenses on line 9 and are not required to file Form 4562 for this business. See the instructions for line 13 to find out if you must file Form 4562.

43 When did you place your vehicle in service for business purposes? (month, day, year) ▶ *01/ 01 /2014*

44 Of the total number of miles you drove your vehicle during 2014, enter the number of miles you used your vehicle for:

a Business *5,407* b Commuting (see instructions) *3,000* c Other *6,000*

45 Was your vehicle available for personal use during off-duty hours? . . . ☑ Yes ☐ No

46 Do you (or your spouse) have another vehicle available for personal use?. . . ☐ Yes ☑ No

47a Do you have evidence to support your deduction? . . . ☑ Yes ☐ No

b If "Yes," is the evidence written? . . . ☑ Yes ☐ No

Part V **Other Expenses.** List below business expenses not included on lines 8–26 or line 30.

48 **Total other expenses.** Enter here and on line 27a	48	

Schedule C (Form 1040) 2014

Self-Study Problem 3.6

Lodging	$1,200
Transportation	350
Meals (50% of $200)	100
Books	175
Tuition	550
Total Deduction	$2,375

The cost of the weekend trip to the Grand Canyon is not deductible.

Self-Study Problem 3.7

1. Deductible
2. Deductible
3. Not Deductible
4. Deductible
5. Not Deductible

Self-Study Problem 3.8

Safety shoes and orange vest	$ 650
Climbing equipment, etc.	275
Total Special Clothing Deduction	$ 925

Self-Study Problem 3.9

1. Mr. Jones	$ 20
2. Mr. Brown	25
3/4. Mrs. and Mr. Green	25
5. Ms. Gray	0
6. Mr. Edwards	75
7. Various customers	140
Total Business Gift Deduction	$285

Self-Study Problem 3.10

1. Business
2. Nonbusiness
3. Nonbusiness
4. Business
5. Nonbusiness

Self-Study Problem 3.11

Gross income	$ 2,800
Less: interest and taxes	(2,100)
Balance	$ 700
Less: maintenance, utilities, and cleaning ($1,400) limited to	(700)
Net income	$ 0

Self-Study Problem 3.12

1. F NOL deductions are carried back 2 years and then forward 20 years.
2. F Generally, NOLs are only from the operation of a trade or business, casualty and theft losses, or confiscation losses.
3. T
4. T
5. F In 2014, the NOL is carried back 2 years and forward 20 years, unless an election is made to forgo the 2-year carryback.

Self-Study Problem 3.13

The maximum amount of expenses that can be deducted is $250, the amount of income from the hobby activity. The expenses of $250 are deductible as a miscellaneous itemized deduction, subject to the 2 percent of adjusted gross income limitation. The sales must be reported as miscellaneous income even though the 2 percent of AGI limitation may prevent the expenses from being deducted.

CHAPTER 4 BUSINESS INCOME AND EXPENSES, PART II

Self-Study Problem 4.1

See Schedule E on Pages E-15 and E-16.

Self-Study Problem 4.2

See Form 8582 on Page E-17.

Self-Study Problem 4.3

$20,700 = $15,000 + $2,000 + $3,000 + $700 (limited by age)

Self-Study Problem 4.4

1. $6,550
2. $0 A plan with no deductible does not qualify.
3. $2,000
4. $0 Individuals are not allowed to make contributions to an HSA after age 65 and qualify for Medicare.

Self-Study Problem 4.5

See Form 3903 on Page E-18.

Self-Study Problem 4.6

a. $\$4{,}950 = \$5{,}500 \times \frac{\$70{,}000 - \$61{,}000}{\$10{,}000}$

b. $\$4{,}400 = \frac{\$129{,}000 - \$117{,}000}{\$15{,}000} \times \$5{,}500$

Self-Study Problem 4.7

$10,000, the lesser of $10,000 (20% of $50,000) or $52,000

Self-Study Problem 4.1

SCHEDULE E (Form 1040)

Department of the Treasury
Internal Revenue Service (99)

Supplemental Income and Loss

(From rental real estate, royalties, partnerships, S corporations, estates, trusts, REMICs, etc.)

▶ **Attach to Form 1040, 1040NR, or Form 1041.**

▶ **Information about Schedule E and its separate instructions is at *www.irs.gov/schedulee*.**

OMB No. 1545-0074

2014

Attachment Sequence No. **13**

Name(s) shown on return: *Janet Randolf*

Your social security number

DRAFT AS OF June 6, 2014 DO NOT FILE

Part I **Income or Loss From Rental Real Estate and Royalties** **Note.** If you are in the business of renting personal property, use **Schedule C** or **C-EZ** (see instructions). If you are an individual, report farm rental income or loss from **Form 4835** on page 2, line 40.

A Did you make any payments in 2014 that would require you to file Form(s) 1099? (see instructions) ☐ Yes ☐ No

B If "Yes," did you or will you file required Forms 1099? ☐ Yes ☐ No

1a	Physical address of each property (street, city, state, ZIP code)
A	*14 Randolf St., San Diego , CA 92111*
B	
C	

1b	Type of Property (from list below)	**2** For each rental real estate property listed above, report the number of fair rental and personal use days. Check the **QJV** box only if you meet the requirements to file as a qualified joint venture. See instructions.		**Fair Rental Days**	**Personal Use Days**	**QJV**
A	2		**A**	365		☐
B			**B**			☐
C			**C**			☐

Type of Property:
1 Single Family Residence 3 Vacation/Short-Term Rental 5 Land 7 Self-Rental
2 Multi-Family Residence 4 Commercial 6 Royalties 8 Other (describe)

Income:	**Properties:**		**A**	**B**	**C**
3	Rents received	**3**	6,000		
4	Royalties received	**4**			
Expenses:					
5	Advertising	**5**			
6	Auto and travel (see instructions)	**6**			
7	Cleaning and maintenance	**7**			
8	Commissions	**8**			
9	Insurance	**9**	225		
10	Legal and other professional fees	**10**			
11	Management fees	**11**			
12	Mortgage interest paid to banks, etc. (see instructions)	**12**	1,700		
13	Other interest	**13**			
14	Repairs	**14**			
15	Supplies	**15**			
16	Taxes	**16**	600		
17	Utilities	**17**	900		
18	Depreciation expense or depletion	**18**	545		
19	Other (list) ▶	**19**			
20	Total expenses. Add lines 5 through 19	**20**	3,970		
21	Subtract line 20 from line 3 (rents) and/or 4 (royalties). If result is a (loss), see instructions to find out if you must file **Form 6198**	**21**	2,030		
22	Deductible rental real estate loss after limitation, if any, on **Form 8582** (see instructions)	**22**	( )	( )	( )

23a	Total of all amounts reported on line 3 for all rental properties	**23a**	6,000
b	Total of all amounts reported on line 4 for all royalty properties	**23b**	
c	Total of all amounts reported on line 12 for all properties	**23c**	1,700
d	Total of all amounts reported on line 18 for all properties	**23d**	545
e	Total of all amounts reported on line 20 for all properties	**23e**	3,970
24	**Income.** Add positive amounts shown on line 21. **Do not** include any losses	**24**	2,030
25	**Losses.** Add royalty losses from line 21 and rental real estate losses from line 22. Enter total losses here	**25**	( )
26	**Total rental real estate and royalty income or (loss).** Combine lines 24 and 25. Enter the result here. If Parts II, III, IV, and line 40 on page 2 do not apply to you, also enter this amount on Form 1040, line 17, or Form 1040NR, line 18. Otherwise, include this amount in the total on line 41 on page 2	**26**	2,030

Self-Study Problem 4.1

Schedule E (Form 1040) 2014 — Attachment Sequence No. 13 — Page 2

Name(s) shown on return. Do not enter name and social security number if shown on other side. — **Your social security number**

Janet Randolf

Caution. The IRS compares amounts reported on your tax return with amounts shown on Schedule(s) K-1.

Part II Income or Loss From Partnerships and S Corporations **Note.** If you report a loss from an at-risk activity for which **any** amount is **not** at risk, you **must** check the box in column **(e)** on line 28 and attach **Form 6198.** See instructions.

DRAFT AS OF June 6, 2014 DO NOT FILE

27 Are you reporting any loss not allowed in a prior year due to the at-risk, excess farm loss, or basis limitations, a prior year unallowed loss from a passive activity (if that loss was not reported on Form 8582), or unreimbursed partnership expenses? If you answered "Yes," see instructions before completing this section. ☐ Yes ☐ No

28	(a) Name	(b) Enter P for partnership; S for S corporation	(c) Check if foreign partnership	(d) Employer identification number	(e) Check if any amount is not at risk
A			☐		☐
B			☐		☐
C			☐		☐
D			☐		☐

	Passive Income and Loss		Nonpassive Income and Loss		
	(f) Passive loss allowed (attach Form 8582 if required)	(g) Passive income from Schedule K-1	(h) Nonpassive loss from Schedule K-1	(i) Section 179 expense deduction from Form 4562	(j) Nonpassive income from Schedule K-1
A					
B					
C					
D					
29a Totals					
b Totals					

30	Add columns (g) and (j) of line 29a	30	
31	Add columns (f), (h), and (i) of line 29b	31	( )
32	**Total partnership and S corporation income or (loss).** Combine lines 30 and 31. Enter the result here and include in the total on line 41 below	32	

Part III Income or Loss From Estates and Trusts

33	(a) Name	(b) Employer identification number
A		
B		

	Passive Income and Loss		Nonpassive Income and Loss	
	(c) Passive deduction or loss allowed (attach Form 8582 if required)	(d) Passive income from Schedule K-1	(e) Deduction or loss from Schedule K-1	(f) Other income from Schedule K-1
A				
B				
34a Totals				
b Totals				

35	Add columns (d) and (f) of line 34a	35	
36	Add columns (c) and (e) of line 34b	36	( )
37	**Total estate and trust income or (loss).** Combine lines 35 and 36. Enter the result here and include in the total on line 41 below	37	

Part IV Income or Loss From Real Estate Mortgage Investment Conduits (REMICs)—Residual Holder

38 (a) Name	(b) Employer identification number	(c) Excess inclusion from Schedules Q, line 2c (see instructions)	(d) Taxable income (net loss) from Schedules Q, line 1b	(e) Income from Schedules Q, line 3b

39	Combine columns (d) and (e) only. Enter the result here and include in the total on line 41 below	39	

Part V Summary

40	Net farm rental income or (loss) from **Form 4835**. Also, complete line 42 below	40	
41	**Total income or (loss).** Combine lines 26, 32, 37, 39, and 40. Enter the result here and on Form 1040, line 17, or Form 1040NR, line 18 ▶	41	
42	**Reconciliation of farming and fishing income.** Enter your **gross** farming and fishing income reported on Form 4835, line 7; Schedule K-1 (Form 1065), box 14, code B; Schedule K-1 (Form 1120S), box 17, code V; and Schedule K-1 (Form 1041), box 14, code F (see instructions)	42	
43	**Reconciliation for real estate professionals.** If you were a real estate professional (see instructions), enter the net income or (loss) you reported anywhere on Form 1040 or Form 1040NR from all rental real estate activities in which you materially participated under the passive activity loss rules	43	

Self-Study Problem 4.2

Form **8582** — Department of the Treasury, Internal Revenue Service (99)

Passive Activity Loss Limitations

► See separate instructions.
► Attach to Form 1040 or Form 1041.
► Information about Form 8582 and its instructions is available at *www.irs.gov/form8582*.

OMB No. 1545-1008 | **2013*** | Attachment Sequence No. 88

Name(s) shown on return: *Sherry Moore* | Identifying number:

Part I — 2013 Passive Activity Loss

Caution: *Complete Worksheets 1, 2, and 3 before completing Part I.*

Rental Real Estate Activities With Active Participation (For the definition of active participation, see **Special Allowance for Rental Real Estate Activities** in the instructions.)

Line	Description	Box	Amount	Box	Amount
1a	Activities with net income (enter the amount from Worksheet 1, column (a))	1a			
b	Activities with net loss (enter the amount from Worksheet 1, column (b))	1b	(*21,000*)		
c	Prior years unallowed losses (enter the amount from Worksheet 1, column (c))	1c	( )		
d	Combine lines 1a, 1b, and 1c			1d	*(21,000)*

Commercial Revitalization Deductions From Rental Real Estate Activities

Line	Description	Box	Amount	Box	Amount
2a	Commercial revitalization deductions from Worksheet 2, column (a)	2a	( )		
b	Prior year unallowed commercial revitalization deductions from Worksheet 2, column (b)	2b	( )		
c	Add lines 2a and 2b			2c	( )

All Other Passive Activities

Line	Description	Box	Amount	Box	Amount
3a	Activities with net income (enter the amount from Worksheet 3, column (a))	3a			
b	Activities with net loss (enter the amount from Worksheet 3, column (b))	3b	(*15,000*)		
c	Prior years unallowed losses (enter the amount from Worksheet 3, column (c))	3c	( )		
d	Combine lines 3a, 3b, and 3c			3d	*(15,000)*
4	Combine lines 1d, 2c, and 3d. If this line is zero or more, stop here and include this form with your return; all losses are allowed, including any prior year unallowed losses entered on line 1c, 2b, or 3c. Report the losses on the forms and schedules normally used			4	*(36,000)*

If line 4 is a loss and:
- Line 1d is a loss, go to Part II.
- Line 2c is a loss (and line 1d is zero or more), skip Part II and go to Part III.
- Line 3d is a loss (and lines 1d and 2c are zero or more), skip Parts II and III and go to line 15.

Caution: *If your filing status is married filing separately and you lived with your spouse at any time during the year,* ***do not*** *complete Part II or Part III. Instead, go to line 15.*

Part II — Special Allowance for Rental Real Estate Activities With Active Participation

Note: *Enter all numbers in Part II as positive amounts. See instructions for an example.*

Line	Description	Box	Amount	Box	Amount
5	Enter the **smaller** of the loss on line 1d or the loss on line 4			5	*21,000*
6	Enter $150,000. If married filing separately, see instructions	6	*150,000*		
7	Enter modified adjusted gross income, but not less than zero (see instructions)	7	*102,000*		
	Note: *If line 7 is greater than or equal to line 6, skip lines 8 and 9, enter -0- on line 10. Otherwise, go to line 8.*				
8	Subtract line 7 from line 6	8	*48,000*		
9	Multiply line 8 by 50% (.5). **Do not** enter more than $25,000. If married filing separately, see instructions			9	*24,000*
10	Enter the **smaller** of line 5 or line 9			10	*21,000*

If line 2c is a loss, go to Part III. Otherwise, go to line 15.

Part III — Special Allowance for Commercial Revitalization Deductions From Rental Real Estate Activities

Note: *Enter all numbers in Part III as positive amounts. See the example for Part II in the instructions.*

Line	Description	Box	Amount
11	Enter $25,000 reduced by the amount, if any, on line 10. If married filing separately, see instructions	11	
12	Enter the loss from line 4	12	
13	Reduce line 12 by the amount on line 10	13	
14	Enter the **smallest** of line 2c (treated as a positive amount), line 11, or line 13	14	

Part IV — Total Losses Allowed

Line	Description	Box	Amount
15	Add the income, if any, on lines 1a and 3a and enter the total	15	*0*
16	**Total losses allowed from all passive activities for 2013.** Add lines 10, 14, and 15. See instructions to find out how to report the losses on your tax return	16	*21,000*

For Paperwork Reduction Act Notice, see instructions. Cat. No. 63704F Form **8582** (2013)

***The 2014 version of this form was not available as we went to press. Please check the IRS website for updates.**

Self-Study Problem 4.5

Form **3903** Department of the Treasury Internal Revenue Service (99)	**Moving Expenses** ▶ Information about Form 3903 and its instructions is available at *www.irs.gov/form3903*. ▶ Attach to Form 1040 or Form 1040NR.	OMB No. 1545-0074 2014 Attachment Sequence No. 170
Name(s) shown on return *Maureen Motsinger*		**Your social security number**

Before you begin: ✓ See the **Distance Test** and **Time Test** in the instructions to find out if you can deduct your moving expenses.
✓ See **Members of the Armed Forces** in the instructions, if applicable.

DRAFT AS OF July 3, 2014 DO NOT FILE

1	Transportation and storage of household goods and personal effects (see instructions)	1	4,100	
2	Travel (including lodging) from your old home to your new home (see instructions). **Do not** include the cost of meals	2	1,282	(a)
3	Add lines 1 and 2	3	5,382	
4	Enter the total amount your employer paid you for the expenses listed on lines 1 and 2 that is **not** included in box 1 of your Form W-2 (wages). This amount should be shown in box 12 of your Form W-2 with code **P**	4	5,382	
5	Is line 3 **more than** line 4? ☐ **No.** You **cannot** deduct your moving expenses. If line 3 is less than line 4, subtract line 3 from line 4 and include the result on Form 1040, line 7, or Form 1040NR, line 8. ☐ **Yes.** Subtract line 4 from line 3. Enter the result here and on Form 1040, line 26, or Form 1040NR, line 26. This is your **moving expense deduction**	5		

For Paperwork Reduction Act Notice, see your tax return instructions. Cat. No. 12490K Form **3903** (2014)

(a) $650 for lodging plus 2,689 mileage × $0.235 per mile. Meals are not deductible.

Self-Study Problem 4.8

a. $8,000, lesser of 20% × $40,000 or $17,500 (annual dollar limit effective for 2014)
b. $17,500 (annual dollar limit effective for 2014)

Self-Study Problem 4.9

a. $150,000
b. $120,000 ($150,000 − 20% × $150,000)
c. August 30, 20XX, unless the hardship waiver provisions apply
d. $150,000

CHAPTER 5 ITEMIZED DEDUCTIONS AND OTHER INCENTIVES

Self-Study Problems 5.1 through 5.6

See Schedule A and Form 4684 on Pages E-21 to E-23.
Line 1 of Schedule A is computed as follows:

Medical insurance	$425
Prescription medicines and drugs	364
Hospital bills	2,424
Doctor bills	725
Eyeglasses for Frank's dependent mother	75
Doctor bills for Betty's sister, who is claimed as a dependent by Frank and Betty	220
Medical transportation in personal vehicle (610 miles * $0.235)	143
Total	$2,956
Less reimbursement	($1,420)
Medical and dental expenses	$2,956

Line 5 of Schedule A—The $225 refund is included on Line 10 of Form 1040 as gross income.
Line 14 of Schedule A—Investment interest is deductible only to the extent of net investment income of $1,000.
Line 16 of Schedule A—The Mexican Red Cross is not a qualified recipient.

Self-Study Problem 5.7

1. DFROM — The employer does not have an accountable plan. The actual $950 of expenses are treated as miscellaneous itemized deductions subject to the 2 percent of adjusted gross income limitation.
2. DFROM — Employee business expenses which are not reimbursed are treated as miscellaneous itemized deductions subject to the 2 percent of adjusted gross income limitation.
3. DFOR — The employer has an accountable reimbursement plan and the employee substantiates the expenses on a timely basis.

Self-Study Problem 5.8

(Note: Due to the expiration of the tuition deduction, solutions use the 2013 phase-out thresholds.)

a. $0
b. $2,000. Henry's AGI is under $95,000 so there is no phase-out.

Self-Study Problem 5.9

Elvis and Greta may deduct $26,505 of the $30,000. The reduction is calculated as the lesser of: $3,495 = 3% × ($421,550 − $305,050) or
$8,000 = 80% × ($30,000 − $20,000)
Deduction allowed = $26,505 = $30,000 − $3,495

CHAPTER 6 CREDITS AND SPECIAL TAXES

Self-Study Problem 6.1

a. $2,000. Two children under the age of 17 at $1,000 each, no phase-out.
b. $1,200. Two children under the age of 17 at $1,000 each less $800 phase-out.

$$\frac{\$125{,}400 - \$110{,}000}{\$1{,}000} = 15.4$$

16 (rounded) × $50 = $800 reduction

Self-Study Problem 6.2

See worksheet on Page E-25.

Self-Study Problem 6.3

See Form 2441 on Page E-27.

Self-Study Problem 6.4A

See Page E-28.

Self-Study Problem 6.4B

See Page E-28.

Self-Study Problem 6.5

a. $1,900 = 100% up to $2,000
b. $1,040 = 20% × $5,200 ($10,000 maximum)

Self-Study Problem 6.6

Country A	$10,000 × 20% =	$ 2,000	
Country B	$20,000 × 50% =	10,000	
		$12,000	Total foreign taxes paid

Overall limitation:

$$\frac{\$30{,}000}{\$90{,}000} \times \$20{,}000 = \$6{,}667$$

The foreign tax credit is limited to $6,667.

Self-Study Problem 6.7

See Form 8839 on Pages E-29 and E-30.

Self-Study Problem 6.8

a. $7,500. The Nissan Leaf qualifies for the full $7,500 credit.
b. $3,000 (30% × $10,000). The solar system for the hot tub is not an allowed cost for the credit.

Self-Study Problem 5.1, 5.2, 5.3, 5.4, and 5.6

SCHEDULE A (Form 1040)
Department of the Treasury Internal Revenue Service (99)

Itemized Deductions

▶ Information about Schedule A and its separate instructions is at *www.irs.gov/schedulea*.
▶ Attach to Form 1040.

OMB No. 1545-0074
2014
Attachment Sequence No. 07

Name(s) shown on Form 1040 | Your social security number

DRAFT AS OF August 15, 2014 DO NOT FILE

Section	Line	Description	Box	Amount	Box	Total
Medical and Dental Expenses		**Caution.** Do not include expenses reimbursed or paid by others.				
	1	Medical and dental expenses (see instructions)	1	2,956		
	2	Enter amount from Form 1040, line 38 [2] 25,400				
	3	Multiply line 2 by 10% (.10). But if either you or your spouse was born before January 2, 1950, multiply line 2 by 7.5% (.075) instead	3	1,905		
	4	Subtract line 3 from line 1. If line 3 is more than line 1, enter -0-			4	1,051
Taxes You Paid	5	State and local a ☑ Income taxes b ☐ RESERVED	5	1,050		
	6	Real estate taxes (see instructions)	6	825		
	7	Personal property taxes	7	85		
	8	Other taxes. List type and amount ▶	8			
	9	Add lines 5 through 8			9	1,960
Interest You Paid	10	Home mortgage interest and points reported to you on Form 1098	10	9,250		
Note. Your mortgage interest deduction may be limited (see instructions).	11	Home mortgage interest not reported to you on Form 1098. If paid to the person from whom you bought the home, see instructions and show that person's name, identifying no., and address ▶	11			
	12	Points not reported to you on Form 1098. See instructions for special rules	12			
	13	RESERVED	13			
	14	Investment interest. Attach Form 4952 if required. (See instructions.)	14	1,000		
	15	Add lines 10 through 14			15	10,250
Gifts to Charity	16	Gifts by cash or check. If you made any gift of $250 or more, see instructions	16	335		
If you made a gift and got a benefit for it, see instructions.	17	Other than by cash or check. If any gift of $250 or more, see instructions. You **must** attach Form 8283 if over $500	17	150		
	18	Carryover from prior year	18	800		
	19	Add lines 16 through 18			19	1,285
Casualty and Theft Losses	20	Casualty or theft loss(es). Attach Form 4684. (See instructions.)			20	500
Job Expenses and Certain Miscellaneous Deductions	21	Unreimbursed employee expenses—job travel, union dues, job education, etc. Attach Form 2106 or 2106-EZ if required. (See instructions.) ▶ *Dues, Journals, Job Hunting*	21	1,700		
	22	Tax preparation fees	22	450		
	23	Other expenses—investment, safe deposit box, etc. List type and amount ▶ *Safe Deposit, Bank Trust fees*	23	1,080		
	24	Add lines 21 through 23	24	3,230		
	25	Enter amount from Form 1040, line 38 [25] 35,000				
	26	Multiply line 25 by 2% (.02)	26	700		
	27	Subtract line 26 from line 24. If line 26 is more than line 24, enter -0-			27	2,530
Other Miscellaneous Deductions	28	Other—from list in instructions. List type and amount ▶			28	
Total Itemized Deductions	29	Is Form 1040, line 38, over $152,525? ☐ **No.** Your deduction is not limited. Add the amounts in the far right column for lines 4 through 28. Also, enter this amount on Form 1040, line 40. ☐ **Yes.** Your deduction may be limited. See the Itemized Deductions Worksheet in the instructions to figure the amount to enter.			29	
	30	If you elect to itemize deductions even though they are less than your standard deduction, check here ▶ ☑				

Self-Study Problem 5.5

Form **4684** Department of the Treasury Internal Revenue Service

Casualties and Thefts

▶ Information about Form 4684 and its separate instructions is at *www.irs.gov/form4684*.
▶ Attach to your tax return.
▶ Use a separate Form 4684 for each casualty or theft.

OMB No. 1545-0177 **2014** Attachment Sequence No. **26**

DRAFT AS OF June 12, 2014 DO NOT FILE

Name(s) shown on tax return	Identifying number
Vivian Walker	

SECTION A—Personal Use Property (Use this section to report casualties and thefts of property **not** used in a trade or business or for income-producing purposes.)

1 Description of properties (show type, location, and date acquired for each property). Use a separate line for each property lost or damaged from the same casualty or theft.

Property **A** *Coin collection, 2005*
Property **B**
Property **C**
Property **D**

		Properties A	B	C	D
2 Cost or other basis of each property	2	*6,000*			
3 Insurance or other reimbursement (whether or not you filed a claim) (see instructions)	3	*2,900*			
Note: *If line 2 is **more** than line 3, skip line 4.*					
4 Gain from casualty or theft. If line 3 is **more** than line 2, enter the difference here and skip lines 5 through 9 for that column. See instructions if line 3 includes insurance or other reimbursement you did not claim, or you received payment for your loss in a later tax year	4				
5 Fair market value **before** casualty or theft	5	*9,000*			
6 Fair market value **after** casualty or theft	6	*0*			
7 Subtract line 6 from line 5	7	*9,000*			
8 Enter the **smaller** of line 2 or line 7	8	*6,000*			
9 Subtract line 3 from line 8. If zero or less, enter -0-	9	*3,100*			

10 Casualty or theft loss. Add the amounts on line 9 in columns A through D	10	*3,100*
11 Enter the **smaller** of line 10 or $100	11	*100*
12 Subtract line 11 from line 10	12	*3,000*
Caution: *Use only one Form 4684 for lines 13 through 18.*		
13 Add the amounts on line 12 of all Forms 4684	13	*3,000*
14 Add the amounts on line 4 of all Forms 4684	14	*0*
15 • If line 14 is **more** than line 13, enter the difference here and on Schedule D. **Do not** complete the rest of this section (see instructions). • If line 14 is **less** than line 13, enter -0- here and go to line 16. • If line 14 is **equal** to line 13, enter -0- here. **Do not** complete the rest of this section.	15	*0*
16 If line 14 is **less** than line 13, enter the difference	16	*3,000*
17 Enter 10% of your adjusted gross income from Form 1040, line 38, or Form 1040NR, line 37. Estates and trusts, see instructions	17	*2,500*
18 Subtract line 17 from line 16. If zero or less, enter -0-. Also enter the result on Schedule A (Form 1040), line 20, or Form 1040NR, Schedule A, line 6. Estates and trusts, enter the result on the "Other deductions" line of your tax return	18	*500*

For Paperwork Reduction Act Notice, see instructions. Cat. No. 12997O Form **4684** (2014)

Self-Study Problem 5.5

Form 4684 (2014) Attachment Sequence No. **26** Page **2**

Name(s) shown on tax return. Do not enter name and identifying number if shown on other side.	**Identifying number**

DRAFT AS OF June 12, 2014 DO NOT FILE

SECTION B—Business and Income-Producing Property

Part I Casualty or Theft Gain or Loss (Use a separate Part I for each casualty or theft.)

19 Description of properties (show type, location, and date acquired for each property). Use a separate line for each property lost or damaged from the same casualty or theft. **See instructions if claiming a loss due to a Ponzi-type investment scheme and Section C is not completed.**

Property **A** ____________________

Property **B** ____________________

Property **C** ____________________

Property **D** ____________________

		Properties A	Properties B	Properties C	Properties D
20 Cost or adjusted basis of each property	20				
21 Insurance or other reimbursement (whether or not you filed a claim). See the instructions for line 3	21				
Note: *If line 20 is* ***more*** *than line 21, skip line 22.*					
22 Gain from casualty or theft. If line 21 is **more** than line 20, enter the difference here and on line 29 or line 34, column (c), except as provided in the instructions for line 33. Also, skip lines 23 through 27 for that column. See the instructions for line 4 if line 21 includes insurance or other reimbursement you did not claim, or you received payment for your loss in a later tax year	22				
23 Fair market value **before** casualty or theft	23				
24 Fair market value **after** casualty or theft	24				
25 Subtract line 24 from line 23	25				
26 Enter the **smaller** of line 20 or line 25	26				
Note: *If the property was totally destroyed by casualty or lost from theft, enter on line 26 the amount from line 20.*					
27 Subtract line 21 from line 26. If zero or less, enter -0-	27				

28 Casualty or theft loss. Add the amounts on line 27. Enter the total here and on line 29 **or** line 34 (see instructions) | 28 | ______

Part II Summary of Gains and Losses (from separate Parts I)

	(a) Identify casualty or theft		(b) Losses from casualties or thefts: (i) Trade, business, rental or royalty property	(b) Losses from casualties or thefts: (ii) Income-producing and employee property	(c) Gains from casualties or thefts includible in income
	Casualty or Theft of Property Held One Year or Less				
29			( )	( )	
			( )	( )	
30	Totals. Add the amounts on line 29	30	( )	( )	
31	Combine line 30, columns (b)(i) and (c). Enter the net gain or (loss) here and on Form 4797, line 14. If Form 4797 is not otherwise required, see instructions			31	
32	Enter the amount from line 30, column (b)(ii) here. Individuals, enter the amount from income-producing property on Schedule A (Form 1040), line 28, or Form 1040NR, Schedule A, line 14, and enter the amount from property used as an employee on Schedule A (Form 1040), line 23, or Form 1040NR, Schedule A, line 9. Estates and trusts, partnerships, and S corporations, see instructions			32	
	Casualty or Theft of Property Held More Than One Year				
33	Casualty or theft gains from Form 4797, line 32			33	
34			( )	( )	
			( )	( )	
35	Total losses. Add amounts on line 34, columns (b)(i) and (b)(ii)	35	( )	( )	
36	Total gains. Add lines 33 and 34, column (c)			36	
37	Add amounts on line 35, columns (b)(i) and (b)(ii)			37	
38	If the loss on line 37 is **more** than the gain on line 36:				
a	Combine line 35, column (b)(i) and line 36, and enter the net gain or (loss) here. Partnerships (except electing large partnerships) and S corporations, see the note below. All others, enter this amount on Form 4797, line 14. If Form 4797 is not otherwise required, see instructions			38a	
b	Enter the amount from line 35, column (b)(ii) here. Individuals, enter the amount from income-producing property on Schedule A (Form 1040), line 28, or Form 1040NR, Schedule A, line 14, and enter the amount from property used as an employee on Schedule A (Form 1040), line 23, or Form 1040NR, Schedule A, line 9. Estates and trusts, enter on the "Other deductions" line of your tax return. Partnerships (except electing large partnerships) and S corporations, see the note below. Electing large partnerships, enter on Form 1065-B, Part II, line 11			38b	
39	If the loss on line 37 is **less** than or **equal** to the gain on line 36, combine lines 36 and 37 and enter here. Partnerships (except electing large partnerships), see the note below. All others, enter this amount on Form 4797, line 3			39	

Note: *Partnerships, enter the amount from line 38a, 38b, or line 39 on Form 1065, Schedule K, line 11. S corporations, enter the amount from line 38a or 38b on Form 1120S, Schedule K, line 10.*

Form **4684** (2014)

Self-Study Problem 6.2

Worksheet A—2014 EIC—Lines 66a and 66b

Keep for Your Records

Before you begin: √ Be sure you are using the correct worksheet. Use this worksheet only if you answered "No" to Step 5, question 2. Otherwise, use Worksheet B.

DRAFT AS OF October 8, 2014

Part 1

All Filers Using Worksheet A

1. Enter your earned income from Step 5. *(Wages, Salaries)* — **1** 15,800

2. Look up the amount on line 1 above in the EIC Table (right after Worksheet B) to find the credit. Be sure you use the correct column for your filing status and the number of children you have. Enter the credit here. — **2** 3,305

If line 2 is zero, STOP You cannot take the credit. Enter "No" on the dotted line next to line 66a.

3. Enter the amount from Form 1040, line 38. *(Adjusted Gross Income)* — **3** 15,900

4. Are the amounts on lines 3 and 1 the same?

☐ **Yes.** Skip line 5; enter the amount from line 2 on line 6.

☒ **No.** Go to line 5.

Part 2

Filers Who Answered "No" on Line 4

5. If you have:

- No qualifying children, is the amount on line 3 less than $8,150 ($13,550 if married filing jointly)?
- 1 or more qualifying children, is the amount on line 3 less than $17,850 ($23,300 if married filing jointly)?

☒ **Yes.** Leave line 5 blank; enter the amount from line 2 on line 6.

☐ **No.** Look up the amount on line 3 in the EIC Table to find the credit. Be sure you use the correct column for your filing status and the number of children you have. Enter the credit here. — **5**

Look at the amounts on lines 5 and 2.
Then, enter the **smaller** amount on line 6.

Part 3

Your Earned Income Credit

6. This is your earned income credit. — **6** 3,305

Enter this amount on Form 1040, line 66a.

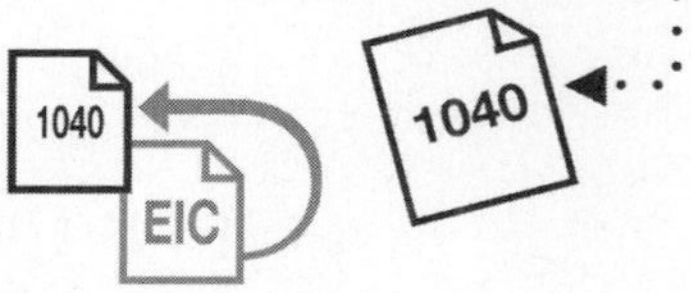

Reminder—

√ If you have a qualifying child, complete and attach Schedule EIC.

CAUTION *If your EIC for a year after 1996 was reduced or disallowed, see* Form 8862, who must file, *earlier, to find out if you must file Form 8862 to take the credit for 2014.*

Self-Study Problem 6.3

Form **2441** Department of the Treasury Internal Revenue Service (99)

Child and Dependent Care Expenses

▶ Attach to Form 1040, Form 1040A, or Form 1040NR.

▶ Information about Form 2441 and its separate instructions is at *www.irs.gov/form2441*.

OMB No. 1545-0074 | 2014 | Attachment Sequence No. 21

1040 / 1040A / 1040NR / 2441

DRAFT AS OF July 2, 2014 DO NOT FILE

Name(s) shown on return: *Julie Brown* | Your social security number

Part I **Persons or Organizations Who Provided the Care**—You **must** complete this part. (If you have more than two care providers, see the instructions.)

1 (a) Care provider's name	(b) Address (number, street, apt. no., city, state, and ZIP code)	(c) Identifying number (SSN or EIN)	(d) Amount paid (see instructions)
ABC Childcare	*11 Elm Street* *Anywhere, USA*	*95-3333333*	*1,500*
XYZ Adultcare	*19 Maple Street* *Anywhere, USA*	*95-4444444*	*2,400*

Did you receive **dependent care benefits?**
- **No** ▶ Complete only Part II below.
- **Yes** ▶ Complete Part III on the back next.

Caution. If the care was provided in your home, you may owe employment taxes. If you do, you cannot file Form 1040A. For details, see the instructions for Form 1040, line 60a, or Form 1040NR, line 59a.

Part II **Credit for Child and Dependent Care Expenses**

2 Information about your **qualifying person(s).** If you have more than two qualifying persons, see the instructions.

(a) Qualifying person's name — First	Last	(b) Qualifying person's social security number	(c) **Qualified expenses** you incurred and paid in 2014 for the person listed in column (a)
Child	*Brown*	*123-33-3333*	*1,500*
Mother	*Brown*	*456-66-6666*	*2,400*

Line	Description	Box	Amount
3	Add the amounts in column (c) of line 2. **Do not** enter more than $3,000 for one qualifying person or $6,000 for two or more persons. If you completed Part III, enter the amount from line 31	3	*3,900*
4	Enter your **earned income.** See instructions	4	*90,000*
5	If married filing jointly, enter your spouse's earned income (if you or your spouse was a student or was disabled, see the instructions); **all others**, enter the amount from line 4	5	*90,000*
6	Enter the **smallest** of line 3, 4, or 5	6	*3,900*
7	Enter the amount from Form 1040, line 38; Form 1040A, line 22; or Form 1040NR, line 37.	7	*90,000*
8	Enter on line 8 the decimal amount shown below that applies to the amount on line 7	8	X. *20*

If line 7 is:

Over—But not over	Decimal amount is	Over—But not over	Decimal amount is
$0—15,000	.35	$29,000—31,000	.27
15,000—17,000	.34	31,000—33,000	.26
17,000—19,000	.33	33,000—35,000	.25
19,000—21,000	.32	35,000—37,000	.24
21,000—23,000	.31	37,000—39,000	.23
23,000—25,000	.30	39,000—41,000	.22
25,000—27,000	.29	41,000—43,000	.21
27,000—29,000	.28	43,000—No limit	.20

Line	Description	Box	Amount
9	Multiply line 6 by the decimal amount on line 8. If you paid 2013 expenses in 2014, see the instructions	9	*780*
10	Tax liability limit. Enter the amount from the Credit Limit Worksheet in the instructions.	10	*6,209*
11	**Credit for child and dependent care expenses.** Enter the **smaller** of line 9 or line 10 here and on Form 1040, line 49; Form 1040A, line 31; or Form 1040NR, line 47	11	*780*

For Paperwork Reduction Act Notice, see your tax return instructions. Cat. No. 11862M Form **2441** (2014)

Solution Self-Study Problem 6.4A:

1. $238.50. Income of $34,000 − $10,150 = $23,850 × 1% = $238.50. The flat amount is $95. The greater of the two is the income amount of $238.50. This is below the cost of a bronze plan.
2. $0. Jill was without MEC for only 2 consecutive months and thus can use one of the exceptions to avoid the individual shared responsibility.
3. $39.58. Joint income of $21,000 − $20,300 = $700 × 1% = $7. The flat amount of $95 is for Ted only since Carlos has MEC all year. Ted's monthly amount is $95/12 = $7.92 per month × 5 months without MEC = $39.58. The greater of the two is $39.58 which is well below the bronze plan premium level for 2014.
4. $3,197. Income of $340,000 − $20,300 = $319,700 × 1% = $3,197. The flat amount is $380 since the actual flat amount ($95 × 2 + $47.50 × 4) is greater than the 2014 family maximum. The greater of the two amounts is $3,197. The maximum bronze premium for a family of 5 or more is $1,020 per month or $12,240 in 2014.

Solution to Self-Study Problem 6.4B

1. Modified household income is $44,000 + $22,000 + $2,000 = $68,000
   The FPL for a family of four (the non-dependent child is not included) is $23,550.
   The Killington's income is $68,000 ÷ $23,550 = 2.89 or 289% of the FPL.
   The applicable amount is (289 − 250)/(300 − 250) × (9.5 − 8.05) = 1.131 + 8.05 = 9.181
   Thus the deemed premium is $68,000 × .09181 = $6,243
   The cost of a silver plan for a four-person household in South Carolina is $9,800 thus the actual premium tax credit is $9,800 − $6,243 = $3,557.
2. The advanced premium tax credit amount was $5,800 thus the repayment amount before any limitation is $5,800 − $3,557 = $2,243.
3. However, the limitation for households between 200% and 300% of the FPL is $1,500 thus the Killingtons will treat the $1,500 as additional tax due on their 2014 tax return.

Self-Study Problem 6.7

Form **8839** | Department of the Treasury, Internal Revenue Service (99)

Qualified Adoption Expenses

▶ Attach to Form 1040 or 1040NR.

▶ For information about Form 8839 and its separate instructions, see *www.irs.gov/form8839*.

OMB No. 1545-0074 | **2014** | Attachment Sequence No. **38**

Name(s) shown on return | **Your social security number**

DRAFT AS OF August 12, 2014 DO NOT FILE

Part I **Information About Your Eligible Child or Children**—You **must** complete this part. See instructions for details, including what to do if you need more space.

1	(a) Child's name — First	Last	(b) Child's year of birth	(c) born **before** 1997 and disabled	(d) a child with special needs	(e) a foreign child	(f) Child's identifying number	(g) Check if adoption became final in 2014 or earlier
Child 1	*Allison*	*Anderson*	*2014*	☐	☐	☐	*466-47-3311*	☑
Child 2				☐	☐	☐		☐
Child 3				☐	☐	☐		☐

Caution. If the child was a foreign child, see **Special rules** in the instructions for line 1, column (e) before you complete Part II or Part III. If you received **employer-provided adoption benefits,** complete Part III on the back next.

Part II **Adoption Credit**

Line	Description		Child 1	Child 2	Child 3
2	Maximum adoption credit per child	2	$13,190 00	$13,190 00	$13,190 00
3	Did you file Form 8839 for a prior year for the same child? ☑ **No.** Enter -0-. ☐ **Yes.** See instructions for the amount to enter.	3			
4	Subtract line 3 from line 2	4	*13,190*		
5	**Qualified adoption expenses** (see instructions). **Caution.** Your qualified adoption expenses may not be equal to the adoption expenses you paid in 2014.	5	*17,000*		
6	Enter the **smaller** of line 4 or line 5	6	*13,190*		

Line	Description		Amount
7	Enter modified adjusted gross income (see instructions)	7	*200,360*
8	Is line 7 more than $197,880? ☐ **No.** Skip lines 8 and 9, and enter -0- on line 10. ☐ **Yes.** Subtract $197,880 from line 7	8	*2,480*
9	Divide line 8 by $40,000. Enter the result as a decimal (rounded to at least three places). Do not enter more than 1.000	9	× *.062*

Line	Description		Child 1	Child 2	Child 3
10	Multiply each amount on line 6 by line 9	10	*818*		
11	Subtract line 10 from line 6	11	*12,372*		

Line	Description		Amount
12	Add the amounts on line 11	12	*12,372*
13	Credit carryforward, if any, from prior years. See your Adoption Credit Carryforward Worksheet in the 2013 Form 8839 instructions	13	
14	Add lines 12 and 13	14	*12,372*
15	Enter the amount from line 5 of the Credit Limit Worksheet in the instructions	15	
16	**Adoption Credit.** Enter the smaller of line 14 or line 15 here and on Form 1040, line 54, or Form 1040NR, line 51. Check box **c** on that line and enter **"8839"** in the space next to box **c**. If line 15 is smaller than line 14, you may have a credit carryforward (see instructions)	16	*12,372*

For Paperwork Reduction Act Notice, see your tax return instructions. Cat. No. 22843L Form **8839** (2014)

Self-Study Problem 6.7

Form 8839 (2014) Page **2**

Part III Employer-Provided Adoption Benefits

			Child 1	Child 2	Child 3		
17	Maximum exclusion per child	17	$13,190 00	$13,190 00	$13,190 00		
18	Did you receive employer-provided adoption benefits for a prior year for the same child? ☑ **No.** Enter -0-. ☐ **Yes.** See instructions for the amount to enter.	18	*0*				
19	Subtract line 18 from line 17	19	*13,190*				
20	Employer-provided adoption benefits you received in 2014. This amount should be shown in box 12 of your 2014 Form(s) W-2 with code **T**	20	*4,000*				
21	Add the amounts on line 20					21	*4,000*
22	Enter the **smaller** of line 19 or line 20. But if the child was a child with special needs and the adoption became final in 2014, enter the amount from line 19	22	*4,000*				
23	Enter modified adjusted gross income (from the worksheet in the instructions)	23	*200,360*				
24	Is line 23 more than $197,880? ☐ **No.** Skip lines 24 and 25, and enter -0- on line 26. ☑ **Yes.** Subtract $197,880 from line 23	24	*2,480*				
25	Divide line 24 by $40,000. Enter the result as a decimal (rounded to at least three places). Do not enter more than 1.000	25	× *.062*				
26	Multiply each amount on line 22 by line 25	26	*248*				
27	**Excluded benefits.** Subtract line 26 from line 22	27	*3,752*				
28	Add the amounts on line 27					28	*3,752*
29	**Taxable benefits.** Is line 28 more than line 21? ☑ **No.** Subtract line 28 from line 21. Also, include this amount, if more than zero, on line 7 of Form 1040 or line 8 of Form 1040NR. On the dotted line next to line 7 of Form 1040 or line 8 of Form 1040NR, enter "AB." ☐ **Yes.** Subtract line 21 from line 28. Enter the result as a negative number. Reduce the total you would enter on line 7 of Form 1040 or line 8 of Form 1040NR by the amount on Form 8839, line 29. Enter the result on line 7 of Form 1040 or line 8 of Form 1040NR. Enter "SNE" on the dotted line next to the entry line. . .					29	*248*

DRAFT AS OF August 12, 2014 DO NOT FILE

TIP

You may be able to claim the adoption credit in Part II on the front of this form if any of the following apply.

- You paid adoption expenses in 2013, those expenses were not fully reimbursed by your employer or otherwise, and the adoption was not final by the end of 2013.
- The total adoption expenses you paid in 2014 were not fully reimbursed by your employer or otherwise, and the adoption became final in 2014 or earlier.
- You adopted a child with special needs and the adoption became final in 2014.

Form **8839** (2014)

Self-Study Problem 6.9

Form **6251** Department of the Treasury Internal Revenue Service (99)

Alternative Minimum Tax—Individuals

▶ Information about Form 6251 and its separate instructions is at *www.irs.gov/form6251*.
▶ Attach to Form 1040 or Form 1040NR.

OMB No. 1545-0074 **2014** Attachment Sequence No. **32**

DRAFT AS OF August 4, 2014 DO NOT FILE

Name(s) shown on Form 1040 or Form 1040NR: *Harold Brown* | **Your social security number**

Part I Alternative Minimum Taxable Income (See instructions for how to complete each line.)

1	If filing Schedule A (Form 1040), enter the amount from Form 1040, line 41, and go to line 2. Otherwise, enter the amount from Form 1040, line 38, and go to line 7. (If less than zero, enter as a negative amount.)	1	106,000
2	Medical and dental. If you or your spouse was 65 or older, enter the **smaller** of Schedule A (Form 1040), line 4, **or** 2.5% (.025) of Form 1040, line 38. If zero or less, enter -0-	2	
3	Taxes from Schedule A (Form 1040), line 9	3	50,000
4	Enter the home mortgage interest adjustment, if any, from line 6 of the worksheet in the instructions for this line	4	
5	Miscellaneous deductions from Schedule A (Form 1040), line 27	5	10,000
6	If Form 1040, line 38, is $152,525 or less, enter -0-. Otherwise, see instructions	6	( )
7	Tax refund from Form 1040, line 10 or line 21	7	( )
8	Investment interest expense (difference between regular tax and AMT)	8	
9	Depletion (difference between regular tax and AMT)	9	
10	Net operating loss deduction from Form 1040, line 21. Enter as a positive amount	10	
11	Alternative tax net operating loss deduction	11	( )
12	Interest from specified private activity bonds exempt from the regular tax	12	
13	Qualified small business stock (7% of gain excluded under section 1202)	13	
14	Exercise of incentive stock options (excess of AMT income over regular tax income)	14	
15	Estates and trusts (amount from Schedule K-1 (Form 1041), box 12, code A)	15	
16	Electing large partnerships (amount from Schedule K-1 (Form 1065-B), box 6)	16	
17	Disposition of property (difference between AMT and regular tax gain or loss)	17	
18	Depreciation on assets placed in service after 1986 (difference between regular tax and AMT)	18	
19	Passive activities (difference between AMT and regular tax income or loss)	19	
20	Loss limitations (difference between AMT and regular tax income or loss)	20	
21	Circulation costs (difference between regular tax and AMT)	21	
22	Long-term contracts (difference between AMT and regular tax income)	22	
23	Mining costs (difference between regular tax and AMT)	23	
24	Research and experimental costs (difference between regular tax and AMT)	24	
25	Income from certain installment sales before January 1, 1987	25	( )
26	Intangible drilling costs preference	26	
27	Other adjustments, including income-based related adjustments	27	
28	**Alternative minimum taxable income.** Combine lines 1 through 27. (If married filing separately and line 28 is more than $242,450, see instructions.)	28	166,000

Part II Alternative Minimum Tax (AMT)

29 Exemption. (If you were under age 24 at the end of 2014, see instructions.)

IF your filing status is . . .	**AND line 28 is not over . . .**	**THEN enter on line 29 . . .**
Single or head of household	$117,300	$52,800
Married filing jointly or qualifying widow(er)	156,500	82,100
Married filing separately	78,250	41,050

If line 28 is **over** the amount shown above for your filing status, see instructions. — **29** 40,625

30	Subtract line 29 from line 28. If more than zero, go to line 31. If zero or less, enter -0- here and on lines 31, 33, and 35, and go to line 34	30	125,375
31	• If you are filing Form 2555 or 2555-EZ, see instructions for the amount to enter. • If you reported capital gain distributions directly on Form 1040, line 13; you reported qualified dividends on Form 1040, line 9b; **or** you had a gain on both lines 15 and 16 of Schedule D (Form 1040) (as refigured for the AMT, if necessary), complete Part III on the back and enter the amount from line 64 here. • **All others:** If line 30 is $182,500 or less ($91,250 or less if married filing separately), multiply line 30 by 26% (.26). Otherwise, multiply line 30 by 28% (.28) and subtract $3,650 ($1,825 if married filing separately) from the result.	31	32,598
32	Alternative minimum tax foreign tax credit (see instructions)	32	
33	Tentative minimum tax. Subtract line 32 from line 31	33	32,598
34	Add Form 1040, line 44 (minus any tax from Form 4972), and Form 1040, line 46. Subtract from the result any foreign tax credit from Form 1040, line 48. If you used Schedule J to figure your tax on Form 1040, line 44, refigure that tax without using Schedule J before completing this line (see instructions)	34	21,750
35	**AMT.** Subtract line 34 from line 33. If zero or less, enter -0-. Enter here and on Form 1040, line 45	35	10,848

Self-Study Problem 6.9

See Form 6251 on Page E-31.

Line 1 of Form 6251 is computed as follows:

Adjusted gross income		$200,000
Less itemized deductions:		
Home mortgage interest expense	$23,000	
Contributions	11,000	
Property taxes	10,000	
State income taxes	40,000	
Miscellaneous	10,000	(94,000)
Taxable income before personal exemption		$106,000

Line 29 of Form 6251 is computed as follows:

Line 28—AMTI	$166,000
Less:	
Line 29 maximum for Single	$117,300
	$48,700
Phase-out—25%	$12,175
Deducted from minimum for Single	$52,800
Exemption	$40,625

Self-Study Problem 6.10

Step 1:

Unearned income	$3,000
Less: greater of $1,000 (standard deduction) or investment expenses	(1,000)
Less: amount taxed at 10%	(1,000)
Net unearned income, taxed at parents' rates	$1,000

Step 2:

Parents' taxable income	$46,050
Plus: child's net unearned income	1,000
Revised taxable income	$47,050
Tax from tax table on revised taxable income ($47,050)	$ 6,154
Less: tax from tax table on regular taxable income ($46,050)	(6,004)
Parental tax	$ 150

Step 3:

Regular tax (at 10% assumed rate)	$ 100
Parental tax	150
Total tax liability	$ 250

Self-Study Problem 6.11

a. Tom's salary (50 percent)	$20,000
Rachel's salary (50 percent)	15,000
Dividends, Rachel's property (100 percent)	3,000
Interest (50 percent)	2,000
Total	$40,000
b. Tom's salary (50 percent)	$20,000
Rachel's salary (50 percent)	15,000
Dividends, Tom's property (50 percent)	2,500
Dividends, Rachel's property (50 percent)	1,500
Interest (50 percent)	2,000
Total	$41,000

CHAPTER 7 ACCOUNTING PERIODS AND METHODS AND DEPRECIATION

Self-Study Problem 7.1

Step 1:

Annualize the income	$48,000 × $^{12}/_{10}$ = $57,600

Step 2:

Tax on annualized income	15% × $50,000 = $ 7,500
	25% × 7,600 = 1,900
	9,400

Step 3:

Short-period tax	$9,400 × $^{10}/_{12}$ = $ 7,833

Self-Study Problem 7.2A

Business income	$ 63,000
Less: business expenses	(42,000)
Operating income	$ 21,000
Add: rent received	9,000
Add: prepaid interest received	12,000
Less: rent expense for one month ($7,200/6)	(1,200)
Net income	$ 40,800

Self-Study Problem 7.2B

1. Yes
2. Yes
3. No
4. Yes, assuming this is a personal service corporation.

Self-Study Problem 7.3

Year	***Depreciation Deduction***
20X1	$ 583
20X2	700
20X3	700
20X4	700
20X5	700
20X6	117
Total	$3,500

Self-Study Problem 7.4

a. See Form 4562 on Pages E-35 and E-36.

b. 7-year property, 24.49% × $14,000	$3,429
Office building, 2.564% × $175,000	$4,487

Self-Study Problem 7.5

Cost	$37,500
Section 179	(25,000)
	12,500
MACRS	× 0.1429
	1,786
Section 179	25,000
Total depreciation (including election to expense)	$26,786

Self-Study Problem 7.4

Form **4562** — Department of the Treasury, Internal Revenue Service (99)

Depreciation and Amortization

(Including Information on Listed Property)

▶ Attach to your tax return.

▶ Information about Form 4562 and its separate instructions is at *www.irs.gov/form4562*.

OMB No. 1545-0172 — **2014** — Attachment Sequence No. 179

Name(s) shown on return	Business or activity to which this form relates	Identifying number
Mary Moser		

DRAFT AS OF June 10, 2014 DO NOT FILE

Part I Election To Expense Certain Property Under Section 179

Note: *If you have any listed property, complete Part V before you complete Part I.*

1	Maximum amount (see instructions)	1	
2	Total cost of section 179 property placed in service (see instructions)	2	
3	Threshold cost of section 179 property before reduction in limitation (see instructions)	3	
4	Reduction in limitation. Subtract line 3 from line 2. If zero or less, enter -0-	4	
5	Dollar limitation for tax year. Subtract line 4 from line 1. If zero or less, enter -0-. If married filing separately, see instructions	5	

6	(a) Description of property	(b) Cost (business use only)	(c) Elected cost

7	Listed property. Enter the amount from line 29	7	
8	Total elected cost of section 179 property. Add amounts in column (c), lines 6 and 7	8	
9	Tentative deduction. Enter the **smaller** of line 5 or line 8	9	
10	Carryover of disallowed deduction from line 13 of your 2013 Form 4562	10	
11	Business income limitation. Enter the smaller of business income (not less than zero) or line 5 (see instructions)	11	
12	Section 179 expense deduction. Add lines 9 and 10, but do not enter more than line 11	12	
13	Carryover of disallowed deduction to 2015. Add lines 9 and 10, less line 12 ▶	13	

Note: *Do not use Part II or Part III below for listed property. Instead, use Part V.*

Part II Special Depreciation Allowance and Other Depreciation (Do not include listed property.) (See instructions.)

14	Special depreciation allowance for qualified property (other than listed property) placed in service during the tax year (see instructions)	14	
15	Property subject to section 168(f)(1) election	15	
16	Other depreciation (including ACRS)	16	

Part III MACRS Depreciation (Do not include listed property.) (See instructions.)

Section A

17	MACRS deductions for assets placed in service in tax years beginning before 2014	17	
18	If you are electing to group any assets placed in service during the tax year into one or more general asset accounts, check here ▶ ☐		

Section B—Assets Placed in Service During 2014 Tax Year Using the General Depreciation System

(a) Classification of property	(b) Month and year placed in service	(c) Basis for depreciation (business/investment use only—see instructions)	(d) Recovery period	(e) Convention	(f) Method	(g) Depreciation deduction
19a 3-year property						
b 5-year property						
c 7-year property		14,000	7 years	HY	200 DB	2,001
d 10-year property						
e 15-year property						
f 20-year property						
g 25-year property			25 yrs.		S/L	
h Residential rental property			27.5 yrs.	MM	S/L	
			27.5 yrs.	MM	S/L	
i Nonresidential real property	03/30/2014	175,000	39 yrs.	MM	S/L	3,558
				MM	S/L	

Section C—Assets Placed in Service During 2014 Tax Year Using the Alternative Depreciation System

(a) Classification of property	(b)	(c)	(d)	(e)	(f)	(g)
20a Class life					S/L	
b 12-year			12 yrs.		S/L	
c 40-year			40 yrs.	MM	S/L	

Part IV Summary (See instructions.)

21	Listed property. Enter amount from line 28	21	
22	**Total.** Add amounts from line 12, lines 14 through 17, lines 19 and 20 in column (g), and line 21. Enter here and on the appropriate lines of your return. Partnerships and S corporations—see instructions	22	5,559
23	For assets shown above and placed in service during the current year, enter the portion of the basis attributable to section 263A costs	23	

Self-Study Problem 7.4

Form 4562 (2014) Page **2**

Part V Listed Property (Include automobiles, certain other vehicles, certain aircraft, certain computers, and property used for entertainment, recreation, or amusement.)

Note: *For any vehicle for which you are using the standard mileage rate or deducting lease expense, complete **only** 24a, 24b, columns (a) through (c) of Section A, all of Section B, and Section C if applicable.*

Section A—Depreciation and Other Information (Caution: *See the instructions for limits for passenger automobiles.*)

24a Do you have evidence to support the business/investment use claimed? ☐ **Yes** ☐ **No** **24b** If "Yes," is the evidence written? ☐ **Yes** ☐ **No**

(a) Type of property (list vehicles first)	(b) Date placed in service	(c) Business/ investment use percentage	(d) Cost or other basis	(e) Basis for depreciation (business/investment use only)	(f) Recovery period	(g) Method/ Convention	(h) Depreciation deduction	(i) Elected section 179 cost
25 Special depreciation allowance for qualified listed property placed in service during the tax year and used more than 50% in a qualified business use (see instructions) .						25		
26 Property used more than 50% in a qualified business use:								
		%						
		%						
		%						
27 Property used 50% or less in a qualified business use:								
		%				S/L –		
		%				S/L –		
		%				S/L –		
28 Add amounts in column (h), lines 25 through 27. Enter here and on line 21, page 1 .						28		
29 Add amounts in column (i), line 26. Enter here and on line 7, page 1							29	

DRAFT AS OF June 10, 2014 DO NOT FILE

Section B—Information on Use of Vehicles

Complete this section for vehicles used by a sole proprietor, partner, or other "more than 5% owner," or related person. If you provided vehicles to your employees, first answer the questions in Section C to see if you meet an exception to completing this section for those vehicles.

	(a) Vehicle 1		(b) Vehicle 2		(c) Vehicle 3		(d) Vehicle 4		(e) Vehicle 5		(f) Vehicle 6	
30 Total business/investment miles driven during the year (**do not** include commuting miles) .												
31 Total commuting miles driven during the year												
32 Total other personal (noncommuting) miles driven												
33 Total miles driven during the year. Add lines 30 through 32												
	Yes	**No**	**Yes**	**No**	**Yes**	**No**	**Yes**	**No**	**Yes**	**No**	**Yes**	**No**
34 Was the vehicle available for personal use during off-duty hours?												
35 Was the vehicle used primarily by a more than 5% owner or related person? . .												
36 Is another vehicle available for personal use?												

Section C—Questions for Employers Who Provide Vehicles for Use by Their Employees

Answer these questions to determine if you meet an exception to completing Section B for vehicles used by employees who **are not** more than 5% owners or related persons (see instructions).

	Yes	**No**
37 Do you maintain a written policy statement that prohibits all personal use of vehicles, including commuting, by your employees?		
38 Do you maintain a written policy statement that prohibits personal use of vehicles, except commuting, by your employees? See the instructions for vehicles used by corporate officers, directors, or 1% or more owners . .		
39 Do you treat all use of vehicles by employees as personal use?		
40 Do you provide more than five vehicles to your employees, obtain information from your employees about the use of the vehicles, and retain the information received?		
41 Do you meet the requirements concerning qualified automobile demonstration use? (See instructions.) . . .		
Note: *If your answer to 37, 38, 39, 40, or 41 is "Yes," do not complete Section B for the covered vehicles.*		

Part VI Amortization

(a) Description of costs	(b) Date amortization begins	(c) Amortizable amount	(d) Code section	(e) Amortization period or percentage	(f) Amortization for this year
42 Amortization of costs that begins during your 2014 tax year (see instructions):					
43 Amortization of costs that began before your 2014 tax year				43	
44 **Total.** Add amounts in column (f). See the instructions for where to report				44	

Form **4562** (2014)

Self-Study Problem 7.6

1. Yes — Qualified business use does not include investment use.
2. No — Qualified business use is more than 50 percent; therefore, Laura may use the accelerated method of depreciation.
3. Yes — Since the computer was acquired for Vicky's own convenience, not the convenience of her employer, qualified business use does not include use of the property in performing services as an employee.

Self-Study Problem 7.7

2014: ($26,000 × 20%) × 90% = $4,680, but limited to $3,160 × 90% = $2,844.

Self-Study Problem 7.8

1. 15-year Amortization.	5. 15-year Amortization.
2. Useful Life.	6. Not Amortizable.
3. Useful Life.	7. 15-year Amortization.
4. 15-year Amortization.	8. Not Amortizable.

Self-Study Problem 7.9

1. 56%; 40% owned directly and 16% (80% × 20%) through X Corporation.
2. 40%; 20% owned directly plus 20% as Gene's brother.
3. 40%; 20% owned directly plus 20% as Frank's brother.
4. $0; since they are related parties, the loss would be disallowed.

CHAPTER 8 CAPITAL GAINS AND LOSSES

Self-Study Problem 8.1

1. No — Inventory is specifically excluded from the definition of a capital asset.
2. Yes
3. No — Property held by the creator is specifically excluded from the definition of a capital asset.
4. No — Accounts receivable are specifically excluded from the definition of a capital asset.
5. Yes
6. No — Section 1231 assets (depreciable property and real estate used in a trade or business) are specifically excluded from the definition of a capital asset.
7. Yes
8. Yes
9. Yes
10. Yes
11. No — Inventory is specifically excluded from the definition of a capital asset.
12. Yes

Self-Study Problem 8.2

1. Short-term
2. Long-term
3. Short-term
4. Long-term

Self-Study Problem 8.3

1. Adjusted basis = $11,000
2. Capital improvements = $2,000
3. Accumulated depreciation = $15,000
4. Original cost = $23,000

Self-Study Problem 8.4

Net long-term ($12,000 − $4,000) + ($14,000 − $17,500) =	$ 4,500
Net short-term	(1,800)
Net capital gains	$ 2,700
Capital gains rate	× 15%
Tax	$ 405

Self-Study Problem 8.5

See Schedule D, Form 8949, and the worksheet on Pages E-39 through E-43.

Self-Study Problem 8.6

See Form 4797 on Pages E-44 and E-45.

Self-Study Problem 8.7

1. $12,000 − $7,000 = $5,000
2. $5,000 + $7,000 = $12,000
3. $12,000 − $5,000 = $7,000
4. $6,000 − $5,000 = $1,000
5. $1,000, the lesser of the amounts in (3) or (4) above.
6. $1,000 (gain realized) − $1,000 (Section 1245 ordinary income) = $0. All of the gain is Section 1245 ordinary income.

Self-Study Problem 8.8

Step 1: Compute separate casualty gains and losses

		Casualty Gain or (Loss)
Furniture	$2,000, lesser of adjusted basis or decrease in fair market value, less $1,600 insurance reimbursement, less $100 floor	$ (300)
Jewelry	$2,500 insurance reimbursement, less $1,800, adjusted basis	700
Business machinery	$14,000, adjusted basis, less $10,000 insurance reimbursement	(4,000)

Step 2: Net all personal casualty gains and losses

$(300) + $700 = $400 net casualty gain

Step 3: Determine nature of casualty gains and losses

a. Personal casualty gains and losses — Since an overall gain results, the gain or loss on each item of personal property is treated as a capital gain or loss as follows:

Furniture — Short-term capital loss	$ (300)
Jewelry — Long-term capital gain	$ 700

(This problem is continued on Page E-46.)

Self-Study Problem 8.5

SCHEDULE D (Form 1040)
Department of the Treasury
Internal Revenue Service (99)

Capital Gains and Losses

▶ Attach to Form 1040 or Form 1040NR.
▶ Information about Schedule D and its separate instructions is at *www.irs.gov/scheduled*.
▶ Use Form 8949 to list your transactions for lines 1b, 2, 3, 8b, 9, and 10.

OMB No. 1545-0074
2014
Attachment Sequence No. **12**

Name(s) shown on return: *Gerry Appel*
Your social security number

DRAFT AS OF June 9, 2014 DO NOT FILE

Part I Short-Term Capital Gains and Losses—Assets Held One Year or Less

See instructions for how to figure the amounts to enter on the lines below. This form may be easier to complete if you round off cents to whole dollars.	(d) Proceeds (sales price)	(e) Cost (or other basis)	(g) Adjustments to gain or loss from Form(s) 8949, Part I, line 2, column (g)	(h) Gain or (loss) Subtract column (e) from column (d) and combine the result with column (g)
1a Totals for all short-term transactions reported on Form 1099-B for which basis was reported to the IRS and for which you have no adjustments (see instructions). However, if you choose to report all these transactions on Form 8949, leave this line blank and go to line 1b				
1b Totals for all transactions reported on Form(s) 8949 with **Box A** checked	*12,000*	*19,200*		*(7,200)*
2 Totals for all transactions reported on Form(s) 8949 with **Box B** checked				
3 Totals for all transactions reported on Form(s) 8949 with **Box C** checked				

4 Short-term gain from Form 6252 and short-term gain or (loss) from Forms 4684, 6781, and 8824	4	
5 Net short-term gain or (loss) from partnerships, S corporations, estates, and trusts from Schedule(s) K-1	5	
6 Short-term capital loss carryover. Enter the amount, if any, from line 8 of your **Capital Loss Carryover Worksheet** in the instructions	6	( )
7 **Net short-term capital gain or (loss).** Combine lines 1a through 6 in column (h). If you have any long-term capital gains or losses, go to Part II below. Otherwise, go to Part III on the back	7	*(7,200)*

Part II Long-Term Capital Gains and Losses—Assets Held More Than One Year

See instructions for how to figure the amounts to enter on the lines below. This form may be easier to complete if you round off cents to whole dollars.	(d) Proceeds (sales price)	(e) Cost (or other basis)	(g) Adjustments to gain or loss from Form(s) 8949, Part II, line 2, column (g)	(h) Gain or (loss) Subtract column (e) from column (d) and combine the result with column (g)
8a Totals for all long-term transactions reported on Form 1099-B for which basis was reported to the IRS and for which you have no adjustments (see instructions). However, if you choose to report all these transactions on Form 8949, leave this line blank and go to line 8b				
8b Totals for all transactions reported on Form(s) 8949 with **Box D** checked	*43,000*	*33,500*		*9,500*
9 Totals for all transactions reported on Form(s) 8949 with **Box E** checked				
10 Totals for all transactions reported on Form(s) 8949 with **Box F** checked				

11 Gain from Form 4797, Part I; long-term gain from Forms 2439 and 6252; and long-term gain or (loss) from Forms 4684, 6781, and 8824	11	
12 Net long-term gain or (loss) from partnerships, S corporations, estates, and trusts from Schedule(s) K-1	12	
13 Capital gain distributions. See the instructions	13	
14 Long-term capital loss carryover. Enter the amount, if any, from line 13 of your **Capital Loss Carryover Worksheet** in the instructions	14	( )
15 **Net long-term capital gain or (loss).** Combine lines 8a through 14 in column (h). Then go to Part III on the back	15	*9,500*

Self-Study Problem 8.5

Schedule D (Form 1040) 2014 Page **2**

Part III **Summary**

16	Combine lines 7 and 15 and enter the result	**16**	*2,300*
	• If line 16 is a **gain,** enter the amount from line 16 on Form 1040, line 13, or Form 1040NR, line 14. Then go to line 17 below. • If line 16 is a **loss,** skip lines 17 through 20 below. Then go to line 21. Also be sure to complete line 22. • If line 16 is **zero,** skip lines 17 through 21 below and enter -0- on Form 1040, line 13, or Form 1040NR, line 14. Then go to line 22.		
17	Are lines 15 and 16 **both** gains? ☑ **Yes.** Go to line 18. ☐ **No.** Skip lines 18 through 21, and go to line 22.		
18	Enter the amount, if any, from line 7 of the **28% Rate Gain Worksheet** in the instructions . . ▶	**18**	*0*
19	Enter the amount, if any, from line 18 of the **Unrecaptured Section 1250 Gain Worksheet** in the instructions . . . . ▶	**19**	*0*
20	Are lines 18 and 19 **both** zero or blank? ☐ **Yes.** Complete the **Qualified Dividends and Capital Gain Tax Worksheet** in the instructions for Form 1040, line 44 (or in the instructions for Form 1040NR, line 42). **Do not** complete lines 21 and 22 below. ☐ **No.** Complete the **Schedule D Tax Worksheet** in the instructions. **Do not** complete lines 21 and 22 below.		
21	If line 16 is a loss, enter here and on Form 1040, line 13, or Form 1040NR, line 14, the **smaller** of: • The loss on line 16 or • ($3,000), or if married filing separately, ($1,500) }	**21**	( )
	Note. When figuring which amount is smaller, treat both amounts as positive numbers.		
22	Do you have qualified dividends on Form 1040, line 9b, or Form 1040NR, line 10b? ☐ **Yes.** Complete the **Qualified Dividends and Capital Gain Tax Worksheet** in the instructions for Form 1040, line 44 (or in the instructions for Form 1040NR, line 42). ☐ **No.** Complete the rest of Form 1040 or Form 1040NR.		

DRAFT AS OF June 9, 2014 DO NOT FILE

Self-Study Problem 8.5

Form **8949** Department of the Treasury Internal Revenue Service

Sales and Other Dispositions of Capital Assets

▶ Information about Form 8949 and its separate instructions is at *www.irs.gov/form8949.*
▶ File with your Schedule D to list your transactions for lines 1b, 2, 3, 8b, 9, and 10 of Schedule D.

OMB No. 1545-0123 **2014** Attachment Sequence No. **12A**

Name(s) shown on return	Social security number or taxpayer identification number
Gerry Appel	

Before you check Box A, B, or C below, see whether you received any Form(s) 1099-B or substitute statement(s) from your broker. A substitute statement will have the same information as Form 1099-B. Either may show your basis (usually your cost) even if your broker did not report it to the IRS. Brokers must report basis to the IRS for most stock you bought in 2011 or later (and for certain debt instruments you bought in 2014 or later).

Part I **Short-Term.** Transactions involving capital assets you held 1 year or less are short term. For long-term transactions, see page 2.

Note. You may aggregate all short-term transactions reported on Form(s) 1099-B showing basis was reported to the IRS and for which no adjustments or codes are required. Enter the total directly on Schedule D, line 1a; you are not required to report these transactions on Form 8949 (see instructions).

You *must* check Box A, B, *or* C below. Check only one box. If more than one box applies for your short-term transactions, complete a separate Form 8949, page 1, for each applicable box. If you have more short-term transactions than will fit on this page for one or more of the boxes, complete as many forms with the same box checked as you need.

☑ **(A)** Short-term transactions reported on Form(s) 1099-B showing basis was reported to the IRS (see **Note** above)
☐ **(B)** Short-term transactions reported on Form(s) 1099-B showing basis was **not** reported to the IRS
☐ **(C)** Short-term transactions not reported to you on Form 1099-B

DRAFT AS OF June 12, 2014 DO NOT FILE

1 (a) Description of property (Example: 100 sh. XYZ Co.)	(b) Date acquired (Mo., day, yr.)	(c) Date sold or disposed (Mo., day, yr.)	(d) Proceeds (sales price) (see instructions)	(e) Cost or other basis. See the **Note** below and see *Column (e)* in the separate instructions	Adjustment, if any, to gain or loss. If you enter an amount in column (g), enter a code in column (f). See the separate instructions. (f) Code(s) from instructions	(g) Amount of adjustment	(h) Gain or (loss). Subtract column (e) from column (d) and combine the result with column (g)
Rose Stock	*04/18/2014*	*12/07/2014*	*12,000*	*19,200*			*(7,200)*
2 Totals. Add the amounts in columns (d), (e), (g), and (h) (subtract negative amounts). Enter each total here and include on your Schedule D, **line 1b** (if **Box A** above is checked), **line 2** (if **Box B** above is checked), or **line 3** (if **Box C** above is checked) ▶			*12,000*	*19,200*			*(7,200)*

Note. If you checked Box A above but the basis reported to the IRS was incorrect, enter in column (e) the basis as reported to the IRS, and enter an adjustment in column (g) to correct the basis. See *Column (g)* in the separate instructions for how to figure the amount of the adjustment.

Self-Study Problem 8.5

Form 8949 (2014) Attachment Sequence No. **12A** Page **2**

Name(s) shown on return. Name and SSN or taxpayer identification no. not required if shown on other side | **Social security number or taxpayer identification number**

Before you check Box D, E, or F below, see whether you received any Form(s) 1099-B or substitute statement(s) from your broker. A substitute statement will have the same information as Form 1099-B. Either may show your basis (usually your cost) even if your broker did not report it to the IRS. Brokers must report basis to the IRS for most stock you bought in 2011 or later (and for certain debt instruments you bought in 2014 or later).

Part II **Long-Term.** Transactions involving capital assets you held more than 1 year are long term. For short-term transactions, see page 1.

Note. You may aggregate all long-term transactions reported on Form(s) 1099-B showing basis was reported to the IRS and for which no adjustments or codes are required. Enter the total directly on Schedule D, line 8a; you are not required to report these transactions on Form 8949 (see instructions).

DRAFT AS OF June 12, 2014 DO NOT FILE

You *must* check Box D, E, *or* F below. Check only one box. If more than one box applies for your long-term transactions, complete a separate Form 8949, page 2, for each applicable box. If you have more long-term transactions than will fit on this page for one or more of the boxes, complete as many forms with the same box checked as you need.

- ☑ **(D)** Long-term transactions reported on Form(s) 1099-B showing basis was reported to the IRS (see **Note** above)
- ☐ **(E)** Long-term transactions reported on Form(s) 1099-B showing basis was **not** reported to the IRS
- ☐ **(F)** Long-term transactions not reported to you on Form 1099-B

1 (a) Description of property (Example: 100 sh. XYZ Co.)	(b) Date acquired (Mo., day, yr.)	(c) Date sold or disposed (Mo., day, yr.)	(d) Proceeds (sales price) (see instructions)	(e) Cost or other basis. See the **Note** below and see *Column (e)* in the separate instructions	Adjustment, if any, to gain or loss. If you enter an amount in column (g), enter a code in column (f). **See the separate instructions.** (f) Code(s) from instructions	(g) Amount of adjustment	(h) **Gain or (loss).** Subtract column (e) from column (d) and combine the result with column (g)
Purple Stock	*06/21/2005*	*08/15/2014*	*18,000*	*12,500*			*5,500*
Blue Stock	*12/18/2006*	*10/02/2014*	*25,000*	*21,000*			*4,000*
2 Totals. Add the amounts in columns (d), (e), (g), and (h) (subtract negative amounts). Enter each total here and include on your Schedule D, **line 8b** (if **Box D** above is checked), **line 9** (if **Box E** above is checked), or **line 10** (if **Box F** above is checked) ▶			*43,000*	*33,500*			*9,500*

Note. If you checked Box D above but the basis reported to the IRS was incorrect, enter in column (e) the basis as reported to the IRS, and enter an adjustment in column (g) to correct the basis. See *Column (g)* in the separate instructions for how to figure the amount of the adjustment.

Form **8949** (2014)

Self-Study Problem 8.5

Qualified Dividends and Capital Gain Tax Worksheet—Line 44

Keep for Your Records

Before you begin:
- ✓ See the earlier instructions for line 44 to see if you can use this worksheet to figure your tax.
- ✓ Before completing this worksheet, complete Form 1040 through line 43.
- ✓ If you do not have to file Schedule D and you received capital gain distributions, be sure you checked the box on line 13 of Form 1040.

Line	Description		Amount		Amount
1.	Enter the amount from Form 1040, line 43. However, if you are filing Form 2555 or 2555-EZ (relating to foreign earned income), enter the amount from line 3 of the Foreign Earned Income Tax Worksheet . *(Taxable income)*	**1.**	*59,000*		
2.	Enter the amount from Form 1040, line 9b* *Qualified dividends*	**2.**			
3.	Are you filing Schedule D?* ☒ **Yes.** Enter the **smaller** of line 15 or 16 of Schedule D. If either line 15 or line 16 is blank or a loss, enter -0- ☐ **No.** Enter the amount from Form 1040, line 13	**3.**	*2,300*		
4.	Add lines 2 and 3	**4.**	*2,300*		
5.	If filing Form 4952 (used to figure investment interest expense deduction), enter any amount from line 4g of that form. Otherwise, enter -0-	**5.**	*0*		
6.	Subtract line 5 from line 4. If zero or less, enter -0-	**6.**	*2,300*		
7.	Subtract line 6 from line 1. If zero or less, enter -0-	**7.**	*56,700*		
8.	Enter: $36,900 if single or married filing separately, $73,800 if married filing jointly or qualifying widow(er), $49,400 if head of household.	**8.**	*36,900*		
9.	Enter the smaller of line 1 or line 8	**9.**	*36,900*		
10.	Enter the smaller of line 7 or line 9	**10.**	*36,900*		
11.	Subtract line 10 from line 9. This amount is taxed at 0%	**11.**	*0*		
12.	Enter the smaller of line 1 or line 6	**12.**	*2,300*		
13.	Enter the amount from line 11	**13.**	*0*		
14.	Subtract line 13 from line 12	**14.**	*2,300*		
15.	Enter: $406,750 if single, $228,800 if married filing separately, $457,600 if married filing jointly or qualifying widow(er), $432,200 if head of household.	**15.**	*406,750*		
16.	Enter the smaller of line 1 or line 15	**16.**	*59,000*		
17.	Add lines 7 and 11	**17.**	*56,700*		
18.	Subtract line 17 from line 16. If zero or less, enter -0-	**18.**	*2,300*		
19.	Enter the smaller of line 14 or line 18	**19.**	*2,300*		
20.	Multiply line 19 by 15% (.15)			**20.**	*345*
21.	Add lines 11 and 19	**21.**	*2,300*		
22.	Subtract line 21 from line 12	**22.**	*0*		
23.	Multiply line 22 by 20% (.20)			**23.**	*0*
24.	Figure the tax on the amount on line 7. If the amount on line 7 is less than $100,000, use the Tax Table to figure the tax. If the amount on line 7 is $100,000 or more, use the Tax Computation Worksheet			**24.**	*10,038*
25.	Add lines 20, 23, and 24			**25.**	*10,383*
26.	Figure the tax on the amount on line 1. If the amount on line 1 is less than $100,000, use the Tax Table to figure the tax. If the amount on line 1 is $100,000 or more, use the Tax Computation Worksheet			**26.**	*10,613*
27.	**Tax on all taxable income.** Enter the **smaller** of line 25 or line 26. Also include this amount on Form 1040, line 44. If you are filing Form 2555 or 2555-EZ, do not enter this amount on Form 1040, line 44. Instead, enter it on line 4 of the Foreign Earned Income Tax Worksheet			**27.**	*10,383*

**If you are filing Form 2555 or 2555-EZ, see the footnote in the Foreign Earned Income Tax Worksheet before completing this line.*

Self-Study Problem 8.6

Form **4797**

Department of the Treasury
Internal Revenue Service

Sales of Business Property

(Also Involuntary Conversions and Recapture Amounts Under Sections 179 and 280F(b)(2))

▶ Attach to your tax return.
▶ Information about Form 4797 and its separate instructions is at *www.irs.gov/form4797.*

OMB No. 1545-0184
2014
Attachment Sequence No. 27

Name(s) shown on return: *Gary Farmer*
Identifying number: *74-8976432*

1 Enter the gross proceeds from sales or exchanges reported to you for 2014 on Form(s) 1099-B or 1099-S (or substitute statement) that you are including on line 2, 10, or 20 (see instructions) . . . 1

Part I **Sales or Exchanges of Property Used in a Trade or Business and Involuntary Conversions From Other Than Casualty or Theft—Most Property Held More Than 1 Year** (see instructions)

DRAFT AS OF June 13, 2014 DO NOT FILE

2 (a) Description of property	(b) Date acquired (mo., day, yr.)	(c) Date sold (mo., day, yr.)	(d) Gross sales price	(e) Depreciation allowed or allowable since acquisition	(f) Cost or other basis, plus improvements and expense of sale	(g) Gain or (loss) Subtract (f) from the sum of (d) and (e)
Land	*12/03/2003*	*01/05/2014*	*37,000*		*24,500*	*12,500*
Computer	*04/05/2011*	*05/02/2014*	*14,000*	*5,175*	*25,875*	*(6,700)*

3	Gain, if any, from Form 4684, line 39 . . .	3	
4	Section 1231 gain from installment sales from Form 6252, line 26 or 37 . . .	4	
5	Section 1231 gain or (loss) from like-kind exchanges from Form 8824 . . .	5	
6	Gain, if any, from line 32, from other than casualty or theft. . . .	6	
7	Combine lines 2 through 6. Enter the gain or (loss) here and on the appropriate line as follows: . . .	7	*5,800*

Partnerships (except electing large partnerships) and S corporations. Report the gain or (loss) following the instructions for Form 1065, Schedule K, line 10, or Form 1120S, Schedule K, line 9. Skip lines 8, 9, 11, and 12 below.

Individuals, partners, S corporation shareholders, and all others. If line 7 is zero or a loss, enter the amount from line 7 on line 11 below and skip lines 8 and 9. If line 7 is a gain and you did not have any prior year section 1231 losses, or they were recaptured in an earlier year, enter the gain from line 7 as a long-term capital gain on the Schedule D filed with your return and skip lines 8, 9, 11, and 12 below.

8	Nonrecaptured net section 1231 losses from prior years (see instructions) . . .	8	
9	Subtract line 8 from line 7. If zero or less, enter -0-. If line 9 is zero, enter the gain from line 7 on line 12 below. If line 9 is more than zero, enter the amount from line 8 on line 12 below and enter the gain from line 9 as a long-term capital gain on the Schedule D filed with your return (see instructions) . . .	9	*5,800*

Part II **Ordinary Gains and Losses** (see instructions)

10 Ordinary gains and losses not included on lines 11 through 16 (include property held 1 year or less):

11	Loss, if any, from line 7 . . .	11	( )
12	Gain, if any, from line 7 or amount from line 8, if applicable . . .	12	*0*
13	Gain, if any, from line 31 . . .	13	
14	Net gain or (loss) from Form 4684, lines 31 and 38a . . .	14	
15	Ordinary gain from installment sales from Form 6252, line 25 or 36 . . .	15	
16	Ordinary gain or (loss) from like-kind exchanges from Form 8824. . . .	16	
17	Combine lines 10 through 16 . . .	17	
18	For all except individual returns, enter the amount from line 17 on the appropriate line of your return and skip lines a and b below. For individual returns, complete lines a and b below:		
a	If the loss on line 11 includes a loss from Form 4684, line 35, column (b)(ii), enter that part of the loss here. Enter the part of the loss from income-producing property on Schedule A (Form 1040), line 28, and the part of the loss from property used as an employee on Schedule A (Form 1040), line 23. Identify as from "Form 4797, line 18a." See instructions . .	18a	
b	Redetermine the gain or (loss) on line 17 excluding the loss, if any, on line 18a. Enter here and on Form 1040, line 14	18b	

Self-Study Problem 8.6

Form 4797 (2014) Page **2**

Part III Gain From Disposition of Property Under Sections 1245, 1250, 1252, 1254, and 1255 (see instructions)

19 (a) Description of section 1245, 1250, 1252, 1254, or 1255 property:	(b) Date acquired (mo., day, yr.)	(c) Date sold (mo., day, yr.)
A		
B		
C		
D		

DRAFT AS OF June 13, 2014 DO NOT FILE

These columns relate to the properties on lines 19A through 19D. ▶		Property A	Property B	Property C	Property D
20 Gross sales price (**Note:** *See line 1 before completing.*)	20				
21 Cost or other basis plus expense of sale	21				
22 Depreciation (or depletion) allowed or allowable	22				
23 Adjusted basis. Subtract line 22 from line 21	23				
24 Total gain. Subtract line 23 from line 20	24				
25 If section 1245 property:					
a Depreciation allowed or allowable from line 22	25a				
b Enter the **smaller** of line 24 or 25a	25b				
26 If section 1250 property: If straight line depreciation was used, enter -0- on line 26g, except for a corporation subject to section 291.					
a Additional depreciation after 1975 (see instructions)	26a				
b Applicable percentage multiplied by the **smaller** of line 24 or line 26a (see instructions)	26b				
c Subtract line 26a from line 24. If residential rental property **or** line 24 is not more than line 26a, skip lines 26d and 26e	26c				
d Additional depreciation after 1969 and before 1976	26d				
e Enter the **smaller** of line 26c or 26d	26e				
f Section 291 amount (corporations only)	26f				
g Add lines 26b, 26e, and 26f	26g				
27 If section 1252 property: Skip this section if you did not dispose of farmland or if this form is being completed for a partnership (other than an electing large partnership).					
a Soil, water, and land clearing expenses	27a				
b Line 27a multiplied by applicable percentage (see instructions)	27b				
c Enter the **smaller** of line 24 or 27b	27c				
28 If section 1254 property:					
a Intangible drilling and development costs, expenditures for development of mines and other natural deposits, mining exploration costs, and depletion (see instructions)	28a				
b Enter the **smaller** of line 24 or 28a	28b				
29 If section 1255 property:					
a Applicable percentage of payments excluded from income under section 126 (see instructions)	29a				
b Enter the **smaller** of line 24 or 29a (see instructions)	29b				

Summary of Part III Gains. Complete property columns A through D through line 29b before going to line 30.

30 Total gains for all properties. Add property columns A through D, line 24	30	
31 Add property columns A through D, lines 25b, 26g, 27c, 28b, and 29b. Enter here and on line 13	31	
32 Subtract line 31 from line 30. Enter the portion from casualty or theft on Form 4684, line 33. Enter the portion from other than casualty or theft on Form 4797, line 6	32	

Part IV Recapture Amounts Under Sections 179 and 280F(b)(2) When Business Use Drops to 50% or Less (see instructions)

		(a) Section 179	(b) Section 280F(b)(2)
33 Section 179 expense deduction or depreciation allowable in prior years	33		
34 Recomputed depreciation (see instructions)	34		
35 Recapture amount. Subtract line 34 from line 33. See the instructions for where to report	35		

b. Business casualty gains and losses — Machinery — Ordinary loss	$(4,000)

The capital gain and capital loss are netted with other capital gains and losses for the year. Since personal casualty gains exceed personal casualty losses, the loss recognized on the furniture is not subject to the 10 percent of adjusted gross income limitation.

Self-Study Problem 8.9

Cash	$ 20,000
Add: buyer's note	100,000
Selling price	$120,000
Less: the adjusted basis ($80,000 − $26,000)	(54,000)
Total gain realized	$ 66,000
Contract price ($20,000 + $100,000)	$120,000
Taxable gain in 2014 = $66,000 / $120,000 × $20,000	$ 11,000

Self-Study Problem 8.10

Calculation of gain recognized:

Fair market value of new truck	$ 22,000
Add: liability assumed by the buyer	8,000
Total amount realized	30,000
Less: the adjusted basis of the property given up	(18,000)
Gain realized	$ 12,000
Boot received (liability assumed by the buyer)	$ 8,000
Gain recognized (the lesser of the gain realized or the boot received)	$ 8,000
Basis of the property received:	
Basis of property given up	$ 18,000
Less: boot received	(8,000)
Add: the gain recognized	8,000
Basis of the property received	$ 18,000

Self-Study Problem 8.11

1. Insurance proceeds	$150,000
Less: the adjusted basis of the property	(70,000)
Gain realized	$ 80,000
Insurance proceeds	$150,000
Less: the cost of the replacement store	(135,000)
Proceeds not reinvested	$ 15,000
Gain recognized (the lesser of the gain realized or the proceeds not reinvested)	$ 15,000
2. Cost of the new store	$135,000
Less: the gain deferred ($80,000 − $15,000)	(65,000)
Basis of the new store	$ 70,000

Self-Study Problem 8.12

a. Sales price	$350,000
Basis	30,000
Realized Gain	$320,000
Exclusion	250,000
Recognized Gain	$ 70,000

b. $0. The $500,000 exclusion for joint filers exceeds the $320,000 realized gain.

c. $25,000 = ($350,000 − $200,000) − (½ × $250,000)

CHAPTER 9 WITHHOLDING, ESTIMATED PAYMENTS, AND PAYROLL TAXES

Self-Study Problem 9.1

1. Monthly salary	$3,000.00
Less: exemptions ($329.20 × 5)	(1,646.00)
Income subject to withholding	$ 1,354.00
Withholding:	
$75.60 + [($1,354.00 − $944.00) × 15%]	$ 137.10

2. From Appendix C, withholding = $145.00

Self-Study Problem 9.2

Form **1040-ES** Department of the Treasury Internal Revenue Service | **2014 Estimated Tax** | **Payment Voucher 1** | OMB No. 1545-0074

File only if you are making a payment of estimated tax by check or money order. Mail this voucher with your check or money order payable to **"United States Treasury."** Write your social security number and "2014 Form 1040-ES" on your check or money order. Do not send cash. Enclose, but do not staple or attach, your payment with this voucher.

Calendar year—Due April 15, 2014

Amount of estimated tax you are paying by check or money order. Dollars: 1,380 Cents:

Print or type

Your first name and initial	Your last name	Your social security number
Ray	Adams	466-47-1131
If joint payment, complete for spouse		
Spouse's first name and initial	Spouse's last name	Spouse's social security number
Address (number, street, and apt. no.)		
City, state, and ZIP code. (If a foreign address, enter city, also complete spaces below.)		
Foreign country name	Foreign province/county	Foreign postal code

For Privacy Act and Paperwork Reduction Act Notice, see instructions. **Form 1040-ES (2014)**

Self-Study Problem 9.3

Debbie:	Soc. Sec. — 6.2% × $117,000	$ 7,254.00
	Medicare — 1.45% × $125,000	1,825.50
	Total employee FICA tax	$ 9,066.50
Debbie's employer:	Soc. Sec. — 6.2% × $117,000	$ 7,254.00
	Medicare — 1.45% × $125,000	1,812.50
	Total employer FICA tax	$ 9,066.50
Total FICA tax		$ 18,133.00

Self-Study Problem 9.4

See Form 941 on Page E-50.

Self-Study Problem 9.5

22222	a Employee's social security number 464-74-1132	OMB No. 1545-0008

b Employer identification number (EIN) 95-1234567	1 Wages, tips, other compensation 16,150.00	2 Federal income tax withheld 2,422.00
c Employer's name, address, and ZIP code Big Bank P.O. Box 12344 San Diego, CA 92101	3 Social security wages 16,150.00	4 Social security tax withheld 1001.30
	5 Medicare wages and tips 16,150.00	6 Medicare tax withheld 234.18
	7 Social security tips	8 Allocated tips
d Control number	9	10 Dependent care benefits
e Employee's first name and initial: Mary / Last name: Jones / Suff.	11 Nonqualified plans	12a Code
6431 Gary Street San Diego, CA 92115	13 Statutory employee ☐ Retirement plan ☐ Third-party sick pay ☐	12b Code
	14 Other	12c Code
f Employee's address and ZIP code		12d Code

15 State	Employer's state ID number	16 State wages, tips, etc.	17 State income tax	18 Local wages, tips, etc.	19 Local income tax	20 Locality name
CA	800 4039250 092	16,150.00	969.00			

Form **W-2** Wage and Tax Statement **2014** Department of the Treasury—Internal Revenue Service

Copy 1—For State, City, or Local Tax Department

☐ VOID ☐ CORRECTED

PAYER'S name, street address, city or town, state or province, country, ZIP or foreign postal code, and telephone no. Big Bank P.O. Box 12344 San Diego, CA 92101	Payer's RTN (optional)	OMB No. 1545-0112 **2014** Form **1099-INT**	**Interest Income**
	1 Interest income $ 461.00		
	2 Early withdrawal penalty $		**Copy 1** **For State Tax Department**
PAYER'S federal identification number 95-1234567 / RECIPIENT'S identification number 464-74-1132	3 Interest on U.S. Savings Bonds and Treas. obligations $		
RECIPIENT'S name Mary Jones	4 Federal income tax withheld $	5 Investment expenses $	
Street address (including apt. no.) 6431 Gary Street	6 Foreign tax paid $	7 Foreign country or U.S. possession	
City or town, state or province, country, and ZIP or foreign postal code San Diego, CA 92115	8 Tax-exempt interest $	9 Specified private activity bond interest $	
	10 Market discount $	11 Bond premium $	
Account number (see instructions)	12 Tax-exempt bond CUSIP no.	13 State / 14 State identification no.	15 State tax withheld $ $

Form **1099-INT** www.irs.gov/form1099int Department of the Treasury - Internal Revenue Service

Self-Study Problem 9.6

See Schedule SE on Pages E-51 and E-52.

Self-Study Problem 9.7

See Form 940 on Pages E-53 and E-54.

Self-Study Problem 9.8

See Schedule H on Pages E-55 and E-56.

Self-Study Problem 9.9

a. $450 = 0.9% × ($250,000 − $200,000)

b. $450 refund – Since Marcia has no earnings, their joint income does not exceed the $250,000 threshhold so they are not subject to the 0.9% surtax.

CHAPTER 10 PARTNERSHIP TAXATION

Self-Study Problem 10.1

1.	Yes	
2.	No	A corporation is not a partnership, but a separate type of entity.
3.	No	The mere joint ownership of property does not constitute a partnership; the owners must engage in some type of business activity.
4.	Yes	The marketing of oil qualifies the venture as a partnership.
5.	Yes	

Self-Study Problem 10.2

1.	None	
2.	$36,000	The amount of cash contributed.
3.	None	
4.	$17,500	The same as Linda's basis in the equipment contributed to the partnership.
5.	$17,500	The same as Linda's basis in the equipment contributed.

Self-Study Problem 10.3

See Form 1065 and Schedule K-1 on Pages E-57 to E-62.

Self-Study Problem 10.4

1. Partnership income before guaranteed payments	$ 32,000
Less: guaranteed payments	(36,000)
Partnership loss after guaranteed payments	$ (4,000)
Jim's income:	
Guaranteed payments	$ 36,000
50% of the $4,000 partnership loss	(2,000)
Total income	$ 34,000
2. Jack's income (loss): 50% of the $4,000 partnership loss	$(2,000)

(The next self-study problem is on Page E-63.)

Self-Study Problem 9.4

Form **941 for 2014: Employer's QUARTERLY Federal Tax Return** 950114
(Rev. January 2014) Department of the Treasury — Internal Revenue Service OMB No. 1545-0029

Employer identification number (EIN) [ ][ ] – [ ][ ][ ][ ][ ][ ][ ]

Name (not your trade name) *Rita O'Miya*

Trade name (if any)

Address
Number Street Suite or room number
City State ZIP code
Foreign country name Foreign province/county Foreign postal code

Report for this Quarter of 2014
(Check one.)

- [x] 1: January, February, March
- [ ] 2: April, May, June
- [ ] 3: July, August, September
- [ ] 4: October, November, December

Instructions and prior year forms are available at *www.irs.gov/form941*.

Read the separate instructions before you complete Form 941. Type or print within the boxes.

Part 1: Answer these questions for this quarter.

1	Number of employees who received wages, tips, or other compensation for the pay period including: *Mar. 12* (Quarter 1), *June 12* (Quarter 2), *Sept. 12* (Quarter 3), or *Dec. 12* (Quarter 4)			1	2
2	Wages, tips, and other compensation			2	9,600 .
3	Federal income tax withheld from wages, tips, and other compensation			3	995 .
4	If no wages, tips, and other compensation are subject to social security or Medicare tax			☐	Check and go to line 6.
		Column 1		**Column 2**	
5a	Taxable social security wages	9,600 .	× .124 =	1190 .	
5b	Taxable social security tips	.	× .124 =	.	
5c	Taxable Medicare wages & tips	9,600 .	× .029 =	278 .	
5d	Taxable wages & tips subject to Additional Medicare Tax withholding	.	× .009 =	.	
5e	Add Column 2 from lines 5a, 5b, 5c, and 5d			5e	1,468 .
5f	Section 3121(q) Notice and Demand—Tax due on unreported tips (see instructions)			5f	.
6	**Total taxes before adjustments.** Add lines 3, 5e, and 5f			6	2,463 .
7	Current quarter's adjustment for fractions of cents			7	.
8	Current quarter's adjustment for sick pay			8	.
9	Current quarter's adjustments for tips and group-term life insurance			9	.
10	**Total taxes after adjustments.** Combine lines 6 through 9			10	2,463 .
11	Total deposits for this quarter, including overpayment applied from a prior quarter and overpayments applied from Form 941-X, 941-X (PR), 944-X, 944-X (PR), or 944-X (SP) filed in the current quarter			11	2,467 .
12	**Balance due.** If line 10 is more than line 11, enter the difference and see instructions			12	.

13 **Overpayment.** If line 11 is more than line 10, enter the difference 4 . Check one: [x] Apply to next return. [ ] Send a refund.

▶ **You MUST complete both pages of Form 941 and SIGN it.** Next ▶

For Privacy Act and Paperwork Reduction Act Notice, see the back of the Payment Voucher. Cat. No. 17001Z Form **941** (Rev. 1-2014)

Self-Study Problem 9.6

SCHEDULE SE (Form 1040) Department of the Treasury Internal Revenue Service (99)	**Self-Employment Tax** ► **Information about Schedule SE and its separate instructions is at *www.irs.gov/schedulese*.** ► **Attach to Form 1040 or Form 1040NR.**	OMB No. 1545-0074 **2014** Attachment Sequence No. **17**

Name of person with **self-employment** income (as shown on Form 1040 or Form 1040NR)	Social security number of person with **self-employment** income ►
Robert Boyd	

Before you begin: To determine if you must file Schedule SE, see the instructions.

DRAFT AS OF May 14, 2014 DO NOT FILE

May I Use Short Schedule SE or Must I Use Long Schedule SE?

Note. Use this flowchart **only if** you must file Schedule SE. If unsure, see *Who Must File Schedule SE* in the instructions.

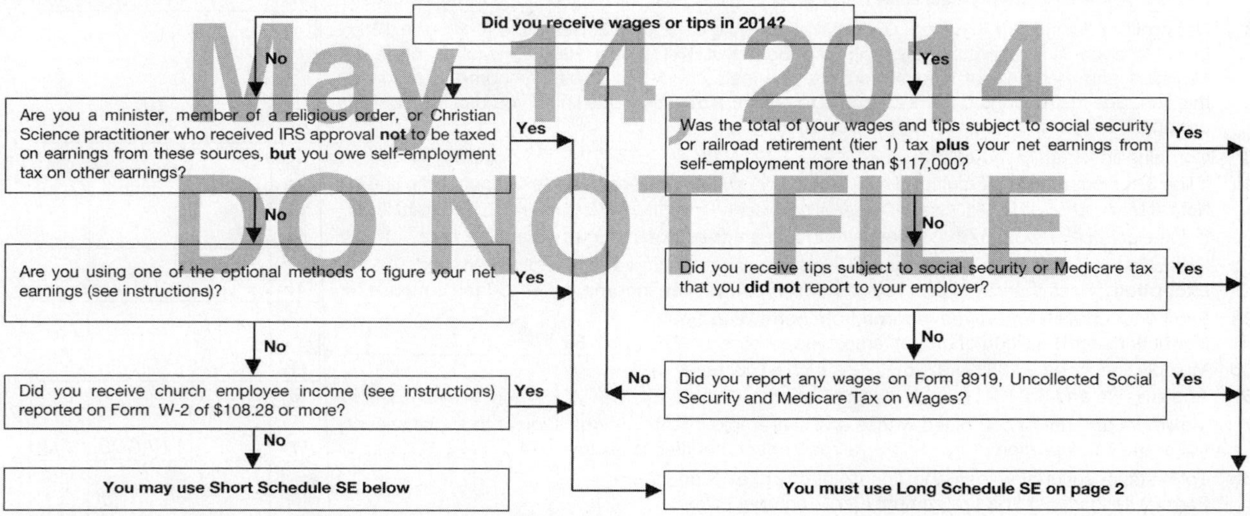

Section A—Short Schedule SE. Caution. Read above to see if you can use Short Schedule SE.

1a	Net farm profit or (loss) from Schedule F, line 34, and farm partnerships, Schedule K-1 (Form 1065), box 14, code A	**1a**	
b	If you received social security retirement or disability benefits, enter the amount of Conservation Reserve Program payments included on Schedule F, line 4b, or listed on Schedule K-1 (Form 1065), box 20, code Z	**1b**	( )
2	Net profit or (loss) from Schedule C, line 31; Schedule C-EZ, line 3; Schedule K-1 (Form 1065), box 14, code A (other than farming); and Schedule K-1 (Form 1065-B), box 9, code J1. Ministers and members of religious orders, see instructions for types of income to report on this line. See instructions for other income to report	**2**	*27,450*
3	Combine lines 1a, 1b, and 2	**3**	*27,450*
4	Multiply line 3 by 92.35% (.9235). If less than $400, you do not owe self-employment tax; **do not** file this schedule unless you have an amount on line 1b . . . . . ►	**4**	*25,350*
	Note. If line 4 is less than $400 due to Conservation Reserve Program payments on line 1b, see instructions.		
5	**Self-employment tax.** If the amount on line 4 is: • $117,000 or less, multiply line 4 by 15.3% (.153). Enter the result here and on **Form 1040, line 57,** or **Form 1040NR, line 55** • More than $117,000, multiply line 4 by 2.9% (.029). Then, add $14,508 to the result. Enter the total here and on **Form 1040, line 57,** or **Form 1040NR, line 55**	**5**	*3,879*
6	**Deduction for one-half of self-employment tax.** Multiply line 5 by 50% (.50). Enter the result here and on **Form 1040, line 27,** or **Form 1040NR, line 27** . . . . . **6** | *1,940*		

For Paperwork Reduction Act Notice, see your tax return instructions. Cat. No. 11358Z **Schedule SE (Form 1040) 2014**

Self-Study Problem 9.6

Schedule SE (Form 1040) 2014 | Attachment Sequence No. **17** | Page **2**

Name of person with **self-employment** income (as shown on Form 1040 or Form 1040NR)	Social security number of person with **self-employment** income ▶	

Section B—Long Schedule SE

Part I Self-Employment Tax

Note. If your only income subject to self-employment tax is **church employee income,** see instructions. Also see instructions for the definition of church employee income.

DRAFT AS OF May 1, 2014 DO NOT FILE

A	If you are a minister, member of a religious order, or Christian Science practitioner **and** you filed Form 4361, but you had $400 or more of **other** net earnings from self-employment, check here and continue with Part I . . . . ▶ ☐			
1a	Net farm profit or (loss) from Schedule F, line 34, and farm partnerships, Schedule K-1 (Form 1065), box 14, code A. **Note.** Skip lines 1a and 1b if you use the farm optional method (see instructions)	1a		
b	If you received social security retirement or disability benefits, enter the amount of Conservation Reserve Program payments included on Schedule F, line 4b, or listed on Schedule K-1 (Form 1065), box 20, code Z	1b	( )	
2	Net profit or (loss) from Schedule C, line 31; Schedule C-EZ, line 3; Schedule K-1 (Form 1065), box 14, code A (other than farming); and Schedule K-1 (Form 1065-B), box 9, code J1. Ministers and members of religious orders, see instructions for types of income to report on this line. See instructions for other income to report. **Note.** Skip this line if you use the nonfarm optional method (see instructions) . . .	2		
3	Combine lines 1a, 1b, and 2 . . .	3		
4a	If line 3 is more than zero, multiply line 3 by 92.35% (.9235). Otherwise, enter amount from line 3 **Note.** If line 4a is less than $400 due to Conservation Reserve Program payments on line 1b, see instructions.	4a		
b	If you elect one or both of the optional methods, enter the total of lines 15 and 17 here . .	4b		
c	Combine lines 4a and 4b. If less than $400, **stop**; you do not owe self-employment tax. **Exception.** If less than $400 and you had **church employee income,** enter -0- and continue ▶	4c		
5a	Enter your **church employee income** from Form W-2. See instructions for definition of church employee income . . . **5a**			
b	Multiply line 5a by 92.35% (.9235). If less than $100, enter -0- . . .	5b		
6	Add lines 4c and 5b . . .	6		
7	Maximum amount of combined wages and self-employment earnings subject to social security tax or the 6.2% portion of the 7.65% railroad retirement (tier 1) tax for 2014 . . .	7	117,000	00
8a	Total social security wages and tips (total of boxes 3 and 7 on Form(s) W-2) and railroad retirement (tier 1) compensation. If $117,000 or more, skip lines 8b through 10, and go to line 11 **8a**			
b	Unreported tips subject to social security tax (from Form 4137, line 10) **8b**			
c	Wages subject to social security tax (from Form 8919, line 10) **8c**			
d	Add lines 8a, 8b, and 8c . . .	8d		
9	Subtract line 8d from line 7. If zero or less, enter -0- here and on line 10 and go to line 11 . ▶	9		
10	Multiply the **smaller** of line 6 or line 9 by 12.4% (.124) . . .	10		
11	Multiply line 6 by 2.9% (.029) . . .	11		
12	**Self-employment tax.** Add lines 10 and 11. Enter here and on **Form 1040, line 57,** or **Form 1040NR, line 55**	12		
13	**Deduction for one-half of self-employment tax.** Multiply line 12 by 50% (.50). Enter the result here and on **Form 1040, line 27,** or **Form 1040NR, line 27** . . . **13**			

Part II Optional Methods To Figure Net Earnings (see instructions)

Farm Optional Method. You may use this method **only** if **(a)** your gross farm income[1] was not more than $7,200, **or (b)** your net farm profits[2] were less than $5,198.

14	Maximum income for optional methods . . .	14	4,800	00
15	Enter the **smaller** of: two-thirds (2/3) of gross farm income[1] (not less than zero) **or** $4,800. Also include this amount on line 4b above . . .	15		

Nonfarm Optional Method. You may use this method **only** if **(a)** your net nonfarm profits[3] were less than $5,198 and also less than 72.189% of your gross nonfarm income,[4] **and (b)** you had net earnings from self-employment of at least $400 in 2 of the prior 3 years. **Caution.** You may use this method no more than five times.

16	Subtract line 15 from line 14 . . .	16		
17	Enter the **smaller** of: two-thirds (2/3) of gross nonfarm income[4] (not less than zero) **or** the amount on line 16. Also include this amount on line 4b above . . .	17		

[1] From Sch. F, line 9, and Sch. K-1 (Form 1065), box 14, code B.

[2] From Sch. F, line 34, and Sch. K-1 (Form 1065), box 14, code A—minus the amount you would have entered on line 1b had you not used the optional method.

[3] From Sch. C, line 31; Sch. C-EZ, line 3; Sch. K-1 (Form 1065), box 14, code A; and Sch. K-1 (Form 1065-B), box 9, code J1.

[4] From Sch. C, line 7; Sch. C-EZ, line 1; Sch. K-1 (Form 1065), box 14, code C; and Sch. K-1 (Form 1065-B), box 9, code J2.

Self-Study Problem 9.7

Form **940 for 2014: Employer's Annual Federal Unemployment (FUTA) Tax Return** 850113

Department of the Treasury — Internal Revenue Service OMB No. 1545-0028

DRAFT AS July 9, 2014 DO NOT FILE

Employer identification number (EIN) 9 4 – 0 0 0 1 1 1 2

Name *(not your trade name)* *Rhus Company*

Trade name *(if any)*

Address
Number Street Suite or room number
City State ZIP code
Foreign country name Foreign province/county Foreign postal code

Type of Return (Check all that apply.)

- ☐ **a.** Amended
- ☐ **b.** Successor employer
- ☐ **c.** No payments to employees in 2014
- ☐ **d.** Final: Business closed or stopped paying wages

Instructions and prior-year forms are available at *www.irs.gov/form940.*

Read the separate instructions before you complete this form. Please type or print within the boxes.

Part 1: Tell us about your return. If any line does NOT apply, leave it blank.

1a	**If you had to pay state unemployment tax in one state only, enter the state abbreviation**	1a	C A
1b	**If you had to pay state unemployment tax in more than one state, you are a multi-state employer**	1b	☐ Check here. Complete Schedule A (Form 940).
2	**If you paid wages in a state that is subject to CREDIT REDUCTION**	2	☐ Check here. Complete Schedule A (Form 940).

Part 2: Determine your FUTA tax before adjustments for 2014. If any line does NOT apply, leave it blank.

3	**Total payments to all employees**	3	113,000 .
4	**Payments exempt from FUTA tax**	4	.
	Check all that apply: 4a ☐ Fringe benefits; 4b ☐ Group-term life insurance; 4c ☐ Retirement/Pension; 4d ☐ Dependent care; 4e ☐ Other		
5	**Total of payments made to each employee in excess of $7,000**	5	39,000 .
6	**Subtotal** (line 4 + line 5 = line 6)	6	39,000 .
7	**Total taxable FUTA wages** (line 3 – line 6 = line 7) (see instructions)	7	74,000 .
8	**FUTA tax before adjustments** (line 7 x .006 = line 8)	8	444 .

Part 3: Determine your adjustments. If any line does NOT apply, leave it blank.

9	**If ALL of the taxable FUTA wages you paid were excluded from state unemployment tax, multiply line 7 by .054** (line 7 × .054 = line 9). Go to line 12	9	.
10	**If SOME of the taxable FUTA wages you paid were excluded from state unemployment tax, OR you paid ANY state unemployment tax late** (after the due date for filing Form 940), complete the worksheet in the instructions. Enter the amount from line 7 of the worksheet	10	.
11	**If credit reduction applies,** enter the total from Schedule A (Form 940)	11	.

Part 4: Determine your FUTA tax and balance due or overpayment for 2014. If any line does NOT apply, leave it blank.

12	**Total FUTA tax after adjustments** (lines 8 + 9 + 10 + 11 = line 12)	12	444 .
13	**FUTA tax deposited for the year, including any overpayment applied from a prior year**	13	444 .
14	**Balance due** (If line 12 is more than line 13, enter the excess on line 14.) • If line 14 is more than $500, you must deposit your tax. • If line 14 is $500 or less, you may pay with this return. (see instructions)	14	0 .
15	**Overpayment** (If line 13 is more than line 12, enter the excess on line 15 and check a box below.)	15	0 .

▶ You **MUST** complete both pages of this form and **SIGN** it. Check one: ☐ Apply to next return. ☐ Send a refund.

Next ▶

For Privacy Act and Paperwork Reduction Act Notice, see the back of Form 940-V, Payment Voucher. Cat. No. 11234O Form **940** (2014)

Self-Study Problem 9.7

850212

Name *(not your trade name)* | **Employer identification number (EIN)**

Part 5: **Report your FUTA tax liability by quarter only if line 12 is more than $500. If not, go to Part 6.**

16 **Report the amount of your FUTA tax liability for each quarter; do NOT enter the amount you deposited. If you had no liability for a quarter, leave the line blank.**

16a	**1st quarter** (January 1 – March 31)	16a	150 .
16b	**2nd quarter** (April 1 – June 30)	16b	156 .
16c	**3rd quarter** (July 1 – September 30)	16c	66 .
16d	**4th quarter** (October 1 – December 31)	16d	72 .
17	**Total tax liability for the year** (lines 16a + 16b + 16c + 16d = line 17)	17	444 .

Total must equal line 12.

DRAFT AS OF July 9, 2014 DO NOT FILE

Part 6: **May we speak with your third-party designee?**

Do you want to allow an employee, a paid tax preparer, or another person to discuss this return with the IRS? See the instructions for details.

☐ **Yes.** Designee's name and phone number

Select a 5-digit Personal Identification Number (PIN) to use when talking to IRS

☐ **No.**

Part 7: **Sign here. You MUST complete both pages of this form and SIGN it.**

Under penalties of perjury, I declare that I have examined this return, including accompanying schedules and statements, and to the best of my knowledge and belief, it is true, correct, and complete, and that no part of any payment made to a state unemployment fund claimed as a credit was, or is to be, deducted from the payments made to employees. Declaration of preparer (other than taxpayer) is based on all information of which preparer has any knowledge.

✗ **Sign your name here**

Print your name here

Print your title here

Date / /

Best daytime phone

Paid Preparer Use Only

Check if you are self-employed . ☐

Preparer's name

PTIN

Preparer's signature

Date / /

Firm's name (or yours if self-employed)

EIN

Address

Phone

City

State

ZIP code

Self-Study Problem 9.8

SCHEDULE H (Form 1040)
Department of the Treasury
Internal Revenue Service (99)

Household Employment Taxes
(For Social Security, Medicare, Withheld Income, and Federal Unemployment (FUTA) Taxes)
▶ **Attach to Form 1040, 1040NR, 1040-SS, or 1041.**
▶ **Information about Schedule H and its separate instructions is at *www.irs.gov/scheduleh*.**

OMB No. 1545-1971
2014
Attachment Sequence No. **44**

Name of employer: *Susan Green*
Social security number
Employer identification number

DRAFT AS OF
June 13, 2014
DO NOT FILE

Calendar year taxpayers having no household employees in 2014 do not have to complete this form for 2014.

A Did you pay **any one** household employee cash wages of $1,900 or more in 2014? (If any household employee was your spouse, your child under age 21, your parent, or anyone under age 18, see the line A instructions before you answer this question.)

☑ **Yes.** Skip lines B and C and go to line 1.
☐ **No.** Go to line B.

B Did you withhold federal income tax during 2014 for any household employee?

☐ **Yes.** Skip line C and go to line 7.
☐ **No.** Go to line C.

C Did you pay **total** cash wages of $1,000 or more in **any** calendar **quarter** of 2013 or 2014 to **all** household employees? (**Do not** count cash wages paid in 2013 or 2014 to your spouse, your child under age 21, or your parent.)

☐ **No. Stop.** Do not file this schedule.
☐ **Yes.** Skip lines 1-9 and go to line 10.

Part I **Social Security, Medicare, and Federal Income Taxes**

1 Total cash wages subject to social security tax	1	2,250		
2 Social security tax. Multiply line 1 by 12.4% (.124)			2	279
3 Total cash wages subject to Medicare tax	3	2,250		
4 Medicare tax. Multiply line 3 by 2.9% (.029)			4	65
5 Total cash wages subject to Additional Medicare Tax withholding	5			
6 Additional Medicare Tax withholding. Multiply line 5 by 0.9% (.009)			6	
7 Federal income tax withheld, if any			7	
8 **Total social security, Medicare, and federal income taxes.** Add lines 2, 4, 6, and 7			8	344

9 Did you pay **total** cash wages of $1,000 or more in **any** calendar **quarter** of 2013 or 2014 to **all** household employees? (**Do not** count cash wages paid in 2013 or 2014 to your spouse, your child under age 21, or your parent.)

☑ **No. Stop.** Include the amount from line 8 above on Form 1040, line 60a. If you are not required to file Form 1040, see the line 9 instructions.

☐ **Yes.** Go to line 10.

For Privacy Act and Paperwork Reduction Act Notice, see the instructions. Cat. No. 12187K **Schedule H (Form 1040) 2014**

Self-Study Problem 9.8

Schedule H (Form 1040) 2014 Page **2**

Part II Federal Unemployment (FUTA) Tax

			Yes	No
10	Did you pay unemployment contributions to only one state? (If you paid contributions to a credit reduction state, see instructions and check "No.")	10		
11	Did you pay all state unemployment contributions for 2014 by April 15, 2015? Fiscal year filers see instructions	11		
12	Were all wages that are taxable for FUTA tax also taxable for your state's unemployment tax?	12		

Next: If you checked the **"Yes"** box on **all** the lines above, complete Section A.
If you checked the **"No"** box on **any** of the lines above, skip Section A and complete Section B.

DRAFT AS OF June 13, 2014 DO NOT FILE

Section A

13 Name of the state where you paid unemployment contributions ▶ ____________

14 Contributions paid to your state unemployment fund 14

15 Total cash wages subject to FUTA tax 15

16 **FUTA tax.** Multiply line 15 by .6% (.006). Enter the result here, skip Section B, and go to line 25 . . . 16

Section B

17 Complete all columns below that apply (if you need more space, see instructions):

(a) Name of state	(b) Taxable wages (as defined in state act)	(c) State experience rate period From	(c) To	(d) State experience rate	(e) Multiply col. (b) by .054	(f) Multiply col. (b) by col. (d)	(g) Subtract col. (f) from col. (e). If zero or less, enter -0-.	(h) Contributions paid to state unemployment fund

18 Totals 18

19 Add columns (g) and (h) of line 18 19

20 Total cash wages subject to FUTA tax (see the line 15 instructions) 20

21 Multiply line 20 by 6.0% (.060) 21

22 Multiply line 20 by 5.4% (.054) 22

23 Enter the **smaller** of line 19 or line 22
(Employers in a credit reduction state must use the worksheet on page H-7 and check here) . ☐ 23

24 **FUTA tax.** Subtract line 23 from line 21. Enter the result here and go to line 25 24

Part III Total Household Employment Taxes

25 Enter the amount from line 8. If you checked the "Yes" box on line C of page 1, enter -0- 25

26 Add line 16 (or line 24) and line 25 26

27 Are you required to file Form 1040?

☐ **Yes. Stop.** Include the amount from line 26 above on Form 1040, line 60a. **Do not** complete Part IV below.

☐ **No.** You may have to complete Part IV. See instructions for details.

Part IV Address and Signature— Complete this part **only** if required. See the line 27 instructions.

Address (number and street) or P.O. box if mail is not delivered to street address | Apt., room, or suite no.

City, town or post office, state, and ZIP code

Under penalties of perjury, I declare that I have examined this schedule, including accompanying statements, and to the best of my knowledge and belief, it is true, correct, and complete. No part of any payment made to a state unemployment fund claimed as a credit was, or is to be, deducted from the payments to employees. Declaration of preparer (other than taxpayer) is based on all information of which preparer has any knowledge.

▶ Employer's signature ▶ Date

Paid Preparer Use Only	Print/Type preparer's name	Preparer's signature	Date	Check ☐ if self-employed	PTIN
	Firm's name ▶			Firm's EIN ▶	
	Firm's address ▶			Phone no.	

Schedule H (Form 1040) 2014

Self-Study Problem 10.3

Form **1065** Department of the Treasury Internal Revenue Service

U.S. Return of Partnership Income

For calendar year 2014, or tax year beginning ________, 2014, ending ________, 20____.
▶ Information about Form 1065 and its separate instructions is at *www.irs.gov/form1065*.

OMB No. 1545-0123 **2014**

DRAFT AS OF August 4, 2014 DO NOT FILE

A Principal business activity	Name of partnership: *Malus Valley Partnership*	D Employer identification number
B Principal product or service	Type or Print — Number, street, and room or suite no. If a P.O. box, see the instructions.	E Date business started: *2014*
C Business code number	City or town, state or province, country, and ZIP or foreign postal code	F Total assets (see the instructions) $ *257,750*

G Check applicable boxes: (1) ☑ Initial return (2) ☐ Final return (3) ☐ Name change (4) ☐ Address change (5) ☐ Amended return (6) ☐ Technical termination - also check (1) or (2)

H Check accounting method: (1) ☐ Cash (2) ☑ Accrual (3) ☐ Other (specify) ▶

I Number of Schedules K-1. Attach one for each person who was a partner at any time during the tax year ▶

J Check if Schedules C and M-3 are attached ☐

Caution. *Include **only** trade or business income and expenses on lines 1a through 22 below. See the instructions for more information.*

Income	1a Gross receipts or sales	1a	255,600		
	b Returns and allowances	1b			
	c Balance. Subtract line 1b from line 1a			1c	255,600
	2 Cost of goods sold (attach Form 1125-A)			2	
	3 Gross profit. Subtract line 2 from line 1c			3	255,600
	4 Ordinary income (loss) from other partnerships, estates, and trusts (attach statement)			4	
	5 Net farm profit (loss) (attach Schedule F (Form 1040))			5	
	6 Net gain (loss) from Form 4797, Part II, line 17 (attach Form 4797)			6	
	7 Other income (loss) (attach statement)			7	
	8 **Total income (loss).** Combine lines 3 through 7			8	255,600
Deductions (see the instructions for limitations)	9 Salaries and wages (other than to partners) (less employment credits)			9	168,000
	10 Guaranteed payments to partners			10	
	11 Repairs and maintenance			11	
	12 Bad debts			12	
	13 Rent			13	12,000
	14 Taxes and licenses			14	6,100
	15 Interest			15	
	16a Depreciation (if required, attach Form 4562)	16a	9,250		
	b Less depreciation reported on Form 1125-A and elsewhere on return	16b		16c	9,250
	17 Depletion **(Do not deduct oil and gas depletion.)**			17	
	18 Retirement plans, etc.			18	
	19 Employee benefit programs			19	
	20 Other deductions (attach statement)			20	
	21 **Total deductions.** Add the amounts shown in the far right column for lines 9 through 20			21	195,350
	22 **Ordinary business income (loss).** Subtract line 21 from line 8			22	60,250

Sign Here

Under penalties of perjury, I declare that I have examined this return, including accompanying schedules and statements, and to the best of my knowledge and belief, it is true, correct, and complete. Declaration of preparer (other than general partner or limited liability company member manager) is based on all information of which preparer has any knowledge.

▶ Signature of general partner or limited liability company member manager ▶ Date

May the IRS discuss this return with the preparer shown below (see instructions)? ☐ Yes ☐ No

Paid Preparer Use Only

Print/Type preparer's name	Preparer's signature	Date	Check ☐ if self-employed	PTIN
Firm's name ▶			Firm's EIN ▶	
Firm's address ▶			Phone no.	

For Paperwork Reduction Act Notice, see separate instructions. Cat. No. 11390Z Form **1065** (2014)

Self-Study Problem 10.3

Form 1065 (2014) Page **2**

Schedule B **Other Information**

DRAFT AS OF August 4, 2014 DO NOT FILE

		Yes	No
1	What type of entity is filing this return? Check the applicable box: a ☑ Domestic general partnership b ☐ Domestic limited partnership c ☐ Domestic limited liability company d ☐ Domestic limited liability partnership e ☐ Foreign partnership f ☐ Other ▶		
2	At any time during the tax year, was any partner in the partnership a disregarded entity, a partnership (including an entity treated as a partnership), a trust, an S corporation, an estate (other than an estate of a deceased partner), or a nominee or similar person?		✔
3	At the end of the tax year:		
a	Did any foreign or domestic corporation, partnership (including any entity treated as a partnership), trust, or tax-exempt organization, or any foreign government own, directly or indirectly, an interest of 50% or more in the profit, loss, or capital of the partnership? For rules of constructive ownership, see instructions. If "Yes," attach Schedule B-1, Information on Partners Owning 50% or More of the Partnership		✔
b	Did any individual or estate own, directly or indirectly, an interest of 50% or more in the profit, loss, or capital of the partnership? For rules of constructive ownership, see instructions. If "Yes," attach Schedule B-1, Information on Partners Owning 50% or More of the Partnership	✔	
4	At the end of the tax year, did the partnership:		
a	Own directly 20% or more, or own, directly or indirectly, 50% or more of the total voting power of all classes of stock entitled to vote of any foreign or domestic corporation? For rules of constructive ownership, see instructions. If "Yes," complete (i) through (iv) below		✔

(i) Name of Corporation	(ii) Employer Identification Number (if any)	(iii) Country of Incorporation	(iv) Percentage Owned in Voting Stock

		Yes	No
b	Own directly an interest of 20% or more, or own, directly or indirectly, an interest of 50% or more in the profit, loss, or capital in any foreign or domestic partnership (including an entity treated as a partnership) or in the beneficial interest of a trust? For rules of constructive ownership, see instructions. If "Yes," complete (i) through (v) below . .		✔

(i) Name of Entity	(ii) Employer Identification Number (if any)	(iii) Type of Entity	(iv) Country of Organization	(v) Maximum Percentage Owned in Profit, Loss, or Capital

		Yes	No
5	Did the partnership file Form 8893, Election of Partnership Level Tax Treatment, or an election statement under section 6231(a)(1)(B)(ii) for partnership-level tax treatment, that is in effect for this tax year? See Form 8893 for more details		✔
6	Does the partnership satisfy **all four** of the following conditions?		
a	The partnership's total receipts for the tax year were less than $250,000.		
b	The partnership's total assets at the end of the tax year were less than $1 million.		
c	Schedules K-1 are filed with the return and furnished to the partners on or before the due date (including extensions) for the partnership return.		
d	The partnership is not filing and is not required to file Schedule M-3		✔
	If "Yes," the partnership is not required to complete Schedules L, M-1, and M-2; Item F on page 1 of Form 1065; or Item L on Schedule K-1.		
7	Is this partnership a publicly traded partnership as defined in section 469(k)(2)?		✔
8	During the tax year, did the partnership have any debt that was cancelled, was forgiven, or had the terms modified so as to reduce the principal amount of the debt?		✔
9	Has this partnership filed, or is it required to file, Form 8918, Material Advisor Disclosure Statement, to provide information on any reportable transaction?		✔
10	At any time during calendar year 2014, did the partnership have an interest in or a signature or other authority over a financial account in a foreign country (such as a bank account, securities account, or other financial account)? See the instructions for exceptions and filing requirements for FinCEN Form 114, Report of Foreign Bank and Financial Accounts (FBAR). If "Yes," enter the name of the foreign country. ▶		✔

Form **1065** (2014)

Self-Study Problem 10.3

Form 1065 (2014) Page **3**

Schedule B Other Information *(continued)*

		Yes	No
11	At any time during the tax year, did the partnership receive a distribution from, or was it the grantor of, or transferor to, a foreign trust? If "Yes," the partnership may have to file Form 3520, Annual Return To Report Transactions With Foreign Trusts and Receipt of Certain Foreign Gifts. See instructions		✔
12a	Is the partnership making, or had it previously made (and not revoked), a section 754 election? See instructions for details regarding a section 754 election.		✔
b	Did the partnership make for this tax year an optional basis adjustment under section 743(b) or 734(b)? If "Yes," attach a statement showing the computation and allocation of the basis adjustment. See instructions		✔
c	Is the partnership required to adjust the basis of partnership assets under section 743(b) or 734(b) because of a substantial built-in loss (as defined under section 743(d)) or substantial basis reduction (as defined under section 734(d))? If "Yes," attach a statement showing the computation and allocation of the basis adjustment. See instructions		✔
13	Check this box if, during the current or prior tax year, the partnership distributed any property received in a like-kind exchange or contributed such property to another entity (other than disregarded entities wholly owned by the partnership throughout the tax year) ▶ ☐		
14	At any time during the tax year, did the partnership distribute to any partner a tenancy-in-common or other undivided interest in partnership property?		✔
15	If the partnership is required to file Form 8858, Information Return of U.S. Persons With Respect To Foreign Disregarded Entities, enter the number of Forms 8858 attached. See instructions ▶		
16	Does the partnership have any foreign partners? If "Yes," enter the number of Forms 8805, Foreign Partner's Information Statement of Section 1446 Withholding Tax, filed for this partnership. ▶		✔
17	Enter the number of Forms 8865, Return of U.S. Persons With Respect to Certain Foreign Partnerships, attached to this return. ▶		
18a	Did you make any payments in 2014 that would require you to file Form(s) 1099? See instructions		✔
b	If "Yes," did you or will you file required Form(s) 1099?		
19	Enter the number of Form(s) 5471, Information Return of U.S. Persons With Respect To Certain Foreign Corporations, attached to this return. ▶		
20	Enter the number of partners that are foreign governments under section 892. ▶		

Designation of Tax Matters Partner (see instructions)

Enter below the general partner or member-manager designated as the tax matters partner (TMP) for the tax year of this return:

Name of designated TMP ▶		Identifying number of TMP ▶	
If the TMP is an entity, name of TMP representative ▶		Phone number of TMP ▶	
Address of designated TMP ▶			

Form **1065** (2014)

DRAFT AS OF August 4, 2014 DO NOT FILE

Self-Study Problem 10.3

Form 1065 (2014) Page **4**

DRAFT AS OF August 4, 2014 DO NOT FILE

Schedule K		Partners' Distributive Share Items			Total amount
Income (Loss)	1	Ordinary business income (loss) (page 1, line 22)		1	60,250
	2	Net rental real estate income (loss) (attach Form 8825)		2	
	3a	Other gross rental income (loss)	3a		
	b	Expenses from other rental activities (attach statement)	3b		
	c	Other net rental income (loss). Subtract line 3b from line 3a		3c	
	4	Guaranteed payments		4	
	5	Interest income		5	
	6	Dividends: a Ordinary dividends		6a	
		b Qualified dividends	6b		
	7	Royalties		7	
	8	Net short-term capital gain (loss) (attach Schedule D (Form 1065))		8	
	9a	Net long-term capital gain (loss) (attach Schedule D (Form 1065))		9a	
	b	Collectibles (28%) gain (loss)	9b		
	c	Unrecaptured section 1250 gain (attach statement)	9c		
	10	Net section 1231 gain (loss) (attach Form 4797)		10	
	11	Other income (loss) (see instructions) Type ▶		11	
Deductions	12	Section 179 deduction (attach Form 4562)		12	
	13a	Contributions		13a	1,500
	b	Investment interest expense		13b	
	c	Section 59(e)(2) expenditures: (1) Type ▶ (2) Amount ▶		13c(2)	
	d	Other deductions (see instructions) Type ▶		13d	
Self-Employment	14a	Net earnings (loss) from self-employment		14a	60,250
	b	Gross farming or fishing income		14b	
	c	Gross nonfarm income		14c	
Credits	15a	Low-income housing credit (section 42(j)(5))		15a	
	b	Low-income housing credit (other)		15b	
	c	Qualified rehabilitation expenditures (rental real estate) (attach Form 3468, if applicable)		15c	
	d	Other rental real estate credits (see instructions) Type ▶		15d	
	e	Other rental credits (see instructions) Type ▶		15e	
	f	Other credits (see instructions) Type ▶		15f	
Foreign Transactions	16a	Name of country or U.S. possession ▶			
	b	Gross income from all sources		16b	
	c	Gross income sourced at partner level		16c	
		Foreign gross income sourced at partnership level			
	d	Passive category ▶ e General category ▶ f Other ▶		16f	
		Deductions allocated and apportioned at partner level			
	g	Interest expense ▶ h Other ▶		16h	
		Deductions allocated and apportioned at partnership level to foreign source income			
	i	Passive category ▶ j General category ▶ k Other ▶		16k	
	l	Total foreign taxes (check one): ▶ Paid ☐ Accrued ☐		16l	
	m	Reduction in taxes available for credit (attach statement)		16m	
	n	Other foreign tax information (attach statement)			
Alternative Minimum Tax (AMT) Items	17a	Post-1986 depreciation adjustment		17a	
	b	Adjusted gain or loss		17b	
	c	Depletion (other than oil and gas)		17c	
	d	Oil, gas, and geothermal properties—gross income		17d	
	e	Oil, gas, and geothermal properties—deductions		17e	
	f	Other AMT items (attach statement)		17f	
Other Information	18a	Tax-exempt interest income		18a	
	b	Other tax-exempt income		18b	
	c	Nondeductible expenses		18c	
	19a	Distributions of cash and marketable securities		19a	50,000
	b	Distributions of other property		19b	
	20a	Investment income		20a	
	b	Investment expenses		20b	
	c	Other items and amounts (attach statement)			

Form **1065** (2014)

Self-Study Problem 10.3

Form 1065 (2014) Page **5**

Analysis of Net Income (Loss)

1	Net income (loss). Combine Schedule K, lines 1 through 11. From the result, subtract the sum of Schedule K, lines 12 through 13d, and 16l	1	58,750

2	Analysis by partner type:	(i) Corporate	(ii) Individual (active)	(iii) Individual (passive)	(iv) Partnership	(v) Exempt Organization	(vi) Nominee/Other
a	General partners		58,750				
b	Limited partners						

DRAFT AS OF August 4, 2014 DO NOT FILE

Schedule L — Balance Sheets per Books

	Assets	Beginning of tax year (a)	(b)	End of tax year (c)	(d)
1	Cash		Initial Return		27,000
2a	Trade notes and accounts receivable			10,000	
b	Less allowance for bad debts				10,000
3	Inventories				
4	U.S. government obligations				
5	Tax-exempt securities				
6	Other current assets (attach statement)				
7a	Loans to partners (or persons related to partners)				
b	Mortgage and real estate loans				
8	Other investments (attach statement)				
9a	Buildings and other depreciable assets			115,000	
b	Less accumulated depreciation			9,250	105,750
10a	Depletable assets				
b	Less accumulated depletion				
11	Land (net of any amortization)				115,000
12a	Intangible assets (amortizable only)				
b	Less accumulated amortization				
13	Other assets (attach statement)				
14	Total assets				257,750
	Liabilities and Capital				
15	Accounts payable				29,750
16	Mortgages, notes, bonds payable in less than 1 year				
17	Other current liabilities (attach statement)				
18	All nonrecourse loans				
19a	Loans from partners (or persons related to partners)				187,750
b	Mortgages, notes, bonds payable in 1 year or more				
20	Other liabilities (attach statement)				
21	Partners' capital accounts				40,250
22	Total liabilities and capital				257,750

Schedule M-1 — Reconciliation of Income (Loss) per Books With Income (Loss) per Return

Note. The partnership may be required to file Schedule M-3 (see instructions).

1	Net income (loss) per books	58,750	6	Income recorded on books this year not included on Schedule K, lines 1 through 11 (itemize):	
2	Income included on Schedule K, lines 1, 2, 3c, 5, 6a, 7, 8, 9a, 10, and 11, not recorded on books this year (itemize):		a	Tax-exempt interest $	
3	Guaranteed payments (other than health insurance)		7	Deductions included on Schedule K, lines 1 through 13d, and 16l, not charged against book income this year (itemize):	
4	Expenses recorded on books this year not included on Schedule K, lines 1 through 13d, and 16l (itemize):		a	Depreciation $	
a	Depreciation $		8	Add lines 6 and 7	0
b	Travel and entertainment $		9	Income (loss) (Analysis of Net Income (Loss), line 1). Subtract line 8 from line 5	
5	Add lines 1 through 4	58,750			58,750

Schedule M-2 — Analysis of Partners' Capital Accounts

1	Balance at beginning of year	0	6	Distributions: a Cash	50,000
2	Capital contributed: a Cash	31,500		b Property	
	b Property		7	Other decreases (itemize):	
3	Net income (loss) per books	58,750			
4	Other increases (itemize):		8	Add lines 6 and 7	50,000
5	Add lines 1 through 4	90,250	9	Balance at end of year. Subtract line 8 from line 5	40,250

Form **1065** (2014)

Self-Study Problem 10.3

651113

☐ Final K-1 ☐ Amended K-1 OMB No. 1545-0123

Schedule K-1 (Form 1065) **2014**

Department of the Treasury
Internal Revenue Service

For calendar year 2014, or tax year beginning ____________, 2014 ending ____________, 20____

Partner's Share of Income, Deductions, Credits, etc. ▶ See back of form and separate instructions.

DRAFT AS OF July 11, 2014 DO NOT FILE

Part I Information About the Partnership

A Partnership's employer identification number

B Partnership's name, address, city, state, and ZIP code

Malus Valley Partnership

C IRS Center where partnership filed return

D ☐ Check if this is a publicly traded partnership (PTP)

Part II Information About the Partner

E Partner's identifying number

F Partner's name, address, city, state, and ZIP code

Robert Conrad

G ☒ General partner or LLC member-manager ☐ Limited partner or other LLC member

H ☐ Domestic partner ☐ Foreign partner

I1 What type of entity is this partner? *Individual*

I2 If this partner is a retirement plan (IRA/SEP/Keogh/etc.), check here ☐

J Partner's share of profit, loss, and capital (see instructions):

	Beginning	Ending
Profit	0 %	50 %
Loss	0 %	50 %
Capital	0 %	50 %

K Partner's share of liabilities at year end:

Nonrecourse	$
Qualified nonrecourse financing	$
Recourse	$ 108,750

L Partner's capital account analysis:

Beginning capital account	$ 0
Capital contributed during the year	$ 15,750
Current year increase (decrease)	$ 29,375
Withdrawals & distributions	$ (25,000)
Ending capital account	$ 20,125

☒ Tax basis ☐ GAAP ☐ Section 704(b) book
☐ Other (explain)

M Did the partner contribute property with a built-in gain or loss?
☐ **Yes** ☒ **No**
If "Yes," attach statement (see instructions)

Part III Partner's Share of Current Year Income, Deductions, Credits, and Other Items

Line	Item	Amount
1	Ordinary business income (loss)	30,125
2	Net rental real estate income (loss)	
3	Other net rental income (loss)	
4	Guaranteed payments	
5	Interest income	
6a	Ordinary dividends	
6b	Qualified dividends	
7	Royalties	
8	Net short-term capital gain (loss)	
9a	Net long-term capital gain (loss)	
9b	Collectibles (28%) gain (loss)	
9c	Unrecaptured section 1250 gain	
10	Net section 1231 gain (loss)	
11	Other income (loss)	
12	Section 179 deduction	
13	Other deductions	A 750
14	Self-employment earnings (loss)	30,125
15	Credits	
16	Foreign transactions	
17	Alternative minimum tax (AMT) items	
18	Tax-exempt income and nondeductible expenses	
19	Distributions	A 25,000
20	Other information	

*See attached statement for additional information.

For IRS Use Only

Self-Study Problem 10.5

12 months × $1,000 per month guaranteed payment	$12,000
Add: Robert's distributive share of income	21,000
Total income	$33,000

The $1,500 per month received in September, October, November, and December of 2014 will be reported on Robert's 2015 income tax return. The guaranteed payments received are reported for the partnership tax year that ends with or within the partner's tax year, in the same manner as a distributive share of the partnership income.

Self-Study Problem 10.6

1. Maxwell has a $5,000 realized loss ($70,000 − $75,000), but the loss is not recognized since he is a more-than-50 percent partner, 50 percent directly and 50 percent indirectly from his daughter.
2. The daughter has a $15,000 gain ($40,000 − $25,000). Since she is a more-than-50 percent partner (50 percent directly and 50 percent indirectly), and the car is not a capital asset to the partnership, the gain is ordinary income.

Self-Study Problem 10.7

1. $45,000, his amount at risk in the activity.
2. Profit $ 31,000

2. Profit	$ 31,000
Less: carryover of disallowed loss from the prior year ($60,000 − $45,000)	(15,000)
Taxable income for 2015	$ 16,000

Self-Study Problem 10.8

1. False — An election must be made to be treated like a corporation for tax purposes.
2. False
3. True
4. True
5. True

CHAPTER 11 THE CORPORATE INCOME TAX

Self-Study Problem 11.1

$22,250 + (39% × [$275,000 − $100,000]) = $90,500

Self-Study Problem 11.2

$22,250 + (39% × [$110,000 − $100,000]) = $26,150

None of the capital losses may be used to offset current year ordinary income. The capital losses may be carried back 3 years and forward 5 years to offset capital gains, if any, recognized during those years.

Self-Study Problem 11.3

The dividends received deduction is equal to the lesser of \$56,000 = 80% × \$70,000; or \$48,000 = 80% × \$60,000 (\$90,000 + \$70,000 − \$100,000). Therefore, \$48,000 is the amount of the deduction.

Self-Study Problem 11.4

Schedule M-1 Reconciliation of Income (Loss) per Books With Income per Return
Note: The corporation may be required to file Schedule M-3 (see instructions).

1	Net income (loss) per books	104,000	7	Income recorded on books this year not included on this return (itemize): Tax-exempt interest $ 4,700	
2	Federal income tax per books	41,000			
3	Excess of capital losses over capital gains	9,100			4,700
4	Income subject to tax not recorded on books this year (itemize):		8	Deductions on this return not charged against book income this year (itemize):	
5	Expenses recorded on books this year not deducted on this return (itemize):		a	Depreciation $ 4,000	
a	Depreciation $		b	Charitable contributions $	
b	Charitable contributions $				
c	Travel and entertainment $				4,000
			9	Add lines 7 and 8	8,700
6	Add lines 1 through 5	154,100	10	Income (page 1, line 28)—line 6 less line 9	145,400

Self-Study Problem 11.5

See Form 1120 on Pages E-65 to E-69. The calculation of tax for Aspen Corporation is as follows: 15% × \$12,000 taxable income = \$1,800 total tax. Net income per the books is equal to \$17,200, \$19,000 net income before income tax expense − \$1,800 income tax expense.

Self-Study Problem 11.6

See Form 1120S and Schedule K-1 on Pages E-70 to E-76.

Self-Study Problem 11.7

Tammy's realized gain is \$125,000 + \$34,000 − \$75,000 = \$84,000.

Tammy's recognized gain is \$0.

Tammy's basis in her stock is \$75,000 − \$0 + \$0 − \$34,000 = \$41,000.

The corporation's basis in the real estate is \$75,000 + \$0 = \$75,000.

Self-Study Problem 11.8

15% × \$190,000 = \$28,500

Only \$190,000 (\$340,000 − \$150,000) is subject to the accumulated earnings tax.

Self-Study Problem 11.9

Regular taxable income	\$ 70,000
Corporate tax preference items	55,000
Alternative minimum taxable income	\$125,000
Less: exemption	(40,000)
Alternative minimum tax base	\$ 85,000
Tax rate	× 20%
Gross alternative minimum tax	\$ 17,000
Less: regular tax	(12,500)
Alternative minimum tax liability	\$ 4,500

(The next self-study problem is on Page E-77.)

Self-Study Problem 11.5

Form **1120** — Department of the Treasury, Internal Revenue Service

U.S. Corporation Income Tax Return

For calendar year 2014 or tax year beginning ________, 2014, ending ________, 20 ____

▶ Information about Form 1120 and its separate instructions is at *www.irs.gov/form1120*.

OMB No. 1545-0123 — **2014**

DRAFT AS OF June 25, 2014 DO NOT FILE

A Check if:
- 1a Consolidated return (attach Form 851) ☐
- b Life/nonlife consolidated return ☐
- 2 Personal holding co. (attach Sch. PH) ☐
- 3 Personal service corp. (see instructions) ☐
- 4 Schedule M-3 attached ☐

TYPE OR PRINT

Name: *Aspen Corporation*

Number, street, and room or suite no. If a P.O. box, see instructions.

City or town, state, or province, country and ZIP or foreign postal code

B Employer identification number

C Date incorporated: *01/01/2014*

D Total assets (see instructions): $ *183,000*

E Check if: (1) ☑ Initial return (2) ☐ Final return (3) ☐ Name change (4) ☐ Address change

Section	Line	Description	Sub-line	Sub-amount	Line no.	Amount
Income	1a	Gross receipts or sales	1a	285,000		
	b	Returns and allowances	1b			
	c	Balance. Subtract line 1b from line 1a			1c	285,000
	2	Cost of goods sold (attach Form 1125-A)			2	80,000
	3	Gross profit. Subtract line 2 from line 1c			3	205,000
	4	Dividends (Schedule C, line 19)			4	10,000
	5	Interest			5	
	6	Gross rents			6	
	7	Gross royalties			7	
	8	Capital gain net income (attach Schedule D (Form 1120))			8	
	9	Net gain or (loss) from Form 4797, Part II, line 17 (attach Form 4797)			9	
	10	Other income (see instructions—attach statement)			10	
	11	**Total income.** Add lines 3 through 10 ▶			11	215,000
Deductions (See instructions for limitations on deductions.)	12	Compensation of officers (see instructions—attach Form 1125-E) ▶			12	90,000
	13	Salaries and wages (less employment credits)			13	82,000
	14	Repairs and maintenance			14	8,000
	15	Bad debts			15	
	16	Rents			16	
	17	Taxes and licenses			17	11,000
	18	Interest			18	
	19	Charitable contributions			19	
	20	Depreciation from Form 4562 not claimed on Form 1125-A or elsewhere on return (attach Form 4562)			20	5,000
	21	Depletion			21	
	22	Advertising			22	
	23	Pension, profit-sharing, etc., plans			23	
	24	Employee benefit programs			24	
	25	Domestic production activities deduction (attach Form 8903)			25	
	26	Other deductions (attach statement)			26	
	27	**Total deductions.** Add lines 12 through 26 ▶			27	196,000
	28	Taxable income before net operating loss deduction and special deductions. Subtract line 27 from line 11.			28	19,000
	29a	Net operating loss deduction (see instructions)	29a			
	b	Special deductions (Schedule C, line 20)	29b	7,000		
	c	Add lines 29a and 29b			29c	7,000
Tax, Refundable Credits, and Payments	30	**Taxable income.** Subtract line 29c from line 28 (see instructions)			30	12,000
	31	Total tax (Schedule J, Part I, line 11)			31	1,800
	32	Total payments and refundable credits (Schedule J, Part II, line 21)			32	2,000
	33	Estimated tax penalty (see instructions). Check if Form 2220 is attached ▶ ☐			33	
	34	**Amount owed.** If line 32 is smaller than the total of lines 31 and 33, enter amount owed			34	
	35	**Overpayment.** If line 32 is larger than the total of lines 31 and 33, enter amount overpaid			35	200
	36	Enter amount from line 35 you want: **Credited to 2015 estimated tax** ▶ 200 **Refunded** ▶			36	

Sign Here

Under penalties of perjury, I declare that I have examined this return, including accompanying schedules and statements, and to the best of my knowledge and belief, it is true, correct, and complete. Declaration of preparer (other than taxpayer) is based on all information of which preparer has any knowledge.

▶ Signature of officer — Date — ▶ Title

May the IRS discuss this return with the preparer shown below (see instructions)? ☐ Yes ☐ No

Paid Preparer Use Only

Print/Type preparer's name — Preparer's signature — Date — Check ☐ if self-employed — PTIN

Firm's name ▶ — Firm's EIN ▶

Firm's address ▶ — Phone no.

For Paperwork Reduction Act Notice, see separate instructions. Cat. No. 11450Q Form **1120** (2014)

Self-Study Problem 11.5

Form 1120 (2014) Page **2**

DRAFT AS OF June 25, 2014 DO NOT FILE

Schedule C	**Dividends and Special Deductions** (see instructions)	**(a)** Dividends received	**(b)** %	**(c)** Special deductions **(a)** × **(b)**
1	Dividends from less-than-20%-owned domestic corporations (other than debt-financed stock)	10,000	70	7,000
2	Dividends from 20%-or-more-owned domestic corporations (other than debt-financed stock)		80	
3	Dividends on debt-financed stock of domestic and foreign corporations		see instructions	
4	Dividends on certain preferred stock of less-than-20%-owned public utilities		42	
5	Dividends on certain preferred stock of 20%-or-more-owned public utilities		48	
6	Dividends from less-than-20%-owned foreign corporations and certain FSCs		70	
7	Dividends from 20%-or-more-owned foreign corporations and certain FSCs		80	
8	Dividends from wholly owned foreign subsidiaries		100	
9	**Total.** Add lines 1 through 8. See instructions for limitation			7,000
10	Dividends from domestic corporations received by a small business investment company operating under the Small Business Investment Act of 1958		100	
11	Dividends from affiliated group members		100	
12	Dividends from certain FSCs		100	
13	Dividends from foreign corporations not included on lines 3, 6, 7, 8, 11, or 12			
14	Income from controlled foreign corporations under subpart F (attach Form(s) 5471)			
15	Foreign dividend gross-up			
16	IC-DISC and former DISC dividends not included on lines 1, 2, or 3			
17	Other dividends			
18	Deduction for dividends paid on certain preferred stock of public utilities			
19	**Total dividends.** Add lines 1 through 17. Enter here and on page 1, line 4 ▶	10,000		
20	**Total special deductions.** Add lines 9, 10, 11, 12, and 18. Enter here and on page 1, line 29b ▶			7,000

Form **1120** (2014)

Self-Study Problem 11.5

Form 1120 (2014) Page **3**

Schedule J **Tax Computation and Payment** (see instructions)

Part I–Tax Computation

1	Check if the corporation is a member of a controlled group (attach Schedule O (Form 1120)) ▶ ☐				
2	Income tax. Check if a qualified personal service corporation (see instructions) ▶ ☐			2	1,800
3	Alternative minimum tax (attach Form 4626)			3	
4	Add lines 2 and 3			4	1,800
5a	Foreign tax credit (attach Form 1118)	5a			
b	Credit from Form 8834 (see instructions)	5b			
c	General business credit (attach Form 3800)	5c			
d	Credit for prior year minimum tax (attach Form 8827)	5d			
e	Bond credits from Form 8912	5e			
6	**Total credits.** Add lines 5a through 5e			6	
7	Subtract line 6 from line 4			7	1,800
8	Personal holding company tax (attach Schedule PH (Form 1120))			8	
9a	Recapture of investment credit (attach Form 4255)	9a			
b	Recapture of low-income housing credit (attach Form 8611)	9b			
c	Interest due under the look-back method—completed long-term contracts (attach Form 8697)	9c			
d	Interest due under the look-back method—income forecast method (attach Form 8866)	9d			
e	Alternative tax on qualifying shipping activities (attach Form 8902)	9e			
f	Other (see instructions—attach statement)	9f			
10	**Total.** Add lines 9a through 9f			10	
11	**Total tax.** Add lines 7, 8, and 10. Enter here and on page 1, line 31			11	1,800

Part II–Payments and Refundable Credits

12	2013 overpayment credited to 2014			12	
13	2014 estimated tax payments			13	2,000
14	2014 refund applied for on Form 4466			14	( )
15	Combine lines 12, 13, and 14			15	2,000
16	Tax deposited with Form 7004			16	
17	Withholding (see instructions)			17	
18	**Total payments.** Add lines 15, 16, and 17			18	2,000
19	Refundable credits from:				
a	Form 2439	19a			
b	Form 4136	19b			
c	Form 8827, line 8c	19c			
d	Other (attach statement—see instructions)	19d			
20	**Total credits.** Add lines 19a through 19d			20	
21	**Total payments and credits.** Add lines 18 and 20. Enter here and on page 1, line 32			21	2,000

DRAFT AS OF June 25, 2014 DO NOT FILE

Schedule K **Other Information** (see instructions)

		Yes	No
1	Check accounting method: a ☐ Cash b ☑ Accrual c ☐ Other (specify) ▶		
2	See the instructions and enter the:		
a	Business activity code no. ▶		
b	Business activity ▶		
c	Product or service ▶		
3	Is the corporation a subsidiary in an affiliated group or a parent-subsidiary controlled group? If "Yes," enter name and EIN of the parent corporation ▶		✓
4	At the end of the tax year:		
a	Did any foreign or domestic corporation, partnership (including any entity treated as a partnership), trust, or tax-exempt organization own directly 20% or more, or own, directly or indirectly, 50% or more of the total voting power of all classes of the corporation's stock entitled to vote? If "Yes," complete Part I of Schedule G (Form 1120) (attach Schedule G)		✓
b	Did any individual or estate own directly 20% or more, or own, directly or indirectly, 50% or more of the total voting power of all classes of the corporation's stock entitled to vote? If "Yes," complete Part II of Schedule G (Form 1120) (attach Schedule G)		✓

Form **1120** (2014)

Self-Study Problem 11.5

Form 1120 (2014) Page **4**

Schedule K **Other Information** *continued* (see instructions)

		Yes	No
5	At the end of the tax year, did the corporation:		
a	Own directly 20% or more, or own, directly or indirectly, 50% or more of the total voting power of all classes of stock entitled to vote of any foreign or domestic corporation not included on **Form 851,** Affiliations Schedule? For rules of constructive ownership, see instructions. If "Yes," complete (i) through (iv) below.		✔

(i) Name of Corporation	(ii) Employer Identification Number (if any)	(iii) Country of Incorporation	(iv) Percentage Owned in Voting Stock

		Yes	No
b	Own directly an interest of 20% or more, or own, directly or indirectly, an interest of 50% or more in any foreign or domestic partnership (including an entity treated as a partnership) or in the beneficial interest of a trust? For rules of constructive ownership, see instructions. If "Yes," complete (i) through (iv) below.		✔

(i) Name of Entity	(ii) Employer Identification Number (if any)	(iii) Country of Organization	(iv) Maximum Percentage Owned in Profit, Loss, or Capital

		Yes	No
6	During this tax year, did the corporation pay dividends (other than stock dividends and distributions in exchange for stock) in excess of the corporation's current and accumulated earnings and profits? (See sections 301 and 316.) If "Yes," file **Form 5452,** Corporate Report of Nondividend Distributions. If this is a consolidated return, answer here for the parent corporation and on Form 851 for each subsidiary.		✔
7	At any time during the tax year, did one foreign person own, directly or indirectly, at least 25% of **(a)** the total voting power of all classes of the corporation's stock entitled to vote or **(b)** the total value of all classes of the corporation's stock? For rules of attribution, see section 318. If "Yes," enter: **(i)** Percentage owned ▶ ______ and **(ii)** Owner's country ▶ ______ **(c)** The corporation may have to file **Form 5472,** Information Return of a 25% Foreign-Owned U.S. Corporation or a Foreign Corporation Engaged in a U.S. Trade or Business. Enter the number of Forms 5472 attached ▶ ______		✔
8	Check this box if the corporation issued publicly offered debt instruments with original issue discount ▶ ☐ If checked, the corporation may have to file **Form 8281,** Information Return for Publicly Offered Original Issue Discount Instruments.		
9	Enter the amount of tax-exempt interest received or accrued during the tax year ▶ $ ______		
10	Enter the number of shareholders at the end of the tax year (if 100 or fewer) ▶ ______		
11	If the corporation has an NOL for the tax year and is electing to forego the carryback period, check here ▶ ☐ If the corporation is filing a consolidated return, the statement required by Regulations section 1.1502-21(b)(3) must be attached or the election will not be valid.		
12	Enter the available NOL carryover from prior tax years (do not reduce it by any deduction on line 29a.) ▶ $ ______		
13	Are the corporation's total receipts (page 1, line 1a, plus lines 4 through 10) for the tax year **and** its total assets at the end of the tax year less than $250,000? If "Yes," the corporation is not required to complete Schedules L, M-1, and M-2. Instead, enter the total amount of cash distributions and the book value of property distributions (other than cash) made during the tax year ▶ $ ______		✔
14	Is the corporation required to file Schedule UTP (Form 1120), Uncertain Tax Position Statement (see instructions)? If "Yes," complete and attach Schedule UTP.		✔
15a	Did the corporation make any payments in 2014 that would require it to file Form(s) 1099?	✔	
b	If "Yes," did or will the corporation file required Forms 1099?	✔	
16	During this tax year, did the corporation have an 80% or more change in ownership, including a change due to redemption of its own stock?		✔
17	During or subsequent to this tax year, but before the filing of this return, did the corporation dispose of more than 65% (by value) of its assets in a taxable, non-taxable, or tax deferred transaction?		✔
18	Did the corporation receive assets in a section 351 transfer in which any of the transferred assets had a fair market basis or fair market value of more than $1 million?		✔

DRAFT AS OF June 25, 2014 DO NOT FILE

Form **1120** (2014)

Self-Study Problem 11.5

Form 1120 (2014) Page 5

Schedule L — Balance Sheets per Books

Assets		Beginning of tax year (a)	(b)	End of tax year (c)	(d)
1	Cash		Initial Return		35,000
2a	Trade notes and accounts receivable			10,000	
b	Less allowance for bad debts	( )		( )	10,000
3	Inventories				
4	U.S. government obligations				
5	Tax-exempt securities (see instructions)				
6	Other current assets (attach statement)				
7	Loans to shareholders				
8	Mortgage and real estate loans				
9	Other investments (attach statement)				
10a	Buildings and other depreciable assets			125,000	
b	Less accumulated depreciation	( )		(5,000)	120,000
11a	Depletable assets				
b	Less accumulated depletion	( )		( )	
12	Land (net of any amortization)				18,000
13a	Intangible assets (amortizable only)				
b	Less accumulated amortization	( )		( )	
14	Other assets (attach statement)				
15	Total assets				183,000
	Liabilities and Shareholders' Equity				
16	Accounts payable		Initial Return		25,800
17	Mortgages, notes, bonds payable in less than 1 year				
18	Other current liabilities (attach statement)				
19	Loans from shareholders				
20	Mortgages, notes, bonds payable in 1 year or more				
21	Other liabilities (attach statement)				
22	Capital stock: a Preferred stock				
	b Common stock			140,000	140,000
23	Additional paid-in capital				
24	Retained earnings—Appropriated (attach statement)				
25	Retained earnings—Unappropriated				17,200
26	Adjustments to shareholders' equity (attach statement)				
27	Less cost of treasury stock		( )		( )
28	Total liabilities and shareholders' equity				183,000

DRAFT AS OF June 25, 2014 DO NOT FILE

Schedule M-1 — Reconciliation of Income (Loss) per Books With Income per Return

Note: The corporation may be required to file Schedule M-3 (see instructions).

1	Net income (loss) per books	17,200	7	Income recorded on books this year not included on this return (itemize): Tax-exempt interest $	
2	Federal income tax per books	1,800			
3	Excess of capital losses over capital gains				
4	Income subject to tax not recorded on books this year (itemize):		8	Deductions on this return not charged against book income this year (itemize):	
5	Expenses recorded on books this year not deducted on this return (itemize):		a	Depreciation $	
a	Depreciation $		b	Charitable contributions $	
b	Charitable contributions $				
c	Travel and entertainment $		9	Add lines 7 and 8	
6	Add lines 1 through 5	19,000	10	Income (page 1, line 28)—line 6 less line 9	19,000

Schedule M-2 — Analysis of Unappropriated Retained Earnings per Books (Line 25, Schedule L)

1	Balance at beginning of year	0	5	Distributions: a Cash	
2	Net income (loss) per books	17,200		b Stock	
3	Other increases (itemize):			c Property	
			6	Other decreases (itemize):	
			7	Add lines 5 and 6	
4	Add lines 1, 2, and 3	17,200	8	Balance at end of year (line 4 less line 7)	17,200

Form **1120** (2014)

Self-Study Problem 11.6

Form **1120S** — Department of the Treasury, Internal Revenue Service

U.S. Income Tax Return for an S Corporation

▶ Do not file this form unless the corporation has filed or is attaching Form 2553 to elect to be an S corporation.
▶ Information about Form 1120S and its separate instructions is at *www.irs.gov/form1120s.*

OMB No. 1545-0123 — **2014**

DRAFT AS OF August 1, 2014 DO NOT FILE

For calendar year 2014 or tax year beginning , 2014, ending , 20

A S election effective date: *01/01/2014*

B Business activity code number (see instructions)

C Check if Sch. M-3 attached ☐

TYPE OR PRINT — Name: *Aspen Corporation*
Number, street, and room or suite no. If a P.O. box, see instructions.
City or town, state or province, country, and ZIP or foreign postal code

D Employer identification number

E Date incorporated: *01/01/2014*

F Total assets (see instructions): $ *183,000*

G Is the corporation electing to be an S corporation beginning with this tax year? ☑ Yes ☐ No If "Yes," attach Form 2553 if not already filed

H Check if: (1) ☐ Final return (2) ☐ Name change (3) ☐ Address change (4) ☐ Amended return (5) ☐ S election termination or revocation

I Enter the number of shareholders who were shareholders during any part of the tax year ▶

Caution. Include **only** trade or business income and expenses on lines 1a through 21. See the instructions for more information.

Section	Line	Description	Sub-line	Sub-amount	Line	Amount
Income	1a	Gross receipts or sales	1a	*285,000*		
	b	Returns and allowances	1b			
	c	Balance. Subtract line 1b from line 1a			1c	*285,000*
	2	Cost of goods sold (attach Form 1125-A)			2	*80,000*
	3	Gross profit. Subtract line 2 from line 1c			3	*205,000*
	4	Net gain (loss) from Form 4797, line 17 (attach Form 4797)			4	
	5	Other income (loss) (see instructions—attach statement)			5	
	6	**Total income (loss).** Add lines 3 through 5 ▶			6	*205,000*
Deductions (see instructions for limitations)	7	Compensation of officers (see instructions—attach Form 1125-E)			7	*90,000*
	8	Salaries and wages (less employment credits)			8	*82,000*
	9	Repairs and maintenance			9	*8,000*
	10	Bad debts			10	
	11	Rents			11	
	12	Taxes and licenses			12	*11,000*
	13	Interest			13	
	14	Depreciation not claimed on Form 1125-A or elsewhere on return (attach Form 4562)			14	*5,000*
	15	Depletion **(Do not deduct oil and gas depletion.)**			15	
	16	Advertising			16	
	17	Pension, profit-sharing, etc., plans			17	
	18	Employee benefit programs			18	
	19	Other deductions (attach statement)			19	
	20	**Total deductions.** Add lines 7 through 19 ▶			20	*196,000*
	21	**Ordinary business income (loss).** Subtract line 20 from line 6			21	*9,000*
Tax and Payments	22a	Excess net passive income or LIFO recapture tax (see instructions)	22a			
	b	Tax from Schedule D (Form 1120S)	22b			
	c	Add lines 22a and 22b (see instructions for additional taxes)			22c	*0*
	23a	2014 estimated tax payments and 2013 overpayment credited to 2014	23a			
	b	Tax deposited with Form 7004	23b			
	c	Credit for federal tax paid on fuels (attach Form 4136)	23c			
	d	Add lines 23a through 23c			23d	*0*
	24	Estimated tax penalty (see instructions). Check if Form 2220 is attached ▶ ☐			24	
	25	**Amount owed.** If line 23d is smaller than the total of lines 22c and 24, enter amount owed			25	
	26	**Overpayment.** If line 23d is larger than the total of lines 22c and 24, enter amount overpaid			26	*0*
	27	Enter amount from line 26 **Credited to 2015 estimated tax** ▶ **Refunded** ▶			27	

Sign Here — Under penalties of perjury, I declare that I have examined this return, including accompanying schedules and statements, and to the best of my knowledge and belief, it is true, correct, and complete. Declaration of preparer (other than taxpayer) is based on all information of which preparer has any knowledge.

▶ Signature of officer — Date ▶ Title

May the IRS discuss this return with the preparer shown below (see instructions)? ☐ Yes ☐ No

Paid Preparer Use Only

Print/Type preparer's name	Preparer's signature	Date	Check ☐ if self-employed	PTIN
Firm's name ▶			Firm's EIN ▶	
Firm's address ▶			Phone no.	

Self-Study Problem 11.6

Form 1120S (2014) Page 2

Schedule B **Other Information** (see instructions)

		Yes	No
1	Check accounting method: a ☐ Cash b ☑ Accrual c ☐ Other (specify) ▶		
2	See the instructions and enter the: a Business activity ▶ b Product or service ▶		
3	At any time during the tax year, was any shareholder of the corporation a disregarded entity, a trust, an estate, or a nominee or similar person? If "Yes," attach Schedule B-1, Information on Certain Shareholders of an S Corporation		✔
4	At the end of the tax year, did the corporation:		
a	Own directly 20% or more, or own, directly or indirectly, 50% or more of the total stock issued and outstanding of any foreign or domestic corporation? For rules of constructive ownership, see instructions. If "Yes," complete (i) through (v) below		✔

(i) Name of Corporation	(ii) Employer Identification Number (if any)	(iii) Country of Incorporation	(iv) Percentage of Stock Owned	(v) If Percentage in (iv) is 100%, Enter the Date (if any) a Qualified Subchapter S Subsidiary Election Was Made

DRAFT AS OF August 1, 2014 DO NOT FILE

		Yes	No
b	Own directly an interest of 20% or more, or own, directly or indirectly, an interest of 50% or more in the profit, loss, or capital in any foreign or domestic partnership (including an entity treated as a partnership) or in the beneficial interest of a trust? For rules of constructive ownership, see instructions. If "Yes," complete (i) through (v) below		✔

(i) Name of Entity	(ii) Employer Identification Number (if any)	(iii) Type of Entity	(iv) Country of Organization	(v) Maximum Percentage Owned in Profit, Loss, or Capital

		Yes	No
5 a	At the end of the tax year, did the corporation have any outstanding shares of restricted stock?		✔
	If "Yes," complete lines (i) and (ii) below.		
	(i) Total shares of restricted stock ▶		
	(ii) Total shares of non-restricted stock ▶		
b	At the end of the tax year, did the corporation have any outstanding stock options, warrants, or similar instruments?		✔
	If "Yes," complete lines (i) and (ii) below.		
	(i) Total shares of stock outstanding at the end of the tax year ▶		
	(ii) Total shares of stock outstanding if all instruments were executed ▶		
6	Has this corporation filed, or is it required to file, **Form 8918,** Material Advisor Disclosure Statement, to provide information on any reportable transaction?		✔
7	Check this box if the corporation issued publicly offered debt instruments with original issue discount ▶ ☐ If checked, the corporation may have to file **Form 8281,** Information Return for Publicly Offered Original Issue Discount Instruments.		
8	If the corporation: **(a)** was a C corporation before it elected to be an S corporation **or** the corporation acquired an asset with a basis determined by reference to the basis of the asset (or the basis of any other property) in the hands of a C corporation **and (b)** has net unrealized built-in gain in excess of the net recognized built-in gain from prior years, enter the net unrealized built-in gain reduced by net recognized built-in gain from prior years (see instructions) ▶ $		
9	Enter the accumulated earnings and profits of the corporation at the end of the tax year. $		
10	Does the corporation satisfy **both** of the following conditions?		
a	The corporation's total receipts (see instructions) for the tax year were less than $250,000		
b	The corporation's total assets at the end of the tax year were less than $250,000		✔
	If "Yes," the corporation is not required to complete Schedules L and M-1.		
11	During the tax year, did the corporation have any non-shareholder debt that was canceled, was forgiven, or had the terms modified so as to reduce the principal amount of the debt?		✔
	If "Yes," enter the amount of principal reduction $		
12	During the tax year, was a qualified subchapter S subsidiary election terminated or revoked? If "Yes," see instructions		✔
13a	Did the corporation make any payments in 2014 that would require it to file Form(s) 1099?	✔	
b	If "Yes," did the corporation file or will it file required Forms 1099?	✔	

Form **1120S** (2014)

Self-Study Problem 11.6

Form 1120S (2014) Page 3

Schedule K Shareholders' Pro Rata Share Items

Section	Line	Item			Line	Total amount
Income (Loss)	1	Ordinary business income (loss) (page 1, line 21)			1	9,000
	2	Net rental real estate income (loss) (attach Form 8825)			2	
	3a	Other gross rental income (loss)	3a			
	b	Expenses from other rental activities (attach statement)	3b			
	c	Other net rental income (loss). Subtract line 3b from line 3a			3c	
	4	Interest income			4	
	5	Dividends: a Ordinary dividends			5a	10,000
		b Qualified dividends	5b	10,000		
	6	Royalties			6	
	7	Net short-term capital gain (loss) (attach Schedule D (Form 1120S))			7	
	8a	Net long-term capital gain (loss) (attach Schedule D (Form 1120S))			8a	
	b	Collectibles (28%) gain (loss)	8b			
	c	Unrecaptured section 1250 gain (attach statement)	8c			
	9	Net section 1231 gain (loss) (attach Form 4797)			9	
	10	Other income (loss) (see instructions) Type ▶			10	
Deductions	11	Section 179 deduction (attach Form 4562)			11	
	12a	Charitable contributions			12a	
	b	Investment interest expense			12b	
	c	Section 59(e)(2) expenditures (1) Type ▶ (2) Amount ▶			12c(2)	
	d	Other deductions (see instructions) Type ▶			12d	
Credits	13a	Low-income housing credit (section 42(j)(5))			13a	
	b	Low-income housing credit (other)			13b	
	c	Qualified rehabilitation expenditures (rental real estate) (attach Form 3468, if applicable)			13c	
	d	Other rental real estate credits (see instructions) Type ▶			13d	
	e	Other rental credits (see instructions) Type ▶			13e	
	f	Biofuel producer credit (attach Form 6478)			13f	
	g	Other credits (see instructions) Type ▶			13g	
Foreign Transactions	14a	Name of country or U.S. possession ▶				
	b	Gross income from all sources			14b	
	c	Gross income sourced at shareholder level			14c	
		Foreign gross income sourced at corporate level				
	d	Passive category			14d	
	e	General category			14e	
	f	Other (attach statement)			14f	
		Deductions allocated and apportioned at shareholder level				
	g	Interest expense			14g	
	h	Other			14h	
		Deductions allocated and apportioned at corporate level to foreign source income				
	i	Passive category			14i	
	j	General category			14j	
	k	Other (attach statement)			14k	
		Other information				
	l	Total foreign taxes (check one): ▶ ☐ Paid ☐ Accrued			14l	
	m	Reduction in taxes available for credit (attach statement)			14m	
	n	Other foreign tax information (attach statement)				
Alternative Minimum Tax (AMT) Items	15a	Post-1986 depreciation adjustment			15a	
	b	Adjusted gain or loss			15b	
	c	Depletion (other than oil and gas)			15c	
	d	Oil, gas, and geothermal properties—gross income			15d	
	e	Oil, gas, and geothermal properties—deductions			15e	
	f	Other AMT items (attach statement)			15f	
Items Affecting Shareholder Basis	16a	Tax-exempt interest income			16a	
	b	Other tax-exempt income			16b	
	c	Nondeductible expenses			16c	
	d	Distributions (attach statement if required) (see instructions)			16d	
	e	Repayment of loans from shareholders			16e	

DRAFT AS OF August 1, 2014 DO NOT FILE

Form **1120S** (2014)

Self-Study Problem 11.6

Form 1120S (2014) Page 4

Schedule K **Shareholders' Pro Rata Share Items** (continued)

				Total amount
Other Information	17a	Investment income	17a	
	b	Investment expenses	17b	
	c	Dividend distributions paid from accumulated earnings and profits	17c	
	d	Other items and amounts (attach statement)		
Recon-ciliation	18	**Income/loss reconciliation.** Combine the amounts on lines 1 through 10 in the far right column. From the result, subtract the sum of the amounts on lines 11 through 12d and 14l	18	19,000

Schedule L **Balance Sheets per Books**

	Assets	Beginning of tax year (a)	(b)	End of tax year (c)	(d)
1	Cash		*Initial Return*		35,000
2a	Trade notes and accounts receivable			10,000	
b	Less allowance for bad debts	( )		( )	10,000
3	Inventories				
4	U.S. government obligations				
5	Tax-exempt securities (see instructions)				
6	Other current assets (attach statement)				
7	Loans to shareholders				
8	Mortgage and real estate loans				
9	Other investments (attach statement)				
10a	Buildings and other depreciable assets			125,000	
b	Less accumulated depreciation	( )		(5,000)	120,000
11a	Depletable assets				
b	Less accumulated depletion	( )		( )	
12	Land (net of any amortization)				18,000
13a	Intangible assets (amortizable only)				
b	Less accumulated amortization	( )		( )	
14	Other assets (attach statement)				
15	Total assets				183,000
	Liabilities and Shareholders' Equity				
16	Accounts payable				24,000
17	Mortgages, notes, bonds payable in less than 1 year				
18	Other current liabilities (attach statement)				
19	Loans from shareholders				
20	Mortgages, notes, bonds payable in 1 year or more				
21	Other liabilities (attach statement)				
22	Capital stock				140,000
23	Additional paid-in capital				
24	Retained earnings				19,000
25	Adjustments to shareholders' equity (attach statement)				
26	Less cost of treasury stock		( )		( )
27	Total liabilities and shareholders' equity				183,000

Form **1120S** (2014)

DRAFT AS OF August 1, 2014 DO NOT FILE

Self-Study Problem 11.6

Form 1120S (2014) Page **5**

Schedule M-1 **Reconciliation of Income (Loss) per Books With Income (Loss) per Return**

Note. The corporation may be required to file Schedule M-3 (see instructions)

1	Net income (loss) per books	*19,000*	5	Income recorded on books this year not included on Schedule K, lines 1 through 10 (itemize): a Tax-exempt interest $	
2	Income included on Schedule K, lines 1, 2, 3c, 4, 5a, 6, 7, 8a, 9, and 10, not recorded on books this year (itemize)				
3	Expenses recorded on books this year not included on Schedule K, lines 1 through 12 and 14l (itemize): a Depreciation $ b Travel and entertainment $		6	Deductions included on Schedule K, lines 1 through 12 and 14l, not charged against book income this year (itemize): a Depreciation $	
			7	Add lines 5 and 6	
4	Add lines 1 through 3	*19,000*	8	Income (loss) (Schedule K, line 18). Line 4 less line 7	*19,000*

Schedule M-2 **Analysis of Accumulated Adjustments Account, Other Adjustments Account, and Shareholders' Undistributed Taxable Income Previously Taxed** (see instructions)

		(a) Accumulated adjustments account	(b) Other adjustments account	(c) Shareholders' undistributed taxable income previously taxed
1	Balance at beginning of tax year	*0*		
2	Ordinary income from page 1, line 21	*9,000*		
3	Other additions	*10,000*		
4	Loss from page 1, line 21	( )		
5	Other reductions	( )	( )	
6	Combine lines 1 through 5	*19,000*		
7	Distributions other than dividend distributions			
8	Balance at end of tax year. Subtract line 7 from line 6	*19,000*		

Form **1120S** (2014)

DRAFT AS OF August 1, 2014 DO NOT FILE

Self-Study Problem 11.6

671113

☐ Final K-1 ☐ Amended K-1 OMB No. 1545-0123

Schedule K-1 (Form 1120S) **2014**
Department of the Treasury
Internal Revenue Service

For calendar year 2014, or tax year beginning ____________, 2014 ending ____________, 20____

Shareholder's Share of Income, Deductions, Credits, etc. ► See back of form and separate instructions.

DRAFT AS OF July 8, 2014 DO NOT FILE

Part I Information About the Corporation

A Corporation's employer identification number

B Corporation's name, address, city, state, and ZIP code

Aspen Corporation

C IRS Center where corporation filed return

Part II Information About the Shareholder

D Shareholder's identifying number

E Shareholder's name, address, city, state, and ZIP code

Janet Nall

F Shareholder's percentage of stock ownership for tax year . . . . *100* %

For IRS Use Only

Part III Shareholder's Share of Current Year Income, Deductions, Credits, and Other Items

1	Ordinary business income (loss) *9,000*	13	Credits
2	Net rental real estate income (loss)		
3	Other net rental income (loss)		
4	Interest income		
5a	Ordinary dividends *10,000*		
5b	Qualified dividends *10,000*	14	Foreign transactions
6	Royalties		
7	Net short-term capital gain (loss)		
8a	Net long-term capital gain (loss)		
8b	Collectibles (28%) gain (loss)		
8c	Unrecaptured section 1250 gain		
9	Net section 1231 gain (loss)		
10	Other income (loss)	15	Alternative minimum tax (AMT) items
11	Section 179 deduction	16	Items affecting shareholder basis
12	Other deductions		
		17	Other information

* See attached statement for additional information.

DRAFT AS OF July 8, 2014 DO NOT FILE

This list identifies the codes used on Schedule K-1 for all shareholders and provides summarized reporting information for shareholders who file Form 1040. For detailed reporting and filing information, see the separate Shareholder's Instructions for Schedule K-1 and the instructions for your income tax return.

1. Ordinary business income (loss). Determine whether the income (loss) is passive or nonpassive and enter on your return as follows:

	Report on
Passive loss	See the Shareholder's Instructions
Passive income	Schedule E, line 28, column (g)
Nonpassive loss	Schedule E, line 28, column (h)
Nonpassive income	Schedule E, line 28, column (j)

		Report on
2.	**Net rental real estate income (loss)**	See the Shareholder's Instructions
3.	**Other net rental income (loss)**	
	Net income	Schedule E, line 28, column (g)
	Net loss	See the Shareholder's Instructions
4.	**Interest income**	Form 1040, line 8a
5a.	**Ordinary dividends**	Form 1040, line 9a
5b.	**Qualified dividends**	Form 1040, line 9b
6.	**Royalties**	Schedule E, line 4
7.	**Net short-term capital gain (loss)**	Schedule D, line 5
8a.	**Net long-term capital gain (loss)**	Schedule D, line 12
8b.	**Collectibles (28%) gain (loss)**	28% Rate Gain Worksheet, line 4 (Schedule D instructions)
8c.	**Unrecaptured section 1250 gain**	See the Shareholder's Instructions
9.	**Net section 1231 gain (loss)**	See the Shareholder's Instructions

10. Other income (loss)

Code		
A	Other portfolio income (loss)	See the Shareholder's Instructions
B	Involuntary conversions	See the Shareholder's Instructions
C	Sec. 1256 contracts & straddles	Form 6781, line 1
D	Mining exploration costs recapture	See Pub. 535
E	Other income (loss)	See the Shareholder's Instructions

11. Section 179 deduction — See the Shareholder's Instructions

12. Other deductions

A	Cash contributions (50%)	See the Shareholder's Instructions
B	Cash contributions (30%)	See the Shareholder's Instructions
C	Noncash contributions (50%)	See the Shareholder's Instructions
D	Noncash contributions (30%)	See the Shareholder's Instructions
E	Capital gain property to a 50% organization (30%)	See the Shareholder's Instructions
F	Capital gain property (20%)	See the Shareholder's Instructions
G	Contributions (100%)	See the Shareholder's Instructions
H	Investment interest expense	Form 4952, line 1
I	Deductions—royalty income	Schedule E, line 19
J	Section 59(e)(2) expenditures	See the Shareholder's Instructions
K	Deductions—portfolio (2% floor)	Schedule A, line 23
L	Deductions—portfolio (other)	Schedule A, line 28
M	Preproductive period expenses	See the Shareholder's Instructions
N	Commercial revitalization deduction from rental real estate activities	See Form 8582 instructions
O	Reforestation expense deduction	See the Shareholder's Instructions
P	Domestic production activities information	See Form 8903 instructions
Q	Qualified production activities income	Form 8903, line 7b
R	Employer's Form W-2 wages	Form 8903, line 17
S	Other deductions	See the Shareholder's Instructions

13. Credits

A	Low-income housing credit (section 42(j)(5)) from pre-2008 buildings	See the Shareholder's Instructions
B	Low-income housing credit (other) from pre-2008 buildings	See the Shareholder's Instructions
C	Low-income housing credit (section 42(j)(5)) from post-2007 buildings	See the Shareholder's Instructions
D	Low-income housing credit (other) from post-2007 buildings	See the Shareholder's Instructions
E	Qualified rehabilitation expenditures (rental real estate)	See the Shareholder's Instructions
F	Other rental real estate credits	See the Shareholder's Instructions
G	Other rental credits	See the Shareholder's Instructions
H	Undistributed capital gains credit	Form 1040, line 73, box a
I	Biofuel producer credit	See the Shareholder's Instructions
J	Work opportunity credit	See the Shareholder's Instructions
K	Disabled access credit	See the Shareholder's Instructions
L	Empowerment zone employment credit	See the Shareholder's Instructions
M	Credit for increasing research activities	See the Shareholder's Instructions
N	Credit for employer social security and Medicare taxes	See the Shareholder's Instructions
O	Backup withholding	See the Shareholder's Instructions
P	Other credits	See the Shareholder's Instructions

14. Foreign transactions

Code		*Report on*
A	Name of country or U.S. possession	Form 1116, Part I
B	Gross income from all sources	Form 1116, Part I
C	Gross income sourced at shareholder level	Form 1116, Part I
	Foreign gross income sourced at corporate level	
D	Passive category	Form 1116, Part I
E	General category	Form 1116, Part I
F	Other	Form 1116, Part I
	Deductions allocated and apportioned at shareholder level	
G	Interest expense	Form 1116, Part I
H	Other	Form 1116, Part I
	Deductions allocated and apportioned at corporate level to foreign source income	
I	Passive category	Form 1116, Part I
J	General category	Form 1116, Part I
K	Other	Form 1116, Part I
	Other information	
L	Total foreign taxes paid	Form 1116, Part II
M	Total foreign taxes accrued	Form 1116, Part II
N	Reduction in taxes available for credit	Form 1116, line 12
O	Foreign trading gross receipts	Form 8873
P	Extraterritorial income exclusion	Form 8873
Q	Other foreign transactions	See the Shareholder's Instructions

15. Alternative minimum tax (AMT) items

A	Post-1986 depreciation adjustment	See the Shareholder's Instructions and the Instructions for Form 6251
B	Adjusted gain or loss	See the Shareholder's Instructions and the Instructions for Form 6251
C	Depletion (other than oil & gas)	See the Shareholder's Instructions and the Instructions for Form 6251
D	Oil, gas, & geothermal—gross income	See the Shareholder's Instructions and the Instructions for Form 6251
E	Oil, gas, & geothermal—deductions	See the Shareholder's Instructions and the Instructions for Form 6251
F	Other AMT items	See the Shareholder's Instructions and the Instructions for Form 6251

16. Items affecting shareholder basis

A	Tax-exempt interest income	Form 1040, line 8b
B	Other tax-exempt income	See the Shareholder's Instructions
C	Nondeductible expenses	See the Shareholder's Instructions
D	Distributions	See the Shareholder's Instructions
E	Repayment of loans from shareholders	See the Shareholder's Instructions

17. Other information

A	Investment income	Form 4952, line 4a
B	Investment expenses	Form 4952, line 5
C	Qualified rehabilitation expenditures (other than rental real estate)	See the Shareholder's Instructions
D	Basis of energy property	See the Shareholder's Instructions
E	Recapture of low-income housing credit (section 42(j)(5))	Form 8611, line 8
F	Recapture of low-income housing credit (other)	Form 8611, line 8
G	Recapture of investment credit	See Form 4255
H	Recapture of other credits	See the Shareholder's Instructions
I	Look-back interest—completed long-term contracts	See Form 8697
J	Look-back interest—income forecast method	See Form 8866
K	Dispositions of property with section 179 deductions	See the Shareholder's Instructions
L	Recapture of section 179 deduction	See the Shareholder's Instructions
M	Section 453(l)(3) information	See the Shareholder's Instructions
N	Section 453A(c) information	See the Shareholder's Instructions
O	Section 1260(b) information	See the Shareholder's Instructions
P	Interest allocable to production expenditures	See the Shareholder's Instructions
Q	CCF nonqualified withdrawals	See the Shareholder's Instructions
R	Depletion information—oil and gas	See the Shareholder's Instructions
S	Reserved	See the Shareholder's Instructions
T	Section 108(i) information	See the Shareholder's Instructions
U	Net investment income	See the Shareholder's Instructions
V	Other information	See the Shareholder's Instructions

CHAPTER 12 TAX ADMINISTRATION AND TAX PLANNING

Self-Study Problem 12.1

1.	False	The IRS has nine major services and enforcement offices.
2.	True	
3.	False	The commissioner of internal revenue is appointed by the president.
4.	False	The IRS is part of the Treasury Department.
5.	True	

Self-Study Problem 12.2

1.	True	
2.	False	An office audit is conducted at the IRS office.
3.	True	
4.	True	
5.	False	Audits can be appealed to the next level of the IRS.

Self-Study Problem 12.3

Part a.	Failure-to-pay penalty:		
	$3,000 × 0.5% × 2 months		$ 30
	Failure-to-file penalty:		
	$3,000 × 5% × 2 months	$ 300	
	Less: failure-to-pay penalty	(30)	
			270
	Total		$300
Part b.	20% × $10,000	$2,000	
Part c.	75% × $10,000	$7,500	

Self-Study Problem 12.4

1.	True	
2.	False	For bad debts, the statute of limitations is 7 years.
3.	False	There is no statute of limitations for fraudulent returns.
4.	True	
5.	True	

Self-Study Problem 12.5

1.	False	Lawyers and enrolled agents may also represent taxpayers before the IRS.
2.	False	A college degree is not required.
3.	False	Anyone may prepare corporate tax returns.
4.	True	
5.	True	
6.	True	
7.	False	The burden of proof is on the IRS.
8.	False	The burden of proof remains on the taxpayer.
9.	True	
10.	True	
11.	True	

Self-Study Problem 12.6

1. True
2. True
3. True Publication 1 directs the reader to Publication 594.
4. True
5. True
6. True

Self-Study Problem 12.7

1. 20.35% = $18,113 / $89,000
2. 20.43% = $18,383 / $90,000
3. 27% = ($18,383 − $18,113) / ($90,000 − $89,000)

GLOSSARY OF TAX TERMS

NOTE: The words and phrases appearing below have been defined to reflect their conventional use in the field of taxation. Such definitions may, therefore, be incomplete for other purposes.

Accelerated Cost Recovery System (ACRS)
For tax years after 1980, a rapid write-off of the cost of a capital asset is allowed by this system, which was later modified in 1986 and renamed Modified Accelerated Cost Recovery System (MACRS). The minimum number of years over which the asset may be depreciated and the applicable percentage of the asset's cost that may be deducted each year depend on the class of the property.

Accelerated death benefits
Early payouts of life insurance, also called accelerated death benefits or viatical settlements, are excluded from gross income for certain terminally or chronically ill taxpayers. The taxpayer may either collect an early payout from the insurance company or sell or assign the policy to a viatical settlement provider.

Accident and health benefits
Employee fringe benefits provided by employers through the payment of health and accident insurance premiums, or the establishment of employer-funded medical reimbursement plans. Employers generally are entitled to a deduction for such payments, whereas employees generally exclude the fringe benefits from gross income.

Accounting method
The method which determines when income and expenses are reported for tax purposes. Major accounting methods include the cash basis, the accrual basis, and the hybrid method.

Accounting period
The period of time, usually a year, used by a taxpayer for the determination of taxable income and tax liability. Unless a fiscal year is chosen, taxpayers must determine and pay their income tax liability using the calendar year (i.e., January 1 through December 31) as the period of measurement. An example of a fiscal year is July 1 through June 30. A change in accounting periods (e.g., from a calendar year to a fiscal year) generally requires the consent of the IRS.

Accrual method
A method of accounting that reflects expenses incurred and income earned for any one tax year. In contrast to the cash basis of accounting, expenses do not have to be paid to be deductible, nor does income have to be received to be taxable. Unearned income (e.g., prepaid interest and rent) generally is taxed in the year of receipt, regardless of the method of accounting used by the taxpayer.

Adjusted basis
The cost or other basis of property reduced by depreciation allowed or allowable and increased by capital improvements. See *Basis*.

Adjusted gross income (AGI)
A determination peculiar to individual taxpayers used as the basis to calculate limitations on the amount of certain expenses which may be deductible, including medical expenses, charitable contributions, personal casualty losses, and certain miscellaneous deductions. Generally, adjusted gross income represents gross income less certain business expenses and expenses attributable to the production of rent or royalty income.

Adoption expenses
Adoption fees, court costs, attorney fees, and other expenses directly related to the legal adoption of an eligible child.

Affordable Care Act (ACA)
Also referred to as Obamacare, ACA is a federal law providing for a fundamental reform of the U.S. healthcare and health insurance system, signed by President Barack Obama in 2010.

Alimony payments
Payments from one spouse or former spouse, to the other, required as a result of a divorce or separation agreement, which meet certain statutory requirements. Alimony and separate maintenance payments, but not child support payments, are included in the gross income of the recipient and are deducted by the payor.

American Opportunity credit
Previously referred to as the HOPE credit, a tax credit available for the first 4 years of postsecondary education expenses.

Amortization
The allocation (and charge to expense) of the cost or other basis of an intangible asset over its estimated useful life. Some intangible assets which have an indefinite life are amortizable. Examples of amortizable intangibles include patents, copyrights, and goodwill.

Amount realized
The amount received by a taxpayer on the sale or exchange of property less the cost incurred to transfer the property. The measure of the amount received is the sum of the cash and the fair market value of any property or services plus any relieved liability of the taxpayer. Determining the amount realized is the starting point for arriving at a realized gain or loss.

Annuity
A fixed sum payable at specified intervals for a specific period of time or for life. Payments represent a partial return of capital and a return (interest income) on the capital investment. An exclusion ratio is generally used to compute the amounts of nontaxable and taxable income.

Automobile expenses
Automobile expenses are generally deductible only to the extent the automobile is used in business or for the production of income. Personal commuting expenses are not deductible. The taxpayer may deduct actual expenses (including depreciation and insurance), or the standard mileage rate may be used.

Bad debts
An ordinary deduction is permitted if a business debt, such as an account receivable, subsequently becomes worthless (uncollectible), provided the income arising from the debt was previously included in taxable income. The deduction is allowed only in the year of worthlessness. A nonbusiness bad debt deduction is allowed as a

short-term capital loss when a debt which did not arise in connection with the creditor's trade or business activities becomes worthless. Loans between related parties (family members) generally are classified as nonbusiness debts.

Basis

The amount assigned to an asset for income tax purposes. For assets acquired by purchase, the basis would be the cost of the asset plus any direct costs incidental to the purchase. Special rules govern the basis of property received as a result of another's death or by gift.

Boot

Cash or property of a type other than that permitted to be received tax free in a nontaxable like-kind exchange. The receipt of boot will cause an otherwise tax-free transfer to become taxable to the extent of the lesser of the fair market value of such boot or the realized gain on the transfer.

Business gifts

Business gifts are deductible only to the extent that each gift does not exceed $25 per person per year. Exceptions are made for promotional gifts and for certain employee awards.

Capital asset

All assets are capital assets except those specifically excluded by the tax law. Major categories of noncapital assets include property held for resale in the normal course of business (i.e., inventory), trade accounts and notes receivable, depreciable property, and real estate used in a trade or business.

Capital expenditure

An expenditure, the amount of which should be added to the basis of the property improved. For income tax purposes, this generally precludes a deduction for the full amount of the expenditure in the year paid or incurred. Any tax deduction has to come in the form of cost recovery or depreciation.

Capital gain

The gain from the sale or exchange of a capital asset. See *Capital asset.* Gain from a property held 12 months or less is deemed to be a short-term capital gain. If the property is held more than 12 months then the gain is deemed to be long-term.

Capital loss

The loss from the sale or exchange of a capital asset. See *Capital asset.* A loss from a property held 12 months or less is deemed to be a short-term capital loss. If the property is held more than 12 months, then the loss is deemed to be long-term.

Cash basis

A method of accounting under which income is reported when received and expenses are deductible when paid by the taxpayer. Prepaid rent and prepaid interest must be deducted using the accrual method.

Casualty loss

A casualty is defined as the complete or partial destruction of property resulting from an identifiable event of a sudden, unexpected or unusual nature (e.g., floods, shipwrecks, storms, fires, automobile accidents). Individuals may deduct a casualty loss only if the loss is incurred in a trade or business; is incurred in a transaction entered into for profit; or arises from fire, storm, shipwreck, or other casualty or from theft. Personal casualty losses are deductible as itemized deductions subject to a $100 nondeductible floor and only to the extent that the taxpayer's total losses from personal-use property (net of the $100 floor) exceed 10 percent of adjusted gross income. Special rules are provided for the netting of certain casualty gains and losses.

Change in accounting method

A change in the taxpayer's method of accounting (e.g., from the FIFO to the LIFO inventory method) generally requires prior approval from the IRS. In some instances, the permission for change will not be granted unless the taxpayer agrees to certain adjustments prescribed by the IRS.

Change in accounting period

A taxpayer must obtain the consent of the IRS before changing his or her tax year. Income for the short period created by the change must be annualized.

Charitable contributions

Contributions are deductible (subject to various restrictions and ceiling limitations) if made to qualified nonprofit charitable organizations. A cash basis taxpayer is entitled to a deduction in the year of payment. Accrual basis corporations may accrue contributions at year-end if payment is authorized properly prior to the end of the year and payment is made on or before the fifteenth day of the third month following the end of the tax year.

Child and dependent care credit

This credit is available to individuals who are employed on a full-time basis and maintain a household for a dependent child or disabled spouse or dependent. The amount of the credit is equal to a percentage of the cost of employment-related child and dependent care expenses, up to a stated maximum amount.

Child support payments

Payments for child support do not constitute alimony, and are, therefore, not included in gross income by the recipient or deducted as alimony by the payor.

Child tax credit

A direct reduction in tax liability granted for each qualifying child under age 17. The child tax credit is phased out based on the level of modified adjusted gross income.

Community property

Community property is all property, other than separate property, owned by a married couple. The income from community property is generally split equally between spouses. The classification of property as community property is important in determining the separate taxable income of married taxpayers.

Deferred compensation

Compensation which will be taxed when received or upon the removal of certain restrictions and not when earned. An example would be contributions by an employer to a qualified pension or profit-sharing plan on behalf of an employee. Such contributions will not be taxed to the employee until the funds are made available or distributed to the employee (e.g., upon retirement). See *Qualified pension or profit-sharing plan.*

Depreciation

The write-off for tax purposes of the cost or other basis of a tangible asset over its estimated useful life or recovery period as specified in ACRS or MACRS tables. Depreciation does not necessarily mean physical deterioration or loss of value of the asset.

Earned income
Income from personal services as distinguished from income generated by property.

Earned income credit
The earned income credit is a refundable credit available to qualifying individuals with income and AGI below certain levels.

Education expenses
Employees may deduct education expenses if such items are incurred either (1) to maintain or improve existing job-related skills or (2) to meet the express requirements of the employer or the requirements imposed by law to retain employment status. Such expenses are not deductible if the education is required to meet the minimum educational requirements for the taxpayer's job or the education qualifies the individual for a new trade or business.

Educational Savings Accounts
Taxpayers may contribute a specified amount for themselves, a spouse, a child, or a grandchild. The contributions are non-deductible, but earnings may be accumulated and distributed tax free if used to pay qualified higher education expenses. Contributions cannot be made after the beneficiary reaches 18. Educational savings accounts are also known as Coverdell Education Savings Accounts.

Entertainment expenses
Such expenses are deductible only if they are directly related to or associated with a trade or business. Various restrictions and documentation requirements have been imposed upon the deductibility of entertainment expenses to prevent abuses by taxpayers.

Exemptions
An exemption is a deduction allowed for individual taxpayers in arriving at taxable income. There are two basic types of exemptions, personal and dependency. The personal exemption is available for the taxpayer and his or her spouse. The dependency exemption is available for qualified dependents of the taxpayer.

Fair market value
The amount at which property would change hands between a willing buyer and a willing seller, neither being under any compulsion to buy or sell, and both having reasonable knowledge of the relevant facts.

First in, first out (FIFO)
An accounting method for determining the cost of inventories. Under this method, the first merchandise acquired is the first to be sold. Thus, the cost of inventory on hand is deemed to be the cost of the most recently acquired merchandise.

Foreign tax credit or deduction
Both U.S. individual taxpayers and U.S. corporations may claim a foreign tax credit on income earned and subject to tax in a foreign country or U.S. possession. As an alternative to the credit, a deduction may be taken for the foreign taxes paid. The purpose of this credit is to eliminate double taxation on income earned in a foreign country.

Gift
A transfer of property for less than adequate consideration. Gifts usually occur in a personal setting (such as between members of the same family) and are generally excluded from taxable income.

Goodwill
The ability of a business to generate income in excess of a normal rate on assets due to superior managerial skills, market position, new product technology, etc. In the purchase of a business, goodwill is the difference between the purchase price and the value of the net assets. Goodwill is an intangible asset which possesses an indefinite life; however, it is amortized over 15 years for federal income tax purposes.

Gross income
All income from whatever source derived except that which is specifically excluded by tax law. Gross income does not include income such as interest on municipal bonds. In the case of a manufacturing or merchandising business, gross income means gross profit (i.e., gross sales or gross receipts less cost of goods sold).

Head of household
An unmarried individual who maintains a household for another and satisfies certain conditions. Such status enables the taxpayer to use income tax rates lower than those applicable to other unmarried individuals (single) but higher than those applicable to surviving spouses (widow(er)) and married persons filing a joint return.

Hobby loss
A nondeductible loss arising from a personal hobby as contrasted with an activity engaged in for profit. Generally, the law provides a presumption that an activity is engaged in for profit if profits are earned during any 3 or more years in a 5-year period.

Holding period
The period of time property has been held by the taxpayer. The holding period is of significance in determining whether gains or losses from the sale or exchange of capital assets are classified as long-term or short-term.

HOPE tax credit
A HOPE Scholarship tax credit is available for postsecondary education expenses. For tax years 2009 through 2017, the Hope credit has been modified and is referred to as the American Opportunity credit.

Hybrid method
A method of accounting that involves the use of both the cash and accrual methods of accounting. The tax law permits the use of a hybrid method, provided the taxpayer's income is clearly reflected by the method.

Individual shared responsibility
Under the Affordable Care Act, individuals are required to maintain minimum essential health coverage (known as minimum essential coverage or MEC) for each month or qualify for an exemption in order to avoid a tax designated as the individual shared responsibility.

Installment method
A method of accounting enabling a taxpayer to spread the recognition of gain on the sale of property over the payment period. Under this procedure, the seller computes the gross profit percentage from the sale (i.e., the gain divided by the contract

price) and applies the percentage to each payment received to arrive at the gain to be recognized.

Internal Revenue Code

Sometimes referred to as the Tax Code, the comprehensive set of tax laws enacted as Title 26 of the United States Code of Congress. The Code is organized according to topic, and covers all relevant rules pertaining to income, gift, estate sales, payroll, and excise taxes. The Internal Revenue Service (IRS) is the implementing agency of the Internal Revenue Code.

Internal Revenue Service (IRS)

A United States government agency that is responsible for the enforcement of the Internal Revenue Code and collection of taxes. The IRS was established in 1862 by President Lincoln and operates under the authority of the United States Department of the Treasury.

Involuntary conversion

The loss or destruction of property through theft, casualty, or condemnation. If the owner reinvests any proceeds received within a prescribed period of time in property that is similar or related in service or use, any gain realized on an involuntary conversion can, at the taxpayer's election, be deferred for federal income tax purposes.

Itemized deductions

Personal expenditures allowed by the Internal Revenue Code as deductions from adjusted gross income. Itemized deductions include certain medical expenses, interest on home mortgages, real and personal property taxes, charitable contributions, personal casualty losses, and other miscellaneous expenses.

Last in, first out (LIFO)

An accounting method for determining the cost of inventories. Under this method, the most recently acquired goods are sold first and the cost of inventory on hand consists of the earliest purchased merchandise (goods).

Life insurance proceeds

Generally, life insurance proceeds paid to a beneficiary upon the death of the insured are exempt from federal income tax. An exception exists when a life insurance contract has been transferred for valuable consideration to another individual who assumes ownership rights. In such a case, the proceeds are income to the assignee to the extent that the proceeds exceed the amount paid for the policy (cash surrender value at the time of transfer) plus any subsequent premiums paid.

Lifetime learning credit

The lifetime learning credit may be used in any tax year the American Opportunity credit (previously the HOPE credit) is not used for expenses paid for education. Unlike the American Opportunity credit, the lifetime learning credit may be claimed for an unlimited number of tax years.

Like-kind exchange

An exchange of property held for productive use in a trade or business or for investment (except inventory and stocks and bonds) for property of the same type. Unless different property is received (i.e., "boot"), the exchange will be completely nontaxable.

Limited Liability Company (LLC)

Business organizations usually treated as partnerships for tax purposes but offering the limited liability of a corporate stockholder to all members.

Listed property

Listed property are those types of assets which lend themselves to personal use and include computer and peripheral equipment, unless used exclusively at a regular business establishment, passenger automobiles, property used for transportation, and property used for entertainment, recreation, or amusement. The depreciation of listed property is subject to certain limitations.

Medical expenses

Medical expenses of an individual, spouse, and dependents are allowed as an itemized deduction to the extent that total medical expenses, less insurance reimbursements, exceed limitations based on the taxpayer's AGI.

Medicare surtax

Beginning after Dec. 31, 2012, the ACA imposed a Medicare surtax at a rate of 0.9 percent to wages, compensation, and self-employment income above an annual threshold amount.

Minimum essential coverage

The individual shared responsibility provision calls for each individual to have minimum essential health coverage (known as minimum essential coverage or MEC) for each month or qualify for an exemption, otherwise taxpayers must pay the individual shared responsibility.

Modified Accelerated Cost Recovery System (MACRS)

See *Accelerated Cost Recovery System (ACRS).*

Moving expenses

A deduction in arriving at adjusted gross income is permitted to employees and self-employed individuals provided certain tests are met (e.g., the taxpayer's new job must be at least 50 miles farther from the former residence than the former residence was from the former place of work).

Necessary

Appropriate and helpful in furthering the taxpayer's business or income-producing activity. See *Ordinary.*

Net investment income tax

The ACA imposed 3.8 percent Medicare tax on certain net investment income of individuals that have net investment income or modified adjusted gross income above the annual statutory threshold amounts.

Net operating loss

To mitigate the effect of the annual accounting period, taxpayers are allowed to use a net loss resulting from operations, as a deduction from net income in past or future years. A carryback period of 2 years and a carryforward period of 20 years are allowed.

Nonbusiness bad debts
A bad debt loss not incurred in connection with a taxpayer's trade or business. Such loss is deductible as a short-term capital loss and will only be allowed in the year the debt becomes entirely worthless. In addition to family loans, many investor losses fall into the classification of nonbusiness bad debts.

Nonrecourse debt
An obligation on which the endorser is not personally liable. An example of a nonrecourse debt is a mortgage on real estate acquired by a partnership without the assumption of any liability on the mortgage by the partnership or any of the partners. The acquired property generally is pledged as collateral for the loan.

Office-in-the-home expenses
Employment and business-related expenses attributable to the use of a residence (e.g., den or office) are allowed only if the portion of the residence is used exclusively and on a regular basis as the taxpayer's place of business or as a place of business which is used by patients, clients, or customers. If the expenses are employment related, the use must be for the convenience of the employer as opposed to being merely appropriate and helpful.

Ordinary
Common, accepted, and legitimate in the general industry or type of activity in which the taxpayer is engaged. It comprises one of the tests for the deductibility of expenses incurred or paid in connection with a trade or business: for the production or collection of income; for the management, conservation, or maintenance of property held for the production of income; or in connection with the determination, collection, or refund of any tax. See *Necessary.*

Organizational expenses
Organizational expenses are associated with the formation of a business prior to the beginning of operation. A corporation may amortize organizational expenses over a period of 180 months.* Certain expenses related to starting a company do not qualify for amortization (e.g., expenses connected with issuing or selling stock or other securities).

Partnerships
Partnerships are conduit, reporting entities, that engage in some type of business or financial activity, and are not subject to taxation. Various items of partnership income, expenses, gains, and losses flow through to the partners and are reported on their income tax returns.

Passive losses
Passive losses are deductible only to the extent of passive income. Losses from actively-managed rental real estate may be deducted up to $25,000. Unused passive losses carry forward indefinitely (until the activity which generated the losses is disposed of) and can be used by taxpayers to offset passive income in future years.

Patents
A patent is an intangible asset which may be amortized over its life. The sale of a patent usually results in long-term capital gain treatment.

Personal expenses
Expenses of an individual incurred for personal reasons which are not deductible unless specifically allowed under the tax law.

Personal property
Generally, all property other than real estate. It is sometimes designated as "personalty" while real estate is termed "realty." Personal property can also refer to property not used in a taxpayer's trade or business or held for the production or collection of income. When used in this sense, personal property could include both realty (e.g., a personal residence) and personalty (e.g., personal effects such as clothing and furniture).

Personal residence
The sale of a personal residence may result in the recognition of capital gain (but not loss). Taxpayers may permanently exclude $250,000 ($500,000 if married) of gain on the sale of their personal residence from income provided certain requirements are met, but generally not more than once every two years.

Points
Loan origination fees generally deductible as interest expense by a buyer of property. A seller of property who pays points is required to reduce the selling price, and, therefore, does not receive an interest deduction.

Portfolio income
Portfolio income includes dividends, interest, royalties, annuities, and realized gains or losses on the sale of assets producing portfolio income.

Premium tax credit
Lower income individuals who obtain health insurance coverage may be eligible for the premium tax credit to assist in covering the cost of health care premiums. Eligible individuals can choose to receive the credit paid in advance or claim the total credit when filing their tax return. If an individual chooses to have the credit paid in advance, the individual will reconcile the amount paid in advance with the actual credit computed when filing their tax return.

Prizes and awards
The fair market value of a prize or award generally is included in gross income.

Qualified pension or profit-sharing plan
An employer-sponsored plan that meets certain requirements. If these requirements are met, none of the employer's contributions to the plan will be taxed to the employee until distributed to him or her. The employer will be allowed a deduction in the year the contributions are made.

Realized gain or loss
The difference between the amount realized upon the sale or other disposition of property and the adjusted basis of such property.

Recognized gain or loss
The portion of realized gain or loss that is subject to income taxation. See *Realized gain or loss.*

Rollover
Transfer of pension funds from one plan or trustee to another. The transfer may be a direct transfer or a rollover distribution.

Roth IRAs
The Roth IRA allows nondeductible contributions. Although the contributions to a Roth IRA are not deductible, earnings

accumulate tax free, and qualified distributions are generally not included in income when received.

S corporation

A small business corporation whose shareholders have filed an election permitting the corporation to be treated in a manner similar to partnerships for income tax purposes. Of major significance are the facts that S corporations usually avoid the corporate income tax and that corporate losses can be claimed by the shareholders, limited to individual shareholder's adjusted basis.

Scholarships

Scholarships are generally taxable income to the recipient except for amounts received for tuition, fees, books, and course-required supplies and equipment.

Section 401(k) plan

A Section 401(k) plan is a qualified retirement plan which grants employee participants a deferral of income for employer contributions to the plan. The plan allows taxpayers to elect to receive compensation or to have the employer make a contribution to the retirement plan. The plan may be structured as a salary reduction plan. There is a maximum annual dollar limitation, as well as a limitation based on the employee's compensation. Some employers match employee contributions up to a certain limit in order to encourage participation.

Section 1231 assets

Section 1231 assets include depreciable assets and real estate used in a trade or business, held for the long-term holding period. Under certain circumstances, the classification also includes timber, coal, domestic iron ore, livestock (held for draft, breeding, dairy, or sporting purposes), and unharvested crops. Gains may be treated as long-term capital gains while losses in some cases may be deducted as ordinary losses.

Self-employment income

Self-employment income is the taxpayer's net earnings from self-employment, which includes gross income from a taxpayer's trade or business, less trade or business deductions. Self-employment income also includes the taxpayer's share of income from a partnership trade or business.

Self-employment tax

The self-employment tax consists of two components: the Social Security portion and the Medicare portion, together known as FICA. The Social Security portion of the self-employment tax consists of a tax of 12.4 percent imposed on an individual's net earnings from self-employment, up to a maximum which changes yearly. The Medicare portion of the tax consists of a tax of 2.9 percent imposed on the individual's net earnings from self-employment, with no maximum. In calculating the self-employment tax, a deduction is allowed for one-half of the otherwise applicable self-employment tax. This deduction is calculated by multiplying the taxpayer's self-employment income, before the self-employment tax deduction, by one-half of the total self-employment tax rate. If a self-employed individual also receives wages subject to FICA, the maximum Social Security tax base on the self-employed earnings is reduced. If a person has self-employment income of less than $400, he/she does not need to calculate self-employment taxes.

Separate property

Separate property is property, other than community property, acquired by the spouse before marriage or after marriage as a gift or inheritance.

Standard deduction

Taxpayers can deduct the larger of the standard deduction or their itemized deductions in calculating taxable income. An extra standard deduction amount is allowed for elderly and blind taxpayers. The standard deduction amounts may change annually.

Tax home

Since travel expenses of a taxpayer are deductible only if the taxpayer is away from home, the deductibility of such expenses rests upon the definition of "tax home." The IRS position is that the "tax home" is the business location, post, or station of the taxpayer. If the taxpayer is temporarily reassigned to a new post for a period of 1 year or less, the taxpayer's home should be his or her personal residence and the travel expenses should be deductible.

Trade or business expenses

Deductions for AGI which are attributable to a taxpayer's business or profession. The expenses must be ordinary and necessary to that business.

Transportation expenses

Transportation expenses for a taxpayer include only the costs of transportation (taxi fares, automobile expenses, etc.) in the course of employment where the taxpayer is not "away from home" in a travel status. Commuting expenses are not deductible.

Travel expenses

Travel expenses include meals (50 percent deductible), lodging, and transportation expenses while away from home in the pursuit of a trade or business (including that as an employee).

Unearned income

For tax purposes, unearned income (e.g., rent) is taxable in the year of receipt. In certain cases involving advance payments for goods and services, income may be deferred.

Vacation home

The Internal Revenue Code places restrictions upon taxpayers who rent their residence or vacation home for part of the tax year. The restrictions may result in the limitation of certain expenses related to the vacation home.

INDEX

A

Abandoned spouse, 1–10
ACA. *See* Affordable Care Act (ACA)
Accelerated Cost Recovery System (ACRS), 1–2, 7–6, 7–10. *See also* Modified Accelerated Cost Recovery System (MACRS)
Accelerated death benefits, 2–15
Accelerated depreciation, 7–7
Accident insurance, gross income and, 2–17
Accountable plan, 5–23, 9–15
Accounting income *vs.* taxable income, 11–6 to 11–7
Accounting periods and methods
- accounting methods, 7–3 to 7–5
- accounting periods, 7–2 to 7–3
- comprehensive problems, 7–34 to 7–35
- corporation tax years, 7–2
- cumulative software problem for, 7–36
- individual tax years, 7–2
- key points for, 7–24 to 7–25
- partnership tax years, 7–2
- questions and problems for, 7–26 to 7–33, 7–37 to 7–50
- self-study problems for, 7–3, 7–4, 7–5
- solutions to self-study problems for, E–34 to E–37
- writing assignment, 7–34

Accrual accounting method, 7–3, 7–4
Accumulated earnings tax, 11–25
Accuracy-related penalty, 12–12
Acquisition debt, 5–9 to 5–10
ACRS (Accelerated Cost Recovery System), 1–2, 7–6, 7–10
Actual cost method, 3–12 to 3–13
Additional comprehensive tax return problems, D–1
- comprehensive problem one, D–2 to D–5
- comprehensive problem two, D–6 to D–9
- Form 1040 for, D–11 to D–12
- Form 2441 for, D–24
- Form 8814 for, D–25
- Form 8949 for, D–19 to D–20
- Qualified Dividends and Capital Gain Tax Worksheet—Line 44, D–21
- Schedule A, Itemized Deductions for, D–13
- Schedule B, Interest and Ordinary Dividends for, D–14
- Schedule C, Profit or Loss From Business for, D–15 to D–16
- Schedule D, Capital Gains and Losses for, D–17 to D–18
- Schedule E, D–22
- Schedule SE, Self-Employment Tax for, D–23

Adjusted basis, 1–21, 8–4 to 8–6
Adjusted gross income (AGI)
- deductions for, 1–6
- individual retirement accounts and, 4–19 to 4–20
- for individuals, 1–6
- modified, 2–23

Adjustments, AMT, 6–22 to 6–23
- corporate, 11–26

Administration. *See* Internal Revenue Service (IRS); Tax administration and planning
Adoption
- credit, 6–16 to 6–18, 6–19 to 6–20
- domestic multiyear, 6–17
- employer-provided assistance for, 6–16, 6–17 to 6–18
- exclusion, 6–18
- expenses, 6–19 to 6–20
- expenses, qualified, 6–18
- foreign multiyear, 6–17

ADRs (Asset depreciation ranges), 7–7
Affordable Care Act (ACA), 6–6 to 6–12
- individual shared responsibility, 6–9 to 6–10
- Medicare surtax in, 1–24, 2–6, 8–7, 9–26 to 9–28
- Medicare taxes under, 1–23 to 1–24
- penalty for lack of coverage, 6–9
- premium assistance credit, 4–10
- premium tax credits, 6–10 to 6–12
- self-study problems for, 6–10, 6–12
- solutions to self-study problems for, E–27

AFTA (Annual Federal Tax Refresher) courses, 12–16
Age
- of dependent child, 1–13
- standard deduction and, 1–6, 1–19

AGI. *See* Adjusted gross income (AGI)
Alimony, 2–6 to 2–10
- defined, 2–6
- recapture of, 2–9

Allowances, 9–2, 9–5
Alternative minimum tax (AMT), 6–22 to 6–26
- adjustments, 6–22 to 6–23
- corporate, 11–25 to 11–26
- exemption allowance, 6–23
- preferences, 6–22 to 6–23
- rates, 6–24
- self-study problems for, 6–25, 6–27
- solution to self-study problem for, E–33

American Opportunity credit, 5–27, 5–28, 6–12 to 6–13, 6–14
American Taxpayer Relief Act (ATRA), 1–23, 1–24
Amortization of organizational costs, 11–5
Amount realized, in capital gains, 1–21, 8–4
Amounts at risk (AAR), 10–17
AMT. *See* Alternative minimum tax (AMT)
Annual contribution limits to IRAs, 4–19 to 4–21
Annual Federal Tax Refresher (AFTR) courses, 12–16
Annual Filing Season Program (AFSP), 12–16
Annualized period, 7–2
Annuities, 2–12 to 2–14
Annulled marriages, 2–10
Appeals process for the IRS, 12–7, 12–9
Asset, capital, defined, 8–2
Asset depreciation ranges (ADRs), 7–7
Assistance, with tax return, 1–22
Athletic facilities, 2–22
ATRA (American Taxpayer Relief Act), 1–23, 1–24
At-risk rule, 10–17 to 10–18
Audits
- appeals process for, 12–7, 12–9
- correspondence, 12–6
- field, 12–6
- office, 12–6
- process of, 12–6 to 12–10
- selection of returns for, 12–7

Automobiles
- business gain or loss on, 8–31
- in casualty losses, 5–17
- electric, credit for, 6–21
- luxury, depreciation limitations on, 7–17 to 7–19

Average tax rates, 12–22
Awards, 2–11

B

Backup withholding, 9–7
Bad debt, 3–22 to 3–23
Barter, 2–2
Bill of Rights, Taxpayer, 12–18 to 12–21
Blindness, standard deduction and, 1–6, 1–19
Bona fide business discussion, 3–16
Bonus depreciation, 7–10
Book income, 11–6
"Boot," 8–29
Bounced check, penalty for, 12–14
Brackets, 1–11
"Bubbles," in corporate income tax rates, 11–2
Burden of proof, 12–17
Business income. *See also* Schedule C
- bad debt and, 3–22 to 3–23
- comprehensive problems, 3–44 to 3–47, 4–42 to 4–44
- cumulative software problems, 3–47 to 3–48, 4–44
- dues and, 3–19 to 3–20
- educational expenses and, 3–17 to 3–19
- entertainment and, 3–16 to 3–17, 3–21
- home office and, 3–23 to 3–25
- inventories and, 3–7 to 3–11
- key points for, 3–29 to 3–30, 4–29 to 4–31
- meals and, 3–16 to 3–17
- net operating losses and, 3–26 to 3–27
- publications and, 3–19 to 3–20
- questions and problems, 3–31 to 3–43, 4–32 to 4–42, 4–45 to 4–55
- rental income and expenses, 4–2 to 4–5
- self-study problems on, part I, 3–7, 3–9 to 3–10, 3–11, 3–13, 3–16, 3–17, 3–19, 3–20, 3–21, 3–22, 3–23, 3–25, 3–27, 3–28
- self-study problems on, part II, 4–5, 4–9, 4–10, 4–11, 4–14, 4–16, 4–23, 4–24, 4–27, 4–28
- solutions to self-study problems on, part I, E–11 to E–12
- solutions to self-study problems on, part II, E–14 to E–16
- subscriptions and, 3–19 to 3–20
- transportation and, 3–11 to 3–13
- travel expenses and, 3–14 to 3–16
- writing assignment, 3–44, 4–42

Business property, casualty gains and losses from, 8–24 to 8–25
Business purpose test, 3–2

C

Campus Processing Sites, 1–7, 12–2
Capital assets, 1–21, 8–2
Capital expenditures as medical expenses, 5–3 to 5–4
Capital gains and losses. *See also* Losses
- adjusted basis in, 1–21, 8–4 to 8–6
- American Taxpayer Relief Act and, 1–24
- amount realized in, 1–21, 8–4
- and bad debts, 3–22
- calculation of, 8–3 to 8–6
- capital assets, defined, 8–2
- and casualty gains and losses, 8–22 to 8–25
- comprehensive problems, 8–53 to 8–55
- contract price in, 8–26 to 8–29
- corporate, 11–3
- cumulative software problem, 8–55
- depreciation recapture in, 8–12 to 8–22
- distributions as, 2–5
- exchanges in, 8–3 to 8–4

Capital gains and losses. *See also* Losses (*continued*)
holding period in, 8–3
installment sales in, 8–25 to 8–29
involuntary conversions in, 8–31 to 8–32
key points for, 8–36 to 8–37
like-kind exchanges in, 8–29 to 8–31
long-term, 8–3, 8–7
net capital gains in, 8–7 to 8–9
net capital losses in, 8–9 to 8–11
net capital position calculation of, 8–8 to 8–9
ordering rules for, 8–8, 8–10 to 8–11
overview of, 1–21 to 1–22
personal residence sales in, 8–32 to 8–34
personal-use property casualty gains and losses in, 8–22 to 8–23
questions and problems, 8–38 to 8–52, 8–57 to 8–77
sales in, 8–3 to 8–4
Section 1231, 8–11 to 8–12, 8–24 to 8–25
Section 1245 depreciation recapture and, 8–12 to 8–21
Section 1250 depreciation recapture and, 8–21
self-study problems for, 1–23, 8–2, 8–3, 8–6, 8–9, 8–11, 8–12, 8–13 to 8–20, 8–22, 8–25, 8–29, 8–31, 8–32, 8–35
short-term, 8–3, 8–7
solutions to self-study problems for, E–37 to E–47
tax rates for, 1–21, 8–7
tax worksheet, 2–8
on unrecaptured depreciation, 8–21 to 8–22
writing assignment, 8–52 to 8–53
Capital improvements, 8–4
Capital loss carryovers, 8–9
Capone, Al, 2–2
Carrybacks of net operating losses, 3–26 to 3–27
Carryovers
capital loss, 8–9
charitable contributions and, 5–15
net operating losses, 3–26
Cars. *See* Automobiles
Cash receipts and disbursements method, 7–3, 7–4 to 7–5
Casualty and theft losses, deductibility of, 5–17 to 5–18, 5–21
Casualty gains and losses
from business property, 8–24 to 8–25
as capital gains and losses, 8–22 to 8–25
from investment property, 8–24 to 8–25
as itemized deductions, 5–17 to 5–18, 5–21
from personal-use property, 8–22 to 8–23
Catch-up contributions
to health savings accounts, 4–13
to individual retirement accounts, 4–19
CD (Certificate of deposit), 2–4
Cell phones and gross income, 2–22
Certificate of deposit (CD), 2–4
Character and tax planning, 12–23
Charities. *See* Contributions, charitable
Child and dependent care credit, 6–3 to 6–6
qualified expenses for, 6–5
Child(ren)
adoption credit for, 6–16 to 6–18
as dependents, 1–13 to 1–14, 1–15
earned income credit and, 6–3
unearned income of, 6–26 to 6–30
Child support, 2–9 to 2–10
Child tax credit, 6–2
Citizenship test, 1–14
Civil War, 1–2
Closed transactions, 12–21
Clothing, special, 3–20 to 3–21
Collectibles, 1–21
Collections, IRS, 12–5 to 12–6
Community property, 6–30 to 6–34
and married filing separately status, 1–10
self-study problem for, 6–34
solution to self-study problem for, E–33
Computation, of tax, 1–11 to 1–12, A–3
Confidentiality privilege, 12–17 to 12–18
Constitution, 1–2
Consumer interest, 5–8, 5–9 to 5–10
Contract price, in capital gains and losses, 8–26 to 8–29
Contribution limits to IRAs, 4–19 to 4–21
Contributions, charitable
acknowledgment of, 5–15
by corporations, deduction of, 11–5 to 11–6
as itemized deductions, 5–12 to 5–16
percentage limitations on, 5–13 to 5–15
quid pro quo, 5–15, 5–16
substantiation of, 5–15 to 5–16
valuation of, 5–13
of vehicles, 5–16
Conventions in depreciation
half-year, 7–7 to 7–8
mid-month, 7–11
mid-quarter, 7–9
Conversions
involuntary, in capital gains and losses, 8–31 to 8–32
Roth IRA, 4–21
Corporate income tax
accumulations and, 11–25
alternative minimum tax, 11–25 to 11–26
capital gains and losses, 11–3
charitable contribution deduction in, 11–5 to 11–6
comprehensive problems for, 11–34 to 11–48
corporate formation and, 11–17 to 11–18
dividends received deduction, 11–4
estimated payments in, 11–7 to 11–8
filing requirements, 11–7 to 11–8
key points for, 11–27 to 11–28
organizational expenditures deduction, 11–4 to 11–5
personal holding company tax, 11–25
on qualified personal service corporation, 11–2
questions and problems, 11–29 to 11–34
rates, 11–2 to 11–3
Schedule M-1 for, 11–6 to 11–7
for S corporations, 11–15 to 11–17
self-study problems for, 11–3, 11–6, 11–7, 11–8 to 11–13, 11–17, 11–18, 11–19 to 11–24, 11–25, 11–26
solutions to self-study problems for, E–61 to E–73
special deductions in, 11–3 to 11–6
special limitations in, 11–3 to 11–6
start-up costs deduction in, 11–4 to 11–5
Corporations. *See also* Corporate income tax
accounting income *vs.* taxable income for, 11–6 to 11–7
basis in property contributed, 11–18
charitable contributions, 11–5 to 11–6
formation of, 11–17 to 11–18
liabilities of, 11–17
S corporations, 1–4, 11–15 to 11–17
shareholder stock basis, 11–18
tax returns and, 1–4
tax years, 7–2
Correspondence audits, 12–6. *See also* Audits
Cost of goods sold, 3–5 to 3–6, 3–7 to 3–8
Coverdell Educational Savings Accounts, 5–28 to 5–29
Credits
adoption, 6–16 to 6–18, 6–19 to 6–20
American Opportunity, 5–27, 5–28, 6–12 to 6–13, 6–14
child, 6–2
child and dependent care, 6–3 to 6–6
comprehensive problems, 6–49 to 6–50
cumulative software problem, 6–51
defined, 6–1
disabled access, 6–22
earned income, 6–2 to 6–3
economic goals of, 1–2
education, 6–12 to 6–15
elderly or disabled, 6–22
electric vehicle, 6–21
employer-provided child care, 6–22
energy, 6–18 to 6–21
foreign tax, 6–15 to 6–16
general business, 6–22
key points for, 6–34 to 6–37
lifetime learning, 6–13 to 6–14
low-income housing, 6–22
Low Income Retirement Plan Contribution, 4–26 to 4–27
premium assistance credit, 4–10
questions and problems for, 6–37 to 6–48, 6–53 to 6–64
refundable, 6–2, 6–13
research activities, 6–22
residential energy-efficient property (REEP), 6–21
self-study problems for, 6–2, 6–4, 6–6, 6–15, 6–16, 6–18, 6–19 to 6–20, 6–21
small employer health insurance, 6–22
social goals of, 1–2
solutions to self-study problems for, E–20, E–25 to E–33
work opportunity, 6–22
writing assignment, 6–48
Criminal Investigation department of IRS, 12–4
Current distributions in partnerships, 10–15

D

Debt
acquisition, 5–9 to 5–10
at-risk rule and, 10–17 to 10–18
bad, 3–22 to 3–23
deductibility of interest on, 5–8
interest on, 5–8 to 5–11
life insurance and, 2–15
mortgage, interest on, 4–2
mortgages, 5–8
statute of limitations for deduction of, 12–15
Deductions. *See also* Itemized deductions; Standard deductions
for adjusted gross income, 1–6
bad debt, 3–22 to 3–23
blindness and, 1–6, 1–19
in business, 3–2 to 3–3
clothing, special, 3–20 to 3–21
corporate charitable contribution, 11–5 to 11–6
dues, 3–19 to 3–20
educational expenses, 3–17 to 3–19
education loan interest, 5–10 to 5–11
entertainment, 3–16 to 3–17, 3–21
gifts, business, 3–21
health insurance for self-employed, 4–9 to 4–10, 5–3
health savings accounts, 4–13 to 4–14
home office, 3–23 to 3–25
inventories and, 3–7 to 3–11
Keogh plans, 4–23
meals, 3–16 to 3–17
moving expenses, 4–14 to 4–16, 4–17
net operating losses, 3–26 to 3–27
organizational expenditures, for corporations, 11–4 to 11–5
passive loss, 4–5 to 4–9, 4–11

Deductions. *See also* Itemized deductions; Standard deductions (*continued*)
  publications, 3–19 to 3–20
  rental expenses, 4–2
  retirement plans and, 4–24 to 4–27
  special corporate, 11–3 to 11–6
  standard, 1–6, 1–19 to 1–20
  start-up costs, for corporations, 11–4 to 11–5
  subscriptions, 3–19 to 3–20
  transportation, 3–11 to 3–13
  travel expenses, 3–14 to 3–16
  uniforms, 3–20 to 3–21
Defense of Marriage Act (DOMA), 1–10, 6–34
Deferred income, withholding and, 9–6
Defined benefit plans, 4–25
Defined contribution plans, 4–25
De minimis fringe benefits, 2–21 to 2–22
Dependent care accounts, 2–20
Dependents
  child tax credit for, 6–2
  exemptions for, 1–13 to 1–18
  filing requirements and, 1–8
  filing status and, 1–11
  qualifying child, 1–13 to 1–14, 1–15
  qualifying relative as, 1–14 to 1–17
  standard deduction for, 1–20
  widow(er) with, 1–11
Depreciation, 7–5 to 7–6. *See also* Modified Accelerated Cost Recovery System (MACRS)
  in adjusted basis, 8–4
  bonus, 7–10
  defined, 7–5
  economic goals of tax law and, 1–2
  election to expense, 7–12 to 7–14
  expense reporting, 7–11
  of intangible assets, 7–20
  listed property and, 7–14 to 7–17
  of luxury automobiles, 7–17 to 7–19
  of real estate, 7–10 to 7–11
  recapture, 8–12 to 8–22
  of rental property, 4–2, 4–3 to 4–4
  self-study problems for, 7–6, 7–12, 7–14, 7–15 to 7–16, 7–17, 7–19, 7–21
  solutions to self-study problems for, E–34 to E–37
  straight-line, 7–5 to 7–6, 7–8 to 7–9, 7–11 to 7–12, 7–20
  unrecaptured, on real estate, 8–21 to 8–22
  of vacation home, 4–3
DIF (Discriminant Function System), 12–7
Direct transfers, from retirement plans, 4–27
Disabled access credit, 6–22
Disaster areas, 1–2
Discounts, employee, 2–21
Discriminant Function System (DIF), 12–7
Distributions
  Health Savings Accounts (HSAs), 4–14
  individual retirement accounts, 4–22
  rollovers, 4–27 to 4–28
Dividend income, 2–5 to 2–6, 2–7, 2–8
Dividends received deduction, for corporations, 11–4
Divorce and filing status, 1–11
DOMA (Defense of Marriage Act), 1–10, 6–34
Domestic multiyear adoptions, 6–17
Domicile test, 1–13
Drugs, as medical expense, 5–3
Dues, 3–19 to 3–20

E

Early withdrawals from IRAs, 4–22
Earned income credit (EIC), 6–2 to 6–3
  table, B–3 to B–11
  worksheet, B–2
Economic goals, of tax system, 1–2
Economic performance, 7–4
Educational expenses
  business income and, 3–17 to 3–19
  credits for, 6–12 to 6–15
  qualified, 5–28
  required by employer or law, 3–18
  for skills maintenance or improvement, 3–18
  travel and, 3–18 to 3–19
Educational incentives, 5–24 to 5–30
Educational Savings Accounts, 5–27, 5–28 to 5–29
Education loan interest, 5–10 to 5–11
Education tax credits, 6–12 to 6–15
Educator expenses, 3–19
EFTPS (Electronic Federal Tax Payment System), 9–12
EIC. *See* Earned income credit (EIC)
Elderly or disabled credit, 6–22
Election to expense, 7–12 to 7–14
  qualification for, 7–12
Electric vehicle credits, 6–21
Electronic Federal Tax Payment System (EFTPS), 9–12
Electronic filing, 1–31
Employees
  annuities, 2–14
  business expenses, 5–23 to 5–24
  discounts, 2–21
  fringe benefits, 2–20 to 2–22
Employee Stock Ownership Plans (ESOPs), 4–25
Employer-provided benefits
  adoption assistance, 6–16, 6–17 to 6–18
  child care, 6–22
  retirement planning fringe benefits, 2–22
  retirement plans, 4–24 to 4–27
  spending accounts, 2–20
Employer reporting requirements, 9–15 to 9–17
Encumbered property, 10–17 to 10–18
Energy credits, 6–18 to 6–21
Entertainment, business income and, 3–16 to 3–17, 3–21
Entity and tax planning, 12–23
ESOPs (Employee Stock Ownership Plans), 4–25
Estimated tax
  for corporations, 11–7 to 11–8
  payments, 9–8 to 9–9
  penalties, 12–14
  self-study problem for, 9–9
  solution to self-study problem for, E–47
Exchanges
  in capital gains, 8–3 to 8–4
  like-kind, 8–29 to 8–31
Exclusions
  accident insurance and, 2–17
  adoption, 6–18
  annuities and, 2–12 to 2–14
  defined, 2–2
  employee fringe benefits, 2–20 to 2–22
  from gross income, 2–3
  health insurance and, 2–17
  life insurance and, 2–15
  for meals and lodging, 2–18, 2–21
  municipal bond interest and, 2–19
  personal residence, sale of, 8–32 to 8–33
  prize money and, 2–11
  scholarships, 2–16
  Social Security benefits and, 2–23 to 2–26
Exemption allowance, AMT, 6–23
Exemptions, 1–6
  dependency, 1–13 to 1–18
  personal, 1–13, 5–31
  phase out for high-income taxpayers, 5–31
Expenses. *See also* Educational expenses; Medical expenses
  adoption, 6–19 to 6–20
  adoption, qualified, 6–18
  employee business, 5–23 to 5–24
  investment, 5–19
  job-hunting, 5–19 to 5–20
  moving, 4–14 to 4–16, 4–17
  rental, 4–2
  self-employment, 3–4 to 3–5, 3–6
  tax preparation, 5–19
  travel, 3–14 to 3–16, 9–15

F

Failure-to-file penalty, 12–11
Failure-to-pay penalty, 12–11
Fair market value of charitable contributions, 5–13
Federal disaster areas, 5–17
Federal Insurance Contributions Act (FICA), 9–9. *See also* FICA tax
Federal poverty line, 6–10 to 6–11
Federal Tax Court, 12–7
Federal tax deposit system, 9–11 to 9–14
Federal Unemployment Tax Act (FUTA), 9–19. *See also* FUTA tax
FICA tax, 9–9 to 9–11
  defined, 9–1
  federal tax deposit system and, 9–11 to 9–14
  "nanny" tax and, 9–25
  overpayment of, 9–11
  rates, 9–9, 9–10
  for self-employed individuals, 3–6 to 3–7, 9–17 to 9–19
  self-study problem for, 9–11
  solution to self-study problem for, E–47
Field audits, 12–6. *See also* Audits
FIFO (First in, first out) inventory valuation, 3–8, 3–11
50 percent limitation, 5–13
Filing requirements
  corporate income tax, 11–7 to 11–8
  dependents, 1–8
  individual taxpayers, 1–7 to 1–9
  self-employment, 1–7
Filing status, 1–9 to 1–12, 9–2
  with deceased spouse, 1–10
  head of household, 1–10 to 1–11
  married filing jointly, 1–10
  married filing separately, 1–10, 6–30
  Qualifying widow(er) with dependent child, 1–11
  single, 1–9 to 1–10
First in, first out (FIFO) inventory valuation, 3–8, 3–11
Fiscal year, 7–2
Foreign multiyear adoptions, 6–17
Foreign tax credit, 6–15 to 6–16
Foreign travel, 3–14
Forms
  872, 12–15
  940, 9–20, 9–26, 9–29 to 9–30
  941, 9–12, 9–13 to 9–14, 9–26
  944, 9–12
  970, 3–8
  1040, 1–3, 1–4, 6–9
  1040A, 1–3, 1–4, 6–9
  1040-ES, 9–9
  1040-EZ, 1–3, 1–4, 6–9
  1040X, 1–3, 1–4
  1041, 1–4
  1065, 1–4, 10–5, 10–7 to 10–9
  1095 (A, B and C), 6–9
  1096, 9–16
  1098, 5–48, D–5
  1098-C, 5–16
  1099, 2–2, 9–7
  1099-B, 9–16, D–9

Forms (*continued*)
1099-DIV, 9–16, D–4
1099-INT, 9–16, D–9
1099-K, 9–16, 10–6
1099-MISC, 9–16, D–5
1099-R, 9–16, D–9
1099-S, 9–16
1116, 6–15
1120, 1–4, 11–7, 11–9 to 11–13
1120S, 1–4, 11–7, 11–19 to 11–22
2106, 5–24
2106-EZ, 5–25
2210, 9–8
2441, 6–7
3903, 4–17
4562, 7–11, 7–15 to 7–16
4684, 5–21
4797, 8–19 to 8–20
4868, 1–7
6251, 6–22, 6–23, 6–27
6252, 8–25, 8–27
7004, 11–7
8283, 5–15
8582, 4–11
8814, 6–31
8824, 8–29
8829, 3–25
8839, 6–19 to 6–20
8867, 6–3
8889, 4–13
8949, 8–15 to 8–16
8959, 1–27
8960, 1–25
8965, 6–9
W-2, 9–15, 9–17, D–4
W-2G, 9–16
W-3, 9–15
W-4, 9–2, 9–3 to 9–4, 9–5
W-4P, 9–6
Formula, tax, for individuals, 1–5 to 1–6
401(k) plans, 4–25 to 4–27
Fraud penalty, 12–12 to 12–13
Fringe benefits, 2–20 to 2–22
Frivolous returns, 12–13
FUTA tax, 9–19 to 9–20
defined, 9–1
"nanny" tax and, 9–25

G

Gains. *See* Capital gains and losses
Gambling losses, 3–6
Gambling winnings, 3–6, 9–16
General business credit, 6–22
General Rule for annuities, 2–14
Gifts
business, 3–21
gross income and, 2–16
Goals, of tax system, 1–2
Going-concern value, 7–20
Goodwill, 7–20
Gross income, 2–2 to 2–4. *See also* Adjusted gross income (AGI)
accident insurance and, 2–17
alimony in, 2–6 to 2–10
annuities in, 2–12 to 2–14
comprehensive problems, 2–39 to 2–42
cumulative software problem, 2–42 to 2–43
defined, 2–2
dividends in, 2–5 to 2–6, 2–7, 2–8
employee fringe benefits, 2–20 to 2–22
exclusions, 2–3
gifts and, 2–16
health insurance and, 2–17
inclusions, 2–3
for individuals, 1–5
inheritances and, 2–16
interest and dividends, 2–4 to 2–6
key points for, 2–27 to 2–28
life insurance in, 2–15 to 2–16
lodging and, 2–18
meals and, 2–18, 2–21
municipal bond interest in, 2–19
prizes and awards in, 2–11
questions and problems, 2–29 to 2–39
scholarships, 2–16 to 2–17
self-study problems on, 2–4, 2–6, 2–10, 2–11, 2–14, 2–16, 2–17, 2–18, 2–19, 2–20, 2–22, 2–26
Social Security benefits and, 2–23 to 2–26
solutions to self-study problems on, E–7 to E–11
unemployment compensation in, 2–19
writing assignment, 2–39
Gross Income Limitation for home office, 3–24 to 3–25
Gross tax liability, 1–6
Group term life insurance, 2–21
Guaranteed payments in partnerships, 10–15

H

Half-year convention, 7–7 to 7–8
Hand, Learned, 12–21
Hatch, Richard, 2–11
Head of household, 1–10 to 1–11
Health insurance
gross income and, 2–17
health savings accounts, 4–13 to 4–14
as medical expense, 5–3
penalties for lack of, 6–9
self-employed deduction for, 4–9 to 4–10, 5–3
Health Savings Accounts (HSAs)
catch-up contributions to, 4–13
deductions for contributions to, 4–13
distributions from, 4–14
High-deductible medical insurance, 4–13
Higher education expenses deductions, 5–29 to 5–30
High-income taxpayers
defined, 1–23
Medicare surtax for, 1–24, 2–6, 8–7, 9–26 to 9–28
Medicare tax, additional for, 1–23 to 1–24
phase outs for, 5–31
special rules for, 1–23 to 1–29
High-Low Method, for travel expenses, 3–15
History and objectives of tax system, 1–2
Hobby income and losses, 3–27 to 3–28
Holding company tax, 11–25
Holding period, for capital assets, 8–3
Homebuyer Assistance and Improvement Act of 2010, 3–13
Home equity interest, deductibility, 5–9 to 5–10
Home office, 3–23 to 3–25
Home office allocation, 3–25
Home sale, gain on, 1–2
HOPE credit, 6–12
Household employer
defined, 9–25
"nanny tax," 9–25 to 9–26
H&R Block, 1–30, 1–31
HSAs. *See* Health Savings Accounts (HSAs)
Hybrid accounting method, 7–3, 7–4

I

Illegal income, 2–2
Inclusions in gross income. *See* Gross income
Income. *See* Adjusted gross income (AGI); Business income; Gross income; Rental income and expenses
Income taxes, deductible, 5–5 to 5–7
Individual
as tax entity, 1–3
tax formula for, 1–5 to 1–6
Individual retirement accounts (IRAs), 4–16 to 4–23
annual contributions to, 4–19 to 4–21
distributions from, 4–22
low income retirement plan contribution credit for, 4–26
nondeductible traditional contribution, 4–20 to 4–21
rollovers, 4–27 to 4–28
Roth, 4–16, 4–21, 4–22
simplified employee pensions, 4–24
traditional, 4–16, 4–22
Individual shared responsibility, 6–9 to 6–10
Information returns, 9–16
Inheritances
capital gains from, 8–6
gross income and, 2–16
Inmate Fraud Prevention Act, 3–13
Installment agreements for tax payments, 12–6
Installment sales, in capital gains and losses, 8–25 to 8–29
Insurance. *See also* Health insurance
accident, 2–17
casualty and theft losses and, 5–18
deduction, in self-employment, 4–9 to 4–10, 5–3
life, 2–15 to 2–16, 2–21
on rental property, 4–2
Intangible assets, 7–20
Interest
consumer, 5–8, 5–9 to 5–10
education loan, 5–10 to 5–11
home equity, 5–9 to 5–10
income, 2–4 to 2–5, 2–7
investment, 5–11
as itemized deduction, 5–8 to 5–11
mortgage, 4–2, 5–8
municipal bond, 2–19
prepaid, 5–9
qualified residence, 5–9 to 5–10
on underpayment of taxes, 12–10
Internal Revenue Service (IRS), 12–2 to 12–6
audit process of, 12–6 to 12–10
Campus Processing Sites, 1–7, 12–2
collections by, 12–5 to 12–6
organizational structure of, 12–2 to 12–4
records examination authority of, 12–5
Wage and Investment (W&I) department, 12–5
website, 1–29 to 1–30
International travel, 3–14
Internet, 1–29 to 1–30, 2–25
Inventories, 3–7 to 3–11
Investment expenses, deductibility, 5–19
Investment income
dividends and, 2–5 to 2–6
Medicare tax on, 1–23 to 1–24
Investment interest, as itemized deduction, 5–11
Investment property, casualty gains and losses from, 8–24 to 8–25
Involuntary conversions, 8–31 to 8–32
IRAs. *See* Individual retirement accounts (IRAs)
IRS. *See* Internal Revenue Service (IRS)
IRS.gov, 1–29 to 1–30
IRS Restructuring Act of 1998, 12–2 to 12–4, 12–17
Itemized deductions. *See also* Deductions; Schedule A
casualty losses, 5–17 to 5–18, 5–21
comprehensive problems, 5–47 to 5–49
contributions, charitable, 5–12 to 5–16
cumulative software problem, 5–49 to 5–50

Itemized deductions. *See also* Deductions; Schedule A (*continued*)
- educational incentives, 5–24 to 5–30
- employee business expenses, 5–23 to 5–24
- home equity interest, 5–9 to 5–10
- income taxes, 5–6
- in individual returns, 1–6
- interest as, 5–8 to 5–11
- investment expenses, 5–19
- investment interest, 5–11
- job-hunting expenses, 5–19 to 5–20
- key points for, 5–32 to 5–33
- medical expenses, 5–2 to 5–4
- miscellaneous, 5–19 to 5–20
- mortgage interest, 5–8
- personal property taxes, 5–7
- phase-out for high-income taxpayers, 5–30 to 5–31
- prepaid interest, 5–9
- property taxes, 5–6 to 5–7
- purposes of, 5–1
- questions and problems, 5–34 to 5–46, 5–51 to 5–59
- residence interest, 5–9 to 5–10
- sales taxes, 5–6
- self-study problems on, 5–5, 5–7, 5–12, 5–16, 5–19, 5–20, 5–21, 5–24, 5–30, 5–31
- social goals of, 5–1
- solutions to self-study problems for, E–19 to E–20, E–21 to E–24
- taxes as, 5–5 to 5–7
- tax return preparation fees, 5–19
- theft losses, 5–17 to 5–18, 5–21
- writing assignment, 5–46 to 5–47

J

Job-hunting expenses deductibility, 5–19 to 5–20
Joint return test, 1–13
Jurisdiction and tax planning, 12–23

K

Keogh plans, 4–23
"Kiddie tax," 6–29

L

Large Business and International (LB&I) department of IRS, 12–4
Last in, first out (LIFO) inventory valuation, 3–8, 3–11
Liens and levies, 12–6
Life insurance, 2–15 to 2–16, 2–21
Lifetime learning credit, 5–27, 5–28, 6–13 to 6–14
LIFO (Last in, first out) inventory valuation, 3–8, 3–11
Like-kind exchanges, 8–29 to 8–31
Like-kind property, 8–30 to 8–31
Limited liability company (LLC), 10–2, 10–19
- defined, 10–1

Limited liability partnership (LLP), 10–1, 10–2, 10–19. *See also* Partnerships
Limited partnerships, 10–2. *See also* Partnerships
Listed property, 7–14 to 7–17
LLC. *See* Limited liability company (LLC)
LLP. *See* Limited liability partnership (LLP)
Lodging
- gross income and, 2–18
- as medical expense, 5–4

Long-term capital gains and losses, 8–3, 8–7
Long-term care premium limitations, 4–10, 5–3
Long-term gains and losses, 1–21 to 1–22
Losses. *See also* Capital gains and losses
- at-risk rule and, 10–17 to 10–18
- casualty, 5–21, 8–22 to 8–25
- deduction limitations, 5–18
- hobby, 3–27 to 3–28
- limitations on, 3–28
- net capital, 8–9 to 8–11
- net operating, 3–26 to 3–27
- ordering rules for, 8–10 to 8–11
- in partnerships, 10–5
- passive, 4–5 to 4–9, 4–11
- personal capital, 8–10
- related parties and, 7–21
- in S corporations, 11–16
- Section 1231, 8–11 to 8–12, 8–24 to 8–25
- theft, 5–17 to 5–18, 5–21, 8–24

Low-income housing credit, 6–22
Low Income Retirement Plan Contribution Credit, 4–26 to 4–27
Luxury automobiles, depreciation limitation on, 7–17 to 7–19

M

MACRS. *See* Modified Accelerated Cost Recovery System (MACRS)
MAGI (Modified adjusted gross income), 2–23
Maintenance expenses, 7–5
Marginal tax rates, 12–22
Marijuana as medical expenses, 5–3
Marriage
- annulment of, 2–10
- community property and, 6–30 to 6–34
- personal residence, sale of, 8–33
- same-sex couples, 1–10

Married filing jointly, 1–10
Married filing separately, 1–10, 6–30
Meals
- business income and, 3–16 to 3–17
- gross income and, 2–18, 2–21

Meals and Incidental Expenses (M&IE) method, for travel expenses, 3–15
Medical expenses
- capital expenditures as, 5–3 to 5–4
- drugs as, 5–3
- as itemized deduction, 5–2 to 5–4
- lodging as, 5–4
- marijuana as, 5–3
- medical insurance as, 5–3
- medicine as, 5–3
- qualifying, 5–2 to 5–3
- transportation as, 5–4

Medical flexible spending accounts, 2–20
Medical insurance. *See* Health insurance
Medicare surtax, 1–24, 2–6, 8–7, 9–26 to 9–28
Medicare taxes
- additional, for high- income taxpayers, 1–23 to 1–24
- calculation of, 9–9 to 9–10
- for self-employed individuals, 3–6 to 3–7

Medicine as medical expenses, 5–3
Member of household test, 1–14
Merchant card and third-party payments, 10–6
Mid-month convention, 7–11
Mid-quarter convention, 7–9
Mileage rate, 3–12 to 3–13
Minimum essential coverage (MEC), 6–9
Minimum required distributions, 4–22
Modified Accelerated Cost Recovery System (MACRS), 7–1, 7–6 to 7–12
- election to expense, 7–13
- half-year convention in, 7–7 to 7–8
- mid-month convention for, 7–11
- mid-quarter convention for, 7–9
- recovery periods in, 7–7

Modified adjusted gross income (MAGI), 2–23
Mortgage interest, 4–2
- deductibility of, 5–8

Moving expenses, 4–14 to 4–16, 4–17
Mud slide in Washington, 1–2
Municipal bond interest, 2–19

N

"Nanny" tax, 9–25 to 9–26
"Negative" income tax, 6–2
Net capital gains, 8–7 to 8–9
Net capital losses, 8–9 to 8–11
- personal, 8–10
- treatment of, 8–9 to 8–10

Net capital position, calculation of, 8–8 to 8–9
Net investment income tax, 1–24
Net operating losses, 3–26 to 3–27
No-additional-cost services, 2–21
Nonaccountable plan, 9–15
Nondeductible traditional IRAs, 4–20 to 4–21
Nonqualified recipients, 5–13
Nonrecourse liabilities, 10–17 to 10–18
Nontaxable distributions, 2–5

O

OASDI (Old Age, Survivors, and Disability Insurance), 9–9
Obamacare. *See* Affordable Care Act (ACA)
Offer in compromise, 12–6
Office, home, 3–23 to 3–25
Office audits, 12–6. *See also* Audits
Office of Online Services of IRS, 12–4
Office of Professional Responsibility (OPR) of IRS, 12–4
Offshore accounts, 6–16
Old Age, Survivors, and Disability Insurance (OASDI), 9–9. *See also* FICA tax
Open transactions, 12–21
Operating losses, net, 3–26 to 3–27
Optional safe harbor method for home offices, 3–25
Ordering rules
- for capital gains, 8–8
- for capital losses, 8–10 to 8–11

Ordinary and necessary test, 3–2
Ordinary dividends, 2–5
Ordinary gains and losses, 1–21
Organizational expenditures deduction, 11–4 to 11–5

P

Parental tax rate, 6–26
Partnerships, 1–4
- advantages of, 10–1
- at-risk rule and, 10–17 to 10–18
- basis in, 10–3 to 10–4
- comprehensive problem, 10–27 to 10–38
- current distributions with, 10–15
- defined, 10–2
- disadvantages of, 10–1
- formation of, 10–3 to 10–5
- guaranteed payments and, 10–15
- income reporting, 10–5 to 10–14
- key points for, 10–20 to 10–21
- limited-liability, 10–1, 10–2, 10–19
- losses in, 10–5
- merchant card and third-party payments, 10–6
- questions and problems, 10–22 to 10–26
- self-study problems for, 10–3, 10–5, 10–6 to 10–14, 10–15, 10–16, 10–17, 10–18, 10–19
- solutions to self-study problems for, E–49, E–55 to E–61
- taxation of, 10–2 to 10–3
- tax years and, 10–16
- transactions between partners and, 10–16 to 10–17

Partnership tax years, 7–2
Passive income and losses, 4–5
Passive loss limitations, 4–5 to 4–9, 4–11
Pass-through items, 11–16
Payroll taxes. *See* FICA tax; Withholding and payroll taxes

Penalties, 12–10 to 12–14
- accuracy-related, 12–12
- early withdrawal from IRAs, 4–22
- failure-to-file, 12–11
- failure-to-pay, 12–11
- fraud, 12–12 to 12–13
- health insurance, lack of, 6–9
- mortgage interest prepayment, 5–8
- for tax preparers, 12–16 to 12–17
- underpayment of taxes, 9–8
- waiver program for first-time, 12–12

Pensions, 4–24 to 4–27
- rollovers, 4–27 to 4–28
- withholding and, 9–6

Percentage limitations on charitable contributions, 5–13 to 5–15
Per diem substantiation, for travel expenses, 3–15 to 3–16
Personal capital assets, 8–10
Personal capital losses, 8–10
Personal exemptions, 1–13, 5–31
Personal holding company tax, 11–25
Personal property taxes, deductible, 5–7
Personal residence, sale of, 8–32 to 8–34
Personal residence exclusion, 8–32 to 8–33
Personal service corporation, 11–2
Personal-use property casualty gains and losses, 8–22 to 8–23
Planning, 12–21 to 12–23. *See also* Tax administration and planning
- defined, 12–21
- tax rate terminology in, 12–22

Plug-in electric vehicle credits, 6–21
PMI (Private mortgage insurance), 5–8
Practitioners, tax, 12–15. *See also* Preparers
Preferences, AMT, 6–22 to 6–23
- corporate, 11–26

Premium assistance credit, 4–10
Premium tax credits, 6–10 to 6–12
Prepaid interest, deductibility of, 5–9
Preparers
- confidentiality privilege with, 12–17 to 12–18
- penalties, 12–16 to 12–17

Preparer tax identification number (PTIN), 12–16
Private mortgage insurance (PMI), 5–8
Prizes, 2–11
Profit-sharing plans, 4–25
Property. *See* Real estate
Property taxes, deductible, 5–6 to 5–7
Property transfers
- alimony and, 2–9
- as gift, 2–16

Protest returns, 12–13
PTIN (Preparer tax identification number), 12–16
Publications, 3–19 to 3–20
Public transportation benefits, 2–20

Q

QTP (Qualified Tuition Program), 5–24 to 5–28
Qualified Dividends and Capital Gain Tax Worksheet, 2–8, 8–17
Qualified employee discounts, 2–21
Qualified expenses for child and dependent care credit, 6–5
Qualified home equity debt, 5–9 to 5–10
Qualified nonrecourse financing, 10–18
Qualified personal service corporations, 11–2
ualified plan award, 2–11
alified recipients, 5–12
lified residence acquisition debt, 5–9 to 5–10
ified residence Interest, 5–9 to 5–10
ied retirement plans, 4–24 to 4–27
d Tuition Program (QTP), 5–24 to 5–28
g child, 1–13 to 1–14, 1–15
Qualifying dividends, 2–6
Qualifying relative, 1–14 to 1–17
Qualifying widower with dependent child, 1–11
Quarterly federal taxes, 9–12, 9–13 to 9–14
Quid pro quo contributions, charitable, 5–15, 5–16

R

Rates. *See* Tax rates
Real estate
- adjusted basis of, 8–4 to 8–6
- and at-risk rules, 10–18
- casualty gains and losses from, 8–24 to 8–25
- depreciation of, 7–10 to 7–11
- personal residence, sale of, 8–32 to 8–34
- rental, as trade or business, 4–6 to 4–9
- taxes, as rental deduction, 4–2
- unrecaptured depreciation on, 8–21 to 8–22

Reasonableness test, 3–2 to 3–3
Recapture, depreciation, 8–12 to 8–21
REEP (Residential energy-efficient property) credit, 6–21
Refundable credits, 6–2, 6–13
Registered Tax Return Preparer (RTRP), 12–16
Regular Federal Rate Method, for travel expenses, 3–15
Rehabilitation expenditures credit, 6–22
Related parties, 7–21 to 7–23
- losses and, 7–21
- relationships in, 7–22 to 7–23
- self-study problem for, 7–23
- solution to self-study problem for, E–37
- unpaid expenses and interest, 7–22

Relationships and related parties, 7–22 to 7–23
Relationship test
- for dependent children, 1–13
- for dependent relative, 1–14

Relative, as dependent, 1–14 to 1–17
Rental income and expenses, 4–2 to 4–5
- passive loss limitations, 4–5 to 4–9

Replacement property, 8–31
Required annual payments, 9–8
Required minimum distributions, 4–22
Research activities credit, 6–22
Residence interest, deductibility, 5–9 to 5–10
Residential energy-efficient property (REEP) credit, 6–21
Retirement planning fringe benefits, 2–22
Retirement plans, 4–24 to 4–27
- rollovers, 4–27 to 4–28
- withholding and, 9–6

Return Preparer Office of IRS, 12–4
Rollovers, 4–27 to 4–28
Roth IRAs, 4–16
- conversions, 4–21
- distributions, 4–22

Roth 401(k) contributions, 4–26
RTRP (Registered Tax Return Preparer), 12–16

S

Sale or exchange of assets, 8–3 to 8–4
Sales
- in capital gains, 8–3 to 8–4
- installment, 8–25 to 8–29
- of personal residence, 8–32 to 8–34

Sales taxes, deductible, 5–6
Same-sex couples
- community property and, 6–34
- marriage of, 1–10

Saver's Credit, 4–26 to 4–27
Savings accounts, educational, 5–27, 5–28 to 5–29
Savings bonds, 2–5
Schedule A, 1–3, 1–4. *See also* Itemized deductions
Schedule B, 1–3, 1–4, 2–7
Schedule C, 1–3, 1–4, 3–2 to 3–7, 3–9 to 3–10
- cost of goods sold, 3–5 to 3–6, 3–7 to 3–8
- expenses, 3–4 to 3–5, 3–6
- income, 3–4
- trade or business in, 3–2
- vehicle information, 3–6

Schedule C-EZ, 3–3
Schedule D, 1–3, 1–4, 8–13 to 8–14
Schedule E, 1–4, 4–2, 4–7
Schedule F, 1–3, 1–4
Schedule H, 9–25, 9–31 to 9–32
Schedule K, 10–10 to 10–11
Schedule K–1, 1–4, 10–5, 10–13 to 10–14, 11–23 to 11–24
Schedule M–1, 11–6 to 11–7
Schedule SE, 3–6, 9–21 to 9–24
Schedule UTP, 11–7
Scholarships, 2–16 to 2–17
S corporations, 1–4
- characteristics of, 11–15
- losses, 11–16
- pass-through items in, 11–16
- reporting income in, 11–15 to 11–16
- special taxes for, 11–16

Section 179 expenses, 7–12, 7–13, 7–14, 7–18
Section 197 intangibles, 7–20
Section 267, 7–21 to 7–23
Section 401(k) plans, 4–25 to 4–27
Section 529 tuition plan, 5–24, 5–28
Section 1231 assets, 8–2
Section 1231 gains and losses, 8–11 to 8–12, 8–24 to 8–25
Section 1245 depreciation recapture, 8–12 to 8–21
Section 1250 depreciation recapture, 8–21
Self-employment. *See also* Business income
- accounting methods, 7–3
- defined, 4–10
- estimated tax payments in, 9–8 to 9–9
- filing requirement for, 1–7
- health insurance deduction, 4–9 to 4–10, 5–3
- income, 1–3
- Keogh plans and, 4–23
- Medicare surtax and, 9–27
- self-study problems for, 9–19
- solution to self-study problem for, E–51 to E–52
- tax, 3–6 to 3–7, 9–17 to 9–19

Self-support test, 1–14
Separate property, 6–30
SEPs (Simplified Employee Pensions), 4–24
Services and Enforcement arm of IRS, 12–4
Short-period taxable income, 7–2 to 7–3
Short-term capital gain or loss, 8–3, 8–7
Short-term gains and losses, 1–21
Simplified Employee Pensions (SEPs), 4–24
Simplified Method for annuities, 2–12 to 2–13
Single filing status, 1–9 to 1–10
Sixteenth Amendment, 1–2, 2–19
Small Business/Self-Employed (SB/SE) Division of IRS, 12–4 to 12–5
Small corporations, 11–25
Small employer health insurance credit, 6–22
Social goals
- of itemized deductions, 5–1
- of tax system, 1–2

Social Security benefits, taxation of, 2–23 to 2–26
Social Security taxes. *See* FICA tax
Solutions to self-study problems
- accounting periods and methods and depreciation, E–34 to E–37
- business income and expenses, part I, E–9 to E–14
- business income and expenses, part II, E–16 to E–19
- capital gains and losses, E–37 to E–48
- corporate income tax, E–61 to E–73

Solutions to self-study problems (*continued*)
credits and special taxes, E–20, E–25 to E–33
gross income and exclusions, E–7 to E–11
individual income tax return, E–1 to E–6
itemized deductions and other incentives, E–19 to E–20, E–21 to E–24
partnership taxation, E–48, E–55 to E–61
tax administration and tax planning, E–74 to E–75
withholding, estimated payments, and payroll taxes, E–46 to E–48, E–49 to E–54
Special withholding allowances, 9–2
Spending accounts, 2–20
Standard deductions
age and, 1–6, 1–19
blindness and, 1–6, 1–19
of dependents, 1–20
in individual return, 1–6
ineligibility for, 1–19 to 1–20
vs. itemized deductions, 5–10
Standard mileage rate, 3–12 to 3–13
Start-up costs deduction, for corporations, 11–4 to 11–5
Statute of limitations, 12–14 to 12–15
Stock bonus plans, 4–25
Straight-line depreciation, 7–5 to 7–6, 7–8 to 7–9, 7–11 to 7–12, 7–20
Students, unearned income of certain, 6–26 to 6–30
Subscriptions, 3–19 to 3–20
Substantiation requirements
charitable contributions, 5–15 to 5–16
employee business expenses, 5–23
entertainment expenses and gifts, 3–21
travel expenses, 3–15 to 3–16, 9–15

T

Taxable entities, 1–3 to 1–4
Tax administration and planning
burden of proof in, 12–17
confidentiality and, 12–17 to 12–18
defined, 12–1
interest in, 12–10 to 12–14
Internal Revenue Service, 12–2 to 12–6
key points for, 12–24 to 12–25
penalties in, 12–10 to 12–14
questions and problems, 12–26 to 2–31
self-study problems for, 12–6, 12–10, 12–14, 12–15, 12–18, 12–21, 12–24
solutions to self-study problems for, E–74 to E–75
statute of limitations and, 12–14 to 12–15
Taxpayer Bill of Rights, 12–18 to 12–21
tax planning, 12–21 to 12–23
Taxes, deductible, 5–5 to 5–7
Tax Exempt & Government Entities (TE/GE) department of IRS, 12–4
Tax home, 3–14
Tax law, goals of, 1–2
Tax liens and levies, 12–6
Taxpayer Bill of Rights, 12–18 to 12–21
Taxpayer Compliance Measurement Program (TCMP), 12–7
Tax practitioners, 12–15. *See also* Preparers
Tax rates
alternative minimum tax, 6–24
"bubbles" in corporate tax, 11–2
for capital gains and losses, 1–21, 8–7
corporate, 11–2 to 11–3
for corporations, 1–4
for dividends, 2–5 to 2–6
planning and, 12–22
schedules, A–2
table, A–3 to A–15
Tax returns
comprehensive problems, 1–43 to 1–45
corporations and, 1–4
cumulative software problem, 1–45
electronic filing of, 1–31
history and objectives of tax system and, 1–2
key points for, 1–32 to 1–33
partnerships and, 1–4
preparation fees, 5–19
questions and problems, 1–34 to 1–42
reporting in, 1–3 to 1–4
self-study problems on, 1–3, 1–5, 1–7, 1–9, 1–12, 1–18, 1–20, 1–23, 1–29, 1–31
solutions to self-study problems on, E–1 to E–6
taxable entities and, 1–3 to 1–4
who must file, 1–7 to 1–9
writing assignment, 1–43
Tax years
as accounting periods, 7–2 to 7–3
partnerships and, 10–16
TCMP (Taxpayer Compliance Measurement Program), 12–7
Teacher expenses, 3–19
Temporary tax code provisions, 7–23
Theft losses, 5–17 to 5–18, 5–21, 8–24
30 percent limitation, 5–14
TIGTA (Treasury Inspector General for Tax Administration), 2–9
Timing for tax planning, 12–22 to 12–23
Tip reporting, 9–6 to 9–7
Trade or business, 3–2
Traditional IRAs, 4–16, 4–22
nondeductible contributions, 4–20 to 4–21
Transportation. *See also* Automobiles
as business expense, 3–11 to 3–13
as medical expense, 5–4
Travel expenses
business income and, 3–14 to 3–16
for education, 3–18 to 3–19
substantiation requirements, 3–15 to 3–16, 9–15
Treasury Inspector General for Tax Administration (TIGTA), 2–9
Trustee-to-trustee transfers, 4–27
Tuition. *See also* Education tax credits
employee benefit of, 2–22
20 percent limitation, 5–14

U

Ulvaeus, Bjorn, 3–21
Unearned income
of children and students, 6–26 to 6–30
self-study problem for, 6–30
solution to self-study problem for, E–33
Unemployment compensation, 2–19
Uniforms, 3–20 to 3–21
Unpaid expenses and interest, related parties and, 7–22
Unrecaptured depreciation, on real estate, 8–21 to 8–22
U.S. General Accounting Office, 1–19

V

Vacation homes, 4–2 to 4–5
primarily personal use of, 4–3
primarily rental use of, 4–3 to 4–4
rental/personal use of, 4–4 to 4–5
Vehicle information, business expense, 3–6
Viatical settlements, 2–15
Volunteer Income Tax Assistance (VITA) Program, 1–22

W

Wage and Investment (W&I) Division, 12–5
Waiver program for first-time penalties, 12–12
Wealthy taxpayers. *See* High-income taxpayers
Websites for tax support, 1–29 to 1–30
Whistleblower Office (WO) of IRS, 12–4
Who must file, 1–7 to 1–9
Widow(er) and filing status, 1–11
Will Yancey's Home Page, 1–30
Winnings, 2–11
Withholding and payroll taxes
backup, 9–7
comprehensive problem, 9–45 to 9–61
computing, 9–5 to 9–6
deferred income and, 9–6
employer reporting requirements, 9–15 to 9–17
estimated tax payments in, 9–8 to 9–9
federal tax deposit system and, 9–11 to 9–14
FICA tax, 9–9 to 9–11
Form W-4 for, 9–2, 9–3 to 9–4, 9–5
key points for, 9–33 to 9–34
married persons monthly payroll period table, C–6 to C–7
methods for withholding, 9–2 to 9–7
"nanny" tax and, 9–25 to 9–26
penalties, 12–13
pension and, 9–6
percentage method tables for, C–2 to C–3
questions and problems, 9–35 to 9–45
self-employment tax and, 9–17 to 9–19
self-study problems for, 9–8, 9–12 to 9–14, 9–16 to 9–17, 9–19, 9–20 to 9–24, 9–26, 9–28 to 9–32
single persons monthly payroll period table, C–4 to C–5
solutions to self-study problems for, E–46 to E–50, E–49 to E–54
tip reporting and, 9–6 to 9–7
writing assignment, 9–45
Working condition fringe benefits, 2–21
Work opportunity credit, 6–22

LIST OF FORMS

Form 940	Employer's Annual Federal Unemployment (FUTA) Tax Return	9-29, E-53
Form 941	Employer's QUARTERLY Federal Tax Return	9-13, E-50
Form 1040	U.S. Individual Income Tax Return	2-49, 3-49, 3-57, 4-45, 4-51, 5-51, 5-55, 6-53, 6-59, 7-43, 8-57, 8-67, 9-49, D-11
Form 1040A	U.S. Individual Income Tax Return	1-49, 2-45
Form 1040-ES	2014 Estimated Tax Payment Voucher	9-9, 9-42, E-47
Form 1040EZ	Income Tax Return for Single and Joint Filers with No Dependents	1-47
Form 1065	U.S. Return of Partnership Income	10-7, 10-29, E-57
Form 1098	Mortgage Interest Statement	5-48, D-5
Form 1099-B	Proceeds From Broker and Barter Exchange Transactions	8-54, D-9
Form 1099-MISC	Miscellaneous Income	9-44, D-5
Form 1099-INT	Interest Income	2-40, 9-17, D-9, E-48
Form 1099-DIV	Dividends and Distributions	2-40, D-4
Form 1099-R	Distributions From Pensions, Annuities, Retirement or Profit-Sharing Plans, IRAs, Insurance Contracts, etc.	D-9
Form 1120	U.S. Corporation Income Tax Return	11-9, 11-37, E-65
Form 1120S	U.S. Income Tax Return for an S Corporation	11-19, 11-43, E-70
Form 2106-EZ	Unreimbursed Employee Business Expenses	5-25
Form 2441	Child and Dependent Care Expenses	6-7, 6-57, D-24, E-27
Form 3903	Moving Expenses	4-17, 4-48, 4-49, E-18
Form 4562	Depreciation and Amortization	7-15, 7-37, 7-41, E-35
Form 4684	Casualties and Thefts	5-21, 5-43, 5-59, E-23
Form 4797	Sales of Business Property	8-19, 8-47, E-44
Form 6251	Alternative Minimum Tax—Individuals	6-27, 6-63, E-31
Form 6252	Installment Sale Income	8-27, 8-49, 8-77
Form 8582	Passive Activity Loss Limitations	4-11, 4-39, 4-55, E-17
Form 8814	Parents' Election to Report Child's Interest and Dividends	6-31, D-25
Form 8829	Expenses for Business Use of Your Home	3-63
Form 8839	Qualified Adoption Expenses	6-19, E-29
Form 8949	Sales and Other Dispositions of Capital Assets	3-55, 7-49, 8-15, 8-45, 8-63, 8-73, 9-57, D-19, E-41
Form 8959	Additional Medicare Tax	1-27, E-4
Form 8960	Net Investment Income Tax	1-25, E-3
Form W-2	Wage and Tax Statement	1-44, 1-44, 9-17, 9-43, D-4, E-48
Form W-4	Employee's Withholding Allowance Certificate	9-3, 9-37, 9-39

LIST OF SCHEDULES

Schedule A	Itemized Deductions	5-53, 5-57, 6-55, 6-61, 7-45, 8-59, 8-69, 9-51, D-13, E-21
Schedule B	Interest and Ordinary Dividends	2-7, 2-33, 3-59, 5-54, 5-58, 6-56, 6-62, 7-46, 8-60, 8-70, D-14, E-7
Schedule C	Profit or Loss from Business	3-9, 3-41, 3-51, 3-61, 7-39, 9-53, D-15, E-11
Schedule D	Capital Gains and Losses	3-53, 7-47, 8-13, 8-43, 8-61, 8-71, 9-55, D-17, E-39
Schedule E	Supplemental Income and Loss	4-7, 4-47, 4-53, D-22, E-15
Schedule EIC	Earned Income Credit	6-45
Schedule H	Household Employment Taxes	9-31, E-55
Schedule K-1 (Form 1065)	Partner's Share of Income, Deductions, Credits, etc.	10-13, 10-35, 10-37, E-62
Schedule K-1 (Form 1120S)	Shareholder's Share of Income, Deductions, Credits, etc.	11-23, 11-47, E-75
Schedule SE	Self-Employment Tax	9-21, 9-23, 9-47, 9-59, D-23, E-52

W9-BXY-092

Income Tax FUNDAMENTALS

GERALD E. WHITTENBURG
San Diego State University

MARTHA ALTUS-BULLER
San Diego, California

STEVEN L. GILL
San Diego State University

CENGAGE Learning

Australia • Brazil • Japan • Korea • Mexico • Singapore • Spain • United Kingdom • United States